Essays and Reviews

"The 'Essays and Reviews' Appeal Case—The Rev. Mr. Wilson Arguing His Own Case before the Judicial Committee of the Privy Council." Engraving by William McConnell from the *Illustrated Times* (11 July 1863).

Courtesy of the British Library.

Essays and Reviews
The 1860 Text and Its Reading

Edited by
VICTOR SHEA
and
WILLIAM WHITLA

University Press of Virginia
Charlottesville and London

The University Press of Virginia

Printed in the United States of America

First published in 2000

♾ The paper used in this publication meets the minimum requirements of the American National Standard for Information Sciences—Permanence of Paper for Printed Library Materials, ANSI Z39.48-1984.

Library of Congress Cataloging-in-Publication Data

Essays and reviews : the 1860 text and its reading / edited by Victor Shea and William Whitla.
p. cm. — (Victorian literature and culture series)
Includes bibliographical references and indexes.
ISBN 0-8139-1869-3 (hardcover : alk. paper)
1. Liberalism (Religion)—Great Britain. I. Shea, Victor, 1960– II. Whitla, William, 1934– III. Series.

BR1616.E88 1999
230'.3—dc21

99-046751

Contents

Illustrations

Preface

ESSAYS AND REVIEWS crystallized many partisan positions on social movements and their cultural discourses around disputed topics in mid-century Victorian England. Numerous writers have alluded to the publication of the volume as a pivotal moment in ideas and institutional practices, indicating shifts in allegiances, transitions in thought and action—in fields as diverse as theology, religious and ecclesiastical history, biblical studies, education, law, science, politics, and literary criticism. The essays by the "Seven Against Christ" (as they were scornfully labeled) is, like Darwin's *On the Origin of Species* that it followed by four months, one of the Victorian books most often referred to by scholars; unlike the *Origin*, however, it is very likely one of the least read. The reasons are not hard to find.

Bristling with difficulties, the volume is not very friendly toward its readers. The essays are very different in subject matter and presentation and methods of scholarly documentation, and they encompass a wide range of learned allusion. They are scholarly treatises, written to promote discussion of contemporary academic issues: C. W. Goodwin positions his case against a series of long, scholarly quotations on Genesis and creation; Rowland Williams, H. B. Wilson, and Mark Pattison quote sources in Greek, Hebrew, Latin, French, and German, none translated; Baden Powell challenges the reigning authorities on the demonstration of religious truth by means of evidence; Frederick Temple draws elaborate analogies between human education, ethnographic development, and religious knowledge; and Benjamin Jowett addresses contemporary biblical hermeneutics in a highly referential and complex argument. Such knowledge and allusions, while resonant for many Victorian readers, are not familiar at the end of the twentieth century. *"Essays and Reviews": The 1860 Text and Its Reading* has been edited as "a social text" (McGann 1991, 2). Our title indicates that our task has been two-fold: first, to establish a critical text in a scholarly edition, and second, to stress that text's "reading"—in numerous Victorian evaluations of *Essays and Reviews*, in a wide range of contemporaneous documents and popular agitation, and finally, for modern readers, through our annotations and commentaries.

We had originally thought that the project could be completed in at most two years; it has taken nine. The University Press of Virginia, especially Janet Anderson, Cathie Brettschneider, Deborah A. Oliver, Ellen Satrom, and Boyd Zenner have been very patient and helpful. Gerald Trett has provided expert editorial guidance.

Financial support and release time have come from a Research Grant from the Social Sciences and Humanities Research Council of Canada and Supplementary Research Grants from the Faculty of Graduate Studies at York University.

For permissions to use copyright materials we wish to thank the Jowett Copyright Trustees for allowing us to publish all of the Jowett materials in the perpetual copyright of Balliol College, Oxford; the archbishop of Canterbury and Lambeth Palace Library for materials from the Court of Arches; the dean and

Chapter of Westminster for materials related to Samuel Wilberforce; the British Library; Oxford University Press for materials on Baden Powell; Longman Group UK Limited for material in its printing archives; the National Portrait Gallery, London, for illustrations in their copyright as specified; Imperial College for documentation from the Huxley Papers; and Francis Baden-Powell for a photograph of Baden Powell.

The staffs of many libraries have provided helpful guidance and assistance: in London, the British Library (Gladstone papers; Lubbock papers, amongst others); the British Library Newspaper Library at Colindale; Lambeth Palace Library and sublibrarian and archivist, Melanie Barber (Tait, Longley, Golightly, and Arches papers); the Office of the Privy Council and the Registrar, D. H. O. Owen; the National Portrait Gallery Archives (especially Jill Springall and Lesley Bradshaw); the Warburg Institute of the University of London (especially J. B. Trapp); and the Imperial College of Science and Technology (Huxley papers); in Oxford, All Souls College (Codrington Library); Balliol College Library (and Dr. Penelope A. Bulloch, librarian, for special access to the Jowett papers, then in process of recataloguing); the Bodleian Library (especially the Pattison, Wilberforce, and Oxford Diocesan papers); and Pusey House (and the Rev. Michael Knight, custodian, for the Pusey and Hamilton papers); in Reading, the University of Reading (especially Michael Bott, keeper of Archives and Manuscripts, for the Longman Archives); in Hawarden, Wales, Clwyd (Welsh) Record Office (especially J. C. Williams for access to the Glynne-Gladstone MSS. at St. Deiniol's Library, Hawarden); St. Deiniol's Residential Library (Gladstone papers and the collection of printed books); in Toronto, the University of Toronto libraries, including the Bora Laskin Law Library, Emmanuel College Library, Knox College Library, Massey College (Robertson Davies Library), Pontifical Institute of Mediaeval Studies Library, Robarts Library (especially Terence Correia), Science and Medicine Library, St. Michael's College (J. M. Kelly Library), Sigmund Samuel Library; the Thomas Fisher Rare Books Library (and its director, Richard Landon); Victoria College (Pratt Library); and Wycliffe College (Leonard Library). Special mention must be made of the Trinity College Library for its collections of nineteenth-century theology, the SPCK, and the John Strachan collections, and thanks especially to Linda Corman, Elsie Del Bianco, Linda Yarema, and Gabbi Zaldin. Also in Toronto the Scott Library at York University was particularly helpful (especially Mary Lehane and the interlibrary loan staff).

We also wish to thank some specific individuals who have helped us at crucial stages of our work. For assistance with photography, John Dawson; for helping solve problems with translations, matters of technical knowledge, and sources of information: John Coleman, Gwenda Echard, William Echard, Baruch Halpern, Richard Helmstadter, Martin Lockshin, Steven Mason, Daniel Norman, Hugh Parry, Elliott Rose, Abe Shenitzer, Mark Webber, William Wright; for reading sections of the text: Sydney Eisen, Paul Fayter, Norman Feltes, Baruch Halpern, Bernard Lightman, Herbert F. Tucker, and Nancy Whitla; for classroom feedback,

Herbert F. Tucker and Sydney Eisen; Stephen M. Waddams for making the proofs of his book on Stephen Lushington available to us before its publication; Terry Brown and Sydney Eisen for extended loan of editions of *Essays and Reviews* and related materials; Secretarial Services and the Academic Technology Support Group in the Faculty of Arts at York University (particularly Pat Cates and Charlie Mitchell) for computer scanning and data processing assistance. Richard Craswell of the University of Chicago helped with some thorny computer and typographical problems. For making available our research assistants, the Graduate Programme in English at York University and Kathleen Pye, Jean Noble, and Joseph Furfaro. Jerome McGann and the anonymous but very well informed and helpful external appraisers for the University Press of Virginia deserve special thanks.

In Oxford, Merton College provided helpful accommodation. Ross King and Lynn Avery kindly provided us with friendly hospitality in London. In London and Oxford Ross King gave invaluable research help. Glovana O'Brien merits special mention as one who helped the project along in many useful ways.

The frontispiece (from the *Illustrated Times* of 11 July 1863) was originally published with the following text:

> Our artist has sketched the Committee of the Privy Council during the hearing of the appeal of Mr. Wilson against this decision [of the Court of Arches]. . . . On the first day, at least, the space allotted to the spectators was well filled and some notabilities were present, among them Mr. Heath, who has himself got into trouble for preaching what has been considered unsound doctrine, and had doubtless a fellow-feeling for the reverent appellants; and Mr. Monckton Milnes, who paid great attention to the proceedings at their beginning, and then perhaps imagining himself to be in the House of Commons, fell into a delightfully sound and lengthened slumber.
>
> The proceedings were anything but lively, and those who came with a desire to hear the result had plenty of time for sleep. As Mr. Wilson stood up to state his case and call for a revocation of Dr. Lushington's decision he must have felt that he had not a very encouraging audience to address. As he stood at the foot of the long table at which the Committee sat he had on his immediate right Lord Chelmsford, whose appearance was rather that of a sportsman than a theologian; next to him sat the Bishop of London [A. C. Tait], who had certainly said some liberal things about the "Essays and Reviews," but who is not likely to be accused of sympathising with their teaching; while on his Lordship's right sat the Archbishop of York [William Thomson] who has not only written an article but an entire volume of articles in refutation of the offending volume; and *his* nearest neighbour was the Archbishop of Canterbury [Charles Thomas Longley], who has, doubtless, as little sympathy with the appellants as he has with Bishop Colenso. The occupants of the other side of the table might not appear so formidable. Four better-tempered gentlemen, to look at, are seldom seen together than Lord Kingsdown (who sat at the foot of the table on Mr. Wilson's left), and Lord

> Cranworth, the Lord Chancellor [Lord Westbury], and Lord Granville (who occupied the succeeding seats); but they had all a strictly orthodox appearance; and it was hardly to be wondered at that Mr. Wilson, when he rose, displayed much nervous excitement, if not fear and trembling. He probably envied the position of Dr. Williams, whose turn had not yet come, and who sat quietly among the spectators, with "spectacles on nose," and a lady on each side of him. . . . The first appearance of the bulky manuscript from which he [Mr. Wilson] read must have appalled the Queen's Advocate (Sir Robert Phillimore), who appeared on the other side, and who sat a little to the rear of Mr. Wilson, on his right. But, besides the manuscript, the reverend gentleman had a little load of books behind him, under the care of a formidably bearded and whiskered clergyman, and the reading of the manuscript and of quotations from the books occupied him some three days (23).

"Essays and Reviews": The 1860 Text and Its Reading has been prepared by the editors in camera-ready copy using Corel WordPerfect 8; it is set in Adobe Garamond expert collection fonts.

Dylani, Tashiana, and Danny Shea, and Becca, Michael, and Nancy Whitla have lived with "E and R" so long that they have long since realized that those initials do not always refer to entertainment and relaxation. It is a pleasure to record their sympathetic interest, puzzled tolerance, and continuous support.

Editorial Procedures

Copytext

We have followed the principles of Greetham (1988), Cohen (1991), and McGann (1991) to establish a copytext and rationale of emendations on the basis of a "social text," taking into account the historical, literary, and theological controversies in which the volume was enmeshed as well as publishers' printing-house practice and the interactions of authors with printing technology (see Dooley 1992, 159–76).

The first edition contains errors, misprintings, wrong numbers, and misspellings, some of which were subsequently corrected, others not, and subsequent editions introduced new variants in accidentals, in spelling, punctuation, and capitalization, as well as rearrangements of passages, realignments of type on the page to accommodate added or removed materials, changes within footnotes, and the addition of new footnotes. No edition from the second to the final English edition of 1869 can be claimed as representing the last or best stage of authorial intention, even were such an editorial principle still unquestioned. It is also impossible to establish an eclectic version of *Essays and Reviews* based on final authorial intention, as advocated by W. W. Greg, Fredson Bowers, and especially G. Thomas Tanselle (1976, 1980, and 1991).

Even were it still theoretically justifiable, it would not be possible to project an ideal or perfect text of *Essays and Reviews* to conform to either original or final authorial intention, especially when there are at least seven authorial intentions involved. This point is unequivocally made (and later both repudiated and defended in the ecclesiastical court) in the preface entitled "To the Reader." But other complex issues undermine the notion of intentionality: the lack of manuscript materials (partial drafts exist only for Pattison and Jowett's essays), the obscure editorial role of Wilson, the interventions of at least three of the Essayists (Powell, Williams, and Wilson) in the text of their contributions, the role of the publisher, William Parker, together with the conventions of his publishing house, the transference of publication from him to William Longman in 1861, the revisions and changes in the text, and the effects on the text of the trials and appeals in the courts.

Problems in establishing a copytext for *Essays and Reviews* include such matters as its multiple authorship, its concealed editor, the lack of manuscript materials upon which the volume was based, the change in publishers, and the relative dearth of examinable copies from all editions and issues. Except for early drafts by Pattison and Jowett, both fragmentary, and the few emendations added by Powell to his copy of the first edition, all of the manuscripts of *Essays and Reviews*, including press copies and proof sheets, have disappeared.

Either the first or second edition was read by those who first propelled the volume to notoriety and brought the legal suits against it and who prepared the quoted extracts, prompting the initial responses and tirades. It was the fourth and following editions that circulated widely, partly through Mudie's Select Circulating Library that had seven hundred copies in circulation in February 1861. Later editions (after 1865) responded to the increased readership during the sensational heresy trials by printing new prefatory explanations and having the passages cited in the heresy trials of Williams and Wilson marked in the text. For these historical and textual reasons the present scholarly edition, *"Essays and Reviews": The 1860 Text and Its Reading*, follows the first edition (1860) as copytext with respect to punctuation and orthography throughout, but also includes the added materials relative to the heresy trials as printed in the twelfth and thirteenth editions.

Variants and Emendations

No consistent editorial hand governed the revisions of the text. Wilson could be more properly called the compiler than editor on the basis of his actual editorial decisions. He was certainly the one who negotiated with the publisher, making the decisions about the conditions of publication, and he scrutinized the changes in format carefully, asking for copies of the changes in the prelims for the thirteenth edition to be sent to him; but he refrained from substantial interference with the content of the essays, very much conducting himself according to the conditions of the preface entitled "To the Reader." When the largest number of editions was published between 1861 and 1863, both he and Williams were occupied with the preparation of their cases before the Court of Arches and the Privy Council, so Wilson had little time for further editorial work. The other authors of *Essays and Reviews* did not place much importance on revising their texts for republication; indeed, with the exception of Powell in the second edition, they appear to have resisted it: certainly Pattison and Temple did. Williams introduced various changes into his text, at Wilson's suggestion, for the twelfth edition; and at the same time Wilson introduced a few to his own text, but by then the appeal in the Judicial Committee had been won. Goodwin and Jowett changed nothing.

Many changes, including added materials, were introduced with the publication of the smaller and cheaper tenth edition (1862); in the twelfth edition (1865) the passages cited in the Court of Arches trial and the Privy Council appeal were marked, necessitating considerable respacing of material to accommodate the introduction of single and double quotation marks at the beginning of each line (in nineteenth-century typographical custom) of the cited passages. Furthermore, there are other textual variants between the tenth and eleventh editions.

Most of these variants (the exceptions being the substantive changes from Powell, Williams, and Wilson noted above), so far as we can discover, have no authorial mandate that can be ascribed clearly to any specific source. The format of *Essays and Reviews* and its use of scholarly conventions (stylistic form for citation, placement of numbers, abbreviations, punctuation, and so on) are not consistent throughout the volume, partly the result of the shift from one house style to another in the move from Parker to Longman, but partly also in the insistence that each of the authors speak for himself, down to the point of the conventions of footnoting. To illustrate the inconsistencies, for instance, within a few lines of Pattison's essay (¶12) the terminal punctuation is sometimes included within the parenthesis for citations references, sometimes not. Such practices are highly inconsistent in the volume, as, to give another example, in Pattison ¶28. All of these inconsistencies were left in place by the publishers who reset the type for each edition by following a press copy from the previous edition. Each edition introduced new variants, at least some of which were contributed by the authors. The exceptions are the sixth to ninth editions of March 1861 that were printed from the standing type of the fifth edition of February, though some formes were lifted and changed, as we explain in the details of the publishing history, section 2 of our Introduction below. All other editions, including the first two issues of the tenth edition of 1862, introduced changes. Our list of variants aims to be comprehensive but not exhaustive: we have examined copies, usually multiple copies, of each of the editions and have included variants from these editions in the Textual Notes.

Substantive variants are noted in the textual apparatus. The copytext has been emended in the following ways:

1. To enable a reader to make easy reference to sections of the text in relation to the outline and for cross-referencing, paragraph numbers have been added for each essay in square brackets. Such numbers are not included in the first edition.

2. Following the twelfth edition (1865), the passages cited in the legal proceedings against Williams and Wilson in the Court of Arches and in the appeal before the Judicial Committee of the Privy Council are indicated in this edition. Under the instruction of Wilson, they were shown in the twelfth edition by single quotation marks for passages charged for heresy and withdrawn or rejected in the Arches trial, and double quotation marks for those sustained and carried forward to the Judicial Committee of the Privy Council where they were either withdrawn or rejected. We have used single and double underlinings to replace the single and double quotation marks of the twelfth edition. Occasionally there are some inconsistencies between the markings in the twelfth edition and the formal legal documents of the courts; such discrepancies are noted in the text by annotation, but in every instance we have followed the twelfth edition as the copytext for these markings.

In addition, the Preface to the Twelfth Edition, which explains this procedure to readers in 1865, has been added to our edition as part of the prelims. We print it preceding the preface of the first edition, entitled "To the Reader," as in the twelfth edition. Details concerning the ordering of the prelims in each of the editions are given in the Textual Notes. Since the preface "To the Reader" was cited in the Court of Arches and was withdrawn in the Judicial Committee, it was marked with double quotation marks in the twelfth edition, and is here printed with double underlining in the prelims to our edition. The date line of "*March*, 1860" was added in the twelfth edition, and has been retained here.

3. Emendations proposed or prepared by the contributors have been incorporated in this edition. Powell's marked copy of the first edition indicates changes he proposed that were introduced into the second edition. Furthermore, Wilson initiated discussions with the authors concerning changes before the tenth edition was published in smaller format and at a cheaper price, issued in the midst of the Court of Arches trial. There are also changes in Williams's and Wilson's essays in the twelfth edition.

We have included references to Powell's eleven manuscript corrections in his copy of the first edition (now in the Bodleian Library, shelfmark Baden Powell 122), corrections that were incorporated into each subsequent edition of *Essays and Reviews*; they are added to the Textual Notes, and are also specified in the annotations. Pattison's emendations, far more substantial, were part of his rethinking concerning the essay, possibly when he was preparing it as part of his larger project of the history of European rationalism. We have incorporated those annotations into the appendix after the notes to his essay. They did not find their way into subsequent editions of the full text of *Essays and Reviews*. Leslie Stephen's additions to Pattison's text were printed in Henry Nettleship's republication of Pattison's collected essays, as we note in detail in the introduction to Pattison's essay. Those annotations are also included in our notes to the essay, but are not included in this textual appendix. Some other alterations in the published text from edition to edition are factual, relating to the death of Baron Bunsen (Williams's correction in the twelfth edition to the note he appended to the volume), the death of Powell, the departure of Williams from Lampeter College, and the election of Pattison as Rector of Lincoln College—all recorded in the changes in the table of contents and in the Textual Notes.

4. Spelling and punctuation throughout conform to the copytext both in the text of *Essays and Reviews* and in the Essayists' notes, except for the following instances. In fifteen instances single quotation marks in internal quotations have been raised to double quotations marks. The sections in Jowett's essay have been renumbered in proper numerical sequence, leaving the first section unnumbered, as in the first edition. We have also inserted five missing quotations marks, one missing period, one semicolon, and one parenthesis and have removed the italics for one author's name in Pattison ¶ 21 (Ferguson). One wrong word, *that*, has been changed to *than* on the basis of a later edition. All of these emendations have been identified in the Textual Notes. All of the Essayists' and others' æ and œ digraphs have been converted to ae and oe.

5. The Essayists' notes are highly idiosyncratic, lacking consistency with respect to location of note numbering (often in midsentence), citation conventions,

abbreviation, spelling, and punctuation. All such variations have been retained in our edition. The format of the book, however, clearly indicated to its nineteenth-century readers that this was a scholarly text, replete with footnotes, citations in English, French, German, Greek, Hebrew, and Latin, and many parenthetical references throughout to biblical passages. The Essayists' own footnotes appear in the sequence of editors' endnotes and are identified and numbered throughout. An asterisk used as a footnote reference in Jowett's essay has been changed to an arabic number.

6. All italics and small caps in the first edition are retained in our edition, except for the small caps following the drop cap for the first word of each essay. The first and subsequent editions used small caps for only the first word. We have not attempted to produce a type-facsimile, imitating the smaller sizes of type in the first edition for the Essayists' footnotes, or other typographical details. We have added the author's name to the first page of each essay (from which we have also removed the terminal punctuation and the rule between the title and the text). In the first edition both recto and verso had the same running title (though a change in the actual title is recorded in the variants of Wilson's essay). Running heads in the present edition use each author's name instead of each essay's title.

7. We have retained the standard British convention of single quotation marks for direct quotation as used by both Parker and Longman in their printings of *Essays and Reviews*. This practice becomes confusing to modern readers when single quotation marks are also used for internal quotation marks as in the first edition. Accordingly, we have changed internal quotation marks from single to double in the fifteen instances where they occur. All are recorded in the Textual Notes. Missing quotation marks from the first edition have been added in six instances, with the authority of later editions for five of them, as recorded in the Textual Notes.

Annotation

The authors of *Essays and Reviews* annotated their own essays extensively. We have preserved their annotation and have added our own annotations and commentary to assist modern readers. As Peter Shillingsburg remarks, "Scholarly editions should trace and respect the development and transmogrification of the text by the succession of entities that have appropriated the work for publication," including the fact that texts are the "product of an unwritten but . . . recognizable social contract in which authors, editors, printers, publishers, booksellers, book buyers, and readers are all caught up in varying degrees of willingness" (1991, 26, 25). Behind such a view is McGann's assertion that textual authority is "a social nexus, not a personal possession. . . . It takes place within the conventions and enabling limits that are accepted by the prevailing institutions of literary production" (1983,

48; see also D. F. McKenzie 1986). This "social nexus" constitutes the "*Reading*" in our title. By its annotation, documentation, and other finding aids, *"Essays and Reviews": The 1860 Text and Its Reading* provides for modern readers the materials that were added in successive editions in response to contemporary controversy, with an indication in every instance of when and where such changes were introduced.

But *Essays and Reviews* also relies extensively upon other texts, chiefly the Bible and the classics, and commentaries on them, and in a sense the volume is itself an annotation of them, a commentary on hermeneutical method, and a gloss on their texts and commentaries. In a further sense, annotation is a central concern to *Essays and Reviews*, since its methodologies presume a historic and continuous tradition of commentary, stretching back much earlier than such canonized texts as the *Glossa ordinaria* (a compilation of patristic biblical commentary dating from the ninth century). One of the sources for the controversy the book aroused was the fact that the Essayists were annotating canonical texts with often noncanonical or disputed commentaries, a general concern addressed by recent theorists of annotation (see Middleton 1990 and Nichols 1991), and other recent editions (see Carlyle [1841] 1993). One aim of the present edition is to bring to the surface some of these secondary discourses of reference and allusion. While *Essays and Reviews* derives from a relatively homogeneous culture in which disciplinary discourses frequently overlap, current readers will use it in a variety of disciplinary and interdisciplinary contexts, and some of these historic configurations, too often hidden or buried, need to be brought to light.

In the interests of compression and coherence, and to avoid the continuous breaking up of argument, we have tried, so far as possible, to gather together several annotated items at the end of a sentence or a paragraph (except for the Essayists' notes, which are left where they occur in the first edition). In a number of places, however, the quantity of information made it necessary to locate our notes in sequence within a paragraph. Information in the endnotes is ordered according to its sequence in the text of the essay. Summations of parts of the cited works are occasionally given in the notes to indicate their relevance to the argument in the essay. Since the Essayists often put paraphrases in quotation marks or misquote their references, exact reference to editions the Essayists used, or to precise locations of cited material, is not always possible. We have left their references as in the first edition, but in our annotation have referred to standard editions where possible.

References for Greek and Latin authors are normally made to the texts and translations in the Loeb Classical Library as those most readily accessible. References to the Bible are to book, chapter, and verse according to the numbering of the Authorized (King James) Version, the one most commonly used in 1860. We have retained throughout the essays and the Essayists' notes any inconsistencies in abbreviations of the books of the Bible. Patristic references are to the translations in the *Ante-Nicene Fathers* (*ANF*), and the two series of the *Nicene and Post-Nicene Fathers of the Christian Church* (*NPNCF1*; *NPNCF2*). Citations to classical and patristic writers and to other literary or philosophical sources normally also include standard references to book and chapter; Shakespearean references are to act, scene, and line. Where possible we have cited editions that were contemporaneous with the Essayists, such as that of Gibbon by Milman (1858), or that of Calvin's *Institutes* by Beveridge (1863).

Passages in a foreign language in an essay are translated in the endnotes. So far as possible, translations from classical and patristic writings are given from standard sources; otherwise the translations are our own. We have translated titles in foreign languages in parentheses, except in the list of Works Cited. Where an English translation has been published we have referred to it. The index of persons identifies people mentioned by the Essayists and in the editors' commentary and annotations. For most names the editors have supplied biographical dates along with an identifying phrase. Such information is not repeated in the notes.

Abbreviations

The editors have followed the *Chicago Manual of Style* (14th ed. 1993) for abbreviations for the books of the Bible (Authorized Version), months, and other details. Exceptions are those abbreviations included in our list that the Essayists use, without consistency within an essay, or from essay to essay. To assist readers we have generally given fuller citations than those proposed in the *Chicago Manual of Style* for classical and other authors' names and works, making use of abbreviations where appropriate.

abp.	archbishop
ANF	*Ante-Nicene Fathers*. [1867–83] 1885. Ed. Alexander Roberts and James Donaldson. 10 vols., with the particular author, work, and translator specified
ap	Lat. *apud*, at, in the writings of (used by the Essayists)
art.	article (used by Essayists)
AV	Authorized (King James) Version of the Bible
B.	Ger. *Band*, volume (used by the Essayists)
b.	born
BAAS	British Association for the Advancement of Science
B.C.E.	Before the Common Era. No abbreviation after a date signifies the Common Era
BCP	*Book of Common Prayer* (1662)
B.D.	Bachelor of Divinity (used by the Essayists)
bk.	book (plural bks.)
BL	British Library
BLC	*British Library General Catalogue of Printed Books to 1975*. 1979–87. London: Bingley, 360 vols. with supplements
bp.	bishop
c.	Lat. *circa*, about, around; chapter (used by the Essayists)
cap.	Lat. *capitulum*, chapter, article in a legal document
cent.	century (used by Essayists)
cf.	Lat. *confer*, compare
ch.	chapter (used by the Essayists)
chap.	chapter (plural chaps.)
C. of E.	Church of England
comp.	compare (used by the Essayists)
d.	died
D.D.	Doctor of Divinity (used by the Essayists)
Dial.	Dialogue (used by the Essayists)
DNB	*Dictionary of National Biography*. 1908–9. Ed. Leslie Stephen and

	Sidney Lee. London: Smith, Elder. 22 vols.
EB	*Encyclopaedia Britannica*. 1910–11. 11th ed. New York: Encyclopaedia Britannica Company. 29 vols.
ERE	*Encyclopaedia of Religion and Ethics*. 1908–26. Ed. James Hastings. New York: Scribners. 13 vols.
Esq.	Esquire (used by the Essayists)
fol.	folio (plural fols.)
frag.	fragment
F.R.S.	Fellow of the Royal Society
F.R.S.E.	Fellow of the Royal Society, Edinburgh (used by the Essayists)
Ger.	German
Gk.	Greek
Heb.	Hebrew
ib.	Lat. *ibidem*, the same (used by the Essayists)
Ital.	Italian
JBC	*The New Jerome Bible Commentary*. Ed. Raymond E. Brown, Joseph A. Fitzmyer, and Roland E. Murphy. Englewood Cliffs: Prentice-Hall. 1990.
κ.τ.λ.	Gk. καὶ τὰ λείπόμενα (*kai ta leipomena*), and the rest; same as Lat. *et cetera* (used by the Essayists)
l.	line (plural ll.); pound or pounds
Lat.	Latin
Loeb	*Loeb Classical Library*. 1912–. Cambridge, Mass.: Harvard Univ. Press, with the particular author, work, and translator specified
LXX	Septuagint
NPNF1	*A Select Library of the Nicene and Post-Nicene Fathers of the Christian Church*. 1886–90. Ed. Philip Schaff and Henry Wace, 1st Series, 14 vols.
NPNF2	*A Select Library of the Nicene and Post-Nicene Fathers of the Christian Church*. 1890–1900. Ed. Philip Schaff, 2d Series, 14 vols.
NT	New Testament
OED	The Oxford English Dictionary. [1884–1928] 1933–86. Ed. James A. H. Murray et al. Oxford: Clarendon Press. 12 vols. 4 vols. *Supplement*
op.	Lat. *opus*, work (used by the Essayists)
OT	Old Testament
p.	page (plural pp.; used by the Essayists); penny or pence
𝔓	papyrus (used by textual critics of the Bible to designate specific papyrus fragments)
pass.	Lat. *passim*, throughout
QC	Queen's Counsel
quest.	question (as in a section of a philosophical or theological work)
RSV	Revised Standard Version of the Bible
S.	Saint (used by the Essayists)

s.	shilling or shillings
seq.	Lat. *sequentes* or *sequentia*, the following (used by the Essayists)
serm.	sermon (used by the Essayists)
st.	stanza
s.v.	Lat. *sub verbo*, under the word
Theil.	Used by Essayists for Ger. *Teil*, part
TLS	*Times Literary Supplement*
v.	volume, Ger. *Volumen* (used by the Essayists); verse (plural vv.); verso of a folio leaf; versus
¶	Paragraph, a reference to one of the editors' added paragraph numbers, inserted in square brackets in the margins in each of the essays (plural ¶s)
[?]	data or manuscript transcription queried by editors, usually following a queried date or word
§	section (used by the Essayists)

Part One

Reading "An Epoch in the History of Opinion"

1 From Clerical Culture to Secularized Anglicanism: Positioning *Essays and Reviews* in Victorian Social Transformation

The seven articles collected as *Essays and Reviews* (1860) engaged the relations between religious faith and mid-Victorian discussion about education, theology, science, history, literature, biblical studies, politics, and philosophy. For a decade after its publication it provoked intense controversy in the church, the university, the press, the government, and the courts, both ecclesiastical and secular. To students and scholars of nineteenth-century Britain the book is well known by name, and many have commented on its intellectual importance. Perhaps many fewer have persevered beyond one or two of the essays that almost a century and a half later remain difficult to follow or contextualize. The book has continued to be cited as a crucial document, not just by Victorian specialists, but by cultural historians. In a vast and prestigious book exhibition of 1963, *Essays and Reviews* was one of 102 nineteenth-century European books that exemplify "the impact of printing on the mind of Western man. . . . Although little read now, its influence, enormous at the time, has persisted to this day" (*Printing* 1963, 98). Despite these claims to the book's significance, no scholarly edition of *Essays and Reviews* has ever been produced.

Frederic Harrison in the *Westminster Review* (Oct. 1860), often cited as inaugurating the book's notoriety, announced its advent decisively: "A book has appeared which may serve to mark an epoch in the history of opinion. The latest phase of religion at length has developed its creed" (Harrison 1860, 157). Writing at the turn of the century in a comprehensive survey of English rationalism, Alfred Benn maintained the book's transformative significance: "Its appearance is perhaps the most important single event in the history of the Church of England during the last two hundred years, and certainly the most important in the history of English rationalism in the nineteenth century" (1906, 2:114).

In the mid-twentieth century, interest in the volume was renewed, primarily by Basil Willey in *More Nineteenth-Century Studies: A Group of Honest Doubters* (1956), in which *Essays and Reviews* is an example of "the loss of faith" or "the re-interpretation of current orthodoxy in the light of nineteenth century canons of historical and scientific criticism" (5). A. O. J. Cockshut followed suit in *Anglican Attitudes: A Study of Victorian Religious Controversies* (1959). Subsequent studies locate *Essays and Reviews* within nineteenth-century ecclesiastical liberalism, in a narrative that traces the loss of faith and the triumphant rise of scepticism and doubt in a series of controversies: the appointment of R. D. Hampden as bishop of Hereford (1847), the Gorham trial on baptism (1847–50), the Colenso affair (1862–65), the publication of J. R. Seeley's *Ecce Homo* (1865), the publication of the essays edited by Charles Gore, *Lux Mundi* (1889), and even, one hundred years after *Essays and Reviews*, in the controversy surrounding the publication of J. A. T. Robinson's *Honest to God* (1963). Such studies include Alec R. Vidler's *The Church in an Age of Revolution, 1789 to the Present Day* (1961), Desmond Bowen's *The Idea of the Victorian Church* (1968), M. A. Crowther's *Church Embattled: Religious Controversy in Mid-Victorian England* (1970), and Owen Chadwick's *The Victorian Church* (1966–70).

Two major monographs on *Essays and Reviews* by specialists in Victorian ecclesiastical history have recently been published. Ieuan Ellis in *Seven against Christ: A Study of "Essays and Reviews"* (1980) claims the book caused "the greatest religious crisis of the Victorian age." Furthermore, citing one of the Essayists, Mark Pattison, he argues that the volume was "the touchstone for a larger conflict, between a new liberal vision of society, scholarly in approach and European in sympathy, and an opposing conservative movement which drew on the most reactionary and anti-intellectual elements in the nation" (ix). In *Anatomy of a Controversy: The Debate over "Essays and Reviews," 1860–1864* (1994), Josef L. Altholz describes *Essays and Reviews* as a "suitable trigger" (142) for "the greatest crisis of Victorian faith" (1994, ix), and the "prototype of Victorian controversies" (1). Both studies have considerable strengths: Ellis explains the theological implications and doctrinal disputes that, to a late twentieth-century reader, are either baffling or invisible; Altholz carefully documents how the controversy was played out in the periodical press, pamphlet wars, and the ecclesiastical, secular, and academic courts.

Despite this scholarly consensus about the book's importance, and although there are several good studies of individual Essayists (Crowther 1970, Barr 1982 and 1983, and Corsi 1988), few have discussed the essays themselves in any detail. As M. A. Crowther has put it, the volume, despite its notable impact on Victorian society, is "now unread and almost unreadable" (1970, 8). There are at least two reasons for this condition: except for a reprint in 1971, no edition of *Essays and Reviews* has been published since the American edition of 1874; second, its unreadability results chiefly from a failure in cultural translation: what stirred such trouble from 1860 to 1870 is easily passed over by modern readers, for whom the then-radical ideas have become normalized. This edition provides a critical text based on the first edition as copytext, but also attempts to render its cultural assumptions and appropriations available to modern readers in contexts that foreground the controversies in which they were embedded, with annotation and documentation that stress the role of the volume as a social, intellectual, and political document.

The general title for the volume, *Essays and Reviews*, is consistent with both the concept of the formal essay through which teaching was conducted at Oxford and Cambridge (and exemplified in a more developed form in the volumes of *Cambridge Essays* and *Oxford Essays*) and with the notion of the review, both a review of a body of knowledge and a review of a specific book or collection of books. It was this genre and model that dominated theological discussion in England and for which the volumes of *Tracts for the Times* provided important precursors for the seven Essayists and Reviewers. Book reviewing throughout the nineteenth century in the periodical press was less a summary and positioning of a book's contents and more a point of departure for a reviewer's particular interests in general topics prompted by the subject matter of the book being noticed. In *Essays and Reviews* Rowland Williams's discussion of Bunsen's writings is the only one of the essays that concentrates on a single book or author; H. B. Wilson's brief treatment of a collection of essays on the Genevan church and C. W. Goodwin's survey of three recent books attempting to reconcile Genesis and geology would qualify within the conventions of the nineteenth century as a review. Each of these, however, uses particular books to launch a broad-ranging discussion on contemporaneous issues of contention. Goodwin also follows the convention in Victorian reviewing of quoting substantial passages interspersed with short comments; Williams adopts the convention of paraphrase. Except for Williams, then, all of the other studies are primarily "essays" within the nineteenth-century sense of the term.

The seven studies were compiled, rather than edited (for there was no consistent editorial policy or controlling hand to ensure any kind of stylistic or conceptual consistency), by Wilson. He also devised the preface to the volume, declaring that each writer argued independently. But while they wrote on diverse topics, there is a consistency to their arguments that suggests a similarity of purpose and theological perspective, a challenge to orthodoxy derived from the liberal, or Broad Church, party of Anglicanism. Wilson's claim, that each of the writers has a "free handling, in a becoming spirit, of subjects peculiarly liable to suffer by the repetition of conventional language, and from traditional methods of treatment," is borne out by the range of topics and methods of analysis used by the Essayists.

The early reviews either praised the volume or criticized its tone and theology, largely on the basis that a number of the Essayists were already comparatively well known. By midsummer 1860, the weeklies and monthlies were almost unanimously opposed to *Essays and Reviews*. The first of the major quarterlies to review the volume was the radical *Westminster Review* (Oct. 1860), in which Frederic Harrison accused the writers of a concerted effort to undermine the Anglican establishment and to redefine Christianity in England as "Neo-Christianity," while the hierarchy in the institutions of learning and the church, in which the Essayists and Reviewers held positions of authority, remained silent and ineffectual.

Samuel Wilberforce, no stranger to political controversy having weathered the storm of Tractarianism, took up Harrison's challenge, addressing his clergy on 7 November 1860. In his episcopal charge he warned them of the dangers of the book's rationalism. In January 1861 Wilberforce published an anonymous article in the *Quarterly Review* in which he declared that the book threatened "to shake the foundations" of the Church of England by its repudiation of biblical inspiration, prophecy, validity of the atonement, and the eternal damnation of the reprobate.

By February local clergy associations mobilized their resources, requesting concerted episcopal direction and action in the light of the Essayists' challenges to orthodoxy. Under Wilberforce's guidance, the bishops produced an Episcopal Manifesto which condemned the Essayists in general, without naming them individually or citing any offending passages. To mediate in this dispute, a long-standing friend and associate of the Essayists, A. P. Stanley, published a long article in the *Edinburgh Review* in April 1861. While he sought to mitigate the episcopal and clerical censure of his friends, his essay had the effect of intensifying it, since he was seen by many, including some of the Essayists, to be a liberal attacking his own. By midsummer, after clerical signatures on declarations and manifestos had been gathered across the nation, the controversy moved into the courts.

Williams and Wilson were arraigned according to ecclesiastical law in the court of the archbishop of Canterbury, the Court of Arches in December 1861, charged by Walter Kerr Hamilton, the bishop of Salisbury, and James Fendall of the diocese of Ely. They were found guilty in the ecclesiastical court and immediately appealed the decision to the Judicial Committee of the Privy Council, the highest court of appeal in the realm. In doing so, they moved the controversy from ecclesiastical to secular jurisdiction, thereby ensuring that their appeal would be judged by a different standard of law. Simultaneously, Jowett was subjected to opposition at Oxford led by E. B. Pusey, who brought Jowett to trial in the Chancellor's Court at Oxford in February 1863, seeking to have him silenced and demanding that he recant his heterodoxy. The episode ended when the case against him was thrown out on procedural grounds but without Jowett's having a chance to defend himself.

The appeals of Williams and Wilson were heard in the Privy Council in the spring and summer of 1863. When the Privy Council granted their appeals on 8 February 1864, the judgment of Lord Westbury in their favor was said to have "dismissed hell with costs," and taken away from every Englishman "his right to eternal damnation." The bishops and clergy mobilized once again against the Essayists and the Judicial Committee. Their action consisted of issuing a solemn synodical condemnation of *Essays and Reviews*, what the secular court of appeal had refused to do. The clergy, to the number of almost 12,000, issued a declaration affirming their belief in the literal inspiration of the Bible and eternal damnation. The last phase of the notoriety of the volume occurred when one of the Essayists, Frederick Temple, was appointed bishop of Exeter in October 1869. As with the actions against Williams, Wilson, and Jowett, the opponents of Temple were ultimately unsuccessful in bringing the weight of ecclesiastical and secular legal censure against him (for these legal episodes, see Part 2: Trials and Appeals and Temple and the Exeter Controversy).

Essays and Reviews is one of a series of texts published in the decade questioning the authority and control of the Anglican Church in the Victorian social formation: Mill's *On Liberty* (1859), Darwin's *On the Origin of Species* (1859), Colenso's *The Pentateuch and Book of Joshua Critically Examined* (1862), Huxley's *Man's Place in Nature* (1863), Lyell's *Antiquity of Man* (1863), the translation of Renan's *Vie de Jésus*

(1863), Newman's *Apologia Pro Vita Sua* (1864), Seeley's *Ecce Homo* (1865), Arnold's *Culture and Anarchy* (1869), and Darwin's *Descent of Man* (1871). Each of these works challenged the widely assumed hegemony of Anglican values and orthodoxies in a broad range of public discourses and unsettled the controlling power of "clerical culture," as Frank Turner calls it (1993, 43), in Victorian society. *Essays and Reviews* challenged that cultural dominance intellectually just as the abolition of the Test Acts (1828) did so politically, and the many efforts to disestablish the Church of England did so institutionally. One of the greatest impediments in understanding the profound impact of *Essays and Reviews* on the institutional and intellectual life of the second half of the nineteenth century is that so much of what was contested fiercely in the decade following its publication is now widely accepted in the conventions of literary, historical, and biblical studies. By the end of the century its arguments had already become accepted, and its political and theological distinctions naturalized. Even the Essayists had risen into the respected ranks of the Victorian sages, as masters of Oxford Colleges (Jowett and Pattison), or the religious orthodoxy of the archbishop of Canterbury (Temple).

The Essayists belonged to the Broad Church party of Anglicanism, a loose affiliation of liberals who wanted changes in doctrine and reform in institutions based on the advances in new fields of knowledge, including modern biblical hermeneutics. Their volume is often seen as the culminating statement of that party's position (see, for instance, Crowther 1970, 30; Waddams 1992, 310–11; and Altholz 1994, 1, 3–8). In significant ways these Broad Church liberals opposed both the High and Low Church parties. The High Church party in the Church of England stressed the historic institution of the church, its hierarchy and sacraments, and was bound to the Tories. It was transformed, somewhat uncomfortably, by the Tractarian movement after 1833, led by J. H. Newman, John Keble, and E. B. Pusey. Its main theological interest was the restoration of the worship, ritual, devotional practice, and doctrine of historic Christianity (advocated in the ninety *Tracts for the Times* published between 1833 and 1841 which gave a name to the movement) under the influence of the Church Fathers and seventeenth-century Anglican divines whom the Tractarians published (see Church 1891 and Geoffrey Faber 1954). The Low Church party, or Evangelicals, placed a stress on personal religion, the state of an individual's soul, and the relation of the individual to the atoning death of Christ. The Low Church party was in 1860 the stronger party in terms of numbers of clergy and weight on the episcopal bench. Such views were shared by some Nonconformists outside the Church of England, especially the Methodists, who, under the earlier leadership of John and Charles Wesley, emphasized religious conversion, repentance, turning from sin, and ensuing righteousness of life. Another group was historically derived from Calvinism and included the Presbyterian and Free Church tradition in Scotland and various Baptist and Reformed Calvinist churches in England and as well exercised an influence on some members of the Low Church party. They placed emphasis on election, predestination, and the sufficiency of the Bible as the rule of faith and life.

The smaller Roman Catholic Church was in the process of re-establishing its hierarchy in a hostile antipopery climate.

All of these groups were united in holding that the Bible was and contained the word of God, that its inspiration was both plenary (extending uniformly throughout the whole Bible) and verbal (applying to every word in its original tongues), and that biblical criticism was, if not the work of the devil, at least of his associates, namely, those who sought to use the inappropriate methods of historical, literary, and scientific study to undermine the truth of the sacred book and the religious life of individuals and the nation.

Before the publication of *Essays and Reviews*, liberal theology had been attacked by charges against individual writers and their works, including four of the Essayists, Powell, Williams, Wilson, and Jowett. With the publication of the volume, however, the small Broad Church movement gained a manifesto: the Essayists were branded as radicals, or worse, as heretics, by both High and Low Church parties whose united opposition against a common foe overcame their theological and political differences. Many factors magnified the threat posed by liberal theology: most significant was the presence of the requirement of a nominal adherence to the Church of England for attendance at Oxford or Cambridge and the omnipresence of at least a formal acknowledgment of the Bible as the literal and inspired word of God. To question the link between education and the Church of England was to challenge the terms of the Elizabethan settlement of church and state. To question the literal interpretation of the Bible was to reject the grounds on which the Establishment was founded, namely, the Anglican Formularies. In their challenging of dominant methods of biblical interpretation, the Essayists were accused of shaking the very foundations of society.

With the increase of literacy, the advent of the steam press, and the reduction of the paper tax, Bibles became cheaper and more widely read. But the reading of that text led precipitately into a literary and theological minefield. One problem was the shifting line between popular and scholarly study of the Bible, between teaching and preaching as pastoral functions for the cure of souls, and academic research on the Bible and religious history. What might pass in the study was often stopped in the pulpit. The Sunday sermon taught practical interpretation and application of the Bible; each scholarly work was in competition with hundreds of others for purchase by the thousands of curates who needed help with just that process of interpretation when the clamor of controversy was gaining strength in the wake of the Oxford Movement and the advent of Broad Church theology. The country parson's sermons on obscure texts might be delivered without fear of question or controversy. But J. H. Newman's sermons at St. Mary's in Oxford were heard with attention by adoring undergraduates and anxious tutors as Heads of Colleges tried to spot creeping Puseyism. One of the charges frequently brought against *Essays and Reviews* was that it too was dangerous in bringing critical methods of reading the Bible to the common man, for without proper supervision such methods would undermine not only personal religious belief but the entire social fabric. It is ironical that while the Essayists were indeed attempting to popularize German biblical criticism, contemporary developments in science, and new methods of historical investigation, their formulation of these new developments alienated them from many potential readers by their references in French, German, Greek, Latin, and Hebrew, their scholarly annotations, and their attempts to situate their challenges to orthodoxy on the cutting edge of seven diverse fields of knowledge.

Uniting the concerns of all seven Essayists were new developments in biblical hermeneutics, in general the practice and theory of interpretation, more narrowly only the latter, paying particular attention to the conditions in which biblical interpretation is possible and accurate. Exegesis, the practical "reading out" of meaning from the text in a process of interpretation, depends upon the recovery, establishment, and reliability of the text (lower criticism) and upon the literary analysis of its genres, forms, and sources (higher criticism). Hermeneutics places exegesis within the larger context of theories of interpretation generally, in relating it to textual, linguistic, historical, and cultural studies, and provides the principles and methods whereby the interpretation may proceed. A conventional notion of nineteenth-century biblical hermeneutics as actually practiced in everyday commentary, sermon preparation, and catechizing was that the Bible was the inspired word of God. Hence, the acceptance of its literal truth in detail as well as in doctrine involved a number of corollaries. The history of interpretation placed the Bible in the general context of religious history and made it an object of discussion and contention around which various sectarian pronouncements erected standards of orthodoxy.

These standards sanctioned three methods of interpretation that dominated nineteenth-century hermeneutics: a reading of the Bible that was at the same time literal and mystical (and yielded allegorical, typological, and prophetic or predictive interpretations); a moral interpretation whereby the Bible is prescriptive of individual and social conduct as both regulatory code and ideal pattern; and an interpretation based on doctrinal assumptions or to derive doctrinal positions.[1] Behind each of these methods of interpretation are two assumptions. First, it was held that all parts of the Bible are in harmony (because of divine inspiration), reconciling all differences of chronology, allusion, or contradiction, and hence allowing any part of the Bible to be used to interpret any other part. Second, it was held that all parts of the Bible may be accommodated to the conditions of historic and contemporary life, and their application to current events or issues was accepted as an unquestioned convention of homiletic technique and popular religion. In England the basis for these standards included the Thirty-nine Articles of Religion which specified the canonicity of the Bible and determined some matters concerning its interpretation, though with a fairly wide latitude.

Limitations were invoked when three particular boundaries of orthodoxy were crossed: when the concept of inspiration was challenged; when the prophetical or predictive aspect of interpretation was questioned; or when the proof in the Bible for contemporary doctrinal positions was disputed. In each of these instances, matters of party affiliation, interpretive traditions, and political alignments came quickly into play, greatly increasing the stakes for legitimacy and approval or rejection of the supposedly offending interpretation.

It was in this context that the impact of the study of the classics and of the Bible in Germany came with such shattering results. When F. A. Wolf in 1795 rejected the notion of a single author for Homer and suggested that the Homeric epics grew as accretions from archaic poems in the hands (or lyres) of the rhapsodes, and when Barthold Georg Niebuhr declared that the early history of Rome was derived from legendary lays, the stability of classical culture seemed threatened. But the effect was devastating when, at the same time, Johann Gottfried Eichhorn and others read in the Pentateuch the "primitive" and multiform traditions of ancient Israel, brought together under the authority of Moses' name but not authorship, and, somewhat later, D. F. Strauss perceived in the gospels the awe of the early church in creating a body of hagiographic legends around the figure of a sainted hero. By the mid-nineteenth century "German rationalism" was a derogatory reference to all German higher criticism that sought to establish the interpretation of the Bible upon hermeneutical principles that had become normative for the classics (see Kümmel 1972; Knight and Tucker 1985; and Epp and MacRae 1989); indeed, German rationalism was often used in condemning *Essays and Reviews* in the aftermath of its publication.

2 "To Inaugurate a New Era": The Origin and Publication of *Essays and Reviews*

One of the primary purposes of *Essays and Reviews* was to disseminate new ideas from Broad Church scholars at Oxford and Cambridge in a work which would, in John Chapman's phrase in a letter to Pattison of 17 April 1860, "inaugurate a new era" of public discussion of crucial matters concerning church and state (Letter 18). The Essayists set out to capture public interest by bringing forward for reasoned discussion what Williams called "grave issues of biblical criticism and of religious truth" (Letter 32).

Essays and Reviews was anticipated by a number of publications. Wilson had already worked with the London publisher John W. Parker from 1855 to 1858, editing four volumes of essays produced by members and graduates of Oxford University. In the first volume of *Oxford Essays* (1855) the anonymous Advertisement, or preface, very likely by Wilson, set out its purpose in terms similar to the preface to *Essays and Reviews*: "This volume of *Oxford Essays* is not intended to advocate any particular set of opinions, theological, social, or political. Each writer is responsible for his own opinions, and for none but his own; and no attempt has been made to give a general unity of thought to the publication. The tie that unites the different contributors is not that they think alike, but that they belong to the same University. And in accordance with the independent character of the separate contributions, the names of the writers have been affixed in the Table of Contents to the several Essays. It is hoped that the undertaking may meet with sufficient encouragement to warrant its being continued in succeeding years" (*Oxford* 1855, v). The publishing of a volume of essays by a different authors with their names attached was unusual. The publishing convention of the mid-nineteenth century stressed collections of essays by popular single authors, such as Macaulay or Carlyle. In the periodical press only *Macmillan's Magazine* published signed articles in 1860, having begun to do so only in 1859 (Altholz 1977). Contributors to *Oxford Essays* over its four years included four of the Essayists of 1860, three writing on a theme related to their eventual contribution to *Essays and Reviews*: Temple ("National Education" in 1856), Powell ("The Burnett Prizes" in 1857), and Wilson ("Schemes of Christian Comprehension" in 1857); Pattison wrote on "Oxford Studies" in 1855. Other contributors to *Oxford Essays* included several who were invited to contribute to *Essays and Reviews* as well as to a proposed sequel but who did not in the end do so: Max Müller ("Comparative Mythology" in 1856) and Alexander Grant ("Ancient Stoics" in 1858). Other writers included the historians J. A. Froude, Goldwin Smith, and E. A. Freeman and the classicists John Conington and the future prime minister W. E. Gladstone.

Four volumes of *Cambridge Essays* were also published during the same period (1855–58). In the Preface to the first volume, the editor, William George Clark, quoted from the Oxford Advertisement, adding: "Each contributor, by signing his name, becomes answerable for his own work. We are thus spared the affectation of a perfect conformity of views, which does not, and cannot, exist; though the nearest possible approximation to it is most likely to be found among men whose youth has been subject to the same influences, and passed within the same walls" (*Cambridge* 1855, v). The same Preface refers to the expected readership, "the general public of educated men" (v). Among the Cambridge essayists were Fitzjames Stephen ("The Relations of Novels to Life" in 1855 and "The Characteristics of English Criminal Law" in 1857), who defended Williams and Wilson in the Court of Arches; and F. J. A. Hort ("Coleridge" in 1856), who declined an invitation to contribute to *Essays and Reviews*. In the fourth volume of 1858, Goodwin published on Egyptian "Hieratic Papyri," making him the fifth of the Essayists and Reviewers to have contributed to the Oxford and Cambridge volumes.

While many recent historians have traced the origin of *Essays and Reviews* directly to these volumes (see, for instance, Altholz 1994, 9–14), a quite different story is told by Williams: "It is an entire fiction and delusion to suppose that they were in any way connected with the Oxford and Cambridge Essays. It only so happened that Wilson wrote in that series and in this volume. Still more, it is utterly untrue that any of our Essays were written for that series. The two things were as independent and as utterly unconnected as the *Quarterly* and *Edinburgh* are, or as Freeman's *Norman Conquest* is with the *Guardian* or the *Fortnightly*" (see Letter 346). On the other hand, Temple's recollection strongly supports the connection of *Essays and Reviews* to the *Oxford Essays* as a model: "The *Oxford Essays* had suggested the publication. And these new essays were supposed to be, and as regards composition actually were, as independent of each other as the different papers in the *Oxford Essays*" (see Letter 262).

Whatever the actual influence, opponents of the volume asserted that the format of the Oxford and Cambridge volumes, as well as the liberal positions they advocated, served as models for *Essays and Reviews.* This attack was made by the *Christian Remembrancer* (Oct. 1860), in the opening paragraph of its fifty-eight-page review. If the connection with the other sets of essays was a link reviewers thought it worthwhile to note, the supposed "lack of unity of purpose and connection" among the essays was to be seriously challenged in the same month in the opening pages of Harrison's review in the *Westminster.* He declared it to be a "joint production" with a "virtual unity in the purpose," with each writer "morally responsible for the tendency of the whole" (1860, 293)—with such disastrous results from the ensuing legal prosecutions on to the appointment of Temple as bishop in 1869, when the same accusations were raised (John Percival Fitzgerald 1870, 10–11). On the other hand, Temple claimed he "did not know [the editor] till he wrote to ask me for my paper. There was neither plan nor organisation" (Letter 262).

The preparations for the volume can be traced to Williams's assertion that Wilson "first projected a Theological Review, to be of the Liberal, but chiefly literary, type. He got promises of help from Jowett and myself. . . . finding we should not be commercially strong enough for the staff of a Review, we agreed on a volume. Jowett got Temple to join, I got Charles Goodwin" (Letter 346). Such an assertion is substantiated in Wilson's letter to Pattison of 27 January 1858, the year of the last of the *Oxford* and *Cambridge Essays,* in which he invited Pattison to join in the discussions that he and Williams had already had about establishing a quarterly journal of their own: "I am now more and more convinced that if theological and kindred subjects are to receive a fair treatment and yet be approached, as you say, in a reverent spirit it must be done by an organ in the hands of those who have been 'hewn out of our own pit' [Isa. 51:1]. . . . It would not do—as it seems to me—for a new periodical intended to carry weight with laity as well as clergy—to be over balanced with theology. General topics must be treated ably" (Letter 2).

When preparing his *Hints to My Counsel* in 1861, Williams explains: "The Defendant takes this opportunity of explaining his 'scope, object, and design' in writing his own Essay, and in endeavoring to get similar Essays written. He wishes to see bridged that chasm between the learned and the unlearned, which in England is so wide as to prejudice Christian ingenuousness. He feels ashamed that the world should often go before the Church, not only in intelligence, but in good works of freedom and humanity." Williams touches upon "reconciling the old conflict between Science and Faith," which he thinks "impossible, so long as men oppose Faith to Reason," and describes the Essayists' goal as fostering new thinking about inspiration, prophecy, and the historical sense of the Bible (Ellen Williams 1874,

2:25–26). Williams continued to contribute to the theological formation of the ideas for the project, whether journal or volume, but from January 1858 Wilson and Pattison assumed the organization of the project, with Williams taking part by letter, but unable to meet with the others because of his teaching duties at Lampeter College in Wales.

Two months later, in March 1858, Wilson reported again to Pattison: "J. W. Parker might perhaps be disposed to merge the Oxford & Cam[bridge]. Essays in a new Theological organ. . . . Dr. Rowland Williams w[d] be very happy to cooperate with the design in that shape or indeed in any shape that we may fix upon. . . . I did not consult Williams & Temple any further. They would, however, be very ready to *publish* a liberal theological organ in any shape we might determine upon. A new Quarterly is probably beyond our means—both commercially and otherwise—There could not be much risk in an annual Volume of Essays with Appendix" (Letter 3). By this point Wilson assumed Pattison had consulted with and conscripted some of his friends in Oxford, and Temple was also committed. On 7 April the prospective publisher advised caution: "Of course the establishment of a new Quarterly would be a very difficult and serious matter & we should not be inclined to go into the question unless we saw our way to success. At present I do not see that there are the elements of success before us" (Letter 5).

Toward the end of the summer of 1858, the concept of a journal had been abandoned in favor of a single volume. By then the contributors were lined up and were being cajoled to write. The exchange of letters among the contributors and their friends alludes to a series of deferrals extended and deadlines broken. Jowett had already been conscripted and wrote on 15 August 1858 to ask A. P. Stanley to join the enterprise. Although Stanley refused (Letter 7), the plan went forward, conscripting Alexander Grant and Max Müller. Others who were solicited but refused included F. J. A. Hort, William Thomson, and G. D. Boyle (Ellis 1980, 51).

When at least five of the Essayists had their papers more or less ready (Williams completed his paper in the Christmas vacation of 1858; see Letter 124), Pattison and Jowett remained recalcitrant. Powell, the last writer to be enlisted, submitted his essay on 10 February 1859 to Wilson, but added to it some contemporary references after November 1859, very likely to the proofs in January 1860 (Corsi 1988, 216–17). Parker thought that he was on sufficiently secure ground to advertise the volume in February 1859 (Altholz 1977, 144; 1994, 14), but the first mention of the title occurs in Wilson's letter to Pattison of 4 July 1859: "The projected Volume of Essays & Reviews now holds for October" (Letter 8). Parker, however, was premature with his advertisement since some Essayists who had been solicited for contributions were still abandoning the project. By 3 October 1859 Wilson wrote Pattison that their numbers were reduced to the final seven as he coaxed and importuned the tardy to produce (Letter 10). Wilson became even more anxious by the early summer of 1859, when it seemed as though Parker would go ahead only with the essays he had in hand. Wilson informed Pattison on 4 July 1859 that the title was then fixed and that he desperately needed his essay, a request repeated with increasing urgency to both Pattison and Jowett. Wilson implied that the rest of the volume was close to ready (Letter 8). Further letters entreat Pattison on 27 September to inform Wilson even "what his subject might be" (Letter 9), and again on 3 October 1859 he wrote under a threat of further postponements: "The delay in your Essay will surely affect the whole Volume as to itself but carries a risk that some other contributor may delay the final revision of his own or take offence or drop off from some other accident" (Letter 10).

In his essay Powell makes reference to contemporary publications, to the review by Whately and others of his *Order of Nature* in the October 1859 number of the *Quarterly Review*, and to Darwin's *On the Origin of Species* that was not published until 24 November 1859 (see Powell ¶s 116–17 and 126 and notes). On 21 November, Wilson continued "gently to apply the whip," informing Pattison that he wanted an article of at least forty pages; Pattison eventually supplied seventy-six. On 13 January 1860 Pattison sent Parker the first sixty manuscript pages, completing the article and sending the rest on 17 January (Bodley MS. Pattison 130). By that time Parker's compositors had already begun to set the text in type. But his was not the last essay submitted.

Jowett had been delayed by preparing the second edition of *The Epistles of St. Paul*, published early in 1859. One of the pieces left over was "The Interpretation of Scripture" that he was possibly intending for a book on the Gospel of John (Geoffrey Faber 1957, 232–33). He had responded positively to Wilson and Pattison's proposals in March 1858 about the volume, had solicited Stanley in midsummer, but had been unable to work on his essay until the winter vacation of 1859 when he visited the Tennysons on the Isle of Wight. By 2 March 1860 it still had not been submitted, but must have been completed within the next two weeks (Bodley, MS. Pattison 130). The publisher continued to postpone the date of publication to accommodate these late contributors. In the *Athenaeum* it was announced on 10 March as appearing "next week," even though it was not finally published until Wednesday, 21 March 1860, when Parker's advertisement in the *Guardian,* listing the titles of the essays and their authors, announced it as appearing "this day."

Thirteen editions were published in England by 1869, as well as an authorized edition for the Continent published by Bernhard Tauchnitz (1862), giving its authors and publishers a handsome profit and making the book a notable best-seller. In North America five pirated editions were published in Boston and New York, the final American edition appearing in 1874, the last issued in the nineteenth century.

The first edition was published as a demy 8⁰ volume in a run of 1,000 copies, selling for the relatively expensive price of ten shillings and sixpence. The volume consists of eight pages of preliminaries: the title page and publishing information; a preface entitled "To the Reader"; the table of contents listing the title of each of essays, followed by the names of the authors, their degrees, and institutional affiliation. Two of the contributors have no institutional affiliation listed, Goodwin, a lawyer, Egyptologist, and journal editor, then hoping for a colonial appointment, and Pattison, then a tutor at Lincoln College, Oxford. The essays follow on 433 pages. The final page, unnumbered, contains the "'Note on Bunsen's Biblical Researches," an additional note to Williams's essay, very likely received at the last minute after the early essays were set in type, when there was no space to insert it after the essay. Six pages of publisher's advertisements complete the final gathering, printed on the same demy sheets as the preliminaries. The whole volume is set in a 12-point modern face, identical to Miller and Richards Pica New, No. 4. (see *Miller & Richards* 1873).[2]

The publisher of the first three British editions was John William Parker. Having risen through the London publishing firm of William Clowes to become its manager, Parker was appointed printer for the Society for Promoting Christian Knowledge (1832) and for the Cambridge University Press (1836–54), actively promoting the printing of cheap Bibles and thereby provoking the hostility of the Bible Society (see Howsam 1991). His advocacy of free trade and cheap prices in books (1852) gained the support of many Victorian authors, including Carlyle, Dickens, Kingsley, Lewes, Mill, and Tennyson, many of whom were persuaded to publish with him (see James J. Barnes 1964). In 1843 his eldest son, John William Parker Jr., and very likely another son, Frederick Parker, joined the renamed establishment, John W. Parker and Sons. Under the managership of John William Parker Jr. the firm became "a major bastion within the London printing establishment of liberal Christianity and eventually of Christian socialism" (Dean 1991, 234). As manager Parker also took over the editorship of *Fraser's Magazine* (from 1847), recruiting Carlyle, Clough, George Eliot, Froude, and others to write for it (*Wellesley Index* 2:310). He oversaw the publishing of both *Oxford Essays* and *Cambridge Essays* (1855–58) and his booklists included Buckle, Froude, J. S. Mill, and other writers associated with the *Westminster Review* and liberal movements in the church and politics. It was with William Parker Jr. that H. B. Wilson, having already worked with him on *Oxford Essays*, negotiated the publication of the first edition of *Essays and Reviews* (see Letters 3–5).

By late May brisk sales and increasing notoriety indicated the need for a second edition. The hostility of the religious press, both Anglican and Nonconformist, ensured a steady demand, and Parker even advertised the new edition on 30 May in the *Guardian*, a week after the paper had severely criticized the book. On 6 June the *Guardian* advertised the second edition as published "this day" (512). Williams entered the comment in his journal on 2 June that the "second [edition] is now in press," and on 11 June Wilson wrote Pattison that it was out (Letter 23). From this edition through the twelfth edition (and the thirteenth, still numbered the twelfth) the number of each edition is stated on the title page under the woodblock ornament (up to the third edition) and under the typographical ornament in subsequent editions. Other changes are introduced on the title page (changing "The authors reserve" to "The author reserves" the "right of Translation"); further changes are introduced on the contents page, in that the "&c. &c" printed after

Powell's degrees and his membership in the Royal Society ("F.R.S.") are omitted with other changes in spacing. It was on the day Wilson wrote to Pattison (11 June) that Powell died, though that fact ("Late Savilian Professor of Geometry") is not recorded on the contents page until the twelfth edition in 1865. However, there was time to incorporate Powell's own revisions into the second edition which was reset from a copy of the first edition. Because the second edition and all subsequent English editions were printed either from newly composed type or from standing type, as we discuss below, there was ample opportunity for similar changes to be introduced into all printings after the first, as we set out in the Textual Notes and Publisher's Records.[3] No notice of any such changes is made in the volume, however, until the smaller format of the tenth edition, and the marking of the passages cited in the Arches trials and appeals in the twelfth edition.

By mid-July 1860 Wilson was so encouraged with interest and sales that he was actively planning a second volume, a project that was pursued sporadically over the next ten years but that never was realized. As he reported to Pattison on 25 July 1860, some 300 copies of the second edition had been sold, and he conjectured that if the *Times* noticed the volume favorably, they would "soon get rid of the second edition" (Letter 25). Even without such a fillip there was sufficient demand, stimulated by reviews in the weeklies and monthlies, for yet another reprinting in the late autumn. At this juncture the publisher's son, John William Parker Jr., died on 9 November 1860. Thereafter his father brought out only one more edition, the third, very likely in December, bearing the date on the title page of 1860.[4] Again typographical changes were introduced in the preliminaries: the number of the edition from second to third and the line at the bottom of the title page concerning the rights of translation were revised. Other minor changes were made: in punctuation (the addition of missing parentheses), spelling ("develop" to "develope"), the addition of a missing page number, and the revision of the numbering of the sections of Jowett's essay to put them into numerical sequence. The publication of Harrison's bombshell review in the *Westminster* in October signaled a shift in the controversy from the religious weeklies to the national secular quarterlies, and while ensuring an even greater sale, this widespread public notice might also have been a factor, together with the changes in the firm with the death of his son, to induce the sixty-nine-year-old Parker to sell the rights to *Essays and Reviews* to Longman.

The publishing house of Longman had a long and distinguished history. Established in 1724, it had published Johnson's *Dictionary* (1755), and the works of Coleridge, Scott, Southey, and Wordsworth. In 1836 it took on the *Edinburgh Review,* and published Disraeli and Macaulay, both best-selling authors. In 1860 Longman took over some of the titles of J. W. Parker and the rest of their publications in 1863, including *Fraser's Magazine* and the works of Froude and Mill. Longman had a highly respectable reputation, specializing in popular and scholarly studies in history, literature, religion, and philosophy (see Cox and Chandler 1925 and Briggs 1974).

The preservation of the Longman archives enables the publishing history from the fourth edition on to be chronicled in some detail. From early January 1861, Longman had the rights to *Essays and Reviews*, and entered into a new contract with Wilson and the other contributors, to publish the fourth and all subsequent English editions during copyright. Wilson corresponded with one of the new publishers, William Longman, drawing up a new contract:

> This Agreement, made this *Twelfth* day of *January 1861*, between *The Revd Henry Bristow Wilson, of the Vicarage, Great Staughton, St. Neots for himself and the other contributors* on the One Part, and Messrs. LONGMAN, GREEN, LONGMAN, and ROBERTS, of Paternoster Row, London, on the Other Part.
>
> It is Agreed that the said Messrs. LONGMAN and Co. shall publish at their own expense and risk *the fourth edition of a volume of Essays & Reviews by the said Revd Henry Bristow Wilson, and other Contributors*—and after deducting from the produce of the Sale thereof all the Expenses of Printing, Paper, Advertising, and other incidental expenses, the Profits remaining of every Edition that may be printed of the Work, during the legal term of Copyright, are to be divided into ~~two equal~~ *three*/ Parts, ~~one Moiety~~ *Two-Thirds*/ to be paid to the said *Revd Henry Bristow Wilson and the other contributors* and the other ~~Moiety~~ *one-third*/ to belong to the Messrs. LONGMAN and Co.
>
> ~~Corrections above per sheet to be charged to the Author, and deducted from his share of the Profits~~
>
> The Books to be accounted for at the Trade-Sale Price, twenty-five as twenty-four, unless it be thought advisable to dispose of Copies, or of the Remainder, at a lower price, which is left to the judgment and discretion of Messrs. LONGMAN and Co. Accounts to be made up annually at Midsummer, and delivered on or before October 1, and settled by Bill at Two Months, dated October 1.
>
> *It is also agreed that the Contributors to the said volume of Essays and Reviews or any of them reserve to himself or themselves the right of re-publishing hereafter their or his Essay or Essays in any volume or volumes consisting wholly of the works of such contributor, but not otherwise, nor in any separate form.*
>
> [signed]
> *Longman & Co*
> *H. B. Wilson*[5]

The fourth edition, the first under the terms of this new contract, was advertised by Longman in the *Athenaeum* as ready "*in a few days*" (26 Jan. 1861:109), and the reset edition was published on 29 January 1861 in a run of 1,000 copies (Longman Archive 34). The day before Wilson had written to Pattison that Longman informed him "there are a great many enquiries for it" (Letter 36). On the title page Parker's printer's device is replaced with a pair of typographical ornaments above and below "*THE FOURTH EDITION.*" The name of the new publisher, Longman, Green, Longman, and Roberts, replaces the name of Parker's firm. The pasted-down endpapers contain advertisements for Longman's publications, for James Whiteside's *Italy in the Nineteenth Century* at the front end, and at the back, Agnes Strickland's *Lives of the Queens of England*, and Mary Anne Everett Green's *Lives of the Princesses of England*. The binding cloth is changed from blue to dark violet. The collation is identical to the first edition, but again the position of the signatures is different from each of the earlier editions. Longman's publisher's catalogue of three leaves (6 pages) is added to complete the gathering FF. In addition, a further Longman's catalogue of twenty-four numbered pages, dated October 1860, is bound in. Some accidentals conforming to house style are introduced in this edition, such as the capitalization of "Church" when it is used as a noun, but not as an adjective (though without consistency); changes in spelling (such as "contemporaries" for the earlier "cotemporaries," "primeval" for "primæval," though not for all occurrences, and "medieval" for "mediæval" throughout, except in cited book titles, "Sydney Smith" for "Sidney Smith," "panic" for "pannic"); and the changing of numbering conventions in Jowett's essay. A number of substantive changes were also introduced. In Wilson's essay, for instance, "future recompense" is changed to "future reward" (¶ 23); "nor, if it be" is changed to "much less, if it be" (¶ 35); "applied to the canonical books" is changed to "applied collectively to the canonical books" (¶ 37); as well as a rewriting of a sentence of Jowett's (¶ 59) (see Textual Notes).

The fifth edition of 2,000 copies was published on 19 February 1861, and sales continued to rise dramatically, bolstered by Wilberforce's strongly adversarial review in the *Quarterly* of January, and the Episcopal Manifesto published in the *Times* on 16 February. Like the fourth edition, the text was again set by the compositors, following a copy of the fourth edition, and, as usual, with different locations for the signatures. But some further changes were also introduced. In the table of contents Pattison's election in January 1861 as Rector of Lincoln College is indicated; a correction is made to a biblical reference in Goodwin's essay, and in Jowett's essay there is a change of asterisked to numbered footnotes; there are also a number of minor corrections in spelling and punctuation. At the end of the run, the publishers anticipated a continuing demand and did not distribute the type but left it standing in formes. According to Ellen Williams, "The fifth edition of two thousand was all sold in a fortnight; Mudie [Lending Library] taking, it was said, seven hundred copies. It became difficult for the publishers to supply quickly enough the demand, and all other work had for the time to be set aside" (1874, 2:35–36).

The next four editions, the sixth through the ninth, were printed in less than a month, in runs of 3,000 copies each. The sixth was published on 8 March 1861, and after a run of 3,000 the title page was reset to read "*THE SEVENTH EDITION*" and a further 3,000 were run off, with the same date listed in Longman's chronological registers. The impression register accords with that information, since no cost was incurred for reading, correcting, or lifting the formes. The eighth edition is dated

22 March and the ninth, 5 April. Each of these editions was printed from the same standing type as used in the fifth edition. But again, certain costs were involved: for the sixth those costs involved proofreading, correcting, and ensuring that the required modifications were successfully completed. Among such modifications were the changing of a book title in a footnote in Wilson's essay. Extra time was needed from the workers, since the publisher had to pay for nightwork to complete the edition, as also was required for the seventh and eighth editions. No cost was incurred for rereading or correcting the seventh, eighth, or ninth editions since each was printed from the same type and formes. The movement of *Essays and Reviews* into best-seller status was impressive, with 15,000 copies issued by Longman in the first four months of 1861, but even so, as Wilson commented to Pattison, the number of copies issued was "rather exaggerated in some papers," so he had to give him the exact publication record on which his royalties would be based (Letter 103). But sales dropped after April, according to Wilson, because of Stanley's "unfortunate article" in the April *Edinburgh* (Letter 136).

The tenth edition was published in a smaller and cheaper format, in foolscap 8^0, selling for five shillings, less than half the price of the earlier editions. As Wilson wrote to Pattison on 18 November 1861, the proposal came from Longman: "They incline to think that the book should now appear in a more portable form at a price of 5/—which is a matter chiefly for the publisher's consideration" (Letter 142). While various alterations had occurred in the text in earlier printings, the prospect of an entire resetting in a different format presented the possibility of more extensive emendations or revisions, as Wilson wrote to Pattison on 18 November 1861: "But there is another subject of importance for the authors—in which will you be so good as to give me your express opinion—that is whether any alterations or additions should be admitted in the Volume in a further edition. Of course if any author is allowed to make alterations or explanations surely all must have the same liberty—and it would be difficult to set any bounds to it. And under present circumstances perhaps every essayist might [wish?] to have the new matter in every other's Essay submitted to him—and have a veto upon it. I confess it seems to me that we should never get through such a process—& it could be at variance with our original principle of limited liability. Of course I write to the other contributors for their opinion on this point" (Letter 142). By the end of the week, Wilson had heard from Temple who was adamant in resisting changes: "Temple protests actively against any alteration whatsoever—you see the difficulty in this—Longman can under the usual business agreement go on publishing the work as it now stands during the legal term of Copyright. But if any alteration were made in which every one of us did not fully concur it might throw us all into confusion. The only way I see to avoid this is to make none, however we might otherwise like it. I think if alterations, even verbal ones, are to be allowed—each man's Essay would have to be submitted for his sanction *to every other man*—and I do not think even that would meet Temple's strong objection to it. He considers the book as a starting point with which we must now be content and would rather have it broken up than alterations allowed—that however could not come under the bookseller's agreement. Talk it over with Jowett" (Letter 143). Although few alterations were introduced, Wilson himself took advantage of the resetting, and introduced a number of changes in his own essay in the gatherings O and P, for which extra costs were incurred for proofing and correcting.

The tenth edition was published in three issues, in January 1862, on 13 March, and on 6 May, each in a run of 1,000 copies.[6] Other composing was required in the second issue for Wilson's four sheets, and extra was also required for setting Greek. Each issue of this new edition was set up for printing on the same smaller foolscap paper, with smaller margins, and with small pica modern-style typeface.[7] As with the previous full-sized editions, the type was largely kept standing and stored between runs so that after the first issue only limited costs were incurred for composition.

The eleventh edition of 500 copies was published almost a year later, in March 1863.[8] Wilson wrote on 5 December 1862 to Pattison that the last issue of the tenth edition was selling slowly (Letter 164). This edition followed after Lushington's final judgment in the Court of Arches (15 December 1862), with its stipulation that Williams and Wilson not promulgate "any erroneous strange or heretical doctrines in any way contrary or repugnant to the doctrine and teaching of the Church of England." Since they had appealed to the Privy Council, the sentence was not acted upon. The eleventh edition also followed the suit in the Chancellor's Court in Oxford against Jowett (beginning on 13 February 1863).

The twelfth edition was published on 28 February 1865 in an edition of 1,000 copies, for the first time indicating typographically the passages that had been cited in the Court of Arches and appealed in the Judicial Committee in June 1863. This innovation was explained to readers in the new Preface to the Twelfth Edition. Both of these sets of materials have been incorporated into our edition, as set out in our Editorial Procedures. The profits were now to be divided equally between the authors and the publisher.

The thirteenth edition was published on 16 November 1869, five weeks after Temple was informed that he was to be bishop of Exeter, and when the controversy about his appointment had aroused all of the old animosity about his essay published nine years earlier. Shortly after his nomination Wilson had foreseen the possibility of yet another public demand for copies, so that on 1 November 1869 he wrote to Longman: "I have sent to all the Contributors . . . and as yet have received only one answer from Mr Pattison—who says 'Further reading has made me so dissatisfied with my Essay on the 18th century that I shall not be willing to republish.' . . . I do not anticipate any objections from any other quarter than Mr. Pattison—and I consider that can stand for nothing. I apprehend our position to be this—that we are bound to the public and to the publishers to reproduce the book as long as it is demanded and without alteration. Only it was right under the circumstances to consult Dr. Temple before issuing another edition at the present moment" (Letter 314). Having learned of the dangers of canvassing the Essayists about introducing revisions into the tenth edition, Wilson only raised the issue of a new edition. Both Pattison and Williams were against republication: the former was not happy with his essay, and the latter thought the book should be broken up into the separate essays, but not reprinted as a whole.

In the same letter Wilson added his printing instructions in a postscript. This new edition should continue to include the passages cited in the trial and the appeal marked in single and double quotation marks, or "inverted commas": "The next edition should be printed from the last with the inverted commas &c. I have a copy with me here and will read the sheets if you will send them to me—I suppose you have considered whether an edition of the larger size could be printed with safety" (Letter 314). The next day Wilson telegraphed Longman to proceed with the printing, having secured the approval of Temple in a letter he received that morning. But Longman was told not to call it a new edition, thereby suggesting to booksellers and buyers that the supply came from continuing stock that the publisher still had on hand from four years earlier, in which only the title page had been redated.[9] This suggestion came from Temple himself in his letter to Wilson, who sent it on to Longman on 2 November 1869: "What I should wish about Essays & Reviews is this. At present to take no marked step either way—it would be a marked step one way to stop the publication; another way to print a new Edition. Would it be possible to print some more to meet the demand without calling it a new Edition? . . . After the present excitement is over I think it would be best to print no more and let the book die out" (Letter 316).

This proposal was particularly ironic given the demands from hostile critics that Temple as bishop-elect should repudiate his role in the volume, and in particular that he should give an undertaking that his essay would not be republished. After his consecration as bishop Temple was forced into a public promise in Convocation that he would not republish it, knowing full well, of course, that it had been successfully republished according to his plan. Wilson followed his telegram to Longman with a letter. To make the plan work, it was essential that the new edition not be advertised by Longman as a new printing or edition, instructions that Wilson first delivered along with a copy of Temple's letter on 2 November and repeated on 4 and 12 November: "Advertise exactly as you would have done if there had been no break in the supply of copies—and without *now ready—this day* or the like. If the public want the book they will soon find out that it is to be had—but the understanding is that *we* do not draw special attention to it apropos of present circumstances" (Letter 322). The act of deception was therefore a collaborative effort, committed at the suggestion of Temple, planned by Wilson, and carried out by Longman in what was indeed a new edition. Wilson proposed a run of 1,000, but in fact it was twice that. Wilson read the proofs only for the prelims (Letter 314). Its publication date was five days after the hotly contested election of Temple by the Exeter cathedral chapter, the action that confirmed that the rest of the process for his consecration as bishop would take place. In the publisher's Impression Book the edition is not listed as the thirteenth, though in all other respects it is treated like any other edition, set in type afresh from a copy of the twelfth edition. Advertisements for the volume were also handled discretely, as Wilson had asked of Longman. In the *Guardian*, so active in earlier attacks on *Essays and Reviews* but now more moderate in the Exeter controversy, the back page of the issue of 24 November 1869 (1251) consists of Longman's advertisement, most of it in large-type promotions of current books. Tucked into a side column amongst miscellaneous books is a small-type notice for *Essays and Reviews*, "the twelfth edition." The stock from the thirteenth edition continued in the warehouse until the last copies were sold, the 12 remaining in June 1873 being sold by June 1874, when the midsummer accounting and payment to authors was undertaken according to the terms of the contract of 1861, the last copies of the total run in England of 24,250.

This subterfuge gave rise to the ghosts of the fourteenth and fifteenth editions. Ellen Williams also reports on French and Gujarati editions that also appear to be ghosts: "A French Protestant translated the book into French, and a learned Parsee was sent over from Bombay to translate it into his own language" (1874, 2:36). The *Athenaeum* reported the same story: "We are informed that the 'Essays and Reviews' are now in process of translation into Gujerattee by a Parsee gentleman at present in London, who takes interest in the subject discussed by the seven authors, and intends publishing his translation for the use of inquiring minds among his countrymen in India" (7 Sept. 1861, 321). It appears doubtful, however, that either of these efforts reached publication. The "French Protestant" translation probably refers to a volume that was advertised by Walker, Wise, and Company, the Boston publishers of the American edition of *Essays and Reviews*. Their advertising copy reads: "*French* 'Essays and Reviews' / *The Progress of Religious Thought as Illustrated / in the Protestant Church of France; / Being Essays and Reviews, Bearing on the Chief Religious Questions of the Day*. Translated from the French; with an Introductory Essay on the 'Oxford Essays and Reviews,' by the Editor, John R. Beard, D. D." This volume was jointly advertised with their publication of *Recent Inquiries in Theology* (that is, *Essays and Reviews*) in such publications as *Tracts for Priests and People* (1862).

It was also alleged that a separate "library [was] got up for the circulation" of *Essays and Reviews* from which individual essays "were let out separately at twopence a day" (Ellen Williams 1874, 2:36). In the proceedings in the Court of Arches it was also alleged by the prosecution that separated essays, or perhaps even separately printed essays, were being sold in Leeds for a penny each, to which Dr. Deane reported for Williams and Wilson that detectives hired to investigate these allegations found no evidence for them (see "Trials and Appeals").

On 26 April 1862 Longman sold to Bernhard Tauchnitz for £20 the right of translation into German, a right that the authors had maintained on the title page from the first edition (see Appendix A, Longman Archives D7). It seems certain, however, that these were the rights for Tauchnitz not to translate it into German but to publish the volume in Leipzig as a "Copyright Edition," as he claims on his title page, as volume 613 in their "Collection of British Authors." It was a 16⁰ volume of 374 pages.

Five pirated American editions were also published. Unlike the Tauchnitz edition for the Continent, nothing was paid to the English publishers or to the authors for the rights of American publication. The first American edition was published in late October or early November, 1860.[10] The 12⁰ volume is retitled *Recent Inquiries in Theology, by Eminent English Churchmen; being "Essays and Reviews"* and was edited with an introduction by the Rev. Frederic H. Hedge (1805–1890), Unitarian clergyman, poet, and translator, who traveled and studied in Germany before completing his theological training at Harvard. Influenced by Kant, Hegel, and Schelling, he introduced German idealism into the United States, assisting in establishing the Transcendental Club in 1836, which included Ralph Waldo Emerson and Margaret Fuller. The edition was published by the "Boston Unitarian firm" (Ellis 1980, 183) of Walker, Wise, and Company and was printed by the Boston printer John Wilson and Son, selling for $1.25. It consisted of the Preface entitled "To the Reader" and table of contents as in the English editions, followed by an introduction to the American Edition by Hedge. Thereafter the text is printed on pages 1–480. The "Note on Bunsen's Biblical Researches" is moved in the American editions to follow Williams's essay (on page 105). The edition claims to be reprinted from the "Second London Edition," but none of Powell's corrections made in the second English edition of June 1860 (except for one punctuation change, very likely made independently) has been incorporated. For each instance the reading in the American first edition follows the English first. However, the American editions introduced a large number of variants, largely changes in accidentals, typographical conventions, and printing-house practice, such as changes in capitalization to ensure greater conformity from essay to essay; the omission and addition of punctuation (on the whole the American edition is more heavily punctuated, sometimes with as many as fifteen to twenty changes per page); the use of double quotation marks for single quotation marks; and the replacing of brackets with parentheses. Typographical and printing-house conventions are very likely responsible for the changing of footnote numbers to symbols and the typesetting of long quotations as indented passages in reduced type; signature numbers are not letters (as in the English editions), but arabic numbers. As well, the name of the author is included as a byline under the title on the first page of each essay. None of these variants, however, carries any weight in suggesting an emendation to the copytext of the first English edition: none is either authorial or connected to the English publishers in any way that we have determined, except that a copy was used for editorial preparation by Hedge. A selection of representative variants in the Textual Notes indicates both a firmer and more interventionist editorial hand on the part of Hedge in ensuring consistency in spelling, citation practice, and accidentals throughout the volume than Wilson apparently exercised; such variants also display different linguistic and publishing conventions between England and America in the mid-nineteenth century.

The second American edition was published in January 1861, the date of the Publishers' Note." Wilson wrote to Pattison on 28 January 1861 that to meet the demand for *Essays and Reviews* in England, the new owner of the rights, Longman, had just published the fourth edition, but the American edition could not circulate in England (Letter 36). The Publishers' Note also provides information about the volume's circulation in America and about new material added to the edition: "The first edition of 'Recent Inquiries' was absorbed almost immediately after publication. To the present edition is added an *Appendix*, containing a valuable note by the American Editor, and Dr. Temple's admirable Sermon delivered before the University of Oxford, during the meeting of the British Association" (vi). The note is on the Phalaris Controversy, incorporated in the present edition in Pattison ¶47 n. 160. Temple's sermon, *The Present Relations of Science to Religion* (not included in this edition), was preached in the University Church of St. Mary the Virgin on "Act Sunday," 1 July 1860, the day after the Huxley-Wilberforce debate on Darwin's *Origin* at the meeting of the British Association for the Advancement of Science.

A number of changes were introduced between the first and the second American editions. For instance, the Preface "To the Reader" is reset with different line-endings; the Introduction to the American Edition has been reset with thirty-one instead of thirty-three lines to the page. In the dedicatory poem to Bunsen that concludes Williams's essay, the seventh line ends in all copies of the English editions with the word "Tongue" followed by a semicolon; in the first American edition the word is "tongue" with a semicolon; in the second and following American editions the word is "tongues" followed by a comma. Other changes in accidentals, several to a page, mostly increased punctuation, indicate that there were numerous interventions in the text between the first and second American editions, along with additional prefatory material and new appendixes.

The imprint page of the second American edition indicates that the book continued to be published by Walker, Wise, and Company, but a different printer was used, the "University Press, Cambridge: Stereotyped and Printed by Welch, Bigelow, & Co" (the press for Harvard University Press). This firm made the stereotype plates that were used to print the reset second edition and all subsequent American editions through to the fifth. The signature numbers are in identical positions throughout from the second American edition on, and the texts are identical, except for the resetting of the advertising page from the publisher facing the title page and the preliminaries in the fifth edition. The title page in each edition indicates the number of the edition and the date. That is, the second to the fourth American editions are identical from the imprint page and other preliminaries (iv–xiv) through to the last page of the text (498); the fifth edition has reset the preliminaries but otherwise is identical, using the same plates for the text from signature 1 on. The third American edition was published in 1861, the fourth in 1862.

In November 1874 the fifth American edition was published by Henry Holt and Company of New York. A number of changes to the preliminaries were made in this edition. A new title was used: *Essays and Reviews by Eminent English Churchmen*, and the title page indicated that the volume contained "A New Introduction Written Expressly for This Edition by Rev. Frederic Hedge, D.D." The edition was also misnumbered the Third American Edition on the title page, leading to some cataloguing confusion. The Publishers' Note is removed. The introduction is retitled "Introduction to the First American Edition" and a new Preface to the Third American Edition, that is, to the fifth, is added. It is signed by Hedge and is dated 26 October 1874. Hence, all of the preliminaries are reset, including the table of contents page. Nothing, however, was done to the rest of the text, which was printed from the same set of stereoplates used for the second to fourth editions with the same signature numbers and locations.

In 1970 Gregg International published a photoreproduction of the first edition. It consists of the preliminaries and the text of the first edition, except that the publisher's data concerning Gregg International have replaced those of the printers Savill and Edwards on the imprint page. Furthermore, the artist's monogram signature to Parker's woodblock device, and the line concerning the authors' reserving the right of translation, have been removed.

Only two of the seven essays have been reproduced separately and completely. Pattison's essay was republished after his death in *Essays by the Late Mark Pattison* (1889, 2:42–118) by Henry Nettleship, his literary executor. Nettleship handed the editing of Pattison's essay to Stephen, who added only a few bibliographical notes, to which we have made reference in our annotations. Jowett's essay was republished three times in its entirety, first in the third edition (1894) of Jowett's *The Epistles of St. Paul* (2:1–101), prepared by his executor, Lewis Campbell. Campbell also reprinted it in *Scripture and Truth* (1907, 1–114), a collection of "dissertations" mostly derived from the second volume of Jowett's study of St. Paul. It also was reprinted from the fifth edition in *The Interpretation of Scripture and Other Essays*, with a life of Jowett by Leslie Stephen (1906, 1–76). Campbell added topical headings in the 1894 reprinting that we have incorporated into our outline of Jowett's essay. Some extracts from the essays were published both in the nineteenth and twentieth centuries: for example, a short selection from Temple (¶s 7–8) is printed in *Helps to Godly Living*, a collection of his devotional writings (1899, 41–42); five short extracts from Jowett's essay (from ¶s 41–42, 45, 61, and 91–92) are printed in J. F. C. Harrison 1965, 255–58; the third section of Jowett's essay (¶s 39–56) is printed in James Moore 1988, 26–33 and in Drury 1989, 139–51.

The sensation provoked in England by *Essays and Reviews* also promoted its large sales. The circulation numbers are consistent with claiming best-seller status for it: according to the *Spectator* (3 Jan. 1863) it sold over 20,000 copies in its first two years (Supplement, 17; see Altick 1957, 381–90), numbers borne out by the publishers' records. The total run in England from 1860 to the thirteenth edition of 1869 was 24,250 copies. Such numbers compare favorably with popular novelists, for instance with the normal first thirty-thousand run of Dickens's novels. His *Little Dorrit* sold 35,000 in 1855 but had much greater sales over several years. The sales numbers for *Essays and Reviews* greatly exceeded Kingsley's *Westward Ho!*, which sold only 8,000 in the first two years of publication (1855–57). The nine-year publishing success of *Essays and Reviews* may also be compared with the work of another Broad Church writer, Thomas Hughes, whose very popular *Tom Brown's School Days* (1857) sold 28,000 copies in six years. To extend the comparison, using Altick's figures, Samuel Smiles's *Self-Help* (1859) sold 20,000 copies in one year; George Eliot's *The Mill on the Floss* (1860), 6,000 in three months. But all of these, with the exception of *Self-Help*, were novels. A more instructive comparison can be drawn with Darwin's *On the Origin of Species* (1859) that sold 17,000 copies in seventeen years (Himmelfarb 1968, 253).

Such sales meant substantial profits for the publishers as well as each of the Essayists. A total of 2,750 copies of *Essays and Reviews* was printed in the first three editions published by Parker. Wilson's letters to Pattison (Letters 143 and 145) set out the profits for the second and third, making it possible to extrapolate a total of about £37.14.7 per author. According to their Stock and Cost Ledgers, the editions published by Longman (fourth to thirteenth) produced a total profit of about £2,733.3.4 (Longman Archives D7, fol. 1), giving some £390 as the share for each author. Therefore the total profits for the first to thirteenth editions were about £2,998, about £428 per author. The most profitable year by far was 1861, when each author received £304.10.3 (Letter 142). To put these profits in perspective, in a contemporaneous novel, Anthony Trollope's *The Warden* (1855), the impoverished clergyman Mr. Quiverful, rector of Puddingdale, raises twelve children on a total income of £400 annually.

By way of contrast, the total cost for the litigants in the trial in the Court of Arches and the appeal in the Judicial Committee of the Privy Council was substantially higher than any profits realized from the book. Williams and Wilson were condemned to pay jointly for the costs in the Court of Arches trial, but in the appeal to the Judicial Committee that decision was changed, so that each of the parties, the two prosecutors and the two defendants, had to pay his own costs. Williams and Wilson were awarded the costs in the appeal, and so James Fendall and Bishop Hamilton had to pay not only for the appeal but also approximately one-quarter of the costs in the Arches trial. Letters to the papers concerning contributions for Fendall's costs indicate that he had to pay £1,250 in total (*Guardian*, 8 June 1864). Hamilton's costs were £2,308 (Pusey House, Hamilton Papers, Hony to Hamilton, 28 July 1864).

The profits realized from the book had repercussions, being used against the Essayists in subsequent controversies. For instance, Temple was attacked in 1870 for receiving tainted money: "Supposing the copyright of the book *not* to have been sold to the publisher, the profits derivable from the sale of twelve editions must have been of course much larger. But whether large or small, such profits are the 'wages of unrighteousness'; they are JUDAS's 'pieces of silver.' Even the first publisher of the book retreated, as we hear, from the responsibility of printing so many infidel treatises. We wonder that so respected a firm ever agreed to issue it.

Another publisher, apparently indifferent to the poison he may circulate, took their place" (Fitzgerald 1870, 12–13).

Two further volumes of *Essays and Reviews* were projected, neither of which materialized. Just after the second edition was published, Wilson wrote to Pattison on 11 June 1860 that Parker would be willing to undertake a second volume, but by July it had been postponed until the following year (Letter 23). Harrison's review in the *Westminster* in October, followed by several months of agitation culminating in the Episcopal Manifesto in February 1861 and the charges in the ecclesiastical courts in May, put the Essayists in a position more of defense and retreat than continuation and attack.

Eight years later the matter was resumed: in July 1869 the prospect of a second volume was raised again in discussions between Wilson and Jowett. Jowett wrote to Florence Nightingale concerning the proposed list of contributors that included himself, Wilson, Lewis Campbell, and Alexander Grant. Grant decided not to jeopardize his appointment as chair of the Scottish Education Board by joining them (Letter 248). In the Jowett papers a list, very likely drawn up with Wilson, sets out the topics that they considered still needed to be addressed from a Broad Church perspective in a changing theological climate. The first essay, by Stanley, was to be on "The Reformation of the Liturgy." The second essay, unassigned, was to be on the relations of church and state in the multifaith condition of nineteenth-century England, "The Relation of the Church of England to other Churches." Wilson was to take up "The Principle of Protestantism," a topic related to his other writings on continental ecumenical projects. The fourth essay, by Lewis Campbell, was on "The Mistranslations and Misreadings of the New Testament." Edward Caird was to take up a topic that Adolph von Harnack and others had been publishing on in Germany, "The History of Doctrine, Protestant and Catholic." Pattison was to extend his eighteenth-century study into "The Religious History of the Nineteenth Century in England." Jowett had the seventh essay, elaborating the arguments of Temple and Powell from the first volume, "The Evidence for Miracles: the Reign of Law, the Moral and Historical Nature of Religion." Max Müller, who had been solicited for the first volume, was to write on his specialty, comparative philology and mythology in "The Eastern Religions." "The True Conception of Religious Education" was proposed for the ninth essay assigned to W. H. Fremantle. The tenth essay, on "Christian Mission," was assigned first to Alexander Grant, but he withdrew. To replace Grant's contribution, Jowett added the names of three of his former students as possible contributors, the jurists Albert Venn Dicey and James Bryce, and a "Green," very likely the historian J. R. Green. Two final topics on the "Dates of the Books of Scripture," and the "Composition of the Gospels" were unassigned (Balliol, MS. Jowett E 20, fol. 6).

Delayed by the controversy over Temple's appointment as bishop of Exeter, by 28 January 1870 the plan was more firmly in place: Jowett wrote in detail to Edward Caird anticipating publication on 1 January 1871 (Letter 348). Caird was eventually asked to write on "Morality, Religion, Theology." Wilson and Jowett also hoped to have Williams contribute, but with his death (18 January 1870), the proposed volume was to contain obituaries of him and Powell. Other contributors were to include C. S. C. Bowen on the Church of England and disestablishment and Samuel Davidson on the translation of the Old Testament. Others considered included Emanuel Oscar Deutsch and Jowett's old friend Gilbert Elliot.

Temple had resolved not to have his essay republished after the thirteenth edition of 1869 and decided to avoid further polemic and controversy after his appointment to the episcopal bench. Pattison was grumpy about the "absence of a professional public" so that "a real theology cannot exist in England," and resolved "to wash my hands of theology and even of Church history, seeing that there existed in England no proper public for either" (Pattison 1885a, 317). It seems probable that he refused the offer to contribute. Goodwin was removed from the scene by being appointed a judge in Shanghai. Of the original Essayists, only Jowett and Wilson remained possible contributors, but Wilson suffered a paralyzing stroke in 1870. In the same year Jowett was elected Master of Balliol College and took on his new responsibilities enthusiastically. The plans for a new *Essays and Reviews* were set aside, never to be resumed.[11]

3 Reception and Response: "The Progress of Ideas" Raises "The Dust of Theological Strife"

HARRISON'S PHRASES ABOUT PROGRESS and strife from the opening paragraph of his review in the *Westminster* of October 1860 both summarized the earlier reception of *Essays and Reviews* and also prophesied its direction. The volume was reviewed first and positively within two weeks of its publication in the *Spectator* (7 Apr. 1860, 331–33), and a week later by the *Literary Gazette* (14 Apr. 1860, 459–60), both weeklies, the latter a journal that C. W. Goodwin had taken over as editor. The latter predicted the "wide celebrity" the volume would achieve because of its radical treatment of "the most difficult subjects," pleading for "tolerance and respect." But a quite different tone was announced in the *Press*, identifying the Essayists with the scepticism of Voltaire, as many other reviewers would do later, along with the scepticism and politics of Hume and Paine: "The appearance of this volume cannot be regarded with indifference. Did its entire contents represent but the opinions of even one of the eminent men whose names are prefixed to it, still it would be a sign of the times which we should not be able to overlook." The review specified the eminent positions of the Essayists and reflected that the fact that the seven "should have combined to publish these reflections is a circumstance of such gravity as almost to constitute an epoch in our religious history. . . . Their reckless, if courageous adoption of advanced sceptical theories reminds us painfully of the error committed by the ancient French noblesse" (21 Apr. 1860, 386). The Anglican Low Church press noticed it in the *Record* (21 May 1860), and the High Church weekly, the *Guardian,* in the same week (23 May 1860). Both weeklies were used throughout the controversy by means of articles and reviews, the printing of documents, and voluminous letters to the editor to keep readers aware of the latest proceedings concerning *Essays and Reviews* (on the religious press see Altholz 1989). In its review, the *Guardian* singled out Temple's and Pattison's essays as containing "nothing which will needs give pain or occasion surprise," unlike the others, such as Jowett's, which "is directly subversive of the doctrinal system of our Church," proposing that the scriptures are "no doctrinal standard at all," and even suggesting (in one of the up-to-date Darwinian references) that the human race "may have originated through the development of species" (473): "We observe . . . two or three of them unhesitatingly embracing Mr. Darwin's theory of the development of species, though it is well known that that theory, so far from being as yet substantiated by proper scientific evidence, is held to be unsound by the greatest living authority on such a point—Professor Owen" (474).

Outside Anglicanism, the Methodist *London Review* lamented the "Oxford Essayists'" contribution to "the steady onward and downward course of latitudinarianism, scepticism, infidelity, and the darkness without" (July 1860, 536), while the Congregationalist *Eclectic Review* in two articles on "The Oxford School" in July and August 1860 concluded that "not only is Revelation treated with the utmost irreverence, but there is such a degree of assumption, illogical statement, and unfounded assertion, as to fill us with a perfect amazement . . . [at the Essayists'] pride of intellect" (Aug. 1860, 126). Also in August a quarterly associated with the Scottish Free Church, the *North British Review*, published a long review of what it called "the manifestation, if not the manifesto" of the Broad Church position, attacking Powell and Jowett particularly (Aug. 1860, 217).

The first of the secular monthlies to notice the volume was *Fraser's Magazine* (Aug. 1860) in which W. D. Watson published a generally enthusiastic review. The politically liberal journal was edited by W. J. Parker Jr., one of the publishers of *Essays and Reviews,* and the review was in many ways typical in that Watson singled out Temple's and Pattison's essays as having "little or no controversial bearing" (228), though Temple came in for at least his fair share of criticism and demands that he separate himself from association with the rest of the seven. Similarly the *Christian Remembrancer*, the only Anglican quarterly, commented in a review (that had been ready in May but was delayed until printed in an expanded version in October) that the same "two of these essays . . . strike us as being quite out of place in the companionship in which they appear . . . because we do not detect in them any direct attack upon miracle or prophecy; they neither attempt to show that the Old Testament is altogether incredible, nor that the New Testament must be explained away to suit the prejudices or meet the claims of the philosophy of the nineteenth century" (Oct. 1860, 351).

In the same month came the first of the national and secular quarterlies, the

Westminster Review with Frederic Harrison's trenchant critique, so that *Essays and Reviews* suddenly was brought before a national readership. Thereafter virtually every periodical publication undertook a review, published letters to the editor, or reported on the temperature of the established church as fears of heretical fever caught from *Essays and Reviews* gripped the nation. These critical notices aroused sufficient interest at the time and subsequently that the reviews of *Essays and Reviews* have themselves become objects of study (see Vogeler 1979 and 1984; Ellis 1980, 104–45; Altholz 1982, 1986, and 1994, 34–49). By mid-century the *Westminster Review* was the leading radical journal, long associated with Utilitarianism, and under the editorship of John Chapman, a friend of Pattison's, who was himself editor of a section on new books in philosophy and theology from 1855 to 1870 (Ellis 1980, 20). The review had been suggested to Harrison by a colleague of Jowett's at Balliol, William Lambert Newman, and Chapman confirmed the agreement (Letters 27, 30, 31). Harrison was aware of his responsibility to set out the book's importance and defects: "The more I read the book, the more I felt its real importance as a manifesto of latitudinarianism, and its cynical insincerity, shallowness, and muddle-headedness" (Harrison 1911, 1:206). The publication of this review led to considerable interest concerning its anonymous authorship; appreciative letters from T. H. Huxley and John Tyndall were forwarded to Harrison by Chapman (Harrison 1911, 1:207). Huxley was appreciative perhaps because Harrison's review contains an oblique reference to Huxley's debate with Wilberforce at Oxford in May 1860 at the annual meeting of the BAAS (Harrison 1860, 308) and the use throughout of the notions of growth, development, and evolution in relation to the human mind and morality. Chapman had to assert to Pattison that Harriet Martineau was not the author. Jowett knew of the authorship by the time that Harrison's article was attacked by Stanley (Letters 113 and 116), when he wrote to offer support to Harrison. Harrison republished his review as "Septem Contra Fidem" (1907, 95–157). See figure 1.

Harrison's extensive attack on Temple in the opening pages goes to a central issue in the volume, the concept of the historical method that pervades all of the analyses. Harrison rightly saw that both Temple and Pattison were deeply implicated in the same project with the other Essayists, to force the formulation of theological doctrine and biblical interpretation to take account of the critical-historical method that had been advanced in Germany: "A book has appeared which may serve to mark an epoch in the history of opinion. The latest phase of religion at length has developed its creed. The vigour and the candour of this volume would raise it above the dust of theological strife; but its origin gives it a place in the record of religious thought. The subject, the form, and the authorship are all alike significant. It is no work of a single or isolated thinker; nor of unconnected thoughts upon secondary questions." He highlighted the importance of the book's appearance: "It is a manifesto from a body of kindred or associated thinkers; if it be not rather an outline of the principles of a new school of English theology. But whatever be the intention of its authors, those who watch the prog-

Figure 1. "An Apostle of Positivism" (Frederic Harrison). Watercolor by "Ape" (Carlo Pellegrini) for Vanity Fair (23 Jan. 1886). Courtesy of the National Portrait Gallery, London.

ress of opinion must look upon its appearance, and still more upon its reception, as full of significance and instruction. When seven theologians, teachers and professors in our universities or schools, combine their strength to deal with the great questions of modern inquiry, the public may justly infer that it has a test of the progress of ideas within the pale of the Church" (293). Harrison rejected outright the notion that the volume was the product of seven individual intentions: "We speak of this book as a joint production, and not as a mere collection of essays; for such, notwithstanding its outward form, it undoubtedly is. We are quite aware that there is no formal connexion in the argument; and we read in the preface that it has been written without concert or comparison. But it cannot escape the most casual reader; first, that there is a virtual unity in the purpose of the whole; secondly, that each writer receives a weight and an authority from all the rest of his associates. . . . It would be . . . idle to pretend that each writer is not morally responsible for the general tendency of the whole" (294).

To Harrison the book was "aggressive," "in direct antagonism to the whole system of popular belief," and "incompatible with the religious belief of the mass of the Christian public, and the broad principles on which the Protestantism of Englishmen rests" (295). After discussing each of the essays in some detail (though Jowett gets only brief mention), Harrison points to the main principles of the book: first, its use of the concept of the development or evolution of human thought and morality (305–9); second, its deployment of the modern German historical and literary-critical method (often used in the treatment of the classics) in criticism of the scriptures and creeds (310–15); and third, the moral implications of surrendering vacated notions of the inspiration and inerrancy of the scriptures to the claims of scientific truth (315–26). Harrison concludes by pointing out that the Essayists still retain their positions of influence: "No authorized rebuke has been put forward. They have been left to the bark of the toothless watchdogs of orthodoxy. . . . Professors, tutors, fellows, and pupils are conscious of this wide-spread doubt. In silence they watch and respect each other's thoughts, and silently work out their own. Above them sit unconscious dignitaries and powers vaguely condemning pantheism and neology, or piecing the articles together with scraps of accommodating texts. . . . How long shall this last?" (330–31). Of all the recent attempts to relate religious thought to moral feeling and faith to science, *Essays and Reviews* is "at once the most able, the most earnest, and—the most suicidal" (322).

His call provoked an immediate national outrage against the volume, a call responded to most vigorously in a denunciation of the book's heresy by Samuel Wilberforce in the *Quarterly Review.* In his diary entry for 2 January 1861, Wilberforce writes: "Dined at home & till late at night @ Review of Essays"; and on 3 January, "at work till 12 on Essays." By 6 January it was completed as he "sent off Review of Essays" to be published anonymously (Bodley, MS. Dep. e. 328/1). Wilberforce was no stranger to this kind of polemic. He had been involved in it with the effort to exclude R. D. Hampden from the see of Hereford in 1847. In July 1860 he had written against Darwin's *On the Origin of Species* in an article in the

Quarterly Review, vilifying his theology, and making him also responsible for the opinions of his grandfather, Erasmus Darwin. The substance of that article was delivered a few days before publication in the famous Wilberforce-Huxley exchange on 30 June 1860 at a meeting in Oxford of the British Association (see J. R. Lucas 1979; Gilley 1981; and Gilley and Loudes 1981). And in the conservative *Quarterly Review* for January 1861, Wilberforce did what Harrison demanded—he denounced the Essayists for their unorthodoxy and for their collusion. The caricature by Ape (Carlo Pellegrini), drawn in 1869 for *Vanity Fair* and entitled "Not a Brawler," captures Wilberforce as the consummate ecclesiastical politician, slippery (earning him the soubriquet "Soapy Sam") in argument and pugnacious in debate, characteristics well exercised in the famous encounter with Huxley over Darwin in the same year that *Essays and Reviews* was published, and renewed in his attacks on the volume and its authors in the following ten years. See figure 2.

Unlike Harrison, Wilberforce found no good in the volume at all. The whole book was full of what was singled out against Powell: "scarcely veiled Atheism," "German rationalism," and "moral dishonesty." Sensationalist polemic combined powerfully with ad hominem denunciation in Wilberforce's rhetoric, and on the matter of a combined purpose he was clear: all were involved in using individual human reason, the "verifying faculty," to test the Bible and find it wanting, to push the Articles of Religion and find them movable, to question the Formularies and find them inadequate. Beginning by attacking *Essays and Reviews* for its "mere literary merits" which display "nothing which is really new . . . either by way of amplification, illustration, or research" (248), Wilberforce then attacks the writers as abusing their position of power, prestige, and privilege in the church by uttering such doctrines (249). Their writing, despite occasional passages of "beauty and attractiveness," is filled with "uncertainty and ambiguity in their expressions, a haziness and indefiniteness" in their arguments yielding "a thick fog of words" or "inky obscurity" (252). Wilberforce perceives several "canons" or rules which govern the book's arguments. First, "a remorseless criticism" is to be pursued to bring the "'strangeness of the past into harmony with the present'" (Williams ¶1; Wilberforce 1861, 254) so that criticism becomes "a universal solvent" to dissolve away the difficult parts of the Bible, or those in seeming conflict with one another, or those incompatible with historical or scientific evidence (255). The second canon, the application of what Williams calls "the verifying faculty" (Williams ¶28), settles, according to Wilberforce, what is true or authentic in the biblical record not by an appeal to "external revelation" but to "internal consciousness" (256), not to the doctrines of inerrancy, inspiration, or the teaching office of the church, but to individual opinion, "THE idea of the whole volume" (255), itself summed up in Jowett's phrase that Wilberforce pillories, "'Interpret the Scripture like any other book'" (Jowett ¶s 10, 42, 45), the "great principle of their Hermeneutics" (258). He ridicules their treatment of the Bible for substituting "rationalizing ideology" for a historical Adam and Eve (260); for replacing "a personal Creator" with "the misty hieroglyphics of the Atheist" (262); for depicting the stories of Abraham and Moses

Figure 2. "Not a Brawler" (Samuel Wilberforce). Watercolor by "Ape" (Carlo Pellegrini) for *Vanity Fair* (24 July 1869). Courtesy of the National Portrait Gallery, London.

as fables (263); for explaining away predictive prophecy (265); for rejecting miracles (269); and for treating the whole of the New Testament as "the report of ordinary bystanders" to the "utter destruction of all notion of inspiration" (267). In sum, Wilberforce follows Harrison closely in arguing that following these interpretive principles, the Bible "becomes a medley of legend, poetry, and oral tradition, compiled, remodelled, and interpolated by a priestly order centuries after the times of its supposed authors" (Harrison 1860, 310). Wilberforce writes that the Bible comprises "—embedded in the crust of earlier legends, oral traditions, poetical licences, and endless parables,—a certain residuum [a word Harrison also uses, 303], which may be considered, in a certain sense, as the record of a revelation; whilst what is legend, and what the more noble residuum, must be determined for himself by every man; for that in this adult age of humanity every one who will, may possess the needful intellectual power by his own inherent 'verifying faculty'" (269). Several pages are devoted to specific attacks on the "mistiness" of Jowett (270–72); Wilson is given extended treatment (272–82), and is accused of "Jesuitry" for "holding one thing as true and teaching another thing as to be received" (275) and "a dreamy vagueness of pantheistic pietism, which is but the shallow water leading on to a profounder and darker atheism"; as well his views are associated, like those of Jowett and Williams, with the major heresies: Arianism, Sabellianism, and Socinianism (273, 287). To Wilberforce the fact that the Essayists maintain such views while retaining "the status and emolument of Church of England clergymen is simply moral dishonesty" (274); the Essayists merely reproduce the "rational views of Paine and Voltaire" (284); the Essayists' "whole apparatus is drawn bodily from the German Rationalists" (293); and behind them lurk "our own Deists in the last century [to whom] belongs the real shame of originating this attack upon the faith" (294). The orthodoxy of the conservative German Lutheran biblical critic E. W. Hengstenberg is invoked as the authority who has "already abundantly repelled [the] objections and fallacies of German rationalism" with which the book is replete (299).

Wilberforce concludes with a summons to deal with the "moral dishonesty" of the disbelieving Essayists who should be challenged concerning their beliefs and their positions, and all devout members of the Church of England should return to a faith position that does not question disputed matters too closely but leaves them as "mysteries": "We have felt bound to express distinctly our conviction that, holding their views, they cannot, consistently with moral honesty, maintain their posts as clergymen of the Established Church. We see more danger in the shape of wide-spread suspicion and distrust likely to arise from their continuance as teachers of that Church, whilst clearly disbelieving her doctrines, than from their lucubrations themselves. . . . We cannot believe that they will exert any wide-spread influence in the Church of our land, or amongst our people. The English mind is too calm, too sound, too essentially honest to be widely or deeply affected by such speculations as these—and more especially from such mouths. The flattering appeal which they make to unassisted human reason, and the gratification which they afford to the natural pride of the human heart, may win for them a certain following, but the great body of Church-of-England men will stand aloof from them." He cites the opposition to the volume as destroying its rational basis: "All the schools, then, of theological opinion amongst us are opposed to the Essayists. On the one side stand in their way the recent growth of higher views of the authority of the Church and a juster value of all the great dogmas of the Catholic faith; on the other, the fact that the special points assailed by them are those which are the dearest to the school which has been least affected by the Church movement, such as the doctrines of original sin, justification by faith, and, above all, that of the Atonement" (302–3).

His final emphasis is "on that momentous subject of inspiration, on which, as we said at first, is the brunt of their whole attack." He expounds a notion of plenary inspiration and the "impenetrable barriers against that proud curiosity which evermore leads men on to seek to be as gods, knowing good and evil" (305). To the observant, Wilberforce revealed his authorship by his insistence, so often maintained in public pronouncements, that the Essayists must hang or fall together: despite their disclaimer in the Preface entitled "To the Reader," the Essayists "all combine in the great common lines of thought which pervade the whole volume . . . the abandonment of the Church's ancient position of certainty or truth" (251); they "admit a unity," construct a "common volume," enter into a "co-partnership," and must assume "joint liability" (250): "The book must be taken as a whole, and, if condemned, it must condemn every writer in it who does not, by some after act, visibly separate himself from the fellowship of opinions to which he is here committed" (251). It was this approach that F. D. Maurice, in a letter to Stanley before Wilberforce's authorship was known, but was suspected, found "very shocking," since he was attacking "his own clergy anonymously" (Letter 48), and it was this line that Wilberforce pursued indefatigably against Temple to the day of his consecration ten years later in which Wilberforce refused to take part. But the popularity of such attacks was unquestioned. The January number of the *Quarterly* containing Wilberforce's article had to be reprinted five times to meet the demand (Ashwell and Wilberforce 1880–82, 3:2; on 3 Apr. the *Guardian* advertised the fifth edition [328]). The publication earned Wilberforce 100 guineas (Altholz 1994, 156) and quickly made him an authority on the volume, his authorship being assumed even though the pretense of anonymity was maintained (Letter 49). Thereafter he assumed leadership in the House of Bishops against *Essays and Reviews*. Stanley, suspecting Wilberforce's authorship, was strong in his condemnation of the review's limitations, since it "displayed or affected the most astonishing ignorance of all that had passed in theological literature, in this and other countries, since the beginning of this century" (1861a, 466). Stanley was not alone in his censure. Wilberforce's anonymous article was roundly attacked by the Cambridge scientist Henry Sidgwick in the *Times* (Letter 62), in the Convocation of Canterbury, and then in the legal proceedings by Dr. Deane, on behalf of Williams and Wilson, because of its "singular ignorance" of what was "perfectly well known to everyone who has the slightest tincture not only of theological literature, but really of the floating literature of the day," making the charges against the volume of "'neology'—mysticism, rationalism, and, of course, scepticism" particularly foolish since they are far from new or unknown (British Library: *Court of Arches: Bishop of Salisbury v. Williams,* 5155 k.11, 1:fols. 5–6). Wilberforce reprinted the essay in the first volume of his own collection of reviews and essays that he contributed to the *Quarterly Review* (Wilberforce 1874).

It was left for a rebuttal in a journal that moderated between the radical and the conservative positions of the *Westminster* and the *Quarterly.* The liberal *Edinburgh Review* was then edited by Henry Reeve, who was the registrar of the Privy Council and also a political leader writer for the *Times,* both of which gave him a significant insight into the matters raised by *Essays and Reviews.* Stanley had been a friend of Jowett's and Temple's since undergraduate days at Balliol College, and they had continued in close association in advocating general Broad Church principles (see Letter 1). Stanley continued for more than ten years to fight for the increase of Jowett's stipend as Regius Professor of Greek. But when asked, he had refused to contribute to *Essays and Reviews* (Letters 6 and 7). At the time of the Episcopal Manifesto he was involved in a correspondence with Tait, the bishop of London, in support especially of Temple and Jowett (Letters 54–55, 58–59). He wrote to Pattison on 12 April that his anonymous review would appear the next day in the *Edinburgh* and on 14 April Chapman wrote Pattison that he had read it, and was pleased that the reviewer "defends them" (Letters 108, 110). Tait, on the other hand, thought its logic "very poor" and, except for the defense of Temple and Jowett, "powerless" as a defense of the whole book (Letter 112). Jowett wrote about it apologetically to Harrison concerning Stanley's remarks about Harrison's "Neo-Christianity" review, while Williams felt he and Wilson had been dropped "in the mud" by Stanley (Letters 113, 115–16). To mediate between the *Westminster* and the *Quarterly* Stanley adopted the policy of prefacing his review with his inside information concerning the sources and origins of the volume, while setting it historically within the course of the controversy it had aroused, laying particular blame on the *Westminster* for stirring up the "whirlwind." He also defends the volume by citing lists of earlier writers who argued views similar to those of the Essayists. None of these efforts proved to be sufficient to stem the tide against the volume that was quickly moving toward the charges in the ecclesiastical court (see Altholz 1994, 45–49). The photograph of Stanley by Charles Lutwidge Dodgson (Lewis Carroll) was taken just two years before the publication of *Essays and Reviews,* when Stanley was already closely identified with the Oxford liberals through the work of the Oxford University Commission and his support of an increase in Jowett's stipend as professor of Greek. At the time the photograph was taken Stanley was professor of Ecclesiastical History and had just been appointed a canon of Christ Church. See figure 3.

Stanley attempted to accomplish an impossible feat: to pick a careful path of reconciliation between Harrison and Wilberforce, to offer serious critique balanced

Figure 3. A. P. Stanley (c. 1858). Photograph by Charles Lutwidge Dodgson (Lewis Carroll). Courtesy of the National Portrait Gallery, London.

with praise, to mediate in the deepening crisis without tipping his political hand, to avoid alienating Evangelicals or High Church supporters, to mollify the Liberals and the Broad Church—and all of this from one who had been asked to contribute to the volume but had declined and who remained a personal friend of the first and last Essayists. As he said to Pattison, he wrote the review "with the intention of supporting you & your colleagues through this storm" (Letter 108). But he had wider purposes too—to take on the question of theological collaboration to advance a single radical position; to show by extensive quotation how the views of the Essayists and Reviewers could be supported by extensive quotation from leading Anglican theologians of the past; and to demonstrate how the comprehensive nature of the established church, and the broad interpretation of the Articles of Religion and the Formularies, could tolerate widespread diversity of opinion, even on what seemed to be fundamentals.

Stanley's interleaved, annotated, and corrected galleys of the review are at Lambeth Palace (H 5155/4.108, #20), in which he expanded the section on Harrison's review in the *Westminster* (463–64). Stanley republished his review in his collection *Essays and Church and State* (1870, 46–96), excising his attack on Harrison. He also added headings that set out the structure of his essay: an opening section entitled "Religious panics," followed by four divisions: the first on publication and agitation; the second on the "Nature of the Word"; the third on "Questions involved" in which he indicates three (biblical creation, the value of internal evidence, and dogmatic theology); and the final division on the "Liberty of Clergy to Inquire."

Beginning by alluding to the origins of the volume in the *Oxford* and *Cambridge Essays*, Stanley then addressed the origins of the controversy about its orthodoxy, laying the blame, in a passage he added to his manuscript in the galley stage, but later omitted from its republished version, on Harrison for having fanned into flame the widespread but unfocused outrage. Harrison was labeled as one who "repudiated all belief in Christian Revelation, and who combined with a profound ignorance of nearly all that had been written on the questions at issue an almost fanatical desire to inveigle those who stood on more secure positions to the narrow ledge of the precipice on the midway of which he himself was standing" (1861a, 464). According to Stanley, Harrison was "poisoned by a sinister intention too transparent to have escaped the notice of any but those who were willingly deceived." His methods "first parodied the book by exaggeration, by amplification, by suppression, by making every writer responsible for what every other writer had said or not said, either on the subjects discussed or not discussed, and then raised a cry of mingled exultation and remonstrance to the phantasm which he had conjured up,—of exultation at the supposed novelty of what he was pleased to call a system of Neo-Christianity" (464). According to Stanley, the impact of Harrison's article was decisive in whipping up the "coming whirlwind": "Partly in genuine alarm, partly in greedy delight at finding such an unlooked-for confirmation of their own uneasy suspicions and dislikes, the partisans of the two chief theological schools in the country caught up and eagerly echoed the note of the infidel journal. They extolled the eloquence and ability of the article; they made its conclusions their own; they discerned, through its inquisitorial gaze, tendencies which, up to that moment, had escaped even their own keen scent for the track of heresy. Gradually the heterogeneous series began to assume that mystified form which it has worn ever since in the public eye" (464–65). Stanley then turned to Wilberforce's anonymous "invective" in the *Quarterly*, hinting at its author as "a powerful ecclesiastical influence at work" who was eager for "crushing not merely the book, but the writers themselves," though from a standpoint that showed "a carelessness . . . of the general facts of history and science," citing Wilberforce's notion of Buddhism and his assertion that the Copernican system had "'wholly passed away'" (466). Other events are described in sequence: the partisan party alignments against Max Müller for his liberal theology and German nationality in the election for the Chair of Sanskrit at Oxford, the issuing of the Episcopal Manifesto, the debate in the Convocation of the Province of Canterbury, and the "Protest of the Clergy" (465–71).

In the second part of his review, Stanley points to the nature of the volume, including its limitations: that the notion of "composite work" was "a decided blunder," as was its "negative character" and "disparaging tone," and its general accessibility to a wide reading public, both clerical and lay, because it was not written in a learned language (Latin or German), but adopted popular conventions in both title and form (471–73). After brief mention of Powell and Goodwin, Stanley praises the ecclesiastical position of the remaining five, and then gives brief attention to each of their essays (475–79). In his third section Stanley concentrates on three large issues, "the proper mode of studying and interpreting the Bible, and, closely allied with it, the relative value of the internal and external evidences of Religion. To which may perhaps be added a third, of less general interest, the relation of dogmatical theology to the Bible and to history" (479). Stanley demonstrates how the Essayists' positions on each of them has ample German and especially English precedent in theologians of note. Among the latter Stanley mentions Coleridge, who "led the way," followed by Thomas Arnold, Hare, Thirlwall, Alford, Milman, Westcott, Lord Arthur Hervey, the much praised *Dictionary of the Bible* edited by William Smith (1860–1865), and even Pusey, who came under the "Germanising influence" (480–81). He also alludes to ancient, medieval, and modern theologians, from Justin Martyr and Anselm to Cudworth and Butler. In a final section Stanley defends the right of the clergy to engage in "free discussion" on matters of biblical interpretation and doctrine where the Articles of Religion and the Formularies are silent—as, for instance, on inspiration or on internal and external evidence, a point that received much attention in subsequent legal actions: "Great indeed would have been the calamity to the Church and country, if the recent agitation had succeeded in the attempt to stifle free discussion and research on theological subjects. There is danger in all such inquiries, but there is a still greater danger in the suppression of inquiry" (496).

Stanley's general impact was much dulled by his recourse to faint praise for Temple and Jowett, so that A. C. Tait wrote in his diary: "Read over again the article in the *Edinburgh* on Essays and Reviews. Its logic is very poor—the writing forcible. It would be a good defence of Temple and perhaps of Jowett, if they stood alone or only with Pattison. As a defence of the book generally it is quite powerless" (Letter 112). Stanley's remarks made precarious Harrison's tenure of his fellowship at Wadham College. Jowett too was surprised, and wrote an irenic letter to Harrison, whom he did not know, to offer regrets for any pain which Stanley's article might have caused him (Letter 113; see also Letter 116). Williams did not read Stanley's article with such equanimity: "A. P. Stanley has written an article in the *Edinburgh* trying to bring off his friends Dr. Temple and Jowett, and to drop Wilson and myself in the mud, particularly poor me. This is ridiculously unfair. . . . The half friendly tone of the *Edinburgh* will do us more harm than the *Quarterly*, with its avowed hostility" (Letter 115).

After the book was reviewed by Harrison and Wilberforce delivered his Charge in November 1860, and as the controversy was being taken up in the ecclesiastical governing body, Convocation, two of the Essayists, Temple and Jowett in succession, visited Archibald Campbell Tait, bishop of London, at Fulham Palace, in late January or early February 1861. The exchange that followed demonstrates the strain that the *Essays and Reviews* controversy put on the network of liberal clergymen, but also points to the delicate line between public functions and private friendships. Temple asked Tait for his views on the book as a whole, and on his own opinion of Temple's essay in particular. Tait replied that he had serious reservations about certain aspects of some of the essays that he considered to have transgressed the limits of theological toleration in the Church of England, and had misgivings about the wisdom of Temple's participating in the publication. He did not find anything in Temple's essay that transgressed the doctrine acceptable to the church. Tait may have thought he implied or even stated that he disagreed with some aspects of Temple's essay—a point that became contentious later; however, he urged Temple to dissociate himself from the rest of the Essayists, and subsequently said more or less the same things to Jowett, but gave Jowett "the impression that he agreed" with him (Letter 85).

By 16 February Tait had affixed his name to the Episcopal Manifesto that Wilberforce drafted for the archbishops and bishops to approve. When it was published, Temple was furious at Tait's apparent treachery. Tait gave an explanation in Convocation: "I have known Dr. Temple, as I have said, for many years in the intimacy of private friendship. The particular essay which he has written certainly does not express my views. I believe it was first preached as a University Sermon in St. Mary's Church, Oxford. I dislike it, but, in my estimation, it is totally different in character from other passages which occur in this volume; and I cannot conceive by what motive the author could be restrained—if it should prove that he is restrained—from publicly declaring that he does not approve of various things which are to be found in this unfortunate book. . . . Let it be distinctly understood that we, the Bishops of the Church of England, looking at the book as a whole, believe that it is likely to do great and grievous harm; but separating, as I trust I shall ever be able to do throughout my whole life, the individuals from their opinions, hoping even against hope that these individuals may return, however far they may have gone astray. . . . I for one shall not permit myself to doubt of their honesty, and I shall not trouble myself about their consistency" (*Chronicle* 1859–64; 28 Feb. 1861:461, 467; quoted in Davidson and Benham 1891, 1:302–3). When this explanation was published, Temple was all the more angry (Letter 80). Tait's rear-guard explanations to Temple of his motives, in agreeing to the general condemnation of the Episcopal Manifesto without citing any particular theological infringement and without specifying any particular passages as heterodox, left no grounds of recourse or appeal and condemned all of the Essayists equally. In Temple's view this was an act of "treachery," not mitigated by Tait's prolonged protestation that he acted in the church's and Temple's best interests. Furthermore, his effort to have Temple, Jowett, and Pattison distance themselves from the general condemnation by urging them to issue public statements that showed each wrote without knowledge of the others' essays, was, at best, an effort to save his friends before the fire engulfed them, while committing the rest to the flames.

Tait's letters to Temple are filled with legal rhetoric that shows that court proceedings were probable, even immanent: he refers to "condemnation" and to judges and judgment throughout, and clearly anticipates that the *Essays and Reviews* will soon be brought to trial in the ecclesiastical courts. Accordingly, Tait wished the three to distance themselves from probable litigation. The bitterness of the correspondence between Temple and Tait, a rift in their long personal friendship, was a significant indication of the severe and diverse tests the publication of *Essays and Reviews* enforced upon both public and private consciences, driving wedges of disagreement between not only established party and doctrinal positions but also between old associations based on educational background, ecclesiastical sympathies, and personal friendships (Letters 65–67; 70; 72; 76; 80; 82; and 85–86).

The outcry against the volume was made more urgent by ongoing controversies such as the actions taken against Colenso and the publication of Ernest Renan's *Vie de Jésus*. Almost 400 pamphlets, tracts, lectures, sermons, and charges were published as attacks on *Essays and Reviews*. A few others were in praise of, or at least in sympathy with, the views of the Essayists. Most of the attacks were either superficial diatribes directed against the book as a whole or took as their primary object one of the Essayists whom they sought to answer in detail. A few polemicists like Anthony George Denison published a series of essays dealing with the book systematically. A list of these publications, doubtless not complete since many of these publications were both ephemeral in production and local in distribution, not always making their way into the copyright libraries, is given in the bibliography of responses (see also the analysis of this material in Ellis 1980, 102–56; and Altholz 1994, 64–84).

Two major volumes of collected essays were published as the Establishment's answer to *Essays and Reviews*, each edited by a bishop, thereby meeting Harrison's demand for a serious intervention and correction from the episcopacy to show the Essayists' theological errors. Both publications were announced for 1861 but appeared early in January 1862 (Altholz 1994, 76). In addition Westcott and Hort projected a volume of essays to be called *Revelation and History*, "a mediating volume" between the Broad Church theology of *Essays and Reviews* and the other church parties (Letter 52), though it was never brought to completion. Hort's biographer remarks that the "joint volume" mentioned in this letter "came to nothing." His essay, called "Doctrine, Human and Divine," remained uncompleted, but the Hulsean lectures of 1871, *The Way, the Truth, and the Life* (published in 1893) "were in some sense a realisation of this long-cherished hope" (A. F. Hort 1896, 1:375–76). At the same time as Hort and Westcott projected their volume, in March 1861, F. D. Maurice and Thomas Hughes planned and published a series of *Tracts for Priests and People*, "bearing upon the religious questions treated of in 'Essays and Reviews' but considered from a strictly positive point of view" (Maurice 1884, 2:386). Seven of the tracts in the first series were issued, both separately and as a bound volume. Hort's biographer notes that he thought that the tracts were "inadequate" as a defense of *Essays and Reviews*.

Wilberforce either edited or oversaw *Replies to "Essays and Reviews"* and wrote the preface, in which he describes the theology of the volume as "a tricked out Atheism" disguised as "Pantheism." There followed an attack on each individual essay. In the first essay Temple's precursor at Rugby, E. M. Goulburn, asserts that Temple has confused the analogy of nature with the analogy of faith: to treat the "progress of the Church in divine knowledge" on the same level as the "progress of the species by civilization" is to secularize the entire process of revelatory history (*Replies* 1862, 21). Henry John Rose wrote on "Bunsen, the Critical School, and Dr. Williams," in which first, Bunsen is dismissed as a marginal thinker; second, the "critical school" is denigrated as under attack in Germany from such traditionalist theologians as Hengstenberg; and third, Williams is repudiated as a falsifier, both of German scholarship and of inspiration and prophecy in the Bible. Powell's essay is addressed by C. A. Heurtley writing on "Miracles," in which he defends a traditionalist view, that the causality of natural law is simply suspended in the case of attested miracles for which there are reliable witnesses whose recorded testimony is documented in an inspired book and whose evidential authenticity is appealed to by Jesus Christ, thereby giving miracles a divine sanction. Writing against Wilson, W. J. Irons stresses the moral and spiritual condition and conscience of the individual believer, who alone must account for his or her stewardship at the day of judgment, rather than the "Generalized Christianity" of "multitudinism" that Wilson advocates. The response to Goodwin by G. Rorison appeals to the meaning of "the Creative Week," as he titled his essay, in which God is a final cause who created by fiat out of nothing. In order to preserve both the natural order as divinely created and human beings as special creations, Rorison attacks modes of biological evolution as viable explanations for human development. This process is recorded in the "oldest and sublimest poem," the first chapter of Genesis. A. W. Haddan's essay on "Rationalism" argues that Pattison is exempt from theological error in writing a historical account of an episode in ecclesiastical history. However, by making rationalism so much a part of that history and the experience of the church, he has unwittingly contributed to a climate in which scepticism is rendered more tolerable. Finally, Christopher Wordsworth answers Jowett, ridiculing his "erroneous principles" (409), his "serene self-sufficiency" (419), and his lack of originality (431). His views are associated with those of a prominent Unitarian, William Rathbone Greg, whom Jowett is all but accused of plagiarizing (432). Jowett's essay is said to be both unclear and unscholarly in that it "teems with insinuations" making a "whispering gallery of indistinct sounds muttering evil" (465). Most of the writers of *Replies to "Essays and Reviews"* also published separate attacks on the Essayists. The volume as a whole is constructed upon denial of the Essayists' arguments and assertions of a traditionalist position; the kind of serious discussion that Wilberforce had anticipated in his preface was not met by the volume's tone of strident adversarial polemic.

It was a different matter with the second major volume of essays, *Aids to Faith: A Series of Theological Essays*, edited by William Thomson who the year previously had become bishop of Gloucester and Bristol, thereby delaying the publication of the volume that Murray had announced as ready "shortly" as early as March 1861 (Ethel Thomson 1919, 117–26). The volume makes an elaborate bow to *Essays and Reviews* in the preface explaining its own means of compilation: the authors of *Aids to Faith* declare, as had the Essayists two years earlier, no common purpose or collusion other than to offer a sustained critique of the offending volume. The contributors to *Aids to Faith* were more prestigious intellectually and institutionally than those writing in *Replies to "Essays and Reviews"* that boasted only Wilberforce, Heurtley, and Goulburn as notables. *Aids to Faith*, on the other hand, contained nine essays, two by bishops (Thomson of Gloucester and Bristol, and William Fitzgerald of Cork, who had been professor of moral philosophy, and then of ecclesiastical history at Trinity College, Dublin, and who was a well-known editor of Butler's *Analogy*); five by professors; and one by the examining chaplain for the bishop of Lincoln. The professors included H. L. Mansel, (Waynflete Professor of Moral and Metaphysical Philosophy, Oxford), Alexander McCaul (Hebrew and Old Testament Exegesis, King's College, London), George Rawlinson (Camden Professor of Ancient History, Oxford), Edward Harold Browne (Norissian Professor of Divinity, Cambridge), and Charles John Ellicott (professor of Divinity, King's College, London). This group of scholars drew on four institutions and a range of disciplines far broader than those of the Essayists, and their ecclesiastical affiliations linked them to Exeter, Ireland, Lincoln, and St. Paul's, London. Two of them, Browne and Ellicott, later became bishops. *Aids to Faith* went through four editions, with about 7,000 copies in circulation (Ethel Thomson 1919, 127).

On the whole, the contributors to *Aids to Faith* take one or more of three positions. First, they criticize the Essayists on the basis of philosophical objections or take up quarrels with their logic. Second, they object to them on the basis of a faulty view of history that ignores empirical data. Third, they take up particular doctrinal positions or points of biblical exegesis. H. L. Mansel adopts the first position, arguing that Powell's view of evidence is defective philosophically because of a limited notion of proof, testimony, and theories of verification. Such philosophical objections are resumed later in the volume by F. C. Cook, attacking the concept of "ideology" in Wilson as one of the dominant intellectual notions that underlies the whole book and that provides the basis for what a number of the writers call the Essayists' "system," an overriding allegiance to Straussian idealism (William Thomson 1861, 133). While other essays in *Aids to Faith* did not generally refute the Essayists with such an artillery of philosophical nuance, the strategy of argumentation is a far cry from the denial and assertion of *Replies*. The second strategy for refuting the Essayists, attacking their handling of empirical and historical data, may be exemplified by William Fitzgerald's appeal to "fact" as the basis for Christianity. While he too addresses the problem of evidence, he appeals fundamentally to an empiricist notion of history, arguing that Christianity is a religion rooted in "fact" whose usefulness in contemporary culture can be measured, weighed, and described accurately with respect to the progress of the human race and the integrity of the responses of moral conscience. This elaborate justification of Christianity on the basis of "fact" is directed especially at Powell's rejection of miracles as undeniably convincing evidence of truth. As well, Fitzgerald is attacking the "verifying faculty" in Williams or the "truth of the human heart" in Jowett, unprovable appeals that in his view depend on romantic theories of emotion, imagination, and understanding derived from Coleridge. The third position common to many of the essays in *Aids to Faith*, the assertion of particular points of interpretation, may be demonstrated by Alexander McCaul in his treatment of doctrine and exegesis. McCaul's two contributions particularly address the exegetical methods of Williams and Powell, controverting their questioning of accepted translations and interpretations of disputed passages. McCaul adopts the technique of the variorum commentary, in bringing forward various explications as though dispassionately chosen from wide-ranging contemporary and historical sources; however, he carefully selects his authorities to bolster the traditionalist readings he advocates, drawing on the Church Fathers, the rabbis like Rashi, Reformation thinkers like Luther, and finally various contemporary critics, such as Ferdinand Hitzig. These authorities are assembled to show that Williams especially, but other Essayists as well, have wrongly devalued the predictive element of prophecy. The result is that they have identified themselves with the German rationalists, and it is for them that McCaul reserves his real scorn (William Thomson 1861, 112). The other writers in *Aids to Faith* addressed other aspects of *Essays and Reviews*. Writing on the Pentateuch, Rawlinson denied that it was a product of multiple sources, affirming the Mosaic authorship for the whole five books, and upholding the universality of the flood. On inspiration Browne rightly saw inspiration as a problem fundamental to the whole volume; Thomson returned to earlier disputes by attacking Jowett on the atonement, and the last essay, by Ellicott, attempted to answer Jowett section by section, rejecting his canons of interpretation outright in favor of a method that would preserve a kind of literal historicism: "Interpret grammatically, historically, contextually, and minutely" (439) but "interpret according to the analogy of Faith" (443). Less polemical and adversarial than *Replies*, *Aids to Faith* attempted to provide a moderate and careful general answer to *Essays and Reviews* by readdressing the topics of the Essayists from a position of comprehensive doctrinal orthodoxy to reassure those whose faith had been shaken. However, the contributors, both Low and High Church, were not unified by party affiliations in the church or by doctrinal consistency and they slipped into direct responses as well as refutational arguments. They set their faces against advances in science and literary study of the evolution of the biblical narrative. While this re-presentation of differing orthodoxies was welcomed by the Essayists' opponents, it was late in appearing on the scene, it gathered its own subcontroversial collection of attacks (Ellis 1980, 121), and it failed to advance the Essayists' arguments to a new level of theological discussion, falling back instead on the reiterated conventional pieties and positions of thirty years earlier.

Thomson, as editor of the volume, was widely known to be an opponent of the Essayists. When he was appointed archbishop of York in 1862, he was necessarily involved in the doctrinal cases that came before the Judicial Committee of the Privy Council. When Williams and Wilson appealed their cases, Thomson was one of the ecclesiastical lords who heard it in the Judicial Committee, disagreed with the unanimous judgment over the issue of inspiration, and followed up that judgment with continued attacks in his Pastoral Letter of 1864.

Opposition to *Essays and Reviews* in the ensuing controversy took many forms and operated on many different social levels. The fact that so many oppositional voices could be united in their vehement condemnation of the volume speaks to the many facets of a text that challenged religious orthodoxy in general and Anglican hegemony in particular.

4 The Essayists, the Essays, and Their Contexts

Frederick Temple, Victorian Education, and the Cycles of History

Frederick Temple (1821–1902) was born in the Ionian Islands, educated at Blundell's School, Tiverton, and at Balliol College, Oxford. Among his tutors were Benjamin Jowett, just beginning his teaching career, A. C. Tait, and William G. Ward, the Tractarian. Interested in the Oxford Movement, Temple never attached himself to their party and gradually became an ecclesiastical liberal. In 1850 he submitted evidence before the Oxford University Reform Commission headed by Gladstone, and he continued to play an active role in educational and social reform. In 1857 he was appointed headmaster of Rugby School, succeeding Tait and E. M. Goulburn, both of whom had followed Thomas Arnold (died 1842). Both Tait and Goulburn became involved subsequently in the *Essays and Reviews* controversy, the former as one of the Privy Councillors, and the latter as one of the early attackers of Temple's essay. Dean's photograph shows Temple a year after his appointment as headmaster of Rugby and two years before the publication of his essay in *Essays and Reviews.* See figure 4.

Following the publication of the volume, Temple came under sustained attack. Despite public and private pressure on him to resign the Rugby headmastership because of his essay, he continued to direct the affairs of the school until 1869. In that year he was offered the bishopric of Exeter by Gladstone, a nomination that was contested by fierce opposition generated by the widespread vilification of Temple's appointment. In 1885 he was appointed bishop of London, and in 1897 was made archbishop of Canterbury. His last speech in the House of Lords (4 Dec. 1902) was in support of Balfour's education bill, but during it he collapsed and died three weeks later.

Temple's writings include the Bampton Lectures on *The Relations between Religion and Science* (1884) and *Sermons Preached in Rugby School Chapel* (1861–71, 3 vols.). The standard biography is E. G. Sandford (ed.), *Memoirs of Archbishop Temple by Seven Friends* (Sandford 1906) and Sandford, *The Exeter Episcopate of Archbishop Temple, 1869–1885* (Sandford 1907).

"The Education of the World" is a treatise on religious education. His culminating argument, that the Bible is the chief instrument for the education of the human race, is appropriate both to his position as the headmaster of Rugby College and to his earlier writings on education, such as his contribution on "National Education" to *Oxford Essays* (1856). This argument is also part of mid-Victorian debate on the role of the Bible as a historical instrument of conversion and colonization. Two contexts for the essay must be stressed: educational reform, particularly the movements at Oxford and Cambridge that had been in process from the early 1850s, as well as the nineteenth-century movement for state-funded elementary education; and historiography, especially the theories of history as moving in cycles of gradual progression that organize the essay to make it consistent with the imperial aspirations of Britain.

Throughout the 1850s some members of the Oxford establishment, including a number of Broad Church supporters, were pushing for educational reform. Powell, Jowett, and Pattison were instrumental in changing the curriculum, teaching, and responsibilities of fellows at Oxford, and, despite a profound commitment to the classics, were also resolved to introduce the modern study of history and the sciences. Educational reform of the universities, as well as of public education, culminating in the Forster Education Bill (1870), demonstrates the links

Figure 4. Frederick Temple (1858). Engraving by Emery Walker from a photograph by Dean & Son. Frontispiece in E. G. Sandford, ed., *Memoirs of Archbishop Temple by Seven Friends.* London: Macmillan, 1906.

between schools and universities and various political and technological changes in mid-nineteenth-century Britain (see Mack 1971 and 1973; and Stephens 1987). In "The Education of the World" Temple barely touches any issues regarding social or political reform; instead, he focuses largely on the role of religion as the central component in education. Such a focus places Temple in opposition to the main direction being taken by educational theory and practice in the nineteenth century. According to recent historians, "Increasingly after 1860 some masters did not favour or encourage religion" (Digby and Searly 1981, 21). In other work Temple displays a knowledge of the practical side of education and took a lead in such reforms. His essay on "National Education" (1856) surveys contemporary legislative debate regarding the leveling of school taxes and national standards for education; Temple gave evidence before the Newcastle Commission in 1860, and was a member of the Schools' Inquiry Commission from 1864 to 1868.

Temple's essay is based upon theories of cyclical history, beliefs in progress, and Eurocentric ethnology. Cyclical history stresses either endless repetition or repetition with variation and is differentiated from linear chronologies of progression and regression. Such cyclical theories draw parallels or analogies between the supernatural order and the three temporal orders: cosmic, natural, and human. The major historiographer of a cyclic theory of history is Giovanni Battista Vico, who published *The New Science* in 1725 (see Day 1964 and Rossi 1984), in which he differentiates three similar orders, the gods, heroes, and humans, the last of which go through courses (*ricorsi*) of social relationships and institutions that are retraced on new planes of self-consciousness or they are annihilated. In the nineteenth century Vico had an impact on Jules Michelet and others (see Hayden White 1973, 160). Cyclical history in the study of classical cultures was revived in Barthold Georg Niebuhr's *Römische Geschichte* (1812; 1827–28; 1832; trans. Julius Hare and Connop Thirlwall, *Roman History*, 1847–51; the first two volumes in 1828 and 1832). Thomas Arnold studied Niebuhr in the preparation of *Thucydides* (1830–35) and his lectures at Oxford published as *History of Rome* (1838–42). In Temple's essay, each cycle of history represents a forward movement in the progress of the "human race." Race is a term used for general humanity ("human race"), and to draw distinctions between what he designates as civilized and barbarian, European and Asiatic, and British and other. Temple's notion of race accords with nineteenth-century theories of ethnology, in placing these racial groups on an evolutionary scale with the white European "race" as its acme. This evolutionary scale forms the basis of Temple's historiography of progress (for nineteenth-century and especially Victorian historiography see Hayden White 1973; Burrow 1981; Culler 1985; Jann 1985; and Von Arx 1985).

According to A. P. Stanley (1861a, 477), the immediate source for this essay was a University Sermon that Temple preached in 1859 in the University Church of St. Mary, Oxford, on "the Fulness of Time" (Gal. 4:4): "When preached before the authorities and the students of Oxford, it was heard with approbation, it might be said, with enthusiasm, by most of his hearers, with acquiescence by all" (Stanley

1861a, 471). A. C. Tait corroborates Stanley's claim (Davidson and Benham 1891, 1:302). Temple's biographer asserts that sermon was expanded from one delivered first at Rugby (Sandford 1906, 2:280). No copy of that sermon has been located. Not all of his fellow Essayists were pleased with his recasting of a sermon into an essay for the volume. On 25 July 1860 Wilson wrote to Pattison about the sermon that he preached at the meeting of the British Association in Oxford: "Temple preached a better sermon at St. Mary's the other day than he gave us in réchauffé in the Volume and it was far better than I expected from him" (Letter 25).

Temple recasts "The Education of the World" (he claimed it took him ten days: see Letter 262) as a comparison between the education of the individual and the education or preparation of the world for the coming of Christ and its effect on subsequent history. His argument is as an extended elaboration of a biblical passage, one of the accepted organizational modes for the mid-Victorian sermon. The text to which he makes most frequent reference, and on which the chief metaphors of the sermon depend, is Galatians 4:1–7. Besides the Bible, which is quoted extensively throughout, contemporary commentators alluded to two kinds of sources for Temple's ideas: various forms of philosophy, such as the thought of Auguste Comte (for the allusion to the education of the "colossal man" to which Frederic Harrison draws attention [1860, 161]); G. E. Lessing's treatise *On the Education of the Human Race* (which E. M. Goulburn noted in his published reply to Temple [*Replies* 1862, 1]); and, most importantly, Blaise Pascal (who in his fragmentary preface to *The Treatise on the Vacuum* [1647] draws an elaborate analogy between the history of humankind and the life cycle of an individual [Pascal 1978, 54]). Indirect reference is made in one of the first notices of *Essays and Reviews* in the weekly edited by C. W. Goodwin, the *Literary Gazette*, to Temple's having "developed his line of thought from a celebrated passage of Pascal" (14 Apr. 1860, 459); in his published charge of 1863 Connop Thirlwall refers explicitly to the passage from Pascal and quotes it (1877, 2:26–27).

A. P. Stanley too was one of the sources for some of Temple's ideas, particularly his distinctions between Eastern and Western thought forms in a narrative of development. In his *Lectures on the History of the Eastern Church*, Stanley aligns East and West with conventional norms of thought and experience (see, for instance, Stanley [1861] 1924, 76). Temple maintains this conventional distinction throughout "The Education of the World," as well as others—the notion of law, both religious and secular, and especially the Mosaic law and the law of conscience (to which Powell, Pattison, and other Essayists return in their discussions of natural law; see also Temple [1861–71] 1896, 91). The correspondences he asserts between an individual's intentional purpose, the development of human life, and natural law, correspondences aligning with God's will, are maintained throughout "The Education of the World," where cosmic patterns provide the grounds for the analogy between the natural and spiritual orders. Consistent with the genre of sermon, his essay does not attempt to provide rational grounds for these analogies; instead they take as their point of departure an assumption of divine purpose as it unfolds in the natural order and human life in both its collective form as nation and its individual form as "man."

Perhaps the most important contemporary sources for Temple's argument, however, are the educational writings and sermons of the founding headmaster of Rugby, Thomas Arnold. For instance, in reforming public schools education, Arnold stressed the importance of the older boys and the masters as examples (Stanley 1844, 1:118; Thomas Arnold 1844, 4:369). Temple extends this notion of example from Arnold as one of the central structuring principles of his essay. Even more importantly for the purposes of "The Education of the World," Arnold (1844, 2:106) had preached on Galatians 3:24 ("The law was our schoolmaster to bring us unto Christ"). In effect, for Arnold, as for Temple, Christ becomes the schoolmaster as example to all humanity. The role of law, as Arnold says in another sermon, is to teach "the rudiments of the world," developing the analogy between law and gospel, set in the context of the development of the human race in moral education (Thomas Arnold 1844, 2:314–15). Temple draws on Arnold's pattern of historical development and the analogy between the history of human growth and racial progress, and also makes use of Arnold's concepts of moral education, the shifts from law to obedience and service, the use of rules in childhood, and the dominating metaphor of the law as a schoolmaster. As our notes indicate, Thomas Arnold's theories of education and historical development, as well as his theology, permeate Temple's essay (for Thomas Arnold see Eugene Williamson 1964 and McCrum 1989).

Temple's essay is constructed on an analogy, drawing a comparison between the human development of an individual from childhood through youth to maturity and the collective development of humankind from a primitive to a civilized state. Education in moral and spiritual principles functions as the causative impulse in this development, so that the analogy is seen under two aspects, one of moral or spiritual development, and the other in historical exemplification. The analogy is articulated for each of the three divisions of the essay: first the education of the child according to the rules and principles of law, demanding obedience, with its analogical application morally and historically to the four major cultures Temple specifies: Judea, Rome, Greece, and Asia. Second, comes the education of the youth, according to the model or example in Christ, with the moral analogue in the mixture of restraint and liberty, the development of friendship, and with the historical analogue in the "three Companions" of Greece, Rome, and the early church. The third stage, that of the adult with an active conscience, has its moral analogy in the development of codes of conduct and intellect, and with a historical analogy in the development from the early church through the early medieval folk-migrations, and the Protestant Reformation, which Temple describes as a transition from medieval discipline to the freedom of conscience. Finally, as a conclusion to the essay, the Bible, if rightly read (according to this analogy), may function as an authority to the child, as an example to youth, and as a guide to conscience for the adult, whether viewed as an individual or as a collective. Such education of the world, he argues, will yield the toleration that is the mark of Christianity and of civilization, read as synonymous.

To many Broad Churchmen, biblical truth, together with the evidences of the natural world (as in Paley's *Evidences of Christianity*, 1794, and *Natural Theology*, 1802), mediates the correspondences between the divine and human orders and is communicated through figures of speech and analogies. The empirical facts of the natural world, including the ethnographic data of the human race and the historic data of human societies, may be read analogically as revelatory of God's nature and as indexes of the indirect action of God in the world. It is this history of the world, particularly of the Jews, Romans, Greeks, and Asians before Christ, which Temple reads as an analogue to individual development.

Temple uses the language of distinctions: science, empirical data, proof, and fact. The utilitarian epistemology of "fact" is constantly under attack in such works as Dickens's *Hard Times* (1854) and Browning's *The Ring and the Book* (1868–69). Temple aligns himself with contemporaneous science in his emphasis on the denotative function of language that relegates figures of speech to the role of ornament; however, he joins in this undermining of an absolute reliance upon scientific data as the sole ground of truth in two significant ways, first by questioning the dependence of Victorian science on empirical data and the related proofs of scientific method in favor of an organicist theory of human and natural development, and, second, by asserting of the discovery of a truth greater than empirical fact, the truth in the human heart.

To literalist Evangelicals, the natural world is a snare and delusion, participating in the deleterious effects of the Fall; to Broad Churchmen, the empirical facts of the natural world are read analogically as revelatory of the God's nature and the divine plan for the world. Temple aligns himself with the Broad Church position, with analogical readings both of the Bible and of the relations between the secular world and divine revelation; however, the Broad Church position locates the analogies not in the relation between the design of the world and the divine nature but in correspondences between human life and experience and aspects of the divine order, ultimately between the human heart and the divine spirit. Reading such correspondences aright is revelatory; it is in this process that Temple locates "the education of the world" and that Jowett designates the "interpretation of Scripture."

Notwithstanding the early praise of the *Literary Gazette* for the "very noble and profound essay" of Temple (14 Apr. 1860, 459), contemporary reviewers were broadly dismissive of it. Stanley, Wilberforce, and the anonymous reviewer for the *Christian Remembrancer* did not take offense at anything Temple writes, but neither did they see much exceptional in it. Stanley calls "almost the whole" of Temple's essay (and "a large portion" of Jowett's) "eminently conservative" (1861a, 472), but nevertheless claims the two of them to "stand far above the others" in the volume (477). According to Stanley, "The elaborate analogy between the individual and the race" could not be justified, "but the general theological position of the writer can only be shaken by impugning the sacred text on which the sermon was founded" (1861a, 477–78). Wilberforce, in discussing the "mere literary quality of the volume" as "below what we should have been led to expect from the names of the seven essayists," singles out "The Education of the World" as empty and prolix (1861, 248). The *Christian Remembrancer* compares Temple's essay with Pattison's, on the grounds of their not being offensive to "miracle or prophecy"; nor do they "attempt to show that the Old Testament is altogether incredible, nor that the New Testament must be explained away to suit the prejudices or meet the claims of philosophy of the nineteenth century." The review also states that both writers do not contradict "their present positions in the Church of England" (*Christian* 1861, 351).

In the *Westminster Review*, Harrison took exception to Temple's more than any other essay in the volume, devoting some seven columns to it in his review. In this scathing attack, Temple "strikes . . . the key-note of the whole by reducing the teaching of the Hebrews to the level of that of Greece and Rome" (1860, 300). To Harrison, Temple's essay is used as to demonstrate more general faults of the clergy and the universities: "The whole essay is a mere mystification. Dr. Temple does not adopt, and scarcely, perhaps, comprehends, the notion of the life of the human race, or its growth by invariable laws. His views of the colossal man is a mere rhetorical phrase recklessly borrowed and loosely adapted. . . . It is a flagrant instance of the habit now prevalent amongst Churchmen (though rare in this book) of snatching up the language or the ideas of really free-thinking, and using them for their purposes in a way which is utterly thoughtless or shamefully dishonest. The pedantic education and shuffling morality of the Universities, too often leads them to adopt the principles of hostile criticism, in the spirit of the rhetorician or the sophist. They turn criticism into apology by trope, and twist an axiom of science to support a popular error" (1860, 309).

Wilberforce in the *Quarterly* singles out Temple for particular mention as inflicting "deepest pain" for his collaboration in the volume, partly because his essay, while it contains no "such sophistries or scepticisms as abound throughout the rest," must still "be construed in connection with them" (1861, 251), all of which makes Wilberforce "tremble, not only for the faith, but for the morals of his pupils" (256). Temple is particularly reprehensible since his essay is the "portal" to the rest of the edifice (251). A number of other writers use Temple's name to pun on the general attack of these critics on the fabric and orthodoxy of the church in constructing a "temple of Infidelity" (Close 1861, 59), and "the pantheistic temple of English liberalism" (Woodgate 1861, 4). E. M. Goulburn, Temple's precursor as headmaster of Rugby, objects to Temple's use of analogy, particularly the parallel between the progress of the individual human mind and the mind of the church (1861, 19). The same line is taken by James Buchanan: Temple's notion of progressive development of the child from infancy to maturity presupposes a similar course and causality in the successive development of law, example, and principle, three of his governing ideas; but such notions are not, according to Buchanan, successive or progressive, but "synchronous" and so the analogy fails (1861, 57). In another pamphlet, W. E. Jelf similarly attacked Temple at each point in his analogy, attempting to show that his turn from the collective progress of the human race to the condition of the individual is flawed (1861, 26). Jelf, like many, including Temple's old friend and colleague Tait, urged him repeatedly to dissociate himself from the rest of the Essayists and Reviewers, an action that he resolutely resisted (Letters 64, 66–67, 70, 72, 76, 80, 82, and 85–86).

When Temple was appointed bishop of Exeter in 1869, all of the old arguments concerning his complicity in the volume as a whole, his liberalism if not worse, and his refusal to distance himself from the other Essayists brought many attacks crashing on his still unmitred head. As usual, the resolute and litigious defender of orthodoxy George Anthony Denison headed the lists in attacking Temple by republishing his 1861 tract against him with the renewed aim of "dispelling the vulgar fallacy that Dr. Temple is responsible for his own Essay only; a fallacy born either of ignorance or of dishonesty. For the general issue, which the intellectual fanaticism of Mr. Gladstone has made possible, I have this to say:—If a writer in a Book, condemned *without reservation* by a Synodical Judgment, may, without retraction, or explanation, or disavowal, or remission or qualification of Sentence, be raised to the Episcopate, then the Church of England, *as by Law established*, is a profane absurdity" (Denison 1869, 4).

Rowland Williams, German Historical Criticism, and Biblical Chronology

Rowland Williams (1817–1870) was born at Haklyn, Flintshire, in Wales. He was educated at Eton College and King's College, Cambridge, winning a scholarship in his first year, later returning to King's as a classics tutor for eight years. He read extensively in German theology, especially the works of C. C. J. von Bunsen and the Old Testament critic H. G. A. Ewald, both of whom he knew and visited. As well he read widely in the group of theologians influenced by the philosophical theology of F. D. E. Schleiermacher, stressing the role of intuition and feeling in religious experience. This group was known from 1828 as the *Vermittlungstheologie* (mediating theology) school, between the old confessional orthodoxies from reformation Lutheranism and the more radical critics such as I. A. Dorner, J. A. W. Neander, and F. A. G. Tholuck, all read by Williams.

In 1849 Williams was appointed to St. David's College, Lampeter, in Wales (founded in 1822 to prepare Welsh students for ordination, but poorly endowed both financially and academically). In 1850 he became vice-principal and professor of Hebrew, publishing a series of public lectures from Cambridge, *Rational Godliness* (1855), and *Christianity and Hinduism* (1856, an expansion of his Muir Prize essay), and was awarded the Cambridge D. D. (1857). Williams was invited by H. B. Wilson to contribute to *Essays and Reviews*: it was his essay, together with Wilson's, that provoked the heresy charges that led to their trial, first, in the Court of Arches, presided over by Dr. Stephen Lushington. He was charged by Walter Kerr Hamilton, bishop of Salisbury, and was convicted in December 1862 in a decision that deprived him of his parochial office and benefits, that inhibited him from publishing and teaching for a year, and that led to his reluctant resignation from Lampeter (1862). The sentence, suspended while he appealed to the Judicial Committee of the Privy Council, wound its way through the courts. When Lord Westbury, the Lord Chancellor, pronounced sentence in 1864, Williams was formally acquitted and retained his offices, and benefits (but not the position at Lampeter). In the meantime the strain on his health was too great: he retired to his parish duties at Broad Chalke. Williams died on 18 January 1870. His biography, edited by his wife Ellen, was published in 1874.For a photograph of Williams taken about the time of the publication of *Essays and Reviews*, see figure 5.

Williams's essay, and the vehement responses it provoked, must be read in the context of the hostile reception in Britain to German higher criticism. In 1825 Hugh James Rose delivered four sermons to the university at Cambridge that he subsequently published as *The State of the Protestant Religion in Germany*, in which he attacks the historical method of Eichhorn and J. S. Semler for leveling a weapon at the gospels to encompass "the destruction of Christianity" and at H. E. G. Paulus for his perpetration of rationalistic "trash" (1825, 68–69). Pusey, who had himself studied at Göttingen in 1825, responded with *An Historical Enquiry into the Probable Causes of the Rationalist Character Lately Predominant in the Theology of Germany* (1828), correcting Rose's excesses by a far more sober account, greatly extending the dimensions of rationalism back to the Reformation, and greatly complicating its history from Rose's simplistic attack by setting out a principle of "crisis" in religious history that enables religion to progress when traditional belief encounters new forms of thought. Pusey also provided a context within which some German theologians could be labeled "rationalist," and he drew important connections with English deism and the replacement of doctrine with morality that such Essayists as Pattison and Wilson would, in his view, later exemplify. On the other hand, Pusey and other traditionalists were quick to align themselves with the conservative side of German scholarship (in people like E. W. Hengstenberg) in which the streams of orthodoxy ran deep, untroubled by, or at least well sand-bagged against, the eroding floods of their radical colleagues.

Two factors made the academic situation in Germany different from England: first, Germany had many more universities—twenty-one to England's four (Oxford, Cambridge, Durham, and London), and the normal system of instruction in Germany made extensive use of lecturing by professors who were published experts in their fields, speaking to students who were expected to attend and take notes since examinations were based on such elaborations of the fields, often with the most up-to-date scholarship; and second, German scholars also did not have to subscribe to doctrinal statements as English university teachers did. Of course theo-

Figure 5. Rowland Williams (c. 1860). From an engraving, frontispiece in Ellen Williams, *The Life and Letters of Rowland Williams, D.D.,* 1874.

logical faculties often reacted negatively to extremes of doctrine by resorting to censures or expulsions, but in general the German professor "had great liberty of religious opinion" (Crowther 1970, 41).

Broad Church theologians opposed English traditionalist interpretations of the Formularies by importing contemporary German scholarship. By such means they pushed the ecclesiastical establishments either to recognize and accept their scholarly arguments, methods, and applications, or to resist them by imposing the strictures of the Formularies. The German challenge was set out three years before *Essays and Reviews* in Mark Pattison's assessment of the "Present State of Theology in Germany" (1857) in the *Westminster Review*: "For in this country, it is hardly necessary to say, a very unfavourable opinion of the state of theology in Germany is widely prevalent. We welcome eagerly their historical and critical labours; the scholars in our universities are content . . . to sit at the feet of German professors in Greek, and in general Philology. But German Theology has been long under a ban" (1889, 2:211). To Pattison, "critical theology" is "the theological movement of the age," equal in importance to the Ecumenical Councils, scholasticism, and the Reformation, and is best represented in the "historico-critical" method of the Tübingen school under F. C. Baur in applying historical methods to the development of biblical documents and doctrine (Pattison 1889, 2:235). The relations between England and Germany in the study of the classics and the Bible, linked disciplines that fostered each other in terms of textual and literary study, are complex and involve a range of political and ecclesiastical interests, as such recent scholars as W. R. Ward have pointed out (Helmstadter and Lightman 1990, 55–62). English classicists and biblical scholars were indebted to German scholars for texts of both the classics and the Bible used in teaching and study. At the same time, the onslaughts of higher criticism, the literary-critical study of the Bible and of the classics, raised many serious problems in the area of truth claims and personal or public belief since similar methods were applied to each. The text "as a historical and an anthropological document" (Wolf [1795] 1985, 20) was being applied to other documents: to the early history of Rome by Niebuhr and to ancient Israel by Henry Hart Milman. Göttingen and Tübingen historians and critics were being studied by such scholars as Thomas Arnold, Julius Hare, John Sterling, and Connop Thirlwall. All read Eichhorn, Wolf, and Niebuhr, and all reacted positively, not agreeing with everything, but accepting that ancient texts had to be treated as historical documents, studied in relation to the various times of their creation, inscription, and reception. The second generation of Broad Church theologians continued this association with contemporary German theology: Stanley and Jowett knew Bunsen and through him met Neander; Temple and Jowett read Kant and began a translation of Hegel's *Logic*; Temple used Lessing in his essay; and Pattison was in many ways the best read of all of them in German theology and philosophy.

A far more controversial dimension was given to biblical study in the mythologizing biography of Jesus published by D. F. Strauss as *Leben Jesu* ([1835]

1846). Strauss argued that the gospels represent a collection of legendary stories based on the knowledge of a Galilean teacher and leader who lived a pure life and whose holiness brought him into heroic conflict with the religious authorities. After his death, his deeds prompted the stories that gathered around him in the early Christian communities, conferring miraculous deeds upon him to indicate his status and as fulfillments of Messianic prophesies. By 1850 the public awareness of "Germanism," "rationalism," and "Straussianism" was so extensive that Robert Browning could assume a response from his readers with the references in *Christmas-Eve and Easter-Day* (1850) to "this Myth of Christ" (ll. 859; 866–75). It was into this atmosphere of threat concerning German theology that *Essays and Reviews*, as one of the first wide-scale applications of German methodology to general questions of criticism, made such an impression and within which Williams's essay, focusing on the work of one German theologian, was a primary instance of affront; however, by the end of the century, virtually all of the claims made by the heretics and their associates were accepted quietly into the theology of a changing orthodoxy. In the 1850s and 1860s, however, these differences between Germany and England were particularly important when an English theologian, such as Williams, sought to represent the work of a German theologian, such as Bunsen, to an English readership in a positive light.

Williams's essay is a review of the works of Baron Bunsen, and the identification of his views with or separation of them from those of Bunsen was particularly difficult to ascertain (see Letter 168). He declared Bunsen to be a point of synthesis among a number of sources he wished to identify: "Best of all for me . . . is that conscientious freedom of inquiry, tinged with metaphysics, and reverential from habit, which may be called the converging result of Neander, Bunsen, Stier, Jowett, and Robertson, coming upon plentiful doses of Coleridge, with some study of the Christian Fathers, in the spirit in which they are unfolded by Bunsen in his *Hippolytus and his Age*" (Ellen Williams 1874, 2:96). English Broad Church theologians such as Arnold, Hare, Maurice, and Thirlwall beat a steady path to Bunsen in Rome and Switzerland, Jowett and Stanley to him in Berlin, while Williams visited him in 1857 and Pattison offered to translate his *Gott in der Geschichte* (God in history) when Susanna Winkworth questioned her competence to finish it (Crowther 1970, 68–69). Bunsen was, then, in many respects an appropriate and suitable theologian for Williams to discuss. His range of writings was broad and was influenced by the leading new historian of the day, Niebuhr, and as well he had an important association with the English and German establishments as a mediating figure in diplomacy, ecclesiastical politics, and theological affiliations.

Christian Charles Josias, baron von Bunsen, was a Prussian diplomat and scholar. He was educated at Marburg and Göttingen, becoming a specialist in comparative philology and in ancient, near eastern, and other languages (Hebrew, Arabic, Persian, and Norse, as well as Italian, French, and English). When the historian Niebuhr was appointed Prussian envoy to the Vatican, he had Bunsen appointed secretary of the embassy, and as such he became responsible for negotiations concerning the re-establishment of the Catholic hierarchy in Prussia, continuing to work in Rome for twenty-one years. In 1838 he moved to England with his English wife (whom he had married in Rome), and at the request of the Prussian king, Frederick Wilhelm IV, assisted England and Prussia in the establishment of the Jerusalem bishopric. The move was controversial since it involved the cooperation of the Church of England with the German Lutheran Church, but it was negotiated and completed in six months in the summer of 1841. Queen Victoria selected him from among three proposed by Prussia as ambassador to England in 1842. In Stanley's *Life and Correspondence of Thomas Arnold* (1844), Bunsen was singled out as one of the German theologians Arnold admired and often wrote to.

From 1845 Bunsen published long monographs in German, soon translated into English, on Egypt and universal history, the history of the early church, historiography, comparative philology, and biblical interpretation and commentary: *Egypt's Place in Universal History* (1848–67, 5 vols.), *Hippolytus and His Age* (1852, 2 vols.), *Outlines of the Philosophy of Universal History, Applied to Language and Religion* (1854, 2 vols.), and *God in History* (1868–70, 3 vols.), as well as a Bible translation and commentary unfinished at his death (see Owen 1924 and Rogerson 1984, 121–37).

Bunsen's study of *Egypt's Place in Universal History* concentrates on documentary evidence, especially the disputed chronologies of the Pharaohs, hieroglyphic inscriptions, and the recent publications of Egyptian antiquities after Napoleon's incursions into Egypt. Drawing on such scholars as Champollion and Lepsius, both of whom he knew, Bunsen paid particular attention to the writings of the German historians of ancient Israel in relating the narratives of the captivity of the Israelites in Egypt to the Egyptian chronologies and archaeological records. The implications were important in relating Egyptian records to Abraham, Jacob, Moses, and the exodus, still problematically dated in English Bibles in 1491 B.C.E., only some 2,513 years from the creation of the world and of Adam according to Ussher's date of 4004 B.C.E.

In *Hippolytus* Bunsen traces the development of Christianity from the apostolic age through seven generations of the early church, from 29 to 264, in each generation outlining the course of theological debate in a selection of patristic writers. The volume concludes with five lengthy letters addressed to his friend Julius Charles Hare, on a new Hippolytus manuscript. The second volume, dedicated to Thomas Arnold, includes translations of documents: first, second-century treatises on church and daily life; second, on liturgy and canon law; and third, on the theology of the early church. After each document, Bunsen discusses its place in early church life ("the Picture"), its ramifications for nineteenth-century religious practice in Germany and England ("the Reflex"), and its implications for the future of the church ("the Practical Application"). In each section Bunsen criticizes the Christianity of his own time, urging religious toleration and broad latitude in religious practice and doctrine. He claims that such inclusiveness was characteristic of the early church, along with a belief in the universalism of the Christian message and the interiority of the religious life, as opposed to exclusiveness and ritual externals.

Bunsen's *God in History*, applies various aspects of Hegelian dialectic to the role of providence in history, especially in ancient Israel. He also began a new multivolume translation into German of a "Bible for the people" with commentaries that relate the study of the Bible to current movements in scholarship. It was while he was engaged on this project that he died. The publication of *A Memoir of Baron Bunsen* by his widow (1868, 2 vols.) brought forth a number of reviews, including those by F. D. Maurice (1868), Margaret Oliphant (1868), and Henry Alford (1868). Alford, then dean of Canterbury, drew the customary distinction between the influential, much-applauded, and well-liked diplomatist and convivial host and the controversial theologian who so influenced Broad Church theology: "Any future historian of the religious struggles of the nineteenth century in this country will have to take account of his personal influence as one of its representative men" (Alford 1868, 136). Alford sets out in summary form the points in Bunsen that "startle many English minds, and grieve many devout hearts," the same points Williams develops that led to his prosecution: "In his [Bunsen's] views as to the date and authorship of books of the Old and New Testament, in his admission of a 'mythical deposit in the Gospel history,' in his exclusion, at first partial, and afterwards complete, of any historical predictions from the work of the prophets of the Old or New Testament, in his criticism on the growth of the creeds and organization of the Church . . . there is much against which . . . to . . . protest" (136–37). The protest, beginning in the year after Bunsen's death, was directed primarily at Williams as one of his English reviewers and champions.

In his review, begun at Christmas 1858, Williams deals extensively with three of Bunsen's works, each relating to an important aspect of his biblical criticism and to important areas of Williams's own theological interest. After an introduction on an enlarged notion of revelation in contemporary thought that includes advances in science and history and that implies continuous and even progressive revelation, Williams addresses Bunsen's work on Egypt. The comparative study of the cultures of the ancient Near East, the use of archaeological and philological evidence, and the testimony of the ancient historians all lead, in Williams's view (ventriloquizing Bunsen), to doubts being cast on the historical reliability of the narrative of the Egyptian portion of the history of Israel as recorded in the Pentateuch.

Williams's review of *God in History* raises the issues of the Hebrew prophets, their chronology, and the meaning and interpretation of prophecy in general. In treating the prophets historically Williams invokes his long-standing appeal to the "verifying faculty" of reason, linking it to Bunsen's concept that the Bible is "the expression of devout reason," showing the divine government of the world. Focusing closely on Bunsen's discussion of Isaiah and Daniel, Williams concludes that the predictive concept of prophecy cannot be supported out of these texts, either as alluding to events that are "foretold" concerning the events in the New Testament or as events in the subsequent history of the church. Instead the prophetic message concerns the moral nature of human beings and the providential plan of God in history to bring in the rule of justice and peace that the Bible calls "the kingdom of God."

Having already struck serious blows at the historicity of the Pentateuch, especially at the formative event of the exodus, and by implication at the Mosaic law, and at the prophetical function of the Hebrew scriptures as Messianic predictions of the life of Jesus or of the church, Williams had already placed himself in jeopardy. In the section of the review dealing with *Hippolytus and His Age*, Williams addresses Bunsen's chronology of the New Testament, the order and dating of the canon, and the sequence of the first centuries compared with the contemporary controversies in Germany and England and concerning the place of ecclesiology and doctrine in the early church. A key moment is the Council at Jerusalem and the issue of inclusivity or exclusivity of the Gentile world on the basis of conformity in doctrine and propriety in morality, points similar to those to be brought up in Wilson's essay.

Williams's strategy throughout is to use Bunsen as a mouthpiece for his own views and to blur the distinctions between his views and those of the German scholar. This tactic was quickly condemned in the trials where Williams's voice was said to be identical to Bunsen's, with no distinction drawn between his views and those of Bunsen. Williams often tried to defend himself on this point, but his admiration for Bunsen, his use of Bunsen's arguments, and their common use of the same sources made it difficult to distinguish between them.

Williams also provoked his critics by advocating a number of doctrines that English theologians consistently attacked in German theologians and biblical interpreters: a denial of plenary and literal inspiration for all parts of the Bible equally in favor of some parts as inspired, others as historical accounts, and still others as flawed and erroneous; a questioning of the authorship of some of the books of the Bible, and an assertion that such traditional ascriptions should be revised; and an acceptance of a too-Lutheran view of justification (that it should be interpreted morally, not literally), and a too–Broad Church view of propitiation, aligning him with Jowett on the atonement. Behind his critics' attacks lurked a suspicion of Bunsen on the part of the High Church party. His work in establishing the Jerusalem bishopric with German Lutherans raised questions concerning the apostolic succession, and his writings on Hippolytus suggested that the priesthood developed later than the New Testament documents could assert; both implied attacks in Williams on Tractarian sacerdotalism. On the other hand, Low Church theologians were deeply suspicious that both Williams and Bunsen held inclusivist views of the church, denied the literal and plenary inspiration of the Bible, and stressed the moral impact of miracles and prophecy rather than their traditional evidential and predictive roles.

Fundamentally, Williams makes a conventional distinction between historical and critical methods of analysis. The former, based on such Broad Church theologians and historians as Arnold, Thirlwall, Hare, and Milman, places history within the cycles of human development, and as such is open to rational understanding. Critical analysis is related to the ideas of Kant and their elaboration by Coleridge. In Coleridge the distinction between understanding and reason is first set out in *Biographia Literaria* ([1817] 1983, 1:173–75). Quoting Milton, Coleridge adds to Kant's notion of the role of reason, arguing against Kant that it can give accurate knowledge of spiritual truth, and so can lead to reading the Bible as the "expression of devout reason," a phrase judged so adversely because Williams's opponents saw reason as a revived eighteenth-century deistic error or as a version of nineteenth-century German rationalism. It was precisely on these grounds that Williams's review was cited for heresy in the Court of Arches.

Several reviewers drew connections among the various treatments of passages from the Pentateuch in the Essayists, and on this point Williams was particularly susceptible. For instance, the reviewer in the *Christian Remembrancer* notes that while Goodwin attacks the Mosaic account of creation on philosophical and scientific grounds, rendering Moses liable to be "charged with the accusation of palming upon an ignorant multitude for political purposes a pure invention" (1860, 330), Williams attacks Moses on historical grounds, casting doubt on both the "fierce ritual" of the Abraham and Isaac story and the idea of the exodus as the march of a group of Bedouin nomads. But, as with other reviewers, the *Christian Remembrancer* is particularly severe on Williams's view of prophecy as descriptions of contemporary events instead of conjectures about the future (332–35). Harrison in the *Westminster* argues that what Temple had done for history, Williams had done for the historians: "Dr. Temple has thus reduced the national position of the Hebrews to the level of the Romans, and Dr. Williams has reduced the critical authority of the Bible to the level of Livy" (1860, 302); he has subjected, according to the historical and literary critical method, "the entire Scripture to a process which combines that pursued by Niebuhr upon Livy, with that of Wolf upon Homer. In short, the truth of the narrative and the identity of the authors disappear together. It becomes a medley of legend, poetry, and oral tradition, compiled, remodelled, and interpolated by a priestly order centuries after the times of its supposed authors" (310). Wilberforce in the *Quarterly* accuses Williams of being a literary puppeteer as he ventriloquizes Bunsen, "sheltering himself behind the burly lay figure whose limbs he moves at will," while uttering "his utmost fancies through another's mouth" (1861, 253). Such dishonest gestures, according to Wilberforce, are futile since the absolute equation of Williams's views with those of Bunsen is manifest throughout his essay: the dominance of the "verifying faculty" or rationalism that is "THE idea of the whole volume, the connecting-link between all its writers" (255). Furthermore, it is Williams's notion of the "verifying faculty" in the individual that is the key link among the essays and the source of the destruction of the doctrine of inspiration that they advocate (244–45). Stanley in the *Edinburgh*, attempting reconciliatory gestures, singled out Williams for some of his harshest remarks: "Conclusions arrived at by the life-long labours of a great German theologian are pitchforked into the face of the English public, who never heard of them before, with hardly a shred of argument to clothe their repulsive forms" (1861a, 474). Williams himself is marked by "a pugnacity and an irritability" in controversy that is ascribed to his "Welsh blood," and his review has a "flippant and contemptuous tone" (479)—all remarks which led Williams to complain that Stanley had dropped "Wilson and myself in the mud, particularly poor me. This is ridiculously unfair" (Letter 115).

Williams tried to provoke Connop Thirlwall into an attack on him in *An Earnestly Respectful Letter to the Lord Bishop of St. David's, on the Difficulty of Bringing Theological Questions to an Issue* (1860). Williams quotes passages from their letters, alleging that the bishop's imputing of heterodoxy against him in 1857 had never been addressed in such a way that Williams could clear himself. Thirlwall resisted a theological response until his charge of 1863, but by then Walter Kerr Hamilton, bishop of Salisbury, in whose diocese Williams was in charge of the parish of Broad Chalke, had initiated the accusations of heresy that wound their way through the ecclesiastical and civil courts from 1861 to 1864.

Baden Powell, Inductive Science, and the Evidence of Miracles

Baden Powell (1796–1860) was born in Kent. His early education was under the influence of the "Hackney Phalanx," a group of Anglican clergy in South London (three of them his uncles) who supported the constitutional links between the established church and the state. Powell graduated from Oriel College, Oxford, in 1817 with a first-class degree in mathematics. Between 1822 and 1825 he published thirteen articles on scientific subjects and on theology in the journal of the Phalanx, the *British Critic*. In 1827 he was appointed Savilian Professor of Geometry at Oxford, devoting the rest of his life to teaching and writing, on differential calculus, radiant heat, optics, the geometry of curves, and the history and philosophy of science; he also engaged in debate concerning the theological questions of his day. Powell died on June 11, 1860, a little over two months after his essay was published in *Essays and Reviews* and just weeks after correcting his copy for the second edition (for his biography see Corsi 1988). See figure 6.

The topic of miracles and evidences was of lively interest in England when Powell was writing his essay. The theological climate had already pitted varying positions against each other. On the one hand were such old-fashioned liberals as Trench, who in 1846 published *Notes on the Miracles of Our Lord*, a popular work which, by 1856, had reached its fifth edition, with a substantial 100-page Preliminary Essay setting out the New Testament terms for miracles, relating the miracles to the general laws of nature, and drawing on a wide range of patristic writing to

Figure 6. Baden Powell (c. 1860). Photograph courtesy of Francis Baden-Powell. Used with permission.

establish the authority of miracles as evidence in the early church. His position anticipated Powell's later rejection of miracles as compelling evidence for the truth claims of Christianity, and he also admitted the role of prior religious faith in determining belief in the miracles. On the other hand, some scientists, like the authors of the Bridgewater Treatises (see Helmstadter and Lightman 1990 and Topham 1993), revisited the relation of the evidences and natural theology through the new sciences.

William Whewell's Bridgewater Treatise, *Astronomy and General Physics Considered with Reference to Natural Theology* (1833), the first of the series to be published, was cited opposite the title page of Darwin's *On the Origin of Species,* reapplying the language attacking miracles to new data: "But with regard to the material world, we can at least go so far as this—we can perceive that events are brought about not by insulated interpositions of Divine power, exerted in each particular case, but by the establishment of general laws" (Whewell 1833, 356). Darwin argues, together with Whewell, that "insulated interpositions of Divine power," or miracles, are subsumed in the enactment and functioning of "general laws" over epochs of modification.

Such views were opposed by other natural theologians, such as Thomas Chalmers, the Scots Evangelical, who also issued a Bridgewater Treatise in 1833, *On the Power, Wisdom, and Goodness of God as Manifested in the Adaptation of External Nature to the Moral and Intellectual Constitution of Man.* In 1836, in *Natural Theology,* he uses "interposition," the same term as Whewell, with reference to the "miracle" of creation: "We hold the week of the first chapter of Genesis to have been literally a week of miracles—the period of a great creative interposition, during which, by so many successive evolutions, the present economy was raised out of the wreck and materials of the one which had gone before it" (1836, 1:230). Hence, in the decades before *Essays and Reviews* scientists and theologians differed, even amongst themselves, about the relation of science to natural theology and of both to evidentiary arguments.

A number of writers in the 1850s and 1860s dealt with the question of miracles in relation to more general problems in epistemology. For instance, H. L. Mansel had delivered the Bampton Lectures in 1858 on *The Limits of Religious Thought Examined.* He followed Kant's view that the noumenal world cannot be known, arguing that human beings know of God's nature only through divine revelation, including miracles. F. D. Maurice attacked this view in *What Is Revelation?* (1859), asserting that miracles are signs of the manifestation or coming of the kingdom of Christ, not evidential proofs of Christ's authority. In 1859 George Rawlinson delivered the Bampton Lectures on *The Historical Evidences of the Truth of the Scripture Records Stated Anew, with Special Reference to the Doubts and Discoveries of Modern Times,*[12] and in the same year Brooke Foss Westcott, one of Maurice's followers, published a collection of Cambridge sermons, *Characteristics of the Gospel Miracles.* In 1865 J. B. Mozley delivered the Bampton Lectures on *Eight Lectures on Miracles.* The topic, particularly the question of whether miracles continued in the church after the death of the Apostles, the issue of "ecclesiastical miracles," also arose in controversy between Anglicans and Roman Catholics. Newman wrote about this matter in his *Lectures on the Present Position of Catholics in England* (1851), and in 1858 the issue was sensationalized as a result of the appearances of the Virgin Mary to Bernadette Soubirous at Lourdes in the south of France.

The phrase prefixed to Powell's essay—"On the Study of"—indicates that his topic is neither "evidence" nor "miracles" in and of themselves; rather, it foregrounds the theory of miracles within the traditional divisions of systematic theology. A student in the nineteenth century began the systematic study of religion with natural theology, in which God's effects in nature provide the basis for the demonstration and description of the divine attributes. "Natural theology" in this context is "the science which treats of the being, attributes, and will of God, as evincible from the various phenomena of created objects" (Buck 1851, 746; see also 504–9; and Dorner 1885, 2:155). But natural theology was seen as defective in dealing with the problems of evil, human sin and error, and the notion of forgiveness, requiring the "*necessity for some direct revelation from God*" (*Encyclopaedia Metropolitana*, 2:863), the second major category of theology, the evidential proofs for the truth claims of the Bible as revelation. The study of the "evidences," then, derives from natural theology but particularly applies to the study of revealed religion and miracles. According to the argument from design, the natural universe provides natural theology with "external evidence" of God's attributes. The Bible, in turn, provides "formal evidence" of the validity of revealed religion through testimony to miracles (sometimes referred to as the "external evidence" of miracles as recorded in the Bible). Finally, human consciousness and moral conduct attest to that validity through the "internal evidence" of feeling and conviction.

The analogy of the "external evidences" from nature was elaborated throughout the eighteenth century chiefly in controversy between Christian apologists and the deists on the one hand and philosophical scepticism on the other. The deists maintained that there are innate ideas concerning the existence of God, that God should be worshipped, chiefly through a life of virtue, that repentance for sin is a duty, and upon such conduct will depend a future life of rewards and punishments. Such views, as advanced by Lord Herbert of Cherbury in *De Veritate* (1624; Concerning truth), were much modified by later deists. John Toland in *Christianity Not Mysterious* (1696) argued that Christianity is wholly conformable to the dictates of reason and has no need of special revelation or miraculous interventions, views that emphasized God's omnipotence and unchangeableness, active at creation but with no role in the providential governing of nature and human life. Christian apologists, then, had to convince the deists of the role of providence in governing nature and moral actions, as in Robert Boyle's *The Excellence of Theology Compared with Natural Philosophy* (1664) and John Ray's *The Wisdom of God Manifested in the Works of Creation* (1691); and second, to convince them of special revelation. In both arguments the role of the evidences was central: external evidence of nature whereby God could be known as active providentially through effects, and the evidence of miracles in revelation as testimony to the truth of the Gospels.

In Britain discussion of miracles in relation to philosophical scepticism derives from John Locke. In *The Reasonableness of Christianity* (1695) Locke establishes the "reasonable" grounds on which faith can be constructed, basing the reliability of revelation on the degree of assent which may be accorded to Christ as the emissary of that revelation in two respects: the fulfilment of prophecies and the performance of miracles. In *A Discourse of Miracles*, published posthumously in 1706, Locke defines a miracle as "a sensible operation, which, being above the comprehension of the spectator, and in his opinion contrary to the established course of nature, is taken by him to be divine" (Locke [1695] 1958, 79). Hence, Locke locates the data for a miracle not in the truth claims of an infallible book or person but in the empirical sensations of an observer, while, at the same time, placing the performance of a miracle in the context of divine power (Locke [1695] 1958, 83). Such power is not comparable to coercive power in the state, as Locke argued in *A Third Letter Concerning Toleration* but is a compelling power that is recognized by the understanding when it functions intuitively in perceiving the agreement of ideas in the mind. Hence, the perception of miracles as "strong marks of an extraordinary divine power" ([1695] 1958, 83) stresses them as empirical evidences, a point David Hume was to reject.

Hume defines miracles as violations of the laws of nature by the specific will or interposition of a deity or invisible agent ([1748] 1964, 93). But miracles to Hume are unknowable empirically. Miracles violate the sacrosanct order and uniformity of natural law. Witnesses' testimony concerning miracles is contradictory, partial, and partisan, and hence is invalid and must be repudiated. In "Of Miracles" he argues "no human testimony can have such force as to prove a miracle, and make it a just foundation for any . . . system of religion" ([1748] 1964, 105). Dismissing all truth claims for religion on the basis of reason, he recuperates religion at the end of his essay on the basis of faith (108). Hume's attack on miracles and testimony to them sets the agenda for Christian apologists for the next 100 years, but it remains, as our annotation of Powell's essay demonstrates, one of the monuments of eighteenth-century reason to which later commentators continually had to return.[13]

Natural theology and its relation to miracles for the eighteenth and earlier nineteenth century are set out chiefly in *The Analogy of Religion, Natural and Revealed, to the Constitution and Course of Nature* (1736) by Joseph Butler, a response to the attacks of the deists; and in *View of the Evidences of Christianity* (1794) and *Natural Theology* (1802) by William Paley, responses to the attacks by Hume and consolidations of earlier theological opinion on the evidences. Each of these treatises was prescribed reading for the examination of undergraduates at Oxford and Cambridge at the time when *Essays and Reviews* was published (see Powell ¶s 24, 105, and notes).[14] Butler and Paley respond to both the deists and the philosophical empiricists that the physical world and the miracles are reliable "evidences"; the physical world is read as evidentiary of the "power, wisdom, and goodness of God," in the words of the Bridgewater Treatises (1833–37). Similarly the Gospel miracles are read as evidentiary of the role of Jesus as the prophesied Messiah (Paley [1794] 1850, pt. 1, chap. 10; "Recapitulation"), contradicting Hume's attack, that the evidence and so the credibility of the Gospel witnesses cannot be tested or believed. To Paley the credibility of such testimony can be evaluated by any reader in terms of its truth or falsity, using commonsense experience to judge its value. All of these points are raised by Powell in his discussion of miracles and their evidential role in the defense of Christianity, and even the title of his own essay alludes to Paley's work of 1794.

Victorian reaction against Paley and Butler was symptomatic of the shift in the location of the burden of proof for the argument from design. Stanley, for instance, commented: "The attempts of Paley to rest Christianity solely upon its external evidences have in our time, been rejected by a higher and more comprehensive philosophy" (1850, 1:310). Paley's pre-eminence continued to be advocated, however, by Richard Whately in *Historic Doubts* (1819) and *Christian Evidences* (1838) and by Renn Dickson Hampden in *Philosophical Evidence of Christianity* (1827). But with the development of the new sciences, particularly geology, the argument from design and the role of evidence in the analogy of nature shifts away from stress on complexity of design. The testimony of the Bible, and especially of the chronology of Genesis, is subordinated to the much longer chronology displayed in the testimony of the rocks and the origin and evolution of species.

The evidentiary value of the miracles was also questioned by German higher criticism of the Bible. To German idealist theologians such as Eichhorn, Paulus, and Strauss, miracles are events in nature that cannot be explained according to other events in human experience, and so are relegated to misunderstood or misinterpreted natural occurrences, conditioned by the mental or moral superiority of the miracle-worker, or the credulous state of mind of the witnesses, or the rhetorical purposes of the gospel narrators.

Powell wrote on miracles and the evidences at least six times before *Essays and Reviews*: in *Connexion of Natural and Divine Truth* (1838), a review of J. H. Newman's *Miracles* (1843) in the *British and Foreign Review* (1844), an article in the *Edinburgh Review* (1847), an essay on "The Burnet Prizes" (1857), the third section of *The Order of Nature* (1859), and an essay on "Testimony" in *Chambers' Edinburgh Journal* (1859). In the last of these he discusses the different kinds of evidence allowed in different fields of knowledge in the light of "the scientific scepticism of our age" (1). He gives what is in many respects a summation of "On the Study of the Evidences of Christianity": "It so happens that the religion which the most enlightened nations of the earth have received and profess, rests on a series of occurrences which took place between eighteen and thirty-six centuries ago, and which have been recorded in historical narratives. Many persons having doubted these alleged facts, a set of writers well affected to the Christian religion have come forward as its apologists or defenders; and a leading part of their works on the subject consists in a treatment of the laws of evidence as to facts, resulting in a conclusion that the occurrences in question, though of a nature not merely extraordinary, but apparently supernatural, being vouched for by a sufficient number of credible witnesses, ought to be implicitly believed" (1859b, 4–5). Powell differentiates verification of facts or witnesses through Baconian principles of experimentation and an unproblematic theory of commonsense observation, just as he would one year later in *Essays and Reviews*: "No contrast could well be more complete. In the one case, testimony regarding assumedly natural, though novel facts and occurrences, is treated with a rigour which *would enable us to battle off anything whatever that we did not wish to receive*, if it could not be readily subjected to experiment, or immediately shewn in a fresh instance—and perhaps even then. In the other, the power and inclination of men to observe correctly any palpable fact, and report it truly, is asserted without exception or reserve; and, on this ground, even facts assumed to be miraculous, or beyond the ordinary routine of nature, are held as triumphantly substantiated. It is plain that one or other of these two views of testimony may be wholly, or, in a great degree, erroneous, as they are quite at issue with each other. It becomes of importance, both with regard to our progress in philosophy and our code of religious beliefs, to ascertain which it is that involves the greatest amount of truth" (1859b, 6). "On the Study of the Evidences of Christianity" addresses these topics in a similar way, making use of the extended treatment in his earlier essay of his examples (in Powell ¶s 119–22).

Much of Powell's essay is constructed on the basis of two "parties," not the usual High and Low Church, but comprised of how they respond to "intuition and evidence" (Powell ¶69), together with related institutional affiliations in both church and state. Intuitionists argue that an appeal to the validity of scriptural miracles is an appeal to commonly shared religious feelings, emotions, and ideas whose apologetic value is internal. Their genealogy derives from German theology and philosophy (especially Kant and Schelling) and from emphasis on the inductive method (as in William Whewell's *Philosophy of the Inductive Sciences*, 1840). Intuitionists, with whom Powell has more sympathy, include English and American transcendentalists (like R. W. Emerson) and Unitarians and theists (like F. W. Newman and Theodore Parker; see especially Powell ¶s 11 and 52). The evidentialists hold that miracles are external, empirical events which prove a supernatural interposition in the natural order; their genealogy, deriving from Locke's empiricism, includes Samuel Clarke, Joseph Butler, and William Paley. Their chief spokesperson in the mid-nineteenth century was Richard Whately, but the evidentialists also included J. H. Newman, R. C. Trench, and H. L. Mansel (see especially Powell ¶s 55, 67–70, and notes).

Powell's discussion of miracles in relation to the traditional discussion of the "evidences" and to new scientific discoveries and the higher criticism of the Bible also takes place within the larger context of debate about freedom of speech and open discussion of political and theological matters (see, for instance, J. S. Mill in chap. 2 of *On Liberty* [1859], "Of the Liberty of Thought and Discussion"). Powell brings up the same notion by his use of "toleration" in *Essays and Reviews*. He argues that "external" evidences, especially the evidence of gospel miracles, are no compelling proof of the claims of Christianity, since they are always conditioned by the "deep prejudices" of the age in which they occur and by the prior faith positions of the witnesses, the apologist, and the inquirer. He pleads for liberty of interpretation on the subject of miracles, just as the other Essayists plead for liberty in biblical interpretation, church dogma, and ecclesiastical affiliation. Powell argues that miracles must be subjected to the "interior" moral position of belief, where the rights of conscience and free choice, however conditioned by external and material forces, must be determinative.

Powell deals extensively with the English and German traditions from the seventeenth century on, especially in the notes, but only to historicize the points in his own argument. Major attention is given to the aftermath of Paley's treatment of evidences. Paley begins his treatise by asserting that "in miracles adduced in support of revelation there is not any such antecedent improbability as no testimony can surmount," in opposition to Hume's objection "that it is contrary to experience that a miracle should be true, but not contrary to experience that testimony should be false" ([1794] 1851, 2). Paley's terms in this passage set the frame for the defense of evidence and miracles in nineteenth-century theology.

Many of these arguments concern the notion of "antecedent improbability," the prior assumption of the governance of the natural world by a system of universal laws within which the extraordinary occurrence of the miraculous suspension or overriding of those laws must be explained or accommodated. "Antecedent" depends upon its use in logic, as "the statement upon which any consequence logically depends" (*OED*). The *OED* cites Paley's *Evidences* for this use of the adjective with the meaning of "previous to investigation, presumptive, *a priori*." In his essay Powell refers to the problems of antecedent improbability nine times and credibility repeatedly, employing terms that Paley also uses in the "Preparatory Considerations" section of *Evidences of Christianity* (for Powell's discussion of "antecedent" see ¶s 22, 25, 28–29, 48–50, and 109–10). Powell and Paley both use "antecedent improbability" to refer to the premise or presumption of an ordered and uniform physical world, so fully and completely governed by antecedent laws, that it is improbable to the point of impossibility that a miracle, whether a suspension or a violation of those laws, could occur. But while Paley asserts that divine interpositions, attested to by reliable witnesses, overcome that presumption, Powell argues that only an antecedent credibility on the part of the biblical witnesses or contemporary readers can reconcile the evidence with the laws of nature.

A second important consideration in these debates is the notion of "testimony." Assessing the reliability of the testimony of witnesses of an alleged miracle is part of testing the reliability and validity of the evidence itself. Two discourses, the language and practices of the law courts as well as systems of logic, are invoked concerning testimony. Rules of evidence are formulated in legal terms, and arguments must be valid logically by procedures that include the testing of syllogisms as well as witnesses for the status of their testimony. Testimony for the evidence of physical nature consists of the empirical data of the senses, together with the logic of natural phenomena, their conformity to the laws of nature derived from Newton and eighteenth-century science. Testimony for the evidence of biblical miracles consists of the reliability of the witnesses whose reactions are reported in the biblical records. In both discourses, the forensic and the scientific, the possibility for interpretation at variance with the received orthodoxies of the Christian Establishment was greatly expanded in the nineteenth century, first with the advances in the sciences, especially astronomy, geology, and biology, and secondly in the fields of biblical interpretation, especially the historical and higher critical study of the Bible. The testimony of witnesses, particularly those recorded in the Bible, is the object of Hume's attack on their knowledge, veracity, and objectivity, on the immediacy of their experience, on their interpretation of what it was they experienced, on their recording of the experience whether directly, or by narrative, with all of the possibilities of the corruption of the narrative to which historical and higher critical methods drew attention. Powell admits the narrative record in the Bible as a historical document, but holds that the miracles as recorded are not susceptible to scientific proof. They are acceptable on the grounds of the antecedent credibility of the witnesses, but even more so on the predispositions of readers in subsequent ages. The miracles are not coercive but confirmatory, functioning to validate the doctrine that is being promulgated. As such, they belong not to the realm of reason but to the realm of faith.

Powell historicizes testimony by positing three phases of the evidential argument (Powell ¶s 17–24): in the early and medieval church as common enough manifestations of divine power authorized by the all-powerful ruler of the created world; at the time of the Reformation and immediately afterwards as rare events that interrupt the functioning of divine and natural law; and in the modern period as events whose explanation as rational occurrences draws on various disciplines of knowledge. Introducing his demand for a tolerant assessment of the debate about miracles, Powell places the question of belief in them within the larger discussion of the evidence of the natural world for the character of God, a natural world whose ordered evolution of species (with specific reference to Darwin's *Origin*) excludes the miraculous. He rejects the traditional definitions of miracle, as "something at variance with nature and law," an "arbitrary interposition" (¶36) in the natural order that is inconceivable in the present day and that, as evidenced in the scriptural records, is only believable under certain conditions. To Powell miracles from the time of Christ can be objects of belief only if they are preconditioned by religious belief itself. He insists that arguments from reason and externals must be augmented with the prior appeal to religious feeling and internal conviction. Miracles in the Bible cannot, therefore, compel faith, but are convincing only according to the observing subject's intellectual and religious disposition. The gospel miracles are particularly aimed at the social and intellectual milieu in which they occurred and are always "objects" of faith, not evidences, in the sense that they are related to the point of doctrine being asserted in the biblical text and in its historical context. The appeal to miracles in the present age, according to Powell, is not fortified with antecedent belief but with antecedent disbelief, the general questioning of all empirical data that is one of the legacies of the Enlightenment. Hence, such appeals are usually futile.

The relations of science and philosophy with religion have to clarify the kinds of truth claims that each is properly making. When religion makes empirical truth claims concerning scientific data that cannot be corroborated with scientific evidence, the truth claims have to be questioned. That is precisely the condition of the argument concerning the natural theology and the relationship between miracles and the theology of evidence. To recuperate such a theology on the basis of a scientific appeal to physical evidence is, according to Powell, fruitless. Such had been the procedure of the evidentialists, whose time, according to him, was over. On the other hand, the intuitionists, with whom he is more sympathetic but critical, should recognize the spiritual nature of Christianity in which the conscience and morality will, in his view, lead to an acknowledgment of Christianity as a revelation of God, uncompelled by external evidence.

Powell's rhetoric throughout stresses the significance of natural law—and of laws generally—as in the juridical language of testimony, witness, argument, pleading, and judgment. In the final third of his essay, as he turns from the discussion of evidence to the spiritual claims of Christianity, his language accords with the universalizing of human nature in line with the essentialist Broad Church position on virtues and truth in the human heart that are found in other Essayists, especially Temple and Jowett.

There is little doubt that Powell, had he not died and been called to "a higher Tribunal," as Phillimore sarcastically put it (*Case Whether Professor Jowett* 1862, 3), would have been attacked in the university, if not the church courts (where he was very likely ineligible, like Jowett, to be prosecuted). To Wilberforce, it was clear where Powell stood in terms of religious orthodoxy: in his review, he refers to "the scarcely-veiled Atheism of Mr. Baden Powell" (1861, 251).

One of the first of the reviews, that in the *Literary Gazette* of 14 April 1860, made preliminary and hostile remarks on Powell: "Despite the decorous use of orthodox phraseology, the article, if it means anything, means both a powerful and subtle assault on the possibility of miracles." On this point, of course, Powell's chief argument is missed or misunderstood, namely, the difficulty of assigning a positive role to miracles as evidence for a faith position when there is a condition of antecedent improbability. As in many other reviews, Powell's position is identified with Hume's (459). To the *Guardian* Powell regards miracles, prophecy, and supernatural governance of human affairs as "purely mythical" and his general position "indistinguishable from Atheism" (23 May 1860, 474).

In the major quarterlies Powell was also singled out. Harrison argues that Powell repudiates miracles "not on the general objections of Hume and his school" but rather on the basis of a universal law predicated upon natural sciences: "This rule of law is not carried far enough. It is sufficient now to observe that the whole supernatural element is eliminated from belief" (1860, 162). The general problem of miracles for the nineteenth century is an important epistemological precondition for Powell as for Harrison: "Miracles, indeed, in the popular acceptation of something at variance with nature and law, are repudiated" (302). Later in his essay, Harrison returns to the notion of law and links it to evolution and to Darwin in biology and Buckle in morals: "Step by step the notion of evolution by law is transforming the whole field of our knowledge and opinion. It is not one order of conceptions which comes under its influence, but the whole sphere of our ideas, and with them the whole system of our actions and conduct. . . . The principle of development in the moral as in the physical, has been definitely admitted; and something like one grand analogy through the whole sphere of knowledge has almost become a part of popular opinion. . . . Just as Mr. Darwin has introduced the principle of growth, in one of the most rigid laws of the physical world; so the reception given to the book of Mr. Buckle has proved that public opinion was ripe for the admission of regular laws in the moral. . . . Everywhere we hear of the development of the constitution, of public law, of public opinion, of institutions, of forms of society, of theories of history" (1860, 322–23). Returning to the arguments of the Essayists, and especially to Powell on this point, Harrison links this evolutionary narrative discernible in public institutions to their position in the structures of knowledge: "The history of religion shows a progress by intelligible laws. The analogy of the material and the intellectual domain is extended to that of faith" (1860, 327).

Attacks on Powell continued over the next several years in articles, pamphlets, and books. For instance, the *Christian Remembrancer* condemns what is said to be Powell's separation of the physical and spiritual realms, simultaneously asserting that science belongs to the former, faith to the latter, an unacceptable compartmentalized epistemology and spirituality (1861, 157). In the two major book responses to *Essays and Reviews*, Powell is accorded lavish critique. H. L. Mansel, Waynflete Professor of Moral and Metaphysical Philosophy at Oxford, headed the list with the first essay in *Aids to Faith* (1861), "On Miracles as Evidences of Christianity," Mansel draws a distinction between the potential unreliability of *spectators* to alleged miracles and the declared intention and claims of the *performer* of an alleged miracle. One instance of the latter, he maintains, "is enough to show that the series of events with which it is connected is one which the Almighty has seen fit to mark by exceptions to the ordinary course of His Providence" (William Thomson 1861, 8). Hence, the reader tends to be placed in the position of admitting one miracle and admitting all, or of denying one and denying all, an uncomfortable binary that would not win widespread assent to either side. The second essay, by William Fitzgerald, bishop of Cork, continues the attack on Powell for his repudiation of the facticity of evidence (for a discussion of the responses to Powell see Himrod 1977). Neither response, however, ended the debate on miracles nor silenced Powell's questions about the compulsive power of miracles without a prior faith position or in the face of antecedent improbability.

H. B. Wilson, the National Church, and the Politics of Church and State

Henry Bristow Wilson (1803–1888) was born in London into a family of clergy and academics. In 1821 he went to St. John's College, Oxford, taking his B.A. in 1825, the same year that he was elected a fellow. He was Rawlinson Professor of Anglo-Saxon from 1839 to 1844. Along with Archibald Campbell Tait, T. T. Churton, and John Griffiths, Wilson wrote "Protest of the Four Tutors," a public letter to J. H. Newman on 8 March 1841 protesting his efforts in *Tract XC* to reconcile the wording of the Articles of Religion with Catholicism. Their condemnation of Newman's "liberty in interpreting the formularies" was later used to attack Tait and Wilson in the *Essays and Reviews* trials (Kennard 1888, 38–39). Wilson continued as a fellow of St. John's College until 1850, when he was appointed by his college (as patron) to the parish of Great Stoughton in Huntingdonshire, in the diocese of Ely, where he remained for the rest of his life. He suffered a paralytic stroke in 1870 and had to resign his parish duties, living on almost unknown for the next eighteen years, though Jowett and other loyal friends kept in touch with him. His former student R. B. Kennard defended him in a book on *Essays and Reviews* (1863) and also published a short memorial of his life (1888).

Wilson's intellectual interests continued during his life as a parish priest. From 1855 to 1870 he wrote extensively for the *Westminster Review*, where he was editor of the philosophy and theology section (Ellis 1980, 20). He often noted that while the impact of German literature, music, philosophy, science, and classical studies was widely known and accepted in England, only German theology was repudiated. In 1855 he became the editor for a series of signed articles that were specially solicited for annual volumes of *Oxford Essays* on controversial topics of the day of interest to a broad readership, written by graduates of the university. He continued this publication until 1858 and joined to it other volumes of *Cambridge Essays*. Both were published by John Parker. Wilson then urged his Broad Church colleagues, Jowett, Pattison, Rowland Williams, and others, to establish a journal to promote their views but eventually accepted the more modest goal of a single volume, *Essays and Reviews*. Wilson assumed the editorship, though his role continued throughout the whole of the legal trials and following controversy to be a matter of complete secrecy except to the publisher and the other Essayists so that no one person could be held especially guilty for the volume. He argued his own case before the Privy Council where he was learned and arcane to the point of antiquarianism, as his published speech demonstrates (see frontispiece).

Wilson's essay explores the contemporary crisis in the relations between the Victorian church and state. The reform of the established church in Ireland in 1833, abolishing two archbishoprics and eight bishoprics, as well as confiscating their incomes, brought about a strong reaction in England (Owen Chadwick 1966–70, 1:47–60; Cook and Keith 1984, 221). John Keble had preached his Assize sermon on

"National Apostasy" against the suppression of the Irish bishoprics in 1833, thereby inaugurating the Oxford Movement, with its entirely different agenda for the relations of church and state. If Parliament could so interfere with the Church of Ireland, many asked, how close were the prospects concerning disestablishment in England? (see Brent 1987).

The financial and pastoral conditions in England were, it was generally agreed, in need of urgent reform. Because tithes were paid by all residents of a parish, Anglicans or not, to the patron of the parish, who gave a small fraction to the clergyman he appointed to do the work, clerical incomes were grossly inequitable. According to Hastings Robinson, of the 7,659 incumbents and 4,254 curates in the Church of England, some 4,361 received less than £150 a year, and two-thirds of them less than £100. At the same time the income of the bishop of London was between £12,000 and £14,000 annually and some well-endowed parishes paid as much as £4,000 or £5,000 a year (Robinson 1833, 13).

Such economic inequalities were exacerbated by pastoral abuses: most nonresident rectors who had the income or patronage of a parish rarely or never visited their parishes but forced impoverished curates whom they hired to engage in another abuse, pluralism (the holding of more than one benefice) in order to augment their frugal incomes. According to Robinson one-quarter of the clergy held only one benefice, but another quarter held two, and some had as many as five. Two further problems complicated these temporal injustices—patronage (most of the clerical appointments were not under church control, but were in the hands of the laity—the Crown, universities and colleges, and lay patrons); and nepotism, the appointment of relatives of the higher clergy to lucrative positions (see Owen Chadwick 1966–70, 1:53; Machin 1978, 28–74, 299–319; and Brent 1987). In the face of this crisis, Peel's new Tory government established an Ecclesiastical Commission to begin the reform of the church. It made its first report in 1835 proposing an equalization of stipends, and in 1836 indicated gross inequities in the distribution of churches, where, in the industrial midlands, thousands of workers had no parish churches or clergy at all. Other attempts at reform by the government, such as the redefinition of diocesan boundaries, the establishment of new dioceses, and regulations on absentee clergy and pluralism, but these met resistance from within the established church (Gilbert 1976, 128–32). At the same time specific concessions from the established church to Dissenters, a broad term that included Methodists, Presbyterians, Congregationalists, Baptists, and Roman Catholics, were made in the repeal of the Test and Corporation Acts and the passing of the Catholic Emancipation Act in 1828–29 that allowed them access to public office.

A second matter that pitted the church and state against each other as contesting authorities involved the way that doctrinal disputes interfered with clerical appointments, particularly in two notable legal cases. Renn Dickson Hampden was offered the Oxford regius professorship of divinity by Melbourne in 1836, and the bishopric of Hereford by Russell in 1847. Both appointments were opposed strenuously by the High Church party on the grounds of Hampden's heterodoxy (he was a liberal in doctrine and politics), and more importantly, on the matter of state appointments of church officials. As a result Hampden was condemned by Convocation at Oxford and by thirteen bishops, and in the press questions were asked about the political patronage involved in appointing bishops, and the more general role of the custodial power of Parliament and the officers of the Crown in caring for the "spiritualities" of the realm (see Thomas Arnold 1836; and Owen Chadwick 1966–70, 112–26). In the second case, in 1847 the Rev. G. C. Gorham was appointed by the Lord Chancellor (in whose gift was the living) to a vicarage in the diocese of Exeter. The bishop, Henry Phillpotts, also later to have an important role in the *Essays and Reviews* affair, was a High Church Tory, in sympathy with the ideals of the Tractarians and a staunch resistor of all efforts to compromise church authority. He refused to institute Gorham into his living on the grounds that he did not believe in baptismal regeneration. The ensuing legal battles eventually wound their way to the Judicial Committee of the Privy Council, where it was decided in 1850 in Gorham's favor, but the doctrinal battles, pamphleteering, and political alignments of opponents (once again Pusey and Keble were against the liberals) continued in attacks on state authority and the use of the judicial system for the settling of such disputes, which, as Phillpotts pronounced, he did "solemnly repudiate" (Nias 1951, 117; see also Wilson ¶76 and n. 124).

A third area of dispute concerned the theoretical basis on which the other two matters, the disposition of the temporalities and the spiritualities of the church, depended, namely, the theory and legal status of church and state. In England a series of legal enactments dating from the reigns of Henry VIII and Elizabeth I maintained continuity with the past and transformed the conditions of the medieval church into a Reformation arrangement of interdependence and reciprocal responsibility, pastoral administration, and financial jurisdiction. The Act of Supremacy (1534) conferred on Henry VIII and his successors the title of "the only supreme head in earth of the Church of England," thereby removing the pope from that position. Henry's act was renewed under Elizabeth as the first act of her reign (1559) with somewhat different wording, declaring her the "only supreme governor of this realm . . . as well in all spiritual or ecclesiastical things or causes as temporal." An oath of obedience to the Crown was required of all clergy. Four Acts of Uniformity (1549, 1552, 1559, and 1662, the last amended but still in effect) determined the forms of service and the doctrinal Formularies established by law in the *Book of Common Prayer*. Hence, the Tudor settlement of church and state was a complicated compromise in which the Crown assumed responsibilities for the appointment of archbishops and bishops under specified conditions, and they in turn have places in the civil government in the House of Lords. The diocesan and parochial boundaries have both civil and ecclesiastical functions (in the Poor Laws, for example), and church endowments in the mid-nineteenth century as now were a complicated arrangement of legal entails, rights, successions, and privileges. Furthermore, the monarch was bound in the Coronation oath to uphold and defend the "the settlement of the Church of England, and the doctrine, worship, discipline, and government thereof, as by law established in England" (Ratcliff 1953, 38). It was this set of interactive relations that Richard Hooker set out in *Of the Laws of Ecclesiastical Polity* (1594–97).

In the nineteenth century three concepts of the relations between the church and the state dominated the period from the 1830s to the 1850s, each associated with the political and ecclesiastical interests and affiliations of the religious parties, Low Church, High Church, and Broad Church. The Low Church position was stated early in the century in the Bampton lectures of 1820 by Godfrey Faussett, *The Claims of the Established Church to Exclusive Attachment and Support* and at mid-century by Thomas Rawson Birks in *The Christian State* (1847), republished as *Church and State* (1869). Low Church theory of the Church of England stressed its Protestantism as an inheritance from the Reformation, its reliance upon a "Scriptural Truth," a stress upon moral conversion and earnestness in personal piety, and the facilitation of all of these objects by means of a "National Church," a divinely sanctioned "true Religion and Polity" (Birks [1847] 1869, xi). While this theory of the church shared a great deal doctrinally with the Protestant side of dissent, it also maintained that the episcopacy was needed for the good of the church (*bene esse*) if not for its ontological existence (*esse*), and similarly the state is a condition of national existence providentially arranged to facilitate the objects of religion (see Nicholls 1967). The High Church position, largely the product of the Oxford Movement, laid stress on the church as a body of believers united invisibly with the believers of the past in an unbroken association of faith and piety, confirmed in the continuity with the church of the New Testament through apostolic succession, and maintained in the three orders of ministry. According to this view bishops are the guardians of religious truth and the means whereby ministerial succession was maintained. Such a view was expressed in the first of the *Tracts for the Times*, "Thoughts on the Ministerial Commission" (1833) by J. H. Newman, really a defense of apostolic succession. Newman's views were applied in a complex discussion by W. E. Gladstone in *The State and Its Relations with the Church* (1838). According to the Tractarian view, the episcopacy, despite its faults, was of the *esse*, the essential being of the church, and so to stress the historical continuity of the church by means of apostolical succession was a vital part of its definition (see Butler 1982). A far more extreme statement was made by William George Ward in *The Ideal of a Christian Church* (1844), taking a sacramental and often pro-Roman Catholic view of the doctrine of the church and its ecclesiology. Ward's publication anticipated the turmoil caused by the efforts of Nicholas Wiseman and others to reinstitute the Roman Catholic hierarchy in England, and the ensuing charges of papal aggression in the no-popery riots. Ward was publicly humiliated by having his book condemned at Oxford in 1844, an event that R. W. Church claimed inaugurated the Broad Church movement and had a decisive impact on the crisis of church and state in the 1850s.

The Broad Church theory of church and state relied on the philosophical restatement of Hooker in S. T. Coleridge's *On the Constitution of the Church and*

State (1829). Coleridge's position was reformulated by Thomas Arnold in *Principles of Church Reform* (1833) and again by F. D. Maurice in *The Kingdom of Christ: or, Hints to a Quaker Respecting the Principles, Constitution and Ordinances of the Catholic Church* (1838). It was chiefly in relation to these thinkers that Wilson elaborated his position.

Coleridge's "idea" of a national church distinguishes it from both the abstract church of Christ as the body of believers continuous through time and universal in the world and also from the established Church of England caught in the exigencies of time, place, and historical circumstance. He refers to "a third form," the Roman Catholic Church, "which is neither national nor Christian, but irreconcileable with and subversive of both" ([1829] 1976, 12). His distinctions among a nation, a people, and a state influenced Broad Church theologians throughout the nineteenth century. According to Coleridge, a state is "a body politic, having the principle of unity within itself, whether by concentration of its forces, as a constitutional or pure Monarchy, which, however, has hitherto continued to be *ens rationale* [a rational entity], unknown in history . . .—or—with which we alone are concerned—by equipoise and interdependency" (23). A nation is the "Unity of the successive generations of a people" and it is marked by two opposite interests, permanence and progression. When these interests of the nation are brought into a relationship with religion, Coleridge resists their combination into a union. Instead he advocates a relationship of "equipoise and interdependency," a mutuality between the interests of the reserved and commonly shared property wealth, or the "commonwealth," and the intellectual resources of the nation. The latter is in effect a third estate (after the landowners and the mercantile class), the purpose of which is "to preserve the stores, to guard the treasures, of past civilization, and thus to bind the present with the past, to perfect and add to the same, and thus to connect the present with the future; but especially to diffuse through the whole community . . . that quantity and quality of knowledge which was indispensable for the understanding of those rights, and for the performance of the duties correspondent" (43–44).

To this body of the intelligentsia Coleridge gives the name "National Clerisy": "The Clerisy of the nation or national church, in its primary acceptation and original intention comprehended the learned of all denominations:—the sages and professors of the law and jurisprudence; of medicine and physiology; of music, of military and civil architecture; of the physical sciences; with the mathematical as the common *organ* of the preceding; in short, all the so-called liberal arts and sciences, the possession and application of which constitute the civilization of a country as well as the Theological" (46). To the "Clerisy," or the national church (what Peter Allen calls "the class of cultural experts" [1985, 90]), is assigned the endowment of the "Nationalty," and upon them devolves the function of teaching "civility," namely, "all the qualities essential to a citizen, and devoid of which no people or class of the people can be calculated on by the rulers and leaders of the state for the conservation or promotion of its essential interests" (54). Hence, the clerisy has to be differentiated from the clergy of the national church; and the national church from the established Church of England. The latter category in each pair is a particular religious institution with its hierarchy, but the former functions for the entire people of the state in and through the economic and political orders.

Thomas Arnold, like Coleridge, argued for a balancing tendency in the relations between church and state as based on the doctrine of the royal supremacy—"the very corner stone of all my political belief" (Stanley 1844, 2:188; and Thomas Arnold 1845, 98–99). He defines this coterminous church and state as a reciprocal relationship in which the "true notion of the Church of Christ [is] 'a society for the putting down of moral evil,' or 'for the moral improvement of mankind.'" Such a comprehensive society is characterized by the term on which Wilson hinges his argument: it is "a multitude," by which Arnold means as inclusive a Christian community as possible based not on doctrinal exclusions or articles of faith but rather on a shared Bible and a commitment to moral action (1845, 24, 27–28). Arnold applies this notion to arguments favoring the repeal of the Test Acts (1828), the abolition of subscription to the Thirty-nine Articles of Religion required for matriculation at Oxford and Cambridge, a point that recurs in the second half of Wilson's essay as a deterrent to the multitudinism of the church.

Wilson draws extensively upon both Coleridge and Thomas Arnold in his scheme for the national church: he takes up Coleridge's notion of the "nationalty," to which he directly refers (¶59). He retains Arnold's extension of Coleridge's concept of a national church, especially with respect to its comprehension. But to Wilson the nationalty is still to be an institution of religion, not, as in Coleridge, composed of the third estate of the clerisy. Its function, as in Coleridge, is to cultivate and nurture the moral sense of human beings in pursuing the social and collective objectives of the state. Its comprehensiveness includes all of the contributions of Dissenters, and so breaks up the Anglican hegemony that has retained power and position through the imposition of doctrinal justifications and distinctions.

Before writing in *Essays and Reviews* on "The National Church," Wilson had completed two other treatments of the theory of church and state. In *The Communion of Saints*, the Bampton Lectures of 1851, he deliberately used a title that, in a phrase drawn from the Apostles' Creed, drew on the spirituality of the Tractarians in order to controvert it. Wilson rejects three arguments about the divine foundation of church polity and authority: the Tractarian appeal to the church as "the mystical body of Christ," a union of all the living and dead who share the doctrine "once delivered to the saints" (a theory not traceable earlier than Augustine and the fourth century [1851, 7, 14–15]); Calvin and Luther's appeal to private judgment (a view limited by a relativist theory of knowledge, attacked by Wilson through Kant and Schleiermacher's *Christian Faith* [1821–22]); and a ground for polity based on a theory of grace, whether individualist or receptionist, or by divine interposition in conversion or sacraments (1851, 126). Hence, Wilson argues that the church is the establishment by Christ in the world of an institution based upon the moral order of the universe and human beings (as argued by Kant), and is intended to bring them all to their highest development (1851, 238). In "Schemes of Christian Comprehension," contributed to *Oxford Essays* in 1857, he explores his topic in four sections: first, a general discussion with examples of various denominational schemes for Christian unity based on the theory of discovering agreed-upon fundamentals; second, a discussion of Jean Alphonse Turretin, a Swiss Reformed theologian who proposed a theory for defining and selecting fundamentals; third, a discussion of Francis Blackburn, an eighteenth-century Anglican theologian who rejected clerical subscription to the Articles of Religion as a way of retaining unity of faith as prescriptive and impinging on individual judgment, conscience, and scruple; and finally, a discussion of the notion of the one fundamental, the appeal to the Bible, on the basis of the probability of evidential value rather than its absolute certainty. Such considerations lead to Wilson's peroration on the "principle of probables" that governs the transmission of historical texts (1857, 115), upon which he wishes to base a wide toleration of doctrinal differences, a resistance to exclusivist formulations, and a repudiation of subscription on which either membership or ministry might depend. It was to these points that he returned in his essay on "Séances historiques de Genève: the National Church."

Ostensibly a review of *Le Christianisme au quatrième siècle*, the second of the series of historical lectures given at Geneva, *Séances historiques de Genève* (1858), but in fact using only one concept from the lectures of M. Bungener, the "multitudinisme" of the early church and of Genevan Protestantism, Wilson's essay addresses the question of the composition and nature of the English religious establishment.[15] Two contrary impulses appeared to be in tension in the first three centuries of Christianity (that Bungener addressed), those of individualism (what later was called by both the reformers and by Wilson "private judgment"), and "multitudinism" (the term that Wilson appropriates to describe the pluralism he wished to see incorporated in his Coleridgean-Arnoldean version of the national church). It encompasses both the sectarian difference and the "moral alienation" that Arnold described, but it also includes the plurality of accepted belief—to overcome the alienation—that Wilson advocates. Hence, in only the most tenuous and formal way is Wilson's study a "review"—certainly not in the sense of Williams's essay. He merely uses the concepts that the "*Séances historiques*" introduce to position his own argument concerning the prospects for the relations between church and state in a pluralist society. Accordingly, he addresses the comprehensiveness of the church in England on several levels: the alienation of all classes from organized religion, the implications of such disaffection on both the present relations of church and state and the future condition of the disaffected after the final judgment; the distinctions between the doctrinal and the moral teaching of Christianity and its consequences in the present moral condition of England and the crisis in church and state; and the derivation of the doctrinal and moral teachings from the Bible, and the role of biblical interpretation in making these teachings known. To accomplish this "condition of England" argument seen from the perspective of moral decay and religious disaffection, the customary remedy of traditional biblical interpretation and conventional missionary activity (such as the preaching of the fear of hell as a certain cure for spiritual lukewarmness) is depicted as woefully inadequate. A study of the conditions of apostolical Christianity casts light on the notions of inclusivity, a national church, and religious diversity.

Pattison too had drawn attention to the contribution of the Genevan church in "Calvin at Geneva" (1858), tracing "two results which have accrued to modern Europe, and are unmistakably traceable to the Reformation of the sixteenth century. The first lies in the domain of intelligence, and is known as the Right of Free Inquiry. The second, a consequence of the foregoing, is a fact of politics, and is known as Liberty of Conscience, or Toleration" (Pattison 1889, 2:4). Wilson uses this historic role to position his own inquiry into these "two results" in determining what would be fundamental for a national church in England: free inquiry, untrammeled by subscription to doctrinal formulas, and toleration of doctrinal difference in the interest of the moral development of the state.

Wilson begins with the Genevan church discussions concerning individualism and multitudinism in the first three centuries of the Christian church. He compares the historic Erastianism of Geneva with England in their reliance upon Reformation formulas and dogmatic prescriptions that lay on the present churches both an important historical inheritance and a doctrinal burden in changed political conditions. A resolution of the doctrinal disputes of the past is urgently needed in the face of growing doubt and scepticism, both in England and overseas in the competition of the denominations in missionary activity. Resolution of old disputes is inhibited by widespread misunderstandings about the Christian communities depicted in the New Testament and their reliance upon inclusivist or exclusionist doctrinal orthodoxy (Wilson ¶s 16–25). Wilson's tentative conclusion is that the New Testament does not sanction exclusion from the comprehensiveness of the church community on the basis of either doctrinal irregularity or moral transgression.

To Wilson the national church has one primary purpose, to teach the importance of the moral conduct of life within a comprehensive or multitudinist national church, as mandated by the apostolic churches (Wilson ¶s 26–36). The block in England to the realization of this ideal has been an exclusionary interpretation of the Formularies that should ensure liberty of conscience and interpretation (Wilson ¶s 37–58). The Thirty-nine Articles of Religion should guarantee the liberty of a national church that declares itself to be founded on the "Word of God," but, because of clerical subscription, and a literalist interpretation of the articles and of the Bible, such a guarantee has been abrogated in the interests of a restrictive orthodoxy. The opposite should be true: that liberty of conscience and freedom of interpretation should be the hallmarks of the "Nationality," those who are enabled by the endowments of the church to pursue informed and disinterested biblical and historical study to lead the people toward moral virtues (Wilson ¶s 59–71).

The chief means of undertaking such a study is by using what Wilson calls "ideology," by which he means a system of knowledge directed at the ultimate aim, meaning, or purpose of a text or action (its "ideal"), a notion derived from German philosophy by way of Coleridge. The ideological method when applied to the study of the Bible, church history, and doctrine considers both historic and purposive meanings derived from the community in which the texts are both records and products, and so mediates between a pietistic literalism and an outright sceptical rationalism. Hence, this ideology allows for inclusivity in biblical interpretation and is a means of ensuring the kind of multitudinism on which the future of the national church depends. Wilson concludes by reverting to the pressing urgency of solving the organizational, doctrinal, and pastoral needs of the church, and of making the message of the national church available to the total citizenry of the state. He argues that all intellectual contributions from a reconstituted clergy (close to Coleridge's clerisy) are needed for this purpose, and nothing, such as doctrinal impediments or enforced subscription to narrow Formularies, should interfere with a national purpose which is caught up in a larger purpose, the ultimate salvation of all. This turn toward universal salvation was the final breaking point for many of Wilson's orthodox readers, and his exoneration on this point led to the quip that the Lord Chancellor "dismissed hell with costs."

Wilson focuses on the "pivot articles" on which his argument hinges, citing the Thirty-fourth Article, "Of the Traditions of the Church," which concludes: "Every particular or national church hath authority to ordain, change, and abolish ceremonies or rites of the church ordained only by man's authority so that all things be done to edifying" (*BCP*). The relations of church and state are set out here in terms of traditions and practices with roots in the past, together with the capability of a national church to change the relationship with that past by redefinition. At the same time, the notion of national sovereignty asserts the independence of the church as a national institution free from foreign intervention, such as the pope. Finally, the notion of national uniformity of practice and doctrine has a particular purpose that is not exclusionary but beneficial, existing for the edification of the entire nation.

At the same time, the role of the spiritual leaders is under scrutiny. Besieged with the claims of apostolic succession and hierarchical authority on the Tractarian side and the moral corrosion of sin and the double predestination of both the elect and the reprobate on the side of Calvinist Protestantism, the clergy in England were forced into subscription according to a very narrow interpretation of the Thirty-nine Articles of Religion. Subscription in the "literal and grammatical sense" was required of every ordinand, as well as for matriculation at Oxford and Cambridge. The uttering of potentially heretical opinions could result in reprimand or demands for resubscription, as happened to Jowett on the publication of *The Epistles of St. Paul* in 1855 (Letter 1). Testing the limits of orthodoxy and heresy concerning the articles was matched by testing the limits of inspiration in the Bible—and both had recently been pursued through the ecclesiastical and civil courts over the question of baptismal regeneration in the case of *Gorham v. the Bishop of Exeter*. And within a year of his *Essays and Reviews* article, Wilson published a long discussion of inspiration that provoked further attacks (Wilson 1861). Hence, for the clergy the issue involved freedom of interpretation, the "liberty" of the church in open discussion of those matters on which fixed opinion was not required. The article that brought these two matters together, was the sixth, one that Wilson calls "the pivot Article of the Church," linking inspiration to the authority of subscription.

Wilson's rhetorical strategy depends upon a series of linked parallel concepts, between Geneva and England, between the "national character" and the individual "English citizen," between the "national church" and the "English Churchman," and between "the freedom of opinion" and "the multitudinist principle." He concludes that if the first item in the series of parallels is conceded, the second also follows. Just as the national character in English citizens involves endorsing freedom of opinion, so the national church represented by English Churchmen should follow a multitudinist principle and should equally endorse freedom of opinion. It is a question of how much "liberty of opinion" is conceded in law and how much is restricted by the Formularies. Even there, the principle of liberty should be invoked for a breadth or latitude of interpretation, and, furthermore, the requirement that the Articles of Religion should be subscribed to as an exclusionary doctrinal policy by a policing hierarchy should be abolished.

In perhaps the most important responses to Wilson's essay, Archbishop Longley of Canterbury and Archbishop Thomson of York condemned his views on biblical infallibility and the prospect of eternal damnation. Both claimed, in charges to their diocese (Longley 1864; William Thomson 1864), that Wilson's arguments threatened the collapse of the general social structure of England in which the church is subordinate to the Crown and Parliament in a very delicate balance. Wilson's essay was also cited as performing a particular political action. Just as J. H. Newman had read the Articles of Religion in *Tract XC* to obliterate distinctions between Anglican and Catholic—often interpreted unsympathetically as Roman—doctrine and practice, so Wilson's "pioneer essay" was, in the words of the *Christian Remembrancer* (Oct. 1860), reading the articles to obliterate distinctions between Anglican and rationalist doctrines ([Review of] "*Essays and Reviews*", 341).

On a more explicitly political level, there were a number of attacks on Wilson's inclusive, or "multitudinist," views of the national church and its relation to the state. From the early notice in the *Eclectic* (Aug. 1860), Wilson's equation of "multitudinism" with the "entire population" was open to ridicule and rejection. Woodgate condemns Wilson as having the same "notions of social science" as J. S. Mill (1861, 152), but a more sustained attack is mounted by James Weyland Joyce in his pamphlet of 1861. Wilson's essay alone is considered, largely because it is judged to be destructive of the social fabric. Aside from his theological vagaries, such as denying the veracity of the Bible and his replacing faith and belief with "ideology," Wilson's view of "multitudinism" threatens the character of the church and its relation to the state by removing its exclusivity as an authoritative spiritual presence (1861, 50–77).

On the other hand, to a critic like Harrison, Wilson's essay was "very able" precisely for his insight into the political and social implications of a multitudinist church: "That which distinguishes his view is the strength with which he grasps the social aspect of the question. He sees religion in its relation to the State and to nations" (Harrison 1860, 302–3). A quite different tack was taken by Wilberforce in the *Quarterly,* where Wilson's essay receives ten pages of scathing comment for his "Jesuitry" in making the required assertions of subscription to the Articles of Religion while at the same time teaching against them: he is a "stammering, equivocating subscriber" whose past history as one of the Four Tutors' protest against the *Tracts for the Times* in 1841 is summoned up as incriminating evidence: what he called dishonesty in Newman then must now fall on his own head for his attack on the doctrines of the creeds, special revelation, the atonement, the inspiration of the Bible, and even the notion of a church which maintains the necessity of subscription to articles of belief (1861, 278–82). Other critics, like the anonymous pamphleteer of *The Idea of a National Church,* went further, accusing Wilson outright of Comteanism or Christian Socialism. In one sentence this pamphleteer draws direct connections between Wilson's essay and the entire edifice of civilization, mediated only by the relations of church and state (*Idea* 1861, 207–8). Such a sweeping gesture was commonly followed in the reviews of Wilson's essay, using Wilson as a means of dismissing all criticism of the Establishment, from Comteanism to Christian Socialism, and using his notion of ideology to align it with Germanism and Germanism with rationalism, dismissing the lot. Although this pamphleteer was very likely outside access to opinion-making bodies such as the major quarterlies, his generalization suggests why Wilson's essay aroused such vehement reactions. The lines between theology, ecclesiastical politics, and practical arrangements of church and state that Wilson touched upon were delicate matters in 1860: his manner of straightforward attack on such an issue as subscription, and his references to universal salvation at the very end of his essay, seem almost calculated to irritate his opponents, and those points are usually the very items that the responses take up with such disapproval.

Charles Wycliffe Goodwin, Geology, and the Problem of Genesis

Charles Wycliffe Goodwin (1817–1878) was born in King's Lynn and educated at St. Catharine's Hall, Cambridge, in 1834, taking his B.A. in Classics with high honors. He received his M.A. in 1842. Although he was elected to a fellowship at St. Catharine's and intended to study for ordination, changes in his religious opinions caused him to reconsider and to resign his fellowship, which was tenable only by clergy. He was called to the bar at Lincoln's Inn in 1843 and continued to practice law for the rest of his career. He published several legal studies, and in 1859 combined his legal interest with his interest in philology and Egyptology, publishing "Curiosities of Law" anonymously in the *Law Magazine*, translations of the Coptic deeds of a monastery located near Thebes in Egypt. He also had an active life as a journalist and editor, succeeding John Morley as editor for the weekly *Literary Gazette* in 1860. In April 1862 Goodwin renamed it the *Pantheon*; within two months, however, he wrote: "My journal . . . has come to an untimely end" (BL Add. MS. 56,273, fol. 59). In 1862 he was appointed a judge in the Supreme Court for China and Japan by the Foreign Office and left for Shanghai in 1865. He was later transferred to Yokahama, where he died in 1878. On receiving a telegram about his death, Derby wrote that he appreciated "the manner in which Mr. Goodwin has discharged his arduous duties, and I have to express my sense of the great loss which has been sustained by Her Majesty's Service" (BL Add. MS. 56,273, fol. 118).

Goodwin's intellectual accomplishments included languages and science, specifically botany and geology. He was trained in classics, but in addition had worked on Hebrew throughout his university career. He also knew Coptic and Anglo-Saxon, and later in life was familiar with a number of the languages of East Asia, including Chinese and Japanese. His chief scholarly interest, however, was in Egyptology: he published several works which gained for him a world-reputation in the field. He was an avid amateur geologist as well, devoting "each long vacation for nine years from 1851 onwards to geological researches" (Ellis 1980, 28). He also contributed to several biblical commentaries including *The Speaker's Commentary* (1871) and was consulted by Ellicott, Lightfoot, and others for the revision of the New Testament undertaken in 1870. For the only extended biography see Warren Dawson 1934. For a portrait-sketch of Goodwin by his sister, see figure 7.

Goodwin's topic in "On the Mosaic Cosmogony" is the relations between literalist readings of the creation narrative in Genesis and contemporary geology. As Tennyson in *In Memoriam* (sec. 56, ll. 1–4; 16–20) and Ruskin in a letter to Henry Acland (24 May 1851; 1903–12, 36:115) testify, the "dreadful hammers" of nineteenth-century geology undermined conventional frames of temporality and beliefs in the eternal verities. Writing around the mid-century, both Tennyson and Ruskin were responding to the geological paradigm laid out in Robert Chambers's anonymously published *Vestiges of the Natural History of Creation* (1844), which argued a developmental hypothesis against the theological views of a special creation. *Vestiges* went through ten editions in ten years to 1854, selling 24,000 copies (Chambers [1844] 1969, 31–32). Chambers negotiated the conflicts between traditional biblical interpreters from the seventeenth and eighteenth centuries who relied on the dating of creation, including the geological record, in the year 4004 B.C.E., according to the chronology of Archbishop James Ussher. Other thinkers,

Figure 7. Charles Wycliffe Goodwin (1853). Drawing by Fanny Wycliffe Goodwin. Frontispiece in Warren R. Dawson, *Charles Wycliffe Goodwin 1817–1878: A Pioneer in Egyptology.* Oxford: Oxford Univ. Press, 1934. Used with permission of Oxford University Press.

like Thomas Burnet, who published *The Sacred Theory of the Earth* (1681), were less interested in the date of creation than assigning to the universe a precise historical moment of origin. William Whiston (to whom Pattison gives some attention in his essay) in *A New Theory of the Earth* (1696) argued that the biblical creation and flood could be explained scientifically. Whiston had referred to the "Mosaick Cosmogony," and the term was subsequently applied to attempts to reconcile the findings of science with the account of the origin of the cosmos in the biblical narrative.

The debate between Genesis and geology had been given a new direction in 1795 with the publication of James Hutton's *Theory of the Earth, with Proofs and Illustrations*, and its popularization by John Playfair in *Illustrations of the Huttonian Theory* (1802). They abandoned the cosmogonists' obsession with historical origins in favor of descriptions of geological evidence, the "testimony of the rocks" (supplemented with fossil evidence supplied by J. B. Lamarck). This shift replaced a transcendental cause with natural processes, a historicism coincident with Whig views of history and increasingly widespread models of progress and development, both in the natural world and in human affairs. The "natural causes," however, were also in dispute: some geologists, the catastrophists, argued that a series of cataclysmic upheavals disturbed the sedimentation of the rocks. Those who sought biblical source texts found them in the account of Noah's flood. Others, the uniformitarians, extended Hutton's views into a theory of unbroken development.

From Hutton to the publication of *Vestiges*, geology was increasingly established as a science with its institutions (the Geological Society of London, the first in Europe, established 1807), professorial chairs (Cambridge, 1818; Oxford, 1819), the establishment of the Geological Survey of Great Britain (1835), the publication of textbooks that summarized current knowledge (such as Charles Lyell's *Elements of Geology* [1838]), and the work of an army of geological amateurs, organized nationally in 1858 as the Geologists' Association (Brock 1981, 107–8). Against this movement were those who continued to reject this scientific evidence or who attempted to reconcile it with a literalist reading of Genesis. Writing at the end of the nineteenth century, one historian explained: "The cosmogonists were not disconcerted when phenomena were appealed to that contradicted their theories, for they usually never saw such phenomena, and when they did, they easily explained them away. Some of these writers were divines . . . bound to suit their speculations to the received interpretation of the books of Moses" (Geike 1905, 65–66). One of the enemics to the divines was Sir Charles Lyell, who in *Principles of Geology* (1830–33) sought to set the study of the rocks upon the theoretical basis of uniformitarianism, the gradual and regular working of geological causes over vast periods of time. Responding to such challenges, the biblical reconcilers, such as those writers whom Goodwin quotes (William Buckland and Hugh Miller, for instance), continued to attempt a fresh accommodation of the chronology of geology to that of Genesis. After the publication of Chambers's *Vestiges*, this controversy became one of the popular topics of the day (see Millhauser 1959 and

Chambers 1994). For instance, the popularizer Mrs. John Wright drew on Lyell, Buckland, Miller, and Bakewell to show that "a close investigation of facts . . . [will be] found to harmonize with the Bible statements of the character and works of God" (1854, v). Her "geological chart" (fig. 8) sets out the widely used but still contested relationship of the geological strata and periods to the relevant biological forms to which Goodwin and others refer.

In 1859 in a review article of several recent works on geology, J. B. Jukes indicates the extent of the popular interest in the topic: the "object we propose to ourselves in this article is to endeavour to explain to non-geological readers what is the present state of geology, both theoretical and practical,—what it is that the geologists of the present day profess to know, and what it is that they profess to do" (1859, 139). In many ways this readership is the same as that of Goodwin, whose argument in *Essays and Reviews* is put forward on grounds that by 1860 had been well established in the scientific community. His focus is "Cosmogony," defined by his contemporary David Page as "reasoning or speculation as to the origin or creation of the universe. Distinct from Geology, whose object is to unfold the *history* of our globe as far only as fact and observation will permit of sound deduction" (Page 1859, s.v. "Cosmogony"). The absolute distinction drawn by Page may be found at the beginning of *Principles,* where Lyell attempts to rationalize the grounds upon which the new science will be founded. He addresses "this controverted question," the relation of science to the doctrine of cosmogony: "It was long ere the distinct nature and legitimate objects of geology were fully recognized and it was at first confounded with many other branches of inquiry, just as the limits of history, poetry, and mythology were ill-defined in the infancy of civilization. . . . But the identification of its objects with those of Cosmogony has been the most common and serious source of confusion. . . . We shall attempt in the sequel of this work to demonstrate that geology differs as widely from cosmogony, as speculations concerning the creation of man differ from history" (Lyell 1830, 1:4). One year previous to the publication of *Principles,* Lyell had written to Murchison (August 1829) that "the age will not stand my anti-Mosaical conclusions" (in Brooks 1978, 45).

Fifteen years after the publication of *Principles,* in the *Encyclopaedia Metropolitana,* William Phillips comments on the "fatal error" of arguing "that all the strata superimposed on one another in the crust of the Earth, with all their included myriads of fossil animals and plants, were deposited by one general flood, 'the Deluge!'" Phillips's discussion of this "error," the "stumbling-block" of seventeenth-century geologists such as Burnet, Woodward, and Whiston, demonstrates not only the discrepancy in mid-Victorian Britain between scientists and the general public but also the consequences of this discrepancy: "The progress of Geology in England was still retarded by the fettered condition of other Sciences, and by a peculiarly unhappy conjunction of Truth and fiction. . . . Though discarded by every sound Geologist, it ["the fatal error"] remains a serious impediment to the diffusion of correct general principles" ([1817–45] 1849, 6:532). It is precisely within this "pecu-

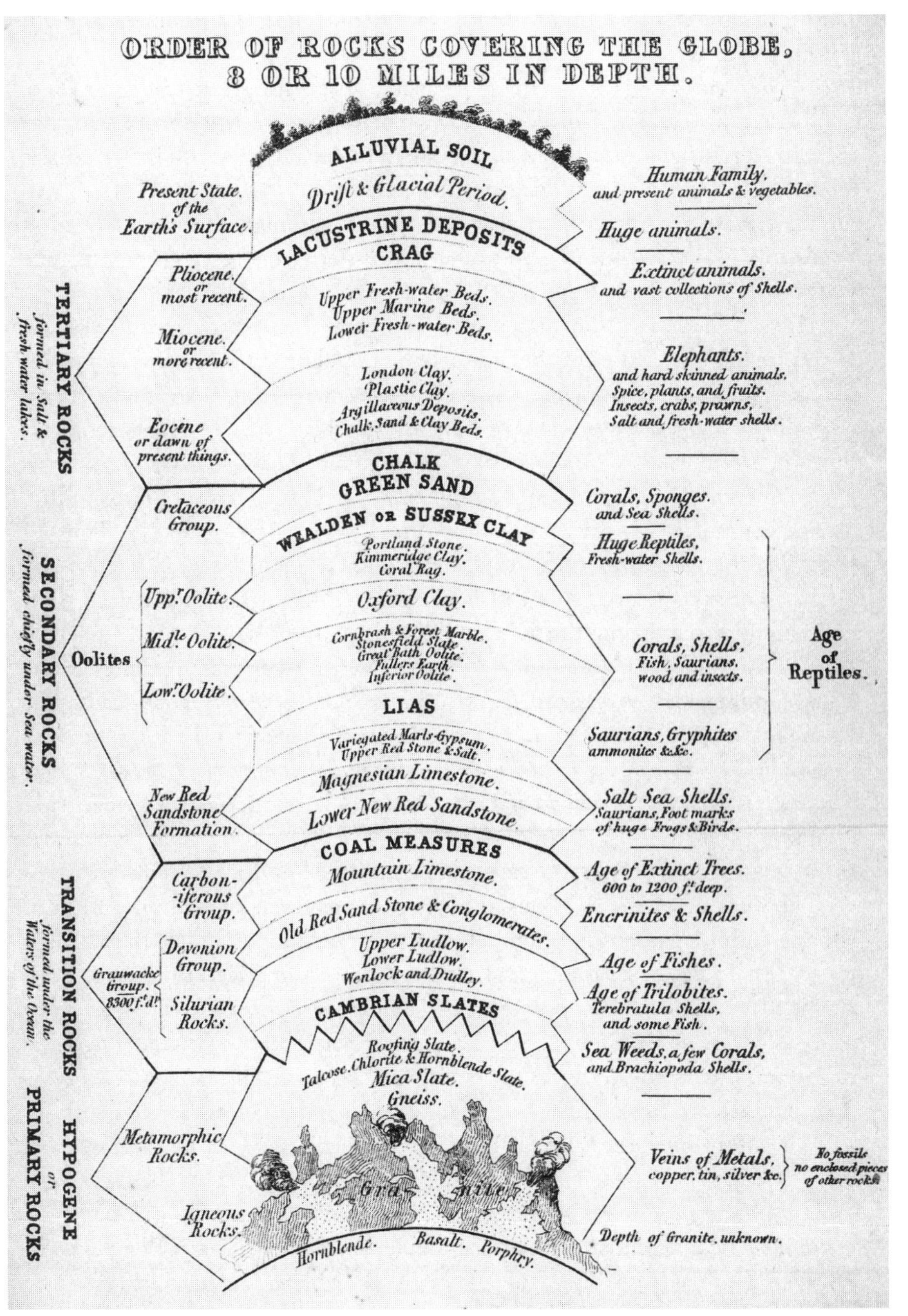

Figure 8. Geological Chart (1854). From Mrs. John Wright, *The Globe Prepared for Man: A Guide to Geology,* 1854. Courtesy of the Sigmund Samuel Library, University of Toronto.

liarly unhappy conjunction of Truth and fiction" that Goodwin locates his argument.

Besides the popularized geology available to an informed reader in 1860, Goodwin draws on two main sources to formulate his argument: three reconcilers of geology and Genesis (Hugh Miller, William Buckland, and J. H. Pratt); and, as with all the other Essayists of *Essays and Reviews*, the ideas and methods of German biblical critics. The three reconcilers are quoted, summarized, and analyzed at length to show that their methods and conclusions are "at variance with one another and mutually destructive" (Warren Dawson 1934, 35).

Hugh Miller was a stonemason who later became a Victorian man of letters, an upward mobility caused by the success of his popularizing works in geology: *The Old Red Sandstone or New Walks in an Old Field* (1841); *Foot-Prints of the Creator; or the Asterolepis of Stromness* (1847; a reply to Chambers's *Vestiges*); his autobiography, *My School and Schoolmasters* (1852); and finally *The Testimony of the Rocks* (drawn upon by Goodwin throughout his essay), published posthumously in 1857 after he committed suicide by shooting himself on 23 December 1856. This last work, like the *Foot-Prints*, deals extensively with relations between science and religion, the two discourses that Miller negotiated throughout his writings; his failure to reconcile them ultimately led to his despair and suicide.

William Buckland, geologist and dean of Westminster, was appointed to the chair of mineralogy in Oxford in 1813, and the same year was elected to the Geological Society in London. In 1818 he was elected Fellow of the Royal Society. His two best-known works are *Reliquae Diluvianae, or Observations on the Organic Remains . . . Attesting the Action of a Universal Deluge* (1823), and his Bridgewater Treatise of 1836, *Geology and Mineralogy Considered with Reference to Natural Theology* (2 vols.). By 1858 this treatise had been issued in three editions.

The work of Miller and Buckland was extremely well known; the author of Goodwin's third major source, John Henry Pratt, was not. Appointed the chaplain of the East India Company in 1838, and archdeacon of Calcutta in 1850, Pratt combined his ministerial duties with an avid interest in science, publishing *Scripture and Science Not at Variance* in 1856; he also published *Mathematical Principles of Mechanical Philosophy* (1836) and a revision, *Treatise on Attractions, La Place's Functions, and the Figure of the Earth* (1860).

The effort to reconcile Genesis and geology had been denounced publicly as early as 1830 by Adam Sedgwick in his "Address of the President" to the Geological Society (Cannon 1960, 39); nevertheless, the reconcilers that serve as Goodwin's source must be differentiated from scriptural geologists like George Bugg, who in *Scriptural Geology* (1826) used conspiracy in his explanations of scientists, "the adversaries of *Revelation*," who "have turned our Geology against the Bible, and made us pay dearly for our unwise confidence and credulity" (1826, 2:314, 355). Although G. L. Davies has called Buckland "the last British geologist of note to relate the discovery of modern geology to the Mosaic writings" (1969, 215), he and Goodwin's other sources do not denounce geology or fundamentally reject its major premises; instead, each attempts to reconcile the discrepancies between the account of creation told in Genesis with interpretive problems, primarily of time and agency, that were introduced by consideration of the scientific evidence.

To pry open their attempts at reconciliation, Goodwin draws upon the higher criticism of Genesis that questioned its attribution to Moses by proposing multiple sources and the compilation of conventional literary genres. In 1753 Jean Astruc published *Conjectures sur les mémoires originaux dont it paroît que Moyse se servit pour composer le livre de la Genèse* (Conjectures on the original records which it appears that Moses made use of in writing the book of Genesis), in which he was the first to argue that Genesis is composed from two different sources identified by two different names for God, Yahweh and Elohim. Eichhorn in his *Einleitung ins Alte Testament* (1780–83; Introduction to the Old Testament) developed the same line, setting out "the foundations of the later Documentary Hypothesis" (Rogerson 1984, 19). His pupil, Heinrich Ewald, in *Geschichte des Volkes Israel* (1843; History of Israel), attributed the first chapter of Genesis to one of the collections of documents he designated "The Book of Origins." Peter von Bohlen published *Introduction to Genesis, with a Commentary on the Opening Portion* (trans. 1855 2 vols.; original Ger. 1835), following Ewald in denying the Mosaic authorship and attributing its organization to a redaction of the eighth century B.C.E., in which the traditions of J(ahweh) and E(lohim) could be perceived. Finally, Ewald's pupil Julius Wellhausen, who published *Prolegomena zur Geschichte Israels* (1883; trans. *Prolegomena to the History of Ancient Israel*, 1885), and Karl Heinrich Graf formulated the documentary hypothesis for Genesis, reading the first chapter of Genesis as part of the Priestly (or P) source.

In England, Alexander Geddes published *Critical Remarks on the Hebrew Scriptures . . . Containing Remarks on the Pentateuch* (1800), in which he denied Mosaic authorship, dated the Pentateuch at the time of Solomon, and accepted Astruc's notion of the two traditions based on the names for God, but not as two sources; instead he advocated a fragmentary hypothesis, compiled by a redactor. German higher critical scholarship of Genesis, such as that of Ewald and Bohlen, was under attack in England from Pusey in *Historical Enquiry into the Probable Causes of the Rationalist Character lately Predominant in the Theology of Germany* (1828) and from Henry John Rose in *The Law of Moses*, his Hulsean Lectures published in 1834. In 1856 Samuel Davidson published as volume 2 of the tenth edition of Horne's *Introduction to the Critical Study . . . of the Holy Scriptures* (to which Goodwin refers) his summary and synthesis of German higher-critical scholarship, *The Text of the Old Testament* (republished 1859). Davidson was forced to resign his teaching position (1857), partly for arguing against the Mosaic authorship of the Pentateuch, and partly for seeming to deny literal inspiration and conservative interpretation. (Davidson 1859, 576–77; see also Rogerson 1984, 198 and Goodwin ¶6 and Jowett ¶12 and n. 20).[16]

James R. Moore, in placing the problem of "interpreting the book of Genesis within the history and philosophy of hermeneutics" specifically in relation to the

German higher criticism as it was imported into nineteenth-century England, indicates the contemporary importance of Goodwin's topic: "What is at stake . . . in the interpretation of Genesis cannot be merely the historicity of ancient narratives, or the doctrine of biblical inspiration, or even the systems of theology based on an inspired historical record of Creation, Fall, and Deluge. From a critical perspective it can be argued that the ultimate issue is nothing less than the social order, its character and sanctions, as dependent on human nature, created and corrupt" (1979, 327). One instance of Goodwin's head-on attack on the scriptural reconcilers (and through them on the even more conservative scriptural geologists as well) will serve to demonstrate the delicacy with which the topic had to be handled. On the one hand Goodwin rejects Genesis as a valid geological document. On the other, his argument is on the grounds of philology: he is careful not to deny in formal terms the authenticity of Genesis as a scriptural document, but denies by implication its attribution to Moses. He uses the name "Moses" only once, distancing himself by locating Moses in others' narratives with the phrase "we are told"; elsewhere the references to Moses occur only in cited passages. He also uses the phrase "Hebrew cosmogonist . . . Hebrew writer" (¶41), a reference to Moses that denies the Mosaic authorship of Genesis, without doing so directly.

More generally, Goodwin isolates "two modes of conciliation" (¶28), the "great-gap theory" and the "day-period theory" as the primary targets of his attack. He begins his essay by constructing an analogy between nineteenth-century resistance to geology and seventeenth-century persecution of astronomy, particularly the condemnation of Galileo. He then elaborates a narrative of the earth's geological history, reading the rocks as marking different phases of that history. He then turns to the creation story in Genesis, focusing first on discrepancies between the two accounts of creation found there. Finally, Goodwin moves to the attempts to reconcile the problems introduced by geology to a literalist belief in Genesis. He attacks the reconcilers through extensive quotation, locating contradictions at specific points of their arguments and pulling on them until the reconciliation comes apart.

Throughout the essay, Goodwin often deploys a rhetoric of dismissal, consistent with what John M. Robson has recently outlined in his discussion of the rhetoric of the Bridgewater Treatises (Helmstadter and Lightman 1990, 94–100). Assertions like "no well-instructed person now doubts" (¶6), "a plain statement of fact" (¶26), and "the plain meaning of language" (¶67) function not only in the place of demonstration but also mark out the points where Goodwin is asserting one side of a controverted point. His means of argument introduces a host of problems related to extensive quotation: specifically, they open the essay to charges of distorting his opponents through simplification, limited range of selectivity, misquotation, and distortion through the setting of faulty comparisons and contrasts. This essay is unique in *Essays and Reviews* in its method: long quotations, sometimes with little commentary, are often left to speak for themselves. Goodwin fails to provide any historical context for his account of geology: he makes no mention of Lyell, Hutton, and the uniformitarians who also deny harmonizing strategies; nor does he adequately situate his opponents in the context of contemporary geology. This lack of historical context may be contrasted to the ways in which Powell and Pattison argue. Opposed to their methods of scholarly argumentation, Goodwin often relies on the conventions of the popular naturalist and popular textbooks that conform to general expectations for science about 1860.

Goodwin discusses the Hebrew terms for the days of creation and the narrative problems of Genesis in a scholarly fashion. Indeed, his biographer has commented that he was "well qualified to write on the subject of the cosmogony of Genesis" (Warren Dawson 1934, 35). He had made an intense study of Hebrew from his childhood on, and was "a competent Hebraist by the time he left Cambridge" and was also skilled in comparative philology. His "considerable knowledge of geology" was that of an up-to-date reader in the field, based again on studies dating back to his early life: "Few scholars, if any, could have been found who were conversant at the same time with the Hebrew language and with the advances of scientific geology" (36). Nevertheless, Goodwin's reference to a single biblical commentator (Pusey) suggests that in theology as well as geology his argument here, though well informed, up-to-date, and accurate in his use of Hebrew and geological scholarship, should be considered less as a scholarly treatment and more as a commonsense attack for a popular audience on the facile harmonization of Genesis and geology.

Discussing recent historians of science who have regrounded their historiographic models away from warfare metaphors and positivistic narratives of progress, L. J. Jordanova and Roy S. Porter stress that one of the important breaks with this tradition is "from the traditional interpretations (of *Genesis* and geology, or geologists struggling with Moses) in not isolating *religious* from other forms of general philosophical belief about the nature of the universe and man's place within it" (1979, xiv). In traditional arguments structured on the narrative of progress, science is the good force; religion, the bad: mediating social discourses tend to be silenced. To a certain extent, Goodwin follows this paradigm. Our annotation attempts to provide a position from which to read against the grain of this tendency by placing specific points of Goodwin's argument on contemporary geological controversy in a broader social context. Perhaps the greatest barrier in reading this essay is the reliance Goodwin and the writers he quotes place on technical language. Our annotation relies heavily on David Page's *Handbook of Geological Terms* (1859), according to the *DNB* "a useful one in its day" (s.v. "Page, David"), to provide readers not only with definitions, but indications that the very geological terms used transparently by Goodwin were often under contestation in 1859. Furthermore, in his definitions Page indicates a utilitarian, technological, or industrial function for the geological phenomena under consideration; such a function is never considered by Goodwin (or most other writers on Genesis and geology). Page's definitions indicate that the science was driven by strong economic concerns along with the so-called disinterested pursuit of knowledge or the search for proof of a divine creator, whose record of creation is found in Genesis.

As part of the debate concerning Genesis and geology Goodwin's essay has a minor but significant place. Because he was a layman, he was not susceptible to prosecution under the Church Discipline Act, and since he did not have the responsibility for teaching what were seen as antibiblical or rationalist views to the young, and since he left the country to take up his legal position in Shanghai, he was effectively removed from the controversy in a directly personal sense.

To some extent, that removal also protected him from the most stringent critical attack. Of the major reviews, Harrison barely mentions Goodwin, claiming "the defenders of the Mosaic cosmogony scarcely needed or deserved so remorseless an exposure" (Harrison 1860, 302). Stanley is equally dismissive and equally brief: "Mr. Goodwin's contribution may also be considered as practically defunct. . . . Except that the style of his Essay is needlessly offensive and irritating, there is nothing in it which needs further notice than any of the other attempts which have been made to adjust the relations of Genesis and geology" (1861a, 475–76). Wilberforce also quickly dismisses Goodwin's essay, but for entirely different reasons from those of Harrison and Stanley. He compares Goodwin's "cavils against the Mosaic cosmogony" to "such speculations as those of . . . Powell," declaring them to be the result of an inability to interpret properly the relations between science and revelation: "In spite of Mr. Goodwin's minute special pleading, we assert, first, that in all this there is a marvellous agreement with the record with which the science of geology is daily furnishing us; and secondly, that it does in truth involve a far higher difficulty to suppose that the writer of the book of Genesis, without Divine enlightenment, rose so far above his age as to invent the cosmogony which he is hinted to fraudulently have palmed upon mankind as a revelation, than to suppose that higher discoveries of science will manifest to all the essential truthfulness of the Mosaic account of Creation" (Wilberforce 1861, 292).

At the same time, there were a number of particular responses to Goodwin. One of the earliest reviews, that in the *Guardian*, asserts that to Goodwin "the Mosaic narrative of the Creation is utterly irreconcileable with the discoveries of modern science" (23 May 1860, 474). A review article in the *Christian Remembrancer* in April 1861 points to the apparent calm and innocence of Goodwin's essay, but perceives a threat within: "Among the *Essays and Reviews*, now unhappily so notorious, is one which, unless the fallacy of it is exposed without loss of time, bids fair to do more mischief than all the rest. . . . With the air of a practised counsel, confident in the possession of a strong case, the writer fairly and dispassionately reviews all that has been said on the other side, and, having closed his brief, sits down in calm and not unimpressive expectation of a verdict" (402). Goodwin is condemned for his illogical literalism (how could the days be marked before the sun and moon were created?), for the neglect of the great gap of time between the first verse of Genesis and the rest of the chapter, and for ignoring the instrumentality of Satan and the "spiritual agencies" which are to be accounted as equal in importance with assumptions of science, such as "gravitation or the inductive principle" (408). Others, such as the scientist Robert Main (1861), who declares himself to be unsympathetic with literalism, were critical of Goodwin for attacking the fundamentals of the Genesis narrative as a scientific account and the biblical geologists along with the Bible without offering an alternative explanation.

In *Aids to Faith* (1861) McCaul attacks Goodwin for distinguishing between the Jahwist and Elohist versions that use different names for God. In a swift overview of German scholarship McCaul concludes that the commentators from Astruc and Eichhorn to Ewald and his contemporaries adopt various versions of the one-, two-, or three-document theory for the creation and other narratives in the first chapters of Genesis: such lack of unanimity renders "valueless their conclusions! With such facts can any sane person talk of the results of modern criticism as regards the book of Genesis? or be willing to give up the belief of centuries for such criticism as this" (William Thomson 1861, 193). His argument is both beside Goodwin's chief point, the attack on the biblical geologists, but even so, his listing of the conflicting theories concerning the document theories about the first chapters of Genesis was, in hindsight, an account of the gradual process of shifting the documentary materials and problems for Genesis that contemporary scholarship does indeed largely agree upon. Finally, J. H. Pratt, one of the reconcilers of geology and Genesis that Goodwin quotes extensively (¶s 44–47), expanded his condemnation of the Essayists, including Goodwin, in the sixth edition of *Scripture and Science Not at Variance* (1871), though without taking on Goodwin's arguments in detail. And there the matter rested, uncomfortably, as debates between Genesis and geology smoldered on throughout the nineteenth century (see J. R. Moore 1979 and Eisen and Lightman 1984), bursting into flames a hundred years after *Essays and Reviews* with the creationism controversies (see Ruse 1982; Larson 1985; and J. H. Brooke 1991).

Mark Pattison and the Intellectual History of the Eighteenth Century

THE ELDEST OF TWELVE CHILDREN, Mark Pattison (1813–1884) was born at Hornby, Yorkshire, and was educated at home by his father, Mark James Pattison, an evangelical clergyman. He took his B.A. in 1836 at Oriel College, Oxford. Forsaking his childhood evangelicalism, he came under the influence of Tractarianism from 1838 to 1848, moving into Newman's house and helping in the translation of Thomas Aquinas's *Catena Aurea*. He was eventually elected to a fellowship at Lincoln College (1839). The college was then strongly anti-Tractarian, but he was able to make a strong impression, improving the College's reputation with his teaching. In 1843 he was ordained priest and was also appointed a tutor at Lincoln College, requiring him to prepare lectures on Aristotle's *Ethics*, on logic, and the classics. In 1848 he was appointed public examiner in Classics for the university.

Although he had been assisting with the administration of Lincoln College and was widely considered to be the most likely candidate for appointment as the new rector (the equivalent of master or provost) when the post became vacant in 1851, he lost the election through a common-room intrigue that pitted him and the serious teachers who supported him against those who regarded the college as a comfortable sinecure. After this loss, Pattison suffered a severe depression for about a year but then gradually recovered and renewed his scholarly life: "Since the year 1851, I have lived wholly for study. There can be no vanity in making this confession, for, strange to say, in a university ostensibly endowed for the cultivation of science and letters, such a life is hardly regarded as a creditable one" (1885a, 331). He began his research on the history of European humanism that he continued until his death, first working on Isaac Casaubon, the seventeenth-century French classical scholar. He continued with his literary activities, writing articles on the general topic of the history of classical scholarship since the Renaissance. Over his lifetime Pattison published in a wide range of periodicals from the conservative *Quarterly Review* to the radical *Westminster*, of which he was one of the book review editors for a number of years. He was appointed in 1854 to succeed George Eliot and managed the theology and philosophy sections, also enlisting the help of H. B. Wilson in this project. In 1861, in the year following the publication of *Essays and Reviews*, Pattison was elected Rector of Lincoln College, and had his photograph taken for the occasion. See figure 9.

Pattison published chiefly on Renaissance humanism, eighteenth-century classical scholarship, and the religion, literature, and philosophy of those periods. He published the biographies of *Isaac Casaubon* (1875) and *Milton* (1879), and also prepared editions of English poetry, Pope's *Essay on Man* (1869) and *Satires and Epistles* (1872), and Milton's *Sonnets* (1883). Pattison served as a delegate of the Oxford University Press, and on the committees of the Bodleian and London libraries. He had the largest private library in Oxford in his day, numbering about 14,000 volumes, chiefly strong in the sixteenth, seventeenth, and eighteenth centuries. He died in 1884. Pattison is alleged to be one of the models for Casaubon in Eliot's *Middlemarch* (1872), Professor Forth in Rhoda Broughton's *Belinda* (1883), and Squire Wendover in Mary Ward's *Robert Elsmere* (1888) (Badger 1945, 438–47). For biographies see his own *Memoirs* (Pattison 1885a); V. H. H. Green 1957; and Sparrow 1967.

"Tendencies of Religious Thought in England, 1688–1750" is on a subject that Pattison studied throughout his life. He defines his historical period as extending from the Glorious Revolution of 1688 to the midpoint of the eighteenth century. The terminal date, two-thirds of the way through the reign of George II, coincides with a number of important dynastic and political events. The Hanoverians secured the English throne by putting down the Second Jacobite Rebellion (1745–46), thus finally ending Stuart claims on the throne of England that had dragged on from the reign of Charles II. Internationally, the War of the Austrian Succession, in which England was aligned with Austria against the claims of Prussia, ended with the

Figure 9. Mark Pattison (c. 1861). Engraving by W. G. Davey from a photograph by Maull & Fox. In Mark Pattison, "Life of St. Edmund, Archbishop of Canterbury." Vol. 6 of *The Lives of the English Saints.* Philadelphia: J. B. Lippincott, 1901.

treaty of Aix-la-Chapelle (1748) with Britain on the defeated side; furthermore, the war with Spain (1739–48) had ended, exacerbated by political acrimony at home among the dominant Whigs after the fall of Sir Robert Walpole in 1742.

The ecclesiastical establishment immediately after the Glorious Revolution was preoccupied with the problems inherited from the last days of the Stuart monarchy in which many constraints on Nonconformists, both Protestant and Roman Catholic, were established. These included the Test Act of 1673, requiring all persons holding public office to take the oath of supremacy and the sacrament of communion in the Church of England, and to make a declaration against transubstantiation. Anti–Roman Catholic emotions had culminated in the "Popish Plot" of 1678. In the aftermath various Roman Catholics were executed. When the Roman Catholic James II succeeded to the throne in 1685 he was conciliatory at first, but when seven bishops refused to publish his Declaration of Liberty of Conscience (1688) (an act ostensibly to ensure specific freedoms for all Dissenters but especially designed to favor James's coreligionists) there was a public outcry. The bishops' public trial and acquittal provoked popular support, and an invitation was issued to William of Orange as heir presumptive to take the English throne. With the Declaration of Rights (1689) the Protestant succession was ensured, along with the rights of Parliament, the courts, and the established church (see J. Miller 1973). A continuing problem in the relations of church and state was the Nonjurors, the clergy and laity who refused to take the Oath of Allegiance to William and Mary, having already done so to James II and his successors.

The condition of the established church by 1750 was not sound. Its pastoral and economic base had been continually eroded from the time of Henry VIII, and its hold on the changing demography of England had failed to meet the religious needs of the whole of English society. Clerical appointments and income in thousands of parishes were assigned to lay patrons (local squires or absent landlords) or corporations (such as colleges or cathedrals) who pocketed most of the income and used a pittance to hire a curate to perform the parish duties. This "plunder of the Church" (Hill 1956, 14) resulted in the decay of church buildings and parochial neglect, clerical ignorance, overwork, and ill-health. The Church of England still had access to enormous wealth and influence, vast property holdings, and powerful political and educational affiliations and duties; nevertheless, popular religion in England was in a serious decline: large numbers of people were alienated from the established church, partly the result of this economic spoilation and the concomitant intellectual decay among the parochial clergy, partly from the changes in the Stuart and Hanoverian policies of toleration that allowed the development of dissent, and partly the results of shifting agricultural and industrial labor during the beginnings of the Industrial Revolution. When Whitefield was ordained in 1736, the same year that John and Charles Wesley returned from Georgia and set up their Methodist societies and began their tours of the west country, Wales, and the north of England, the failures of the Church of England to be the church for the whole nation had reached a crisis (see Gilbert 1976).

By Pattison's terminal date of 1750 important social shifts help to explain the collapse in popular religion and account for the rise of Methodism. In particular he stresses the conditions that fostered rationalism and deism and those that facilitated the emergence of Methodism and a renewed evangelicalism in the Church of England. Pattison describes his period as one that emphasized the internal proofs for Christianity, the reasonable nature of religion, the grounds for religious belief in human reason, and a greater interest in morality than in sacraments. He distinguishes this period from the one that follows it (from 1750 to 1830), from the rise of science to the Oxford Movement, when philosophical emphasis was placed upon the external proofs for Christianity, especially on the evidence from the natural order (the argument from design) in Paley and Whately, on the evidence of divine interventions in human affairs (evidenced in the biblical miracles), on piety and sentiment rather than morality, and on the historic traditions of the church and sacraments. Rationalism in religion was not very effective in meeting the great pastoral needs that the plunder of the church had made so critical; natural theology gave little succor to popular religion and did little to attract the unchurched.

Pattison organizes his essay according to this characterization of the period from 1688 to his own time in ¶s 1–11. He gives brief attention to the Romanist controversy (1688–99), and the Bangorian controversy (1717), placing most attention in the first half of his essay on the deist controversy concerning the tenets and implications for Christianity of natural religion in the two decades from 1720 to 1740 (¶s 12–39). The second half of the essay discusses, first, the nature of theological debate in the period of the dominance of rationalist religion, with its rhetorical emphasis on polemic (¶s 40–57), and second, on the function of theology and metaphysics in this period (¶s 58–73). He concludes that the rise of Evangelicalism and the success of Methodist preaching occurred precisely because of the vacuum in public morality and civic virtue resulting from the failure of the prudential ethics of rationalist theology.

Pattison defines the assumptions of both deists and Christians concerning the role of reason and natural religion in describing their common ground and develops the relations of deists to revelation, the Bible, and morality (¶s 21–24). Deism refers to the religious movement from the mid-seventeenth to mid-eighteenth centuries that stressed the possibility of a rational knowledge of a supreme being or God who exists, who is the author of the natural world, including human existence, and who is the source for human morality. At the same time, all notions about the role of the supernatural in human life were rejected, and especially the theological doctrines of Christianity and the idea of a divine revelation in the Bible. Reliance upon human reason as the basis for "natural religion" was sufficient, they maintained, for the religious needs of human beings.

The orthodox but rationalist Christians of the period, according to Pattison, have much in common with the deists, agreeing with them about the primary notion, that it is reason that characterizes human existence and that by the exercise of reason the existence of God can be determined. There, according to Pattison, they part company, the orthodox maintaining that the character of this God can only be known through revelation, the deists asserting that they can go no further. Pattison contends that such philosophical and theological positions overdetermine all religious debate in the period, on every side of the issue, and lead to various direct effects in popular preaching and piety and in the practices and defects of individual morality and public virtue.

Deism was part of a larger context in European thought that placed increasing emphasis on rationalism from the later sixteenth and through the eighteenth centuries, as, for instance, in the writings and influence of René Descartes. In England deism was one center of religious controversy among several for about 100 years, that is, from the first attack on deism in William Stillingfleet's *Letter to a Deist* (1677) to David Hume's *Dialogues concerning Natural Religion* (1779). The first English deist is usually taken to be Lord Herbert of Cherbury,[17] but his erudite philosophy, written for the learned in Latin, became much better known through the satiric attack on the deists by the poet laureate John Dryden in his poem *Religio Laici* (1682; for his summary of Herbert's five main points, see Dryden 1958, 1:312–13; ll. 42–61). The last sustained attack on deism as though it were still alive in its eighteenth-century form appears to be Edward Chichester's *Deism Compared with Christianity* (1821 3 vols.). Of course many of the notions of deism continued to be adopted by individual adherents of establishment churches and were appropriated in part by such religious denominations as the Unitarians (for discussions of deism see Lovejoy 1932; Heineman, 1950; Don Cameron Allen 1964; Waring 1967; Byrne 1989; and Baird 1992).

Pattison's account positions John Locke as one of the philosophical precursors to deism: the role of human understanding of natural religion leads in Locke to an assertion of the reasonableness of Christianity. Using the conventions and practices of public debate, pulpit oratory, and popular religion Pattison sets in opposition the chief proponents for deism, John Toland, Anthony Collins, Matthew Tindal, and Thomas Woolston, against their orthodox opponents, including Edward Stillingfleet, William Warburton, and Thomas Sherlock. The philosophers and theologians George Berkeley and Joseph Butler are counterpoises to Locke, though on the side of orthodoxy. For modern readers it is particularly difficult to follow the complicated alignments during the various philosophical and theological debates, associations made all the more complex because of their direct political implications. For instance, the Bangorian controversy is on one level a debate about the role of authority in the church and on another concerns the relations between church and state and the relative power of the Crown and Parliament. And throughout all of these debates, as Pattison repeatedly emphasizes, the thread of rationalism unites all writers in their drawing fine lines of definition, sharp distinctions, and demarcations between loyal supporters and bitter enemies (for discussions of Toland and Collins see O'Higgins 1970 and Robert E. Sullivan 1982).

Charles Blount was a transitional figure between Herbert and the deists of the last decade of the seventeenth century. His response to Dryden's attack on deism in *Religio Laici* inaugurated the intense debate that followed to about 1700, to which he contributed *A Summary Account of the Deist's Religion* (1693). Among the philosophers, Thomas Hobbes in *Leviathan* (1651) had argued that all knowledge is derived from reason and sense experience, and that the Bible is not contrary to reason, while John Locke in *The Reasonableness of Christianity* (1695) maintained the conformity of the Bible to the rules of reason, and that reason is the determining instrument in assessing the validity of the miracles as proofs for the divine origin of the Bible. In Pattison's account there were four major contributors to the arguments for deism: John Toland in *Christianity Not Mysterious* (1696) argued that God and revelation can be comprehended by human reason, that the supposed mysteries of Christianity are pagan borrowings or priestly interventions, and that Christianity did not introduce anything that was previously not known. Anthony Collins, a friend of Locke's, in *A Discourse of Freethinking* (1723), argued that free inquiry, independent of revelation and authority, was the only means of achieving truth; it was followed by the biblical writers and was enjoined by them as a method to be followed. Matthew Tindal in *Christianity as Old as the Creation* (1730) maintained that all rational creatures are subject to a law of nature, namely, reason, which is eternal, perfect, and unchangeable, and the Bible is not to add to this law, nor to take from it, but is to be tested by it, and so is enabled to be an instrument in freeing people from superstition. Finally, Thomas Woolston in *Six Discourses on the Miracles of Our Saviour* (1729) followed the allegorizing methods of biblical interpretation of Origen but extended them to assert that all of the New Testament miracles were not factual but symbolic, especially the virgin birth and the resurrection.

It was impossible for the views of the deists and their adherents to be freely disseminated in a kingdom where the state church controlled the lives of most citizens, at least formally, with a complex systems of church taxes, tithes, courts, canon law, and patronage (Hill 1969, 74–77), but with the beginnings of the Civil War, the Puritan revolution demanded drastic administrative and political transformation in the alignments and procedures of the established church. The political and religious disputes of the seventeenth century made deist views politically, as well as religiously, suspicious. The conflicts of the English Civil War (1642–46), the theological and military opposition of Charles I and Oliver Cromwell, the Commonwealth (1649–60), and the Restoration under Charles II constructed political oppositions in which the antagonism of Puritan and cavalier was reenforced with theological enmity and ecclesiastical repression on both sides. Accordingly, the ideas of the deists and of other free thinkers were overdetermined by political affiliations and became instruments in the struggles for control of the ecclesiastical establishment, the appointment of bishops and other administrative positions in church, government, and university. Rather than being considered as items for discussion in philosophical debate, deist ideas became weapons in religious controversy. The deists and their sympathizers tended to support republican forms of government, and radical positions in church reform; increasingly they became anticlerical in their attacks, especially after 1688, when the succession of the English throne was settled on William and Mary, and James II fled to France.

The task of the Christian apologists, whom Pattison discusses at length, was first to convince the deists of the role of providence in governing nature and moral actions in such works as Robert Boyle's *The Excellence of Theology Compared with Natural Philosophy* (1664) and John Ray's *The Wisdom of God Manifested in the Works of Creation* (1691). Their second task was to convince the deists of special revelation. In both arguments the role of the "evidences" was central, both the external evidence of nature whereby God could be known as active providentially through effects and also the evidence of miracles in revelation as testimony to the truth of the Gospels. Never a widely popular, consistent, or coordinated religious movement, deism shifted through the eighteenth century from a conscious philosophical position with respect to natural religion to a term of abuse for any free-thinking tendencies in religious thought. By 1860 the study of deism was not a matter of religious polemic or apologetic but had become part of the study of the history of religious thought. Pattison's is the first study in a series of examinations of late seventeenth and eighteenth century religion in Britain that continued over the next decade and a half with A. S. Farrar's *Critical History of Free Thought* (1862); John Tulloch's *Rational Theology and Christian Philosophy in England in the Seventeenth Century* (1872, 2 vols.); John Hunt's *Religious Thought in England from the Reformation to the End of the Last Century* (1873, 3 vols.); and Leslie Stephen's *English Thought in the Eighteenth Century* (1876, 2 vols.).

As Pattison describes the writing of "Tendencies of Religious Thought in England 1688–1750" in his *Memoirs*, his work on the history of religious thought was groundbreaking: "The movement of theological sentiment in modern Europe had long had a peculiar charm for me. It was a subject, too, that had never been touched by any English writer, with the exception of one Unitarian sketch by J. J. Tayler—*Retrospect of the Religious Life of England*—a volume not known beyond Unitarian circles. I saw the impossibility of attempting, as Tayler had done, to survey the whole course of religious thought in England." To overcome the enormity of the task, he explains, "I therefore selected a special period which had peculiarly definite limits. It had always struck me as a surprising fact that Deism, which had been the prevailing form of thought among the educated classes in England during the first half of the eighteenth century, should have abruptly disappeared somewhere about 1760, giving place to a revived Puritanism in the form of Methodism and Evangelicalism. I saw clearly that the usual solution offered by the orthodox, viz. that Deism had been triumphantly refuted in argument, did not explain the fact. I attempted an original inquiry, of a kind new in this country, into the philosophical causes of the sudden rise and as sudden extinction of Deism in the last century." He describes the difficulties in having such a study understood: "So wholly extinct is scientific theology in the Church of England that the English public could not recognise such a thing as a neutral and philosophic inquiry into the causes of the form of thought existing at any period. Our clergy knew only of pamphlets which must be either for or against one of the parties in the Church."

This "scientific history of the self-development of opinion," which he claims took him two years to research, was "singularly unsuccessful": "To judge from the reviews, it never occurred to any of our public instructors that such a conception was possible. Clerical or anti-clerical, from the *Westminster Review* to the *Guardian*, they were all busily occupied in finding or making contradictions between the writer's words and the thirty-nine articles." Despite these British critics, the essay, according to Pattison, was well received on the Continent: "The Protestant historian—[Isaac August] Dorner—going over the same ground a few years afterwards, accepted the essay for what it was intended to be—a history, and not a party manifesto. Dorner's chapter, 'Der streitende und siegende Deismus' [The struggle and victory of deism], makes much use and ample acknowledgment of my essay." The absence of an atmosphere of "free discussion and contradiction," which became increasingly apparent with the reception of *Essays and Reviews*, led him to despair: "No topic excites the English world more than a religious topic, yet there is no public in this country for a scientific treatment of theology. This absence of a professional public and not the restraints of our formularies, seems to me the true reason why a real theology cannot exist in England. . . . For myself, I refused to attempt any defence or to enter into controversy with my critics. We were at cross purposes, and there was an end. But I resolved to wash my hands of theology and even of Church history, seeing that there existed in England no proper public for either" (Pattison 1885a, 312–17).

Pattison had been writing for the *Westminster Review* as the editor of the philosophical section from October 1854 as the replacement for George Eliot. John Chapman, the publisher, wrote him a number of letters early in 1854 in which he asked Pattison to write in the series of articles on "the Religious Condition of England": "I think you would render essential service by continuing it" (Bodley MS. Pattison 50, fol. 304). In January 1857 Pattison published "The Present State of Religion in Germany" in the *Westminster*, and proposed following it with a companion piece, "The Religious State of England," the topic Chapman had proposed three years earlier. However, because of Chapman's restriction imposed on the *Westminster* of only one theological treatise per issue, Pattison was told his contribution had to be postponed until July 1858 (MS. Pattison 51, fols. 386–98), though in fact it was never published in the *Westminster* (see Francis 1974, 802–7). Very likely it was the work on this essay that eventually issued in Pattison's contribution to *Essays and Reviews*. Pattison's remark in his *Memoirs* that his essay was "hastily written" (1885a, 313) is borne out by the fact that Wilson was trying to pry it, or even its title, from him in November, when all of the other essays were apparently ready except his and Jowett's (Letter 12); and in the aftermath of the appointment of Temple to the see of Exeter in 1869, during the plans to republish the thirteenth edition of *Essays and Reviews*, again Pattison complains of his accomplishment: "Further reading has made me so dissatisfied with my Essay on the 18th century that I shall not be willing to republish" (Letter 314). Part of that dissatisfaction is reflected, perhaps, in the bibliographical and other additions that he made to it over many years.

Despite his claims to never again enter into religious controversy, nor to ever want the essay republished, he certainly worked through his text repeatedly, and was very likely preparing it for republication, though it is not clear from the surviving correspondence whether he acceded in the project for a second volume of *Essays and Reviews* in 1869–70. Among the Pattison papers in the Bodleian Library, Oxford, two manuscripts bear directly on the text of Pattison's "Tendencies of Religious Thought in England 1688–1750." Bodley MS. Pattison 106 consists of a disbound copy of the printed text of the tenth edition of his essay, interfoliated with blank leaves to make it into a notebook in which Pattison added, in different ink at different times, some 150 references, illustrations, quotations, and citations from late seventeenth- and eighteenth-century religious controversy and from recent philosophical studies of rationalism in English, French, and German. He has also edited all of his internal references in pencil, with the instruction that each is to be printed as a footnote in the revision he was very likely planning. All of the annotations from this manuscript are given in the appendix following the endnotes to Pattison's essay. A second manuscript, Bodley MS. Pattison 109, is an undated draft of "Tendencies of Religious Thought in England 1688–1750." It consists of 45 folios of unwatermarked paper measuring 9 x 11 1/4 inches. Fol. 1 contains an outline of the essay, fol. 1^{v} has a paragraph on the future of rationalism; fol. 2 a paragraph on Berkeley and a quotation from F. W. Newman's *Phases of Faith*; fol. 2^{v} is blank. Fols. 3–10^{v} are written on both sides of the sheets in continuous text, and thereafter most sheets are written on the recto only. The MS. leaves space throughout for quotations to be added; references are frequently added interlinearly. A study of this manuscript indicates that it was revised to add data (dates, names, works, and illustrative references), integrating such information into the argument to demonstrate its pertinence, and expanding historical, theological, and philosophical argument by means of extension and qualification.

The sources for Pattison's essay and for these extensive revisions are drawn from four kinds of materials. First he read widely in the voluminous sermons of the period, of preachers as different as the archbishops of Canterbury, Edward Stillingfleet and John Tillotson, and little-known country rectors, such as Thomas Bartlett and Edward Chichester. On the basis of an analysis of this homiletical material he draws conclusions concerning the public discussion of religious topics, the style of pulpit oratory, and its role in the theological disputes of the ecclesiastical parties. A second body of material relates to dominant philosophical positions, especially those concerning rationalism in religion in the writings of Locke, Berkeley, and Butler. A third group of sources is seventeenth- and eighteenth-century tracts and other ephemeral literature of religious controversy, particularly the deists and their associates, as well as their orthodox opponents. A fourth range of sources consists of mostly German discussions of the history of philosophical and theological movements in the period. Pattison's resources included his own large library and the Bodleian Library in Oxford (he added Bodley shelf-marks to some annotations in MS. Pattison 106). His accomplishment in drawing this body of material together for analysis, with little precedent in the historical analyses of his own or earlier periods, is still praised by a recent historian of the deists as a "classic, luminous essay" (Rupp 1986, 257).

Critical responses to Pattison were generally puzzled or favorable. Many of his friends wrote to him praising his treatment of a neglected period of intellectual history. The early review in the *Literary Gazette* praises "a vigorous and racy essay, and, we suspect, the most readable and popular of the set. It is a brilliant and philosophical review of the theology of the seventeenth century" (14 April 1860, 460). Later reviewers, however, would find him guilty by association with the other condemned writers. Then grounds had to be manufactured, usually based on the fact that his rather sympathetic treatment of the deists and his criticism of the moral and intellectual laxity of many of the clergy in the late seventeenth and early eighteenth century, were, by extension, an affiliation with German neology and a criticism of the morality and intellectual accomplishments of the clergy in the present. But the reviewers had little knowledge of the period of which they were writing. Their knowledge of Butler and Paley was limited to what they had studied at Oxford or Cambridge, and the history and aftermath of deism was a little-known topic.

In an early review in the *Guardian*, Pattison's essay is praised as a "very able tractate [that] is almost entirely of a historical character, and affords little opportunity for discussing and enforcing any peculiar opinions which the writer himself may hold. . . . He is one of those patient thinkers and painstaking writers who carefully possess themselves of the phenomena belonging to the subject before them . . . and endeavour to derive their theories from a strict examination of facts and documents. . . . It is perhaps for solid and durable worth the most important literary contribution of the whole seven" (23 May 1860, 473). In the *North British Review* it is described as "an extended but interesting sketch" but its description of the rationalism of the eighteenth century is applied to Broad Church theology: "Mr Pattison leaves us to infer that this reaction is to be found in the religious movement of which this volume is an indication" (Aug. 1860, 223). A number of reviews, like the *Christian Remembrancer*, consider that because of the descriptive and historical nature of Pattison's essay it does not belong in a volume that was considered to be polemical; it is "a very remarkable specimen both of extensive research and logical thought. It is singularly interesting and contains a really valuable addition to the literature of the day" (Oct. 1860, 353). In the major quarterlies, Pattison is either praised or ignored. Harrison, for instance, praises it as "an admirable page in the history of doctrine . . . an inquiry so patiently and candidly conducted. . . . It is remarkable, first, as expressing the discredit into which the Analogy of Butler has lapsed in Oxford; secondly as an unanswerable and suggestive repudiation of a long line of conflicting apologists" (1860, 304); but Wilberforce and Stanley have little to say about it.

At the time of its publication it was also recognized as groundbreaking: "There is no other summary of that part of the literature of the eighteenth century which bears upon religious subjects in which so much information is found, or which will enable the Churchman to form so true an estimate of this dark portion of the history of the Church of England" (*Christian Remembrancer*, Oct. 1860, 353). Pattison is praised for his "most masterly analysis of the course of religious thought from the Revolution to the first publication of the Tracts for the Times" (352–53). At the same time he is condemned for not appreciating "the connexion of faith with the state of the heart and the affections [which] appears here for the first time explicitly, and it may be well to observe that it gives its tone to the whole of the essay" (355). Such shifts from his arguments to ad hominem attacks gave Pattison grounds for asserting that the reception of his essay was often testy at the time of its publication, and for the ensuing ten years. The presence in the volume of *Essays and Reviews* of what he calls "a scientific treatment of theology" and "a neutral and philosophic inquiry into the causes of the form of thought" puzzled critics, reviewers, and readers. Later historians, such as W. E. H. Lecky (1838–1903), writing almost twenty years after Pattison in *The History of England in the Eighteenth Century* (1878–90, 8 vols.), continued to characterize the period from 1688 to 1750 in the same terms that Pattison uses (and distances himself from) in ¶2: "The essential and predominating characteristics of the prevailing theology were the prominence that was given to external morality as distinguished both from dogma and from all forms of emotion, and the assiduity with which the preachers laboured to establish the purely rational character of Christianity" (Lecky 2:562). Beginning his chapter on the deists, Gordon Rupp in a recent volume in the *Oxford History of the Christian Church* refers in his opening sentence to Pattison's essay as "classic" (1986, 257) and in his extensive bibliography he cites it as one of only three studies of "rationalists and moralists" written before 1954.

Benjamin Jowett and Biblical Hermeneutics

BENJAMIN JOWETT (1817–1893) was born in the south-London district of Camberwell into a piously evangelical family. He was educated at St. Paul's School, where he became expert in "double translation," retranslating into Greek or Latin the passages that he had just translated into English. He also began his lifelong habit of memorizing long selections from the Greek and Latin poets, and from the Bible. In 1835 he won a "blue-ribbon" scholarship to Balliol College, Oxford, entering in October 1836, and remaining there until his death almost sixty years later.

When he entered Balliol College, Oxford University was in the throes of the turmoil over the Tractarian Movement and in particular was debating the controversial appointment of R. D. Hampden as regius professor of divinity. Among Jowett's friends were A. P. Stanley, three years his senior at Balliol, and Frederick Temple, two years his junior. At the same time John Ruskin was at Christ Church and J. A. Froude at Oriel, where Mark Pattison was a young tutor. At Balliol, one of his tutors was A. C. Tait. Most of these associates were to have significant roles in the history of *Essays and Reviews*. Jowett was elected a fellow after competitive examination over 29 other candidates, most much senior to him, while still an undergraduate, and before taking his first-class degree in 1839.

In 1855 Jowett became Regius Professor of Greek, an appointment that aroused controversy, as did most of Jowett's public activities for the next ten years. The Greek Professorship was disputed as inappropriate because of Jowett's theological views, just published in *The Epistles of St. Paul to the Thessalonians, Galatians, and Romans* (1855). His colleagues at Oxford raised so many questions about his religious orthodoxy that he was humiliated by being forced to appear before the vice-chancellor to subscribe again to the Thirty-nine Articles (Letter 1). It is in relation to his appointment as Professor of Greek that Jowett is still well known. His classical learning made him the leading Platonist of Victorian England, and his monumental translation of Plato (1871, 4 vols.) still is published by the Jowett Trust and Oxford University Press. His introduction to Plato shaped the course of Greek study for generations of Oxford students. He also published translations of Thucydides (1881, 2 vols.) and Aristotle's *Politics* (1885).

After being attacked over *Essays and Reviews* by his trial in the Chancellor's Court in Oxford (February 1863), he gave up writing on theology except for sermons, published only after his death. He was elected master of Balliol in 1870, and although he contemplated working with H. B. Wilson and others of the earlier Essayists on another volume, it came to naught. From 1882 to 1886 he was vice-chancellor of Oxford University. Jowett died in 1893. For biographies see Abbott and Campbell 1897; Geoffrey Faber 1957; and Hinchliff 1987. The portrait of Jowett (fig. 10) by the distinguished Victorian photographer Julia Margaret Cameron was taken after 1865, perhaps when Jowett was making one of his visits to Tennyson at Freshwater on the Isle of Wight, where the Camerons had a place close by.

According to his biographers, Jowett had first contemplated an essay on the interpretation of the Bible in 1847 when he was planning with A. P. Stanley their commentary on the New Testament, of which only the commentaries by each of them on the letters of Paul were published. Geoffrey Faber asserts (1957, 230) that the essay was to be a part of the commentary on John's gospel and part of it was then written. In the Jowett manuscripts in Balliol College there are preliminary drafts of parts of the essay in notebooks along with other parts of the commentary on Paul (Balliol, MS. Jowett H14 fols. 75–84 [four pages written out in an early draft, the rest in notes]; H16 fols. 1–11; H21 fols. 23v–38v [miscellaneous jottings in a small notebook]). However, the essay was not included in the first edition of 1855.

Figure 10. Benjamin Jowett (1866). Photograph by Julia Cameron. Private Collection. Courtesy of the National Portrait Gallery, London.

When the second edition of *The Epistles of St. Paul* was being prepared in 1857, he again considered using it, but he was unable to finish it because of his "constant headaches" (Abbott and Campbell 1897, 1:251, 273). Jowett visited Tennyson annually, and on the visit to him in the Isle of Wight in December 1859 he was working on the essay (Abbott and Campbell 1897, 1:276), but it took more time than he anticipated. When Wilson was trying desperately to assemble the volume, he wrote to Pattison for his article, urging him not to tell Jowett how late he was, so as not to allow him to procrastinate further (Letters 10 and 12). Finally, Jowett sent it in pieces, the first 60 pages on 17 Jan. 1860, but the rest only after 2 March, when Parker was already setting the volume in type for publication less than three weeks later. "On the Interpretation of Scripture" aroused great indignation among Jowett's contemporaries, in particular because of his views on inspiration and atonement, but more generally because of his extensive use of German higher criticism.

Traditional literary study among Jowett's contemporaries (from at least the mid-eighteenth century) consisted first, in the recovery and establishment of reliable texts of the classics and the Bible (lower criticism), and second, of interpreting those texts according to widely accepted general principles: the structural and theological unity of the Bible (so that any part of the Bible could be used to interpret any other part, all being the writing of one divine author, God); the harmonization of its parts, especially the Old and New Testaments on the basis of prophecy and fulfilment; a mystical or allegorical mode of interpretation (related to the notion of harmonization) that reads typologically not only in general prophecy but in minute detail; a moralizing of theological content to yield prescriptions for human action, in which particular narratives are read to function as dictating good and bad behavior; and a hermeneutics located in a dogmatic or apologetic tradition, so that the interpretation of the Bible justifies later theological and institutional positions, and the interpreter becomes an apologist for those institutions. Two further facts about the prevailing modes of biblical study should be noted: there was a general neglect of literary genres or forms, and the notion of harmonization tended to allow any kind of anachrony. Hence, the practices of much later periods and cultures were read back into earlier ones within the context of the Bible, and such anachronism even extended to postbiblical periods, so that credal and Christological debates of the fourth and fifth centuries were read back into New Testament documents, and the medieval developments and elaborations of the orders of ministry (bishops, priests, and deacons) were read back unproblematically into the documents of the apostolic church.

Jowett's method of interpretation rejects each of these positions in some detail, in ways that are amplified in the annotations to his essay. He denied that traditional methods that yielded orthodox readings acceptable to specific denominations were beyond questioning. Further than that, he asserted that many traditional meanings and interpretive implications are without foundation in both the text and historical-critical methodology. Such a position strikes directly at the literalists' common assumption and frequent assertion that the Bible is in some way dictated by God. Jowett has two presuppositions: first, that the textual difficulties have been or can be settled as far as is possible by following up-to-date biblical scholarship and the most recent work on the manuscript traditions, and second, that any interpretation must be reliant upon exegetical models that take into account the specific grammatical, syntactical, and philological usage of the author and the time of composition or circulation. Hence, the act of interpretation, already begun in the determination of textual readings and exegesis, continues with the "reading" of the text according to principles of common sense: the Bible is to be "read like any other book" (that is, without preconceptions concerning dogmatical, doctrinal, or institutional positions, or without assumptions concerning divine authorship), in order that its one meaning may emerge from a thorough investigation of the circumstances of its composition, construction, and reception.

In *The Epistles of St. Paul* Jowett discusses what he means by the "modern criticism" of the classics and of the Bible: "Modern criticism, in the sense here meant, may be described shortly as the spirit of inquiry into historical facts. Its course has been hitherto in some degree to discredit the value of historical testimony, and this in two ways; first, by bringing to light its inconsistencies; and, secondly, by indicating the manner in which, though false, it may without falsehood have sprung up, in the course of nature, by the workings or impressions of the human mind itself" ([1855] 1859, 1:108). Modern criticism, then, is a mode of formulating a critique of historical facts, especially "facts of Scripture" which hitherto had been accepted as uncontroverted points of interpretation, as part of the "historical testimony" or "evidences" which conferred on classical and biblical writings their authority. In the case of the Bible, this "historical testimony" is appealed to as guaranteeing its inspired authority as, in some measure, the direct word of God mediately spoken. "Modern criticism" as a term, then, raised theoretical questions that were metahistorical, concerning the validity or the truth claims of both exegesis and interpretation. According to Jowett, modern criticism enables a critique of this evidence, first by using literary-critical methods to examine the inconsistencies in the documents under scrutiny, whether biblical or classical, and secondly, to account for these inconsistencies through a phenomenological or psychological analysis of them, including the conditions of their production and reception. Such principles were known in England through the translations by Herbert Marsh of J. D. Michaelis's *Introduction to the New Testament* (1793–1801) and the work of the biblical critic Samuel Davidson, whose *Sacred Hermeneutics, Developed and Applied* (1843), revised as *A Treatise on Biblical Criticism* (1852), brought him to the center of the field in England. Hermeneutics, according to Davidson, is the relating of detailed commentary on the text from a linguistic and historical point of view (exegesis), to the placement of the specific text within a larger argument, the book as a whole, and the text in its historical setting and culture. Hence, hermeneutics as the theory and mode of interpretation consists in formulating its rules, conditions, methods, and goals, drawing on a broad range of scholarship—literary, historical, philosophical, linguistic, and sociological.[18]

Such cross-disciplinary scholarship had been arousing much controversy in Germany. In *Prolegomena ad Homerum* (1795), F. A. Wolf had provoked disputes when he argued there was no single poet, Homer, but that the "Homeric" poems were redactions of folk lays. The overlap of such controversies into biblical discussions concerning Moses and the Pentateuch, as in the works of Eichhorn, led to attacks on him for charlatanism and heresy. The higher criticism of Homer and the Bible had an impact on Coleridge, who took Eichhorn's philological seminar in Göttingen in 1798, as E. S. Shaffer (1975) has shown in detail, and through him Eichhorn penetrated throughout Victorian literary culture. Hence, the term *modern criticism*, introduced with such apparent innocence by Jowett in his commentary on the Pauline epistles, invokes notions that are diametrically opposite to contemporary reading and interpretive strategies that relied upon concepts of literal or plenary inspiration, biblical harmony, and typological reading that saw the figures, events, and persons of the Hebrew scriptures as the types of the New Testament, and as prophetic, in which the events of the past are predictive of the events of the Gospels and early Christian history, as well as of events in subsequent ages up to modern times. Such views of interpretation (literary, mystical—including allegorical, typological, and prophetic—and moral) were commonplaces in textbooks and other introductions to biblical study (see Horne [1818] 1828, 2:281–86). To introduce the word "criticism" with its Kantian connotations of German analysis, quite apart from the suggestion that it conceals an implied attack, and to use it with the adjective "modern," suggesting that new methods have overthrown old values in some sense, was problem enough; but because its contemporary usage implied being up-to-date with German classical and biblical scholarship, "modern criticism" was certainly to declare for a liberal, if not radical, politics of reading.

The most detailed nineteenth-century treatment of hermeneutics was elaborated in the lectures given in Berlin by F. E. D. Schleiermacher (Jowett had his collected works: see Hinchliff 1987, 79). In a statement of first principles, Schleiermacher writes: "The question arises whether on account of the Holy Spirit the Scriptures must be treated in a special way. This question cannot be answered by a dogmatic decision about inspiration, because such a decision itself depends upon interpretation" (Schleiermacher [1838] 1977, 107). Schleiermacher argues that the interpretation of the Bible must be placed within the general rules and principles for interpretation applied to all texts: "In the dispute over the historical interpretation of the New Testament there emerged the curious view that there are several different kinds of interpretation. To the contrary, only historical interpretation can do justice to the rootedness of the New Testament authors in their time and place" (103–4). Schleiermacher's philosophical approach, then, aided by the use of the grammatical-historical method, requires the interpreter to "put oneself both objectively and subjectively in the position of the author." In order to do so, emphasis is placed on "knowing the language as the author knew it. But this is a more specific task than putting oneself in the position of the original readers, for they too had to identify with the author. On the subjective side this requires knowing the inner and the outer aspects of the author's life" ([1838] 1977, 113). Schleiermacher's stress on "knowing" (derived from Kant's concept of understanding [*Verstand* in *Critique of Pure Reason*, 1781] as bringing the diversity of sense experience into a unified apprehension) is grounded in language in a specific historical context that includes a text's formation in the mind of the author and its reception by its audience, all concepts later picked up by Jowett.

In common with his Broad Church contemporaries, Jowett had been introduced to new methods of historical study by the work of Niebuhr on Rome and Ewald on the history of Israel. Niebuhr's *History of Rome*, first published in 1812, much revised and expanded in 1827–28, had a great impact on German as well as English historiography, especially as interpreted through the eyes of the English Broad Church followers of Niebuhr (themselves under the influence of a revived Viconian view of the cycles of history), such as Thomas Arnold, Connop Thirlwall, Julius Hare, and Henry Hart Milman (Frank M. Turner 1981, 25–27 and 418–19). Arnold had reviewed Niebuhr in the *Quarterly* in June 1825, and the next year Hare and Thirlwall began the translation of the first two volumes of Niebuhr into English (1828, 1832). Niebuhr had re-examined the early history of Rome, and by the use of contemporary studies in ethnography and mythology was able to construct new views of class relations in ancient Rome, and as well to argue that the legendary history of Rome as recorded in Livy and the other historians, was, like Homer, based on folk lays. The implication was clear—if that were true of Homer and the Roman historians, so too it could be true of Moses and the Pentateuch.

While Jowett is sometimes disparaged for knowing little of, and perhaps caring less for, the work of biblical critics in Germany (Rogerson 1984, 27 and Hinchliff 1987, 74–75), the background to his allusions and his direct references suggest a broader knowledge and use of contemporary biblical scholarship than he has been given credit for.[19] Jowett's hermeneutical principles were quite conventional in continental, and especially German scholarship, and had been conventional since the late eighteenth century, but it is his way of stating them as though newly minted, and putting them in the double context of comparison with classical literature and with points disputed in the Bible, together with a clear rejection of literalism, that provoked his biblicist readers. In Germany, aided by the work of Michaelis, Eichhorn, and De Wette, the study of the Bible, especially the five books of Moses, the prophets, and the gospels, became throughout the nineteenth century largely a matter of determining the applicability of the historical-critical methods. From them Jowett, as well as Frederick Temple, adopted a modified Viconian notion of cycles of human development perceived in nations, resembling the stages of human growth, maturing, and decay. Such a model opposed that of progress in a linear development: rather than having God as the prime mover in history, providentially influencing it at crucial stages in its more or less uniform progressive course, a cyclical view perceives the design of providence in both progression and regression, in cycles of development and of decay.

Thomas Arnold in "Essay on the Right Interpretation and Understanding of Scripture" articulates a number of interpretive principles that closely resemble those laid out in "On the Interpretation of Scripture." These principles together make the interpretation of the Bible a hermeneutics of distinctions or the making of choices between absolute and relative truth claims, thereby conveying the choice to the individual reader rather than deferring to an authoritative church or interpretive tradition. This Broad Church interpretive position is therefore at variance with the widely held and conventional concept of inspiration that was both literal and plenary (full, complete, without any admixture of error): "From his own early education, from the practice of the Church, from the common language of Christians, a young man . . . is led to regard the volume of the Old and New Testaments as containing God's revelation of himself to mankind;—he is taught that all its parts are of equal authority: but in what sense the revelation of the Old and New Testament is *one*, and all its parts of equal authority, he has probably never clearly apprehended nor thought of inquiring" (Arnold [1832] 1844, 2:377). Against such a unitary reading of the Bible "as *one* . . . all composed at one time and addressed to persons similarly situated" (2:377), Arnold posits some hermeneutical principles to guide interpretation. First, "a command given to one man, or to one generation of men, is, and can be, binding upon other men, and other generations, only so far forth as the circumstances in which both are placed are similar" (2:379). Such commands may be of "eternal and universal obligation" relating "to points in which all men at all times are alike," or may be of a "transitory nature" and so are binding only upon "particular persons, or at particular times" (2:378–80). Such an argument seems to throw readers into complete moral relativism, from which Arnold tries to rescue them with the doctrine of analogy: "From knowing what was God's will under such and such circumstances, we may gather, by parity of reasoning, what it will be, in all other circumstances; namely, the same when the circumstances are the same; analogous when the circumstances are analogous; and absolutely contrary, when they also are contrary" (2: 379–80).

Arnold posits a gradualism or development in revelation, which he calls "the famous doctrine of *accommodation*" (a term much used by Jowett): "The revelations of God to man were gradual and adapted to his state at the several periods when they were successively made. . . . In any communication between a Being of infinite knowledge and one of finite, it is obvious that the former must speak sometimes according to the views of the latter, unless it be his pleasure to raise him almost to his own level" (2:382–83). Accommodation functions, according to Arnold, not only in the act of communication from infinite to finite being, but also "in the very message itself," while leaving untouched the faculties of the finite being who is the medium of the communication, "except so far as regards the especial message with which he is entrusted" (2:383). Such a view strikes at the plenary inspiration of the prophet, at the prophetic voice, and at every utterance of the prophet. It constantly demands an interpretative intervention on the part of a reader. This view is then generalized on the basis of linguistic signification and epistemology: "The very means by which we receive all our knowledge, that is, language, and the observations of our senses, are themselves so imperfect, that they could not probably convey to the mind other than imperfect notions of truth" (2:384). Arnold's principles of interpretation, as well as the fundamental presuppositions of German "modern criticism," are inscribed in the central arguments of Jowett's "On the Interpretation of Scripture."

Jowett's three major interpretive principles are set out first in a kind of thesis statement in ¶10. The first is to interpret "the book itself [which] remains as at the first unchanged" with its corollary: the task of the interpreter of the book is "to recover the original meaning." The second principle is to read scripture based on "a knowledge of the text itself." The third principle is "to read Scripture like any other book." Full treatment of these concepts is reserved until later in the essay and in a reverse order (¶s 45–65). In ¶10 his first principle cannot refer to the notion of an unchanging biblical *text*, since he was well aware of the new editions and discoveries such as those by Karl Lachmann (his revision of the *textus receptus* in 1831 based on the oldest Greek MSS.) and Constantin Tischendorf (his edition of the Codex Ephraemi in 1843–45 and other texts and his discovery of the fourth-century MS. of the Greek Bible, the Codex Sinaiticus, in 1859). Furthermore he cannot be referring to some theory of an unchanging canon, since he argues throughout that the compilation of the biblical books was not a single moment of creation of the total text, but an elaborate institutional process of siftings, approvals, agreements, and legal or synodical procedures. Hence, "the book . . . as at the first unchanged" refers to a kind of idealized and transcendental notion of the Bible as, in some undefined sense, a divine or supernatural Hegelian event, a manifestation of the Absolute Idea, a static document as a completed text independent of theories as to its sources, compilation, and variants. It is the recovery of that event that constitutes one of the first principles of interpretation which he then states in another way.

Jowett's reformulation of this first principle in ¶10 is the corollary of the "book . . . unchanged," what he understands to be the major task of the interpreter, namely "to recover the original" or singular meaning of the words as "they first struck . . . those who heard and read them," a kind of historicized receptionism. This concept was elaborated by Swiss and German Enlightenment biblical critics in an effort to establish the historical conditions in which the biblical books were written and read. Such a methodology accords with what Spinoza in the *Tractatus Theologico-Politicus* (1670) defined as "the environment of all the prophetic books extant; that is the life, the conduct, and the studies of the author of each book, who he was, what was the occasion, and the epoch of his writing, whom did he write for, and in what language. Further, it should inquire into the fate of each book: how it was first received, into whose hands it fell, how many different versions of it there were, by whose advice it was received into the Bible, and, lastly, how all the books now universally accepted as sacred, were united into a single whole" ([1670] 1951,

103). In his lectures *De Sacrae Scripturae interpretandae methodo* (1728; Concerning the method of interpreting sacred scripture), Jean Alphonse Turretin (or Turretini) sets out a principle in words strikingly like Jowett's: "One must put oneself into the times and into the surroundings in which they [the sacred writers] wrote, and one must see what (concepts) could arise in the souls of those who lived at that time. This rule is of the greatest importance for the understanding of Scripture; and, despite it, theologians and interpreters commonly proceed quite contrariwise." Fundamental to this recovery is the laying aside of "the ideas of all the opinions and systems of our day. . . . An empty head, if I may so express myself, must be brought to Scripture; one's head must be, as it were a *tabula rasa* if it is to comprehend the true and original meaning of Scripture" (in Kümmel 1972, 59). Similarly, Johann Jakob Wettstein in an introductory essay "On the Interpretation of the New Testament" in his edition of the New Testament (1751–52, 2 vols.) advocated an act of mental identification: "Put yourself in the place of those to whom they [the books of the Bible] were first delivered by the apostles. . . . Transfer yourself in thought to that time and that area where they were first read" (in Kümmel 1972, 50). So also another critic, Karl August Gottlieb Keil, in *De historica librorum interpretatione* (1788; On the historical interpretation of the books), writes: "In the case of the sacred (writers) . . . they can be understood in no other way than as human (authors). And also the interpretation of their books will be historical to the extent that in their explication one must ask at any given place what the sacred writers themselves thought and what their readers for whom their books were first destined were intended to think" (in Kümmel 1972, 109). Such a principle was designated the *usus loquendi* (usage according to speech or in speaking): "the meaning affixed to [any word] by those for whom [any biblical writer] *immediately* wrote" (Horne [1818] 1828, 2:287). This proto-historical procedure is not unlike part of the method advocated by St. Ignatius Loyola in the *Exercitia Spiritualia* (1548; Spiritual exercises) in which the first stage of meditation is the composition or imaging of the scene and circumstances where the biblical events took place (see Gardner 1952). It was a method widely known and used in the poetry of Donne and his school (Martz 1954) and became, after a series of epistemological shifts, a part of German romantic hermeneutics in Schleiermacher's lectures ([1838] 1977, 113) and, more generally, part of a reader's sympathetic identification with a descriptive scene in romantic poetry (Abrams 1971). The concept of the reader's placing him- or herself imaginatively in a biblical scene enables the reader to interpret many aspects of the context in a different light, a procedure still widely used in meditation and Bible study. This approach of personalized meditation should be distinguished from a historical reinterpretation of the context, or the *Sitz im Leben* (situation in life—the social and cultural milieu, later important in form-criticism in determining what literary forms were current in a particular community), of a passage of the Bible, later incorporated more formally into the historico-critical method of German Higher Criticism. The notion of one "original" and "true" meaning of the Bible is returned to often by Jowett, as in ¶s 15, 35, 42–43, 51, 73–78, 82, and 88.

Jowett's second principle is that the interpretation of the Bible is to be based on "a knowledge of the text itself" (¶10), mentioned at several important turning points in his argument (¶s 36, 63, and 70). The major discussion is given to it in ¶s 49–56. While the idea was current in Homeric scholarship in the eighteenth century, the idea derives from the Reformation, and especially the Lutheran and Calvinist doctrine, of *sola scriptura*—that the Bible alone is the guide to salvation, rather than the Bible as interpreted by the church or clergy, or through any other mediation. Luther's phrase, that "scripture is its own interpreter" (see Jowett ¶49 and n. 87), summarizes this position, and it, in turn, is related to a strongly Augustinian position, that the sense of the Bible is located in the Bible (see Jowett ¶16 and n. 29). This principle as a method of hermeneutics is not intentionally solipsistic, but is designed to be exclusionary in two respects: it excludes the interpretation of the Bible from an interested position within a sect or credal community; and it excludes the activities of the harmonizers for whom the Bible often functions as a realm of free association governed only by a verbal echo quite independent of any other considerations. The principle of the "knowledge of the text itself," then, is governed by the corollary that Jowett defines as "interpretation of like by like": one Testament is used to interpret material from that Testament, one author is to explain other passages from that author, one kind or genre of writing is used to interpret other passages from that genre of writing—all to ensure consistency in reading and application, uniformity or at least similarity of language, historical context, and philosophical or theological ideas. In hermeneutical theory, Wettstein in 1751–52, for instance, had set out the same principle: "We get to know the meaning of words and sentences in the first instance from other passages by the same author, then from the rest of the sacred writings, as well as from the version of the seventy translators [the LXX], then from the authors who lived about the same time and in the same region, and finally from common usage" (in Kümmel 1972, 50).

Jowett's third interpretive principle in ¶10 is his cardinal rule in ¶45, that the Bible is to be read "like any other book." This principle occurs in some of the same German and Swiss biblical critics quoted above; as a principle of hermeneutics, however, it has a longer genealogy. Spinoza, for example, had argued against those who demanded "beforehand, as a foundation for the study and true interpretation of Scripture, the principle that it is in every passage true and divine. Such a doctrine should be reached only after strict scrutiny and thorough comprehension of the Sacred Books" ([1670] 1951, 8). Instead biblical hermeneutics should be based, in his view, on three principles: the Bible should be interpreted in the way that nature is examined, according to its history, definitions, axioms, and fundamental principles; its contents and doctrines should be sought in the Bible (the Bible should be used to interpret itself); and his "universal rule" should be applied: "to accept nothing as an authoritative Scriptural statement which we do not perceive very clearly when we examine it in the light of its history" ([1670] 1951, 98–101). For this reason Leo Strauss claims Spinoza as one of the ancestors of Jowett's third notion: "In our time scholars generally study the Bible in the manner in which they study any other book and it is generally admitted Spinoza more than any other man laid the foundation for this kind of Biblical study" ([1930] 1965, 35). From Spinoza the principle passed into widespread use, and is cited by Turretin in his formulation of hermeneutical principles: "Let us keep the fact firmly in view that the Scriptures are to be explained in no other way than other books. . . . That is clearly the way in which all books, as well as all discourses, are understood; since God wished to teach us by means of books and discourses, though not in a different way, it is therefore clearly evident thereby that the Holy Scripture is not to be understood otherwise than are other books" (in Kümmel 1972, 58). Wettstein too follows Turretin's principle in the preparation of his edition of the Greek New Testament: "Since we read with the same eyes the sacred books and the laws given by decrees of the princes, as well as all ancient and modern books, so also the same rules are to be applied in the interpretation of the former as we use for an understanding of the latter" (in Kümmel 1972, 50). In *Institutio interpretis Nove Testamenti* (1761; Instruction for the interpreter of the New Testament) Johann August Ernesti made a similar argument: "And since all these things are common to divine and human books, it is evident that the sense of the words in the sacred books cannot be sought or found in any other way, so far as human effort is involved, than that which is customary or necessary in (the study of) human (books)" (in Kümmel 1972, 61). Jowett's position, then, was in close conformity with all of these continental theorists of interpretation, and, indeed, these views were already naturalized (quite inoffensively because of their assertions of plenary inspiration and literalism) in England by the early nineteenth century by T. H. Horne and others.[20] Moses Stuart, who translated Ernesti as *Elements of Interpretation* (1822)—and a copy was in Pusey's library (Barr 1983, 43)—also wrote on the same topic in his article "Are the Same Principles of Interpretation to Be Applied to the Scripture as to Other Books?" in *The Biblical Repository* (Stuart 1832). This approach to the Bible on the same terms as to any other document became widely influential through the *Einleitung in das Neue Testament* (1804–27, 5 vols; Introduction to the New Testament) of Eichhorn (4:67–68; in Kümmel 1972, 87) and through Schleiermacher's lectures ([1838] 1977, 107). In England the same notion is advocated by S. T. Coleridge, derived in part from his reading of Schleiermacher and other German biblical critics, in *Confessions of an Inquiring Spirit* ([1840] 1988, 59). Jowett discusses this notion in ¶s 42, 45, and 49.[21] While Jowett accepts that the Bible is read like any other book to determine its one, true, and original meaning, his assumptions are very different, of course, from apparently similar principles (if not methods) of interpretation posited by Horne and are much closer to those of Turretin, Ernesti, and Schleiermacher. Jowett challenged Horne's assumptions. Such ongoing but partly hidden battles over interpretation flared into open warfare as Jowett was attacked, for instance, about the eight matters of contemporary controversy raised in ¶27 of his essay.

Such principles of interpretation, which apply equally to classical as to biblical literature, had to be carried to one further and final level. Their truth claims have to be attested to not only in the court of reason but also, according to Jowett and other Broad Church theologians, in the "human heart." Jowett appeals to the human heart as a hermeneutical principle of interpretation, and in the second half of his essay it is used repeatedly ("heart" is used 31 times). The discussion is focused particularly in ¶42, although the "light in the human heart," and the "truth" of the human heart, are frequently appealed to as a ground for belief (¶s 4, 22, 25, 79, 80, and 91). His argument that knowledge is based not only on rational thought in the mind but in the psychological affirmation of subjective and even objective knowledge in the human heart appears at first to be a strictly romantic notion, indebted to Wordsworth and Coleridge. One biblical source for such a method, apart from the many references to having the law of love inscribed on the heart, or the Kingdom of God within (Luke 17:21), is the postresurrection appearance of Jesus to the disciples on the road to Emmaus (Luke 24:13–53). There are also philosophical and theological sources for this notion in the nineteenth century. Fundamentally it is derived from the Kantian philosopher Jakob Friedrich Fries, who taught at Jena and Heidelberg and published *Neue oder anthropologische Kritik der Vernunft* (1807; New or anthropological critique of reason). Kant argues that the first task of philosophy is the analysis of the faculty of knowledge, and particularly of the a priori categories whereby the mind organizes the knowledge of sense experience. Fries tries to reconcile the critical philosophy of Kant with the thought of Friedrich Heinrich Jacobi. Jacobi stresses the role of belief (Ger. *Glaube*) in the perception of mediate thoughts through the reason or understanding, as well as the consciousness of immediate truth or "real facts" directly, argued in his *David Hume über den Glauben, oder Idealismus und Realismus* (1797; David Hume on belief or idealism and realism). Fries uses Jacobi to interrogate Kant's notion that the ordering of sense experience is a function of the synthetic nature of the mind, by means of the principles a priori—that is, the principles or categories which are independent from and prior to experience given in the experiencing subject itself and by which the mind structures experience. To Fries the issue of how we know that we have knowledge of the principles a priori demands further investigation; he argues that we only know these principles through inner or psychical experience—not, as in Kant, as transcendental factors of all experience, but as conditioned and necessary elements in our inner experience. Hence, the analysis of this psychological inner experience is the precondition of philosophy, called by Fries "anthropological critique." W. M. L. De Wette had studied with Fries at Heidelberg, incorporating his ideas on the role of belief in interpretation, and the sources of subjective and objective truth in the human heart, in *Über Religion und Theologie* (1815; On religion and theology) and *Das Wesen des christlichen Glaubens* (1846; The nature of Christian belief). For nineteenth-century discussions of this principle see Lichtenberger 1889; and Pfleiderer 1893, 97–102.

The idea of interpreting texts according to the insight of the heart was a widespread notion in nineteenth-century literary aesthetics. Carlyle advised it for readers of *Sartor Resartus* ([1833–34] 1937, 13). By transference and extension interpreting by the heart involved also entering into the "heart" of the text and of the author. For instance, in *Of King's Treasuries* (1864), Ruskin, after a detailed exposition of lines from Milton's *Lycidas*, advised his listeners to enter into not only the "thoughts" of the "great teachers" but also their "hearts," so that "you may share at last their just and mighty Passion" (1903–12, 18). Such views depend also upon romantic theories of poetry and language. In a famous passage of the Preface to *Lyrical Ballads* (1800), Wordsworth argues against "personifications of abstract ideas" in favor of the "language of men" that will allow a sympathetic identification between reader and text on an emotional level (1974, 130). By bringing language "near to the language of men" the hermeneutic possibility in Jowett's reading the Bible like any other book, as a book speaking directly to the heart, becomes possible.

Jowett's general approach in the essay is to define the topic, to analyze its categories, and to take up each with examples for illustration, comparison, and contrast. Rhetorically, he proceeds often by indirection, stating his argument in terms of negation, citing negative evidence, or positions that he will contradict, leaving the reader, oftentimes, to draw the conclusion that he has demonstrated obliquely. Hence, because of his references to many biblical passages as controverted (without stating what the controversies are that attach to them or what the theological or institutional affiliations are of those who espouse them), and his references to both general and particular points of doctrinal controversy, his method is highly referential but also unspecific. Where Williams and Pattison had carefully documented their sources, Jowett contents himself with only a handful of references. On the other hand, he is generally quite specific with respect to his biblical references where he is making an interpretive point (less so when he simply echoes the Bible in a phrase). Jowett conceals his indebtedness to a wide range of scholarship; his allusive method refers to it, but in such a way that a contemporary reader would have had to refer to guides and handbooks to make sense of him. Many of his allusions are to points of biblical interpretation that are firmly attached to doctrinal arguments that were flourishing when he wrote—but that, alas, are much less readily accessible to modern readers. He often uses the passive voice to make reference to a position held by unspecified opponents; or he uses it to make a point without specifying it in the rhetoric of common sense: "It has often been said"; "Everyone who is acquainted would agree. . . ." There is room for various ghosts here, such as unnamed opponents or old doctrinal scores to be settled, rather than individual grievances to be addressed or current controversies to be dissected. Without some kind of gloss, such ghosts would have to flit past the reader unidentified; our annotations here have tried to identify them as clearly as possible, but the task is sometimes frustrating because of Jowett's resistance to precise identification.

Another strategy is to pose a rhetorical question (as in ¶s 26, 35–36, 50, 73, and 95), and then to respond to it by a series of further rhetorical questions, each a response that pushes the question further, rising in a climax to a series of principles for further reflection or action. Jowett also uses classical rhetoric to set out a concept, to pursue its categories of definition according to the conventional strategies of "invention" in classical rhetoric (for instance, in Cicero's various writings on oratory). Invention, the notion of finding or "inventing" arguments for any subject, consisted of arranging an argument, usually according to five categories of common topics: definition, comparison, relationship (showing the relationships of cause and effect, antecedent or consequent relationships, or relationships of contraries or contradictions), circumstance, and, finally, testimony or evidence. For instance, Jowett often presents his evidence by means of enumeration. He gives a list of items as evidence of a particular issue, and then devotes an extended discussion to each item (as, for example, in ¶s 27–28). Another instance involves a central thematic concern of his essay, inspiration. At the beginning of the essay (¶s 1–9) Jowett shows how there are different views of interpretation, the sources from which these differences arise (the authority of the Bible in the church and in the human mind), whether such views of interpretation are general (applying to all literature) or restrictive (to the Bible only), and finally he tests his argument with an example (suppose Plato or Aristotle were interpreted like the Bible).

Such concepts, however, are not merely enumerated and elaborated in order to settle on a final choice. Instead the principles of adjudication by which one exemplar is more viable than another depends upon the relationships among truth claims within and across the disciplines of knowledge. For instance, Jowett continues his discussion of inspiration in ¶17 by asserting that it must conform to the "well-ascertained facts of history or science." Here he refers to geology and astronomy, relating their "conditions" or "severer" standards of scientific proof to those demanded in theology, as he advocates different kinds of "proof" for different categories of knowledge. In ¶19 he addresses the standards of proof in history. Having shown that the creeds, whether ancient and historic, or contemporary, cannot be used anachronistically to read back dogmatic definitions into the Bible or to derive a mode of hermeneutics from the Bible (¶s 22–24), Jowett then turns to a second proposed kind of accommodation that a biblical hermeneutics is wrongly tempted to undertake: to read the conditions of the real world (both social and ecclesiastical), whether at the time of the writing of the biblical documents, or in the present era, as determinative of the "ideal" for human life presented in the Bible.

We have included in our annotation commentary from Jowett's *The Epistles of St. Paul*, as well as from the work of such Broad Church theologians as Stanley. To demonstrate the controversial nature of these positions, we also include other commentaries that are either more traditionally orthodox or that make special arguments. As an example of a standard learned commentary on the New Testament we have made frequent use of Henry Alford's four-volume commentary, *The Greek Testament*, which he had published in 1848 and revised frequently, issuing his fifth edition in 1863. Alford's scholarship, exactly overlapping with the work of Jowett and Stanley, provides a scholarly but conservative balance to Jowett's comments, and often gives a contemporary gloss on the Greek text that supplements Jowett's comments.[22] Other references to other kinds of commentaries, such as those of Horne and Davidson, are also included in the annotation. Such comments give a kind of "interpretation" of the context of the production and reception of Jowett's text, making it possible to see some of the reasons why his contemporaries reacted so strongly to his application of modern criticism to the Bible.

In the religious press Jowett was widely attacked for his views of inspiration and interpretation: from the early notice in the *Guardian,* for instance, it was alleged that he held the Bible to be "of all books the most deceitful" (23 May 1860, 474), that he himself was "untrustworthy," and that his was "the most dangerous essay in the series" in which he denied both the divine authorship of the books of the Bible and their plenary inspiration and inerrancy (*Christian Remembrancer*, Oct. 1860, 360, 372–73). As well, Jowett was aligned with three popular objects of attack, German rationalist theologians, English radical political philosophers, particularly those associated with J. S. Mill and the *Westminster Review,* and a group affiliated with them, the Comtean positivists, especially those later connected with Frederic Harrison. Henry Woodgate, for instance, in his pamphlet of 1861, claims that "Mr. Jowett's views of practical Christianity do not differ materially . . . from those of Mr. Mill" (1861, 152). To Wilberforce, Jowett is guilty of "mistiness" in his argument and of "an absolute lack of all perception of what sin is, and so of what atonement is" (1861, 273), long-standing subjects of accusation against him. On the other hand, it is not surprising that Jowett should be praised, along with Temple, in Stanley's review of his old friends in the *Edinburgh Review.* To Stanley, Jowett's essay is "a valuable supplement" to his work on St. Paul, and his "indirect" style in the last pages reaches a "lofty tone" (1861a, 478).

Jowett's principles of interpretation were attacked generally by such exegetes as Alford in his commentary on the New Testament, but more extendedly and directly by C. J. Ellicott in his essay on "Scripture and its Interpretation" in *Aids to Faith* (1861): "What . . . can really be more illusory than to lay down the rule that we are 'to interpret the Scripture like any other book,' when, in the merest rough and outside view, the Scripture presents such striking differences from any book that the world has ever seen" (William Thomson 1861, 391). Ellicott set down four hermeneutical canons to oppose those of Jowett: "*Ascertain as clearly as it may be possible the literal and grammatical meaning of the words*" (427); "*Illustrate, wherever possible, by reference to history, topography, and antiquities*" (430); "*Develop and enunciate the meaning under the limitations assigned by the context*, or, in other words, *Interpret contextually*" (432); and, "*In every passage elicit the full significance of all details*" (435). All four of these may be summarized as "Interpret grammatically, historically, contextually, minutely" (439). Finally he comes to his overriding principle, "the true and vital principle of all really Scriptural exegesis,—*interpret according to the analogy of Faith*" (443). Ellicott qualifies Jowett's principle that the

Bible should interpret itself, finding it inadequate because it is too solipsistic. Hence, where there are exegetical problems, and after all of the other methods have been tried, doctrinal allusions, hints, and references, must, according to him, invoke the analogy of faith to solve them, a view that Jowett had rejected as eisegetical, importing a doctrinal or credal position (which is precisely what Ellicott demands) back into the text anachronistically, but defended on the basis of "analogy" (1861, 443–47). In *Replies to "Essays and Reviews"* Christopher Wordsworth also attacked Jowett's view: "He *has* treated the Bible like a common book. He tells us that it is of no importance to him whether the Bible is inspired or no" (1862, 459).

After their publication in *Essays and Reviews* Jowett's three principles are often incorporated into current methodologies for interpreting the Bible, or for meditation. The rapid process by which Jowett's phrase "like any other book" became a critical commonplace is indicated by its incorporation without attribution in the Bampton lectures of 1893, *Inspiration* by William Sanday, one of Jowett's students and Lady Margaret Professor of Divinity at Oxford: "We must recognise the fact that a change has come over the current way of thinking on this subject of the authority of the Bible. The maxim that the Bible must be studied 'like any other book' has been applied. For good or for evil, the investigations to which it has given rise are in full swing, and it would be hopeless to attempt to stop them, even if it were right to do so. . . . When once it was decided that the Bible was to be read like any other book, it lay near at hand to assume that it must be like any other book. . . . Let us by all means study it if we will like any other book, but do not let us beg the question that it must be wholly like any other book, that there is nothing in it distinctive and unique" ([1893] 1896, 1–2). On the other hand, Jowett was still being attacked in the introduction to C. W. Dugmore's *The Interpretation of the Bible* (1944) for his rationalist liberalism in reading the Bible like any other book. More recently, J. Philip Hyatt has written: "There is a basic principle of the modern approach to the Bible . . . *we must read and study the Bible as we would any other book*. . . . We can seek to place ourselves in the position of the first hearers or readers of various parts of the Bible, and determine what the words meant to them. This is the best way to begin to understand what the words can say to us in the twentieth century" (1964, 18, 27). The same phrase is still cited within quotation marks but without attribution in a recent dictionary of biblical interpretation (Coggins and Houlden 1990, 285; s.v. "Historical-Critical Method").[23]

For all of the controversy Jowett aroused in his own day, he is still appealed to as an authority. For instance, in a book that attempts to be "a guide to the major hermeneutical approaches and perspectives on interpreting the Bible," David Steinmetz begins by citing Jowett's "justly famous essay," mentioning several of its principles, including the notion of reaching "one meaning—the meaning which it had in the mind of the Prophet or Evangelist who first uttered or wrote, to the hearers or readers who first received it." Steinmetz comments that "the quarrel between modern biblical scholarship and Benjamin Jowett is less a quarrel over his hermeneutical theory that it is a disagreement with him over the application of that theory in his exegetical practice. Biblical scholarship still hopes to recover the original intention of the author of a biblical text, and still regards the precritical exegetical tradition as an obstacle to the proper understanding of the true meaning of that text" (1986, iii and 65–66). While Steinmetz distances himself from this view, there are others who agree that Jowett's view approaches either modern orthodoxy or modern rationalism. William Abraham introduces the topic of his book on biblical inspiration with Jowett: "No summary of the matter can improve on that provided by the celebrated Benjamin Jowett in 1861 [*sic*; the first three sentences of Jowett ¶15 are quoted]. . . . Jowett not only reports succinctly the confusion that existed in his day, he also epitomizes the root cause of that confusion. Acquainted with the rise of critical scholarship, especially German scholarship, Jowett argued that the Bible should be studied like any other book. Today few would argue with this, for it enshrines insights that are invaluable if the riches of scripture are to be identified and appropriated" (1981, 14).

5 The Broad Church Compromise

ESSAYS AND REVIEWS controverted accepted orthodoxies concerning history and biblical hermeneutics in a profound way. The even tentative introduction of German higher criticism, partly through the work of Baron Bunsen in Williams's essay, the advocacy of a very different kind of hermeneutics by Jowett, the questioning of the predictive function of prophecy and the historicity of miracles by Williams and Powell, the rejection of linear history in favor of cycles by Temple and Jowett, the attack on the literal meaning of Genesis by Goodwin, and the reformulation of the relations between church and state in contravention of traditional biblical interpretation and the formulations of the Elizabethan settlement by Wilson—each of these, and all of them overwhelmingly when taken together, were an affront to the Establishment doctrines of church and state alike. Their challenges to orthodoxy, however, are limited in important ways: in effect the Essayists neutralize their power by strategies of accommodation and compromise.

Although the Essayists aroused strong reactions from numerous quarters, they still remained within the pale of acceptability—barely. In a letter to Stanley inviting him to join the project, two years before the volume's publication, Jowett anticipates the boundaries of Anglican hegemony within which the controversy over *Essays and Reviews* would be played out: "Wilson wishes me to write to you respecting a volume of Theological Essays which he has already mentioned. . . . The object is to say what we think freely within the limits of the C[hurch] of England. A notice will be prefixed that no one is responsible for any notions but his own. It is however an essential part of the plan that names shall be given, partly for the additional weight which the articles will have if the authors are known & also from the feeling that on such subjects as Theology it is better not to write anonymously. We do not wish to do anything rash or irritating to the Public or the University, but we are determined not to submit to this abominable system of terrorism which prevents the statement of the plainest facts and makes true theology or theological education impossible" (Letter 6). This notion of freedom is carefully circumscribed as being "within limits" defined by the established church. The freedom is aligned with a rejection of what Jowett calls the "terrorism" of orthodoxy, which has stultified critical reading; however, the weight of this "abominable system" is acknowledged as caution is urged to avoid "anything rash or irritating." Hence, Jowett's comments to Stanley map out succinctly the extensions and limitations of the Broad Church position, and place *Essays and Reviews* within the context of Victorian cultural transformation.

By balancing the two dominant traditions of English theology, rationalism and the role of feeling, *Essays and Reviews* managed to strike out a new line in historiographical analysis and simultaneously managed to alienate almost everyone. In part the alienation resulted not from the arguments advanced but from the perceived sources of the arguments, a combination of English empiricism, French rationalism, German philosophy and theology, rationalist biblical analysis (that is, higher criticism), and an attenuated English romanticism combined with continental piety. Such views were called "neology," the application of new terms and rationalistic concepts to theological discourse, since the 1830s a term of opprobrium. In the first major review in the quarterlies Harrison entitles his article "Neo-Christianity," signaling a new configuration of theology and institutional position. He discusses the ecclesiastical establishment as "unconscious dignities and powers vaguely condemning pantheism and neology" (1860, 177), referring in the last phrase to both the emotional and rational aspects of Broad Church theology. This line is picked up by Samuel Wilberforce in his review, attacking the Essayists' "dreamy vagueness of pantheistic pietism, which is but the shallow water leading on to a profounder and darker atheism" (1861, 373). The juggling of these two factors, the emotional, located in the truth of the human heart, and the rational, located in the critical faculties of the mind analyzing history and language, comprise what we term the Broad Church compromise.

While the Essayists placed considerable stress on the new historiography from Niebuhr and Thomas Arnold, on the congruence of religion and science as two parallel modes of revelation, and on philological and textual studies for their hermeneutics, they were more or less opposed to the empiricist claims of the evidentialists with their insistence on the pre-eminence of fact. Instead, like a number of their contemporaries, they espoused the principles of the inductive method. William Whewell had written extensively on it in relation to science and philosophy, and in literary and biblical criticism too the method was significant. The inductive method, the gathering of specific data from which a general hypothesis can be drawn, and the adjustment of the general hypothesis according to the discovery of new evidence, may be parallelled to the progressive revelation advocated in Broad Church theology. Just as empirical science presupposes a discoverable reality, free from human interpretation, so too Broad Church theology presupposes a deity outside human time and space. In both science and theology the totality of this discoverable reality can never be known from a human perspective. But in both science and theology the gradual gathering of evidence leads to progressive shifts in the state of knowledge. The Essayists' discussion of history and archaeology—that is, the relation of present knowledge to the past—impacts on the present not by encompassing the whole of time in a presupposed totality of knowledge but rather by relating the events of the past to a progressive apprehension of the role of providence in that totality.

The Essayists generally argue in two dominant modes, drawing relations of difference and of identity. When arguing difference, they cite contradictions and inconsistencies in the biblical record and point out difficulties in translating components of one language to another. They resist reconciling these differences. In doing so they display comprehensive knowledge of the German higher criticism, controversies concerning language, recent historical and archaeological discoveries, the state of textual criticism, and other contemporary fields such as geology and education. They also argue by drawing identities, or collapsing these differences onto an originary point. In Jowett and Temple, for instance, this turn is directed toward an interior space, the truth of the human heart, reflected in the Bible, which, in the developmental theology of progressive revelation, is spun out over time, so that the disagreements pointed out, for example, in contemporary biblical criticism, historical discoveries, and philology, are swept away as ultimately only of secondary, little, or no importance. Pattison rarely makes this gesture to locate truth claims in the inward life, although he acknowledges it in some of the theological controversies with which he deals, such as the Cambridge Platonists' notion of the inner light. Wilson locates this identity in a notion of nationalism in a much more process-oriented argument: the agents of the national identity, the clerisy, are continually shaping and working toward the notion of a national church; simultaneously, he invokes the concept of a universal parent, discussing identity in universalizing language similar to the other Essayists' gestures toward the truth of the human heart.

On the theological level, the Broad Church compromise acknowledges difference but places it under careful controls. Questions of doubt are dealt with extensively in the Essayists' elaborated attacks on literalist readings of the Bible; ultimately, however, these discrepancies are swept away and a faith position is asserted, rendering the bulk of the argumentation insignificant with respect to the Essayists' final faith position. Politically, the Broad Church compromise acknowledges difference with toleration, but within a rigid notion of race and class. Disraeli's two nations are acknowledged and the poor and working classes are to be given charity, as well as education, especially religious and moral instruction. When the differences become extreme, however, and the poor nation begins to demand as rights what were considered privileges, the tendency in the Broad Church compromise is to repress. Wilson, for instance, extends sympathy to the working classes and articulates means for their advancement under carefully controlled conditions; however, his comments on the French Revolution and the overturning of social forms, those institutions and customs which maintain class differences within manageable limits, indicate the political limits of a Broad Church position generally, and, more specifically, how this balance between identity and difference works as a justification of liberal politics. In terms of race and the politics of empire, several Essayists posit relations of identity with peoples in other parts of the world: Wilson dismisses the notion that non-Christians are damned a priori; Temple calls for the education of non-Europeans through missionary work; Jowett refers to the holy books of Buddhism as comparable to those of Christianity; and Powell refers to the ingenuity of the Australian aboriginal for inventing the boomerang. The universalist grid that other ethnic groups are placed upon, however, positions them as primitive and barbarous as opposed to Europeans as advanced and progressive. This racialist grid corresponds with that of a progressive historical revelation. Historical revelation presupposes a development in knowledge wherein previous stages of knowledge are accommodated to the more advanced by being filtered through a faith position. Eurocentric Christian missionary work and, comparatively, the education of the working classes at home, presuppose an advanced stage within which the more primitive groups must be accommodated.

Increasingly after *Essays and Reviews* the Broad Church compromise relied not on religious faith to achieve this accommodation but rather on education and culture. Hence, whereas Frank M. Turner (1993) describes the process of Victorian cultural transformation from 1830 to 1870 as one that moves from an Anglican hegemony to a "secularized Anglicanism" dominated by Arnoldian notions of culture, we locate *Essays and Reviews* in a moment when this transition was arrested, when the Broad Church compromise held diverse forces together for a decade.

Notes to Reading "An Epoch in the History of Opinion"

1. According to Thomas Hartwell Horne's much-reprinted *Introduction to the Critical Study of the Holy Scriptures*, the conventional modes of interpretation of the Bible include the following:

> 1. The LITERAL SENSE of any place of Scripture is that which the words signify, or require, in their natural and proper acceptation, without any trope, metaphor, or figure, and abstracted from any mystic meaning. . . . The literal sense has also been termed the *grammatical* sense. . . . Further, the literal sense has been called the HISTORICAL SENSE, as conveying the meaning of the words and phrases used by a writer at a certain time. . . . Interpreters now speak of the true sense of a passage, by calling it the GRAMMATICO-HISTORICAL SENSE: and exegesis, founded on the nature of language, is called grammatico-historical. The object in using this compound name is, to show that both grammatical and historical considerations are employed in making out the sense of a word or passage.
>
> 2. Where, besides the direct or immediate significance of a passage, whether literally or figuratively expressed, there is attached to it a more remote or recondite meaning, this is termed the MEDIATE, SPIRITUAL, or MYSTICAL SENSE: and this sense is founded, not on a transfer of words from one signification to another, but on the entire application of the matter itself to a different subject. . . .
>
> > (1.) The ALLEGORICAL SENSE is, when the Holy Scriptures, besides the literal sense, signify any thing belonging to faith or *spiritual doctrine*. . . .
> >
> > (2.) The TYPICAL SENSE is, when under external objects or prophetical visions, secret things, whether present or future, are represented; especially when certain transactions in the Old Testament presignify or adumbrate those related in the New Testament.
> >
> > (3.) The PARABOLICAL SENSE is, when besides the plain and obvious meaning of the thing related, an occult or spiritual sense is intended. As this chiefly occurs in passages of a moral tendency, the parabolic has by some writers been termed the *moral* or tropological sense. . . .
>
> 3. The MORAL SENSE or interpretation, advocated by the late Professor Kant, of Berlin . . . consists in setting aside the laws of grammatical and historical interpretation, and attributing a moral meaning to those passages of Scripture. . . . According to this hypothesis, nothing more is necessary, than that it be *possible* to attach a moral meaning to the passage:—it is of little moment, how forced or unnatural it may be ([1818] 1828, 2:281–86).

2. The pages measure 5⅝ x 8¾ inches, and the type 3⅝ x 6⅝. It was bound in blue pressed cloth-covered boards, embossed with frame on the front and back covers, enclosing a vine border, with a Greek cross in the corners, and with a wavy grain overall. The spine reads "ESSAYS | AND | REVIEWS." and at the base of the spine: "1860."

The collation of signatures is: 8^0: π^4 B–Z^8 2A–$2E^8$ $2F^4$; 224 leaves (the omitted letters for the gatherings are conventional: J, U, W; V is printed as U; π = prelims with no signature, as usual; superscript numbers indicate the number of leaves in a gathering: hence, ^{8} = 8 leaves or 16 pages: 1 leaf of text and 3 leaves [6 pages] of publisher's advertisements to complete the gathering FF, printed with the prelims).

The collation consists of the following: [i half-title:] ESSAYS AND REVIEWS. [ii blank] [iii title page:] ESSAYS AND REVIEWS. | [ornament: double circle, within the outer the motto, PER ASPERA AD ARDUA TENDO, and within the inner a shield with the intertwined letters, JWP; signed monogram outside the double circle] | LONDON: | JOHN W. PARKER AND SON, WEST STRAND | 1860. | [*The Authors reserve the right of Translation.*] [iv printer's information:] LONDON: | SAVILL AND EDWARDS, PRINTERS, CHANDOS STREET, | COVENT GARDEN [v] TO THE READER. | [rule] | [printed text] [vi blank] [vii] CONTENTS. | [rule] | [text] [viii blank] [pages of text, numbered 1–433] [434, unnumbered:] NOTE ON BUNSEN'S BIBLICAL RESEARCHES. [6 pages of publisher's advertisements].

The printer's device on the title page consists of a double circle, enclosing the Latin proverb: PER ASPERA AD ARDUA TENDO, framing an inner circle with a floriated background. Placed on this circle is a plain heraldic shield, bearing the entwined monogram JWP, the initials of the printer and publisher. The artist's monogram signature is printed outside the double circle. From the fourth edition on, when Longman took over Parker's firm, the device is replaced by a printer's ornamental arabesque.

The Latin motto, "Through the rough places I

strive toward the heights," a variant of the proverb, *per aspera ad astra*, (through hardship to the stars), echoes Seneca's line from *Hercules Furens*: "*Non est ad astra mollis e terris via*" ("There is no easy way to the stars from earth," l. 437; trans. Frank J. Miller, *Loeb* 1:40–41). John W. Parker used variants of this monogram from about 1855. It was well known to the Victorian reading public, from its use, for instance, on the title page of *Fraser's Magazine* (see Landauer 1926, 71). The printer's device is signed with the initials FP in an artist's monogram outside the ornament to the lower right. The artist is probably Frederick Parker, the son of the publisher and a wood-engraver (see Redgrave 1878, 320 and Engen 1985, 200).

3. Altholz's claim that the first nine editions "were identical in text and pagination" is based on the belief that "the same plates were used through the ninth edition" (1982, 312); however, a primary indicator of recomposition, shifted locations for the signature letters, is evident in all editions from the second to the seventh. The signature letters in the second edition are located not in the center of the page (as in the first edition) but close to the right-hand margin. Moreover, none of the tests proposed by Shillingsburg for stereotype plates in nineteenth-century books proved positive (1975, 2–3). Finally, the stereotype catalogues in the Longman archive indicate that no stereotype plates were made for *Essays and Reviews*, nor are there charges for stereotyping in any of their ledgers; instead, the costs for new composition or for lifting the already-set formes are set out in detail (see Publishers' Records).

4. Ellis states that it was "in the shops by November" (1980, 116), in an edition of 1,000; Altholz says that 750 copies were published in January 1861 (1981, 312; following Ellen Williams 1874, 2:30). On the basis of Wilson's recapitulation to Pattison (Letter 103) of the sales for the first three months of 1861, in which he makes no mention of the third edition, as well as the 1860 date on the title page, it must have been published in late 1860. That the run was indeed 750 copies is proved from Wilson's letter of 23 November 1861 to Pattison (Letter 143).

5. Reading MS. Longman 43, fols. 1–1ᵛ. The passages in the contract that are handwritten in ink are italicized; printed passages that are scored out in ink are so marked.

6. The collation for the tenth edition is as follows: 8^{0}: π^{4} B–Z^{8} 2A–2L^{8}; 265 leaves. The size of each page is 4¼ x 6¾ inches, and the size of type 3⅓ x 5½ inches.

7. The fact that the tenth edition was printed in three issues led Ellen Williams to record them as separate editions, the tenth, eleventh, and twelfth, as Altholz has rightly noticed (1982, 312; Ellen Williams 1874, 2:61). Ellen Williams's slip resulted in Ellis's misnumbering of the editions, so that he collapses some of the characteristics of the twelfth and thirteenth editions, such as the marking of the cited passages, onto what in fact are the second and third issues of tenth edition (Ellis 1980, 183). By continuing Ellen Williams's numbering, he creates two ghosts, the fourteenth and fifteenth editions (200).

8. Altholz claims that the eleventh edition was 1,500 copies and included the markings of the passages cited in the Court of Arches and in the appeal to the Judicial Committee (1982, 312; 1994, 100). The Publisher's Records show that the run was 500. The cited passages were not so marked until the twelfth edition.

9. The circumstances surrounding the thirteenth edition have been a source of scholarly confusion. For instance, Altholz says that in 1869 "Longmans re-issued the book in what should have been the thirteenth edition but was erroneously re-numbered the twelfth, which thus bears two dates . . . . Evidently the plates of the actual twelfth edition were used. The only change is the new date and the description of Temple in the Table of Contents as Bishop Elect of Exeter" (1982, 312; see also Altholz 1994, 136). We have been unable to corroborate that the table-of-contents page for the thirteenth edition was modified, since the only located copy, in the Bodleian Library, prints the same wording for Temple as in the twelfth and earlier editions. Furthermore, the letters of November 1869 between Wilson and Longman indicate that the labeling of the thirteenth edition as the twelfth was not erroneous but intentional in order to capitalize on the controversy around Temple's appointment as bishop of Exeter while not seeming either to exploit it or to put him in a vulnerable position. The Longman ledgers also indicate that no stereoplates existed, as the publisher paid to have the volume reset. Another source for confusion is Ellis's claim that the thirteenth edition is really the fifteenth, an accounting he arrives at by counting the second and third issues of the tenth edition as separate editions (1980, 200).

10. A page of quotations from English reviews of *Essays and Reviews* is printed opposite the title page in the first American edition. It includes a citation from Harrison's review in the *Westminster* of October 1860 and also one from the *Christian Examiner* for November, said to be printed "from advance sheets." The Introduction is dated 14 August 1860.

11. Several of these proposed essays were eventually published: W. H. Fremantle published "Convocation, Parliament, and the Prayer-book," an examination of the disestablishment of the Church of England, in the *Edinburgh Review* in 1874 (140:427–71). Lewis Campbell published "On the Revision of the English New Testament" in the *Contemporary Review* in 1876 (27 [May]: 848–61; 28 [June]: 93–109; 28 [Aug.]: 462–94). Samuel Davidson published an extended version of his proposed topic in *On a Fresh Revision of the English Old Testament*

(1873). Deutsch published an essay on the Talmud in the *Quarterly Review* in 1867 (123 [Oct.]: 417–64). Jowett had worked on a number of manuscripts, some of which may have been drafts for one or other of the essays he was proposing for himself. He left some thirty pages of a manuscript on "The religions of the world," only fragments of which have been published, as well as other materials on the future of religion (Abbott and Campbell 1897, 2:13, 15; Jowett 1902b, 156–58; 170–72; 180–81).

12. Other Bampton Lectures were delivered on the subject of the Christian "evidences": Edward Nares, *A View of the Evidences of Christianity at the Close of the Pretended Age of Reason* (1805); Henry Hart Milman, *The Character and Conduct of the Apostles Considered as an Evidence of Christianity* (1827); Thomas William Lancaster, *The Popular Evidence of Christianity, Stated and Examined* (1831); Frederick Nolan, *The Analogy of Revelation and Science Established* (1833); and R. Michell, *The Nature and Comparative Value of the Christian Evidences Considered Generally* (1849).

13. For instance, J. S. Mill's *A System of Logic* (1843) examines Hume's doctrine of miracles (bk. 3, chap. 25), showing that Hume's rejection is not a full proof because that would require a complete induction.

14. Butler's and Paley's works were required reading for examination for all undergraduates at Oxford and Cambridge in 1860. Butler's *Sermons* and the *Analogy of Religion* were among the set books at Cambridge from 1802; at Oxford, Butler was required for finals and was often used in comparison with Aristotle's *Nichomachean Ethics*. R. D. Hampden lectured on Butler in the 1830s. Paley's *Moral and Political Philosophy* (1785) was used for examinations at Cambridge from 1787, becoming a required text from 1802 to 1857. The *Evidences* was prescribed at Cambridge in 1822, required for the "Previous Examinations" for all candidates for a first degree. It continued in the syllabus until 1920 (see Winstanley 1947, 144–45; and Clarke 1974, 127–29). Both Butler and Paley continued to be required reading for all undergraduates at Oxford until 1864, when Pattison was instrumental in having Butler removed from the general Examination Statute (Farrar 1856, 26–28; Montagu Burrows 1860, 12–15, 128; W. R. Ward 1965, 214; Ellis 1980, 272–75). In 1848 Pattison and Jowett had proposed substituting Butler's *Analogy* with Adam Smith and David Ricardo. In Moderations and in final School examinations in Divinity at Oxford (the examinations at the end of the first year of study and at the end of the three-years' course of study), Butler continues to be required reading for examination purposes.

15. The Avertissement in *Le Christianisme* (1858, vi) states the purpose of the series of lectures in terms not unlike the preface "To the Reader" affixed to the beginning of *Essays and Reviews*: "*Ces séances, comme celles de l'année dernière, ont été organisées par l'*UNION CHRÉTIENNE DE JEUNES GENS *de Genève. Les orateurs, ayant été invités à parler avec une entière indépendance et une pleine liberté, ne sont engagés à aucune solidarité les uns vis-à-vis des autres. Chacun d'eux est donc seul responsable des opinions et des sentiments exprimés dans ses discours.*" (These lectures, like those of last year, have been organized by the Christian Union of Young People of Geneva. The speakers, having been invited to talk with a complete independence and a full liberty, are not engaged in any solidarity of purpose of one with the other. Each of them is therefore alone responsible for the opinions and sentiments expressed in these discourses).

16. For an assessment of the history of the higher-critical source theories for Genesis, an account of the weaknesses of the view, and some discussion of the contribution of Form Criticism, see the article on Genesis by R. K. Harrison in Bromiley 1982, 2:431–43.

17. He outlined his views in five "common notes" (*notitiae communes*) of all religions in *De Veritate*: (1) "there is a Supreme God" whose "attributes" (blessed, the ultimate goal, the final cause, providential, eternal, good, just, and wise) are known through innate ideas and are "manifest daily in his works"; (2) "this Sovereign Deity ought to be worshipped"; (3) worship consists in "the connection of Virtue with Piety," an obligation to live a life of virtue; (4) it is a duty to repent of sin: "our crimes may be washed away by true penitence, and . . . we can be restored to new union with God"; and (5) upon such conduct will depend "Reward or Punishment after this life" ([1624] 1937, 291–307).

18. The view of Jowett and his contemporaries, then, is different from the so-called "new hermeneutics" and "philosophical hermeneutics" that developed in the 1960s, in the work of Martin Heidegger, Hans-Georg Gadamer, and Jürgen Habermas (see Mueller-Vollmer 1987 and Weinsheimer 1991). The application of some of these methods to biblical study has resulted in a new interest in the theory of interpretation in relation to exegesis (see McKim 1986), particularly in using phenomenological modes of literary criticism that concentrate on the process of "hearing" or "reading" a text—stressing the "essential elements in the reader's response" as a means of becoming "open to the intentionality of what is heard." The "language-event" is the "reality" that creates the experience for the reader (William A. Beardslee in Epp and MacRea 1989, 177).

19. Hinchliff goes to some lengths to demonstrate Jowett's awareness of the German philosophical tradition in his ownership of 23 volumes of Schleiermacher in Lücke's edition, 6 of Hegel, 10 of the Kant edition of 1838, some Schelling, and 8 volumes of Fichte, as well as the 7 volumes of the theological and philosophical writings of Karl Daub (1987, 79). He was instrumental in helping to make

Hegel known in England (Geoffrey Faber 1957, 178 ff.).

20. It is highly likely that Jowett knew the works on hermeneutics by Turretin, and Ernesti. He refers to the latter in his correspondence and borrowed his New Testament from the Balliol library (Hinchliff 1987, 78). The others were available in Oxford and were standard authorities cited in hermeneutical methodology. To Jowett they were also available in extensive citation in the widely available textbook of T. H. Horne ([1818] 1828, 2:281–86). Furthermore, Jowett and H. B. Wilson were friends of Samuel Davidson, the reviser of the tenth edition of Horne's *Introduction* (1856). Jowett refers to Davidson in his essay (¶12 and note). Horne himself comments on reading the Bible "like any other book": "As the same method and the same principles of interpretation are common both to the sacred volume and to the productions of uninspired man, consequently the signification of words in the Holy Scriptures must be sought precisely in the same way in which the meanings of words in other works usually is or ought to be sought. . . . We must endeavour to find out that *one true sense* precisely in the same manner as we would investigate the sense of Homer or any other antient writer" ([1818] 1828, 2:286).

21. On this topic see the two articles by James Barr (1982 and 1983), who argues that "Jowett's kind of biblical research rested only slightly upon the foundations of historical research, and much more upon literary, dramatic and philosophical foundations" (1983, 3; see also 3–5; 7–13). Barr reads Jowett's principles not as "an essentially *historical* approach to the Bible" but "literary, dramatic and philosophical . . . as one reads Plato or Scott or as one watches a play of Shakespeare" (1982, 433–34). According to Barr, Jowett tried to return to the "original" meaning not in a historical sense but to determine "the sense of the text itself" by ridding the Bible of accumulated interpretations, often pious and devotional, determined by later doctrinal, apologetic, or institutional positions, where word-meanings are colored by later definitions and controversies. Hence, Jowett's methods and principles are, according to Barr, comparable to those of the schools of "biblical theology" and "canonical criticism" that developed in Europe after World War Two and that involved reading "the Bible as literature . . . in the complete biblical books as they stand" rather than in "their previous sources and original forms" (1983, 26–27).

22. Commenting on the deleterious impact of Jowett's view of interpretation and its application in *The Epistles of St. Paul*, Alford in the fifth edition of his commentary on the Greek New Testament writes: "I must enter my protest against the views of Professor Jowett on points which lie at the very root of the Christian life: views as unwarranted by any data furnished in the Scriptures of which he treats, as his reckless and crude statement of them is pregnant with mischief to minds unaccustomed to biblical research. Among the various phaenomena of our awakened state of apprehension of the characteristics and the difficulties of the New Testament, there is none more suggestive of saddened thought and dark foreboding, than the appearance of such a book as Professor Jowett's." He goes on to apply the book to a general fear: "Our most serious fears for the Christian future of England, point, it seems to me, just in this direction: to persons who allow fine aesthetical and psychological appreciation, and the results of minute examination of spiritual feeling and mental progress in the Epistles, to keep out of view that other line of testimony to the fixity and consistency of great doctrines, which is equally discoverable in them." Explaining the rational for a part of his commentary, he claims: "I have endeavoured below, in speaking of the matter and style of our Epistle [to the Thessalonians] to meet some of Professor Jowett's assertions and inferences of this kind" ([1849] 1863, 3:43]).

23. The degree to which Jowett is accommodated to accepted orthodoxy, even evangelical orthodoxy concerning inspiration, can be determined by noting how often his words are used without attribution as, for instance, in D. P. Fuller's article on "Interpretation" in the *International Standard Bible Encyclopedia* (1982): "Thus one thesis of this article is that even though the Bible is the verbally inspired Word of God, it is nevertheless to be interpreted like any other book, i.e. by recourse to the literary-historical method" (2:864).

Part Two

Essays and Reviews

ESSAYS AND REVIEWS.

LONDON:

JOHN W. PARKER AND SON, WEST STRAND

1860.

[*The Authors reserve the right of Translation.*]

Figure 11. Title page of *Essays and Reviews,* first ed., 1860. Courtesy of the Thomas Fisher Rare Books Library, University of Toronto.

PREFACE TO THE TWELFTH EDITION

THE opportunity is taken of a new edition of *Essays and Reviews* being required, to indicate those portions of the Volume against which certain Charges were brought in the Ecclesiastical Court, as being contrary to, or inconsistent with, the doctrines of the Church of England. The whole of those Charges, as is well known, failed to be sustained. Those brought against the passages included within single commas were withdrawn or rejected in the Court of Arches. The Charges against the passages within double commas, admitted in the Court of Arches, were in like manner either withdrawn during the hearing before the Judicial Committee of the Privy Council, or rejected in their Lordships' final Judgment.

February, 1865.

TO THE READER

[Single quotation marks (see Preface to the Twelfth Edition, p. 133) were used to indicate passages charged for heresy and withdrawn or rejected in the Arches trial, and double quotation marks for passages sustained and carried forward to the Judicial Committee of the Privy Council where they were either withdrawn or rejected. The present edition uses single underlining for the material in single quotations, and double underlinings for the material before the Judicial Committee. See also Editorial Procedures p. xv and Textual Notes. Similar marked passages are also found in the following essays by Williams and by Wilson.]

It will readily be understood that the Authors of the ensuing Essays are responsible for their respective articles only. They have written in entire independence of each other, and without concert or comparison.

The Volume, it is hoped, will be received as an attempt to illustrate the advantage derivable to the cause of religious and moral truth, from a free handling, in a becoming spirit, of subjects peculiarly liable to suffer by the repetition of conventional language, and from traditional methods of treatment.

[*March*, 1860.]

CONTENTS

1 *Frederick Temple*

The Education of the World

IN A WORLD OF MERE PHENOMENA, where all events are bound to one another by a rigid law of cause and effect, it is possible to imagine the course of a long period bringing all things at the end of it into exactly the same relations as they occupied at the beginning.[1] We should, then, obviously have a succession of cycles rigidly similar to one another, both in events and in the sequence of them. The universe would eternally repeat the same changes in a fixed order of recurrence, though each cycle might be many millions of years in length. Moreover, the precise similarity of these cycles would render the very existence of each one of them entirely unnecessary. We can suppose, without any logical inconsequence, any one of them struck out, and the two which had been destined to precede and follow it brought into immediate contiguity.

This supposition transforms the universe into a dead machine. The lives and the souls of men become so indifferent, that the annihilation of a whole human race, or of many such races, is absolutely nothing. Every event passes away as it happens, filling its place in the sequence, but purposeless for the future. The order of all things becomes, not merely an iron rule, from which nothing can ever swerve, but an iron rule which guides to nothing and ends in nothing.

Such a supposition is possible to the logical understanding: it is not possible to the spirit. The human heart refuses to believe in a universe without a purpose. To the spirit, all things that exist must have a purpose, and nothing can pass away till that purpose be fulfilled. The lapse of time is no exception to this demand. Each moment of time, as it passes, is taken up in the shape of permanent results into the time that follows, and only perishes by being converted into something more substantial than itself. A series of recurring cycles, however conceivable to the logical understanding, is inconceivable to the spirit; for every later cycle must be made different from every earlier by the mere fact of coming after it and embodying its results. The material world may possibly be subject to such a rule, and may, in successive epochs, be the cradle of successive races of spiritual beings. But the world of spirits cannot be a mere machine.[2]

In accordance with this difference between the material and the spiritual worlds, we ought to be prepared to find progress in the latter, however much fixity there may be in the former. The earth may still be describing precisely the same orbit as that which was assigned to her at the creation. The seasons may be precisely the same. The planets, the moon, and the stars, may be unchanged both in appearance and in reality. But man is a spiritual as well as a material creature, must be subject to the laws of the spiritual as well as to those of the material world, and cannot stand still because things around him do. Now, that the individual man is capable of perpetual, or almost perpetual, development from the day of his birth to that of his death, is obvious of course. But we may well expect to find something more than this in a spiritual creature who does not stand alone, but forms a part of a whole world of creatures like himself. Man cannot be considered as an individual. He is, in reality, only man by virtue of his being a member of the human race. Any other animal that we know would probably not be very different in its nature if brought up from its very birth apart from all its kind. A child so brought up becomes, as instances could be adduced to prove, not a man in the full sense at all, but rather a beast in human shape, with human faculties, no doubt, hidden underneath, but with no hope in this life of ever developing those faculties into true humanity.[3] If, then, the whole in this case, as in so many others, is prior to the parts, we may conclude, that we are to look for that progress which is essential to a spiritual being subject to the lapse of time, not only in the individual, but also quite as much in the race taken as a whole. We may expect to find, in the history of man, each successive age incorporating into itself the substance of the preceding.[4]

[5] This power, whereby the present ever gathers into itself the results of the past, transforms the human race into a colossal man, whose life reaches from the creation to the day of judgment.[5] The successive generations of men are days in this man's life. The discoveries and inventions which characterize the different epochs of the world's history are his works. The creeds and doctrines, the opinions and principles of the successive ages, are his thoughts. The state of society at different times are his manners. He grows in knowledge, in self-control, in visible size, just as we do. And his education is in the same way and for the same reason precisely similar to ours.

[6] All this is no figure but only a compendious statement of a very comprehensive fact. The child that is born to-day may possibly have the same faculties as if he had been born in the days of Noah; if it be otherwise, we possess no means of determining the difference. But the equality of the natural faculties at starting will not prevent a vast difference in their ultimate development.[6] That development is entirely under the control of the influences exerted by the society in which the child may chance to live. If such society be altogether denied, the faculties perish, and the child (as remarked above) grows up a beast and not a man; if the society be uneducated and coarse, the growth of the faculties is early so stunted as never afterwards to be capable of recovery; if the society be highly cultivated, the child will be cultivated also, and will show, more or less, through life the fruits of that cultivation.[7] Hence each generation receives the benefit of the cultivation of that which preceded it. Not in knowledge only but in development of powers the child of twelve now stands at the level where once stood the child of fourteen, where ages ago stood the full-grown man. The discipline of manners, of temper, of thought,

of feeling, is transmitted from generation to generation, and at each transmission there is an imperceptible but unfailing increase. The perpetual accumulation of the stores of knowledge is so much more visible than the change in the other ingredients of human progress, that we are apt to fancy that knowledge grows, and knowledge only. I shall not stop to examine whether it be true (as is sometimes maintained) that all progress in human society is but the effect of the progress of knowledge. For the present, it is enough to point out that knowledge is not the only possession of the human spirit in which progress can be traced.[8]

We may, then, rightly speak of a childhood, a youth, and a manhood of the world. The men of the earliest ages were, in many respects, still children as compared with ourselves, with all the blessings and with all the disadvantages that belong to childhood. We reap the fruits of their toil, and bear in our characters the impress of their cultivation. Our characters have grown out of their history, as the character of the man grows out of the history of the child. There are matters in which the simplicity of childhood is wiser than the maturity of manhood, and in these they were wiser than we. There are matters in which the child is nothing, and the man everything, and in these we are the gainers. And the process by which we have either lost or gained corresponds, stage by stage, with the process by which the infant is trained for youth, and the youth for manhood.

This training has three stages. In childhood we are subject to positive rules which we cannot understand, but are bound implicitly to obey. In youth we are subject to the influence of example, and soon break loose from all rules unless illustrated and enforced by the higher teaching which example imparts. In manhood we are comparatively free from external restraints, and if we are to learn, must be our own instructors. First come Rules, then Examples, then Principles. First comes the Law, then the Son of Man, then the Gift of the Spirit. The world was once a child under tutors and governors until the time appointed by the Father. Then, when the fit season had arrived, the Example to which all ages should turn was sent to teach men what they ought to be. Then the human race was left to itself to be guided by the teaching of the Spirit within.[9]

The education of the world, like that of the child, begins with Law. It is impossible to explain the reasons of all the commands that you give to a child, and you do not endeavour to do so. When he is to go to bed, when he is to get up, how he is to sit, stand, eat, drink, what answers he is to make when spoken to, what he may touch and what he may not, what prayers he shall say and when, what lessons he is to learn, every detail of manners and of conduct the careful mother teaches her child, and requires implicit obedience. Mingled together in her teaching are commands of the most trivial character and commands of the gravest importance; their relative value marked by a difference of manner rather than by anything else, since to explain it is impossible. Meanwhile to the child obedience is the highest duty, affection the highest stimulus, the mother's word the highest sanction. The conscience is alive, but it is, like the other faculties at that age, irregular, undeveloped, easily deceived. The mother does not leave it uncultivated, nor refuse sometimes to explain her motives for commanding or forbidding; but she never thinks of putting the judgment of the child against her own, nor of considering the child's conscience as having a right to free action.[10]

[10] As the child grows older the education changes its character, not so much in regard to the sanction of its precepts as in regard to their tenor. More stress is laid upon matters of real duty, less upon matters of mere manner. Falsehood, quarrelling, bad temper, greediness, indolence, are more attended to than times of going to bed, or fashions of eating, or postures in sitting. The boy is allowed to feel, and to show that he feels, the difference between different commands. But he is still not left to himself: and though points of manner are not put on a level with points of conduct, they are by no means neglected. Moreover, while much stress is laid upon his deeds, little is laid upon his opinions; he is rightly supposed not to have any, and will not be allowed to plead them as a reason for disobedience.

[11] After a time, however, the intellect begins to assert a right to enter into all questions of duty, and the intellect accordingly is cultivated. The reason is appealed to in questions of conduct: the consequences of folly or sin are pointed out, and the punishment which, without any miracle, God invariably brings upon those who disobey His natural laws—how, for instance, falsehood destroys confidence and incurs contempt; how indulgence in appetite tends to brutal and degrading habits, how ill-temper may end in crime, and must end in mischief.[11] Thus the conscience is reached through the understanding.

[12] Now, precisely analogous to all this is the history of the education of the early world. The earliest commands almost entirely refer to bodily appetites and animal passions. The earliest wide-spread sin was brutal violence. That wilfulness of temper,—those germs of wanton cruelty, which the mother corrects so easily in her infant, were developed in the earliest form of human society into a prevailing plague of wickedness. The few notices which are given of that state of mankind do not present a picture of mere lawlessness, such as we find among the medieval nations of Europe, but of blind, gross ignorance of themselves and all around them. Atheism is possible now, but Lamech's presumptuous comparison of himself with God is impossible, and the thought of building a tower high enough to escape God's wrath could enter no man's dreams. We sometimes see in very little children a violence of temper which seems hardly human: add to such a temper the strength of a full-grown man, and we shall perhaps understand what is meant by the expression, that the earth was filled with violence.[12]

[13] Violence was followed by sensuality. Such was the sin of Noah, Ham, Sodom, Lot's daughters, and the guilty Canaanites.[13] Animal appetites—the appetites which must be subdued in childhood if they are to be subdued at all—were still the temptation of mankind. Such sins are, it is true, prevalent in the world even now. But the peculiarity of these early forms of licentiousness is their utter disregard of every kind of restraint, and this constitutes their childish character.

[14] The education of this early race may strictly be said to begin when it was formed into the various masses out of which the nations of the earth have sprung

The world, as it were, went to school, and was broken up into classes.[14] Before that time it can hardly be said that any great precepts had been given. The only commands which claim an earlier date are the prohibitions of murder and of eating blood.[15] And these may be considered as given to all alike. But the whole lesson of humanity was too much to be learned by all at once. Different parts of it fell to the task of different parts of the human race, and for a long time, though the education of the world flowed in parallel channels, it did not form a single stream.

[5] The Jewish nation, selected among all as the depository of what may be termed, in a pre-eminent sense, religious truth, received, after a short preparation, the Mosaic system. This system is a mixture of moral and positive commands: the latter, precise and particular, ruling the customs, the festivals, the worship, the daily food, the dress, the very touch; the former large, clear, simple, peremptory.[16] There is very little directly spiritual. No freedom of conduct or of opinion is allowed. The difference between different precepts is not forgotten; nor is all natural judgment in morals excluded. But the reason for all the minute commands is never given. Why they may eat the sheep and not the pig they are not told. The commands are not confined to general principles, but run into such details as to forbid tattooing or disfiguring the person, to command the wearing of a blue fringe, and the like.[17] That such commands should be sanctioned by divine authority is utterly irreconcileable with our present feelings. But in the Mosaic system the same peremptory legislation deals with all these matters, whether important or trivial. The fact is, that however trivial they might be in relation to the authority which they invoked, they were not trivial in relation to the people who were to be governed and taught.

[6] The teaching of the Law was followed by the comments of the Prophets.[18] It is impossible to mistake the complete change of tone and spirit. The ordinances indeed remain, and the obligation to observe them is always assumed. But they have sunk to the second place. The national attention is distinctly fixed on the higher precepts. Disregard of the ordinances is, in fact, rarely noticed, in comparison with breaches of the great human laws of love and brotherly kindness, of truth and justice. There are but two sins against the ceremonial law which receive marked attention—idolatry and sabbath-breaking; and these do not occupy a third of the space devoted to the denunciation of cruelty and oppression, of maladministration of justice, of impurity and intemperance.[19] Nor is the change confined to the precepts enforced: it extends to the sanction which enforces them. Throughout the Prophets there is an evident reference to the decision of individual conscience, which can rarely be found in the Books of Moses. Sometimes, as in Ezekiel's comment on the Second Commandment, a distinct appeal is made from the letter of the law to the voice of natural equity. Sometimes, as in the opening of Isaiah, the ceremonial sacrifices are condemned for the sins of those who offered them. Or, again, fasting is spiritualized into self-denial. And the tone taken in this teaching is such as to imply a previous breach, not so much of positive commands, as of natural morality. It is assumed that the hearer will find within himself a sufficient

sanction for the precepts. It is no longer, as in the law, 'I am the Lord;' but, 'Hath not he showed thee, O man, what is good?'[20] And hence the style becomes argumentative instead of peremptory, and the teacher pleads instead of dogmatizing. In the meanwhile, however, no hint is ever given of a permission to dispense with the ordinances even in the least degree. The child is old enough to understand, but not old enough to be left to himself. He is not yet a man. He must still conform to the rules of his father's house, whether or not those rules suit his temper or approve themselves to his judgment.

[17] The comments of the Prophets were followed in their turn by the great Lesson of the Captivity.[21] Then for the first time the Jews learned, what that Law and the Prophets had been for centuries vainly endeavouring to teach them, namely, to abandon for ever polytheism and idolatry. But though this change in their national habits and character is unmistakeable, it might seem at first sight as if it were no more than an external and superficial amendment, and that their growth in moral and spiritual clearness, though traceable with certainty up to this date, at any rate received a check afterwards. For it is undeniable that, in the time of our Lord, the Sadducees had lost all depth of spiritual feeling, while the Pharisees had succeeded in converting the Mosaic system into so mischievous an idolatry of forms, that St. Paul does not hesitate to call the law the strength of sin.[22] But in spite of this it is nevertheless clear that even the Pharisaic teaching contained elements of a more spiritual religion than the original Mosaic system. Thus, for instance, the importance attached by the Pharisees to prayer is not be found in the law. The worship under the law consisted almost entirely of sacrifices. With the sacrifices we may presume that prayer was also offered, but it was not positively commanded; and, as a regular and necessary part of worship, it first appears in the later books of the Old Testament, and is never even there so earnestly insisted upon as afterwards by the Pharisees. It was in fact in the captivity, far from the temple and the sacrifices of the temple, that the Jewish people first learned that the spiritual part of worship could be separated from the ceremonial, and that of the two the spiritual was far the higher. The first introduction of preaching and the reading of the Bible in the synagogues belong to the same date. The careful study of the law, though it degenerated into formality, was yet in itself a more intellectual service than the earlier records exhibit. And this study also, though commencing earlier, attains its maximum after the captivity; the Psalmists who delight in the study of the law are all, or nearly all, much later than David; and the enthusiasm with which the study is praised increases as we come down. In short, the Jewish nation had lost very much when John the Baptist came to prepare the way for his Master; but time had not stood still, nor had that course of education whereby the Jew was to be fitted to give the last revelation to the world.[23]

[18] The results of this discipline of the Jewish nation may be summed up in two points—a settled national belief in the unity and spirituality of God, and an acknowledgment of the paramount importance of chastity as a point of morals.

[19] The conviction of the unity and spirituality of God was peculiar to the Jews

among the pioneers of civilization. Greek philosophers had, no doubt, come to the same conclusion by dint of reason.[24] Noble minds may often have been enabled to raise themselves to the same height in moments of generous emotion. But every one knows the difference between an opinion and a practical conviction—between a scientific deduction or a momentary insight and that habit which has become second nature. Every one, also, knows the difference between a tenet maintained by a few intellectual men far in advance of their age, and a belief pervading a whole people, penetrating all their daily life, leavening all their occupations, incorporated into their very language. To the great mass of the Gentiles, at the time of our Lord, polytheism was the natural posture of the thoughts into which their minds unconsciously settled when undisturbed by doubt or difficulties. To every Jew, without exception, monotheism was equally natural. To the Gentile, even when converted, it was, for some time, still effort to abstain from idols; to the Jew it was no more an effort than it is to us. The bent of the Jewish mind was, in fact, so fixed by their previous training that it would have required a perpetual and difficult strain to enable a Jew to join in such folly. We do not readily realize how hard this was to acquire, because we have never had to acquire it: and in reading the Old Testament we look on the repeated idolatries of the chosen people as wilful backslidings from an elementary truth within the reach of children, rather than as stumblings in learning a very difficult lesson—difficult even for cultivated men.[25] In reality, elementary truths are the hardest of all to learn, unless we pass our childhood in an atmosphere thoroughly impregnated with them; and then we imbibe them unconsciously and find it difficult to perceive their difficulty.

It was the fact that this belief was not the tenet of the few, but the habit of the nation, which made the Jews the proper instruments for communicating the doctrine to the world. They supported it, not by arguments, which always provoke replies, and rarely, at the best, penetrate deeper than the intellect; but by the unconscious evidence of their lives. They supplied that spiritual atmosphere in which alone the faith of new converts could attain to vigorous life. They supplied forms of language and expression fit for immediate and constant use. They supplied devotions to fill the void which departed idolatry left behind. The rapid spread of the Primitive Church, and the depth to which it struck its roots into the decaying society of the Roman empire, are unquestionably due, to a great extent, to the body of Jewish proselytes already established in every important city, and to the existence of the Old Testament as a ready-made text-book of devotion and instruction.[26]

Side by side with this freedom from idolatry there had grown up in the Jewish mind a chaster morality than was to be found elsewhere in the world. There were many points, undoubtedly, in which the early morality of the Greeks and Romans would well bear a comparison with that of the Hebrews. In simplicity of life, in gentleness of character, in warmth of sympathy, in kindness to the poor, in justice to all men, the Hebrews could not have rivalled the best days of Greece. In reverence for law, in reality of obedience, in calmness under trouble, in dignity of self-respect, they could not have rivalled the best days of Rome. But the sins of the flesh corrupted both these races, and the flower of their finest virtues had withered before the time of our Lord. In chastity the Hebrews stood alone; and this virtue, which had grown up with them from their earliest days, was still in the vigour of fresh life when they were commissioned to give the Gospel to the nations. The Hebrew morality has passed into the Christian church, and sins of impurity (which war against the soul) have ever since been looked on as the type of all evil; and our Litany selects them as the example of deadly sin.[27] What sort of morality the Gentiles would have handed down to us, had they been left to themselves, is clear from the Epistles. The excesses of the Gentile party at Corinth (1 Cor. v. 2), the first warning given to the Thessalonians (1 Thes. iv. 3), the first warning given to the Galatians (Gal. v. 19), the description of the Gentile world in the Epistle to the Romans, are sufficient indications of the prevailing Gentile sin. But St. James, writing to the Hebrew Christians, says not a word upon the subject, and St. Peter barely alludes to it.[28]

[22] The idea of monotheism and the principle of purity might seem hardly enough to be the chief results of so systematic a discipline as that of the Hebrews. But, in reality, they are the cardinal points in education. The idea of monotheism outtops all other ideas in dignity and worth. The spirituality of God involves in it the supremacy of conscience, the immortality of the soul, the final judgment of the human race. For we know the other world, and can only know it, by analogy, drawn from our own experience. With what, then, shall we compare God? With the spiritual or the fleshly part of our nature? On the answer depends the whole bent of our religion and of our morality. For that in ourselves which we choose as the nearest analogy of God, will, of course, be looked on as the ruling and lasting part of our being. If He be one and spiritual, then the spiritual power within us, which proclaims its own unity and independence of matter by the universality of its decrees, must be the rightful monarch of our lives; but if there be Gods many and Lords many, with bodily appetites and animal passions, then the voice of conscience is but one of those wide-spread delusions which, some for a longer, some for a shorter period, have, before now, misled our race. Again, the same importance which we assign to monotheism as a creed, we must assign to chastity as a virtue.[29] Among all the vices which it is necessary to subdue in order to build up the human character, there is none to be compared in strength, or in virulence, with that of impurity. It can outlive and kill a thousand virtues; it can corrupt the most generous heart; it can madden the soberest intellect; it can debase the loftiest imagination. But, besides being so poisonous in character, it is above all others most difficult to conquer. And the people whose extraordinary toughness of nature has enabled it to outlive Egyptian Pharaohs, and Assyrian kings, and Roman Caesars, and Mussulman caliphs, was well matched against a power of evil which has battled with the human spirit ever since the creation, and has inflicted, and may yet inflict, more deadly blows than any other power we know of.[30]

[23] Such was the training of the Hebrews. Other nations meanwhile had a training parallel to and contemporaneous with theirs. The natural religions, shadows

projected by the spiritual light within shining on the dark problems without, were all in reality systems by Law, given also by God, though not given by revelation but by the working of nature, and consequently so distorted and adulterated that in lapse of time the divine element in them had almost perished. The poetical gods of Greece, the legendary gods of Rome, the animal worship of Egypt, the sun worship of the East, all accompanied by systems of law and civil government springing from the same sources as themselves, namely, the character and temper of the several nations, were the means of educating these people to similar purposes in the economy of Providence to that for which the Hebrews were destined.

4] When the seed of the Gospel was first sown, the field which had been prepared to receive it may be divided into four chief divisions, Rome, Greece, Asia, and Judea.[31] Each of these contributed something to the growth of the future Church. And the growth of the Church is, in this case, the development of the human race. It cannot indeed yet be said that all humanity has united into one stream; but the Christian nations have so unquestionably taken the lead amongst their fellows, that although it is likely enough the unconverted peoples may have a real part to play, that part may be plainly quite subordinate; subordinate in a sense in which neither Rome, nor Greece, nor perhaps even Asia, was subordinate to Judea.

5] It is not difficult to trace the chief elements of civilization which we owe to each of the four. Rome contributed her admirable spirit of order and organization. To her had been given the genius of government. She had been trained to it by centuries of difficult and tumultuous history. Storms which would have rent asunder the framework of any other polity only practised her in the art of controlling popular passions; and when she began to aim consciously at the Empire of the World, she had already learned her lesson. She had learned it as the Hebrews had learned theirs, by an enforced obedience to her own system. In no nation of antiquity had civil officers the same unquestioned authority during their term of office, or laws and judicial rules the same reverence. That which religion was to the Jew, including even the formalism which encrusted and fettered it, law was to the Roman. And law was the lesson which Rome was intended to teach the world. Hence the Bishop of Rome soon became the Head of the Church.[32] Rome was, in fact, the centre of the traditions which had once governed the world; and their spirit still remained; and the Roman Church developed into the papacy simply because a head was wanted, and no better one could be found. Hence again in all the doctrinal disputes of the fourth and fifth centuries the decisive voice came from Rome.[33] Every controversy was finally settled by her opinion, because she alone possessed the art of framing formulas which could hold together in any reasonable measure the endless variety of sentiments and feelings which the Church by that time comprised. It was this power of administering law which enabled the Western Church, in the time of Charlemagne, to undertake, by means of her bishops, the task of training and civilizing the new population of Europe.[34] To Rome we owe the forms of local government which in England have saved liberty and elsewhere have mitigated despotism. Justinian's laws have penetrated into all modern legislation, and almost all improvements bring us only nearer to his code. Much of the spirit of modern politics came from Greece; much from the woods of Germany.[35] But the skeleton and framework is almost entirely Roman. And it is not this framework only that comes from Rome. The moral sentiments and the moral force which lie at the back of all political life and are absolutely indispensable to its vigour are in great measure Roman too. It is true that the life and power of all morality will always be drawn from the New Testament; yet it is in the history of Rome rather in the Bible that we find our models and precepts of political duty, and especially of the duty of patriotism. St. Paul bids us follow whatsoever things are lovely, whatsoever things are of good report.[36] But except through such general appeals to natural feeling it would be difficult to prove from the New Testament that cowardice was not only disgraceful but sinful, and that love of our country was an exalted duty of humanity. That lesson our consciences have learnt from the teaching of Ancient Rome.

[26] To Greece was entrusted the cultivation of the reason and the taste. Her gift to mankind has been science and art. There was little in her temper of the spirit of reverence. Her morality and her religion did not spring from the conscience. Her gods were the creatures of imagination not of spiritual need. Her highest idea was, not holiness, as with the Hebrews, nor law, as with the Romans, but beauty. Even Aristotle, who assuredly gave way to mere sentiment as little as any Greek that ever lived, placed the Beautiful (τὸ καλόν) at the head of his moral system, not the Right, nor the Holy.[37] Greece, in fact, was not looking at another world, nor even striving to organize the present, but rather aiming at the development of free nature. The highest possible cultivation of the individual, the most finished perfection of the natural faculties, was her dream. It is true that her philosophers are ever talking of subordinating the individual to the state. But in reality there never has been a period in history nor a country in the world, in which the peculiarities of individual temper and character had freer play. This is not the best atmosphere for political action; but it is better than any other for giving vigour and life to the impulses of genius, and for cultivating those faculties, the reason and taste in which the highest genius can be shown. Such a cultivation needs discipline less than any. And of all the nations Greece had the least of systematic discipline, least of instinctive deference to any one leading idea. But for the reason the cultivation required less time than any other; and the national life of Greece is the shortest of all. Greek history hardly begins before Solon, and it hardly continues after Alexander, barely covering 200 years.[38] But its fruits are eternal. To the Greeks we owe the logic which has ruled the minds of all thinkers since. All our natural and physical science really begins with the Greeks, and indeed would have been impossible had not Greece taught men how to reason. To the Greeks we owe the corrective which conscience needs to borrow from nature. Conscience, startled at the awful truths which she has to reveal, too often threatens to withdraw the soul into gloomy and perverse asceticism: then is needed the beauty which Greece taught us to admire, to show us another aspect of the Divine Attributes.[39] To the Greeks

we owe all modern literature. For though there is other literature even older than the Greek, the Asiatic for instance, and the Hebrew, yet we did not learn this lesson from them; they had not the genial life which was needed to kindle other nations with the communication of their own fire.[40]

27] The discipline of Asia was the never-ending succession of conquering dynasties, following in each other's track like waves, an ever moving yet never advancing ocean. Cycles of change were successively passing over her, and yet at the end of every cycle she stood where she had stood before, and nearly where she stands now. The growth of Europe has dwarfed her in comparison, and she is paralysed in presence of a gigantic strength younger but mightier than her own.[41] But in herself she is no weaker than she ever was. The monarchs who once led Assyrian, or Babylonian, or Persian armies across half the world impose on us by the vast extent and rapidity of their conquests; but these conquests had in reality no substance, no inherent strength.[42] This perpetual baffling of all earthly progress taught Asia to seek her inspiration in rest. She learned to fix her thoughts upon another world, and was disciplined to check by her silent protest the over-earthly, over-practical tendency of the Western nations. She was ever the one to refuse to measure Heaven by the standard of earth. Her teeming imagination filled the church with thoughts 'undreamt of in our philosophy.' She had been the instrument selected to teach the Hebrews the doctrine of the Immortality of the Soul; for whatever may be said of the early nations on this subject, it is unquestionable that in Babylon the Jews first attained the clearness and certainty in regard to it which we find in the teaching of the Pharisees.[43] So again, Athanasius, a thorough Asiatic in sentiment and in mode of arguing, was the bulwark of the doctrine of the Trinity.[44] The Western nations are always tempted to make reason not only supreme, but despotic, and dislike to acknowledge mysteries even in religion. They are inclined to confine all doctrines within the limits of spiritual utility, and to refuse to listen to dim voices and whispers from within, those instincts of doubt, and reference, and awe which yet are, in their place and degree, messages from the depths of our being. Asia supplies the corrective by perpetually leaning to the mysterious. When left to herself, she settles down to baseless dreams, and sometimes to monstrous and revolting fictions.[45] But her influence has never ceased to be felt, and could not be lost without serious damage.

] Thus the Hebrews may be said to have disciplined the human conscience, Rome the human will, Greece the reason and taste, Asia the spiritual imagination. Other races that have been since admitted into Christendom also did their parts. And others may yet have something to contribute; for though the time for discipline is childhood, yet there is no precise line beyond which all discipline ceases. Even the grey-haired man has yet some small capacity for learning like a child; and even in the maturity of the world the early modes of teaching, may yet find a place. But the childhood of the world was over when our Lord appeared on earth. The tutors and governors had done their work. It was time that the second teacher of the human race should begin his labour. The second teacher is Example.[46]

[29] The child is not insensible to the influence of example. Even in the earliest years the manners, the language, the principles of the elder begin to mould the character of the younger. There are not a few of our acquirements which we learn by example without any, or with very little, direct instruction—as, for instance, to speak and to walk. But still example at that age is secondary. The child is quite conscious that he is not on such an equality with grown-up friends as to enable him to do as they do. He imitates, but he knows that it is merely play, and he is quite willing to be told that he must not do this or that till he is older. As time goes on, and the faculties expand, the power of discipline to guide the actions—and to mould the character decreases, and in the same proportion the power of example grows. The moral atmosphere must be brutish indeed which can do deep harm to a child of four years. But what is harmless at four is pernicious at six, and almost fatal at twelve. The religious tone of a household will hardly make much impression on an infant; but it will deeply engrave its lessons on the heart of a boy growing towards manhood.[47] Different faculties within us begin to feel the power of this new guide at different times. The moral sentiments are perhaps the first to expand to the influence; but gradually the example of those among whom the life is cast lays hold of all the soul, of the tastes, of the opinions, of the aims, of the temper. As each restraint of discipline is successively cast off, the soul does not gain at first a real, but only an apparent freedom. The youth, when too old for discipline, is not yet strong enough to guide his life by fixed principles. He is led by his emotions and impulses. He admires and loves, he condemns and dislikes, with enthusiasm. And his love and admiration, his disapproval and dislike, are not his own, but borrowed from his society. He can appreciate a character, though he cannot yet appreciate a principle. He cannot walk by reason and conscience alone; he still needs those 'supplies to the imperfection of our nature' which are given by the higher passions.[48] He cannot follow what his heart does not love as well as his reason approve; and he cannot love what is presented to him as an abstract rule of life, but requires a living person. He needs to see virtue in the concrete, before he can recognise her aspect as a divine idea. He instinctively copies those whom he admires, and in doing so imbibes whatever gives the colour to their character. He repeats opinions without really understanding them, and in that way admits their infection into his judgment. He acquires habits which seem of no consequence, but which are the channels of a thousand new impulses to his soul. If he reads, he treats the characters that he meets with in his book as friends or enemies, and so unconsciously allows them to mould his soul. When he seems most independent, most defiant of external guidance, he is in reality only so much the less master of himself, only so much the more guided and formed, not indeed by the will, but by the example and sympathy of others.[49]

[30] The power of example probably never ceases during life. Even old age is not wholly uninfluenced by society; and a change of companions acts upon the character long after the character would appear incapable of further development.

The influence, in fact, dies out just as it grew; and as it is impossible to mark its beginning, so is it to mark its end. The child is governed by the will of its parents; the man by principles and habits of his own. But neither is insensible to the influence of associates, though neither finds in that influence the predominant power of his life.

1] This, then, which is born with our birth and dies with our death, attains its maximum at some point in the passage from one to the other. And this point is just the meeting point of the child and the man, the brief interval which separates restraint from liberty. Young men at this period are learning a peculiar lesson. They seem to those who talk to them to be imbibing from their associates and their studies principles both of faith and conduct. But the rapid fluctuations of their minds show that their opinions have not really the nature of principles. They are really learning, not principles, but the materials out of which principles are made. They drink in the lessons of generous impulse, warm unselfishness, courage, self-devotion, romantic disregard of worldly calculations, without knowing what are the grounds of their own approbation, or caring to analyse the laws and ascertain the limits of such guides of conduct. They believe, without exact attention to the evidence of their belief; and their opinions have accordingly the richness and warmth that belongs to sentiment, but not the clearness or firmness that can be given by reason. These affections, which are now kindled in their hearts by the contact of their fellows, will afterwards be the reservoir of life and light with which their faith and their highest conceptions will be animated and coloured. The opinions now picked up, apparently not really, at random, must hereafter give reality to the clearer and more settled convictions of mature manhood. If it were not for these, the ideas and laws afterwards supplied by reason would be empty forms of thought, without body or substance; the faith would run a risk of being the form of godliness without the power thereof. And hence the lessons of this time have such an attractiveness in their warmth and life, that they are very reluctantly exchanged for the truer and profounder, but at first sight colder wisdom which is destined to follow them. To almost all men this period is a bright spot to which the memory ever afterwards loves to recur; and even those who can remember nothing but folly—folly too which they have repented and relinquished—yet find a nameless charm in recalling such folly as that. For indeed even folly itself at this age is sometimes the cup out of which men quaff the richest blessings of our nature—simplicity, generosity, affection. This is the seed time of the soul's harvest, and contains the promise of the year. It is the time for love and marriage, the time for forming lifelong friendships.[50] The after life may be more contented, but can rarely be so glad and joyous. Two things we need to crown its blessings—one is, that the friends whom we then learn to love, and the opinions which we learn to cherish, may stand the test of time, and deserve the esteem and approval of calmer thoughts and wider experience; the other, that our hearts may have depth enough to drink largely of that which God is holding to our lips, and never again to lose the fire and spirit of the draught. There is nothing more beautiful than a manhood surrounded by the friends, upholding the principles, and filled with the energy of the spring-time of life. But even if these highest blessings be denied, if we have been compelled to change opinions, and to give up friends, and the cold experience of the world has extinguished the heat of youth, still the heart will instinctively recur to that happy time, to explain to itself what is meant by love and what by happiness.[51]

[32] Of course, this is only one side of the picture. This keen susceptibility to pleasure and joy implies a keen susceptibility to pain. There is, probably, no time of life at which pains are more intensely felt; no time at which the whole man more 'groaneth and travaileth in pain together.'[52] Young men are prone to extreme melancholy, even to disgust with life. A young preacher will preach upon afflictions much more often than an old one. A young poet will write more sadly. A young philosopher will moralize more gloomily. And this seems unreal sentiment, and is smiled at in after years. But it is real at the time; and, perhaps, is nearer the truth at all times than the contentedness of those who ridicule it. Youth, in fact, feels everything more keenly; and as far as the keenness of feeling contributes to its truth, the feeling, whether it is pain or pleasure, is so much the truer. But in after life it is the happiness, not the suffering of youth, that most often returns to the memory, and seems to gild all the past.

[33] The period of youth in the history of the world, when the human race was, as it were, put under the teaching of example, corresponds, of course, to the meeting point of the Law and the Gospel. The second stage, therefore, in the education of man was the presence of our Lord upon earth. Those few years of His divine presence seem, as it were, to balance all the systems and creeds and worships which preceded, all the Church's life which has followed since. Saints had gone before, and saints have been given since; great men and good men had lived among the heathen; there were never, at any time, examples wanting to teach either the chosen people or any other. But the one Example of all examples came in the 'fulness of time,' just when the world was fitted to feel the power of His presence. Had His revelation been delayed till now, assuredly it would have been hard for us to recognise His Divinity; for the faculty of Faith has turned inwards, and cannot now accept any outer manifestations of the truth of God.[53] Our vision of the Son of God is now aided by the eyes of the Apostles, and by that aid we can recognise the Express Image of the Father. But in this we are like men who are led through unknown woods by Indian guides. We recognise the indications by which the path was known, as soon as those indications are pointed out; but we feel that it would have been quite vain for us to look for them unaided. We, of course, have, in our turn, counterbalancing advantages. If we have lost that freshness of faith which would be the first to say to a poor carpenter—Thou art the Christ, the Son of the Living God—yet we possess, in the greater cultivation of our religious understanding, that which, perhaps, we ought not to be willing to give in exchange.[54] The early Christians could recognise, more readily than we, the greatness and beauty of the Example set before them; but it is not too much to say, that we know better

than they the precise outlines of the truth. To every age is given by God its own proper gift. They had not the same clearness of understanding as we; the same recognition that it is God and not the devil who rules the world; the same power of discrimination between different kinds of truth; they had not the same calmness, or fixedness of conduct; their faith was not so quiet, so little tempted to restless vehemence. But they had a keenness of perception which we have not, and could see the immeasurable difference between our Lord and all other men as we could never have seen it. Had our Lord come later, He would have come to mankind already beginning to stiffen into the fixedness of maturity. The power of His life would not have sunk so deeply into the world's heart; the truth of His Divine Nature would not have been recognised. Seeing the Lord, would not have been the title to Apostleship.[55] On the other hand, had our Lord come earlier, the world would not have been ready to receive Him, and the Gospel, instead of being the religion of the human race, would have been the religion of the Hebrews only. The other systems would have been too strong to be overthrown by the power of preaching. The need of a higher and purer teaching would not have been felt. Christ would have seemed to the Gentiles the Jewish Messiah, not the Son of Man. But He came in the 'fulness of time,' for which all history had been preparing, to which all history since has been looking back.[56] Hence the first and largest place in the New Testament is assigned to His Life four times told. This life we emphatically call the Gospel. If there is little herein to be technically called doctrine, yet here is the fountain of all inspiration. There is no Christian who would not rather part with all the rest of the Bible than with these four Books. There is no part of God's Word which the religious man more instinctively remembers. The Sermon on the Mount, the Parables and the Miracles, the Last Supper, the Mount of Olives, the Garden of Gethsemane, the Cross on Calvary—these are the companions alike of infancy and of old age, simple enough to be read with awe and wonder by the one, profound enough to open new depths of wisdom to the fullest experience of the other.[57]

4] Our Lord was the Example of mankind, and there can be no other example in the same sense. But the whole period from the closing of the Old Testament to the close of the New was the period of the world's youth—the age of examples; and our Lord's presence was not the only influence of that kind which has acted upon the human race. Three companions were appointed by Providence to give their society to this creature whom God was educating; Greece, Rome, and the Early Church. To these three mankind has ever since looked back, and will ever hereafter look back, with the same affection, the same lingering regret, with which age looks back to early manhood. In these three mankind remembers the brilliant social companion whose wit and fancy sharpened the intellect and refined the imagination; the bold and clever leader with whom to dare was to do, and whose very name was a signal of success; and the earnest, heavenly-minded friend, whose saintly aspect was a revelation in itself.

Greece and Rome have not only given to us the fruits of their discipline, but the companionship of their bloom. The fruits of their discipline would have passed into our possession, even if their memory had utterly perished; and just as we know not the man who first discovered arithmetic, nor the man who first invented writing—benefactors with whom no other captains of science can ever be compared—so, too, it is probable that we inherit from many a race, whose name we shall never hear again, fruits of long training now forgotten.[58] But Greece and Rome have given us more than any results of discipline in the never-dying memory of their fresh and youthful life. It is this, and not only the greatness or the genius of the classical writers which makes their literature pre-eminent above all others. There have been great poets, great historians, great philosophers in modern days. Greece can show few poets equal, none superior to Shakespeare. Gibbon, in many respects, stands above all ancient historians. Bacon was as great a master of philosophy as Aristotle.[59] Nor, again, are there wanting great writers of times older, as well as of times later, than the Greek, as, for instance, the Hebrew prophets. But the classics possess a charm quite independent of genius. It is not their genius only which makes them attractive. It is the classic life, the life of the people of that day. It is the image, there only to be seen, of our highest natural powers in their freshest vigour. It is the unattainable grace of the prime of manhood. It is the pervading sense of youthful beauty. Hence, while we have elsewhere great poems and great histories, we never find again that universal radiance of fresh life which makes even the most commonplace relics of classic days models for our highest art. The common workman of those times breathed the atmosphere of the gods. What are now the ornaments of our museums were then the every-day furniture of sitting and sleeping rooms. In the great monuments of their literature we can taste this pure inspiration most largely; but even the most commonplace fragments of a classic writer are steeped in the waters of the same fountain. Those who compare the moderns with the ancients, genius for genius, have no difficulty in claiming for the former equality, if not victory. But the issue is mistaken. To combine the highest powers of intellect with the freshness of youth was possible only once, and that is the glory of the classic nations. The inspiration which is drawn by the man from the memory of those whom he loved and admired in the spring-time of his life, is drawn by the world now from the study of Greece and Rome. The world goes back to its youth in hopes to become young again, and delights to dwell on the feats achieved by the companions of those days. Beneath whatever was wrong and foolish it recognises that beauty of a fresh nature which never ceases to delight. And the sin and vices of that joyous time are passed over with the levity with which men think of their young companions' follies.[60]

[36] The Early Church stands as the example which has most influenced our religious life, as Greece and Rome have most influenced our political and intellectual life. We read the New Testament, not to find there forms of devotion, for there are few to be found; nor laws of church government, for there are hardly any; nor creeds, for there are none; nor doctrines logically stated, for there is no attempt at logical precision. The New Testament is almost entirely occupied with

two—the life of our Lord and the life of Early Church.[61] Among the Epistles there are but two which seem, even at first sight, to be treatises for the future instead of letters for the time—the Epistle to the Romans and the Epistle to the Hebrews. But even these, when closely examined, appear, like the rest, to be no more than the fruit of the current history. That early church does not give us precepts, but an example. She says, Be ye followers of me, as I also am of Christ. This had never been said by Moses, nor by any of the prophets. But the world was now grown old enough to be taught by seeing the lives of saints, better than by hearing the words of prophets. When afterwards Christians needed creeds, and liturgies, and forms of church government and systems of theology, they could not find them in the New Testament. They found there only the materials out of which such needs could be supplied. But the combination and selection of those materials they had to provide for themselves. In fact, the work which the early church had to do was peculiar. Her circumstances were still more peculiar. Had she legislated peremptorily for posterity, her legislation must have been set aside, as, indeed, the prohibition to eat things strangled and to eat blood has been already set aside. But her example will live and teach for ever. In her we learn what is meant by zeal, what by love of God, what by joy in the Holy Ghost, what by endurance for the sake of Christ. For the very purpose of giving us a pattern, the chief features in her character are, as it were, magnified into colossal proportions. Our saints must chiefly be the saints of domestic life, the brightness of whose light is visible to very few. But their saintliness was forced into publicity, and its radiance illumines the earth. So on every page of the New Testament is written, Go and do thou likewise.[62] Transplant into your modern life the same heavenly-mindedness, the same fervour of love, the same unshaken faith, the same devotion to your fellow-man. And to these pages accordingly the church of our day turns for renewal of inspiration. We even busy ourselves in tracing the details of the early Christian life, and we love to find that any practice of ours comes down from apostolic times. This is an exaggeration. It is not really following the early church, to be servile copyists of her practices. We are not commanded to have all things in common, because the church of Jerusalem once had; nor are we to make every supper a sacrament, because the early Christians did so. To copy the early church is to do as she did, not what she did. Yet the very exaggeration is a testimony of the power which that church has over us. We would fain imitate even her outward actions as a step towards imitating her inner life. Her outward actions were not meant for our model. She, too, had her faults: disorders, violent quarrels, licentious recklessness of opinion, in regard both to faith and practice. But these spots altogether disappear in the blaze of light which streams upon us when we look back towards her. Nay, we are impatient of being reminded that she had faults at all. So much does her youthful holiness surpass all that we can show, that he who can see her faults seems necessarily insensible to the brightness of her glory. There have been great saints since the days of the apostles. Holiness is as possible now as it was then. But the saintliness of that time had a peculiar beauty which we cannot copy; a beauty not confined to the apostles or great leaders, but pervading the whole church. It is not what they endured, nor the virtues which they practised, that so dazzle us. It is the perfect simplicity of the religious life, the singleness of heart, the openness, the child-like earnestness.[63] All else has been repeated since, but this never. And this makes the religious man's heart turn back with longing to that blessed time when the Lord's service was the highest of all delights, and every act of worship came fresh from the soul. If we compare degrees of devotion, it may be reckoned something intrinsically nobler, to serve God and love Him now when religion is colder than it was, and when we have not the aid of those thrilling heart-stirring sympathies which blessed the early church. But even if our devotion be sometimes nobler in itself, yet theirs still remains the more beautiful, the more attractive. Ours may have its own place in the sight of God, but theirs remains the irresistible example which kindles all other hearts by its fire.

[37] It is nothing against the drift of this argument, that the three friends whose companionship is most deeply engraven on the memory of the world were no friends one to another. This was the lot of mankind, as it is the lot of not a few men. Greece, the child of nature, had come to full maturity so early as to pass away before the other two appeared; and Rome and the Early Church disliked each other. Yet that dislike makes little impression on us now. We never identify the Rome of our admiration with the Rome which persecuted the Christian, partly, indeed, because the Rome that we admire was almost gone before the church was founded; but partly, too, because we forget each of these while we are studying the other. We almost make two persons of Trajan, accordingly as we meet with him in sacred or profane history.[64] So natural is it to forget in after life the faulty side of young friends' characters.

[38] The susceptibility of youth to the impression of society wears off at last. The age of reflection begins. From the storehouse of his youthful experience the man begins to draw the principles of his life. The spirit or conscience comes to full strength and assumes the throne intended for him in the soul. As an accredited judge, invested with full powers, he sits in the tribunal of our inner kingdom, decides upon the past, and legislates upon the future without appeal except to himself. He decides not by what is beautiful, or noble, or soul-inspiring, but by what is right. Gradually he frames his code of laws, revising, adding, abrogating, as a wider and deeper experience gives him clearer light. He is the third great teacher and the last.[65]

[39] Now the education by no means ceases when the spirit thus begins to lead the soul; the office of the spirit is in fact to guide us into truth, not to give truth. The youth who has settled down to his life's work makes a great mistake if he fancies that because he is no more under teachers and governors his education is therefore at an end. It is only changed in form. He has much, very much, to learn, more perhaps than all which he has yet learned; and his new teacher will not give it to him all at once. The lesson of life is in this respect like the lessons whereby we learn any ordinary business. The barrister, who has filled his memory with legal forms and imbued his mind with their spirit, knows that the most valuable part of his

education is yet to be obtained in attending the courts of law. The physician is not content with the theories of the lecture-room, nor with the experiments of the laboratory, nor even with the attendance at the hospitals; he knows that independent practice, when he will be thrown upon his own resources, will open his eyes to much which at present he sees through a glass darkly. In every profession, after the principles are apparently mastered, there yet remains much to be learnt from the application of those principles to practice, the only means by which we ever understand principles to the bottom. So too with the lesson which includes all others, the lesson of life.[66]

40] In this last stage of his progress a man learns in various ways. First he learns unconsciously by the growth of his inner powers and the secret but steady accumulation of experience. The fire of youth is toned down and sobered. The realities of life dissipate many dreams, clear up many prejudices, soften down many roughnesses. The difference between intention and action, between anticipating temptation and bearing it, between drawing pictures of holiness or nobleness and realizing them, between hopes of success and reality of achievement, is taught by many a painful and many an unexpected experience. In short, as the youth puts away childish things, so does the man put away youthful things.[67] Secondly, the full-grown man learns by reflection. He looks inwards and not outwards only. He re-arranges the results of past experience, re-examines by the test of reality the principles supplied to him by books or conversation, reduces to intelligible and practical formulas what he has hitherto known as vague general rules. He not only generalizes—youth will generalize with great rapidity and often with great acuteness—but he learns to correct one generalization by another. He gradually learns to disentangle his own thoughts, so as not to be led into foolish inconsistency by want of clearness of purpose. He learns to distinguish between momentary impulses and permanent determinations of character. He learns to know the limits of his own powers, moral and intellectual; and by slow degrees and with much reluctance he learns to suspend his judgment and to be content with ignorance where knowledge is beyond his reach. He learns to know himself and other men, and to distinguish in some measure his own peculiarities from the leading features of humanity which he shares with all men.[68] He learns to know both the worth and the worthlessness of the world's judgment and of his own. Thirdly, he learns much by mistakes, both by his own and by those of others. He often persists in a wrong cause till it is too late to mend what he has done, and he learns how to use it and how to bear it. His principles, or what he thought his principles, break down under him, and he is forced to analyse them in order to discover what amount of truth they really contain. He comes upon new and quite unexpected issues of what he has done or said, and he has to profit by such warnings as he receives. His heirs often force him, as it were, to go back to school; not now with the happy docility of a child, but with the chastened submission of a penitent. Or, more often still, his mistakes inflict a sharp chastisement which teaches him a new lesson without much effort on his own part to learn. Lastly, he learns much by contradiction. The collision of society compels him to state his opinions clearly; to defend them; to modify them when indefensible; perhaps to surrender them altogether, consciously or unconsciously; still more often to absorb them into larger and fuller thoughts, less forcible but more comprehensive. The precision which is thus often forced upon him always seems to diminish something of the heartiness and power which belonged to more youthful instincts. But he gains in directness of aim, and therefore in firmness of resolution. But the greatest of his gains is what seems a loss: for he learns not to attempt the solution of insoluble problems, and to have no opinion at all on many points of the deepest interest. Usually this takes the form of an abandonment of speculation; but it may rise to the level of a philosophical humility which stops where it can advance no further, and confesses its own weakness in the presence of the mysteries of life.

[41] But throughout all this it must not be supposed that he has no more to do either with that law which guided his childhood or with any other law of any kind. Since he is still a learner, he must learn on the one condition of all learning—obedience to rules; not indeed, blind obedience to rules not understood, but obedience to the rules of his own mind—an obedience which he cannot throw off without descending below the childish level. He is free. But freedom is not the opposite of obedience, but of restraint. The freeman must obey, and obey as precisely as the bondman; and if he has not acquired the habit of obedience he is not fit to be free. The law in fact which God makes the standard of our conduct may have one of two forms. It may be an external law, a law which is in the hands of others, in the making, in the applying, in the enforcing of which we have no share; a law which governs from the outside, compelling our will to bow even though our understanding be unconvinced and unenlightened; saying you must, and making no effort to make you feel that you ought; appealing not to your conscience, but to force or fear, and caring little whether you willingly agree or reluctantly submit. Or, again, the law may be an internal law; a voice which speaks within the conscience, and carries the understanding along with it; a law which treats us not as slaves but as friends, allowing us to know what our Lord doeth; a law which bids us yield not to blind fear or awe, but to the majesty of truth and justice; a law which is not imposed on us by another power, but by our own enlightened will. Now the first of these is the law which governs and educates the child; the second the law which governs and educates the man. The second is in reality the spirit of the first. It commands in a different way, but with a tone not one whit less peremptory; and he only who can control all appetites and passions in obedience to it can reap the full harvest of the last and highest education.[69]

[42] This need of law in the full maturity of life is so imperative that if the requisite self-control be lost or impaired, or have never been sufficiently acquired, the man instinctively has recourse to a self-imposed discipline if he desire to keep himself from falling. The Christian who has fallen into sinful habits often finds that he has no resource but to abstain from much that is harmless in itself because he has associated it with evil. He takes monastic vows because the world has proved too

much for him. He takes temperance pledges because he cannot resist the temptations of appetite. There are devils which can be cast out with a word; there are others which go not out but by (not prayer only, but) fasting. This is often the case with the late converted. They are compelled to abstain from, and sometimes they are induced to denounce, many pleasures and many enjoyments which they find unsuited to their spiritual health. The world and its enjoyments have been to them a source of perpetual temptation, and they cannot conceive any religious life within such a circle of evil. Sometimes these men are truly spiritual enough and humble enough to recognise that this discipline is not essential in itself, but only for them and for such as they. The discipline is then truly subordinate. It is an instrument in the hands of their conscience. They know what they are doing and why they do it. But sometimes, if they are weak, this discipline assumes the shape of a regular external law. They look upon many harmless things, from which they have suffered mischief as absolutely, not relatively, hurtful. They denounce what they cannot share without danger, as dangerous, not only for them, but for all mankind, and as evil in itself. They set up a conventional code of duty founded on their own experience which they extend to all men. Even if they are educated enough to see that no conventional code is intellectually tenable, yet they still maintain their system, and defend it, as not necessary in itself, but necessary for sinful men. The fact is, that a merciful Providence, in order to help such men, puts them back under the dominion of the law. They are not aware of it themselves—men who are under the dominion of the law rarely are aware of it. But even if they could appeal to a revelation from heaven, they would still be under the law; for a revelation speaking from without and not from within is an external law and not a spirit.[70]

For the same reason a strict and even severe discipline is needed for the cure of reprobates. Philanthropists complain sometimes that this teaching ends only in making the man say, 'the punishment of crime is what I cannot bear;' not, 'the wickedness of crime is what I will not do.' But our nature is not all will: and the fear of punishment is very often the foundation on which we build the hatred of evil. No convert would look back with any other feeling than deep gratitude on a severity which had set free his spirit by chaining down his grosser appetites.[71] It is true that the teaching of mere discipline, if there be no other teaching, is useless. If you have *only* killed one selfish principle by another you have done nothing. But if while thus killing one selfish principle by another you have also succeeded in awaking the higher faculty and giving it free power of self-exertion, you have done everything.

This return to the teaching of discipline in mature life is needed for the intellect even more than for the conduct. There are many men who though they pass from the teaching of the outer law to that of the inner in regard to their practical life, never emerge from the former in regard to their speculative. They do not think; they are contented to let others think for them and to accept the results. How far the average of men are from having attained the power of free independent thought is shown by the staggering and stumbling of their intellects when a completely new subject of investigation tempts them to form a judgment of their own on a matter which they have not studied. In such cases a really educated intellect sees at once that no judgment is yet within its reach, and acquiesces in suspense. But the uneducated intellect hastens to account for the phenomenon; to discover new laws of nature, and new relations of truth; to decide, and predict, and perhaps to demand a remodelling of all previous knowledge. The discussions on table-turning, a few years ago, illustrated this want of intellects able to govern themselves. The whole analogy of physical science was not enough to induce that suspension of judgment which was effected in a week by the dictum of a known philosopher.[72]

[45] There are, however, some men who really think for themselves. But even they are sometimes obliged, especially if their speculations touch upon practical life, to put a temporary restraint upon their intellects. They refuse to speculate at all in directions where they cannot feel sure of preserving their own balance of mind. If the conclusions at which they seem likely to arrive are very strange, or very unlike the general analogy of truth, or carry important practical consequences, they will pause, and turn to some other subject, and try whether if they come back with fresh minds they still come to the same results. And this may go further, and they may find such speculations so bewildering and so unsatisfactory, that they finally take refuge in a refusal to think any more on the particular questions. They content themselves with so much of truth as they find necessary for their spiritual life; and, though perfectly aware that the wheat may be mixed with tares, they despair of rooting up the tares with safety to the wheat, and therefore let both grow together till the harvest. All this is justifiable in the same way that any self-discipline is justifiable. That is, it is justifiable if really necessary. But as is always the case with those who are under the law, such men are sometimes tempted to prescribe for others what they need for themselves, and to require that no others should speculate because they dare not. They not only refuse to think, and accept other men's thoughts, which is often quite right, but they elevate those into canons of faith for all men, which is not right.[73] This blindness is of course wrong; but in reality it is a blindness of the same kind as that with which the Hebrews clung to their law; a blindness, provided for them in mercy, to save their intellects from leading them into mischief.

[46] Some men, on the other hand, show their want of intellectual self-control by going back not to the dominion of law, but to the still lower level of intellectual anarchy. They speculate without any foundation at all. They confound the internal consistency of some dream of their brains with the reality of independent truth.[74] They set up theories which have no other evidence than compatibility with the few facts that happen to be known; and forget that many other theories of equal claims might readily be invented. They are as little able to be content with having no judgment at all as those who accept judgments at second hand. They never practically realize that when there is not enough evidence to justify a conclusion, it is wisdom to draw no conclusion. They are so eager for light that they will rub

their eyes in the dark and take the resulting optical delusions for real flashes. They need intellectual discipline—but they have little chance of getting it, for they have burst its bands.

47] There is yet a further relation between the inner law of mature life and the outer law of childhood which must be noticed. And that is, that the outer law is often the best vehicle in which the inner law can be contained for the various purposes of life. The man remembers with affection, and keeps up with delight the customs of the home of his childhood; tempted perhaps to over-estimate their value, but even when perfectly aware that they are no more than one form out of many which a well-ordered household might adopt, preferring them because of his long familiarity, and because of the memories with which they are associated. So, too, truth often seems to him richer and fuller when expressed in some favourite phrase of his mother's, or some maxim of his father's. He can give no better reason very often for much that he does every day of his life than that his father did it before him; and provided the custom is not a bad one the reason is valid. And he likes to go to the same church. He likes to use the same prayers. He likes to keep up the same festivities. There are limits to all this. But no man is quite free from the influence; and it is in many cases, perhaps in most, an influence of the highest moral value. There is great value in the removal of many indifferent matters out of the region of discussion into that of precedent. There is greater value still in the link of sympathy which binds the present with the past, and fills old age with the fresh feelings of childhood. If truth sometimes suffers in form, it unquestionably gains much in power; and if its onward progress is retarded, it gains immeasurably in solidity and in its hold on men's hearts.

8] Such is the last stage in the education of a human soul, and similar (as far as it has yet gone) has been the last stage in the education of the human race. Of course, so full a comparison cannot be made in this instance as was possible in the two that preceded it. For we are still within the boundaries of this third period, and we cannot yet judge it as a whole. But if the Christian Church be taken as the representative of mankind it is easy to see that the general law observable in the development of the individual may also be found in the development of the Church.

] Since the days of the Apostles no further revelation has been granted, nor has any other system of religion sprung up spontaneously within the limits which the Church has covered. No prophets have communicated messages from Heaven. No infallible inspiration has guided any teacher or preacher. The claim of infallibility still maintained by a portion of Christendom has been entirely given up by the more advanced section.[75] The Church, in the fullest sense, is left to herself to work out, by her natural faculties, the principles of her own action. And whatever assistance she is to receive in doing so, is to be through those natural faculties, and not in spite of them or without them.

From the very first, the Church commenced the task by determining her leading doctrines and the principles of her conduct. These were evolved, as principles usually are, partly by reflection on past experience, and by formularizing the thoughts embodied in the record of the Church of the Apostles, partly by perpetual collision with every variety of opinion. This career of dogmatism in the Church was, in many ways, similar to the hasty generalizations of early manhood. The principle on which the controversies of those days were conducted is that of giving an answer to every imaginable question. It rarely seems to occur to the early controversialists that there are questions which even the Church cannot solve—problems which not even revelation has brought within the reach of human faculties. That the decisions were right, on the whole—that is, that they always embodied, if they did not always rightly define, the truth—is proved by the permanent vitality of the Church as compared with the various heretical bodies that broke from her. But the fact that so vast a number of the early decisions are practically obsolete, and that even many of the doctrinal statements are plainly unfitted for permanent use, is a proof that the Church was not capable, any more than a man is capable, of extracting, at once, all the truth and wisdom contained in the teaching of the earlier periods. In fact, the Church of the Fathers claimed to do what not even the Apostles had claimed—namely, not only to teach the truth, but to clothe it in logical statements, and that not merely as opposed to then prevailing heresies (which was justifiable), but for all succeeding time. Yet this was, after all, only an exaggeration of the proper function of the time. Those logical statements were necessary. And it belongs to a later epoch to see 'the law within the law' which absorbs such statements into something higher than themselves.[76]

[51] Before this process can be said to have worked itself out, it was interrupted by a new phenomenon, demanding essentially different management. A flood of new and undisciplined races poured into Europe, on the one hand supplying the Church with the vigour of fresh life to replace the effete materials of the old Roman Empire, and, on the other carrying her back to the childish stage, and necessitating a return to the dominion of outer law. The Church instinctively had recourse to the only means that would suit the case—namely, a revival of Judaism. The Papacy of the Middle Ages, and the Papal Hierarchy, with all its numberless ceremonies and appliances of external religion, with its attention fixed upon deeds and not on thoughts, or feelings, or purposes, with its precise apportionment of punishments and purgatory, was, in fact, neither more nor less than the old schoolmaster come back to bring some new scholars to Christ.[77] Of course, this was not the conscious intention of the then rulers of the Church; they believed in their own ceremonies as much as any of the people at large. The return to the dominion of law was instinctive, not intentional. But its object is now as evident as the object of the ancient Mosaic system. Nothing short of a real system of discipline, accepted as Divine by all alike, could have tamed the German and Celtic nature into the self-control needed for a truly spiritual religion. How could Chlovis, at the head of his Franks, have made any right use of absolute freedom of conscience? Nor was this a case in which the less disciplined race could have learned spirituality from the more disciplined. This may happen when the more disciplined is much the more

vigorous of the two. But the exhausted Roman Empire had not such strength of life left within it. There was no alternative but that all alike should be put under the law to learn the lesson of obedience.[78]

[52] When the work was done, men began to discover that the law was no longer necessary.[79] And of course there was no reason why they should then discuss the question whether it ever had been necessary. The time was come when it was fit to trust to the conscience as the supreme guide, and the yoke of the medieval discipline was shaken off by a controversy which, in many respects, was a repetition of that between St. Paul and the Judaizers.[80] But, as is always the case after a temporary return to the state of discipline, Christendom did not go back to the position or the duty from which she had been drawn by the influx of the barbarian races.[81] The human mind had not stood still through the ages of bondage, though its motions had been hidden. The Church's whole energy was taken up in the first six centuries of her existence in the creation of a theology. Since that time it had been occupied in renewing by self-discipline the self-control which the sudden absorption of the barbarians had destroyed. At the Reformation it might have seemed at first as if the study of theology were about to return. But in reality an entirely new lesson commenced—the lesson of toleration. Toleration is the very opposite of dogmatism. It implies in reality a confession that there are insoluble problems upon which even revelation throws but little light. Its tendency is to modify the early dogmatism by substituting the spirit for the letter, and practical religion for precise definitions of truth.[82] This lesson is certainly not yet fully learnt. Our toleration is at present too often timid, too often rash, sometimes sacrificing valuable religious elements, sometimes fearing its own plainest conclusions. Yet there can be no question that it is gaining on the minds of all educated men, whether Protestant or Roman Catholic, and is passing from them to be the common property of educated and uneducated alike. There are occasions when the spiritual anarchy which has necessarily followed the Reformation threatens for a moment to bring back some temporary bondage, like the Roman Catholic system. But on the whole the steady progress of toleration is unmistakeable. The mature mind of our race is beginning to modify and soften the hardness and severity of the principles which its early manhood had elevated into immutable statements of truth. Men are beginning to take a wider view than they did. Physical science, researches into history, a more thorough knowledge of the world they inhabit, have enlarged our philosophy beyond the limits which bounded that of the Church of the Fathers. And all these have an influence, whether we will or no, on our determinations of religious truth. There are found to be more things in heaven and earth than were dreamt of in the patristic theology. God's creation is a new book to be read by the side of His revelation, and to be interpreted as coming from Him.[83] We can acknowledge the great value of the forms in which the first ages of the Church defined the truth, and yet refuse to be bound by them; we can use them, and yet endeavour to go beyond them, just as they also went beyond the legacy which was left us by the Apostles.

[53] In learning this new lesson, Christendom needed a firm spot on which she might stand, and has found it in the Bible. Had the Bible been drawn up in precise statements of faith, or detailed precepts of conduct, we should have had no alternative but either permanent subjection to an outer law, or loss of the highest instrument of self-education. But the Bible, from its very form, is exactly adapted to our present want. It is a history; even the doctrinal parts of it are cast in a historical form, and are best studied by considering them as records of the time at which they were written, and as conveying to us the highest and greatest religious life of that time. Hence we use the Bible—some consciously, some unconsciously—not to over-ride, but to evoke the voice of conscience. When conscience and the Bible appear to differ, the pious Christian immediately concludes that he has not really understood the Bible. Hence, too, while the interpretation of the Bible varies slightly from age to age, it varies always in one direction. The schoolmen found purgatory in it. Later students found enough to condemn Galileo. Not long ago it would have been held to condemn geology, and there are still many who so interpret it. The current is all one way—it evidently points to the identification of the Bible with the voice of conscience.[84] The Bible, in fact, is hindered by its form from exercising a despotism over the human spirit; if it could do that, it would become an outer law at once; but its form is so admirably adapted to our need, that it wins from us all the reverence of a supreme authority, and yet imposes on us no yoke of subjection. This it does by virtue of the principle of private judgment, which puts conscience between us and the Bible, making conscience the supreme interpreter, whom it may be a duty to enlighten, but whom it can never be a duty to disobey.

[54] This recurrence to the Bible as the great authority has been accompanied by a strong inclination, common to all Protestant countries, to go back in every detail of life to the practices of early times, chiefly, no doubt, because such a revival of primitive practices, wherever possible, is the greatest help to entering into the very essence, and imbibing the spirit of the days when the Bible was written. So, too, the observance of the Sunday has a stronger hold on the minds of all religious men because it penetrates the whole texture of the Old Testament. The institution is so admirable, indeed so necessary in itself, that without this hold it would deserve its present position. But nothing but its prominent position in the Bible would have made it, what it now is, the one ordinance which all Christendom alike agrees in keeping.[85] In such an observance men feel that they are, so far, living a scriptural life, and have come, as it were, a step nearer to the inner power of the book from which they expect to learn their highest lessons. Some, indeed, treat it as enjoined by an absolutely binding decree, and thus at once put themselves under a law. But short of that, those who defend it only by arguments of Christian expediency, are yet compelled to acknowledge that those arguments are so strong that it would be difficult to imagine a higher authority for any ceremonial institution. And among those arguments one of the fore-most is the sympathy which the institution fosters between the student of the Bible and the book which he studies.

55] This tendency to go back to the childhood and youth of the world has, of course, retarded the acquisition of that toleration which is the chief philosophical and religious lesson of modern days.[86] Unquestionably as bigoted a spirit has often been shown in defence of some practice for which the sanction of the Bible had been claimed, as before the Reformation in defence of the decrees of the Church. But no lesson is well learned all at once. To learn toleration well and really, to let it become, not a philosophical tenet but a practical principle, to join it with real religiousness of life and character, it is absolutely necessary that it should break in upon the mind by slow and steady degrees, and that at every point its right to go further should be disputed, and so forced to logical proof. For it is only by virtue of the opposition which it has surmounted that any truth can stand in the human mind. The strongest argument in favour of tolerating all opinions is that our conviction of the truth of an opinion is worthless unless it has established itself in spite of the most strenuous resistance, if necessary. Toleration itself is no exception to the universal law; and those who must regret the slow progress by which it wins its way, may remember that this slowness makes its final victory the more certain and complete. Nor is that all. The toleration thus obtained is different in kind from what it would otherwise have been. It is not only stronger, it is richer and fuller. For the slowness of its progress gives time to disentangle from dogmatism the really valuable principles and sentiments that have been mixed up and entwined in it, and to unite toleration, not with indifference and worldliness, but with spiritual truth and religiousness of life.

56] Even the perverted use of the Bible has therefore not been without certain great advantages. And meanwhile how utterly impossible it would be in the manhood of the world to imagine any other instructor of mankind. And for that reason, every day makes it more and more evident that the thorough study of the Bible, the investigation of what it teaches and what it does not teach, the determination of the limits of what we mean by its inspiration, the determination of the degree of authority to be ascribed to the different books, if any degrees are to be admitted, must take the lead of all other studies. He is guilty of high treason against the faith who fears the result of any investigation, whether philosophical, or scientific, or historical. And therefore nothing should be more welcome than the extension of knowledge of any and every kind—for every increase in our accumulations of knowledge throws fresh light upon these the real problems of our day. If geology proves to us that we must not interpret the first chapters of Genesis literally; if historical investigations shall show us that inspiration, however it may protect the doctrine, yet was not empowered to protect the narrative of the inspired writers from occasional inaccuracy; if careful criticism shall prove that there have been occasionally interpolations and forgeries in that Book, as in many others; the results should still be welcome.[87] Even the mistakes of careful and reverent students are more valuable now than truth held in unthinking acquiescence. The substance of the teaching which we derive from the Bible will not really be affected by anything of this sort. While its hold upon the minds of believers, and its power to stir the depths of the spirit of man, however much weakened at first, must be immeasurably strengthened in the end, by clearing away any blunders which may have been fastened on it by human interpretation.

[57] The immediate work of our day is the study of the Bible. Other studies will act upon the progress of mankind by acting through and upon this. For while a few highly educated men here and there who have given their minds to special pursuits may think the study of the Bible a thing of the past, yet assuredly, if their science is to have any effect upon the men in the mass, it must be by affecting their moral and religious convictions—in no other way have men been, or can men be, deeply and permanently changed. But though this study must be for the present and for some time the centre of all studies, there is meanwhile no study of whatever kind which will not have its share in the general effect. At this time, in the maturity of mankind, as with each man in the maturity of his powers, the great lever which moves the world is knowledge, the great force is the intellect. St. Paul has told us 'that though in malice we must be children, in understanding we ought to be men.'[88] And this saying of his has the widest range. Not only in the understanding of religious truth, but in all exercise of the intellectual powers, we have no right to stop short of any limit but that which nature, that is, the decree of the Creator, has imposed on us. In fact, no knowledge can be without its effect on religious convictions; for if not capable of throwing direct light on some spiritual questions, yet in its acquisition knowledge invariably throws light on the process by which it is to be, or has been, acquired, and thus affects all other knowledge of every kind.

[58] If we have made mistakes, careful study may teach us better. If we have quarrelled about words, the enlightenment of the understanding is the best means to show us our folly. If we have vainly puzzled our intellects with subjects beyond human cognizance, better knowledge of ourselves will help us to be humbler. Life, indeed, is higher than all else; and no service that man can render to his fellows is to be compared with the heavenly power of a life of holiness. But next to that must be ranked, whatever tends to make men think clearly and judge correctly. So valuable, even above all things (excepting only godliness) is clear thought, that the labours of the statesman are far below those of the philosopher in duration, in power, and in beneficial results. Thought is now higher than action, unless action be inspired with the very breath of heaven. For we are now men, governed by principles, if governed at all, and cannot rely any longer on the impulses of youth and the discipline of childhood.

1 Notes to Frederick Temple

1. For "The Education of the World" see Gotthold Ephraim Lessing, *Die Erziehung des Menschengeschlechts* (1777–80; trans. D. W. Robertson, *The Education of the Human Race*, 1858), a collection of 100 aphoristic paragraphs concerning the spiritual evolution of humanity that develops an analogy between the intellectual development of the human species and that of an individual from childhood through youth to maturity. Pascal uses a similar notion in his fragmentary preface to the *Treatise on the Vacuum* (1647; Pascal 1978, 54). Temple uses the same three stages to structure his argument (see ¶8).

In *Self-Help* (1859) Samuel Smiles refers to "that finishing instruction as members of society, which Schiller designated 'the education of the human race,' consisting in action, conduct, self-culture, self-control,—all that tends to discipline a man truly, and fit him for the proper performance of the duties and business of life,—a kind of education not to be learnt from books, or acquired from any amount of mere literary training" ([1859] 1906, 7).

2. Jowett makes a similar argument in *The Epistles of St. Paul* ([1855] 1859, 2:625; quoted in Jowett ¶25 note). For "mere machine" see Browning, *Christmas-Eve and Easter-Day* (1850; sec. 5, l. 40), who makes a similar distinction between "the material world" and "the world of spirits." The distinction is a commonplace of Victorian poetry: see, for instance, Tennyson's "Locksley Hall" (1842; ll. 119–94); Matthew Arnold's *Empedocles on Etna* (1852; 1.2.77–426); and Browning's "Cleon" (1855; ll. 221–72) and "Caliban upon Setebos" (1864; ll. 231–40).

Carlyle in "Signs of the Times" (1829) made the same distinction: "Were we required to characterise this age of ours by any single epithet, we should be tempted to call it, not an Heroical, Devotional, Philosophical, or Moral Age, but, above all others, the Mechanical Age. It is the Age of Machinery, in every outward and inward sense of that word" (Carlyle 1896–99, 27:59). For a recent discussion of this distinction see Sussman 1968.

3. The "beast . . . hidden underneath . . . [the] true humanity" of the "child" may be read in the context of nineteenth-century concepts of acculturation and education. Two instances of the so-called wild child from the early nineteenth century were well known. Victor, the *enfant sauvage*, or wolf-boy, found in central France in 1799, became the subject of the educational experiments of Jean-Marc-Gaspard Itard, one of the precursors to the Montessori schools. He published *Rapports sur le sauvage de l'Aveyron* (1801; trans. *Reports of the Savage of Aveyron*, 1807). Kaspar Hauser, locked in a cellar from his birth without access to speech, appeared in Nuremberg in 1828 and was gradually acculturated. For studies of these cases see Singh and Zingg 1966; Malson 1972; and Maclean 1977.

More generally, the "beast" may be contrasted to the corrupting influence of civilization on the noble savage, exalted by Rousseau and in romantic fiction, such as Chateaubriand's *Atala* (1801) and *René* (1805), and James Fenimore Cooper's *The Last of the Mohicans* (1826). R. M. Ballantyne's *The Coral Island* (1857) inverts the pattern of the wild child's acculturation, demonstrating the ways in which ideas of the savage and education are closely linked to Eurocentric theories of race and progress that structure Temple's argument.

4. Temple's argumentation may be compared with Sir Henry Maine's contemporaneous account of the transition from status to contract in *Ancient Law: Its Connection with the Early History of Society and Its Relation to Modern Ideas* (1861). In drawing continuities between ancient and modern law, Maine also uses a concept of the individual and a principle of collective progress mediated by the law: "The movement of the progressive societies has been uniform in one respect. Through all its course it has been distinguished by the gradual dissolution of family dependency and the growth of individual obligation in its place. The individual is steadily substituted for the family, as the unit of which civil laws take account" ([1861] 1931, 139).

5. In this paragraph Temple conflates the communion of saints ("reaches from the creation to the day of judgment") with the "colossal man," a synecdoche for collective humanity as the body politic. The idea derives from the vast statue of a human being as Apollo, the Colossus of Rhodes, one of the seven wonders of the ancient world (Gibbon [1776–88] 1858, 5:219; chap. 61). The "colossal man" is often associated with political hegemony encapsulated in a single individual, and hence is a threat to the body politic. For example, see Shakespeare, *Julius Caesar* (1.1.134); in the nineteenth century the image as a summary "example . . . colossal" of English virtue is applied to the duke of Wellington in Tennyson's *Ode on the Duke of Wellington* (1852, ll. 220–21). The frontispiece in Thomas Hobbes, *Leviathan, or the Matter, Forme and Power of a Commonwealth, Ecclesiastical or Civil* (1651), depicts a "colossal man" citing the description of the primeval sea monster, Leviathan, associated with political chaos and tyranny in

Job 41. See Williams ¶4, n. 7.

In the philosophy of positivism of Auguste Comte, the "religion of humanity" is located in the past, present, and future of humanity conceived as a "Great Being" (*Cours de philosophie positive* [1830–42, 6 vols. Trans. Harriet Martineau, *Course of Positive Philosophy*. 1853, 2 vols.]). Interpreting the image in this context, Frederic Harrison in the *Westminster Review* placed particular emphasis on Temple's use of "colossal man": "The theory is adopted from Auguste Comte, without acknowledgment and possibly unconsciously. . . . He adopts the positivist conception of mankind as a colossal man possessing life, and growth, and mind. This principle we regard as the most profound truth contained in this entire volume, and we ask no other with which to judge and to test it" (Oct. 1860, 300–305).

6. The generations from Noah (Gen. 10) recount the dispersal of the nations after the destruction of humanity by the flood (Gen. 6–9). The flood demarcates the difference between ante- and post-diluvian time.

"Equality" and "natural faculties" have complex implications that relate both to theology and politics. According to Aristotle in *Politics*, "Equality means, for persons who are alike, [the] identity of status" (bk. 7 chap. 13; trans. H. Rackham, *Loeb* 21:603). Equality as a nineteenth-century political construct, and its relation to education and what Temple calls "development," receives extensive treatment in political and social writers in Britain from the time of the French Revolution. See for instance Mill's *On Liberty* (1859) and *On Representative Government* (1863) and Matthew Arnold's "Equality" (1879). In these essays the limits of "equality" are explicitly drawn: in Mill, the geographical and racial boundaries of Western culture exclude the "East" from what Temple calls "ultimate development"; and in Arnold, the "ultimate development" of the working classes is continually deferred.

Paul extends equality into universalism (Gal. 3:28). As a theological concept, it is further influenced by Augustine's notions of grace, free will, and predestination in *Enchiridion on Faith, Hope and Charity* (chaps. 30–32; trans. J. B. Shaw, *NPNF1* 3:237–76). Equality is redefined by Calvin in *Institutes of the Christian Religion*: "All are not created on equal terms, but some are preordained to eternal life, others to eternal damnation" (bk. 3, chap. 21, sec. 5; [1536] 1957, 2:206).

In Locke's *Essay concerning Human Understanding* (1690) "natural faculties" are among the matters treated which undermine both the basis of traditional Calvinist notions of inequality grounded in predestination, as well as the political and economic basis for inequality derived from hereditary and social factors (bk. 2, chap. 11, sec. 14; chap. 21, secs. 17, 20; [1690] 1975, 161–62, 242, 243–44). The development of the "natural faculties" is a keystone of Arnoldian educational theory. In discussing the reforms to public school education Thomas Arnold brought to Rugby, Stanley writes: "'Can the change from childhood to manhood be hastened, without prematurely exhausting the faculties of body or mind?' was one of the chief questions on which his mind was constantly at work" (Stanley 1844, 1:107–8; citing Arnold's sermon 1 on Christian life, Arnold 1844, 4:19).

7. "Cultivation" by society as a benevolent teacher counterbalances or places "under control" the random operation of "chance." Society and nature as the two scenes of cultivation were conventional from the late seventeenth and eighteenth centuries. For instance, Voltaire's *Candide* (1749) concludes with the communal activity of the reconstituted society cultivating the garden to ensure survival and happiness. The metaphor is used by Stanley in describing Thomas Arnold's concepts of education: "In proportion as he disliked the assumption of a false manliness in boys, was his desire to cultivate in them true manliness, as the only step to something higher, and to dwell on earnest principle and moral thoughtfulness, as the great and distinguishing mark between good and evil" (Stanley 1844, 1:108). For "cultivation" see also Wilson ¶62 and note.

The notion of "chance" as alien to the notion of human reason and the rational order evident in the natural creation under the benevolent control of God is a Victorian commonplace. In Thomas Hardy's "Hap" (1866) a figure of chance, "Crass Casualty" (l. 11), is the determining power in a universe without a supreme being. John M. Robson has recently demonstrated that "chance," the concept used by science to challenge theology over the issue of providential control, is ruled "out in no uncertain terms" throughout the Bridgewater Treatises of 1833–36 (1990, 81): The "idea of chance seems too monstrous to be entertained for a moment by an irrational being" (Prout 1834, 89); "It must be borne in mind that nothing really happens by chance, or is the result of an accidental concourse of fortuitous events" (William Kirby 1835, 1:54); "To say that [effects] are the results of chance conveys no information; and is equivalent to the assertion that they are wholly without a cause" (Roget 1834, 1:20). Darwin's conclusion to *On the Origin of Species* posits laws of progressive development that limit "chance" in the process of the cultivation of species: the "elaborately constructed forms" of the "tangled bank" are cultivated by the operation of "laws acting around us," "powers . . . originally breathed" by a "Creator" ([1859] 1964, 489–90).

8. For "knowledge grows, and knowledge only" compare Tennyson, "Locksley Hall" (1842): "Knowledge comes, but wisdom lingers, and I linger on the shore,/And the individual withers, and the world is more and more" (ll. 141–42).

9. The argument throughout this paragraph parallels the extended passage from Gal. 3:23–4:6. A

cluster of biblical allusions constructs the second half of the paragraph: for "Law" see Rom. (passim); Gal. 3:24; "Son of Man," Ezek. 2:1 ff.; Matt. 8:20 (and passim); "Gift of the Spirit," Acts 3:38, 10:45; "tutors and governors" and "time appointed," Gal. 4:2; "fit seasons," Eccles. 3:1; Luke 12:42; Mark 1:15; Gal. 3:24; "Example . . . ought to be," John 13:15; "to teach men," John 16:13; "Spirit within," Ps. 51:10; Isa. 63:11; Ezek. 11:19.

Temple's discussion of law in the schooling of the child in ¶s 8–14 and notes expands a sentence in Calvin's *Institutes of the Christian Religion*: "'The law of the Lord,' says he [the Psalmist], 'is perfect, converting the soul . . . ' (Psalm xix. 1–9). For though the law has other uses besides . . . the general meaning is, that it is the proper school for training the children of God; the invitation given to all nations, to behold him in the heavens and earth, proving of no avail" ([1536] 1957, 1:67). God as schoolmaster, tutor, and governor was a commonplace in English theology, as, for instance, in William Warburton's *Divine Legation of Moses Demonstrated* (1737–41): "God himself, and not human Reason, was our first Schoolmaster in the rudiments of Speech. . . . Here we have the most natural and familiar image of a Teacher and a learner; where the abilities of the Scholar are *tried* before they are *assisted* . . . [by the] Moral Governor of the World" (bk. 9. chap. 1; Warburton 1811, 6:244–46). Warburton's last phrase, echoed by Temple, was especially familiar through its repeated use in Butler's *Analogy* (1736): see Butler 1896, 1:47–63; and Pattison ¶36 and note. Temple's account may be compared with Gladstone's treatment of Homer and the Bible as religious teachers. Gladstone argues that Homer teaches the role of providence and the capabilities of human nature, while the Bible provides "the moral law, written on the tables of stone, [that] was in one sense a schoolmaster to bring us to Christ" (1858, 2:528). See also Temple's reference in ¶51 to the laws of the medieval church as a "schoolmaster" to bring "some new scholars to Christ."

Commenting on Gal. 3:24 in *The Epistles of St. Paul*, Jowett writes: "The English associations of the word schoolmaster have introduced ideas which have no place in his thoughts. He is not speaking of the part which the law bore in the education of the human race, or of the manner in which the Old Testament prepared the way for the New. He regards the law in one point only, as the slave to whose severe discipline we were subject in the days of our pupilage, nothing differing from slaves in our own condition. To this is opposed the freedom and sonship of the Gospel. In our inferior state, while we were unable to take care of ourselves, the law was our tutor 'for' or 'unto' Christ" ([1855] 1859, 1:330). Note the similarity of Jowett's phrase "the education of the human race" and Temple's title. The dedication of the second edition of Jowett's *The Epistles of St. Paul* is "affectionately inscribed" to Temple.

Temple extends the conventional opposition of the OT and NT, the old and new dispensations, to include a third term, establishing a Trinitarian pattern based on the analogy of human development or growth over time. The Trinity of Father, Son, and Holy Spirit is reformulated in terms of law ("Rules," "Law" of Moses), gospel ("Examples," "Son of Man," Christ's person and actions), and church ("Principles," "the Gift of the Spirit" at Pentecost, taken as the inception of the church).

10. Temple uses a number of ideas from Thomas Arnold's theories of education in his discussion of the role of obedience to rules and law in childhood. For instance, in Arnold's sermon on Gal. 3:24, he develops the notion of the law as a schoolmaster to bring children to Christ (Thomas Arnold 1844, 2:105–15); or in his sermon on 1 Tim. 1:9, he traces the move from law to gospel: "Now all this applies exactly to that earlier and, as it were, preparatory life, which ends not in death, but in manhood. The state of boyhood begins under a law. It is a great mistake to address always the reason of a child, when you ought rather to require his obedience. But we should desire and endeavour to see this state of law succeeded by something better; we should desire so to unfold the love of Christ as to draw the affections towards him" (1844, 4:105).

11. As a theological concept, natural law inheres in human nature to regulate conduct toward God, others, and self: see, for instance, Rom. 2:14; and the discussion of law in Thomas Aquinas, *Summa Theologica* (c. 1270; bk. 2. pt. 1. chap. 90 ff., especially chap. 94).

12. Several biblical allusions underlie this paragraph: for "the earliest wide-spread sin" see the story of Cain, Gen. 4:1–15; 6:11–13; "plague of wickedness," Gen. 6:5; "Lamech's presumptuous comparison," Gen. 4:19–24; "building a tower," Gen. 11:1–9.

13. For "the sin of Noah, Ham" and the "guilty Canaanites" see Gen. 9:20–27; "the sin of . . . Sodom," Gen. 13:13, 19:5; "the sin of . . . Lot's daughter," Gen. 19:30–38.

14. In Gen. 10 and 11 the "nations of the earth" are said to be derived both from the generations of the descendants of Noah, and from the separation into languages resulting from the building of the tower of Babel (Gen. 11:1–9).

For "the world . . . went to school" see Gal. 3:23–25; Eph. 6:4. The idea was a cliché in children's books of moral instruction: see, for instance, Ellinor Fenn, *School Dialogues for Boys* (1783) where she writes of the boy who leaves his mother's side to go "into that LITTLE WORLD, a SCHOOL"; and Elizabeth Sandham, *The School-Fellows* (1818): "The school may be styled the world in miniature" (cited in Pickering 1993, 31; see also chap. on "School Stories," 31–57). See also Temple ¶51 and note.

15. For "prohibitions of murder" see Gen. 9:5–6; Exod. 20:13; for "prohibitions . . . of eating blood,"

Gen. 9:4; Lev. 17:10–16; Deut. 12:16.

16. On the "Jewish nation" see Wilson ¶s 30–32. The "Mosaic system" includes both the "moral" precepts of the Decalogue or Ten Commandments (Exod. 20:1–17) and the "positive" or ceremonial and other ordinances. These are set out in the code of Deuteronomy, concerning the rituals of worship, daily life, and moral conduct. For the "customs" see Deut. 12–26; "festivals," Deut. 16:1–17; "worship," Deut. 12:1–13:19; "daily food," Deut. 14:1–21; "the dress," Deut. 22:5; "the very touch," Deut. 25:11–12. For modern and recent discussions of the "Mosaic system" see Welch 1932; Reider 1937; Nicholson 1967; and Weinfeld 1991.

17. For "the sheep and not the pig" see Lev. 11:7; Deut. 14:4–8; "tattooing" and "disfiguring," Lev. 19:28; "disfiguring," Deut. 23:1; "blue fringe," Num. 15:38–39.

18. This canonical and generic distinction between the "Law" (the Pentateuch) and the "Prophets" (the major prophets, Isa., Jer., and Ezek., and the twelve minor prophets, from Hos. to Mal.) is traditional in biblical interpretation, based partly on Matt. 5:17 and 22:40.

19. For examples of the many occurrences of the topics referred to by Temple see the following: "idolatry," the second commandment (Exod. 20:4–5); "sabbath-breaking," the fourth commandment (Exod. 20:8–11; Neh. 13:15–22; Jer. 17:21–27); "cruelty and oppression," Ezek. 18:7–18; "justice," Isa. 59:4–14; 1 Kings 21:1–22:40; "impurity," the seventh and tenth commandments (Exod 20:14, 17); "intemperance," Jer. 9:20–27; 23:14–15.

20. For "Ezekiel's comment" see Ezek. 8:1–18; 11:14–21; "I am the Lord," Exod. 6:2–8; "Hath not he showed thee," Mic. 6:8.

21. Part of the kingdom of Judah was taken into captivity, or exile, in Babylon in the sixth century B.C.E. The captivity is recounted in 2 Kings 24 and 25 as the punishment of God upon the infidelity of the kings of Israel and Judah both to the obligations of the covenant (with Abraham and Moses) and to the worship of the temple (see 1 Kings 11; 2 Kings 17:7–23). The exile is often interpreted as another banishment from paradise, and was understood by the early church as a type of the Fall, just as the exodus and the return from exile are interpreted typologically as figures of the resurrection and baptism. For a recent discussion of the captivity see Newsome 1979.

22. The Sadducees and Pharisees (along with the Essenes from Qumran, whose writings have survived in the Dead Sea Scrolls) were sects of Judaism (second century B.C.E. to the end of the first century). Specialists in the observance and interpretation of the law and ritual purity, the Sadducees and Pharisees were often linked in the gospels in opposition to Jesus: see Matt. 3:7; 16:6. The Sadducees did not believe in life after death, in angels or spirits, while the Pharisees did (Acts 23:8; Mark 12:18); their beliefs are detailed in Josephus' *Antiquities* (c. 94). The later rabbinic tradition followed the Pharisees. For "strength of sin" see 1 Cor. 15:56.

23. This paragraph continues the contrast between the "Mosaic system" (in Temple ¶15), with its ritual observance of the law and the deuteronomic code, and the Gospel. Paul draws out this contrast in Rom. 3 and Rom. 7:1–25. In developing the contrast, Temple alludes to the transition from the formal observance of the law, ritual, and sacrifice in pre-exilic times. He also refers to the development of religious practice in the exilic and postexilic periods, interpreting it as a loss in formal observance, but a growth in spiritual insight and practice, part of the providential preparation for the coming of Christ that he reads into the history and worship of Israel. Such views were widely accepted when Temple was writing, as in Brook Foss Westcott's *Introduction to the Study of the Gospels*: "The history of the Jews thus becomes as it were the key to the history of the world; and, by regarding the various stages through which it passed, it is possible to distinguish the various constituents which combined to form the character of the Apostles and to prepare men for their teaching" ([1851] 1888, 48).

Temple alludes in particular to daily temple ritual (Lev. 6:8–23; Exod. 30:7–36; Lev. 24:1–4), the rituals of animal and cereal sacrifice (Lev. 1:1–7:38), and the study of the Bible, especially the law. Prayer is not an enjoined part of worship in the Pentateuch, and is only mentioned for the priestly benediction (Num. 6:24–26) and the prayer over the first fruits and tithes (Deut. 26:3–15). The prophets stressed the significance of spiritual rather than ritual purity, and the importance of prayer over sacrifice in the context of altruistic motives and ethical observance (Isa. 1:15–17; Hos. 6:6; Amos 5:21–24; Mic. 6:8). This paragraph spans more than a millennium, from the monarchy of David in the tenth century B.C.E. to the fall of Jerusalem in the first century. David ruled Israel (1 Sam. 16:13–1 Kings 2:12) from 1010–970 B.C.E. The first temple was erected in the tenth century B.C.E. under David's son, Solomon; it was destroyed during the Babylonian conquest of Judah (586 B.C.E.), during which it is conjectured synagogue worship, including the reading of the law, was begun (Ezek. 11:16; 14:1; Neh. 6; 1 Macc. 3:48). The temple was rebuilt (520–515 B.C.E.), and was enlarged as the Third Temple (37 B.C.E.–4). This temple was destroyed during the siege of Jerusalem (70). For discussion of the temple and its worship see Parrot 1957; and Haran 1978.

The whole of the book of Psalms is attributed to David in the title of the book in the AV, but only seventy-three psalms are specifically identified as "a Psalm of David" (and fourteen more in the LXX; Ps. 72:18–19 is a coda that consists of a conclusion or closing of the Davidic psalter, except for Ps. 86). The book of Psalms is composed of five collections, with different titles and ascriptions (for instance, to the sons or guild of Korah, Ps. 42–49; 84–85; 87–88; or of Asaph, Ps. 50; 73–83). The attribution to "David" as the traditional founder of Hebrew poetry is also connected to a guild of psalm-writers under the patronage of David (1 Sam. 16:18; Amos 6:5). Personal references concerning the life of David (for instance, in the title of Ps. 3) are qualified by other references to later dates (in Ps. 3:5, "my holy mountain" refers to a period after the building of the Temple of Solomon). Many of these and other psalms are dated as long as half a millennium after David, from the exilic period when temple worship was impossible, or from the postexilic period when the temple was rebuilt about 538 B.C.E. (Ezra 3:1–13) and when the study of the law and temple sacrifice were renewed (Ezra 7:10, 25 and Neh. 8:1–8). Ps. 119 is especially concerned with the praise of the law.

John the Baptist, who "came to prepare the way" for Jesus, preached repentance for sin and baptized his followers in the Jordan, including Jesus (Matt. 3:1–17). He was beheaded by command of Herod Antipas, tetrarch of Galilee (Matt. 14:1–12 and parallels).

24. Paul discusses "the unity and spirituality of God" in Greek philosophy in his sermon on Mars Hill at the Acropolis of Athens, referring to the Greek philosophers and poets Aratus and Cleanthes, both of the third century B.C.E. (Acts 17:28). Browning cites the same passage as the epigraph to "Cleon" (1854), a poem on an imaginary Greek philosopher-poet who hears Paul preach.

25. For "the repeated idolatries" see 2 Kings 21:11–21; Ezek. 6; 20:7–19.

26. "Primitive Church" is used to describe the earliest, and ostensibly the purest, state of the Christian church: the Christian community of the first century, both as the organic inheritor of Judaism and as a new movement amongst the non-Jewish, or Gentile, communities of the Hellenistic culture of the Mediterranean, dominated by the Roman Empire under Augustus (27 B.C.E.–14) and his immediate successors to Nero (54–68), Vespasian (69–79), and Titus (79–81). The term is used in the *BCP* in the Commination service: "Brethren, in the primitive Church there was a godly discipline, that, at the beginning of Lent, such persons as were notorious Sinners, were put to open penance and punished in this world, that their souls might be saved in the day of the Lord." This text was used as early as 1549 in the *First Prayer Book of Edward VI.* "Primitive Church" was used widely in the seventeenth and eighteenth centuries to indicate a reforming program of return to first principles, free from later corrupting practices and the complications of theological debate, as in William Whiston's *Primitive Christianity Revived* 1711, 4 vols.) and Edmund Burke's comment in 1795, I wish very much to see . . . an image of a primitive Christian Church" (1844, 4:285). The Primitive Methodist Church was established in 1811 as a breakaway group claiming a return to foundational principles in both the Wesleys and the early church. For a contemporary account see Petty 1860. For modern studies of the primitive church, Streeter 1929; and Goguel 1964.

27. For "sins of the flesh" see Col. 2:11; "war against the soul," 1 Pet. 2:11. For "sins of the flesh" and "deadly sin" see the Litany (*BCP*): "From fornication, and all other deadly sin; and from all the deceits of the world, the flesh, and the devil, good Lord deliver us." The terms *type* and *example* are closely linked here, a point to which Temple returns in ¶s 28–29 and 33.

28. The Epistle of James is written "to the twelve tribes which are scattered abroad" (James 1:1). Peter alludes to his readers' "former lusts" (1 Pet. 1:13) and "fleshly lusts, which war against the soul" (1 Pet. 2:12).

29. Both the Apostles' (its title first found in a letter of Ambrose, c. 390) and the Nicene creeds (325), summarizing the beliefs of the early church, begin with a profession of monotheism. For recent discussions of Israel and the development of monotheism see Lang 1983; and *Monotheism* 1985. For "chastity" see Exod. 20:14.

30. Temple's alignment of "monotheism" with "discipline" and "conscience" in the religious traditions of the Hebrews is a commonplace of nineteenth-century cultural debates. Matthew Arnold gives this association a canonical formulation in *Culture and Anarchy* (1867), setting up oppositions between "the Greek" and "the Hebrew," between Hellenism and Hebraism, between "beauty" and "conscience." Beauty and Reason ("sweetness" and "light") structure Arnold's first chapter; Hebraism and Hellenism, the fourth (see M. Arnold 1960–77, 5:165, 168–69). Temple sets up the same opposition in ¶26.

The series of oppressors of the "Hebrews" spans 3,000 years: from the Pharaohs of the slavery of the Israelites in Egypt under Sety I and Rameses II (thirteenth century B.C.E.); the Assyrian kings of the exile, Tiglath-Pileser III and Shalmaneser V (eighth century B.C.E.); the Roman Caesars from Titus to Nero (first century); the Muslim caliph Omar, who conquered Syria and Palestine (637–41), to the continuation of Muslim control under the Ottoman Turks until the Treaty of Paris (30 Mar. 1856), which ended the Crimean War (1854–56); and Turkish hegemony over Palestine, Syria, and other areas of the eastern Mediterranean that continued until the end of World War I.

31. For "seed . . . first sown" see the parable of the sower, Matt. 13:3–20.

In aligning national characteristics to racial traits in four chief divisions, Temple is consistent with the historiography of Thomas Arnold and others. In reference to Arnold's *History of Rome* (1838–42, 3 vols.), Rosemary Jann argues: "He follows the romantic historians lead in seeking 'national personality' in phenomena such as race, language, religion and institutions" (1985, 24). Temple's treatment of each of these characteristics is dealt with in separate notes below.

32. Rome was both the administrative and legal center of the Roman Empire as well as an important locus of early Christianity. Roman legislative power and ideals of government vested in the authority of the Roman emperors were gradually assumed by the bishops of Rome in their government of church affairs in the western Mediterranean. Their claims to power were fortified on four grounds: first, Rome was the traditional site of the martyrdom of Peter and Paul whose deaths were interpreted as a sanctification of the early Christian community; second, the committing of the "keys" of heaven and earth to Peter by Christ (Matt. 16:19) gave to Rome and to the successors of Peter pre-eminence among early Christian communities; third, the martyrdoms of Christian leaders such as Ignatius in the Roman persecutions under Nero and his successors provided a testimonial basis for Roman church doctrine; and fourth, the writings of Roman bishops such as the first and second epistles of Clement (c. 96) re-enforced the assertions of headship in the church. For discussion of the establishment of the "Bishop of Rome" as "the Head of the Church" see Vaillancourt 1980; and Cheetham 1983, 8–20.

In England the designation "Head of the Church" has connotations that refer less to the papal authority than to the break with Rome, when by the Act of Supremacy (1534) Henry VIII was declared to be "the only supreme head in earth of the Church of England."

33. These "doctrinal disputes," largely concerned with the definition of the nature of Christ, occupied the theological agenda of the church from the Council of Nicaea (325), presided over by Constantine, to the Council of Chalcedon (451). At Chalcedon the theological problems were resolved by the orthodox *Tome* of Leo I, whose authority was expressed in the maxim: "Peter has spoken through Leo." For a comprehensive survey of these disputes see Young 1983.

34. Charlemagne, crowned first emperor of the Holy Roman Empire on Christmas Day, 800 by Pope Leo III, established an efficient centralized government for the administration of law throughout the empire by capitularies enforced by special imperial emissaries. His educational reforms were carried out by his court scholars presided over by Alcuin of York.

35. Temple alludes to three conventional historical sources for English "liberty" and "modern politics": first, the codification of Roman "laws" under Justinian I in 529, the impact of which is summarized in Gibbon's *Decline and Fall* (chap. 44); second, the "spirit of modern politics" as derived "from Greece," generally attributed by Victorian writers to Athenian democracy summarized in the funeral oration of Pericles, delivered in 431 B.C.E. for those who died in the Peloponnesian War, as well as in the Athenian constitution (see Frank M. Turner 1981, 187–264); and third, "the woods of Germany," a reference to the Germanic peoples who invaded the Roman Empire from as early as the third century. According to Gibbon: "The most civilized nations of modern Europe issued from the woods of Germany; and in the rude institutions of those barbarians we may still distinguish the original principles of our present laws and manners" ([1776–88] 1858, 1:250). For a discussion of the "freedom" of the "Teutonic Churches" see Wilson ¶35 and note.

Temple is again consistent with the historiography of Thomas Arnold. According to Rosemary Jann, in Arnold's *History of Rome* (1838–42, 3 vols.) he "follows his contemporaries in assuming that certain political traits were innate to certain 'races.' The love of institutions and order, the reverence for law, and the subordination of individual to social good characterized the Greeks and the Romans, needing only the addition of Teutonic morality and domestic virtue to produce a racial mixture uniquely suited to promote Arnold's ideal Christian democracy" (1985, 24).

36. For "whatsoever things" see Phil. 4:8.

37. At the beginning of *Nichomachean Ethics* Aristotle sets out "the Beautiful (τὸ καλόν [*to kalon*])" or the good as the aim of every study: "Every art and every investigation, and likewise every practical pursuit or undertaking, seems to aim at some good: hence it has been well said that the Good [*to kalon*] is that at which all things aim. . . . Now our treatment of this science [Ethics] will be adequate, if it achieves that amount of precision which belongs to its subject matter. . . . The subjects studied by political science are Moral Nobility [*kalon*] and Justice" (bk. 1, chap. 1, sec. 1; chap. 3, sec. 1–2; trans. H. Rackham, *Loeb* 19:3–7). Similarly, in the *Poetics* Aristotle's opening sentence outlines his topic as a study of the kinds and functions of poetry and of how poetic plots must be constructed to be beautiful (*kalos*) (chap. 1; trans. W. Hamilton Fyfe, *Loeb* 5). Temple's qualification—"even Aristotle"—indicates that the canonical site for classical discussion on *kalon* is elsewhere. Plato discusses the beautiful as a mode of knowledge. In the *Symposium*, for instance, beauty is a means of ascending toward the highest good: all are said to desire the beautiful (*kalos*) and to possess it, and so may come "to know the very essence of beauty," the highest good (207c ff.; trans. W. R. M. Lamb, *Loeb* 5:211). Making reference to these same passages, and to Plato's *Alcibiades II* (145c), George Berkeley draws out the moral implications of the beautiful as the good in his treatise *Alciphron* of 1732 (Berkeley 1948–56, 3:118).

38. Solon inaugurated a reform of the Athenian

constitution from 594 B.C.E. Alexander consolidated his power as the ruler of Greece (334 B.C.E.) and defeated the Persians in 333 B.C.E. These boundaries, "barely covering 200 years," with the Periclean age as the culmination of Greek culture, were being contested by Temple's contemporaries: for instance, George Grote argues in *A History of Greece* (1846–56) that there was no empirical evidence for the history of Greece before the First Olympiad in 776 B.C.E., while Gladstone emphasizes prehistoric and protohistoric aspects of Greek culture in *Homer and the Homeric Age* (1858). For recent discussions of these issues and the Victorian debate on Homer see Jenkyns 1980, 73–77 and Frank M. Turner 1981, 187–264.

39. For a discussion of the opposition between the Greek and the Hebrew in Victorian culture, see Temple ¶22 and note. For an analysis of this opposition see Delaura 1969.

40. Temple uses a transferred epithet, taking the notion of Greek "fire," a combustible substance used in naval encounters by the Byzantine Greeks in the seventh century, and applying it to the ways in which classical Greek culture is communicated to "kindle other nations." A recent book on classical civilization, published as a companion piece to a popular television series, conveys a similar notion with its title: see Taplin 1989.

41. Temple's earlier opposition between "Greek" and "Hebrew" is now subsumed into a general category, "Europe," which is then opposed to "Asia." This opposition constructs "Europe" as a natural principle of dynamic progress with which he aligns his readers, and "Asia" as one of static subjugation. As a transparent category assumed by many nineteenth-century writers, "Asia" suppresses all differences. "Asia," or "the East," or "the Orient" as an ahistorical concept collapses vast geographical spaces and six or seven millennia, with highly diverse cultural and religious affiliations, into a single entity. Edward Said calls this process "Orientalism" ([1978] 1979).

A. P. Stanley uses an almost identical construction in his 1857 lectures on the Eastern Church: "The Eastern Church was, like the East, stationary and immutable; the Western, like the West, progressive and flexible. . . . [The] peculiar corruptions [of the 'Oriental Church'] have been such as are consequent not on development but on stagnation; its peculiar excellences have been such as belong to the simplicity of barbarism, not to the freedom of civilisation" ([1861] 1924, 75–76).

42. Temple alludes to the "monarchs" of secular history: the empire of Assyria on the upper Tigris with its capital at Nineveh (c. 1000–612 B.C.E.) under Tiglath-Pileser III (745–727 B.C.E.); the empire of Babylon in the sixth century B.C.E. under Nebuchadnezzar II; and the empire of Persia in the sixth and fifth centuries B.C.E. under Darius I and Xerxes. The Persian empire was defeated by the Greeks at Marathon (490 B.C.E.) and Salamis (480 B.C.E.); see Herodotus, *History* (bk. 3 chap. 89; bk. 7, chap 7; trans. A. D. Godley, *Loeb* 2:116–17; 306–9); and Aeschylus, *Persae* (472 B.C.E.). This sequence is paralleled in the biblical accounts of these conquests: Assyria (2 Kings 15), Babylon and the destruction of Jerusalem and the exile (2 Kings 25; Jer. 39), and Persia (Dan. 10), with the desecration of the temple (Dan 5:31) under the Graeco-Syrian king Antiochus IV Epiphanes (Dan 11:31).

Temple groups these Mesopotamian empires together primarily as the ancient Asian conquerors of the Hebrews, but also within the typology of the Oriental despot, aligning nineteenth-century Europe with the ancient Hebrews by relating their oppression as a cultural imposition "on us." For this type and its political implications in historical and social theory see Lichtheim 1967, 62–93.

43. For "undreamt of in our philosophy" see Shakespeare, *Hamlet* (1.5.167). In the Hebrew scriptures the connection between the body and the spirit is not severed at death (Gen. 3:9). The notion of an afterlife for the soul developed among the Hebrews during the Babylonian exile of the sixth century B.C.E. Its clearest statements are in the collective restoration of the remnant of Israel (Jer. 31), the clothing of the dry bones with flesh after the exile (Ezek. 37), and individual immortality (Dan. 12:1–2; Wisd. 1:12–3:19). For a discussion of the Hebrew notion of the afterlife see Nickelsburg 1972; and Gowan 1986. For a discussion of Hebrew wisdom literature and its relation to Greek concepts of immortality see Reese 1970, 62–71.

Hellenistic Greek influence on Jewish thought derives from earlier Greek discussions of the "doctrine of the Immortality of the Soul." For instance, see Plato, especially in *Phaedo* (63e–69e; 80c–84b; trans. H. N. Fowler, *Loeb* 1:221–41; 279–93). Jowett's edition of *The Dialogues of Plato* has a long commentary on the immortality of the soul in Plato, the Bible, and modern philosophy ([1871] 1875, 1:409–28). For a survey of nineteenth-century thought on the Platonic notion of immortality Gaye 1904; for a recent discussion see Bostock 1986, 21–41.

The Pharisees are associated, as in Dan. 12:1–2 and 1 Macc. 2–4, with the time of Judas Maccabeus and his revolt against Antiochus Epiphanes IV (167 B.C.E.). Their beliefs in immortality are discussed by Josephus in *Jewish Wars* (bk. 2, chaps. 162–66) and *Antiquities* (bk. 18, chaps. 11–22); and are referred to at Acts 23:6–9 and Mark 12:18–27.

44. Athanasius led the orthodox Christians in defining the divinity of Christ and Trinitarian theology against Arianism at the Councils of Nicaea (325) and Alexandria (362). The heresy named after Arius held that Christ was not, as Athanasius maintained, co-eternal and co-equal with the person of the Father, but was a separate creation, brought into being to be the instrument for the creation of the world. He had sonship conferred on him by God because of his

righteousness. Arianism stressed Christ's humanity and mutability against the idea implied in Athanasius' famous term *homoousios* (Gk. of the same substance), asserting that Christ was of the "same substance," or consubstantial with the Father and the Holy Spirit. Athanasius is the subject of lecture 7 of Stanley's *Lectures on the History of the Eastern Church*, delivered in 1857 (Stanley [1861] 1924, 227–53).

45. "Asia" as "mysterious" is a commonplace among Temple's contemporaries. In Disraeli's *Tancred, or the New Crusade* (1847), the young hero goes to the Holy Land "to penetrate the great Asian mystery" (chaps. 17, 22; Disraeli 1904, 15:160, 213), in order to find answers to his questions: "What is duty, and what is faith? What ought I to do, and what ought I to believe?" (chap. 7; 1904, 15:70). In the lecture on Constantine in *Le Christianisme au quatrième siècle*, Gasparin (discussed in Wilson ¶2) writes that "L'Orient s'est toujours distingué par une tendance théologique, par une aspiration à l'explication des mystères" (The Orient is itself always distinguished by a theological tendency, by an aspiration toward the explication of mysteries; *Le Christianisme* 1858, 29). In 1857 Stanley comments on the "distinction" between "the speculative tendency of the Oriental and the practical tendency of the Western Church," between "the savage energy and freedom of Europe, and the intellectual repose and apathy of Asia" ([1861] 1924, 71).

Temple's emphasis upon the "mysteries" of Asia, his qualified dismissal or relegation of Asiatic culture to "baseless dreams" and "monstrous and revolting fictions," may be read in the context of discussions concerning the imperial role of Great Britain. In the "Minute on Indian Education" (1835), Macaulay, unlike Temple, dismisses outright all of Sanskrit and Arabic literature: "All the historical information which has been collected from all the books written in the Sanskrit language is less valuable than what may be found in the most paltry abridgments used at preparatory schools in England." He argues that no one "could deny that a single shelf of a good European library was worth the whole native literature of India and Arabia": European "intrinsic superiority" extends "from works of imagination to works in which facts are recorded and general principles investigated," where "the superiority of the Europeans becomes absolutely immeasurable." Macaulay goes on to use phrases similar to Temple's, referring to "monstrous superstitions" and "false history, false astronomy, false medicine, . . . [and] false religion" (Macaulay 1972, 241–43; 248).

46. Temple's argument now shifts from pre-Christian history to emphasize the history of the individual child: in ¶33 the transition from childhood to adolescence is made analogous ("corresponds, of course") to that from the Hebrew to the Christian scriptures. "Discipline" is used to educate in childhood, "example" in adolescence. The term "discipline" occurs thirty-four times in Temple's essay, usually related, as in the last phrase of the essay, to the education of childhood, or with respect to some period in the history of the human race that Temple considers to be the childhood of humanity. He is making use of two related notions here. The first is the Puritan notion of the role of discipline in the education of children by curbing the will. C. John Sommerville discusses "this problem of training without crushing the will that made discipline the central feature of the child-rearing manuals," such as Robert Cleaver's *A Godly Form of Household Government* (1598), the most-frequently reprinted parental handbook for the guidance of parents in the seventeenth century (1992, 95–96). The same ideas concerning discipline occur in Anglican sources, such as Richard Allestree's *The Whole Duty of Man* (1677), and in secular treatises such as John Locke's *Some Thoughts concerning Education* (1693).

The second notion, for older children and adolescents, is the use of "example" (used twenty-five times by Temple throughout this essay) upon which to model behavior. "Example" occurs a number of times in the NT to translate one of two Greek words, ὑπόδειγμα (*hupodeigma*) or τύπος (*tupos*). The former refers to that which is set forth as a document, proof, model or paradigm, as in John 13:15; the latter derives from the word for a blow or strike: hence, an impression, an image or figure, a pattern as in Heb. 8:5; 1 Cor. 10:6, 11; and 1 Tim. 4:12. For a discussion of these biblical terms see Kittel 1964–76, 2:32–33; 8:246–59. In ¶29 Temple uses both senses, first as an active process in which the child initiates the action: "he imitates" and "he . . . copies"; in the second, where the child is acted upon: "it will deeply engrave" and "among whom the life is cast."

Locke writes on the impact of "Example" on the education of children in *Some Thoughts concerning Education* [1693] 1989, sec. 71. Throughout the eighteenth and nineteenth centuries, children's books were full of "examples" or models of moral virtue and warnings against worldly vice, as, for instance, Thomas Day's *History of Sandford and Merton* (1783–89, frequently reprinted throughout the nineteenth century), Mary Pilkington's *Biography for Boys, or Characteristic Histories Calculated to Impress the Youthful Mind with an Admiration of Virtuous Principles and a Detestation of Vicious Ones* (1809), and Elizabeth Somerville, *The History of Little Charles and His Friend Frank Wilful* (1808). For a discussion of the didactic example in children's literature see Pickering 1993.

The notion of teaching by example is one of the concepts of public-school education that Temple derived from Thomas Arnold: "But the danger of the intermediate state between childhood and manhood is often this, that whilst in the one point of teachableness, the change runs on too fast, in the other three of wisdom, of unselfishness, and of thoughtfulness, proceeds much too slowly: that the faults of childhood thus remain in the character, whilst that quality by means of which these faults are meant to be corrected,—namely, teachableness,—is at the same time diminishing." (1844, 4:16–17). The example or pattern of such teachableness and of life is Christ: "It hardly matters what particular chapter of the Gospels we open, for Christ's life is in every part of it more or less our pattern. . . . And therefore, Christ's example is the more needed" (1844, 3:29).

The concept of example as the "best teacher" was the method upon which Samuel Smiles structured *Self-Help* as a manual that helped young people to both discover and accept their place in English society through the method of exemplification. The citation of hundreds of examples of success stories, overwhelmingly of men, also provided a strong incentive for self-improvement. "Examples—Models" (chap. 12) begins: "Example is one of the most potent of instructors, though it teaches without a tongue. It is the practical school of mankind, working by action, which is always more forcible than words" ([1859] 1906, 423). For a recent discussion of the role of *Self-Help* in the sociology of cultural controls in Victorian England see Royden Harrison 1968, 261–75.

For "tutors and governors" see Gal 4:6.

47. In his sermon on Gal. 3:24 to Rugby schoolboys, Thomas Arnold discusses the "character of the young": "Unquestionably, the time of life at which you are arrived, and more particularly the younger boys among you, is, in itself, exceedingly dangerous. It is just the time, beyond all others in life, when temptation is great, and the strength of character to resist it exceedingly small. Earlier, under your parents' roof, the taint of evil reached you with far less virulence,—you were surrounded with all influences of good. Later, you will be exposed, indeed, to enough of evil, but you will have gained at least more experience, and more strength of mind, to resist it" (Thomas Arnold 1844, 2:112). Arnold goes on to discuss what Temple calls "the moral atmosphere . . . brutish indeed": "The system [of unreformed Public School education] also was too much one of fear and outward obedience; the obedience of the heart and the understanding was little thought of" (Thomas Arnold 1844, 2:113–14).

48. For "supplies to the imperfection" see Horace, *Ars Poetica* (l. 351; trans. H. R. Fairclough, *Loeb* 479).

49. The transition from childhood to youth and to manhood, from rules or law to example and to principle, is expounded in a number of places in the writings of Thomas Arnold, for instance in his sermon on Luke 21:36, commenting on the transition from childhood to youth and manhood, "when principle takes the place of innocence. . . . And, then, this second beginning of life, resting on faith and conscious principle, and not on mere passive innocence, stands sure for the middle and the end [of life]" (1844, 4:117–19).

50. For "the form of godliness without the power thereof" see 2 Tim. 3:5. For "a bright spot to which the memory . . . loves to recur," compare William Wordsworth's discussion of the "spots of time" in *The Prelude* (1850), where "memory" functions not only to give pleasure, but also to re-enforce the hegemony of reason (bk. 12, ll. 208–25). For "seed time" see Gen. 8:22; and compare *The Prelude* (1850; bk. 1, ll. 301–2, occurring at the point of transition between childhood and the poet's going to Hawkshead Grammar School); "promise of the year . . . crown its blessings," Ps. 65:11; "the time for . . . ," Eccles. 3.

51. The relationship between friendship and happiness is discussed by Aristotle in *Nichomachean Ethics* (bks. 8 and 9) and by Cicero in *De Amicitia* (c. 44 B.C.E.; On friendship): "Friendship was given to us by nature as the handmaid of virtue. . . . In such a partnership, I say, abide all things that men deem worthy of pursuit—honour and fame and delightful tranquillity of mind; so that when these blessings are at hand life is happy, and without them it cannot be happy" (chap. 22, secs. 83–84; trans. W. A. Falconer, *Loeb* 20:191). For "heat of youth" see Tennyson, *In Memoriam* (1850; sec. 53, l. 10).

52. See Rom. 8:22.

53. The passage from ¶33, "The faculty of faith . . . truth of God," was cited as one of the "false and dangerous statements, and reasonings at variance with the teaching of the Church of England" that comprised the grounds for the Synodical Condemnation of *Essays and Reviews* on 21 June 1864. As well, Temple's general argument in this paragraph is condemned as "denying the probability of the recognition of the Divinity of our Lord in the more matured age of the world . . . [involving a] denial of all miracles as historical facts" (*Chronicle* 1859–64:1864, Session 66, 1657).

54. For "'fulness of time'" see Gal. 4:4; "Express Image," Heb. 1:3; "Thou art the Christ," Matt. 16:16.

55. For "the title" see Paul's claim to Apostleship for having been one of those who had seen Jesus in his vision on the road to Damascus (Acts 9; 1 Cor. 9:1; 15:8).

56. Temple is adopting a widespread Victorian convention of reading history according to the model of typological interpretation of the Bible, wherein secular history is marked by a division between the history of the Jews and the advent of Christ. He locates the originary moment for Western Christian civilization at the conventional mark between the pre- and post-Christian eras (summarized in the traditional dating practices of "B.C." and "A.D."). Within this convention, history before Christ, and especially as recorded in the Hebrew scriptures, is read as the *preparatio evangelium*, the preparation for the Gospel, as Eusebius of Caesarea titled his treatise on this subject written in the early fourth century. Westcott

titles the first chapter of his introductory handbook "The Preparation for the Gospel," in which he writes: "Even when the divine power was withdrawn from visible operation, it was no less certainly engaged in bringing within its control new powers, and opening new fields for its future work. The end itself came only with the *fulness of time.*" He concludes: "A missionary nation was waiting to be charged with the heavenly commission, and a world was unconsciously prepared to welcome it" ([1851] 1888, 51–52; 84).

The division of time and history at the moment of Christ's birth is also a division between promise and fulfillment, referring to a particular mode of reading by typologies: the Hebrew scriptures are interpreted as a prefiguration or foreshadowing, as signifiers whose true signified is unknown except prophetically until "the fulness of time" in the life of Christ and the church. The point concerning fulfillment is made at the beginning of Mark (1:14–15). Sanction for such typological readings is given in the NT through the use of the word *pattern* (Gk. τύπος, *tupos*; see Temple ¶28 and note) as at Heb. 8:5.

Rowland Williams reacts against such typological readings, citing passages from Justin Martyr and Irenaeus that interpret the prophecies in Isaiah as detailed prefigurations of events in the life of Christ (Williams ¶13). For a recent discussion of periodization and the division of time before and after Christ, first used in the Easter calculations of Dionysius Exiguus (525) and popularized by the Venerable Bede, see Shepherd 1968.

57. Temple refers to the four Gospels that tell the life of Christ. The first three, Matthew, Mark, and Luke are said to be "synoptic" in that they recount Christ's life from birth to death and resurrection. John's gospel begins with a prologue on the divine word or *logos*, and then introduces his narrative of Christ's last years, beginning with the miracle at the marriage feast at Cana. Each gospel has an accounts of parables and miracles, and each tells the passion story from the "Last Supper" to "Calvary," though with differences, particularly between the synoptics and John. The "Sermon on the Mount," however, is recounted only in Matt. 5–7. The much shorter parallel in Luke (6:17, 20–49) locates the sermon on a plain; Mark and John have no parallel sermon.

58. Plato in *Phaedrus* gives a legendary account of the invention of arithmetic and writing and of how they were taught to the human race by Theuth, an Egyptian god (274c; trans. H. N. Fowler, *Loeb* 1:561–63).

For "captains of science" compare Carlyle who uses the phrase "Captain of Industry" to describe his industrialist, Plugson of Undershot, in *Past and Present* ([1843] 1977, 193, 267–73).

59. Temple makes conventional general comparisons eulogizing Shakespeare and Gibbon above the Greek and Roman poets and historians. The specific comparison placing Francis Bacon above Aristotle, is based, perhaps, on Bacon's several qualifications of Aristotelianism in *The Advancement of Learning*; see, for instance, the discussion of "natural history" (bk. 1, chap. 4, sec. 10; Bacon [1605] 1973, 29).

60. The comparison between "the moderns" and "the ancients" invokes the late seventeenth- and early eighteenth-century battle over literary models, in the context of a similar struggle that involved the reform of curriculum at Oxford and Cambridge in the nineteenth century. In France the long-standing rivalry of classical and modern writers as authorities became a subject of literary controversy. The *Querelle des anciens et des modernes* (Quarrel of the ancients and the moderns) was inaugurated by the defense of the moderns by Charles Perrault in *Le Siècle de Louis le Grand* (1687; The century of Louis the great), comparing his age favorably against that of Augustus. His position, extended in *Parallèle des anciens et des modernes* (1688–97; Parallel of the ancients and the moderns), was supported by Bernard de Fontenelle in *La Digression sur les anciens et les modernes* (1688; Digression on the ancients and the moderns). The case for the classical writers was argued by Jean de la Fontaine in *L'Épître à Huet* (1687; Letter to Huet) and by Nicolas Boileau in *Reflexions critique sur quelques passages du rhétor Longin* (1694; Critical reflections on some passages in Longinus). In England the more temperate dialogue of Dryden in *An Essay of Dramatic Poesy* (1668) also became controversial when Sir William Temple published *Essay upon the Ancient and Modern Learning* (1690) defending the classical writers. He was attacked by William Wotton in *Reflections upon Ancient and Modern Learning* (1694) and *A Defense of Reflections* (1697), an exchange that eventually involved many writers in concerning the dating and works of Phalaris. This exchange was satirized by Jonathan Swift in *The Battle of the Books* (1704). For the *querelle* see Richard Foster Jones 1975; and Levine 1991. See also Pattison ¶47 and note.

Powell, Jowett, and Pattison were all involved in reform of the curriculum, teaching, and responsibilities of fellows at Oxford, and, despite a profound commitment to the classics, were also resolved to introduce the modern study of history and the sciences. Stanley too was involved, as the secretary to the Gladstone Commission for reform at Oxford (1852). For contemporary accounts of these debates at Oxford and Cambridge see Pattison 1855; and Grote 1856. For recent accounts see Clarke 1959; W. R. Ward 1965, 180–234; and Brink 1985, 114–50.

61. "Early Church" is a general term to designate the Christian church of the first several centuries

of the Christian era, sometimes divided into the "primitive" church (see Temple ¶54), encompassing the community described in the Christian scriptures (to c. 100), and the early church, to the end of the conciliar period at the Council of Chalcedon (451). For a history of the early church see Henry Chadwick 1967. Temple links the life of Christ and the life of the church, a link established in the Pauline writings through the trope of the church as the body of Christ (see, for instance, Rom. 12:5; 1 Cor. 12:12–30; Eph. 4:4–6, 5:23; Col. 1:18–24).

62. For "be ye followers" see 1 Cor. 4:6; "I also am of Christ," 1 Cor. 11:1; "the work . . . was peculiar," Titus 2:14; 1 Pet. 2:9; "prohibition to eat things strangled," Acts 15:29; "zeal," 2 Cor. 7:11; "love of God," Rom. 5:5 and passim; "joy in the Holy Ghost," Rom. 14:17; 1 Thess. 1:6; "the sake of Christ," 2 Cor. 12:10; "go and do thou likewise," Luke 10:37.

63. Temple praises early Christian practices of sharing possessions and food, such as apostolic communism ("all things in common," see Acts 2:44) and the shared meal or love feast ("nor are we to make every supper," 1 Cor. 11: 20–21), to be distinguished from the "Lord's supper"; he contrasts them with disputes and controversies in the apostolic church, such as those referred to in Eph. 4–5 and Col., arguing that the latter are dissipated by the "saintliness of that time." For "brightness of her glory" see Heb. 1:3; "simplicity," 2 Cor. 1:12; "singleness of heart," Acts 2:46; Eph. 6:5; Col. 3:22.

64. Trajan, Roman emperor from 98 to 117, revised the imperial administration and conducted an extensive rebuilding program in Rome, culminating in the Forum and column which bear his name. His "two persons" are those of the "profane" classical historians (like Pliny), who praise his military, civil, administrative and architectural achievements for the Roman Empire, and the "sacred" historians (like Eusebius), who condemn his continuing the persecution of Christians.

The distinction between sacred and profane history extends Temple's dualism of biblical and classical cultures, of church and state. The "Sub-introduction . . . Of the Claims and Uses of Sacred History" to the volumes on history in the *Encyclopaedia Metropolitana* asserts: "Sacred History is that narrative of events, commencing from the creation of the world, which is recorded in the Bible, and is so called, because it is assumed to be written under divine superintendence, and is evidently associated with the being, perfections, and plans of Deity. All other History details facts simply, but Sacred History combines them with the doctrine of providence and demonstrates the event to be coincident with the purposes of an infinite mind" ([1817–1845] 1849, 9:73). The major influence on Western historiographic constructions of the sacred and profane is Augustine's *City of God*, distinguishing between the two cities, one earthly, the other heavenly. For a recent discussion of the concept see Oort 1991.

65. As opposed to the more conventional body-soul dualism, Temple is alluding to the tripartite division of body, soul, and spirit, as in 1 Thess. 5:23 and Heb. 4:12). The biblical distinction between the spirit (Gk. πνεῦμα, *pneuma*; Heb. רוח, *ruach*; Job 27:3) as the rational human self (or conscience or mind), and life or soul (Gk. ψυχή, *psyche*; Heb. נפש, *nephesh*; Gen. 2:7) as individual human life animating a fleshly body, is elaborated by Henry Alford, drawing on Plato's distinctions in *Republic* (434d–441c). Commenting on 1 Thess. 5:23, Alford refers to his opposition to Jowett's commentary on the same passage, asserting that *pneuma* "is the Spirit, the highest and distinctive part of man, the immortal and responsible *soul*, in our common parlance"; while the *psyche* "is the lower or animal soul, containing the passions and desires . . . which we have in common with the brutes, but which in *us* is ennobled and drawn up by the *pneuma*. That St. Paul had these distinctions in mind, is plain (against Jowett) from such places as 1 Cor. ii. 14" (Alford [1849] 1863, 3:282). Jowett had commented on this same verse that Paul "is not writing a treatise on the soul, but pouring forth from the fulness of his heart, a prayer for his converts. Language thus used should not be too closely analysed. His words may be compared to similar expressions among ourselves: *e.g.* 'with my heart and soul.' Who would distinguish between the two? Neither did the age in which St. Paul lived admit of any great accuracy in speaking of the human soul" (Jowett [1855] 1859, 1:105). For a recent discussion of the dualism see Kittel 1967–76, 6:332–455; 9:608–66).

66. For "the spirit . . . guide us into truth' see John 16:13; "through a glass darkly," 1 Cor. 13:12. Temple takes the latter out of context, making it refer to knowledge before and after education; according to Alford, in Paul it refers to the "contrast between our present sight and knowledge,—and those in the future perfect state" (Alford [1849] 1863, 2:588). Commenting on Thomas Arnold's theory of education, David Newsome writes: "To imply that one should not teach boys the supreme *lessons of life* at the age at which they were most teachable would have seemed to him culpable negligence" (1961, 31; see Thomas Arnold 1844, 4:13).

Temple's differentiation between theory and practice in "every profession" may be read in the context of nineteenth-century class distinctions. In 1857 H. Byerley Thomson wrote in *The Choice of a Profession*: "The importance of the professions and the professional classes can hardly be overrated, they form the head of the great English middle class, maintain its tone of independence, keep up to the mark its standard of morality, and direct its intelligence" (quoted in Reader 1966, 1). W. J. Reader begins his study of Victorian "professional men" with a discussion of "Divinity, Physic and Law": "The three 'liberal professions' of the eighteenth century were the nucleus about which the professional class of the nineteenth century was to form. . . . Their broad and ill-defined functions covered much that later would crystallize out into new, specialized, occupations: . . . each, ultimately, derived much of its standing from its connection with the established order in the State. . . . It was this connection with the State, as well as their reputation for polite learning, which made the professions generally acceptable as occupations fit for gentlemen, and for that reason especially attractive to the rising middle class" (Reader 1966, 23–24). Sociologists have read the professionalization of the middle classes in Victorian Britain as a measure of social change, and the acceptance of science as a way of measuring the legitimation of secular thought (Barnes and Shapin 1979, 92). Significantly, Temple does not indicate the newer professions related to trade, science, or technology. Instead he draws entirely upon two of the three traditionally professions for the middle class, law and medicine, omitting his own, the clergy.

67. For "childish things" see 1 Cor. 13:11.

68. The inscription "Know Thyself" (Gr. γνῶθι σαυτόν, *gnothi sauton*) was inscribed on the Temple of Apollo at Delphi (Plato, *Protagoras* 343b; trans. W. R. M. Lamb, *Loeb* 4:196–99). Those who sought the Delphic Oracle for advice were thus counseled to know the limits of their own knowledge and capabilities before interpreting the enigmatic predictions of the prophetess. This counsel of self-knowledge is related to the Greek ideal of *sophrosyne*, or moderation, whereby human limits and boundaries are recognized and followed. Moderation is related by Basil and other Church Fathers to Deut. 4:9 and Song of Sol. 2:56 (Wilkins [1917] 1980, 1–11; 89–99).

"Know Thyself" became a cliché in neoclassical views of human nature, as in Pope, "Essay on Man" (bk. 2, ll. 1–2). In *Sartor Resartus* Carlyle distances himself from such rationalism and from its results in romantic introspection and Byronic despair: "Our Works are the mirror wherein the spirit first sees its natural lineaments. Hence, too, the folly of that impossible Precept, *Know thyself*; till it be translated into this partially possible one, *Know what thou canst work at*" (bk. 2, chap. 7; Carlyle [1833–34] 1937, 162–63).

69. In this paragraph the analogy between the education of the child and moral growth of the world is developed through a series of biblical references. A contrast is drawn between the enforced bondage of obedience to external rules (the commandments and the ritual observance of Mosaic rules), necessary in human infancy, and freedom in willing obedience to the inner law of conscience (the law written in the heart, or the gospel of Christ active in the conscience). Such views are elaborated in Paul's writings contrasting the Mosaic law on tables of stone and the Christian law in the heart, especially in Rom. 2:15 ff. and 2 Cor. 3:3.

For "learning" and "obedience" see Heb 5:8; "obedience," "the law," and the heart, Rom. 6:16–17; "his own mind," Rom. 14:5; "voice within," "understanding," and "internal law," Job 38:36; "voice which speaks" in the "conscience," Acts 26:14; Rom. 2:15; "not as slaves but as friends," John 15:13–15. The extended analogy of "freeman" and "bondman" is developed in Gal. 4:23–5:1.

Pusey in his correspondence to the *Times* appeals to the "majesty of truth and justice" and its relation to "law" in the Oxford trial of Jowett (Letters 175–78); see also Part 3, Satires for Carroll's poem on the same topic.

70. Throughout his essay, Temple stresses the notions of self-control (the term is used five times), self-discipline (twice), self-respect, and self-education. Samuel Smiles's *Self-Help* (1859) uses the same terms to promote the elevation of the mind and character of the young boy ([1859] 1906, 387 and 458).

For "keep himself from falling" see Jude 24. The three "monastic vows" are poverty, chastity, and obedience, set out in chapters 5 and 33 of the *Rule* of St. Benedict (c. 525). "Temperance," the classical virtue of moderation, was identified with teetotalism by Victorian temperance societies, such as the United Kingdom Alliance (established 1853), the British Temperance League (1854), and the National Temperance League (1856) whose members took the pledge of "temperance." For "(not prayer only, but) fasting" see Matt. 17:21; "dominion of the law," Rom. 7:1; 1 Cor. 9:20–27.

71. For "reprobates" see 2 Cor. 13:5–7; for the contrast between "the punishment" and "the wickedness" Gen. 4:13; "grosser appetites," Shakespeare, *Troilus and Cressida* (2.2.180–83).

72. "Table-turning" became popular in England in 1852 with the visit of a Boston medium, Mrs. Hayden. In 1855 the American medium Daniel Dunglas Home arrived in England and gave widely reported séances, including one with Queen Victoria. These included "table-turning." Robert Browning and Elizabeth Barrett Browning attended one in the same year, which Robert thought to be a hoax and which he later described in "Mr. Sludge, the 'Medium'" (1864). For contemporary discussion of the phenomenon see Carpenter 1853, 1857, and 1858.

The "known philosopher" was very likely Michael Faraday, who published his "dictum" on the subject in a letter to the *Times*, arguing that the table-turning was caused by the unconscious movement of the participants' hands placed on it: "The effect produced by table-turners has been referred to [many causes which] . . . the natural philosopher can investigate. . . . I think the system of education that could leave the mental condition of the public body in a state in which this subject has found it must have been greatly deficient in some very important principle" (30 June 1853, 8). On Faraday see Cantor 1991.

73. For "tares" and "wheat" see the parable of the sower, Matt. 13:3–23. "Faith for all men" echoes the canon of faith of Vincent of Lérins in its appeal to universality or ecumenicity (*universitas*), as well as antiquity (*antiquitas*) and consent (*consensio*), a summary statement of the criteria for canonicity: "*quod ubique, quod semper, quod ab omnibus creditum est*" ("we hold that faith which has been believed everywhere, always, by all"; chap. 2, sec. 6; trans. C. A. Heurtley, *NPNF2* 11:132).

74. For "dream of their brains" see Shakespeare, *Romeo and Juliet* (1.4.97).

75. "Infallibility" is the assurance of being without doctrinal error because of the direct influence of God. On the one hand the concept is appealed to by biblical literalists who generally use the term *inerrancy* to denote the infallible accuracy of the Bible, guaranteed by the operation of the Holy Spirit's inspiring the writers and the text (see Preface, AV, 1611). On the other hand, it is appealed to by Roman Catholics who hold the infallible teaching authority of the church in matters of doctrine on the basis of the Petrine claims (Matt. 16:18) and the guidance of the Holy Spirit (John 16:13). In 1854 the promulgation by Pope Pius IX of the Immaculate Conception of the Virgin Mary as a teaching requiring universal assent provoked controversy in England concerning claims to infallibility: see, for instance, Cheney 1855; for the Catholic position see J. M. Capes 1849; and J. H. Newman 1859. The Dogma of Papal Infallibility was promulgated by Pius IX at the Vatican Council in 1870. On infallibility in relation to the Bible and the church see Jowett ¶s 14, 15, and notes.

76. For "'the law within the law'" see Tennyson, "The Two Voices" (1842; l. 141).

77. Temple collapses several centuries of the history of the migrations into the Roman empire (*Völkerwanderung*, Ger. wandering or migration of the peoples), and reads "Judaism," the emphasis on the formal observance of the Mosaic law, as the typological precursor of the "outer law" of the medieval Roman church. The collapse of several centuries is then made analogous to the childish stage of the development of the individual, the remedy for which is the application of the "outer law," or "discipline," to the individual.

The migration of the "new and undisciplined races," which Temple specifies as "German and Celtic," began as early as the fourth century B.C.E. Their clashes with the "effete" Roman Empire are a commonplace in ancient and modern history (see, for instance, Tacitus' *Annals*, bk. 1, chap. 4; trans. John Jackson, *Loeb* 3:249 and bk. 1, chap. 54; *Loeb* 3:335).

Encounters between the Germans and the Romans began in the first century B.C.E., as the Germanic Cimbri and Teutons overran the frontiers of the Empire and advanced into Italy. Unable to continue the wars of aggression as Trajan had done, later emperors resorted to the building of defenses against their incursions and to define the borders of the empire, such as the wall built across England by Hadrian from 121 to 127. Over the next four hundred years various Germanic tribes, the Goths, Vandals, Burgundians, Alemanni and others, assaulted the northern boundaries of the empire: Rome was sacked by Alaric the Visigoth in 410 and by the Vandals in 455; the Roman Empire in the West fell to Odoacer in 476. For a discussion on the Celts and the empire see Rankin 1987, 103–53; see also Wallace-Hadrill 1952; and Hodgkin 1967.

The medieval church elaborated its "outer law" through its "ceremonies" in the various collections of ritual texts like the Leonine Sacramentary (seventh century) and the Gregorian Sacramentary (sixth to eighth centuries); its moral prescriptions, discipline, and "precise apportionment of punishments" in the penitential books of the fifth and sixth centuries; and its emphasis on "appliances," such as relics and miracles, and on "punishments and purgatory," in such writings as the *Dialogues* of Gregory the Great (Pope from 590–604).

For "scholars to Christ" see Gal. 3:24.

78. King Clovis of the Franks was converted to Christianity in 496. Gibbon describes how Clovis "tamed the German and Celtic nature" by a "system of discipline," and how the "exhausted countries" were made obedient ([1776–88] 1858, 3:569, 573).

Temple's remarks on "German and Celtic nature" are a commonplace in ancient and Victorian history. For instance, regarding Tacitus, H. D. Rankin argues: "Nothing he says ever suggests he had any interest in non-Roman peoples in their own right. In the time in which he lived, there was no romantic idea that there was something intrinsically stimulating or intrinsically attractive about the barbarian nations." He goes on to argue that "the Irish Classical scholar J. P. Mahaffy . . . himself possessed of a Gaelic name, had nothing but vociferous contempt for Gaelic language and culture" (1987, 147). J. P. Mahaffy was professor of ancient history at Trinity College, Dublin from 1871 to 1900. For another discussion of this commonplace see Curtis 1968.

79. The ambiguous phrase "when the work was done" collapses together at least four different aspects of the conversion of the "barbarian races."

The first two aspects involve the interaction between Rome and the Germanic tribes from the first through fifth centuries—the barbarizing of Rome and the Romanizing of the barbarians—which Thomas Arnold alludes to in his *History of Rome*: "The inhabitants of the left or eastern bank of the Rhone were . . . no longer to be considered barbarians, but were become Romans both in their customs and in their language" (1842, 2:364).

The third and fourth aspects involve the acceptance of Christianity by both groups, a process extending from Paul to the baptism of Clovis in 496. By encompassing such diverse movements in a single phrase, Temple smooths out all variations and exceptions. The Goths were converted in the fourth century by Ulfilas, whose Arianism continued among his converts for several centuries until the Visigoths, then in Spain, embraced Catholicism in the reign of Recared (586–601). Remigius baptized Clovis with many of his Frankish followers, to which Temple refers. For recent discussions of the conversion of the Roman empire to Christianity see Benko 1984; MacMullen 1984; and *Christianity* 1986.

80. Temple draws a parallel between Paul's controversy with the Judaizers and the Protestant Reformation, Luther's break with Rome between 1516 and 1520. Paul's "controversy" is set out in his letter to the Galatians, concerning ritual and moral observances, whether conscience (the law of Christ written in the inward heart) or pre-existent Jewish law should govern conduct for the converted Christian. The controversy culminated in the Jerusalem Conference (c. 50) that decided not to require circumcision of converts (Gal. 2:1–10; Acts 15:1–21). Luther, in his commentaries on Romans and Galatians (1516 and 1517), and in *The Liberty of the Christian Man* (1520), develops the view that salvation does not depend on good works, nor on conformity to the sacramental and ecclesiastical system as the "medieval discipline" of the Roman Catholic Church required, but on justification by faith based on the free choice of individual conscience.

81. "Barbarian" is used in Rom. 1:5, 14 (cf. 1 Cor. 14:11) to draw a distinction between Greek and non-Greek, a distinction earlier used by Strabo in *Geography* (c. 20; bk. 14, chap. 2, sec. 28; trans. Horace L. Jones, *Loeb* 6:302–7). Paul's distinction is particularized to Greek and Jew and then is collapsed into an accommodation of "all nations" in the "new man," Christ (Col. 3:11).

A wide range of pejorative connotations for "barbarian" were commonplace in Victorian England; for example, see Thomas Arnold: "I believe with you that *savages* could never civilize themselves, but *barbarians* I think might; and there are some races, e.g. the Keltic, the Teutonic, and the Hellenic, that we cannot trace back to a savage state, nor does it appear that they ever were savages. With regard to such races as have been found in a savage state, if it be admitted that all mankind are originally one race, then I should say that they must have degenerated . . . . The races of mankind [are] divided into those improveable by themselves, and those improveable only by others" (Stanley 1844, 1:408–9). A. P. Stanley in *Sinai and Palestine* (1856) writes of "the imperceptible boundary between civilisation and barbarism." "Barbarians" in Matthew Arnold's *Culture and Anarchy* (1867) refers to a discredited English aristocracy (1960–77, 5:140–41). Darwin uses the phrase in *On the Origin of Species* (1859) to superimpose a theory of human development on a history of genetic preservation of racial characteristics. First, the term is used concerning laws pertaining to genetic contamination from imports in "rude and barbarous periods of English history"; then it is applied to "savages so barbarous" who did not think of the preservation of the inherited characteristics of their animals; and finally, it designates the moral status of people: "We see the value set on animals even by the barbarians of Tierra del Fuego, by their killing and devouring their old women, in times of death, as of less value than their dogs" ([1859] 1964, 33–36).

82. For "spirit for the letter" see Rom. 2:29; 2 Cor. 3:6.

83. For "heaven and earth" see Shakespeare, *Hamlet* (1.5.166); and Temple ¶27. "Patristic theology," the theological writings of the Church Fathers, such as Ambrose, Jerome, Augustine, Basil, and John Chrysostom, was republished in the nineteenth century by the Tractarians in *The Library of the Fathers of the Holy Catholic Church, Anterior to the Division of the East and West* (1838–85, 48 vols.). The series, planned by Pusey in 1836, was very popular, having 3,600 subscribers.

The "new book" of "creation" to be read with that of "revelation" is discussed by Richard Hooker in *Of the Laws of Ecclesiastical Polity*: "It sufficeth therefore that Nature and Scripture do serve in such full sort, that they both jointly and not severally either of them be so complete, that unto everlasting felicity we need not the knowledge of any thing more than these two may easily furnish our minds with on all sides" ([1594–1662] 1954, 1:218). Francis Bacon, in *The Advancement of Learning* (1605), argues in similar terms: "Let no man upon a weak conceit of sobriety or an ill-applied moderation think or maintain, that a man can search too far, or be too well studied in the book of God's word, or in the book of God's works; divinity or philosophy: but rather let men endeavour an endless progress or proficience in both . . . and again, that they do not unwisely mingle or confound these learnings together" (bk. 1, chap. 1, sec. 3; Bacon [1605] 1973, 8). Part of this passage is printed opposite the titlepage in Darwin's *On the Origin of Species* (1859). Bacon also argues: "For our Saviour saith, *You err, not knowing the scriptures, nor the power of God* [Matt. 22:29]; laying before us two books or volumes to study, if we will be secured from error; first the scriptures, revealing the will of God, and then the creatures expressing his power; whereof the latter is a key unto the former" (bk. 1, chap. 6, sec 16; 1973, 41–42). For a recent discussion of the doctrine of the two books see A. R. Peacocke's first Bampton lecture of 1978 (1979, 1–49).

84. Temple locates various occasions in history when "the voice of conscience" overdetermines the "interpretation of the Bible": first among the scholastic theologians concerning the doctrine of purgatory,

then the shift from the Ptolemaic to the Copernican world order, and finally the questioning by geology of the literalist reading of Genesis as a creation in six days. Each of these occasions in Temple's argument resembles a paradigm shift in the sense used in Kuhn 1962.

"Schoolmen" refers to the medieval scholastics, flourishing first in the schools (at Chartres, Oxford, and St. Victor, the modified Cistercian abbey in Paris) and then in the universities. Following Anselm's notion, faith seeking knowledge (*fides quaerens intellectum*) through the exercise of reason, and relying on the newly discovered texts of Aristotle, Thomas Aquinas elaborated the most extensive scholastic treatment of medieval theology. Besides Dante's *Purgatorio*, the most detailed treatment of "purgatory" is found in Thomas Aquinas's *Commentary on the Sentences of Peter Lombard* (bk. 4, distinction 21, quest. 1). The biblical passages frequently cited on purgatory include Matt. 12:31 ff.; 1 Cor. 3:11–15; and 2 Macc. 12:39–45.

Galileo Galilei repudiated the Ptolemaic system in favor of the Copernican in his publications from *The Starry Messenger* (1610) to the *Dialogue concerning the Two Chief World Systems* (1632). In 1633 he was summoned to a trial before the Inquisition that showed him the instruments of torture to elicit a recantation and to force him to declare the earth to be the center of the universe and immoveable, to publish nothing, and to remain silent for the rest of his life under house arrest. Goodwin (¶s 1–2) and Jowett (¶88) also use Galileo as an example of a victim of biblical literalists in their discussions of geology and the Bible.

Many who held that the Bible condemns geology, or at least is of greater truth than the facts of geology, attacked Goodwin's views in *Essays and Reviews*. One such attack was the first chapter of J. Bayley's *Twelve Discourses on Essays and Reviews* (1862), "Genesis and Geology." Robert Jamieson in his commentary on Genesis adds a long note on "Geological Eras," attacking liberal theologians' views: "so Moses, when he wrote of the days of creation, was led unconsciously to use language which, while it was plain and literal, was at the same time symbolical of vast epochs. By putting such a liberal construction on the inspired record, they hope to adapt its brief and general statements . . . to the views of an advanced state of society, and to show that beneath its archaic simplicity of style there underlies a store of philosophic truths, which, when unfolded, place the testimony of God in the volume of revelation in exact accordance with that which He has given in the book of nature" (1868–71, 1:10). But later in the commentary Jamieson seems to adopt a somewhat more accepting position on geology: "We accept the facts which geology has established as certain and universal truths, and consider that we are bound, in the spirit of sound Biblical criticism, to accommodate our interpretation of the written record in accordance with the manifest testimony of the rocks. But geology has not yet attained the character of a perfect science, nor are the opinions of all [of] even her most eminent cultivators to be admitted as principles: and in no respect do we hesitate so much to receive their dogmas as in that of days meaning extended periods of creation" (1:15). Other conservative exegetes, such as Harold Browne, glossed Gen. 1:1–31 to the effect that when there was an apparent conflict between geology and Genesis, the spiritual meaning of the Bible would remove all difficulties. Citing Hugh Miller's *Testimony of the Rocks* (1857) favorably, he writes: "In the present condition of geological science, and with the great obscurity of the record of creation . . . it may be wise not to attempt an accurate comparison of the one with the other. . . . This is the course of creation as popularly described in Genesis, and the rocks give their testimony, at least in the general, to the same order and progress (in Cook 1871–88, 1:36).

85. The observation of the Sabbath (Saturday) is enjoined upon the Jews in the Ten Commandments (Exod. 20:8–11) with respect to the cessation of required work in recognition of God's resting on the seventh day of creation (Gen. 2:1–3). In the Christian scriptures Jesus is lax on the subject of Sabbath-observation (Matt. 12:1–8), but he is also affirmed as the Lord of the Sabbath (Mark 2:8). Sunday as the weekly memorial of the resurrection became the day of special observation for Christians from the fourth century onwards.

In England Nicholas Bound's *True Doctrine of the Sabbath* (1495) identified the Christian Sunday with the Jewish Sabbath, and this view was extended in the civil realm by James I, and even more pervasively throughout the Puritan revolution. The Lord's Day Act of 1781 made the observance of Sunday a requirement of law. The Sabbatarian movement in Victorian England enforced by legal means the strict observation of Sunday as a day of churchgoing, rest, and a limited range of activities. It was the special interest of the Evangelical Lord's Day Observance Society (founded 1831) and was associated with revivalism, teetotalism, "and other restrictive practices" (John Kent 1978, 93). In *Little Dorrit* (1857) Dickens gives a sketch of a "Sunday evening in London, gloomy, close, and stale. . . . In every thoroughfare, up almost every alley, and down almost every turning, some doleful bell was throbbing, jerking, tolling, as if the Plague were in the city and the dead-carts were going round. Everything was bolted and barred that could by possibility furnish relief to an overworked people. No pictures, no unfamiliar animals, no rare plants or flowers, no natural or artificial wonders of the ancient world—all *taboo* with that enlightened strictness" (bk. 1, chap. 3; [1857] 1988, 67). Dickens also wrote against the "enlightened strictness" of the Sabbatarians in *House-*

hold Words (see for instance 4 Aug. and 13 Oct. 1855). Just months before the publication of *Essays and Reviews*, J. A. Hessey delivered the Bampton Lectures, *Sunday: Its Origins, History, and Present Obligation* (1860). For other contemporary discussions see Hickson 1850; "Sunday in Great Britain" 1856; and "The Christian Sabbath" 1857.

86. For "youth of the world" see Francis Bacon, "*Antiquitas saeculi juventus mundi*" (Ancient times were the youth of the world) in *De Dignitate et Augmentis Scientiarum* (1623; Concerning the worth and growth of science; bk. 1, chap. 8, sec. 81). Gladstone used this phrase in the title of his second book on Homer: *Juventus Mundi: The Gods and Men of the Heroic Age* (1869).

87. "Criticism" is a technical term used in reference to two methodologies of biblical scholarship: first to lower criticism, the establishment of a critical or reliable text of the Bible; and second to higher criticism, the application of literary and historical analysis to that text. Both methods sought to establish the text and interpretation of the Bible, but both also aroused controversy by questioning the authority of authorized biblical translations, received interpretations, and the notion of inspiration.

Such criticism raised problems about possible interpolations in the biblical text, for instance, about two or more different narrative traditions in Genesis, depending on the use of the terms for God, and the references to the priestly code; about the unity of some of the biblical books, like Isaiah; about the genealogies of Jesus (in Matt. and Luke) traced through Joseph in a tradition that ignores the narrative of the Virgin birth; about the end of Mark's gospel (Mark 16:8b–20) which does not appear in any of the earliest surviving manuscripts from the fourth century; or about John 7:53–8:11 which appears variously in the earliest MSS. after Luke 21:38, John 7:36, John 21:24 or does not appear at all. For recent discussions of the role of lower and higher criticism see Frei 1974; and Rogerson 1984.

The most notorious forgeries connected with the church are those known as the "False Decretals" (a set of documents that included the "Donation of Constantine," giving territorial sovereignty to the Papacy throughout Italy on the basis of ancient claims for papal supremacy). They purported to be written by Isidore of Seville (d. 636), but were actually written in France about 850, as was demonstrated by Lorenzo Valla in 1440, using textual criticism to establish their later dating. The most notorious contemporary case of "interpolations and forgeries" involving Genesis concerned Konstantinos Simonides. In 1853 he offered to sell some manuscripts to the librarian of the British Museum. Eventually some that were determined to be genuine were bought by the museum. Some others were forgeries and were sold to collectors. In 1860 he deciphered some papyri owned by Joseph Mayer, a Liverpool antiquary, including fragments of Matthew, the epistles of St. James and St. Jude, the ten commandments, and parts of Genesis—all attacked as forgeries, and shown to be so in 1863 (see *Codex Sinaiticus*, 1982).

88. For "lever which moves the world" see Archimedes: "Give me a place to stand and I will move the world"; quoted in Pappus of Alexandria, *Synagogue* (Collections; bk. 8, chap. 10, sec. 11). For "though in malice" see 1 Cor. 14:20.

2 *Rowland Williams*

Bunsen's Biblical Researches

When geologists began to ask whether changes in the earth's structure might be explained by causes still in operation, they did not disprove the possibility of great convulsions, but they lessened the necessity for imagining them. So, if a theologian has his eyes opened to the Divine energy as continuous and omnipresent, he lessens the sharp contrast of epochs in Revelation, but need not assume that the stream has never varied in its flow.[1] Devotion raises time present into the sacredness of the past; while Criticism reduces the strangeness of the past into harmony with the present. Faith and Prayer (and great marvels answering to them), do not pass away: but, in prolonging their range as a whole, we make their parts less exceptional. We hardly discern the truth, for which they are anxious, until we distinguish it from associations accidental to their domain. The truth itself may have been apprehended in various degrees by servants of God, of old, as now. Instead of, with Tertullian, *what was first is truest,* we may say, what comes of God is true, and He is not only afar, but nigh at hand; though His mind is not changed.[2]

Questions of miraculous interference do not turn merely upon our conceptions of physical law, as unbroken, or of the Divine Will, as all-pervading: but they include inquiries into evidence, and must abide by verdicts on the age of records. Nor should the distinction between poetry and prose, and the possibility of imagination's allying itself with affection, be overlooked. We cannot encourage a remorseless criticism of Gentile histories and escape its contagion when we approach Hebrew annals; nor acknowledge a Providence in Jewry without owning that it may have comprehended sanctities elsewhere. But the moment we examine fairly the religions of India and of Arabia, or even those of primeval Hellas and Latium, we find they appealed to the better side of our nature, and their essential strength lay in the elements of good which they contained, rather than in any Satanic corruption.[3]

Thus considerations, religious and moral, no less than scientific and critical, have, where discussion was free, widened the idea of Revelation for the old world, and deepened it for ourselves; not removing the footsteps of the Eternal from Palestine, but tracing them on other shores; and not making the saints of old orphans, but ourselves partakers of their sonship.[4] Conscience would not lose by exchanging that repressive idea of revelation, which is put over against it as an adversary, for one to which the echo of its best instincts should be the witness. The moral constituents of our nature, so often contrasted with Revelation, should rather be considered parts of its instrumentality. Those cases in which we accept the miracle for the sake of the moral lesson prove the ethical element to be the more fundamental. We see this more clearly if we imagine a miracle of cruelty wrought (as by Antichrist) for immoral ends; for then only the technically miraculous has its value isolated; whereas by appealing to *good* 'WORKS' (however wonderful) for his witness, Christ has taught us to have faith mainly in goodness.[5] This is too much overlooked by some apologists. But there is hardly any greater question than whether history shows Almighty God to have trained mankind by a faith which has reason and conscience for its kindred, or by one to whose miraculous tests their pride must bow; that is, whether His Holy Spirit has acted through the channels which His Providence ordained, or whether it has departed from these so signally that comparative mistrust of them ever afterwards becomes a duty. The first alternative, though invidiously termed philosophical, is that to which free nations and Evangelical thinkers tend; the second has a greater show of religion, but allies itself naturally with priestcraft or formalism; and not rarely with corruptness of administration or of life.

[4] In this issue converge many questions anciently stirred, but recurring in our daylight with almost uniform[6] accession of strength to the liberal side. Such questions turn chiefly on the law of growth, traceable throughout the Bible, as in the world; and partly on science, or historical inquiry: but no less on the deeper revelations of the New Testament, as compared to those of the Old. If we are to retain the old Anglican foundations of research and fair statement, we must revise some of the decisions provisionally given upon imperfect evidence; or, if we shrink from doing so, we must abdicate our ancient claim to build upon the truth; and our retreat will be either to Rome, as some of our lost ones have consistently seen, or to some form, equally evil, of darkness voluntary. The attitude of too many English scholars before the last Monster out of the Deep is that of the degenerate senators before Tiberius.[7] They stand, balancing terror against mutual shame. Even with those in our universities who no longer repeat fully the required Shibboleths, the explicitness of truth is rare.[8] He who assents most, committing himself least to baseness, is reckoned wisest.

[5] Bunsen's enduring glory is neither to have paltered with his conscience nor shrunk from the difficulties of the problem; but to have brought a vast erudition, in the light of a Christian conscience, to unroll tangled records, tracing frankly the Spirit of God elsewhere, but honouring chiefly the traditions of His Hebrew sanctuary. No living author's works could furnish so pregnant a text for a discourse on Biblical criticism. Passing over some specialties of Lutheranism, we may meet in the field of research which is common to scholars; while even here, the sympathy, which justifies respectful exposition, need not imply entire agreement.[9]

[6] In the great work upon Egypt,[10] the later volumes of which are now appearing

in English, we do not find that picture of home life which meets us in the pages of our countryman, Sir G. Wilkinson.[11] The interest for robust scholars is not less, in the fruitful comparison of the oldest traditions of our race, and in the giant shapes of ancient empires, which flit like dim shadows, evoked by a master's hand. But for those who seek chiefly results, there is something wearisome in the elaborate discussion of authorities; and, it must be confessed, the German refinement of method has all the effect of confusion. To give details here is impossible (though the more any one scrutinizes them, the more substantial he will find them), and this sketch must combine suggestions, which the author has scattered strangely apart, and sometimes repeated without perfect consistency. He dwells largely upon Herodotus, Eratosthenes, and their successors, from Champollion and Young to Lepsius.[12] Especially the dynastic records of the Ptolemaic priest, Manetho,[13] are compared with the accounts of the stone monuments. The result, if we can receive it, is to vindicate for the civilized kingdom of Egypt, from Menes downward, an antiquity of nearly four thousand years before Christ. There is no point in which archaeologists of all shades were so nearly unanimous as in the belief that our Biblical chronology was too narrow in its limits; and the enlargement of our views, deduced from Egyptian records, is extended by our author's reasonings on the development of commerce and government, and still more of languages, and physical features of race. He could not have vindicated the unity of mankind if he had not asked for a vast extension of time, whether his petition of twenty thousand years be granted or not. The mention of such a term may appear monstrous to those who regard six thousand years as a part of Revelation.[14] Yet it is easier to throw doubt on some of the arguments than to show that the conclusion in favour of a vast length is improbable. If pottery in a river's mud proves little, its tendency may agree with that of the discovery of very ancient pre-historic remains in many parts of the world. Again, how many years are needed to develope modern French out of Latin, and Latin itself out of its original crude forms? How unlike is English to Welsh, and Greek to Sanskrit—yet all indubitably of one family of languages![15] What years were required to create the existing divergence of members of this family! How many more for other families, separated by a wide gulf from this, yet retaining traces of a primaeval aboriginal affinity, to have developed themselves, either in priority or collaterally? The same consonantal roots, appearing either as verbs inflected with great variety of grammatical form, or as nouns with case-endings in some languages, and with none in others, plead as convincingly as the succession of strata in geology, for enormous lapses of time. When, again, we have traced our Gaelic and our Sanskrit to their inferential pre-Hellenic stem, and when reason has convinced us that the Semitic languages which had as distinct an individuality four thousand years ago as they have now, require a cradle of larger dimensions than Archbishop Ussher's chronology, what farther effort is not forced upon our imagination, if we would guess the measure of the dim background in which the Mongolian and Egyptian languages, older probably than the Hebrew, became fixed, growing early into the type which they retain? Do we see an historical area of nations and languages extending itself over nearly ten thousand years: and can we imagine less than another ten thousand, during which the possibilities of these things took body and form? Questions of this kind require from most of us a special training for each: but Baron Bunsen revels in them, and his theories are at least suggestive. He shows what Egypt had in common with that primaeval Asiatic stock, represented by Ham, out of which, as raw material, he conceives the divergent families, termed Indo-European[16] and Semitic (or the kindreds of Europe and of Palestine) to have been later developed. Nimrod is considered as the Biblical representative of the earlier stock, whose ruder language is continued, by affiliation or by analogy, in the Mongolian races of Asia and in the negroes of Africa.

[7] The traditions of Babylon, Sidon, Assyria, and Iran, are brought by our author to illustrate and confirm, though to modify our interpretation of, Genesis. It is strange how nearly those ancient cosmogonies[17] approach what may be termed the philosophy of Moses, while they fall short in what Longinus called his 'worthy conception of the divinity.' <u>Our deluge takes its place among geological phenomena, no longer a disturbance of law from which science shrinks, but a prolonged play of the forces of fire and water, rendering the primaeval regions of North Asia uninhabitable, and urging the nations to new abodes. We learn approximately its antiquity, and infer limitation in its range, from finding it recorded in the traditions of Iran and Palestine (or of Japhet and Shem) but unknown to the Egyptians and Mongolians, who left earlier the cradle of mankind. In the half ideal half traditional notices</u>[18] <u>of the beginnings of our race, compiled in Genesis, we are bid notice the combination of documents, and the recurrence of barely consistent genealogies.</u> As the man Adam begets Cain, the man Enos begets Cainan. Jared and Irad, Methuselah and Methusael, are similarly compared. Seth, like El, is an old deity's appellation, and MAN was the son of Seth in one record, as Adam was the son of God in the other. One could wish the puzzling circumstance, that the etymology of some of the earlier names seems strained to suit the present form of the narrative had been explained. That our author would not shrink from noticing this, is shown by the firmness with which he relegates the long lives of the first patriarchs to the domain of legend, or of symbolical cycle. He reasonably conceives that the historical portion begins with Abraham, where the lives become natural, and information was nearer.[19] A sceptical criticism might, indeed, ask, by what right he assumes that the moral dimensions of our spiritual heroes can not have been idealized by tradition, as he admits to have been the case with physical events and with chronology rounded into epical shape. But the first principles of his philosophy, which fixes on personality (or what we might call force of character) as the great organ of Divine manifestation in the world, and his entire method of handling the Bible, lead him to insist on the genuineness, and to magnify the force, of spiritual ideas, and of the men who exemplified them. Hence, on the side of religion, he does not intentionally violate that reverence with which Evangelical thinkers view the fathers of our faith. To Abraham and Moses, Elijah and Jeremiah, he renders grateful honour. Even in archaeology his scepticism does not outrun the

suspicions often betrayed in our popular mind; and he limits, while he confirms these, by showing how far they have ground. But as he says, with quaint strength, 'there is no chronological element in Revelation.'[20] Without borrowing the fifteen centuries which the Greek Church and the Septuagint would lend us, we see, from comparing the Bible with the Egyptian records and with itself, that our common dates are wrong, though it is not so easy to say how they should be rectified.[21] The idea of bringing Abraham into Egypt as early as 2876 B.C. is one of our author's most doubtful points, and may seem hardly tenable. But he wanted time for the growth of Jacob's family into a people of two millions, and he felt bound to place Joseph under a native Pharaoh, therefore, before the Shepherd Kings. He also contends that Abraham's horizon in Asia is antecedent to the first Median conquest of Babylon in 2234. A famine, conveniently mentioned under the twelfth dynasty of Egypt, completes his proof. Sesortosis, therefore, is the Pharaoh to whom Joseph was minister; the stay of the Israelites in Egypt is extended to fourteen centuries; and the date 215 represents the time of oppression. Some of these details are sufficiently doubtful to afford ground of attack to writers whose real quarrel is with our author's Biblical research, and its more certain, but not therefore more welcome, conclusions. It is easier to follow him implicitly when he leads us, in virtue of an overwhelming concurrence of Egyptian records and of all the probabilities of the case, to place the Exodus as late as 1320 or 1314.[22] The event is more natural in Egypt's decline under Menephthah, the exiled son of the great Ramses, than amidst the splendour of the eighteenth dynasty.[23] It cannot well have been earlier, or the Book of Judges must have mentioned the conquest of Canaan by Ramses; nor later, for then Joshua would come in collision with the new empire of Ninus and Semiramis.[24] But Manetho places, under Menephthah, what seems the Egyptian version of the event, and the year 1314, one of our alternatives, is the date assigned it by Jewish tradition. Not only is the historical reality of the Exodus thus vindicated against the dreams of the Drummonds and the Volneys, but a new interest is given it by its connexion with the rise and fall of great empires.[25] We can understand how the ruin on which Ninus rose made room in Canaan for the Israelites, and how they fell again under the satraps of the New Empire, who appear in the Book of Judges as kings of the provinces.[26] Only, if we accept the confirmation, we must take all its parts. Manetho makes the conquerors before whom Menephthah retreats into Ethiopia Syrian shepherds, and gives the human side of an invasion, or war of liberation;[27] Baron Bunsen notices the 'high hand' with which Jehovah led forth his people, the spoiling of the Egyptians, and the lingering in the peninsula, as signs, even in the Bible, of a struggle conducted by human means. Thus, as the pestilence of the Book of Kings becomes in Chronicles the more visible angel, so the avenger who slew the firstborn may have been the Bedouin host, akin nearly to Jethro, and more remotely to Israel.[28]

So in the passage of the Red Sea, the description may be interpreted with the latitude of poetry: though, as it is not affirmed that Pharaoh was drowned, it is no serious objection that Egyptian authorities continue the reign of Menephthah later.

A greater difficulty is that we find but three centuries thus left us from the Exodus to Solomon's Temple. Yet less stress will be laid on this by whoever notices how the numbers in the Book of Judges proceed by the eastern round number of forty, what traces the whole book bears of embodying history in its most popular form, and how naturally St. Paul or St. Stephen would speak after received accounts.

[9] It is not the importance severally, but the continual recurrence of such difficulties, which bears with ever-growing induction upon the question, whether the Pentateuch is of one age and hand, and whether subsequent books are contemporary with the events, or whether the whole literature grew like a tree rooted in the varying thoughts of successive generations, and whether traces of editorship, if not of composition, between the ages of Solomon and Hezekiah, are manifest to whoever will recognise them. Baron Bunsen finds himself compelled to adopt the alternative of gradual growth. He makes the Pentateuch Mosaic, as indicating the mind and embodying the developed system of Moses, rather than as written by the great lawgiver's hand. Numerous fragments of genealogy, of chronicle, and of spiritual song go up to a high antiquity, but are imbedded in a crust of later narrative, the allusions of which betray at least a time when kings were established in Israel. Hence the idea of composition out of older materials must be admitted; and it may in some cases be conceived that the compiler's point of view differed from that of the older pieces, which yet he faithfully preserved. If the more any one scrutinizes the sacred text, the more he finds himself impelled to these or like conclusions respecting it, the accident of such having been alleged by men more critical than devout should not make Christians shrink from them. We need not fear that what God has permitted to be true in history can be at war with the faith in Himself taught us by His Son.[29]

[10] As in his *Egypt* our author sifts the historical date of the Bible, so in his *Gott in der Geschichte*,[30] he expounds its directly religious element. Lamenting, like Pascal, the wretchedness of our feverish being, when estranged from its eternal state, he traces, as a countryman of Hegel, the Divine thought bringing order out of confusion.[31] Unlike the despairing school, who forbid us trust in God or in conscience, unless we kill our souls with literalism, he finds salvation for men and States only in becoming acquainted with the Author of our life, by whose reason the world stands fast, whose stamp we bear in our forethought, and whose voice our conscience echoes.[32] In the Bible, as an expression of devout reason, and therefore to be read with reason in freedom, he finds record of the spiritual giants whose experience generated the religious atmosphere we breathe. For, as in law and literature, so in religion we are debtors to our ancestors; but their life must find in us a kindred apprehension, else it would not quicken; and we must give back what we have received, or perish by unfaithfulness to our trust. Abraham, the friend of God, Moses the inspired patriot, Elijah the preacher of the still small voice, and Jeremiah the foreseer of a law written on the conscience, are not ancestors of Pharisees who inherit their flesh and name, so much as of kindred spirits who put trust in a righteous God above offerings of blood, who build up free nations by

wisdom, who speak truth in simplicity though four hundred priests cry out for falsehood, and who make self-examination before the Searcher of hearts more sacred than the confessional.[33] When the fierce ritual of Syria, with the awe of a Divine voice, bade Abraham slay his son, he did not reflect that he had no perfect theory of the absolute to justify him in departing from traditional revelation, but trusted that the Father, whose voice from heaven he heard at heart, was better pleased with mercy than with sacrifice; and this trust was his righteousness.[34] Its seed was sown from heaven, but it grew in the soil of an honest and good heart. So in each case we trace principles of reason and right, to which our heart perpetually responds, and our response to which is a truer sign of faith than such deference to a supposed external authority as would quench these principles themselves.

[11] It may be thought that Baron Bunsen ignores too peremptorily the sacerdotal element in the Bible, forgetting how it moulded the form of the history. He certainly separates the Mosaic institutions from Egyptian affinity more than our Spencer and Warburton would permit; more, it seems, than Hengstenberg considers necessary.[35] But the distinctively Mosaic is with him, not the ritual, but the spiritual, which generated the other, but was overlaid by it. Moses, he thinks, would gladly have founded a free religious society, in which the primitive tables written by the Divine finger on man's heart should have been law; but the rudeness or hardness of his people's heart compelled him to a sacerdotal system and formal tablets of stone. In favour of this view, it may be remarked, that the tone of some passages in Exodus appears less sacerdotal than that of later books in the Pentateuch. But, be this as it may, the truly Mosaic (according to our author) is not the Judaic, but the essentially human; and it is not the Semitic form, often divergent from our modes of conception, but the eternal truths of a righteous God, and of the spiritual sacrifices with which He is pleased, that we ought to recognise as most characteristic of the Bible; and these truths the same Spirit which spoke of old speaks, through all variety of phrase, in ourselves.[36]

[12] That there was a Bible before our Bible, and that some of our present books, as certainly Genesis and Joshua, and perhaps Job, Jonah, Daniel, are expanded from simpler elements, is indicated in the book before us rather than proved as it might be. Fuller details may be expected in the course of the revised *Bible for the People*,[37] that grand enterprise of which three parts have now appeared. So far as it has gone, some amended renderings have interest, but are less important than the survey of the whole subject in the Introduction. The word Jehovah has its deep significance brought out by being rendered The Eternal. The famous Shiloh (Gen. xlix. 10) is taken in its local sense, as the sanctuary where the young Samuel was trained; which, if doctrinal perversions did not interfere, hardly any one would doubt to be the true sense. The three opening verses of Genesis are treated as *side*-clauses (*when* God created, &c.), so that the first direct utterance of the Bible is in the fourth verse, '*God said*, Let there be light.' Striking as this is, the Hebrew permits, rather than requires it. Less admissible is the division after verse 4 of the 2nd chapter, as if 'This is the history' was a summary of what precedes, instead of an

announcement of what follows. But the 1st verse of the 2nd chapter belongs properly to the preceding. Sometimes the translator seems right in substance but wrong in detail. He rightly rejects the perversions which make the cursing Psalms evangelically inspired; but he forgets that the bitterest curses of Psalm 109 (from verse 6 to 19) are not the Psalmist's own, but a speech in the mouth of his adversary. These are trifles, when compared with the mass of information, and the manner of wielding it, in the prefaces to the work.[38] There is a grasp of materials and a breadth of view from which the most practised theologian may learn something, and persons least versed in Biblical studies acquire a comprehensive idea of them. Nothing can be more dishonest than the affectation of contempt with which some English critics endeavoured to receive this instalment of a glorious work. To sneer at demonstrated criticisms as 'old,' and to brand fresh discoveries as 'new,' is worthy of men who neither understand the Old Testament nor love the New. But they to whom the Bible is dear for the truth's sake will wish its illustrious translator life to accomplish a task as worthy of a Christian statesman's retirement as the Tusculans of Cicero were of the representative of Rome's lost freedom.[39]

[13] Already in the volume before-mentioned Baron Bunsen has exhibited the Hebrew Prophets as witnesses to the Divine Government. To estimate aright his services in this province would require from most Englishmen years of study. Accustomed to be told that modern history is expressed by the Prophets in a riddle, which requires only a key to it, they are disappointed to hear of moral lessons, however important. Such notions are the inheritance of days when Justin could argue, in good faith, that by the riches of Damascus and the spoil of Samaria were intended the Magi and their gifts, and that the King of Assyria signified King Herod (!);[40] or when Jerome could say, '*No one doubts that by Chaldeans are meant Demons*,'[41] and the Shunammite Abishag could be no other than heavenly wisdom, for the honour of David's old age[42]—not to mention such things as Lot's daughters symbolizing the Jewish and Gentile Churches.[43] It was truly felt by the early fathers that Hebrew prophecy tended to a system more spiritual than that of Levi;[44] and they argued unanswerably that circumcision and the Sabbath[45] were symbols for a time, or means to ends. But when, instead of using the letter as an instrument of the spirit, they began to accept the letter in all its parts as their law, and twisted it into harmony with the details of Gospel history, they fell into inextricable contradictions; the most rational interpreter among them is Jerome, and the perusal of his criticisms is their ample confutation.[46] Nor could the strong intellect of Augustine compensate for his defect of little Greek, which he shared with half, and of less Hebrew, which he shared with most of the Fathers.[47] But with the revival of learning began a reluctant and wavering, yet inevitable, retreat from the details of patristic exposition, accompanied with some attempts to preserve its spirit. Even Erasmus looked that way; Luther's and Calvin's strong sense impelled them some strides in the same direction; but Grotius, who outweighs as a critic any ten opposites, went boldly on the road.[48] In our own country each successive defence of the prophecies, in proportion as its author was able, detracted something from

the extent of literal prognostication; and either laid stress on the moral element, or urged a second, as the spiritual sense. Even Butler foresaw the possibility, that every prophecy in the Old Testament might have its elucidation in contemporaneous history; but literature was not his strong point, and he turned aside, endeavouring to limit it, from an unwelcome idea. Bishop Chandler is said to have thought twelve passages in the Old Testament directly Messianic;[49] others restricted this character to five. Paley ventures to quote only one. Bishop Kidder[50] conceded freely an historical sense in Old Testament texts remote from adaptations in the New. The apostolic Middleton pronounced firmly for the same principle; Archbishop Newcome[51] and others proved in detail its necessity. Coleridge, in a suggestive letter, preserved in the memoirs of Cary, the translator of Dante, threw secular prognostication altogether out of the idea of prophecy.[52] Dr. Arnold, and his truest followers, bear, not always consistently, on the same side. On the other hand, the declamatory assertions, so easy in pulpits or on platforms, and aided sometimes by powers, which produce silence rather than conviction, have not only kept alive but magnified with uncritical exaggeration, whatever the Fathers had dreamt or modern rhetoric could add, tending to make prophecy miraculous. Keith's edition of Newton need not be here discussed. Davison, of Oriel, with admirable skill, threw his argument into a series as it were of hypothetical syllogisms, with only the defect (which some readers overlook) that his minor premise can hardly in a single instance be proved.[53] Yet the stress which he lays on the moral element of prophecy atones for his sophistry as regards the predictive. On the whole, even in England, there is a wide gulf between the arguments of our genuine critics, with the convictions of our most learned clergy, on the one side, and the assumptions of popular declamation on the other. This may be seen on a comparison of Kidder with Keith.[54] But in Germany there has been a pathway streaming with light, from Eichhorn to Ewald, aided by the poetical penetration of Herder and the philological researches of Gesenius, throughout which the value of the moral element in prophecy has been progressively raised, and that of the directly predictive, whether secular or Messianic, has been lowered. Even the conservatism of Jahn amongst Romanists, and of Hengstenberg amongst Protestants, is free and rational, compared to what is often in this country required with denunciation, but seldom defended by argument.[55]

To this inheritance of opinion Baron Bunsen succeeds. Knowing these things, and writing for men who know them, he has neither the advantage in argument of unique knowledge, nor of unique ignorance. He dare not say, though it was formerly said, that David foretold the exile, because it is mentioned in the Psalms. He cannot quote Nahum denouncing ruin against Nineveh, or Jeremiah against Tyre, without remembering that already the Babylonian power threw its shadow across Asia, and Nebuchadnezzar was mustering his armies.[56] If he would quote the book of Isaiah, he cannot conceal, after Gesenius, Ewald, and Maurer have written, that the book is composed of elements of different eras. Finding Perso-Babylonian, or new-coined words, such as *sagans* for officers, and Chaldaic forms of the Hebrew verb, such as *Aphel* for *Hiphil*, in certain portions, and observing that the political horizon of these portions is that of the sixth century, while that of the elder or more purely Hebraic portions belonged to the eighth, he must accept a theory of authorship and of prediction, modified accordingly.[57] So, if under the head of Zechariah he finds three distinct styles and aspects of affairs, he must acknowledge so much, whether he is right or wrong in conjecturing the elder Zechariah of the age of Isaiah to have written the second portion, and Uriah in Jeremiah's age the third.[58] If he would quote Micah, as designating Bethlehem for the birthplace of the Messiah, he cannot shut his eyes to the fact, that the Deliverer to come from thence was to be a contemporary shield against the Assyrian. If he would follow Pearson in quoting the second Psalm, *Thou art my Son*;[59] he knows that Hebrew idiom convinced even Jerome[60] the true rendering was, worship *purely*. He may read in Psalm xxxiv. that, 'not a bone of the righteous shall be broken,' but he must feel a difficulty in detaching this from the context, so as to make it a prophecy of the crucifixion. If he accepts mere versions of Psalm xxii. 17, he may wonder how 'piercing the hands and the feet' can fit into the whole passage; but if he prefers the most ancient Hebrew reading, he finds, instead of '*piercing*,' the comparison 'like a lion,' and this corresponds sufficiently with the 'dogs' of the first clause; though a morally certain emendation would make the parallel more perfect by reading the word 'lions' in both clauses.[61] In either case, the staring monsters are intended, by whom Israel is surrounded and torn. Again he finds in Hosea that the Lord loved Israel when he was young, and called him out of Egypt to be his son; but he must feel, with Bishop Kidder, that such a citation is rather accommodated to the flight of Joseph into Egypt, than a prediction to be a ground of argument. Fresh from the services of Christmas, he must sincerely exclaim, *Unto us a child is born*; but he knows that the Hebrew translated *Mighty God*, is at least disputable, that perhaps it means only Strong and Mighty One, Father of an Age; and he can never listen to any one who pretends that the Maiden's Child of Isaiah vii. 16, was not to be born in the reign of Ahaz, as a sign against the Kings Pekah and Rezin.[62] In the case of Daniel, he may doubt whether all parts of the book are of one age, or what to the starting point of the seventy weeks; but two results are clear beyond fair doubt, that the period of weeks ended in the reign of Antiochus Epiphanes, and that those portions of the book, supposed to be specially predictive, are a history of past occurrences up to that reign. When so vast an induction on the destructive side has been gone through, it avails little that some passages may be doubtful, one perhaps in Zechariah, and one in Isaiah, capable of being made Messianic, and a chapter possibly in Deuteronomy foreshadowing the final fall of Jerusalem. Even these few cases, the remnant of so much confident rhetoric, tend to melt, if they are not already melted, in the crucible of searching inquiry. If our German ignored all that the masters of philology have proved on these subjects, his countrymen would have raised a storm of ridicule, at which he must have drowned himself in the Neckar.[63]

[15] Great then is Baron Bunsen's merit, in accepting frankly the belief of scholars, and yet not despairing of Hebrew Prophecy as a witness to the kingdom of God.

The way of doing so left open to him, was to show, pervading the Prophets, those deep truths which lie at the heart of Christianity, and to trace the growth of such ideas, the belief in a righteous God, and the nearness of man to God, the power of prayer, and the victory of self-sacrificing patience, ever expanding in men's hearts, until the fullness of time came, and the ideal of the Divine thought was fulfilled in the Son of Man.[64] Such accordingly is the course our author pursues, not with the critical finish of Ewald, but with large moral grasp. Why he should add to his moral and metaphysical basis of prophecy, a notion of foresight by vision of particulars, or a kind of *clairvoyance*, though he admits it to be[65] a natural gift, consistent with fallibility, is not so easy to explain. One would wish he might have intended only the power of seeing the ideal in the actual, or of tracing the Divine Government in the movements of men. He seems to mean more than presentiment or sagacity; and this element in his system requires proof.[66]

6] The most brilliant portion of the prophetical essays is the treatment of the later Isaiah.[67] With the insertion of four chapters concerning Hezekiah from the histories of the kings, the words and deeds of the elder Isaiah apparently close. It does not follow that all the prophecies arranged earlier in the book are from his lips; probably they are not; but it is clear to demonstration,[68] that the later chapters (xl., &c.,) are upon the stooping of Nebo, and the bowing down of Babylon, when the Lord took out of the hand of Jerusalem the cup of trembling; for the glad tidings of the decree of return were heard upon the mountains; and the people went forth, not with haste or flight, for their God went before them, and was their rereward (ch. lii). So they went forth with joy and were led forth with peace (ch. liv). So the arm of the Lord was laid bare, and his servant who had foretold it was now counted wise, though none had believed his report.[69] We cannot take a portion out of this continuous song, either by dividing it as a chapter, separate its primary meaning from what precedes and follows. The servant in chapters lii. and liii. must have relation to the servant in chapters xlii. and xlix. Who was this servant, that had foretold the exile and the return, and had been a man of grief, rejected of his people, imprisoned and treated as a malefactor? The oldest Jewish tradition, preserved in Origen,[70] and to be inferred from Justin,[71] said the chosen people—in opposition to heathen oppressors—an opinion which suits ch. xlix. ver. 3. Nor is the[72] later exposition of the Targum altogether at variance; for though Jonathan speaks of the Messiah, it is in the character of a Judaic deliverer: and his expressions about '*the holy people's being multiplied*,' and seeing their sanctuary rebuilt, especially when he calls the holy people a *remnant*,[73] may be fragments of a tradition older than his time. It is idle, with Pearson,[74] to quote Jonathan as a witness to the Christian interpretation, unless his conception of the Messiah were ours. But the idea of the Anointed One, which in some of the Psalms belongs to Israel, shifted from time to time, being applied now to people, and now to king or prophet, until at length it assumed a sterner form, as the Jewish spirit was hardened by persecutions into a more vindicative hope. The first Jewish expositor who loosened, without breaking Rabbinical fetters, R. Saadiah,[75] in the 9th century, named Jeremiah as the man of grief, and emphatically the prophet of the return, rejected of his people. Grotius, with his usual sagacity, divined the same clue; though Michaelis says upon it, *pessimè Grotius.*[76] Baron Bunsen puts together, with masterly analysis, the illustrative passages of Jeremiah; and it is difficult to resist the conclusion to which they tend. Jeremiah compares his whole people to sheep going astray,[77] and himself to 'a lamb or an ox, brought to the slaughter.'[78] He was taken from prison;[79] and his generation, or posterity, none took account of;[80] he interceded for people in prayer:[81] but was not the less despised, and a man of grief, so that no sorrow was like his;[82] men assigned his grave with the wicked,[83] and his tomb with the oppressors; all who followed him seemed cut off out of the land of the living,[84] yet his seed prolonged their days;[85] his prophecy was fulfilled,[86] and the arm of the Eternal laid bare; he was counted wise on the return; his place in the book of Sirach[87] shows how eminently he was enshrined in men's thoughts as the servant of God; and in the book of Maccabees[88] he is the gray prophet, who is seen in vision, fulfilling his task of interceding for the people.

[17] This is an imperfect sketch, but may lead readers to consider the arguments for applying Isaiah lii. and liii to Jeremiah. Their weight (in the master's hand) is so great, that if any single person should be selected, they prove Jeremiah should be the one. Nor are they a slight illustration of the historical sense of that famous chapter, which in the original is a history.[89] Still the general analogy of the Old Testament which makes collective Israel, or the prophetic remnant, especially the servant of Jehovah, and the comparison of c. xlii., xlix. may permit us to think the oldest interpretation the truest; with only this admission, that the figure of Jeremiah stood forth amongst the Prophets, and tinged the delineation of the true Israel, that is, *the faithful remnant* who had been disbelieved—just as the figure of Laud or Hammond might represent the Caroline Church in the eyes of her poet.[90]

[18] If this seems but a compromise, it may be justified by Ewald's phrase, '*Die wenigen Treuen im Exile, Jeremjah und andre,*'[91] though he makes the servant idealized Israel.

[19] If any sincere Christian now asks, is not then our Saviour spoken of in Isaiah; let him open his New Testament, and ask therewith John the Baptist, whether he was Elias? If he finds the Baptist answering *I am not*, yet our Lord testifies that in spirit and power this was Elias; a little reflexion will show how the historical representation in Isaiah liii. is of some suffering prophet or remnant, yet the truth and patience, the grief and triumph, have their highest fulfilment in Him who said, 'Father, not my will, but thine.'[92] But we must not distort the prophets, to prove the Divine WORD incarnate, and then from the incarnation reason back to the sense of prophecy.

[20] Loudly as justice and humanity exclaim against such traditional distortion of prophecy as makes their own sacred writings a ground of cruel prejudice against the Hebrew people, and the fidelity of this remarkable race to the oracles of their fathers a handle for social obloquy, the cause of Christianity itself would be the greatest gainer, if we laid aside weapons, the use of which brings shame. Israel would be

acknowledged, as in some sense still a Messiah, having borne centuries of reproach through the sin of the nations; but the Saviour who fulfilled in his own person the highest aspiration of Hebrew seers and of mankind, thereby lifting the ancient words, so to speak, into a new and higher power, would be recognised as having eminently the unction of a prophet whose words die not, of a priest in a temple not made with hands, and of a king in the realm of thought, delivering his people from a bondage of moral evil, worse than Egypt or Babylon.[93] If already the vast majority of the prophecies are acknowledged by our best authorities to require some such rendering, in order to Christianize them, and if this acknowledgment has become uniformly stronger in proportion as learning was unfettered, the force of analogy leads us to anticipate that our Isaiah too must require a similar interpretation. No new principle is thrust upon the Christian world, by our historical understanding of this famous chapter; but a case which had been thought exceptional, is shown to harmonize with a general principle.

Whether the great prophet, whose triumphant thanksgiving on the return from Babylon forms the later chapters of our Isaiah, is to remain without a name, or whether Baron Bunsen has succeeded in identifying him with BARUCH, the disciple, scribe, and perhaps biographer or editor of Jeremiah, is a question of probability. Most readers of the argument for the identity will feel inclined to assent; but a doubt may occur, whether many an unnamed disciple of the prophetic school may not have burnt with kindred zeal, and used diction not peculiar to any one; while such a doubt may be strengthened by the confidence with which our critic ascribes a recasting of Job, and of parts of other books, to the same favourite Baruch. Yet, if kept within the region of critical conjecture, his reasons are something more than ingenious. It may weigh with some Anglicans, that a letter ascribed to St. Athanasius mentions Baruch among the canonical prophets.[94]

In distinguishing the man Daniel from our book of Daniel, and in bringing the latter as low as the reign of Epiphanes, our author only follows the admitted necessities of the case.[95] Not only Macedonian words, such as *symphonia*[96] and *psanterion*, but the texture of the Chaldaic, with such late forms as לֵכוֹן, הֵן and אִלֵן the pronominal ם and ה having passed into ן, and not only minute description of Antiochus's reign, but the stoppage of such description at the precise date 169 B.C., remove all philological and critical doubt as to the age of the book.[97] But what seems peculiar to Baron Bunsen, is the interpretation of the four empires' symbols with reference to the original Daniel's abode in Nineveh: so that the winged lion traditionally meant the Assyrian empire; the bear was the Babylonian symbol; the leopard that of the Medes and Persians; while the fourth beast represented, as is not uncommonly held, the sway of Alexander.[98] A like reference is traced in the mention of Hiddekel, or the Tigris, in ch. x; for, if the scene had been Babylon under Darius, the river must have been the Euphrates.[99] The truth seems, that starting like many a patriot bard of our own, from a name traditionally sacred, the writer used it with no deceptive intention, as a dramatic form which dignified his encouragement of his countrymen in their great struggle against Antiochus. The original place of the book,[100] amongst the later Hagiographa of the Jewish canon and the absence of any mention of it by the son of Sirach, strikingly confirm this view of its origin; and, if some obscurity rests upon details, the general conclusion, that the book contains no predictions, except by analogy and type, can hardly be gainsaid. But it may not the less, with some of the latest Psalms, have nerved the men of Israel, when they turned to flight the armies of the aliens; and it suggests, in the Godless invader, no slight forecast of Caligula again invading the Temple with like abomination, as well as of whatever exalts itself against faith and conscience, to the end of the world. It is time for divines to recognise these things, since, with their opportunities of study, the current error is as discreditable to them, as for the well-meaning crowd, who are taught to identify it with their creed, it is a matter of grave compassion.[101]

[23] It provokes a smile on serious topics to observe the zeal with which our critic vindicates the personality of Jonah, and the originality of his hymn (the latter being generally thought doubtful), while he proceeds to explain that the narrative of our book, in which the hymn is imbedded, contains a late legend,[102] founded on misconception. One can imagine the cheers which the opening of such an essay might evoke in some of our own circles, changing into indignation as the distinguished foreigner developed his views. After this, he might speak more gently of mythical theories.

[24] But, if such a notion alarms those who think that, apart from omniscience belonging to the Jews, the proper conclusion of reason is atheism; it is not inconsistent with the idea that Almighty God has been pleased to educate men and nations, employing imagination no less than conscience, and suffering His lessons to play freely within the limits of humanity and its shortcomings.[103] Nor will any fair reader rise from the prophetical disquisitions without feeling that he has been under the guidance of a master's-hand. The great result is to vindicate the work of the Eternal Spirit; that abiding influence, which as our church teaches us in the Ordination Service, underlies all others, and in which converge all images of old time and means of grace now; temple, Scripture, finger, and hand of God; and again, preaching, sacraments, waters which comfort, and flame which burns.[104] If such a Spirit did not dwell in the Church the Bible would not be inspired, for the Bible is, before all things, the written voice of the congregation. Bold as a theory of inspiration may sound, it was the earliest creed of the Church, and it is the only one to which the facts of Scripture answer. The sacred writers acknowledge themselves men of like passions with ourselves, and we are promised illumination from the Spirit which dwelt in them.[105] Hence, when we find our Prayer-book constructed on the idea of the Church being an inspired society, instead of objecting that every one of us is fallible, we should define inspiration consistently with the facts of Scripture, and of human nature. These would neither exclude the idea of fallibility among Israelites of old, nor teach us to quench the Spirit in true hearts for ever. But if any one prefers thinking the Sacred Writers passionless machines, and calling

Luther and Milton 'uninspired,' let him cooperate in researches by which his theory, if true, will be triumphantly confirmed. Let him join in considering it a religious duty to print the most genuine text of those words which he calls Divine; let him yield no grudging assent to the removal of demonstrated interpolations in our text or errors in our translation; let him give English equivalents for its Latinisms, once natural, but now become deceptive; let him next trace fairly the growth of our complex doctrines out of scriptural germs, whether of simple thought or of Hebrew idiom; then, if he be not prepared to trust our Church with a larger freedom in incorporating into her language the results of such inquiry and adapting one-sided forms to wider experience, he will a least have acquired such a knowledge of this field of thought as may induce him to treat labourers in it with respect. A recurrence to first principles, even of Revelation, may, to minds prudent or timid, seem a process of more danger than advantage; and it is possible to defend our traditional theology, if stated reasonably, and with allowance for the accidents of its growth. But what is not possible, with honesty, is to uphold a fabric of mingled faith and speculation, and in the same breath to violate the instinct which believed, and blindfold the mind which reasoned. It would be strange if God's work were preserved, by disparaging the instruments which His wisdom chose for it.

On turning to the *Hippolytus*[106] we find a congeries of subjects, but yet a whole, pregnant and suggestive beyond any book of our time. To lay deep the foundations of faith in the necessities of the human mind, and to establish its confirmation by history, distinguishing the local from the universal, and translating the idioms of priesthoods or races into the broad speech of humanity, are amongst parts of the great argument. Of those wonderful aphorisms, which are further developed in the second volume of *Gott in der Geschichte*, suffice it here, that their author stands at the farthest pole from those who find no divine footsteps in the Gentile world. He believes in Christ, because he first believes in God and in mankind. In this he harmonizes with the church Fathers before Augustine, and with all our deepest Evangelical school. In handling the New Testament he remains faithful to his habit of exalting spiritual ideas, and the leading characters by whose personal impulse they have been stamped on the world. Other foundation for healthful mind or durable society he suffers no man to lay, save that of Jesus, the Christ of God. In Him he finds brought to perfection that religious idea, which is the thought of the Eternal, without conformity to which our souls cannot be saved from evil. He selects for emphasis such sayings as, *'I came to cast fire upon the earth, and how I would it were already kindled! I have a baptism to be baptized with, and how am I straitened until it be accomplished!'* In these he finds the innermost mind of the Son of Man, undimmed by the haze of mingled imagination and remembrance, with which his awful figure should scarcely fail to be at length invested by affection. The glimpses thus afforded us into the depth of our Lord's purpose, and his law of giving rather than receiving, explain the wonder-working power with which he wielded the truest hearts of his generation and correspond to his life and death of self-sacrifice.[107]

[26] This recognition of Christ as the moral Saviour of mankind may seem to some Baron Bunsen's most obvious claim to the name of Christian. For, though he embraces with more than orthodox warmth New Testament terms, he explains them in such a way, that he may be charged with using Evangelical language in a philosophical sense. But in reply he would ask, what proof is there that the reasonable sense of St. Paul's words was not the only which the Apostle intended? Why may not justification by faith have meant the peace of mind, or sense of Divine approval, which comes of trust in a righteous God, rather than a fiction of merit by transfer? St. Paul would then be teaching moral responsibility, as opposed to sacerdotalism; or that to obey is better than sacrifice. Faith would be opposed, not to the good deeds which conscience requires, but to works of appeasement by ritual. Justification would be neither an arbitrary ground of confidence, nor a reward upon condition of disclaiming merit, but rather a verdict of forgiveness upon our repentance, and of acceptance upon the offering of our hearts.[108] It is not a fatal objection, to say that St. Paul would thus teach Natural Religion, unless we were sure that he was bound to contradict it; but it is a confirmation of the view, if it brings his hard sayings into harmony with the Gospels and with the Psalms, as well as with the instincts of our best conscience. If we had dreamed of our nearest kindred in irreconcilable combat, and felt anguish at the thought of opposing either, it could be no greater relief to awaken, and find them at concord, than it would be to some minds to find the antagonism between Nature and Revelation vanishing[109] in a wider grasp and deeper perception of the one, or in a better balanced statement of the other.

[27] If our philosopher had persuaded us of the moral nature of Justification, he would not shrink from adding that Regeneration is a correspondent giving of insight, or an awakening of forces of the soul.[110] By Resurrection he would mean a spiritual quickening. Salvation would be our deliverance, not from the life-giving God, but from evil and darkness, which are His finite opposites, (ὁ ἀντικείμενος.) Propitiation would be the recovery of that peace, which cannot be while sin divides us from the Searcher of hearts.[111] The eternal is what belongs to God, as spirit, therefore the negation of things finite and unspiritual, whether world, or letter, or rite of blood. The hateful fires of the vale of Hinnom, (Gehenna,) are hardly in the strict letter imitated by the God who has pronounced them cursed, but may serve as images of distracted remorse.[112] Heaven is not a place, so much as fulfilment of the love of God. The kingdom of God is no more Romish sacerdotalism than Jewish royalty, but the realization of the Divine Will in our thoughts and lives. This expression of spirit, in deed and form, is generically akin to creation, and illustrates the incarnation. For though the true substance of Deity took body in the Son of Man, they who know the Divine Substance to be Spirit, will conceive of such embodiment of the Eternal Mind very differently from those who abstract all Divine attributes, such as consciousness, forethought, and love, and then imagine a material *residuum*, on which they confer the Holiest name. The Divine attributes are[113] consubstantial with the Divine essence. He who abides

in love, abides in God, and God in him. Thus the incarnation becomes with our author as purely spiritual, as it was with St. Paul. The son of David by birth is the Son of God by the spirit of holiness. What is flesh, is born of flesh, and what is spirit, is born of spirit.[114]

28] If we would estimate the truth of such views, the full import of which hardly lies on the surface, we find two lines of inquiry present themselves as criteria: and each of these divides itself into two branches. First, as regards the subject matter, both spiritual affection and metaphysical reasoning forbid us to confine revelations like those of Christ to the first half century of our era, but show at least affinities of our faith existing in men's minds, anterior to Christianity, and renewed with deep echo from living hearts in many a generation. Again, on the side of external criticism, we find the evidences of our canonical books and of the patristic authors nearest to them, are sufficient to prove illustration in outward act of principles perpetually true; but not adequate to guarantee narratives inherently incredible, or precepts evidently wrong. Hence we are obliged to assume in ourselves a verifying faculty, not unlike the discretion which a mathematician would use in weighing a treatise on geometry, or the liberty which a musician would reserve in reporting a law of harmony.[115] Thus, as we are expressly told, we are to have the witness in ourselves. It is not our part to dictate to Almighty God, that He ought to have spared us this strain upon our consciences; nor in giving us through His Son a deeper revelation of His own presence, was He bound to accompany His gift by a special form of record.[116] Hence, there is no antecedent necessity that the least rational view of the gospel should be the truest, or that our faith should have no human element, and its records be exempt from historical law. Rather we may argue, the more Divine the germ, the more human must be the development.

9] Our author then believes St. Paul, because he understands him reasonably. Nor does his acceptance of Christ's redemption from evil bind him to repeat traditional fictions about our canon, or to read its pages with that dullness which turns symbol and poetry into materialism. On the side of history lies the strength of his genius. His treatment of the New Testament is not very unlike the acute criticism of De Wette, tempered by the affectionateness of Neander.[117] He finds in the first three gospels divergent forms of the tradition, once oral, and perhaps catechetical, in the congregations of the apostles. He thus explains the numerous traces characteristic of a traditional narrative. He does not ascribe the quadruple division of record to the four churches of Jerusalem, Rome, Antioch, and Alexandria, on the same principle as liturgical families are traced; but he requires time enough for some development, and for the passing of some symbol into story.[118] By making the fourth gospel the latest of all our genuine books, he accounts for its style (so much more Greek than the Apocalypse), and explains many passages. The verse, 'And no man hath ascended, up to Heaven, but he that came down,'[119] is intelligible as a free comment near the end of the first century; but has no meaning in our Lord's mouth at a time when the ascension had not been heard of. So the Apocalypse, if taken as a series of poetical visions, which represent the outpouring of the vials of wrath upon the city where the Lord was slain, ceases to be a riddle. Its horizon answers to that of Jerusalem already threatened by the legions of Vespasian, and its language is partly adapted from the older prophets, partly a repetition of our Lord's warnings as described by the Evangelists, or as deepened into wilder threatenings in the mouth of the later Jesus,[120] the son of Ananus. The Epistle to the Hebrews, so different in its conception of faith, and in its Alexandrine rhythm, from the doctrine, and the language of St. Paul's known Epistles, has its degree of discrepance explained by ascribing it to some[121] companion of the apostle's; and minute reasons are found for fixing with probability on Apollos. The second of the Petrine Epistles, having alike external and internal evidence against its genuineness, is necessarily surrendered as a whole; and our critic's good faith in this respect is more certain than the ingenuity with which he reconstructs a part of it.[122] The second chapter may not improbably be a quotation; but its quoter, and the author of the rest of the epistle, need not therefore have been St. Peter. Where so many points are handled, fancifulness in some may be pardoned; and indulgence is needed for the eagerness with which St. Paul is made a widower, because some fathers[123] misunderstood the texts, 'true yoke-fellow,' and 'leading about a sister.'

[30] After a survey of the Canon; the working as of leaven in meal, of that awakening of mankind which took its impulse from the life of Christ, is traced through the first seven generations of Christendom. After Origen, the first freedom of the Gospel grows faint, or is hardened into a system more Ecclesiastical in form, and more dialectical in speculation, the fresh language of feeling or symbol being transferred to the domain of logic, like Homer turned into prose by a scholiast.[124] It need not, to a philosophical observer, necessarily follow that the change was altogether a corruption; for it may have been the Providential condition of religious feeling brought into contact with intellect, and of the heavenly kingdom's expansion in the world. The elasticity with which Christianity gathers into itself the elements of natural piety, and assimilates the relics of Gentile form and usage, can only be a ground of objection with those who have reflected little on the nature of revelation. But Baron Bunsen, as a countryman of Luther, and a follower of those *Friends of God* whose profound mysticism appears in the *Theologia Germanica*,[125] takes decided part with the first freshness of Christian freedom, against the confused thought and furious passions which disfigure most of the great councils. Those who imagine that the laws of criticism are arbitrary (or as they say, subjective), may learn a different lesson from the array of passages, the balance of evidence, and the estimate of each author's point of view, with which the picture of Christian antiquity is unrolled in the pages of the *Hippolytus*. Every triumph of our faith, in purifying life, or in softening and enlightening barbarism, is there expressed in the lively records of Liturgies and Canons; and again the shadows of night approach, with monkish fanaticism and imperial tyranny, amidst intrigues of bishops who play the parts, alternately, of courtier and of demagogue.

[31] The picture was too truly painted for that ecclesiastical school which appeals loudest to antiquity, and has most reason to dread it. While they imagine a system

of Divine immutability, or one in which, at worst, holy fathers unfolded reverently Apostolic oracles, the true history of the Church exhibits the turbulent growth of youth; a democracy, with all its passions, transforming itself into sacerdotalism, and a poetry, with its figures, partly represented by doctrine, and partly perverted.[126] Even the text of Scripture fluctuated in sympathy with the changes of the Church, especially in passages bearing on asceticism, and the fuller development of the Trinity. The first Christians held that the heart was purified by faith; the accompanying symbol, water, became by degrees the instrument of purification. Holy baptism was at first preceded by a vow, in which the young soldier expressed his consciousness of spiritual truth; but when it became twisted into a false analogy with circumcision, the rite degenerated into a magical form, and the Augustinian notion, of a curse inherited by infants, was developed in connexion with it.[127] Sacrifice, with the Psalmist, meant not the goat's or heifer's blood-shedding, but the contrite heart expressed by it. So, with St. Paul, it meant the presenting of our souls and bodies, as an oblation of the reason, or worship of the mind. The ancient liturgies contain prayers that God would make our sacrifices 'rational,' that is spiritual. Religion was thus moralized by a sense of the righteousness of God and morality transfigured into religion, by a sense, of His holiness. Vestiges of this earliest creed yet remain in our communion service.[128] As in life, so in sacrament, the first Christians offered themselves in the spirit of Christ; therefore, in his name. But when the priest took the place of the congregation, when the sacramental signs were treated as the natural body, and the bodily sufferings of Christ enhanced above the self-sacrifice of his will even to the death of the cross, the centre of Christian faith became inverted, though its form remained.[129] Men forgot that the writer to the Hebrews exalts the blood of an *everlasting*, that is, of a spiritual covenant; for what is fleshly, vanishes away. The angels who hover with phials, catching the drops from the cross, are pardonable in art, but make a step in theology towards transubstantiation.[130] Salvation from evil through sharing the Saviour's spirit, was shifted into a notion of purchase from God through the price of his bodily pangs. The deep drama of heart and mind became externalized into a commercial transfer, and this effected by a form of ritual. So with the more speculative fathers, the doctrine of the Trinity was a profound metaphysical problem, wedded to what seemed consequences of the incarnation. But in ruder hands, it became a materialism almost idolatrous, or an arithmetical enigma.[131] Even now, different accepters of the same doctrinal terms hold many shades of conception between a philosophical view which recommends itself as easiest to believe, and one felt to be so irrational, that it calls in the aid of terror. 'Quasi non unites, *irrationaliter* collecta, haeresin faciat; et Trinitas *rationaliter* expensa, veritatem constituat,' said Tertullian.[132]

] The historian of such variations was not likely, with those whose theology consists of invidious terms, to escape the nickname of Pelagian or Sabellian.[133] He evidently could not state Original Sin in so exaggerated a form as to make the design of God altered by the first agents in his creation, or to destroy the notion of moral choice and the foundation of ethics. Nor could his Trinity destroy by inference that divine Unity which all acknowledge in terms. The fall of Adam represents with him ideally the circumscription of our spirits in limits of flesh and time, and practically the selfish nature with which we fall from the likeness of God, which should be fulfilled in man. So his doctrine of the Trinity ingenuously avoids building on texts which our Unitarian critics from Sir Isaac Newton to Gilbert Wakefield have impugned, but is a philosophical rendering of the first chapter of St. John's Gospel. The profoundest analysis of our world leaves the law of thought as its ultimate basis and bond of coherence. This thought is consubstantial with the Being of the Eternal I AM.[134] Being, becoming, and animating, or substance, thinking, and conscious life, are expressions of a Triad, which may be also represented as will,[135] wisdom, and love, as light, radiance, and warmth, as fountain, stream, and united flow, as mind, thought, and consciousness, as person, word, and life, as Father, Son, and Spirit. In virtue of such identity of Thought with Being the primitive Trinity represented neither three originant principles nor three transient phases, but three eternal inherencies in one Divine Mind. 'The unity of God, as the eternal Father, is the[136] fundamental doctrine of Christianity.' But the Divine Consciousness or Wisdom, consubstantial with the Eternal Will, becoming personal in the Son of man, is the express image of the Father; and Jesus actually, but also mankind ideally, is the Son of God. If all this has a Sabellian or almost a Brahmanical sound, its impugners are bound, even on patristic grounds, to show how it differs from the doctrine of Justin Martyr, Tertullian, Hippolytus, Origen, and the historian Eusebius.[137] If the language of those very fathers who wrote against different forms of Sabellianism, would, if now first used, be condemned as Sabellian, are we to follow the ancient or the modern guides? May not a straining after orthodoxy, with all the confusion incident to metaphysical terms, have led the scholars beyond their masters? We have some authorities, who, if Athanasius himself were quoted anonymously, would neither recognise the author nor approve his doctrine. They would judge him by the creed bearing his name, the sentiments of which are as difficult to reconcile with his genuine works as its Latin terms are with his Greek language. Baron Bunsen may admire that creed as little as Jeremy Taylor[138] and Tillotson did, without necessarily contradicting the great Father to whom it is ascribed. Still more, as a philosopher, sitting loose to our Articles, he may deliberately assign to the conclusions of councils a very subordinate value; and taking his stand on the genuine words of Holy Scripture, and the immutable laws of God to the human mind, he may say either the doctrine of the Trinity agrees with these tests, or, if you make it disagree, you make it false. If he errs in his speculation, he gives us in his critical researches the surest means of correcting his errors; and his polemic is at least triumphant against those who load the church with the conclusions of patristic thought, and forbid our thinking sufficiently to understand them. As the coolest heads at Trent said, Take care lest in condemning Luther you condemn St. Augustine; so if our defenders of the faith would have men believe the doctrine of the Trinity, they had better not forbid metaphysics, nor even sneer at Realism.[139]

3] The strong assertions in the *Hippolytus* concerning the freedom of the human will, may require some balance from the language of penitence and of prayer. They must be left here to comparison with the constant language of the Greek Church, with the doctrine of the first four centuries, with the schoolmen's practical evasions of the Augustinian standard which they professed, and with the guarded, but earnest protests and limitations of our own ethical divines from Hooker and Jeremy Taylor to Butler and Hampden.[140]

4] On the great hope of mankind, the immortality of the soul, the *Hippolytus* left something to be desired. It had a Brahmanical, rather than a Christian, or Platonic, sound. But the second volume of *Gott in der Geschichte* seems to imply that, if the author recoils from the fleshly resurrection and Judaic millennium of Justin Martyr, he still shares the aspiration of the noblest philosophers elsewhere, and of the firmer believers among ourselves, to a revival of conscious and individual life, in such a form of immortality as may consist with union with the Spirit of our Eternal life-giver. Remarkable in the same volume is the generous vindication of the first Buddhist Sakya against the misunderstandings which fastened on him a doctrine of atheism and of annihilation. The penetrating prescience of Neander seems borne out on this point by genuine texts against the harsher judgment of recent Sanskrit scholars. He judged as a philosopher, and they as grammarians.[141]

It would be difficult to say on what subject Baron Bunsen is not at home. But none is handled by him with more familiar mastery than that of Liturgies, ancient and modern.[142] He has endeavoured to enlarge the meagre stores of the Lutheran Church by a collection of evangelical songs and prayers.[143] Rich in primitive models, yet adapted to Lutheran habits, this collection might be suggestive to any Nonconformist congregations which desire to enrich or temper their devotions by the aid of common prayers. Even our own Church, though not likely to recast her ritual in a foreign mould, might observe with profit the greater calmness and harmony of the older forms as compared with the amplifications which she has in some cases adopted.[144] Our Litany is hardly equal to its germ. Nor do our collects exhaust available stores. Yet if it be one great test of a theology, that it shall bear to be prayed, our author has hardly satisfied it.[145] Either reverence, or deference, may have prevented him from bringing his prayers into entire harmony with his criticisms; or it may be that a discrepance, which we should constantly diminish, is likely to remain between our feelings and our logical necessities. It is not the less certain, that some reconsideration of the polemical element in our Liturgy, as of the harder scholasticism in our theology, would be the natural offspring of any age of research in which Christianity was free; and if this, as seems but too probable, is to be much longer denied us, the consequence must be a lessening of moral strength within our pale, and an accession to influences which will not always be friendly. But to estrange our doctrinal teaching from the convictions, and our practical administration from the influence, of a Protestant Laity, are parts of one policy, and that not always a blind one. Nor is doctrinal narrowness of view without practical counterpart in the rigidity which excludes the breath of prayer from our churches for six days in seven, rather than permit a clergyman to select such portions as devotion suggests, and average strength permits.

[36] It did not fall within the scope of this Essay to define the extent of its illustrious subject's obligations (which he would no doubt largely acknowledge) to contemporary scholars, such as Mr. Birch, or others.[146] Nor was it necessary to touch questions of ethnology and politics which might be raised by those who value Germanism so far as it is human, rather than so far as it is German. Sclavonians might notice the scanty acknowledgment of the vast contributions of their race to the intellectual wealth of Germany.[147] Celtic scholars might remark that triumph in a discovery which has yet to be proved, regarding the law of initial mutations in their language, is premature.[148] Nor would they assent to our author's ethical description of their race. So, when he asks: 'How long shall we bear this fiction of an *external* revelation,'—that is, of one violating the heart and conscience, instead of expressing itself through them—or when he says, 'All this is delusion for those who believe it; but what is it in the mouths of those who teach it?'—or when he exclaims, 'Oh the fools! who, if they do see the imminent perils of this age, think to ward them off by narrow-minded persecution!' and when he repeats, 'Is it not time, in truth, to withdraw the veil from our misery? to tear off the mask from hypocrisy, and destroy that sham which is undermining all real ground under our feet? To point out the dangers which surround, nay, threaten already to engulph us?'—there will some who think his language to vehement for good taste. Others will think burning words needed by the diseases of our time. They will not quarrel on points of taste with a man who in our darkest perplexity has reared again the banner of truth, and uttered thoughts which give courage to the weak, and sight to the blind. If Protestant Europe is to escape those shadows of the twelfth century, which with ominous recurrence are closing round as, to Baron Bunsen will belong a foremost place among the champions of light and right. Any points disputable, or partially erroneous, which may be discovered in his many works, are as dust in the balance, compared with the mass of solid learning, and the elevating influence of a noble and Christian spirit.[149] Those who have assailed his doubtful points are equally opposed to his strong ones. Our own testimony is, where we have been best able to follow him, we have generally found most reason to agree with him. But our little survey has not traversed his vast field, nor our plummet sounded his depth.

[37] Bunsen, with voice, like sound of trumpet born,
Conscious of strength, and confidently bold,
Well feign the sons of Loyola the scorn
Which from thy books would scare their startled fold—
To thee our Earth disclosed her purple morn,
And Time his long-lost centuries rolled;
Far Realms unveiled the mystery of their Tongue;
Thou all their garlands on the Cross hast hung.

My lips but ill could frame thy Lutheran speech,
    Nor suits thy Teuton vaunt our British pride—
But ah! not dead my soul to giant reach,
    That envious Eld's vast interval defied;
And when those fables strange, our hirelings teach,
    I saw by genuine learning cast aside,
Even like Linnaeus kneeling on the sod,
For faith from falsehood severed, thank I GOD.[150]

Note on Bunsen's Biblical Researches

SINCE the Essay on Bunsen's Biblical Researches was in type, two more parts of the '*Bible for the People*' have reached England. One includes a translation of Isaiah, but does not separate the distinguishable portions in the manner of Ewald, or with the freedom which the translator's criticisms would justify. The other part comprehends numerous dissertations on the Pentateuch, entering largely on questions of its origin, materials, and interpretation. There seems not an entire consistency of detail in these dissertations, and in the views deducible from the author's Egypt, but the same Spirit and breadth of treatment pervade both. The analysis of the Levitical laws, by which the Mosaic germs are distinguished from subsequent accretions, is of the highest interest. The Ten Plagues of Egypt are somewhat rationalistically handled, as having a true historical basis, but as explicable by natural phenomena, indigenous to Egypt in all ages. The author's tone upon the technical definition of miracles, as distinct from great marvels and wonders, has acquired a firmer freedom, and would be represented by some among ourselves as 'painfully sceptical.' But even those who hesitate to follow the author in his details must be struck by the brilliant suggestiveness of his researches, which tend more and more, in proportion as they are developed, to justify the presentiment of their creating a new epoch in the science of Biblical criticism.[151]

R. W.

2. Notes to Rowland Williams

1. This analogy aligns Broad Church theology with the latest developments in geology. Catastrophism, the belief that "great convulsions" such as Noah's flood caused the elimination of species (the view held by the "scriptural geologists" who took Genesis literally), was advocated by Georges Cuvier in *Discours sur les révolutions de la surface du globe* (1825; trans. *A Discourse on the Revolutions of the Surface of the Globe*, 1829). This view was opposed by uniformitarianists, who explained "changes in the earth's structure" by "causes still in operation." This position was advanced principally by Lyell in *The Principles of Geology* (1830–33). Gradualism in the formation of the surface of the earth and in continuous revelation characterizes new science and new theology: Williams's attack on "convulsions" in geology parallels attacks on miracles in theology, as well as various versions of the apocalypse ("sharp contrast of epochs and Revelation"). For a discussion of the uniformitarian-catastrophist debate see Cannon 1960. See also Goodwin ¶38 and n. 49.

2. Tertullian wrote *The Prescription against Heretics* (c. 200), concerning the derivation of doctrine: "It is in the same degree manifest that all doctrine which agrees with the apostolic churches—those moulds and original sources of the faith must be reckoned for truth" (chap. 21: trans. Peter Holmes, *ANF* 3:252). For "nigh at hand" see Joel 2:1; Luke 21:31.

3. The contrast drawn by Williams between different cultures and between the "better side of our nature" and "Satanic corruption" may be exemplified in statements of Friedrich Schlegel and Thomas Babington Macaulay. In 1808 Schlegel published *Über die Sprache und Weisheit der Indier* (trans. "On the Indian Language, Literature, and Philosophy" [1849]), in which he argues that just as the rediscovery of classical learning led to the renewal of European culture in the Renaissance, so "the Indian study, if embraced with equal energy, will prove no less grand and universal in its operation, and have no less influence on the sphere of European intelligence" (1849, 427). On the other hand, in the "Minute on Indian Education" (1835), Macaulay argues that studying Sanscrit is not "entitled to peculiar encouragement" because the language is "fruitful of monstrous superstitions." In wanting to eliminate such teaching he asks, "Can we reasonably and decently bribe men out of the revenues of the state to waste their youth in learning how they are to purify themselves after touching an ass, or what text of the Vedas they are to repeat to expiate the killing of a goat?" (1972, 248).

4. For the metaphor of the divine footprints in England compare William Blake, Preface to *Milton* (1804, ll. 1–4). Williams uses the metaphor again in ¶25.

5. For "good works" see Matt. 5:16; John 6:28–29; Rom. 13:3.

6. It is very remarkable that, amidst all our Biblical illustration from recent travellers, Layard, Rawlinson, Robinson, Stanley, &c., no single point has been discovered to tell in favour of an irrational supernaturalism; whereas numerous discoveries have confirmed the more liberal (not to say, rationalizing) criticism which traces Revelation historically within the sphere of nature and humanity. Such is the moral, both of the Assyrian discoveries, and of all travels in the East, as well as the verdict of philologers at home. Mr. G. Rawlinson's proof of this is stronger, because undesigned [Williams's note].

Sir Austen Henry Layard, excavator of Nineveh, published *Illustrations of the Monuments of Nineveh* (1848) and *Nineveh and its Remains* (1849, 2 vols.). His excavations from Nineveh are the core of the Assyrian collection of the British Museum. Sir Henry Creswicke Rawlinson excavated at Nineveh with Layard and at Baghdad and deciphered cunieform from the Behistun stone in 1846. He donated his collections to the British Museum. Edward Robinson traveled to Palestine in 1837–40 and published *Biblical Researches* (1841), an early work on biblical geography. A. P. Stanley toured Egypt and the Holy Land in 1852–53, publishing *Sinai and Palestine* (1856). George Rawlinson delivered the 1859 Bampton Lectures: *The Historical Evidence of the Truth of the Scripture Records, Stated Anew, with Special Reference to the Doubts and Discoveries of Modern Times.* On the development in the 1860s of ethnographical studies of "primitive and oriental peoples" as a result of more professionalized institutional study of antiquity see Burrow 1966, 80.

7. For the "Monster out of the Deep," or Leviathan, see Job 41; Ps. 104:25–26; Isa. 27:1; Rev. 13:1; 17:1–8. Williams identifies the "last" Leviathan with the Roman Catholic Church as the goal for Anglican converts following J. H. Newman's secession in 1845. See also Temple ¶5, n. 5. The Roman emperor Tiberius pretended great reluctance to succeed Augustus in 14, and only acquiesced, according to Tacitus, before the "abject supplications" of the Senate (*Annals*, bk. 1, chaps. 11–14; trans. John Jackson, *Loeb* 3:267).

8. The pronunciation of the Hebrew "shibbo-

leth" ("ear of grain" or "flood") was a password used by Jephthah's sentries (Judg. 12:6) to determine whether those crossing the Jordan were Gileadites, since the Ephraimites mispronounced it and were slain.

Williams's application is to the subscription to the Thirty-nine Articles of Religion that were "required" by students at Oxford for admission and at Cambridge for graduation. In 1834 a number of fellows at both Oxford and Cambridge sent a petition to Parliament, asking that submission to the articles be removed; the resulting bill to admit Dissenters was defeated in the House of Lords on 1 August 1834. The next year F. D. Maurice issued the pamphlet *Subscription No Bondage*, arguing that the articles were not exclusionary religious tests but instruments of education. The University of London was established in 1836 partly to admit students without religious tests. Dissenters were admitted to Oxford in the Oxford University Reform Act of 1854 without subscribing to the articles: Powell, Jowett, and Stanley were active opponents of required subscription. Jowett gave extended testimony to the Select Committee of the House of Lords on University Tests in 1871 (Abbott and Campbell 1899, 19–39). See also Wilson ¶s 43–58, and notes.

Controversy about clerical subscription continued through the nineteenth century, exacerbated by evangelical expositions of the Articles of Religion (see Laurence [1804] 1853), and Tractarian views of them advocated by Newman in *Tract XC*. Wilson alludes to the difficulty of subscription for those with a historical sense of the ways in which the articles were tied to theological debates in the reformation church; he also notes the fact that while subscription is required of those who seek ordination in the church, the meaning of that assent is not set out (see also Wilson ¶s 44–47, 51, 45–57, and notes). In 1865 the Clerical Subscription Act changed the forms used by priests and deacons in subscribing to the articles and the *BCP* at the time of ordination: while previously there were two separate oaths required by Elizabeth I and Charles II, obliging unfeigned assent to every word of the articles and *BCP* as containing "nothing contrary" to the "Word of God," the new formula required assent that they were "agreeable" to the word of God (see *Subscription* 1968, 29–40). In 1871 religious tests were abolished as conditions for receiving the M.A. at Oxford and Cambridge (see Hardwick 1904, 219–36 and W. R. Ward 1965, 235–62).

9. By "some specialties of Lutheranism" Williams refers to Bunsen's Lutheran liturgies, his diplomatic work in 1841 on behalf of Frederick William IV of Prussia to establish the Anglo-Prussian Bishopric in Jerusalem in cooperation with Anglicans and German Lutherans, and his views on inclusivity in the church and religious toleration according to the tenets of Lutheranism, set out in *The Constitution of the Church of the Future* (1847) where the "minute points" were, according to Maurice, "nearly uninteresting, scarcely intelligible anywhere else" (1861, 377). Bunsen's *Life of Martin Luther*, first written as an entry for the *Encyclopaedia Britannica* (8th ed. 1853–60), was republished in 1859. One of his translators, Susanna Winkworth, comments: "After the Apostle Paul, Luther was and always remained the first hero in his Pantheon of Christian Humanity" (quoted in Ralph Owen 1924, 67).

10. *Egypt's Place in Universal History*, by Christian C. J. Bunsen, &c. London. 1848, vol. i. 1854, vol. ii [Williams's note].

Aegyptens Stelle in der Weltgeschichte (1845–57, 5 vols.); trans. Charles H. Cottrell (1848–67, 5 vols.; vol. 1, 1848; vol. 2, 1854; vol. 3, 1859; vol. 4, 1860; vol. 5, 1867); 2d English ed. 1867, with additions by Samuel Birch.

11. Sir John Gardner Wilkinson published *The Topography of Thebes and General Survey of Egypt* (1835), *Manners and Customs of the Ancient Egyptians* (1837), *Architecture of Ancient Egypt* (1850), *A Popular Account of the Ancient Egyptians* (1858) and a facsimile of the Turin papyrus (1851), which had been edited previously by Karl Richard Lepsius. Bunsen refers to "Wilkinson's valuable edition" (Bunsen 1854, 2:xiii).

12. Herodotus includes in *The History of the Persian Wars* a long account of the history of Egypt (bk. 2). Eratosthenes of Cyrene wrote a treatise surviving in fragments that dates events in universal history. Jean François Champollion, part of Napoleon's team of archaeological experts taken to Egypt (1798–99), deciphered the Rosetta Stone, the key to the reading of the Egyptian archaeological records, publishing his findings in *Précis du système hiéroglyphique* (1823; Precis of the hieroglyphic system) and *Description de l'Egypte* (1802–25). He is eulogized by Bunsen in a poem in *Egypt* (1848–67, 3:v–vii). Thomas Young began to decipher the demotic text of the Rosetta Stone in 1814, publishing *Account of the Recent Discoveries in Hieroglyphic Literature and Egyptian Antiquities* (1823). Karl Richard Lepsius, a Prussian friend of Bunsen, succeeded Champollion as the foremost European archaeological researcher on Egypt. He published *Denkmäler aus Ägypten und Äthiopien* (1845–59, 12 vols.; Monuments from Egypt and Ethiopia). Bunsen describes this work in detail (1848–67, 3:3–7).

13. See an account of him, and his tables, in the Byzantine Syncellus, pp. 72–145, vol. i., ed. Dind., in the *Corpus Historiae Byzantinae*, Bonn, 1829. But with this is to be compared the Armenian version of Eusebius's Chronology, discovered by Cardinal Mai. The text, the interpretation, and the historical fidelity, are all controverted. Baron Bunsen's treatment of them deserves the provisional acceptance due to elaborate research, with no slight concurrence of probabilities; and if it should not ultimately win a favourable verdict from Egyptologers, no one who

summarily rejects it as arbitrary or impossible can have a right to be on the jury [Williams's note].

Manetho's *Aegyptiaca*, a history of Egypt from legendary times, from Menes, (fl. 3200 B.C.E.) to 323 B.C.E., the reign of Artaxerxes III, King of Persia (d. 338 B.C.E.). Menes, founder of the First Dynasty of the kings of Egypt, united Upper and Lower Egypt under one monarch. Long considered the legendary founder of Memphis, his historicity was established by archaeological discoveries in the Valley of the Kings in the nineteenth century. Bunsen dates his reign earlier, about 3620 B.C.E. (Bunsen 1848–67, 4:14). Manetho divides his Egyptian history into thirty dynasties, still largely accepted by scholars. His work, written in Greek, survives only in fragments, partly in *Against Apion* of Josephus (bk. 1, chaps. 14–16, 26–33; trans. H. St. J. Thackeray, *Loeb* 1:191–205, 255–85); and partly in the *Chronicle* of Eusebius. Lepsius published a study of Manetho's chronologies *Über die Manethonische Bestimmung des Umfangs der aegyptischen Geschichte* (1857, On the Manethan determination of the range of Egyptian history); and Wilhelm Kellner published *De fragmentis manethonianis quae apud Josephum contra Apionem I.14 et I.26 sunt* (1859, On the fragments of Manetho in Josephus' *Against Apion*, bk. 1, chaps. 14, 26).

Georgius Syncellus wrote *Chronographia* (c. 800), a chronology of the history of the world from the creation to the end of the reign of the Roman emperor Diocletian (313), using many sources, including Manetho. Syncellus' chronology was edited in 1829 by Karl Wilhelm Dindorf for August Immanuel Bekker's *Corpus Scriptorum Historiae Byzantinae* (Collection of the writings of the history of Byzantium, 25 vols.). The librarian of the Vatican, Cardinal Angelo Mai, recovered lost classical works by deciphering palimpsests, including the Armenian version of Eusebius' *Chronicle*. He published it with a Latin translation (1818), including many otherwise unknown fragments of Manetho. In 1825 Mai published *Scriptorum Veterum nova Collectio* (Of ancient writings newly collected), including fragments of Hippolytus that Bunsen refers to in *Hippolytus* (1854, 1:483–85).

14. "Six thousand years" refers to the dating of the events in the Bible by James Ussher in *Annales Veteris et Novae Testamenti* (1650–55; Annals of the Old and New Testament; trans. as *Annals of Creation* [1662]). Ussher's chronology, refined by John Lightfoot and incorporated in the folio AV (1701), was printed in many Bibles as marginal dates, beginning with creation on 22 October, 4004 B.C.E. It was not challenged until the late eighteenth and early nineteenth centuries by geologists such as Lyell (see ¶1 and note), James Hutton, and William Smith.

15. According to Williams, Bunsen established the antiquity of the Egyptian dynasties to 4,000 years before Christ, thereby challenging Ussher's dating of creation in 4004 B.C.E. Williams extends the attack on Ussher by drawing parallels between geology and recent developments in comparative philology. Bunsen also uses geological metaphors to argue for gradual philological development over millennia: "If we find almost 4,000 years before our era, a mighty empire, possessing organic members of very ancient type, a peculiar written character, and national art and science, we must admit that it required thousands of years to bring them to maturity in the retired valley of the Nile. If, again, its language be shown to be a deposit of Asiatic life, and by no means the oldest formation, it will be admitted, upon reflection, to be a sober conclusion, that we require some 20,000 years to explain the beginnings of the development of man" (Bunsen 1848–67, 4:21).

The "new," or Germanic, philology was introduced into England by the work of Franz Bopp in his essay "Analytical Comparison of the Sanskrit, Greek, Latin and Teutonic Languages" in the *Annals of Oriental Literature* (1820), and in the 1830s by Benjamin Thorpe and John Mitchell Kemble. It was consolidated by the establishment of the Philological Society in 1842, by theologians such as Thomas Arnold, Stanley, Trench, Thirlwall, and Whewell (Aarsleff [1966] 1983, 211–15). Controversy around the new discipline ensued in England throughout the 1840s. Chambers's *Vestiges* uses ethnographical philology to argue for an extended period of geological development by attributing similarly vast periods of time to the development of human languages and cultures ([1844] 1969, 283–94). Whewell responded, claiming a divine origin for language by republishing "Origin of Languages" from *Philosophy of the Inductive Sciences* (1840) in *Indications of the Creator* (1845). Debate between supporters of the divine and the human origins of language culminated at the 1847 meeting of the BAAS in Oxford where five papers on ethnographical philology were given; "the *pièce de résistance* was Christian Bunsen's ponderous report" (Aarsleff [1966] 1983, 225).

Comparative ethnographic philology raised questions about a single Adamic language. It also unsettled Victorian conventions of racial and linguistic superiority by identifying Sanskrit, the classical language of India, as a relative of English and by suggesting that language follows laws of development independent of human control. Further, "modern French" has taken over two thousand years to develop from Latin, and Latin, Greek, Sanskrit, English, and Welsh are relatives in one linguistic family, having developed over many millennia from a common Indo-European ancestor. According to Williams, different linguistic families, including "Semitic languages" ("Hebrew"), the Ural-Altaic ("Mongolian") and the Hamitic ("Egyptian") carry "traces of a primaeval aboriginal affinity." The developments of such distinct language groups, Williams states, took place over 20,000 years. In his account of Bunsen's argument, Williams suggests an evolution in the history of language analogous to the evolution of the rocks: the development of language pleads "as convincingly as the succession of strata in geology, for enormous lapses of time." See also Crystal 1987, 288–303.

16. The common term was Indo-Germanic. Dr. Prichard, on bringing the Gael and Cymry into the same family, required the wider term Indo-European. Historical reasons, chiefly in connexion with Sanskrit, are bringing the term Aryan (or Aryas) into fashion. We may adopt whichever is intelligible, without excluding, perhaps, a Turanian or African element surviving in South Wales. Turanian means nearly Mongolian [Williams's note].

Ham, the second son of Noah, is the father of Cush (Ethiopia), Mizraim (Egypt), Phut (Libya), and Canaan (Gen. 10:6–20). Nimrod, the son of Cush, is associated with Babel and Nineveh (Gen. 10:8–12). The Egyptian language belongs to the Hamitic, or Khamitic, family. Bunsen discusses the relations between Khamitic and Semitic language groups (1848–67, 4:71–73, 125, 424–28).

James Cowles Prichard published *Physical Researches into the History of Man* (1813, 2 vols.; rev. 1826, 5 vols.), demonstrating the affiliations of the Celtic languages with other Indo-European languages: "By some the term of Indo-European, by others that of Indo-German dialects, has been applied to the whole class of idioms which are found to be thus allied. The former of these terms is preferable to the latter, and indeed to any other, as being most general" (1826, 1:491). Pritchard's *Eastern Origin of the Celtic Nations* (1831) examined relations between Celtic and Sanskrit languages, and *Natural History of Man* (1843) argues for the primitive unity of the human species. In his 1847 address at the BAAS Prichard referred to Indian and Iranian subfamilies of Indo-European as "Aryan," recognizing that some writers used the term for the entire family (1847, 241). "Turanian" refers to the Ural-Altaic linguistic family, including Mongolian, as argued by Bunsen (1854, 6:64) and by Max Müller in 1859 (1861, 1:276). For relations between Indo-European and other language families see Crystal 1987, 304–25.

17. *Aegypten's Stelle in der Weltgeschichte*, pp. 186–400; B. v. 1–3. Gotha. 1856 [Williams's note].

For the cited references see Bunsen 1848–67, 3:457–70; 4:149–428.

18. *Aegypten's Stelle*, &c., B. v. 4–5, pp. 50–142. Gotha. 1857 [Williams's note].

For Longinus see *On the Sublime*, where Genesis is cited as an instance of the sublime: "So too, the lawgiver of the Jews [Moses], no ordinary man, having formed a worthy conception of divine power, gave expression to it at the very threshold of his *Laws*, where he says: 'God said'—what? '"Let there be light," and there was light'" (bk. 9, chap. 9; trans. W. Hamilton Fyfe, *Loeb* 149). Japhet and Shem are Noah's other sons (Gen. 10). Bunsen distinguishes between time before and after the flood (prehistoric and postdiluvian), using various ancient literatures for stories of floods and migrations of the Iranians or Arians from their "primeval country" in north Asia, as well as of others leaving the "cradle of mankind," Mesopotamia (Bunsen 1848–67, 3:461–70).

19. For "Adam begets" see Gen. 4:18–26; 5:1–20; for "Seth, like El," Gen. 4:25–5:8. Bunsen discusses various ancient names for God: "The most prominent name here is SET or SETH. It must be the oldest authentic name of this God. . . . We find this primitive name of God indicated in the list of patriarchs, where Set is the father of Enosh, i.e. the Man (synonymous with Adam)" (Bunsen 1848–67, 4:208). "El" is the title for 'god' in ancient Semitic languages and also is attributed to the chief god in the pantheon of Canaan and Israel. It is used in Gen. 33:20, throughout Job, and in combinations: Elohim, a plural form (Gen. 1:1) and El-Shaddai, God of the mountain, translated in the LXX as "God the Almighty" (Exod. 6:3). For Abraham see Gen. 11:27 ff.

20. Williams does not accurately represent Bunsen's argument. Bunsen suggests a complex relationship between chronology and revelation rather than an opposition: "Whoever adopts as a principle that chronology is a matter of revelation, is precluded from giving effect to any doubt that may cross his path, as involving a virtual abandonment of his faith in revelation." On the other hand, an exclusivist principle of historical inevitability is limiting in other ways: "He who . . . neither believes in an historical tradition as to the eternal existence of man, nor admits an historical and chronological element in revelation, will either contemptuously dismiss the inquiry, or by prematurely rejecting its more difficult elements, fail to discover those threads of the research which lie beneath the unsightly and time-worn surface, and which yet may prove the thread of Ariadne (Bunsen 1848–67, 1:161–62; see also 1:159–66).

21. "Septuagint" (abbreviated LXX) refers to the translation (between 250–100 B.C.E.) of the Hebrew scriptures into Greek for the use of Hellenistic Jews in the diaspora. According to legend, seventy-two (Lat. *septuaginta et duo*) Jewish scholars were brought to Alexandria in Egypt by Ptolemy II and translated the Hebrew Bible in seventy-two days. The LXX, still used by the Greek Orthodox Church, preserves a textual tradition different from that of the received or Masoretic text, with thousands of minor variants and some major ones. Many of its readings are corroborated by the Hebrew and Greek MSS. in the Dead Sea Scrolls found since 1947 at Qumran (Frank More Cross 1992, 144–45).

22. For Abraham's journey into Egypt see Gen. 12:10–20; see also Bunsen 1848–67, 3:340. Williams outlines Bunsen's argument that harmonizes discrepancies between biblical and Egyptian chronologies. The family of Jacob, son of Isaac who was the son of

Abraham, multiplied in Egypt (according to Bunsen) during the Fifteenth and Sixteenth Dynasties (c. 1667–1559 B.C.E.) when the Asiatic Hyksos, or shepherd kings, moved into Egypt and ruled there (see Gen. 25–35). Bunsen's Egyptian chronology is taken from Manetho as cited in Josephus, *Against Apion* (bk. 1, chaps. 14–16, 26–33; trans. H. St. J. Thackeray, *Loeb* 1:191–205, 255–85). For Manetho in the light of archaeological and other evidence see Van Seters 1966; and Redford 1992, 98–122. The "Medes" (or Kassites to modern scholars) were a group of Indo-European peoples living southwest of the Caspian Sea in the first millennium B.C.E., involved in the struggles with Assyria (see Culican 1965; Redford 1992, 447–69). The Medes participated in the overthrow of Assyria and are identified with the prophecies against Babylon (see Isa. 13:17; Jer. 51:11, 28; Dan. 5:31; 9:1; 11:1). "Sesortosis" (or Sesostris) is a semilegendary pharaoh, perhaps of the Twelfth Dynasty (Redford 1992, 257–58; for different calculations of Bunsen and comparisons with Ewald see Rogerson 1984, 125).

The Jews' oppression in Egypt after Joseph (Gen. 37 ff.) began , according to Bunsen, 215 years before the exodus (*Egypt* 1848–67, 3:350–60). Ussher dates the exodus 1491 B.C.E.; Bunsen dates the chief oppression at the end of the fourteenth and beginning of the thirteenth centuries B.C.E. under Rameses II, and the exodus under his son Menephthah (or Merneptah) in the thirteenth century B.C.E., rather than the traditional dating (1450 B.C.E.) under Thutmose III (Bunsen 1848–67, 3:xii–xxii, 194–205, 258, 260–63; 5:73–74). Traditional biblical scholarship harmonizes biblical chronologies and narratives with other evidence: see, for instance, Bright 1959; Noth 1962; Herrmann 1975, 56–68 and Thomas L. Robinson 1992.

Modern scholars use a wide range of historical, archaeological, textual, and socioeconomic evidence concerning Mesopotamia and Egypt to contextualize the biblical narrative. See Halpern 1983 and 1988; Van Seters 1983; Ahlström 1986; Miller and Hayes 1986; and Coote and Whitelam 1987. Redford, who argues that "the Sojourn and Exodus narrative is an adaptation by Israel of an earlier Canaanite tradition," perhaps connected with the West-Semitic Hyksos occupation and expulsion, gives extensive references to the controversies on the issue (1992, 257–63, 408–22).

23. Menephthah (or Merneptah), the son of Rameses II, ruled Egypt from 1322 B.C.E. according to Bunsen (1848–67, 3:xiii; 24–25; 188–205), or from about 1237 B.C.E. according to modern scholars (Redford 1992, 247). Siegfried Herrmann comments: "The usual formula that Rameses II was the Pharaoh of the oppression and his successor Merneptah the 'Pharaoh of the Exodus' rests on a combination of passages in the Book of Exodus which is not compelling. . . . Still we can begin from the fact that the exodus took place at the end of the thirteenth century BC" (1975, 62). Bunsen relies on Lepsius's *Book of the Kings of Egypt* (1858) for the dating of Menephthah's reign. Lepsius also published the relevant archaeological data in *Monuments of Egypt and Ethiopia* (1859, 12 vols.; see Bunsen 1848–67, 3:3–7). Many of Lepsius's findings were disputed later. Israel is mentioned only once in any ancient Egyptian inscription, on a granite stele from Menephthah's mortuary chapel at Thebes, now in the Cairo Museum (see Herrmann 1975, 51).

24. Ninus is the eponymous founder of Nineveh, capital of the Assyrian Empire. In Babylonian mythology Semiramis, a queen of Assyria, left her husband to marry Ninus. Bunsen dates both, the first year of the rule of Ninus in 1273 B.C.E. (Bunsen 1848–67, 3:442), followed by the Assyrian conquest of Egypt and Palestine (Bunsen 1848–67, 3:269–71, 443), and the death of Semiramis, in 1222 B.C.E. (Bunsen 1848–67, 3:289).

The problem of dating Ninus and Semiramis is a historical conundrum traceable back to classical authors: "Most of the early Greek authors, and those who have followed them . . . agree in assigning to the first kings of Nineveh the remotest antiquity. . . . Their united testimony even tends to identify or to confound Ninus, the first king, with Nimrod himself, or with one of the immediate descendants of the scriptural Noah" (Layard 1849, 2:177). Stanley Cook comments on this confused Assyrian chronology: "The old classical writers contain so many discrepant and confused statements and figures that little reliance can be placed upon their unsupported testimony. . . . Semiramis (the Sammuramat of history) is the famous Assyrian queen of classical legend. She has a prominent position in the traditional lists of Assyrian kings extending from the legendary Ninus, the founder of Nineveh, to the equally notorious Sardanapalus, who is placed at the age of a Median invasion or, otherwise, in the time of Nebuchadrezzar (c. 600 B.C.E.). To this Assyrian empire is attributed a duration varying from 520 years (Herodotus, bk. 1, chap. 96) to ten or even fourteen centuries. It looks, therefore, as though the scheme of Berosus [third-century B.C.E. who wrote a chronology of Babylonian or Chaldean history] has introduced the Assyrian empire together with the Babylonian, and that his list contains dynasties that were really contemporary" ([1923] 1928, 1:152–53).

25. Bunsen locates "Jewish tradition" in Flavius Josephus, the "historian of his nation" (Bunsen 1848–67, 1:185–94). For Josephus see Williams n. 120.

Williams dismisses the "dreams of the Drummonds and Volneys" as futile prognostications. Henry Drummond with Edward Irving were founders of the Catholic Apostolic, or Irvingite, Church. Drummond published on the interpretation of prophecy in *Dialogues on Prophecy* (1827). Constantin François Chasseboeuf, comte de Volney, spent four years in Egypt and Syria, and published *Voyage en Egypt et en Syrie* (1787; Voyage to Egypt and Syria). His *Les Ruines, ou méditations sur la révolution des empires* (1791; The ruins, or meditations on the upheaval of empires; trans. *The Ruins of Empires*, 1792) advanced a philosophy of history which predicted the final union of all religions by the recognition of the common truth underlying them. The Monster in Mary Shelley's *Frankenstein* (1818) learned the history of the world by overhearing a reading of Volney's *Ruins*.

26. Since satraps were provincial governors at the time of the Achaemenid Persians (c. 550–330 B.C.E.), much later than the period Williams is discussing, "satrap" is an anachronism. The Persian term is used in both the Hebrew and Greek Bible, but not in the AV, where it is translated as "princes" (Dan. 3:2 and 6:1). Williams refers to the Israelites' legendary military exploits against the rulers of the local nations about Iron 1 (1200–1000 B.C.E.); see Judg. 1:1–10; 3:10 and 6:1–8:35. "New Empire" is Bunsen's term for the New Kingdom Period in the history of Ancient Egypt (Eighteenth to Twentieth Dynasties, c. 1550–1070 B.C.E.), at the start of which the so-called Hyksos, or shepherd kings, were driven from their capital Avaris in the Nile delta. The New Kingdom includes the period of the exodus under Menephthah (Bunsen 1848–67, 2:499–506; 3:194–205). Williams follows Bunsen (1848–59, 3:271–6) in arguing that the rise of Assyria under "Ninus," another "New Empire," coincided with the time of the Judges, after 1273 B.C.E., during which local kings continued as "tributaries" (Bunsen 1848–67, 3:289) or "satraps."

27. νόμον ἔθετο μήτε προσκυνεῖν Θεοὺς . . . . συνάπτεσθαι δὲ μηδενὶ πλὴν τῶν συνωμοσμένων. αὐτὸς δὲ . . . . ἔπεμψε πρέσβεις πρὸς τοὺς ὑπὸ Τεθμώσεως ἀπελαθέντας ποιμένας . . . . καὶ ἠξίου συνεπιστρατεύειν κ.τ.λ. Manetho, apud Jos. c. Apion. The whole passage has the stamp of genuine history [Williams's note].

(Gr. "By his first law he ordained that they should not worship the gods [of the Egyptians] . . . . and that they should have no connexion with any save members of their own confederacy. Then . . . he sent an embassy to the shepherds who had been expelled by Tethmosis . . . and inviting them to join in an united expedition [against Egypt]"). This passage from Manetho's *Aegyptiaca* is cited in Josephus' *Against Apion* (bk. 1, chap. 26; trans. H. St. J. Thackeray *Loeb* 1:261) and is quoted by Bunsen (1854, 2:562–67). It recounts the revolt of the Israelite captives who were working in the stone quarries of Tura, in Egypt east of the Nile, led by Osarsêph, a priest of Heliopolis, later identified with Moses.

28. Williams uses Bunsen's chronologies (Egyptian, Greek, Hebrew, and Christian) that record a datable account of Moses' struggle to lead the Hebrews out of slavery. Bunsen argues that at the time of the exodus an invasion of "Palestinians" (Bedouins) entered Egypt, and that human rather than divine instrumentality, except in the Hebrew sources, explains the exodus events (Bunsen 1848–67, 3:263–69; 4:587–89). For "high hand" see Exod. 14:8; "pestilence," 1 Kings 8:37; "angel," 1 Chron. 12–30; and "Jethro," Exod. 2:16–22; 18:1–12.

29. In ¶s 7 and 8 Williams makes use of Bunsen's argument about multiple sources from varying dates for the Pentateuch to locate gaps and contradictions in the biblical chronologies. Such gaps call into question the unity of the Pentateuch (the first five books of the Bible ascribed to Moses) and notions of its single authorship.

Bunsen raises the following problems: Pharaoh and his armies, according to Exod. 14, were drowned in the Red Sea, but there is no break in the Egyptian chronologies of the pharaohs (Bunsen 1848–67, 3:263–69); the 480 years between the exodus and the Temple (1 Kings 6:1) are set against Bunsen's chronology of 300 years from the exodus in 1320 B.C.E. to the Temple in 1014 B.C.E. (Bunsen 1848–67, 3:422) or 1004 B.C.E. (Bunsen 1848–67, 5:74). Drawing on Bunsen (1848–67, 1:194–95), Williams proposes different ways of counting years in Judges (Judg. 3:11; 5:31; 8:28), the use of forty as a symbolic number (Gen. 6:12; Num. 14:20–23; Exod. 2:11; Mark 1:12), and different datings for the exodus in the NT given by Paul (Acts 13:16–20) and Stephen (Acts 7:2–47). Finally, Williams uses such apparent inconsistencies between Bunsen's chronologies and the biblical text (Bunsen 1848–67, 1:159–94; 3:415–38) to question the ascription of the Pentateuch to Moses and his age, instead of to later periods and several compilers, in the period between Solomon, king over Israel in the late tenth century B.C.E., and Hezekiah, king of Judah in the late eighth century B.C.E. In 1862 John William Colenso began to publish *The Pentateuch and Book of Joshua Critically Examined* (1862–79), in which he makes use of Williams's essay to challenge traditional authorship and dating of these books (Hinchliff 1964, 90).

30. *Gott in der Geschichte* (i.e. the Divine Government in History). Books i. and ii. Leipzig. 1857 [Williams's note].

Books 1 and 2 are published in vol. 1. A. P. Stanley wrote the preface for the translation of 1868–70. Reviewing the translation, F. D. Maurice writes: "God in history seemed to him [Bunsen] the capital interpreter of all the acts which history records, the root on which human unity must rest; [and] the end after which all human beings in all the bounds of their habitations are seeking" (1868, 149).

31. Blaise Pascal published *Pensées* (1670; Thoughts), the second section of which is entitled "The Misery of Man without God." G. W. F. Hegel's *Phenomenology of Spirit* (1807) argues that an absolute Spirit orders history by the continual self-

affirmation of its presence. A similar argument is made in his *Philosophy of History* (1837).

32. For "Author of life" see Heb. 5:9; 12:2.

33. Bunsen's concept of the Bible "as an expression of devout reason" was ascribed to Williams as a condemned belief in the trial in the Court of Arches. Williams, like Jowett and other Broad Church theologians, used Kant's distinction between understanding and reason, elaborated and qualified by Coleridge in *Biographia Literaria* ([1817] 1983, 1:173–75). The work of the practical intellect, or understanding, sifts the qualities and quantities of time and space, especially concerning history and the details of language; reason involves the intuitive and synthetic grasp of eternal relationships.

Bunsen discusses Abraham, Moses, Elijah, and Jeremiah in "The Four Leading Persons in the History of the Hebrew Religious Consciousness" (Bunsen 1857, 1: bk. 2, chap. 2). For "friend of God" see James. 2:23; "still small voice," 1 Kings 19:12; "law written on the conscience," Jer. 31:33; "speak truth," Jer. 9:5; "four hundred priests," 1 Kings 18:18–29; "the Searcher of hearts," Jer. 17:10.

34. For "Abraham slay his son" see Gen. 22:10; "mercy than with sacrifice," Hos. 6:6; "trust was his righteousness," Ezek. 33:13.

The passage from ¶10, "When the fierce ritual . . . sacrifice," was cited as "false and dangerous" in the Synodical Condemnation of *Essays and Reviews* on 21 June 1864 because Williams attempts "to explain away supernatural agency, even when its presence is directly asserted in Holy Scripture. That which is explicitly declared therein to be the immediate intervention of God is here attributed to the mere action of the human mind" (*Chronicle* 1859–64:1864, Session 66, 1657).

35. Bunsen discusses Mosaic institutions in "The Religious Consciousness of the Hebrews as Manifested in Their Political Institutions and Their Philosophic Thought" (Bunsen 1857, 1: bk. 2, chap. 6).

John Spencer published *De Legibus Hebraeorum* (1685; Concerning the laws of the Hebrews) relating the Jewish religious laws to those of other semitic peoples. William Warburton published *The Divine Legation of Moses Demonstrated on the Principles of a Religious Deist* (1737–41, 2 vols.), arguing for the divine origin of the Mosaic Law against the deists. Ernst Wilhelm Hengstenberg edited a conservative religious journal, *Evangelische Kirchenzeitung* (Evangelical Church Times), from 1827 to 1869 which defended orthodox methods of reading the Bible. He also published a treatise on Moses and Egypt (1841) and *Dissertations on the Genuineness of the Pentateuch* (1847). Mark Pattison in 1857 suspected Hengstenberg of having a network of spies that reported on rationalist ideas among the German clergy (Pattison 1857, 354–59; see Crowther 1970, 45, 51–52).

36. For "Divine finger" see Exod. 31:18; "people's heart . . . formal tablets of stone," 2 Cor. 3:3; "spiritual sacrifices with which He is pleased," 1 Pet. 2:5; Heb. 13:16. For the use of "sacerdotal" in a different context, compare ¶31.

37. *Bibel-werk für die Gemeinde*. I. and II. Leipzig. 1858 [Williams's note].

Bunsen describes his *Vollständiges Bibel-werk für die Gemeinde* (1858–72, 9 vols.; Complete Bible for the People) in his *Memoirs* as "a corrected translation, with parallel passages, and comprehensive explanations of the sense and its connection, below the text—to the exclusion of all systems" (Frances Bunsen 1868, 2:238). He discusses "the Bible before our Bible" in "The Hebrew Theory of Providence during the Two Centuries before Christ" (Bunsen 1857, 1: bk. 2, chap. 8).

38. Williams cites five textual or interpretative cruxes on which Bunsen comments, offering his own qualifications on them, but relegating them to "trifles" in comparison with Bunsen's overall accomplishments. These cruxes are: the spelling of the most common biblical name of God; the sanctuary of Shiloh; the opening verses of Genesis; the chapter and verse divisions in the Bible; and the so-called "cursing" psalms. Jehovah is a hybrid word, composed of the four Hebrew consonants (YHWH), the sacred "tetragrammaton" (Gk. four letters) of the name of God (Exod. 3:15; 7:2), considered too holy to be uttered, and so the circumlocution "Lord" (Heb. *'adonai*) was substituted. "Jehovah" combines the consonants of the former with the vowels of the latter. In the AV this Hebrew conflation was misunderstood, so that "Jehovah" is rendered by the small capitals Lord as at Gen. 21:33, "the Lord, the everlasting GOD" (Heb. YHWH El-Olam). Shiloh in Gen. 49:10 ("until Shiloh come"), usually interpreted in the nineteenth century as a Messianic prophesy, was an ancient religious center of Israel in the twelfth century B.C.E. (Josh. 18:1). The opening verses of Genesis raise the question of the meaning of the Hebrew *bereshit*: "in the beginning God created" or "in the beginning of God's creating," and so also raise the problem of whether creation is out of nothing, and whether the climactic moment of the opening verses is the creation of light. The division of the books of the Bible into chapters became common in thirteenth-century MS. Bibles and was continued in the first printed Bibles, such as the 42-line Bible of Johannes Gutenberg (c. 1455); biblical verse-divisions were first set out and numbered in the NT published in Greek in Paris in 1550 by Robert Estienne, and for the whole Bible in his Latin Vulgate (1555). For other cursing psalms see Ps. 58:6–9; 69:23–29.

39. Cicero wrote *Tusculanae Disputationes* (45–44 B.C.E.; Tusculan disputations) on fear, grief, death, and human happiness; it was composed at his "retirement" villa at Tusculum at the outbreak of the civil war that marked the transition from Republican to Imperial Rome ("Rome's lost freedom").

In the 12th edition (1865) a new note was added here in brackets: "See Note at the end of the volume." It refers to Williams's "Note on Bunsen's Biblical Researches" printed on p. 434 in the 1st edition, revised for the 12th edition to include information concerning Bunsen's death, and making specific reference to this paragraph. In the present edition the note follows Williams's essay on p. 204.

40. Isaiah viii. 4. Trypho §77, 8, 9. Well might Trypho answer, that such interpretations are strained, if not blasphemous [Williams's note].

Justin Martyr wrote *Dialogue . . . with Trypho* (c. 135). In chaps. 77–79 he argues that the details of Isa. 8:4 are prophetic of the infancy narrative of Christ and the Magi (Matt. 2), and Trypho responds that Justin's explanations are "mere contrivances . . . nay, even blasphemies" (trans. G. Reith, *ANF* 1:237–38). Tiglath-Pileser III was "King of Assyria" at the time of its greatest power, when Ahaz was king of Judah. Tiglath-Pileser III conquered the territories west of the Euphrates and seized Damascus in 732 B.C.E. and carried off its "riches . . . and the spoil of Samaria," as well as that of Jerusalem (2 Kings 16). The parallel to this passage in Isa. 8 is interpreted typologically by Justin as the gold of the Magi. The oracles of Isaiah, pronounced against Ahaz, prophesy destruction and a coming restoration under an ideal monarch (Isa. 9). This proclamation is interpreted by Christian commentators as a Messianic prophecy of Jesus; accordingly, Ahaz as the puppet ruler is read typologically as Herod.

41. On Isaiah xliii. 14–15, and again, on ch. xlviii. 12–16. He also shows on xlviii. 22, that the Jews of that day had not lost the historical sense of their prophecies; though mystical renderings had already shown themselves. But the later mysticists charitably prayed for Hillel, because his expositions had been historical. (See Pearson's Notes on Art. iii.) When will *our* mysticists show as Christian a temper as the Jewish ones? *Condonet Dominus hoc R. Hillel!* [Williams's note].

Jerome wrote a series of biblical commentaries, including a *Commentary on Isaiah,* to which Williams alludes (bks. 12, 13). Hillel the Elder was the leader of the Pharisees in Jerusalem and one of the most distinguished teachers of his day (c. 30 B.C.E.). His sayings are recorded in *Maxims.* John Pearson published *Exposition of the Creed* (1659), to which Williams alludes in reference to the third article of the Apostles' Creed, "Which was conceived by the Holy Ghost, born of the Virgin Mary." Pearson adds the same reference to Hillel to which Williams also refers: "It is the known saying of Hillel. . . . *There is no Messias to the Israelites, because they have already enjoyed him in the days of Hezekiah.* Divers of the later Rabbins endeavour to mollify these words of Hillel by their several expositions, but in vain. And R[abbi]. Joseph understood him better, who thought he took away all expectation of a Messias, and therefore fairly prayed for him" (1849, 324; cross-referenced to 172 of the standardized pagination of the 1669 edition). Pearson gives the citation as *Sanhedrin* c. Chelek, fol. 98, col. 2. Pearson then gives the Latin quotation cited by Williams: May the Lord pardon this Rabbi Hillel!

42. To Nepotian. Letter 52 [Williams's note].

Jerome's Letter 52 (c. 384), on the nature of the clerical life, is addressed to the priest Nepotian. It begins with a discussion of Abishag's relationship with King David and her typological role as wisdom (1 Kings 1:4, 15).

43. Presbyteri apud Irenaeum [Williams's note].

(Lat. The priests in Irenaeus). Irenaeus' *Adversus omnes haereses* (c. 180; Against all heresies) interprets the story of Lot's daughters who lie with him (Gen. 19:30–38) as types of the Jerusalem temple with its "priests," as contrasted with the Christian church (bk. 4, chap. 31, secs. 1–2).

44. Levi Ben Gershon (Gersonides) wrote a commentary on the Pentateuch as well as a philosophical treatise, *Milchamoth Adonai* (c. 1340; The wars of the Lord), dealing with the soul, prophecy, divine foreknowledge, creation, and miracles.

45. Trypho §41-43. This tract of Justin's shows strikingly a transition from the utmost evangelical freedom, with simplicity of thought, to a more learned, but confused speculation and literalism. He still thinks reason a revelation, Socrates a Christian, prophecy a necessary and perpetual gift of God's people, circumcision temporary, *because not natural*; and lustral washings, which he contrasts with mental baptism, superstitious. His view of the Sabbath is quite St. Paul's. His making a millennial resurrection the Christian doctrine, as opposed to the heathen immortality of the soul, is embarrassing, but perhaps primitive. But his Scriptural interpretations are dreams, and his charge against the Jews of corrupting the Prophets as suicidal as it is groundless [Williams's note].

For "circumcision and the Sabbath" see *Dialogue . . . with Trypho* (chaps. 16–21; trans. G. Reith *ANF* 1:202–5). See also Augustine: "From the time that circumcision was instituted among the people of God it was a 'seal of the righteousness of faith' [Rom. 4:11] and availed for old and young for the purging of original and former sin; just as baptism began to avail for the restoration of man from the time when it was instituted" (*De Nuptiis et concupiscentia* [On marriage and concupiscence, bk. 2, chap. 11, sec. 24], quoted in Fairweather 1956, 341). Justin also discusses the other matters to which Williams refers: for reason and revelation see *Apology* in *ANF* 1:166–67; "Socrates a Christian," *Second Apology* in *ANF* 1:191; prophecy and "corrupting the Prophets," *Apology* 1:173–74; resurrection and immortality, *Apology* 1:168–69. For Paul's "view of the Sabbath" as a human observance (Mark 2:27) that prefigures the coming messianic feast see Col. 2:16.

46. Thus he makes Isaac's hundredfold increase, Gen. xxvi. 12. mean 'multiplication of virtues,' because no grain is specified! *Quaest. Hebraic. in Gen.* ch. xxvi. When Jerome Origenises, he is worse than Origen, because he does not, like that great genius, distinguish the historical from the mystical sense [Williams's note].

Jerome wrote *Quaestiones Hebraicorum* (c. 388; Questions of the Hebrews on Genesis). Origen uses the allegorical rather than historical methods of reading in his commentaries on the Bible; he also produced the *Hexapla* edition of the OT (begun c. 231) with the Hebrew text in Hebrew and Greek characters, and four other parallel Greek texts.

47. Augustine's *Confessions* (c. 400) tell of his education in Latin rhetoric at Carthage and Milan. He learned "little Greek" and "less Hebrew." (bk. 1 secs. 13–14; trans. J. G. Pilkington, *NPNF*1 1:51–53). R. S. Pine-Coffin, discussing problems of translating Augustine's versions of the Psalms, comments: "Saint Augustine is known to have had a profound distaste for Greek and it is doubtful whether he had any knowledge of Hebrew" (Pine-Coffin 1961, 17). Ambrose, Augustine's teacher, was proficient in both Latin and Greek; Jerome knew both Greek and Hebrew. The term *Fathers* was used from the fourth century to refer to a restricted group of Christian authors whose writings on church doctrine, the "patristic expositions" (of Williams's next sentence), are accepted as authoritative. Williams's phrase echoes Ben Jonson's remark that Shakespeare had "small Latin and less Greek" ("To the Memory of My Beloved, the Author, Mr. William Shakespeare").

48. Erasmus's edition of the Greek text of the NT with a retranslation into "classical" Latin (1516) challenged the authority of the Latin Vulgate version of Jerome. He also edited the Church Fathers (including Ambrose, Augustine, and Jerome). Luther published a translation of the Bible into German (1521) and a series of commentaries and sermons on the Bible. Calvin published *Christianae Religionis Institutio* (1536; trans. Henry Beveridge *Institutes of the Christian Religion*, 1845–46) and a large number of biblical commentaries. Hugo Grotius defended Christianity on the basis of both natural theology and a devotional reading of the gospels in *De Veritate Religionis Christianae* (1627; On the truth of the Christian religion); he also published biblical commentaries.

49. In the 12th edition (1865) a new note was added here in brackets:

[He is stated by Hey to have alleged as many as twelve passages from the Old Testament as directly Messianic; it seems, he said he could have alleged more.]

Joseph Butler's *The Analogy of Religion* (1736) discusses "prophecy" and "contemporaneous history" (pt. 2, chap. 7, secs. 53–60; 1896, 1:345–51). John Hey published his lectures (1796, 4 vols.); they were republished in 1841 (2 vols.). In "Of Prophecies" (bk. 1, chap. 17, secs. 18–19) he discusses Chandler (1841, 1:181–89). Samuel Chandler published *Vindication of . . Daniel's Prophesies* (1728), *Vindication of the History of the Old Testament* (1740), and *Witnesses of the Resurrection of Jesus Re-Examined* (1744). Hey refers to Chandler's *Defence of the Prime Ministry and Character of Joseph* (1743). Though he follows Hey, Williams's title of "Bishop Chandler" is incorrect: although Chandler was offered preferment in the church, he refused, retaining his Presbyterian affiliation.

50. Collected in the *Boyle Lectures* [Williams's note].

William Paley's *Evidences of Christianity* (1794) and *Natural Theology* (1802), both draw an analogy based on the argument of design between the mechanical operations of nature and revelation. In *Evidences* (pt. 2, chap. 1) Paley discusses Isa. 52:13–53:12 as the one example of Messianic prophecy from the Hebrew scriptures (Paley [1794] 1851, 148–56). Richard Kidder delivered the Boyle Lectures on *Demonstration of the Messias* (1693) as part of the project to convert Jews in England to Christianity, but they were also directed against the deists. The Boyle Lectures were instituted from the legacy of Robert Boyle who left £50 to endow eight lectures to be given in a London church proving the Christian religion against "'notorious infidels, viz. atheists, theists, pagans, Jews, and Mahommedans,' with the proviso that controversies between Christians were not to be mentioned" (*EB*, 4:355). For a recent study of Boyle see Jacob 1977.

51. *A Literal Translation of the Prophets, from Isaiah to Malachi*, with Notes, by Lowth, Blayney, Newcome, Wintle, Horsley, &c. London. 1836. A book unequal, but useful for want of a better, and of which a revision, if not an entire recast, with the aid of recent expositors, might employ our Biblical scholars [Williams's note].

Conyers Middleton discusses history in relation to prophecy and miracles in *An Introductory Discourse to a Larger Work . . . concerning the Miraculous Powers Which are Supposed to have Subsisted in the Christian Church from the Earliest Ages* (1747) and *Remarks on Two Pamphlets* (1748). A work by the title cited by Williams has not been located; probably he is referring to William Newcome's *An Attempt towards an Improved Version . . . of the Twelve Minor Prophets Now Greatly Enlarged and Improved, with Comments by Blayney, Horsley etc.*, ed. J. Harrison (1836). The annotators cited in the title Williams gives were all prominent scholars and ecclesiastics. Robert Lowth published *Lectures on the Sacred Poetry of the Hebrews* (Latin 1753; trans. 1787) and *Isaiah: A New Translation* (1778). Benjamin Blayney prepared a corrected edition of the AV for the Clarendon Press. Thomas Wintle published *Daniel, an Improved Version* (1792) and *A Dissertation on the Vision Contained in the*

Second Chapter of Isaiah (1797). Samuel Horsley published an edition of *Hosea* (1801); he was also secretary of the Royal Society (1773–84), and edited the collected works of Newton (1779–85, 5 vols.). Williams's desideratum of a "better" commentary on the prophets, not met in his view by E. B. Pusey's *The Minor Prophets, with a Commentary Explanatory and Practical* (1860), was supplied by his own edition: *The Hebrew Prophets, Translated Afresh from the Original* (1866–71, 2 vols.).

52. 'Of prophecies in the sense of *prognostication* I utterly deny that there is any instance delivered by one of the illustrious Diadoche, whom the Jewish church comprised in the name *Prophets*—and I shall regard *Cyrus* as an exception, when I believe the 137th Psalm to have been composed by David . . . .

Nay, I will go farther, and assert that the contrary belief, the hypothesis of prognostication, is in irreconcileable oppugnancy to our Lord's declaration, that the *times* hath the Father reserved to Himself.'—*Memoir of Cary*, vol. ii. p. 180 [Williams's note].

Henry Francis Cary translated Dante's *Divine Comedy* into blank verse (1805–14); his son, Henry Cary, published his father's *Memoir* (1847) where the letter of Coleridge is printed. "Diadoche" means succession: here it refers to the sequence of the Hebrew prophets. For "Cyrus" see Isa. 44:28; for his being credited with having allowed the Jews to rebuild the Temple after the return from captivity in Babylon, see the end of 2 Chron. and beginning of Ezra. Psalm 137 is an exilic psalm which, if written during the Exile in the sixth century B.C.E. (because of its references to Babylon), cannot have been written by David who reigned 300 years earlier (c. 1010–970 B.C.E.). For "*times* hath the Father reserved to Himself" compare Acts 1:7.

53. Thomas Arnold published *Two Sermons on Prophecy, with Notes* (1838). Alexander Keith's *Sketch of the Evidence from Prophecy . . . with an Appendix, Extracted from Sir Isaac Newton's Observations on the Prophecies* (1823) sold forty editions by 1873 and became a standard work on evidence and prophecy. The thirty-seventh edition, published in 1859, includes "A Refutation of A. P. Stanley's Poetical Interpretations." Isaac Newton's *Observations on the Prophecies of Daniel and the Apocalypse of St. John* (1733) was published posthumously. For a recent study of Newton's theology see Force and Popkin 1990. John Davison delivered the Warburtonian Lectures on *Discourses on Prophecy, in Which are Considered Its Structure, Use, and Inspiration* (1824), stressing the moral element contained in prophecy and the progressive condition of its revelation. The Warburtonian Lectures, founded in 1768 by William Warburton, were delivered at Lincoln's Inn "to prove the truth of revealed religion . . . from the completion of the prophecies of the Old and New Testament which relate to the Christian Church, especially to the apostacy of Papal Rome" (*EB*, 28:318).

54. Amongst recent authors, Dr. Palfrey, an American scholar, has expounded in five learned volumes the difficulties in current traditions about prophecy; but instead of remedying these by restricting the idea of revelation to Moses and the Gospels, he would have done better to seek a definition of revelation which would apply to the Psalms, and Prophets, and Epistles.

Mr. Francis Newman, in his *Hebrew Monarchy*, is historically consistent in his expositions, which have not been controverted by any serious argument; but his mind seems to fail in the *Ideal* element; else he would see, that the typical ideas (of patience or of glory) in the Old Testament, find culminating fulfilment in the New.

Mr. Mansel's *Bampton Lectures* must make even those who value his argument, regret that to his acknowledged dialectical ability he has not added the rudiments of Biblical criticism. In all his volume not one text of Scripture is elucidated, nor a single difficulty in the evidences of Christianity removed. Recognised mistranslations, and misreadings, are alleged as arguments, and passages from the Old Testament are employed without reference to the illustration, or inversion, which they have received in the New. Hence, as the eristic arts of logic without knowledge of the subject-matter become powerless, the author is a mere gladiator hitting in the dark, and his blows fall heaviest on what it was his duty to defend. As to his main argument (surely a strange parody of Butler), the sentence from Sir W. Hamilton prefixed to his volume, seems to me its gem, and its confutation. Of the *reasoning*, which would bias our interpretation of Isaiah, by telling us Feuerbach was an atheist, I need not say a word.

We are promised from Oxford farther elucidations of the Minor Prophets by the Regius Professor of Hebrew, whose book seems launched sufficiently to catch the gales of friendship, without yet tempting out of harbour the blasts of criticism. Let us hope that, when the work appears, its interpretations may differ from those of a *Catena Aurea*, published under high auspices in the same university, in which the narrative of Uriah the Hittite is improved by making David represent Christ, and Uriah symbolize the devil; so that the grievous crime which 'displeased the Lord,' becomes a typical prophecy of Him who was harmless and undefiled! [Williams's note].

For modifications to this note in the 10th (1862) and 12th editions (1865) see the Textual Notes. At the end of his note in the 10th ed. Williams added: "This comes from Anselm on St. Matthew, ch. i." Williams refers to Anselm's comments on Matt. 1 quoted in the *Catena Aurea* (1841). In the 12th edition Williams tempers the sarcasm directed at Pusey.

The American Unitarian John Gorham Palfrey published *Academical Lectures on the Jewish Scriptures and Antiquities* (1838–52; in 4 vols., not 5, as Williams states). F. W. Newman's anonymous *History of the Hebrew Monarchy* (1847) applies German higher criticism to the history of early Israel. Henry Longueville Mansel's Bampton Lectures, *The Limits of Religious Thought Examined* (1858), develop an agnostic approach to religious thought by a reading of Kant's philosophy, derived from Sir William Hamilton. Hamilton published *Philosophy of the Unconditioned* (1829) with the following epigraph: "No difficulty emerges in theology, which had not previously emerged in philosophy." Ludwig Feuerbach published an attack on Christianity, *Das Wesen des Christentums* (1841, trans. George Eliot, *The Essence of Christianity*, 1854). E. B. Pusey published *The Minor Prophets, with a Commentary Explanatory and Practical* (1860). The *Catena Aurea* (1261, "Golden Chain") refers to Thomas Aquinas's compilation of the commentary of the Church Fathers on the four gospels, undertaken at the request of Pope Urban IV (1261–64); A translation was published in 1841 as part of *The Library of Fathers*; Pattison did Matthew (see Pattison ¶3 and n. 5). For Uriah the Hittite see 2 Sam. 11:9 ff.; "displeased the Lord," 2 Sam. 11:27.

55. Williams paraphrases Bunsen's comments on the debt owed to "the German school of critics" (see Bunsen 1868–70, 1:69, where the same names are referred to).

Johann Gottfried Eichhorn promoted the higher criticism of the Bible and comparative study of biblical and other Semitic texts in *Einleitung ins Alte Testament* (1790; Introduction to the Old Testament). Heinrich Georg August Von Ewald opposed the theology of F. C. Baur and the Tübingen school that interpreted the NT and early Christian history and dogma according to the model of Hegelian dialectical development. He published his *Geschichte des Volkes Israël* (1843–55, 5 vols.; trans. Russell Martineau and J. Estlin Carpenter, *History of Israel*, 1867–74, 5 vols.), developing the notion of the education of the human race from Lessing and Herder, reading Israel's place in universal history as providential and culminating in Christ. Johann Gottfried Herder published studies on, among other things, folksong and Shakespeare, as well as *Vom Geist der hebräischen Poesie* (1782–83; From the spirit of Hebrew poetry). Heinrich Friedrich Wilhelm Gesenius, a student of Eichhorn's at Göttingen before teaching at Halle from 1810, was attacked as a rationalist by Hengstenberg for teaching Hebrew philology comparatively with other Semitic languages, and, as much as possible, free of theological partisanship. He published a Hebrew grammar (1813) and a commentary on Isaiah (1820–29). The conservative theologian Johann Jahn was professor of Biblical Archaeology and Oriental Languages at the University of Vienna from 1789. In 1806 he resigned under pressure from Cardinal Migazzi for theological positions taken in *Einleitung ins Alte Testament* (1792, 2 vols.; Introduction to the Old Testament), especially for his reading of Job, Jonah, Tobit, and Judith as didactic poems rather than prophecies.

Opposing attacks upon his *Rational Godliness* (1855) in an open letter to Alfred Ollivant, Williams refers to rationalism in the same context: "What first strikes me [about Ollivant's attack] is *the want of any clear Definition of Terms*, even when the weight of the question hinges upon terms. You have not defined *Rationalism*, though you ascribe it to Dr Jahn, and impute a knowledge of his works to me as a fault. But neither in the strictest, nor in the most usual, sense of the word can Dr Jahn be termed a Rationalist. He taught within the rigid limits of the Roman Catholic Church. His works have been reprinted at Oxford. . . . If you know any better work on Biblical Criticism, pray recommend it to me. I wish to use the most trustworthy authorities" (1857, 23).

56. Bunsen discusses the role and limitations of prediction and prophecy in *God in History*: (1868–70, 1: bk. 1, chap. 1, secs. 2–5). For "David" see Ps. 137; "Nineveh," Nah. 1:1 ff.; "Tyre," Jer. 47:4. The reference to Tyre is an oracle associated with Nebuchadnezzar's sack of Ashkelon as part of his punitive campaign against Judah in 594 B.C.E. (see Bunsen 1848–67, 4:601–06).

57. Isaiah was a prophet in Jerusalem under the rule of Uzziah, Jotham, Ahaz, and Hezekiah, from c. 740–701 B.C.E. While "Isaiah" is the title of a single book in the biblical manuscripts (including the two Isaiah scrolls discovered in 1947 amongst the Dead Sea Scrolls), it has been assigned to two different historical periods since Johann Christoph Döderlein's demonstration in 1775, popularized by Eichhorn in 1783. The argument was continued by Gesenius, Ewald, and Maurer, who published in Latin a commentary on the Hebrew scriptures in 1832–34, and *In Jesaiam Commentarius* (1836; Commentary on Isaiah). The first section of Isaiah (chaps. 1–39) dates from the Assyrian period (c. 700 B.C.E.) and deals with the threat of attack on the kingdom of Judah in 701 B.C.E. The second section (chaps. 40–66), often called "Deutero-Isaiah," dates from the Persian period (sixth and fifth centuries), the period of the rebuilding of the Temple in Jerusalem under Cyrus II (Isa. 44:28). Sometimes the second part is divided into two: Isa 40–56 just before the Babylonian exile, and Isa. 56–66 after the return.

Williams follows Bunsen in using philological differences between Aramaic and Hebrew to date Isaiah's separate parts and to address its textual problems. Aramaic was the lingua franca of the Persian empires and the diplomatic language of the Babylonians. "Chaldee" (on the supposition that "Chaldee" was the language used in Babylon, rather than Assyrian) is the usual term in nineteenth-century biblical scholarship for Aramaic, as in parts of Ezra (4:8–6:18; 7:12–26) and Daniel (2:4–7:28), or in reference to the targums, the Aramaic translations of the OT. Williams cites two examples. First, for "sagans" (Heb. [Aramaic] סְגָנִים, *seganim*) see Isa. 41:25, the only occurrence of the term in Isaiah. *Gesenius's Lexicon* notes the Chaldaic (Aramaic) derivation for the word, meaning a Babylonian prefect, magistrate, or local prince (Gesenius 1846, 578–79). "Sagans" therefore dates from the Babylonian period and cannot refer to the Assyrian period 200 years earlier. Second, Semitic languages have a causative mode for verb conjugations: for instance, in the *hiphil*, or causative conjugation, the verb *kwn*, "to be firm," means to cause to be firm, to establish. *Aphel* rather than *hiphil* is the causative conjugation in Aramaic. *Aphel* forms have been identified in Deutero-Isaiah.

58. Bunsen discusses the visions of divine government in Isaiah and Jeremiah in *God in History* (1868–70, 1: bk. 2, chap. 1, sec. 6; chap. 3, secs. 3, 4, 5). Zechariah 1–8 concerns events datable to the second year of the reign of the Persian king Darius I the Great (520 B.C.E.), specifically the restoration of the Temple and a series of visions. Zechariah 9–11 deals with none of these concerns and may be contemporaneous with Deutero-Isaiah (see Isa. 53; 64:18–24). Zechariah 12–14 comprises yet another section; both Zechariah 9–11 and 12–14 are often associated with the prophet Malachi on linguistic grounds, but their placement in the Hebrew canon together with Zechariah 1–8 is perhaps prompted by a compulsion to complete the symbolic number of the twelve minor prophets (see R. Mason 1977). Williams alludes to Bunsen's attribution of the third section to Uriah the prophet (c. 600 B.C.E.) and to his argument that Uriah's attacks on Jehoiakim (Jer. 26:20–23) make the writing of Zechariah 12–14 contemporaneous with Jeremiah (Bunsen 1848–67, 4:605–6).

59. Bunsen discusses Micah as a prophet of the eighth century in *God in History* (1868–70, 1: bk. 2, chap. 3, sec. 1). For "Bethlehem" see Mic. 5:2; "Assyrian," Mic. 7:1–7. Pearson refers to "Thou art my Son" (Ps. 2:7) in *Exposition of the Creed* when commenting on Article 2 ("And in Jesus Christ, His only Son, Our Lord") and Article 5 ("He descended into Hell: the third day He rose again from the dead"). In the first passage, Pearson alludes to these difficulties in the Hebrew text ([1659] 1849, 256, 474, cross-referenced to 136, 259 of the standardized pagination of the 1669 edition).

60. Cavillatur . . . . quod posuerim, ... *Adorate purè* . . . . ne violentus viderer interpres, et Jud. locum darem.—*Hieron. c. Ruffin.* §19 [Williams's note].

The elided passage from Jerome's *Apology. . . against Ruffinus* (bk. 1) cited by Williams reads: "I am told that he [Ruffinus] also carps at me for the translation I have given of a phrase in the Second Psalm. In the Latin it stands: "Learn discipline," in the Hebrew it is written Nescu Bar; and I have given it in my commentary, Adore the Son; and then, when I translated the whole Psalter into the Latin language, as I had forgotten my previous explanation, I put "Worship purely." No one can deny, of course, that these interpretations are contrary to each other; and we must pardon him for being ignorant of the Hebrew writing when he is so often at a loss even in Latin. . . . What sin have I committed, then, when a word is thus uncertain in its meaning, if I have rendered it differently in different places. . . so that I should not be thought to translate capriciously or give grounds for cavil on the part of the Jews" (trans. W. H. Fremantle, *NPNF2* 3:493). Jerome's self-defense against his former school friend Ruffinus, a translator of Greek theological works into Latin, consists of prolonged argument over fine points of scriptural interpretation, including the opening of Ps. 2:12: "Kiss the son." W. O. E. Oesterley comments on this textual crux: "The use of the Aramaic word for 'son' (*bar*), after the Hebrew, *ben*, has been used previously (*v.* 7), is unprecedented. . . . The Septuagint and the [Latin] Vulgate have, instead of 'kiss the son,' the rendering, 'take hold of correction'; similarly the Targum. Jerome had the present text before him, but translated it *adorate pure*, taking *bar* in an adverbial sense from the root *barar* 'to purify'" (1955, 126).

61. By reading כלביאים for כלבים. The Septuagint version may have arisen from הקיפוני, taken as from נקף [Williams's note].

Bunsen discusses cosmology in the Psalms in *God in History* (1868–70, 1: bk. 2, chaps. 4–5). Williams refers to the Hebrew text which reads "like a lion my hands and my feet." The passage is translated in the AV, following a marginal gloss in the LXX, "they pierced my hands and my feet." Such a reading is possible because the Hebrew letters for "like a lion" (כָּאֲרִי, *ka-ariy*, Ps. 22:16) are close to the word for "bind" (אָסַר, *asar*, as at Ps. 149:8), and the parallel verb in the preceding stich can be construed to mean "pierced." The problems Williams specifies are related to the LXX and Targum variants on Ps. 22:16 (17), *kelebyaym* ("roaring like a lioness," *ki-leba'iym*, as at Isa. 5:29), derived by emendation from *keleb/kalebim* (dog/s) at the beginning of the verse. Williams further conjectures that perhaps the LXX derives the notion of "piercing" with strength (*taqqiyph*, mightier) from the verb to strike, beat, or enclose (*naqaph*).

62. Bunsen discusses Pekah and Rezin in *God in History* (1868–70, 1: bk. 2, chap. 3, sec. 3). For "called him out of Egypt" see Hos. 11:1; "Unto us a child is born," Isa. 9:6. In the *BCP*, Isa. 9 is to be read at Morning Prayer at "the services of Christmas." The Hebrew *'el gibbor* is translated in the AV as "The mighty God" (Isa 9:6) without warranty for the definite article and its capitalization. Modern scholars relate the oracle of Isa. 9:1–6 to an ideal king

in the Davidic succession, sometimes to the occasion of the ritual coronation of King Hezekiah (in 715 or 725 B.C.E.); see Alt 1966, 241–59. Pekah was king of Israel (2 Kings 15:27) and was allied with Rezin of Damascus in an anti-Assyrian coalition against Tiglath-Pileser III in 732 B.C.E.; earlier Ahaz of Judah refused to join and the allies seized part of his territory (Isa. 7:1–10). Ahaz successfully appealed to Tiglath-Pileser to intervene. Williams is mocked for reviving old cavils with Hebrew translations such as "kiss the son" and "The mighty God" in *Aids to Faith* (William Thomson 1861, 83–84).

63. In his discussion of Daniel in *God in History* Bunsen argues: "It is one of the finest triumphs and most useful achievements of modern criticism to have succeeded in proving that the book of Daniel is to be referred to that age [of the Maccabees]. Thus alone can the stain of intentional deceit be removed from the book; for we are now, by means of the cuniform inscriptions, sufficiently acquainted with the Chaldean language as it was at the time of Nebuchadnezzar, to be able to affirm that the language of the Book of Daniel is no more Chaldee of the sixth century B.C. than it is the Hebrew" (1868–70, 1:191).

The unity of the book of Daniel is a matter of scholarly and theological dispute, relating to whether the book is to be read prophetically or historically. Arguing in favor of multiple authorship on historical grounds, Williams maintains that the first part of Daniel (1–6) refers to the conflation of three figures, Nebuchadnezzar, Belshazzar (the son of Nabonidus, not of Nebuchadnezzar, who did not actually rule; see Dan. 5:1–11), and to a fictitious ruler, Darius the Mede (Dan. 5:30). The references in Daniel 1–5 are to Nebuchadnezzar II (son of Nabopolassar, founder of the Chaldean dynasty). Williams summarizes Bunsen's argument that Daniel, rather than prophetic of the Babylonian exile (597–81 B.C.E.), was written considerably after it. The reference to "seventy weeks of years" (Dan. 9:24) signals the displacement of 490 years from the Exile to a period in the second century B.C.E., in particular to Antiochus IV Epiphanes who became the king of Syria in 175 B.C.E. Williams then addresses other textual cruxes: Zech. 12:10; Isa. 9:6; and Deut. 13, especially 13–17.

The Neckar is a river in Germany, a tributary of the Rhine that passes by Tübingen; hence, the reference in general is to German higher criticism. Here, however, it refers particularly to Bunsen, who retired from public life in 1854 to a villa on the Neckar near Heidelberg.

The last three sentences of ¶14, "When so vast an induction. . . . in the Neckar," were cited as "false and dangerous" in the Synodical Condemnation of *Essays and Reviews* on 21 June 1864. To Convocation, Williams rejected "the Prophesies of the Old Testament" as "the direct prediction of future events" (*Chronicle* 1859–64:1864, Session 66, 1657).

64. For "fullness of time" see Mark 1:15. The phrase "Son of Man" (Aramaic *ben nasha*) is used by Jesus of himself some eighty times in the Gospels, echoing the frequent use of the phrase (Heb. *ben Adam*) in Ezekiel.

65. 'Die Kraft des Schauens, die im Menschen verborgen liegt, und, von der Naturnothwendigkeit befreit, im hebräischen Prophetenthum sich zur wahren Weltanschauung erhoben hat . . . . ist der Schlüssel,' &c. *Gott in der Geschichte*, p. 149.

'Jene Herrlichkeit besteht nicht in dem Vorhersagen . . . . Dieses haben sie gemein mit manchen Aussprüchen der Pythia, ... und mit vielen Weissagungen der Hellseherinnen dieses Jahrhunderts . . . *id.* p. 151 [Williams's note].

Both quotations, the second slightly misquoted, are on the cited pages of Bunsen 1857. The first is translated: "The faculty of clairvoyance or open vision, which is latent in our nature, and which, in the case of the Hebrew prophets, released from the yoke of physical necessity, rose to a true intuition of the universe—that is to say, to a perception of the moral order of the world—forms the key to a considerable part of the prophetic writings, as well as to the influence which they exerted on their age" (Bunsen 1868–70, 1:70); and the second: "Thus that which renders the Hebrew prophecy unique is not merely the ethical tone of its thought. Similar moral reflections are to be found likewise in the sermons of divinely enlightened Christian orators, in all ages of the Church; nay, they meet us again in substance, and in a yet more perfect form, in the lyrical poetry of the Greeks, and the mythical verse of Jelaleddeen Rumi and his successors. Nor does their singular majesty consist in their prediction of external historical events; this they have in common with many of the Pythian oracles which have been handed down to us from antiquity in a perfectly trustworthy manner, and with many predictions of the clairvoyantes of this century" (Bunsen 1868–70, 1:72).

Rūmi, the pre-eminent Sufic poet of Persia, is celebrated for his mystical verse in *Mathnawī* (1273). A selection of his poems was translated into German verse by V. von Rosenzweig in 1838. The Pythia is the priestess of the temple of Apollo at Delphi, one of the sibyls, or inspired women, who uttered prophecies or oracles while in a religious trance.

66. The last three sentences of ¶15, "Why he should add to his moral. . . . requires proof," were cited as "false and dangerous" in the Synodical Condemnation of *Essays and Reviews* on 21 June 1864 because they reject "the Prophesies of the Old Testament" as "the direct prediction of future events" (*Chronicle* 1859–64:1864, Session 66, 1657).

67. In the next six paragraphs Williams discusses Bunsen's "brilliant" treatment of Isa. 42–54 (see ¶14 and note). Williams develops his earlier argument about the two parts of Isaiah. The first, chapters 1–39, is pre-exilic (eighth century B.C.E.),

includes oracles of judgment against Judah and Assyria, and concludes (Isa. 38–39) with an account of the reign of Hezekiah, king of Judah (727–698 B.C.E.) and a vassal of Assyria. Second Isaiah, chapters 40–66, is postexilic, dating from the time of Cyrus of Persia (c. 539 B.C.E.) just before and after the fall of Babylon. Second Isaiah prophesies the joyful return of the exiles. Williams interprets the "suffering servant" in the historical context of the sixth century B.C.E. on the basis of philological analysis and historical exegesis, making reference to both rabbinic and patristic sources. Rather than reading the "suffering servant" prophetically as a messianic deliverer, according "to the Christian interpretation . . . of the Messiah," Williams, following Bunsen, identifies the "suffering servant" as a collective term referring to the particular situation of the "faithful remnant" in Israel and in captivity. To do so, Bunsen quotes from Jeremiah, Lamentations, and Psalms. This reading breaks up the unity of Isaiah as a book of single authorship, dating, and referentiality, aligning the "remnant" with the postexilic period and denying the prophetical and messianic reading characteristic of Christian literalism and typological interpretation.

68. To prove this, let any one read Jerome's arguments against it; if the sacred text itself be not sufficient proof. '*Go ye forth of Babylon,*' &c., ch. xlviii. 20 [Williams's note].

Jerome discusses the problems of interpreting and translating the Bible in *Apology . . . against Ruffinus* (*NPNF*2 3:516; with the chapters given in summary); for the complete text, and Jerome's view of the LXX translators, see Jerome (1965, 143–59); for Jerome's comment specifically on Isaiah see bk. 2, chap. 32 (1965, 156–57). For "Go ye forth" see Isa. 48:20.

69. For "stooping of Nebo" see Isa. 46:1; "bowing down of Babylon," Isa. 47:1; "cup of trembling," Isa. 51:17, 22; "the arm of the Lord was laid bare," Isa. 53:1.

70. *C. Celsum*, i. 55. (Quoted by Pearson) [Williams's note].

Williams alludes again to Pearson's *Exposition of the Creed* (1659). In a discussion of Article 4 of the Apostles' Creed ("Suffered under Pontius Pilate, was crucified, dead, and buried") Pearson refers to "the ancient Rabbins" (Williams's "oldest Jewish tradition") and quotes Origen: "The shift of the Jews, turning these expressions off from the Messias [with quotations from the prophets, especially Isa. 53:4 concerning the Suffering Servant's bearing of 'our griefs and. . . sorrows'], and attributing of them to the people as to one, is something ancient: for we find that Origen was urged with that exposition, in a disputation with the Jews." Pearson then quotes Origen, *Against Celsus* (Pearson [1659] 1849, 344–45; cross-referenced to 182 of the standardized pagination of the 1669 edition). For Origen see *Against Celsus* (bk. 1, chap. 55; trans. Frederick Crombie, *ANF* 4:420–21).

71. For, in making the Gentiles mean *Proselytes*, they must have made the servant Israel. ἀλλὰ τί; οὐ πρὸς τὸν νόμον λέγει, καὶ τοὺς φωτιζομένους ὑπ' αὐτôυ, κ.τ.λ.—*Trypho*, §122 [Williams's note].

"But what? does He [Christ, read prophetically in the passage from Isa. 42:3] not refer to the law, and to those illumined by it?" (*Dialogue with Trypho*, trans. G. Reith, *ANF* 1:260–61). Justin Martyr is trying to convince Trypho that the Gentile "proselytes" are not converts to Judaism but to Christianity, not to the law but to the Gospel; hence, he argues, they are the true Israel as the children of the new covenant.

72. Later, because it implies the fall of Jerusalem. It is thought to have been compiled in the fourth century of our era. It is very doubtful, whether the Jewish schools of the middle ages had (except in fragments) any Hermeneutic tradition so old as what we gather from the Church Fathers, however unfairly this may be reported. My own belief is clear, that they had not [Williams's note].

Hermeneutics, the theory and practice of interpretation, was codified by Rabbi Hillel of Jerusalem (c. 55 B.C.E.–30) into seven rules for establishing interpretive norms (*middôt*), later extended to thirteen by Rabbi Ishmael Ben Elisha at Hebron (c. 100–150); for Hillel's rules see Metzger and Coogan 1993, 305–9. The hermeneutic tradition among the Church Fathers emerged into two clearly distinguished approaches from the late second century. One, associated with Alexandria (Clement and Origen) stressed allegorical interpretation; the other, associated with Antioch (Theodore of Mopsuestia and John Chrysostom), stressed literalism and typological interpretation. Recent studies on patristic and other traditions of hermeneutics include Robert Grant and Tracy [1948] 1984; Drury 1989; and Mark S. Burrows and Rorem 1991.

73. יסגון תולדת קודשא, and ית שארא דעמיה.—*Targum on Isaiah* liii [Williams's note].

The two passages from the *Targum on Isaiah* in Aramaic read: "the holy lineage increases" and "there is a remnant of the people": "*Yet before the* Lord *it was a pleasure to refine and* to *cleanse the remnant of his people, in order to purify their* soul *from sins; they* shall see *the kingdom of their Messiah, they shall increase sons and daughters. . . .* (Targum on Isaiah, 53:10 in Chilton 1987, 104–5).

The Targum (Aramaic: "translation") is the translation of the Hebrew Bible into Aramaic (c. 250 B.C.E.–300) for reading in the synagogues when Aramaic came to be spoken throughout the Mediterranean after the return of the exiles from Babylon. Targum versions, then, contain many readings at variance from the Masoretic and LXX texts, depending on their manuscript tradition. The Masoretes [Heb. transmitters], tracing their tradition back to the time of the rebuilding of the Temple under Ezra, flourished in Babylonia and Tiberias in the fifth century, and continued until the tenth century. They assumed the task of preserving the most accurate consonantal text of the Hebrew scriptures, the Masoretic text. To do so they introduced systems of vowels and so fixed pronunciation and interpretation.

The targum of the prophets (comprising both the "Former Prophets," the historical books of the OT and the "Latter Prophets") is ascribed erroneously in the Talmud, the commentaries on the Mishnah, or code, of rabbinic law, to Jonathan Ben Uzziel. From the fourteenth century the initial letters were taken to refer to Targum Jonathan, as it came to be known, instead of *Targum Yerushalmi*. Jonathan was a pupil of Rabbi Hillel the Elder in Jerusalem, in the early first century. Recent discussions of the collective authorship and dating of the *Targum on Isaiah* suggest that it was compiled in the first and second centuries, with redactions to the fourth century as "successive generations took up the work of earlier interpreters" (Chilton 1987, xxiv–xxv). See also Smolar and Aberbach 1983.

74. In Pearson's hands, even the Rabbins become more Rabbinical. His citations from Jonathan and from Jarchi are most unfair; and in general he makes their prose more prosaic [Williams's note].

Pearson refers to Rabbi Jonathan Ben Uzziel twice ([1659] 1849, 155, 552; cross-referenced to 82 and 296 of the standardized pagination of the 1669 edition). Jarchi is a thirteenth-century mistranslation of the Hebrew name of one of the most famous medieval Jewish theologians, Rashi. He established an academy at Troyes in France and wrote a commentary on the whole Bible except Chronicles. Pearson refers to Jarchi twice ([1659] 1849, 163–64, n. 1; 256, n. 2; cross-referenced to 87 and 136 of the standardized pagination of the 1669 edition). In both cases Pearson sets the rabbinic commentators in the context of grammatical quibbles concerning disputed points of prophecy. Williams considers Pearson's qualifications "more Rabbinical" and "most unfair"; similar derogatory comments are made by A. P. Stanley: "Josephus . . . refers throughout to sources of information not contained in the Old Testament, yet free from the grotesqueness and absurdity of the Rabbinical interpretation" ([1856] 1860, 32).

75. Titularly styled Gaon, as president of the Sora school [Williams's note].

Rabbi Shaadiah, Gaon (Heb. excellency), head of the rabbinical academy at Sura in Babylonia, translated the Bible into Arabic, and wrote biblical commentaries. For "man of sorrows" see Isa. 53:3.

76. In *God in History* Bunsen writes: "Hugo Grotius came very close to this idea, yet did not establish it by proof"; to which is added a note: "I have to thank my learned friend, Professor Jacob Bernays of Breslau, for communicating to me the words of Aben Ezra (1168) in his Commentary on Jeremiah, according to which it appears that Rabbi Saadia, the great head of the Babylonian College at Sura (892–942 A.D.), has already unfolded a similar view based on the life and words of Jeremiah" (1868–70, 1:119).

Johann David Michaelis published an annotated version of the Hebrew scriptures (1769–91, 13 vols.), and *Mosäisches Recht* (1770–75, 6 vols.; Mosaic justice; trans. 1840, 4 vols.), arguing that the Bible should be interpreted in the context of contemporary Near Eastern life, thereby anticipating the historical approach of German Higher Criticism. "*Pessimè Grotius*": Lat. So much for Grotius.

77. Jer. xxiii. 1–2; l. 6–17; xii. 3 [Williams's note].

In this and the following eleven notes, Williams cites the biblical passages adduced by Bunsen in *God in History* to link the "suffering servant" of Second Isaiah to the "faithful remnant" of Jeremiah's account of the exile. See Bunsen's discussion of Jeremiah as "the Servant of the Lord" (1868–70, 1: bk. 2, chap. 3, sec. 4).

78. Jer. xi. 19 [Williams's note].

79. Jer. xxxviii. 4–6, 13; xxxvii. 16 [Williams's note].

80. Jer. xi. 19–23; xx. 10; xxxvi. 19; xlv. 2–3 [Williams's note].

81. Jer. xviii. 20; xiv. 11; xv. i [Williams's note].

Williams's last reference is corrected to Jer. xv.1 in the 12th ed. (1865). See the Textual Notes.

82. Jer. xviii. 18; xx. 9–17; Lam. iii. 1–13 [Williams's note].

83. Lam. iii. 52, 53, 54; Jer. xxvi. 11–15, 23; xliv. 15, 16; i. 18, 19 [Williams's note].

84. Jer. xlv. 1–3; xi. 19; xli. 2–3; with xli. 9–10 [Williams's note].

85. Psalm cxxvi. 1; Isaiah xliii. 1–5, 10–14 [Williams's note].

86. Lam. i. 17; Jer. xvi. 15; xxx. 1, 2, 3, 10, 18; xxxi. 6–12; Isaiah xliv. 7–8; xlvi. 1–9, 10; l. 5–6; lii. 10–13 [Williams's note].

87. Eccles. xlix. 6–7, and Jer. i [Williams's note].

The "book of Sirach" is the Apocryphal book, "The Wisdom of Jesus, the Son of Sirach, or Ecclesiasticus" (Ecclus. 49:6–7).

88. 2 Macc. xv. 13, 14 [Williams's note].

89. The tenses from verse 2 onward are rather historical than predictive; and in ver. 8, for *he was stricken*, the Hebrew is, נגע למו, the *stroke was upon them*; i.e. on the generation of the faithful, which was cut off; when the blood of the Prophets was shed on every side of Jerusalem [Williams's note].

The Hebrew is *nega'* (the stroke) *lamo* (upon them) (Isa. 53:8). Biblical Hebrew has no tenses, but indicates temporality by verbal sequences taken as a whole. To limit this prophetical sense to the descriptive mode, Williams interprets verbs usually understood by biblical conservatives as prophetic in an aspectual or atemporal mode.

90. The theologians of the "Caroline Church" advocated High Church principles of worship, polity, and theology during the reigns of Charles I (1625–49) and Charles II (1660–85). William Laud established the professorships of Hebrew and Arabic at Oxford, imposed liturgical uniformity on the church, and proclaimed the divine right of kings in the new canons of 1640, thereby arousing Puritan hostility. Impeached by the Long Parliament, he was imprisoned in the Tower (1641), tried, and beheaded. Henry Hammond supported Charles I as his chaplain while the king was imprisoned by Parliament. In 1647 he too was imprisoned for ten weeks. The reference to the poet of the Caroline Church is to George Herbert whom Laud ordained and appointed to the parish of Bemerton (1630). His poems were published posthumously in *The Temple* (1633). For a recent study of the "Caroline Church" see Julian Davies 1992.

91. *Die Propheten, d. A. B.* 2ter Band. pp. 438–453 [Williams's note].

The cited passage reads: "The few faithful ones in exile, Jeremiah and others." Ewald published *Die Propheten des alten Bundes* (1840–41, 2 vols.; trans. J. Frederick Smith, *Commentary on the Prophets of the Old Testament*, 1875–81, 5 vols.).

92. For the references to "Elias," or Elijah, in relation to John the Baptist and Jesus see John 1:21; Matt. 11:14; Luke 1:17; "Father, not my will," Luke 22:42.

93. The three Messianic roles of prophet, priest, and king structure Christian typological interpretations of the Hebrew scriptures; see, for instance, Mark 14:62; 15:2, 26; Matt. 21:10–11; Heb. 9:23–28. For "temple not made with hands" see Heb. 9:11.

94. 'Ιερεμίας, καὶ σὺν αὐτῷ Βαρούχ, Θρῆνοι, 'Επιστολὴ καὶ μετ' αὐτὸν 'Ιεζεκιήλ, κ.τ.λ.—*Ep. Fest.* [Williams's note].

The cited passage from the *Festal Epistles*, listing the canonical books of the Hebrew scriptures, reads: "[Then Isaias,] Jeremias, and with him Baruch, Lamentations, and the epistle; afterwards, Ezekiel" (Athanasius 1854, 138; letter 39). Bunsen discusses Baruch as Jeremiah's successor (1868–70, 1: bk. 2, chap. 2, sec. 4). Baruch, a scribe under Jehoiakim and his successors, was the amanuensis of Jeremiah (Jer. 36:32) and inscribed the prophecies of Jeremiah in a scroll (Jer. 36:4). He went to Egypt with Jeremiah after a dispute over submitting to the Chaldeans at the time of Zedekiah's revolt (Jer. 43–46). He is credited with the Book of Baruch in the Apocrypha, found in the LXX. Anglicans accept Baruch and other Apocryphal books "for example of life and instruction of manners" (Sixth Article). The reference to "some Anglicans" is perhaps an allusion to the Tractarians, who published Athanasius' *Festal Epistles* in their *Library of the Fathers* (vol. 38), and thereby laid claim to patristic authority for the canonicity of Baruch.

95. Auberlen indeed defends, but says, 'Die Unächtheit Daniels ist in der modernen Theologie zum Axiom geworden.'—*Der Prophet Daniel.* Basel. 1854 [Williams's note].

Karl August Auberlen published *Der Prophet Daniel und die Offenbarung Johannis* (1854); trans. Adolph Sapir, *The Prophecies of Daniel and the Revelations of St. John* (1856). The cited passage is in the Preface: "The ungenuineness of Daniel has become an axiom in modern theology" (Auberlen 1856, v–vi). For the general dating and textual problems of Daniel see Auberlen 1856, 9–13. Williams uses linguistic and historical evidence to support a late date for Daniel.

The "man Daniel" is depicted as a Jew exiled in the Babylonian captivity of the sixth century B.C.E. He interprets the dreams of Nebuchadnezzar and the vision of Belshazzar and is preserved from death in the den of lions (Dan. 1–6). The second part of the book refers to events of the second century B.C.E., during the reign of Antiochus IV Epiphanes, who is presented as the "little horn" in a vision (Dan. 8), a phrase used to identify him elsewhere (1 Macc. 1:10; see Josephus, *Antiquities*, bk. 10, chap. 11, sec. 7; trans. Ralph Marcus, *Loeb* 6:309–10, where the identification is explicit).

Pusey's biographers specify that "because Dr. Williams had asserted that recent criticism had proved that the book was written at a very late date" (Liddon 1893–97, 4:71), Pusey chose Daniel for undergraduate lectures, beginning work in early 1862 on *Daniel the Prophet* (1864). He writes in the Preface: "I selected the book of Daniel because unbelieving critics considered their attacks upon it to be one of their greatest triumphs. . . . The exposure of the weakness of criticism, where it thought itself most triumphant, would, I hoped, shake the confidence of the young in their would-be misleaders. True! Disbelief of Daniel had become an axiom in the unbelieving critical school. Only they mistook the result of unbelief for the victory of criticism. They overlooked the historical fact that the disbelief had been antecedent to the criticism. Disbelief had been the parent, not the offspring, of their criticism, their starting-point, not the winning-post of their course" (quoted in Liddon 1893–97, 4:71). See also Jowett ¶38 and n. 74.

96. Compare 'Philosophy of Universal History' (part of the *Hippolytus*), vol. i. pp. 217–219, with *Gott in der Geschichte*, 1str Theil. pp. 514–540 [Williams's note].

"*Symphonia*" (Heb. סומפניא, *sumponeyah*) is translated as "dulcimer," and "*psanterion*" (Heb. פסנתרין, *pesanteriyn*) as "psaltery" at Dan. 3:5, 10, 15 (AV). These words are loan words, transliterations from Macedonian Greek into Hebrew, which could only have been incorporated into a semitic language after the dissemination of Greek culture by the military campaigns of Alexander the Great (356–323

B.C.E.).

97. Daniel is written in two different languages, Hebrew (1:1–2:4 and 8–12) and Aramaic (2:4–7:28). The Hebrew text makes reference to the court language of Nebuchadnezzar II as "Chaldean" (Dan. 1:4), the learned language of the astronomers, sages, and officials, but in fact Aramaic became common as a court language only under the Persian Empire (c. 550–330 B.C.E.), and was widespread as the legal and official language throughout Palestine (see Williams, n. 57). In *Geography* Strabo makes reference to the Chaldeans: "In Babylonia a settlement is set apart for local philosophers, the Chaldaeans, as they are called, who are concerned mostly with astronomy" (bk. 16. chap. 1. sec. 6; trans. H. L. Jones, *Loeb* 7:200–3). Dan. 8:11 refers to the actions of Antiochus IV Epiphanes: first, his deposing in 175 B.C.E. of the legitimate high priest Onias III in favor of his brother, Jason, who purchased the right to the high priesthood (1 Macc. 4:8); and second, his ordering of the cessation of Temple sacrifice, the defilement of the Temple sanctuary, and the erection of the "abomination of desolation," the statue of Baal or Zeus in 169/8 B.C.E. (Dan. 8:13; 9:27; 11:31; 12:11; see also 1 Macc. 1:34; 1 Macc. 1:44–51; 4:42, 47).

Williams argues that the use of Greek terms for musical instruments and late Eastern Aramaic terms in Daniel is an index of the book's production at the height of the influence of the Hellenistic period. For instance, the term לכון (*lechon*, to you) occurs at Dan. 3:4; דֵּן (*den*, this, in the form דְּנָה, *denah*) at Dan 2:18 and nineteen other occurrences in the same book; and אִלֵּין (*'illeyn*, these) as at Dan. 6:7. The suffix letters mem (ם) and he (ה) have been modified into the terminal nun (ן) in each of these pronouns. Williams's point is supported by the references and explications in Tregelles's edition of *Gesenius's Hebrew and Chaldee Lexicon* (Gesenius 1846).

98. Bunsen discusses these "symbols" in "The Maccabees and the Book of Daniel" (1868–70, 1: bk. 2, chap. 7, sec. 1). For "empires' symbols" see Dan. 7:4–7; modern scholars are in general agreement with Bunsen and Williams in identifying them with the successive empires of the Babylonians, Medes, Persians, and Macedonian-Greeks (Rowley 1935 and Arthur Jeffery 1956, 453–56).

99. For Hiddekel as the Tigris River, see Gen. 2:14; Dan. 10:4. Williams turns to geographical contradictions in Daniel. The Euphrates is usually referred to in the OT as "the great river." But in the Peshitta, the Syriac version of the Hebrew scriptures, the reading of Dan. 10:6 is "Euphrates." The Euphrates is associated with Babylon and Persia ("under Darius" the Mede), one of the mythical successors of Nebuchadnezzar in the sixth century. But at Dan. 10:4 the mention of the Akkadian term *Hiddekel* for the Tigris connotes a different association—with Assyria, Nineveh, and later with the conquest of Babylon by the Seleucids and the reign of Antiochus IV in the second century B.C.E.

100. The saying that later Jews changed the place of the book in the canon, seems to rest on no evidence [Williams's note].

Bunsen discusses the canon in "The Fixing of the Canon of Scripture" (1868–70, 1: bk. 2, chap. 8, sec. 4). The different placement of Daniel in the Hebrew and Christian canons of the Bible is used by Williams, drawing on Bunsen, to continue his distinction between Daniel as seer and as prophet. In the Greek (LXX) and Latin Bibles, and in the AV, Daniel is placed with the prophets. However, in the "Jewish canon" it is placed late in the "Hagiographa" [Gk. writings], as a part of the Wisdom tradition, whereby Daniel is read as an interpreter or sage. The Hebrew canon locates Daniel at the time of its purported events, about 600 B.C.E., but its placement within the Hagiographa rather than the prophets is an acknowledgment of its late appearance in the canon, after the closing of the canon of the prophets. The "son of Sirach" (Jesus Ben Sirach, writing c. 200 B.C.E.) lists all of the other prophetical books, but not Daniel (Ecclus. 49), so supporting by this negative evidence that Daniel was composed after 200 B.C.E. On the other hand, in the "predictive" tradition that Williams rejects, Daniel is understood to date historically from the time of the captivity in Babylon, so the prophecies foresee a series of later historical events: first, Antiochus IV Epiphanes and the Maccabean revolt (Dan. 11:34); second, the coming of "Messiah the Prince" (Dan. 9:25) to restore power to Israel (Matt. 24:15; Mark 13:14); third, the wish of Caligula to erect his own statue in the Temple in Jerusalem (the "abomination" of desolation of Dan. 12:11, set up c. 40); and fourth, the destruction of the Temple by Titus in 70. Christian apocalyptists read Daniel as prophetic of the coming of Jesus as Messiah at the last day (2 Thess. 2:2–4).

The allusion to "many a patriot bard of our own" refers to Williams's part in the nineteenth-century revival of Welsh nationalism and culture that included appeals to the "sacred" bards of Welsh legend (Aneurin and Taliessin), the revival of the Eisteddfod (1819) as a bardic congress (especially the archaic festival of 1858 [*EB* 9:136–37]), Williams's publication of a translation of Goronva Camlan's *Owen Glendower: A Dramatic Biography: Being a Contribution to the Genuine History of Wales* (1870), and the "patriotic enthusiasm" Williams drew on in preparing Welsh clergy at Lampeter (*DNB* 21:451).

In the context of British imperialism Williams's juxtaposition of "a patriot bard of our own" with Daniel aligns the "quiet struggle" of the Maccabean nationalists against Antiochus' imperial power with Welsh resistance to English domination. The symbolic event in that resistance was the English conquest of Wales under Edward I (1282) and the tradition that he ordered the execution of the Welsh bards, an event popularized in Augustan and romantic poetry and painting (especially Thomas Gray's *The Bard* [1757], illustrated by William Blake [1797] and by John Martin [1817]). Anti-Welsh prejudice against Williams for his intemperate letters is even voiced by such collaborators as Jowett in Letters 134 and 153.

101. Williams positions Bunsen's historical contextualizing of Daniel against the Protestant tradition of reading Daniel as predictive prophecy. Among eighteenth- and nineteenth-century Protestant interpreters, the "Abomination of Desolation" foretold the abuses of the Roman Catholic church, whose destruction would occur at the end of time when Christ appears as the Messiah predicted in Dan. 9:25. Such apocalyptic interpretations often conflate Daniel and Revelation so that the Roman Catholic church is equated with both the mark of the beast and the Whore of Babylon as in Calvin's *Commentarie on the Book of the Prophet Daniel* (1571; trans. Thomas Myers, 1852, 2 vols.). In 1829 Edward Irving published *The Church and State Responsible to Christ and to One Another: A Series of Discourses on Daniel's Vision of the Four Beasts,* which warns of "the three great forms of Antichrist—the Papal, the Mohammedan, and the infidel" (170). In 1848 William White published *Providence, Prophecy, and Popery as Exhibited in the First Seven Chapters of Daniel*; and in 1858 Samuel Sparkes published *A Historical Commentary on the Eleventh Chapter of Daniel, Extending from the Days of Cyrus to the Crimean War, Receiving Its Ultimate Accomplishment in the Fall of the Turkish Ottoman Empire.* Daniel is sometimes still read as explicit anti-Roman Catholic propaganda (for example Ulrich Smith 1944, 60 ff.; 707 ff.). For English millenarianism see Oliver 1978.

102. The present writer feels excused from repeating here the explanation given in the appendix to his *Sermon on Christian Freedom.* London, 1858 [Williams's note].

For Jonah's hymn see Jon. 2:2–8. In a letter which supplements *Christian Freedom,* Williams argues against the charge by Alfred Ollivant that he had "'dogmatically asserted' the Book of Jonah to be an allegory": "You there extract some strongly worded sentences from a work published by the learned Dr. Donaldson in 1857. . . . On turning to Rosenmüller's *Commentaries,* I find some dozen critics who resolve the narrative of Jonah either into an allegory, or into a poetical tale. . . . I cannot refuse what a profound harmonist [Donaldson] of the Gospels had lately observed, that, on collation of all the passages, we may suppose our Lord's genuine words to have made the parallel consist merely in threatening a great city with destruction, the door of repentance being left open to each. The same eminent writer thinks, that the disputed hymn in Jonah is the genuine germ, around which clustered a parasitical growth of the later narrative, embodying a prosaic misconception of the figures of song" (Williams 1857, 47–8).

John William Donaldson published *Christian Orthodoxy Reconciled with the Conclusions of Modern Biblical Learning* (1857). Ernst Friedrich Carl Rosenmüller published *Commentationes Theologicae* (1825, 2 vols.).

103. Williams's Broad Church argument concerning the role of "reason" and "conscience" in interpreting the Bible may be paralleled to that of Bunsen: "Reason is summoned by Christ and His Apostles to apply her powers even to the investigation of the divine nature, of which the human mind is the finite mirror and evolution; but all her operations are so intimately connected with the dictates of Conscience, that they cannot be understood, still less exert an active, freeing, regenerating influence, without the recognition of the law of conscience. . . . The history of mankind is the development of a divine plan of progress from instinct to reason, from impulse to conscious principles, which is all summed up in the expression—transition from physical necessity to moral freedom, from unconscious nature to conscious spirit in nature" (Bunsen 1852b, 1:305–6).

Williams returns to this argument repeatedly throughout the essay. In first discussing *Gott in der Geschichte,* he argues that the Bible is the "expression of devout reason" (¶10). He reiterates the reciprocal necessity of reason as the interpreter, in the light of "the Eternal Spirit," of continuous revelation (¶22). The instrumentality of that interpretation is the Bible "within the limits of humanity," that is, written by fallible authors and interpreted by fallible scholars using informed reason. The issue of infallibility was a major consideration in Williams's condemnation in the Court of Arches. His views aroused widespread popular disapproval. For a contemporary review of twenty books concerning biblical infallibility see Cairns 1852; see also Paton 1858 and Jowett ¶s 15–16 and n. 24–30; for a recent study see Cameron, 1987.

104. The Ordination Service in the *BCP* enjoins the singing of the tenth-century hymn *Veni Creator Spiritus* ("Come, Holy Ghost, our souls inspire, / Enlighten with celestial fire") immediately before the ordination of priests. The hymn contains the references alluded to by Williams.

105. For "Spirit which dwelt in them" see John 16:13.

106. *Hippolytus and his Age,* by Chr. C. J. Bunsen, &c. London, 1852. 2nd edition, recast London, 1854. The awakening freshness of the first edition is hardly replaced by the fullness of the second. It is to be wished that the Biblical portions of the *Philosophy of Universal History,* vol. ii. pp. 149–338, were reprinted in a cheap form [Williams's note].

Bunsen's *Outlines of a Philosophy of a Universal History* was originally a part of the first edition of *Hippolytus* (1852b), but its separate and "improved" form (1854, 1:v) traces the principles of progress in universal history, applying them "to Language and Religion as the two universal and primitive manifestations of the human mind, upon which all subsequent social and national development is based" (1854, 1:1–2). Hippolytus, the second-century Roman priest and theologian (and bishop according to Bunsen), wrote about the doctrinal controversies of his age in *Refutation of All Heresies*; however, the authenticity of other works attributed to him is disputed.

107. For "I came to cast fire" see Luke 12:49–50 (discussed in Bunsen 1852b, 1:221); "giving rather than receiving," Acts 20:35. The latter is one of the remarks of Jesus not recorded in the Gospels.

108. The term *justification* (Gk. δικαίωμα, Rom. 5:16) means being declared just or righteous by acquittal from guilt. In Reformation theology, especially in Lutheranism, humans are justified by faith alone: sinful humans are reconciled with God through faith in the divine offer of forgiveness, whereby the righteousness or merit of Christ is imputed or counted to the sinner through faith, establishing a new relationship between the individual and God (Rom. 4:3–22). No priest or church need intervene with their systems of hierarchy and authority ("sacerdotalism" to Bunsen and Williams) or their rights to guard or allocate "the fiction of merit or transfer" of grace. Merit is the right to be rewarded by God for good works (Matt. 5:3–12; James 2:24), but Protestant reformers denied that human beings had any right to merit of their own after the Fall. Hence, they opposed the scholastic theologians who argue that justification comes through faith as a supernatural virtue infused by God into the soul. Late medieval Roman Catholicism stressed the prescriptive conditions under which merit could be obtained or transferred from the "treasury" of Christ or the saints who have stored up abundant merit and grace or through the performance of such good works as the devout reception of the sacraments. For medieval, Reformation, Anglican, and Roman Catholic views of merit and grace see Leeming 1960, 76–93. Bunsen elaborates Paul's concept of "justification by faith" (Rom. 5:1–18; Gal. 2:16; 3:8–24), drawing on this Lutheran tradition, elaborating "Evangelical language in a philosophical sense" (Bunsen 1852b, 1:71).

Justification had been contentious in England at the time of the Reformation; one of the Homilies, "On Justification," sets out the theological position of the Elizabethan settlement but the doctrine continued to arouse controversy in nineteenth-century England—a point of dispute between Tractarians and Evangelicals. The 1669 treatise of George Bull attacking Protestant theories of justification was republished in the Tractarian *Library of Anglo-Catholic Theology* as *Harmonia Apostolica; or, The Mutual Agreement of St. Paul and St. James, Comprising a Complete View of Christian Justification and the Deficiency of Former Commentaries* (1842, 2 vols.). In 1838 J. H. Newman delivered his thirteen *Lectures on Justification*, reacting against Calvinists and Lutherans on the one hand and Romanists on the other. In *Tract XC* (1841), Newman again addressed "Justification by Faith Alone," arguing that as the doctrine was presented in the Eleventh Article of Religion it was "not uncatholic." On the evangelical side, and as a direct attack on Tractarian theology, Charles Pettit M'Ilvaine published *Oxford Divinity, Compared with That of the Romish and Anglican Churches: With a Special View to the Illustration of the Doctrine of Justification by Faith as It Was Made of Primary Importance by the Reformers; and as It Lies at the Foundation of All Scriptural Views of the Gospel of Our Lord Jesus Christ* (1841). The next year, Francis Whaley Harper published *A Few Observations on the Teaching of Dr. Pusey and Mr. Newman concerning Justification* (1842); in 1845 Charles Heurtley, an Evangelical, delivered the Bampton Lectures on *Justification*; and in 1853 E. B. Pusey published *Justification* from a Tractarian point of view. False views of "justification" were charged to Dunbar Isidore Heath in his trial before the Court of Arches in 1861 (see Williams ¶27 and n. 110). On justification see McGrath 1986; and Seifrid 1992; see also Jowett ¶s 2 (n. 5) and 34 (n. 67). For "to obey is better than sacrifice" see 1 Sam. 15:2.

The notion of imputed righteousness, against which Williams is reacting, was widely understood in the nineteenth century as a purely legal verdict of acquittal from sin, quite apart from any amendment of life. Commenting on justification by transferred merit as a "fiction" in *Broadchalke Sermon-Essays* (1867), Williams writes: "'Deus *non* facit salvos *fictè* peccatores' [God does not make the saved fictively sinners] are the famous words of Luther. 'Deus non facit salvos fictè *justos*' [God does not make the saved fictively justified] might be a restored summary of Dr. Newman's lectures on Justification. *Figment* is the word with Bishop Bull, and with some of the Oxford school; *fiction*, with Whately and F. Robertson. That a grave tribunal went out of its way to call one of the common-places of Divines on all sides 'unbecoming,' is difficult to explain in any complimentary manner" (iv; and quoted in Ellen Williams 1874, 2:149). Williams's reference to the "grave tribunal" is to the Court of Arches' admission of this passage for condemnation. In a retraction made on 15 December 1862 before the final judgment was pronounced in the Court of Arches, Williams offered to "suppress in future editions" this passage, along with that on propitiation in ¶27. He argues that these "two Bunsenian sentences. . . were unconnected with the main tenor of the Essay" but "had been held to entangle me in the Articles." The prosecution did not accept this offer (Ellen Williams 1874, 2:78–81).

109. 'The doctrine of the Fall, the doctrine of

Grace, and the doctrine of the Atonement, *are grounded in the instincts of mankind.*'—Mozley *on Predestination*, chap. xi. p. 331 [Williams's note].

James Bowling Mozley was the joint editor of the *Christian Remembrancer* but resigned in 1855 because of his agreement with the decision on the Gorham case (1847–49); see Wilson ¶76 and n. 124. On this controversy he published *A Treatise on the Augustinian Doctrine of Predestination* (1855) and two other works: *On the Primitive Doctrine of Baptismal Regeneration* (1856) and *A Review of the Baptismal Controversy* (1862). Mozley was also one of the earliest supporters of the *Guardian*, a High Church weekly.

110. Having introduced "justification" in the previous paragraph, Williams now turns to other "New Testament terms," giving a brief definition of each in the light of Bunsen's argument in *Hippolytus* about the belief of the early church. Each term or doctrine provoked controversy between Evangelicals and High Church Anglicans in England (especially in controversy about baptism, sin, and grace), and often between Anglicans and continental Protestant theology (especially as represented in German higher criticism). Furthermore, in the trial of Heath in the Court of Arches (*Burder vs. Heath*) similar theological problems arose. Heath's contested book, *Sermons on Important Subjects*, carried some of the views of F. D. Maurice to extremes, arguing that justification by faith means that God would do justice to the whole human race by putting everyone in the proper place according to Christ's trust in the future and that justification is not faith in Christ, but Christ's own faith (against the Eleventh Article of Religion). Further, he argued that Christ's death as atonement was not a propitiation of God's wrath against sinful humans; that forgiveness of sins has nothing to do with the gospel, and that a number of traditional and still current theological terms such as *guilt of sin*, *satisfaction*, *merit*, and *necessary for salvation* are modern terms with no sanction in the Bible. Although Heath's book was published in the same year as *Essays and Reviews*, his trial in the Court of Arches (1861) and his appeal before the Privy Council (1862) proceeded those of Williams and Wilson; hence, the treatment of such terms by Heath and the courts turned out to be an important precedent against Williams. The clergy of the Isle of Wight petitioned the bishop, Charles Richard Sumner of Winchester, to prosecute him, and the case was heard by Stephen Lushington in the Court of Arches in 1861. Lushington's judgment (2 Nov. 1861) declared him to have forfeited his pastoral charge under the statute of 13 Eliz. c. 12. Heath appealed to the Judicial Committee which on 6 June 1862 confirmed the decision of the Court of Arches. See Trials and Appeals for Heath's case as precedent (especially n. 21).

According to Williams, "Regeneration" (Gk. παλινγενεσία, Matt. 19:28; Titus 3:5), new or spiritual rebirth, is associated with baptism, whereby the believer is incorporated into the church through the infusion of grace to allow for spiritual growth (see also the Twenty-seventh Article: "Baptism is . . . a sign of Regeneration or new Birth"). Evangelicals argued such regeneration was the result of conversion and worthy reception of the sacrament; High Church theologians, that it always accompanied baptism. The Gorham case (1849) turned on the issue of belief in baptismal regeneration, whereby the High Church view, upheld in the Court of Arches, was overturned by the Judicial Committee of the Privy Council. On baptism, see also Wilson ¶76 and note 124 and Jowett ¶34 and note.

Resurrection (Gk. ἀνάστασις, Acts 2:22–36; 1 Pet. 1:3; 1 Cor. 15:1–7; Mark. 16:1–8) refers primarily to the rising of Jesus from the dead after the crucifixion. Nineteenth-century controversies about resurrection included D. F. Strauss's attack on the visionary experiences of the NT witnesses (Strauss [1835] 1846), as well as the question of the general resurrection at the last judgment and the fate of Christians according to their faith and deeds (1 Cor. 15:12–29). E. M. Goulburn delivered the Bampton Lectures on *The Doctrine of the Resurrection of the Body, as Taught in Holy Scripture* (1850).

"Salvation" (Gk. σωτηρία, Rom. 1:16, and frequently elsewhere in the NT) means "deliverance," especially spiritual deliverance from the bondage of sin, achieved through repentance and faith in Christ (as in the apostolic preaching in Acts 4:12 and Paul, as in Rom. 1:16).

"Propitiation" (Gk. ἱλαστήριον and cognates, Rom. 3:25; 1 John 2:2; 4:10) is formally an act (Christ's death) of appeasement or reconciliation, mitigating the wrath of God against human sin. The emphasis of this term is upon the anger of the deity that must be appeased. This view of propitiation is related to both the juridical theory of the atonement (the reconciliation of human beings to God through Christ's death on the Cross, from Anselm's view that Christ died to satisfy the honor of God as a kind of feudal lord) and also to the sacrificial theory of atonement, from the Jewish notion of sacrifice of the sin-offering, that Christ died as both perfect high priest and as sinless sin-offering. Broad Church theologians tended to reject both the juridical and the sacrificial views in favor of "expiation" (the word does not occur in the AV, but is used by some explicators instead of propitiation), placing emphasis on the one who seeks to appease or make satisfaction (whether the willing suffering of Christ, or the act of repentance for sin and guilt made by the individual Christian), the position Williams advances in making reference to the "Searcher of hearts."

The Broad Church position concerning "the eternal" (Gk. αἰώνιος, 2 Cor. 4:18, Heb. 5:9 and elsewhere) is the next issue Williams discusses. Frederick Denison Maurice in *The Kingdom of Christ* (1836) outlines "eternal life" and repudiates th everlasting punishment of the damned (as in the "hateful fires" of 2 Thess. 1:8–9; see also Matt. 10: 28; Luke 12: 4), also a matter of contemporaneous controversy, aroused by Maurice's *Theological Essays* (1853), particularly in the concluding essay, "On Eternal Life and Eternal Death." These essays provoked Maurice's removal as professor from King's College, London. See Wheeler 1990.

Williams's paragraph concludes with references to the three fundamental doctrines of Christianity. "Creation" is controversial especially in relation to Genesis and geology. Williams states two opposing views of the "incarnation": first, the Hellenistic *logos* doctrine whereby the divine reason, mind, or word becomes flesh as stated in the prologue to John's gospel, a belief tending to the heresy of docetism (see Bunsen 1852b, 1:243), in which Christ is God in the appearance of man; and second, the Jewish Ebionite belief (from the sect of Ebionites of the first and second centuries) who conferred the dignity of God's name on Christ's humanity, often at his baptism (Bunsen 1852b, 1:125–34). The third doctrine Williams discusses is the Trinity, stressing the three persons' "consubstantiality," the Latin term for the Greek ὁμοούσιος (*homoousios*), used in the Nicene Creed (325) to settle the controversy concerning the Arian heresy that denied the divinity of Christ. The classic Anglican defense of the Nicene faith is George Bull's *Defensio Fidei Nicaenae* (1685; Defense of the Nicene Faith), translated into English and republished in the *Library of Anglo-Catholic Theology* (1851). It contains a separate discussion of "Consubstantiality." Other works current on the Trinity indicate the range of the controversy: in 1829 Edward Burton gave the Bampton Lectures on *An Enquiry into the Heresies of the Apostolic Age*, and in 1837 Thomas Vogan delivered them on *The Principle Objections against the Doctrine of the Trinity.*

111. For "ὁ ἀντικείμενος" [the adversary] see Luke 13:17; 1 Cor. 16:9; Phil. 1:28; 2 Thess. 2:4; 1 Tim. 5:14. This sentence was admitted before the Court of Arches as heretical concerning propitiation, and was explicated by Lushington in the light of the two sentences which precede it. Williams offered to suppress it, along with the passage on "justification" in ¶26, in his retraction on 15 December 1862. The condemnation of this sentence was withdrawn without argument or protest in the appeal before the Judicial Committee of the Privy Council in June 1863.

112. For "one who searches and judges" see John 8:50; "the hateful fires," see 2 Thess. 1:8–9; "Hinnom," see 2 Chron. 28:3; 33:6; Jer. 7:31–32.

113. On this point, the summary of St. Augustine at the end of his 15th book, '*On the Trinity,*' is worth reading [Williams's note].

The "summary" (bk. 15, chaps. 27, 28) concludes *On the Trinity* (c. 419): "Since the Spirit of both is a kind of consubstantial communion of Father and Son, He is not called . . . the Son of both. . . . Yet that light [of God] shows to thee these three things in thyself, wherein thou mayest recognize an image of the highest Trinity itself. . . . There is in the mind's eye of the thinker an image resembling that thought which the memory contained, will or love as a third combining these two as parent and offspring. And . . . this will proceeds indeed from thought . . . yet is not an image of the thought: and so that there is insinuated in this intelligible thing a sort of difference between birth and procession since to behold by thought is not the same as to desire, or even to enjoy will. . . . May I remember Thee, understand Thee, love Thee . . . O Lord the one God, God the Trinity" (*NPNF*1 3:227–28).

114. 'Neque sermo aliud quam Deus neque caro aliud quam homo,' and 'ex carne homo, ex spiritu Deus.'—Tertullian *adv. Prax.* c. xxvii. Comp. Romans i. 1–3 [Williams's note].

The cited passages read: "The word is nothing else but God, and the flesh nothing else but Man"; and "[Of them Jesus consists:] Man, of the flesh, of the spirit, God" (*Against Praxeas*; trans. Peter Holmes, *ANF* 3:624). Tertullian quotes the passage from John 3:6. In *Against Praxeas* (c. 217) he argues for an orthodox theology of the Trinity against the Christological and Trinitarian heresies of Praxeas. Williams alleges that Bunsen sides with the view that the incarnation is a form of docetism, in which Christ's person is a spiritual mode of Godhead, and the flesh of Christ is a veil for divinity. Rom. 1:1–4 depicts the lineage of Christ as from David according to the flesh and from God, according to the spirit. For "abides in love . . . God in him" see 1 John 4:16.

115. The passage from ¶28, "Again, on the side of external criticism. . . . law of harmony," was cited as "false and dangerous" in the Synodical Condemnation of *Essays and Reviews* on 21 June 1864. Williams presupposes that on the basis of human reason passages of the Bible may be rejected as unbelievable or wrong (*Chronicle* 1859–64:1864, Session 66, 1658).

116. Butler's *Analogy*. Part ii. ch. iii. Hooker, *Eccl. Pol.* Books i. ii [Williams's note].

The cited chapter of Butler's *Analogy* is entitled: "Of our Incapacity of Judging, what were to be Expected in a Revelation; and the Credibility, from Analogy, that it must Contain Things Appearing Liable to Objections" (1896, 1:221). Richard Hooker published *Laws of Ecclesiastical Polity* (1594–97, bks 1–5; 1648–62, bks 6–8, posthumous). Hooker writes: "Now forasmuch as there hath been reason alleged sufficient to conclude, that all things necessary unto salvation must be made known, and that God himself hath therefore revealed his will, because otherwise men could not have known so much as is necessary; his surceasing to speak to the world, since the publishing of the Gospel of Jesus Christ and the delivery of the same in writing, is unto us a manifest token that the way of salvation is now sufficiently opened, and that we need no other means for our full instruction than God hath already furnished us withal" ([1594–1662] 1954, 1:217).

117. Wilhelm Martin Leberecht de Wette published *Beiträge zur Einleitung in das Alte Testament* (1806–7, 2 vols.; Contribution toward an introduction to the Old Testament) and *Lehrbuch der historisch-kritischen Einleitung in die Bibel* (1817; Compendium for the historical-critical introduction to the Bible), arguing that the Pentateuch is composed of diverse documents very different in age, composition, and purpose. Johann August Wilhelm Neander published *Allgemeine Geschichte der christlichen Religion und Kirche* (1825–52, 6 vols.; trans. J. Torrey, *General History of the Christian Religion and Church*, 1850–58), arguing that Christianity has tolerated divergent views simultaneously.

118. Each Gospel is traditionally associated with a particular place of origin, Matthew with Jerusalem, Mark with Rome, Luke with Antioch, and John with Alexandria (Alford [1849] 1863, 1:1–64). The "liturgical families" of the early church derive from the practices of particular locations: the Syrian liturgies associated with the Liturgy of St. James at Jerusalem; the Roman liturgical tradition with Clement of Rome (in the Clementine liturgies in the *Apostolic Constitutions* VIII) and through him with St. Peter; the liturgy in the *Apostolic Tradition of Hippolytus* (in 1860 known only through the *Apostolic Constitutions* and fragments), with Antioch (and giving rise to the liturgies of St. Basil and St. John Chrysostom); and the Hispano-Gallican liturgies (in the nineteenth century called "Ephesine" and linked to St. John and Ephesus, through Irenaeus, bp. of Lyons, who derived it from Polycarp, the disciple of John), which are associated with Alexandria. Bunsen discovered and published some fragments of these liturgies in *Analecta Ante-Nicaena* (1852b, 3:263–66; reissued in an expanded form in *Christianity and Mankind*, 1854, vols. 5–7).

119. John iii. 13 [Williams's note].

Bunsen discusses the first three Gospels in 1852b, 1:35–43; and John in 1852b, 1:48–52.

120. Josephus *B. J.* b. vi. c. v. §3 [Williams's note].

For "Apocalypse" see Rev. 15:7; 16:1. Titus Flavius Vespasian led the suppression of the Jewish rebellion in 67 in which Josephus was captured and imprisoned. Vespasian had largely completed the task except for Jerusalem when the death of Nero in 69 led to his acclamation as emperor (Josephus' prophesy of this event led to his release and his adoption of the emperor's name). Vespasian's son Titus (for whom Josephus was an interpreter) took over the seige of Jerusalem, destroying the third Temple, that of Herod, in 70. The warnings in the Apocalypse against Jerusalem echo those of the prophets (Jer. 13:27; Ezek. 4:7; 9:8), and of Jesus in the Gospels (Matt. 23:37; Luke 13:34; 23:28). In the section of Josephus' *The Jewish War* (cited by Williams as *B. J.* or *Belli Judaeorum*), Jesus the son of Ananias goes about the city for seven years predicting its destruction: "A voice from the east, a voice from the west, a voice from the four winds, a voice against Jerusalem and the sanctuary, a voice against the bridegroom and the bride, a voice against all the whole people"; and later, "Woe to Jerusalem!" (bk. 6, chap. 5, sec. 3; trans. H. St. J. Thackeray, *Loeb* 3:463–5). For Josephus see Rhoads 1976 and Mason 1991.

121. In my own judgment, the Epistle bears traces of being *post*-apostolic. iii. 14; xiii. 7; ii. 3; x. 2, 25–32 [Williams's note].

Though the book of Hebrews was attributed to Paul in the formation of the NT canon, Bunsen, following Luther, attributes it to Apollos, pointing out its links with Alexandria and the Judaizing party amongst the Christians there. Its polished Greek style ("Alexandrine rhythm") is quite different from the language and theological interests of Paul (Bunsen 1854, 33–4). Apollos, a Jewish Christian from Alexandria, went to Ephesus and Corinth where he came to know Paul. There was some rivalry between the two as Christian leaders (Acts 18:24–19:1; 1 Cor. 16:12).

122. Bunsen discusses the historical and textual problems of 2 Peter, reconstructing what he believes to be an authentic short letter (2 Pet. 1:1–11), to which he thinks the apostle refers at 1 Pet. 5:12 (1852b, 1:24–25).

123. Clement and Origen, amongst others [Williams's note].

Clement of Alexandria wrote "On Marriage," (c. 200) in which he argues: "Even Paul did not hesitate in one letter to address his consort. The only reason why he did not take her about with him was that it would have been an inconvenience for his ministry. Accordingly, he says in a letter, 'Have we not a right to take about with us a wife that is a sister like the other apostles?'" (chap. 6, sec. 53; Owen Chadwick 1954, 64–65). Origen studied under Clement in the catechetical school at Alexandria. Bunsen discusses Origen extensively in *Hippolytus* (1852b, 1:279–300). For "true yoke-fellow" see Phil. 4:3; "lead about a sister," 1 Cor. 9:5.

124. The Homeric scholia are collections of notes on prosody and grammar that were produced in the second century B.C.E. in the Alexandrian school of Homeric criticism by Aristarchus and others who refer to the Homeric tradition of annotation that had begun a century earlier with Zenodotus, the first librarian of Alexandria. The scholia survived in the MSS. of Homer's *Iliad* at Venice known as *Venetus A* and *B*. The translation of Homer was a subject of considerable controversy for the Victorians: for instance, the Matthew Arnold and F. W. Newman debates were contemporaneous with the publication of *Essays and Reviews*.

125. "*Friends of God*" (Ger. *Gottesfreunde*) were a group of fourteenth-century mystics of the Rhine-

land and Switzerland who emphasized spiritual transformation and union with God. Their *Theologia Germanica,* a fourteenth-century mystical treatise, was printed under Martin Luther's supervision (1518; trans. Susanna Winkworth [1854] with a preface by Charles Kingsley and an introductory letter by Bunsen).

126. Bunsen uses the metaphor of "the picture" throughout *Hippolytus* (vol. 1) to explicate "the age" of the early Christians. The "ecclesiastical school which appeals loudest to antiquity" refers to the Tractarians, about whom Bunsen writes: "We may now form a more just estimate of the Catholicizing tendency which has unfortunately become so prominent in a certain school in England, whenever attention has been turned to the defects in the National Liturgy" (1852b, 2:203). "Sacerdotalism" is church polity and doctrine under the control of "caste of the priesthood" (Bunsen 1852b, 2:203), associated by Williams at the end of ¶30 with the medieval church ("monkish fanaticism," "imperial tyranny," "intrigues of bishops"), and by implication with the attractions of the Roman Catholicism to the Tractarians (see also Bunsen 1852b, 2:201, 203). The term "sacerdotalism" was first used pejoratively in 1847 (*OED*). For other connotations see ¶11.

127. For "purified by faith" see Acts 15:9. Bunsen discusses the theology, ritual, and formularies concerning baptism in the early church (Bunsen 1852b, 2:115–17), making reference to all the points Williams alludes to, including the analogy with circumcision and the baptismal theology of Augustine (Bunsen 1852b, 2:118–28). Augustine's views on the inheritance of original sin by every child are set out in *De Baptismo* (c. 401; Concerning baptism). To Catholicism, baptism is a "good work," but to Luther and his followers it required subsequent conversion and justification by faith. In nineteenth-century England, controversy on baptism aligned Tractarians against Evangelicals: the former argued that baptism is efficacious in communicating the grace of God provided the prescribed form, matter, and intention are valid and that regeneration accompanies baptism; the latter stressed repentance and the devout worthiness of the receiver for baptism to have an effect. In *Tract LXXVII: Scriptural Views of Holy Baptism* (1835), Pusey discusses the issues in "The Meaning of Baptismal Regeneration" (chap. 2). Baptismal regeneration was the doctrinal issue of the Gorham controversy (1847–49), eventually decided by the Privy Council in favor of a latitudinarian position (see ¶27 and note). Robert Halley delivered the Congregational Lectures in 1854 on Baptism entitled *The Sacraments: An Enquiry into the Nature of the Symbolic Institutions of the Christian Religion.* Bunsen discusses "the Scholastic Doctrine of Baptismal Regeneration" in *Christianity* (1854, 2:xxv; 113–17). In the ensuing discussion, Williams positions himself in relation to the notion of penitence and conversion ("the contrite heart"), and with a particular Broad Church approach to Baptism, that it is the "oblation of the reason." Sacrifice in the early church and its relation to "rational" or "spiritual" worship is discussed in the three essays "On the Christian Sacrifice" that Bunsen appends to *Hippolytus* (1852b, 2:357–94). See also Wilson ¶76 and note; Jowett ¶s 28, 34, and notes.

128. For "contrite heart" see Ps. 51:17; "worship of the mind," Rom. 12:1. The Prayer of Oblation after communion (*BCP*) contains the phrase "reasonable, holy, and lively sacrifice," an echo of Rom. 12:1. Bunsen discusses sacrifice and the eucharist referring to "the 'reasonable service' of the Apostles" (1852b, 2:201) and to the discussion of Rom. 12:1 in Augustine's *City of God* (bk. 10, chap. 6) in relation to the eucharist and sacrifice (Bunsen 1852b, 2:389–90).

129. For "Christ became obedient" see Phil. 2:8. Williams summarizes Bunsen's argument that the evolution of the Roman eucharistic liturgy shifted the oblation of self-sacrifice of praise and thanksgiving in a materialistic direction, as "propitiatory" (Council of Trent, Session 22, 1562); such views characterize nineteenth-century Roman Catholic theology: "Great stress. . . is laid upon such forms as gradually drew off the consciousness of the Church . . . from the Thank-offering of the believers to the repetition of the Sacrifice of Atonement. . . . The whole celebration of the Roman mass is the act of the priest, who sacrifices the Lord's body, and thereby repeats the propitiatory sacrifice of Christ" (Bunsen 1852b, 2:172–3). Two Tractarians had recently written on the eucharist and sacrifice: Robert Isaac Wilberforce, *The Doctrine of the Holy Eucharist* (1853) and Pusey, *The Doctrine of the Real Presence, as Contained in the Fathers* (1855).

130. For "blood . . . *everlasting*" see Heb. 13:20; "vanishes away," 1 Cor. 13:8; Heb. 8:13. The "angels who hover" refers to the fresco by the thirteenth-century Florentine painter Giotto, in the Arena Chapel in Padua. In 1854 John Ruskin published *Giotto and His Works in Padua,* with a commentary on a series of woodcuts of the frescoes.

Transubstantiation refers to the conversion of the entire "substance" (or inner reality) of the bread and wine in the eucharist into the whole "substance" of the body and blood of Christ. The term *substance* is a technical and philosophical term, contrasting with "accidents." The constitutive element, "reality," or "substance" of the bread and wine is converted into the "substance" of Christ's body and blood, though the "accidents" or external forms, species, or "appearances," such as consistency, taste, or color, remain unchanged. This distinction between substance and accidents is derived from Aristotle and is developed in the scholastic philosophy of the twelfth century, especially in Thomas Aquinas (*Summa Theologica,* bk. 3, chaps. 75–77). The term *transubstantiation* was defined in this sense at the fourth

Lateran Council (1215) and at the Council of Trent as official Catholic teaching (1551; session 13, canon 2). In the C. of E. the twenty-eighth Article of Religion rejects "transubstantiation" as "overthrowing the nature of a sacrament," a position adopted in the light of late medieval nominalism.

Williams alludes to the "real presence" controversy in Victorian England. The Tractarians affirmed the real presence of Christ in the sacrament, the Evangelicals affirmed a presence by receptionism, depending on the spiritual state of the receiver. Newman defended transubstantiation in its scholastic sense as appropriate for Anglicans in his criticism of the twenty-eighth Article of Religion in *Tract XC* (sec. 8), and on 14 May 1843 Pusey preached a University Sermon in Oxford in which he implied a belief in transubstantiation (Faber 1954, 407). The Lancelot Andrewes–Cardinal Bellarmine debate of 1608–10 on transubstantiation (see Pattison ¶32 and n. 98) was republished in the Tractarian *Library of Anglo-Catholic Theology* (1851). Among other contemporaneous writings on the controversy are Charles S. Bird, *Transubstantiation Tried by Scripture and Reason; Addressed to the Protestant Inhabitants of Reading* (1839); T. J. O'Connell, *A Letter to the Reverend Doctor Pusey, on the True Mode of the Real Presence, or Transubstantiation* (1843); Robert Isaac Wilberforce, *The Doctrine of the Holy Eucharist* (1853); and Robert Maquire, *Transubstantiation a Tractarian Doctrine; Suggested by Archdeacon Wilberforce on the Holy Eucharist* (1854). Bunsen discusses the early views of the presence of Christ in the eucharist and its later development, especially attacking the Tractarian and Roman Catholic positions (1852b, 2:158, 170–73; 199–204). In ¶49 Williams argues for the eucharistic theology of the earliest liturgical formularies. See also Pattison ¶32 and n. 98; and Jowett ¶34.

131. See this shown, with just rebuke of some Oxford sophistries, in the learned Bishop Kaye's *Council of Nicaea*, London, 1853; a book of admirable moderation, though hardly of speculative power. See pp. 163, 168, 194, 199, 219, 226, 251, 252 [Williams's note].

John Kaye published posthumously *Some Account of the Council of Nicaea in Connexion with the Life of Athanasius* (1853). The cited pages are in "Some Account of the Four Orations of Athanasius against the Arians." In each case, Kaye disagrees with a particular "Oxford translator" or "Oxford annotator." *Selected Treatises of S. Athanasius. . . in Controversy with the Arians*, translated and annotated by J. H. Newman, was published in *The Library of the Fathers* (1842, 2 vols.).

132. *Adv. Prax.* c. iii [Williams's note].

"They are constantly throwing out against us that we are preachers of two gods and three gods, while they take to themselves pre-eminently the credit of being worshippers of the One God; just as if the Unity itself with irrational deductions did not produce heresy, and the Trinity rationally considered constitute the truth" (*Against Praxeas*; trans. Peter Holmes, *ANF* 3:599).

133. Williams refers to two classical heresies concerning the person of Christ. Pelagius, a British monk teaching at Rome, denied original sin, argued that human beings are responsible for their own moral acts and that they can act virtuously and achieve salvation without the need for divine grace. He was attacked by Augustine (*Against the Pelagians* c. 419–20, and other writings). Jowett, commenting on Rom. 5:12–21 in *The Epistles of St. Paul*, declares in a long discussion of Pelagianism that it is the one heresy that will "last as long as the world itself" because it involves "the relation of God to man" ([1855] 1859, 2:170). See also Jowett ¶s 2, 3, and notes. Sabellianism, named after the third-century heretic Sabellius, held that God is one nature with three distinct names and modes of revelation. Sabellianism was attacked by Origen and later by Athanasius.

134. Sir Isaac Newton established the laws of motion, gravity, and differential calculus. In *Principia Mathematica* (1687), he acknowledged his belief in God as transcendent power and perfection, evinced through the order of creation. As a Unitarian, however, he denied belief in the Christian Trinity as inaccessible to reason. Gilbert Wakefield resigned his Anglican orders to become professor of Classics at the Unitarian College at Hackney. He published *The Internal Evidence of the Christian Religion* (1789) and *The Spirit of Christianity, Compared with the Spirit of the Times in Great Britain* (1794). For "I AM" see Exod. 3:14.

135. 'Anima hominis naturâ suâ in se habet Ss. Trinitatis simulacrum; in se enim tria complectitur, Mentem, Intellectum, et Voluntatem; . . . cogitat . . . percipit . . . vult.'—Bede i. 8. Copying almost verbally St. Augustine [Williams's note].

Williams appeals to seven analogies to construct an orthodox base in early Christianity for definitions of the Trinity that avoid the problems that later Latin Christianity had with prescriptive formulations of the relations between one "substance" and three "persons." Five of the analogies are drawn from Augustine's tripartite structuration of the human soul. In the *Confessions* (bk. 13. chap. 11) Augustine discusses being, knowing, and willing; in *On the Trinity*, mind, knowledge, and love (bk. 9, chaps. 1–3); will, wisdom, love (bk. 9. chaps. 5, 8); and memory, understanding, and will (bk. 10. chap. 1). The distinction between the sun as object, as ray, and as heat, is developed in Tertullian (*Apology*, bk. 21, chaps. 10–14; *On the Prescription of Heretics*, chap. 8; and *Against Praxeas*, chaps. 8, 27), along with other analogies (water, and the functions of the soul). The modes of existence for water are developed as an analogy for the Trinity in Anselm of Canterbury, in the letter *De Incarnatione Verbi* (On the incarnation of the word, chap. 13). The passage from Bede has not been located.

136. *Hippolytus*, vol. ii. p. 46. 1st ed [Williams's note].

Bunsen 1852b, 2:46.

137. Brahmanism denotes a system of Hindu religious institutions. The Brahmins are the sacerdotal caste who interpret the sacred scriptures of Hinduism, the Vedas, Upanishads, and other writings. Brahman is also the term for the supreme soul, divine essence, or ultimate reality, the source and goal of all existence. From this term is derived the term *Brahma*, one of the three hypostases of that essence whose creative aspect he represents: Brahma, as creator, with Vishnu as preserver, and Shiva as destroyer. The heresy of Sabellianism and Brahmanism are aligned on the basis of their stressing the unity of God, who is revealed under three modes, or essences. The trinitarian doctrines of Justin, Tertullian, Hippolytus, Origen, and Eusebius stress the unity of God (monism), while sustaining some distinction in the separate persons of the Trinity.

Two passages from ¶32, "Being, becoming . . . and Spirit" and "The Divine consciousness or wisdom . . . image of the Father" were cited as "false and dangerous" in the Synodical Condemnation of *Essays and Reviews* on 21 June 1864. Williams's Trinitarianism is condemned for using the term "Person" only of the Father, and not of Jesus Christ or the Holy Spirit (*Chronicle* 1859–64:1864, Session 66, 1658).

138. '*Liberty of Prophesying*,' pp. 491–2; vol. vii. ed. Heber. Burnet's '*Own Times*.' Letter from Tillotson at the end [Williams's note].

Williams uses historical and linguistic evidence to question the orthodoxy of attribution and unity of authorship of the so-called Athanasian Creed, or Quicumque vult (Lat. Whosoever wishes [to be saved], from the first words of the text). As was demonstrated by G. J. Voss in 1642, this statement of orthodox Trinitarianism was actually written in Latin in Gaul (c. 420) for the use of the Western Church, some time after the death of Athanasius (373) who had been largely responsible for the Nicene creed (325), and whose name bestowed an aura of orthodoxy on this later production. Particularly objectionable in the nineteenth-century controversy concerning this creed were the damnatory clauses or anathemas (verses 2, 42) that condemn disbelievers to "perish eternally," offensive to Broad Church notions of universal salvation. In the *BCP* the Athanasian Creed is enjoined to be recited on specific days throughout the year and is required of assent in the Eighth Article of Religion, but it had been attacked sporadically throughout the eighteenth century (see the references in Pattison ¶4 and n. 15). During the 1850s and 1860s it came under special attack and from 1867 there were efforts to have it removed. For instance, C. Neoptolemus (pseud.) published *A Letter to the Rev. Walter F. Hook, D.D. on His Defence and Exposition of the Damnatory Clauses of the Athanasian Creed* (1838). George Hale published *The Athanasian Creed Weighed and Found Wanting* (1858). The controversy concerning the creed continued for the twelve years following the publication of *Essays and Reviews*, coming to a crisis in 1872 with *Memorials to the Primates and Petition to Convocation, Signed by Nearly 3,000 Clergymen Praying for Some Changes Either in the Compulsory Rubric or in the Damnatory Clauses* (1872), to which the committee of bishops responded in *Revision of the Text and Translation of the Athanasian Creed* (1872). The *BLC* lists scores of publications occasioned by the controversy (13:119–24). See also Wilson ¶7 and n. 17.

Jeremy Taylor published *Liberty of Prophesying* (1647), a plea for toleration. His letter is published in *History of My Own Time* (1723–34) by Gilbert Burnet. John Tillotson wished to be rid of the Athanasian Creed in the 1689 revision of the *BCP*.

139. The Council of Trent (1545–64) made no doctrinal concessions to Protestantism, reasserting the central role of the seven sacraments, the interpretation of the Bible according to the traditional teaching function of the church, justification by both faith and works, and the central role of the priesthood. Williams refers to the ambivalent role of Augustine in the proceedings: on the one hand, the Council of Trent used Augustine to define its position that grace is prevenient as a gift of God before justification and the conferring of sanctifying grace in baptism; on the other, Luther, a former Augustinian monk, relied heavily on Augustine for his doctrine of justification and grace and the fallen state of the human will and its loss of freedom because of original sin. For a general history of the Council of Trent see Jedin 1961; for the role of Augustine, see especially 1:166–77; 2:144–57. For the relations between the C. of E. and Trent see Symonds 1933.

140. In *Hippolytus* Bunsen draws on Luther's stress on the importance of the freedom of the will, as set out in *On Christian Liberty* (1520) and in the controversy with Erasmus (*On the Bondage of the Will*, 1525). As an Augustinian, Luther makes use of the "Augustinian standard" concerning the relation between free will and the necessity of divine grace to make the right choices, a view Augustine explores in *On Grace and Free Will*, *On Free Choice*, and elsewhere, especially in controverting the doctrines of Pelagius who taught that human beings make their first movements toward God out of free will, without divine aid. See Vernon Bourke on "the Augustinian distinction between free choice (*liberum arbitrium*) and a higher freedom (*libertas*)" (Augustine 1964, 176).

Each of the "ethical divines" referred to by Williams writes on free will. Richard Hooker in *Ecclesiastical Polity* writes of "Man's Will, which is the first thing that the Laws of action are made to guide" (title of bk. 1, chap. 7; Hooker [1594–1662]

1954, 1:264–76), citing medieval scholastics and their use of Augustine. Jeremy Taylor's *Unum Necessarium, or the Doctrine and Practice of Repentance* (1655) criticizes current teaching on original sin that laid all of the blame on Adam's fall from grace; he alleges that humans can freely choose to do what is commanded and abstain from what is forbidden, a view that led to his being accused of Pelagianism. In *Fifteen Sermons Preached at the Rolls Chapel* (1726) Joseph Butler argues that moral conduct depends upon acting in accord with human nature, and especially in accord with self-love, benevolence, and conscience. Renn Dickson Hampden's Bampton Lectures *The Scholastic Philosophy, Considered in Its Relation to Christian Theology* (1832) argue that the "schoolmen" had elaborated systems concerning the sacraments and doctrinal tradition that were at variance with the Bible and the moral truths of human nature. His appointments at Oxford and as bp. of Hereford were supported by Baden Powell and other Broad Churchmen but were opposed by Newman, Pusey, and the Tractarians, who disagreed with his theological liberalism (see Desmond Bowen 1968, 67–83).

141. Concluding his discussion (¶29–34) of Bunsen's *Hippolytus,* Williams continues his earlier distinction between "flesh" and "spirit" (¶27) by applying it to distinctions between immortality and resurrection. Citing Platonic, Christian, and Buddhist writings, he argues that "immortality," involving "union with the Spirit of our Eternal life-giver," may reconcile these differences. In *God in History* Bunsen discusses Judaism and the consciousness of God (bk. 2) and Buddhism (bk. 3, chap. 7). On the immortality of the soul in Plato, see *Phaedrus* 245c; *Laws* 10. 194–95; 12. 959a; and *Timaeus* 41a. Christian notions of the afterlife are elaborated especially in 1 Cor. 15. See also the last clauses of the Nicene Creed ("I believe . . . in the life of the world to come"). The "Brahmanical" writings of Hinduism are textbooks of ritual and prayer dating from about 600 B.C.E. For a comparative discussion of "immortality" in the Buddhist and Christian traditions see Streeter 1932, 266–305.

The "fleshly resurrection" of the body after the thousand years ("Judaic millennium") preceding Christ's second coming is based chiefly on Jewish and Christian apocalyptic (2 Esd., Rev. 20, and the apocryphal book of Enoch). Early Christian writings in the NT argue for an immanent eschatology, that the last days would come directly (1 Cor.). After the period of Hippolytus and the martyrs of the first and second centuries, belief in the immanence of the last day dissipated, so that the last day, coming at the end of time, would be the occasion for the general resurrection of the dead. Such a view was conflated with the millennium or thousand years of peace before the judgment (see Justin Martyr, *Apology,* chap. 52; *Dialogue with Trypho* chap. 40, sec. 4; chap. 80, sec. 5; chap. 81. sec. 4).

One of the "noblest philosophers elsewhere" who argued for "the immortality of the soul" is the "first Buddhist Sakya." "Sakya" is the name of the clan to which the Buddha belonged; in later legend he was given the name of Sakyamuni, or sage of the Sakya clan.

Throughout this paragraph, Williams is drawing on a recent controversy involving Max Müller. In April 1857 Müller published "Buddhist Pilgrims" (1876, 2:232–75), in which he argues that Nirvana meant not a "union and communion with God" but rather "utter annihilation." In a letter to the *Times* (24 Apr. 1857) Francis Barham objected to this interpretation. Müller replied citing a number of "recent Sanskrit scholars" to refute the "second-hand" knowledge of Barham's chief authority, Neander. For Neander's comparison of Christianity and Buddhism see Neander [1825–52] 1850–58, 2:6–7.

Williams took part in Sanskrit studies in the field of comparative religion, publishing *Christianity and Hinduism* in 1856. Bunsen read the work, and on 22 April 1857 wrote to a friend: "Rowland Williams has written a highly remarkable, philosophical, and learned book, 'Christianity and Hinduism,'—being called upon to do so by another uncommon man, Mr. Muir, late of the Bengal Civil Service, who had offered 500£ for a work which should in an intelligible manner afford the Brahmins and the learned Buddhists a comparison of those two systems of religion with Christianity. This prize Rowland Williams has gained by writing a volume of 500 pages, which cost him ten years' labour, from 1847–56; which volume Muir sent to me and I received three weeks ago, just as I had worked through the self-same enquiry. Imagine my surprise, to find, under the form of a perfectly framed Platonic Dialogue, a representation more nearly similar to my own than any other than has been made in England or in Germany" (Frances Bunsen 1868, 2:282–83). On 27 April 1857 Bunsen wrote to Max Müller praising Williams for both *Christianity and Hinduism* and *Rational Godliness* (Müller 1876, 3:480–81).

142. Bunsen published his collection of liturgical texts in *Analecta Ante-Nicaena,* issued in *Christianity and Mankind* (1854, vols. 5–7); *Christianity* also included the second edition of *Hippolytus* (vols. 1–2). In *Hippolytus* (vol. 2) there is considerable discussion of liturgical developments from the period of early Christianity to the mid-nineteenth century, with particular attention given to Lutheran and Anglican Formularies. Bunsen also issued *Die heilige Leidensgeschichte und die stille Woche* (1841, 2 vols.; The holy passion-history and holy week), a study of the holy week liturgies and music.

143. *Gesang-und Gebet-buch.* Hamburgh. 1846 [Williams's note].

Bunsen published *Versuch eines allgemeinen evangelischen Gesang- und Gebetbuchs* (1833; Trial toward a general evangelical song and prayer book). A selection was published at Rugby as *Hymns* (1842, trans. H. J. Buckoll); The standard selection and translation by Catherine Winkworth was *Lyra Germanica: Hymns for the Sundays and Chief Festivals of the Christian Year* (1855) that had six editions by 1859. A second series (1858) had five editions by 1863.

144. The terms *ritual* and *liturgy* refer to the ritualist controversies in England that began in the 1840s, and continued throughout the rest of the nineteenth century. The Tractarians looked to "recast her ritual in a foreign mould," that is, to the early and medieval church in the reforming of public worship. The English Church Union, formed in 1860, supported High Church doctrine and ritual practices; in opposition to it, the Evangelical Church Association was established in 1865, taking an active role in prosecuting clergy for ritual offenses. Almost contemporaneous with the publication of *Essays and Reviews* there was a riot involving 3,000 people at St. George's-in-the-East in London over precisely these issues (*Times*, 30 Jan. 1860, 3). In 1867 a Royal Commission was appointed, consisting of Longley, Tait, and Wilberforce, to make recommendations. Their work resulted in the Public Worship Regulation Act of 1874, that attempted to control the spread of ritualistic practices, and under which several clergy were prosecuted and jailed.

145. The Litany (*BCP*) is a responsive supplication used on specific days in the year; it was first published in 1544. Its "germ" is the Sarum Litany (from Salisbury). Though he calls the Anglican Litany "a most beautiful and impressive prayer in itself," Bunsen is critical of such formal prayers as departures from the supplications of the early church. He also alludes to the responsive intercession (*preces*) used in Morning and Evening Prayer in the *BCP* as "a short intercessory prayer. . . the greater part of which is also old" (Bunsen 1852b, 2:178–79). For "the test of theology. . . be prayed" see the maxim of the early church, *lex orandi, lex credendi* (Lat. the law of prayer is the law of belief). The Collects of the *BCP*, the short prayers, assigned to each Sunday and to saint's days, that precede the biblical readings in the eucharist, derive in large measure from medieval sources. Bunsen is critical of the formal nature of these prayers, lamenting the loss of silent and free prayer (1852b, 2:175) and suggesting that "the post-Nicene, Greek Church, and the Roman Catholic Church also in some points, especially in her collects, offer much valuable material and many instructive hints to the investigator, who, with Christian freedom, follows up the thought of worship in the intervening fifteen centuries" (1852b, 2:205). Bunsen also suggests that the freer use of psalms and hymns, as in the Lutheran liturgies, would be an asset to the English liturgy (1852b, 2:176–77).

146. Samuel Birch was appointed in 1836 to the Antiquities Department of the British Museum and soon became head of the Egyptian and Assyrian Branch. He published a grammar and dictionary of hieroglyphics, a translation of the *Book of the Dead*, and many guides and handbooks on the collections. He would subsequently supply "notes and additions" to the second edition of Bunsen's *Egypt's Place in Universal History* (1867).

147. One might ask, whether the experience of our two latest wars encourages our looking to Germany for any unselfish sympathy with the rights of nations? Or has she not rather earned the curse of Meroz? [Williams's note].

Germany, as a nation-state emerged throughout the 1860s, being consolidated, after the Franco-Prussian War (1870–71), between the North German Federation and the south German states. "Sclavonians" is a collective noun derived from the archaic *Sclaveni*, the term by which Gothic and Byzantine writers of the sixth century referred to Slavs. The "two latest wars" are the one with China (1857–58), when the British (allied with France) fought over access to ports for trade and missionary work, and the Crimean War (1854–56), when Britain (allied with France and Turkey) opposed Russian aggression against the Baltic Slavs. On 20 April 1854, ten days after the Crimean War was declared, Austria and Prussia entered a defensive alliance guaranteeing each other's territory for the war's duration. Meroz is a town cursed in the Song of Deborah (Judg. 5:23) for failing to join the Israelites in their fight against Sisera, the leader of the Philistine hosts.

148. So the vaunted discovery of Professor Zeuss, deriving Cymry from an imaginary word 'Combroges,' is against the testimony of the best Greek geographers [Williams's note].

Johann Kaspar Zeuss, founder of Celtic philology, published *Grammatica Celtica* (1853). The "law of initial mutations," explained in 1838 by Franz Bopp, showed that in Welsh the changes in initial sounds of words in sentence combinations prove links between Welsh and other Indo-European languages.

149. For "courage. . . and sight" see Luke 4:18; "dust in the balance," Isa. 40:15.

150. Williams follows the model Bunsen set in opening and closing his volumes with a dedicatory poem. For instance, in *Egypt's Place in Universal History* (1848–57) he included dedicatory poems to Manetho and to Niebuhr (1:lvii); to Eratosthenes (2:v); to Champollion (3:vi–vii); and to Schelling (4:3–10). A poem in honor of Julius Hare follows the dedicatory page of the first volume in the second edition of *Hippolytus* (Bunsen 1854); one in honor of Thomas Arnold appears in the second volume. Bunsen wrote the poem on the occasion of Arnold's death in 1842, and after attending the funeral at Rugby sent a copy of the poem in a letter to Hare (Frances Bunsen 1868, 2:10–12; with English trans.).

St. Ignatius Loyola was the founder of the

Society of Jesus, or Jesuits (1534), officially recognized by Paul III in 1540, whose task was to reform the church from within, especially in opposition to the emerging Protestantism. The Jesuits placed particular stress on education and the sacraments, being active particularly in missionary work and in combating heresy. The power of the order, and their ability to make fine moral (casuistic) and theological distinctions, led to the application of the term and its derivatives to deceitful or equivocating practices in argument or conduct, and especially to the practice of making mental reservations concerning truth. Williams uses "sons of Loyola" here to refer to the Jesuits in particular, but more generally to Roman Catholic opponents of the Lutheran Bunsen.

Carl von Linné ("Linnaeus") defined the differences between species, but gave names to the order, genus, and species of each, compiling the categories together into a taxonomy of nature in his *Systema Naturae* (1735). As a botanist he published *Genera Plantarum* (1737) and many other works, collected and named hundreds of plants, assisted in the extension of botanical gardens in Holland, England, and Sweden, and undertook a number of botanical explorations in northern Europe.

151. [The prayer expressed at page 75, which a higher Wisdom saw not fit to grant, was the offspring of a presentiment destined too soon to be fulfilled. Baron de Bunsen died at Bonn in the morning of Nov. 28th, 1860. His end was full of trust and peace.

It will, of course, be understood that subsequent continuations of his Commentary, left by him in I know not how prepared a state, could form no part of the subject-matter of the Review contained in this volume.] [Williams's note].

This additional note was incorporated in the twelfth edition of *Essays and Reviews*. The reference to "page 75" refers to the last sentence of ¶12 of Williams's essay. The "Note on Bunsen's Biblical Researches" was printed on the unnumbered p. 434 of the first edition, at the end of the volume. It was followed in the first and subsequent editions with the phrase "THE END." For the convenience of readers the "Note" has been placed at the conclusion of the essay. See Textual Notes.

For Bunsen's *Vollständiges Bibelwerk für die Gemeinde* [Bible for the people] see Williams ¶12 and note. Both F. D. Maurice (1861, 379) and Margaret Oliphant (1868, 306) praise this work in the context of the translations of Luther and nineteenth-century German nationalism.

3 *Baden Powell*

On the Study of the Evidences of Christianity

THE INVESTIGATION of that important and extensive subject which includes what have been usually designated as 'The Evidences of Revelation,' has prescriptively occupied a considerable space in the field of theological literature, especially as cultivated in England. There is scarcely one, perhaps, of our more eminent divines who has not in a greater or less degree distinguished himself in this department, and scarcely an aspirant for theological distinction who has not thought it one of the surest paths to that eminence, combining so many and varied motives of ambition, to come forward as a champion in this arena. At the present day it might be supposed the discussion of such a subject, taken up as it has been successively in all its conceivable different bearings, must be nearly exhausted. It must, however, be borne in mind, that, unlike the *essential doctrines* of Christianity, 'the same yesterday, to-day, and for ever,' these *external accessories* constitute a subject which of necessity is perpetually taking somewhat at least of a new form, with the successive phases of opinion and knowledge.[1] And it thus becomes not an unsatisfactory nor unimportant object, from time to time, to review the condition in which the discussion stands, and to comment on the peculiar features which at any particular epoch it most prominently presents, as indicative of strength or weakness—of the advance and security of the cause—if, in accordance with the real progress of enlightenment, its advocates have had the wisdom to rescind what better information showed defective, and to substitute views in accordance with higher knowledge; or, on the other hand, inevitable symptoms of weakness and inefficiency, if such salutary cautions have been neglected. To offer some general remarks of this kind on the existing state of these discussions will be the object of the present Essay.

Before proceeding to the main question we may, however, properly premise a brief reflection on the spirit and temper in which it should be discussed. In writings on these subjects it must be confessed we too often find indications of a polemical acrimony on questions where a calm discussion of arguments would be more becoming, as well as more consistent with the proposed object; the too frequent assumption of the part of the special partisan and ingenious *advocate*, when the character to be sustained should be rather that of the unbiassed *judge*; too much of hasty and captious objection on the one hand, or of settled and inveterate prejudice on the other; too strong a tendency not fairly to appreciate, or even to keep out of sight, the broader features of the main question, in the eagerness to single out particular salient points for attack; too ready a disposition to triumph in lesser details, rather than steadily to grasp more comprehensive principles, and leave minor difficulties to await their solution, or to regard this or that particular argument as if the entire credit of the cause were staked upon it.[2]

[3] And if on the one side there is often a just complaint that objections are urged in a manner and tone offensive to religious feeling and conscientious prepossessions, which are, at least, entitled to respectful consideration; so, on the other, there is too often evinced a want of sympathy with the difficulties which many so seriously feel in admitting the alleged evidences, and which many habitual believers do not appreciate, perhaps because they have never thought or enquired deeply on the subject; or, what is more, have believed it wrong and impious to do so.

[4] Any appeal to *argument* must imply perfect freedom of conviction. It is a palpable absurdity to put *reasons* before a man, and yet wish to *compel* him to adopt them, or to anathematize him if he find them unconvincing; to repudiate him as an unbeliever, because he is careful to find satisfactory grounds for his belief; or to denounce him as a sceptic, because he is scrupulous to discriminate the truth; to assert that his honest doubts evince a moral obliquity; in a word, that he is no judge of his own mind; while it is obviously implied that his instructor is so—or, in other words, is omniscient and infallible. When serious difficulties have been felt and acknowledged on any important subject, and a writer undertakes the task of endeavouring to obviate them, it is but a fair demand that, if the reader be one of those who do not feel the difficulties, or do not need or appreciate any further argument to enlighten or support his belief, he should not cavil at the introduction of topics, which may be valuable to others, though needless, or distasteful to himself. Such persons are in no way called upon to enter into the discussion, but they are unfair if they accuse those who do so of agitating questions of whose existence *they* have been unconscious; and of unsettling men's minds, because their *own* prepossessions have been long settled, and they do not perceive the difficulties of others, which it is the very aim of such discussion to remove.

[5] Perhaps most of the various parties who have at all engaged in the discussion of these subjects are agreed in admitting a wide distinction between the influences of feeling and those of reason; the impressions of conscience and the deductions of intellect; the dictations of moral and religious sense, and the conclusions from evidence; in reference especially to the questions agitated as to the grounds of belief in Divine revelation. Indeed, when we take into account the nature of the *objects* considered, the distinction is manifest and undeniable; when a reference is made to matters of *external fact* (insisted on as such) it is obvious that reason and intellect can alone be the proper judges of the evidence of such facts. When, on the other hand, the question may be as to points of moral or religious doctrine, it is equally

clear, other and higher grounds of judgment and conviction must be appealed to.

In the questions now under consideration, *both* classes of argument are usually involved. It is the professed principle of at least a large section of those who discuss the subject, that the question is materially connected with the truth and evidence of certain external alleged historical facts: while again, all will admit that the most essential and vital portion of the inquiry refers to matters of a higher—of a more internal, moral, and spiritual kind.

But while this distinction is clearly implied and even professedly acknowledged by the disputants, it is worthy of careful remark, how extensively it is overlooked and kept out of sight in practice; how commonly—almost universally, we find writers and reasoners taking up the question, even with much ability and eloquence, and arguing it out sometimes on the one, sometimes on the other ground, forgetful of their own professions, and in a way often quite inconsistent with them.

Thus we continually find the professed advocates of an external revelation and historical evidence, nevertheless making their appeal to conscience and feeling, and decrying the exercise of reason; and charging those who find critical objections in the evidence with spiritual blindness and moral perversity; and on the other hand we observe the professed upholders of faith and internal conviction as the only sound basis of religion, nevertheless regarding the external facts as not less essential truth which it would be profane to question. It often seems to be rather the want of clear apprehension in the first instance of the distinct kind and character of such inquiries, when on the one side directed to the *abstract* question of evidence, and when on the other pointing to the *practical* object of addressing the moral and religious feelings and affections, which causes so many writers on these subjects to betray an inconsistency between *their professed purpose* and their *mode* of carrying it out. They avow matter-of-fact inquiry—a question of the critical evidence for alleged events—yet they pursue it as if it were an appeal to moral sentiments; in which case it would be a virtue to assent, and a crime to deny: if it be the one, it should not be proposed as the other.

Thus it is the common language of orthodox writings and discourses to advise the believer, when objections or difficulties arise, not to attempt to offer a precise answer, or to argue the point, but rather to look at the whole subject as of a kind which ought to be exempt from critical scrutiny and be regarded with a submission of judgment, in the spirit of humility and faith. This advice may be very just in reference to practical impressions; yet if the question be one (as is so much insisted on) of external facts, it amounts to neither more nor less than a tacit surrender of the claims of external evidence and historical reality. We are told that we ought to investigate such high questions rather with our affections than with our logic, and approach them rather with good dispositions and right motives, and with a desire to find the doctrine true; and thus shall discover the real assurance of its truth in obeying it; suggestions which, however good in a *moral* and *practical sense*, are surely inapplicable if it be made a question of *facts*.

If we were inquiring into historical evidence in any other case (suppose *e.g.* of

Caesar's landing in Britain) it would be little to the purpose to be told that we must look at the case through our desires rather than our reason, and exercise a believing disposition rather than rashly scrutinize testimony by critical cavils.[3] Those who speak thus on the question of religious belief, in fact shift the basis of all belief from the alleged evidence of facts to the influence of an internal persuasion; they virtually give up the evidential proof so strongly insisted on, and confess that the whole is, after all, a mere matter of feeling and sentiment, just as much as those to whose views they so greatly object as openly avowing the very same thing.

[11] We find certain forms of expression commonly stereotyped among a very large class of Divines, whenever a critical difficulty or a sceptical exception is urged, which are very significant as to the prevalent view of religious evidence. Their reply is always of this tenor: 'These are not subjects on which you can expect demonstrative evidence; you must be satisfied to accept such general proof or probability as the nature of the question allows: you must not inquire too curiously into these things; it is sufficient that we have a general moral evidence of the doctrines; exact critical discussion will always rake up difficulties, to which perhaps no satisfactory answer can be at once given. A precise sceptical caviller will always find new objections as soon as the first are refuted. It is in vain to seek to convince reason unless the conscience and the will be first well-disposed to accept the truth.' Such is the constant language of orthodox theologians. What is it but a mere translation into other phraseology, of the very assertions of the sceptical transcendentalist?[4]

[12] Indeed, with many who take up these questions, they are almost avowedly placed on the ground of practical expediency rather than of abstract truth. Good and earnest men become alarmed for the *dangerous* consequences they think likely to result from certain speculations on these subjects, and thence in arguing against them, are led to assume a tone of superiority, as the guardians of virtue and censors of right, rather than as unprejudiced inquirers into the matters-of-fact on which, nevertheless, they professedly make the case rest. And thus a disposition has been encouraged to regard any such question as one of *right or wrong*, rather than one of *truth or error*: to treat all objections as profane, and to discard exceptions unanswered as shocking and immoral.

[13] If indeed the discussion were carried on upon the professed ground of spiritual impression and religious feeling, there would be a consistency in such a course; but when *evidential* arguments are avowedly addressed to the *intellect*, it is especially preposterous to shift the ground, and charge the rejection of them on *moral* motives; while those who impute such bad motives fairly expose themselves to the retort, that their own belief may be dictated by other considerations than the love of truth.

[14] Again, in such inquiries there is another material distinction very commonly lost sight of; the difference between discussing the *truth* of a conclusion, or opinion, and the *mode* or *means* of arriving at it; or the *arguments* by which it is supported. Either may clearly be impugned or upheld without implicating the other. We may have the best evidence, but draw a wrong conclusion from it; or we may support a

incontestible truth by very fallacious arguments.

[15] The present discussion is not intended to be of a controversial kind, it is purely contemplative and theoretical; it is rather directed to a calm and unprejudiced survey of the various opinions and arguments adduced, whatever may be their ulterior tendency, on these important questions; and to the attempt to state, analyse, and estimate them just as they may seem really conducive to the high object professedly in view.

[16] The idea of *a positive external Divine revelation* of some kind has formed the very basis of all hitherto received systems of Christian belief.[5] The Romanist indeed regards that revelation as of the nature of a standing oracle accessible in the living voice of the Church; which being infallible, of course sufficiently accredits all the doctrines it announces, and constitutes them Divine. A more modified view has prevailed among a considerable section of Anglican theologians, who ground their faith on the same principles of Church authority, divested of its divine and infallible character. Most Protestants, with more or less difference of meaning, profess to regard revelation as once for all announced, long since finally closed, permanently recorded, and accessible only in the written Divine word contained in the Scriptures. And the discussion with those outside the pale of belief has been entirely one as to the validity of those external marks and attestations by which the truth of the alleged fact of such communication of the Divine will, was held to be substantiated.

[17] The scope and character of the various discussions raised on 'the evidences of religion,' have varied much in different ages, following of course both the view adopted of revelation itself, the nature of the objections which for the time seemed most prominent, or most necessary to be combated, and stamped with the peculiar intellectual character, and reasoning tone, of the age to which they belonged.

[18] The early apologists were rather defenders of the Christian cause generally; but when they entered on evidential topics, naturally did so rather in accordance with the prevalent modes of thought, than with what would now be deemed a philosophic investigation of alleged facts and critical appreciation of testimony in support of them.[6]

[19] In subsequent ages, as the increasing claims of infallible Church authority gained ground, to discuss evidence became superfluous, and even dangerous and impious; accordingly, of this branch of theological literature (unless in the most entire subjection to ecclesiastical dictation) the mediaeval church presented hardly any specimens.[7]

[20] It was not perhaps till the 15th century, that any works bearing the character of what are now called treatises on 'the evidences' appeared; and these were probably elicited by the sceptical spirit which had already begun to show itself, arising out of the subtilties of the schoolmen.[8]

[21] But in modern times, and under Protestant auspices, a greater disposition to follow up this kind of discussion has naturally been developed. The sterner genius of Protestantism required definition, argument, and proof, where the ancient

church had been content to impress by the claims of authority, veneration, and prescription, and thus left the conception of truth to take the form of a mere impression of devotional feeling or exalted imagination.

[22] Protestantism sought something more definite and substantial, and its demands were seconded and supported, more especially by the spirit of metaphysical reasoning which so widely extended itself in the 17th century, even into the domains of theology; and divines, stirred up by the allegations of the Deists, aimed at formal refutations of their objections, by drawing out the idea and the proofs of revelation into systematic propositions supported by logical arguments. In that and the subsequent period the same general style of argument on these topics prevailed among the advocates of the Christian cause. The appeal was mainly to the miracles of the Gospels, and here it was contended we want merely the same testimony of eye-witnesses which would suffice to substantiate any ordinary matter of fact; accordingly, the narratives were to be traced to writers at the time, who were either themselves eye-witnesses, or recorded the testimony of those who were so, and the direct transmission of the evidence being thus established, everything was held to be demonstrated. If any antecedent question was raised, a brief reference to the Divine Omnipotence to work the miracles, and to the Divine goodness to vouchsafe the revelation and confirm it by such proofs, was all that could be required to silence sceptical cavils.

[23] It is true, indeed, that some consideration of the *internal* evidence derived from the excellence of the doctrines and morality of the Gospel was allowed to enter the discussion, but it formed only a subordinate branch of the evidences of Christianity. The main and essential point was always the consideration of external facts, and the attestations of testimony offered in support of them. Assuming Christianity to be essentially connected with certain outward and sensible events, the main thing to be inquired into and established, was the historical evidence of those events, and the genuineness of the records of them; if this were satisfactorily made out, then it was considered the object was accomplished. The external facts simply substantiated, the intrinsic doctrines and declarations of the Gospel must by necessary consequence be Divine truths.

[24] If we compare the general tone, character, and pretensions of those works which, in our schools and colleges, have been regarded as the standard authorities on the subject of 'the evidences,' we must acknowledge a great change in the taste or opinions of the times from the commencement of the last century to the present day; which has led the student to turn from the erudite folios of Jackson and Stillingfleet, or the more condensed arguments of Clarke *On the Attributes*, Grotius *de Veritate*, and Leslie's *Method with the Deists*, the universal text-books of a past generation, to the writings of Lardner and Paley; the latter of whom, in the beginning of the present century, reigned supreme, the acknowledged champion of revelation, and the head of a school to which numerous others, as Campbell, Watson, and Douglas, contributed their labours. But more recently, these authors have been in an eminent degree superseded, by a recurrence to the once compara-

tively neglected resources furnished Bishop Butler; of so much less formal, technical, and positive a kind, yet offering wider, and more philosophical views of the subject; still, however, confessedly not supplying altogether that comprehensive discussion which is adapted to the peculiar tone and character of thought and existing state of knowledge in our own times.[9]

[25] The state of opinion and information in different ages is peculiarly shown in the tone and character of those discussions which have continually arisen, affecting the *grounds* of religious belief. The particular species of difficulty or objection in the reception of Christianity, and especially of its external manifestations, which have been found most formidable, have varied greatly in different ages according to the prevalent modes of thought and the character of the dominant philosophy. Thus, the difficulties with respect to miraculous evidence in particular, will necessarily be very differently viewed in different stages of philosophical and physical information. Difficulties in the idea of suspensions of natural laws, in former ages were not at all felt, canvassed, or thought of. But in later times they have assumed a much deeper importance. In an earlier period of our theological literature, the critical investigation of the question of *miracles* was a point scarcely at all appreciated. The attacks of the Deists of the 17th and early part of the 18th century were almost wholly directed to other points. But the speculations of Woolston, and still more the subsequent influence of the celebrated Essay of Hume, had the effect of directing the attention of divines more pointedly to the precise topic of miraculous evidence; and to these causes was added the agitation of the question of the ecclesiastical miracles, giving rise to the semi-sceptical discussions of Middleton, which called forth a more exact spirit of examination into such distinctions as were needed to preserve the miracles of the Gospels from the criticisms applied to those of the Church.[10] This distinction, in fact, involves a large part of the entire question; and towards marking it out effectually, various precautionary rules and principles were laid down by several writers. Thus, Bishop Warburton suggested as a criterion the *necessity* of the miracles to the ends of the dispensation,[11] which he conceived answered the demands of Middleton. Bishop Douglas made it the test—to connect miracles with inspiration in those who wrought them; this, he thought, would exclude the miracles of the Church.[12]

6] But it was long since perceived that the argument from *necessity* of miracles is at best a very hazardous one, since it implies the presumption of constituting ourselves judges of such necessity, and admits the fair objection—when were miracles more needed than at the present day, to indicate the truth amid manifold error, or to propagate the faith? And again, in the other case, how is the inspiration to be ascertained apart from the miracles? or, if it be, what is the use of the miracles? In fact, in proportion as external evidence to facts is made the professed demand, it follows that we can only recur to those grounds and rules by which the intellect always proceeds in the satisfactory investigation of any questions of fact and evidence, especially those of *physical* phenomena. By an adherence to those great principles on which all knowledge is acquired—by a reference to the fixed laws of belief, and our convictions of established order and analogy—we estimate the credibility of alleged events and the value of testimony, and weigh them more carefully in proportion as the matter may appear of greater moment or difficulty.

[27] In appreciating the evidence for *any* events of a striking or wonderful kind, we must bear in mind the extreme difficulty which always occurs in eliciting the truth, dependent not on the uncertainty in the transmission of testimony, but even in cases where we were ourselves witnesses, on the enormous influence exerted by our prepossessions previous to the event, and by the momentary impressions consequent upon it. We look at all events, through the medium of our prejudices, or even where we may have no prepossessions, the more sudden and remarkable any occurrence may be, the more unprepared we are to judge of it accurately or to view it calmly; our after representations, especially of any extraordinary and striking event, are always at the best mere recollections of our impressions, of ideas dictated by our emotions at the time, of surprise and astonishment which the suddenness and hurry of the occurrence did not allow us time to reduce to reason, or to correct by the sober standard of experience or philosophy.[13]

[28] Questions of this kind are often perplexed for want of due attention to the laws of human thought and belief, and of due distinction in ideas and terms. The proposition 'that an event may be so incredible intrinsically as to set aside any degree of testimony,' in no way applies to or affects the *honesty* or *veracity* of that testimony, or the reality of the *impressions* on the minds of the witnesses, so far as it relates to the matter of *sensible fact* simply.[14] It merely means this: that from the nature of our antecedent convictions, the probability of *some* kind of mistake or deception *somewhere*, though we know not *where*, is greater than the probability of the event really happening in *the way* and from the *causes* assigned.

[29] This of course turns on the general grounds of our antecedent convictions. The question agitated is not that of mere testimony, of its value, or of its failures. It refers to those *antecedent* considerations which must govern our entire view of the subject, and which being dependent on higher laws of belief, must be paramount to all *attestation*, or rather belong to a province distinct from it. What is alleged is a case of the supernatural; but no testimony can reach to the supernatural; testimony can apply only to apparent sensible facts; testimony can only prove an extraordinary and perhaps inexplicable occurrence or phenomenon: that it is due to supernatural causes is entirely dependent on the previous belief and assumptions of the parties.

[30] If at the present day any very extraordinary and unaccountable fact were exhibited before the eyes of an unbiassed, educated, well-informed individual, and supposing all suspicion of imposture put out of the question, his only conclusion would be that it was something he was unable at present to explain; and if at all versed in physical studies, he would not for an instant doubt either that it was really due to some natural cause, or that if properly recorded and examined, it would at some future time receive its explanation by the advance of discovery.

[31] It is thus the prevalent conviction that at the present day miracles are not to be

expected, and consequently alleged marvels are commonly discredited.[15]

[32] But as exceptions proving the rule, it cannot be denied that amid the general scepticism, instances sometimes occur of particular persons and parties who, on peculiar grounds, firmly believe in the occurrence of certain miracles even in our own times. But we invariably find that this is only in connexion with their own particular tenets, and restricted to the communion to which they are attached. Such manifestations of course are believed to have a religious object, and afford to the votaries a strong confirmation of their belief, or are regarded as among the high privileges vouchsafed to an earnest faith. Yet even such persons, almost as a matter of course, utterly discredit all such wonders alleged as occurring within the pale of any religion except their own; while those of other communions as unhesitatingly reject the belief in theirs.

[33] To take a single instance, we may refer to the alleged miraculous 'tongues' among the followers of the late Mr. Irving some years ago.[16] It is not, and was not, a question of *records* or *testimony*, or fallibility of *witnesses*, or exaggerated or fabulous *narratives*. *At the time*, the matter was closely scrutinized and inquired into, and many perfectly unprejudiced, and even sceptical persons, themselves witnessed the effects, and were fully convinced, as, indeed, were most candid inquirers at the time, that after all reasonable or possible allowance for the influence of delusion or imposture, beyond all question, *certain extraordinary manifestations did occur*. But just as little as the *mere fact* could be disputed, did any sober-minded person, except those *immediately interested*, or *influenced by peculiar views*, for a moment believe those effects to be *miraculous*. Even granting that they could not be explained by any known form of nervous affection, or on the like physiological grounds, still that they were in some way to be ascribed to natural causes, as yet perhaps little understood, was what no one of ordinarily cultivated mind, or dispassionate judgment, ever doubted.

[34] On such questions we can only hope to form just and legitimate conclusions from an extended and unprejudiced study of the laws and phenomena of the natural world. The entire range of the inductive philosophy is at once based upon, and in every instance tends to confirm, by immense accumulation of evidence, the grand truth of the universal order and constancy of natural causes, as a primary law of belief; so strongly entertained and fixed in the mind of every truly inductive inquirer, that he can hardly even conceive the possibility of its failure.[17] Yet we sometimes hear language of a different kind. There are still some who dwell on the idea of Spinoza, and contend that it is idle to object to miracles as violations of natural laws, because we know not the extent of nature; that all inexplicable phenomena are, in fact, miracles, or at any rate mysteries; that we are surrounded by miracles in nature, and on all sides encounter phenomena which baffle our attempts at explanation, and limit the powers of scientific investigation; phenomena whose causes or nature we are not, and probably never shall be, able to explain.[18]

[35] Such are the arguments of those who have failed to grasp the positive scientific idea of the power of the inductive philosophy, or the *order of nature*.[19] The

boundaries of nature exist only where our *present* knowledge places them; the discoveries of to-morrow will alter and enlarge them. The inevitable progress of research must, within a longer or shorter period, unravel all that seems most marvellous, and what is at present least understood will become as familiarly known to the science of the future, as those points which a few centuries ago were involved in equal obscurity, but are now thoroughly understood.

[36] None of these, or the like instances, are at all of the same kind, or have any characteristics in common with the idea of what is implied by the term 'miracle,' which is asserted to mean something at variance with nature and law; there is not the slightest analogy between an unknown or inexplicable phenomenon, and a supposed suspension of a known law: even an exceptional case of a known law is included in some larger law. Arbitrary interposition is wholly different in kind; no argument from the one can apply to the other.

[37] The enlarged critical and inductive study of the natural world, cannot but tend powerfully to evince the inconceivableness of imagined interruptions of natural order, or supposed suspensions of the laws of matter, and of that vast series of dependent causation which constitutes the legitimate field for the investigation of science, whose constancy is the sole warrant for its generalizations, while it forms the substantial basis for the grand conclusions of natural theology. Such would be the grounds on which our convictions would be regulated as *to marvellous events at the present day*; such the rules which we should apply to *the like cases narrated in ordinary history.*

[38] But though, perhaps, the more general admission at the present day of critical principles in the study of history, as well as the extension of physical knowledge, has done something to diffuse among the better informed class more enlightened notions on this subject, taken abstractedly, yet they may be still much at a loss to apply such principles in all cases: and readily conceive that there are possible instances in which *large exceptions must be made.*

[39] The above remarks may be admitted in respect to events at the *present day* and those narrated in *ordinary history*; but it will be said there may be, and there are, cases which are, *not like those of* the present times nor of *ordinary history.*

[40] Thus if we attempt any uncompromising, rigid scrutiny of the Christian miracles, on the same grounds on which we should investigate any ordinary narrative of the supernatural or marvellous, we are stopped by the admonition not to make an irreverent and profane intrusion into what ought to be held sacred and exempt from such unhallowed criticism of human reason.

[41] Yet the champions of the 'Evidences' of Christianity have professedly rested the discussion of the miracles of the New Testament on the ground of precise evidence of witnesses, insisting on the *historical* character of the Gospel records, and urging the investigation of the truth of the facts on the strict principles of criticism, as they would be applied to any other historical narrative. On these grounds, it would seem impossible to exempt the miraculous parts of those narratives, from such considerations as those which must be resorted to in regard to marvellous or

supposed supernatural events in general. Yet there seems an unwillingness to concede the propriety of such examination, and a disposition to regard this as altogether an *exceptional case*. But in proportion as it is so regarded, it must be remembered its strictly *historical* character is forfeited, or at least tampered with; and those who would shield it from the criticisms to which history and fact are necessarily amenable, cannot in consistency be offended at the alternative involved, of a more or less mythical interpretation.

[42] In history generally our attention is often called to narratives of the marvellous: and there is a sense in which they may be viewed with reference to its general purport and in connexion with those influences on human nature which play so conspicuous a part in many events. Thus it has been well remarked by Dean Milman—'History to be true must condescend to speak the language of legend; the belief of the times is part of the record of the times; and though there may occur what may baffle its more calm and searching philosophy, it must not disdain that which was the primal, almost universal motive of human life.'[20]

[43] Yet in a more general point of view, when we consider the strict office of the critical historian, it is obvious that such cases are fair subjects of analysis, conducted with the view of ascertaining their real relation to nature and fact.

[44] From the general maxim that all history is open to criticism as to its grounds of evidence, no *professed history* can be exempt without forfeiting its *historical* character; and in its contents, what is properly historical, is, on the same grounds, fairly to be distinguished from what may appear to be introduced on other authority and with other objects. Thus, the general credit of an historical narrative does not exclude the distinct scrutiny into any statements of a supernatural kind which it may contain; nor supersede the careful estimation of the value of the testimony on which they rest—the directness of its transmission from eye-witnesses, as well as the possibility of misconception of its tenor, or of our not being in possession of all the circumstances on which a correct judgment can be formed.

[45] It must, however, be confessed that the propriety of such dispassionate examination is too little appreciated, or the fairness of weighing well the improbabilities on one side, against possible openings to misapprehension on the other.

[46] The nature of the laws of all human belief, and the broader grounds of probability and credibility of events, have been too little investigated, and the great extent to which all testimony must be modified by antecedent credibility as determined by such general laws, too little commonly understood to be readily applied or allowed.

[47] Formerly (as before observed) there was no question as to general credibility. But in later times the most orthodox seem to assume that interposition would be *generally* incredible; yet endeavour to lay down rules and criteria by which it may be rendered probable, in cases of great emergency. Miracles were formerly the *rule*, latterly the *exception*.

[48] The arguments of Middleton and others, all assume the antecedent incredibility of miracles in general, in order to draw more precisely the distinction that in

certain cases of a very special nature that improbability may be removed, as in the case of authenticating a revelation. Locke[21] expressly contends that it is the very extraordinary nature of such an emergency which renders an extraordinary interposition requisite and therefore credible.

[49] The belief in Divine interposition must be essentially dependent on what we *previously* admit or believe with respect to the *Divine attributes.*

[50] It was formerly argued that every Theist must admit the credibility of miracles; but this, it is now seen, depends on the *nature* and *degree* of his Theism, which may vary through many shades of opinion. It depends, in fact, on the precise view taken of the Divine attributes; such, of course, as is attainable *prior* to our admission of revelation, or we fall into an argument in a vicious circle. The older writers on natural theology, indeed, have professed to deduce very exact conclusions as to the Divine perfections, especially *Omnipotence*; conclusions which, according to the physical argument already referred to, appear carried beyond those limits to which reason or science are competent to lead us; while, in fact, all our higher and more precise ideas of the Divine perfections are really derived from that very revelation, whose evidence is the point in question. The Divine Omnipotence is entirely an inference *from the language of the Bible*, adopted *on the assumption* of a belief in revelation. That 'with God nothing is impossible,' is the very declaration of Scripture; yet on this, the whole belief in miracles is built, and thus, with the many, that belief is wholly the *result*, not the *antecedent* of faith.[22]

[51] But were these views of the Divine attributes, on the other hand, ever so well established, it must be considered that the Theistic argument requires to be applied with much caution; since most of those, who have adopted such theories of the Divine perfections, on abstract grounds, have made them the basis of a precisely opposite belief, rejecting miracles altogether; on the plea, that our ideas of the Divine perfections must directly discredit the notion of occasional interposition; that it is derogatory to the idea of Infinite power and wisdom, to suppose an order of things so imperfectly established that it must be occasionally interrupted and violated when the necessity of the case compelled, as the emergency of a revelation was imagined to do. But all such Theistic reasonings are but one-sided, and if pushed further must lead to a denial of all active operation of the Deity whatever; as inconsistent with unchangeable, infinite perfection.[23] Such are the arguments of Theodore Parker,[24] who denies miracles *because* 'everywhere I find law the constant mode of *operation of an infinite God*,' or that of Wegscheider,[25] that the belief in miracles is irreconcilable with the idea of an *eternal God consistent with himself*, &c.

[52] Paley's grand resource is 'once believe in a God, and all is easy.'[26] Now, no men have evinced a more deep-seated and devout belief in the Divine perfections than the writers just named, or others differing from them by various shades of opinion, as the late J. Sterling, Mr. Emerson, and Professor F. W. Newman.[27] Yet these writers have agreed in the inference that the entire view of Theistic principles, in their highest spiritual purity, is utterly at variance with all conception of suspensions of the laws of nature, or with the idea of any kind of external manifestation

addressed to the senses, as overruling the higher, and as they conceive, sole worthy and fitting convictions of moral sense and religious intuition.

3] We here speak impartially and disinterestedly, since we are far from agreeing in their reasonings, or even their first principles. But we think it deeply incumbent on all who would fairly reason out the case of miraculous evidence at the present day, to give a full and patient discussion to this entire class of arguments which now command so many adherents.

4] In advancing from the argument *for* miracles to the argument *from* miracles; it should, in the first instance, be considered that the evidential force of miracles (to whatever it may amount) is wholly *relative* to the apprehensions of the parties addressed.

5] Thus, in an 'evidential' point of view, it by no means follows, supposing we at this day were able to explain what in an ignorant age was regarded as a miracle, that therefore that event was not equally *evidential* to those immediately addressed. Columbus's prediction of the eclipse to the native islanders was as true an argument *to them* as if the event had really been supernatural.[28]

6] It is a consideration adopted by some eminent divines that in the very language of the Gospels the distinction is always kept up between mere 'wonders' (τέρατα) and 'miracles' or 'signs' (σημεια); that is to say, the latter were occurrences not viewed as mere matters of wonder or astonishment, but regarded as indications of other truths, specially adapted to convince those to whom they were addressed in their existing stage of enlightenment.[29]

] Archbishop Whately, besides dwelling on this distinction, argues that 'the apostles would not only not have been believed but not even *listened* to, if they had not first *roused men's attention* by working, as we are told they did, special (remarkable) miracles.'[30] (Acts xix. 11.)

] Some have gone further, and have considered the application of miracles as little more than is expressed in the ancient proverb, 'Θαύματα μώροις'—which is supposed to be nearly equivalent to the rebuke, 'an evil generation seeketh a sign, &c.'[31] (Matt. xii. 38.)

] Schleiermacher regards the miracles as only relatively or apparently such, to the apprehensions of the age.[32] By the Jews we know such manifestations, especially the power of healing, were held to constitute the distinctive marks of the Messiah, according to the prophecies of their Scriptures.[33] Signs of an improper or irrelevant kind were refused, and even those which were granted were not necessarily nor universally conclusive. With some they were so, but with the many the case was different. The Pharisees set down the miracles of Christ to the power of evil spirits; and in other cases no conviction[34] was produced, not even on the apostles.[35] Even Nicodemus, notwithstanding his logical reasoning, was but half convinced. While Jesus himself, especially to his disciples in private, referred to his works as only secondary and subsidiary to the higher evidence of his character and doctrine,[36] which was so conspicuous and convincing even to his enemies as to draw forth the admission, 'Never man spake like this man.'

[60] The later Jews adopted the strange legend of the *'Sepher Toldeth Yehsu'* (Book of the Generation of Jesus), which describes his miracles substantially as in the Gospels, but says that he obtained his power by hiding himself in the Temple, and possessing himself of the secret ineffable name, by virtue of which such wonders could be wrought.[37]

[61] All moral evidence must essentially have respect to the parties to be convinced. 'Signs' might be adapted peculiarly to the state of moral or intellectual progress of one age, or one class of persons, and not be suited to that of others. With the cotemporaries of Christ and the Apostles, it was not a question of testimony or credibility; it was not the mere occurrence of what they all regarded as a supernatural event, as such, but the particular character to be assigned to it, which was the point in question. And it is to the entire difference in the ideas, prepossession, modes, and grounds of belief in those times that we may trace the reason why miracles, which would be incredible *now*, were not so in the age and under the circumstances in which they are stated to have occurred.

[62] The force and function of all moral evidence is nullified and destroyed if we seek to apply that *kind* of argument which does not find a response in the previous views or impressions of the individual addressed; all evidential reasoning is essentially an adaptation to the conditions of mind and thought of the parties addressed, or it fails in its object. An evidential appeal which in a long past age was convincing as made to the state of knowledge in that age, might have not only no effect, but even an injurious tendency, if urged in the present, and referring to what is at variance with existing scientific conceptions; just as the arguments of the present age would have been unintelligible to a former.

[63] In his earlier views of miracles Dr. J. H. Newman[38] maintained (agreeing therein with Paulus and Rosenmüller,)[39] that most of the Christian miracles could only be evidential *at the time* they were wrought, and are not so at present, a view in which a religious writer of a very different school, Athanase Coquerel,[40] seems to concur, alleging that they can avail only in founding a faith—not in preserving it.

[64] This was also the argument of several of the Reformers, as Luther, Huss, and others[41] have reasonably contemplated the miracles as a part of the peculiarities of the first outward manifestation and development of Christianity; like all other portions of the Divine dispensations specially adapted to the age and the condition of those to whom they were immediately addressed: but restricted apparently to those ages, and at any rate, not in the same form continued to subsequent times, when the application of them would be inappropriate.

[65] The force of the appeal to miracles must ever be essentially dependent on the preconceptions of the parties addressed. Yet even in an age, or among a people, entertaining an indiscriminate belief in the supernatural, the allegation of particular miracles as evidential may be altogether vain; the very extent of their belief may render it ineffective in furnishing proofs to authenticate the communications of any teacher as a Divine message. The constant belief in the miraculous may neutralize

all evidential distinctions which it may be attempted to deduce. Of this we have a striking instance on record, in the labours of the missionary, Henry Martyn, among the Persian Mahometans.[42] They believed readily all that he told them of the Scripture miracles, but directly paralleled them by wonders of their own; they were proof against any argument from the resurrection, because they held that their own Sheiks had the power of raising the dead.

[66] It is also stated that the later Jewish Rabbis, on the same plea that miracles were believed to be wrought by so many teachers, of the most different doctrines, denied their evidential force altogether.[43]

[67] By those who take a more enlarged survey of the subject, it cannot fail to be remarked how different has been the spirit in which miracles were contemplated as they are exhibited to us in the earlier stages of ecclesiastical literature, from that in which they have been regarded in modern times; and this especially in respect to that particular view which has so intimately connected them with precise 'evidential arguments;' and by a school of writers, of whom Paley may be taken as the type, and who regard them as the sole external proof and certificate of a Divine revelation.

[68] But at the present day this 'evidential' view of miracles as the sole or even the principal external attestation to the claims of a Divine revelation, is a species of reasoning which appears to have lost ground even among the most earnest advocates of Christianity. It is now generally admitted that Paley took too exclusive a view in asserting that we cannot conceive a revelation substantiated in any other way. And it has been even more directly asserted by some zealous supporters of Christian doctrine that the external evidences are altogether inappropriate and worthless.

[69] Thus by a school of writers of the most highly orthodox pretensions, it is elaborately argued, to the effect, that revelation ought to be believed though destitute of strict evidence, either internal or external; and though we neither see it nor know it.[44] And again, 'We must be as sure that the bishop is Christ's appointed representative, as if we actually saw him work miracles as St. Peter and St. Paul did.'[45] Another writer of the same school exclaims, 'As if *evidence* to the Word of God were a thing to be tolerated by a Christian; except as an additional condemnation for those who reject it, or as a sort of exercise and indulgence for a Christian understanding.'[46] Thus while the highest section of Anglican orthodoxy does not hesitate openly to disavow the old evidential argument; referring everything to the authority of the Church, the more moderate virtually discredit it by a general tone of vacillation between the antagonistic claims of reason and faith;—intuition and evidence;—while the extreme 'evangelical' school, strongly asserting the literal truth of the Bible, seeks its evidence wholly in spiritual impressions, regarding all exercise of the reason as partaking in the nature of sin. But even among less prejudiced thinkers, we find indications of similar views;[47] thus a very able critic writing in *express defence* of the Christian cause, speaks of 'that accumulation of historical testimonies,' 'which the last age erroneously denominated the evidences of

Christianity.' And the poet Coleridge, than whom no writer has been more earnest in upholding and defending Christianity, even in its most orthodox form, in speaking of its external attestations, impatiently exclaims, 'Evidences of Christianity! I am weary of the word: make a man feel the want of it . . . and you may safely trust it to its own evidence.'[48]

[70] But still further: Paley's well-known conclusion to the 5th book of his *Moral Philosophy*, pronounced by Dr. Parr to be the finest prose passage in English literature, more especially his final summing up of the evidential argument in the words, 'He alone discovers who proves: and no man can prove this point (a future retribution), but the teacher who testifies by miracles that his doctrine comes from God,'—calls forth from Coleridge an emphatic protest against the entire principle, as being at variance with that moral election which he would make the essential basis of religious belief;[49] to which he adds, in another place, 'The cordial admiration with which I peruse the preceding passage as a masterpiece of composition would, could I convey it, serve as a measure of the vital importance I attach to the convictions which impelled me to animadvert on the same passage as doctrine.'[50]

[71] Some of the most strenuous assertors of miracles have been foremost to disclaim the notion of their being the *sole certificate* of Divine communication, and have maintained that the true force of the Christian evidences lies in the *union* and *combination* of the *external* testimony of miracles, with the *internal* excellence of the doctrine; thus, in fact, practically making *the latter the real test of the admissibility of the former.*[51]

[72] The necessity for such a combination of the evidence of miracles with the test of the doctrine inculcated is acknowledged in the Bible, both under the old and the new dispensations. We read of false prophets who might predict signs and wonders, which might come to pass; but this was to be of no avail if they led their hearers 'after other gods.'[52]

[73] In like manner, 'if an angel from heaven' preached any other gospel to the Galatians, they were to reject it.[53] And even according to Christ's own admonitions, *false* Christs and false prophets should show signs and wonders such as might 'deceive, if possible, the very elect.'[54]

[74] According to this view, the main ground of the admissibility of external attestations is the worthiness of their object—the doctrine; its unworthiness will discredit even the most distinctly alleged apparent miracles, and such worthiness or unworthiness appeals solely to our moral judgment.

[75] No man has dwelt more forcibly on miraculous evidence than Archbishop Whately; yet in relation to the character of Christ as conspiring with the external attestations of his mission, he strongly remarks (speaking of some who would ascribe to Christ an unworthy doctrine, an equivocal mode of teaching), 'If I could believe Jesus to have been guilty of such subterfuges. . . . . . I not only could not acknowledge him as sent from God, but should reject him with the deepest moral indignation.'[55]

[76] Dean Lyall enters largely into this important qualification in his defence of the miraculous argument, applying it in the most unreserved manner to the ecclesiastical miracles,[56] which he rejects at once as having no connexion with doctrine. We have also on record the remark of Dr. Johnson: —'Why, sir, Hume, taking the proposition simply, is right; but the Christian revelation is not proved by miracles alone, but as connected with prophecies and with the doctrines in confirmation of which miracles were wrought.'[57]

[77] This has, indeed, been the common argument of the most approved divines; it is that long ago urged by Dr. S. Clarke,[58] and recently supported by Dean Trench.[59] Yet what is it but to acknowledge the right of an appeal, superior to that of all miracles, to our own moral tribunal, to the principle that 'the human mind is competent to sit in moral and spiritual tribunal on a professed revelation,' in virtue of which Professor F. Newman, as well as many other inquirers, have come to so very opposite a conclusion.[60]

[78] Again, it has been strongly urged by the last-named writer, if miracles are made the sole criterion, then amid the various difficulties attending the scrutiny of evidence, and the detection of imposture, an advantage is clearly given to the shrewd sceptic over the simple-minded and well-disposed disciple, utterly fatal to the purity of faith.[61]

[79] The view of miraculous evidence which allows it to be taken only in connexion with, and in fact in subserviency to, the moral and internal proof derived from the character of the doctrine, has been pushed to a greater extent by the writer last named; who asks, What is the value of 'faith at second hand?'—Ought any external testimony to overrule internal conviction? Ought any *moral* truth to be received in mere obedience to a miracle of *sense*?[62] and observes that a miracle can only address itself to our external senses, and that *internal and moral impressions* must be deemed of a kind paramount to *external* and *sensible*.

[80] If it be alleged that this internal sense may be delusive, not less so, it is replied, may the external senses deceive us as to the world of sense and external evidence. The same author however expressly allows that the claims of 'the historical' and 'the spiritual,' the proofs addressed to 'reason' and to the 'internal sense,' may each be properly entertained in their respective provinces—the danger lies in confounding them or mistaking the one for the other.

[81] Even in the estimation of external evidence, everything depends on our *preliminary* moral convictions, and upon deciding in the first instance whether, on the one hand, we are 'to abandon moral conviction at the bidding of a miracle,' or, on the other, to make conformity with moral principles the sole test both of the evidences and of the doctrines of revelation.[63]

[82] In point of fact, he contends that the main actual appeal of the Apostles, especially of St. Paul, was not to outward testimony or logical argument, but to spiritual assurances:—that even when St. Paul does enter on a sort of evidential discussion, his reasoning is very unlike what a Paley would have exacted:—that all real evidence is of the spirit—which alone can judge of spiritual things; that the

Apostles did not go about proclaiming *an infallible book*, but the convert was to be convinced by his own internal judgment, not called on to resign it to a systematized and dogmatic creed.[64] And altogether the reasoning of the Apostles (wherever they enter upon the department of reasoning), was not according to our logic, but only in accordance with the knowledge and philosophy of the age.

[83] Thus in this fundamental assumption of internal evidence, some of the most orthodox writers are in fact in close agreement with those nominally of a very opposite school.

[84] It was the argument of Döderlein, that 'the truth of the doctrine does not depend on the miracles, but we must *first* be convinced of the doctrine by its internal evidence.'[65]

[85] De Wette and others of the rationalists expressly contend, that the real evidence of the divinity of any doctrine can only be its accordance with the dictations of this moral sense, and this, Wegscheider further insists, was in fact the actual appeal of Christ in his teaching.[66]

[86] In a word, on this view, it would follow that all external attestation would seem superfluous if it concur with, or to be rejected if it oppose, these moral convictions.[67] Thus a considerable school have been disposed to look to the intrinsic evidence *only*, and to accept the declarations of the Gospel *solely* on the ground of their intrinsic excellence and *accordance* with our best and highest moral and religious convictions; a view which would approach very nearly to rejecting its peculiarities altogether.

[87] Thus considerations of a very different nature are now introduced from those formerly entertained; and of a kind which affect the *entire primary conception* of 'a revelation' and its authority, and not merely any alleged *external* attestations of its truth. Thus any discussion of the 'evidences' at the present day, must have a reference equally to the influence of the various systems whether of ancient precedent or of modern illumination, which so widely and powerfully affect the state of opinion or belief.

[88] In whatever light we regard the 'evidences' of religion, to be of any effect, whether external or internal, they must always have a special reference to the *peculiar capacity and apprehension of the party addressed.* Points which may be seen to involve the greatest difficulty to more profound inquirers, are often such as do not occasion the least perplexity to ordinary minds, but are allowed to pass without hesitation. To them all difficulties are smoothed down, all objections (if for a moment raised) are at once answered by a few plausible commonplace generalities, which to their minds are invested with the force of axiomatic truths, and to question which they would regard as at once idle and impious.

[89] On the other hand, exceptions held forth as fatal by the shallow caviller are seen by the more deeply reflecting in all their actual littleness and fallacy. But for the sake of all parties, at the present day, especially those who at least profess a disposition for pursuing the serious discussion of such momentous subjects, it becomes imperatively necessary, that such views of it should be suggested as may

be really suitable to better informed minds, and may meet the increasing demands of an age pretending at least to greater enlightenment.

[90] Those who have reflected most deeply on the nature of the argument from external evidence, will admit that it would naturally possess very different degrees of force as addressed to different ages; and in a period of advanced physical knowledge the reference to what was believed in past times, if at variance with principles now acknowledged, could afford little ground of appeal: in fact, would damage the argument rather than assist it.

[91] Even some of the older writers assign a much lower place to the *evidence of miracles*, contrasting it with the conviction of *real faith*, as being merely a preparatory step to it. Thus, an old divine observes: —

[92] 'Adducuntur primum ratione exteri ad fidem, et quasi praeparantur; . . . signis ergo et miraculis via fidei per sensus et rationem sternitur.'[68]

[93] And here it should be especially noticed, as characteristic of the ideas of his age, that this writer classes the *sensible* evidence of miracles along with the convictions of *reason*, the very opposite to the view which would now be adopted, indicative of the difference in physical conceptions, which connects miracles rather with faith as they are seen to be inconceivable to reason.

[94] These prevalent tendencies in the opinions of the age cannot but be regarded as connected with the increasing admission of those broader views of physical truth and universal order in nature, which have been followed out to higher contemplations, and point to the acknowledgment of an overruling and all-pervading supreme intelligence.

[95] In advancing beyond these conclusions to the doctrines of revelation, we must recognise both the due claims of science to decide on points properly belonging to the world of *matter*, and the independence of such considerations which characterizes the disclosure of *spiritual* truth, as such.

[96] All reason and science conspire to the confession that beyond the domain of physical causation and the possible conceptions of *intellect* or *knowledge*, there lies open the boundless region of spiritual things, which is the sole dominion of *faith*. And while intellect and philosophy are compelled to disown the recognition of anything in the world of matter at variance with the first principle of the laws of matter—the universal order and indissoluble unity of physical causes—they are the more ready to admit the higher claims of divine mysteries in the invisible and spiritual world. Advancing knowledge, while it asserts the dominion of science in physical things, confirms that of faith in spiritual; we thus neither impugn the generalizations of philosophy, nor allow them to invade the dominion of faith, and admit that what is not a subject for a problem may hold its place in a creed.

[97] In an evidential point of view it has been admitted by some of the most candid divines that the appeal to miracles, however important in the early stages of the Gospel, has become less material in later times, and others have even expressly pointed to this as the reason why they have been withdrawn; whilst at the present day the most earnest advocates of evangelical faith admit that outward marvels are

needless to spiritual conviction, and triumph in the greater moral miracle of a converted and regenerate soul.[69]

[98] They echo the declaration of St. Chrysostom—'If you are a believer as you ought to be, and love Christ as you ought to love him, you have no need of miracles, for these are given to unbelievers.'[70]

[99] After all, the *evidential* argument has but little actual weight with the generality of believers. The high moral convictions often referred to for internal evidence are, to say the least, probably really felt by very few, and the appeal made to miracles as *proofs* of *revelation* by still fewer; a totally different feeling actuates the many, and the spirit of faith is acknowledged where there is little disposition to reason at all, or where moral and philosophical considerations are absolutely rejected on the highest religious grounds, and everything referred to the sovereign power of divine grace.

[100] Matters of clear and positive fact, investigated on critical grounds and supported by exact evidence, are properly matters of knowledge, not of faith. It is rather in points of less definite character that any exercise of faith can take place; it is rather with matters of religious belief belonging to a higher and less conceivable class of truths, with the mysterious things of the unseen world, that faith owns a connexion, and more readily associates itself with spiritual ideas, than with external evidence, or physical events: and it is generally admitted that many points of important religious instruction, even conveyed under the form of fictions (as in the instances of doctrines inculcated through parables) are more congenial to the spirit of faith than any relations of historical events could be.

[101] The more knowledge advances, the more it has been, and will be, acknowledged that Christianity, as a real religion, must be viewed apart from connexion with physical things.

[102] The first dissociation of the spiritual from the physical was rendered necessary by the palpable contradictions disclosed by astronomical discovery with the letter of Scripture. Another still wider and more material step has been effected by the discoveries of geology. More recently the antiquity of the human race, and the development of species, and the rejection of the idea of 'creation,' have caused new advances in the same direction.

[103] In all these cases there is, indeed, a direct discrepancy between what had been taken for revealed truth and certain undeniable existing monuments to the contrary.

[104] But these monuments were interpreted by science and reason, and there are other deductions of science and reason referring to alleged events, which, though they have left no monuments or permanent effects behind them, are not the less legitimately subject to the conclusions of positive science, and require a similar concession and recognition of the same principle of the independence of spiritual and of physical truth.

[105] Thus far our observations are general: but at the present moment some recent publications on the subject seem to call for a few more detailed remarks. We have

before observed that the style and character of works on 'the evidences,' has of necessity varied in different ages. Those of Leslie and Grotius have, by common consent, been long since superseded by that of Paley. Paley was long the text-book at Cambridge; his work was never so extensively popular at Oxford—it has, of late, been entirely disused there.[71] By the public at large however once accepted, we do not hesitate to express our belief, that before another quarter of a century has elapsed it will be laid on the shelf with its predecessors; not that it is a work destitute of high merit—as is pre-eminently true also of those it superseded, and of others again anterior to them; but they have all followed the irreversible destiny that a work, suited to convince the public mind at any one particular period, must be accommodated to the actual condition of knowledge, of opinion, and mode of thought of that period. It is not a question of *abstract excellence*, but of *relative adaptation*.[72]

6] Paley caught the prevalent tone of thought in his day. Public opinion has now taken a different turn; and, what is more important, the style and class of difficulties and objections *honestly* felt has become wholly different. New modes of speculation—new forms of scepticism—have invaded the domain of that settled belief which a past age had been accustomed to rest on the Paleyan syllogism.[73] Yet, among several works which have of late appeared on the subject, we recognise few which at all meet these requirements of existing opinion. Of some of the chief of these works, even appearing under the sanction of eminent names, we are constrained to remark that they are altogether behind the age; that amid much learned and acute remark on matters of detail, those material points on which the modern difficulties chiefly turn, as well as the theories advanced to meet them, are, for the most part, not only ignored and passed over without examination or notice, but the entire school of those writers who, with infinitely varied shades of view, have dwelt upon these topics and put forth their attempts, feeble or powerful as the case may be—to solve the difficulties—to improve the tone of discussion, to reconcile the difficulties of reason with the high aspirations and demands of faith—are all indiscriminately confounded in one common category of censure; their views dismissed with ridicule as sophistical and fallacious, abused as infinitely dangerous, themselves denounced as heretics and infidels, and libelled as scoffers and atheists.

] In truth, the majority of these champions of the evidential logic betray an almost entire unconsciousness of the advance of opinion around them. Having their own ideas long since cast in the stereotyped mould of the past, they seem to expect that a progressing age ought still to adhere to the same type, and bow implicitly to a solemn and pompous, but childish parade and reiteration, of the one-sided dogmas of an obsolete school, coupled with awful denunciations of heterodoxy on all who refuse to listen to them.

Paley clearly, as some of his modern commentators do *avowedly*, occupied the position of an *advocate*, not of a *judge*. They professedly stand up on one side, and challenge the counsel on the other to reply. Their object is not truth, but their client's case. The whole argument is one of special pleading;[74] we may admire the ingenuity, and confess the adroitness with which favourable points are seized, unfavourable ones dropped, evaded, or disguised; but we do not find ourselves the more impressed with those high and sacred convictions of truth, which ought to result rather from the wary, careful, dispassionate summing-up on both sides, which is the function of the impartial and inflexible judge.

[109] The one topic constantly insisted on as essential to the grounds of belief, considered as based on outward historical evidence, is that of *the credibility of external facts as supported by testimony.* This has always formed the most material point in the reasonings of the evidential writers of former times, however imperfectly and unsatisfactorily to existing modes of thought they treated it. And to this point, their more recent followers have still almost as exclusively directed their attention.

[110] In the representations which they constantly make, we cannot but notice a strong apparent tendency and desire to uphold the mere assertion of *witnesses* as the *supreme* evidence of *fact*, to the utter disparagement of all general grounds of reasoning, analogy, and antecedent credibility, by which that testimony may be modified or discredited. Yet we remark, that all the *instances* they adduce, when carefully examined, *really tend* to the very conclusion they are so anxious to set aside. Arguments of this kind are sometimes deduced from such cases as, *e.g.*, the belief accorded on very slight ground of probability in all commercial transactions dependent on the assumed credit and character of the negotiating parties; from the conclusions acted upon in life assurances, notwithstanding the proverbial instability of life;—and the like: in all which we can see no other real drift or tendency than to *substantiate* instead of *disparage* the necessity for *some* deeply-seated conviction of *permanent order* as the basis of all probability.

[111] A great source of misapprehension in this class of arguments has been the undue confusion between the force of *testimony* in regard to *human* affairs and events in *history*, and in regard to *physical* facts. It may be true that some of the most surprising occurrences in ordinary history are currently, and perhaps correctly accepted, on but slight grounds of real testimony; but then they relate to events of a kind which, however singular in their particular concomitant circumstances, are not pretended to be beyond natural causes, or to involve higher questions of intervention.

[112] The most seemingly improbable events in *human* history may be perfectly credible, on sufficient testimony, however contradicting ordinary experience of human motives and conduct—simply because we cannot assign any limits to the varieties of human dispositions, passions, or tendencies, or the extent to which they may be influenced by circumstances of which, perhaps, we have little or no knowledge to guide us. But no such cases would have the remotest applicability to alleged violations of the laws of *matter*, or interruptions the course of *physical* causes.

[113] The case of the alleged external attestations of Revelation, is one essentially

involving considerations of *physical* evidence. It is not one in which such reflexions and habits of thought as arise out of a familiarity with human history, and moral argument, will suffice. These no doubt and other kindred topics, with which the scholar and the moralist are familiar, are of great and fundamental importance to our general views of the whole subject of Christian evidence; but the particular case of *miracles*, as such, is one specially bearing on purely *physical* contemplations, and on which no general moral principles, no common rules of evidence or logical technicalities, can enable us to form a correct judgment. It is not a question which can be decided by a few trite and commonplace generalities as to the moral government of the world and the belief in the Divine Omnipotence—or as to the validity of human testimony, or the limits of human experience. It involves, and is essentially built upon, those grander conceptions of the order of nature, those comprehensive primary elements of all physical knowledge, those ultimate ideas of universal causation, which can only be familiar to those thoroughly versed in cosmical philosophy in its widest sense.

4] In an age of physical research like the present, all highly cultivated minds and duly advanced intellects have imbibed, more or less, the lessons of the inductive philosophy, and have at least in some measure learned to appreciate the grand foundation conception of universal law—to recognise the impossibility even of *any two material atoms* subsisting together without a determinate relation—of any action of the one on the other, whether of equilibrium or of motion, without reference to a physical cause—of any modification whatsoever in the existing conditions of material agents, unless through the invariable operation of a series of eternally impressed consequences, following in some necessary chain of orderly connexion—however imperfectly known to us.[75] So clear and indisputable indeed has this great truth become—so deeply seated has it been now admitted to be, in the essential nature of sensible things and of the external world, that not only do all philosophical inquirers adopt it, as a primary principle and guiding maxim of all their researches—but, what is most worthy of remark, minds of a less comprehensive capacity, accustomed to reason on topics of another character, and on more contracted views, have at the present day been constrained to evince some concession to this grand principle, even when seeming to oppose it.

Among writers on these questions, Dean Trench has evinced a higher view of physical philosophy than we might have expected from the mere promptings of philology and literature, when he affirms that 'we continually behold lower laws held in restraint by higher; mechanic by dynamic—chemical by vital, physical by moral;' remarks which, if only followed out, entirely accord with the conclusion of universal subordination of causation; though we must remark in passing that the meaning of 'moral laws controlling physical,' is not very clear.[76]

It is for the most part hazardous ground for any general moral reasoner to take, to discuss subjects of evidence which essentially involve that higher appreciation of *physical truth* which can be attained only from an accurate and comprehensive acquaintance with the connected series of the physical and mathematical sciences.

Thus, for example, the simple but grand truth of the law of conservation, and the stability of the heavenly motions, now well understood by all sound cosmical philosophers, is but the type of the universal self-sustaining and self-evolving powers which pervade all nature. Yet the difficulty of conceiving this truth in its simplest exemplification was formerly the chief hindrance to the acceptance of the solar system—from the prepossession of the peripatetic dogma that there must be a constantly acting moving force to keep it going. This very exploded chimera, however, by a singular infatuation, is now actually revived as the ground of argument for miraculous interposition by redoubtable champions who, to evince their profound knowledge of mechanical philosophy, inform us that 'the whole of nature is like a mill, which cannot go on without the continual application of a moving power!'[77]

[117] Of these would-be philosophers, we find many anxiously dwelling on the topic, so undeniably just in itself, of the danger of incautious conclusions—of the gross errors into which men fall by over-hasty generalizations. They recount with triumph the absurd mistakes into which some even eminent philosophers have fallen in prematurely denying what experience has since fully shown to be true, because in the then state of knowledge it seemed incredible.[78] They feel an elevating sense of superiority in putting down the arrogance of scientific pretensions by alleging the short-sighted dogmatism with which men of high repute in science have evinced a scepticism in points of vulgar belief, in which, after all, the vulgar belief has proved right. They even make a considerable display of reasoning on such cases; but we cannot say that those reasonings are particularly distinguished for consistency, force, or originality. The philosopher (for example) denies the credibility of alleged events professedly in their nature *at variance with all physical analogy*. These writers, in reply, affect to make a solemn appeal to the bar of analogy, and support it by instances which precisely defeat their own conclusion. Thus they advance the novel and profoundly instructive story of an Indian who denied the existence of ice as at variance with experience; and still more from the contradiction that being solid, it could not float in water.[79] In like manner they dwell upon other equally interesting stories of a butterfly, who from the experience of his ephemeral life in summer, denied that the leaves were ever brown or the ground covered with snow; of a child who watched a clock made to strike *only* at noon, through many hours, and therefore concluded it could never strike; of a person who had observed that fish are organized to *swim*, and therefore concluded there could be no such animals as *flying* fish.

[118] These, with a host of other equally recondite, novel, startling, and conclusive instances are urged in a tone of solemn wisdom, to prove—what? That water is converted into ice by a regular *known law*; that it has a specific gravity less than water by *some law* at present but imperfectly understood; that without *violation of analogy*, fins may be modified into wings; that it is part of the *great law* of climate that in winter leaves are brown and the ground sometimes white—that machinery may be made with action intermitting by *laws as regular* as those of its more

ordinary operations. In a word, that the philosopher who looks to an endless subordinating series of laws of successively higher generality, is inconsistent in denying events at variance with that subordination!

19] It is indeed curious to notice the elaborate multiplication of instances adduced by some of the writers referred to, all really tending to prove the subordination of *facts* to *laws*, clearly evinced as soon as the cases were well understood, though, till then, often regarded in a sceptical spirit; while of that scepticism they furnish the real and true refutation in the principle of *law* ultimately established, under whatever appearance and semblance of marvellous discordance from all law. It would be beyond our limits to notice in detail such instances as are thus dwelt upon, and apparently regarded as of sovereign value and importance, to discredit philosophical generalization:—such as the disbelief in the marvels recounted by Marco Polo; of the miracle of the martyrs who spoke articulately after their tongues were cut out; the angel seen in the air by 2000 persons at Milan; the miraculous balls of fire on the spires at Plausac; Herodotus's story of the bird in the mouth of the crocodile; narratives of the sea-serpent, marvels of mesmerism and electro-biology; all discredited formerly as fables; vaccination observed and attested by peasants,[80] but denied and ridiculed by medical men:—

20] These and the like cases are all urged as triumphant proofs, of what?—that some men have always been found of unduly sceptical tendencies; and sometimes of a rationally cautious turn; who have heard strange, and, perhaps, exaggerated narratives, and have maintained sometimes a wise, sometimes an unwise, degree of reserve and caution in admitting them; though they have since proved in accordance with *natural causes.*

21] Hallam and Rogers are cited as veritable witnesses to the truth of certain effects of mesmerism in their day generally disbelieved; and for asserting which they were met with all but an imputation of 'the lie direct.'[81] They admitted, however, that their assertion was founded on 'experience so rare as to be had only once in a century;' but that experience has been since universally borne out by all who have candidly examined the question, and the *apparently isolated and marvellous cases* have settled down into examples of *broad and general laws*, now fully justified by experience and analogy.

22] Physiological evidence is adduced (which we will suppose well substantiated) to show that the excision of the *whole tongue* does not take away the power of speech, though that of the *extremity* does so; hence the denial of the story from imperfect experience. So of other cases: the angel at Milan was the aerial reflexion of an image on a church; the balls of fire, at Plausac, were electrical; the sea-serpent was a basking shark, or a stem of sea-weed. A committee of the French Academy of Sciences, with Lavoisier at its head, after a grave investigation, pronounced the alleged fall of aërolites to be a superstitious fable.[82] It is, however, now substantiated, *not* as a miracle, but as a well-known *natural* phenomenon. Instances of undue philosophical scepticism are unfortunately common; but they are the errors, not the correct processes, of inductive inquiry.

[123] Granting all these instances, we merely ask—what do they prove?—except the real and paramount dominion of the rule of *law* and *order*, of *universal subordination* of *physical causes*, as the sole principle and criterion of proof and evidence in the region of physical and sensible truth; and nowhere more emphatically than in the history of marvels and prodigies, do we find a verification of the truth, 'opinionum commenta delet dies, naturae judicia confirmat.'[83]

[124] This in fact is the sole real result of all the profound parallelisms and illustrative anecdotes so confidently but unconsciously adduced by these writers with an opposite design.

[125] What is the *real* conclusion from the far-famed *Historic Doubts* and the *Chronicles of Ecnarf?*[84] but simply this—*there is a rational solution*, a *real* conformity to *analogy and experience*, to whatever extent a partially informed inquirer might be led to reject the recounted apparent wonders on imperfect knowledge, and from too hasty inference; these delightful parodies on Scripture (if they prove anything), would simply prove that the Bible narrative is no more properly *miraculous* than the marvellous exploits of Napoleon I., or the paradoxical events of recent history.

[126] Just a similar scepticism *has been* evinced by nearly all the first physiologists of the day, who have joined in rejecting the development theories of Lamarck and the *Vestiges*;[85] and while they have strenuously maintained successive creations, have denied and denounced the alleged production of organic life by Messrs. Crosse and Weekes, and stoutly maintained the impossibility of spontaneous generation,[86] on the alleged ground of contradiction to experience. Yet it is now acknowledged under the high sanction of the name of Owen,[87] that 'creation' is only another name for our ignorance of the mode of production; and it has been the unanswered and unanswerable argument of another reasoner that new species *must* have originated *either*, out of their inorganic elements, *or* out of previously organized forms; *either* development *or* spontaneous generation *must be* true: while a work has now appeared by a naturalist of the most acknowledged authority, Mr. Darwin's masterly volume on *The Origin of Species* by the law of 'natural selection,'—which now substantiates on undeniable grounds the very principle so long denounced by the first naturalists,—*the origination of new species by natural causes*: a work which must soon bring about an entire revolution of opinion in favour of the grand principle of the self-evolving powers of nature.[88]

[127] By parity of reason it might just as well be objected to Archbishop Whately's theory of civilization, we have only for a few centuries known anything of savages; how then can we pretend to infer that they have *never* civilized themselves? never, in all that enormous length of time which modern discovery has now indisputably assigned to the existence of the human race! This theory, however, is now introduced as a comment on Paley in support of the credibility of revelation; and an admirable argument no doubt it is, though perhaps many would apply it in a sense somewhat different from that of the author. If the use of fire, the cultivation of the soil, and the like, were Divine revelations, the most obvious inference would be that so likewise are printing and steam. If the boomerang was divinely

communicated to savages ignorant of its principle, then surely the disclosure of that principle in our time by the gyroscope, was equally so.[89] But no one denies revelation in this sense; the philosophy of the age does not discredit the inspiration of Prophets and Apostles, though it may sometimes believe it in poets, legislators, philosophers, and others gifted with high genius. At all events, the revelation of civilization does not involve the question of *external miracles*, which is here the sole point in dispute. The main assertion of Paley is that it is impossible to conceive a revelation given except by means of miracles.[90] This is his primary axiom; but this is precisely the point which the modern turn of reasoning most calls in question, and rather adopts the belief that a revelation is then most credible, when it appeals least to violations of natural causes. Thus, if miracles were in the estimation of a former age among the chief *supports* of Christianity, they are present among the main *difficulties*, and hindrances to its acceptance.

28] One of the first inductive philosophers of the age, Professor Faraday, has incurred the unlimited displeasure of these profound intellectualists, because he has urged that the mere contracted experience of the senses is liable to deception, and that we ought to be guided in our conclusions—and, in fact, can only correct the errors of the senses—by a careful recurrence to the consideration of natural laws and extended analogies.[91] In opposition to this heretical proposition, they[92] set in array the dictum of two great authorities of the Scottish school, Drs. Abercrombie and Chalmers, that 'on a certain amount of testimony we might believe any statement, however improbable;'[93] so that if a number of respectable witnesses were to concur in asseverating that on a certain occasion they had seen two and two make five, we should be bound to believe them!

9] This, perhaps, it will be said, is an extreme case. Let us suppose another:—if a number of veracious witnesses were to allege a *real* instance of witchcraft at the present day, there might no doubt be found some infatuated persons who would believe it; but the strongest of such assertions to any educated man would but prove either that the witnesses were cunningly imposed upon, or the wizard himself deluded. If the most numerous ship's company were all to asseverate that they had seen a mermaid, would any rational persons at the present day believe them? That they saw something which *they believed* to be a mermaid, would be easily conceded. No amount of attestation of innumerable and honest witnesses, would ever convince any one versed in mathematical and mechanical science, that a person had squared the circle or discovered perpetual motion. Antecedent credibility depends on antecedent knowledge, and enlarged views of the connexion and dependence of truths; and the value of any testimony will be modified or destroyed in different degrees to minds differently enlightened.[94]

] Testimony, after all, is but a second-hand assurance;—it is but a blind guide; testimony can avail nothing against reason. The essential question of miracles stands quite apart from any consideration of *testimony*; the question would remain the same, if we had the evidence of our own senses to an alleged miracle, that is, to an extraordinary or inexplicable fact. It is not the *mere fact*, but the *cause* or *explanation* of it, which is the point at issue.

[131] The case, indeed, of the *antecedent* argument of miracles is very clear, however little some are inclined to perceive it. In nature and from nature, by science and by reason, we neither have nor can possibly have any evidence of a *Deity working miracles*;—for that, we must go out of nature and beyond reason.[95] If we could have any such evidence *from nature*, it could only prove extraordinary *natural* effects, which would not be *miracles* in the old theological sense, as isolated, unrelated, and uncaused; whereas no *physical* fact can be conceived as unique, or without analogy and relation to others, and to the whole system of natural causes.

[132] To conclude,[96] an alleged miracle can only be regarded in one of two ways;—either (1) abstractedly as a physical event, and therefore to be investigated by reason and physical evidence, and referred to physical causes, possibly to *known* causes, but at all events to some higher cause or law, if at present unknown; it then ceases to be supernatural, yet still might be appealed to in support of religious truth, especially as referring to the state of knowledge and apprehensions of the parties addressed in past ages; or (2) as connected with religious doctrine, regarded in a sacred light, asserted on the authority of inspiration. In this case it ceases to be capable of investigation by reason, or to own its dominion; it is accepted on religious grounds, and can appeal only to the principle and influence of faith.

[133] Thus miraculous narratives become invested with the character of articles of faith, if they be accepted in a less positive and certain light, or perhaps as involving more or less of the parabolic or mythic character; or at any rate as received in connexion with, and for the sake of the doctrine inculcated.[97]

[134] Some of the most strenuous advocates of the Christian 'evidences' readily avow, indeed expressly contend, that the attestation of miracles is, after all, not irresistible; and that in the very uncertainty which confessedly remains lies the 'trial of faith,'[98] which it is thus implied must really rest on some other independent moral conviction.

[135] In the popular acceptation, it is clear the Gospel miracles are always *objects*, not *evidences* of faith; and when they are connected specially with doctrines, as in several of the higher mysteries of the Christian faith, the sanctity which invests the point of faith itself is extended to the external narrative in which it is embodied; the reverence due to the mystery renders the external events sacred from examination, and shields them also within the pale of the sanctuary; the *miracles* are merged in the *doctrines* with which they are connected, and associated with the declarations of spiritual things which are, as such, exempt from those criticisms to which physical statements would be necessarily amenable.

[136] But even in a reasoning point of view, those who insist most on the positive external proofs, allow that *moral* evidence is distinguished from *demonstrative*, not only in that it admits of *degrees*, but more especially in that the *same* moral argument is of *different force* to *different minds*. And the advocate of Christian evidence triumphs in the acknowledgment that the strength of Christianity lies in the *variety* of its evidences, suited to all varieties of apprehension; and, that, amid

all the diversities of conception, those who cannot appreciate some one class of proofs, will always find some other satisfactory, is itself the crowning evidence.

[137] With a firm belief in constant supernatural interposition, the cotemporaries of the Apostles were as much blinded to the reception of the gospel, as, with an opposite persuasion, others have been at a later period. Those who had access to living Divine instruction were not superior to the prepossessions and ignorance of their times. There never existed an 'infallible age' of exemption from doubt or prejudice. And if to later times records written in the characters of a long past epoch are left to be deciphered by the advancing light of learning and science,—the spirit of faith discovers continually increasing attestation of the Divine authority of the truths they include.

138] The '*reason* of the hope that is in us' is not restricted to *external* signs, nor to any one kind of evidence, but consists of such assurance as may be most satisfactory to each earnest individual inquirer's own mind.[99] And the true acceptance of the entire revealed manifestation of Christianity will be most worthily and satisfactorily based on that assurance of 'faith,' by which the Apostle affirms 'we stand,' (2 Cor. ii. 24), and which, in accordance with his emphatic declaration, must rest, 'not in the wisdom of man, but in the power of God.' (1 Cor. ii. 5.)

3 Notes to Baden Powell

1. For "the same yesterday" see Heb. 13:8.

2. The phrase "or to regard this" is emended to "and to regard this" by Powell in ink in his copy of the first edition (Bodley: Baden Powell 122, p. 95). This and all ten subsequent emendations by Powell were incorporated in the second and following editions of *Essays and Reviews.*

3. Powell's emphasis on fact from ¶s 5 to 10 is part of the Victorians' love of empirical validity; at the same time fact was also under widespread attack, from the oft-cited opening of Dickens's *Hard Times* (1854) to the opening of Matthew Arnold's "The Study of Poetry" (1880): "Our religion has materialized itself in the fact, in the supposed fact; it has attached itself and its emotion to the fact, and now the fact is failing it" (1860–77, 9:161). Powell returns to a systematic questioning of the truth claims of fact later in his essay (see, for example, ¶s 109–19). See also Temple ¶6; Wilson ¶46 and n. 82 and ¶s 72–75; Goodwin (where the conflict between the facts of Genesis and the facts of geology is addressed, as in ¶s 1–9); and Jowett, from the first sentence to the second-to-last paragraph; see especially ¶14 and n. 23.

Although the Romans did not conquer Britain until the expedition under Claudius in 43, Julius Caesar landed near Dover in 55 B.C.E. to punish the Britons for their aid to the Gauls, and with a larger army in 54 B.C.E. he enforced submission and tribute. See Caesar *De Bello Gallico* (bk. 4, chaps. 20–37; On the Gallic War).

4. "Sceptical" refers to doubts concerning the validity of both intuitive and empirical knowledge, but here it aligns theologians with the religious questioning attributed to German idealism. A transcendentalist posits true knowledge as intuitive and supernatural, derived from feelings and ideas, emphasizing the limitedness of what can be perceived by the senses. Transcendentalism as deriving from the idealism of Kant and Schelling is discussed by Carlyle in "Natural Supernaturalism" in *Sartor Resartus* (1833–34). In America it was associated with Henry David Thoreau and the Transcendentalist Club of Boston, founded (1836) by Emerson and Frederic Henry Hedge, the editor of the American editions of *Essays and Reviews.* To Powell the term *transcendentalist* designates a group of his friends, London Unitarians and theological radicals, associated with the *Westminster Review* (Corsi 1988, 146–47; 201–8). Powell refers to them (including Emerson) in ¶52.

5. Powell's comprehensive definition of the Christian religion in four terms refers to two branches of theology that operate complementarily in "all . . . systems of Christian belief." "Positive" theology, as distinguished from natural theology, deals with matters of historic fact in the Bible as well as church history and practice, appealing "to the testimonies of the fathers, the decrees or canons of councils, &c." (Buck 1851, 747). "External" refers to outward features of such evidence, rather than to inward or spiritual meanings or truth claims.

The following paragraph aligns three external elements: "the living voice of the Church," the "word contained in the Scriptures," and "the Divine will," each of which is named "Divine" on the basis of different institutional authority. In each case, "revelation" is located in the "positive" aspects of three theological positions. To Roman Catholics, the pope as "infallible" expresses the "voice of the Church" as an "external Divine revelation" under specific conditions: when speaking *ex cathedra,* on a matter of faith and morals. To Anglicans, "Church authority" is located in the externals of religion, including the Bible and the early church councils (as specified in the twentieth and twenty-first Articles of Religion). To Protestants, "positive external Divine revelation" is located in a closed canon of the Bible. Finally Powell refers to unbelievers amongst whom proselytizing has been undertaken on the basis of external evidence, whether in positive or natural theology.

6. The "apologists" were Christian writers of the second and third centuries, such as Justin Martyr, Tertullian, and Origen, who in controversy with the authorities of the Roman Empire, wrote arguments in defense of Christianity that addressed the objections of both Jewish and pagan thinkers. *Corpus Apologetarum* (The collection of the Apologists), a critical edition of their writings in nine volumes, began to appear at Jena in 1847 under the editorship of J. C. T. Otto. The word "apology" may mean an excuse for some kind of fault or failure; it may also mean a speech made in defense, especially in defense of Christianity, as in Browning's "Bishop Blougram's Apology" (1855) in which the bishop, modeled on Cardinal Wiseman after his elevation as archbishop of Westminster (1850) makes his self-defense. J. H. Newman defended his religious position in *Apologia Pro Vita Sua* (1864). William Paley (see ¶24 and note) cites Justin, Tertullian, and Origen, "the class of ancient *apologists,* whose declared design it was to defend Christianity, and to give the reasons of their adherence to it" ([1794] 1851, 281–82). "Apologetics" is a branch of theology, the study of the doctrinal defense of Christianity. For the apologists and miracles see Anthony Grant 1952 and Lampe 1965.

See also Jowett ¶21 and n. 34.

7. Medieval discussions of miracles include Augustine's *Contra Faustum Manichaeum* (397–98; Reply to Faustus the Manichaean): "There is, however, no impropriety in saying that God does a thing contrary to nature, when it is contrary to what we know of nature. For we give the name nature to the usual common course of nature; and whatever God does contrary to this, we call a prodigy, or a miracle" (bk. 26, sec. 3; trans. Southert, *NPNF*1 4:321–22); and Thomas Aquinas, who defines a miracle as "being full of wonder; as having a cause hidden from all" (*Summa theologica* [1265–] 1962–64, bk. 1, quest. 105, art. 7); see also *Summa contra Gentiles* (1259–64; bk. 3, pt. 2, chap. 103). For medieval concepts of miracles see Benedicta Ward 1982. For recent studies of NT miracles see Kee 1983 and 1986; Theissen 1983; and Hendrickx 1987.

8. Several such treatises are enumerated and described by Eichhorn. See Hallam's *Lit. of Europe*, i. p. 190. [Powell's note].

Johann Gottfried Eichhorn published *Einleitung in das Alte Testament* (1780–83, 3 vols.; Introduction to the Old Testament), where in the opening pages he introduces the term "*höheren Kritik*" (higher criticism) to biblical studies. On the cited page Hallam alludes to "numerous vindications of Christianity written in the fifteenth century. Eichhorn, after referring to several passages in the works of Petrarch, mentions defenses of religion by Marsilius Ficinus, Alfonso de Spina, a converted Jew, Savonarola, Aeneas Silvius, Picus of Mirandola. He gives an analysis of the first, which, in the course of argument, differs little from modern apologies of the same class" (1837–39, 1:190).

9. Thomas Jackson published *Commentaries upon the Apostles' Creed* in his *Collected Works* (1672–73, 3 vols.). Edward Stillingfleet published *Irenicum* (1659) where he expresses Latitudinarian views, urging union between the Anglicans and the Presbyterians on the basis of separation of church and state. He also published *Origines Sacrae* (1662; Sacred origins) on the authority of the Bible, and *Rational Account of the Grounds of the Protestant Religion* (1664). Samuel Clarke delivered two sets of Boyle Lectures in 1704–5, defending rational theology against the empiricism of John Locke, published as *A Discourse concerning the Being and Attributes of God, the Obligations of Natural Religion, and the Truth and Certainty of the Christian Revelation, in Opposition to Hobbes, Spinoza, the Author of the Oracles of Reason, and Other Deniers of Natural and Revealed Religion* (1716). Hugo Grotius was a strong advocate of Christian reunion and religious toleration, earning him the criticism of Calvinist authorities in Holland and leading eventually to his imprisonment. After escaping, he lived in France and Germany, publishing *De Veritate Religionis Christianae* (1623; Concerning the truth of the Christian religion), a missionary handbook based on the evidences of natural theology. Charles Leslie published *A Short and Easy Method with the Deists, Wherein the Certainty of the Christian Religion is Demonstrated by Infallible Proof from Four Rules, Which Are Incompatible to Any Imposture That Ever Yet Has Been, or That Can Possibly Be* (1698). These "Four Rules" (relevant to Powell's argument) are, first, the judgment of the "evidence" of Christianity according to the empirical sensations of sight and hearing; second, the public disclosure of the evidence; third, the observance of the evidence in public monuments and outward religious practice; and fourth, the determination that such monuments and practices are contemporaneous with the evidence. Nathaniel Lardner published *The Credibility of the Gospel History* (1727–57, 14 vols.), using patristic commentaries to ascertain the dates and authorship of NT documents and to establish critical methodologies in the study of early Christian literature. William Paley published *Principles of Moral and Political Philosophy* (1785), *Horae Paulinae* (1790), *A View of the Evidences of Christianity* (1794), and *Natural Theology* (1802), all of which became standard works in their fields (see ¶105). George Campbell published *Dissertation on Miracles* (1763) against Hume's "Of Miracles," asserting that the NT miracles are evidential because they are susceptible to proof by testimony. Richard Watson published *Apology for the Bible* (1796), answering the attacks on Christianity by Tom Paine. John Douglas published *The Criterion or Rules by Which the True Miracles Recorded in the New Testament Are Distinguished from the Spurious Miracles of Pagans and Papists* (1752), an attack on Hume. Joseph Butler answered the deists in *The Analogy of Religion, Natural and Revealed, to the Constitution and Course of Nature* (1736) where he establishes a conformity between natural and revealed religion. Knowledge "in our own times" (that is, the nineteenth century) contained extensive presentations of the "evidences," especially in their relations to the developing physical sciences, as, for instance, in the major theological lecture series (Bampton, Boyle, and Hulsean), and particularly in the Bridgewater Treatises on *The Power, Wisdom, and Goodness of God as Manifested in the Creation* (1832–40). On this context see Robson's essay in Helmstadter and Lightman 1990.

The word "confessedly" is emended to "altogether" and then both words were scored out by Powell in ink in his copy of the first edition of *Essays and Reviews* (Bodley: Baden Powell 122, p. 104), a change incorporated in the second edition.

10. Thomas Woolston published six *Discourses on the Miracles of Our Saviour* from 1727 to 1729, for which he was tried and imprisoned. He denied proof of revelation by miracles, arguing instead for an allegorical or typological reading of the Bible. David Hume wrote "Of Miracles" as an essay for *A Treatise of Human Nature* (1739–40, 3 vols.), but excised it

before publication: "I am at present castrating my Work . . . [so] it shall give as little Offence as possible; before which I cou'd not pretend to put it into the Drs [Butler's] hands" (quoted in Mossner 1980, 112). It was published in *Philosophical Essays concerning Human Understanding* (1748). To Hume a miracle is "*a transgression of a law of nature by a particular volition of the Deity, or by the interposition of some invisible agent*" (Hume [1748] 1964, 93).

11. *Div. Leg.* ix. 5 [Powell's note].

William Warburton published *Divine Legation of Moses Demonstrated on the Principles of a Religious Deist* (1737–41, 2 vols.), where he accepts the deists' position that the Mosaic law does not contain reference to eternal life, but turns their argument against them by maintaining the divine origin of the Mosaic law. Warburton also wrote on miracles in *A Critical and Philosophical Enquiry into the Causes of Prodigies and Miracles as Related by Historians* (1727), arguing that the distinction between credible and incredible miracles, to be tested by their historical context, is overdetermined by the psychological emotion of "admiration" whereby one believes in the wonderful. The problem of "necessity" depends on the kinds of evidence adduced and the authority of the judge in determining such necessity, a point Powell turns to in the next paragraph. Conyers Middleton argued in *A Free Inquiry into the Miraculous Powers* (1748) that the "ecclesiastical" miracles after the New "dispensation" must be accepted or rejected as a whole. Middleton distinguished between early Christianity's extensive testimony to miracles but very limited credibility concerning them. John Davison published his Warburtonian Lectures as *Discourses on Prophecy in Which Are Considered Its Structure, Use, and Inspiration* (1824). Powell reviewed Davison in the *British Critic* (Powell 1824).

12. *Criterion*, pp. 239, 241 [Powell's note].

In *Criterion* (1752) Douglas accepted the authenticity of the biblical miracles, but rejected ecclesiastical miracles, including contemporary Jansenist healings in France and Queen Anne's alleged healings by the royal touch, because the recorded accounts appeared long after the supposed events. He attributed other healings to fraud or to the psychosomatic state of the patient. Powell probably cites the edition of 1824, abridged by William Marsh. On the cited pages, Douglas discusses "the vast multitudes of Christian martyrs during the persecutions of the three first centuries. . . . He, I say, who can suppose, that this venerable host of holy confessors, could have braved death with a fortitude so uncommon, if God had not, by his invisible agency, interposed to comfort and strengthen their minds under such distress, will believe a miracle greater than any of those to which we Christians appeal."

13. The words "of surprise and astonishment" are emended to "by the surprise and astonishment" by Powell in ink in his copy of the first edition of *Essays and Reviews* (Bodley: Baden Powell 122, p. 106), a change incorporated in the second edition.

14. On the opposite side, Paley writes: "We assert only, that in miracles adduced in support of revelation there is not any such antecedent improbability as no testimony can surmount" (Paley [1794] 1851, 2).

15. The passage from ¶s 29–31, "What is alleged. . . . commonly discredited," was cited as one of the "false and dangerous statements, and reasonings at variance with the teaching of the Church of England" that comprised the grounds for the Synodical Condemnation of *Essays and Reviews* on 21 June 1864 on the basis of a denial of miracles as historical fact (*Chronicle* 1859–64:1864, Session 66, 1656–57).

16. Edward Irving was rejected by the Church of Scotland because of his views of prophecy and Christ's humanity, and founded the Catholic Apostolic Church in 1832. He practiced faith healings from 1828 and many at his gatherings spoke in tongues (the phenomenon of glossolalia; see Acts 2:4–11; 1 Cor. 14), uttering apparently unintelligible sounds in states of ecstatic excitement. For contemporary discussions of Irving's miracles see Empson 1831, Sewall 1838 (where mention is made of "Mr. Irving's delusions and the Unknown Tongues" [303]), and Margaret Oliphant 1858.

17. The phrase "can hardly even conceive" is emended to "cannot even conceive" by Powell in ink in his copy of the first edition of *Essays and Reviews* (Bodley: Baden Powell 122, p. 109), a change incorporated in the second edition.

18. Benedict de Spinoza published *Tractatus Theologico-Politicus* (1670) where, in "Of Miracles" (chap. 6), he argues rather differently than Powell suggests. Spinoza defines a "miracle" as "an event of which the causes cannot be explained by the natural reason through a reference to ascertained workings of nature" ([1670] 1951, 84). Writing within the long tradition of relating miracles to limited human knowledge of the laws of nature, Spinoza identifies those laws with the decrees of God: "Whatever comes to pass, comes to pass according to laws and rules which involve eternal necessity and truth; nature, therefore, always observes laws and rules . . . although they may not all be known to us, and therefore she keeps a fixed and immutable order" (83). Similarly, Augustine refers to "inexplicable phenomena [as] . . . miracles," arguing that "whatever God does contrary to this [law of nature], we call a prodigy, or a miracle. But against the supreme law of nature, which is beyond the knowledge both of the ungodly and of weak believers, God never acts, any more than He acts against Himself" (*Contra Faustum Manichaeum* [Against Faustus the Manichaean] bk. 26, sec. 3; trans. Southert, *NPNF*1 4:321–2). Jean-Jacques Rousseau, in his third "Letter from the Mountain," draws comparable attention to

such limited "attempts at explanation": "*Les découvertes continuelles qui se font dans les loix de la nature, celles qui probablement se feront encore . . . ; les diverses bornes que donnent les peuples à l'ordre des possibles selon qu'ils sont plus ou moins éclairés; tout nous prouve que nous ne pouvons connoître ces bornes*" (*Lettre* iii; Rousseau [1763] 1964, 4:744; The continual discoveries that are made in the laws of nature, those that probably will yet come to be . . . ; the different bounds that people set to the order of the possible according as they have more or less knowledge; all proves to us that we are not able to know these limits).

19. Powell published *The Order of Nature Considered in Reference to the Claims of Revelation* (1859); the third essay is "The Rationalistic and other Theories of Miracles."

20. *Latin Christianity*, vol. i. p. 388 [Powell's note].

Milman draws distinctions throughout his study among Latin, Greek, and Eastern forms of Christianity, and parallels between Latin and Teutonic Christianity (1855).

21. *Essay*, Book i. ch. xvi. § 13 [Powell's note].

John Locke published *An Essay concerning Human Understanding* (1690). The reference, uncorrected in subsequent editions of *Essays and Reviews*, is actually to bk. 4, chap. 16, par. 13.

22. For "with God nothing . . . " see Matt. 19:26; Mark 10:27.

23. See Mansel, *Bampt. Lect.* p. 185 [Powell's note].

Henry Longueville Mansel published his Bampton Lectures on *The Limits of Religious Thought Examined* (1858). Following Kant and the Scottish philosopher Sir William Hamilton, he denied suprasensuous knowledge, arguing that consciousness involves knowledge of both the self and the external world; however, knowledge of the nature of God is derived only from supernatural revelation, and not from the evidences of natural theology or from direct intuition. Mansel was attacking English transcendental Unitarians such as F. W. Newman and W. R. Greg, as well as materialist philosophers such as J. S. Mill (Corsi 1988, 202–13); see Lightman 1979.

"But all such Theistic reasonings are but one sided, and if pushed further must lead" is emended to "All such Theistic reasonings, in fact, if pushed to their consequences, must lead" by Powell in ink in his copy of the first edition of *Essays and Reviews* (Bodley: Baden Powell 122, p. 114), a change incorporated in the second edition with added punctuation.

24. *Theism*, &c. p. 263, comp. p. 113 [Powell's note].

The cited passage is from Theodore Parker's *Sermons on Theism, Atheism and the Popular Theology* (1853). The passage to be compared is "In Nature God is the only Cause, the only Providence, the only power; the law of nature, that is, the constant mode of action of the forces of the material world—represent the modes of action of God Himself, his thought made visible" (113). Powell reviewed Parker's *Discourse of Matters Pertaining to Religion* (1842), along with J. H. Newman's *Essay on the Miracles Recorded in Ecclesiastical History* (1843) and William Palmer's *Doctrine of Development and Conscience Considered in Relation to the Evidences of Christianity* (1846) (Powell 1847). Alfred Ollivant uses the first citation from Parker to attack Rowland Williams: "Distressing as it is for Christian lips to repeat such vile and blasphemous sentiments, I shall not scruple to cite a passage of one who may be regarded as the Corypheus of this once exploded, but lately revived Spiritualism, in which features of the system in all their native hideousness, are presented to our view" (1857, 37).

25. 'Persuasio de supernaturali et miraculosa eademque immediata Dei revelatione, haud bene conciliari videtur cum idea Dei aeterni, semper sibi constantis, &c.'— Wegscheider, *Instit. Theol.* § 12 [Powell's note].

(Lat. An argument concerning the supernatural and miraculous and the same immediate revelation of God does not seem to congrue easily with the idea of an eternal God who is always existing for himself). Julius August Ludwig Wegscheider published *Institutiones teologicae dogmaticae* (1815; Institutes of dogmatic theology).

26. In the "Preparatory Considerations" of the *Evidences*, Paley writes: "In a word, once believe that there is a God, and miracles are not incredible" (Paley [1794] 1850, 5); and in "The Conclusion": "once fix upon our minds the belief of a God, and after that all is easy" (305).

27. The three cited authors were well-known theists, John Sterling, Ralph Waldo Emerson, and Francis William Newman. In their theism all leaned toward Unitarianism. F. W. Newman was a close friend of Powell's.

28. During his third and final voyage, Columbus was in Jamaica from June 1503 to June 1504 when his followers so alienated the inhabitants that they withheld supplies. Columbus's prediction of the eclipse on the evening of 29 February 1504 helped to overcome their hostility.

29. Powell follows conventional biblical terminology concerning miracles. Trench, for instance, distinguishes between three terms: *wonders* (τέρατα, *terata*), in which "the effect of astonishment, which the work produces upon the beholders, is transferred to the work itself" (Mark 2:13); *signs* (σημεῖα, *semeia*), "a token and indication of the near presence of God, . . . pledges of something more than and beyond themselves" (John 3:2), and hence an appeal to intelligent understanding of the purpose or final cause of the miracle; and a *power* or *mighty work* (δυνάμεις, *dynameis*), the instrumentality, or efficient cause, pointing "to new powers that have

entered, and are working in, this world" (Matt. 11:20). The word for "marvel" (θαυμάσιον, *thaumasion*) occurs only once in the NT (Matt. 21:15) (Trench [1846] 1856, 2–7; on "the vocabulary of miracles" see also Moule 1965, 235–38).

30. *Lessons on Evidences*, vii. § 5 [Powell's note].

Richard Whately published *Lessons on Christian Evidences* in the *Saturday Magazine* 11 (15 July, 23 Dec. 1837) and 12 (20 Jan., 3 Feb. 1838); and as a book in 1838. It quickly became a standard text and during Whately's lifetime was translated into more than a dozen languages.

31. *Letter and Spirit*, by Rev. J. Wilson, 1852, p. 21 [Powell's note].

(Gk. wonders to the foolish). This erroneous reference was corrected in the sixth edition of *Essays and Reviews* to "*The Letter and Spirit of Scripture*, by the Rev. Thomas Wilson, M.A., 1852, p. 21." On the cited page Wilson gives the Greek and biblical quotation, and the qualification Powell paraphrases.

32. Friedrich Schleiermacher published *Der christliche Glaube nach den Grundsätzen de evangelischen Kirche* (1821–22; The Christian faith according to the principles of the Evangelical Church), where miracles are discussed in sec. 103 (see Colin Brown 1984, 114–9).

33. In the Hebrew scriptures miracles were wrought by such figures as Moses (Exod. 4:1–9; 7:1–13; 14:16–27), Joshua (Josh. 3:7–17; 6:1–20; 10:12–14), Elijah (1 Kings 17), and Elisha (2 Kings 2:13–24). For examples of miraculous healing, see Elisha's raising of the dead son of the Shunammite woman (2 Kings 4:18–37), and his healing of Naaman's leprosy (5:1–19), to both of which reference is made by Jesus (Luke 4:27).

34. As, *e.g.*, John xi. 46; vi. 2–30; Matt. xii. 39 [Powell's note].

Powell refers to the controversy between Jesus and the Pharisees concerning the power of miracles to produce scepticism or faith (see also Matt. 9:34 and 12:24).

35. Matt. xvi. 9; Luke xxiv. 21–25 [Powell's note].

Matt. 16:9 indicates that the apostles did not recall the miraculous event of the feeding of the multitudes. Luke 24:21–25 refers to the post-resurrection appearance of Jesus to two disciples on the road to Emmaus whose faith in the miracles was not sufficient to overcome their despair at Jesus' death and their frustrated hope in the redemption of Israel from oppression.

36. John xiv. 11 [Powell's note].

Jesus demands belief first on the basis of his relationship to God, and second because of the "works" he had done. For Nicodemus see John 3 and 7:50–52; for "Never man spake," John 7:46.

37. Orobio, a Jewish writer, quoted by Limborch *(De Verit.* p. 12-156), observes:—'Non crediderunt Judaei non quia opera illa quae in Evangelio, narrantur a Jesu facta esse negabant; sed quia iis se persuaderi non sunt passi ut Jesum crederent Messiam.' Celsus ascribed the Christian miracles to magic (Origen *cont. Cels.* i. 38; ii. 9.) as Julian did those of St. Paul to superior knowledge of nature. (*Ap. Cyr.* iii. 100.) The general charge of magic is noticed by Tertullian, *Ap.* 23. See also Dean Lyall, *Propaedia Prophetica*, 439. Neander, *Hist.* i. 67 [Powell's note].

(Lat. The Jews had not believed not because they denied that those works which are narrated in the gospels were in fact done by Jesus, but because they did not allow themselves to be persuaded that they should believe that Jesus was the Messiah). Isaac Orobio de Castro, professor of metaphysics at Salamanca, was arrested by the Inquisition and confessed his Judaism under torture, subsequently escaping to Amsterdam in 1662. There he met Philip van Limborch, a Dutch friend of John Locke. The treatise *De Veritate Religionis Christianae amica collatio cum erudito Judaeo* (1687; Concerning the truth of the Christian religion: a friendly collation with an erudite Jew) records the debate between Orobio and Limborch in Locke's presence.

Origen's *Contra Celsum* (c. 250; Against Celsus) answers Celsus' Ἀληθὴς Λόγος [c. 178; True discourse), the earliest known attack on Christianity and especially on miracles. In the *Apology against Julian* Cyril of Alexandria (d. 444) attacked the persecution of Christianity by the emperor Julian the Apostate. Tertullian's *Apologeticum* (c. 197; Apology) was addressed to the prefects of the Roman provinces, relegating as absurd the charges brought against Christianity. William Rowe Lyall, a friend of Powell's from about 1820 (Corsi 4), published *Propaedia Prophetica: The Preparation of Prophecy* (1840). On the cited page Lyall refers to "Sepher Toldoth Jeshu (The book of the Generation of Jesus" (1674), dating it in the thirteenth century. The Jewish *Toldot Yeshu* (Life of Jesus) exists in nine medieval versions, the earliest dating from the tenth century. They have been edited by Samuel Krauss in *Das Leben Jesu nach jüdischen Quellen* (1904; The life of Jesus according to Jewish sources). Lyall also refers to the "ineffable name," to the deceptions, and makes reference to both Celsus and Origen as well as to the passage from Orobio quoted by Powell, and the reference to Limborch. Johann August Wilhelm Neander published *Allgemeine Geschichte der christlichen Religion und Kirche* ([1825–52] 1850–58).

38. *Essay on Miracles*, &c. p. 107 [Powell's note].

J. H. Newman wrote an essay on biblical and ecclesiastical miracles for the *Encyclopaedia Metropolitana* (1825–26). The essay was reprinted in *Two Essays on Biblical and on Ecclesiastical Miracles* (Newman [1825–26; 1842–43; 1870] 1969).

39. Heinrich Eberhard Gottlob Paulus published *Exegetisches Handbuch über dei drei ersten*

Evangelien (1830–33, 3 vols.; Exegetical handbook on the first three Gospels), where he attempts to reconcile belief in the accuracy of the gospel narratives with disbelief in the miracles and the supernatural. Ernst Friedrich Karl Rosenmüller published a number of editions of the Hebrew scriptures, and a *Handbook für die Literatur der biblischen Kritik und Exegese* (1797–1800, 4 vols.; Handbook for the literature of biblical criticism and exegesis).

40. *Christianity,* &c. Davison's transl. 1847, p. 226 [Powell's note].

Athanase Laurent Charles Coquerel published *Le Christianisme experimental,* translated by David Davison as *Christianity: Its Perfect Adaptation to the Mental, Moral and Spiritual Nature of Man* (1847).

41. See Seckendorf's *Hist. Luther.,* iii. 633 [Powell's note].

Veit Ludwig Von Seckendorf published *Commentarius historicus et apologeticus de Lutheranismo sive de Reformatione* (1692, 3 vols.; Historical and apologetical commentary on Lutheranism, or more accurately, on the Reformation). For Luther's discussion of miracles, see particularly *Sermons on the Gospel of John, Chapters 14–16* (Luther 1961, 24:283–7; 367–75). John Huss published *De Omni Sanguine Christi Glorificato* (1404; Concerning the whole blood of Christ glorified), an attack on forged miracles and ecclesiastical greed, urging Christians to desist from looking for external evidence of Christ's presence, finding it instead in the Bible. Commissioned in 1405 to examine certain reputed miracles at Wilsnack near Wittenberg, he denounced them and as a result all pilgrimages from Bohemia were prohibited by the archbishop on pain of excommunication.

42. Henry Martyn spent most of his life working as a missionary in India. He translated the NT into Hindi and Persian. In 1811 on doctor's orders he left India for Persia where he died. His *Journals and Letters* (1837) were edited and published by Samuel Wilberforce.

43. For some instances of this class of objections, see Dean Lyall's *Propaedia Prophetica,* p. 437 *et seq.* [Powell's note].

On the cited page Lyall writes: "Instead of maintaining that the facts related by the Evangelists did not really happen . . . [the adversaries of Christianity] argued that miracles afforded no evidence of a Divine authority; that they were of common occurrence, and could be performed by thousands, by means of arts which it was a disgrace to practise" (Lyall 1840, 437).

44. See *Tracts for the Times,* No. lxxxv. pp. 85–100 [Powell's note].

Tract LXXXV, by J. H. Newman, published anonymously in 1838, is entitled *Lectures on the Scripture Proofs of the Doctrines of the Church.*

45. *Tract* No. x. p. 4 [Powell's note].

Tract X, by J. H. Newman, published anonymously in 1833, is entitled *Heads of a Week-Day Lecture, Delivered to a Country Congregation in —Shire.*

46. *British Critic,* No. xlviii. p. 304 [Powell's note].

The reference is to Sewell 1838. William Sewell was a Tractarian theologian. The *British Critic,* a journal sponsored by the Hackney Phalanx ceased publication in 1843 in the midst of controversy concerning the Oxford Movement. J. H. Newman was editor from 1838 to 1840. Sewell wrote in defense of orthodox Christian spirituality and the evidence for the Gospel miracles, and against the kinds of spiritualism and hypnotism being practiced by the advocates of healings through mesmerism or animal magnetism. For mesmerism see ¶121 and note.

47. *Edin. Rev.* No. cxli [Powell's note].

Powell refers to an unsigned review of "The Practical Works of Richard Baxter" by James Stephen in the *Edinburgh Review.* According to Stephen, Baxter, a Puritan divine, was the first (except for Hugo Grotius) "to establish the truth of Christianity, by a systematic exhibition of the evidence of the arguments in favour of the divine origins of our faith" (Stephen 1839, 211–12).

48. *Aids to Reflexion,* i. p. 333 [Powell's note].

In *Aids to Reflection* (1825), S. T. Coleridge distinguishes between understanding (generalizing on the basis of sense impressions of the natural world) and reason (through which one can have knowledge of spiritual truth).

49. *Aids to Reflexion,* p. 278 [Powell's note].

Samuel Parr was granted an honorary LL.D. by Cambridge in 1781. Powell quotes the last sentence of "Of Reverencing the Deity" (bk. 5, chap. 9) of Paley's *Principles of Moral and Political Philosophy,* adding his own comment in parentheses.

50. *Ib.* p. 338 [Powell's note].

51. Powell continues to draw on Coleridge, as in *The Friend*: "Is not a true, efficient conviction of a moral truth, is not *the creating of a new heart* . . . the one essential miracle. . . . Is it not that implication of doctrine in the miracle, and of miracle in the doctrine, which is the bridge of communication between the senses and the soul? that predisposing warmth that renders the understanding susceptible of the specific impression from the historic, and from all other outward, seals of testimony? Is not this the one infallible criterion of miracles, by which a man can *know* whether they be of God?" (Coleridge [1809] 1969, 421). This same passage is cited by Trench ([1846] 1856, 90–91).

52. Deut. xiii. 1 [Powell's note].

53. Gal. i. 8 [Powell's note].

This and the previous citation occur in a similar context in Trench [1846] 1856, 25–26.

54. Matt. xxiv. 24 [Powell's note].

55. *Kingdom of Christ,* Essay i. § 12 [Powell's note].

The quoted passage is from Essay 1, sec. 11, "Impiety of attributing double-dealing to our Lord" ([1841] 1842, 47).

56. *Propaedia Prophetica*, p. 441 [Powell's note].

57. Boswell's *Life*, iii. 169. Ed. 1826 [Powell's note].

Johnson's comment is recorded in Boswell's *The Life of Samuel Johnson* (1791) under 22 September 1777.

58. *Evidences of Natural and Revealed Religion*, § xiv [Powell's note].

Samuel Clarke's Boyle Lectures (1704–5) were published in 1716. See ¶24 and note.

59. *Notes on Miracles*, p. 27 [Powell's note].

Richard Chenevix Trench published *Notes on the Miracles of Our Lord* (1846). In the same year he was made examining chaplain to Samuel Wilberforce.

60. F. W. Newman published *Phases of Faith, or Passages from the History of My Creed* (1850), a religious autobiography detailing his passage from Calvinism to theism, in which he writes: "For these [external evidences] also are confessedly moral evidences, to be judged of by our moral faculties. . . . To allege therefore that our moral faculties are not to judge, is to annihilate the evidences for Christianity" (115).

The words "moral and spiritual tribunal" are emended to "moral and spiritual judgement" by Powell in ink in his copy of the first edition of *Essays and Reviews* (Bodley: Baden Powell 122, p. 122), a change incorporated in the second edition with the spelling "judgment."

61. See *Phases of Faith*, p. 154 [Powell's note].

On the cited page F. W. Newman writes: "Faith therefore is essentially *from within*. To assent to a religious proposition *solely* in obedience to an outward miracle, would be Belief; but would not be Faith, any more than is scientific conviction. . . . A really overpowering miraculous proof would have destroyed the moral character of Faith."

62. *Ib.* pp. 82, 108, 201, 1st Ed. [Powell's note].

F. W. Newman entitles the "Fifth Period," or phase, of his religious development "Faith at Second Hand Found to Be Vain." Powell also draws on other phrases of Newman: "We discern moral truth by a something within us" (1850, 82); and "Ought we in any case to receive moral truth in obedience to an apparent miracle of sense?" (1850, 145).

63. Compare F. W. Newman's "No sensible miracle would authorize me to violate my moral perceptions" (F. W. Newman 1850, 150).

64. On spiritual assurances see 1 Thess. 1:5 and Col. 2:2. The most elaborate analogy between nature and faith in St. Paul is 1 Cor. 15:35–49 (see also Heb. 11:1). In introducing a discussion of St. Paul and Paley in *Phases of Faith*, F. W. Newman writes: "We ought to conceive how many questions a Paley would have wished to ask of St. Paul" (1850, 181–83); and subsequently: "Some good people are secretly conscious that the Bible is not an infallible book" (208).

65. Johann Christoph Döderlein published *Opuscula theologica* (1789; Lesser theological works).

66. Jesus ipse doctrinam quam tradidit divinam esse professus est, quantum divina ejus indoles ab homine vere religioso proboque bene cognosci potest atque dijudicari.—Wegscheider, *in Joh.* vii. 17.

Nulla alia ratio et via eas [doctrinas] examinandi datur quam ut illarum placita cum iis quae via naturali rectae rationis de Deo ejusque voluntate ipsi innotuerint diligenter componat et ad normam sine omni superstitione examinet.—Wegscheider, *Instit. Theol. Chris. Dogm.*, § 11. 38 [Powell's note and his interpolation].

(Lat. Jesus professed that the doctrine which he handed down was divine inasmuch as his divine character is able to be well recognized and judged by a man who is truly religious and truly upright); and (Lat. No other method and way is given of examining those [doctrines] than that he should diligently compare their opinions with those which they themselves have taken notice of by a natural path of correct reasoning concerning God and his will, and that he should examine them with respect to the norm without any excessive credulity). Wegscheider published *Einleitung in das Evangelium Johannis* (1806; Introduction to the Gospel of John); Powell also cites *Institutiones teologicae dogmaticae* (1815; Institutes of dogmatic theology) in ¶51.

Wilhelm Martin Leberecht De Wette was an innovator in the historical criticism of the Pentateuch, publishing *Beiträge zur Einleitung in das Alte Testament* (1806–7, 2 vols.; Contribution to the introduction to the Old Testament, trans. Theodore Parker 1843).

67. Such was the argument of the *Characteristics*, vol. ii. p. 334. Ed. 1727 [Powell's note].

Lord Shaftesbury published *Characteristics of Men, Manners, Opinions, Times* (1711, 3 vols.). On the cited page, from Treatise 5 ("The Moralist: A Philosophical Rhapsody," sec. 5, pt. 2), Shaftesbury writes: "To whom therefore the Laws of this Universe and its Government appear just and uniform; to him they speak the Government of one JUST-ONE; to him they *reveal* and witness a GOD: and laying in him the Foundation of this *first* Faith, they fit him for a *subsequent One*. He can then hearken to *Historica Revelation*; and is then fitted (and not till then) fo the Reception of any *Message* or miraculous *Notic* from Above; where he knows beforehand all is jus and true. But this, no Power of Miracles, nor any Power besides his Reason, can make him know, o apprehend."

68. Melchior Canus, *Loci Theol.* ix. 6. abou 1540 [Powell's note].

(Lat. They are led to the faith first from th outside by reason, and just as if they are prepared . . therefore by signs and miracles the way of faith i smoothed out through the senses and the reason)

Melchior Canus or Cano sought greater independence from the Vatican for both his Dominican order and the Spanish church; he published *De locis theologicis* (1563; Concerning the divisions of theology).

69. In this paragraph Powell draws a contrast between eighteenth- and nineteenth-century debates concerning the evidential power of miracles at the time of the Gospels. Hume writes in "Of Miracles": "The *Christian Religion* not only was at first attended with miracles, but at this day cannot be believed by any reasonable person without one. Mere reason is insufficient to convince us of its veracity: And whoever is moved by *Faith* to assent to it, is conscious of a continued miracle in his own person, which subverts all the principles of his understanding, and gives him a determination to believe what is most contrary to custom and experience" (Hume [1748] 1964, 108). In the same year Middleton concluded his Preface to *A Free Inquiry*: "As the benefit of miraculous powers began to be less and less wanted [in apostolic times] . . . so the use and exercise of them began gradually to decline, and as soon as Christianity had gained an establishment in every quarter of the known world they were finally withdrawn, and the Gospel left to make the rest of its way by its own genuine graces . . . faith, hope, and charity" (in Waring 1967, 242). In the nineteenth century, reacting against Paley and Whately's claim that "the truth of Christianity depends upon its leading facts, and upon them alone" (Paley [1794] 1851, 299), deriving from the testimony of credible witnesses to them as miraculous, Coleridge makes a point similar to Middleton's, concerning the "moral miracle" of a "regenerate soul" in *The Friend*. On the withdrawing of miracles from the early church, J. H. Newman writes that "the Scripture miracles" were at their time "evidence of a Divine Revelation" but they "are not so at this day." They "have never been evidence except to those who saw them, and have but held the place of doctrine ever since; like the truths revealed to us about the unseen world, which are matters of faith, not means of conviction" (J. H. Newman [1825–26; 1842–43; 1870] 1969, 231–32). Trench, also distancing himself from Paley, writes: "Few points present greater difficulties than the attempts to fix accurately the moment when these miraculous powers were withdrawn from the Church, and it entered into its permanent state, with only its present miracles of grace and the record of its past miracles of power" (Trench [1846] 1856, 52–53).

70. . . . χρείαν ἔχεις τῶν σημείων ταῦτα γὰρ ἀπίστοις δέδοται.—*Hom.* xxiii. *in Johan.* To the same effect also S. Isidore, 'Tunc oportebat mundum miraculis credere,—nunc vero credentem oportet bonis operibus coruscare,' cited in Huss in defense of Wickliff [Powell's note].

Powell translates the Chrysostom passage in his text. John Chrysostom delivered a series of homilies in 386–98, including one on the Gospel of John, defending literal interpretation of Bible against the allegorists. The quotation comes from Homily 24 (not 23 as Powell specified). Isidore of Pelusium followed in the exegetical tradition of Chrysostom. John Huss wrote *De Ecclesia* (1413; On the church), the first ten chapters copying the *De Ecclesia* (1381) of John Wycliffe: Lat. Then it was appropriate for the world to believe in miracles,—now the true believer should tremble at good works (Huss [1413] 1974).

71. The standard treatises on "evidences," the prescribed texts for examination for students at Oxford and Cambridge were Butler's *Analogy* (1736) and Paley's *A View of the Evidences of Christianity* (1794) and *Natural Theology, or Evidences of the Existence and Attributes of the Deity Collected from the Appearances of Nature* (1802). Paley's *Moral and Political Philosophy* (1875) was used for examinations at Cambridge and was required in 1802. As F. W. Newman wrote in *Phases of Faith*: "The Christian Evidences are an essential part of the course of religious study at Oxford" (1850, 40). In 1850 a new edition of *Evidences* and *Horae Paulinae* was published in Cambridge with these comments in the Preface: "By a Grace of the Senate it was decreed on March 23, 1849, that the Holy Scriptures and the Evidences of Christianity should assume a more important place than formerly in the Previous Examination. It is provided in the new regulations, which will take effect in 1851, that the examination in the Evidences of Christianity shall be extended to three hours. . . . Paley's work has been used in the University, as the authorized text-book on the Evidences, for the last quarter of a century. It was appointed as one of the fixed subjects when the 'Previous Examination' was instituted in 1822" (Paley 1850, v–vi). In their anonymous *Suggestions for an Improvement of the Examination Statute* (1848), Benjamin Jowett and A. P. Stanley proposed substituting Adam Smith's *Wealth of Nations* (1776) and David Ricardo's *Principles of Political Economy and Taxation* (1817) for Butler's *Analogy*. Butler's *Analogy* continued as part of the Examination Statutes for all undergraduates until 1864 when Mark Pattison led the way for its removal (Ellis 1980, 274), though it still continues as one of the examinable texts for the Honours School of Theology. At Cambridge, Paley's *Evidences* continued as a part of the first examination for undergraduates until 1920 (Clarke 1974, 1; 127–29). By 1929 one commentator noted: "Paley had never been much stressed at Oxford; now he is seen losing ground at Cambridge" (Robertson 1929, 1:229). For Leslie and Grotius see ¶24 and note.

72. Because Paley's books were not adequately adapted for survival in the current intellectual environment, Powell's metaphor, adopted from evolutionary biology as well as natural theology, relegates them to an earlier position in the evolutionary succession. Paley did not accept the notion of the

extinction of species; Powell predicts Paley's extinction within twenty-five years. In *Natural Theology* (1802) Paley gives various examples of structures suited to their teleological purposes, such as human organs (chaps. 8 and 9) and animal "contrivances": the oil of birds, the air bladders of fish, the fangs of vipers, and the tongues of woodpeckers (chap. 13). All are evidence of providential design, accomplished by God in one act of creation. On the other hand, Darwin's hypothesis of natural selection in *On the Origin of Species* (1859) is predicated upon a very gradual "adaptation" among species relative to external conditions or environment. Providential design, therefore, cannot be deduced in any simple way from Paley's argument about the appropriateness of the human or animal organs to their function, for without such appropriateness, there would be no survival. Powell's metaphor, then, gestures toward Darwinian methodology to position as outmoded "types" the teleological examples of the evidentialist school drawn from nature and the Bible (see ¶s 62, 67, and 107).

73. Powell gives his version of "Paley's argument" in the essay on "The Burnett Prizes": "design implies a designer: a designer is a person: that person is God" (Powell 1857, 183).

The words "objections *honestly* felt" are emended to "objections *generally* felt" by Powell in ink in his copy of the first edition of *Essays and Reviews* (Bodley: Baden Powell 122, p. 130), a change incorporated in the second edition.

74. "Special pleading" in legal discourse specifies a pleading drawn from a particular reference to circumstances of a case, as opposed to general pleading; used figuratively, it implies a one-sided, disingenuous, or sophistical argument. Wilberforce refers to "Mr. Goodwin's minute special pleading" in his review of *Essays and Reviews* (1861, 292).

75. Powell alludes to the three aspects of the "universal law," the laws of motion formulated by Isaac Newton in *Principia Mathematica* (1687).

76. Trench [1846] 1856, 16.

77. The law of conservation of energy was first enunciated by Hermann Ludwig Ferdinand von Helmoltz in 1847.

Powell paraphrases ("like a mill") a section from Whately's highly critical review of Powell's *The Order of Nature* (1859). The review, by William Fitzgerald, Whitwell Elwin, and Richard Whately, was published in the *Quarterly Review*, in October 1859 (Fitzgerald 1859). It also discussed Powell's *Tradition Unveiled*, 1839, Whately's own *Dr. Paley's Works: A Lecture* (1859) and Fitzgerald's *Cautions for the Times* that Whately edited. Whately identifies Powell as "one of the infidel party" who is "unconscious of his disgrace" and is "so satisfied with his own position, that he warily . . . recommends it also to his brethren" (Fitzgerald 1859, 421). In the article, and in the passage cited from it in his edition of Paley, Whately compares God to "a man who has constructed some such engine as—for instance—a mill, [and who] leaves it usually to *work of itself* (for they forget that there is an external agency which keeps it in motion, and of which the mill-wright has availed himself) but which he has the power of stopping when he sees cause" (Paley [1794] 1859, 18–19; see also Fitzgerald 1859, 443). For "would-be philosophers" Whately writes in his "Annotation" of "some who are called philosophers" (Paley [1794] 1859, 20). For a discussion of Powell's attacks on Whately see Corsi 1988, 216–19.

78. Numerous instances of the kind referred to will be found cited in Mr. R. Chambers's *Essay on Testimony*, &c. Edinburgh Papers, 1859; and in Abp. Whately's Edition of Paley's *Evidences* [Powell's note].

Robert Chambers published *Testimony: Its Posture in the Scientific World* (1859) as the third of his collection of *Edinburgh Papers* (1859–61); he also published (anonymously) *Vestiges of the Natural History of Creation* (1844). Powell was a friend of Chambers in the 1850s (Corsi 1988, 205). Richard Whately edited Paley's *A View of the Evidences of Christianity . . . with Annotations* (1859) and referred to it in his antagonistic review of Powell in the *Quarterly*.

79. Hume added a paragraph and note on "the Indian prince" to the chapter "Of Miracles" in the 1750 edition of *Philosophical Essays concerning Human Understanding*: "No Indian . . . could have experience that water did not freeze in cold climates" (Hume [1748] 1964, 92).

80. Marco Polo (c. 1254–1324) recounted the "marvels" of Kubla Khan's court, wars, and administration. St. Victor (late fifth century) wrote *Historia Persecutionis Africanae Provinciae* (c. 485; The history of the persecutions of the province of Africa), an account of the persecution by the Arian Vandals, including the "miracle of the martyrs" who spoke after their tongues were cut out. The same narrative is discussed by J. H. Newman in *Two Essays on . . . Miracles* ([1825–26; 1842–43; 1870] 1969, 369–87). The angel at Milan has not been located. The miraculous balls of fire are St. Elmo's fire, the discharging of electricity from the atmosphere to a spire as a conductor. Powell's example was recorded in an article on "St. Elmo's Fire" in the *Penny Magazine*: "M. Binon, who was curé of Plauzet during twenty-seven years, informed Mr. Watson the electrician that during great storms accompanied with black clouds and frequent lightnings, the three pointed extremities of the cross of the steeple of that place appeared surrounded with a body of flame" ("St. Elmo's" 1845, 107). Herodotus traveled to Egypt around 450 B.C.E. He writes of the crocodile and bird in his *History* (bk. 2, sec. 68): the sandpiper enters the crocodile's mouth to eat the leeches there to their reciprocal benefit. In 1848, in the *Annual Magazine of Natural*

History, Frank Buckland explains that a reported sea serpent was actually a pair of basking sharks (ser. 2, vol. 2:461). F. Smith reported a large mass of seaweed being harpooned by persons thinking it was a sea serpent (*Times*, Feb. 1858). On mesmerism and electrobiology see Powell ¶122 and note. Vaccination was discovered by Dr. Edward Jenner in 1798. The discovery derived from Gloucestershire peasant stories regarding the antipathy between cowpox and smallpox. Powell discusses Marco Polo, Newman's examples, the same Herodotus passage, sea serpents, electrobiology and Jenner in "Testimony" in *Chambers's Edinburgh Journal* (1859, 13–19).

81. For Hallam see ¶20 and note. Powell very likely refers to Samuel Rogers, who recounts an experience of clairvoyance with a medium in Paris (Rogers 1856, 292). Powell alludes to the Hallam and Rogers episode in Paris in his essay on "Testimony" (1959, 11), also citing a reference to the same episode in the *Daily News* (25 Jan. 1859). Friedrich Anton Mesmer practiced sensational cures through animal magnetism and forms of hypnosis in Paris from 1778 that were investigated and condemned in 1784 by a Government Commission that included Benjamin Franklin and Lavoisier. Animal magnetism, on the analogy of mineral magnetism, assumed that bodily fluids may be controlled by magnets and the magnetic forces of the planets; miraculous cures were claimed by the manipulation of such magnetic forces. In England mesmerism and animal magnetism were subjects of popular interest from the 1830s to the 1850s, especially because of John Elliotson's public demonstrations in 1837 of mesmeric healings at University College Hospital, resulting in his losing his medical position in 1838. Harriet Martineau underwent a mesmeric cure and published her *Letters on Mesmerism* (1844). In 1851 the visit of American mesmerists practising "electrobiology," another name for mesmerism that stressed the electrical charges and affiliations of human subjects and their relations with magnetic or galvanic substances, for purposes of hypnotic trances or healings, provoked renewed public interest and articles in the periodical press. See James White 1837; Samuel Brown 1851; Eagles 1851; Froude 1851; Carpenter 1853; and Brewster 1854. For a recent study see Pattie 1994.

For "The lie direct" see Shakespeare, *As You Like It* 5.4.85–89.

82. In July 1772, Antoine-Laurent Lavoisier and others issued a report on behalf of the French Academy on Abbé Bachelay's meteorite (Guerlac 1961, 63). The *Encyclopaedia Metropolitana* reported that the German scientist Ernst Florent Frédéric Chladni claimed that "it had been proved upon evidence that could not be rejected that masses of stone and iron had repeatedly fallen from the sky; that these masses were identical with fire-balls; and that previous to their fall they did not belong to the earth or its atmosphere. . . . In France, however, Chladni's arguments failed to produce conviction. The doubts of the most sceptical, here and elsewhere, were at last removed by the shower of aerolites that fell at L'Aigle in April, 1803" (s.v. "Stones, Meteoric"). Powell discussed this debate and mentioned Lavoisier and Plausac church in his essay on "Testimony" (1859, 10, 16). Powell also published his annual "Catalogue of Observations of Luminous Meteors" in the *Reports of the British Association* for each year between 1847 and 1851. They are reviewed in Holland 1852.

83. The quotation is from Cicero's *De Natura Deorum* (Concerning the nature of the gods): "The years obliterate the inventions of the imagination, but confirm the judgements of nature" (bk. 2, chap. 2, sec. 5; trans. Rackham, *Loeb*).

84. Richard Whately's *Historic Doubts Relative to Napoleon Buonaparte* was published anonymously in 1819. His authorship was acknowledged in the fourth edition (1831). In the first part of this satire Whately uses the language and style of Hume's "Of Miracles" to ridicule the reliability of newspapers and witnesses as providing reliable testimony concerning the existence of Napoleon. In the second part, using biblical language to recount Napoleon's quasi-miraculous achievements, Whately challenges the rejection of biblical miracles on the basis of archaic language.

He also published the satiric *Historic Certainties Respecting the Early History of America Developed in a Critical Examination of the Book of the Chronicles of the Land of Ecnarf, by Rev. Aristarchus Newlight* (1851). Using biblical language to recount the recent history of the land of Ecnarf, and the convention of spelling proper names backwards, he gives a detailed treatment to "Noel-opan of Akisroc." This satire of recent French history, cast as the primitive history of America, is directed against the higher critics of the Bible who reinterpret the ancient history of Israel and the biblical miracles as historically objective narratives rather than revelation.

85. Jean-Baptiste Antoine De Monet Lamarck published *Histoire naturelle des animaux sans vertèbres* (1815; Natural history of animals without vertebrae). In the Introduction he propounds four laws, the second and fourth of which concern "development theories." The second deals with the production of new organs in response to a new and continuous need. The fourth law concerns the inheritance of these acquired characteristics, to be "conserved by generation and transmitted to the new individuals which proceed from those which have undergone those changes" (Lamarck 1815–22). In the fourteenth chapter of *Vestiges*, entitled "Hypothesis of the Development of the Vegetable and Animal Kingdoms," Robert Chambers writes: "The whole train of animated beings, from the simplest and oldest up to the highest and most recent, are, then, to be regarded as a series of *advances of the principle of development*, which have depended upon external physical circumstances, to which the resulting animals are appropri-

ate" ([1844] 1969, 203–4). By 1860 *Vestiges* had reached the eleventh edition.

86. Andrew Crosse reported in his paper to the BAAS in 1837 on what appeared to be the spontaneous generation of insect life in metallic solutions, supersaturated with muriatic acid through which an electrical current was passed. His report aroused the admiration of naturalists and theological supporters of progressive evolution, and the animus of the scientific community (Crosse 1836–37). William Henry Weekes continued Crosse's experiments and published his results (Weekes 1843).

In a review of Chambers's *Vestiges of Creation* (1844), the experiments of Crosse and Weekes are described as implausible instances of spontaneous generation: "If Mr Crosse or Mr Weekes produce a species of worm by the agency of electricity, it is impossible to say that the germ of life was not previously existing in the fluid through which the electricity passed. . . . The experiments of these gentlemen excite in us no horror or alarm. A Frankenstein who produces nothing worse than a harmless worm, may surely be suffered to go blameless" (William Henry Smith 1845, 452–53). In another 1845 review of *Vestiges* their experiments are considered plausible (Carpenter 1845, 155–81). The author, W. B. Carpenter, was a friend of both F. W. Newman and Powell. On Crosse and Weekes see Corsi 1988, 253–54, 262–64; and Secord 1989. "Spontaneous generation," the idea that life originates independent of a genetically related progenitor, dates from Aristotle and Pliny; in 1860 it was a subject of renewed controversy when a prize was offered in France for a study on spontaneous generation that was won in 1863 by Louis Pasteur. He was opposed in a subsequent debate by F. A. Pouchet, who had published *Hétérogénie, ou Traité de la génération spontanée* (1859; Heterogenesis, or treatise on spontaneous generation).

The words "alleged production" are emended to "asserted production" by Powell in ink in his copy of the first edition of *Essays and Reviews* (Bodley: Baden Powell 122, p. 139), a change incorporated in the second edition.

87. *British Association Address*, 1858 [Powell's note].

Sir Richard Owen, the first director of the British Museum of Natural History, delivered his presidential address to the BAAS on the subject of reptiles; it was published in the *Reports of the British Association* (1859). In April 1860 Owen wrote a harsh review of Darwin's *Origin* in the *Edinburgh Review* (Owen 1860), and in June prepared Samuel Wilberforce for his famous exchange with T. H. Huxley, concerning Darwin and evolution at the meeting of the BAAS in Oxford. Wilberforce introduces his quotation from Powell's ¶126 in his review of *Essays and Reviews* with the phrase: "For he tells us (misrepresenting, as we hold, utterly, the meaning of that true philosopher, Professor Owen)" (Wilberforce 1861, 261). For re-examinations of the Huxley-Wilberforce debate see Himmelfarb 1968, 268–310; J. R. Lucas 1979; Gilley 1981; Gilley and Loades 1981; and Jensen 1991.

88. This is the only direct reference to Darwin's *On the Origin of Species* in *Essays and Reviews.* It is also the first positive evaluation of Darwin from a theologian in a book. The *Origin* was published on 24 November 1859, and the whole of the first edition of 1,250 copies was taken by the booksellers on the first day. It was very likely one of these that Powell acquired, in order to have added this comment to his essay before submitting it to Parker, the publisher, sometime before January 1860, when Pattison handed in his essay (except for Jowett's, the last to be submitted).

89. Whately's annotation to Paley's "Preparatory Considerations" includes a long discussion on "civilization," where he argues: "It appears . . . very doubtful whether men left wholly untaught, would be able to subsist at all, even at the state of the lowest savages. But at any rate, it is plain they could never have risen *above* that state. And consequently the existence of civilization at this day is a kind of *monument* attesting the fact that some instruction from above must, at some time or other, have been supplied to mankind. And the most probable conclusion is, that Man when first created, or very shortly afterwards, was advanced, by the Creator Himself, to a state above that of a mere savage" (Paley [1794] 1859, 25). Hence, the development of civilization, marked by the use of fire and the move from hunting to crop-planting cultures is to Whately an evidence of divine intervention that Powell rejects in favor of progressive revelation, the evolution of cultures according to natural laws, and the accommodation of apologetics to contemporary scientific thought.

Steam printing was first used by the *Times* in 1814 to print 1,100 impressions per hour. While the historic origins of the boomerang as a weapon are impossible to trace, the word enters the English language as a result of colonial encounters between aboriginal peoples in New South Wales and the British. The word, a mistransliteration, is first recorded in 1827. Whately argued in *Introductory Lectures* (1831, 122) and *On the Origin of Civilization* (1854) that the boomerang is God's gift enabling the transition from aboriginal primitivism to civilization. Powell explained to Whately in 1837 the principles of its aerodynamics, beyond the limited capabilities Whately assumed in the indigenous peoples of Australia (Corsi, 1988, 148). The gyroscope was invented in 1852 by Jean Bernard Léon Foucault.

90. "Now in what way can a revelation be made, but by miracles?" (Paley [1794] 1851, 2). Whately annotates this assertion elaborately in his edition of Paley, asserting that a miracle "is a proof, only when it is (as it is commonly called in our

Scriptures) a *Sign*. When any one performs something beyond human power, or foretells something undiscoverable by human sagacity, appealing to this as a *sign* that he is the bearer of a divine message, it is then, and then only, that this becomes miraculous *evidence*" (Paley [1794] 1859, 18–19).

91. *Lecture on Mental Education*. 1854 [Powell's note].

The reference is to Faraday 1854. For Faraday see Cantor 1991 and Temple ¶44 and note.

92. See *Edinburgh Papers*, 'Testimony,' &c., by R. Chambers, Esq., F.R.S.E., &c. [Powell's note].

For Chambers see ¶117 and note.

93. John Abercrombie published *Inquiries concerning the Intellectual Powers and the Investigation of Truth* (1830). The "dictum" relates to the argument in a section on "Testimony" (pt. 2, sec. 3). Thomas Chalmers published *The Evidences and Authority of the Christian Revelation* (1814) and the first of the Bridgewater Treatises, *On the Adaptation of External Nature to the Moral and Intellectual Constitution of Man* (1833). He also published a course of lectures on Paley's *Evidences* and another on Butler's *Analogy* (1839).

94. The last trial for witchcraft in England took place in 1712, when Jane Wenham was convicted but not executed. In Scotland the last trial and execution was in 1722, in Spain in 1782, and in Germany in 1793. In England elaborate manuals stressed the kinds of evidence and testimony to be gathered for judicial conviction of witches (see Elliot Rose [1962] 1989; Langbain 1976; and Ankarloo and Henningsen 1990).

Various nineteenth-century literary works refer to mermaids and mermen: Scott's *Minstrelsy of the Scottish Border* (1802–3), T. C. Croker's *Fairy Legends* (1825–28), Tennyson's "The Mermen and the Mermaid" (1830), Hans Christian Andersen's "The Littlest Mermaid" (1837) and Matthew Arnold's "The Forsaken Merman" (1849). In 1775 the French Academy of Sciences refused to receive schemes for perpetual motion, classing them with other impossibilities such as squaring the circle. The impossibility of squaring the circle, known to the ancient Greeks in the application of Euclidean geometry, involved drawing a square that contains precisely the same area as a circle: the problem consists in the infinite regression of π, the ratio between a circle's circumference and its diameter. Perpetual motion is impossible according to Newtonian physics, since it would require a machine that creates its own energy. Both problems were topics of scientific interest in 1860, as in W. Shanks's *Reification of the Circle* (1853) and Henry Dircks's *Perpetuum Mobile* (1861, 2 vols.).

95. The words "beyond reason" are emended to "beyond science" by Powell in ink in his copy of the first edition of *Essays and Reviews* (Bodley: Baden Powell 122, p. 142), a change incorporated in the second edition.

96. "To conclude," is emended to "To conclude:" by Powell in ink in his copy of the first edition of *Essays and Reviews* (Bodley: Baden Powell 122, p. 142), a change incorporated in the second edition.

97. The words "articles of faith, if they be accepted in a less positive and certain light, or perhaps as involving" are emended by Powell in ink in his copy of the first edition of *Essays and Reviews* (Bodley: Powell 122, p. 142) to "articles of faith, as requiring some suspension of judgement as to their nature & circumstances, if they be accepted in a less positive and certain light, or perhaps as involving." In the second edition the change is incorporated as "articles of faith, if they be accepted in a less positive and certain light, as requiring some suspension of judgment as to their nature and circumstances, or perhaps as involving"; the paragraph break before this phrase is eliminated to accommodate the added words.

The passage from ¶s 132–33, "an alleged miracle. . . . inculcated" was cited as "false and dangerous" in the Synodical Condemnation of *Essays and Reviews* on 21 June 1864, on the basis of a denial of miracles as historical fact (*Chronicle* 1859–64:1864, Session 66, 1656–57).

98. See, *e.g.*, Butler's *Analogy*, pt. ii. ch. 6 [Powell's note].

In the chapter that Powell cites Butler argues: "If, upon consideration of religion, the evidence of it should seem to any persons doubtful, in the highest supposable degree; even this doubtful evidence will, however, put them into a general state of *probation* in the moral and religious sense" (Butler [1736] 1855, 236). For "trial of faith" see 1 Pet. 1:7.

99. For "reason of the hope" see 1 Pet. 3:15.

4 *Henry Bristow Wilson*

Séances historiques de Genève—the National Church

IN THE CITY OF GENEVA, once the stronghold of the severest creed of the Reformation, Christianity itself has of late years received some very rude shocks. But special attempts have been recently made to counteract their effects and to re-organize the Christian congregations upon Evangelical principles.[1] In pursuance of this design, there have been delivered and published during the last few years a series of addresses by distinguished persons holding Evangelical sentiments, entitled *Séances Historiques.* The attention of the hearers was to be conciliated by the concrete form of these discourses; the phenomenon of the historical Christianity to be presented as a fact which could not be ignored, and which must be acknowledged to have had some special source; while, from time to time, as occasion offered, the more peculiar views of the speakers were to be instilled. But before this panorama of historic scenes had advanced beyond the period of the fall of heathenism in the West, there had emerged a remarkable discrepancy between the views of two of the authors, otherwise agreeing in the main.[2]

It fell to the Comte Léon de Gasparin to illustrate the reign of Constantine.[3] He laid it down in the strongest manner, that the individualist principle supplies the true basis of the Church, and that by inaugurating the union between Church and State Constantine introduced into Christianity the false principle of Multitudinism.[4] M. Bungener followed in two lectures upon the age of Ambrose and Theodosius.[5] He felt it necessary, for his own satisfaction and that of others, to express his dissent from these opinions. He agreed in the portraiture drawn by his predecessor of the so-called first Christian emperor, and in his estimate of his personal character.[6] But he maintained, that the multitudinist principle was not unlawful, nor essentially pagan; that it was recognised and consecrated in the example of the Jewish theocracy; that the greatest victories of Christianity have been won by it; that it showed itself under Apostolic sanction as early as the day of Pentecost;—for it would be absurd to suppose the three thousand who were joined to the Church on the preaching of Peter to have been all 'converted' persons in the modern Evangelical sense of the word.[7] He especially pointed out, that the Churches which claim to be founded upon Individualism, fall back themselves, when they become hereditary, upon the multitudinist principle.[8] His brief, but very pertinent observations on that subject were concluded in these words:—

[3] 'Le multitudinisme est une force qui peut, comme toute force, être mal dirigée, mal exploitée, mais qui peut aussi l'être au profit de la vérité, de la piété, de la vie. Les Eglises fondées sur un autre principe ont aidé à rectifier celui-là; c'est un des incontestables services qu'elles ont rendus, de nos jours, à la cause de l'Evangile. Elles ont droit à notre reconnaissance; mais à Genève, qu'elles ne nous demandent pas ce que nous ne pouvons faire, et qu'on me permette de le dire, ce qu'elles ne font pas elles-mêmes. Oui! le multitudinisme genevois est resté vivant chez elles, et certainement elles lui doivent une portion notable de leur consistence au dedans, de leur influence au dehors. Elles font appel, comme nous, à ses souvenirs et à ses gloires; elles forment, avec nous, ce que le monde chrétien appelle et appellera toujours *l'Eglise de Genève.* Nous ne la renions, au fond, pas plus les uns que les autres. Elle a été, elle est, elle restera notre mère à tous.'[9]

[4] Such are the feelings in favour of Nationalism on the part of M. Bungener, a member of the Genevan Church; a Church to which many would not even concede that title, and of which the ecclesiastical renown centres upon one great name; while the civil history of the country presents but little of interest either in ancient or modern times. But the questions at issue between these two Genevans are of wide Christian concern, and especially to ourselves. If the Genevans cannot be proud of their Calvin, as they cannot in all things—and even he is not truly their own—they have little else of which to speak before Christendom.[10] Very different are the recollections which are awakened by the past history of such a Church as ours. Its roots are found to penetrate deep into the history of the most freely and fully developed nationality in the world, and its firm hold upon the past is one of its best auguries for the future. It has lived through Saxon rudeness, Norman rapine, baronial oppression and bloodshed; it has survived the tyranny of Tudors, recovered from fanatical assaults, escaped the treachery of Stuarts; has not perished under coldness, nor been stifled with patronage, nor sunk utterly in a dull age, nor been entirely depraved in a corrupt one. Neither as a spiritual society, nor as a national institution, need there be any fear that the Church of this country, which has passed through so many ordeals, shall succumb, because we may be on the verge of some political and ecclesiastical changes. We, ourselves, cohere with those who have preceded us, under very different forms of civil constitution, and under a very different creed and externals of worship. The 'rude forefathers,' whose mouldering bones, layer upon layer, have raised the soil round the foundations of our old churches, adored the Host, worshipped the Virgin, signed themselves with the sign of the cross, sprinkled themselves with holy water, and paid money for masses for the relief of souls in purgatory. But it is no reason, because we trust that spiritually we are at one with the best of those who have gone before us in better things than these, that we should revert to their old-world practices; nor should we content ourselves with simply transmitting to those who shall follow us, traditions which have descended to ourselves, if we can transmit something better. There is a time

for building up old waste places, and a time for raising fresh structures; a time for repairing the ancient paths, and a time for filling the valleys and lowering the hills in the constructing of new. The Jews, contemporaries of Jesus and his Apostles, were fighters against God, in refusing to accept a new application of things written in the Law, the Prophets, and the Psalms; the Romans in the time of Theodosius were fighters against Him, when they resisted the new religion with an appeal to old customs; so were the opponents of Wycliffe and his English Bible, and the opponents of Cranmer and his Reformation. Meddle not with them that are given to change is a warning for some times, and self-willed persons may 'bring in damnable heresies;' at others, 'old things are to pass away,' and that is erroneously 'called heresy' by the blind, which is really a worshipping the God of the Fathers in a better way.[11]

When signs of the times are beheld, foretelling change, it behoves those who think they perceive them to indicate them to others, not in any spirit of presumption or of haste; and, in no spirit of presumption, to suggest inquiries as to the best method of adjusting old things to new conditions.[12]

Many evils are seen in various ages, if not to have issued directly, to have been intimately linked with the Christian profession—such as religious wars, persecutions, delusions, impositions, spiritual tyrannies; many goods of civilization in our own day, when men have run to and fro and knowledge has been increased, have apparently not the remotest connexion with the Gospel. Hence grave doubts arise in the minds of really well-meaning persons, whether the secular future of humanity is necessarily bound up with the diffusion of Christianity—whether the Church is to be hereafter the life-giver to human society. It would be idle on the part of religious advocates to treat anxieties of this kind as if they were forms of the old Voltairian anti-Christianism. They are not those affectations of difficulties whereby vice endeavours to lull asleep its fears of a judgment to come; nor are they the pretensions of ignorant and presumptuous spirits, making themselves wise beyond the limits of man's wisdom. Even if such were, indeed, the sources of the wide-spread doubts respecting traditional Christianity which prevail in our own day, it would be very injudicious polemic which should content itself with denouncing the wickedness, or expressing pity for the blindness, of those who entertain them. An imputation of evil motives may embitter an opponent and add gall to controversy, but can never dispense with the necessity for replying to his arguments, nor with the advisableness of neutralizing his objections.[13]

If anxieties respecting the future of Christianity, in the office of the Christian Church in time to come, were confined to a few students or speculative philosophers, they might be put aside as mere theoretical questions, if rude criticisms upon the Scriptures, of the Tom Paine kind, proceeding from agitators of the masses, or from uninstructed persons, were the only assaults to which the letter of the Bible was exposed, it might be thought, that further instruction would impart a more reverential and submissive spirit: if lay people only entertained objections to established formularies in some of their parts, a self-satisfied sacerdotalism, confident in a supernaturally transmitted illumination, might succeed in keeping peace within the walls of emptied churches.[14] It may not be very easy by a statistical proof, to convince those whose preconceptions indispose them to admit it, of the fact of a very wide-spread alienation, both of educated and uneducated persons, from the Christianity which is ordinarily presented in our churches and chapels. Whether it be their reason or their moral sense which is shocked by what they hear there, the ordinances of public worship and religious instruction provided for the people of England, alike in the endowed and unendowed churches, are not used by them to the extent we should expect, if they valued them very highly, or if they were really adapted to the wants of their nature as it is.[15] And it has certainly not hitherto received the attention which such a grave circumstance demanded, that a number equal to five millions and a quarter of persons, should have neglected to attend means of public worship within their reach on the census Sunday in 1851; these five millions and a quarter being forty-two per cent. of the whole number able and with opportunity of then attending.[16] As an indication, on the other hand, of a great extent of dissatisfaction on the part of the clergy to some portion, at least, of the formularies of the Church of England, may be taken the fact of the existence of various associations to procure their revision, or some liberty in their use, especially that of omitting one unhappy creed.[17]

[8] It is generally the custom of those who wish to ignore the necessity for grappling with modern questions concerning Biblical interpretation, the construction of the Christian Creed, the position and prospects of the Christian Church, to represent the disposition to entertain them as a disease contracted by means of German inoculation. At other times, indeed, the tables are turned, and theological inquirers are to be silenced with the reminder, that in the native land of the modern scepticism, Evangelical and High Lutheran reactions have already put it down.[18] It may be, that on these subjects we shall in England be much indebted, for some time to come, to the patience of German investigators; but we are by no means likely to be mystified by their philosophical speculations, nor to be carried away by an inclination to force all facts within the sweep of some preconceived comprehensive theory. If the German Biblical critics have gathered together much evidence, the verdict will have to be pronounced by the sober English judgment. But, in fact, the influence of this foreign literature extends to comparatively few among us, and is altogether insufficient to account for the wide spread of that which has been called the negative theology.[19] This is rather owing to a spontaneous recoil, on the part of large numbers of the more acute of our population, from some of the doctrines which are to be heard at church and chapel; to a distrust of the old arguments for, proofs of, a miraculous Revelation; to a misgiving as to the authority, or extent of the authority of the Scriptures. In the presence of real difficulties of this kind, probably of genuine English growth, it is vain to seek to check that open discussion out of which alone any satisfactory settlement of them can issue.

[9] There may be a certain amount of literature circulating among us in a cheap

form, of which the purpose, with reference to Christianity, is simply negative and destructive, and which is characterized by an absence of all reverence, not only for beliefs, but for the best human feelings which have gathered round them, even when they have been false or superstitious.[20] But if those who are old enough to do so would compare the tone generally of the sceptical publications of the present day with that of the papers of Hone and others about forty years ago, they would be reminded, that assaults were made then upon the Christian religion in far grosser form than now, and long before opinion could have been inoculated by German philosophy—long before the more celebrated criticisms upon the details of the Evangelical histories had appeared. But it was attacked then as an institution, or by reason of the unpopularity of institutions and methods of government connected, or supposed to be connected, with it. The anti-christian agitation of that day in England was a phase of radicalism, and of a radicalism which was a terrific and uprooting force, of which the counterpart can scarcely be said to exist among us now.[21]

0] The sceptical movements in this generation are the result of observation and thought, not of passion. Things come to the knowledge of almost all persons, which were unknown a generation ago, even to the well informed. Thus the popular knowledge, at that time, of the surface of the earth, and of the populations which cover it, was extremely incomplete. In our own boyhood the world as known to the ancients was nearly all which was known to ourselves. We have recently become acquainted intimate—with the teeming regions of the far East, and with empires, pagan or even atheistic, of which the origin runs far back beyond the historic records of Judaea or of the West, and which were more populous than all Christendom now is, for many ages before the Christian era. Not any book learning—not any proud exaltation of reason—not any dreamy German metaphysics—not any minute and captious Biblical criticism—suggest questions to those who on Sundays hear the reading and exposition of the Scriptures as they were expounded to our forefathers, and on Monday peruse the news of a world of which our forefathers little dreamed;—descriptions of great nations, in some senses barbarous compared with ourselves, but composed of men of flesh and blood like our own—of like passions, marrying and domestic, congregating in great cities, buying and selling and getting gain, agriculturists, merchants, manufacturers, making wars, establishing dynasties, falling down before objects of worship, constituting priesthoods, binding themselves by oaths, honouring the dead.[22] In what relation does the Gospel stand to these millions? Is there any trace on the face of its records that it even contemplated their existence? We are told, that to know and believe in Jesus Christ is in some sense necessary to salvation. It has not been given to these. Are they—will they be, hereafter, the worse off for their ignorance? As to abstruse points of doctrine concerning the Divine Nature itself, those subjects may be thought to lie beyond the range of our faculties; if one says, aye, no other is entitled to say no to his aye; if one says, no, no one is entitled to say aye to his no.[23] Besides, the best approximative illustrations of those doctrines must be sought in metaphysical conceptions, of which few are capable, and in the history of old controversies with which fewer still are acquainted. But with respect to the moral treatment of His creatures by Almighty God, all men, in different degrees, are able to be judges of the representations made of it, by reason of the moral sense which He has given them. As to the necessity of faith in a Saviour to these peoples, when they could never have had it, no one, upon reflection, can believe in any such thing—doubtless they will be equitably dealt with. And when we hear fine distinctions drawn between covenanted and uncovenanted mercies, it seems either to be a distinction without a difference, or to amount to a denial of the broad and equal justice of the Supreme Being. We cannot be content to wrap this question up and leave it for a mystery, as to what shall become of those myriads upon myriads of non-christian races.[24] First, if our traditions tell us, that they are involved in the curse and perdition of Adam, and may justly be punished hereafter individually for his transgression, not having been extricated from it by saving faith, we are disposed to think, that our traditions cannot herein fairly declare to us the words and inferences from Scripture; but if on examination it should turn out that they have, we must say, that the authors of the scriptural books have, in those matters, represented to us their own inadequate conceptions, and not the mind of the Spirit of God; for we must conclude with the Apostle, 'Yea, let God be true and every man a liar.'[25]

[11] If, indeed, we are at liberty to believe that all shall be equitably dealt with according to their opportunities, whether they have heard or not of the name of Jesus, then we can acknowledge the case of the Christian and non-Christian populations to be one of difference of advantages. And, of course, no account can be given of the principle which determines the unequal distribution of the divine benefits. The exhibition of the divine attributes is not to be brought to measure of numbers or proportions. But human statements concerning the dealings of God with mankind, hypotheses and arguments about them, may very usefully be so tested. Truly, the abstract or philosophical difficulty may be as great concerning a small number of persons unprovided for, or, as might be inferred from some doctrinal statements, not equitably dealt with, in the divine dispensations, as concerning a large one; but it does not so force itself on the imagination and heart of the generality of observers. The difficulty, though not new in itself, is new as to the great increase in the numbers of those who feel it, and in the practical urgency for discovering an answer, solution, or neutralization for it, if we would set many unquiet souls at rest.[26]

[12] From the same source of the advance of general knowledge respecting the inhabitancy of the world issues another inquiry concerning a promise, prophecy, or assertion of Scripture. For the commission of Jesus to his Apostles was to preach the gospel to 'all nations,' 'to every creature;' and St. Paul says of the gentile world, 'But I say have they not heard? Yes, verily, their sound went into all the earth, and their words unto the ends of the world,' (Rom. x. 18), and speaks of the gospel 'which was preached to every nation under Heaven,' (Col. i. 23), when it has never

yet been preached even to the half.[27] Then, again, it has often been appealed to as an evidence of the supernatural origin of Christianity, and as an instance of supernatural assistance vouchsafed to it in the first centuries, that it so soon overspread the world. It has seemed but a small leap of about three hundred years to the age of Constantine, if in that time, not to insist upon the letter of the texts already quoted, the conversion of the civilized world could be accomplished. It may be known only to the more learned, that it was not accomplished to the Roman empire even then; that the Christians of the East cannot be fairly computed at more than half the population, nor the Christians of the West at so much as a third, at the commencement of that emperor's reign. But it requires no learning to be aware that neither then nor subsequently have the Christians amounted to more than a fourth part of the people of the earth; and it is seen to be impossible to appeal any longer to the wonderful spread of Christianity in the three first centuries, as a special evidence of the wisdom and goodness of God.[28]

13] So likewise a very grave modification of an 'evidence' heretofore current must ensue in another respect, in consequence of an increased knowledge of other facts connected with the foregoing. It has been customary to argue that, *a priori*, a supernatural revelation was to be expected at the time when Jesus Christ was manifested upon the earth, by reason of the exhaustion of all natural or unassisted human efforts for the amelioration of mankind. The state of the world, it has been customary to say, had become so utterly corrupt and hopeless under the Roman sway, that a necessity and special occasion was presented for an express divine intervention. Our recently enlarged ethnographical information shows such an argument to be altogether inapplicable to the case. If we could be judges of the necessity for a special divine intervention, the stronger necessity existed in the East. There immense populations, like the Chinese, had never developed the idea of a personal God, or had degenerated from a once pure theological creed, as in India, from the religion of the Vedas.[29] Oppressions and tyrannies, caste-distinctions, common and enormous vices, a polluted and idolatrous worship, as bad as the worst which disgraced Rome, Greece, or Syria, had prevailed for ages.

4] It would not be very tasteful, as an exception to this description, to call Buddhism the gospel of India, preached to it five or six centuries before the Gospel of Jesus was proclaimed in the nearer East.[30] But on the whole it would be more like the realities of things, as we can now behold them, to say that the Christian revelation was given to the western world, because it deserved it better and was more prepared for it than the East. Philosophers, at least, had anticipated in speculation some of its dearest hopes and had prepared the way for its self-denying ethics.

:] There are many other sources of the modern questionings of traditional Christianity which cannot now be touched upon, originating like those which have been mentioned, in a change of circumstances wherein observers are placed; whereby their thoughts are turned in new directions, and they are rendered dissatisfied with old modes of speaking. But such a difficulty as that respecting the souls of heathendom, which must now come closely home to multitudes among us, will disappear, if it be candidly acknowledged that the words of the New Testament, which speak of the preaching of the Gospel to the whole world, were limited to the understanding of the times when they were spoken; that doctrines concerning salvation, to be met with in it, are for the most part applicable only to those to whom the preaching of Christ should come; and that we must draw our conclusions respecting a just dealing hereafter with the individuals who make up the sum of heathenism, rather from reflections suggested by our own moral instincts than from the express declarations of Scripture writers, who had no such knowledge, as is given to ourselves, of the amplitude of the world, which is the scene of the divine manifestations.[31]

[16] Moreover, to our great comfort, there have been preserved to us words of the Lord Jesus himself, declaring that the conditions of men in another world will be determined by their moral characters in this, and not by their hereditary or traditional creeds; and both many words and the practice of the great Apostle Paul, within the range which was given him, tend to the same result.[32] He has been thought even to make an allusion to the Buddhist *Dharmma*, or law, when he said, 'When the gentiles which have not the law do by nature the things contained in the law, these having not the law are a law unto themselves, which show the work of the law written in their hearts,' &c. (Rom. i. 14, 15.)[33] However this may be, it is evident that if such a solution as the above is accepted, a variety of doctrinal statements hitherto usual, Calvinistic and Lutheran theories on the one hand, and sacramental and hierarchical ones on the other, must be thrown into the background, if not abandoned.

[17] There may be a long future during which the present course of the world shall last. Instead of its drawing near the close of its existence, as represented in Millennarian or Rabbinical fables, and with so many more souls, according to some interpretations of the Gospel of Salvation, lost to Satan in every age and in every nation, than have been won to Christ, that the victory would evidently be on the side of the Fiend, we may yet be only at the commencement of the career of the great Spiritual Conqueror even in this world.[34] Nor have we any right to say that the effects of what He does upon earth shall not extend and propagate themselves in worlds to come. But under any expectation of the duration of the present secular constitution, it is of the deepest interest to us, both as observers and as agents, placed evidently at an epoch when humanity finds itself under new conditions, to form some definite conception to ourselves of the way in which Christianity is henceforward to act upon the world which is our own.

[18] Different estimates are made of the beneficial effects already wrought by Christianity upon the secular aspect of the world, according to the different points of view from which it is regarded. Some endeavour, from an impartial standing point, to embrace in one panorama the whole religious history of mankind, of which Christianity then becomes the most important phase; others can only look at such a history from within some narrow chamber of doctrinal and ecclesiastical

prepossessions. And anticipations equally different for like reasons will be entertained by persons differently imbued, as to the form under which, and the machinery by which, it shall hereafter be presented with success, either to the practically unchristianized populations of countries like our own, or to peoples of other countries never as yet even nominally christianized.

[19] Although the consequences of what the Gospel does will be carried on into other worlds, its work is to be done here; although some of its work here must be unseen, yet not all; nor much even of its unseen work without at least some visible manifestation and effects. The invisible Church is to us a mere abstraction. Now it is acknowledged on all hands, that to the multitudinist principle are due the great external victories which the Christian name has hitherto won. On the other hand, it is alleged by the advocates of Individualism, that these outward acquisitions and numerical accessions have always been made at the expense of the purity of the Church; and, also, that Scriptural authority and the earliest practice is in favour of Individualism. Moreover, almost all the corruptions of Christianity are attributed by individualists to the effecting by the Emperor Constantine of an unholy alliance between Church and State.[35] Yet a fair review, as far as there are data for it, of the state of Christianity before the time of that emperor will leave us in at least very great doubt, whether the Christian character was really, in the anterior period, superior on the average to what it has subsequently been. We may appeal to the most ancient records extant, and even to the Apostolic Epistles themselves, to show, that neither in doctrine nor in morals did the primitive Christian communities at all approach to the ideal which has been formed of them. The moral defects of the earliest converts are the subject of the gravest expostulation on the part of the Apostolic writers: and the doctrinal features of the early Church are much more undetermined than would be thought by those who read them only through the ecclesiastical creeds.

[20] Those who belong to very different theological schools acknowledge at times, that they cannot with any certainty find in the highest ecclesiastical antiquity the dogmas which they consider most important. It is customary with Lutherans to represent their doctrine of justification by subjective faith as having died out shortly after the Apostolic age. In fact, it never was the doctrine of any considerable portion of the Church in the time of the Reformation. It is not met with in the immediately post-Apostolic writings, nor in the Apostolic writings, except those of St. Paul, not even in the Epistle to the Hebrews, which is of the Pauline or Paulo-Johannean school. The faith at least of that Epistle, 'the substance of things hoped for,' is a very different faith from the faith of the Epistle to the Romans,— if the Lutherans are correct in representing that to be, a conscious apprehending of the benefits to the individual soul, of the Saviour's merits and passion.[36] Then, on the other hand, it is admitted, even maintained, by a very different body of theologians, as by the learned Jesuit Petavius and many others, that the doctrine afterwards developed into the Nicene and Athanasian, is not to be found explicitly in the earliest Fathers, nor even in Scripture, although provable by it.[37] One polemical value of this view to

those who uphold it, is to show the necessity of an inspired Church to develope Catholic truth.

[21] But although the primitive Christians fell far short both of a doctrinal and ethical ideal, there is this remarkable distinction to be noted between the primitive aspects of doctrine and of ethics. The morals of the first Christians were certainly very far below the estimate which has been formed of them; but the standard by which they were measured was unvarying, lofty, and peculiar; moreover, the nearer we approach to the fountainhead, the more definite do we find the statement of the Christian principle, that the source of religion is in the heart. On the contrary, the nearer we come to the original sources of the history, the less definite do we find the statements of doctrines, and even of the facts from which the doctrines were afterwards inferred. And, at the very first, with our Lord Himself and His Apostles, as represented to us in the New Testament, morals come before contemplation, ethics before theoretics.[38] In the patristic writings, theoretics assume continually an increasingly disproportionate value. Even within the compass of our New Testament there is to be found already a wonderful contrast between the words of our Lord and such a discourse as the Epistle to the Hebrews. There is not wanting, indeed, to this Epistle an earnest moral appeal, but the greater part of it is illustrative, argumentative, and controversial. Our Lord's discourses have almost all of them a direct moral bearing. This character of His words is certainly more obvious in the three first Gospels than in the fourth; and the remarkable unison of those Gospels, when they recite the Lord's words, notwithstanding their discrepancies in some matters of fact, compel us to think, that they embody more exact traditions of what He actually said than the fourth does.[39]

[22] As monuments or witnesses, discrepant in a certain degree as to other particulars, the evidence afforded by the three Synoptics to the Lord's own words is the most precious element in the Christian records. We are thereby placed at the very root of the Gospel tradition. And these words of the Lord, taken in conjunction with the Epistle of St. James, and with the first, or genuine, Epistle of St. Peter, leave no reasonable doubt of the general character of His teaching having been what, for want of a better word, we must perhaps call moral.[40] But to represent the Spirit of Christ as a moral Spirit is not merely to proclaim Him as a Lawgiver, enacting the observance of a set of precepts, but as fulfilled with a Spirit given to Him 'without measure,' of which, indeed, all men are partakers who have a sense of what they 'ought' to be and do; yet flowing over from Him, especially on those who perceive in His words, and in His life, principles of ever-widening application to the circumstances of their own existence; who learn from Him to penetrate to the root of their conscience, and to recognise themselves as being active elements in the moral order of the universe.

[23] We may take an illustration of the relative value in the Apostolic age of the doctrinal and moral principles, by citing a case which will be allowed to be extreme enough. It is evident there were among the Christian converts in that earliest period, those who had no belief in a corporeal resurrection. Some of these had,

perhaps, been made converts from the sect of the Sadducees, and had brought with them into the Christian congregation the same doubts or negative beliefs which belonged to them before their conversion. The Jewish church embraced in its bosom both Pharisees and Sadducees: but our Lord, although he expressly taught a resurrection, and argued with the Sadducees on the subject, never treated them as aliens from Israel because they did not hold that doctrine; is much more severe on the moral defects and hypocrisies of the Pharisees than upon the doctrinal defects of the Sadducees. The Christian Church was recruited in its Jewish branch chiefly from the sect of the Pharisees, and it is somewhat difficult for us to realize the conversion of a Sadducee to Christianity, retaining his Sadducee disbelief or scepticism. But, the 'some among you who say that there is no resurrection of the dead,' (1 Cor. xv. 12, comp. 2 Tim. ii. 18), can leave us in no doubt upon the matter, that there were Christians of Sadducee or Gentile prejudices, like those who mocked or those who hesitated when Paul preached at Athens the resurrection of the dead.[41] But St. Paul argues with such elaborately in that chapter, without expelling them from the Church, although he always represents faith in the resurrection as the corner-stone of the Christian belief. He endeavours rather to conciliate and to remove objections. First, he represents the rising to life again, not as miraculous or exceptional, but as a law of humanity, or at least of Christian and spiritualized humanity; and he treats the resurrection of Christ, not as a wonder, but as a prerogative instance. Secondly, he shows, upon the doctrine of a spiritual body, how the objections against a resurrection from the gross conception of a flesh and blood body, fall to the ground.[42] How, if there might thus be Sadducee, or quasi-Sadducee, Christians in the Church, their Christianity must have consisted in an appreciation of the moral spirit of Jesus, and in an obedience, such as it might be, to the Christian precepts; they could have been influenced by no expectation of a future recompense.[43] Their obedience might or might not be of as high an order as that which is so motived; it might have been a mere legal habit, or an exalted disinterested life. Now, let us compare a person of this description with such as those who are indicated, (1 Cor. xv. 19, 32); and we cannot think that St. Paul is there speaking of himself personally, but of the general run of persons reluctant to exercise self-restraint and to expose themselves to persecution for the Gospel's sake, yet induced to do so by the hope of a future recompense. Let us consider these two descriptions of persons. The one class is defective in the Christian doctrine, and in the most fundamental article of the Apostle's preaching, the other in the Christian moral life; can we say that the one defect was more fatal than the other? We do not find the Apostle excommunicating these Corinthians, who said there was no resurrection of the dead.[44] On the other hand, we know it was only in an extreme case that he sanctioned excommunication for the cause of immorality. And upon the whole, if we cannot effectually compare the person deficient in a true belief of the resurrection, with an immoral or evil liver—if we can only say they were both bad Christians—at least we have no reason to determine that the good liver who disbelieved the resurrection was treated by St. Paul as less of a Christian than the evil liver who believed it. We cannot suppose the evil life always to have brought on the disbelief in the doctrine, nor the disbelief in the doctrine to have issued always in an evil life.[45]

[24] Now, from what has been said we gather two important conclusions:—first, of the at least equal value of the Christian life, as compared with the Christian doctrine; and, secondly, of the retaining within the Church, both of those who were erroneous and defective in doctrine, and of those who were by their lives unworthy of their profession; they who caused divisions and heresies were to be marked and avoided but not expelled, and if any called a brother were a notoriously immoral person, the rest were enjoined, no not to eat with him, but he was not to be refused the name of brother or Christian. (1 Cor. v. 11.)

[25] It would be difficult to devise a description of a multitudinist Church, exhibiting more saliently the worst defects which can attend that form, than this which is taken from the evidence of the Apostolic Epistles. We find the Pauline Churches to have comprised, not only persons of the truest doctrinal insight, of the highest spiritual attainments, of martyr-like self-devotion, but of the strangest and most incongruous beliefs, and of the most unequal and inconsistent practice.[46] The individualist could say nothing more derogatory of any multitudinist Church, not even of a national one; unless, perhaps, he might say this, that less distinction is made within such a Church itself, and within all modern Churches, between their better and worse members, than was made in the Apostolic Churches. Any judicial sentence of excommunication was extremely rare in the Apostolic age, as we have seen, and the distinction between the worthy and unworthy members of the Church was to be marked, not by any public and authoritative act, but by the operation of private conduct and opinion.[47]

[26] The Apostolic Churches were thus multitudinist, and early tended to become National Churches; from the first they took collective names from the localities where they were situate.[48] And it was natural and proper they should, except upon the Calvinistic theory of conversion.[49] There is some show of reasonable independence, some appearance of applying the standard liberty of private judgment, in maintaining the Christian unlawfulness of the union of Church and State, corruption of national establishments, and like propositions. But it will be found, that where they are maintained by serious and religious people, they are parts of a Calvinistic system, and are held in connexion with peculiar theories of grace, immediate conversion, and arbitrary call. It is as merely a Calvinistic and Congregational commonplace to speak of the unholy union of Church and State accomplished by Constantine, as it is a Romish commonplace to denounce the unholy schism accomplished by Henry the Eighth. But in fact both those sovereigns only carried out, chiefly for their own purposes, that which was already in preparation by the course of events; even Henry would not have broken with the Pope if he had not seen the public mind to be in some degree ripe for it, nor would Constantine have taken the first steps towards an establishment of Christianity, unless the empire had already been growing Christian.[50]

27] Unhappily, together with his inauguration of Multitudinism, Constantine also inaugurated a principle essentially at variance with it, the principle of doctrinal limitation. It is very customary to attribute the necessity of stricter definitions of the Christian creed from time to time to the rise of successive heresies. More correctly, there succeeded to the fluid state of Christian opinion in the first century after Christ, a gradual hardening and systematizing of conflicting views; and the opportunity of reverting to the freedom of the Apostolic and immediately succeeding periods, was finally lost for many ages by the sanction given by Constantine to the decisions of Nicaea.[51] We cannot now be very good judges, whether it would have been possible, together with the establishment of Christianity as the imperial religion, to enforce forbearance between the great antagonisms which were then in dispute, and to have insisted on the maxim, that neither had a right to limit the common Christianity to the exclusion of the other.[52] At all events a principle at variance with a true Multitudinism was then recognised. All parties it must be acknowledged were equally exclusive. And exclusion and definition have since been the rule for almost all Churches, more or less, even when others of their principles might seem to promise a greater freedom.

28] That the members of a Calvinistic Church, as in the Geneva of Calvin and Beza, or in the Church of Scotland, should coincide with the members of the State—that 'election' and 'effectual call' should be hereditary, is, of course, too absurd to suppose; and the congregational Calvinists are more consistent than the Calvinists of Established Churches.[53] Of Calvinism, as a system of doctrine, it is not here proposed to say anything, except, that it must of necessity be hostile to every other creed; and the members of a Calvinistic Church can never consider themselves but as parted by an insuperable distinction from all other professors of the Gospel; they cannot stand on a common footing, in any spiritual matter, with those who belong to the world, that is, with all others than themselves. The exclusiveness of a multitudinist Church, which makes, as yet, the ecclesiastical creeds the terms of its communion, may cease when that test or limitation is repealed. But the exclusiveness of a Calvinistic Church, whether free from the creeds or not, is inherent in its principles. There is no insuperable barrier between Congregationalists not being Calvinists, and a multitudinist Church which should liberate itself sufficiently from the traditional symbols. Doctrinal limitations in the multitudinist form of Church are not essential to it; upon larger knowledge of Christian history, upon a more thorough acquaintance with the mental constitution of man, upon an understanding of the obstacles they present to a true Catholicity, they may be cast off. Nor is a multitudinist Church necessarily or essentially hierarchical, in any extreme or superstitious sense; it can well admit if not pure congregationalism, a large admixture of the congregational spirit. Indeed, a combination of the two principles will alone keep any Church in health and vigour. Too great importance attached to a hierarchical order will lead into superstitions respecting Apostolical succession, ministerial illumination, and supernatural sacramental influence; mere congregationalism tends to keep ministers and people at a dead spiritual level. A just recognition and balance of the two tendencies, allows the emerging of the most eminent of the congregation into offices for which they are suited; so that neither are the true hierarchs and leaders of thought and manners drawn down and made to succumb to a mere democracy, nor those clothed in the priests' robe who have no true unction from above.[54] And this just balance between the hierarchy and the congregation would be at least as attainable in the national form of Church and in any other, if it were free from dogmatical tests and similar intellectual bondage. But there are some prejudices against Nationalism which deserve to be farther considered.[55]

[29] It was natural for a Christian in the earliest period to look upon the heathen State in which he found himself as if it belonged to the kingdom of Satan and not to that of God; and consecrated as it was, in all its offices, to the heathen divinities, to consider it a society having its origin from the powers of darkness, not from the Lord of light and life.[56] In the Apostolic writers this view appears rather in the First Epistle of St. John than with St. Paul. The horizon which St. John's view embraced was much narrower than St. Paul's;

> Qui mores hominum multorum vidit et urbes.[57]

If the love felt and inculcated by St. John towards the brethren was the more intense, the charity with which St. Paul comprehended all men was the more ample; and it is not from every point of view we should describe St. John as pre-eminently the Apostle of love. With St. John, 'the whole world lieth in wickedness,' while St. Paul exhorts 'prayers and supplications to be made for all men, for kings, and for all that are in authority.'[58] Taking a wide view of the world and its history, we must acknowledge political constitutions of men to be the work of God Himself; they are organizations into which human society grows by reason of the properties of the elements which generate it.[59] But the primitive Christians could scarcely be expected to see, that ultimately the Gospel was to have sway in doing more perfectly that which the heathen religions were doing imperfectly; that its office should be, not only to quicken the spirit of the individual and to confirm his future hopes, but to sanctify all social relations and civil institutions, and to enter into the marrow of the national life; whereas heathenism had only decorated the surface of it.

[30] Heathendom had its national Churches. Indeed, the existence of a national Church is not only a permissible thing, but is necessary to the completion of a national life, and has shown itself in all nations, when they have made any advance in civilization. It has been usual, but erroneous, to style the Jewish constitution a theocracy in a peculiar and exclusive sense, as if the combination of the religious and civil life had been confined to that people.[60] Even among barbarous tribes the fetish-man establishes an authority over the rest, quite as much from the yearning of others after guidance as from his own superior cunning. Priesthoods have always been products. Priests have neither been, as some would represent, a set of

deliberate conspirators against the free thoughts of mankind; nor, on the other hand, have they been the sole divinely commissioned channels for communication of spiritual truth. If all priests and ministers of religion could at one moment be swept from the face of the earth, they would soon be reproduced. If the human race, or a given people—and a recent generation saw an instance of something like it in no distant nation—were resolved into its elements, and all its social and religious institutions shattered to pieces, it would reconstruct a political framework, and a spiritual organization, re-constituting governors, laws, and magistrates, educators, and ministers of religion.[61]

The distinction between the Jewish people and the other nations, in respect of this so-called theocracy, is but feebly marked on both sides. For the religious element was much stronger than has been supposed in other nationalities, and the priesthood was by no means supreme in the Hebrew State.[62]

Constantly the title occurs in the Hebrew Scriptures, of 'the Lord's people,' with appeals to Jehovah as their Supreme Governor, Protector, and Judge.[63] And so it is with polytheistic nations; they are the offspring of the gods; the deities are their guides and guardians, the authors of their laws and customs; their worship is interwoven with the whole course of political and social life. It will of course be said, the entire difference is no more than this—the object of worship in the one case was the true God, in the other cases idols or demons. But it is very clear to unprejudiced persons, that the conceptions which the Hebrews formed of Jehovah, though far superior to the conceptions embodied in any other national religion, were obscured by figurative representations of Him in accordance with the character of His worshippers. The passions ascribed to Him were not those most base and degrading ones attributed to their deities by the pagans; and on that account it has been less easy to separate the figurative description from the true idea of Him. The better pagans could easily perceive the stories of their gods to have been, at the best, allegories, poetical embellishments, inventions of some kind or other. Jews did not perceive, that the attribution of wrath and jealousy to their God could only be by a figure of speech; and what is worse, it is difficult to persuade many Christians of the same thing, and solemn inferences from the figurative expressions of the Hebrew literature have been crystallized into Christian doctrine.

All things sanctioned among the Jews are certainly not to be imitated by us, nor all pagan institutions to be abhorred. In respect of a State religion, Jew and Gentile were more alike than has been thought. All nations have exhibited, in some form or another, the development of a public religion, and have done so by reason of tendencies inherent in their nationality. The particular form of the religion has been due to various causes. Also in periods of transition there would, for a time, be a breaking in upon this feature of national life. While prophets, philosophers, reformers, were at work, or some new principle winning its way, the national uniformity would be disturbed. So it was at the first preaching of the Gospel; St. Paul and the Lord Jesus himself offered it to the Jews as a nation, on the multitudinist principle; but when they put it from them, it must make progress by kindling a fire in the earth, even to the dividing families, two against three and three against two. Thereupon Christians appear for a while to be aliens from their countries and commonwealths, but only for a while. We must not confound with an essential principle of Christianity that which only resulted from a temporary necessity. The individualist principle may have been the right one for a time, and under certain circumstances, not consequently the right one, under all circumstances, nor even the possible one. In this question, as in that of hierarchy, and in various ceremonial discussions, the appeal to a particular primitive antiquity is only an appeal from the whole experience of Christendom to a partial experience limited to a short period. Moreover, as to the mind of Jesus himself with respect to Nationalism it is fully revealed in those touching words, preserved both in the first and third Gospels, 'How often would I have gathered thy children together, even as a hen gathereth her chickens under her wings, and ye would not.'[64]

[34] Christianity was therefore compelled, as it were against its will, and in contradiction to its proper design, to make the first steps in its progress by cutting across old societies, filtering into the world by individual conversions, showing nevertheless, from the very first, its multitudinist tendencies; and before it could comprehend countries or cities, embracing families and households, the several members of which must have been on very different spiritual levels (Acts xvi. 31-34). The Roman world was penetrated in the first instance by an individual and domestic Christianity, to which was owing the first conversion of our own country; in the second or Saxon conversion, the people were Christianized *en masse.* Such conversions as this last may not be thought to have been worth much, but they were worth the abolition of some of the grossness of idolatry; they effected all of which the subjects of them were for the time capable, and prepared the way for something better in another generation. The conversions operated by the German Apostle, Boniface, were of the same multitudinous kind as those of Austin and Paulinus in Britain, and for a like reason; in both cases the development of Christianity necessarily followed the forms of the national life.[65]

[35] In some people of the West this national and natural tendency was counteracted by the shattering which ensued upon the breaking up of the Roman empire. And in those countries especially which had been longest and most closely connected with Pagan Rome, such as Italy itself, Spain, France, the people felt themselves unable to stand alone in their spiritual institutions, and were glad to lean on some other prop and centre, so far as was still allowed them. The Teutonic Churches were always more free than the Churches of the Latinized peoples, though they themselves had derived their Christianity from Roman Missionaries; and among the Teutonic Churches alone has a freedom from extraneous dominion as yet established itself.[66] For a time even these could only adopt the forms of doctrine and practice which were current in other parts of the West. But those forms were neither of the essence of a national Church, nor even of the essence of a Christian Church. A national Church need not, historically speaking, be Christian, nor, if it be Christian, need it be tied down to particular forms which

have been prevalent at certain times in Christendom. That which is essential to a national Church is, that it should undertake to assist the spiritual progress of the nation and of the individuals of which it is composed, in their several states and stages. Not even a Christian Church should expect all those who are brought under its influence to be, as a matter of fact, of one and the same standard, but should endeavour to raise each according to his capacities, and should give no occasion for a reaction against itself, nor provoke the individualist element into separatism. It would do this if it submitted to define itself otherwise than by its own nationality—if it represented itself as a part rather than a whole, as deriving authority and not claiming it, as imitative and not original.

6] It will do this also, if while the civil side of the nation is fluid, the ecclesiastical side of it is fixed; if thought and speech are free among all other classes, and not free among those who hold the office of leaders and teachers of the rest in the highest things; if they are to be bound to cover up instead of opening; and having, it is presumed, possession of the key of knowledge, are to stand at the door with it, permitting no one to enter, unless by force. A national Church may also find itself in this position, which, perhaps, is our own. Its ministers may become isolated between two other parties—between those on the one hand who draw fanatical inferences from formularies and principles which they themselves are not able or are unwilling to repudiate; and on the other, those who have been tempted, in impatience of old fetters, to follow free thought heedlessly wherever it may lead them. If our own Churchmen expect to discourage and repress a fanatical Christianity, without a frank appeal to reason, and a frank criticism of Scripture, they will find themselves without any actual arms for that combat; or if they attempt to check inquiry by the repetition of old forms and denunciations, they will be equally powerless, and run the especial risk of turning into bitterness the sincerity of those who should be their best allies, as friends of truth. They should avail themselves of the aid of all reasonable persons enlightening the fanatical religionist, making no reserve of any seemingly harmless or apparently serviceable superstitions of their own; they should also endeavour to supply to the negative theologian some positive elements in Christianity, on grounds more sure to him than the assumption of an objective 'faith once delivered to the saints,' which he cannot identify with the creed of any Church as yet known to him.[67]

It has been matter of great boast within the Church of England, in common with other Protestant Churches, that it is founded upon the 'Word of God,' a phrase which begs many a question when applied to the canonical books of the Old and New Testaments, a phrase which is never applied to them by any of the Scriptural authors, and which, according to Protestant principles, never could be applied to them by any sufficient authority from without. In that which may be considered the pivot Article of the Church this expression does not occur, but only 'Holy Scripture,' 'Canonical Books,' 'Old and New Testaments.'[68] It contains no declaration of the Bible being throughout supernaturally suggested, nor any intimation as to which portions of it were owing to a special divine illumination, nor the slightest attempt at defining inspiration, whether mediate or immediate, whether through, or beside, or overruling the natural faculties of the subject of it,—not the least hint of the relation between the divine and human elements in the composition of the Biblical books. Even if the Fathers have usually considered 'canonical' as synonymous with 'miraculously inspired,' there is nothing to show that their sense of the word must necessarily be applied in our own sixth Article. The word itself may mean either books ruled and determined by the Church, or regulative books; and the employment of it in the Article hesitates between these two significations. For at one time 'Holy Scripture' and canonical books are those books 'of whose authority never was any doubt in the Church,'[69] that is, they are 'determined' books; and then the other, or uncanonical books, are described as those which 'the Church doth not apply to establish any doctrine,' that is, they are not 'regulative' books.[70] And if the other principal Churches of the Reformation have gone farther in definition in this respect than our own, that is no reason we should force the silence of our Church into unison with their expressed declarations, but rather that we should rejoice in our comparative freedom.[71]

[38] The Protestant feeling among us has satisfied itself in a blind way with the anti-Roman declaration, that 'Holy Scripture containeth all things necessary to salvation, so that whatsoever is not read therein, nor may be proved thereby, is not to be required of any man, that it should be believed as an article of the faith,' &c., and without reflecting how very much is wisely left open in that Article. For this declaration itself is partly negative and partly positive; as to its negative part it declares that nothing—no clause of creed, no decision of council, no tradition or exposition—is to be required to be believed on peril of salvation, unless it be Scriptural; but it does not lay down, that everything which is contained in Scripture must be believed on the same peril. Or it may be expressed thus:—the Word of God is contained in Scripture, whence it does not follow that it is co-extensive with it. The Church to which we belong does not put that stumbling-block before the feet of her members; it is their own fault if they place it there for themselves, authors of their own offence. Under the terms of the sixth Article one may accept literally, or allegorically, or as parable, or poetry, or legend, the story of a serpent tempter, of an ass speaking with man's voice, of an arresting of the earth's motion, of a reversal of its motion, of waters standing in a solid heap, of witches, and a variety of apparitions. So, under the terms of the sixth Article, every one is free in judgment as to the primeval institution of the Sabbath, the universality of the deluge, the confusion of tongues, the corporeal taking up of Elijah into Heaven, the nature of angels, the reality of demoniacal possession, the personality of Satan, and the miraculous particulars of many events. So the dates and authorship of the several books received as canonical are not determined by any authority, nor their relative value and importance.[72]

[39] Many evils have flowed to the people of England, otherwise free enough, from an extreme and too exclusive Scripturalism. The rudimentary education of a large number of our countrymen has been mainly carried on by the reading of the

Scriptures. They are read by young children in thousands of cases, where no attempt could be made, even if it were desired, to accompany the reading with the safeguard of a reasonable interpretation. A Protestant tradition seems to have prevailed, unsanctioned by any of our formularies, that the words of Scripture are imbued with a supernatural property, by which their true sense can reveal itself even to those who, by intellectual or educational defect, would naturally be incapable of appreciating it. There is no book indeed, or collection of books, so rich in words which address themselves intelligibly to the unlearned and learned alike. But those who are able to do so ought to lead the less educated to distinguish between the different kinds of words which it contains, between the dark patches of human passion and error which form a partial crust upon it, and the bright centre of spiritual truth within.[73]

40] Some years ago a vehement controversy was carried on, whether the Scripture ought to be distributed in this country with or without note and comment. It was a question at issue between two great parties and two great organized societies. But those who advocated the view which was the more reasonable in itself, did so in the interest of an unreasonable theory; they insisted on the authority of the Church in an hierarchical sense, and carried out their commentations in dry catenas of doctrine and precept. On the other side, the views of those who were for circulating the Bible without note or comment were partly superstitious, and partly antagonistic in the way of a protest against the hierarchical claim.[74] The Scriptures have no doubt been received with sufficient readiness by all classes of English people, for there has been something very agreeable to some of the feelings of the Englishman in the persuasion that he possesses, independently of priest or clergyman, the whole matter of his religion bound up in the four corners of a portable book, furnishing him, as he thinks, with an infallible test of the doctrine which he hears from his preacher, with a substitute for all teaching, if he so pleases, and with the complete apparatus necessary, should he desire to become the teacher of other in his turn. But the result of this immense circulation of the Scriptures for many years by all parties, has been little adequate to what might have been expected beforehand, from the circulation of that which is in itself so excellent and divine.[75]

1] It is ill to be deterred from giving expression to the truth or from prosecuting the investigation of it, from a fear of making concessions to revolutionary or captious dispositions. For the blame of this captiousness, when it exists, lies in part at the door of those who ignore the difficulties of others, because they may not feel any for themselves. To this want of wisdom on the part of the defenders of old opinions is to be attributed, that the noting of such differences as are to be found in the Evangelical narratives, or in the books of Kings and Chronicles, takes the appearance of an attack upon a holy thing. The like ill consequences follow from not acknowledging freely the extent of the human element in the sacred books; for if this were freely acknowledged on the one side, the divine element would be frankly recognised on the other. Good men—and they cannot be good without the Spirit of God—may err in facts, be weak in memory, mingle imagination with memory, be feeble in inferences, confound illustration with argument, be varying in judgment and opinion. But the Spirit of absolute Truth cannot err or contradict Himself, if He speak immediately, even in small things, accessories, or accidents. Still less can we suppose Him to suggest contradictory accounts, or accounts only to be reconciled in the way of hypothesis and conjecture. Some things indited by the Holy Spirit may appear to relate to objects of which the whole cannot be embraced by the human intellect, and it may not, as to such objects, be possible to reconcile opposite sides of Divine truth. Whether this is the general character of Scripture revelations is not now the question; but the theory is supposable and should be treated with respect, in regard to some portions of Scripture. To suppose, on the other hand, a supernatural influence to cause the record of that which can only issue in a puzzle, is to lower infinitely our conception of the Divine dealings in respect of a special revelation.[76]

[42] Thus it may be attributed to the defect of our understandings, that we should be unable altogether to reconcile the aspects of the Saviour as presented to us in the three first Gospels, and in the writings of St. Paul and St. John. At any rate, there were current in the primitive Church very distinct Christologies. But neither to any defect in our capacities, nor to any reasonable presumption of a hidden wise design, nor to any partial spiritual endowments in the narrators, can we attribute the difficulty, if not impossibility, of reconciling the genealogies of St. Matthew and St. Luke, or the chronology of the Holy Week or the accounts of the Resurrection; nor to any mystery in the subject-matter can be referred the uncertainty in which the New Testament writings leave us, as to the descent of Jesus Christ according to the flesh, whether by his mother He were of the tribe of Judah, or of the tribe of Levi.[77]

[43] If the national Church is to be true to the multitudinist principle, and to correspond ultimately to the national character, the freedom of opinion which belongs to the English citizen should be conceded to the English Churchman; and the freedom which is already practically enjoyed by the members of the congregation, cannot without injustice be denied to its ministers. A minister may rightly be expected to know more of theology than the generality, or even than the best informed of the laity; but it is a strange ignoring of the constitution of human minds, to expect all ministers, however much they may know, to be of one opinion in theoreticals, or the same person to be subject to no variation of opinion at different periods of his life. And it may be worth while to consider how far a liberty of opinion is conceded by our existing laws, civil and ecclesiastical. Along with great openings for freedom it will be found there are some restraints, or appearances of restraints, which require to be removed.[78]

[44] As far as opinion privately entertained is concerned, the liberty of the English clergyman appears already to be complete. For no ecclesiastical person can be obliged to answer interrogations as to his opinions, nor be troubled for that which he has not actually expressed, nor be made responsible for inferences which other people may draw from his expressions.[79]

[45] Still, though there may be no power of inquisition into the private opinions

either of ministers or people in the Church of England, there may be some interference with the expression of them; and a great restraint is supposed to be imposed upon the clergy by reason of their subscription to the Thirty-nine Articles. Yet it is more difficult than might be expected, to define what is the extent of the legal obligation of those who sign them; and in this case the strictly legal obligation is the measure of the moral one. Subscription may be thought even to be inoperative upon the conscience by reason of its vagueness. For the act of subscription is enjoined, but its effect or meaning nowhere plainly laid down; and it does not seem to amount to more than an acceptance of the Articles of the Church as the formal law to which the subscriber is in some sense subject. What that subjection amounts to, must be gathered elsewhere, for it does not appear on the face of the subscription itself.[80]

46] The ecclesiastical authority on the subject is to be found in the Canons of 1603, the fifth and the thirty-sixth. The fifth, indeed, may be applicable theoretically both to lay and to ecclesiastical persons; practically it can only concern those of whom subscription is really required. It is entitled, *Impugners of the Articles of Religion established in this Church of England censored.* 'Whosoever shall hereafter affirm, that any of the nine and thirty articles, &c., are in any part superstitious or erroneous, or such as he may not with a good conscience subscribe unto, let him be excommunicated, &c.'[81] We need not stay to consider what the effects of excommunication might be, but rather attend to the definition which the canon itself supplies of 'impugning.' It is stated to be the affirming, that any of the Thirty-nine Articles are in any part 'superstitious or erroneous.' Yet an Article may be very inexpedient, or become so; may be unintelligible, or not easily intelligible to ordinary people; it may be controversial, and such as to provoke controversy and keep it alive when otherwise it would subside; it may revive unnecessarily the remembrance of dead controversies—all or any of these, without being 'erroneous;' and though not 'superstitious,' some expressions may appear so, such as those which seem to impute an occult operation to the Sacraments. The fifth canon does not touch the affirming any of these things, and more especially, that the Articles present truths disproportionately, and relatively to ideas not now current.[82]

7] The other canon which concerns subscription is the thirty-sixth, which contains two clauses explanatory to some extent, of the meaning of ministerial subscription, 'That he *alloweth* the Book of Articles, &c.' and 'that he *acknowledgeth* the same to be agreeable to the Word of God.' We 'allow' many things which we do not think wise or practically useful; as the less of two evils, or an evil which cannot be remedied, or of which the remedy is not attainable, or is uncertain in its operation, or is not in our power, or concerning which there is much difference of opinion, or where the initiation of the change does not belong to ourselves, nor the responsibility belong to ourselves, either of the things as they are, or of searching for something better. Many acquiesce in, submit to, 'allow,' a law as it operates upon themselves which they would be horror-struck to have enacted; yet they would gladly and in conscience, 'allow' and submit to it, as part of a constitution under which they live, against which they would never think of rebelling, which they would on no account undermine, for the many blessings of which they are fully grateful—they would be silent and patient rather than join, even in appearance, the disturbers and breakers of its laws. Secondly, he 'acknowledgeth' the same to be agreeable to the Word of God. Some distinctions may be founded upon the word 'acknowledge.' He does not maintain, nor regard it as self-evident, nor originate it as his own feeling, spontaneous opinion, or conviction; but when it is suggested to him, put in a certain shape, when the intention of the framers is borne in mind, their probable purpose and design explained, together with the difficulties which surrounded them, he is not prepared to contradict, and he acknowledges. There is a great deal to be said, which had not at first occurred to him; many other better and wiser men than himself have acknowledged the same thing —why should he be obstinate? Besides, he is young, and has plenty of time to reconsider it; or he is old and continues to submit out of habit, and it would be too absurd, at his time of life, to be setting up as a Church reformer.[83]

[48] But after all, the important phrase is, that the Articles are 'agreeable to the Word of God.' This cannot mean that the Articles are precisely co-extensive with the Bible, much less of equal authority with it as a whole. Neither separately, nor together, do they embody all which is said in it, and inferences which they draw from it are only good relatively and *secundum quid* and *quatenus concordant.* If their terms are Biblical terms, they must be presumed to have the same sense in the Articles which they have in the Scripture; and if they are not all Scriptural ones, they undertake in the pivot Article not to contradict the Scripture. The Articles do not make any assumption of being interpretations of Scripture or developments of it. The greater must include the less, and the Scripture is the greater.[84]

[49] On the other hand, there may be some things in the Articles which could not be contained, or have not been contained, in the Scripture—such as propositions or clauses concerning historical facts more recent than the Scripture itself; for instance, that there never has been any doubt in the Church concerning the books of the New Testament. For without including such doubts as a fool might have, or a very conceited person, without carrying doubts founded upon mere criticism and internal evidence only, to such an extent as a Baur or even an Ewald, there was a time when certain books existed and certain others were not as yet written;—for example, the Epistles of St. Paul were anterior, probably to all of the Gospels, certainly to that of St. John, and of course the Church could not receive without doubt books not as yet composed.[85] But as the canon grew, book after book emerging into existence and general reception, there were doubts as to some of them, for a longer or shorter period, either in their authorship or their authority. The framers of the Articles were not deficient in learning, and could not have been ignorant of the passages in Eusebius where the different books current in Christendom in his time are classified as genuine or acknowledged, doubtful and spurious.[86] If there be an erroneousness in such a statement, as that there never was doubt in the Church concerning the book of the Revelation, the Epistle to the

Hebrews, or the second of St. Peter, it cannot be an erroneousness in the sense of the fifth canon, nor can it be at variance with the Word of God according to the thirty-sixth. Such things in the Articles as are beside the Scripture are not in the contemplation of the canons. Much less can historical questions not even hinted at in the Articles be excluded from free discussion—such as concern the dates and composition of the several books, the compilation of the Pentateuch, the introduction of Daniel into the Jewish canon, and the like with some books of the New Testament—the date and authorship, for instance, of the fourth Gospel.[87]

0] Many of those who would themselves wish the Christian theology to run on in its old forms of expression, nevertheless deal with the opinions of others, which they may think objectionable, fairly as opinions. There will always, on the other hand, be a few whose favourite mode of warfare it will be, to endeavour to gain a victory over some particular person who may hold opinions they dislike, by entangling him in the formularies. Nevertheless, our formularies do not lend themselves very easily to this kind of warfare *Contra retiarium baculo.*[88]

] We have spoken hitherto of the signification of subscription which may be gathered from the canons; there is, also, a statute, a law of the land, which forbids, under penalties, the advisedly and directly contradicting any of them by ecclesiastics, and requires subscription with declaration of 'assent' from beneficed persons. This statute (13 Eliz. c. 12), three hundred years old, like many other old enactments, is not found to be very applicable to modern cases; although it is only about fifty years ago that it was said by Sir William Scott to be *in viridi observantiâ.*[89] Nevertheless, its provisions would not easily be brought to bear on questions likely to be raised in our own days. The meshes are too open for modern refinements. For not to repeat concerning the word 'assent' what has been said concerning 'allow' and 'acknowledge,' let the Articles be taken according to an obvious classification. Forms of expression, partly derived from modern modes of thought on metaphysical subjects, partly suggested by a better acquaintance than heretofore with the unsettled state of Christian opinion in the immediately post-apostolic age, may be adopted with respect to doctrines enunciated in the five first Articles, without directly contradicting, impugning, or refusing assent to them, but passing by the side of them—as with respect to the humanifying of the Divine Word and to the Divine Personalities. Then those which we have called the pivot Articles, concerning the rule of faith and the sufficiency of Scripture, are, happily, found to make no effectual provision for an absolute uniformity, when once the freedom of interpretation of Scripture is admitted; they cannot be considered as interpreting their own interpreter; this has sometimes been called a circular proceeding; it might be resembled to a lever becoming its own fulcrum.[90] The Articles, again, which have a Lutheran and Calvinistic sound, are found to be equally open, because they are, for the most part, founded on the very words of Scripture, and these, while worthy of unfeigned assent, are capable of different interpretations. Indeed, the Calvinistic and Arminian views have been declared by a kind of authority to be both of them tenable under the seventeenth Article; and if the Scriptural terms of 'election' and 'predestination' may be interpreted in an anti-Calvinistic sense, 'faith,' in the tenth and following Articles, need not be understood in the Lutheran. These are instances of legitimate affixing different significations to terms in the Articles, by reason of different interpretations of Scriptural passages.[91]

[52] If, however, the Articles of religion and the law of the Church of England be in effect liberal, flexible, or little stringent, is there any necessity for expressing dissatisfaction with them, any sufficient provocation to change? There may be much more liberty in a Church like our own, the law of which is always interpreted, according to the English spirit, in the manner most favourable to those who are subject to its discipline, than in one which, whether free or not from Articles, might be empowered to develope doctrine and to denounce new heresies. Certainly the late Mr. Irving, if he had been a clergyman of the Church of England, could scarcely have been brought under the terms of any ecclesiastical law of ours, for the expression of opinions upon an abstruse question respecting the humanity of Jesus Christ, which subjected him to degradation in the Presbyterian Church of Scotland.[92] And this transition state may be a state of as much liberty as the Church of England could in any way as yet have been enabled to attain, a state of greater practical liberty than has been attained in Churches supposed to be more free; it is a state of safety and protection to those who use it wisely, under which a farther freedom may be prepared.

[53] But it is not a state which ought to be considered final, either by the Church itself or by the nation. It is very well for provisions which cease to be easily applicable to modern cases to be suffered to fall into desuetude, but after falling into desuetude they should be repealed. Desuetude naturally leads to repeal. Obsolete tests are a blot upon a modern system, and there is always some danger lest an antiquated rule may be unexpectedly revived for the sake of an odious individual application; when it has outlived its general regulative power, it may still be a trap for the weaker consciences; or when it has become powerless as to penal consequences, it may serve to give a point to invidious imputations.

[54] And farther than this, the present apparent stringency of subscription as required of the clergy of the Church of England does not belong to it as part of its foundation, is not even coeval with its reconstruction at the period of the Reformation. For the Canons are of the date 1603, and the Act requiring the public reading of the Thirty-nine Articles, with declaration of assent by a beneficed person after his induction, is the 13th Elizabeth. An enactment prohibiting the bishops from requiring the subscriptions under the third article of the thirty-sixth canon, together with the repeal of 13th Elizabeth, except as to its second section, would relieve many scruples, and make the Church more national, without disturbing its ultimate law. The Articles would then obviously become for the clergy that which they are for the laity of the Church, 'articles of peace, not to be contradicted by her sons,' as the wise and liberal Burnet described them: and there is forcible practical reason for leaving the Thirty-nine Articles as the ultimate law of the Church, not to be contradicted, and for confining relaxation to the abolition of subscription.[93]

55] A large portion of the Articles were originally directed against the corruptions of the Church of Rome, and whatever may be thought of the unadvisableness of retaining tests to exclude opinions which few think of reviving in their old shape, these Roman doctrines and practices are seen to be flourishing in full life and vigour. And considering the many grievous provocations which the people of England have suffered from the Papacy both in ancient and modern times, they would naturally resist any change which might by possibility weaken the barriers between the National Church and the encroachments of the Church of Rome.[94] It is evident, moreover, that the act of signature to the Thirty-nine Articles contributes nothing to the exclusion from the Church of Romish views. For, as it is, opinions and practices prevail among some of the clergy, which are extremely distasteful to the generality of the people, by reason of their Romish character. Those of the Articles which condemn the Romish errors, cannot themselves be made so stringent as to bar altogether the intrusion of some opinion of a Roman tone, which the Reformers, if they could have foreseen it, might have desired to exclude, and which is equally strange and repugnant to the common sense of the nation.[95] No act of subscription can supply this defect of stringency in the formulas themselves. Now it would be impossible to secure the advantages of freedom in one direction without making it equal as far as it goes. We must endeavour to liberate ourselves from the dominion of an unwise and really unchristian principle with the fewest possible risks and inconveniences.

] Considering therefore the practical difficulties which would beset any change, and especially those which would attend, either the excepting of the anti-Romish Articles from repeal or including them in it; any attempt at a relaxation of the clerical test should prudently confine itself in our generation, to an abolition of the act of subscription, leaving the Articles themselves protected by the second section of the Statute of Elizabeth and by the canons, against direct contradiction or impugning.

] For, the act of subscription being abolished, there would disappear the invidious distinction between the clergy and laity of the same communion, as if there were separate standards for each of belief and morals. There would disappear also a semblance of a promissory oath on a subject which a promise is incapable of reaching. No promise can reach fluctuations of opinion and personal conviction.[96] Open teaching can, it is true, if it be thought wise, be dealt with by the law and its penalties; but the law should content itself with saying, you shall not teach or proclaim in derogation of my formularies; it should not require any act which appears to signify 'I think.' Let the security be either the penal or the moral one, not a commingling of the two. It happens continually, that able and sincere persons are deterred from entering the ministry of the national Church by this consideration; they would be willing to be subject to the law forbidding them to teach Arianism or Pelagianism—as what sensible man in our day would desire to teach them?—but they do not like to say, or be thought to say, that they assent to a certain number of anti-Arian and anti-Pelagian propositions.[97] And the absence of vigorous tone—not confined to one party in the Church, which is to be lamented of late years in its ministry, is to be attributed to the reluctance of the stronger minds to enter an Order in which their intellects may not have free play. The very course of preparation for ordination, tied down as it is in one department to the study of the Articles, which must perforce be proved consentaneous to the 'Word of God' according to some, and to 'Catholic antiquity' according to others, has an enervating effect upon the mind, which is compelled to embrace much scholastic matter, not as a history of doctrine, but as a system of truth of which it ought to be convinced.[98]

[58] It may be easy to urge invidiously, with respect to the impediments now existing to undertaking office in the national Church, that there are other sects, which persons dissatisfied with her formularies may join, and where they may find scope for their activity with little intellectual bondage. Nothing can be said here, whether or not there might be elsewhere bondage at least as galling, of a similar or another kind. But the service of the national Church may well be regarded in a different light from the service of a sect. It is as properly an organ of the national life as a magistracy, or a legislative estate. To set barriers before the entrance upon its functions, by limitations not absolutely required by public policy, is to infringe upon the birthright of citizens.[99] And to lay down as an alternative to striving for more liberty of thought and expression within the Church of the nation, that those who are dissatisfied may sever themselves and join a sect, would be paralleled by declaring to political reformers, that they are welcome to expatriate themselves, if they desire any change in the existing forms of the constitution.[100] The supposition of the alternative is an insult; if it could be enforced, it would be a grievous wrong.

[59] There is another part of the subject which may be slightly touched upon in this place—that of the endowment of the national Church. This was well described by Mr. Coleridge as the Nationalty.[101] In a certain sense, indeed, the nation or state is lord paramount over all the property within its boundaries. But it provides for the usufruct of the property in two different ways. The usufruct of private property, as it is called, descends, according to our laws, by inheritance or testamentary disposition, and no specific services are attached to its enjoyment. The usufruct of that which Coleridge called the Nationalty circulates freely among all the families of the nation. The enjoyment of it is subject to the performance of special services, is attainable only by the possession of certain qualifications. In accordance with the strong tendency in England to turn every interest into a right of so-called private property, the nominations to the benefices of the national Church have come, by an abuse, to be regarded as part of the estates of patrons, instead of trusts, as the they really are. No trustee of any analogous property, of a grammar-school for instance, would think of selling his right of appointment; he would consider the proper exercise of the trust his duty; much less would any court of law acknowledge that a beneficial interest in the trust property was an asset belonging to the estate of the trustee. If the nomination to the place of a schoolmaster ought to be considered as purely fiduciary, much more should the nomination of a spiritual

person to his parochial charge. Objections are made against our own national Church founded upon these anomalies, which may in time be rectified. Others are made against the very principle of endowment.[102]

[60] It is said, that a fixed support of the minister tends to paralyse both him and his people—making him independent of his congregation, and drying up their liberality. It would be difficult, perhaps, to say which would be the greater evil, for a minister to be in all things independent of his people, or in all things dependent upon them. But the endowed minister is by no means independent of all restraints, as, for instance, of the law of his Church and, which is much more, of public opinion, especially of the opinion of his own people. The unendowed minister is dependent in all things, both upon the opinion of his people and upon their liberality; and frequent complaints transpire among Nonconformists of the want of some greater fixity in the position and sustentation of their ministers. In the case of a nationally endowed Church, the people themselves contribute little or nothing to its support. The Church of England is said to be the richest Church in Europe, which is probably not true; but its people contribute less to its support than the members of any other Church in Christendom, whether established or voluntary.[103] And if the contributing personally to the support of the ministry were the only form which Christian liberality could take, the stopping up the outflow of it would be an incalculable evil. But it is not so; there are a multitude of other objects, even though the principal minister in a parish or other locality were sufficiently provided for, to give an outlet for Christian liberality. It may flow over from more favoured localities where Churches are sufficiently endowed, into more destitute districts and into distant lands. This is so with ourselves; and those who are familiar with the statistics of the numerous voluntary societies in England for Christian and philanthropic purposes, know to how great an extent the bulk of the support they meet with is derived from the contributions of churchmen. There is reason to think on the other hand, that the means and willingness to give on the part of nonconforming congregations are already mainly exhausted in making provision for their ministers.[104]

[61] Reverting to the general interest in the *Nationalty,* it is evidently twofold. First, in the free circulation of a certain portion of the real property of the country, inherited not by blood, nor through the accident of birth, but by merit and in requital for certain performances. It evidently belongs to the popular interest, that this circulation should be free from all unnecessary limitations and restraints—speculative, antiquarian, and the like, and be regulated, as far as attainable, by fitness and capacity for a particular public service. Thus by means of the national endowment there would take place a distribution of property to every family in the country, *unencumbered by family provisions at each succession*—a distribution in like manner of the best kind of education, of which the effects would not be worn out in one or two generations. The Church theoretically is the most popular, it might be said, the most democratic of all our institutions; its ministers—as a spiritual magistracy—true tribunes of the people.[105] Secondly, the general interest in the

Nationalty as the material means whereby the highest services are obtained for the general good, requires, that no artificial discouragements should limit the number of those who otherwise would be enabled to become candidates for the service of the Church—that nothing should prevent the choice and recruiting of the Church ministers from the whole of the citizens. As a matter of fact we find that nearly one-half of our population are at present more or less alienated from the communion of the national Church, and do not, therefore, supply candidates for its ministry. Instead of securing the excellences and highest attainments from the whole of the people, it secures them, by means of the national reserve, only from one-half; the rest are either not drawn up into the Christian ministry at all, or undertake it in connexion with schismatical bodies, with as much detriment to the national unity, as to the ecclesiastical.[106]

[62] We all know how the inward moral life—or spiritual life on its moral side, if that term be preferred—is nourished into greater or less vigour by means of the conditions in which the moral subject is placed. Hence, if a nation is really worthy of the name, conscious of its own corporate life, it will develop itself on one side into a Church, wherein its citizens may grow up and be perfected in their spiritual nature.[107] If there is within it a consciousness that as a nation it is fulfilling no unimportant office in the world, and is, under the order of Providence, an instrument in giving the victory to good over evil and to happiness over misery, it will not content itself with the rough adjustments and rude lessons of law and police, but will throw its elements, or the best of them, into another mould, and constitute out of them a society, which is in it, though in some sense not of it—which is another, yet the same.[108]

[63] That each one born into the nation is, together with his civil rights, born into a membership or privilege, as belonging to a spiritual society, places him at once in a relation which must tell powerfully upon his spiritual nature.[109] For the sake of the reaction upon its own merely secular interests, the nation is entitled to provide from time to time, that the Church teaching and forms of one age do not traditionally harden, so as to become exclusive barriers in a subsequent one, and so the moral growth of those who are committed to the hands of the Church be checked, or its influences confined to a comparatively few. And the objects of the care of the State and of the Church will nearly coincide; for the former desires all its people to be brought under the improving influence, and the latter is willing to embrace all who have even the rudiments of the moral life.

[64] And if the objects of the care of each nearly coincide, when the office of the Church is properly understood, so errors and mistakes in defining Church-membership, or in constituting a repulsive mode of Church teaching, are fatal to the purposes both of Church and State alike.

[65] It is a great misrepresentation to exhibit the State as allying itself with one out of many sects—a misrepresentation, the blame of which does not rest wholly with political persons, nor with the partisans of sects adverse to that which is supposed to be unduly preferred. It cannot concern a State to develop as part of its own

organization a machinery or system of relations founded on the possession of speculative truth. Speculative doctrines should be left to philosophical schools. A national Church must be concerned with the ethical development of its members. And the wrong of supposing it to be otherwise, is participated by those of the clericalty who consider the Church of Christ to be founded, as a society, on the possession of an abstractedly true and supernaturally communicated speculation concerning God, rather than upon the manifestation of a divine life in man.

[66] It has often been made matter of reproach to the heathen State religions, that they took little concern in the moral life of the citizens. To a certain extent this is true, for the heathens of classical history had not generally the same conceptions of morals as we have.[110] But as far as their conceptions of morals reached, their Church and State were mutually bound together, not by a material alliance, nor by a gross compact of pay and preferment passing between the civil society and the priesthood, but by the penetrating of the whole public and domestic life of the nation with a religious sentiment. All the social relations were consecrated by the feeling of their being entered into and carried on under the sanction—under the very impulse of Deity. Treaties and boundaries, buying and selling, marrying, judging, deliberating on affairs of State, spectacles and all popular amusements, were under the protection of Divinity; all life was a worship. It can very well be understood how philosophers should be esteemed atheists, when they began to speculate upon origins, causes, abstract being, and the like.

[67] Certainly the sense of the individual conscience was not sufficiently developed under those old religions. Their observances, once penetrated with a feeling of present Deity, became, in course of time, mere dry and superstitious forms. But the glory of the Gospel would only be partial and one-sided, if, while quickening the individual conscience and the expectation of individual immortality, it had no spirit to quicken the national life. An isolated salvation, the rescuing of one's self, the reward, the grace bestowed on one's own labours, the undisturbed repose, the crown of glory in which so many have no share, the finality of the sentence on both hands—reflections on such expectations as these may make stubborn martyrs and sour professors, but not good citizens; rather tend to unfit men for this world, and in so doing prepare them very ill for that which is to come.[111]

[68] But in order to the possibility of recruiting any national ministry from the whole of the nation, in order to the operation upon the nation at large of the special functions of its Church, no needless intellectual or speculative obstacles should be interposed. It is not to be expected that terms of communion could be made so large, as by any possibility to comprehend in the national Church the whole of such a free nation as our own. There will always be those who, from a conscientious scruple, or from a desire to define, or from peculiarities of temper, will hold aloof from the religion and the worship of the majority; and it is not desirable that it should be otherwise, so long as the national unity and the moral action of society are not thereby seriously impaired. No doubt, speaking politically, and regarding merely the peacefulness with which the machinery of ordinary executive govern-

ment can be carried on, it has proved very advantageous to the State, that an Established Church has existed in this country, to receive the shafts which otherwise might have been directed against itself. Ill-humour has evaporated harmlessly in Dissent, which might otherwise have materially deranged the body politic; and village Hampdens have acquired a parochial renown, sufficient to satisfy their ambition, in resistance to a Church-rate, whose restlessness might have urged them to dispute, even to prison and spoiling of their goods, the lawfulness of a war-tax.[112] But whatever root of conscientiousness and truth-seeking there has been in non-conformity, whatever amount of indirect good is produced by the emulation of the different religious bodies, whatever safety to social order by the escapement for temper so provided—the moral influence of the better people in their several neighbourhoods is neutralized or lost for want of harmony and concentration, when the alienation from the national Church reaches the extent which it has done in our country. Even in the more retired localities, industry, cleanliness, decency in the homes of the poor, school discipline and truthfulness, are encouraged far less than they might otherwise be, by reason of the absence of religious unanimity in the superior classes.[113] And if the points of speculation and of form which separate Dissenters from the Church of England were far more important than they are, and the approximative truth preponderatingly upon the side of Dissent, it would do infinitely more harm by the dissention which it creates, than it possibly could accomplish of good, by a greater correctness in doctrine and ecclesiastical constitution. If this statement concerns Dissent itself on one side, it concerns the Church on the other, or rather those who so limit the terms of its communion as to provoke, and—as human beings are constituted—to necessitate separation from it. It is stated by Neal,[114] that if the alterations in the Prayer-book, recommended by the Commissioners of 1689 had been adopted, it would 'in all probability have brought in three parts in four of the Dissenters.' No such result could be expected from any 'amendments' or 'concessions' now. Much less could anything be hoped for, by means of a 'Conference.' But it concerns the State, on the highest grounds of public policy, to rectify, as far as possible, the mistakes committed in former times by itself or by the Church under its sanction; and without aiming at an universal comprehension, which would be Utopian, to suffer the perpetuation of no unnecessary barriers excluding from the communion or the ministry of the national Church.

[69] There are, moreover, besides those who have joined the ranks of Dissent, many others holding aloof from the Church of England, by reason of its real or supposed dogmatism—whose co-operation in its true work would be most valuable to it—and who cannot become utterly estranged from it, without its losing ultimately its popular influence and its national character. If those who distinguish themselves in science and literature cannot, in a scientific and literary age, be effectually and cordially attached to the Church of their nation, they must sooner or later be driven into a position of hostility to it. They may be as indisposed to the teaching of the majority of Dissenters as to that which they conceive to be the teaching of the

Church; but the Church, as an organization, will of necessity appear to be the most damaged by a scientific criticism of a supposed Christianity common to it with other bodies. Many personal and social bonds have retarded hitherto an issue which from time to time has threatened a controversy between our science and our theology. It would be a deplorable day, when the greatest names on either side should be found in conflict; and theology should only learn to acknowledge, after a defeat, that there are no irreconcileable differences between itself and its opponents.[115]

70] It is sometimes said with a sneer, that the scientific men and the men of abstractions will never change the religions of the world; and yet Christianity has certainly been very different from what it would have been without the philosophies of a Plato and an Aristotle; and a Bacon and a Newton exercise an influence upon the Biblical theology of Englishmen.[116] They have modified, though they have not made it. The more diffused science of the present day will farther modify it. And the question seems to narrow itself to this—How can those who differ from each other intellectually in such variety of degrees as our more educated and our less educated classes, be comprised under the same formularies of one national Church—be supposed to follow them, assent to them, appropriate them, in one spirit? If such formularies embodied only an ethical result addressed to the individual and to society, the speculative difficulty would not arise. But as they present a fair and substantial representation of the Biblical records, incorporating their letter and presupposing their historical element, precisely the same problem is presented to us intellectually, as English Churchmen or as Biblical Christians.

71] It does not seem to be contradicted, that when Church formularies adopt the words of Scripture, these must have the same meaning, and be subject to the same questions, in the formularies, as in the Scripture. And we may go somewhat farther and say, that the historical parts of the Bible, when referred to or presupposed in the formularies, have the same *value* in them which they have in their original seat; and this *value* may consist, rather in their significance, in the ideas which they awaken, than in the scenes themselves which they depict. And as Churchmen, or as Christians, we may vary as to their value in particulars—that is, as to the extent of the verbal accuracy of a history, or of its spiritual significance, without breaking with our communion, or denying our sacred name. These varieties will be determined partly by the peculiarities of men's mental constitution, partly by the nature of their education, circumstances, and special studies. And neither should the idealist condemn the literalist, nor the literalist assume the right of excommunicating the idealist.[117] They are really fed with the same truths; the literalist unconsciously, the idealist with reflection. Neither can justly say of the other that he under-values the Sacred Writings, or that he holds them as inspired less properly than himself.

72] The application of ideology to the interpretation of Scripture, to the doctrines of Christianity, to the formularies of the Church, may undoubtedly be carried to an excess—may be pushed so far as to leave in the sacred records no historical residue whatever. On the other side, there is the excess of a dull and unpainstaking acquiescence, satisfied with accepting in an unquestioning spirit, and as if they were literally facts, all particulars of a wonderful history, because in some sense it is from God. Between these extremes lie infinite degrees of rational and irrational interpretation.[118]

[73] It will be observed that the ideal method is applicable in two ways; both to giving account of the origin of parts of Scripture, and also in explanation of Scripture. It is thus either critical or exegetical. An example of the critical ideology carried to excess is that of Strauss, which resolves into an ideal the whole of the historical and doctrinal person of Jesus; so again, much of the allegorizing of Philo and Origen is an exegetical ideology, exaggerated and wild. But it by no means follows, because Strauss has substituted a mere shadow for the Jesus of the Evangelists, and has frequently descended to a minute captiousness in details, that there are not traits in the scriptural person of Jesus, which are better explained by referring them to an ideal than an historical origin: and without falling into fanciful exegetics, there are parts of Scripture more usefully interpreted ideologically than in any other manner—as, for instance, the history of the temptation of Jesus by Satan, and accounts of demoniacal possessions. And liberty must be left to all as to the extent in which they apply the principle, for there is no authority, through the expressed determination of the Church, nor of any other kind, which can define the limits within which it may be reasonably exercised.[119]

[74] Thus some may consider the descent of all mankind from Adam and Eve as an undoubted historical fact; others may rather perceive in that relation a form of narrative, into which in early ages tradition would easily throw itself spontaneously. Each race naturally—necessarily, when races are isolated—supposes itself to be sprung from a single pair, and to be the first, or the only one, of races. Among a particular people this historical representation became the concrete expression of a great moral truth—of the brotherhood of all human beings, of their community, as in other things, so also in suffering and in frailty, in physical pains and in moral 'corruption.' And the force, grandeur, and reality of these ideas are not a whit impaired in the abstract, nor indeed the truth of the concrete history as their representation, even though mankind should have been placed upon the earth in many pairs at once, or in distinct centres of creation. For the brotherhood of men really depends, not upon the material fact of their fleshly descent from a single stock, but upon their constitution, as possessed in common, of the same faculties and affections, fitting them for mutual relation and association; so that the value of the history, if it were a history strictly so called, would lie in its emblematic force and application.[120] And many narratives of marvels and catastrophes in the Old Testament are referred to in the New, as emblems, without either denying or asserting their literal truth—such as the destruction of Sodom and Gomorrah by fire from heaven, and the Noachian deluge. And especially if we bear in mind the existence of such a school as that which produced Philo, or even the author of the Epistle to the Hebrews, we must think it would be wrong to lay down, that

whenever the New Testament writers refer to Old Testament histories, they imply of necessity that the historic truth was the first to them. For their purposes it was often wholly in the background, and the history, valuable only in its spiritual application. The same may take place with ourselves, and history and tradition be employed emblematically, without, on that account, being regarded as untrue. We do not apply the term 'untrue' to parable, fable, or proverb, although their words correspond with ideas, not with material facts; as little should we do so, when narratives have been the spontaneous product of true ideas, and are capable of reproducing them.[121]

[75] The ideologian is evidently in possession of a principle which will enable him to stand in charitable relation to persons of very different opinions from his own, and of very different opinions mutually. And if he has perceived to how great extent the history of the origin itself of Christianity rests ultimately upon *probable* evidence, his principle will relieve him from many difficulties which might otherwise be very disturbing. For relations which may repose on doubtful grounds as matters of history, and, as history, be incapable of being ascertained or verified, may yet be equally suggestive of true ideas with facts absolutely certain. The spiritual significance is the same of the transfiguration, of opening blind eyes, of causing the tongue of the stammerer to speak plainly, of feeding multitudes with bread in the wilderness, of cleansing leprosy, whatever links may be deficient in the traditional record of particular events.[122] Or, let us suppose one to be uncertain, whether our Lord were born of the house and lineage of David, or of the tribe of Levi, and even to be driven to conclude that the genealogies of Him have little historic value; nevertheless, in idea, Jesus is both Son of David and Son of Aaron, both Prince of Peace and High Priest of our profession; as He is, under another idea, though not literally, 'without father and without mother.' And He is none the less Son of David, Priest Aaronical, or Royal Priest Melchizedecan, in idea and spiritually, even if it be unproved, whether He were any of them in historic fact. In like manner it need not trouble us, if, in consistency, we should have to suppose both an ideal origin and to apply an ideal meaning to the birth in the city of David, and to other circumstances of the infancy. So, again, the incarnification of the divine Immanuel remains, although the angelic appearances which herald it in the narratives of the Evangelists may be of ideal origin according to the conceptions of former days. The ideologian may sometimes be thought sceptical, and be sceptical or doubtful, as to the historical value of related facts; but the historical value is not always to him the most important; frequently it is quite secondary. And, consequently, discrepancies in narratives, scientific difficulties, defects in evidence, do not disturb him as they do the literalist.[123]

[76] Moreover, the same principle is capable of application to some of those inferences which have been the source, according to different theologies, of much controversial acrimony and of wide ecclesiastical separations; such as those which have been drawn from the institution of the sacraments. Some, for instance, cannot conceive a presence of Jesus Christ in His institution of the Lord's Supper, unless

it be a corporeal one, nor a spiritual influence upon the moral nature of man to be connected with baptism, unless it be supernatural, quasi-mechanical, effecting a psychical change then and there. But within these concrete conceptions there lie hid the truer ideas of the virtual presence of the Lord Jesus everywhere that He is preached, remembered, and represented, and of the continual force of His spirit in His words, and especially in the ordinance which indicates the separation of the Christian from the world.[124]

[77] The same may be said of the concrete conceptions of an hierarchy described by its material form and descent; also of millenarian expectations of a personal reign of the saints with Jesus upon earth, and of the many embodiments in which from age to age has reappeared the vision of a New Jerusalem shining with mundane glory here below. These gross conceptions, as they seem to some, may be necessary to others, as approximations to true ideas. So, looking for redemption in Israel was a looking for a very different redemption, with most of the Jewish people, from that which Jesus really came to operate, yet it was the only expectation which they could form, and was the shadow to them of a great reality.

> 'Lo, the poor Indian, whose untutored mind,
> Sees God in clouds, or hears Him in the wind.'[125]

Even to the Hebrew Psalmist, He comes flying upon the wings of the wind; and only to the higher Prophet is He not in the wind, nor in the earthquake, nor in the fire, but in 'the still small voice.' Not the same thoughts—very far from the same thoughts—pass through the minds of the more and the less instructed on contemplating the same face of the natural world. In like manner are the thoughts of men various, in form at least, if not in substance, when they read the same Scripture histories and use the same Scripture phrases. Histories to some, become parables to others; and facts to those, are emblems to these. The 'rock' and the 'cloud' and the 'sea' convey to the Christian admonitions of spiritual verities; and so do the ordinances of the Church and various parts of its forms of worship.[126]

[78] Jesus Christ has not revealed His religion as a theology of the intellect, nor as an historical faith; and it is a stifling of the true Christian life, both in the individual and in the Church, to require of many men a unanimity in speculative doctrine, which is unattainable, and a uniformity of historical belief, which can never exist. The true Christian life is the consciousness of bearing a part in a great moral order, of which the highest agency upon earth has been committed to the Church. Let us not oppress this work nor complicate the difficulties with which it is surrounded; 'not making the heart of the righteous sad, whom the Lord hath not made sad, nor strengthening the hands of the wicked by promising him life.'[127]

[79] There is enough indeed to sadden us in the doubtful warfare which the good wages with the evil, both within us and without us. How few, under the most favourable conditions, learn to bring themselves face to face with the great moral law, which is the manifestation of the Will of God! The greater part can only detect

the evil when it comes forth from them, nearly as when any other might observe it. We cannot, in the matter of those who are brought under the highest influences of the Christian Church, any more than in the case of mankind viewed in their ordinary relations, give any account of the apparently useless expenditure of power—of the apparent overbearing generally of the higher law by the lower—of the apparent poverty of result from the operation of a wonderful machinery—of the seeming waste of myriads of germs, for the sake of a few mature growths. 'Many are called but few chosen'—and under the privileges of the Christian Church, as in other mysteries,—

πολλοὶ μὲν ναρθηκοφόροι, βάκχοι δέ γε παῦροι.[128]

o] Calvinism has a keen perception of this truth; and we shrink from Calvinism and Augustinianism, not because of their perceiving how few, even under Christian privileges, attain to the highest adoption of sons; but because of the inferences with which they clog that truth—the inferences which they draw respecting the rest, whom they comprehend in one mass of perdition.[129]

] The Christian Church can only tend on those who are committed to its care, to the verge of that abyss which parts this world from the world unseen. Some few of those fostered by her are now ripe for entering on a higher career: the many are but rudimentary spirits—germinal souls. What shall become of them? If we look abroad in the world and regard the neutral character of the multitude, we are at a loss to apply to them, either the promises, or the denunciations of revelation. So, the wise heathens could anticipate a reunion with the great and good of all ages; they could represent to themselves, at least in a figurative manner, the punishment and the purgatory of the wicked; but they would not expect the reappearance in another world, for any purpose, of a Thersites or an Hyperbolos—social and poetical justice had been sufficiently done upon them. Yet there are such as these, and no better than these, under the Christian name—babblers, busy-bodies, livers to get gain, and mere eaters and drinkers. The Roman Church has imagined a limbus infantium; we must rather entertain a hope that there shall be found, after the great adjudication, receptacles suitable for those who shall be infants, not as to years of terrestrial life, but as to spiritual development—nurseries as it were and seed-grounds, where the undeveloped may grow up under new conditions—the stunted may become strong, and the perverted be restored. And when the Christian Church, in all its branches, shall have fulfilled its sublunary office, and its Founder shall have surrendered His kingdom to the Great Father—all, both small and great, shall find a refuge in the bosom of the Universal Parent, to repose, or be quickened into higher life, in the ages to come, according to his Will.[130]

4 Notes to Henry Bristow Wilson

1. In 1815 the Congress of Vienna restored the sovereignty of Switzerland: in the same year the canton of Geneva was admitted into the Swiss confederacy. In the ensuing years there was continual struggle between the Protestant cantons (such as Geneva) and the Catholic cantons, which were aligned with the restoration of the power of the Jesuits and the former secular authorities. Hence, the "rude shocks . . . of late years" Wilson refers to are both political and ecclesiastical.

In 1842 the city of Geneva got a liberal constitution; in 1845 seven Catholic cantons organized as a *Sonderbund* (league of protection) to oppose the liberals. A one-month war ensued in 1847, in which the European powers, France, Austria, and Prussia, sided with the Catholic cantons. Britain, on the other hand, supported the Protestants: Lord Palmerston, the British foreign secretary, took control of the European nations' policy against Switzerland, so that, by delaying tactics, he prevented military intervention until the war was over. On 12 September 1848 a new constitution replaced the pact of 1815, organizing Switzerland as a federal union.

The Neuchâtel problem, concerning the relations between that canton and the royalist claims to the territory by the Prussian ruler, Friedrich Wilhelm IV, continued from 1848 to 1857 as a struggle between the republicans and the monarchists and was finally settled when the absolute independence of Neuchâtel from Prussia was assured at the Conference of Paris in 1857.

Throughout all of this period Britain, together with France and Prussia, was involved in these "rude shocks." Baron von Bunsen had been Prussian ambassador in Switzerland and was active as ambassador in London in both furthering the Prussian cause as well as supporting the British government's policy of nonintervention to maintain Switzerland as a control for the balance of power among the European nations. Switzerland, on the other hand, had to muster military strength to protect the neutrality of its borders frequently during the period, as, for example, during the Italian war of 1859. For Anglo-Swiss relations between 1845–60 in relation to Switzerland's political neutrality, see Imlah 1966.

The "severest creed of the Reformation" refers to Calvinism, the theological and ecclesiastical version of Christianity that John Calvin introduced into Geneva from 1536 to 1538. As Wilhelm Oechsli comments, his religious and political prescriptions were embodied in the Ordinances of 1541 that established Geneva as a theocracy under his leadership: "The purpose of the State was to secure purity both of doctrine and of morals, since to think wrongly and to act wrongly were alike rebellion against God. The moral laws enacted under his influence exceeded in severity anything effected in such matters in the other Swiss towns" (1922, 158). For a detailed account of Geneva at the time of Calvin see Monter [1967] 1975.

The Calvinist reformed church in Geneva, and in Switzerland, underwent a "second Reformation" under Jean Alphonse Turretin, its "second founder" (Wilson 1857, 97), in the early eighteenth century, and a third period of reorganization in the early nineteenth century, one that concerned English theologians because of its realignment of the relations between church and state. In *Principles of Church Reform* (1833), Thomas Arnold comments: "At this moment the mischief in Geneva consists in the enforcement of the exclusive principle, not in its abandonment: the Church is now exclusively Arian or Socinian, as it once was exclusively Calvinistic; and Trinitarian ministers are not allowed to teach to their congregations the great and peculiar doctrines of Christianity" ([1833] 1962, 149–50).

"Evangelical principles" here refers to the Lutheran branches of Christianity. The term *evangelical* in the nineteenth century is fraught with contradictions that cross national borders, contradictions that Wilson exploits to score points against political and theological opponents in England. For a recent discussion of relations between Geneva and British Evangelicals see Stunt 1981.

In general, "evangelical" refers to Protestant claims of basing all doctrinal positions on the gospel (Gk. εὐαγγέλιον, *evangelion*). The Evangelical Church (*Evangelische Kirche*) was formed in 1817 in Prussia by the union of Lutheran and Reformed denominations. The reformed churches were those of France and Germany that followed a strictly Calvinist doctrine and ecclesiastical organization. In Germany and Switzerland "evangelical" was associated more closely with the Lutheran groups of Protestant churches, differentiating them from the reformed, or Calvinist, churches. In England "evangelical" is associated with the Methodist movement, and with the Low Church in the C. of E., in opposition to the High Church, or Oxford Movement. The Evangelical Alliance, formed in London in 1846, was an interdenominational and international association of like-minded Protestants; in September 1857 Friedrich Wilhelm IV summoned a meeting of the Alliance in Berlin.

Wilson refers specifically to English Evangelicalism in ¶s 40 ff.

2. The "series of addresses" was published in

three volumes: *Le Christianisme aux trois premiers siècles: Séances historiques données à Genève en Février, Mars et Avril 1857 par MM. Merle d'Aubigné, Bungener, de Gasparin et Viguet* (1857; Christianity in the first three centuries: historical sessions given at Geneva in February, March and April 1857 by . . .); *Le Christianisme au quatrième siècle: Constantin, Ambroise, Augustin. Séances historiques (Seconde Série) données à Genève en Mars 1858 par MM. de Gasparin, Bungener et de Pressensé* (1858; Christianity in the fourth century: Constantine, Ambrose, Augustine. Historical Sessions [Second Series] delivered in Geneva in March 1858 by . . .); and *Le Christianisme au moyen-age: Innocent III: Séances historiques (Troisième Série)* (1859; Christianity in the Middle Ages: Innocent III: Historical Sessions).

The "period of the fall of heathenism" refers to the formal adoption of Christianity in the Roman Empire.

3. Agénor Étienne Léon, comte de Gasparin retired from politics in 1846 and published a series of books on French Protestantism. He contributed a lecture on Constantine to the first series of *Séances historiques* and two lectures on the same topic to the second series. He also published *La Question de Neufchâtel* (1857; The Neuchâtel question).

Constantine (274/288–337), Roman emperor from 312 when he defeated Maxentius at the Milvian Bridge, adopted Christianity as a tolerated religion of the Roman Empire from 313 and sought increasingly to develop close links between Christianity and the state. He presided at the Council of Nicaea (325) to deal with the heresy of Arianism. He was baptized as a Christian on his deathbed. Lecture 6 of A. P. Stanley's *Lectures on the History of the Eastern Church*, given in 1857, is "The Emperor Constantine" ([1861] 1924, 197–225). For discussions of Constantine's conversion see A. H. M. Jones 1948; Dörries 1960; and Timothy David Barnes 1981.

4. The *OED* records this as the first use of "multitudinism" in English: "the principle according to which the interests of multitudes are placed before those of individuals, *esp.* in religion."

Gasparin uses the terms *individualism* and *multitudinism* in a less straightforward manner than Wilson implies, to distinguish personal conversion on "the true basis of the Church" in Christian scripture ("individualism") and the pagan state religions of the Roman Empire, with its bureaucracy and armies ("multitudinism").

5. Laurent Louis Félix Bungener took an active part in the struggles in Geneva, taking the antiliberal side. He published two lectures on Ambrose in *Le Christianisme au quatrième siècle* (1858).

Ambrose is one of the four traditional "doctors" of the Western church. His treatise *De Officiis Ministrorum* (Concerning the office of ministers) converts the Ciceronian and stoical concept of devotion to the state to devotion to God. He is known for having combated paganism, and in his disputes with the Roman authorities, including those with the emperors, he tried to pursue an independent role for the church.

Theodosius I (known as the great) was Roman emperor from 379 to 395. He continued the imperial policies of establishing Christianity as the state religion: Arianism and other heresies became legal offenses and paganism was forbidden. After he perpetrated a massacre at Thessalonica (390), Theodosius submitted to Ambrose as a penitent, an act that has come to symbolize the church's supremacy in morals and religion.

6. For "first Christian emperor," see Stanley's lecture on Constantine "as the first Christian Emperor" ([1861] 1924, 200). Stanley also uses the phrase in citing J. S. Mill: "'It is one of the most tragical facts of all history,' says Mr. Mill, 'that Constantine, rather than Marcus Aurelius was the first Christian Emperor.'" (197).

J. S. Mill in 1859 discussed the differences between Constantine and Marcus Aurelius concerning the latter's persecution of Christianity in *On Liberty* (1963–91, 18:237).

7. "Theocracy," a coinage of Josephus, refers to a political system in which a deity, represented by the monarch, is the ruler of the state. Josephus in *Against Apion* applies the term particularly to the monarchy in ancient Israel under the house of David, which lasted from 931 to 586 B.C.E. (bk. 2, chap. 16; trans. H. St. John Thackeray, *Loeb* 1:358). The term is also associated with Calvin's government in Geneva. Calvin discusses "Civil Government" in the last chapter of *Institutes* (see Calvin [1536] 1957, 2:650–75; bk. 4, chap. 20). "Theocracy" is applied to Cromwell's Commonwealth in England (1649–60) by Milton in the *Defensio Prima* (1651; The first defense, see Milton [1651] 1932, 137).

Acts 2 records "the preaching of Peter" on "the day of Pentecost," the day memorialized for the inauguration of the Christian Church. Immediately the apostles began to preach and to baptize. Peter preached that "whosoever shall call on the name of the Lord shall be saved" (Acts 2:21), urging that such persons "repent, and be baptized" (2:38), without the personal experience of conversion that "modern Evangelical" Christianity advocated as a necessary preliminary step. For "the three thousand" see Acts 2:41; "converted," Acts 3:19.

Wilson's argument and biblical example, as he indicates, are taken directly from Bungener (*Le Christianisme* 1858, 146–54). Gasparin, agreeing with Bungener, argues that from the time that Christianity became an official religion in the Roman Empire, faith did not depend on individual conversion but became collective and hereditary (*Le Christianisme* 1858, 12–13).

8. "Individualism" is the political, social, and religious theory that advocates the organization of

human societies according to the free actions and conduct of individual persons acting independently, as opposed to the agreements and conditions of the collectivity. According to Raymond Williams "the development" of individualism "corresponds to the main movement of liberal political and economic thought" of the nineteenth century (1976, 164). It was first applied in the 1820s by conservative and counter-Revolutionary French thinkers to an Enlightenment appeal to reason and to individual rights and self-interest.

Thomas Arnold, writing on the period 1827–33 in *Fragments on Church and State*, formulates an early Broad Church position on "individualism" in the relations between church, state, and the individual: "Individuals, in a political sense, are necessarily members; as distinct from the body, they are nothing. Against society, they have no political rights whatever, and their belonging to society or not is a matter not of their own choice, but determined for them by their being born and bred members of it" (1845, 52–53).

Contemporaneous with *Essays and Reviews*, J. S. Mill demarcates political individualism based on "Liberty of the will" and his chief subject, "Civil, or Social Liberty: the nature and limits of the power which can be legitimately exercised by society over the individual" (1963–91, 18:217). In the same year Samuel Smiles praised the "energetic individualism which produces the most powerful effects upon the life and actions of others, and really constitutes the best practical education" (Smiles [1859] 1906, 7). For another contemporaneous discussion see Simpson 1858; for recent discussions of Victorian individualism see Swart 1962; and Taylor 1992. In Tocqueville's negative formulation in *Democracy in America* (1835–39), "individualism," distinguished from "egotism," is collapsed not into a sense of the collective (as Wilson argues) but rather with an extreme form of isolation (Pt. 2, bk. 2, chap. 2; 1899, 2:106). For a recent study comparing French and American concepts of individualism see Higonnet 1989.

In nineteenth-century America "individualism" was identified variously and positively with the personalist ideals of the founders, together with Puritanism, the religious and political ideals of Jefferson, the philosophy of natural rights, Emersonian naturalism and transcendentalism, and the notions of personal salvation in evangelical religion. Epitomized in Walt Whitman's *Democratic Vistas* (1871), it came to be aligned with personal success and self-determination (epitomized in the novels of Horatio Alger) and with American business ethic, as in the first chapter of *Individualism versus Socialism* (1907) by Andrew Carnegie and Henry Clews, in which they discussed "that system of Individualism which guards, protects and encourages competition . . . the American Spirit—the love of freedom,—of free industry, free and unfettered opportunity." For a discussion of the American individualism see Arieli 1964.

Theological individualism identifies the theology and practice of the gospels and the early church with acts of individual conversion and profession and stresses the right and duty of the individual to enter into direct communion with God. As a policy of relations between church and state, the term is associated particularly with Alexandre R. Vinet, of the Swiss canton of Vaud, promoter of the Free Church Movement, who advocated a principle of ecclesiastical individualism wherein the church is conceptualized entirely on the basis of volunteer adherence to a confession of faith. See Vinet 1849. For recent discussions of theological individualism see Mouw 1982; Dumont 1982; and Schinder 1989.

In summarizing Bungener, Wilson considerably simplifies the former's argument. Bungener introduces "Multitudinism" with a series of qualifications: "Entre la question historique de l'union de l'Eglise et de l'Empire, telle que l'inaugura Constantin, et la question générale, je ne dis pas de l'Eglise *unie* à l'Etat, mais du nationalisme religieux, ou, pour élargir encore les termes, du *multitudinisme*, comme on dit" (*Le Christianisme* 1858, 147; Between the historical question of the union of the church and the empire, such as Constantine inaugurated it, and the general question; I do not speak of the church *united* to the state, but of religious nationalism, or, to enlarge the terms further, of multitudinism, so to speak). Gasparin, on the other hand, argues that the church under Constantine became united with the state, disappearing "pour se confondre avec le monde, la coïncidence de la société civile et de la société religieuse . . . l'adoption officielle de l'Eglise par l'empereur (*Le Christianisme* 1858, 38; In conforming itself to the world, the coincidence of civil society and of religious society . . . the official adoption of the church by the emperor).

9. *Séances Historiques de Genève—Le Christianisme au 4ième Siècle*, p. 153 [Wilson's note].

Le Christianisme 1858, 153. (Multitudinism is a force that can, like all force, be badly directed and badly exploited, but it is able also to be of profit to the truth, to piety, and to life. The churches founded on another principle have helped to correct the former [bad uses of multitudinism]; that is one of the incontrovertible services that they have rendered, in our times, to the Evangelical cause. They deserve our recognition; but let the Genevan church not ask us what we are not able to do, and, if you will permit me to say it, what they do not themselves do. Yes! Genevan multitudinism remains living among them, and certainly they owe to it a notable part of their internal consistency and their external influence. They make an appeal, like us, to its memories and to its glories: they form, with us, what the Christian world calls and will call always *the Church of Geneva*. We do not renounce her, fundamentally, any more for the one than for the other. She has been, she is, and she will remain for ever the mother of us all).

10. John Calvin was born in Picardy, studied in Paris for the Roman Catholic priesthood, but abandoned it and fled to Basle in Switzerland where he wrote *Institutes of the Christian Religion* (1536). He advocated an extreme form of Lutheran beliefs concerning sin and salvation: that the Bible is the only rule of faith; that free will is abrogated after the Fall of Adam; that justification is accomplished by faith, not by good works; that grace is irresistible; that the elect cannot defect from their vocation; and that the elect are predestined to salvation, the reprobate to damnation. Calvin led the reformation in Geneva, inaugurating strict conformity to his rigorous discipline. Bungener published *Calvin: sa vie, son oeuvre et ses écrits* (1863). For contemporaneous discussions of Calvin see Emil 1849; and Dyer 1855. Mark Pattison published "Calvin at Geneva" in the *Westminster Review* (1858; see Pattison 1889, 2:1–41), a review of Bonnet's edition of Calvin's *Lettres receuillies pour la première fois* (1854) and Gaberel's *Histoire de l' Église de Genève* (1855). Pattison also cites Dyer, as providing "the usual ecclesiastical narrative of these transactions" (1889, 2:11). For recent studies see Bousma 1988; and McGrath 1990.

Among the events for which the Genevans "cannot be proud of their Calvin" was the use he made of excommunication, the suppression of opposition from the *Enfants de Genève* by executions (1555), and the trials conducted for heresy, including that of Michael Servetus, whose burning at the stake "earned immediate notoriety throughout Protestant Europe as a test case in religious persecution" (Monter [1967] 1975, 84). Pattison acknowledges that an "illogical spirit of Protestant tyranny is seen embodied in the person and institutions of Calvin," but argues a "strange paradox, that in the suppression of the liberties of Geneva was sown the seed of liberty in Europe" (1889, 2:5–6).

11. For "'rude forefathers'" see Thomas Gray, "Elegy Written in a Country Churchyard" (1751), l. 16; "a time . . . a time," Eccles. 3:1–17; "building up . . . places," Isa. 58:12; "ancient paths," Jer. 18:15.

To draw parallels between early Christianity and English "nationality," Wilson aligns four oppositional pairs: Jesus and the apostles against their Jewish opponents; the Christians against "the Romans in the time of Theodosius," who opposed Christianity in the Roman Empire; Wycliffe against the opponents of the English Bible; and Cranmer against the opponents of the English Reformation.

John Wycliffe translated the Bible into English with Nicholas of Hereford and John Purvey in the early fifteenth century. The Council of Oxford (1407) forbade translating any portion of the Bible and making use of any translation undertaken "in the times of John Wycliffe or since" without ecclesiastical approval. Thomas Cranmer negotiated the ecclesiastical separation of the Anglican Church from the Church of Rome following the annulment of the marriage of Henry VIII to Katherine of Aragon and his marriage to Anne Boleyn. Cranmer advocated the public reading of the Bible in English, was largely responsible for the Prayer Book of 1549 (the basis of the *B.C.P.* enjoined by the Act of Uniformity, 1662), and drafted the Forty-two Articles of Religion (1553), on which the Thirty-nine Articles (1563) are based. He was burned at the stake in Oxford in 1556 during the reign of Mary Tudor.

For "meddle not . . . change" see Prov. 24:21; "'damnable heresies,'" 2 Pet. 2:1; "'old things are to pass away,'" 2 Cor. 5:17; "'heresy' . . . God of the Fathers," Acts 24:14.

12. For "signs of the times" see Matt. 16:3. Thomas Carlyle published "Signs of the Times" (1829), where he argues: "The thinking minds of all nations call for change. There is a deep-lying struggle in the whole fabric of society; a boundless grinding collision of the New with the Old" (1896–99, 27:82).

13. For "Men have run . . . increased" see Dan. 12:4.

"Well-meaning persons" are the English followers of the positivism of Auguste Comte, who published *Cours de philosophie positive* (1830–42; trans. Harriet Martineau, *Course of Positive Philosophy*, 1853, 2 vols.), advocating the application of the rational principles of empirical science to all aspects of human life in a kind of secular religion. Comte divided human thought into three stages: theology (explaining phenomena on the basis of the supernatural), metaphysics, (explaining them by abstraction), and positive science (explaining by scientific laws), with the transition to the third stage taking place during the nineteenth century. His ideas influenced George Henry Lewes, who introduced positivism into England in *Biographical History of Philosophy* (1845–46), George Eliot, and the group associated with the *Westminster Review*, including Frederic Harrison.

The "grave doubts" Wilson raises here (that the "secular future of humanity" need not have any connection with "the diffusion of Christianity") are the point of departure of Harrison's "Neo-Christianity" review. Hence Harrison asserts that Wilson and the other Essayists are hypocritical in maintaining their privileges within the church without holding any of the church's beliefs (1860, 157–60; 176–78), a point Wilberforce agrees with (1861, 286). Stanley disagreed vehemently, aligning Harrison with "the mixture of Paganism and Catholicism in which the followers of M. Comte have found a refuge" (1861, 464).

Voltaire was influenced by the English deists during his time in England (1726–29). Through *Candide* (1759) and other attacks on traditional Christianity 'Voltaire' became a commonplace for the agnostic. For instance, in *On Heroes and Hero Worship* (1840) Carlyle writes: "Truly, if Christianity be the highest instance of hero-worship, then we may find here in Voltaireism one of the lowest! He whose life was that of a kind of Antichrist, does again on this side exhibit a curious contrast" (1896–99, 5:14). In 1860 William Rathbone Greg referred to Benjamin Constant, French author and friend of Mme. de Staël, as "a second Voltaire . . . profoundly cynical and profoundly sceptical, he loved nothing and believed in nothing" (1853, 1–3). Pattison in his *Memoirs* writes: "If it is against the Church it is a fiction of the Voltairians" (1885a, 212).

For "judgment to come" see Acts 24:25.

14. Wilson positions "anxieties" about Christianity between "rude criticisms . . . of a Tom Paine kind" and "a self-satisfied sacerdotalism," that is, between a radical political view and a High Church religious one. Thomas Paine published *Common Sense* (1776), which called for American independence. Inspired by the French Revolution, he criticized religion from a position of natural reason, developing a system based on science and abstract morality. He also published *The Age of Reason* (1794; 1796, 2 pts.), which was attacked as an atheistic tract but which was accepted by Benjamin Franklin and Thomas Jefferson as the basis of their deism.

For "rude criticisms upon the Scriptures" by Paine, see the compilation *The Theological Writings of Thomas Paine* (London: R. Carlile, 1818), which includes *The Age of Reason: Being Investigation of True and of Fabulous Theology* and "A Reply to the Bishop of Llandaff's Apology for the Bible." In them he introduces his "rude criticisms" of the Bible: "The suspicion that the theory of what is called the Christian church is fabulous is becoming very extensive in all countries; and it will be a consolation to men staggering under that suspicion, and doubting what to believe and what to disbelieve, to see the subject freely investigated. I therefore pass on to an examination of the books called the Old and New Testament" (1989, 216). In *The Age of Reason* Paine argues that all religious institutions are "no other than human inventions set up to terrify and enslave mankind and monopolize power and profit" (1989, 208). For a discussion of Paine's influence on the radical and free thinking traditions in Britain, see Royle 1974, 23–31 and Royle 1976, 1–16.

15. "Endowed and unendowed churches" refers to the complicated systems of church finances, comprised of endowments, as well as tithes, church rates, pew rents, advowsons, and patronage. These interlocking systems, dating back to the medieval landholding of monasteries and the nobility, benefited the patron and his appointee rather than the local cleric who actually conducted the parochial duties.

Endowments were benefactions of land, money, or goods to parishes, the proceeds from which might go to the parish or to the patron; the more endowments, the more wealth and prestige the parish claimed. An unendowed parish would have trouble maintaining its buildings, grounds, and rectory and attracting well-qualified or prestigious clergy. Tithes were the payment by *all* residents of a parish (whether or not members of the C. of E.) of a fixed amount (one-tenth of the annual yield) in produce or money from all lands within the parish to either the rector (two-thirds of the benefices) or to the local lay patron (in vicarages, one-third of the benefices). The clerical appointee, often nonresident, gave a small portion of the income to the parish priest or curate. Church rates were the payment of taxes by all residents to maintain and repair the parish church. Such rates, often deflected to other uses, were a much-hated financial burden, inflicted by the established church on people of other or no religious beliefs. Pew rents were charges required of a family to gain rights to sit in the church. Only a few pews were free for the poor (see Heales 1872). An advowson was the right to appoint a clergyman to a parish or other ecclesiastical benefice, often a friend or relative of the patron, and so was a means of ensuring that income remained under the control of the patron and his appointee. Advowsons were usually in the control of the lay patron, often a local squire or lord, a college, or a corporation. From time to time they were sold to the highest bidder. Patronage involved the holding of an advowson and the possession of the rights to parish income. Thus the patron could appoint an incumbent of his choice, who had to be a priest, but who was not required to live in or ever go near the parish. Once appointed he had possession for life and could not be removed. Most income would then come to the incumbent and patron. From his portion the incumbent could appoint a curate for a fraction of his income, preferably for as little as possible. Curates could be dismissed at the whim of the incumbent. Hence the local curate in a "starvation parish" might have £60 to £150 per annum, while the bishopric of Winchester, to which Samuel Wilberforce was transferred in 1869, had a reputed annual income of £10,500 as one of the richest sees in England (corrected by the *Times* as actually £7,000 [8 Oct. 1869]).

To initiate reform, the Ecclesiastical Commission was established in 1835 to manage the property, estates, and revenues of the C. of E., and so to start to moderate the long-standing abuses of absentee incumbencies, simony (the selling of church offices), and pluralism (the multiplication of such rectorships or curacies to increase income). Between 1840 and 1855 "the Ecclesiastical Commission endowed or augmented 5,300 parishes from [church] offices [or appointments] scheduled for abolition by the Cathedrals Act of 1840" (Desmond Bowen 1968, 22). The policy of the commissioners was to endow where local benefactors would endow an equal amount.

Contemporaneous with *Essays and Reviews*, endowments and church finances are satirized in the

Barchester novels of Anthony Trollope especially in *Barchester Towers* (1857), *Doctor Thorne* (1858), and *Framley Parsonage* (1861).

For a discussion of the background to the financial inequalities of the Victorian Church see Hill 1956, 50–198; on the Ecclesiastical Commission see Best 1964; and Thompson 1970; on the general effect of such financial exploitation and inequalities see Desmond Bowen 1968; and Hammond 1977, 13–43.

16. As part of the national census on 30 March 1851 ("census Sunday"), an inventory was taken in Britain (excluding Ireland) of all those who attended public worship at any time on that day, together with other kinds of information (the date the building was erected, the numbers of free and appropriated sittings, the numbers present, and details concerning endowments of the C. of E.). The results were tabulated by Horace Mann, secretary to the Civil Service Commission, and were published in 1854 as *Report and Tables* in Parliamentary Paper no. 1690: House of Commons 1852–53, vol. 89, and in an abridged form by Routledge. It was reviewed extensively; for instance, see Martineau 1854.

The religious census provoked a considerable controversy concerning the validity of the data and their interpretation and implications. Mann calculated that whereas the population of England and Wales was 17,927,609, there were 11,696,066 attendances—though the last figure does not indicate how many persons attended more than once. Mann devised the formula of counting all of the morning congregation, one-half of the afternoon and one-third of the evening, yielding 7,261,042 "attending." After adjustments were made calculating the numbers who were incapable of attending, Mann concluded that "the most important fact which this investigation as to attendance brings before us is, unquestionably, the alarming number of the non-attendants. Even in the least unfavorable aspect of the figures just presented, and assuming (as no doubt is right) that the 5,288,294 absent every Sunday are not always the same individuals, it must be apparent that a sadly formidable portion of the English people are habitual neglecters of the public ordinances of religion" (Thompson 1978, 257).

"Census Sunday" continues to be an important point of reference for recent historians of Victorian Britain. For instance, G. Kitson Clark organizes his entire chapter "The Religion of the People" by a reading of the 1851 census (1962, 147–206). See also Mills and Pearce 1989. For a discussion of the ideology of census-taking in the context of nineteenth-century colonialism, particularly the identity categories of race and religion, see Benedict Anderson 1991, 164–70.

17. The Formularies of the C. of E. consist of the official documents that contain doctrinal statements regulating religious practice. The chief document is the *Book of Common Prayer* of 1662 that is legally binding on all members of the church according to the terms of the Elizabethan settlement. Throughout the nineteenth and twentieth centuries the legal status of the *BCP* was under continual revision. For an explanation see Williams ¶4 and note and Wilson ¶s 43 ff. and notes. The *BCP* includes particular formulaic statements, such as the three creeds (Apostles', Nicene, and the "one unhappy creed" of St. Athanasius), as well as the ordinal and the catechism. Other documents included in the Formularies are the Thirty-nine Articles of Religion (1562) and the *Book of Canons* (1603). In 1860 it was a matter of dispute whether the two *Books of Homilies* (1547, 1571) were to be included among the Formularies: Stephen Lushington, the judge in the Court of Arches trial of *Essays and Reviews*, considered it an open question whether the Homilies were part of the Formularies (see Waddams 1992, 318). For eighteenth-century controversies concerning the Athanasian Creed see Pattison ¶4 and n. 15; for nineteenth-century contexts see Williams ¶32 and n. 138. Among the "various associations" contemporaneous with *Essays and Reviews* established to seek "revision" of the *BCP* were the Church of England Liturgical Revision Society that issued a "Declaration of Principles and Objects" in 1855 and the Association for Promoting a Revision of the Prayer-Book, active in meetings in 1860, that published a report in 1861.

18. Inoculation, introducing into the body the virus or germs of an infectious disease, applies to vaccination, the intentional introduction of smallpox virus. Edward Jenner discovered the smallpox vaccination in 1798. "Inoculation" is used in the nineteenth century as a figure for the imbuing of someone with emotions or ideas: for example, Byron's *Don Juan*: "The inoculation / Of others with her own opinions" (Canto 15, st. 50) and also as a preventive measure to avoid contagion. As Wilson uses it, "German inoculation" is the contracting of the disease of German rationalism through the introduction of German higher criticism into England.

"Reactions" to "modern scepticism" in Prussia included the unification of the Reformed (Calvinist) and the Lutheran churches to oppose both rationalism and the higher criticism of the Bible. Frederick William III of Prussia initiated this union in 1817. M. A. Crowther comments: "The United Evangelical Church spread through Prussia in spite of fears that it was a covert plan for the State to gain complete control over the Church." Some Lutheran congregations decided to preserve their Lutheranism outside the union, but others, according to Crowther, "accepted it with motives which foreshadowed those of the Tractarians. They opposed a loose union of congregations without definite principles of faith and feared the encroachments of rationalism; this led them to demand a strong Church hierarchy with more power in the hands of the clergy" (1970, 45). These views are what Wilson calls "High Lutheran reactions." Frederick William IV continued to be hostile to "modern scepticism" and the higher critics, refusing to appoint them to important posts in the Evangelical Church.

19. "Negative theology" refers to the critical interpretation of the Bible derived from German higher criticism. John Rogerson has recently explained the term in the context of German universities in the nineteenth century: "The so-called negative criticism could be found at Basel (under de Wette, 1822–49), Halle (under Gesenius, 1811–42 and Hupfeld, 1843–66) and Marburg (at least during Hupfeld's tenure, 1825–43). . . . The so-called negative critics worked within a philosophical framework which was more strictly Kantian, whereas the positive critics were more overtly idealists. Thus de Wette and his closest followers regarded religion as a matter of experience, feeling, and *ahndung* [retribution, punishment], and they looked to the Old Testament to provide examples of religion in these terms. Their so-called negative attitude was based upon their inability to see history as an organic process guided towards an ultimate purpose" (1984, 139–40). Jowett uses the phrase about *Essays and Reviews*: "It is the beginning of a long controversy which has now for the first time taken hold of the Church of England. And I believe it may tend not merely to a negative and critical theology but to the making of religion more natural & effectual" (Letter 109). And to Florence Nightingale he writes of the use and limits of negative theology (Letter 249).

20. Wilson contrasts the "cheap form" of current "negative and destructive" anti-Christian "literature circulating among us" with the "assaults" in the popular press from "forty years ago" when, as Altholz says, English free thought enlisted "in the welter of radical democratic movements stimulated by the French revolution and released into activity after the peace of 1815. The flurry of pamphlets and periodicals that soon appeared attacked both political institutions and organized religion." According to Altholz many radical newspapers refused to pay the newspaper tax, leading to the "War of the Unstamped" in 1830. For instance, George Jacob Holyoake established the Anti-Persecution Union (and its journal, *Movement* [1843–45]) and the Rationalist Society (with the *Herald of Progress* [1845–46], succeeded by the *Reasoner* [1846–61]). Charles Bradlaugh published the *London Investigator* (1854–57) and the *Investigator* (1858–59). See Altholz 1989, 117–21. For a discussion of atheism and radical politics see Royle 1974 and Royle 1976. See also Wilson ¶96 and note; and Jowett ¶30 and note.

21. William Hone, writer and bookseller, was arraigned on charges from the attorney-general to face three separate trials in December 1817. He was accused of injuring public morals and bringing into contempt both religion and the *BCP* for publishing three works: *The Late J. W.'s Catechism of a Ministerial Member* by John Wilkes; *The Political Litany*, a parody of the litany and catechism of the *BCP* and attack on the prince regent; and *The Sinecurist's Creed*, a parody of the Athanasian Creed. All were published with illustrations by George Cruikshank. Hone was acquitted on each of the charges after arguing vigorously in his own defense and was freed by the public's raising of a subscription of £3,000. See Hackwood 1912.

The "celebrated criticisms" of the "Evangelical histories" are the German higher-critical commentaries on the gospels that had begun about the beginning of the nineteenth century to be translated into English. These translations, such as that of Michaelis by Herbert Marsh, published from 1793 to 1801, appeared in England much earlier than Wilson asserts; however, much greater impact was felt from German criticism from the 1820s on. See Thrane 1956; Crowther 1970, 40–65; and Reidy 1971.

Wilson divides English radicalism into two phases, a period ending at the Peterloo massacre of 1819 and middle-class agitation for the vote and parliamentary reform up to 1860. Such a comparison omits consideration of the agitation around the Reform Bill of 1832 and the history of Chartism, ignoring the continuity of the English radical tradition that has been established by recent historians since E. P. Thompson's *The Making of the English Working Class* (1963).

For general histories of nineteenth-century English radicalism see Royle and Walvin 1982; for English radicalism from 1789 to 1815 see R. J. White 1957; Hone 1982; G. Stedman Jones 1983, 102–3; Dickinson 1985; and John Stevenson 1989; for studies of radicalism around 1860 see Biagini and Reid 1991. For a collection of documents relating "anti-Christian agitation" to radicalism from 1791 to 1866 see Royle 1976, 1–89.

22. For "great nations" see Josh. 23:9; Ps. 135:10; Jer. 50:9; Ezek. 31:6; "buying and selling," James 4:13; "flesh and blood," Matt. 16:17; 1 Cor. 15:50; Gal. 1:16; Eph. 6:12; Heb. 2:14; "like passions," Acts 14:15; James 5:17; "great cities," 1 Kings 4:13; "falling down before objects of worship," 1 Cor. 14:25; "constituting priesthoods," Exod. 40:15; "binding themselves by oaths," Num. 30:10; Acts 23:21; "honouring the dead," 2 Chron. 32:33; Rev. 14:13.

The increased availability of "the news" in mid-Victorian Britain can be attributed to several factors, including technological changes in methods of printing, the growth of literacy, and new developments in the communication and distribution of information, such as the telegraph and the railways. The period from 1850 to 1860 was transitional in terms of ownership and government control of the press, as well as the types of "news" that were printed. Alan Lee argues that "discussion of the British press before the 1850s has been in terms of the struggle of a 'free' press to shift government controls to the bourgeoisie's commercial interests in a free and cheap press. This process was aided by "the repeal of what their skilful propagandist opponents called 'the taxes on knowledge'—the Advertisement Duties, abolished in 1853, the Newspaper Stamp Duty in 1855, and the Paper Duties in 1861" (1978, 117). Michael Harris argues that these changes represented "a triumph for radicalism" and "brought about a major shift in the balance of output from London to the provinces, broadened the range of news-carrying publications and substantially altered the character of political involvement with the press" (1986, 107).

Louis Billington has demonstrated that similar types of "popular information" were available in both the secular and religious newspapers of Victorian Britain: "Many of the papers had a . . . format with a leader and news reports under such headings as 'Parliament,' 'Foreign,' 'Agriculture,' 'Markets,' and other standard topics. . . . There was also much denominational and general religious news with extensive reports on the meetings of churches and great religious societies. The more radical papers also provided extensive coverage of political reform movements and of temperance, peace, antislavery, and allied campaigns" (1986, 122–23). Altholz has argued that the missionary press in Britain "supplied much of the Victorians' geographical knowledge and contributed to interest in the Empire" (1989, 123).

For general histories of Victorian newspapers see Harris and Lee 1976; Boyce, Curran, and Wingate 1978; and Brake, Jones, and Madden 1990; for bibliographical studies of Victorian newspapers see Vann and Van Arsdel 1978 and 1989. For the religious press see Altholz 1989.

23. For "necessary to salvation" see Acts 16:31 and the Sixth Article of Religion; "Aye . . . no," Shakespeare, *King Lear* 4.6.100.

24. These last two sentences were admitted in 1862 in the trial in the Court of Arches as heretical with respect to no distinctions' being drawn between covenanted and uncovenanted mercies. In 1863 in the appeal before the Judicial Committee of the Privy Council, the Lord Chancellor (Westbury) indicated that the Judicial Committee was willing to have this passage withdrawn from accusation, provided the prosecuting counsel (Phillimore) did not object. He did not: accordingly, this passage was withdrawn and did not have to be appealed.

"Covenanted mercies" refers to the formal gifts of grace received though entering the church in baptism or through a declaration of faith; that is, the "mercies" follow upon the covenant relationship of promise and obligation in the act of faith. "Uncovenanted mercies" are those that are presumed to be extended freely by God to those persons outside a covenant relationship and so outside the church, whether agnostics, atheists, or the "myriads upon myriads of non-christian races." In commenting on this passage in his interlocutory judgment, Stephen Lushington proposes a definition: "Now covenanted mercy is the mercy promised by our Saviour to those who believe in Him; uncovenanted mercy is that which God may be pleased to bestow, though no promise thereof has been made. Covenanted mercy is matter of absolute certainty, the fulfilment of the promise of the Almighty; uncovenanted mercy is speculation of what may happen upon a human idea of the Divine attributes" (Lushington 1862, 42).

25. Wilson's question of whether the "non-Christian races" are involved in the "curse and perdition of Adam" involved him in charges of heresy. The "curse . . . of Adam" is defined by the Ninth Article of Religion, "Of Original or Birth-Sin": "Original Sin standeth not in the following of *Adam* . . . but it is the fault and corruption of the Nature of every man, that naturally is engendered of the offspring of *Adam* . . . and therefore in every person born into this world, it deserveth God's wrath and damnation" (*BCP*). For "Yea, let God be true" see Rom. 3:4.

The passage from Wilson ¶10, "First, if our traditions. . . . every man a liar," was cited as one of the "false and dangerous statements, and reasonings at variance with the teaching of the Church of England" that comprised the grounds for the Synodical Condemnation of *Essays and Reviews* on 21 June 1864. Wilson was alleged to hold that rational thought can be used to test the veracity of doctrine (*Chronicle* 1859–64:1864, Session 66, 1658).

26. For "unquiet souls" see Matt. 11:29; see also Shakespeare, *Merchant of Venice* 3.2.308.

27. For "all nations" see Matt. 28:19; Mark 13:10; "to every creature," Mark 16:15. Wilson refers to the "Great Commission" of Jesus concerning the evangelizing of the world. British missionary organizations include the Society for Promoting Christian Knowledge (founded 1698), the Society for the Propagation of the Gospel in Foreign Parts (1701), the London Missionary Society (1795), the Church Missionary Society (1799), and the British and Foreign Bible Society (1804). Specialized societies proliferated during the nineteenth century, directing their activities to particular countries as part of the project of colonization. Included among these are the Universities' Mission to Central Africa (1859), established following a Cambridge speech by David Livingstone, who published *Missionary Travels and Researches in South Africa* (1857). Dickens satirizes these societies in *Bleak House* in the figure of Mrs. Jellyby, who neglects her children for her philanthropic endeavors (bk.1, chap. 4; [1853] 1971, 85–86). T. O. Lloyd relates the increased religious proselytizing and expansionist C. of E. to the British imperial project (1984, 135). See also Kiernan's linking of expansionist Christianity and empire in Britain in the nineteenth century and the U. S. A. in the twentieth ([1969] 1972, 64).

28. J. B. Bury argues that the population of the

empire at the time of Constantine was about 70,000,000 (1928, 38); however, such figures (and the certainty with which Wilson makes his assertions) are matters of "supreme difficulty" and cannot command "great confidence in their accuracy" (Boak 1955, 4–5). For a recent study of the problems of determining the population of the Roman Empire see Parkin 1992.

For "wisdom and goodness" compare the title of the Bridgewater Treatises: *On the Power, Wisdom, and Goodness of God, as Manifested in the Creation* (1833–40).

29. The Vedas (Sanskrit, *veda*: sacred knowledge) are sacred books of Brahmanic Hinduism. The oldest, the *Rig-Veda*, written in Vedic (the parent language of Sanskrit) and consisting of over 1,000 hymns in praise of the gods, dates from the Indo-European migrations into India between 1500 and 900 B.C.E. To it were added other Vedic writings on ritual observances (the Brahmanas), as well as the *Upanishads*, dating from the 1500 to 500 B.C.E., philosophical dialogues commenting on the Vedas and expanding their thought. Wilson published "Vedic Religion" in *Westminster Review* (Wilson 1860). For contemporaneous discussions of the religions of China see Capes 1852, 1857, and 1858; Anthony Grant 1853; Huc 1857; Elwin 1857; Donne 1857; and Martineau 1858a. For the religion of India see Kaye 1857; Müller 1859; and Patterson 1859.

30. Buddhism is the religion of the followers of Siddhartha Gautama Buddha. His dates are matters of dispute: 1956 was widely celebrated in Southeast Asia as the 2,500th anniversary of the Buddha's death.

After gaining enlightenment, Gautama preached his first sermon to his followers at Benares, India, urging them to follow the "Four Noble Truths": that life is pervaded with suffering, that the origin of suffering lies in the craving for worldly things and satisfactions, that suffering can be ended by removing craving, and that this goal is possible through the "Noble Eightfold Path" of right knowledge about reality, right aspiration for salvation, right speech, behavior, livelihood, effort, mindfulness, and contemplation. Followers of this teaching can achieve mastery of human passions by renunciation, a state of tranquil compassion in this life, and eventually nirvana, release in extinction from the endless cycle of reincarnation.

Buddhist scriptures derive from the two branches of Buddhism: Hinayana ("lesser vehicle"), or Theravada (teaching of the elders), and Mahayana (the "greater vehicle"). Hinayana scriptures, written in Pali, consist of the *Sutta* (Buddha's sermons, discourses, and life), *Vinaya* (rules for monastic orders of monks and nuns), and *Abhidhamma* (a commentary on Buddhist teaching). Mahayana scriptures, written in Sanskrit, include those that cover some of the materials of the Hinayana Buddhists, as well as other writings, such as the *Lotus Sutra*, or *Lotus of the Good Law*. For contemporaneous discussion see Maurice 1847; E. Vansittart Neale 1856 and 1860; and H. R. Reynolds 1859. For a recent discussion of Buddhism from a European perspective see Harvey 1990.

31. For "preaching the Gospel to the whole world" see Mark 16:15. The instruction of Jesus concerning missionary activity in the entire world (Mark 16:9–20) is of contested authority, not being found in either of the fourth-century codices, MSS. Vaticanus and Sinaiticus. In the RSV it is relegated to footnotes. Instead of raising questions concerning the authenticity of the passage, Wilson directs attention to how it accommodates the limited knowledge of the world available to its supposed hearers.

32. For such a declaration, see the prophecy of the final judgment and the separation of the sheep from the goats, Matt. 25:31–46.

33. "*Dharmma*" (Sanskrit: moral code or decree) in Buddhism refers to the law or the canonical books contained in the *Vinaya* and *Abhidhamma* of Theravada Buddhism.

34. Millenarianism is the belief that there will be a thousand-year (millennium) reign of the saints before the immanent second coming of Christ, a notion based on Jewish and Christian apocalyptic writings, such as Rev. 20:1–7. In 1553 Thomas Cranmer drew up the Forty-two Articles of Religion that received royal assent from Edward VI, forming the basis for the Thirty-nine Articles approved in 1563. Article 41 comments on "Millennarian . . . fables": "Thei that goe aboute to renewe the fable of heretickes called Millenarii, be repugnant . . . to holie Scripture." Thomas Arnold, writing on the moral function of the state in 1831, argues that he did not have "the slightest expectation of what is commonly meant by the Millennium, and I wonder more and more that any one can so understand Scripture as to look for it" (Stanley 1844, 1:302). Millenarianism was one of the central doctrines of the Catholic Apostolic Church established in 1832 by Henry Drummond and Edward Irving. Irving published *The Coming of the Messiah in Glory and Majesty* (1827), a translation of a millenarian work by Manuel de Lacunza y Díaz, a Spanish Jesuit. *Venida del mesías en gloria y majestad* (1812) was banned by the papal office on 6 September 1824 because of its arguments about millenarianism. For millenarianism see also Jowett ¶21 and note.

"Rabbinic fable" refers to allegorical interpretations of the Bible as practiced by the rabbinical school at Alexandria in the Hellenistic period. See Jowett ¶35 and notes and his phrase "Rabbinical fancy" ¶48; see also S. T. Coleridge [1829] 1976, 122, n. 5.

35. The "visible" and "invisible Church" refer to different views of ecclesiology, deriving from the NT writings of Peter in which the church is composed of a visible membership, and those of the Johannine

circle in which the church is invisible and its members are known only to God. The former view is elaborated in the institutions of the church, with conditions of membership based on credal affirmations; the latter depends upon the individual dispositions of the heart.

The differing views may be traced in Calvin and the Formularies of the C. of E. In *Institutes of the Christian Religion*, Calvin argues that the church refers to both, to "the visible Church . . . but also to all the elect of God, including in the number even those who have departed this life. . . . But . . . to God alone must be left the knowledge of his Church, of which his secret election forms the foundation" (bk. 4, chap. 1, sec. 2; [1536] 1957, 1:281–82). The Nineteenth Article of Religion ("Of the Church") states: "The visible Church of Christ is a congregation of faithful men, in which the pure Word of God is preached and the Sacraments be duly ministered according to Christ's ordinance in all those things that of necessity are requisite to the same" (*BCP*).

While many Broad Church liberals tended to stress the invisible church rather than the conditions for formal church membership as marks of the visible church, in this section Wilson argues that the visible church has expanded by "numerical accessions" because of multitudinism, not because of individualism, and not at the expense of loss of purity.

36. Justification is the doctrine of being made just, righteous, or blameless before God, not through any human action (since humans are held to be sinful, not righteous), but through the grace of God, or, in Luther's phrase in *The Liberty of a Christian Man* (1520), by "faith alone" in the efficacy of Christ. In the NT the doctrine of justification is discussed chiefly in Romans and Galatians. Luther came to his position through the interpretation of Rom. 1:17 (Preface to the first volume of the Latin Writings, 1545). At "the time of the Reformation," the Council of Trent commented that faith is "the beginning, foundation, and root of all justification" (session 6, chap. 7). The council did not argue that such faith is "subjective," but rather that it is formed by love. For an extended contemporaneous treatment see Heurtley 1845, the Bampton Lectures for that year; for a more recent treatment see Lampe 1954.

Hebrews is entitled "The Epistle of Paul the Apostle to the Hebrews" in the AV. Wilson disputes this attribution by asserting that it belongs to the "Pauline or Paulo-Johannean school" as other contemporaries argue, such as Henry Alford in a sixty-page commentary on the uncertainty of its authorship while attributing it to the Pauline school (Alford [1849] 1863, 4:1–61).

For "the substance of things hoped for" see Heb. 11:1.

37. Dionysius Petavius published *De theologicis dogmatibus* (1644–50, 4 vols.; Concerning dogmatic theology). George Bull attacked Petavius's criticisms of the orthodoxy of the "Fathers" in *Defensio Fidei Nicaenae* (1685; Defense of the Nicene Creed), which was translated and republished in the Library of Anglo-Catholic Theology in 1851 ([1685] 1851, 1:9).

38. For the "source of religion is in the heart" see Mark 12:33; Acts 8:37; Rom. 6:17; and 2 Cor. 3:3. For the placing of ethics before theoretical doctrine in the NT see, for instance, the beatitudes, Matt. 5:2–12; the whole of Jesus' sermon on the mount, Matt. 5:1–7:28; and the prophecy of the final judgment and the separation of the sheep and goats, Matt. 25:31–46.

39. The fourth Gospel has always been supposed to have been written with a controversial purpose, and not to have been composed till from sixty to seventy years after the events which it undertakes to narrate; some critics, indeed, think it was not of a date anterior to the year 140, and that it presupposes opinions of a Valentinian character, or even Montanist, which would make it later still. At any rate it cannot, by external evidence, be attached to the person of St. John as its author, in the sense wherein moderns understand the word author: that is, there is no proof that St. John gives his voucher as an eye and ear witness of all which is related in it. Many persons shrink from a *bonâ fide* elimination of the 'Gospel question,' because they imagine, that unless the four Gospels are received as perfectly genuine and authentic—that is entirely the composition of the persons whose names they bear, and without any admixture of legendary matter or embellishment in their narratives, the only alternative is to suppose a fraudulent design in those who did compose them. This is a supposition from which common sense, and the moral instinct, alike revolt; but it is happily not an only alternative [Wilson's note].

The principle of religion in the heart (2 Cor. 3:3; Eph 3:17; 1 Pet 3:15; 1 John 3:19-21) is one of Jowett's principles of hermeneutics (see Jowett ¶s 26, 41, 57 and notes).

Wilson in both ¶21 and his note refers to the Johannine Question. There is no external evidence, or testimony from any other NT document, that the apostle John was the author of the fourth gospel. Although accepting the Johannine authorship, Alford comments on the silence of the early church; there is no reference to this gospel in Papias, Polycarp, Barnabas, Clement of Rome, or Ignatius: "In the most ancient circle of ecclesiastical testimony, it appears to be unknown or not recognized" ([1849] 1863, 1:66). For a recent treatment see Hengel 1989.

Among those who had asserted the "controversial purpose" of John were Irenaeus, who asserts John was written to repudiate the errors of Cerinthus (*Against Heretics*, chap. 10, sec. 1); Tertullian, who uses John to oppose Praxeas (*Against Praxeas*, chap. 32); and Jerome and Augustine, both of whom wrote Commentaries on John.

A "Valentinian" was a follower of Valentinus;

a "Montanist," of Montanus. Both movements flourished in the latter half of the second century, hence, after 140. For a discussion of the Valentinians and Montanists in relation to John, see Watkins 1890, 209–10. For recent treatments of the Valentinians see McQuire 1983; Jacqueline A. Williams 1988; and David Dawson 1992. For recent treatments of the Montanists see Goree 1980; and Rottman 1987.

The passage from Wilson ¶21, "embody more exact traditions of what He actually said than the fourth does;" and from the note (above), "admixture of legendary matter or embellishment in their narratives," were cited as "false and dangerous" in the Synodical Condemnation of *Essays and Reviews* on 21 June 1864. Wilson is condemned for declaring that John's gospel does not record the words of Jesus exactly and that the gospels mix legend and embellishment with their narratives (*Chronicle* 1859–64:1864, Session 66, 1659).

40. "Synoptics" refers to the first three gospels, by Matthew, Mark, and Luke that give a more or less chronological account, or "synopsis," of the life of Christ: "The terms *Synoptist, Synoptical,* as applied to the first three Evangelists appear to date from the time of Johann Jakob Griesbach's analysis of their interdependence, printing them in parallel columns in his edition of the Greek NT (1774), though the terms were brought into general use by Neander" (Westcott [1851] 1888, 170). In particular Neander popularized the term in his *Life of Jesus Christ* (1837; English translation, 1848), an answer to D. F. Strauss. Chapter 2 of Neander's Introduction relates the synoptic problem to the Gospel of John. F. C. Baur's *Kritische Untersuchungen über die kanonischen Evangelien* (1847; A critical examination of the canonical gospels), points to the theological and mystical interests of John but denigrates its value as a useful document for the historical reconstruction of a "life" of Jesus. Eichhorn argued for an original gospel (*Urevangelium*) behind Matthew and Luke, but not Mark. Lachmann in 1835 in an article in *Studien und Kritiken* first argued that the *Urevangelium* lay instead behind Mark, a view much developed by Christian Hermann Weisse in *Die evangelische Geschichte kritisch und philosophish bearbeitet* (1838, 2 vols.; A critical and philosophical study of the gospel history) and many others in the mid- and late-nineteenth century. See also Jowett ¶s 13, 37, and 49.

In England the scholarly debate on this issue began with the publication of Marsh's translation in 1793–1801 of Johann David Michaelis's *Einleitung in die göttlichen Schriften des Neuen Bundes* (1750) as *Introduction to the New Testament* (4 vols. in 6). Marsh included his own contribution to the debate, "Dissertation on the Origin and Composition of the First Three Canonical Gospels" (Marsh 1823), an argument for multiple sources for the synoptics. His work was continued by Connop Thirlwall in his translation of Schleiermacher's *Critical Essay on the Gospel of St. Luke* (1817; trans. 1825). Such efforts to harmonize the differences among the synoptics embroiled Marsh and his followers in heated controversy, since they seemed to be rejecting the inspiration of the authors to whom the synoptic Gospels are ascribed. Such harmonizing and source-critical methods were repudiated by Strauss in *Leben Jesu* ([1835] 1846), who took all parallels and contradictions as evidence of the interference of the messianic mythologizing of the early church in order to create their own hero. The contemporaneous state of the synoptic controversy is summarized by B. F. Westcott in *An Introduction to the Study of the Gospels* (1860). See also Jowett ¶13 and n. 21; ¶37, n. 72, 73; and ¶49.

The Epistle of James is one of the most disputed writings in the NT, especially its date, authorship, audience, and theology (notably Jas. 2:14 ff. on justification that seems at variance with the theology of Paul in Romans). It was not a formal part of the NT canon until approved at the Council of Carthage (397). In *Ecclesiastical History,* Eusebius calls it "spurious" and comments that "not many of the ancients have mentioned it" (bk. 3, chap. 25; *Loeb,* trans. Kirsopp Lake 1:257–59); to Luther it is an "epistle of straw." Alford thinks that the apostolic James, the son of Zebedee, "cannot well have written our Epistle" because "the state of things and doctrines which we find in it can hardly have been reached as early as before the execution of that Apostle, related in Acts xii" ([1849] 1863, 4:87). On its genuineness and canonicity Alford writes: "We have before us a question not easily settled, and on which both the ancients and moderns have been much divided" ([1849] 1863, 2:108). See also Davidson 1849, 3:339–45. But 1 Peter, according to Alford, was "universally acknowledged by the ancient church as part of the Christian Scriptures" ([1849] 1863, 4:111).

41. The "illustration" or "case" is the controversy between the Sadducees and Pharisees over the resurrection of the body, in which Jesus sides with the Pharisees doctrinally but condemns them for their moral culpability; he disagrees with the Sadducees doctrinally but does not exclude them on moral grounds; see, for instance, Matt. 22:23–46 and parallel passages.

The "sect of the Sadducees," active from perhaps the second century B.C.E. to about 70, stressed the role of free will in human action, devalued the role of providence, and did not believe in the resurrection of the body. In *The Jewish War* Josephus writes: "As for the persistence of the soul after death, penalties in the underworld, and rewards, they will have none of them" (bk 2, chap 8, sect 14; *Loeb,* trans. H. St. J. Thackeray 2:387). In the NT they are associated with the wealthy, with temple worship in Jerusalem, and with the priests.

The Pharisees, a sect of Judaism active about

the same time as the Sadducees, were skilled interpreters of the Jewish religious and ritual law. Their "philosophy" involved a balance between free will and the rule of providence and a belief in resurrection. In the NT they are the opponents of Jesus and are associated with the "scribes" or students and teachers of the Torah, or Law.

For "Paul preached at Athens" see Acts 17:16–33.

42. So in Luke XX. 27-35, the Sadducees are dealt with in a like argumentative manner. They understood the doctrine of the resurrection to imply the rising of men with such bodies as they now have; the case supposed by them loses its point when the distinction is revealed between the animal and the angelic bodies [Wilson's note].

For Christ as the "corner-stone" see Eph. 2:20; "spiritual body," 1 Cor. 15:44; "animal and the angelic bodies," 1 Cor. 15:35–40.

In 1 Cor. 15:5–8 Christ's resurrection is first attested to by appearances. Paul discusses the general resurrection in relation to the resurrection of Christ chiefly in 1 Cor. 15: the argument, positioned against those who deny the resurrection (1 Cor. 15:12), is not based on the miracle or "wonder" of Christ's resurrection but on it as a "prerogative instance" that establishes, in a legal phrasing, the right of all humanity to resurrection on the basis of Christ's precedent. Subsequently, Paul deals with the resurrection of Christ using the metaphor of the "firstfruits," the first crop of the year that is offered to God, and the crops that are sown a "physical body" and raised a "spiritual body" (1 Cor. 15:20–23; 44). Wilson here alludes to contemporaries who use either an overly legalistic interpretation of the Formularies, particularly the damnatory clauses of the Athanasian Creed, in an exclusionary manner, or who stress a highly physical rather than spiritual resurrection, as in the case of Archdeacon Francis Wrangham who allegedly saved his nail clippings and hair cuttings to be buried with him to save God extra work in reassembling him complete at the general resurrection.

43. For "future recompense" see Luke 14:12–14, where the term refers to God's distribution of rewards and punishments at the final judgment according to good works completed on earth. If the resurrection were denied, as by the Sadducees, there could be no motive for their good works in seeking future rewards, but only "an appreciation of the moral spirit of Jesus." The point is more clearly put from the fourth edition of *Essays and Reviews* on, when the text was changed to read "future rewards."

Wilson rejects those Calvinists who denied the efficacy of good works, and some Evangelicals, who stressed Calvin's view of double predestination, to heaven for the elect and to hell for the reprobate. The issue of "future recompense" was a contemporary issue championed by Broad Church liberals, following the publication of F. D. Maurice's *Kingdom of Christ* (1838) and Jowett's *Commentaries on the Epistles of St. Paul* (1855). Both raise questions about a limited atonement for the elect only and the universal application of "future recompense" to the elect and reprobate. The matter appeared in ecclesiastical controversy and religious trials soon after *Essays and Reviews* with Colenso's publication in October 1861 of *St. Paul's Epistle to the Romans: Newly Translated, and Explained from a Missionary Point of View.* The book extends the lectures Colenso gave to his mission workers in 1854 as " a deliberate statement of doctrinal policy made by the most important missionary in South Africa" (Hinchliff 1964, 79). Hinchliff argues that "contrary to the common opinion, it was *Romans* and not his Old Testament criticism which really brought the attack on Colenso to a head. It was for his doctrine of the atonement that he was again formally delated." Following Maurice on the atonement, Colenso rejected "the penal substitution theory." Maurice "denied that Christ died in order to take upon himself the *punishment* due to human sin . . . [and] that Christ died to placate an angry Father." Colenso went further, denying "that God really has any righteous anger against sin at all," having Christ pay the "debt of nature which sin had the right to demand of Him," and in thus paying the debt to nature once, all people everywhere are redeemed (Hinchliff 1964, 79–81; see Colenso [1861] 1863, 96 ff.). Colenso was condemned, as also was Wilson in the Court of Arches, for denying the "future recompense" of the damned in incurring eternal punishment.

44. St. Paul 'delivered to Satan' (whatever that may mean), Hymenaeus, who maintained the resurrection to be past already, most likely meaning it was only a moral one; but it does not appear it was for this offence he is so mentioned in conjunction with Alexander, and their provocation is not described: where he is said to have taught that the resurrection is past already, he is in companionship with Philetus, and nothing is added of any punishment of either. These strange opinions afterwards hardened into heretical doctrine. Tertull. *de Praescriptione Haer.* c. xxxiii. Paulus in imâ ad Corinthios notat negatores et dubitatores resurrectionis. Haec opinio propria Sadducaeorum: partem ejus usurpat Marcion et Apelles, et Valentinus et si qui alii resurrectionem carnis infringunt—aeque tangit eos qui dicerent factam jam resurrectionem; id de se Valentini adseverant [Wilson's note].

Tertullian, *On the Prescription against Heretics*: "Paul, in his first epistle to the Corinthians, sets his mark on certain who denied and doubted the resurrection. This opinion was the especial property of the Sadducees. A part of it, however, is maintained by Marcion and Apelles and Valentius, and all the impugners of the resurrection" (chap. 100, sec. 33; trans. Peter Holmes, *ANF* 3:259).

Through these ancient doctrinal controversies,

Wilson continues his attack and on his contemporaries' legalistic interpretations of the atonement and exclusion of some people from its redemptive effects. The views of Hymenaeus and his fellow teachers were adopted by the Gnostics and others influenced by them in the next century, such as Marcion (d. c. 160) and his followers. They rejected the OT and the Judaic law in favor of Jesus and the gospels as a new law of love. According to the Marcionites, Jesus in the crucifixion overthrew the Demiurge to reveal God as love, but Jesus did not suffer for human sin, a view condemned as the heresy of Docetism. Marcion was formally excommunicated in 144. Apelles (second century), a disciple of Marcion, founded a Gnostic sect.

Paul does not refer to excommunicating the Christians who deny "the most fundamental article," the resurrection (as in Wilson's discussion of 1 Cor. 15:19, 32; or of Hymenaeus and others in Wilson's footnote). Excommunication is reserved instead for those who commit grievous moral sin. Paul asks that such persons be both "delivered . . . unto Satan" (1 Cor. 5:5) and be excluded from the Christian community (1 Cor. 5:13), in contrast to those who commit lesser moral sins (1 Cor. 5:9–11).

By the phrase "delivered to Satan" (1 Tim. 1:20), Paul advises Timothy to beware of "false teachers" who argue that the "resurrection . . . be past" (2 Tim. 2:18). Hymenaeus, an opponent of Paul, is associated with Alexander (1 Tim. 1:18–20 and 2 Tim. 4:14) and Philetus (2 Tim. 2:14–18), all three of whom hold that the resurrection be "past." While Hymenaeus and Alexander are "delivered to Satan" by Paul for "blasphemy" (1 Tim. 1:20), Paul is silent about exclusion from the community. Wilson's viewpoint is supported by Alford commenting on 1 Tim. 1:20, that delivering to Satan, "an apostolic act, for the purpose of active punishment," did not involve excommunication ([1849] 1863, 3:312).

The effort to discover the "fundamental article of the Apostle's preaching" as a basis for church unity or exclusions on the basis of doctrinal difference was addressed by Wilson in his essay on "Schemes of Christian Comprehension" (1857).

45. The "extreme case" (1 Cor. 5), concerning the man living with his father's wife, raises further problems concerning the composition of the Christian Church in the early centuries, what moral and belief obligations apply inside and outside the Christian community, authority for excommunication, and, for Wilson, inclusion or exclusion in a present and future national church.

46. The "Pauline Churches" attribute their foundation to the missionary work of Paul. Other "Apostolic Churches" were established by various apostles in the Jewish communities in the Roman province of Palestine as recounted in Acts 1–12. Acts 13 describes Paul's journey to Cyprus, Pamphilia, Antioch in Pisidia, and other places in the Mediterranean from about 50 on. At the Jerusalem Conference convened by Peter to consider whether uncircumcised Gentiles should be admitted to the church, Paul's arguments for inclusivity proved persuasive (Acts 15), and his missionary activity was extended to the Gentile world. After the conference, Paul and Barnabas went again to the "brethren in every city where we have preached the word of the Lord" (Acts 15:36). Responding to a visionary request to move from Asia Minor into Greece (Acts 16:9), Paul journeyed through Macedonia, Samothrace, Philippi, Thessalonica, Athens (Acts 16–19), Ephesus, and Corinth. Paul made five missionary journeys as recorded in Acts, eventually going as prisoner to Rome to appeal to Caesar as a Roman citizen (Acts 25). He wrote the letters preserved in the NT to a number of these churches that he founded.

47. Changes in the concept of excommunication, from a method for healing the church (in which offenders are excluded from the sacraments or from the general meetings of Christians) to an instrument of punishment, began in the fourth century. Earlier even the treatment of heretics was considered good for the health of the church. But with the passing of the imperial edict against heresy *De summa trinitate et fide catholica* (On the major doctrine of the Trinity and the Catholic faith) in 380, secular punishments were inflicted on offenders, a practice that escalated when the power to excommunicate passed from the community to local bishops and when the punishment was imposed by secular authorities. For a discussion of excommunication see Storm 1987.

48. Wilson suppresses the ecclesiological and missiological conflict between the nationalist Judaizing position advocated by the Jerusalem church and the universalizing theology of Paul. After Paul's death (c. 62) and the destruction of Jerusalem as the spiritual center of Judaism and Christianity in 70, Christianity was directed by four Christian churches in the Gentile cities of Antioch, Ephesus, Alexandria, and Rome.

Stanley argues similarly to Wilson, that some "Divisions of the Eastern Church" contain "isolated fragments of an earlier Christendom" that must be regarded as "heretical sects" but that are "in fact the National Churches of their respective countries protesting against the supposed innovations of the see of Constantinople, and holding with a desperate fidelity to forms and doctrines of earlier date" ([1861] 1924, 57–58). Gasparin takes an opposite view, that the centralized administration of the Roman Empire turned these "National Churches" into subordinate ecclesiastical provinces coterminous with imperial administrative units (*Le Christianisme* 1858, 38).

49. In Calvinism conversion is a free act of God, independent of the will of the individual. Such a conversion makes one a member of the elect, but election is a secret act, not known either to the individual or to the community. Hence, notwith-

standing Calvin's advocacy of a theocracy in Geneva, conversion cannot be a condition in Calvinism for membership in a national Church. For Calvin's discussion of conversion see Calvin [1536] 1957, 1:255–64; bk. 2, chap. 3, secs. 6–14.

50. To English Dissenters, especially the Anabaptist precursors of the Congregationalists (see also Wilson ¶28 and note), "the adoption of Christianity as the religion of the Empire (under Constantine) marked the 'fall' of the church. Belonging to the church became no longer a matter of decision but of birth and social destiny. The vitality and very essence of the church as a voluntary association was destroyed" (Dillenberger and Welch 1954, 64). For an example of Calvin's denouncing Constantine's "unholy union of Church and State" see Calvin [1536] 1957, 2:373; bk. 4, chap. 7, sec. 10.

In the Preface (1869) to *Culture and Anarchy*, Matthew Arnold denounces English Nonconformity by using Constantine in a manner similar to Wilson (1960–77, 5:250–51).

Roman Catholic polemic against Henry VIII and the Elizabethan Settlement has a long history. For instance, in 1585 Nicholas Sander published *Rise and Growth of the Anglican Schism*, writing in his Preface that "for about a thousand years, none other than the Roman Catholic faith prevailed in England. . . . But Henry VIII . . . changed the faith of Christ, and severed the realm of England from the communion of the Roman pontiff ([1585] 1877, cxlv–cxlvi). In the nineteenth century, the Benedictine historian Francis Gasquet similarly writes: "By 1534 Henry's quarrel with the pope had reached its height, and the severance of the Church in England from its ancient dependence on Rome was complete" ([1887] 1889, 172–73). Stanley also compares the "despotic powers" of Constantine with those of Henry VIII ([1861] 1924, 200).

51. Constantine's policy of tolerating Christianity as one of the religions of the Roman Empire from 313 in the so-called Edict of Milan or Edict of Toleration, interpreted as "multitudinist," or inclusive, by Wilson, is set against his "doctrinal limitations," the imperial prescriptions against heretics. The edict granted "both to the Christians and to all others full authority to follow whatever worship each man has desired" (Stevenson 1957, 300). In both instances the state determines inclusions and exclusions that previously had been under local Christian control.

In 325 Constantine called a general council at Nicaea in Bythinia, south of Constantinople, to oppose Arianism, the view that denied the divinity and eternal nature of Christ. Arius, a priest of Alexandria, argued that Jesus was created from nothing to make the world, and the title "Son of God" was conferred on him because of Jesus' righteousness. After lengthy debate the council condemned Arianism as a heresy, and Constantine agreed with the anti-Arian canons, requiring prompt compliance as he wrote to Dracilian: "The privileges that have been granted in consideration of religion must benefit only the adherents of the Catholic faith. It is Our will moreover, that heretics and schismatics shall not only be alien from these privileges but shall also be bound and subjected to various compulsory public services. 1 September, 326" (Stevenson 1957, 335). Under Athanasius's leadership, Arianism was condemned again at the ecumenical council at Constantinople in 381.

Wilson here agrees with Gibbon's comments in *Decline and Fall*: "The edict of Milan, the great charter of toleration, had confirmed to each individual of the Roman world the privilege of choosing and professing his own religion. But this inestimable privilege was soon violated; with the knowledge of truth, the emperor imbibed the maxims of persecution; and the sects which dissented from the Catholic church were afflicted and oppressed by the triumph of Christianity" ([1776–88] 1858, 2:295). Wilson implies a parallel between Constantine's Edict of Toleration and the English Act of Toleration (1689) as a means of rebuking his contemporaries for their failures to be inclusive in doctrine and ecclesiastical polity in a national church. The Act of Toleration granted some civil and religious rights to Dissenters in order to unite English Protestants against James II.

52. Wilson's summary of the three accomplishments of the Council of Nicaea, the establishment of Christianity as the state religion, the resolution of doctrinal differences in the banishment of Arian heretics by the Catholic orthodox, and finally the "maxim" or principle of toleration, are presented as contradictory goals that cannot easily be harmonized. The maxim concerning toleration was reiterated by Constantine in terms close to Wilson's: "Let those, therefore, who still delight in error, be made welcome to the same degree of peace and tranquillity which they have who believe. For it may be that this restoration of equal privileges to all will prevail to lead them into the straight path" (quoted in Eusebius's *Vita Constantinae* [Life of Constantine] 2.56; Stevenson 1957, 333).

53. Theodore Beza, a friend and follower of Calvin, studied for the Catholic priesthood but abandoned it in favor of Calvinism. Moving to Geneva, he taught and published his editions of the NT, a translation of the Greek text (1556), and an explanation of Calvinist beliefs, *Confession de la foi chrétienne* (1560; Confession of the Christian faith). On the death of Calvin in 1564 he assumed the leadership of the Swiss Calvinists. He also published the first critical edition of the Greek NT based on the collation of a number of MSS. (1565). For recent studies of Beza see Raitt 1981; Lewis 1985; and Marvin W. Anderson 1987.

In Scotland, John Knox, a friend of Calvin, wrote the Calvinistic *Scottish Confession*, adopted by the Scottish Parliament in 1560, establishing "the

Church of Scotland" on Presbyterian principles. In the Solemn League and Covenant (1643), the agreement between Scotland and the Long Parliament, Presbyterianism was confirmed for Scotland and was accepted by the General Assembly of the Church of Scotland in the same year as the established church. It also accepted the reforms instituted by the Westminster Assembly (1643), originally called to reform the C. of E., but after the Solemn League, to reform both England and Scotland in terms of Presbyterianism. The assembly issued the *Westminster Confession* (1646), a revision of the Thirty-nine Articles, in 33 chapters. Wilson makes repeated reference to the *Westminster Confession* as one of the sources for his treatment of Calvinistic doctrines.

For "election" see Rom. 11:5–7; 1 Pet. 2:9–25; "effectual call," Matt. 9:12–13; Rom. 8:28–30. The idea of the "effectual call" or vocation is closely related to the idea of election.

Calvin interpreted vocation in Luther's sense, that all vocations in life are instances of divine calling; but true or effectual calling is the election by God of the individual to salvation (Calvin [1536] 1957, 2:240–50; bk.3, chap. 24, secs. 1–11). Chapter 10 of the *Westminster Confession*, "Of Effectual Calling," extends Calvin's notion to "all those whom God hath predestined unto life" who have been effectually called "by His Word and Spirit." Such an effectual call leads to election, "not by infusing righteousness into them, but by pardoning their sins, and by accounting and accepting their persons as righteous: not for any thing wrought in them, or done by them, but for Christ's sake alone" (chap. 11, "Of Justification").

Wilson argues that membership in an established state church (in Geneva or Scotland) is not a "hereditary" or necessary guarantee of either election or an effectual call, according to Calvinism. Hence Calvinists in congregational polities can be "more consistent" since their membership is not coincidental with state boundaries but is established on the basis of the "effectual call."

54. Wilson advocates a typical Broad Church *via media,* or middle way, argument between Protestantism (especially in a Congregationalist polity) and a Catholic position (with hierarchical authority). Thomas Arnold, writing to James Marshall on 23 January 1840, remarks on the Reformation's "balance of the two tendencies" accomplished by "the doctrine of the King's Supremacy" that asserts "the supremacy of the Church or Christian society over the clergy. . . . I am equally opposed to Popery, High Churchism, and the claims of the Scotch Presbyteries, on the one hand; and to all the Independents, and advocates of the separation, as they call it, of Church and State, on the other; the first setting up a Priesthood in the place of the Church, and the other lowering necessarily the objects of Law and Government, and reducing them to a mere system of police, while they profess to wish to make the Church purer" (Stanley 1844, 2:187–88). For similar articulations of the Broad Church position see S. T. Coleridge [1829] 1976, 32–36.

Congregationalism (see also Wilson ¶27 and note) posits a polity of independence and autonomy for each local church. Its "spirit" of pure democracy is based on the principle that only Christ is the head of the church (Col. 1:18), and that the priesthood consists of all believers (1 Pet. 2:9). Congregationalists trace their origins to the Reformation, particularly to Robert Browne, who published *A Book Which Sheweth the Life and Manner of All True Christians* (1582) and *A Treatise of Reformation without Tarrying for Any* (1582). The number of Congregationalists increased dramatically during the reign of Elizabeth I. During the English revolution they supported Cromwell; the Act of Uniformity (1662) made them Nonconformists; the Act of Toleration (1689) restored their legal rights. In 1832 there was a union of "the Congregational Churches of England and Wales." Their declaration of principles includes the belief that "the power of the Christian church is purely spiritual, and should in no way be corrupted by union with temporal or civil power" (Walker [1893] 1960, 552). Wilson uses "Congregationalism" metonymically for all Dissenting denominations. In *Culture and Anarchy,* Matthew Arnold uses "Nonconformist" in a similar fashion (1960–77, 5:198).

The "barriers" between Congregationalist and Calvinists refer to the Calvinist controversy of 1770–80, in which various English Methodists attempted to distance themselves from Calvinist doctrines of predestination. Foremost among the English Calvinists was Augustus Montague Toplady, who wrote *The Historic Proof of the Doctrinal Calvinism of the Church of England* (1774). See Elliott-Binns 1953, 196–207.

"Apostolical succession" is the doctrine that Christian ministry is derived by direct succession through episcopal consecration and ordination from the time of the apostles. In the first of the *Tracts for the Times,* "Thoughts on the Ministerial Commission" (1833), J. H. Newman defines "apostolical succession": "The Lord Jesus Christ gave His Spirit to His Apostles; they in turn laid their hands on those who should succeed them; and these again on others; and so the sacred gift has been handed down to our present Bishops" (J. H. Newman 1833a, 2). Other tracts also discussed "apostolical succession," including *Tract IV* by John Keble, "Adherence to the Apostolical Succession the Safest Course" (1833), and *Tract XV* by W. Palmer and J. H. Newman, "On the Apostolical Succession in the English Church" (1833c). Henry Cary published *The Apostolical Succession in the Church of England Briefly Deduced, in Answer to Certain Popular Objections* (1836). For a discussion of Thomas Arnold's attack on the Oxford Movement, particularly on "apostolic succession," see

Thomas Arnold [1833] 1962, 49–55.

"Ministerial illumination" refers to the enlightening of priestly character conferred in ordination. The medieval Latin hymn *Veni Creator Spiritus* ("Come Holy Ghost," in the translation by John Cousin, 1627), sung during ordination in the *BCP* (1662), contains the lines "Enable with perpetual light / The dulness of our blinded sight." The efficacy of this "character" is asserted in the Twenty-sixth Article of Religion.

"Supernatural sacramental influence" refers to the notion that the sacraments confer supernatural grace, rather than being human observances of rituals set out in the NT, as the Calvinists argued. In the Catechism in the *BCP* the two sacraments of baptism and the eucharist are defined as "an outward and visible sign of an inward and spiritual grace, given unto us, ordained by Christ himself, as a means whereby we receive the same, and a pledge to assure us thereof." Similarly, in the Twenty-fifth Article the sacraments are said to be "not only badges or tokens of Christian men's profession, but rather they be certain sure witnesses, and effectual signs of grace, and God's good will towards us, by the which he doth work invisibly in us." The "superstitions" associated with these ideas of succession, priestly character, and the sacraments are the "Romish Doctrines" referred to in the Twenty-second Article that treat such matters as either mechanical or physical.

For "priests' robe," based on the robe of the High Priest in temple worship in Israel, see Exod. 28:4 and Lev. 8:7. Wilson alludes to the contemporaneous controversy concerning the application of the "ornaments rubric" of the *BCP* to ecclesiastical vestments (such as the surplice, alb, and chasuble, revived by the Tractarians and their followers) to be worn in the services of the church: "The Ornaments of the Church, and of the Ministers thereof at all times of their Ministration, shall be retained and be in use, as were in the Church of England, by the Authority of Parliament, in the second year of the reign of King Edward the Sixth." The ritualists included such opponents of *Essays and Reviews* as George Anthony Denison, who had defended ritualistic views of the eucharist from 1854 to 1858 and was instrumental with Keble and Pusey in the establishment of the Church of England Protection Society (1859; changed in 1860 to English Church Union), occasioned by the trial of a ritualist priest Bryan King by A. C. Tait (bp. of London). The English Church Union promoted Catholic doctrine and practice in the C. of E. and helped defend clergy prosecuted in the ecclesiastical courts for ritualism. It was supported by such ritualist periodicals as the *Christian Remembrancer* and the *Literary Churchman*. To maintain the Protestant ideals of worship and doctrine in the C. of E., the Church Association was established in 1865 in opposition to the ritualists (see Wilson ¶55 and note).

For "unction from above," the anointing oil used from ancient times in ordination, see the second verse of the *Veni Creator* in the ordination service of the *BCP* (1662): "Thy blessed unction from above / Is comfort, life, and fire of love."

55. Nationalism is the political, social, and religious theory that advocates the nation-state as the governing entity as opposed to both the free action and wills of individual citizens and such universalist polities as those of the Holy Roman Empire or the Roman Catholic Church. The basis of this collectivity is usually established in a common language and race as shared genetic inheritance.

In its nineteenth-century usage, nationalism developed in association with the romantic cultivation of national artistic and literary traditions; it is linked to the emergence of the nation-state, particularly in the American and French revolutions; with the subsequent patriotic responses of separate nation-states to resist the expansionist military policies of Napoleon; and with the European revolutions of 1830 and 1848. Furthermore, it encompasses the unification movements in Germany and Italy, together with such resistance movements as those in Poland and Ireland. E. J. Hobsbawm indicates some of the problems of definition concerning "nationalism" as a European term that was only coming into currency in the 1840s and 1850s ([1975] 1979, 87). For recent discussions of nationalism see Hobsbawm 1992; for nationalism as a religion see Hayes 1966, 93–125.

In a theological sense "nationalism" refers to the divine election or mission of a particular nation. In the OT, Israel is the chosen "nation" (see, for instance, Exod. 19:3–6; Deut. 4:5–8). In the NT, however, Christ is said to have died for "all nations" (John 11:50–52), and the disciples are told to "preach . . . unto all nations" (Matt. 24:14). See also Wilson ¶35 and note. Contemporary religious "prejudices against Nationalism" to which Wilson alludes encompass the Evangelical George S. Faber, and the High Churchman J. H. Newman, both of whom published in the early 1840s. Faber argues against nationalism in that it is not found in the Bible or in the primitive church but is a "system" that intervenes between the individual and God; Newman attempts to sustain the tension between the universal Catholic church and the particular national churches. Faber argues that nationalism, along with other "doctrinal systems," is false: "The several doctrinal Systems, usually denominated *Arminianism* and *Nationalism* and *Calvinism*, were alike unknown to that earliest Church Catholic, which conversed either with the Apostles or with the disciples of the Apostles, and which by them personally was instructed in the real articles of the Christian Faith" (1842, 189).

Newman, on the other hand, argues in "Catholicity in the Anglican Church": "The Anglican view . . . of the Church has ever been this, that its separate portions need not be united together, for their essential completeness, except by the tie of descent from one original. They are like a number of colonies sent out from a mother country, or as the tribes or nations which spring from a common parent. . . . They are in consequence, as Churches, under the supremacy of the state or monarch whom they obey in temporals, and may be used by him as one of the functions of his government, as his ministers of public instruction" ([1840] 1948, 2:58).

Two famous statements on nationalism and nationality contemporaneous with *Essays and Reviews* indicate the extension of religious implications of nation and race into the realm of the political. In the chapter "Of Nationality, as Connected with Representative Government" in *Considerations on Representative Government* (1861), J. S. Mill argues: "A portion of mankind may be said to constitute a Nationality, if they are united among themselves by common sympathies, which do not exist between them and any others. . . . Community of language, and community of religion, greatly contribute to it. Geographical limits are one of its causes. But the strongest of all is identity of political antecedents; the possession of a national history, and consequent community of recollections; collective pride and humiliation, pleasure and regret, connected with the same incidents in the past" (1963–91, 19:546–47). In "Nationality" in the *Home and Foreign Review* (1862), Lord Acton traces an idea of progress and liberty that in many ways is comparable to Wilson's: "Christianity rejoices at the mixture of races, as paganism identifies itself with their differences, because truth is universal, and errors various and particular. In the ancient world idolatry and nationality went together, and the same term is applied in Scripture to both. It was the mission of the Church to overcome national differences. . . . Out of the mediaeval period, and the combined action of the German race and the Church, came forth a new system of nations and a new conception of nationality. Nature was overcome in the nation as well as in the individual . . . and the new principle of self-government, which Christianity imposed, enabled them to live together under the same authority, without necessarily losing their cherished habits, their customs, or their laws. The new idea of freedom made room for different races in one State. . . . A State may in course of time produce a nationality; but that a nationality should constitute a State is contrary to the nature of modern civilisation. The nation derives its rights and its power from the memory of a former independence" (1986, 1:426–27).

56. For "powers of darkness" see Luke 22:53; Col. 1:13; "Lord of light and life," John 1:4; 8:12.

57. Wilson contrasts the little-traveled John with the much-traveled Paul by referring to the latter in the words of Horace: "Who many towns and men and manners saw" (*Ars Poetica*, trans. H. Rushton Fairclough, *Loeb* l. 142). Horace quotes the description of Odysseus in the opening lines of the *Odyssey*. See also Tennyson: "Much have I seen and known; cities of men / And manners." ("Ulysses," 1833, ll. 13–14).

58. For "whole world . . . wickedness" see 1 John 5:19; "prayers . . . authority," 1 Tim. 2:2.

Wilson compares John's doctrine of love as "the more intense" and Paul's "charity" "as the more ample," using the conventional distinction between John and Paul's writings. John, described as the "disciple whom Jesus loved" (John 20:2; 21:7; 21:20), refers in his gospel to Jesus as the incarnation of love (John 3:16) and as teaching a gospel of love (John 13:34–35). A similar doctrine is stated in the epistles of John (for instance, 1 John 4:8–11). Paul's "charity," stressed by Wilson as one that "comprehended all men," involves the notion that love is the fulfilment of the law (Rom. 13:10) and that the inclusivity of love as the highest of the virtues (1 Cor. 13) involves especially the mission to the Gentiles (Acts 13:46–49). At the same time Wilson indicates points of difference in the cited passages regarding the universality of fallen human nature in John and Paul's notion of prayers for all, especially those placed in authority as part of a benevolent order.

59. The dependant relations between "political constitutions" and the "work of God Himself" have a long genealogy. Paul, for instance, writes that "the powers that be are ordained of God" (Rom. 13:1). Cicero in *De Republica* (44) argues that "all those who have preserved, aided, or enlarged their fatherland have a special place prepared for them in the heavens . . . . Their rulers and preservers come from that place, and to that place they return" (bk. 6, sec. 13; trans. Clinton Walker Keyes, *Loeb* 265–67).

Calvin attributes "the task of constituting religion aright to human polity" ([1536] 1957, 2:653; bk. 4, chap. 20, sec. 3). For recent discussions of relations between church and state in Calvin's Geneva see Mueller 1953; Innes 1983; and Gamble 1992.

G. F. W. Hegel explicitly connects the notions of political constitution, the state, and the will of God in the Introduction to *Lectures on the Philosophy of History*: "The State is the Divine Idea as it exists on Earth. . . . The State is an *abstraction*. . . . It is only by a constitution that the *abstraction*—the State—attains life and reality; but this involves the distinction between those who command and those who obey" ([1832] 1881, 41, 45). See also Wilson ¶63 and note.

60. For "all nations," see Matt. 24:15; John 11:50–52.

Thomas Arnold makes the United States of America an exception to "all nations" when discussing the "national churches" of "heathendom" in *Principles of Church Reform*, because there "the evil spirit of sectarianism has wrought his perfect work" ([1833] 1962, 98).

For Wilson's discussion of theocracy see ¶27. For a nineteenth-century discussion that "style[s] the Jewish constitution a theocracy" see Horne [1818] 1828, 1:77–81. According to the *New Catholic Encyclopedia*, other theocratic systems of polity include those of "Tibet, some Buddhist regimes of Japan and China, Islam, the Geneva of John Calvin, Puritan New England, the Papal States, and Mormon Salt Lake Salt City" (s.v. "Theocracy," 14:13).

Wilson refers not to a formal constitution but to the political system of the Jews of which Josephus asserts that Moses set up the "constitution" of Israel, using "the form of what . . . may be termed a 'theocracy,' placing all sovereignty and authority in the hands of God" (*Against Apion*, bk. 2, chap. 16; trans. H. St. J. Thackeray, *Loeb* 1:359).

61. For "the face of the earth" see Jer. 28:16.

In *Principles of Church Reform*, Thomas Arnold makes a similar argument regarding the universality rather than the inevitability (as in Wilson) of priesthood in all cultures, stressing that "all the tendencies of the ministerial office, as such, are wholly beneficial" ([1833] 1962, 95–96).

"No distant nation . . . [whose] institutions [are] shattered to pieces" refers to the French Revolution in terms similar to Thomas Carlyle in *The French Revolution* (1837). For instance, Carlyle writes of the "Constitution Burst in Pieces" (vol. 2, bk. 6, chap. 8; 1896–99, 3:302–8), and of "the Destruction of the Catholic Religion; and indeed, for the time being, of Religion itself" in November 1793 (vol. 3, bk. 5, chap. 4; 1896–99, 4:223–27). While Carlyle's rhetoric is strikingly different from Wilson's, their arguments about the destructiveness of the revolution, and the reconstitution of social authority in the form of a new religion, are similar; Wilson draws political lines concerning democratic reform that align him more with Carlyle than, for instance, with the views of Tom Paine on the revolution (see Wilson ¶7 and note).

62. Previous to the time of the divided kingdom, the Jewish history presents little which is thoroughly reliable. The taking of Jerusalem by 'Shishak' is for the Hebrew history that which the sacking of Rome by the Gauls is for the Roman. And from no facts ascertainable is it possible to infer there was any early period during which the Government by the priesthood was attended with success. Indeed the greater probability seems on the side of the supposition, that the priesthood, with its distinct offices and charge, was constituted by Royalty, and that the higher pretensions of the priests were not advanced till the reign of Josiah. There is no evidence of the priesthood ever having claimed a supremacy over the kings, as if it had been in possession of an oracular power; in the earlier monarchy the kings offer sacrifice, and the rudiments of a political and religious organization, which prevailed in the period of the Judges, cannot be appealed to as pre-eminently a theocracy. At any rate, nothing could be more unsuccessful, as a government, whatever it might be called. Indeed, the theory of the Jewish theocracy, seems built chiefly upon some expressions in 1 Sam. viii., xii. Samuel, however, with whose government the Israelites were dissatisfied, was not a priest but a prophet; and the whole of that part of the narrative is conceived in the prophetical, not in the priestly interest [Wilson's note].

The "divided kingdom," or divided monarchy, refers to the period from 922 to 722 B.C.E., when northern and southern Israel were ruled by different dynasties following the death of Solomon.

For "the taking of Jerusalem by Shishak" see 1 Kings 14:25–29 and 2 Chron. 12:2–9. Shishak, or Shoshenq, was pharaoh of Egypt (945–924 B.C.E.), a contemporary of Solomon. When Palestine was divided into the Northern Kingdom of Israel and Southern Kingdom of Judah after Solomon's death (922 B.C.E.), Shishak invaded Judah, then being ruled by Rehoboam, and captured Jerusalem, taking as tribute the treasures of the temple. For an account of this "Hebrew history" see Josephus, *Jewish Antiquities* (bk. 8, secs. 255–63; trans. H. St. J. Thackeray and Ralph Marcus, *Loeb* 5:711–15), in which Rehoboam is blamed for not preparing a defense of Jerusalem.

The "sacking of Rome by the Gauls" occurred in 390 B.C.E., when Celts under Brennus defeated Roman armies at Allia. The Gauls besieged Rome for seven months, laying hold of the entire city except for the Capitol. See Livy, *History of Rome*, bk. 5, chap. 38–39; trans. B. O. Foster, *Loeb* 3:129–37, where the unpreparedness of the city of Rome for the attack is stressed. Hence Wilson's comparison stresses the weakness of theocratic rule under a priesthood against a superior political and military force.

"The reign of Josiah" began in 639 B.C.E. when at the age of eight, upon the assassination of his father, he was made king of Judah (2 Kings 22:1). During a reign of 31 years Josiah undertook a series of religious reforms (2 Kings 23).

"The period of the Judges" follows the occupation of Canaan under Joshua (Exod. 6–12) to the establishment of the monarchy under Samuel (1 Sam. 9–10). The first cited passage is the people's request to Samuel for a king, after which Samuel delivers a diatribe against the principle of monarchy. In the second, Samuel gives his last speech that marks the end of the period of Judges and a structural break in the narrative of the Deuteronomic history. The expressions Wilson alludes to in 1 Sam. 8 and 12 (as in 1 Sam. 8:5,7 and 12:1, 12) refer to the period when God was king over Israel, giving rise to "the theory of the Jewish theocracy." Contemporaneous commentaries on 1 Sam. 8:7, for instance by Simon Patrick and others, make the same point: "For the supreme Governor of the world was their sovereign; who governed them by judges whom he raised up and extraordinarily inspired. . . . [Josephus] makes it a most distinct sort of government, different from all other; which he truly calls by a new name, Θεοκρατία [*Theokratia*], 'the government of God' (lib. ii)" (1846–49, 2:133). For "the Hebrew State" see also Temple ¶15.

63. For "the Lord's people" see, for example, 2 Chron. 23:16; "Supreme Governor," Ps 8:1, 10 (*BCP* version: "O Lord our Governor"); 1 Pet. 2:13.

64. For "kindling a fire in the earth" see Luke 12:49; "dividing families . . . against two," Luke 12:51–53; "aliens from their . . . commonwealths," Eph. 2:12; Heb. 13:14; "How often . . . would not," Matt. 23:37; Luke 13:34.

For the notion that Paul preached the kingdom of Christ (the word of God) to the Jewish people and, on their rejecting it, to the Gentiles, see Acts 13:46–48, where the word "Gentiles" is a translation of the Greek ἔθνος (*ethnos*, nation); Paul moves from the mission in Palestine into Europe as he crosses over into Macedonia, into the "nations" (Acts 16:9); Jesus speaks in a vision to Paul to go to preach to the nations or the "Gentiles" (Acts 26:14–18). In the Gospels, Jesus offers his kingdom to the Jews but it is rejected (Matt. 21:42–44). The apostolic preaching to the nations or the Gentiles as an individualist matter is stressed in Paul's references to his work amongst families and speaking "privately" (Gal. 2:2).

The connection between the "mind of Jesus" and "Nationalism" is made clearer by Wilson's contemporary, Christopher Wordsworth, who interprets Matt. 23:37 typologically: just as the children of Israel are gathered symbolically into the Temple in Jesus' address to Jerusalem, so also the nations are gathered into the church, whose antetype is the temple (1861, 1:84).

65. In this paragraph Wilson gives a brief history of the missionary activity of the early Christian community from the time of Paul to the time of Charlemagne, suggesting that patterns of conversion increasingly were linked with nationality, particularly when Christianity was adopted by the rulers of particular peoples or "nations," linking Christianity, nation, and race.

After Paul's vision of the request to preach in Macedonia (Acts 16:10), he enters Europe for the first time, going to Philippi in Greece, where he was arrested for preaching and causing a disturbance. In the passage Wilson refers to, his jailor and whole "household" are converted and baptized, an instance of "individual and domestic" extension of Christianity in the Hellenistic world.

During the Roman occupation of Britain from 43 to 401/410, there is evidence of extensive individual conversions, martyrdoms (such as that of St. Alban about 209), and the setting up of ecclesiastical structures (Britain sent three bishops to the Council of Arles in 314). The invasion of Britain by the Picts, Scots (from about 370), and the Saxons, (with the Angles and Jutes from about 450) not only eroded and terminated Roman hegemony but also led to other conversion processes, as whole populations were converted by the Celtic missionaries from Rome and Gaul such as Ninian among the Picts and Scots (c. 400), Patrick among the Irish (c. 450), and the whole of the Franks under Remigius, bishop of Rheims, when their king, Clovis, accepted Christianity in 496. The Saxons, however, were more instrumental in eliminating the last traces of Christianity remaining from the conversions under the Roman occupation, until Ethelbert, king of Kent, accepted Christianity at the hands of Austin (Augustine of Canterbury) who had come to Britain as a missionary in 596. Augustine sent Mellitus to work among the East Saxons near London (c. 604), and Paulinus of York to work in the north where he converted Edwin, king of Northumbria and his people (c. 625). Boniface, the "apostle of Germany," born in Devon, was a missionary in Germany from 716 to his death in 754. The chronological narrative of this history is recounted in Bede's *Ecclesiastical History of the English People*, which covers the period from the invasion of Britain by Julius Caesar until Bede's death in 731.

For a contemporaneous discussion of the Roman occupation see Thomas Wright 1851. For recent treatments of early Christian missions see Talbot 1954; McNeil 1974; Thomas 1981; and Wallace-Hadrill 1988.

66. The consolidation of "Italy itself" under the power of "pagan Rome" occurred about 265 B.C.E. after the three Samnite Wars (342–341 B.C.E.; 327–304 B.C.E.; and 295–290 B.C.E.); the defeat of Pyrrhus (275 B.C.E.); and successful wars against the Umbrians, Picentes, and Sallentini (270–265 B.C.E). Relations between Rome and Spain involve the two Punic Wars (264–241 B.C.E.; and 218–202 B.C.E.). After the latter, the Romans established two provinces in Spain in 197 B.C.E. The conquest of France by the Romans began in 123–121 B.C.E., and was completed by Julius Caesar in 59–54 B.C.E.

"Teutonic" refers to an association of tribal nations in Germany. Wilson is establishing the Germanic element of the English national "character," differentiating it from those countries (Italy, Spain and France) still predominantly Roman Catholic. Henry Soames in his Bampton Lectures of 1830 makes an argument similar to Wilson's: "The Anglo-Saxons . . . were chiefly converted by native missionaries. . . . Our forefathers . . . were not generally converted . . . by Roman missionaries. The heralds of salvation, who routed Christianity in most parts of England, were trained in native schools of theology, and were attached firmly to those national usages which had descended to them from periods of the most venerable antiquity" (1830, 112, 257). For a mid-nineteenth-century discussion of "the resistance offered by the native Churches to Romish Influence" see George Smith 1844, 477–508.

The appeal to Teutonic liberty was a contemporary topic, as in E. A. Freeman's discussion of the British Constitution from "the first Teutonic settlers" to "the Norman Conquest" when "the many small Teutonic kingdoms in Britain had grown into one Teutonic kingdom of England, rich in her barbaric greatness and barbaric freedom, with the germs, but as yet only the germs, of every institution which we most dearly prize" ([1860] 1871, 42). L. P. Curtis relates Teutonic liberty to nineteenth-century "Anglo-Saxonism": "For the Englishman who believed in the superiority of the Anglo-Saxon race and culture over all others in the world, the supreme embodiment of that genius could be found in the English Constitution which had enshrined and preserved over many centuries certain fundamental liberties, sometimes labelled Saxon, Gothic, German, or Teutonic, or ancient liberties, the sum of which accounted for the moral and material progress of the modern English people" (1968, 8). For such an appeal to the "freedom" of the "Teutonic Churches" see Temple ¶25 and note.

67. For "faith once delivered to the saints" see Jude 1:3.

The whole of Wilson ¶36, as well as ¶40, are specified as "false and dangerous" in the Synodical Condemnation of *Essays and Reviews* on 21 June 1864. Wilson is attacked for asserting that it is acceptable to subscribe to the Articles of Religion "without believing them to be true" (*Chronicle* 1859–64:1864, Session 66, 1659).

68. The Sixth Article of Religion, "Of the Sufficiency of the Holy Scriptures for Salvation," is the "pivot Article" to which Wilson refers: "Holy Scripture containeth all things necessary to Salvation: so that whatsoever is not read therein, nor may be proved thereby, is not to be required of any man, that it should be believed as an article of the faith, or be thought requisite or necessary to salvation. In the name of the holy Scripture we do understand those Canonical Books of the Old and New Testament, of whose authority was never any doubt in the Church" (*BCP*).

69. This clause is taken from the Wirtemburg Confession (1552), which proceeds: 'Hanc Scripturam credimus et confitemur esse oraculum Spiritus Sancti, caelestibus testimoniis ita confirmatum, ut *Si Angelus de caelo aliud praedicaverit, anathema sit*' [Wilson's note].

The Würtemberg Confession of thirty-five articles by Johann Brenz, a follower of Philip Melanchthon, who led the Lutheran reformers in the Duchy of Würtemberg, was prepared for the Council of Trent in 1552 to help explain the reformers' positions. The cited passage is from Article 30, on the Bible: "We believe and confess these scriptures to be the oracles of the Holy Spirit, as a testimony confirmed by heaven, so that if an angel from heaven were to were to preach otherwise, let him be accursed." The italicized phrase in Wilson's note echoes Gal. 1:8.

The Würtemberg Confession influenced the Anglican Articles of Religion. Archbishop Matthew Parker revised Thomas Cranmer's *42 Articles* (1552) by using it in a number of places (the second, fifth, sixth, tenth, eleventh, twelfth, and twentieth) in the preparation of the *Thirty-Nine Articles* (1571). The Würtemberg Confession is the basis of the second sentence in the Sixth Article of Religion (see above, n. 68).

70. After listing the canonical books of the OT the Sixth Article of Religion continues: "And the other Books (as *Hierome* saith [in his Preface to the Books of Samuel]) the Church doth read for example of life and instruction of manners; but yet doth it not apply them to establish any doctrine." Then follows the list of the books of the Apocrypha. These books, mostly in Greek and mostly dating from before the fall of Jerusalem in 70, were accepted by the Jews in the diaspora and were included in some versions of the Septuagint. Jerome's Latin "vulgate" version of the fourth century did not include most of these books, but they were added to his vulgate from the earlier Old Latin version and subsequently were included in most Roman Catholic bibles where they were regarded as "sacred and canonical" according to the Council of Trent in a decree of 1546. Luther gathered these books together at the end of the OT in his 1534 Bible, naming the collection "Apocrypha" (Gk: concealed, hidden) on the basis of 2 Esdras 12:37–38 that refers to writing "all these things that thou hast seen in a book, and hid[ing] them."

In the C. of E. the Apocrypha was included in the lectionary and was printed in the AV. The Third Article of the Presbyterian *Westminster Confession* (1648) states that the Apocrypha is "of no authority in the Church of God, nor to be otherwise approved of, or made use of, than other human writings." Largely as a result of the opposition of the (Presbyterian) Church of Scotland, the British and Foreign Bible Society in 1826 omitted the Apocrypha from its publications after a six-year controversy (see Howsam 1991, 13–15).

71. Thus the Helvetic Confession states: 'We believe and profess that the Canonical Scriptures of the Holy Prophets and Apostles, of the Old and New Testaments, *are* the very Word of God, and have sufficient authority from themselves and not from men.' The Saxon Confession refers to the creeds as interpreters of Scripture—nos vera fide amplecti omnia scripta Prophetarum et Apostolorum; et quidem in hac ipsa nativa sententia, quae expressa est in Symbolis, Apostolico, Nicaeno et Athanasiano.—*De Doctrina* [Wilson's note].

Wilson refers to the second Helvetic Confession (1566) by Henry Bullinger, the friend and successor of Ulrich Zwingli. It is the last of the Zwinglian confessions of faith elaborated in German-speaking Switzerland during the Reformation.

Wilson translates the Latin of the first clause of chap. 1. A text is given in Schaff [1877] 1983, 3:237. As Wilson points out in an earlier essay, the reforms of Turretin in the early eighteenth century abolished the requirement that prospective ordinands in the Swiss Reformed Church sign the Helvetic Confession, thereby facilitating progress toward church union (Wilson 1857, 103 ff.).

The Saxon Confession, an elaboration of the Lutheran Augsburg Confession (1530), was written by Philip Melanchthon for discussion at the Council of Trent in 1551. It was printed in 1552 as *Confessio Doctrinae Saxonicarum,* from which Wilson quotes part of the first article: "Our true faith is comprehended in all the scriptures of the Prophets and Apostles, and indeed in these original thoughts is expressed what is in the Apostolic, Nicene, and Athanasian Creeds." The Thirty-nine Articles of Religion did not go so far as these continental confessions in moving beyond canonical to doctrinal claims.

72. Wilson alludes to different methods of interpretation and different generic forms of narrative: literal or allegorical interpretation, and the forms of parable, poetry, legend, and story. Such distinctions were common, as in Horne's chapter on "the Special Interpretation of Scripture" where he discusses "the literal meaning," "Scripture Allegories," "Parables," "Fables," and "Poetical Parts of Scripture" ([1818] 1828, 2: 369–446).

For the "serpent tempter" see Gen. 3; "an ass speaking," Num. 22:28–30; "an arresting of the earth's motion" Josh. 10:12–13; "waters standing . . . heap," Exod. 15:8; "witches," 1 Sam. 28:7–9; Nah. 3:5; "apparitions," Deut. 18:10–11; Isa. 8:19. For "institution of the Sabbath" see Gen. 2:3 and Exod. 20:8–11; "the deluge," Gen. 7:4–8:22; "confusion of tongues," Gen. 11:7; "corporeal taking up of Elijah," 2 Kings 2:11–12; "nature of angels," Ps. 104:4; Luke 2:13; "demoniacal possession," Matt. 4:24; 8:16–33; 9:32. 12:22; the "personality of Satan," Job 1:6–12; Matt. 4.

The passage from Wilson ¶38, "Under the terms of the. . . . of many events," was cited as "false and dangerous" in the Synodical Condemnation of *Essays and Reviews* on 21 June 1864. Wilson is attacked for asserting that rational thought can be used to test the veracity of the Articles of Religion (*Chronicle* 1859–64:1864, Session 66, 1658–59).

73. "Scripturalism," or biblicism, is the doctrine that the Bible is the word of God literally inspired in each word and letter, rejecting any form of the historical critical method of interpretation (see also Wilson ¶41 and note).

The role of the Bible in the "rudimentary education" of "a large number of our countrymen" was partly the result of the Sunday Schools and partly the work of the British and Foreign Bible Society. Robert Raikes established the Sunday School movement in the 1780s, giving major attention to Bible reading in teaching literacy. The Bible Society (founded in 1804) had as its goal the distribution of cheap copies of the Bible to the poor or "unlearned" while the three privileged presses (Oxford, Cambridge, and the Queen's Printer, Eyre and Spottiswoode) produced Bibles, often with parallels, in more expensive editions. For instance, in Manchester in November 1845, the British and Foreign Bible Society was faced with a demand for 20,000 copies for the month: "The superintendents, teachers and senior students of the Sunday Schools, under the supervision of a 'zealous . . . gentleman', sell Bibles and Testaments to the workpeople of the local mills and factories" (Howsam 1991, 162). Ellen Henrietta Ranyard published an account of her work for the Bible Society in distributing cheap copies among the London poor in 1855–57, *The Missing Link; or, Bible-Women in the Homes of the London Poor* (1859).

74. The "controversy" concerned the British and Foreign Bible Society's "fundamental principle," the mandate to reprint the Bible cheaply "without note or comment" as stated in its charter (1804), and in the decision of the administrative Committee of 7 June 1813. This policy was adopted to allay the Apocryphal Controversy (Howsam 1991, 13). The "two great parties" of the C. of E. were the High and Low Church. The latter, also sometimes called "Evangelicals, were aligned with the Dissenters. The "two great organized societies" were the Society for Promoting Christian Knowledge (founded 1698), "an exclusively Anglican organization untouched by the evangelical revival . . . [and] the customary source of Bibles for Anglicans" and its rival in Bible publishing, the British and Foreign Bible Society (Howsam 1991, 4–5).

The tenth and subsequent editions of *Essays and Reviews* (from January 1862 on), and the first American edition, change the phrase "without note and comment" to "without note or comment," thereby conforming to the wording of the Bible Society's stated principle.

75. Biblical "infallibility," or inerrancy is related to the idea of "Scripturalism" (see also Wilson ¶39), arguing that as more and more "truth" is known, the Bible in its autograph, or original, forms (which MSS. are autograph, or original, remains a problem) is true in its entirety and is never false in all matters with which it deals, including the social and physical sciences. Such literalism frequently takes words and passages out of context by free association or echoic resonance to function as "proof" texts or "infallible tests" of a particular point of doctrine, faith, morals, or practice. For a contemporaneous survey see Call 1861. For recent defenses of such views see Warfield [1940] 1960; and Carson and Woodbridge 1983. For recent arguments questioning them see Beegle 1979.

Plenary inspiration, on the other hand, allows some accommodation with secular knowledge. Rather than locating inspiration in the very letters and words of the text, plenary inspiration locates it in the writers of the Bible, in the authors of the specific books, with the assumption that they have been inspired by God. For histories of the concept of biblical inspiration see Burtchaell 1969; Abraham 1981; Cameron 1987; and Fox 1992, 13–49; 155–58; 399–417.

For an extended discussion of inspiration see Jowett ¶14 and notes.

The whole of Wilson ¶40, as well as ¶36, are cited in the Synodical Condemnation. See Wilson ¶36 and note.

76. Wilson's distinction between inspiration and revelation questions how infallible inspiration, under the direct influence of the Holy Spirit as "absolute Truth," can propagate scriptural "puzzles" or biblical inconsistencies, whether real or apparent. Contemporaneously, Westcott writes that inspiration is the correlative of revelation and both imply supernatural extensions of spiritual vision: "By Inspiration we conceive that his natural powers are quickened so that he contemplates with a divine intuition the truth as it exists still among the ruins of the moral and physical worlds. By Revelation we see as it were the dark veil removed from the face of things, so that the true springs and issues of life stand disclosed in their eternal nature" ([1851] 1888, 8).

By "differences . . . in the Evangelical narratives" Wilson alludes to the "synoptic problem," the differences in narratives and detail among the synoptic gospels: "In many cases, as in the genealogies and the narratives of the Passion and the Resurrection, these differences amount to serious difficulties from our ignorance of all the circumstances on which the accounts depend; and even where it is not so, they are distinct and numerous" (Westcott [1851] 1888, 200). Similarly, those who stress differences in the chronologies in Kings and Chronicles that recount events from the same historical periods are alleged to be attacking "a holy thing," namely, the infallibility of the Bible.

77. "Distinct Christologies" refer to different theological positions on the person and work of Christ in the apostolic period. Westcott refers to "The Christology of the Samaritans" in a long note on its relation to the synoptics, the gospel of John ([1851] 1888, 163–64), and the writings of Paul (238–40; 283–96). For "primitive Church" see Temple ¶20 and note.

Wilson alludes to four notable points of difference in the gospels. First, the genealogy of Christ in Matthew (1:1–17), from the Davidic and Solomonic lines of kingship traced through the covenant with Abraham, differs from that in Luke (3:23–38), traced backwards to Adam. Second, what Westcott calls "the difficulties connected with the chronology of the Paschal week . . . acknowledged on all hands to be very considerable" ([1851] 1888, 343), relate to the time and nature of the Last Supper and the day of the week on which Jesus died, in such matters as the "preparation" for the sabbath and the eve of Passover: see Matt. 27; Mark 15; Luke 23; John 19; and different accounts of the inscription on the cross. The "accounts of the Resurrection" are also at variance or record different appearances and actions, as, for example, those of Mary Magdalene (Matt. 28:1–8; Mark 16:1–8; Luke 24:1–12; John 20:1–29). Such discrepancies were explained as complementary narratives, and today are accounted for on the basis of different textual sources. Finally, Wilson alludes to the assertion that Jesus is descended from the tribe of Judah (Matt. 1:2) and from the tribe of Levi (Luke 3:24).

78. Wilson draws an analogy between "the national character" exemplified in the individual "English citizen" and the "national Church" exemplified in the "English Churchman." The analogy depends upon "the freedom of opinion" attributed to the first, and the "multitudinist principle" attributed to the second. Just as national character in an English citizen involves endorsing freedom of opinion, so the multitudinist principles of the national church represented in an English churchman should equally endorse freedom of opinion.

The question of legal rights to and constraints on such "freedom of opinion" was widely discussed in the mid-nineteenth century. In *The Tracts for the Times*, J. W. Bowden wrote *Tracts XXIX* and *XXX* on *Christian Liberty, or Why Should We Belong to the Church of England?* (1834). In *On Liberty* (1859), J. S. Mill connects "freedom of conscience" to "religious freedom" which has "hardly anywhere been practically realized" (1963–91, 18:222). Concluding the first chapter, he writes of the limits to liberty imposed by "the engines of moral repression [which] have been wielded more strenuously against divergence from the reigning opinion" especially in religion where the engines are driven "either by the ambition of a hierarchy, seeking control over every department of human conduct, or by the spirit of Puritanism" (1963–91, 18:226–27). In chapter 2 Mill refers to religious persecution for opinions which are frowned upon or rejected by religious authorities (1963–91, 18:239–40). Mill cites various examples of such persecution, and the cases preferred against Williams, Wilson, and Jowett in the *Essays and Reviews* trials provide further exemplification of Wilson's point.

In his reference to "some restraints" on freedom of opinion, Wilson alludes specifically to the continuing debate about subscription to the Thirty-nine Articles of Religion (See Williams ¶4 and note), and about the kinds of mental reservations that an individual might have in swearing to them.

79. The oath *ex officio* in the ecclesiastical law, is defined to be an oath whereby any person may be obliged to make any presentment of any crime or offence, or to confess or accuse himself or herself of any criminal matter or thing, whereby he or she may

be liable to any censure, penalty, or punishment whatsoever. 4 Jac. 'The lords of the council at Whitehall demanded of Popham and Coke, chief justices, upon motion made by the Commons in Parliament, in what cases the ordinary may examine any person *ex officio* upon oath.' They answered—1. That the ordinary cannot constrain any man, ecclesiastical or temporal, to swear generally to answer such interrogations as shall be administered to him, &c. 2. That no man, ecclesiastical or temporal, shall be examined upon the secret thoughts of his heart, or of his secret opinion, but something ought to be objected against him, which he hath spoken or done. Thus 13 Jac. *Dighton* and *Holt* were committed by the high commissioners because they being convicted for slanderous words against the book of Common Prayer and the government of the Church, and being tendered the oath to be examined, they refused. The case being brought before the K. B. on *Habeas Corpus*, Coke, C. J., gave the determination of the Court. 'That they ought to be delivered, because their examination is made to cause them to accuse themselves of a breach of a penal law, which is against law, for they ought to proceed against them by witnesses, and not inforce them to take an oath to accuse themselves.' Then by 13 Car. 2, c. 12, it was enacted, 'that it shall not be lawful for any person, exercising ecclesiastical jurisdiction, to tender or administer to any person whatsoever the oath usually called the oath *ex-officio*, or any other oath, whereby such person to whom the same is tendered, or administered, may be charged, or compelled to confess, or accuse, or to purge himself, or herself, of any criminal matter or thing,' &c.—Burn's *Eccl. Law,* iii. 14, 15. Ed. Phillimore [Wilson's note].

Wilson cites the standard textbook on the subject, Richard Burn's *The Ecclesiastical Law* ([1760] 1842, 4 vols., 9th ed.) edited by Robert Phillimore (the section on "Oaths: *ex officio*," 3:14), omitting several phrases.

The legal precedent dates from the struggle in 1607–8 involving Sir Edward Coke concerning the jurisdiction and procedures of the Court of High Commission as opposed to the Court of Common Pleas, that is, the ecclesiastical against the secular courts. The chief justices and the House of Commons were ranged against James I and Archbishop Richard Bancroft concerning Puritan clergy who refused to take the oath *ex officio*. That is, they refused to take an oath swearing innocence when charged with a criminal offence—some form of nonconformity to the Articles and Formularies. The oath was widely used in other courts appropriately, since the protestation of innocence was needed before judicial examination, and the precise factual accusation was known to the defendant in a writ. But in the ecclesiastical courts there was no such writ, and what was at issue was not matters of fact and action but matters of private belief and opinion, in which the oath *ex officio* was used for entrapment. In 1607 the House of Commons asked Coke and Sir John Popham, chief justice of the Court of King's Bench, for an opinion on the legality of the oath *ex officio* as used in the ecclesiastical courts. Coke replied: "No man ecclesiastical or temporal shall be examined upon secret thoughts of his heart or of his secret opinion. And the defendant must have, as in Star Chamber and Chancery, the bill [of charges] delivered unto him, or otherwise he need not answer to it. Laymen for the most part are not lettered, wherefore they may easily be inveigled and intrapped and principally in heresy and matters of faith" (Catherine Bowen 1957, 298). In the case of *Edwards*, Coke pronounced: "The Ecclesiastical judge cannot examine any man upon his oath, upon the intention and thought of his heart. *Cogitationis poenam nemo emeret* [No one may merit punishment for his thoughts]. For it hath been said in the Proverb, thought is free" (Catherine Bowen 1957, 310)). The Court of Common Pleas, over which Coke had presided as chief justice since 1606, continued to send forward prohibitions, disallowing such cases to be tried by the ecclesiastical courts. On 6 and 13 November 1608 the common-law judges and the ecclesiastical authorities were summoned by James to meet with the Privy Council at Whitehall, and it was at these meetings that Coke repeated his assertions concerning the limitations exercised by Parliament upon the royal authority and by the secular courts upon the ecclesiastical ones (Catherine Bowen 1957, 301–6).

Coke's pronouncements as cited in Burn are from Coke 1826, 6:227–32. The case of *Dighton and Holt* dates from 1616 in the Court of King's Bench where Coke was presiding as Lord Chief Justice of England (from 1613). It concluded that "no man is bound to take the *ex officio* oath in the Spiritual Court upon any matter which subjects him to a penalty," and did so on two grounds, first, the reason cited in Wilson's note, and second, because they "required a copy of the interrogatories, and were denied them" (*English Reports* 1907, 79:332). Reference is made in the same source to the 1673 decision during the reign of Charles II, cited by Wilson.

Similar kinds of struggles on the part of the archbishops of Canterbury (Longley) and York (Thomson) against the use of secular courts (the Judicial Committee of the Privy Council) in matters that they considered to be of ecclesiastical jurisdiction, and that the plaintiffs (Williams and Wilson) considered to be of freedom of speech were replayed in the *Essays and Reviews* trials of 1861–64.

80. From ¶45 to ¶58 Wilson discusses the contemporary controversy concerning subscription to the Thirty-nine Articles of Religion, first showing that the meaning of subscription is not formally explicated (Wilson ¶45) before discussing the legal requirements for subscription in canon law. Com

menting on the still-unresolved matter more than a hundred years later, and referring to the Clerical Subscription Act, passed five years after the publication of *Essays and Reviews*, the Archbishops' Commission writes that assent as "complete legal acceptance . . . has been variously interpreted. A minimal view, associated with the names of Laud, Bramhall, and Ussher, maintained that the Articles were only Articles of peace and that complete legal acceptance implies no more than an undertaking not to contradict them in public. At the other extreme, there have been those who believed that complete legal acceptance of the Articles implies inward commitment to their every proposition. . . . The Act of 1865 retained the word 'assent,' and it is this, rather than any intentions expressed by individuals in the debates, which has legal force. Thus in law the situation remains essentially as it was" (*Subscription* 1968, 11–12). On subscription as a test see Williams ¶4 and note. See also Jowett's testimony before the Select Committee of the House of Lords, 1871 (Abbott and Campbell 1899, 19–39).

81. The *Constitutions and Canons Ecclesiastical* were drawn up in Latin by Richard Bancroft when he was bishop of London. They were debated and approved at the convocation of Canterbury in 1603–4. The Latin text only was confirmed by Letters Patent from James I under the Great Seal of England, being published in 1604. They were never approved by Parliament. Sometimes they are dated, as by Wilson, from the date of their being first debated in convocation, sometimes from the date of confirmation and publication. Wilson omits data from the fifth canon concerning the legal approval of the Thirty-nine Articles of Religion in 1562, and the final clause: "let him be excommunicated *ipso facto*, and not restored, but only by the Archbishop, after his repentance, and public revocation of such his wicked errors." Canon Five is one of the first group of twelve canons dealing with the relation of the church to the state, with those who attack the state religion ("impugners," including those in Canon Five who attack the Thirty-nine Articles), and with schismatics. The wording of this canon is new, but the precedent for it may be traced to the canon of Thomas Arundel, archbishop of Canterbury from 1396 to 1398, who decreed that no one might disagree openly or privately with what was contained in the decrees and constitutions of synods (see Bullard 1934, 161). Hence it appears, as Wilson points out, that this canon applies to laity as well as clergy.

82. The "effects of excommunication" are discussed in Bullard 1934, 153–57. Excommunication was the penalty imposed in each of canons two to twelve. Excommunication was the issue on which Parliament took exception to the Canons of 1604 because of the loss of civil liberties and rights that followed upon its sentence. More than half of the Parliament was Puritan in sympathy, and if brought under the sway of the canons could have become excommunicate. Civil penalties included exclusion from association with others and the loss of rights to serve on a jury or to appear in court, even to claim loss of goods or property; and, if the bishop brought a suit in the Court of Chancery, excommunication could result in imprisonment. Hence the Commons passed a proposal denying the efficacy of the Canons as punitive measures, but the resolution died in the House of Lords.

"Dead controversies" alludes to the fact that the Articles of Religion, which were laid down for the "establishment of a godly concord and the avoiding of controversies" (The Forty-Two Articles of 1553, in Hardwick 1904, 82), are aimed at disagreements with the Anabaptists and Zwinglians. But the dead controversies were resuscitated, as apparently closed issues like baptismal regeneration were opened up in such Victorian controversies as the Gorham case. "Occult operation" in the sacraments refers to a phrase in Article Twenty-five, that the sacraments are "effectual signs of grace" whereby God "doth work invisibly in us," a possible reference to the function of the sacrament *ex opere operato* (by force of the function itself), whereby the sacramental effect is to mediate the grace appropriate to the sacrament and is not dependent upon the moral worth of the officiant or in a Lutheran sense on the spiritual condition of the recipient (see Leeming 1962, 3–22).

Wilson returns to contradictions between the Articles of Religion and matters of fact again in ¶49.

83. Canon Thirty-six stipulates that no person is to be ordained or licensed "except he shall first subscribe" to the three articles, the first acknowledging the king as the "supreme Governor" in all things "Spiritual or Ecclesiastical" as well as temporal; second, that the *BCP* "containeth in it nothing contrary to the Word of God"; and third, that "he alloweth the Book of Articles of Religion agreed upon by the Archbishops and Bishops of both provinces. . . ; and that he acknowledgeth all and every the Articles therein contained, being in number nine and thirty, besides the Ratification, to be agreeable to the Word of God" (*Book of Sermons or Homilies* [1547, 1563] 1802, 536–37). Wilson alludes to the various meanings of "allow" (praise, approval, acceptance as truth, and permission) and "acknowledge" (the admittance of truth, the conferring of legal assent, and the simple recognition of something). However, nothing in the canon explicates either term. Hence, Wilson argues that if "the intention of the framers" (which might well be diverse) could be ascertained, the potential subscriber might not "contradict" such diversity, but could "acknowledge" it, in whatever sense.

How to reform the Articles of Religion concerned those who resisted subscription. In *Principles of Church Reform*, in the section on "Agents of Reform," Thomas Arnold asks how "the National

Church should be rendered thoroughly comprehensive in doctrine, in government, and in ritual" and who should remodel "the Articles, a measure obviously essential to the proposed comprehension." Arnold argues that the task should be committed to a representative ecclesiastical commission, both clerical and lay ([1833] 1962, 145).

84. Wilson asserts the limited authority of the Articles of Religion in relation to the authority of the Bible. The Latin phrases mean "according to what things" and "how far they agree"; that is, the phrase "agreeable to the Word of God" in Canon 36 means that the Articles of Religion agree with the Bible or do not contradict it only insofar as they speak of those matters using biblical terminology or language. On the limited authority of the Articles see Hardwick (1904, 157).

85. For "never . . . any doubt in the Church" see the Sixth Article of Religion; "doubts as a fool might have," Ps. 14:1.

Ferdinand Christian Baur, one of the founders of the "Tübingen School" of biblical criticism, published the controversial *Paulus, der Apostel Jesu Christi* (1845; trans. Eduard Zeller, *Paul, the Apostle of Jesus Christ*, 1873–75, 2 vols.). Baur denies the authenticity of all of the "Pauline" epistles except Galatians, 1 and 2 Corinthians, and Romans. Heinrich Georg August Ewald studied at Göttingen under Eichhorn. Ewald later rejected the work of his teacher, as well as that of Baur and D. F. Strauss. He succeeded Eichhorn at Göttingen, promoting the study of Semitic languages and publishing *Geschichte des Volkes Israel* (1843–55, 5 vols.; trans. Russell Martineau, *History of Israel*, 1869, 2 vols.).

For contemporaneous arguments that the epistles of Paul were "anterior, probably to all of the Gospels, certainly to that of John," see, for example, Samuel Davidson 1848–51, 1:135–36; 2:106–12); and Bernhard Weiss: "The gospel literature came later than the epistolary. Paul knows nothing as yet of written Gospels, but appeals to oral tradition (1 Cor. xv. 3, etc.)" (1887, 1:30).

86. The gradual growth of the canon of the Bible, with specific inconsistencies, was well known in England in the sixteenth century when the Articles of Religion were drawn up. The canon of Hebrew scriptures was closed at the end of the first century, but controversy over the Apocrypha continued through the Reformation (see Wilson ¶37 and note). Similarly, the canon of the NT grew with the widespread acceptance of the four gospels and the thirteen letters of Paul, partly in reaction to the very limited canons of heretics like Marcion in the second century, who accepted only Luke and a few of Paul's letters, and none of the Hebrew Bible. Eusebius in *Ecclesiastical History* refers to canonical disputes by categorizing the books of the Bible as the "accepted writings . . . disputed writings . . . and the rejected writings" (bk. 3, chap. 25; trans. Arthur Cushman McGiffert, *NPNF2* 1:155–57). The first edition of Eusebius in Greek was published in Paris in 1544, though a Latin version by Ruffinus (402) was in wide circulation throughout the Middle Ages and was printed at Rome in 1476. Eusebius was well known to the Tudor and later divines. For instance, Burnet quotes the cited passage in his commentary on the Thirty-nine Articles ([1699] 1819, 106–7).The "framers" of the Articles of Religion included Thomas Cranmer, who was responsible for drafting the "Forty-Two Articles of Religion" (1553) on which the Thirty-nine Articles are based. The Sixth Article was derived from the fifth of the Forty-Two Articles, though the phrase concerning the canonical books not doubted in the church was introduced by Matthew Parker into the Thirty-nine Articles of Religion in 1563, imported from the Würtemberg Confession (see Wilson ¶37 and note).

87. For "never . . . Church" see the Sixth Article of Religion.

In *Ecclesiastical History* Eusebius refers to a number of biblical books as in "doubt" concerning canonicity, including the three Wilson notes, as well as Jude, James, and 2 and 3 John (bk. 3, chap. 3 and chap. 25; trans. Arthur Cushman McGiffert, *NPNF2* 1:134, 155–57). If they were in "doubt" to Eusebius, the statement in the Sixth Article, that the "Canonical Books . . . [are] those of whose authority was never any doubt in the Church" is contradicted. This contradiction is irreconcilable, except that, assuming the framers of the articles, including the scholarly Parker, to know their Eusebius, and also the framers of the Canons Ecclesiastical to know the articles, such a contradiction cannot be a ground for excommunication under Canon Six (see Wilson ¶46 and note). Hooker addresses the related question of how it is that, if the Bible contains all things necessary to salvation, it does not contain information about what canonical books the Bible is to consist of: "The very chiefest [point] is to know what books we are bound to esteem holy; which point is confessed impossible for the Scripture itself to teach" (bk. 1, chap. 14; [1594–1662] 1954, 1:215).

Other historical questions that the articles do not touch, not being encyclopedic statements concerning faith and morals, are open to free discussion, including such matters as are discussed elsewhere in *Essays and Reviews* and in contemporary biblical criticism. For instance Temple refers to problems with the dating and authorship of the book of Psalms (¶17), and more generally to problems of the composition and dating of the books in ¶56. Williams refers to the compiling of the Pentateuch rather than the ascription of it to the autograph hand of Moses in ¶s 9 and 12, and to the problems concerning the canonical place of the book of Daniel in ¶s 14 and 22. The issue of a late date for John's gospel, raising problems about ascribing it to the Apostle John, is discussed widely: see, for instance, Westcott [1851] 1888, 257–63;

and Alford ([1849] 1863, 1:50–70).

88. For "*Contra . . . baculo*" ("[battling] against a net-caster with a wand," or stick) see Martial, *Epigrams* (bk. 2. Prologue; trans. Walter C. A. Ker, *Loeb* 1:109). The allusion compares experienced litigants entangling neophytes in the legalities of the Formularies to the impossible position of a victim with a walking stick fighting off a trained gladiator armed with a net to entangle the opponent.

89. "13 Eliz. c. 12" is the statue "for the Ministers of the Church to be of Sound Religion" (1571) enjoining that each ordained person "shall . . . declare his assent, and subscribe to all the articles of Religion, which only concern the confession of the true Christian faith and the doctrines of the Sacraments, comprised in a book imprinted, entitled *Articles whereupon it was agreed by the archbishops and bishops of both provinces, and the whole clergy in the Convocation holden at London in the year of our Lord God one thousand five hundred and sixty and two.*" Issues arose concerning whether the word "only" was restrictive or demonstrative, and what version of the articles was referred to (see Hardwick 1904, 147–49; 223–27). The form of subscription was superseded by the *Canons of 1603*.

Sir William Scott, Lord Stowell, was an M.P., an admiralty and ecclesiastical judge. Theologically and judicially conservative, he opposed ecclesiastical reform; he was registrar of the Court of Faculties of the archbishop of Canterbury and chancellor of the Diocese of London. His legal phrase "*in viridi observantiâ*" (Lat. present to the minds of men) suggests that the Elizabethan statute is not only memorable but also current, and hence in some sense applicable in 1860.

90. The first five Articles of Religion concern the Trinity, the person and work of Christ, and the Holy Spirit, largely in the language of the Nicene Creed. Wilson suggests that modern definitions based on contemporary philosophy and historical research concerning the formulations of the early church would avoid the controversies involved in credal language without contradicting it. Despite Wilson's cautious phrasing concerning this matter of freedom of interpretation, this passage was cited in the Court of Arches, just as similar arguments, advanced by F. D. Maurice in *The Kingdom of Christ* (1838), resulted in attacks on him.

The "pivot Articles" are those concerning the Bible, the Sixth and Seventh (see Wilson ¶s 37, 48, and notes).

91. Each Article of Religion echoes biblical language. The Lutheran-sounding articles are those concerning original sin (Ninth Article, based on the Cranmer's Thirteen Articles of 1538, reliant on the Lutheran Augsburg Confession of 1530), free will (Tenth Article, based on Augustine's *On Grace and Free Will* and the Confession of Würtemberg of 1552), justification (Eleventh Article based on the Thirteen Articles and the Augsburg Confession), good works (Twelfth to Fourteenth Articles; the Twelfth added by Parker derived from the Würtemberg Confession), predestination and election (Seventeenth Article, derived from Luther's *Preface to his Commentary on the Epistle to the Romans*, and from Melanchthon), and the sacraments (Twenty-fifth, based on the Thirteen Articles and the Augsburg Confession). Each of these takes an anti-Calvinist position. Cranmer had initiated a series of conferences with the German Lutherans from 1536 to 1538, at some of which Luther, and often Melanchthon, were present, resulting in the particular Lutheran cast to the Thirteen Articles and those deriving from them in the Articles of Religion. See Hardwick 1904, 391–420; and Tjernagel 1965.

The Twenty-eighth Article, "Of the Lord's Supper," has a "Calvinistic sound." It underwent modifications in 1563 under Parker when a substantial group of bishops had come under Zwinglian influence, particularly those sympathizers who had fled England to Switzerland during the religious persecutions under Mary Tudor from 1553 to 1558. An extreme Zwinglian clause, concerning the eucharist as a memorial only and denying Christ's real presence, was removed, but the Zwinglian notion of the Eucharist as a sign of Christian love remains in the opening paragraph.

Jacobus Arminius attacked the deterministic logic of the Calvinists on the predestination of the elect to glory and the reprobate to damnation, as well as the notion of limited atonement—that Christ died only for the elect (see Calvin [1536] 1957, 2:206–8; bk. 3, chap. 21, sect. 5). Arminius argued "that God foresaw from all eternity who among men would make a good use of the grace which is freely offered to all, and that *therefore, i.e.* because He foresaw their future merits, He predestined some to final glory" (Edgar Gibson 1915, 470). The followers of Arminius drew up the Remonstrance at Gouda in 1610 (hence "Remonstrants"), setting out their views in distinction from the Calvinists. The Arminian Seventeenth Article ("Of Predestination and Election") claims in its last clause that "we must receive God's promises in such wise, as they be generally set forth to us in Holy Scripture," and thus predestination is to be interpreted by the Bible, especially by Rom. 8–9 and Eph. 1 which underlie the Seventeenth Article. On the Arminian controversy in England see Pattison ¶5 and n. 16.

The "kind of authority" that permits both "Calvinistic and Arminian views" to be "both of them tenable" is possibly the statement of James I at the Hampden Court Conference, convened in 1604 under his presidency, between the English bishops and the Puritan leaders. On the subject of the Seventeenth Article, James asked that predestination "be very tenderly handled, and with great discretion, lest on the one side, God's omnipotency might be called in question, by impeaching the doctrine of his eternal predestination, or on the other, a desperate presumption might be arreared, by inferring the necessary certainty of standing and persisting in grace" (quoted in Peter White 1992, 145–46). But it seems more likely that the "authority" is Burnet, whom Wilson quotes in ¶54. In his lengthy commentary on the Seventeenth Article, Burnet writes that Calvinist and Arminian views each have "practical advantages": "A Calvinist is taught, by his opinions, to think meanly of himself, and to ascribe the honour of all to God. . . . A Remonstrant, on the other hand, is engaged to awaken and improve his faculties, to fill his mind with good notions, to raise them in himself by frequent reflection, and by a constant attention to his own actions. . . . The Calvinist is tempted to a false security, and sloth: and the Arminian may be tempted to trust too much to himself, and too little to God: so equally may a man of a calm temper, and of moderate thoughts, balance this matter between both the sides" ([1699] 1819, 232–33).

Burnet's view was widely dispersed. In the Bampton Lectures of 1804 Richard Laurence, maintaining that the articles are not Calvinistic, states: "On the one hand it has been contended, that our Articles are consonant with the Creed of Calvin; on the other with that of Arminius" ([1804] 1853, 7). In 1842 the Evangelical G. S. Faber published *The Primitive Doctrine of Election* in which he argued that Calvinism, Arminianism (and Nationalism) are alike rejected in the Seventeenth Article and in a biblical view of predestination. J. B. Mozley saw little difference in Augustinian, Thomistic, and Calvinist views of predestination ([1855] 1883, 393). Commenting on the same issue, H. P. Liddon, writes: "If we shrink from sacrificing God's Sovereignty to man's free will with Arminius, and from sacrificing man's freedom to God's sovereignty with Calvin, we can only express a wise ignorance by saying, that to us they seem like parallel lines which yet must meet at a point in eternity" ([1870] 1904, 188).

"Faith" in the Eleventh Article, derived from the Augsburg Confession, is seemingly defined in a solafideistic Lutheran sense: "That we are justified by faith only, is a most wholesome doctrine." Burnet argued that the definition was not exclusively Lutheran: "By *faith only*, is not to be meant faith as it is separated from the other evangelical graces and virtues; but faith, as it is opposite to the rites of the Mosaical Law" ([1699] 1819, 170). J. H. Newman also showed in *Tract XC* that the phrase was susceptible of non-Lutheran interpretation in that baptism is also a means and instrument of justification: "When, then, Faith is called the sole instrument, this means the sole *internal* instrument, not the sole instrument of any kind" ([1841] 1865, 12).

92. Wilson's argument concerning the liberty conveyed by the Articles, creeds, and Formularies and the legal status of the C. of E. continues through to ¶55. Thomas Arnold similarly argues in *Principles of Church Reform* for inclusivity and toleration in credal statements and Formularies ([1833] 1962, 115).

Edward Irving was excommunicated (1830) and expelled from the Church of Scotland (1833) for allegedly arguing in *The Orthodox and Catholic Doctrine of Our Lord's Human Nature* (1830) that in taking on sinful human nature in the incarnation Christ was sinful. Preaching millenarianism, he was one of the founders of the Catholic Apostolic Church. See Margaret Oliphant 1862; and Edward Miller 1878. F. D. Maurice writes sympathetically of Irving, and on similar grounds to Wilson that the articles would not bear on his case, and, so there would be no grounds for legal action against him if he were in the Anglican Church (1884, 2: 407–8). Maurice also refers to "the late Mr. Irving" in *The Kingdom of Christ* ([1838] 1958, 1:153–55; 2:135–40).

93. Burnet writes: "Some have late thought that they are only *Articles of Union and Peace*; that they are a standard of *doctrine* not to be contradicted, or disputed; that the sons of the Church are only bound to acquiesce silently to them; and that the subscription binds only to a general compromise upon those Articles, so that there may be no disputing nor wrangling about them" ([1699] 1819, 7–8).

94. Among the Articles of Religion directed against "the corruptions of Rome" were the Nineteenth ("the Church of Rome hath erred, not only in their living and manner of ceremonies, but also in matters of faith"), the Twenty-second ("The Romish doctrine concerning purgatory, pardons, worshipping and adoration as well of images, as of relics, and also invocation of Saints, is a fond thing, vainly invented, and grounded upon no warranty of Scripture, but rather repugnant to the Word of God"), the Twenty-eighth (attacking transubstantiation), the Thirty-first ("Wherefore the sacrifices of Masses . . . were blasphemous fables, and dangerous deceits"), and the Thirty-second (attacking required clerical celibacy).

Such practices were "flourishing in full life and vigour" in two contexts, first in the Catholicizing of the Oxford Movement; second, to in the "Papal aggression" of 1850. By "Roman doctrines and practices" Wilson refers to the agitation provoked by the Letters Apostolic (*Universalis Ecclesiae*, 1850: "The power of governing the universal church") in which Pope Pius IX made England and Wales an ecclesiastical province of the Roman Catholic Church. The newly appointed archbishop of Westminster, Nicholas Wiseman, issued an inflammatory pastoral letter, "From the Flaminian Gate at Rome," in which he wrote of governing and exercising administrative jurisdiction over English counties (Beck 1950, 99). Popular "no Popery" agitation culminated in the Ecclesiastical Titles Act (1851; 14 & 15 Vict. cap 60)) that denied Roman Catholics rights to "encroachments," to territorial titles and jurisdiction. In this context J. H. Newman delivered his

Lectures on the Present Position of Catholics in England (1851). J. C. Hare answered Newman directly in *The Contest with Rome: A Charge to the Clergy of the Archdeaconry of Lewes . . . with Notes, Especially in Answer to Dr. Newman's Recent Lecture* (1852). On the anti-Romanist side there were many publications, such as the novel by Catherine Sinclair, *Beatrice, or The Unknown Relatives* (1850); and religious tracts such as her own *Popish Legends, or Bible Truths* (1852); Edward Beecher's *The Papal Conspiracy Exposed* (1855); and James Aitken Wylie's *Rome and Civil Liberty: The Papal Aggression and Its Relation to the Sovereignty of the Queen and the Independence of the Nation* (1865). For a recent survey of this controversy see Norman 1984.

"Grievous provocations" include the persecutions under Mary Tudor (1553–58), the "corruptions of the Church of Rome" in Richard Whately's *Essays on the Errors of Romanism* (1856–57), and such sensationalist revelations as those told in *The Awful Disclosures of Maria Monk* (1836).

95. The Oxford Movement promoted a revival of worship and ceremonial within the Anglican Church that was viewed by many as excessively romanizing (see Ollard 1963). For popular attacks on Tractarian ceremonial, often called Puseyism or ritualism, see Walsh 1898 and Walsh 1900. Walsh lists those who defected to Rome.

"Practices . . . distasteful to the . . . people" is a reference to the antiritualist riots at St. George's-in-the-East, London, in 1859, and the self-justifying publication of *Sacrilege and Its Encouragement* (1860) by the incumbent, Bryan King (see Wilson ¶28 and note). For a recent account see James Bentley 1978.

The phrase "strange and repugnant" was common in heresy trials, as in the Gorham case in relation to doctrinal questions: the decision of the Judicial Committee (1850) was that "the doctrine held by Mr. *Gorham* is not contrary, or repugnant to the declared doctrine of the Church of *England* as by Law established" (William Brooke 1874, 38). It was used also in the Letters of Request under which both Williams and Wilson were arraigned as promoting "erroneous, strange and heretical [opinions] . . . repugnant to the Doctrine" of the C. of E.

The notion of doctrines being "repugnant" to the word of God is a frequent collocation in the Articles of Religion. Wilson turns the phrase as "repugnant to the common sense of the nation." Wilson assigns to the term *common sense* a positive value as in the moral sense given to it by the Scottish philosopher Thomas Reid (*Enquiry into the Human Mind on the Principles of Common Sense*, 1764). The political implications of the phrase are stressed in Thomas Paine's *Common Sense* (1776) advocating American independence. In current usage, the Italian philosopher Antonio Gramsci uses "common sense" in a critical way to signify the concealed and unconscious set of assumptions and beliefs held by any given society (1971, 323–43).

96. A "promissory oath" is an oath that binds "the party to observe a certain course of conduct, or to fulfil certain duties. . . . A solemn appeal to God, or, in a wider sense, to some superior sanction or a sacred or revered person in witness of the inviolability of a promise or undertaking" (Henry Black [1891] 1990, 1071).

Jeremy Taylor in *The Great Exemplar of Sanctity and Holy Life* (1649), commenting on the third commandment, "Thou shalt not take the name of the Lord thy God in vain," argues for "some cases in which the interests of kingdoms and bodies politic, peace and confederacies, require the sanction of promissory oaths" (1847–54, 2:424–25).

Wilson refers to the "promissory oath" enjoined upon the clergy in subscribing to the Thirty-nine Articles of Religion according to the requirement of the Act 13 Elizabeth, chap. 12 (Hardwick 1904, 223), the Oath of Supremacy, and the other requirements of the Canons of 1604. The Thirty-ninth Article is on "a Christian man's oath."

The secular form of such oaths was later determined in the Promissory Oaths Act of 1868. The most notorious case was the refusal of the atheist Charles Bradlaugh to swear judicial oaths in a number of legal cases in his advocacy of the abolition of oaths in his publications, such as the periodicals the *London Investigator* (1854–57) and the *Investigator* (1858–59), and in his refusal to take the parliamentary oath on the Bible on being elected M.P. for Northampton in 1880. He claimed the right to affirm, but was then ejected from the House of Commons, as he was repeatedly over the following months and years after being repeatedly re-elected by his constituents, until he was finally admitted in 1886. For swearing an oath see also Jowett ¶30 and note; for a recent discussion of Bradlaugh see Arnstein 1965.

97. For Arianism see Wilson ¶27 and note.

Pelagianism argues that humans can move toward salvation through their own efforts independently of divine grace. It is named after the British theologian Pelagius, who was teaching at Rome and whose views, though widely popular, were attacked by Augustine and condemned as heretical at the Council of Ephesus in 431. See also Williams ¶32 and notes; and Jowett ¶s 2, 3, and notes.

The Second and Ninth Articles of Religion affirm orthodox Nicaean Christology against the revived Arianism of the Anabaptists in Essex and Kent in the 1550s (Hardwick 1904, 88–90).

Wilson argues that the articles address specific doctrinal positions in the sixteenth century; to require assent to them apart from their historical context in the nineteenth century is a deterrent to ordination candidates. Jowett held that the rejection by the clergy of *Essays and Reviews* indicated problems with subscription: "In a few years there will be no religion in Oxford among intelligent young men, unless religion is shewn to be consistent with criticism" (Letter 47).

98. Preparation for ordination consisted in part of the study of the Articles of Religion, whether from the "Catholic" position of the Tractarian exegetes or the Evangelicals. Such study, instead of presenting the historical context of sixteenth-century doctrinal debates, made appeals to truth claims since subscription was required as a matter of belief before ordination.

The Articles of Religion were subjects for examination at Oxford, Cambridge, and London throughout the nineteenth century. At Cambridge, for instance, Edward Harold Browne published *An Exposition of the Thirty-Nine Articles, Historical and Doctrinal* in two volumes (1850, 1853), and as Norissian Professor of Divinity lectured on the articles for the Voluntary Theological Examinations held by the Board of Theological Studies, established in the same year as his appointment (1854). Browne later joined in the attack on *Essays and Reviews,* publishing in *Aids to Faith.* Later, however, after being appointed bishop of Ely (1864) he participated in the consecration of Temple as bishop of Exeter (1869). In the Preface to the twelfth edition of his *Exposition* (1882), Browne comments that "the book has been accepted and used by almost all the Anglican Bishops, colleges, and universities, in Great Britain, Ireland, the Colonies, and America." For an extended treatment of theological education in Victorian England see Bullock 1955.

99. S. T. Coleridge gives a historical account for the legal grounds for the separation of the "National Church" from the other sects "by having its priesthood *endowed,* . . . by favour of the legislature—that is, by the majority, for the time being, of the two Houses of Parliament" ([1829] 1976, 61). For Thomas Arnold's discussion of "sects" and the "national church" see [1833] 1962, 97–108.

100. Wilson draws out the comparison between the fragmentation of sects into smaller units over doctrinal differences and political affiliation. He makes a contemporary reference to the latter in that the second Derby Ministry, which took office on 25 February 1858, fell on 11 June 1859 after the defeat of a reform bill. For an account of this defeat see Conacher 1959, 170–73.

101. Coleridge defines the "Nationalty" in *On the Constitution of the Church and State*: "It was, I say, common to all the primitive races, that in taking possession of a new country, and in the division of the land into hereditable estates among the individual warriors or heads of families, a reserve should be made for the nation itself. The sum total of these heritable portions, appropriated each to an individual Lineage, I beg leave to name the PROPRIETY; and to call the *reserve* above-mentioned the NATIONALTY" ([1829] 1976, 35). For Thomas Arnold's discussion of church property and endowments see "The Case for a Church Establishment" ([1833] 1962, 92–97).

102. For a discussion of "abuse" of endowments see Wilson ¶7 and note.

In *Principles of Church Reform* Thomas Arnold discusses ecclesiastical endowments, praising them for "reserving," in S. T. Coleridge's phrase, land for public use and placing the effects of private property in historical context, relating them to what Wilson calls "individualism" ([1833] 1962, 93).

Objections to endowments were voiced primarily by advocates of the disestablishment of the Anglican church. On 30 April 1844, Edward Miall founded the British Anti-State Church Society, dedicated to "the liberation of religion from all governmental or legislative interference" (*DNB*, s.v. "Miall, Edward"). In 1853 it was renamed the Society for the Liberation of Religion from State Patronage and Control. In 1861, Miall wrote against endowments and tithe property as an "ancient tax," contrasting Arnold's notion of its "public purpose," as well as Wilson's argument regarding the "inheritance or testamentary disposition . . . of private property" (Miall 1862, 6).

Wilson's analogy between "the place of the schoolmaster" and the "spiritual person" as "purely fiduciary" may be qualified by examining letters to the *National Society Monthly Paper* (Apr. 1851), in which "Pro Bono Publico" argues about the "the inadequate remuneration which schoolmasters receive for their labour" despite the fact that theirs is "the most onerous and responsible position next to that of a clergyman in a country parish" (quoted in Digby and Searby 1981, 190–91).

103. On the endowments and incomes of the C. of E. see Ellens 1983, 24–30. His analysis of the returns in 1832 is as follows: church rates £446,247; county rates £761,901; in 1835 the "total revenues of the Church . . . exclusive of voluntary payments and church rates" were calculated by the Church Commissioners to be £3,738,951 (Ellens 1983, 24). Owen Chadwick refers to the "revenues of the established church" in 1835 as corresponding to "legends of oriental wealth" (1966–70, 1:104).

104. Thomas Arnold writes in *Principles of Church Reform* of the role of endowments in ensuring public access to church land and buildings in the face of property "bought up for private convenience or enjoyment," notwithstanding the unequal distribution of church income from those endowments ([1833] 1962, 93–94). See also Wilson ¶7 and note.

105. Wilson's "spiritual magistrates" resemble S. T. Coleridge's "clerisy." They are "members and ministers of the national clerisy or church . . . preserving, continuing and perfecting, the necessary sources and conditions of national civilization" ([1829] 1976, 54–5).

Thomas Arnold draws on Coleridge to define the relations of the state and a national church which "in their ideal form were not two societies, but one.

. . . This theory had, indeed, already been sanctioned by some of the greatest names in English theology and philosophy, by Hooker in his Ecclesiastical Polity, and in later times by Burke, and in part by Coleridge" (Stanley 1844, 1:220–21).

Michael Young coined the term *meritocracy* to describe the system in which merit, rather than inherited privilege, is "the arbiter, attainment the standard, for entry and advancement in a splendid profession" (1958, 17). Young locates the origin of meritocracy in the 1870 Education Bill, when education was made compulsory in Great Britain. Wilson's argument for the selection of clergy based on merit is similar to that regarding the reform of the civil service in an 1854 *Report* made by Sir Stafford Northcote and Sir Charles Trevelyan (see Young 1958, 153). Jowett was a member of the committee that drafted the *Report.* In *Past and Present* Carlyle had mocked the notion of an "Aristocracy of Talent," concluding that it "seems at a considerable distance yet" ([1843] 1977, 37).

The designation "tribunes of the people" (Lat. *tribuni plebis*) was given to "magistrates" in ancient Rome from 494 B.C.E. whose role was to safeguard the lives and property of the plebian class, often in opposition to the demands of the patricians and in conflict with the Senate. During the period of the Roman Empire the authority of the tribunes was assumed by the emperor. For "tribunes of the people" see also Shakespeare, *Coriolanus* 1.1.258 and elsewhere.

Interest in the tribunes was revived by Edward Bulwer-Lytton's novel *Rienzi, or The Last of the Tribunes* (1835), based on the career of Cola di Rienzi, who in the fourteenth century plotted a popular uprising against the rule of the nobles in Rome, assuming the ancient title of "tribune." Lytton refers to Gibbon's presentation (in chap. 70) and in an appendix he cites the writings of Jean Antoine Du Cerceau on Rienzi (1733). Richard Wagner's opera *Rienzi* (1842) was based on Bulwer-Lytton; Byron also mentioned Rienzi in *Childe Harold's Pilgrimage* (1818, IV.114). *The Red Republican* (19 July 1851) published an anonymous poem, "Rienzi," based on Du Cerceau (268).

106. Wilson's reference to one-half of the population is limited to males and to information collected on Census Sunday (30 Mar. 1851; see ¶7 and note). The excluded half includes Roman Catholics and Dissenters or Nonconformists. The failure to factor women into what he terms "the whole of the people" follows contemporaneous practice. To meet the needs of women for postsecondary education, Girton College was founded at Cambridge in 1869 but it was denied official status by the university. Although women took examinations informally at Cambridge from 1884 they were not admitted as full members of the university able to receive degrees until 1948. Oxford established two women's college in 1879, Lady Margaret Hall and Somerville College. Women were excluded from ordination as priests in the C. of E. until 1994.

107. Wilson's comment may be compared with Gladstone: "The Church and the State have ends reciprocally inclusive. . . . Both of them [have] moral agencies. But the State aims at character through conduct: the Church at conduct through character" (1841, 1:115–16). The metaphor of cultivation and growth with the church as nurturer of the nation's inner life is a Broad Church commonplace: see, for instance, Temple ¶6 and note. Matthew Arnold's "culture" expands the function of the "State Church" to other national institutions by making it "culture's way of working for reason and the will of God" (1960–77, 5:129).

108. For "in the world . . . though in some sense not of it" see John 15:19; 17:14–16.

109. On the relationship between "one born into the nation" and "belonging to a spiritual society" Burke argues for the social contract as "a partnership in all science; a partnership in all art; a partnership in every virtue, and in all perfection. As the ends of such a partnership cannot be obtained in many generations, it becomes a partnership not only between those who are living, but between those who are living, those who are dead, and those who are to be born. . . , connecting the visible and invisible world, according to a fixed compact sanctioned by the inviolable oath which holds all physical and all moral natures, each in their appointed place" ([1790] 1969, 194–96).

110. On the relation between state and morality in Rome, on "the government of the State by virtue," see Cicero, *The Republic* (bk. 1, chap. 34; trans. Walter Keyes, *Loeb* 79).

The separation of "heathen State religions" from Christianity on the basis of the latter's intrinsic superior morality is a Victorian commonplace. On the relations between the heathens and morality in general see Hey [1796] 1841, 1:154. On Rome and its morality see Thomas Arnold ([1833] 1962, 95) and F. D. Maurice (1847, 121–22). Edward Westermarck sums up the Victorian view: "The gods of the Romans were on the whole unsympathetic and lifeless beings. . . . The gods of uncivilised races are to a very large extent of a malevolent character. . . . They as a rule take little interest in any kind of human conduct which does not affect their own welfare and, . . . if they show any signs of moral feelings, they may be guardians of tribal customs in general or only of some special branch of morality" ([1908] 1917, 2:716–17, 728).

111. For "quickening the individual conscience and the expectation of individual immortality," see Rom. 8:11; "grace bestowed on one's own labours," 1 Cor. 15:10; "crown of glory," 1 Pet 5:4; "this world, and . . . that which is to come," Matt. 12:32.

112. For "village Hampdens" see Thomas Gray,

"Elegy Written in a Country Churchyard" (1751; l. 56). John Hampden as a member of Parliament defended civil rights against the policies of Charles I. As a soldier in the Cromwellian army he was killed in a battle at Oxford. His name is a byword for a private person's resistance based on religious principles against the arbitrary exercise of civil authority in collecting an illegal tax (ship-money) in 1638–40. For "to prison and spoiling of their goods" see Heb. 10:34.

The "Church-rate" was a property tax levied on all local rate payers, adherents of the C. of E. and Dissenters alike, to maintain the local parish church buildings of the C. of E. Between the Reform Act of 1832 and the abolition of church rates by Gladstone in 1868, there were many efforts to repeal them, including thirteen separate bills between 1853 and 1859. Church rates were strongly opposed by the Dissenters, many having their goods seized, and some going to prison, including John Thorogood, imprisoned in 1839 for eighteen months (see Machin 1978, 104–5). From the time of the Reform Bill rate payers denied the legitimacy of an ecclesiastical tax. Their political agitation was organized by the Church Rate Abolition Society (established 1836), and by the Anti-State Church Association, which in 1853 was reorganized into the Society for the Liberation of Religion from State Patronage and Control, or the Liberation Society. Such societies were opposed by those who feared that the abolition of church rates would lead to the financial and moral ruin of the C. of E. It was argued in Parliament that "the nationality of the Church of England would be destroyed, and it would be considered as a Church not supported by the nation, but by itself" (*Hansard*: 3 Mar. 1837, 36:1255). Income from church rates in 1832 was £446,247, about 12% of the total revenues of the church (Ellens 1983, 24).

Opponents of the church rate included Edward Miall; supporters included George Anthony Denison, who in 1861 published *Church Rate: What Ought Parliament to Do?* The matter was particularly critical when *Essays and Reviews* was published, since the leaders of the Liberation Society were being attacked for attempting to use church rates as a means of promoting disestablishment and the supporters of church rates were organizing in the Convocation of Canterbury and in Parliament. For contemporaneous arguments for the church rates see Conybeare 1854 and Hayward 1859; for arguments against see Martineau 1858b. For a detailed treatment of church rates in nineteenth-century Britain see Ellens 1983.

The "war-tax" had been a fear during the Crimean War (1854–56), and in fact was imposed by Gladstone as an increase in income tax (see Coode 1853). The war scare of 1859–60 was the result of an imagined French threat under Napoleon III that precipitated a widespread volunteer enlistment and the passing of an enormous defense budget of £26,000,000 as well as an additional £11,000,000 for improvements in fortifications (Hansard, 1859, 155:667–92; Parliamentary Papers 23: *Reports from Commissioners*, 1:2681: Report of the Commissioners Appointed to Consider the Defenses of Great Britain, 442–48). See Greg 1860; Olive Anderson 1967; and Salevouris 1982.

113. Wilson's claims about the continued separation of the social classes are consistent with the Broad Church position that, as Thomas Arnold put it, "the ministry should contain persons taken from all" classes of society, so that "all the great divisions of the nation should have a share in the government" ([1833] 1962, 118). See Gloyn 1942, 109.

114. *Hist. Pur.* iv. p. 618 [Wilson's note].

Daniel Neal published *History of the Puritans, 1517–1688* (1732–38). For the cited passage see Neal [1732–38] 1822, 5:82.

The thirty commissioners were appointed by William III. They proposed that the Athanasian Creed be optional, revised the collects, lectionary, and made many other verbal and ritual changes; however, the whole proposal was rejected by the lower house of Convocation in 1689 and never came to Parliament.

115. Wilson's comments on "the ranks of Dissent" and "national character" resemble Thomas Arnold's argument that the comprehensive union of church and state is compromised by the "faults and errors" of both Dissenters and the C. of E. ([1833] 1962, 166–67).

116. The influence of each of these thinkers on "Biblical theology" was much commented upon throughout the nineteenth century. For instance, F. D. Maurice discusses the relations between Christianity and the philosophy of Greece and Rome in his Boyle Lectures (1847); William Temple, the son of Frederick Temple, and, like him, archbishop of Canterbury, published *Plato and Christianity* (1916). John Stuart Blackie published *Four Phases of Morals: Socrates, Aristotle, Christianity, Utilitarianism* (1871). Newton's *Observations upon the Prophecies of Daniel and the Apocalypse* was published posthumously in 1733. For recent studies of relations between philosophy, science, and theology see Madigan 1988; Force and Popkin 1990; and Wybrow 1991.

117. The term *idealist* is derived from S. T. Coleridge's argument for the "ideal," or national, church. William George Ward published *The Ideal of a Christian Church* (1844) in which he attacked the spiritual laxity of the C. of E. while praising the medieval sanctity still preserved in Roman Catholicism. Further, Ward had flagrantly announced "how utterly . . . inoperative our Articles really are. . . . It is now three years since I, a clergyman of the English Church . . . said plainly, that in subscribing the Articles I renounce no one Roman doctrine: yet I retain my Fellowship which I hold on the tenure of subscription, and have received no ecclesiastical

censure in any shape" (1844, 567). Ward, thenceforward known as "Ideal Ward," was charged before the Vice-Chancellor at Oxford for teaching views inconsistent with the Articles of Religion, and eventually had his degrees removed by Convocation (1845). He was received into the Roman Catholic Church in the same year; hence Wilson's comment on "excommunication."

118. Wilson uses *ideology* to open a series of mediations between a literalist reading of the Bible and the historical ideas and contexts that determine the text and its interpretation. He does not use the term to signify a set of political beliefs but rather a system of knowledge, an epistemology. For a recent discussion of ideology in this sense see Eagleton 1991, 63–93. Wilson's "ideal" and its derivative "ideology" derive from the German and English idealist philosophers, via S. T. Coleridge's *On the Constitution of the Church and State*: "By an *idea*, I mean . . . that conception of a thing, which is not abstracted from any particular state, form, or mode, in which the thing may happen to exist at this or at that time; not yet generalized from any number or succession of such forms or modes; but which is given by knowledge of *its ultimate aim*" [1829] 1976, 12).

119. David Friedrich Strauss published a critical life of Christ, *Leben Jesu* ([1835] 1846]). He adopted a Hegelian dialectic, arguing that the early forms of Christianity represented a synthesis of opposite tendencies, the Jewish elements (Petrine) and the gentile (Pauline). Strauss caused a sensation in Germany, resulting in his failing to win a position at Zürich, and another sensation in England because of his relegation of the historical data of Jesus' life to the realm of myth that developed before the gospels were written down.

Philo Judaeus was an Alexandrian philosopher and biblical commentator who developed an allegorizing method of interpretation that found Greek philosophy in the Hebrew scriptures. For contemporaneous discussions of Philo see Godwin ¶26; see also Caesar Morgan 1853 and Drummond 1888. Origen, another Alexandrian biblical exegete, was a follower of Philo in the allegorical method, writing commentaries on most books of the Bible. Charles Bigg's Bampton Lectures of 1886 were on the work of Origen and his school (Bigg 1886). For recent studies of Strauss see Horton Harris 1973; and Lawler 1986. For Philo see Sandmel 1979; and Berchman 1984. For Origen see Hanson 1959; and Trigg 1983. For a general study of the uses of typology in the nineteenth century see Landow 1980.

For "the temptation of Jesus by Satan" see Matt. 4:1–11; Mark 1:12–13; Luke 4:1–13. For "demoniacal possession" see Matt. 4:24; 8:16, 28, 33; Mark 1:32; 5:15–18; Luke 8:36. For particular instances of healings from possession see Matt. 8:28–33; Mark 5:2–16 (and the parallel passage, Luke 8:26–39).

The passage from ¶73, "But it by no means follows. . . . reasonably exercised," was cited as "false and dangerous" in the Synodical Condemnation of *Essays and Reviews* on 21 June 1864. Wilson was condemned for having applied generally the principle that "instances of supernatural interference recorded in the Bible may be safely rejected as facts" and especially to "the historical life of our blessed Lord, and that liberty must be left to all as to the extent in which they may apply it" (*Chronicle* 1859–64:1864, Session 66, 1657).

120. For "'corruption'" see 2 Pet. 1:4; "brotherhood," 1 Pet. 2:17

Wilson seeks to reconcile the two positions of an ethnographical and anthropological debate of the 1850s and 1860s with a position on the Bible as a historical record in an allegorical or abstract sense. Monogenists held that all of the human races have a common descent from the biblical Adam and Eve as the originary couple; polygenists argued that the different races originated from several or many independent ancestors. Polygenists denied the essentialist and supernatural unity of the human races, as in the work of Josiah Clark Nott: "The only argument left, then, for the advocates of the *unity* of the human species to fall back upon, is that of 'congenital' varieties or peculiarities, which are said to spring up, and be transmitted from parent to child, so as to form new races. . . . Numerous attempts have been made to establish the intellectual equality of the dark races with the white; and the history of the past has been ransacked for examples, but they are nowhere to be found. Can any one recall the name of a negro who has ever written a page worthy of being remembered?" ([1849] 1969, 30–31).

Such views collapse only too easily into the racialism of white superiority: "The time must come when the blacks will be worse than useless to us. What then? *Emancipation* must follow, which, from the lights before us, is but another name for extermination. Look at the free blacks of the North, of the South, of the West Indies, and of Africa. Could several millions of such idle, vicious vagabonds be permitted by our posterity to live and propagate amongst them? It is impossible" (Nott [1849] 1969, 18). Similarly, Robert Knox argued that "race is everything: literature, science, art—in a word—civilization—depends on it" (1850, v). These racialist ideas, together with views of Nordic superiority, were widely propagated by Count Gobineau (Gobineau 1853–55). Nott added an appendix to the first volume of the translation. See also Nott and Gliddon (1854).

The controversy extended to the periodicals: "This quarrel of the mono- and polygenesists . . . is a very pretty one" (*Temple Bar* 5 [1862]: 215); and T. H. Huxley wrote: "Five-sixths of the public are taught this Adamitic Monogenism as if it were an established truth, and believe it" (1865, 273). For recent analysis of the ethnographic debate see Bildiss

1970 and 1976; and Outlaw 1990.

121. For "the destruction of Sodom and Gomorrah" see Gen. 19:24; 2 Pet. 2:6; Jude 1:7; the "Noachian deluge," Gen. 6:17; 2 Pet. 2:5. The same passage in 2 Peter refers also to the throwing of the rebel angels into hell (an interpretation current in the first century of the "sons of God," the angels who consorted with humans and begat a race of giants or *nephilim*, Gen. 6:1–6) and the deliverance of Lot from Sodom (Gen. 19:15 ff.). All are examples that show the punishment of the wicked and are read as typological prophecies of the universal judgment by fire (2 Pet. 3:7). For recent discussions of the allegorical, or "emblematical," method of Philo as it applies to Hebrews, see Sowers 1965; Ronald Williamson 1970; and Dey 1975.

122. For "the transfiguration" of Jesus between Moses and Elijah, see Matt. 17:1–9; Mark 9:2–9; "opening of blind eyes," Mark 8:22–26; 10:46–52; Luke 4:17–21; 18:35–43; John 9:1–39; "causing the tongue of the stammerer to speak plainly," Mark 7:32–37; "feeding the multitude," Matt. 14:14–22; 15:32–39; Mark 8:1–9; Luke 9:12–17; "cleansing leprosy," Matt. 8:2–4; Mark 1:40–45; Luke 5:12–13.

Wilson's "probable evidence," concerning the relations between doctrinal statements and faith, may be compared to Goodwin's "region of uncertainty" (¶10), referring to geological time.

The passage from ¶75: "The ideologian. . . . particular events" was cited as "false and dangerous" in the Synodical Condemnation of *Essays and Reviews* on 21 June 1864. Wilson alleges "that the instances of supernatural interference recorded in the Bible may be safely rejected as facts, provided that we retain the ideas which would have been awakened by the knowledge of such alleged facts, if they had been real" (*Chronicle* 1859–64:1864, Session 66, 1657).

123. For "house and lineage of David" see Luke 2:4; "tribe of Levi," Luke 3: 24, 29; "Son of David," Matt. 1:1 and Matt. passim; Luke 3:31; "Son of Aaron," Heb, 7:11; "Prince of Peace," Isa. 9:6; "High Priest of our profession," Heb. 3:1; "'without father and without mother,'" Heb. 7:3; "Royal Priest Melchizedecan," Heb. 5:6, 10; 6:20–7:21; "birth in the city of David," Luke 2:11; "angelic appearances," Matt. 1:20; Luke 1:28; 2:9–13.

124. For "separated from the world" see James 1:27.

Wilson refers to two notable cases of "controversial acrimony," concerning the real presence of Christ in the eucharist and baptismal regeneration. Pusey had initiated the controversy concerning the "presence of Jesus Christ" in the eucharist in his sermon *The Holy Eucharist, a Comfort to the Penitent* (1843), resulting in Oxford's vice-chancellor's banning him from preaching in the university pulpit for two years. In 1848 Robert Isaac Wilberforce, Tractarian theologian, published *The Doctrine of the Incarnation* in which he discussed Christ's "spiritual presence" (chap. 10, 11), and in 1853 *The Doctrine of the Holy Eucharist*. In 1855 Pusey published *The Doctrine of the Real Presence*. At the same time, from 1854 to 1858, the Tractarian George Anthony Denison was prosecuted and condemned in the Court of Arches for having affirmed, in a series of sermons in Wells cathedral, the real presence of Christ in the Eucharist. He escaped on a legal technicality, but his conviction prompted John Keble to publish *On Eucharistical Adoration* (1857).

Contemporary differences about the theology of baptism centered on the Gorham case that began in 1847 when the bishop of Exeter (Henry Phillpotts) refused to institute the Low Church George Cornelius Gorham as vicar because of his view that baptismal regeneration was conditional upon worthy reception of the sacrament. Phillpotts examined Gorham on baptismal regeneration for five days in December 1847 and three days in March 1848, finding that Gorham rejected the High Church view that baptism confers grace and a change of Christian character and initiates a spiritual rebirth. Gorham was condemned in the Court of Arches (1849), a blow to the Low Church belief that regeneration meant conversion of life, repentance for sin, and the renewal of the heart of the person (already baptized) later in life when the promises made on his behalf were accepted. But the decision was reversed on appeal by Gorham to the Judicial Committee of the Privy Council in 1850. The judgment was taken as a repudiation of High Church, and especially Tractarian theology, and many secessions to Rome followed. Keble, Pusey, and others wrote more than 105 pamphlets on the case. The *Spectator* (25 May 1861) commented on the "taste for discussing half-understood theology": "Every word of the arguments in the Gorham case, every quotation cited, every explanation offered, were perused by men usually content with police reports and the Debate [in the House of Commons]" (555). The Gorham case was an important precedent appealed to by Stephen Lushington in his judgment on Wilson in the Court of Arches decision. See Nias 1951 and Owen Chadwick 1966–70, 1:250–71. For other Essayists' treatments of baptism and the eucharist see Williams ¶s 27 and 31; and Jowett ¶34 and notes.

125. For "rule of the saints . . . upon earth" see Rev. 5:10; "vision of a New Jerusalem," Rev. 21:2; "looking for redemption in Israel," Luke 2:28; "shadow . . . of a great reality," Col. 2:17; Heb. 8:5; 10:1. For "'Lo, the poor Indian" see Pope, "Essay on Man, Epistle 1" (1733; l. 99–100).

126. For "flying . . . wind" see Ps. 18:10; "not in the wind . . . 'voice,'" 1 Kings 19:12. The "spiritual verities" to which Wilson refers consist in reading passages from the Hebrew scriptures typologically as "examples" (1 Cor. 10:6), as references to Christ. All three of the "emblems" cited by Wilson occur in the same passage in 1 Cor. 10:1–4. The "'rock'" struck by

Moses in the wilderness (Exod. 17:6) is read typologically as Christ, the "spiritual rock" (1 Cor. 10:4). The "'cloud'" of Gen. 9:13 is the rainbow of Noah, and that of Exod. 13:21 is the pillar of cloud as God leading Israel in the wilderness. The "sea" is the Red Sea (Exod. 13:18 ff.). In the NT, the cloud and water are brought together at the baptism of Christ in the Jordan (Mark 1:1–11). The connection of these "emblems" and events with Christian baptism as a "spiritual verity" is made in 1 Cor. 10:1–2. On the widespread Victorian use of this typology see Landow 1980, 66–94.

127. In Wilson's Court of Arches trial the 7th original Article of Charge cited the passage "Jesus Christ has not revealed . . . committed to the Church." In the twelfth edition, however, the whole of Wilson ¶78 is (erroneously) marked as cited in the Court of Arches. We have retained the marking of the twelfth edition, following it as our copytext for the passages cited as Articles of Charge in Wilson and Williams.

For "not making the heart . . . life" see Ezek. 13:22.

128. The "great moral law" is the ten commandments (Exod 20:1–17), repeated at Deut. 5:6–21, and summarized in the injunction stated in Deut. 6:4–6. These words are repeated as the "great commandment in the law" on which "hang all the law and the prophets" (Matt. 22:36–40; Mark 12:28–31; Luke 10:25–27). For "many are called but few chosen" see Matt. 20:16. The Greek quotation, a parallel to Matt. 20:16, is from Plato's *Phaedo*: "For the thyrsis-bearers are many, but the mystics few" (69c; trans. H. N. Fowler, *Loeb* 1: 241).

129. Calvin's notion of double predestination articulated here, of the limited number of the elect known only to God who are destined to salvation and of the reprobate who are destined to damnation, contrasts with the idea of universal salvation Wilson argues for in his last paragraph. Calvin's view ([1536] 1957, 2: 202–58; bk. 3, chaps. 21–24) is conflated here with Augustinianism, the Reformation assimilation of Augustine's anti-Pelagian views on predestination (see also Wilson ¶51 and note). In *Institutes of the Christian Religion,* Calvin quotes Augustine in support of his views (bk. 3, chap. 23; [1536] 1957, 2:225–38). J. B. Mozley had argued for the agreements between Calvin and Augustine in his 1855 Bampton Lectures (see Wilson ¶51 and note). Augustine's own position is set out in a number of his anti-Pelagian writings, including the *Letters against the Pelagians* (Trans. Peter Holmes, *NPNCF1* 5:377–434). For "mass of perdition" see Augustine, *Enchiridion*: "The mass of perdition caused by the first man's sin" (chap. 92; trans. J. F. Shaw, *NPNCF1* 3:226; quoted and commented on by Calvin ([1536] 1957, 2:228).

130. [1 Cor. xv. 28] This note was added in the twelfth edition.

The "wise heathens" who expected a reunion with the dead include Plato (*Phaedrus,* 246–49; *Republic,* the Myth of Er, 614–21), Cicero, *The Dream of Scipio,* and Virgil (*Aeneid,* 6:640 ff.). See McDannell and Lang 1988. Thersites, a general in Homer's *Iliad,* mocked Agamemnon and was beaten by Ulysses (2:212 ff.); in Apollodorus he is depicted as mocking Achilles' mourning of Penthisilea, whereupon Achilles killed him with one blow (*Bibliotheca,* bk. 1, chap. 8). Hyperbolos was an Athenian leader of the war party in the Archidamian War. Ostracized in 417, he was murdered on the island of Samos.

For "babblers" see Acts 17:18; "livers to get gain," James 4:13; and "eaters and drinkers," Isa. 22:13; 1 Cor. 10:7.

The "limbus infantium" (Lat. borderland of the infants) was the borderland of Hell where the souls of unbaptized children awaited the final judgment. It was devised to answer the theological dispute concerning the most appropriate time for baptism and the nature of grace before baptism. Before Augustine the Church Fathers held generally that such children were not damned, but were excluded from the beatific vision; Augustine, reacting to the Pelagians, argued that they do share at least to some degree in punishment ("Concerning Merit and the Remission of Sins," trans. Peter Holmes, *NPNCF1* 5:36–37). Thomas Aquinas, arguing against Augustine, maintained that unbaptized infants are in a state of positive natural happiness. Calvinists returned to a strict Augustinian position, but the Roman Catholic position was stated by Pius VI in the bull *Auctorem Fidei* (1794; The author of faith) that infants are not condemned to the fires of hell. For an extended discussion on limbo see G. J. Dyer 1964.

For "surrendered His kingdom to the Great Father" see 1 Cor. 15:24; "refuge," Deut. 33:27; "bosom of the Universal Parent," John 1:18; "quickened into higher life," 1 Cor. 15:36; "according to his Will," 1 John 5:14.

Wilson closes his essay by arguing for universal salvation, based on a theology of hope, a doctrine known as *apocatastasis,* based on Acts 3:21 ("the restitution of all things" at the last judgment). This view was argued by Origen in *De Principiis* (bk. 3, chap. 6) but was condemned at the Synod of Constantinople in 343. After the Reformation it was advocated by the Anabaptists and by F. D. E. Schleiermacher in *The Christian Faith* (1822); in England it was supported by a number of Broad Church thinkers. Such a view was reprehensible to Evangelicals and the High Church alike, who stressed both the fear of hell as a spur to conversion and the everlasting punishment of the damned, as mandated in the condemnatory clauses of the Athanasian Creed. Pusey defended this view vigorously, campaigning against Wilson on this point, and later publishing *What Is of Faith as to Everlasting Punishment?* (1880) against the universalist views of F. W.

Farrar in *Eternal Hope* (1877). For recent studies on the general theological concept see Deák 1977; and Cameron 1992.

The passage from ¶81, "The Christian Church can only tend. . . . according to his Will," was cited as "false and dangerous" in the Synodical Condemnation of *Essays and Reviews* on 21 June 1864. Wilson is condemned for his view on the last judgment (*Chronicle* 1859–64:1864, Session 66, 1659).

5 *Charles Wycliffe Goodwin*

Mosaic Cosmogony

On the revival of science in the 16th century, some of the earliest conclusions at which philosophers arrived were found to be at variance with popular and long-established belief.[1] The Ptolemaic system of astronomy, which had then full possession of the minds of men, contemplated the whole visible universe from the earth as the immovable centre of things. Copernicus changed the point of view, and placing the beholder in the sun, at once reduced the earth to an inconspicuous globule, a merely subordinate member of a family of planets which the terrestrials had until then fondly imagined to be but pendants and ornaments of their own habitation.[2] The Church naturally took a lively interest in the disputes which arose between the philosophers of the new school and those who adhered to the old doctrines, inasmuch as the Hebrew records, the basis of religious faith, manifestly countenanced the opinion of the earth's immobility and certain other views of the universe very incompatible with those propounded by Copernicus.[3] Hence arose the official proceedings against Galileo, in consequence of which he submitted to sign his celebrated recantation, acknowledging that 'the proposition that the sun is the centre of the world and immovable from its place is absurd, philosophically false, and formally heretical, because it is expressly contrary to the Scripture;' and that 'the proposition that the earth is not the centre of the world, nor immovable, but that it moves and also with a diurnal motion, is absurd, philosophically false, and at least erroneous in faith.'[4]

The Romish Church, it is presumed, adheres to the old views to the present day.[5] Protestant instincts, however, in the 17th century were strongly in sympathy with the augmentation of science, and consequently Reformed Churches more easily allowed themselves to be helped over the difficulty, which, according to the views of inspiration then held and which have survived to the present day, was in reality quite as formidable for them as for those of the old faith. The solution of the difficulty offered by Galileo and others was, that the object of a revelation or divine unveiling of mysteries, must be to teach man things which he is unable and must ever remain unable to find out for himself; but not physical truths, for the discovery of which he has faculties specially provided by his Creator. Hence it was not unreasonable that, in regard to matters of fact merely, the Sacred Writings should use the common language and assume the common belief of mankind, without purporting to correct errors upon points morally indifferent. So, in regard to such a text as, 'The world is established, it cannot be moved,' though it might imply the sacred penman's ignorance of the fact that the earth does move, yet it does not put forth this opinion as an indispensable point of faith.[6] And this remark is applicable to a number of texts which present a similar difficulty.

[3] It might be thought to have been less easy to reconcile in men's minds the Copernican view of the universe with the very plain and direct averments contained in the opening chapter of Genesis. It can scarcely be said that this chapter is not intended in part to teach and convey at least some physical truth, and taking its words in their plain sense it manifestly gives a view of the universe adverse to that of modern science. It represents the sky as a watery vault in which the sun, moon, and stars are set. But the discordance of this description with facts does not appear to have been so palpable to the minds of the seventeenth century as it is to us. The mobility of the earth was a proposition startling not only to faith but to the senses. The difficulty involved in this belief having been successfully got over, other discrepancies dwindled in importance. The brilliant progress of astronomical science subdued the minds of men; the controversy between faith and knowledge gradually fell to slumber; the story of Galileo and the Inquisition became a school commonplace, the doctrine of the earth's mobility found its way into children's catechisms, and the limited views of the nature of the universe indicated in the Old Testament ceased to be felt as religious difficulties.[7]

[4] It would have been well if theologians had made up their minds to accept frankly the principle that those things for the discovery of which man has faculties specially provided are not fit objects of a divine revelation. Had this been unhesitatingly done, either the definition and idea of divine revelation must have been modified, and the possibility of an admixture of error have been allowed, or such parts of the Hebrew writings as were found to be repugnant to fact must have been pronounced to form no part of revelation. The first course is that which theologians have most generally adopted, but with such limitations, cautels, and equivocations as to be of little use in satisfying those who would know how and what God really has taught mankind, and whether anything beyond that which man is able and obviously intended to arrive at by the use of his natural faculties.

[5] The difficulties and disputes which attended the first revival of science have recurred in the present century in consequence of the growth of geology. It is in truth only the old question over again—precisely the same point of theology which is involved,—although the difficulties which present themselves are fresh. The school-books of the present day, while they teach the child that the earth moves, yet assure him that it is a little less than six thousand years old, and that it was made in six days.[8] On the other hand, geologists of all religious creeds are agreed that the earth has existed for an immense series of years,—to be counted by millions rather than by thousands; and that indubitably more than six days elapsed from its first creation to the appearance of man upon its surface. By this broad discrepancy between old and new doctrine is the modern

mind startled, as were the men of the sixteenth century when told that the earth moved.

[6] When this new cause of controversy first arose, some writers more hasty than discreet, attacked the conclusions of geologists, and declared them scientifically false.[9] This phase may now be considered past, and although school-books probably continue to teach much as they did, no well-instructed person now doubts the great antiquity of the earth any more than its motion. This being so, modern theologians, forsaking the maxim of Galileo, or only using it vaguely as an occasional make-weight, have directed their attention to the possibility of reconciling the Mosaic narrative with those geological facts which are admitted to be beyond dispute.[10] Several modes of doing this have been proposed which have been deemed more or less satisfactory.[11] In a text-book of theological instruction widely used,[12] we find it stated in broad terms, 'Geological investigations, it is now known, all prove the perfect harmony between scripture and geology, in reference to the history of creation.'

[7] In truth, however, if we refer to the plans of conciliation proposed, we find them at variance with each other and mutually destructive. The conciliators are not agreed among themselves, and each holds the views of the other to be untenable and unsafe. The ground is perpetually being shifted, as the advance of geological science may require. The plain meaning of the Hebrew record is unscrupulously tampered with, and in general the pith of the whole process lies in divesting the text of all meaning whatever. We are told that Scripture not being designed to teach us natural philosophy, it is in vain to attempt to make out a cosmogony from its statements. If the first chapter of Genesis convey to us no information concerning the origin of the world, its statements cannot indeed be contradicted by modern discovery. But it is absurd to call this harmony. Statements such as that above quoted are, we conceive, little calculated to be serviceable to the interests of theology, still less to religion and morality. Believing, as we do, that if the value of the Bible as a book of religious instruction is to be maintained, it must be not by striving to prove it scientifically exact, at the expense of every sound principle of interpretation, and in defiance of common sense, but by the frank recognition of the erroneous views of nature which it contains, we have put pen to paper to analyse some of the popular conciliation theories. The inquiry cannot be deemed a superfluous one, nor one which in the interests of theology had better be let alone. Physical science goes on unconcernedly pursuing its own paths. Theology, the science whose object is the dealing of God with man as a moral being, maintains but a shivering existence, shouldered and jostled by the sturdy growths of modern thought, and bemoaning itself for the hostility which it encounters. Why should this be, unless because theologians persist in clinging to theories of God's procedure towards man, which have long been seen to be untenable? If, relinquishing theories, they would be content to inquire from the history of man what this procedure has actually been, the so-called difficulties of theology would, for the most part, vanish of themselves.

The account which astronomy gives of the relations of our earth to the rest of the universe, and that which geology gives of its internal structure and the development of its surface, are sufficiently familiar to most readers. But it will be necessary for our purpose to go over the oft-trodden ground, which must be done with rapid steps. Nor let the reader object to be reminded of some of the most elementary facts of his knowledge. The human race has been ages in arriving at conclusions now familiar to every child.

[9] This earth apparently so still and steadfast, lying in majestic repose beneath the aetherial vault, is a globular body of comparatively insignificant size, whirling fast through space round the sun as the centre of its orbit, and completing its revolution in the course of one year, while at the same time it revolves daily once about its own axis, thus producing the changes of day and night. The sun, which seems to leap up each morning from the east, and traversing the skyey bridge, slides down into the west, is relatively to our earth motionless. In size and weight it inconceivably surpasses it. The moon, which occupies a position in the visible heavens only second to the sun, and far beyond that of every other celestial body in conspicuousness, is but a subordinate globe, much smaller than our own, and revolving round the earth as its centre, while it accompanies it in yearly revolutions about the sun. Of itself it has no lustre, and is visible to us only by the reflected sunlight. Those beautiful stars which are perpetually changing their position in the heavens, and shine with a soft and moon-like light, are bodies, some much larger, some less, than our earth, and like it revolve round the sun, by the reflection of whose rays we see them. The telescope has revealed to us the fact that several of these are attended by moons of their own, and that besides those which the unassisted eye can see, there are others belonging to the same family coursing round the sun. As for the glittering dust which emblazons the nocturnal sky, there is reason to believe that each spark is a self-luminous body, perhaps of similar material to our sun, and that the very nearest of the whole tribe is at an incalculable distance from us, the very least of them of enormous size compared with our own humble globe. Thus has modern science reversed nearly all the *primâ facie* views to which our senses lead us as to the constitution of the universe; but so thoroughly are the above statements wrought into the culture of the present day, that we are apt to forget that mankind once saw these things very differently, and that but a few centuries have elapsed since such views were startling novelties.[13]

[10] Our earth then is but one of the lesser pendants of a body which is itself only an inconsiderable unit in the vast creation. And now if we withdraw our thoughts from the immensities of space, and look into the construction of man's obscure home, the first question is whether it has ever been in any other condition than that in which we now see it, and if so, what are the stages through which it has passed, and what was its first traceable state. Here geology steps in and successfully carries back the history of the earth's crust to a very remote period, until it arrives at a region of uncertainty, where philosophy is reduced to mere guesses and possibilities, and pronounces nothing definite. To this region belong the speculations which have been ventured upon as to the original concretion of the earth and planets out

of nebular matter of which the sun may have been the nucleus. But the first clear view which we obtain of the early condition of the earth, presents to us a ball of matter, fluid with intense heat, spinning on its own axis and revolving round the sun. How long it may have continued in this state is beyond calculation or surmise. It can only be believed that a prolonged period, beginning and ending we know not when, elapsed before the surface became cooled and hardened and capable of sustaining organized existences. The water which now enwraps a large portion of the face of the globe, must for ages have existed only in the shape of steam, floating above and enveloping the planet in one thick curtain of mist.[14] When the cooling of the surface allowed it to condense and descend, then commenced the process by which the lowest stratified rocks were formed, and gradually spread out in vast layers. Rains and rivers now acted upon the scoriaceous integument, grinding it to sand and carrying it down to the depths and cavities. Whether organized beings co-existed with this state of things we know not, as the early rocks have been acted upon by interior heat to an extent which must have destroyed all traces of animal and vegetable life, if any such ever existed. This period has been named by geologists the Azoic, or that in which life was not. Its duration no one presumes to define.[15]

It is in the system of beds which overlies these primitive formations that the first records of organisms present themselves. In the so-called Silurian system we have a vast assemblage of strata of various kinds, together many thousands of feet thick, and abounding in remains of animal life. These strata were deposited at the bottom of the sea, and the remains are exclusively marine. The creatures whose exuviae have been preserved belong to those classes which are placed by naturalists the lowest with respect to organization, the mollusca, articulata, and radiata. Analogous beings exist at the present day, but not their lineal descendants, unless time can effect transmutation of species, an hypothesis not generally accepted by naturalists. In the same strata with these inhabitants of the early seas are found remains of fucoid or seaweed-like plants, the lowest of the vegetable tribe, which may have been the first of this kind of existences introduced into the world. But, as little has yet been discovered to throw light upon the state of the dry land and its productions at this remote period, nothing can be asserted positively on the subject.[16]

In the upper strata of the Silurian system is found the commencement of the race of fishes, the lowest creatures of the vertebrate type, and in the succeeding beds they become abundant. These monsters clothed in mail who must have been the terror of the seas they inhabited, have left their indestructible coats behind them as evidence of their existence.[17]

Next come the carboniferous strata, containing the remains of a gigantic and luxuriant vegetation, and here reptiles and insects begin to make their appearance. At this point geologists make a kind of artificial break, and for the sake of distinction, denominate the whole of the foregoing period of animated existences the Palaeozoic, or that of antique life.[18]

[14] In the next great geological section, the so-called Secondary period, in which are comprised the oolitic and cretaceous systems, the predominant creatures are different from those which figured conspicuously in the preceding.[19] The land was inhabited by gigantic animals half-toad, half-lizard, who hopped about, leaving often their foot-prints like those of a clumsy human hand, upon the sandy shores of the seas they frequented.[20] The waters now abounded with monsters, half-fish, half-crocodile, the well-known saurians, whose bones have been collected in abundance. Even the air had its tenantry from the same family type, for the pterodactyls were creatures, half-lizard, half-vampyre, provided with membranous appendages which must have enabled them to fly. In an early stage of this period traces of birds appear, and somewhat later those of mammals, but of the lowest class belonging to that division, namely, the marsupial or pouch-bearing animals, in which naturalists see affinities to the oviparous tribes. The vegetation of this period seems to have consisted principally of the lower classes of plants, according to the scale of organization accepted by botanists, but it was luxuriant and gigantic.[21]

[15] Lastly, comes the Tertiary period, in which mammalia of the highest forms enter upon the scene, while the composite growths of the Secondary period in great part disappear, and the types of creatures approach more nearly to those which now exist.[22] During long ages this state of things continued, while the earth was the abode principally of mastodons, elephants, rhinoceroses, and their thick-hided congeners, many of them of colossal proportions, and of species which have now passed away. The remains of these creatures have been found in the frozen rivers of the north, and they appear to have roamed over regions of the globe where their more delicate representatives of the present day would be unable to live. During this era the ox, horse, and deer, and perhaps other animals, destined to be serviceable to man, became inhabitants of the earth. Lastly, the advent of man may be considered as inaugurating a new and distinct epoch, that in which we now are, and during the whole of which the physical conditions of existence cannot have been very materially different from what they are now. Thus, the reduction of the earth into the state in which we now behold it has been the slowly continued work of ages. The races of organic beings which have populated its surface have from time to time passed away, and been supplanted by others, introduced we know not certainly by what means, but evidently according to a fixed method and order, and with a gradually increasing complexity and fineness of organization, until we come to man as the crowning point of all. Geologically speaking, the history of his first appearance is obscure, nor does archaeology do much to clear this obscurity. Science has, however, made some efforts towards tracing man to his cradle, and by patient observation and collection of facts much more may perhaps be done in this direction. As for history and tradition, they afford little upon which anything can be built. The human race, like each individual man, has forgotten its own birth, and the void of its early years has been filled up by imagination, and not from genuine recollection. Thus much is clear, that man's existence on earth is brief, compared

with the ages during which unreasoning creatures were the sole possessors of the globe.

16] We pass to the account of the creation contained in the Hebrew record. And it must be observed that in reality two distinct accounts are given us in the book of Genesis, one being comprised in the first chapter and the first three verses of the second, the other commencing at the fourth verse of the second chapter and continuing till the end. This is so philologically certain that it were useless to ignore it. But even those who may be inclined to contest the fact that we have here the productions of two different writers, will admit that the account beginning at the first verse of the first chapter, and ending at the third verse of the second, is a complete whole in itself. And to this narrative, in order not to complicate the subject unnecessarily, we intend to confine ourselves. It will only be sufficient for our purpose to enquire, whether this account can be shown to be in accordance with our astronomical and geological knowledge. And for the right understanding of it the whole must be set out, so that the various parts may be taken in connexion with one another.[23]

7] We are told that 'in the beginning God created the heaven and the earth.' It has been matter of discussion amongst theologians whether the word 'created' (Heb. *bara*) here means simply shaped or formed, or shaped or formed out of nothing. From the use of the verb *bara* in other passages, it appears that it does not necessarily mean to make out of nothing,[24] but it certainly might impliedly mean this in a case so peculiar as the present. The phrase 'the heaven and the earth,' is evidently used to signify the universe of things, inasmuch as the heaven in its proper signification has no existence until the second day. It is asserted then that God shaped the whole material universe, whether out of nothing, or out of pre-existing matter. But which sense the writer really intended is not material for our present purpose to enquire, since neither astronomical nor geological science affects to state anything concerning the first origin of matter.

] In the second verse the earliest state of things is described; according to the received translation, 'the earth was without form and void.' The prophet Jeremiah[25] uses the same expression to describe the desolation of the earth's surface occasioned by God's wrath, and perhaps the words 'empty and waste' would convey to us at present something more nearly approaching the meaning of *tohu va-bohu*, than those which the translators have used.[26]

] The earth itself is supposed to be submerged under the waters of the deep, over which the breath of God—the air or wind—flutters while all is involved in darkness. The first special creative command is that which bids the light appear, whereupon daylight breaks over the two primaeval elements of earth and water —the one lying still enveloped by the other; and the space of time occupied by the original darkness and the light which succeeded, is described as the first day. Thus light and the measurement of time are represented as existing before the manifestation of the sun, and this idea, although repugnant to our modern knowledge, has not in former times appeared absurd. Thus we find Ambrose (*Hexaemeron* lib. 4, cap. 3) remarking:—'We must recollect that the light of day is one thing, the light of the sun, moon, and stars another,—the sun by his rays appearing to add lustre to the daylight. For before sunrise the day dawns, but is not in full refulgence, for the midday sun adds still further to its splendour.'[27] We quote this passage to show how a mind unsophisticated by astronomical knowledge understood the Mosaic statement; and we may boldly affirm that those for whom it was first penned could have taken it in no other sense than that light existed before and independently of the sun, nor do we misrepresent it when we affirm this to be its natural and primary meaning. How far we are entitled to give to the writer's words an enigmatical and secondary meaning, as contended by those who attempt to conciliate them with our present knowledge, must be considered further on.

[20] The work of the second day of creation is to erect the vault of Heaven (Heb. *rakia*; Gr. στερέωμα; Lat. *firmamentum*) which is represented as supporting an ocean of water above it. The waters are said to be divided, so that some are below, some above the vault. That the Hebrews understood the sky, firmament, or heaven to be a permanent solid vault, as it appears to the ordinary observer, is evident enough from various expressions made use of concerning it. It is said to have pillars (Job xxvi. 11), foundations (2 Sam. xxii. 8), doors (Ps. lxxviii. 23), and windows (Gen. vii. 11). No quibbling about the derivation of the word *rakia*, which is literally something beaten out,[28] can affect the explicit description of the Mosaic writer, contained in the words 'the waters that are above the firmament,' or avail to show that he was aware that the sky is but transparent space.

[21] On the third day, at the command of God, the waters which have hitherto concealed the earth are gathered together in one place—the sea,—and the dry land emerges. Upon the same day the earth brings forth grass, herb yielding seed and fruit trees, the destined food of the animals and of man (v. 29). Nothing is said of herbs and trees which are not serviceable to this purpose, and perhaps it may be contended, since there is no vegetable production which may not possibly be useful to man, or which is not preyed upon by some animal, that in this description the whole terrestrial flora is implied. We wish, however, to call the attention of the reader to the fact, that trees and plants destined for food are those which are particularly singled out here as the earliest productions of the earth, as we shall have occasion to refer to this again presently.

[22] On the fourth day, the two great lights, the sun and moon, are *made* (Heb. *hasah*) and *set* in the firmament of heaven to give light to the earth, but more particularly to serve as the means of measuring time, and of marking out years, days, and seasons. This is the most prominent office assigned to them (v. 14–18). The formation of the stars is mentioned in the most cursory manner. It is not said out of what materials all these bodies were made, and whether the writer regarded them as already existing, and only waiting to have a proper place assigned them, may be open to question. At any rate, their allotted receptacle—the firmament—was not made until the second day, nor were they set in it until the fourth; vegetation, be it observed, having already commenced on the third, and therefore independently of the warming influence of the sun.

23] On the fifth day the waters are called into productive activity, and bring forth fishes and marine animals, as also the birds of the air.[29] It is also said that God created or formed (*bara*) great whales and other creatures of the water and air. On the sixth day the earth brings forth living creatures, cattle, and reptiles, and also 'the beast of the field,' that is, the wild beasts. And here also it is added that God made (*hasah*) these creatures after their several kinds. The formation of man is distinguished by a variation of the creative fiat. 'Let us make man in our image after our likeness.' Accordingly, man is made and formed (*bara*) in the image and likeness of God, a phrase which has been explained away to mean merely 'perfect, sinless,' although the Pentateuch abounds in passages showing that the Hebrews contemplated the Divine being in the visible form of a man.[30] Modern spiritualism has so entirely banished this idea, that probably many may not without an effort be able to accept the plain language of the Hebrew writer in its obvious sense in the 26th verse of the 1st chapter of Genesis, though they will have no difficulty in doing so in the 3rd verse of the 5th chapter, where the same words 'image' and 'likeness' are used. Man is said to have been created male and female, and the narrative contains nothing to show that a single pair only is intended.[31] He is commanded to increase and multiply, and to assume dominion over all the other tribes of beings. The whole of the works of creation being complete, God gives to man, beast, fowl, and creeping thing, the vegetable productions of the earth as their appointed food. And when we compare the verses Gen. i. 29, 30, with Gen. ix. 3, in which, after the Flood, animals are given to man for food in addition to the green herb, it is difficult not to come to the conclusion that in the earliest view taken of creation, men and animals were supposed to have been, in their original condition, not carnivorous. It is needless to say that this has been for the most part the construction put upon the words of the Mosaic writer, until a clear perception of the creative design which destined the tiger and lion for flesh-eaters, and latterly the geological proof of flesh-eating monsters having existed among the pre-adamite inhabitants of the globe, rendered it necessary to ignore this meaning.

4] The 1st, 2nd, and 3rd verses of the second chapter of Genesis, which have been most absurdly divided from their context, conclude the narrative.[32] On the seventh day God rests from His work, and blesses the day of rest, a fact which is referred to in the Commandment given from Sinai as the ground of the observance of Sabbatic rest imposed upon the Hebrews.

] Remarkable as this narrative is for simple grandeur, it has nothing in it which can be properly called poetical. It bears on its face no trace of mystical or symbolical meaning. Things are called by their right names with a certain scientific exactness widely different from the imaginative cosmogonies of the Greeks, in which the powers and phenomena of nature are invested with personality, and the passions and qualities of men are represented as individual existences.[33]

The circumstances related in the second narrative of creation are indeed such as to give at least some ground for the supposition that a mystical interpretation was intended to be given to it. But this is far from being the case with the first narrative, in which none but a professed mystifier of the school of Philo could see anything but a plain statement of facts. There can be little reasonable dispute then as to the sense in which the Mosaic narrative was taken by those who first heard it, nor is it indeed disputed that for centuries, putting apart the Philonic mysticism, which after all did not exclude a primary sense, its words have been received in their genuine and natural meaning.[34] That this meaning is *primâ facie* one wholly adverse to the present astronomical and geological views of the universe is evident enough. There is not a mere difference through deficiency. It cannot be correctly said that the Mosaic writer simply leaves out details which modern science supplies, and that, therefore, the inconsistency is not a real but only an apparent one. It is manifest that the whole account is given from a different point of view from that which we now unavoidably take; that the order of things as we now know them to be, is to a great extent reversed, although here and there we may pick out some general analogies and points of resemblance. Can we say that the Ptolemaic system of astronomy is not at variance with modern science, because it represents with a certain degree of correctness some of the apparent motions of the heavenly bodies?

[27] The task which sundry modern writers have imposed upon themselves is to prove, that the Mosaic narrative, however apparently at variance with our knowledge, is essentially, and in fact true, although never understood properly until modern science supplied the necessary commentary and explanation.

[28] Two modes of conciliation have been propounded which have enjoyed considerable popularity, and to these two we shall confine our attention.[35]

[29] The first is that originally brought into vogue by Chalmers and adopted by the late Dr. Buckland in his Bridgewater Treatise, and which is probably still received by many as a sufficient solution of all difficulties.[36] Dr. Buckland's treatment of the case may be taken as a fair specimen of the line of argument adopted, and it shall be given in his own words. 'The word *beginning*,' he says, 'as applied by Moses in the first verse of the book of Genesis, expresses an undefined period of time which was antecedent to the last great change that affected the surface of the earth, and to the creation of its present animal and vegetable inhabitants, during which period a long series of operations may have been going on; which as they are wholly unconnected with the history of the human race, are passed over in silence by the sacred historian, whose only concern was barely to state, that the matter of the universe is not eternal and self-existent, but was originally created by the power of the Almighty.'[37] 'The Mosaic narrative commences with a declaration that "in the beginning God created the heaven and the earth." These few first words of Genesis may be fairly appealed to by the geologist as containing a brief statement of the creation of the material elements, at a time distinctly preceding the operations of the first day; it is nowhere affirmed that God created the heaven and the earth in the *first day*, but in the *beginning*; this beginning may have been an epoch at an unmeasured distance, followed by periods of undefined duration during which all the physical operations disclosed by geology were going on.'

[30] 'The first verse of Genesis, therefore, seems explicitly to assert the creation of

the universe; the heaven, including the sidereal systems;[38] and the earth, more especially specifying our own planet, as the subsequent scene of the operations of the six days about to be described; no information is given as to events which may have occurred upon this earth, unconnected with the history of man, between the creation of its component matter recorded in the first verse, and the era at which its history is resumed in the second verse; nor is any limit fixed to the time during which these intermediate events may have been going on: millions of millions of years may have occupied the indefinite interval, between the beginning in which God created the heaven and the earth, and the evening or commencement of the first day of the Mosaic narrative.'[39]

1] 'The second verse may describe the condition of the earth on the evening of this first day (for in the Jewish mode of computation used by Moses each day is reckoned from the beginning of one evening to the beginning of another evening).[40] This first evening may be considered as the termination of the indefinite time which followed the primeval creation announced in the first verse, and as the commencement of the first of the six succeeding days in which the earth was to be filled up, and peopled in a manner fit for the reception of mankind. We have in this second verse, a distinct mention of earth and waters, as already existing and involved in darkness; their condition also is described as a state of confusion and emptiness (*tohu bohu*), words which are usually interpreted by the vague and indefinite Greek term chaos, and which may be geologically considered as designating the wreck and ruins of a former world. At this intermediate point of time the preceding undefined geological periods had terminated, a new series of events commenced, and the work of the first morning of this new creation was the calling forth of light from a temporary darkness, which had overspread the ruins of the ancient earth.'[41]

] With regard to the formation of the sun and moon, Dr. Buckland observes, p. 27, 'We are not told that the substance of the sun and moon was first called into existence on the fourth day; the text may equally imply that these bodies were then prepared and appointed to certain offices, of high importance to mankind, "to give light upon the earth, and to rule over the day, and over the night, to be for signs, and for seasons, and for days, and for years." The fact of their creation had been stated before in the first verse.'[42]

] The question of the meaning of the word *bara*, create, has been previously touched upon; it has been acknowledged by good critics that it does not of itself necessarily imply 'to make out of nothing,' upon the simple ground that it is found used in cases where such a meaning would be inapplicable.[43] But the difficulty of giving to it the interpretation contended for by Dr. Buckland, and of uniting with this the assumption of a six days' creation, such as that described in Genesis, at a comparatively recent period, lies in this, that the heaven itself is distinctly said to have been formed by the division of the waters on the second day. Consequently during the indefinite ages which elapsed from the primal creation of matter until the first Mosaic day of creation, there was no sky, no local habitation for the sun, moon, and stars, even supposing those bodies to have been included in the original material. Dr. Buckland does not touch this obvious difficulty, without which his argument that the sun and moon might have been contemplated as pre-existing, although they are not stated to have been set in the heaven until the fourth day, is of no value at all.[44]

[34] Dr. Buckland appears to assume that when it is said that the heaven and the earth were created in the beginning, it is to be understood that they were created in their present form and state of completeness, the heaven raised above the earth as we see it, or seem to see it now. This is the fallacy of his argument. The circumstantial description of the framing of the heaven out of the waters, proves that the words 'heaven and earth,' in the first verse, must be taken either proleptically, as a general expression for the universe, the matter of the universe in its crude and unformed shape, or else the word *bara* must mean formed, not created, the writer intending to say 'God formed the heaven and earth in manner following,' in which case heaven is used in its distinct and proper sense. But these two senses cannot be united in the manner covertly assumed in Dr. Buckland's argument.

[35] Having, however, thus endeavoured to make out that the Mosaic account does not negative the idea that the sun, moon, and stars had 'been created at the indefinitely distant time designated by the word beginning,' he is reduced to describe the primaeval darkness of the first day as 'a temporary darkness, produced by an accumulation of dense vapours upon the face of the deep.' 'An incipient dispersion of these vapours may have readmitted light to the earth, upon the first day, whilst the exciting cause of light was obscured, and the further purification of the atmosphere upon the fourth day, may have caused the sun and moon and stars to re-appear in the firmament of heaven, to assume their new relations to the newly modified earth and to the human race.'[45]

[36] It is needless to discuss the scientific probability of this hypothesis, but the violence done to the grand and simple words of the Hebrew writer must strike every mind. 'And God said, Let there be light—and there was light—and God saw the light that it was good. And God divided the light from the darkness, and God called the light day, and the darkness called he night; and the evening and the morning were the first day.'[46] Can any one sensible of the value of words suppose, that nothing more is here described, or intended to be described, than the partial clearing away of a fog? Can such a manifestation of light have been dignified by the appellation of day? Is not this reducing the noble description which has been the admiration of ages to a pitiful *caput mortuum* of empty verbiage?[47]

[37] What were the *new relations* which the heavenly bodies according to Dr. Buckland's view, assumed to the newly modified earth and to the human race? They had, as we well know, marked out seasons, days and years, and had given light for ages before to the earth, and to the animals which preceded man as its inhabitants, as is shown, Dr. Buckland admits, by the eyes of fossil animals, optical instruments of the same construction as those of the animals of our days, and also by the existence of vegetables in the early world, to the development of which light must have been as essential then as now.[48]

38] The hypothesis adopted by Dr. Buckland was first promulgated at a time when the gradual and regular formation of the earth's strata was not seen or admitted so clearly as it is now. Geologists were more disposed to believe in great catastrophes and sudden breaks.[49] Buckland's theory supposes that previous to the appearance of the present races of animals and vegetables there was a great gap in the globe's history,—that the earth was completely depopulated, as well of marine as land animals; and that the creation of all existing plants and animals was coaeval with that of man. This theory is by no means supported by geological phenomena, and is, we suppose, now rejected by all geologists whose authority is valuable.[50] Thus writes Hugh Miller in 1857—'I certainly did once believe with Chalmers and with Buckland that the six days were simply natural days of twenty-four hours each—that they had comprised the entire work of the existing creation—and that the latest of the geologic ages was separated by a great chaotic gap from our own. My labours at the time as a practical geologist had been very much restricted to the palaeozoic and secondary rocks, more especially to the old red and carboniferous systems of the one division, and the oolitic system of the other; and the long-extinct organisms which I found in them certainly did not conflict with the views of Chalmers. All I found necessary at the time to the work of reconciliation was some scheme that would permit me to assign to the earth a high antiquity, and to regard it as the scene of many succeeding creations. During the last nine years, however, I have spent a few weeks every autumn in exploring the late formations, and acquainting myself with their particular organisms. I have traced them upwards from the raised beaches and old coastlines of the human period, to the brick clays, Clyde beds, and drift and boulder deposits of the Pleistocene era; and again from them, with the help of museums and collections, up through the mammaliferous crag of England to its red and coral crags; and the conclusion at which I have been compelled to arrive is, that for many long ages ere man was ushered into being, not a few of his humbler contemporaries of the fields and woods enjoyed life in their present haunts, and that for thousands of years anterior to even *their* appearance, many of the existing molluscs lived in our seas. That *day* during which the present creation came into being, and in which God, when he had made 'the beast of the earth after his kind, and the cattle after their kind,' at length terminated the work by moulding a creature in His own image, to whom He gave dominion over them all, was not a brief period of a few hours' duration, but extended over, mayhap, millenniums of centuries. No blank chaotic gap of death and darkness separated the creation to which man belongs from that of the old extinct elephant, hippopotamus, and hyaena; for familiar animals, such as the red deer, the roe, the fox, the wild cat, and the badger, lived throughout the period which connected their time with our own; and so I have been compelled to hold that the days of creation were not natural but prophetic days, and stretched far back into the bygone eternity.'[51]

] Hugh Miller will be admitted by many as a competent witness to the untenability of the theory of Chalmers and Buckland on mere geological grounds.

He had, indeed, a theory of his own to propose, which we shall presently consider; but we may take his word that it was not without the compulsion of what he considered irresistible evidence that he relinquished a view which would have saved him infinite time and labour, could he have adhered to it.[52]

[40] But whether contemplated from a geological point of view, or whether from a philological one, that is, with reference to the value of words, the use of language, and the ordinary rules which govern writers whose object it is to make themselves understood by those to whom their works are immediately addressed, the interpretation proposed by Buckland to be given to the Mosaic description will not bear a moment's serious discussion. It is plain, from the whole tenor of the narrative, that the writer contemplated no such representation as that suggested, nor could any such idea have entered into the minds of those to whom the account was first given. Dr. Buckland endeavours to make out that we have here simply a case of leaving out facts which did not particularly concern the writer's purpose, so that he gave an account true so far as it went, though imperfect. 'We may fairly ask,' he argues, 'of those persons who consider physical science a fit subject for revelation, what point they can imagine short of a communication of Omniscience at which such a revelation might have stopped without imperfections of omission, less in degree, but similar in kind, to that which they impute to the existing narrative of Moses? A revelation of so much only of astronomy as was known to Copernicus would have seemed imperfect after the discoveries of Newton; and a revelation of the science of Newton would have appeared defective to La Place: a revelation of all the chemical knowledge of the eighteenth century would have been as deficient in comparison with the information of the present day, as what is now known in this science will probably appear before the termination of another age; in the whole circle of sciences there is not one to which this argument may not be extended, until we should require from revelation a full development of all the mysterious agencies that uphold the mechanism of the material world.'[53] Buckland's question is quite inapplicable to the real difficulty, which is, not that circumstantial details are omitted—that might reasonably be expected,—but that what is told, is told so as to convey to ordinary apprehensions an impression at variance with facts. We are indeed told that certain writers of antiquity had already anticipated the hypothesis of the geologist, and two of the Christian fathers, Augustine and Episcopius, are referred to as having actually held that a wide interval elapsed between the first act of creation, mentioned in the Mosaic account, and the commencement of the six days' work.[54] If, however, they arrived at such a conclusion, it was simply because, like the modern geologist, they had theories of their own to support, which led them to make somewhat similar hypotheses.

[41] 'After all,' says Buckland, 'it should be recollected that the question is not respecting the correctness of the Mosaic narrative, but of our interpretation of it,'[55] a proposition which can hardly be sufficiently reprobated. Such a doctrine, carried out unreservedly, strikes at the root of critical morality. It may, indeed, be sometimes possible to give two or three different interpretations to one and the

same passage, even in a modern and familiar tongue, in which case this may arise from the unskilfulness of the writer or speaker who has failed clearly to express his thought. In a dead or foreign language the difficulty may arise from our own want of familiarity with its forms of speech, or in an ancient book we may be puzzled by allusions and modes of thought the key to which has been lost. But it is no part of the commentator's or interpreter's business to introduce obscurity or find difficulties where none exist, and it cannot be pretended that, taking it as a question of the use of words to express thoughts, there are any peculiar difficulties about understanding the first chapter of Genesis, whether in its original Hebrew or in our common translation, which represents the original with all necessary exactness. The difficulties arise for the first time, when we seek to import a meaning into the language which it certainly never could have conveyed to those to whom it was originally addressed. Unless we go the whole length of supposing the simple account of the Hebrew cosmogonist to be a series of awkward equivocations, in which he attempted to give a representation widely different from the facts, yet, without trespassing against literal truth, we can find no difficulty in interpreting his words. Although language may be, and often has been, used for the purpose, not of expressing, but concealing thought, no such charge can fairly be laid against the Hebrew writer.

42] 'It should be borne in mind,' says Dr. Buckland, 'that the object of the account was, not to state *in what manner*, but *by whom* the world was made.'[56] Every one must see that this is an unfounded assertion, inasmuch as the greater part of the narrative consists in a minute and orderly description of the manner in which things were made. We can know nothing as to the *object* of the account, except from the account itself. What the writer meant to state is just that which he has stated, for all that we can know to the contrary. Or can we seriously believe that if appealed to by one of his Hebrew hearers or readers as to his intention, he would have replied, My only object in what I have written is to inform you that God made the world; as to the manner of His doing it, of which I have given so exact an account, I have no intention that my words should be taken in their literal meaning.

3] We come then to this, that if we sift the Mosaic narrative of all definite meaning, and only allow it to be the expression of the most vague generalities, if we avow that it admits of no certain interpretation, of none that may not be shifted and altered as often as we see fit, and as the exigencies of geology may require, then may we reconcile it with what science teaches. This mode of dealing with the subject has been broadly advocated by a recent writer of mathematical eminence, who adopts the Bucklandian hypothesis, a passage from whose work we shall quote.[57]

4] 'The Mosaic account of the six days' work is thus harmonized by some. On the first day, while the earth was "without form and void," the result of a previous convulsion in nature, "and darkness was upon the face of the deep," God commanded light to shine upon the earth. This may have been effected by such a clearing of the thick and loaded atmosphere, as to allow the light of the sun to penetrate its mass with a suffused illumination, sufficient to dispel the total darkness which had prevailed, but proceeding from a source not yet apparent on the earth. On the second day a separation took place in the thick vapoury mass which lay upon the earth, dense clouds were gathered up aloft and separated by *an expanse* from the waters and vapours below. On the third day these lower vapours, or fogs and mists which hitherto concealed the earth, were condensed and gathered with the other waters of the earth into seas, and the dry land appeared. Then grass and herbs began to grow. On the fourth day the clouds and vapours so rolled into separate masses, or were so entirely absorbed into the air itself, that the sun shone forth in all its brilliancy, the visible source of light and heat to the renovated earth, while the moon and stars gave light by night, and God appointed them henceforth for signs, and for seasons, and for days, and for years, to his creatures whom he was about to call into existence, as he afterwards set or appointed his bow in the clouds, which had appeared ages before, to be a sign to Noah and his descendants. The fifth and sixth days' work needs no comment.[58]

[45] 'According to this explanation, the first chapter of Genesis does not pretend (as has been generally assumed) to be a cosmogony, or an account of the original creation of the material universe. The only cosmogony which it contains, in that sense at least, is confined to the sublime declaration of the first verse, "In the beginning God created the heavens and the earth." The inspired record thus stepping over an interval of infinite ages with which man has no direct concern, proceeds at once to narrate the events preparatory to the introduction of man on the scene; employing phraseology strictly faithful to the *appearances* which would have met the eye of man, could he have been a spectator on the earth of what passed those six days. All this has been commonly supposed to be a more detailed account of the general truth announced in the first verse, in short, a cosmogony: such was the idea of Josephus; such probably was the idea of our translators; for their version, without form and void, points to the primaeval chaos, out of which all things were then supposed to emerge; and these words standing *in limine*, have tended, perhaps more than anything else, to foster the idea of a cosmogony in the minds of general readers to this very day.[59]

[46] 'The foregoing explanation many have now adopted. It is sufficient for my purpose, if it be a possible explanation, and if it meet the difficulties of the case. That it is possible in itself, is plain from the fact above established, that the Scriptures wisely speak on natural things according to their *appearances* rather than their *physical realities*. It meets the difficulties of the case, because all the difficulties hitherto started against this chapter on scientific grounds proceeded on the principle that it is a cosmogony; which this explanation repudiates, and thus disposes of the difficulties. It is therefore an explanation satisfactory to my own mind. I may be tempted to regret that I can gain no certain scientific information from Genesis regarding the process of the original creation; but I resist the temptation, remembering the great object for which the Scripture was given—to

tell man of his origin and fall, and to draw his mind to his Creator and Redeemer. Scripture was not designed to teach us natural philosophy, and it is vain to attempt to make a cosmogony out of its statements. The Almighty declares himself the originator of all things, but he condescends not to describe the process or the laws by which he worked. All this he leaves for reason to decipher from the phenomena which his world displays.[60]

[47] 'This explanation, however, I do not wish to impose on Scripture; and am fully prepared to surrender it, should further scientific discovery suggest another better fitted to meet all the requirements of the case.'

[48] We venture to think that the world at large will continue to consider the account in the first chapter of Genesis to be a cosmogony. But as it is here admitted that it does not describe physical realities, but only outward appearances, that is, gives a description false in fact, and one which can teach us no scientific truth whatever, it seems to matter little what we call it. If its description of the events of the six days which it comprises be merely one of appearances and not of realities, it can teach us nothing regarding them.

[49] Dissatisfied with the scheme of conciliation which has been discussed, other geologists have proposed to give an entirely mythical or enigmatical sense to the Mosaic narrative, and to consider the creative days described as vast periods of time. This plan was long ago suggested, but it has of late enjoyed a high degree of popularity, through the advocacy of the Scotch geologist Hugh Miller, an extract from whose work has been already quoted.[61] Dr. Buckland gives the following account of the first form in which this theory was propounded, and of the grounds upon which he rejected it in favour of that of Chalmers:[62]—

[50] 'A third opinion has been suggested both by learned theologians and by geologists, and on grounds independent of one another—viz., that the days of the Mosaic creation need not be understood to imply the same length of time which is now occupied by a single revolution of the globe, but successive periods each of great extent; and it has been asserted that the order of succession of the organic remains of a former world accords with the order of creation recorded in Genesis. This assertion, though to a certain degree apparently correct, is not entirely supported by geological facts, since it appears that the most ancient marine animals occur in the same division of the lowest transition strata with the earliest remains of vegetables, so that the evidence of organic remains, as far as it goes, shows the origin of plants and animals to have been contemporaneous: if any creation of vegetables preceded that of animals, no evidence of such an event has yet been discovered by the researches of geology. Still there is, I believe, no sound critical or theological objection to the interpretation of the word "day" as meaning a long period.'[63]

Archdeacon Pratt also summarily rejects this view as untenable:[64]—

'There is one other class of interpreters, however, with whom I find it impossible to agree,—I mean those who take the six days to be six periods of unknown indefinite length. This is the principle of interpretation in a work on the

Creation and the Fall, by the Rev. D. Macdonald; also in Mr. Hugh Miller's posthumous work, the *Testimony of the Rocks*, and also in an admirable treatise on the *Prae-Adamite Earth* in Dr. Lardner's *Museum of Science*.[65] In this last it is the more surprising because the successive chapters are in fact an accumulation of evidence which points the other way, as a writer in the *Christian Observer*, Jan. 1858, has conclusively shown. The late M. D'Orbigny has demonstrated in his *Prodrome de Palaeontologie*, after an elaborate examination of vast multitudes of fossils, that there have been at least twenty-nine distinct periods of animal and vegetable existence—that is, twenty-nine creations separated one from another by catastrophes which have swept away the species existing at the time, with a very few exceptions, never exceeding one and a-half per cent. of the whole number discovered which have either survived the catastrophe, or have been erroneously designated.[66] But not a single species of the preceding period survived the last of these catastrophes, and this closed the Tertiary period and ushered in the Human period. The evidence adduced by M. D'Orbigny shows that both plants and animals appeared in every one of those twenty-nine periods. The notion, therefore, that the "days" of Genesis represent periods of creation from the beginning of things is at once refuted. The parallel is destroyed both in the number of the periods (thirty, including the Azoic, instead of six), and also in the character of the things created. No argument could be more complete; and yet the writer of the *Prae-Adamite Earth*, in the last two pages, sums up his lucid sketch of M. D'Orbigny's researches by referring the account in the first chapter of Genesis to the whole creation from the beginning of all things, a *selection* of epochs being made, as he imagines, for the six days or periods.'[67]

[53] In this trenchant manner do theological geologists overthrow one another's theories. However, Hugh Miller was perfectly aware of the difficulty involved in his view of the question, and we shall endeavour to show the reader the manner in which he deals with it.

[54] He begins by pointing out that the families of vegetables and animals were introduced upon earth as nearly as possible according to the great classes in which naturalists have arranged the modern flora and fauna. According to the arrangement of Lindley,[68] he observes—'Commencing at the bottom of the scale we find the thallogens, or flowerless plants, which lack proper stems and leaves—a class which includes all the algae. Next succeed the acrogens, or flowerless plants that possess both stems and leaves—such as the ferns and their allies. Next, omitting an inconspicuous class, represented by but a few parasitical plants incapable of preservation as fossils, come the endogens—monocotyledonous flowering plants, that include the palms, the liliaceae, and several other families, all characterized by the parallel venation of their leaves. Next, omitting another inconspicuous tribe, there follows a very important class, the gymnogens—polycotyledonous trees, represented by the coniferae and cycadaceae. And last of all come the dicotyledonous exogens—a class to which all our fruit and what are known as our forest trees belong, with a vastly preponderating majority of the herbs and flowers that impart

fertility and beauty to our gardens and meadows.'[69] The order in which fossils of these several classes appear in the strata, Hugh Miller states to be as follows:—In the Lower Silurian we find only thallogens, in the Upper Silurian acrogens are added. The gymnogens appear rather prematurely, it might be thought, in the old red sandstone, the endogens (monocotyledonous) coming after them in the carboniferous group. Dicotyledonous exogens enter at the close of the oolitic period, and come to their greatest development in the tertiary.[70] Again, the animal tribes have been introduced in an order closely agreeing with geological divisions established by Cuvier. In the Silurian beds the invertebrate creatures, the radiata, articulata, and mollusca, appear simultaneously.[71] At the close of the period, fishes, the lowest of the vertebrata, appear: before the old red sandstone period had passed away, reptiles had come into existence; birds, the marsupial mammals, enter in the oolitic period; placental mammals in the tertiary; and man last of all.[72]

5] Now, these facts do certainly tally to some extent in the Mosaic account, which represents fish and fowl having been produced from the waters on the fifth day, reptiles and mammals from the earth on the sixth, and man as made last of all. The agreement, however, is far from exact, as according to geological evidence, reptiles would appear to have existed ages before birds and mammals, whereas here the creation of birds is attributed to the fifth day, that of reptiles to the sixth. There remains, moreover, the insuperable difficulty of the plants and trees being represented as made on the third day—that is, more than an age before fishes and birds; which is clearly not the case.

6] Although, therefore, there is a superficial resemblance in the Mosaic account to that of the geologists, it is evident that the bare theory that a 'day' means an age or immense geological period might be made to yield some rather strange results.[73] What becomes of the evening and morning of which each day is said to have consisted? Was each geologic age divided into two long intervals, one all darkness, the other all light? and if so, what became of the plants and trees created in the third day or period, when the evening of the fourth day (the evenings, be it observed, precede the mornings) set in? They must have passed through half a seculum of total darkness, not even cheered by that dim light which the sun, not yet completely manifested, supplied on the morning of the third day.[74] Such an ordeal would have completely destroyed the whole vegetable creation, and yet we find that it survived, and was appointed on the sixth day as the food of man and animals. In fact, we need only substitute the word 'period' for 'day' in the Mosaic narrative to make it very apparent that the writer at least had no such meaning, nor could he have conveyed any such meaning to those who first heard his account read.

'It has been held,' says Hugh Miller, 'by accomplished philologists, that the days of Mosaic creation may be regarded without doing violence to the Hebrew language, as successive periods of great extent.'[75] We do not believe that there is any ground for this doctrine. The word 'day' is certainly used occasionally in particular phrases, in an indefinite manner, not only in Hebrew, but other languages. As for instance, Gen. xxxix. 11—'About this time,' Heb. literally, 'about this day.' But every such phrase explains itself, and not only philology but common sense disclaims the notion, that when 'day' is spoken of in terms like those in the first chapter of Genesis, and described as consisting of an evening and a morning, it can be understood to mean a seculum.

[58] Archdeacon Pratt, treating on the same subject, says (p. 41, note), 'Were there no other ground of objection to this mode of interpretation, I think the wording of the fourth commandment is clearly opposed to it. Ex. xx. 8. 'Remember the Sabbath day to keep it holy. 9. Six days shalt thou labour and do all thy work. 10. But the seventh day is the Sabbath of the Lord thy God. In it thou, shalt not do any work, thou, nor thy son, nor thy daughter, thy manservant, nor thy maidservant, nor thy cattle, nor thy stranger that is within thy gates. 11. For in six days the Lord made heaven and earth, the sea and all that in them is, and rested the seventh day; wherefore the Lord blessed the Sabbath day and hallowed it.'

[59] 'Is it not a harsh and forced interpretation to suppose that the six days in v. 9 do not mean the same as the six days in v. 11, but that in this last place they mean six periods? In reading through the eleventh verse, it is extremely difficult to believe that the seventh day is a long period, and the sabbath day an ordinary day, that is, that the same word day should be used in two such totally different senses in the same short sentence and without any explanation.'[76]

[60] Hugh Miller saw the difficulty; but he endeavours to escape the consequences of a rigorous application of the periodic theory by modifying it in a peculiar, and certainly ingenious manner. 'Waiving,' he says, 'the question as a philological one, and simply holding with Cuvier, Parkinson, and Silliman, that each of the *six* days of the Mosaic account in the first chapter were what is assuredly meant by the *day*[77] referred to in the second, not natural days but lengthened periods, I find myself called on, as a geologist, to account for but three out of the six. Of the period during which light was created, of the period during which a firmament was made to separate the waters from the waters, or of the period during which the two great lights of the earth, with the other heavenly bodies, became visible from the earth's surface—we need expect to find no record in the rocks. Let me, however, pause for a moment, to remark the peculiar character of the language in which we are first introduced in the Mosaic narrative, to the heavenly bodies—sun, moon, and stars. The moon, though absolutely one of the smallest lights of our system, is described as secondary and subordinate to only its greatest light, the sun. It is the apparent, then, not the actual, which we find in the passage—what *seemed* to be, not what *was*; and as it was merely what appeared to be greatest that was described as greatest, on what grounds are we to hold that it may not also have been what *appeared* at the time to be made that has been described as made? The sun, moon, and stars, may have been created long before, though it was not until this fourth day of creation that they became visible from the earth's surface.'[78]

[61] The theory founded upon this hint is that the Hebrew writer did not state facts, but merely certain appearances, and those not of things which really happened as assumed in the explanation adopted by Archdeacon Pratt, but of

certain occurrences which were presented to him in a vision, and that this vision greatly deceived him as to what he seemed to see; and thus, in effect, the real discrepancy of the narrative with facts is admitted. He had in all, seven visions, to each of which he attributed the duration of a day, although indeed each picture presented to him the earth during seven long and distinctly marked epochs. While on the one hand this supposition admits all desirable latitude for mistakes and misrepresentations, Hugh Miller, on the other hand, endeavours to show that a substantial agreement with the truth exists, and to give sufficient reason for the mistakes. We must let him speak for himself.[79] 'The geologist, in his attempts to collate the Divine with the geologic record, has, I repeat, only three of the six periods of creation to account for[80]—the period of plants, the period of great sea-monsters and creeping things, and the period of cattle and beasts of the earth. He is called on to question his systems and formations regarding the remains of these three great periods, and of them only. And the question once fairly stated, what, I ask, is the reply? All geologists agree in holding that the vast geological scale naturally divides into three great parts. There are many lesser divisions—divisions into systems, formations, deposits, beds, strata; but the master divisions, in each of which we find a type of life so unlike that of the others, that even the unpractised eye can detect the difference, are simply three: the palaeozoic, or oldest fossiliferous division; the secondary, or middle fossiliferous division; and the tertiary, or latest fossiliferous division. In the first, or palaeozoic division, we find corals, crustaceans, molluscs, fishes; and in its later formations, a few reptiles. But none of these classes give its leading character to the palaeozoic; they do not constitute its prominent feature, or render it more remarkable as a scene of life than any of the divisions which followed. That which chiefly distinguished the palaeozoic from the secondary and tertiary periods was its gorgeous flora. It was emphatically the period of plants—"of herbs yielding seed after their kind." In no other age did the world ever witness such a flora; the youth of the earth was peculiarly a green and umbrageous youth—a youth of dusk and tangled forests, of huge pines and stately araucarians, of the reed-like calamite, the tall tree-fern, the sculptured sigillaria, and the hirsute lepidodendrons. Wherever dry land, or shallow lakes, or running stream appeared, from where Melville Island now spreads out its icy coast under the star of the pole, to where the arid plains of Australia lie solitary beneath the bright cross of the south, a rank and luxuriant herbage cumbered every foot-breadth of the dank and steaming soil; and even to distant planets our earth must have shone through the enveloping cloud with a green and delicate ray . . . .[81] The geologic evidence is so complete as to be patent to all, that the first great period of organized being was, as described in the Mosaic record, peculiarly a period of herbs and trees "yielding seed after their kind."

'The middle great period of the geologist—that of the secondary division—possessed, like the earlier one, its herbs and plants, but they were of a greatly less luxuriant and conspicuous character than their predecessors, and no longer formed the prominent trait or feature of the creation to which they belonged. The period had also its corals, its crustaceans, its molluscs, its fishes, and in some one or two exceptional instances, its dwarf mammals. But the grand existences of the age—the existences in which it excelled every other creation, earlier or later—were its huge creeping things—its enormous monsters of the deep, and, as shown by the impressions of their foot-prints stamped upon the rocks, its gigantic birds. It was peculiarly the age of egg-bearing animals, winged and wingless. Its wonderful *whales*, not however, as now, of the mammalian, but of the reptilian class,—ichthyosaurs, plesiosaurs, and cetosaurs, must have tempested the deep; its creeping lizards and crocodiles, such as the teliosaurus, megalosaurus, and iguanodon—creatures, some of which more than rivalled the existing elephant in height, and greatly more than rivalled him in bulk—must have crowded the plains, or haunted by myriads the rivers of the period; and we know that the foot-prints of at least one of its many birds are of fully twice the size of those made by the horse or camel.[82] We are thus prepared to demonstrate, that the second period of the geologist was peculiarly and characteristically a period of whale-like reptiles of the sea, of enormous creeping reptiles of the land, and of numerous birds, some of them of gigantic size; and in meet accordance with the fact, we find that the second Mosaic period with which the geologist is called on to deal, was a period in which God created the fowl that flieth above the earth, with moving (or creeping) creatures, both in the waters and on land, and what our translation renders great whales, but that I find rendered in the margin great sea-monsters. The tertiary period had also its prominent class of existences. Its flora seems to have been no more conspicuous than that of the present time; its reptiles occupy a very subordinate place; but its beasts of the field were by far the most wonderfully developed, both in size and numbers, that ever appeared on earth. Its mammoths and its mastodons, its rhinoceri and its hippopotami, its enormous dinotherium, and colossal megatherium, greatly more than equalled in bulk the hugest mammals of the present time, and vastly exceeded them in number.[83] * * * "Grand, indeed," says an English naturalist, "was the fauna of the British Islands in these early days. Tigers as large again as the biggest Asiatic species lurked in the ancient thickets; elephants of nearly twice the bulk of the largest individuals that now exist in Africa or Ceylon roamed in herds; at least two species of rhinoceros forced their way through the primaeval forest; and the lakes and rivers were tenanted by hippopotami as bulky and with as great tusks as those of Africa." The massive cave-bear and large cave-hyaena belonged to the same formidable group, with at least two species of great oxen (*Bos longifrons* and *Bos primigenius*), with a horse of smaller size, and an elk (*Megaceros Hibernicus*) that stood ten feet four inches in height.[84] Truly this Tertiary age—this third and last of the great geologic periods—was peculiarly the age of great "beasts of the earth after their kind, and cattle after their kind."'[85]

[63] Thus by dropping the invertebrata, and the early fishes and reptiles of the Palaeozoic period as inconspicuous and of little account, and bringing prominently forward the carboniferous era which succeeded them as the most characteristic feature of the first great division, by classing the great land reptiles of the secondary

period with the moving creatures of the waters, (for in the Mosaic account it does not appear that any inhabitants of the land were created on the fifth day), and evading the fact that terrestrial reptiles seem to have preceded birds in their order of appearance upon earth the geologic divisions are tolerably well assimilated to the third, fifth, and sixth Mosaic days. These things were represented, we are told, to Moses in visionary pictures, and resulted in the short and summary account which he has given.[86]

[64] There is something in this hypothesis very near to the obvious truth, while at the same time something very remote from that truth is meant to be inferred. If it be said the Mosaic account is simply the speculation of some early Copernicus or Newton who devised a scheme of the earth's formation, as nearly as he might in accordance with his own observations of nature, and with such views of things as it was possible for an unassisted thinker in those days to take, we may admire the approximate correctness of the picture drawn, while we see that the writer, as might be expected, took everything from a different point of view from ourselves, and consequently represented much quite differently from the fact. But nothing of this sort is really intended. We are asked to believe that a vision of creation was presented to him by Divine power, for the purpose of enabling him to inform the world of what he had seen, which vision inevitably led him to give a description which has misled the world for centuries, and in which the truth can now only with difficulty be recognised. The Hebrew writer informs us that on the third day 'the earth brought forth grass, the herb yielding seed after his kind, and the tree yielding fruit, whose seed was in itself, after his kind;' and in the 29th verse, that God on the sixth day said, 'Behold, I have given you every herb bearing seed, which is upon the face of all the earth, and every tree in the which is the fruit of a tree yielding seed, to you it shall be for meat. And to every beast of the earth, and to every fowl of the air, and to everything that creepeth upon the earth, wherein there is life, I have given every green herb for meat.' Can it be disputed that the writer here conceives that grass, corn, and fruit, were created on the third day, and with a view to the future nourishment of man and beast? Yet, according to the vision hypothesis, he must have been greatly deceived; that the luxuriant vegetation which he saw on the third day, consisted not of plants destined for the food of man, but for his fuel. It was the flora of the carboniferous period which he beheld, concerning which Hugh Miller makes the following remark, p. 24:—'The existing plants whence we derive our analogies in dealing with the vegetation of this early period, contribute but little, if at all, to the support of animal life. The ferns and their allies remain untouched by the grazing animals. Our native club-mosses, though once used in medicine, are positively deleterious; the horsetails, though harmless, so abound in silex, which wraps them round with a cuticle of stone, that they are rarely cropped by cattle; while the thickets of fern which cover our hill-sides, and seem so temptingly rich and green in their season, scarce support the existence of a single creature, and remain untouched in stem and leaf from their first appearance in spring, until they droop and wither under the frosts of early winter. Even the insects

that infest the herbaria of the botanist almost never injure his ferns. Nor are our resin-producing conifers, though they nourish a few beetles, favourites with the herbivorous tribes in a much greater degree. Judging from all we yet know, the earliest terrestrial flora may have covered the dry land with its mantle of cheerful green, and served its general purposes, chemical and others, in the well-balanced economy of nature; but the herb-eating animals would have fared but ill, even where it throve most luxuriantly; and it seems to harmonize with the fact of its unedible character that up to the present time we know not that a single herbivorous animal lived amongst its shades.'[87] The Mosaic writer is, however, according to the theory, misled by the mere appearance of luxurious vegetation, to describe fruit trees and edible seed-bearing vegetables as products of the third day.

[65] Hugh Miller's treatment of the description of the first dawn of light is not more satisfactory than that of Dr. Buckland. He supposes the prophet in his dream to have heard the command 'Let there be light' enunciated, whereupon 'straightway a grey diffused light springs up in the east, and casting its *sickly gleam* over a cloud-limited expanse of steaming vaporous sea, journeys through the heavens towards the west. One heavy, sunless day is made the representative of myriads; the faint light waxes fainter,—it sinks beneath the dim, undefined horizon.'[88]

[66] We are then asked to imagine that a second and a third day, each representing the characteristic features of a great distinctly-marked epoch, and the latter of them marked by the appearance of a rich and luxuriant vegetation, are presented to the seer's eye; but without sun, moon, or stars as yet entering into his dream. These appear first in his fourth vision, and then for the first time we have 'a brilliant day,' and the seer, struck with the novelty, describes the heavenly bodies as being the most conspicuous objects in the picture. In reality we know that he represents them (v. 16) as having been *made* and *set* in the heavens on that day, though Hugh Miller avoids reminding us of this.[89]

[67] In one respect the theory of Hugh Miller agrees with that advocated by Dr. Buckland and Archdeacon Pratt. Both these theories divest the Mosaic narrative of real accordance with fact; both assume that appearances only, not facts, are described, and that in riddles, which would never have been suspected to be such, had we not arrived at the truth from other sources.[90] It would be difficult for controversialists to cede more completely the point in dispute, or to admit more explicitly that the Mosaic narrative does not represent correctly the history of the universe up to the time of man. At the same time, the upholders of each theory see insuperable objections in details to that of their allies, and do not pretend to any firm faith in their own. How can it be otherwise when the task proposed is to evade the plain meaning of language, and to introduce obscurity into one of the simplest stories ever told, for the sake of making it accord with the complex system of the universe which modern science has unfolded? The spectacle of able and, we doubt not, conscientious writers engaged in attempting the impossible is painful and humiliating. They evidently do not breathe freely over their work, but shuffle and stumble over their difficulties in a piteous manner; nor are they themselves again

until they return to the pure and open fields of science.

[68] It is refreshing to return to the often-echoed remark, that it could not have been the object of a Divine revelation to instruct mankind in physical science, man having had faculties bestowed upon him to enable him to acquire this knowledge by himself.[91] This is in fact pretty generally admitted; but in the application of the doctrine, writers play at fast and loose with it according to circumstances. Thus an inspired writer may be permitted to allude to the phenomena of nature according to the vulgar view of such things, without impeachment of his better knowledge; but if he speaks of the same phenomena assertively, we are bound to suppose that things are as he represents them, however much our knowledge of nature may be disposed to recalcitrate. But if we find a difficulty in admitting that such misrepresentations can find a place in revelation, the difficulty lies in our having previously assumed what a Divine revelation ought to be. If God made use of imperfectly informed men to lay the foundations of that higher knowledge for which the human race was destined, is it wonderful that they should have committed themselves to assertions not in accordance with facts, although they may have believed them to be true? On what grounds has the popular notion of Divine revelation been built up? Is it not plain that the plan of Providence for the education of man is a progressive one, and as imperfect men have been used as the agents for teaching mankind, is it not to be expected that their teachings should be partial and, to some extent, erroneous? Admitted, as it is, that physical science is not what the Hebrew writers, for the most part, profess to convey, at any rate, that it is not on account of the communication of such knowledge that we attach any value to their writings, why should we hesitate to recognise their fallibility on this head?

[69] Admitting, as is historically and in fact the case, that it was the mission of the Hebrew race to lay the foundation of religion upon the earth, and that Providence used this people especially for this purpose, is it not our business and our duty to look and see how this has really been done? not forming for ourselves theories of what a revelation ought to be, or how we, if entrusted with the task, would have made one, but enquiring how it has pleased God to do it. In all his theories of the world, man has at first deviated widely from the truth, and has only gradually come to see how far otherwise God has ordered things than the first daring speculator had supposed. It has been popularly assumed that the Bible, bearing the stamp of Divine authority, must be complete, perfect, and unimpeachable in all its parts, and a thousand difficulties and incoherent doctrines have sprung out of this theory. Men have proceeded in the matter of theology, as they did with physical science before inductive philosophy sent them to the feet of nature, and bid them learn in patience and obedience the lessons which she had to teach. Dogma and groundless assumption occupy the place of modest enquiry after truth, while at the same time the upholders of these theories claim credit for humility and submissiveness. This is exactly inverting the fact; the humble scholar of truth is not he who, taking his stand upon the traditions of rabbins, Christian fathers, or schoolmen, insists upon

bending facts to his unyielding standard, but he who is willing to accept such teaching as it has pleased Divine Providence to afford, without murmuring that it has not been furnished more copiously or clearly.

[70] The Hebrew race, their works, and their books, are great facts in the history of man; the influence of the mind of this people upon the rest of mankind has been immense and peculiar, and there can be no difficulty in recognising therein the hand of a directing Providence. But we may not make ourselves wiser than God, nor attribute to Him methods of procedure which are not His. If, then, it is plain that He has not thought it needful to communicate to the writer of the Cosmogony that knowledge which modern researches have revealed, why do we not acknowledge this, except that it conflicts with a human theory which presumes to point out how God ought to have instructed man? The treatment to which the Mosaic narrative is subjected by the theological geologists is anything but respectful. The writers of this school, as we have seen, agree in representing it as a series of elaborate equivocations—a story which 'palters with us in a double sense.' But if we regard it as the speculation of some Hebrew Descartes or Newton, promulgated in all good faith as the best and most probable account that could be then given of God's universe, it resumes the dignity and value of which the writers in question have done their utmost to deprive it.[92] It has been sometimes felt as a difficulty to taking this view of the case, that the writer asserts so solemnly and unhesitatingly that for which he must have known that he had no authority. But this arises only from our modern habits of thought, and from the modesty of assertion which the spirit of true science has taught us. Mankind has learnt caution through repeated slips in the process of tracing out the truth.

[71] The early speculator was harassed by no such scruples, and asserted as facts what he knew in reality only as probabilities. But we are not on that account to doubt his perfect good faith, nor need we attribute to him wilful misrepresentation, or consciousness of asserting that which he knew not to be true. He had seized one great truth, in which, indeed, he anticipated the highest revelation of modern enquiry—namely, the unity of the design of the world, and its subordination to one sole Maker and Lawgiver. With regard to details, observation failed him. He knew little of the earth's surface, or of its shape and place in the universe; the infinite varieties of organized existences which people it, the distinct floras and faunas of its different continents, were unknown to him. But he saw that all which lay within his observation had been formed for the benefit and service of man, and the goodness of the Creator to his creatures was the thought predominant in his mind. Man's closer relation to his Maker is indicated by the representation that he was formed last of all creatures, and in the visible likeness of God. For ages, this simple view of creation satisfied the wants of man, and formed a sufficient basis of theological teaching, and if modern research now shows it to be physically untenable, our respect for the narrative which has played so important a part in the culture of our race need be in nowise diminished. No one contends that it can be used as a basis of astronomical or geological teaching, and those who profess to see

in it an accordance with facts, only do this *sub modo,* and by processes which despoil it of its consistency and grandeur, both which may be preserved if we recognise in it, not an authentic utterance of Divine knowledge, but a human utterance, which it has pleased Providence to use in a special way for the education of mankind.[93]

5 Notes to Charles Wycliffe Goodwin

1. In the Table of Contents in the first edition of *Essays and Reviews* Goodwin's essay is titled "On the Mosaic Cosmogony"; the title on the first page of his essay is "Mosaic Cosmogony."

2. Ptolemy published *Syntaxis* (2d century; The arrangement), translated into Arabic as *Almagest* (The greatest composition), its best-known title. It posits the earth as the stationary center of the universe around which the sun and the planets revolve at a uniform rate in circular orbits with epicycles. "The Ptolemaic system" was the received view until the sixteenth century when Copernicus published *De revolutionibus orbium coelestium libri sex* (1543; Six books on the revolutions of the celestial orbs), arguing that the sun was the center of the universe around which the earth revolved. Copernicus's book became an object of attack by the Jesuits and others at the Council of Trent (1545–63); see Olaf Pedersen 1991. In 1616 it was placed on the Roman Catholic index of prohibited books by a decree that also condemned all other books that tried to reconcile the heliocentric system with the Bible. Accordingly, ninety years after the death of Copernicus, Galileo was condemned for teaching the Copernican theory. On Galileo and Copernicus see Fantoli 1994.

3. The "philosophers of the new school" included the sixteenth-century Copernicans, Giordano Bruno, and Johannes Kepler. The advocates of "the old doctrines" included the leaders of the Counter-Reformation, especially those affiliated with the Jesuit Collegio Romano (established 1550), such as Christopher Clavius, Juan de Pineda, and Jean Lorin. For "the Hebrew records" see Westman's discussion of "four specific classes of biblical passages that were relevant to the Copernican issue—references to the stability of the earth, the sun's motion with respect to the terrestrial horizon, the sun at rest, and the motion of the earth" (in Lindberg and Numbers 1986, 90–93). For examples of such passages see Josh. 10:12–13; Ps. 93:1; 104:19; and Eccles. 1:4, 5. Hugh Miller also discusses Copernicus and Galileo in relation to supposed astronomical anomalies in the Hebrew scriptures (1857, 351–82).

4. Galileo Galilei published *Sidereus Nuncius* (1610; The sidereal messenger), containing the results of his investigations of the motions of the planets, his observations of the moon, and his rejection of the Ptolemaic system. In his *Letter to the Grand Duchess Christina* (1632), he discusses the relations between the Bible and astronomy, arguing that where there is a conflict the Bible must be reinterpreted, since God, the author of both nature and the Bible, cannot be a source of contradiction. He published *Dialogo sopra i due Massimi Sistemi del Mondo; Tolemaico, e Copernicano* (1632; Dialogue concerning the two great world systems, Ptolemaic and Copernican) that led directly to a summons before the Inquisition in Rome in 1633. He had been forced on 24 February 1616 to abjure his error of teaching that the earth moves, as Copernican views that the Inquisition had condemned in two propositions and the verdicts on them (in the words Goodwin cites).

These documents, part of the Inquisition's archives recovered in Paris in 1846, were returned to the Vatican Library (Codex 1181) and were published in a truncated form by Marino Marini in 1850. William Whewell also published an account of these discoveries (1857, 57–58); they are printed in full in Favaro 1907, 60–61. Bethune's biography of Galileo discusses "the abjuration of Galileo" (1829, 62–63). An account of Galileo's trial was published in *The Accusation, Condemnation, and Abjuration of Galileo Galilei, before the Holy Inquisition, at Rome, 1633* (1819); for a fuller discussion see Wegg-Prosser 1889; for recent studies see Redordi [1983] 1987; Drake 1990; Biaglioli 1993; and Reston 1994.

5. On 16 June 1734, the Roman Inquisition agreed to a request from the city of Florence to erect a monument over the unmarked tomb of Galileo, who had been quietly buried in the Church of Santa Croce after his death. In a routine re-editing and without announcement, "the 1835 edition of the Catholic Index of Prohibited Books for the first time omits the *Dialogue* from the list" (Whewell 1857, 57). Whewell gives the date as 1818. See also Finocchiaro (1989, 307).

Although different popes presided over various stages of the proceedings, signed various documents of condemnation, and agreed with the decisions, the *New Catholic Encyclopedia* (1967) separates the condemnation of the heliocentric theory and Galileo from infallible teaching but asserts: "The condemnation was the act of a Roman Congregation [of the Index] and in no way involved infallible teaching authority. But the theologians' treatment of Galileo was an unfortunate error; and however it might be explained, it cannot be defended" (s.v. "Galilei, Galileo").

On 10 November 1979 in a speech to the Pontifical Academy of Sciences, John Paul II acknowledged that Galileo suffered unjustly at the hands of the church (Finocchiaro 1989, 308), setting up a commission to inquire into his case. On 31 October 1992 John Paul II, again speaking to the

Pontifical Academy of Sciences, reported their findings, acquitting Galileo of heresy for asserting that the earth revolves around the sun: while his accusers acted in good faith, they were "incapable of dissociating faith from an age-old cosmology" and made "mistakes [which] must be frankly recognized." As a result of these admissions, the Vatican Observatory has recently published a series of new studies of the trial and its implications; see Coyne, Heller and Zycinski 1985; Westfall 1989; Olaf Pedersen 1991; and Fantoli 1994.

6. For "world is established" see Ps. 96:10.

7. *Conflict* is the more common term for the relations between science and religion in the writings of Tyndall and Huxley. The more nuanced term *controversy* implies a debate while *conflict* implies a warfare. The social origins for this model for science and religion in the Victorian England are discussed in Frank M. Turner 1993. On "controversy" in relation to *Essays and Reviews* see Altholz 1994; in geology and religion see Rudwick 1985 and Secord 1986; and in ethnology, Service 1985.

8. For example, Sharon Turner's popular school book, *The Sacred History of the World*, reaching its eighth edition in 1848, argues that the earth is "nearly 6,000 years old" (1832–37, 1:8), was first created as material substance and then was "put into form" (1:13), and was "replenished" on the following "natural days" (1:17).

9. The scriptural geologists maintained the literal veracity of Genesis 1 by denigrating the geological evidence for "the great antiquity of the earth" or by making the discoveries of geology conform to Genesis. They were so named in George Bugg's *Scriptural Geology* (1826). Other such attacks on the validity of the geological evidence include Kidd 1815; Penn 1822; Cole 1834; J. Mellor Brown 1838; and George Young 1838. According to Milton Millhauser, Brown's "was the last major monument of the theological geologists" (1954, 74), but such studies continued to be published throughout the nineteenth century, such as Kinns's *Moses and Geology* (1882) that by 1895 was in its fourteenth edition. Other writers promoting a reconciliation of Genesis and geology included most of the professional geologists and many clergy, such as Buckland (1823), Silliman in his appendix to Bakewell ([1813] 1833), and Powell (1838).

The views of the scriptural geologists have been revived in the twentieth century from George McCready Price's *The New Geology* (1923), arguing that after creation in six solar days a universal deluge within human history was the catastrophe that produced the strata of the rocks. His views were extended by Henry M. Morris and John C. Whitcomb Jr. in *The Genesis Flood* (1961) and led to the establishment (1972) of the Institute for Creation Research to publish such views and to challenge the legality of teaching evolution in schools. On the intellectual background of such creationism see J. R. Moore 1979 and Lindberg and Numbers 1986.

10. The "maxim of Galileo" is very likely his muttered comment, "*e pur si muove*" (Ital. and yet it does move), spoken immediately after having recanted his writings and theory that the sun is the center of the universe and immovable and that the earth moves. The phrase is first attributed to Galileo in 1761 and is cited in Bethune 1829, 63 and Whewell 1857, 58.

11. Benjamin Silliman outlines "the following modes" of accommodating Gen. 1 and geological time: "1. The present earth was formed from the ruins and fragments of an earlier world, re-arranged and set in order during the six days of creation" (Silliman in Bakewell [1813] 1833, 436; see also Goodwin ¶s 18 and 31). "2. The present crust of the planet has been regularly formed between the first creation 'in the beginning,' and the commencement of the first day" (437; see also Goodwin ¶s 29 and 30, quoting Buckland). "3. The days of the creation were periods of time of indefinite length" (439; see also Goodwin ¶s 40 ff.). "4. It has been supposed that the succession of geological events may have happened in the first ages of the world, after the creation of man" (458; see also Goodwin ¶38). "5. It has been supposed that a general deluge will account for all the geological events that have been described" (458; see also Goodwin ¶s 23, 33–34, and 38).

12. Horne's *Introduction to the Holy Scriptures* (1856, tenth Edition) [Goodwin's note].

The cited passage in "Geological investigations" is from Appendix 7, "Alleged Contradictions to Philosophy and the Nature of Things" ([1818] 1872, 1:583). Parts of the tenth edition that Goodwin cites, edited by Samuel Davidson, provoked controversy over Davidson's liberal view of inspiration; he was replaced by John Ayre in the eleventh edition. The Appendix lists fourteen "alleged contradictions" in question and answer format. On Davidson see Jowett ¶6 and note.

13. Goodwin compares contemporary discoveries in geology to the impact in the seventeenth century of optics on astronomy and cosmology, leading to the questioning of received knowledge from the new empirical evidence. The invention of the telescope is attributed both to Italian lensmakers about 1600, and to the Dutch lensmaker, Hans Lippershey (c. 1608); as an astronomical instrument it was first used by Galileo, whose third telescope (1610) had a magnification of thirty-three diameters. For recent discussions of the impact of the telescope see Van Helden 1974; 1977; and 1985.

14. The "region of uncertainty" reference to geological time may be compared to Wilson's "probable evidence" (¶75) concerning the relations between doctrinal statements and faith.

For "thick curtain of mist" compare Hugh Miller's comments on the same geological period: "A continuous stratum of steam, then, that attained to the height of even our present atmosphere, would wrap up the earth in a darkness gross and palpable as that of Egypt of old,—a darkness through which even a single ray of light would fail to penetrate" (1857, 176–77).

15. Scoriaceous," the adjectival form of "scoriae," is "applied to all accumulations of dust, ashes, cinders, and loose fragments of rocks, discharged from active volcanoes. Properly speaking, the term refers to the *scum-like dross* which floats on the surface of molten masses, and which, when cooled down, breaks up into loose cindery fragments and clinkers" (Page 1859, s.v. "Scoriae").

For "Azoic" see Page: "Without life, void of life; a term applied to the lowest or deepest-seated strata in the crust of the globe, such as gneiss, mica-schist, and other crystalline schists, which have yet yielded no fossils or traces of life to palaeontologists. Used by many as synonymous with *Hypozoic, Non-fossiliferous,* and *Metamorphic"* (1859, s.v. "Azoic").

16. It has been stated that a coal-bed, containing remains of land-plants, underlying strata of the lower Silurian class, has been found in Portugal [Goodwin's note].

For "Silurian system" see Page: "The name originally given by Sir Roderick Murchison (and now adopted by all geologists) to that vast suite of fossiliferous strata which lies between the Non-fossiliferous Slaty-schists beneath and the Old Red Sandstone above, from the fact of their being well developed, and first worked out by him, in the district between England and Wales anciently inhabited by the *Silures* under their chief *Caractacus* or Caradoc" (1859, s.v. "Silurian System"). Roderick Impey Murchison described these in *The Silurian System* (1839). See Dean 1981; Secord 1982; Stafford 1989.

For "Exuviae" see Page: "In Zoology this term is applied to the moulted or cast-off coverings of animals, such as the skin of the snake, the crust of the crab, &c. But in Geology it has a somewhat wider sense, and applies to all fossil animal matter or fragments of whatever description" (1859, s.v. "Exuviae").

The three divisions of "mollusca, articulata, and radiata" together comprise in descending order the category of "invertebrata" set out in Georges Cuvier, *Règne animal* (1817; trans. *The Animal Kingdom, Arranged in Conformity with Its Organization, with Additions by Edward Griffith*, 1827–35, 16 vols.). Miller discusses these divisions in relation to the Silurian period (1857, 13–14; see also Goodwin ¶54 and notes). The mollusca include shellfish and others organisms with exoskeletons; articulata have jointed bodies; radiata have their organs disposed around an axis: "Since Cuvier's time, this arrangement has been somewhat modified; and the lower groups of animals which are 'globular' rather than 'rayed' have been erected into an independent class under the title PROTOZOA, which includes such orders as the Rhizopods, Sponges, and Infusoria" (Page 1859, s.v. "Radiata").

"Fucoid" refers to "fungus-like impressions [which] occur in strata of every epoch, from the lower Salurians to the upper tertiaries. Such terms, therefore, as 'fucoidal' sandstones, 'fucoidal' shales, &c., are not unfrequent in geological descriptions" (Page 1859, s.v. "Fucoids").

For "a coal-bed . . . in Portugal" see Philip Lake 1896.

17. Goodwin refers to the fossil remains of the upper Silurian strata that comprise the fourth of Cuvier's divisions of the animal kingdom, the vertebrata, here instanced by "the race of fishes" as the "lowest creatures of the vertebrate type."

For "monsters clothed in mail" compare Miller: "mail-covered fishes of the ancient type" (1857, 89).

18. For "Carboniferous strata" see Page: "that formation, or system of fossiliferous strata which, in order of time, succeeds the Old Red Sandstone, and is in turn surmounted by the Permian or New Red Sandstone of the earlier English geologists. As a system, it constitutes the younger or upper portion of the Palaeozoic cycle, and it derives its importance from being, in Britain, North America, and other countries, the great repository . . . of COAL, so indispensable to the industrial arts and manufactures of modern civilisation" (1859, s.v. "Carboniferous System").

For "Palaeozoic" see Page: "[The term is] applied to the lowest division of stratified groups, as holding the most ancient or earliest known forms of life, in contradistinction to the *Mesozoic* and *Cainozoic*. It includes the Silurian, Devonian, Carboniferous, and Permian systems of British geologists." (1859, s.v. "Palaeozoic, Palaeozoic Formations").

19. For "the so-called Secondary period" see Page: "Originally applied to the fossiliferous strata lying between the Transition and Tertiary of Werner; now employed as equivalent to *Mesozoic*; that is, comprehending the Trias, Lias, Oolite, Wealden, and Chalk formations" (1859, s.v. "Secondary Strata"). Abraham Gottlob Werner advocated Neptunism, the aqueous origin of rocks, precipitated in definite succession from the primeval ocean that covered the globe; see Ospovat 1967 and 1969.

For "oolitic" see Page: "[The term derives] from the prevalence of limestones of an *oolitic texture* as developed in England, or from the *Jura range*, as typically exhibited on the continent of Europe. This system may be said to comprehend the whole of those peculiar limestones, calcareous sandstones, marls, shales, and clays which lie between the New Red Sandstone beneath and the Chalk formation above. . . . With the exception of the higher mammalia, almost every existing order is represented in the fauna of the Oolite, but the forms are all Mesozoic, and died out at the close of the chalk era. The vegetation of the system is extremely varied, but the highest orders appear to be coniferous, and as yet no example of a true exogenous timber tree has been detected" (1859, s.v. "Oolitic or Jurassic System").

For "cretaceous" see Page: "The Cretaceous system—so called from the chalk beds which form its most notable feature—is the last or uppermost of the secondary formations. . . . The entire suite of strata . . . bear evidence of shallow and widespread seas, and of a climate favourable to the growth of cycads and zamias on land, and of corals, gigantic saurians, and turtles in the waters. . . . All the Life-types of the system are strictly Mesozoic, and of the numerous species found in the Trias, Oolite, and Chalk, not one, it is affirmed by Palaeontologists have been detected in Tertiary strata. Industrially, the chief products are chalk and flint" (1859, s.v. "Cretaceous or Chalk System").

20. For "foot-prints . . . upon the sandy shores" see Miller, who quotes Longfellow's "A Psalm of Life" (1839): "And of this scene of things only the foot-prints remain,—'foot-prints on the sands of time'" (Miller 1857, 89). Miller also reproduces illustrations of several fossil footprints (1857, 86–87). In 1847 he published *The Foot-Prints of the Creator: or, the Asterolepis of Stromness*, an argument for successive periods of divine creation, evidence for which is found in the fossil record or "the Foot-prints of the Creator." Miller's work answers the hypothesis of development without divine intervention in Robert Chambers's *Vestiges of the Natural History of Creation* (1844). The debate over the interpretation of the Asterolepis raises significant issues for the relations between Victorian science and religion. While both Chambers and Miller were progressionists, Chambers believed in evolution in the sense of descent-with-modification. To Miller, focusing on the nervous system, the Asterolepis of Stromness represented a highly organized vertebrate, while for Chambers, stressing the skeleton, it was low and primitive in the evolutionary scale. Hence, fossils did not represent unambiguous evidence for evolutionary transformation and were not incontrovertibly susceptible to harmonization with theories of a divinely authored creation. The debates between the discontinuous catastrophists and the progressive creationists over such matters were not simply antithetical to an evolutionist position but contributed positively to both Darwinian and non-Darwinian evolutionary theories. See Chambers [1844] 1994 and Rudwick 1972. For "foot-prints" see also Goodwin ¶62 and note.

21. For "Marsupial . . . oviparous tribes" see Page: "Literally 'pouched animals;' an order of mammalia having a sack or pouch under the belly, in which they carry their young, as the kangaroo, wombat, and opossum. They are sometimes termed *ovo-viviparous* mammals, as being intermediate between the viviparous and the oviparous birds and reptiles" (1859, s.v. "Marsupialia, Marsupiata").

On "pterodactyls" see Buckland 1837, 1:221–33; for an extended nineteenth-century treatment see Seeley 1870 and 1901.

22. For "Tertiary period" see Page: "The earlier geologists, in dividing the stratified crust into primary, secondary, and tertiary formations regarded as *Tertiary* all that occurs above the Chalk. The term is still retained, but the progress of discovery has rendered it necessary to restrict and modify its meaning. Even yet the limits of the system may be said to be undetermined—some embracing under the term all that lies between the Chalk and the Boulder-drift, others including the Drift and every other accumulation in which no trace of man or his works can be detected. Palaeontologically speaking, much might be said in favour of both views; but the difficulty of unravelling the relations of many clays, sands, and gravels, makes it safer to adopt, in the meantime, a somewhat provisional arrangement" (1859, s.v. "Tertiary System").

23. The "two distinct accounts" of creation in Genesis contradict each other concerning the order of creation. The first account, Gen. 1:1–2:3/4a, divides creation according to six specific days of activity. As Goodwin shows, Gen. 1:1 is often interpreted as referring to the creation of primal matter, Gen. 1:2–31 to the six days of creation, and Gen. 2:1–3/4a to the seventh day and the institution of the Sabbath. The first three acts of creation are separations: of light from darkness, of waters from the firmament, and of earth and land, with the creation of plants. Then follow three specific creative acts: the creation of planets and stars, of fishes and fowls, and of animals, including humans. This double set of three actions aligns an act of separation with an act of creation, so that the first day corresponds with the fourth, the second with the fifth, and the third with the sixth. For subsequent discussion of the days of creation see Goodwin ¶61 and note.

The second account of creation begins in the second chapter of Genesis with the separation of heaven and earth (Gen. 2:4), then the creation of a man before the ground can be tilled or the vegetable kingdom is created (Gen. 2:5–9). Subsequently the rivers are created (Gen. 2:10–14), and a prohibition is given concerning the eating of a specific fruit (Gen. 2:15–18); the beasts are "formed" and named (2:19–20), followed by the creation of woman (Gen. 2:21–25). The second account, whose chronological order differs from the first, is not discussed by such geological reconcilers as Miller, Buckland, and Pratt.

By alluding to the distinction between Genesis 1 and 2 as "so philologically certain," Goodwin refers to the well-known arguments that identify the passages as from different sources, on the basis of different names used for God in the two passages, *Elohim* in Gen. 1 and *Yahweh* in Gen 2., different formulaic devices, and the alternating use of different verbs, *bara* (create) and *'asaha* (make). Among the numerous commentaries on Genesis that take into account the documentary and other source and form-critical materials see Brueggemann 1982; Coats 1983, 41–60; Westermann 1984; and Simkins 1994. For a discussion of the relations between Genesis and geology in the seventeenth century, see Porter 1977, 64–70; and in the period 1790–1850 see Gillispie 1959; on the Genesis–geology debate in the United States in the nineteenth century see Sherwood 1969. For an anthropological analysis of Genesis in the nineteenth century see Cunningham 1973a.

24. This appears at once from verse 21, where it is said that God created (*bara*) the great whales; and from verses 26 and 27, in the first of which we read, 'God said, Let us make (*hasah*) man in our image,' and in the latter, 'So God created (*bara*) man in his image.' In neither of these cases, can it be supposed to be implied that the whales, or man, were made out of nothing. In the second narrative, another word is used for the creation of man, *itzer*—to mould; and his formation out of the dust is circumstantially described [Goodwin's note].

For Goodwin's indebtedness to E. B. Pusey for this information see Goodwin ¶30 and note. The Hebrew verb to create (*bara*) occurs ten times in Genesis, always in the priestly materials (designated "P"), and always dating from the exilic period or later: "It can be regarded as certain that *bara'* was introduced into OT literature as a theological idea for the first time in the exilic period. . . . It is used exclusively to denote divine creation . . . in Gen.1:1–2:4a. . . . This verb does not denote an act that somehow can be described, but simply states that, unconditionally, without further intervention, through God's command something comes into being that had not existed before" (Botterweck and Ringgren 1874–86, 1:245–47). Another contemporary commentary, by the conservative biblical critic Edward Harold Browne, explicates "create": "In the first two chapters of Genesis we meet with four different verbs to express the creative work of God, viz. 1, to create; 2, to make; 3, to form; 4, to build. The first is used of the creation of the universe (v. 1); of the creation of the great sea-monsters, whose vastness seems to have excited special wonder (v. 21); and of the creation of man, the head of animated nature, in the image of God (v. 27). Everywhere else we read of God's *making*, as from an already created substance, the firmament, the sun, the stars, the brute creation (vv. 7, 16, 25, &c.); or of His *forming* the beasts of the field out of the ground (ch. ii.19); or lastly, of His *building up* (ii. 22, margin) into a woman the rib which He had taken from man" (in Cook 1871–88, 1:31).

For "to make out of nothing" see *ERE*: "The doctrine of a creation out of nothing—*ex nihilo*—is nowhere expressly taught in Holy Scripture. The first near approach to it occurs in the words of the mother of the Maccabees . . . (2 Macc.7:28), which are too definitely rendered by the Vulgate: *ex nihilo fecit illa Deus*" (4:229). The Latin phrase refers to the heavens and the earth: God made them out of nothing. The same phrase is in quotation marks in Goodwin ¶33.

25. Chap. iv. 33 [Goodwin's note].

Goodwin's citation is incorrect: the "expression" occurs in Jer. 4:23; the reference was corrected in the fifth edition of *Essays and Reviews*.

26. Goodwin extends the discussion of *tohu* and *bohu* in ¶31. To accommodate the Mosaic account of creation in the first verses of Genesis to the Neptunist hypothesis of geological formation (see Goodwin ¶14 and note), Richard Kirwan focused on the different meanings of the Hebrew words: "[For] *without form and void* the Hebrew has *Tohu* and *Bohu*. . . . That is to say, that the earth was partly in a *chaotic* state, and partly full of *empty* cavities" (Kirwan [1799] 1978, 46). In Patrick's *Critical Commentary*, Gen. 1:2 is explicated: "These two words, *tohu vabohu*, are used in Scripture . . . for confusion and emptiness (Isa. xxxiv. 11; Jerem. iv. 23), being a description of that which the ancients called Chaos" (1846–49, 1:2). A recent exegete comments on the passage: "The translations 'formlessness' or 'shapelessness' . . . are not quite accurate. . . . It would be nearer to the sense if the nothingness, the non-existence, were understood as something gruesome. . . . This too is the meaning of the Greek χάος: chasm, abyss, and also darkness. So Hesiod in his cosmogony (*Theogony* 5, 116): 'First of all there arose chaos and later the earth'" (Westermann 1984, 103).

27. The *Hexameron* was delivered as a series of nine homilies by Ambrose in Milan in 387. The cited passage is from Ambrose's *Hexameron: The Six Days of Creation* (bk. 4, chap. 3, para. 8); see Ambrose 1961, 132.

28. The root is generally applied to express the hammering or beating out of metal plates; hence, something beaten or spread out. It has been pretended that the word *rakia* may be translated *expanse*, as merely to mean empty space. The context sufficiently rebuts this [Goodwin's note].

This point is responded to by Alexander McCaul in *Aids to Faith* (William Thomson 1861, 220–30) and in the *Literary Churchman* (1 Apr. 1861, 129), where the first modern translation of the Bible from Hebrew and Greek (into Latin) by Santes Pagninus in the sixteenth century is cited, the Hebrew *rakia* being translated *expansionem*. References to both of these responses are made by Pratt ([1856] 1871, 16–17) in his reply to Goodwin.

29. In the second narrative of creation, in which no distinction of days is made, the birds are said to have been formed out of the ground. Gen. ii [Goodwin's note].

For the creation of the "marine animals" and "the birds of the air" in the first creation story see Gen. 1:20–21; for "the birds" in the second creation story, Gen. 2:19.

30. See particularly the narrative in Genesis xviii [Goodwin's note].

For the creation of the whales and animals see Gen. 1:21, 24–25; the creation of humans "after our likeness," Gen. 1:26. The idea of Adam as "perfect" and "sinless" before the Fall is a theological commonplace, as, for example, in the Ninth Article of Religion. The question of sin and guilt is discussed by Wilson in relation to Calvinist and other interpretations of the articles (see Wilson ¶s 10, 16–28, and especially 51). Gen. 18 recounts God's appearance to Abraham in the "visible form of a man." For "divine . . . visible form of a man" compare William Blake, "the human form divine" in "The Divine Image" (1794).

31. It is in the second narrative of creation that the formation of a single man, out of the dust of the earth, is described, and the omission to create a female at the same time, is stated to have been repaired by the subsequent formation of one from the side of the man [Goodwin's note].

Goodwin argues there are discrepancies between the first and second accounts of human creation. The account in Genesis 1:26–27 concerns the creation of human beings in general, both male and female. Genesis 2:7 is the account of the creation of a single man, followed by the creation of a single woman from the rib of the man (Gen. 2:21–23). The creation of a woman is undertaken to redress a defect: "it is not good that the man should be alone" (Gen. 2:18). In a contemporary commentary Browne explicates Adam's "image": "Many Christian writers think that nothing is meant except that man was created holy and innocent, and that this image of God was lost when Adam fell" (in Cook 1871–88, 1:35). In a longer note, "On the Immediate Creation and Primitive State of Man," Browne argues against Darwin, Lubbock, and evolution, in favor of the sudden emergence of "new and strange forms . . . upon the stage of life, with no previous intimation of their coming." Browne also maintains "the derivation of mankind from a single pair" (1:43), and adds a note on Gen. 5 (the other passage Goodwin alludes to) in a longer comment titled "On the early Civilization of Mankind": "The argument from Geology is really coincident with the testimony of Scripture and of universal primitive tradition, viz. that man, in his original condition, was not a helpless savage, but had at least the rudiments of civilization and intelligence" (1:59).

32. The common arrangement of the Bible in chapters is of comparatively modern origin, and is admitted, on all hands, to have no authority or philological worth whatever. In many cases, the division is most preposterous, and interferes greatly with an intelligent perusal of the text [Goodwin's note].

The divisions of the books of the Bible into chapters, marked by illuminated letters, became common in thirteenth century MS. Bibles and was continued in the first printed Bibles, from the 42-line Bible of Johannes Gutenberg (c. 1455). Verse divisions were first introduced in a printed text in the *Psalterium Quincuplex*, published by Henri Estienne in 1509. Robert Estienne published a folio French Bible in 1553, "the first to use his verse divisions throughout"; this numbering was widely copied and became the standard for biblical references (M. H. Black 1963, 442). See also Williams ¶12 and note.

33. For "imaginative cosmogonies of the Greeks" see the discussion of the "Geology of the Greeks and Romans" in Geike 1905, 1–41.

34. In the first century Philo Judaeus used an allegorical interpretation of the Hebrew scriptures, attempting to reconcile Greek philosophy and Jewish traditional thought, especially in his commentaries on the Pentateuch, including *Quaestiones et Solutiones in Genesim et Exodum* (Questions and solutions in Genesis and Exodus). In "A Treatise on the Account of the Creation of the World, as given by Moses" Philo discusses creation in Gen. 1 chiefly in terms of numerology (Philo 1854, 1:3–37), the analogy of the harmony of music and the musical ratios (1:12–14), ratios in geometry (1:28–29), in human life (1:30–33) and in astronomy (1:34–35). His hermeneutics influenced the Alexandrian school of Christian allegorists, including Clement and Origen. For a general discussion of the exegetical methods of the school of Alexandria see Robert M. Grant [1948] 1965, 57–60; for a more extensive treatment see Sandmel 1979.

35. On the "popularity" of geology in the nineteenth century see Knight 1972, 162–89. Gillispie compares the popularity of Miller with Chambers and Lyell by citing sales figures: "The first ten editions of the *Vestiges* disposed of about twenty-five thousand copies. Each of Lyell's editions ran to about two thousand. By the end of the century, however, Miller's *Testimony of the Rocks* had sold forty-two thousand copies, his *Foot-Prints of the Creator* had been through seventeen editions, and his *Old Red Sandstone* twenty" (1959, 172). In a note Gillispie extends this comparison to Darwin: "By 1876, *On the Origin of Species* had sold 16,000, and Darwin thought this very good indeed" (286, n. 70). Buckland and the other volumes of the Bridgewater Treatises, according to John M. Robson, "sold very well through the middle 1830s, and then less well in the original format. . . . Starting in 1852 the treatises begin to appear in Bohn's Scientific Library in London (with US editions), and continued with reissues and 'new editions' even into the 1880s" (in Helmstadter and Lightman 1990, 74). Lynn Barber states that an edition of Buckland's Treatise, edited by his son Frank in 1858 (two years after Buckland's death), "sold five thousand copies in the first three days" (1980, 144). For a further discussion of the Bridgewater Treatises see Topham 1993. For the "two modes of conciliation" see Goodwin ¶38 and notes.

36. Thomas Chalmers published on the Christian evidences (Chalmers 1814) and the sixth Bridgewater Treatise, *On the Adaptation of External Nature to the Moral and Intellectual Constitution of Man* (1833). On Chalmers, Buckland writes with "great satisfaction" that his views are "in perfect accordance with the highly valuable opinion of Dr. Chalmers, recorded in the following passages of his Evidence of the Christian Revelation, chap. vii.:—'Does Moses ever say, that when God created the heavens and the earth he did more, at the time alluded to, than transform them out of previously existing materials? Or does he ever say that there was not an interval of many ages between the first act of creation described in the first verse of the Book of Genesis, and said to have been performed at the *beginning*, and those more detailed operations, the account of which commences at the second verse, and which are described to us as having been performed in so many days? Or, finally, does he ever make us to understand that the genealogies of man went any farther than to fix the antiquity of the species, and, of consequence, that they left the antiquity of the globe a free subject for the speculation of philosophers?'" (Buckland 1837, 1:19–20).

Rupke has noted other forms of reconciliation between Chalmers and Buckland, drawing comparisons between "geology and political economy," between "Buckland and the English school" of geology and the "Malthusianism . . . championed by Thomas Chalmers" who argued that "Malthusian population dynamics represented a balanced system, and that the poor should not be artificially helped" (Rupke 1983, 255–61). For other recent studies of Chalmers see Stewart Brown 1982 and Cheyne 1985.

37. Buckland 1837, 1:19. Goodwin omits "and revolutions" after "a long series of operations"; and "with them" after "whose only concern." He also omits the information that Buckland is quoting from an earlier lecture he gave at Oxford in 1820.

38. Goodwin omits Buckland's note at this point: "The Hebrew plural word, *shamaim*, Gen. i. 1, translated heaven, means etymologically, the higher regions, all that seems above the earth: as we say, God above, God on high, God in heaven; meaning thereby to express the presence of the Deity in space distinct from this earth.—E. B. Pusey" (Buckland 1837, 1:21).

39. Goodwin omits Buckland's long explanatory note at this point, which was written by E. B. Pusey at Buckland's request (see Rupke 1983, 205). Buckland showed his work to Pusey and others in the ecclesiastical Establishment to ensure the orthodoxy of his theology. Goodwin draws extensively on this note without attribution for his own annotation in ¶17, and uses it again in ¶40:

> I have much satisfaction in subjoining the following note by my friend, the Regius Professor of Hebrew in Oxford, as it enables me to advance the very important sanction of Hebrew criticism, in support of the interpretations, by which we may reconcile the apparent difficulties arising from geological phenomena, with the literal interpretation of the first chapter of Genesis.—"Two opposite errors have, I think, been committed by critics, with regard to the meaning of the word *bara*, created; the one, by those who asserted that it *must* in itself signify 'created out of nothing;' the other, by those who endeavoured, by aid of etymology, to show that it *must* in itself signify 'formation out of existing matter.' In fact, neither is the case; nor am I aware of any language in which there is a word signifying *necessarily* 'created out of nothing;' as of course, on the other hand, no word when used of the agency of God would, *in itself*, imply the previous existence of matter. Thus the English word, create, by which *bara* is translated, expresses that the thing created received its existence from God, without in itself conveying whether God called that thing into existence *out of nothing*, or no; for our very addition of the words 'out of nothing,' shows that the word creation has not, in itself, that force: nor indeed, when we speak of ourselves as creatures of God's hand, do we at all mean that we were *physically* formed out of nothing. In like manner, whether *bara* should be paraphrased by 'created out of nothing' (as far as we can comprehend these words), or, 'gave a new and distinct state of existence to a substance already existing,' must depend upon the context, the circumstances, or what God has elsewhere revealed, not upon the mere force of the word. This is plain, from its use in Gen. i. 27, of the creation of man, who, as we are instructed, chap. ii. 7, was formed out of previously existing matter, the 'dust of the ground.' The word *bara* is indeed so far stronger than *asah*, 'made,' in that *bara* can only be used with reference to God, whereas *asah* may be applied to man. The difference is exactly that which exists in English between the words by which they are rendered, 'created' and 'made.' But this seems to me to belong rather to our mode of conception than to the subject itself; for making, when spoken of with reference to God, is equivalent to creating.
>
> The words accordingly, bara, *created*—asah, *made*—yatsar, *formed*, are used repeatedly by Isaiah, and are also employed by Amos, as equivalent to each other. *Bara* and *asah* express alike the formation of something new (de novo), something whose existence in this new state originated in, and depends entirely upon the will of its creator or maker. Thus God speaks of Himself as the Creator '*boree*' of the Jewish people, *e. g.* Isaiah xliii. 1,

15; and a new event is spoken of under the same term as 'a creation,' Numb. xvi. 30, English version, 'If the Lord make a new thing:' in the margin, Heb. 'create a creature.' Again, the Psalmist uses the same word, Ps. civ. 30, when describing the renovation of the face of the earth through the successive generations of living creatures, thou sendest forth thy spirit, they are *created*; and thou renewest the face of the earth.' The question is popularly treated by Beausobre, Hist. de Manicheisme, tom. ii. lib. 5, c. 4; or, in a better spirit, by Petavius Dogm. Theol. tom. iii. de opificio sex dierum lib. 1, c. 1, §8.

After having continually reread and studied this account, I can come to no other result than that the words 'created' and 'made' are synonymous, (although the former is to us the stronger of the two), and that, because they are so constantly interchanged; as, Gen. i. ver. 21, 'God *created* great whales;' ver. 25, 'God *made* the beast of the earth;' ver. 26, 'Let us *make* man;' ver. 27, 'So God *created* man.' At the same time it is very probable that bara, '*created*,' as being the stronger word, was selected to describe the first production of the heaven and the earth.

The point, however, upon which the interpretation of the first chapter of Genesis appears to me *really* to turn, is, whether the two first verses are merely a summary statement of what is related in detail in the rest of the chapter, and a sort of introduction to it, or whether they contain an account of an act of creation. And this last seems to me to be their true interpretation, first, because there is no other account of the creation of the earth; secondly, the second verse describes the condition of the earth when so created, and thus prepares for the account of the work of the six days; but if they speak of any creation, it appears to me that this creation 'in the beginning' was previous to the six days, because, as you will observe, the creation of each day is preceded by the declaration that God said, or willed, that such things should be ('and God said'), and therefore the very form of the narrative seems to imply that the creation of the first day began when these words are first used, i. e. with the creation of light in ver. 3. The time then of creation in ver. 1 appears to me not to be defined: we are told only what alone we are concerned with, that all things were made by God. Nor is this any new opinion. Many of the fathers (they are quoted by Petavius, *l. c.* c. 11, §i.—viii.) suppose the two first verses of Genesis to contain an account of a distinct and prior act of creation; some, as Augustine, Theodoret, and others, that of the creation of matter; others, that of the elements; others again (and they the most numerous) imagine that, not these visible heavens, but what they think to be called elsewhere 'the highest heavens,' the 'heaven of heavens,' are here spoken of, our visible heavens being related to have been created on the second day. Petavius himself regards the light as the only act of creation of the first day (c. vii. 'de opere primae diei, i. e. luce'), considering the two first verses as a summary of the account of creation which was about to follow, and a general declaration that all things were made by God.

Episcopius again, and others, thought that the creation and fall of the bad angels took place in the interval here spoken of: and misplaced as such speculations are, still they seem to show that it is natural to suppose that a considerable interval may have taken place between the creation related in the first verse of Genesis and that of which an account is given in the third and following verses. Accordingly, in some old editions of the English Bible, where there is no division into verses, you actually find a break at the end of what is now the second verse; and in Luther's Bible (Wittenburg, 1557) you have in addition the figure 1 placed against the third verse as being the beginning of the account of the creation on the first day.

This then is just the sort of confirmation which one wished for, because, though one would shrink from the impiety of bending the language of God's book to any other than its obvious meaning, we can not help fearing lest we might be unconsciously influenced by the floating opinions of our own day, and therefore turn the more anxiously to those who explain Holy Scripture, before these theories existed. You must allow me to add that I would not define further. We know nothing of creation, nothing of ultimate *causes*, nothing of space, except what is bounded by actual existing bodies, nothing of time, but what is limited by the revolution of those bodies. I should be very sorry to appear to dogmatize upon that, of which it requires very little reflection, or reverence, to confess that we are necessarily ignorant. 'Hardly do we guess aright of things that are upon earth, and with labour do we find the things that are before us; but the things that are in heaven who hath searched out?"—Wisdom, ix. 16.—E. B. Pusey (Buckland 1837, 1:22–25).

Isaac de Beausobre published *Histoire critique de Manichée et du Manichéisme* (1734–39, 2 vols.; Critical history of Manes and Manicheism). The cited passage, in the chapter "Whether the creation of matter is taught in the scriptures" (2:204–19), also cites Petavius in the last paragraph. Dionysius Petavius published *De theologicis dogmatibus* (1644–50, 4 vols.; Concerning dogmatic theology). Simon Episcopius wrote an Arminian Confession of Faith (1622); his *Opera theologica* were published posthumously (1650–65, 2 vols.). Augustine discusses the first verses of Genesis with respect to the creation of matter in *Confessions* (bk. 13, chap. 3–9; trans. William Watts, *Loeb* 2:381–93) and in *De Genesi ad litteram* (On Genesis: bk. 1, chap. 15, sect. 29). Theodoret was an active participant in the Christological controversies of the fifth century, and also wrote a series of commentaries on the Bible.

40. The "Jewish mode of computation" of the 24-hour day, beginning at sunset, is based on the antecedence of darkness to light and of night to day (Gen. 1:5), so that the sabbath begins at sunset on Friday.

41. Goodwin omits Buckland's note at this point: "I learn from Professor Pusey that the words '*let there be light*,' *yehi or*, Gen. i. 3, by no means necessarily imply, any more than the English words by which they are translated, that light had *never* existed before. They may speak only of the substitution of light for darkness upon the surface of this our planet: whether light had existed before in other parts of God's creation, or had existed on this earth, before the darkness described in v. 2, is foreign to the purpose of the narrative" (Buckland 1837, 1:26). For the extended quotation in ¶s 29–31 ("The Mosaic narrative commences . . . the ruins of the ancient earth") see Buckland 1837, 1:20–26. Goodwin transcribes "the earth was fitted up" as "the earth was filled up."

For "chaos . . . geologically considered" see Page: "Matter without form or arrangement; according to the poets, the primal condition of the material universe before it was arranged and fashioned into *Cosmos.*—Chaotic, confused; thrown together into a vast heap without any order or arrangement, like the debris resulting from a violent land-flood or debacle" (1859, s.v. "Chaos").

For Buckland's "wreck and ruin of a former world" and "ruins of the ancient earth" see Stackhouse [1737] 1816, 1:6–7 as cited by Buckland: "the wreck of some former system . . . the ruins of a former earth, deposited in the chaotic mass of which Moses informed us that God formed the present system" (Buckland 1837, 1:28–30, n.).

42. The quoted passage occurs on the cited page. Goodwin transcribes "substance of the sun and moon were" as "substance of the sun and moon was"; and "existence upon the fourth day" as "existence on the fourth day." Goodwin conflates the quotations that are separated in Buckland's text by omitting the quotation marks.

For "to give light . . . night" see Gen. 1:17; for "to be for signs . . . and for years," Gen. 1:14.

43. "Good critics" include E. B. Pusey, cited by Buckland 1837, 1:22–26; see Goodwin ¶s 30, 31, and notes.

44. For "local habitation" see Shakespeare, *Midsummer Night's Dream* 5.1.17.

The "obvious difficulty" Goodwin attacks in Buckland is the Aristotelian and scholastic distinction between matter and form in the creation of matter, and the subsequent conferring of form on matter. In contemporaneous physics this distinction was collapsed: matter cannot exist without form. Goodwin argues that in Gen. 1 no location is specified for "the original material," a "difficulty" that Buckland glosses over by separating the description of "the primal creation of matter" in the first verse of Genesis from the conferring of form on the planets, stars, and their satellites in subsequent verses, with an emphasis on the anthropomorphic purpose of such a creation in foregrounding earth and humankind (Buckland 1837, 1:27–28). Buckland cites Gleig: "I am indeed strongly inclined to believe that the *matter* of the corporeal universe was all created at once, though very different portions of it may have been reduced to *form* at very different periods" (Stackhouse [1737] 1816, 1:6).

45. Buckland 1837, 1:29–30. For "upon the face of the deep," set off in quotation marks in Buckland, see Gen. 1:2.

46. For "And God said . . ." see Gen. 1:3–5.

47. A *caput mortuum* (Lat. dead head) is a skull or "worthless residue" (*OED*).

48. In his discussion of the nonmateriality of light, Buckland alludes to the utility of "eyes of fossil animals" and to the heliotropism of the vegetable fossils, even though light was created according to the second verse of Genesis after vast eons of geological time. He refers to John Herschell's article on "Light" in the *Encyclopaedia Metropolitana* (1845), to George Biddell Airy's *Mathematical Tracts on Physical Astronomy* (1831), and to Mary Somerville's *On the Connexion of the Physical Sciences* (1834). See Buckland 1837, 1:32.

49. Goodwin aligns his argument against catastrophists such as Miller and Buckland in support of one aspect of uniformitarianism, "the gradual and regular formation of the earth's strata." This position was advocated by Lyell in *Principles of Geology* (1830–33), and his followers. According to Cannon, "By 1850, it is apparent, it was becoming difficult, in particular problems of geological dynamics, to distinguish a Uniformitarian from a Catastrophist" (1960, 50). Evidence of the effect of the glaciers was accepted by both sides; but the catastrophists required very substantial catastrophes to raise the Alps, ones far greater than the sedimentation allowed for in the Noachian deluge, however long it might have been. On the other hand, the uniformitarians were challenged by the vast evidence of fossil remains that made the task of regular sequence without progression difficult to sustain: "In this situation the Ca-

tastrophists resorted to the Argument from Design. . . . This . . . enabled the Catastrophists to reject not only Lyell's ideas, but also the 'materialistic' Lamarckian notions of steady organic progression as currently presented in the socially and scientifically disreputable *Vestiges of the Natural History of Creation* of 1844" (Cannon 1960, 51). Lyell's two presidential addresses to the Geological Society (1850 and 1851) defended uniformitarianism; in the second he discussed the fossil remains, as argued for by the catastrophists Adam Sedgwick, Richard Owen, and Miller. Lyell's argument was attacked by the next president, the catastrophist William Hopkins, in his presidential address of 1852 (Cannon 1960, 54–55). By 1860 the notion of progressive development in evolutionary biology was accommodated to the uniformitarian position, while the catastrophists still tried to reconcile Genesis and geology: "After 1859, the surviving catastrophists, though they had toyed with ideas of organic progression in the 1830's, were to be solidly behind Wilberforce; while the uniformitarians who were still alive supported Darwin and Huxley" (Gillispie 1959, 135). See Williams ¶1, n. 1.

50. The theory of the "great gap," the presumed vast interval between Gen. 1:1 and 1:2, was advanced by Thomas Chalmers in 1814, republished as "Remarks on Cuvier's Theory of the Earth in Extracts from a Review of That Theory Which Was Contributed to *The Christian Instructor* in 1814." In the chapter "Scepticism of Geologists" in *Evidences* (1814) Chalmers repeats the view that "the early verses of Genesis record not one Creation but two; and the aeons of geology fall between," prompting Millhauser to comment that "this is the first responsible British attempt to face in at all realistic terms the problem posed by the new geology. . . . Chalmers' suggestion was favourably received by theological liberals, and encouraged the rise of a more or less self-conscious party of 'reconciliation.' Its prestige was such that the 'interval' theory presently became almost the official British rival to the continental one that interpreted the Six Days as six creative eras" (Millhauser 1954, 68–69). See also J. R. Moore: "By midcentury nearly everyone who wrote on the subject [of Genesis and modern science] . . . agreed that earth history had been unimaginably vast—the aeons could be interpolated in a pre-Adamic creation (the 'gap theory' again), by extending the Genesis 'days' (the 'day-age theory'), or through loopholes in the genealogies preceding the Flood narrative" (in Lindberg and Numbers 1986, 325). Miller in the following quotation (¶38) refers twice to "chaotic gaps."

51. *Testimony of the Rocks*, p. 10 [Goodwin's note].

The cited passage is part of the address To the Reader (Miller 1857, x–xi). Goodwin generally quotes accurately, changing some punctuation, capitalization, and the occasional word: for Goodwin's "comprised" Miller reads "compressed"; for "late formations," "later formations"; for "from them," "from these"; for "its red and coral crags," "its Red and its Coral crags"; and for "time with their own," "times with their own."

For "old red and carboniferous systems" see Page: "Taking the Coal-Measures as a sort of middle formation, there is generally found in the British Islands one set of reddish sandstones lying beneath, and another lying immediately above them. By the earlier geologists the lower set was designated the *Old Red Sandstone*, and the upper the *New Red Sandstone*. . . . The Old Red Sandstone may therefore be held as embracing the whole series of strata which lies between the Silurian system on the one hand, and the Carboniferous system on the other. Certain portions of the system are peculiarly developed in Devonshire, and contain a copious and varied fossil fauna; hence, the introduction by Murchison and Sedgwick of the term *Devonian*—a term now generally employed as synonymous with the earlier and more descriptive one of "Old Red Sandstone" (1859, s.v. "Old Red Sandstone or Devonian System"). For a recent discussion of this geological discovery see Rudwick 1985.

For "brick clays" see Page: "The familiar term for any clay used in the manufacture of bricks, tiles, and the like. . . . In geological classification, the term 'Brick-clay' is frequently used in contradistinction to that of 'Boulder-clay'—meaning thereby those finely laminated clays of the Pleistocene epoch which immediately overlie the true boulder-clay, and have evidently been derived from it by the wasting and reassorting agency of water" (1859, s.v. "Brick-clay").

"Clyde beds" refer to the distinct layers of rock adjacent to the Clyde, the principal river of Lanarkshire, Scotland.

For "Pleistocene era" see Page: "Literally, 'most recent;' that is, the most recent or uppermost of the Tertiaries, a term implying that the organic remains in such accumulations, belong almost wholly to existing species. Sir Charles Lyell makes use of the word *Post-Pliocene*, and others employ the term *Pleistocene* as equivalent to *Post-Tertiary*; but, properly speaking, the organic remains of the post-tertiaries belong exclusively to species still existing, while those of the pleistocene embrace a few extinct forms" (1859, s.v. "Pleistocene").

For "mammaliferous . . . red and coral crags" see Page: "Shelly tertiary deposits of the Pliocene epoch, occurring in Norfolk and Suffolk, and generally subdivided into three members—viz. the upper or 'Mammaliferous Crag,' the 'Red Crag,' and the lower or 'Coraline Crag'" (1859, s.v. "Crag").

For "beast of the earth . . . their kind" see Gen. 1:25.

Page has an entry on each of mastodon ("the old extinct elephant"), hippopotamus, and hyena, indicating that such extinct species existed in Western Europe in the Pleistocene period. In 1821 a cavern at Kirkdale in Yorkshire was found containing a large number of bones of hyenas, birds, tigers, elephants, rhinoceroses, and hippopotamuses. Buckland visited the cave and sought out similar ones, publishing his conclusions in *Philosophical Transactions* 112 (1822): 171–236, following it with *Reliquae Diluviae* (1823). For an extensive discussion on Buckland's work on the Kirkdale cave see Rupke 1983, 29–109. See also Goodwin ¶62.

52. For "the compulsion of what he considered irresistible evidence" see Miller: "After in some degree committing myself to the other side, I have yielded to evidence which I found it impossible to resist; and such in this matter has been my *inconsistency,*—an inconsistency of which the world has furnished examples in all the sciences, and will, I trust, in its onward progress, continue to furnish many more" (1857, xi). This passage immediately follows the long quotation from Miller cited in Goodwin ¶38, and concludes the prefatory To the Reader.

53. Buckland 1837, 1:15. For Copernicus see Goodwin ¶1 and note. The physicist Pierre Simon Laplace attacked Newton's theological appeal to first causes in *Exposition du système du monde* (1813): "I cannot forgo noting here how Newton strayed on this point [celestial mechanics] from the method that he otherwise used so effectively" (quoted in Lindberg and Numbers 1986, 272). For a recent discussion of Laplace in the context of eighteenth-century science see Hahn 1967; for an extended comparison between Laplace and Newton see Hahn's essay in Lindberg and Numbers 1986.

54. See Dr. Pusey's note—Buckland's *Bridgewater Treatise,* pp. 24, 25 [Goodwin's note].

For "Pusey's note" see Goodwin ¶30 and note.

55. Buckland 1837, 1:33.

56. Buckland 1837, 1:33. Goodwin transcribes "this account" as "the account."

57. *Scripture and Science not at Variance.* By J. H. Pratt, M.A., Archdeacon of Calcutta, 1859. Third edition, p. 34 [Goodwin's note].

John Henry Pratt published *Scripture and Science Not at Variance; with Remarks on the Historical Character, Plenary Inspiration, and Surpassing Importance, of the Earlier Chapters of Genesis* (1856) and *Mathematical Principles of Mechanical Philosophy* (1836). Goodwin's quotation for the next four paragraphs omits a short footnote on "desolation and emptyness" (Pratt [1856] 1859, 34) and a very long note qualifying relations between Genesis and science (Pratt [1856] 1859, 35–38). Throughout the quotation, Goodwin consistently converts capitalized patronymics to lower case.

Pratt included some illustrations from "Bunsen, Homer, Darwin and Goodwin" in the fourth edition of *Scripture and Science Not at Variance* (1861). But in the extensively revised sixth edition (1871) Pratt elaborates his "great gap" theory: "The days [of creation] were literally days of twenty-four hours, [and so] we have but to suppose that an interval of untold duration occurred between the first creation of the heaven and the earth . . . and the preparation of the earth for the reception of man" ([1856] 1871, 77).

In the preface to the sixth edition Pratt declares that he originally wrote his treatise in 1856 "to meet the assertion by the late Professor Baden Powell, that 'all geology is contrary to Scripture'" ([1856] 1871, iii; see also 373–75, citing Powell's *Inductive Philosophy* (1855). Pratt has now greatly increased his text by responding to Powell and Goodwin's essays in *Essays and Reviews,* as well as to Colenso's *The Pentateuch and the Book of Joshua Critically Examined* (1862–79), Darwin's *On the Origin of Species* (1859) and *Descent of Man* (1871), Lyell's *The Geological Evidences for the Antiquity of Man* (1863), Huxley's *Evidence as to Man's Place in Nature* (1863) and *Lay Sermons* (1870), and Lubbock's *Prehistoric Times* (1865) and *The Origin of Civilization and Primitive Condition of Man* (1870). Pratt adds that despite these additions, "the price remains as before" (v).

Other than a brief discussion of Hebrew etymology (see Goodwin ¶s 20 and 26), Pratt's extensive discussion of Gen. 1 and science responds to Goodwin only in general terms ([1856] 1871, 41–86).

58. In the sixth edition Pratt revises this paragraph extensively: for "convulsion in nature" the sixth edition reads "revolution on its surface"; for "separated by *an expanse* . . . below," "separated from the waters and vapours below by an 'expanse,' the word rightly substituted in the margin of our Bibles for 'firmament'"; for "seize . . . appeared," "seize—we may suppose by the upheaval of the ocean-bed in some places—and the dry land appeared"; for "his creatures," "the rational beings"; for "the fifth . . . comment," "on the fifth and sixth days the waters and the earth brought forth living creatures, and man was created" ([1856] 1871, 49–50).

59. For Goodwin's "thus stepping" Pratt reads "then, stepping"; for "infinite ages," "indefinite ages." In this quoted paragraph Pratt asserts the conventional temporal "gap" between Gen. 1:1 and 1:2 by collapsing geological evidence onto a concept of "appearances," as though the narrative of Gen. 1 were perceived by a human observer. The argument is supported by the conflation of Josephus with a supposition about the language of the translators of the AV. For "the idea of Josephus" see *The Antiquities of the Jews*: "The Constitution of the World and the Disposition of the Elements" (bk. 1, chap. 1; quoted by Pratt [1856] 1871, 15). The chair of the "translators" of the AV Genesis was Lancelot Andrewes; their task was to revise the previous versions in the light of the most recent biblical knowledge, and so changed the reading of William Tyndale in his translation of 1530: "the erth was

voyde and emptie."

For "without form and void" see Goodwin ¶s 18, 44, and notes. "*In limine*" (Lat. on or at the threshold) is a legal term for a motion which seeks to exclude prejudicial evidence before that evidence is presented. Pratt excised the passages quoted in ¶s 45 and 46 in his sixth edition, substituting a discussion of perception and appearance concerning the "movement" of the sun ([1856] 1871, 14–40).

60. For Goodwin's "out of its statements" Pratt reads "from its statements" ([1856] 1859, 39).

61. Miller discusses the "mythical or enigmatical sense [of] the Mosaic narrative" in lectures three to six of *Testimony of the Rocks*. For "this plan was long ago suggested" see, for instance, *The Sacred Theory of the Earth* (1684) by Thomas Burnet, who argues that Genesis is not a literal account of creation, but allegorical. For a comparison of Burnet and James Hutton as cosmogonists in relation to Genesis, see Jordanova and Porter 1979, 30–33.

62. *Bridgewater Treatise*, p. 17 [Goodwin's note].

For "in favour of . . . Chalmers" see Goodwin ¶29 and note.

63. Buckland 1837, 1:17–18. For "learned theologians and . . . geologists" see Buckland's note, omitted by Goodwin: "A very interesting treatise on the Consistency of Geology with Sacred History has recently been published . . . by Professor Silliman. . . . The author contends that the period alluded to in the first verse of Genesis, 'In the beginning,' is not necessarily connected with the first day, and that it may be regarded as standing by itself, and admitting of any extension backward in time when the facts seem to require. He is further disposed to consider the six days of creation as periods of time of indefinite length, and that the word 'day' is not of necessity limited to twenty-four hours" (Buckland 1837, 1:18, citing Bakewell [1813] 1833).

For "transition strata" see Page: "In the classification of [Abraham] Werner and his school the transition strata were separated from the primary as being less crystalline, affording unmistakable evidence of their mechanical or sedimentary origin, and containing occasional remains of plants and animals. For these reasons it was assumed they were deposited at a period when the earth or sea were passing into a state fit for the reception of organized beings; and hence the term *Transition*" (1859, s.v. "Transition Rocks or Strata").

64. *Science and Scripture not at Variance*, p. 40, note [Goodwin's note].

Pratt revised this "note" extensively by the sixth edition, excising the references to Macdonald, expanding the discussions of D'Orbigny and Miller. He also cites McCaul's attack on Goodwin from *Aids to Faith* ([1856] 1871, 59–65).

65. Donald Macdonald's *Creation and the Fall* (1856) discusses "days" of creation (92–108). Miller refers to Macdonald's study as "a brief but masterly view of these [Etrurian, Egyptian, Phoenician, and Babylonian] ancient cosmogonies" (1857, 352).

Dionysius Lardner initiated the *Cabinet Encyclopedia* in 1829, for which Baden Powell wrote on natural philosophy and astronomy. John Harris's *The Prae-Adamite Earth, Contributions to Theological Science* (1846) was republished as vol. 12 of Lardner's *Museum of Science and Art* (1856). Harris discusses Gen. 1 in a long note, drawing extensively on Pusey's note in Buckland regarding *bara*, cited in Goodwin ¶30 and note (John Harris 1846, 349–56). *The Prae-Adamite Earth* and Harris's *Man Primeval, or the Constitution and Primitive Condition of the Human Being* (1849) are advertised on the front inside cover of Miller's *Foot-Prints of the Creator* ([1847] 1850): "The object is to reconcile the theology and the geology of the age, by showing what can be proved in regard to the progressive steps of creation, prior to the formation of the first man." For a recent discussion of the pre-Adamite theory see Livingstone 1992.

66. For "few exceptions" Pratt reads "few solitary exceptions" ([1856] 1859, 40). Alcide Dessalines D'Orbigny published *Prodrome de Paléontologie Stratigraphique universelle des animaux mollusques & rayonnés* (1849, 3 vols.; Preamble to universal stratigraphic paleontology concerning molluscs and rayed animals), which included a complex system of classification into twenty-seven stages of creation, some with subdivisions, based on a vast body of fossil evidence arranged according to species: "The result of our labour has been to rely upon all the paleontological evidence: on the unity of formations, on the unity of kinds, on the unity of species, and on the unity of names of species. . . . We will show in consequence that our plan is the natural succession of the earth and of its stages in chronological order. We shall give, therefore, the successive periods and in each of them, in the zoological order by class and by kind, all the species that are well known to us. Hence the periods will succeed each other, comprised in the paleozoic, triassic, jurassic, cretaceous, and tertiary formations" (1:lvi–lix).

67. Pratt's note (see Goodwin ¶51 and note) is much longer: Goodwin resumes it in ¶58.

68. John Lindley published *An Introduction to the Natural System of Botany* (1830), *The Fossil Flora of Great Britain* (1831–37, 3 vols.), and the most complete treatment of his system, *The Vegetable Kingdom, or the Structure, Classification, and Uses of Plants, Illustrated upon the Natural System* (1846). Lindley advocates a system of plant classification following the French botanist Antoine Laurent de Jussieu, who in *Genera plantarum* (1789), arranged the orders according to comparative study of structural and morphological botany, opposed to the Linnaean system. Carl Linnaeus published *Systema naturae* (1735) and *Genera plantarum* (1737), in which he classifies plants on the basis of function, chiefly their

sexual characteristics.

In *A Manual of Botany* John Hutton Balfour acknowledges that "in the important subject of classification, much aid has been derived from the standard work of Lindley" (1855, vii); in another textbook, Balfour refers to *The Vegetable Kingdom* as giving "a full view of all the systems of Natural Classification" (1854, 735). Miller in *Testimony* associates Lindley's botanical classification with the zoological system of Cuvier, adopting Lindley's classification as his own (1857, 7).

69. For the cited passage see Miller 1857, 7–8; for Goodwin's "cycadaceae" Miller reads "cycadacae." Lindley's botanical terms are defined in a general sense by Miller in the passage Goodwin cites. In the Linnaean and subsequent systems of plant classification, "monocotyledonous," "polycotyledonous," and "dicotyledonous" refer to the number (one, many, two) of seed-lobes or first leaves in the embryo (cotyledon), or seed of a plant. "Liliaceae" refers to members of the lily family; "Coniferae," to the cone-bearing family of plant; "Cycadaceae," to the cycas family of palmlike ferns.

70. Goodwin greatly compresses the discussion of "the order in which fossils of these several classes appear," which occupies nine pages in Miller (1857, 7–16).

71. George Cuvier published *Tableau élémentaire de l'histoire naturelle des animaux* (1798, Elementary table of the natural history of animals) and *Règne animal* (1817). For Cuvier's system in which these classes of invertebrata are set out see Goodwin ¶11 and note.

72. For "mammals" see Page: "The general term for all animals that give suck to their young. They constitute the first and highest class of VERTEBRATA, and are usually divided into *Placentalia*, and *Implacentalia*—the former being those that are nourished previous to birth by a uterine network of blood-vessels called the *placenta*, and do not come into the world until they are provided with all their organs; the latter, those that are non-placental, or have no attachment to the uterus, and are brought forth in an imperfect state—the young being received into an external pouch (*marsupium*), and there nourished till their organs are matured. The non-placentals are comparatively few in number, are chiefly confined to the Australasian continent, and are regarded as lower in the scale of being than the placentals. Remains of marsupial mammals have been found in the triassic and oolitic rocks; the higher orders not till the Chalk and Tertiaries" (1859, s.v. "Mammals, Mammalia").

For "and man last of all" compare Miller: "And finally,—last born of creation,—man appears upon the scene" (1857, 15).

73. Equating the Mosaic "day" to the geological "period," Miller writes: "These, taken together, exhaust the geologic scale, and may be named in their order as, *first* the Azoic day or period; *second*, the Silurian and Old Red Sandstone day or period; *third*, the Carboniferous day or period; *fourth*, the Permian and Triassic day or period; *fifth*, the Oolitic and Cretaceous day or period; and *sixth*, the Tertiary day or period" (1857, 175).

74. For "seculum" (Lat. an age) see Page: "Applied in Geology to great natural processes, whose results become appreciable only after the lapse of ages: thus we speak of the 'secular refrigeration' of the globe from some hypothetical state of original igneous fluidity; 'of secular contraction' of the earth's mass, as resulting from its gradual refrigeration, and so on" (1859, s.v. "Secular").

75. *Testimony*, p. 133 [Goodwin's note].

The quoted passage is on the cited page. For Goodwin's "violence of the Hebrew language" Miller reads "violence to the genius of the Hebrew language." Goodwin attacks Miller's philology but omits Miller's disclaimers to philological expertise: "I come before you this evening, not as a philologist, but simply as a student of geological fact. . . . Premising, then, that I make no pretensions to even the slightest skill in philology, I remark further, that it has been held by accomplished philologists . . ." (1857, 132–33). For a recent discussion relating nineteenth-century philology to geology see J. R. Moore in Lindberg and Numbers 1986.

76. Goodwin picks up the same note quoted in ¶52, omitting a paragraph of qualification. Pratt's note continues for three pages ([1856] 1859, 42–44).

77. The expression, Gen. ii. 4, 'In the day that the Lord God created the earth and heaven,' to which Hugh Miller here refers, may possibly mean 'at the time when,' meaning a week, year, or other limited time. But there is not the smallest reason for understanding it to mean 'a *lengthened* period,' *i.e.*, an immense lapse of time. Such a construction would be inadmissible in the Hebrew, or any other language. It is difficult to acquit Hugh Miller of an equivocation here. In real truth, the second narrative is, as we have before observed, of distinct origin from the first, and we incline to the belief that, in this case also, 'day' is to be taken in its proper signification [Goodwin's note].

On Miller's elaboration of the Mosaic day as a geological period see Goodwin ¶s 56, 57, and notes. For Cuvier see Goodwin ¶54 and note. James Parkinson published *Organic Remains of a Former World: An Examination of the Mineralized Remains of the Vegetables* (1804–11, 3 vols.) and *Outlines of Oryctology: An Introduction to the Study of Fossil Organic Remains, Especially Those Found in the British Strata* (1822). In 1850 Gideon Algernon Mantell called the former "a memorable event in the history of British Palaeontology. It was the first attempt to give a familiar and scientific account of the fossil relics of animals and plants" (13). For Silliman see Goodwin ¶50 and note.

78. *Testimony*, p. 134 [Goodwin's note].

The quoted passage is on the cited page. For Goodwin's "Mosaic account" Miller reads "Mosaic narrative"; for "three out of the six," "three of the six"; for "fourth day of creation," "fourth period of creation."

79. The following lengthy quotation in ¶s 61 and 62 is from Miller 1857, 134–38. Goodwin omits two paragraph divisions and a passage indicated by an elision.

80. A very inadmissible assertion. Any one, be he geologist, astronomer, theologian, or philologist, who attempts to explain the Hebrew narrative, is bound to take it with all that really belongs to it. And in truth, if the fourth day really represented an epoch of creative activity, geology would be able to give some account of it. There is no reason to suppose that any intermission has taken place [Goodwin's note].

For the two accounts of creation in Genesis see Goodwin n. 23. Miller asserts that the geological record can present evidence only of the works of the third, fifth, and sixth days.

81. For "umbrageous" see Page: "shady, belonging to the dust; the fourteenth of the fifteen series [of geological formations, named for the time of day] into which Professor H. D. Rogers subdivides the palaeozoic strata of the Appalachian Chain [*Report on Pennsylvania* (1858)]—the 'Dusk' of the North American palaeozoics, and the equivalent, in part, of our Carboniferous Limestone and Lower Coal-Measures" (1859, s.v. "Umbral"; and for Rogers's scheme see Page 1859, s.v. "Palaeozoic").

Miller refers to the "araucarians" (a genus of evergreens, now found in the southern hemisphere, including the monkey-puzzle tree), "calamites" (gigantic reeds fossilized in coal), "sigillaria" (an extinct genus of small-leafed tree with trunks up to several feet in diameter), and "lepidodendron" (an extinct genus of leafy plants, some species of which grew to great size). The entries in Page's *Handbook* for each of these terms of classification are stated to be provisional and the subject of dispute amongst fossil botanists in 1859. For "plains of Australia" see Page: "The *Araucariae* are natives of the Southern Hemisphere, and are all more or less gigantic trees. . . . It is an interesting fact, therefore, to find that trees closely resembling those of Australia and the adjacent islands, should at one period have flourished extensively in the northern latitudes now occupied by Great Britain" (1859, s.v. "Araucarites").

Melville Island is located in the Arctic Ocean, part of the Canadian Northwest Territories (not the Melville Island off Australia), identified by the "icy coast" and the "star of the pole" (the North Star or Polaris); the "cross of the south" refers to the constellation of the Southern Cross (or Crux), visible in the southern hemisphere.

82. For "wonderful *whales*" see Page, who comments on the ichthyosaurus: "a well-known genus of the extinct *Enaliosaurs* or marine saurians, and so called from its combining the characters of saurian reptiles and of fishes with some of the peculiarities of the whales. The ichthyosaurs were in fact the 'reptile-whales' of their period" (1859, s.v. "Ichthyosaurus"). For "the reptilian class" see Page: "The Saurians comprehend the lizards, monitors, iguanas, chameleons, &c., all well-known forms among living species; and the ichthyosaurus, plesiosaurus, deinosaurus, iguanodon, and numerous other extinct and gigantic forms, some of which were marine, others terrestrial—some carnivorous, and others herbivorous" (1859, s.v. "Saurian"). Buckland addressed the Geological Society of London in 1824 on the megalosaurus and Mantell wrote on the iguanodon in *The Fossils of the South Downs* (1822). For recent discussions of Victorian palaeontology see Delaire and Sarjeant 1975; and Desmond 1984.

For "foot-prints of . . . birds . . . fully twice the size" see Page: "Footprints supposed to be those of birds, and found abundantly on the sandstone slabs of the Trias, especially on the sandstones of the Connecticut valley in North America. Many of these are of gigantic size, and would seem to indicate the existence of . . . birds three or four times the size of the existing ostrich" (1859, s.v. "Ornithichnites"). "Ornithichnites" derives from Gr. *ornis*, *ornithes*, a bird, and *ichnon*, a footprint. Buckland also discusses these footprints in detail (1837, 2:9–42, and plates 26a and 26b). "Foot-prints stamped upon the rocks" allow Miller to read fossils in the geological record as evidence for divine creation (see Goodwin ¶14 and note).

83. "In the margin" refers to the marginal emendations, alternative readings, and interpretive comments introduced in Hebrew MSS. of the Bible produced by the Masoretes, the Hebrew scholars entrusted with the transmission of the biblical text. Their chief centers were in Babylonia at Sura and in Palestine at Tiberias, during the period from the fifth to the tenth centuries. Masorah readings were common in MSS. Hebrew Bibles, and were first introduced into the margins of a printed Hebrew Bible in the *Second Rabbinic Bible* printed by Daniel Bomberg at Venice in 1525, becoming the received text of the Masorah and the standard edition of the Hebrew Bible for four hundred years.

For "great whales" see Gen. 1:21; the alternate translation, "sea-monster," is incorporated in the Revised Version (1885).

For "enormous dinotherium, and colossal megatherium" see Page: "A huge proboscidean mammal found in the meiocene tertiaries of Europe and Asia. The zoological position of the *dinothere* (of which there seem to be several species) is not yet distinctly ascertained—the skull, molar teeth, and scapular bone being the only portions yet discovered" (1859, s.v. "Deinotherium"); "A huge edentate mammal whose remains occur abundantly in the upper tertiary or Pampean deposits of South America. In anatomical structure the Megatherium exhibits features intermediate between the Sloths, Armadilloes, and Ant-eaters. . . . Larger than the largest rhinoceros, its length was about nine or ten feet; but its bones were proportionally much more colossal than those either of the rhinoceros or elephant" (1859, s.v. "Megatherium"). Buckland discusses the dinotherium and the megatherium as "affording fresh proofs of the infinitely varied, and inexhaustible contrivances of Creative Wisdom" (1:164). Richard Owen published *Description of the Skeleton of an Extinct Gigantic Sloth* (1842) and *Memoir on the Megatherium; or, Giant Ground-Sloth of America* (1861). For a discussion of Owen's place in Victorian science see Rupke 1994.

84. The "English naturalist" has not been identified. Buckland discusses the fossils of animals once prevalent but now extinct in England, the cave-bear, cave-hyena, and oxen bones found at the Kirkdale cave, in *Reliquae Diluvianae* (1823, 17–18; 20–24). Mantell identifies the "cave-bear" as the "*ursus spelaeus* or bear of the caverns" and also discusses the cave-hyenas (1857, 1:178–80). On the ox Mantell writes: "The Ox-tribe also affords interesting examples of the diminution or total passing away of species from the European area within comparatively modern times. Of four species known as occurring fossils in the post-tertiary deposits of Britain, namely, 1. the *Bison priseus* (or old bison), 2. *Bos primigenius* (ancient ox), 3. *Bos longifrons* (long-fronted ox), and 4. *Bubalus moschatus* (musk-buffalo), the first is now represented by the herds of Aurochs preserved in the royal forests of Lithuania; the second, though apparently well known to the Romans, is now quite extinct; the third survives possibly in the race of short-horned cattle of Wales and the Highlands; while the last is now restricted to the frozen arctic regions of the north" (1857, 1:133–34). For the "elk" see Page: "Literally, the 'great antlered deer of Ireland.' The fossil or sub-fossil gigantic deer of our pleistocene marls and peat-bogs, often, but erroneously, termed the 'Irish Elk'" (1859, s.v. "Megaceros Hibernicus"); "It is usually, but erroneously, termed *Elk*—the creature being a true deer, though far exceeding in magnitude any living species. Skeletons have been found ten feet high from the ground to the point of the antlers. . . . Chronologically, the Irish deer seems to have been antecedent to man in Europe, though some of their species appear also to have been contemporary with him, and to have been extirpated by the earliest hunter tribes that took possession of its plains and forests" (1859, s.v. "Irish Deer"). For a recent discussion of the Irish Elk and of evolutionary theory see Gould 1979, 75–90.

85. Goodwin omits 14 lines at the asterisks in the long quotation in ¶s 61 and 62 (Miller 1857, 134–38). He introduces the following variants: for Goodwin's "them only" Miller reads "these only"; for "three great parts," "*three* great parts"; for "classes give," "classes of organisms give"; for "lepidodendrons," "lepidodendron"; for "shallow lakes," "shallow lake"; for "its icy coast," "its ice wastes"; for "cetosaurs," "cetiosaurs"; for "on land," "on the land"; for "appeared on earth," "appeared upon earth"; for "these early days," "those early days"; and for "and cattle after their kind," "and of cattle after their kind."

86. Miller's fourth lecture of *Testimony of the Rocks* is on "The Mosaic Vision of Creation" (1857, 157–91). Pratt (see ¶s 43 ff.) rejects outright the notion that Genesis is a vision of Moses: "It is difficult to see any good ground for supposing, as some have done, that the revelation of these truths was made to Moses by vision" ([1856] 1871, 55).

87. The passage is quoted from Miller 1857, 24–26. For Goodwin's "unedible character," Miller reads "non-edible character"; for "amongst its shades," "among its shades."

88. For the cited passage see Miller 1857, 187. For Goodwin's "*sickly gleam*," Miller reads "sickly gleam." For Buckland's treatment of light see 1837, 1:29–33; see also Goodwin ¶s 36 and 37.

89. For "a brilliant day" see Miller 1857, 189.

90. Miller discusses the "visual or optical character of *some* of the revelations made to Moses" (1857, 165–72).

91. For an instance of the "often-echoed remark" see the conclusion to Miller's fourth lecture, "The Mosaic Vision of Creation" (1857, 190–91).

92. For "palters . . . sense" see *Macbeth* 5.8.21. René Descartes, one of the founders of French rationalism and scientific method based on deduction, published *Discours de la méthode* (1637).

93. *Sub modo* (Lat. under qualification) is a legal term meaning subject to a restriction or qualification.

6 *Mark Pattison*

Tendencies of Religious Thought in England, 1688–1750

THE THIRTY YEARS OF PEACE which succeeded the Peace of Utrecht (1714), 'was the most prosperous season that England had ever experienced; and the progression, though slow, being uniform, the reign of George II. might not disadvantageously be compared for the real happiness of the community with that more brilliant, but uncertain and oscillatory condition which has ensued. A labourer's wages have never for many ages commanded so large a portion of subsistence as in this part of the 18th century.' (Hallam, *Const. Hist.* ii. 464.)[1]

This is the aspect which that period of history wears to the political philosopher. The historian of moral and religious progress, on the other hand, is under the necessity of depicting the same period as one of decay of religion, licentiousness of morals, public corruption, profaneness of language—a day of 'rebuke and blasphemy.' Even those who look with suspicion on the contemporary complaints from the Jacobite clergy of 'decay of religion' will not hesitate to say that it was an age destitute of depth or earnestness; an age whose poetry was without romance, whose philosophy was without insight, and whose public men were without character; an age of 'light without love,' whose 'very merits were of the earth, earthy.' In this estimate the followers of Mill and Carlyle will agree with those of Dr. Newman.[2]

The Stoical moralists of the second century who witnessed a similar coincidence of moral degradation and material welfare, had no difficulty in connecting them together as effect with cause. 'Bona rerum secundarum optabilia, adversarum mirabilia.' (Seneca, *ad Lucil.* 66.)[3] But the famous theory which satisfied the political philosophers of antiquity, viz., that the degeneration of nations is due to the inroads of luxury, is laughed to scorn by modern economists.[4] It is at any rate a theory which can hardly be adopted by those who pour unmeasured contempt on the 18th, by way of contrast with the revival of higher principles by the 19th century. It is especially since the High Church movement commenced that the theology of the 18th century has become a byeword. The genuine Anglican omits that period from the history of the Church altogether. In constructing his *Catenae Patrum* he closes his list with Waterland or Brett, and leaps at once to 1833, when the *Tracts for the Times* commenced—as Charles II. dated his reign from his father's death.[5] Such a legal fiction may be harmless or useful for purposes of mere form, but the facts of history cannot be disposed of by forgetting them. Both the Church and the world of to-day are what they are as the result of the whole of their antecedents. The history of a party may be written on the theory of periodical occultation; but he who wishes to trace the descent of religious thought, and the practical working of the religious ideas, must follow these through all the phases they have actually assumed. We have not yet learnt, in this country, to write our ecclesiastical history on any better footing than that of praising up the party, in or out of the Church, to which we happen to belong. Still further are we from any attempt to apply the laws of thought, and of the succession of opinion, to the course of English theology. The recognition of the fact, that the view of the eternal verities of religion which prevails in any given age is in part determined by the view taken in the age which preceded it, is incompatible with the hypothesis generally prevalent among us as to the mode in which we form our notions of religious truth.[6] Upon none of the prevailing theories as to this mode is a deductive history of theology possible. 1. The Catholic theory, which is really that of Roman-Catholics, and professedly that of some Anglo-Catholics, withdraws Christianity altogether from human experience and the operation of the ordinary laws of thought. 2. The Protestant theory of free inquiry, which supposes that each mind takes a survey of the evidence, and strikes the balance of probability according to the best of its judgment—this theory, defers indeed to the abstract laws of logic, but overlooks the influences of education. If, without hypothesis, we are content to observe facts, we shall find that we cannot decline to study the opinions of any age only because they are not our own opinions. There is a law of continuity in the progress of theology which, whatever we may wish, is never broken off. In tracing the filiation of consecutive systems, we cannot afford to overlook any link in the chain, any age, except one in which religious opinion did not exist. Certainly we, in this our time, if we would understand our own position in the Church, and that of the Church in the age, if we would hold any clue through the maze of religious pretension which surrounds us, cannot neglect those immediate agencies in the production of the present, which had their origin towards the beginning of the 18th century.[7]

[4] Of these agencies there are three, the present influence of which cannot escape the most inattentive. 1. The formation and gradual growth of that compromise between Church and State, which is called Toleration, and which, believed by many to be a principle, is a mere arrangement between two principles.[8] But such as it is, it is part of our heritage from the last age, and is the foundation, if foundation it can be called, upon which we still continue to build, as in the late Act for the admission of the Jews to Parliament.[9] 2. The great rekindling of the religious consciousness of the people which, without the Established Church, became Methodism, and within its pale has obtained the name of the *Evangelical* movement. However decayed may be the Evangelical party as a party, it cannot be

denied that its influence, both on our religious ideas, and on our church life, has penetrated far beyond those party limits.[10] 3. The growth and gradual diffusion through all religious thinking of the supremacy of reason. This, which is rather a principle, or a mode of thinking, than a doctrine, may be properly enough called *Rationalism.* This term is used in this country with so much laxity that it is impossible to define the sense in which it is generally intended. But it is often taken to mean a system opposed to revealed religion imported into this country from Germany at the beginning of the present century.[11] A person, however, who surveys the course of English theology during the eighteenth century will have no difficulty in recognising that throughout all discussions, underneath all controversies, and common to all parties, lies the assumption of the supremacy of reason in matters of religion. The Kantian Philosophy did but bring forward into light, and give scientific form and a recognised position to, a principle which had long unconsciously guided all treatment of religious topics both in Germany and in England.[12] Rationalism was not an anti-Christian sect outside the Church making war against religion. It was a habit of thought ruling all minds, under the conditions of which all alike tried to make good the peculiar opinions they might happen to cherish. The Churchman differed from the Socinian, and the Socinian from the Deist, as to the number of articles in his creed; but all alike consented to test their belief by the rational evidence for it.[13] Whether given doctrines or miracles were conformable to reason was not disputed between the defence and the assault; but that all doctrines were to stand or fall by that criterion was not questioned. The principles and the priority of natural religion formed the common hypothesis on the ground of which the disputants argued whether anything, and what, had been subsequently communicated to man in a supernatural way. The line between those who believed much and those who believed little cannot be sharply drawn. Some of the so-called Deists were, in fact, Socinians; as Toland, who expressly admits all those parts of the New Testament revelation which are, or seem to him, comprehensible by reason. (*Christianity not Mysterious.*) Nor is there any ground for thinking that Toland was insincere in his profession of rational Christianity, as was insinuated by his opponents—*e.g.* Leland. (*View of the Deistical Writers*, vol. i. p. 49.) A more candid adversary, Leibnitz, who knew Toland personally, is 'glad to believe that the design of this author, a man of no common ability, and as I think, a well-disposed person, was to withdraw men from speculative theology to the practice of its precepts.' (*Annotatiunculae subitaneae.*)[14] Hardly one here and there, as Hume, professed Rationalism in the extent of Atheism; the great majority of writers were employed in constructing a *via media* between Atheism and Athanasianism, while the most orthodox were diligently 'hewing and chiselling Christianity into an intelligible human system, which they then represented, as thus mutilated, as affording a remarkable evidence of the truth of the Bible.' (*Tracts for the Times*, vol. ii. No. 73.) The title of Locke's treatise, *The Reasonableness of Christianity*, may be said to have been the solitary thesis of Christian theology in England for great part of a century.[15]

[5] If we are to put chronological limits to this system of religious opinion in England, we might, for the sake of a convenient landmark, say that it came in with the Revolution of 1688, and began to decline in vigour with the reaction against the Reform movement about 1830. Locke's *Reasonableness of Christianity* would thus open, and the commencement of the *Tracts for the Times* mark the fall of Rationalism. Not that chronology can ever be exactly applied to the mutations of opinion. For there were Rationalists before Locke, *e.g.* Hales of Eton, and other Arminians, nor has the Church of England unanimously adopted the principles of the *Tracts for the Times.* But if we were to follow up Cave's nomenclature, the appellation *Seculum rationalisticum* might be affixed to the eighteenth century with greater precision than many of his names apply to the previous centuries.[16] For it was not merely that Rationalism then obtruded itself as a heresy, or obtained a footing of toleration within the Church, but the rationalizing method possessed itself absolutely of the whole field of theology. With some trifling exceptions, the whole of religious literature was drawn in to the endeavour to 'prove the truth' of Christianity. The essay and the sermon, the learned treatise and the philosophical disquisition, Addison the polite writer, and Bentley the classical philologian (Addison: *Evidences of the Christian Religion*, a posthumous publication. Bentley: *Eight Sermons at Boyle's Lecture*, 1692), the astronomer Newton (*Four Letters, &c.*, Lond. 1756), no less than the theologians by profession, were all engaged upon the same task.[17] To one book of A. Collins, *A Discourse on the Grounds and Reasons of the Christian Religion*, Lond. 1724, are counted no less than thirty-five answers.[18] Dogmatic theology had ceased to exist; the exhibition of religious truth for practical purposes was confined to a few obscure writers. Every one who had anything to say on sacred subjects drilled it into an array of argument against a supposed objector. Christianity appeared made for nothing else but to be 'proved;' what use to make of it when it was proved was not much thought about. Reason was at first offered as the basis of faith, but gradually became its substitute. The mind never advanced as far as the stage of belief, for it was unceasingly engaged in reasoning up to it. The only quality in Scripture which was dwelt upon was its 'credibility.' Even the 'Evangelical' school, which had its origin in a reaction against the dominant Rationalism, and began in endeavours to kindle religious feeling, was obliged to succumb at last. It, too, drew out its rational 'scheme of Christianity,' in which the atonement was made the central point of a system, and the death of Christ was accounted for as necessary to satisfy the Divine Justice.[19]

[6] This whole rationalist age must again be subdivided into two periods, the theology of which, though belonging to the common type, has distinct specific characters. These periods are of nearly equal length, and we may conveniently take the middle year of the century, 1750, as our terminus of division. Though both periods were engaged upon the proof of Christianity, the distinction between them is that the first period was chiefly devoted to the internal, the second to the external, attestations. In the first period the main endeavour was to show that there was nothing in the contents of the revelation which was not agreeable to reason. In the

second, from 1750 onwards, the controversy was narrowed to what are usually called the 'Evidences,' or the historical proof of the genuineness and authenticity of the Christian records. From this distinction of topic arises an important difference of value between the theological produce of the two periods. A great injustice is done to the 18th century, when its whole speculative product is set down under the description of that Old Bailey theology in which, to use Johnson's illustration, the Apostles are being tried once a week for the capital crime of forgery.[20] This evidential school—the school of Lardner, Paley, and Whately—belongs strictly to the latter half only of the period now under consideration.[21] This school, which treated the exterior evidence, was the natural sequel and supplement of that which had preceded it, which dealt with the intrinsic credibility of the Christian revelation. This historical succession of the schools is the logical order of the argument. For when we have first shown that the facts of Christianity are not incredible, the whole burden of proof is shifted to the evidence that the facts did really occur. Neither branch of the argument can claim to be religious instruction at all, but the former does incidentally enter upon the substance of the Gospel. It may be philosophy rather than theology, but it raises in its course some of the most momentous problems which can engage the human mind. On the other hand, a mind which occupies itself with the 'external evidences' knows nothing of the spiritual intuition, of which it renounces at once the difficulties and the consolations. The supply of evidences in what for the sake of a name may be called the Georgian period (1750–1830), was not occasioned by any demands of controversy. The attacks through the press were nearly at an end, the Deists had ceased to be. The clergy continued to manufacture evidence as an ingenious exercise, a literature which was avowedly professional, a study which might seem theology without being it, which could awaken none of the scepticism then dormant beneath the surface of society. Evidences are not edged tools; they stir no feeling; they were the proper theology of an age, whose literature consisted in writing Latin hexameters.[22] The orthodox school no longer dared to scrutinize the contents of revelation. The preceding period had eliminated the religious experience, the Georgian had lost besides, the power of using the speculative reason.

The historical investigation, indeed, of the *Origines* of Christianity is a study scarcely second in importance to a philosophical arrangement of its doctrines.[23] But for a genuine inquiry of this nature the English writers of the period had neither the taste nor the knowledge. Gibbon alone approached the true difficulties, but met only with opponents 'victory over whom was a sufficient humiliation.' (*Autobiography*.)[24] No Englishman will refuse to join with Coleridge in 'the admiration' he expresses 'for the head and heart' of Paley, 'the incomparable grace, propriety, and persuasive facility of his writings.' (*Aids to Reflection*, p. 401.)[25] But Paley had unfortunately dedicated his powers to a factitious thesis; his demonstration, however perfect, is in unreal matter. The case, as the apologists of that day stated it, is wholly conventional. The breadth of their assumptions is out of all proportion to the narrow dimensions of the point they succeed in proving. Of an honest critical enquiry into the origin and composition of the canonical writings there is but one trace, Herbert Marsh's Lectures at Cambridge, and that was suggested from a foreign source, and died away without exciting imitators. That investigation, introduced by a bishop and a professor of divinity, has scarcely yet obtained a footing in the English Church.[26] But it is excluded, not from a conviction of its barrenness, but from a fear that it might prove too fertile in results. This unwholesome state of theological feeling among us, is perhaps traceable in part to the falsetto of the evidential method of the last generation. We cannot justify, but we may perhaps make our predecessors bear part of the blame of, that inconsistency, which while it professes that its religious belief rests on historical evidence, refuses to allow that evidence to be freely examined in open court.

[8] It seems, indeed, a singular infelicity that the construction of the historical proof should have been the task which the course of events allotted to the latter half of the 18th century. The critical knowledge of antiquity had disappeared from the Universities. The past, discredited by a false conservatism, was regarded with aversion, and the minds of men directed habitually to the future, some with fear, others with hope. 'The disrespect in which history was held by the French *philosophes* is notorious; one of the soberest of them, D'Alembert, we believe, was the author of the wish that all record of past events could be blotted out.' (Mill, *Dissertations*, vol. i. p. 426.) The same sentiment was prevalent, though not in the same degree, in this country.[27] Hume writing to an Englishman in 1756, speaks of 'your countrymen' as 'given over to barbarous and absurd faction.' Of his own history the publisher, Millar, told him he had only sold forty-five copies in a twelvemonth. (*My Own Life*, p. 5.)[28] Warburton had long before complained of the Chronicles published by Hearne that 'there is not one that is not a disgrace to letters; most of them are so to common sense, and some even to human nature.' (Parr's *Tracts, &c.*, p. 109.)[29] The oblivion into which the remains of Christian antiquity had sunk, till disinterred by the Tractarian movement, is well known. Having neither the critical tools to work with, nor the historical materials to work upon, it is no wonder if they failed in their art. Theology had almost died out when it received a new impulse and a new direction from Coleridge. The evidence-makers ceased from their futile labours all at once, as beneath the spell of some magician. Englishmen heard with as much surprise as if the doctrine was new, that the Christian faith, the Athanasian Creed, of which they had come to wish that the Church was well rid, was 'the perfection of human intelligence;' that, 'the compatibility of a document with the conclusions of self-evident reason, and with the laws of conscience, is a condition *a priori* of any evidence adequate to the proof of its having been revealed by God,' and that this 'is a principle clearly laid down by Moses and St. Paul;' lastly, that 'there are mysteries in Christianity, but these mysteries are reason, reason in its highest form of self-affirmation.' (*Aids to Reflection*, pref. *Lit. Remains*, iii. 293.)[30] In this position of Coleridge, the rationalist theology of England, which was in the last stage of decay and dotage, seemed to recover a second youth, and to revert at once to the point from which it had started a century before.[31]

Should the religious historian then acknowledge that the impatient contempt with which 'the last century' is now spoken of, is justifiable with respect to the later period, with its artificial monotone of proof that is no proof, he will by no means allow the same of the earlier period 1688–1750. The superiority which the theological writing of this period has over that which succeeded it, is to be referred in part to the superiority of the internal, over the external, proof of Christianity, as an object of thought.[32]

Both methods alike, as methods of argumentative proof, place the mind in an unfavourable attitude for the consideration of religious truth. It is like removing ourselves for the purpose of examining an object to the furthest point from which the object is visible. Neither the external nor the internal evidences are properly theology at all. Theology is—1st, and primarily, the contemplative, speculative habit, by means of which the mind places itself already in another world than this; a habit begun here, to be raised to perfect vision hereafter. 2ndly, and in an inferior degree, it is ethical and regulative of our conduct as men, in those relations which are temporal and transitory. Argumentative proof that such knowledge is possible can never be substituted for the knowledge without detriment to the mental habit. What is true of an individual is true of an age. When an age is found occupied in proving its creed, this is but a token that the age has ceased to have a proper belief in it. Nevertheless, there is a difference in this respect between the sources from which proof may be fetched. Where it is busied in establishing the 'genuineness and authenticity' of the books of Scripture, neglecting its religious lessons, and drawing out instead 'the undesigned coincidences,' Rationalism is seen in its dullest and least spiritual form.[33] When, on the other hand, the contents of the Revelation are being freely examined, and reason as it is called, but really the philosophy in vogue, is being applied to determine whether the voice be the voice of God or not, the reasoner is indeed approaching his subject from a false point of view, but he is still engaged with the eternal verities. The reason has prescribed itself an impossible task when it has undertaken to prove, instead of evolve them; to argue instead of appropriate them. But anyhow, it is handling them; and by the contact is raised in some measure to the 'height of that great argument.'[34]

This acknowledgment seems due to the period now referred to. It is, perhaps, rather thinking of its pulpit eloquence than its controversies, that Professor Fraser does not hesitate to call this 'the golden age of English theology.' (*Essays in Philosophy*, p. 205.)[35] Such language, as applied to our great preachers, was once matter of course, but would now hardly be used by any Anglican, and has to be sought for in the mouth of members of another communion. The names which once commanded universal homage among us—the Souths, Barrows, Tillotsons, Sherlocks,—excite, perhaps, only a smile of pity.[36] Literary taste is proverbially inconstant; but theological is still more so, for here we have no rule or chart to guide us but the taste of our age. Bossuet, Bourdaloue, and Massillon have survived a dozen political revolutions.[37] We have no classical theology, though we have not had a political revolution since 1660. For in this subject matter the most of Englishmen have no other standard of merit than the prejudices of sect. Eminence only marks out a great man for more cordial hatred; every flippant High Church reviewer has learnt to fling at Locke, the father of English Rationalism, and the greatest name among its worthies. Others are, perhaps, only less disliked because less known; '*qui n'a pas de lecteurs, n'a pas d'adversaires*.'[38] The principal writers in the Deistical Controversy, either side of it, have expiated the attention they once engrossed by as universal an oblivion.

[12] The Deistical Controversy, the all-absorbing topic of religious writers and preachers during the whole of this first period, has pretty well-defined limits. Stillingfleet, who died Bishop of Worcester in the last year (1699) of the seventeenth century, marks the transition from the old to the new argument. In the six folios of Stillingfleet's works may be found the latest echoes of the Romanist Controversy, and the first declaration of war against Locke.[39] The Deistical Controversy attained its greatest intensity in the twenties (1720–1740), after the subsidence of the Bangorian controversy, which for a time had diverted attention to itself, and it gradually died out towards the middle of the century.[40] The decay of interest in the topic is sufficiently marked by the fact that the opinions of Hume failed to stimulate curiosity or antagonism. His *Treatise of Human Nature* (1739) 'fell dead-born from the press,' and the only one of his philosophical writings which was received with favour on its first appearance was one on the new topic—*Political Discourses* (1752). Of this he says 'it was the only work of mine which was successful on the first publication, being well received both abroad and at home.' (*My Own Life*.)[41] Bolingbroke, who died in 1751, was the last of the professed Deists. When his works were brought out by his executor, Mallet, in 1754, the interest in them was already gone; they found the public cold or indisposed. It was a rusty blunderbuss, which he need not have been afraid to have discharged himself, instead of 'leaving half-a-crown to a Scotchman to let it off after his death.' (*Boswell*, p. 88.)[42] To talk Deism had ceased to be fashionable as soon as it ceased to attract attention.

[13] The rationalism, which is the common character of all the writers of this time, is a method rather than a doctrine; an unconscious assumption rather than a principle from which they reason. They would, however, all have consented in statements such as the following[43]: Bp. Gibson, *Second Pastoral Letter*, 1730. 'Those among us who have laboured of late years to set up reason against revelation would make it pass for an established truth, that if you will embrace revelation you must of course quit your reason, which, if it were true, would doubtless be a strong prejudice against revelation. But so far is this from being true, that *it is universally acknowledged that revelation itself is to stand or fall by the test of reason*, or, in other words, according as reason finds the evidences of its coming from God to be or not to be sufficient and conclusive, and the matter of it to contradict or not contradict the natural notions which reason gives us of the being and attributes of God.'[44]

[14] Prideaux (Humphrey, Dean of Norwich), *Letter to the Deists*, 1748. 'Let what

is written in all the books of the N. T. be tried by that which is the touchstone of all religions, I mean that religion of nature and reason which God has written in the hearts of every one of us from the first creation; and if it varies from it in any one particular, if it prescribes any one thing which may in the minutest circumstances thereof be contrary to its righteousness, I will then acknowledge this to be an argument against us, strong enough to overthrow the whole cause, and make all things else that can be said for it totally ineffectual for its support.'[45]

5] Tillotson (Archbishop of Canterbury), *Sermons*, vol. iii. p. 485. 'All our reasonings about revelation are necessarily gathered by our natural notions about religion, and therefore he who sincerely desires to do the will of God is not apt to be imposed on by vain pretences of divine revelation; but if any doctrine be proposed to him which is pretended to come from God, he measures it by those sure and steady notions which he has of the divine nature and perfections; he will consider the nature and tendency of it, or whether it be a doctrine according to godliness, such as is agreeable to the divine nature and perfections, and tends to make us like unto God; if it be not, though an angel should bring it, he would not receive it.'[46]

] Rogers (John, D.D.), *Sermons at Boyle's Lecture*, 1727, p. 59. 'Our religion desires no other favour than a sober and dispassionate examination. It submits its grounds and reasons to an unprejudiced trial, and hopes to approve itself to the conviction of any equitable enquirer.'[47]

] Butler, (Jos., Bp. of Durham), *Analogy, &c.*, pt. 2, ch. 1. 'Indeed, if in revelation there be found any passages, the seeming meaning of which is contrary to natural religion, we may most certainly conclude such seeming meaning not to be the real one.' *Ibid.*, ch. 8: 'I have argued upon the principles of the fatalists, which I do not believe; and have omitted a thing of the utmost importance which I do believe: the moral fitness and unfitness of actions, prior to all will whatever, which I apprehend as certainly to determine the divine conduct, as speculative truth and falsehood necessarily determine the divine judgment.'[48]

To the same effect the leading preacher among the Dissenters, James Foster, *Truth and Excellency of the Christian Revelation*, 1731. 'The faculty of reason which God hath implanted in mankind, however it may have been abused and neglected in times past, will, whenever they begin to exercise it aright, enable them to judge of all these things. As by means of this they were capable of discovering at first the being and perfections of God, and that he governs the world with absolute wisdom, equity, and goodness, and what those duties are which they owe to him and to one another, they must be as capable, if they will divest themselves of prejudice, and reason impartially, of rectifying any mistakes they may have fallen into about these important points. It matters not whether they have hitherto thought right or wrong, nor indeed whether they have thought at all; let them but begin to consider seriously and examine carefully and impartially, and they must be able to find out all those truths which as reasonable creatures they are capable of knowing, and which affect their duty and happiness.'[49]

[19] Finally, Warburton, displaying at once his disdain and his ignorance of catholic theology, affirms on his own authority, *Works* iii. p. 620, 'the image of God in which man was at first created, lay in the faculty of reason only.'[50]

[20] But it is needless to multiply quotations. The received theology of the day taught on this point the doctrine of Locke, as clearly stated by himself. (*Essay*, B. iv. ch. 19. §4.) 'Reason is natural revelation, whereby the eternal Father of light and fountain of all knowledge communicates to mankind that portion of truth which he has laid within the reach of their natural faculties; revelation is natural reason enlarged by a new set of discoveries communicated by God immediately, which reason vouches the truth of, by the testimony and proofs it gives, that they come from God. So that he that takes away reason to make way for revelation, puts out the light of both, and does much-what the same as if he would persuade a man to put out his eyes the better to receive the remote light of an invisible star by a telescope.'[51]

[21] According to this assumption, a man's religious belief is a result which issues at the end of an intellectual process. In arranging the steps of this process, they conceived natural religion to form the first stage of the journey. That stage theologians of all shades and parties travelled in company. It was only when they had reached the end of it that the Deists and the Christian apologists parted. The former found that the light of reason which had guided them so far indicated no road beyond. The Christian writers declared that the same natural powers enabled them to recognise the truth of revealed religion. The sufficiency of natural religion thus became the turning point of the dispute. The natural law of right and duty, argued the Deists, is so absolutely perfect that God could not add anything to it. It is commensurate with all the real relations in which man stands. To suppose that God has created artificial relations, and laid upon man positive precepts, is to take away the very notion of morality. The moral law is nothing but the conditions of our actual being, apparent alike to those of the meanest and of the highest capacity. It is inconsistent with this to suppose that God has gone on to enact arbitrary statutes, and to declare them to man in an obscure and uncertain light. This was the ground taken by the great champion of Deism—Tindal, and expressed in the title of the treatise which he published in 1732, when upwards of seventy, *Christianity as old as the Creation; or, the Gospel a Republication of the Religion of Nature.*[52] This was the point which the Christian defenders laboured most, to construct the bridge which should unite the revealed to the natural. They never demur to making the Natural the basis on which the Christian rests, to considering the natural knowledge of God as the starting point both of the individual mind and of the human race. This assumption is necessary to their scheme, in which revelation is an argument addressed to the reason. Christianity is a *résumé* of the knowledge of God already attained by reason, and a disclosure of further truths. These further truths could not have been thought out by reason; but when divinely communicated, they approve themselves to the same reason which has already put us in possession of so much. The new truths are not of another order of ideas, for

'Christianity is a particular scheme under the general plan of Providence,' (*Analogy*, pt. 2, ch. 4,) and the whole scheme is of a piece and uniform.[53] 'If the dispensation be indeed from God, all the parts of it will be seen to be the correspondent members of one entire whole, which orderly disposition of things essential to a religious system will assure us of the true theory of the Christian faith.' (Warburton, *Divine Legation, &c.*, B. ix. Introd. *Works*, vol. iii. p. 600.)[54] 'How these relations are made known, whether by reason or revelation, makes no alteration in the case, because the duties arise out of the relations themselves, not out of the manner in which we are informed of them.' (*Analogy*, pt. 2, ch. 1.)[55] 'Those very articles of belief and duties of obedience, which were formerly natural with respect to their manner of promulgation, are now in the declaration of them also supernatural.' (Ferguson, *Reason in Religion*, 1675, p. 29.)[56] The relations to the Redeemer and the Sanctifier are not artificial, but as real as those to the Maker and Preserver, and the obligations arising out of the one set of relations as natural as those arising out of the other.

[22] The deference paid to natural religion is further seen in the attempts to establish *a priori* the *necessity* of a revelation. To make this out it was requisite to show that the knowledge with which reason could supply us was inadequate to be the guide of life, yet reason must not be too much depressed, inasmuch as it was needed for the proof of Christianity. On the one hand, the moral state of the heathen world prior to the preaching of Christianity, and of Pagan and savage tribes in Africa and America now, the superstitions of the most civilized nations of antiquity, the intellectual follies of the wisest philosophers, are exhibited in great detail. The usual arguments of scepticism on the conscious weakness of reason are brought forward, but not pushed very far. Reason is to be humiliated so far as that supernatural light shall be seen to be necessary, but it must retain its competence to judge of the evidence of this supernatural message. Natural religion is insufficient as a light, and a motive to show us our way and to make us walk in it; it is sufficient as a light, and a motive to lead us to revelation, and to induce us to embrace it. How much of religious truth was contained in natural knowledge, or how much was due to supernatural communication, was very variously estimated. Locke, especially, had warned against our liability to attribute to reason much of moral truth that had in fact been derived from revelation.[57] But the uncertainty of the demarcation between the two is only additional proof of the identity of the scheme which they disclose between them. The whole of God's government and dealings with man form one wide-spread and consistent scheme, of which natural reason apprehends a part, and of which Christianity was the manifestation of a further part. Consistently herewith they treated natural religion, not as an historical dispensation, but as an abstract demonstration. There never was a time when mankind had realized or established an actual system of natural religion, but it lies always potentially in his reason. It held the same place as the social contract in political history. The 'original contract' had never had historical existence, but it was a hypothesis necessary to explain the existing fact of society. No society had, in

fact, arisen on that basis, yet it is the theoretical basis on which all society can be shown to rest. So there was no time or country where the religion of nature had been fully known, yet the natural knowledge of God is the only foundation in the human mind on which can be built a rational Christianity. Though not an original condition of any part of mankind, it is an ever-originating condition of every human mind, as soon as it begins to reason on the facts of religion, rendering all the moral phenomena available for the construction of a scientific theory of religion.[58]

[23] In accordance with this view they interpreted the passages in St. Paul which speak of the religion of the heathen; e.g., Rom. ii. 14. Since the time of Augustine (*De Spir. et Lit.* §27) the orthodox interpretation had applied this verse, either to the Gentile converts, or to the favoured few among the heathen who had extraordinary divine assistance. The Protestant expositors, to whom the words 'do by nature the things contained in the law,' could never bear their literal force, sedulously preserved the Augustinian explanation.[59] Even the Pelagian Jeremy Taylor is obliged to gloss the phrase 'by nature,' thus: 'By fears and secret opinions which the Spirit of God who is never wanting to men in things necessary was pleased to put into the hearts of men.' (*Duct. Dubit.* B. ii. ch. 1, §3.) The rationalists, however, find the expression 'by nature' in its literal sense exactly conformable to their own views, (Wilkins, *Of Nat. Rel.* ii. C. 9) and have no difficulty even in supposing the acceptableness of these works, and the salvability of those who do them. Burnet on Art. xviii., in his usual confused style of eclecticism, suggests both opinions without seeming to see that they are incompatible relics of divergent schools of doctrine.[60]

[24] Consequent with such a theory of religion was their notion of its practical bearings. Christianity was a republication of the moral law—a republication rendered necessary by the helpless state of moral debasement into which the world was come by the practice of vice. The experience of ages had proved that, though our duty might be discoverable by the light of nature, yet virtue was not able to maintain itself in the world without additional sanctions. The disinterestedness of virtue was here a point much debated. The Deists, in general, argued from the notion of morality, that so far as any private regard to my own interest, whether present or future, influenced my conduct, so far my actions had no moral worth. From this they drew the inference that the rewards and punishments of Christianity—these additional sanctions—could not be a divine ordinance, inasmuch as they were subversive of morality. The orthodox writers had to maintain the theory of rewards and punishments in such a way as not to be inconsistent with the theory of the disinterestedness of virtue which they had made part of their theology. Even here no precise line can be drawn between the Deistical and the Christian moralists. For we find Shaftesbury placing in a very clear light the mode in which religious sanctions do, in fact, as society is constituted, support and strengthen virtue in the world, though he does not deny that the principle of virtue in the individual may suffer from the selfish passion being appealed to by the hope of reward or the fear of punishment. (*Characteristicks*, vol. ii. p. 66.)[61] But with

whatever variation in individual disputants, the tone of the discussions is unmistakeable. When Collins was asked, 'Why he was careful to make his servants go to Church?' he is said to have answered, 'I do it that they may neither rob nor murder me.'[62] This is but an exaggerated form of the practical religion of the age. Tillotson's Sermon (*Works*, vol. iii. p. 43) '*On the Advantages of Religion to Societies*,' is like Collins' reply at fuller length.[63] The Deists and their opponents alike assume that the purpose of the supernatural interference of the Deity in revelation must have been to secure the good behaviour of man in this world; that the future life and our knowledge of it may be a means to this great end; that the next world, if it exist at all, bears that relation to the present. We are chiefly familiar with these views from their having been long the butt of the Evangelical pulpit, a chief topic in which was to decry the mere 'legal' preaching of a preceding age. To abstain from vice, to cultivate virtue, to fill our station in life with propriety, to bear the ills of life with resignation, and to use its pleasures moderately—these things are indeed not little; perhaps no one can name in his circle of friends a man whom he thinks equal to these demands. Yet the experience of the last age has shown us unmistakeably that where this is our best ideal of life, whether, with the Deists, we establish the obligation of morality on 'independent' grounds; or, with the orthodox, add the religious sanction—in Mr. Mill's rather startling mode of putting it (*Dissertations*, vol. ii. p. 436), 'Because God is stronger than we, and able to damn us if we don't'—it argues a sleek and sordid epicurism, in which religion and a good conscience have their place among the means by which life is to be made comfortable.[64] To accuse the divines of this age of a leaning to Arminianism is quite beside the mark. They do not intend to be other than orthodox. They did not take the Arminian side rather than the Calvinistic in the old conflict or concordat between Faith and Works, between Justification and Sanctification.[65] They had dropt the terminology, and with it the mode of thinking, which the terms implied. They had adopted the language and ideas of the moralists. They spoke not of sin, but of vice, and of virtue, not of works. In the old Protestant theology actions had only a certain exterior relation to the justified man; 'gute fromme Werke machen nimmermehr einen guten frommen Mann, sondern ein guter frommer Mann macht gute Werke.' (*Luther.*)[66] Now, our conduct was thought of, not as a product or efflux of our character, but as regulated by our understanding; by a perception of relations, or a calculation of consequences. This intellectual perception of regulative truth is religious Faith. Faith is no longer the devout condition of the entire inner man.[67] Its dynamic nature, and interior working, are not denied, but they are unknown; and religion is made to regulate life from without, through the logical proof of the being and attributes of God, upon which an obligation to obey him can be raised.

5] The preachers of any period are not to be censured for adapting their style of address and mode of arguing to their hearers. They are as necessarily bound to the preconceived notions, as to the language, of those whom they have to exhort. The pulpit does not mould the forms into which religious thought in any age runs, it simply accommodates itself to those that exist. For this very reason, because they must follow and cannot lead, sermons are the surest index of the prevailing religious feeling of their age. When we are reminded of the powerful influence of the pulpit at the Reformation, in the time of the Long Parliament, or at the Methodist revival, it must also be remembered that these preachers addressed a different class of society from that for which our classical pulpit oratory was written.[68] If it could be said that 'Sherlock, Hare, and Gibson preach in vain,' it was because the populace were gone to hear mad Henley on his tub.[69] To charge Tillotson or Foster with not moving the masses which Whitefield moved, is to charge them with not having preached to another congregation than that to which they had to preach.[70] Nor did they preach to empty pews, though their carefully-written 'discourses' could never produce effects such as are recorded of Burnet's extempore addresses, when he 'was often interrupted by the deep hum of his audience, and when, after preaching out the hour-glass, he held it up in his hand, the congregation clamorously encouraged him to go on till the sand had run off once more.' (*Macaulay*, vol. ii. p. 177.)[71] The dramatic oratory of Whitefield could not have sustained its power over the same auditors; he had a fresh congregation every Sunday. And in the judgment of one quite disposed to do justice to Whitefield there is nothing in his sermons such as are printed. Johnson (ap. *Boswell*) speaking of the comparisons drawn between the preaching in the Church and that of the Methodists to the disadvantage of the former, says, 'I never treated Whitefield's ministry with contempt; I believe he did good. But when familiarity and noise claim the praise due to knowledge, art, and elegance, we must beat down such pretensions.'[72] It is, however, the substance, and not the manner, of the classical sermons of the eighteenth century which is meant, when they are complained of as cold and barren. From this accusation they cannot be vindicated. But let it be rightly understood that it is a charge not against the preachers but against the religious ideas of the period. In the pulpit, the speaker has no choice but to take his audience as he finds them. He can but draw them on to the conclusions already involved in their premises. He cannot supply them with a new set of principles, and alter their fixed forms of thought. The ideas out of which the Protestant or the Puritan movement proceeded were generated elsewhere than in the pulpit.

[26] The Rationalist preachers of the eighteenth century are usually contrasted with the Evangelical pulpit which displaced them. Mr. Neale has compared them disadvantageously with the mediaeval preachers in respect of Scripture knowledge. He selects a sermon of the eighteenth and one of the twelfth century; the one by the well-known Evangelical preacher John Newton, Rector of St. Mary Woolnoth; the other by Guarric, Abbot of Igniac. 'In Newton's sermon we find nine references to the Gospels, two to the Epistles, nine to the Prophets, one to the Psalms, and none to any other part of Scripture. In the sermon of Guarric we find seven references to the Gospels, one the Epistles, twenty-two to the Psalms, nine to the Prophets, and eighteen to other parts of Scripture. Thus the total number of quotations made by the Evangelical preacher is twenty-one, by Guarric fifty-seven, and this in

sermons of about equal length.' (*Mediaeval Preaching*, Introd. xxvi.)[73] Mr. Neale has, perhaps, not been fortunate in his selection of a specimen sermon. For having the curiosity to apply this childish test to a sermon of John Blair, taken at random out of his four volumes, I found the number of texts quoted thirty-seven.[74] But, passing this by, Mr. Neale misses his inference. He means to show how much more Scripture knowledge was possessed by the preachers of the 'dark ages.' This is very likely, if familiarity with the mere words of the Vulgate version be Scripture knowledge. But it is not proved by the abstinence of the eighteenth century preacher from the use of Biblical phraseology. The fact, so far as it is one, only shows that our divines understood Scripture differently, some will say better, than the Middle Age ecclesiastic. The latter had, in the mystical theology of the Christian Church, a rich store of religious sentiment, which it was an exercise of their ingenuity to find in the poetical books of the Hebrew canon. Great part of this fanciful allegorizing is lost, apart from the Vulgate translation. But of this the more learned of them were quite aware, and on their theory of Scripture interpretation, according to which the Church was its guaranteed expositor, the verbal meanings of the Latin version were equally the inspired sense of the sacred record. It was otherwise with the English divine of the eighteenth century. According to the then received view of Scripture, its meaning was not assigned by the Church, but its language was interpreted by criticism—*i.e.*, by reason. The aids of history, the ordinary rules of grammar and logic, were applied to find out what the sacred writers actually said. *That* was the meaning of Scripture, the message supernaturally communicated. Where each text of Scripture has but one sense, that sense in which the writer penned it, it can only be cited in that sense without doing it violence. This was the turn by which Selden so discomfited the Puritan divines, who, like the Catholic mystics, made Scripture words the vehicle of their own feelings. 'Perhaps in your little pocket Bibles with gilt leaves the translation may be thus, but the Greek or Hebrew signifies otherwise.' (Whitelocke, Johnson's *Life of Selden*, p. 303.)[75] If the preacher in the eighteenth century had allowed himself to make these allusions, the taste of his audience would have rejected them. He would have weakened his argument instead of giving it effect.

[27] No quality of these 'Discourses' strikes us more now than the good sense which pervades them. They are the complete reaction against the Puritan sermon of the 17th century. We have nothing far-fetched, fanciful, allegoric. The practice of our duty is recommended to us on the most undeniable grounds of prudence. Barrow had indulged in ambitious periods, and South had been jocular.[76] Neither of these faults can be alleged against the model sermon of the Hanoverian period. No topic is produced which does not compel our assent as soon as it is understood, and none is there which is not understood as soon as uttered. It is one man of the world speaking to another. Collins said of St. Paul, 'that he had a great respect for him as both a man of sense and a gentleman.'[77] He might have said the same of the best pulpit divines of his own time. They bear the closest resemblance to each other, because they all use the language of fashionable society, and say exactly the proper

thing. 'A person,' says Waterland, 'must have some knowledge of men, besides that of books, to succeed well here; and must have a kind of practical sagacity which nothing but the grace of God joined with recollection and wise observation can bring, to be able to represent truths to the life, or to any considerable degree of advantage.' This is from his recommendatory preface prefixed to an edition of Blair's Sermons (1739); not the Presbyterian Dr. Hugh Blair, but John Blair, the founder and first President of a Missionary College in Virginia, whose 'Sermons on the Beatitudes' were among the most approved models of the day, and recommended by the bishops to candidates for orders.[78] Dr. Hugh Blair's Sermons, which Johnson thought 'excellently written, both as to doctrine and language,' (ap. *Boswell*, p. 528), are in a different taste—that of the latter half of the century, when solid and sensible reasoning was superseded by polished periods and flowery rhetoric.[79] 'Polished as marble,' says Hugh J. Rose, 'but also as lifeless and as cold.' The sermons which Waterland recommends to young students of divinity comprise Tillotson, Sharp, Calamy, Sprat, Blackhall, Hoadly, South, Claggett, and Atterbury.[80] Of these, 'Sharp's, Calamy's, and Blackhall's are the best models for an easy, natural, and familiar way of writing. Sprat is fine, florid and elaborate in his style, artful in his method, and not so open as the former, but harder to be imitated. Hoadly is very exact and judicious, and both his sense and style just, close, and clear. The others are very sound, clear writers, only Scot[81] is too swelling and pompous, and South is something too full of wit and satire, and does not always observe a decorum in his style.' He advises the student to begin his divinity course with reading sermons, because 'they are the easiest, plainest, and most entertaining of any books of divinity; and might be digested into a better body of divinity than any that is yet extant.' (*Advice to a Young Student*, 1730).[82]

[28] Not only the pulpit, but the whole theological literature of the age, takes the same tone of appeal. Books are no longer addressed by the cloistered academic to a learnedly educated class, they are written by popular divines—'men of leisure,' Butler calls them—for the use of fashionable society.[83] There is an epoch in the history of letters when readers and writers change places; when it ceases to be the reader's business to come to the writer to be instructed, and the writer begins to endeavour to engage the attention of the reader. The same necessity was now laid upon the religious writer. He appeared at the bar of criticism, and must gain the wits, and the town. At the debate between the Deists and the Christian apologists the public was umpire. The time was past when Baxter 'talked about another world like one that had been there, and was come as a sort of express from thence to make a report concerning it.' (Calamy, *Life*, i. 220).[84] As the preacher now no longer spake with the authority of a heavenly mission, but laid the state of the argument before his hearers, so philosophy was no longer a self-centered speculation, an oracle of wisdom. The divine went out into the streets, with his demonstration of the being and attributes of God printed on a broadside; he solicits your assent in 'the new court-jargon.'[85] When Collins visited Lord Barrington at Tofts, 'as they were all men of letters, and had a taste for Scripture criticism, it is said to have been their

custom, after dinner, to have a Greek Testament laid on the table.' (*Biog. Brit.* Art. 'Barrington.')[86] These discussions were not necessarily unprofitable. Lord Bolingbroke 'was seldom in the company of the Countess of Huntingdon without discussing some topic beneficial to his eternal interests, and he always paid the utmost respect and deference to her ladyship's opinion.' (*Memoirs of Countess of Hunt.*, i. 180.)[87] Bishop Butler gives his clergy hints how to conduct themselves when 'sceptical and profane men bring up the subject (religion) at meetings of entertainment, and such as are of the freer sort; innocent ones, I mean, otherwise I should not suppose you would be present at them.' (*Durham Charge*, 1751).[88] Tindal's reconversion from Romanism is said to have been brought about by the arguments he heard in the coffee-houses. This anecdote, given in Curll's catchpenny 'Life,' rests, not on the bookseller's authority, which is worthless, but on that of the medical man who attended him in his last illness.[89] It was the same with the controversy on the Trinity, of which Waterland says, in 1723, that it was 'spread abroad among all ranks and degrees of men, and the Athanasian creed become the subject of common and ordinary conversation.' (*Critical Hist. of the Athan. Creed*, Introd.)[90] The Universities were invaded by the spirit of the age, and instead of taking students through a laborious course of philosophy, natural and moral, turned out accomplished gentlemen upon 'the classics' and a scantling of logic. Berkeley's ironical portrait of the modish philosopher is of date 1732. 'Lysicles smiled, and said he believed Euphranor had figured to himself philosophers in square caps and long gowns, but thanks to these happy times, the reign of pedantry was over. Our philosophers are of a very different kind from those awkward students who think to come at knowledge by poring on dead languages and old authors, or by sequestering themselves from the cares of the world to meditate in solitude and retirement. They are the best bred men of the age, men who know the world, men of pleasure, men of fashion, and fine gentlemen. EUPH.: I have some small notion of the people you mention, but should never have taken them for philosophers. CRI.: Nor would any one else till of late. The world was long under a mistake about the way to knowledge, thinking it lay through a tedious course of academical education and study. But among the discoveries of the present age, one of the principal is the finding out that such a method doth rather retard and obstruct, than promote knowledge. LYS.: I will undertake, a lad of fourteen, bred in the modern way, shall make a better figure, and be more considered in any drawing-room, or assembly of polite people, than one at four-and-twenty, who hath lain by a long time at school and college. He shall say better things, in a better manner, and be more liked by good judges. EUPH.: Where doth he pick up this improvement? CRI.: Where our grave ancestors would never have looked for it, in a drawing-room, a coffee-house, a chocolate-late-house, at the tavern, or groom-porter's. In these and the like fashionable places of resort, it is the custom for polite persons to speak freely on all subjects, religious, moral, or political. So that a young gentleman who frequents them is in the way of hearing many instructive lectures, seasoned with wit and raillery, and uttered with spirit. Three or four sentences from a man of quality, spoken with a good air, make more impression, and convey more knowledge, than a dozen dissertations in a dry academical way. . . . You may now commonly see a young lady, or a *petit maître* non-plus a divine or an old-fashioned gentleman, who hath read many a Greek and Latin author, and spent much time in hard methodical study.' (*Alciphron*, Dial. i. §11.)[91]

[29] Among a host of mischiefs thus arising, one positive good may be signalized. If there must be debate, there ought to be fair play; and of this, publicity is the best guarantee. To make the public arbiter in an abstract question of metaphysics is doubtless absurd, yet it is at least a safeguard against extravagance and metaphysical lunacy. The verdict of public opinion on such topics is worthless, but it checks the inevitable tendency of closet speculation to become visionary. There is but one sort of scepticism that is genuine, and deadly in proportion as it is real; that, namely, which is forced upon the mind by its experience of the hollowness of mankind; for 'men may be read, as well as books, too much.'[92] That other logical scepticism which is hatched by over-thinking can be cured by an easy remedy; ceasing to think.

[30] The objections urged against revelation in the course of the Deistical controversy were no chimaeras of a sickly brain, but solid charges; the points brought into public discussion were the points at which the revealed system itself impinges on human reason. No time can lessen whatever force there may be in the objection against a miracle; it is felt as strongly in one century as in another. The debate was not frivolous; the objections were worth answering, because they were not pitched metaphysically high. To a platonizing divine they look trivial; picked up in the street. So Origen naturally thought 'that a faith which could be shaken by such objections as those of Celsus was not worth much.' (*Cont. Cels.*, Pref. §4.)[93] Just such were the objections of the Deists; such as come spontaneously into the thoughts of practical men, who never think systematically, but who are not to be imposed upon by fancies. Persons sneer at the 'shallow Deism' of the last century; and it is customary to reply that the antagonist orthodoxy was at least as shallow. The truth is, the 'shallowness' imputed belongs to the mental sphere into which the debate was for the time transported. The philosophy of the age was not above its mission. 'Philosophy,' thought Thomas Reid, in 1764, 'has no other root but the principles of common sense; it grows out of them, it draws its nourishment from them; severed from this root, its honours wither, its sap is dried up, it dies and rots.' (*Inquiry, &c.*, Intr. §4.)[94] We, in the present generation, have seen the great speculative movement in Germany die out from this very cause, because it became divorced from the facts on which it speculated. Shut up in the Universities, it turned inwards on itself, and preyed on its own vitals. It has only been neglected by the world, because it first neglected the great facts in which the world has, and feels, an interest.

[31] If ever there was a time when abstract speculation was brought down from inaccessible heights and compelled to be intelligible, it was the period from the Revolution to the middle of the last century. Closet speculation had been

discredited; the cobwebs of scholasticism were exploded; the age of feverish doubt and egotistical introspection had not arrived. In that age the English higher education acquired its practical aim; an aim in which the development of the understanding, and the acquisition of knowledge are considered secondary objects to the formation of a sound secular judgment, of the 'scholar and the gentleman' of the old race of schoolmasters. Burke contrasting his own times with the preceding age 'considered our forefathers as deeper thinkers than ourselves, because they set a higher value on good sense than on knowledge in various sciences, and their good sense was derived very often from as much study and more knowledge, though of another sort.' (*Recollections by Samuel Rogers*, p. 81.)[95]

2] When a dispute is joined, e.g. on the origin and composition of the Gospels, it is, from the nature of the case, confined to an inner circle of Biblical scholars. The mass of the public must wait outside, and receive the result on their authority.[96] The religious public were very reluctant to resign the verse 1 John v. 7, but they did so at last on the just ground that after a philological controversy conducted with open doors, it had been decided to be spurious.[97] No serious man would consider a popular assembly a proper court to decide on the doctrine of transubstantiation, or on the Hegelian definition of God, though either is easily capable of being held up to the ridicule of the half-educated from the platform or the pulpit.[98] It is otherwise with the greater part of the points raised in the Deistical controversy. It is not the speculative reason of the few, but the natural conscience of the many, that questions the extirpation of the Canaanites, or the eternity of hell-torments.[99] These are points of divinity that are at once fundamental and popular. Butler, though not approving 'of entering into an argumentative defence of religion in common conversation,' recommends his clergy to do so from the pulpit on the ground that, 'such as are capable of seeing the force of objections, are capable also of seeing the force of the answers which are given to them.' (*Durham Charge*.)[100] If the philosophic intellect be dissatisfied with the answers which the divines of that day gave to the difficulties started, let it show how, on the rationalist hypothesis, these difficulties are removeable for the mass of those who feel them. The transcendental reason provides an answer which possibly satisfies itself; but to the common reason the answer is more perplexing than the difficulty it would clear.

] M. Villemain has remarked in Pascal, 'that foresight which revealed to him so many objections unknown to his generation, and which inspired him with the idea of fortifying and intrenching positions which were not threatened.' The objections which Pascal is engaged with are not only not those of his age, they are not such as could ever become general in any age. They are those of the higher reason, and the replies are from the same inspiration. Pascal's view of human depravity seems to the ordinary man but the despair and delirium of the self-tormenting ascetic. The cynical view of our fallen nature, however, is at least a possible view. It is well that it should be explored, and it will always have its prophets, Calvin or Rochefoucault. But to ordinary men an argument in favour of revelation, founded on such an assumption, will seem to be in contradiction to his daily experience. Pascal's *Pensées* stand alone; a work of individual genius, not belonging to any age.[101] The celebrity which the *Analogy* of Bishop Butler has gained is due to the opposite reason. It is no paradox to say that the merit of the *Analogy* lies in its want of originality. It came (1736) towards the end of the Deistical period. It is the result of twenty years' study—the very twenty years during which the Deistical notions formed the atmosphere which educated people breathed. The objections it meets are not new and unseasoned objections, but such as had worn well, and had borne the rub of controversy, because they were genuine. And it will be equally hard to find in the *Analogy* any topic in reply, which had not been suggested in the pamphlets and sermons of the preceding half century. Like Aristotle's physical and political treatises, it is a *résumé* of the discussions of more than one generation. Its admirable arrangement only is all its own. Its closely packed and carefully fitted order speaks of many years' contrivance. Its substance are the thoughts of a whole age, not barely compiled, but each reconsidered and digested. Every brick in the building has been rung before it has been relaid, and replaced in its true relation to the complex and various whole. In more than one passage we see that the construction of this fabric of evidence, which 'consists in a long series of things, one preparatory to and confirming another from the beginning of the world to the present time,' (*Durham Charge*) was what occupied Butler's attention. 'Compass of thought, even amongst persons of the lowest rank,' (*Pref. to Sermons*), is that form of the reflective faculty to which he is fond of looking both for good and evil. He never will forget that 'justice must be done to every part of a subject when we are considering it.' (*Sermon* iv.)[102] Harmony, and law, and order, he will suppose even where he does not find. The tendency of his reason was that which Bacon indicates; 'the spirit of a man being of an equal and uniform substance doth usually suppose and feign in nature a greater equality and uniformity than is in truth.' (*Advancement of Learning*.)[103] This is, probably, the true explanation of the 'obscurity' which persons sometimes complain of in Butler's style. The reason or matter he is producing is palpable and plain enough. But he is so solicitous to find its due place in the then stage of the argument, so scrupulous to give it its exact weight and no more, so careful in arranging its situation relatively to the other members of the proof, that a reader who does not bear in mind that 'the effect of the whole' is what the architect is preparing, is apt to become embarrassed, and to think that obscurity which is really logical precision. The generality of men are better qualified for understanding particulars one by one, than for taking a comprehensive view of the whole. The philosophical breadth which we miss in Butler's mode of conceiving is compensated for by this judicial breadth in his mode of arguing, which gives its place to each consideration, but regards rather the cumulative force of the whole. Many writers before Butler had insisted on this character of the Christian evidences. Dr. Jenkin, Margaret Professor at Cambridge, whose *Reasonableness and Certainty of the Christian Religion* was the 'Paley' of divinity students then, says, 'there is an excellency in every part of our religion separately considered, but the strength and vigour of each part is in the relation it has to the rest, and the several parts must be taken altogether, if we would have a true knowledge, and make a just estimate of the whole.' (*Reasonableness, &c.* Pt. ii. Pref. 1721.)[104] But Butler does not merely take the hint from others. It is so entirely the guiding rule of his hand and pen that it would appear to have been forced upon him by some peculiar experience of his own. It was in society, and not in his study, that he had learned the weight of the Deistical arguments. At the Queen's philosophical parties, where these topics were canvassed with earnestness and freedom, he must have often felt the impotence of reply in detail, and seen, as he says, 'how impossible it must be, in a cursory conversation, to unite all this into one argument, and represent it as it ought.' (*Durham Charge.*)[105] Hence his own labour to work up his materials into a connected framework, a methodized encyclopaedia of all the extant topics.

34] Not that he did not pay attention to the parts. Butler's eminence over his contemporary apologists is seen in nothing more than in that superior sagacity which rejects the use of any plea that is not entitled to consideration singly. In the other evidential books of the time we find a miscellaneous crowd of suggestions of very various value; never fanciful, but often trivial; undeniable, but weak as proof of the point they are brought to prove. Butler seems as if he had sifted these books, and retained all that was solid in them. If he built with brick, and not with marble, it was because he was not thinking of reputation, but of utility, and an immediate purpose. Mackintosh wished Butler had had the elegance and ornament of Berkeley.[106] They would have been sadly out of place. There was not a spark of the littleness of literary ambition about him. 'There was a certain naturalness in Butler's mind, which took him straight to the questions on which men differed around him. Generally it is safer to prove what no one denies, and easier to explain difficulties which no one has ever felt. A quiet reputation is best obtained in the literary quaestiunculae of important subjects. But a simple and straightforward man studies great topics because he feels a want of the knowledge which they contain. He goes straight to the real doubts and fundamental discrepancies, to those on which it is easy to excite odium, and difficult to give satisfaction; he leaves to others the amusing skirmishing and superficial literature accessory to such studies. Thus there is nothing light in Butler, all is grave, serious, and essential; nothing else would be characteristic of him.' (Bagehot, *Estimates, &c.*, p. 189.)[107] Though he has rifled their books he makes no display of reading. In the *Analogy* he never names the author he is answering. In the *Sermons* he quotes, directly, only Hobbes, Shaftesbury, Wollaston, Rochefoucauld, and Fenelon. From his writings we should infer that his reading was not promiscuous, even had he not himself given us to understand how much opportunity he had of seeing the idleness and waste of time occasioned by light reading. (*Sermons*, Pref.)[108]

] This popular appeal to the common reason of men, which is one characteristic of the rationalist period, was a first effort of English theology to find a new basis for doctrine which should replace those foundations which had failed it. The Reformation had destroyed the authority of the Church upon which Revelation had so long rested. The attempt of the Laudian divines to substitute the voice of the national Church for that of the Church universal had met with only very partial and temporary success. When the Revolution of 1688 introduced the freedom of the press and a general toleration, even that artificial authority which, by ignoring nonconformity, had produced an appearance of unity, and erected a conventional standard of truth and falsehood, fell to the ground. The old and venerated authority had been broken by the Reformation. The new authority of the Anglican establishment had existed in theory only, and never in fact, and the Revolution had crushed the theory, which was now confined to a small band of non-jurors. In reaction against Anglican 'authority,' the Puritan movement had tended to rest faith and doctrine upon the inward light within each man's breast. This tendency of the *new* Puritanism, which we may call Independency, was a development of the *old*, purely scriptural, Puritanism of Presbyterianism.[109] But it was its natural and necessary development. It was a consequence of the controversy with the establishment. For both the Church and Dissent agreed in acknowledging Scripture as their foundation, and the controversy turned on the interpreter of Scripture. Nor was the doctrine of the inner light, which individualized the basis of faith, confined to the Nonconformists. It was shared by a section of the Church, of whom Cudworth is the type, to whom 'Scripture faith is not a mere believing of historical things, and upon artificial arguments or testimonies only, but a certain higher and diviner power in the soul that peculiarly correspondeth with the Deity.' (*Intellectual System*, Pref.)[110] The inner light, or witness of the Spirit in the soul of the individual believer had, in its turn, fallen into discredit through the extravagances to which it had given birth. It was disowned alike by Churchmen and Nonconformists, who agree in speaking with contemptuous pity of the 'sectaries of the last age.' The re-action against individual religion led to this first attempt to base revealed truth on reason. And for the purpose for which reason was now wanted, the higher, or philosophic, reason was far less fitted than that universal understanding in which all men can claim a share. The 'inner light,' which had made each man the dictator of his own creed, had exploded in ecclesiastical anarchy. The appeal from the frantic discord of the enthusiasts to reason must needs be, not to an arbitrary or particular reason in each man, but to a *common* sense, a natural discernment, a reason of universal obligation. As it was to be universally binding, it must be generally recognisable. It must be something not confined to the select few, a gift of the self-styled elect, but a faculty belonging to all men of sound mind and average capacity. Truth must be accessible to 'the bulk of mankind.' It was a time when the only refuge from a hopeless maze, or wild chaos, seemed to be the rational consent of the sensible and unprejudiced. 'Have the bulk of mankind,' writes Locke, 'no other guide but accident and blind chance to conduct them to their happiness or misery? Are the current opinions and licensed guides of every country sufficient evidence and security to every man to venture his great concernments on? Or, can those be the certain and infallible oracles and standards of truth which teach one thing in Christendom, and another in Turkey? Or shall a poor countryman be eternally happy for having the chance to be born in Italy? Or a day labourer be unavoidably lost because he had the ill-luck to be born in England? How ready some men may be to say some of these things, I will not here examine; but this I am sure, that men must allow one or other of these to be true, or else grant that God has furnished men with faculties sufficient to direct them in the way they should take, if they will but seriously employ them that way, when their ordinary vocations allow them the leisure.' (*Essay*, Book iv. ch. 19, §3.)[111]

[36] Such an attempt to secure a foundation in a new consensus will obviously forfeit depth to gain in comprehensiveness. This phase of rationalism—'Rationalismus vulgaris'—resigns the transcendental, that it may gain adherents. It wants, not the elect, but all men. It cannot afford to embarrass itself with the attempt to prove what all may not be required to receive. Accordingly there can be no mysteries in Christianity. The word μυστήριον, as Archbishop Whately points out (*Essays*, 2nd ser., 5th ed., p. 288), always means in the New Testament not that which is incomprehensible, but that which was once a secret, though now it is revealed it is no longer so.[112] Whately, who elsewhere (Paley's *Evidences*, new ed.) speaks so contemptuously of the 'cast-off clothes' of the Deists, is here but adopting the argument of Toland in his *Christianity not Mysterious*. (Cf. Balguy, *Discourses*, p. 237.)[113] There needs no special 'preparation of heart' to receive the Gospel, the evidences of religion are sufficient to convince every unprejudiced inquirer. Unbelievers are blameworthy as deaf to an argument which is so plain that they cannot but understand it, and so convincing that they cannot but be aware of his force. Under such self-imposed conditions religious proof seems to divest itself of all that is divine, and out of an excess of accommodation to the recipient faculty to cease to be a transforming thought. Rationalism can object to the old sacramental system that it degrades a spiritual influence into a physical effect. But rationalism itself, in order to make the proof of revelation universal, is obliged to resolve religion into the moral government of God by rewards and punishments, and especial the latter. It is this anthropomorphic conception of God as the 'Governor of the universe,' which is presented to us in the theology of the Hanoverian divines, a theology which excludes on principle not only all that is poetical in life, but all that is sublime in religious speculation.[114] 'To degrade religion to the position of a mere purveyor of motive to morality is not more dishonourable to the ethics which must ask, than to the religion which will render such assistance.' (A. J. Vaughan, *Essays*, vol. 1. p. 61.)[115] It is this character that makes the reading even of the *Analogy* so depressing to the soul, as Tholuck (*Vermischte Schriften*, i. 193) says of it 'we weary of a long journey on foot, especially through deep sand.'[116] Human nature is not only humbled but crushed. It is a common charge against the 18th century divines that they exalt man too much, by insisting on the dignity of human nature, and its native capacities for virtue. This was the charge urged against the orthodox by the evangelical pulpit. But only very superficial and incompetent critics of doctrine can suppose that man is exalted by being thrown upon his moral faculties. The history of doctrine teaches a very different lesson. Those periods when morals have been represented as the proper

study of man, and his only business, have been periods of spiritual abasement and poverty.[117] The denial of scientific theology, the keeping in the back-ground the transcendental objects of faith, and the restriction of our faculties to the regulation of our conduct, seem indeed to be placing man in the foreground of the picture, to make human nature the centre round which all things revolve. But they do so not by exalting the visible, but by materializing the invisible. 'If there be a sphere of knowledge level to our capacities and of the utmost importance to us, we ought surely to apply ourselves with all diligence to this our proper business, and esteem everything else nothing, nothing as to us, in comparison of it. . . . Our province is virtue and religion, life and manners; the science of improving the temper and making the heart better. This is the field assigned to us to cultivate; how much it has lain neglected is indeed astonishing. . . . He who should find out one rule to assist us in this work would deserve infinitely better of mankind than all the improvers of other knowledge put together.' (*Sermon* xv.)[118] This is the theology of Butler and his contemporaries; a utilitarian theology, like the Baconian philosophy, contemning all employment of mental power that does not bring in fruit. 'Intellectui non plumae,sed plumbum addendum et pondera,' (Bacon, *Nov. Or.*, i. 104,) might be its device.[119]

[37] In the *Analogy* it is the same. His term of comparison, the 'constitution and course of *nature*,' is not what we should understand by that term; not what science can disclose to us of the laws of the *cosmos*, but a narrow observation of what men do in ordinary life. We see what he means by the 'constitution of things,' by his saying (*Sermon* xv.) that 'the writings of Solomon are very much taken up with reflections upon human nature and human life; to which he hath added, in Eccelesiastes, reflections upon the constitution of things.'[120] In Part i. ch. 3, of the *Analogy*, he compares the *moral* government of God with the *natural*—the distinction is perhaps from Balguy (*Divine Rectitude*, p. 39), that is to say, one part of natural religion with another; for the distinction vanishes, except upon a very conventional sense of the term 'moral.'[121] Altogether we miss in these divines not only distinct philosophical conceptions, but a scientific use of terms. Dr. Whewell considers that Butler shunned 'the appearance of technical terms for the elements of our moral constitution on which he speculated,' and thinks that he 'was driven to indirect modes of expression.' (*Moral Philosophy in England*, p. 109.)[122] The truth is that Butler uses the language of his day upon the topics on which he writes. The technical terms, and strict logical forms, which had been adhered to by the writers, small as well as great, of the 17th century, had been disused as pedantic; banished first from literature, and then from education. They did not appear in style, because they did not form part of the mental habit of the writers. Butler does not, as Dr. Whewell supposes, think in one form, and write in another, out of condescension to his readers. He thinks in the same language in which he and those around him speak. Mr. Hort's remark that 'Butler's writings are stoic to the core in the true and ancient sense of the word' (*Cambridge Essays*, 1856, p. 337) must be extended to their style.[123] The English style of philosophical writing in the Hanoverian period is to

the English of the 17th century, as the Greek of Epictetus, Antoninus, or Plutarch, is to that of Aristotle. And for the same reason. The English stoics and their Greek predecessors were practical men who moralized in a practical way on the facts of common life, and in the language of common life. Neither the rhetorical Schools of the Empire, nor the Universities of England, any longer taught the correct use of metaphysical language. To imitate classical Latin was become the chief aim of the University man in his public exercises, and precision of language became under that discipline very speedily a lost art.[124]

[38] Upon the whole, the writings of that period are serviceable to us chiefly as showing what can and what cannot be effected by common-sense thinking in theology. It is of little consequence to inquire whether or not the objections of the Deists and the Socinians were removed by the answers brought to meet them. Perhaps, on the whole, we might be borne out in saying that the defence is at least as good as the attack; and so, that even on the ground of common reason, the Christian evidences may be arranged in such a way as to balance the common-sense improbability of the supernatural—that 'there are three chances to one for revelation, and only two against it.' (*Tracts for the Times*, No. 85.)[125] Had not circumstances given a new direction to religious interests, the Deistical controversy might have gone on indefinitely, and the 'amoebaean strain of objection and reply, et cantare pares et respondere parati'—have been prolonged to this day without any other result.[126] But that result forces on the mind the suggestion that either religious faith has no existence, or that it must be to be reached by some other road than that of the 'trial of the witnesses.'[127] It is a reductio ad absurdum of common-sense philosophy, of home-baked theology, when we find that the result of the whole is that 'it is safer to believe in a God, lest, if there should happen to be one, he might send us to hell for denying his existence.' (Maurice, *Essays*, p. 236.)[128] If a religion be wanted which shall debase instead of elevating, this should be its creed. If the religious history of the eighteenth century proves anything it is this:—That good sense, the best good sense, when it sets to work with the materials of human nature and Scripture to construct a religion, will find its way to an ethical code, irreproachable in its contents, and based on a just estimate and wise observation of the facts of life, ratified by Divine sanctions in the shape of hope and fear, of future rewards and penalties of obedience and disobedience. This the eighteenth century did and did well. It has enforced the truths of natural morality with a solidity of argument and variety of proof which they have not received since the Stoical epoch, if then. But there its ability ended. When it came to the supernatural part of Christianity its embarrassment began. It was forced to keep it as much in the background as possible, or to bolster it up by lame and inadequate reasonings. The philosophy of common-sense had done its own work; it attempted more only to show, by its failure, that some higher organon was needed for the establishment of supernatural truth.[129] The career of the evidential school, its success and failure,—its success in vindicating the ethical part of Christianity and the regulative aspect of revealed truth, its failure in establishing the supernatural and speculative

part, have enriched the history of doctrine with a complete refutation of that method as an instrument of theological investigation.

[39] This judgment, however, must not be left unbalanced by a consideration on the other side. It will hardly be supposed that the drift of what has been said is that common-sense is out of place in religion, or in any other matter. The defect of the eighteenth century theology was not in having too much good sense, but in having nothing besides. In the present day when a godless orthodoxy threatens, as in the fifteenth century, to extinguish religious thought altogether, and nothing is allowed in the Church of England but the formulae of past thinkings, which have long lost all sense of any kind; it may seem out of season to be bringing forward a misapplication of common-sense in a bygone age. There are times and circumstances when religious ideas will be greatly benefited by being submitted to the rough and ready tests by which busy men try what comes in their way; by being made to stand their trial, and be freely canvassed, coram populo.[130] As poetry is not for the critics, so religion is not for theologians. When it is stiffened into phrases, and these phrases are declared to be objects of reverence but not of intelligence, it is on the way to become a useless encumbrance, the rubbish of the past, blocking the road. Theology then retires into the position it occupies in the Church of Rome at present, an unmeaning frostwork of dogma, out of all relation to the actual history of man. In that system, theological virtue is an artificial life quite distinct from the moral virtues of real life. 'Parmi nous,' says Remusat, 'un homme religieux est trop souvent un homme qui se croit entouré d'ennemis, qui voit avec défiance ou scandale les événements et les institutions du siècle, qui se désole d'être né dans les jours maudits, et qui a besoin d'un grand fond de bonté innée pour empêcher ses pieuses aversions de devenir de mortelles haines.'[131] This system is equally fatal to popular morality and to religious theory. It locks up virtue in the cloister, and theology in the library. It originates caste sanctity, and a traditional philosophy. The ideal of holiness striven after may once have been lofty, the philosophy now petrified into tradition may once have been a vital faith, but now that they are withdrawn from public life, they have ceased to be social influences. On the other hand, the eighteenth century exhibits human attainment levelled to the lowest secular model of prudence and honesty, but still, such as it was, proposed to all men as their rule of life. Practical life as it was, was the theme of the pulpit, the press, and the drawing-room. Its theory of life was not lofty, but it was true as far as it went. It did not substitute a factitious phraseology, the past-words of the modern pulpit, for the simple facts of life, but called things by their right names. 'Nullum numen habes si sit prudentia' was its motto, not denying the 'numen,' but bringing him very close to the individual person, as his 'moral governor.'[132] The prevailing philosophy was not a profound metaphysic, but it was a soundly based arrangement of the facts of society; it was not a scheme of the sciences, but a manual for everyday use. Nothing of the wild spirit of universal negation which was spread over the Continent fifty years later belonged to the solid rationalism of this period. The human understanding wished to be satisfied, and did not care to believe that of

which it could not see the substantial ground. The reason was coming slowly to see that it had duties which it could not devolve upon others; that a man must think for himself, protect his own rights, and administer his own affairs. The reason was never less extravagant than in this its first essay of its strength. Its demands were modest, it was easily satisfied; far too easily, we must think, when we look at some of the reasonings which passed as valid.[133]

[10] The habits of controversy in which they lived deceived the belligerents themselves. The controversial form of their theology, which has been fatal to its credit since, was no less detrimental to its soundness at the time. They could not discern the line between what they did, and what they could not, prove. The polemical temper deforms the books they have written. Literature was indeed partially refined from the coarser scurrilities with which the Caroline divines, a century before, had assailed their Romanist opponents.[134] But there is still an air of vulgarity about the polite writing of the age, which the divines adopt along with its style. The cassocked divine assumes the airs of the 'roaring blade,' and ruffles it on the mall with a horsewhip under his arm. Warburton's stock argument is a threat to cudgel anyone who disputes his opinion. All that can be said is that this was a habit of treating your opponent which pervaded society.[135] At a much later period Porson complains, 'in these ticklish times . . . talk of religion it is odds but you have infidel, blasphemer, atheist, or schismatic, thundered in your ears; touch upon politics, you will be in luck if you are only charged with a tendency to treason. Nor is the innocence of your intention any safeguard. It is not the publication that shows the character of the author, but the character of the author that shows the tendency of the publication.' (Luard's 'Porson,' *Camb. Essays*, 1857.)[136] A license of party vituperation in the House of Commons existed, from the time of the opposition to Walpole onwards, which has long been banished by more humane manners. 'The men who took a foremost part seemed to be intent on disparaging each other, and proving that neither possessed any qualification of wisdom, knowledge, or public virtue. . . Epithets of reproach were lavished personally on Lord North, which were applicable only to the vilest and most contemptible of mankind.' (Massey, *Hist. of England*, ii. 218.)[137]

Were this blustering language a blemish of style and nothing more, it would taint their books with vulgarity as literature, but it would not vitiate their matter. But the fault reaches deeper than skin-deep. It is a most serious drawback on the good-sense of the age that it wanted justice in its estimate of persons. They were no more capable of judging their friends than their foes. In Pope's satires there is no medium; our enemies combine all the odious vices, however incongruous; our friends have 'every virtue under heaven.' We hear sometimes of Pope's peculiar 'malignity.' But he was only doing what every one around him was doing, only with a greatly superior literary skill.[138] Their savage invective against each other is not a morally worse feature than the style of fulsome compliment in which friends address each other. The private correspondence of intimate friends betrays an unwholesome insincerity, which contrasts strangely with their general manliness of character. The burly intellect of Warburton displays an appetite for flattery as insatiable as that of Miss Seward and her coterie.[139]

[42] This habit of exaggerating both good and evil the divines share with the other writers of the time. But theological literature, as a written debate, had a form of malignant imputation peculiar to itself. This is one arising out of the rationalistic fiction which both parties assumed, viz., that their respective beliefs were determined by an impartial inquiry into the evidence. The orthodox writers considered this evidence so clear and certain for their own conclusions, that they could account for its not seeming so to others only by the supposition of some moral obliquity which darkened the understanding in such cases. Hence the obnoxious assumption of the divines that the Deists were men of corrupt morals, and the retort of the infidel writers, that the clergy were hired advocates. Moral imputation, which is justly banished from legal argument, seems to find a proper place in theological. Those Christian Deists who, like Toland or Collins, approached most nearly in their belief to Revelation, were treated, not better, but worse, by the orthodox champions; their larger admissions being imputed to disingenuousness or calculated reserve. This stamp of advocacy which was impressed on English theology at the Reformation—its first work of consideration was an 'Apology'—it has not to this day shaken off. Our theologians, with rare exceptions, do not penetrate below the surface of their subject, but are engaged in defending or vindicating it. The current phrases of 'the bulwarks of our faith,' 'dangerous to Christianity,' are but instances of the habitual position in which we assume ourselves to stand. Even more philosophic minds cannot get rid of the idea that theology is polemical. Theological study is still the study of topics of defence. Even Professor Fraser can exhort us 'that by the study of these topics we might not merely disarm the enemies of religion of what, in other times has been, and will continue to be a favourite weapon of assault, but we might even convert that weapon into an instrument of use in the Christian service.' (*Essays in Philosophy*, p. 4.)[140] 'Modern science,' as it is called, is recommended to the young divine, because in it he may find means of 'confuting infidelity.'

[43] A little consideration will show that the grounds on which advocacy before a legal tribunal rests, make it inappropriate in theological reasoning. It is not pretended that municipal law is coextensive with universal law, and therefore incapable of admitting right on both sides. It is allowed that the natural right may be, at times, on one side, and the legal title on the other; not to mention the extreme case where '*communis error facit jus*.'[141] The advocate is not there to supply all the materials out of which the judge is to form his decision, but only one side of the case. He is the mere representative of his client's interests, and has not to discuss the abstract merits of the juridical point which may be involved. He does not undertake to show that the law is conformable to natural right, but to establish the condition of his client relatively to the law. But the rational defender of the faith has no place in his system for the variable, or the indifferent, or the non-natural. He

proceeds on the supposition that the whole system of the Church is the one and exclusively true expression of reason upon the subject on which it legislates. He claims for the whole of received knowledge what the jurist claims for international law, to be a universal science. He lays before us, on the one hand, the traditional canon or symbol of doctrine. On the other hand, he teaches that the free use of reason upon the facts of nature and Scripture is the real mode by which this traditional symbol is arrived at. To show then, that the candid pursuit of truth leads every impartial intellect to the Anglican conclusion was the task which, on their theory of religious proof, their theology had to undertake. The process, accordingly, should have been analogous to that of the jurist or legislator with regard to the internal evidence, and to that of the judge with regard to the external evidence.

4] If theological argument forgets the judge and assumes the advocate, or betrays the least bias to one side, the conclusion is valueless, the principle of free inquiry has been violated. Roman Catholic theologians consistently enough teach that 'apologetics' make no part of theology, as usually conducted as replies to special objections urged, but that a true apologetic must be founded (1) on a discovery of the general principle from which the attack proceeds, and (2) on the exhibition, *per contra*, of that general ground-thought of which the single Christian truths are developments. (Hageman, *Die Aufgabe der Catholischen Apologetik.*)[142]

5] With rare exceptions the theology of the Hanoverian period is of the most violently partisan character. It seats itself, by its theory, in the judicial chair, but it is only to comport itself there like Judge Jefferies.[143] One of the favourite books of the time was Sherlock's *Trial of the Witnesses*. First published in 1729, it speedily went through fourteen editions. It concludes in this way:—

'*Judge*.—What say you? Are the Apostles guilty of giving false evidence in the case of the resurrection of Jesus, or not guilty?

'*Foreman*.—Not guilty.

'*Judge*.—Very well; and now, gentlemen, I resign my commission, and am your humble servant. The company then rose up, and were beginning to pay their compliments to the Judge and the counsel, but were interrupted by a gentleman, who went up to the Judge and offered him a fee. "What is this?" says the Judge. "A fee, sir," said the gentleman. "A fee to a judge is a bribe," said the Judge. "True, sir," said the gentleman; "but you have resigned your commission, and will not be the first judge who has come from the bench to the bar without any diminution of honour. Now, Lazarus's case is to come on next, and this fee is to retain you on his side."[144] One might say that the apologists of that day had in like manner left the bench for the bar, and taken a brief for the Apostles. They are impatient at the smallest demur, and deny loudly that there is any weight in anything advanced by their opponents. In the way they override the most serious difficulties, they show anything but the temper which is supposed to qualify for the weighing of evidence. The astonishing want of candour in their reasoning, their blindness to real difficulty, the ill-concealed predetermination to find a particular verdict, the rise of their style in passion in the same proportion as their argument fails in strength, constitute a class of writers more calculated than any other to damage their own cause with young ingenuous minds, bred in the school of Locke to believe that 'to love truth for truth's sake is the principal part of human perfection in this world, and the seed-plot of all other virtues.' (Locke, aet. 73. *Letter to Collins*.)[145] Spalding has described the moral shock his faith received on hearing an eminent clergyman in confidential conversation with another, who had cited some powerful argument against revelation, say, 'That's truly awkward; let us consider a little how we get out of that;' *wie wir uns salviren*. (*Selbstbiographie*, p. 128.)[146] A truthful mind is a much rarer possession than is commonly supposed, for 'it is as easy to close the eyes of the mind as those of the body.' (Butler, *Sermon* x.)[147] And in this rarity there is a natural limit to the injury which uncandid vindications of revelation can cause. To whatever causes is to be attributed the decline of Deism, from 1750 onwards, the books polemically written against it cannot reckon among them. When Casaubon first visited Paris, and was being shown over the Sorbonne, his guide said, 'This is the hall in which the doctors have *disputed* for 300 years.' 'Aye! and what have they settled?' was his remark.[148]

[46] Some exceptions, doubtless, there are to the inconclusiveness of this debate. Here again the eminent exception is the *Analogy*. Butler, it is true, comes forward not as an investigator, but as a pleader. But when we pass from his inferior brethren to this great master of the art, we find ourselves in the hands of one who knows the laws of evidence, and carefully keeps his statements within them. Butler does not, like his fellow apologists, disguise the fact that the evidence is no stronger than it is. 'If it be a *poor* thing,' to argue in this way, 'the epithet *poor* may be applied, I fear, as properly to great part, or the whole, of human life, as it is to the things mentioned.' (*Analogy*, Part ii. ch. 8.)[149] Archbishop Whately, defining the temper of the rational theologian, says:—'A good man will, indeed, wish to find the evidence of the Christian religion satisfactory; but a wise man will not, for that reason, think it satisfactory, but will weigh the evidence the more carefully on account of the importance of the question.' (*Essays*, 2nd series, p.24.)[150] This character Butler's argument exemplifies. We can feel, as we read, how his judgment must have been offended in his contemporaries by the disproportion between the positiveness of their assertion and the feebleness of their argument. Nor should we expect that Butler satisfied them. They thought him 'a little too little vigorous,' and 'wished he would have spoke more earnestly.' (Byrom's *Journal*, March, 1737.)[151] Men who believed that they were in possession of a 'demonstration' of Christianity were to be satisfied with one who saw so strongly 'the doubtfulness in which things were involved' that he could not comprehend 'men's being impatient out of action or vehement in it.' (*Unpublished Remains, &c.*)[152] Warburton, who has a proof which 'is very little short of mathematical certainty, and to which nothing but a mere physical possibility of the contrary can be opposed' (*Divine Leg.*, b. i. §1), was the man for the age, which did not care to stand higgling with Butler over the degrees of probability. What could the world do with a man who 'designed the search after truth as the business of my life' (*Correspondence with Dr. Clarke*), and

who was so little prepared to dogmatise about the future world that he rather felt that 'there is no account to be given in the way of reason of men's so strong attachments to the present world.' (*Sermon* vii.)[153] Butler's doubtfulness, however, it should be remarked, is not the unsteadiness of the sceptical, but the wariness of the judicial mind; a mind determined for itself by its own instincts, but careful to confine its statements to others within the evidence produced in court. The *Analogy* does not depicture an inward struggle in his own mind, but as 'he told a friend, his way of writing it had been to endeavour to answer as he went along, every possible objection that might occur to any one against any position of his in his book.' (Bartlett's *Life of Butler*, p. 50.)[154] He does not doubt himself, but he sees, what others do not see, the difficulty of proving religion to others. There is a saying of Pitt circulating to the effect that the *Analogy* is 'a dangerous book; it raises more doubts than it solves.'[155] All that is true in this is, that to a mind which has never nourished objections to revelation a book of evidences may be the means of first suggesting them. But in 1736 the objections were everywhere current, and the answers to them were mostly of that truly 'dangerous' sort in which assertion runs ahead of proof. The merit of Butler lies not in the 'irrefragable proof,' which Southey's epitaph attributes to his construction, but in his showing the nature of the proof, and daring to admit that it was less than certain; to own that 'a man may be fully convinced of the truth of a matter and upon the strongest reasons, and yet not be able to answer all the difficulties which may be raised upon it.' (*Durham Charge*, 1751)[156]

Another, perhaps the only other, book of this polemical tribe which can be said to have been completely successful as an answer, is one most unlike the *Analogy* in all its nobler features. This is Bentley's *Remarks upon a late Discourse of Freethinking, by Phileleutherus Lipsiensis*, 1713.[157] Coarse, arrogant, and abusive, with all Bentley's worst faults of style and temper, this masterly critique is decisive. Not, of course, of the Deistical controversy, on which the critic avoids entering. The *Discourse of Freethinking* was a small tract published in 1713 by Anthony Collins. Collins was a gentleman of independent fortune, whose high personal character and general respectability seemed to give a weight to his words, which assuredly they do not carry of themselves. By freethinking, he means liberty of thought—the right of bringing all received opinions whatsoever to the touchstone of reason. Among the grounds or authorities by which he supports this natural right, Collins unluckily had recourse to history, and largely, of course, to the precedent of the Greek philosophers. Collins, who had been bred at Eton and King's, was probably no worse a scholar than his contemporary Kingsmen, and the range of his reading was that of a man who had made the classics the companions of his maturer years. But that scholarship which can supply a quotation from Lucan, or flavour the style with an occasional allusion to Tully or Seneca, is quite incompetent to apply Greek or Roman precedent properly to a modern case.[158] Addison, the pride of Oxford, had done no better. In his *Essay on the Evidences of Christianity*, Addison 'assigns as grounds for his religious belief, stories as absurd as that of the Cocklane ghost, and forgeries as rank as Ireland's *Vortigern*, puts faith in the lie about the thundering legion, is convinced that Tiberius moved the Senate to admit Jesus among the gods, and pronounces the letter of Agbarus, King of Edessa, to be a record of great authority.' (Macaulay: *Essays*.)[159] But the public was quite satisfied with Addison's citations, in which a public, which had given the victory to Boyle in the *Phalaris* controversy, could hardly suspect anything wrong.[160] Collins was not to escape so easily. The Freethinker flounders hopelessly among the authorities he has invoked. Like the necromancer's apprentice, he is worried by the fiends he has summoned but cannot lay, and Bentley, on whose nod they wait, is there like another Cornelius Agrippa hounding them on and enjoying the sport.[161] Collins's mistakes, mistranslations, misconceptions, and distortions are so monstrous, that it is difficult for us now, forgetful how low classical learning had sunk, to believe that they *are* mistakes, and not wilful errors. It is rare sport to Bentley, this rat-hunting in an old rick, and he lays about him in high glee, braining an authority at every blow. When he left off abruptly, in the middle of a 'Third Part,' it was not because he was satiated with slaughter, but to substitute a new excitement, no less congenial to his temper—a quarrel with the University about his fees. A grace, voted 1715, tendering him the public thanks of the University, and 'praying him in the name of the University to finish what remains of so useful a work,' could not induce him to resume his pen.[162] The *Remarks of Phileleutherus Lipsiensis*, unfinished though they are, and trifling as was the book which gave occasion to them, are perhaps the best of all Bentley's performances. They have all the merits of the *Phalaris* dissertation, with the advantage of a far nobler subject. They show how Bentley's exact appreciation of the value of terms could, when he chose to apply it to that purpose, serve him as a key to the philosophical ideas of past times, no less than to those of poetical metaphor. The tone of the pamphlet is most offensive, 'not only not insipid, but exceedingly bad-tasted.' We can only say the taste is that of his age, while the knowledge is all his own. It was fair to show that his antagonist undertook 'to interpret the Prophets and Solomon without Hebrew; Plutarch and Zosimus (Collins spells it Zozimus) without Greek; and Cicero and Lucan without Latin.' (*Remarks*, Part i. No. 3.)[163] But the dirt endeavoured to be thrown on Collins will cleave to the hand that throws it. It may be worth mention that this tract of Bentley contains the original of Sidney Smith's celebrated defence of the 'prizes' in the Church. The passage is a favourable specimen of the moral level of a polemic who was accusing his opponent of holding 'opinions the most abject and base that human nature is capable of.' (Letter prefixed to *Remarks*.)[164]

[48] 'He can never conceive or wish a priesthood either quieter for him, or cheaper, than that of the present Church of England. Of your quietness himself is a convincing proof, who has writ this outrageous book, and has met with no punishment nor prosecution. And for the cheapness, that appeared lately in one of your parliaments, when the accounts exhibited showed that 6,000 of your clergy, the greater part of your whole number, had, at a middle rate one with another, not 50 pounds a year. A poor emolument for so long, so laborious, so expensive an

education, as must qualify them for holy orders. While I resided at Oxford, and saw such a conflux of youth to their annual admissions, I have often studied and admired why their parents would, under such mean encouragements, design their sons for the church; and those the most towardly, and capable, and select geniuses among their children, who must needs have emerged in a secular life. I congratulated, indeed, the felicity of your establishment, which attracted the choice youth of your nation for such very low pay; but my wonder was at the parents, who generally have interest, maintenance and wealth, the first thing in their view, till at last one of your state-lotteries ceased my astonishment. For as in that, a few glittering prizes, 1,000, 5,000, 10,000 pounds among an infinity of blanks, drew troops of adventurers, who, if the whole fund had been equally ticketted, would never have come in; so a few shining dignities in your church, prebends, deaneries, bishopricks, are the pious fraud that induces and decoys the parents to risk their child's fortune in it. Everyone hopes his own will get some prize in the church, and never reflects on the thousands of blanks in poor country livings. And if a foreigner may tell you his mind, from what he sees at home, 'tis this part of your establishment that makes your clergy excel ours [*i.e.*, in Germany, from which *Phileleutherus Lipsiensis* is supposed to write]. Do but once level all your preferments, and you'll soon be as level in your learning. For, instead of the flower of the English youth, you'll have only the refuse sent to your academies, and those, too, cramped and crippled in their studies, for want of aim and emulation. So that, if your Freethinkers had any politics, instead of suppressing your whole order, they should make you all alike; or, if that cannot be done, make your preferments a very lottery in the whole similitude. Let your church dignities be pure chance prizes without regard to abilities, or morals, or letters.' (*Remarks, &c.*, Part ii. §40.)[165]

It has been mentioned that Bentley does not attempt to reply to the argument of the *Discourse on Freethinking*. His tactic is to ignore it, and to assume that it is only meant as a covert attack on Christianity; that Collins is an Atheist fighting under the disguise of a Deist. Some excuse perhaps may be made for a man nourished on pedagogic Latin, and accustomed to launch furious sarcasm at any opponent who betrayed a brutal ignorance of the difference between 'ac' and 'et.' But Collins was not a sharper, and would have disdained practices to which Bentley stooped for the sake of a professorship. When Bentley, in the pride of academic dignity, could thus browbeat a person of Collins's consideration, it was not to be expected that the inferior fry of Deistical writers,—Toland, a writer for the press; Tindal, a fellow of a college; or Chubb, a journeyman glover—met with fairer treatment from their opponents.[166] The only exception to this is the case of Shaftesbury, to whom, as well after his death as in his lifetime, his privileges as a peer seem to have secured immunity from hangman's usage. He is simply 'a late noble author.'[167] Nor was this respect inspired by the Earl's profession of christianity. He does, indeed, make this profession with the utmost unreserve. He asserts his 'steady orthodoxy,' and 'entire submission to the truly Christian and Catholic doctrines of our holy Church, as by law established,' and that he holds 'the mysteries of our religion even in the minutest particulars.' (*Characteristicks*, Vol. iii. p. 315.)[168] But this outward profession would only have brought down upon any other writer an aggravated charge of cowardly malice and concealment of Atheism. If Shaftesbury was spared on account of his rank, the orthodox writers were not altogether wrong in fastening upon this disingenuousness as a moral characteristic of their antagonists. The excuse for this want of manliness in men who please themselves with insinuating unpopular opinions which they dare not advocate openly, is that it is an injustice perpetrated by those who have public feeling on their side. 'They make,' says Mr. Tayler, 'the honest expression of opinion penal, and then condemn men for disingenuousness. They invite to free discussion, but determine beforehand that only one conclusion can be sound and moral. They fill the arena of public debate with every instrument of torture and annoyance for the feeling heart, the sensitive imagination, and the scrupulous intellect, and then are angry that men do not rush headlong into the martyrdom that has been prepared for them.' (*Religious Life of England*, p. 282.)[169]

[50] In days when the pillory was the punishment for common libel, it cannot be thought much that heresy and infidelity should be punished by public opprobrium.[170] And public abhorrence was the most that a writer against revelation had now to fear. Mandeville's *Fable of the Bees*, indeed, was presented as a nuisance by the grand jury of Middlesex, in 1723, as were Bolingbroke's collected '*Works*,' in 1752, and Toland's *Christianity not Mysterious*, in 1699.[171] We find, too, that Toland had to fly from Dublin, and Collins to go out of the way to Holland, for fear of further consequences. But nothing ever came of these presentments. The only[172] prosecution for religious libel was that of Woolston, 2 George II., in which the defendant, who was not of sound mind, provoked and even compelled the law officers of the crown to proceed against him, though they were very reluctant to do so. When thus compelled to declare the law, on this occasion, the Lord Chief Justice (Raymond) 'would not allow it to be doubted that to write against Christianity in general was punishable at common law.' Yet both then and since, judges and prosecutors have shown themselves shy of insisting upon the naked offence of 'impugning the truth of Christianity.' That it is an offence at common law, independent of 9 & 10 William III., no lawyer will deny.[173] But an instinctive sense of the incompatibility of this legal doctrine with the fundamental tenet of Protestant rationalism has always served to keep it in the background. 'The judges seem to have played fast and loose in this matter, in such sort as might enable the future judge to quote the tolerant or the intolerant side of their doctrine as might prove convenient; and while seemingly disavowing all interference with fair discussion, they still kept a wary hold of the precedents of Hale and Raymond, and of the great arcanum of "part and parcel;" "semianimesque micant digiti, ferrumque retractant."' (*Consideration on the Law of Libel*. By John Search, 1833.)[174]

[51] Whatever excuse the Deistical writers might have for their insidious manner of writing, it is more to the present purpose to observe that we may draw from it the conclusion that public opinion was throughout on the side of the defenders of

Christianity. It might seem almost superfluous to say this, were it not that complaints meet us on every side, which seem to imply the very contrary; that in the words of Mr. Gregory, 'the doctrine of our Church is exploded, and our holy religion become only a name which is everywhere spoken against.' (*Pref. to Beveridge's Private Thoughts*, 1709.)[175] Thirty years later Butler writes, that 'it is come to be taken for granted that Christianity is not so much as a subject of inquiry; but that it is now, at length, discovered to be fictitious. Accordingly they treat it as if in the present age this were an agreed point among all people of discernment, and nothing remained but to set it up as a principal subject of mirth and ridicule, as it were by way of reprisals for its having so long interrupted the pleasures of the world.' (*Advertisement, to Analogy*, 1736.)[176] However a loose kind of Deism might be the tone of fashionable circles, it is clear that distinct disbelief of Christianity was by no means the general state of the public mind. The leaders of the Low-church and Whig party were quite aware of this. Notwithstanding the universal complaints of the High-church party of the prevalence of infidelity, it is obvious that this mode of thinking was confined to a very small section of society. The *Independent Whig* (May 4, 1720), in the middle of its blustering and endeavours to terrify the clergy with their unpopularity, is obliged to admit that 'the High-church Popish clergy will laugh in their sleeves at this advice, and think there is folly enough yet left among the laity to support their authority; and will laugh themselves, and rejoice over the ignorance of the Universities, the stupidity of the drunken squires, the pannic of the tender sex, and the never-to-be-shaken constancy of the multitude.'[177] A still better evidence is the confidence and success with which the writers on the side of Revelation appealed to the popular passions, and cowed their Deistical opponents into the use of that indirect and disingenuous procedure with which they then taunted them. The clerical sphere was much more a sphere by itself than it has since become. Notwithstanding the large toleration really practised, strict professional etiquette was still observed in the Church and the Universities. The horizontal hat, the starched band, and the cassock, were still worn in public, and certain proprieties of outward manner were expected from 'the cloth.' The violation of these proprieties was punished by the forfeiture of the offenders' prospects of preferment, a point on which the most extreme sensitiveness existed. In the Balguy and Waterland set an officious spirit of delation seems to have flourished.[178] The general habit of publicly canvassing religious topics was very favourable to this espionage; as, at the Reformation, the Catholics gathered their best calumnies against Luther from his unreserved 'table-talk.'[179]

It was not difficult to draw the unhappy Middleton into 'unguarded expressions' (Van Mildert, *Life of Waterland*, p. 162); and something which had fallen from Rundle in his younger days was used against him so successfully that even the Talbot interest was able to procure him only an Irish bishoprick.[180] Lord Chesterfield, seeing[181] what advantage the High-church party derived from this tactic, endeavoured to turn it against them. He gives a circumstantial account of a conversation with Pope, which would tend to prove that Atterbury was, nearly all his life, a sceptic. The thing was not true, as Mr. Carruthers has shown (*Life of Pope*, 2nd ed. p. 213), and true or false, the weapon in Chesterfield's hands was pointless.[182]

[53] Though the general feeling of the country was sufficiently decided to oblige all who wished to write against Christianity, do so under a mask, this was not the case with attacks upon the Clergy. Since the days of the Lollards there had never been a time when the established ministers of religion were held in so much contempt as in the Hanoverian period, or when satire upon churchmen was so congenial to general feeling.[183] This too was the more extraordinary, as there was no feeling against the Church Establishment, nor was non-conformity as a theory ever less in favour. The contempt was for the persons, manners, and character of the ecclesiastics. When Macaulay brought out his portrait of the clergyman of the revolution period, his critics endeavoured to show that that portrait was not true to life. They seem to have brought out the fact that it was pretty fairly true to literature. The difficult point is to estimate how far the satirical and popular literature of any age may be taken as representative of life. Satire to be popular must exaggerate, but it must be exaggeration of known and recognised facts. Mr. Churchill Babington (*Character of the Clergy, &c., considered*, p. 48) sets aside two of Macaulay's authorities, Oldham and T. Wood, because Oldham was an Atheist and Wood a Deist. Admitting that an Atheist and a Deist can be under no obligation to truth, yet a satirist, who intends to be read, is under the most inevitable engagement to the probable. Satire does not create the sentiment to which it appeals. A portrait of the country parson *temp.* George the Second which should be drawn verbatim from the pamphlets of the day would be no more historical, than is that portrait of the begging friar of the sixteenth century which our historians repeat after Erasmus and the *Epistolae Obscurorum Virorum*. History may be extracted from them, but these caricatures are not themselves history.[184]

[54] One inference which we may safely draw is that public feeling encouraged such representations. It is a symptom of the religious temper of the times, that the same public which compelled the Deist to wear the mask of 'solemn sneer' in his assaults upon Christian doctrine, required no such disguise or reserve when the ministers of the Church were spoken of.[185] Nor does the evidence consist in a few stray extracts from here and there a Deist or a cynic, it is the tone of all the popular writers of that time. The unedifying lives of the clergy are a standard theme of sarcasm, and continue to be so until a late period in the century, when a gradual change may be observed in the language of literature. This antipathy to the clergy visible in the Hanoverian period, admits of comparison with that vein which colours the popular songs of the Wickliffite era. In the fifteenth century, the satire is not indiscriminate.[186] It is against the monks and friars, the bishops and cardinals, as distinct from the 'poor persoun of a toun.' Its point against the organized hypocrisy of the Papal Churchmen is given it by the picture of the ideal minister of 'Christe's Gospel' which always accompanies the burlesque. In the eighteenth century the license of satire goes much beyond this.[187] In the early part

of the century we find clerical satire observing to some extent a similar discrimination. The Tory parson is libelled always with an ostentatious reserve of commendation for the more enlightened and liberal Hanoverian, the staunch maintainer of the Protestant succession. This is the tone of the *Independent Whig*, one of the numerous weekly sheets called into being in imitation of the *Tatler*.[188] It was started in 1720, taking for its exclusive theme the clergy, whom it was its avowed object to abuse. A paper came out every Wednesday. It was not a newspaper, and does not deal in libel or personalities, hardly ever mentioning a name, very rarely quoting a fact, but dilating in general terms upon clerical ignorance and bigotry. This dull and worthless trash not only had a considerable circulation at the time, but was reprinted, and passed through several editions in a collected form.[189] The bishops talked of prohibiting it, but, on second thoughts, acted more wisely in taking no notice of it. The only part of the kingdom into which it could not find entrance was the Isle of Man, where the saintly Wilson combined with apostolic virtues much of the old episcopal claims over the consciences of his flock.[190] The *Independent Whig*, though manifestly written by a man of no religion, yet finds it necessary to keep up the appearance of encouraging the 'better sort' of clergy, and affecting to despise only the political priests, the meddling chaplain, the preferment-hunter, the toper, who is notable at bowls, and dexterous at whisk.[191]

55] As we advance towards the middle of the century, and the French influence begins to mingle with pure English Deism, the spirit of contempt spreads till it involves all priests of all religions. The language now is, 'The established clergy in every country are generally the greatest enemies to all kinds of reformation, as they are generally the most narrow-minded and most worthless set of men in every country. Fortunately for the present times, the wings of clerical power and influence are pretty close trimmed, so that I do not think their opposition to the proposed reformations could be of any great consequence, more of the people being inclined to despise them, than follow them blindly.' (Burgh, *Political Disquisitions*, 1774.)[192] It was no longer for their vices that the clergy were reviled, for the philosopher now had come to understand that 'their virtues were more dangerous' to society. Strictness of life did but increase the dislike with which the clergyman was regarded; his morality was but double-dyed hypocrisy; religious language from his mouth was methodistical cant. Nor did the orthodox attempt to struggle with this sentiment. They yielded to it, and adopted for their maxim of conduct, 'surtout point de zèle.'[193] Their sermons and pamphlets were now directed against 'Enthusiasm,' which became the bugbear of that time.[194] Every clergyman, who wished to retain any influence over the minds of his parishioners, was anxious to vindicate himself from all suspicion of enthusiasm. When he had set himself right in this respect, he endeavoured to do the same good office for the Apostles. But if he were not an 'enthusiast,' he was an 'imposter.' For every clergyman of the Church had against him an antecedent presumption as a 'priest.' It was now well understood, by all enlightened men, that the whole sacerdotal brood were but a set of imposters, who lived by deceiving the people, and who had invented religion for their own benefit. Natural religion needed no 'priests' to uphold it; it was obvious to every understanding, and could maintain itself in the world without any confraternity sworn to the secret.

[56] Again came a change. As the Methodist movement gradually leavened the mass beneath, zeal came again into credit. The old Wickliffite, or Puritan, distinction is revived between the 'Gospel preachers' and the 'dumb dogs.' The antipathy to priests was no longer promiscuous. Popular indignation was reserved for the fox-hunter and the pluralist; the Hophni and Phinehas generation; the men, who are described as 'careless of dispensing the bread of life to their flocks, preaching a carnal and soul-benumbing morality, and trafficking in the souls of men by receiving money for discharging the pastoral office in parishes where they did not so much as look on the faces of the people more than once a year.'[195] In the well-known satire of Cowper, it is no longer irreligious mocking at sacred things under pretence of a virtuous indignation. It becomes again what it was before the Reformation—an earnest feeling, a religious sentiment, the moral sense of man; Huss or Savonarola appealing to the written morality of the Gospel against the practical immorality consecrated by the Church.[196]

[57] Something too of the old anti-hierarchical feeling accompanies this revival of the influence of the inferior clergy; a faint reflection of the bitter hatred which the Lollard had borne to pope and cardinal, or the Puritan to 'Prelacy.'[197] The utility of the episcopal and capitular dignities continued to be questioned long after the evangelical parish pastor had re-established himself in the affections of his flock, and 1832 saw the cathedrals go down amid the general approbation of all classes.[198] In the earlier half of the century the reverse was the case. The boorish country parson was the man whose order was despised then, and his utility questioned. The Freethinkers themselves could not deny that the bench and the stalls were graced by some whose wit, reputation, and learning would have made them considerable in any profession. The higher clergy had with them the town and the court, the country clergy sided with the squires. The mass of the clergy were not in sympathy, either politically or intellectually, with their ecclesiastical superiors. The Tory fox-hunter in the *Freeholder* (No. 22.) thinks 'the neighbouring shire very happy for having scarce a Presbyterian in it except the bishop;' while Hickes 'thanks God that the main body of the clergy are in their hearts Jacobites.'[199] The bishops of George the Second deserved the respect they met with. At no period in the history of our Church has the ecclesiastical patronage of the crown been better directed than while it was secretly dispensed by Queen Caroline. For a brief period, liberality and cultivation of mind were passports to promotion in the Church. Nor were politics a hindrance; the queen earnestly pressed an English see upon Bishop Wilson.[200] The corruption which began with the Duke of Newcastle (1746) gradually deepened in the subsequent reign, as political orthodoxy and connexion were made the tests, and the borough-holders divided the dignities of the Church among their adherents.[201]

[58] Of an age so solid and practical it was not to be expected that its theology and

metaphysics would mount into the more remote spheres of abstraction. Their line of argument was, as has been seen, regulated by the necessity they laid themselves under of appealing to sound sense and common reason. But not only was their treatment of their topic popular, the motive of their writings was an immediate practical necessity. Bishops and deans might be made for merit, but it was not mere literary merit, classical scholarship, or university distinction. The Deistical controversy did not originate, like some other controversies which have made much noise in their time, in speculative fancy, in the leisure of the cloister, or the college. It had a living practical interest in its complication with the questions of the day. The endeavour of the moralists and divines of the period to rationalize religion was in fact an effort to preserve the practical principles of moral and religious conduct for society. It was not an academical disputation, or a contest of wits for superiority, but a life and death struggle of religious and moral feeling to maintain itself. What they felt they had to contend against was moral depravity, and not theological error; they wrote less in the interest of truth than in that of virtue. A general relaxation of manners, in all classes of society, is universally affirmed to be characteristic of that time; and theology and philosophy applied themselves to combat this. A striking instance of this is Bishop Berkeley, the only metaphysical writer of the time, besides Locke, who has maintained a very high name in philosophical history. He forms a solitary—it might seem a singular—exception to what has been said of the prosaic and unmetaphysical character of this moralising age. The two peculiar metaphysical notions which are connected with Berkeley's name, and which, though he did not originate, he propounded with a novelty and distinctness equal to originality, have always ranked as being on the extreme verge of rational speculation, if not actually within the region of unfruitful paradox and metaphysical romance. These two memorable speculations, as propounded by Berkeley in the *Alciphron*, come before us not as a Utopian dream, or an ingenious play of reason, but interwoven in a polemic against the prevailing unbelief. They are made to bend to a most practical purpose, and are Berkeley's contribution to the Deistical controversy.[202] The character of the man, too, was more in harmony with the plain utilitarian spirit of his time than with his own refining intellect. He was not a closet thinker, like his master Malebranche, but a man of the world and of society, inquisitive and well informed in many branches of practical science.[203] Practical schemes, social and philanthropic, occupied his mind more than abstract thinking. In pushing the received metaphysical creed to its paradoxical consequences, as much as in prescribing 'tar-water,' he was thinking only of an immediate 'benefit to mankind.' He seems to have thought nothing of his argument until he had brought it to bear on the practical question of the day.[204]

Were the 'corruption of manners' merely the complaint of one party or set of writers, a cry of factious puritanism, or of men who were at war with society, like the Nonjuring clergy, or of a few isolated individuals of superior piety, like William Law, it would be easily explicable. The 'world' at all times, and in all countries, can be described with truth as 'lying in wickedness,' and the rebuke of the preacher of righteousness is equally needed in every age. There cannot be a darker picture than that drawn by the Fathers of the third century of the morals of the Christians in their time. (See passages in Jewel's *Apology*.)[205] The rigorous moralist, heathen or Christian, can always point in sharp contrast the vices and the belief of mankind. But, after making every allowance for the exaggeration of religious rhetoric, and the querulousness of defeated parties, there seems to remain *some* real evidence for ascribing to that age a more than usual moral licence, and contempt of external restraints. It is the concurrent testimony of men of all parties, it is the general strain of the most sensible and worldly divines, prosperous men who lived with this very world they censure, men whose code of morals was not large, nor their standard exacting. To attempt the inquiry what specific evils were meant by the general expressions 'decay of religion' and 'corruption of manners,' the stereotype phrases of the time, is not within the limits of this paper.[206] No historian, as far as I am aware, has attempted this examination; all have been content to render, without valuation, the charges as they find them. I shall content myself with producing here one statement of contemporary opinion on this point; for which purpose I select a layman, David Hartley. (*Observations on Man*, vol. ii. p. 441.)[207]

[60] 'There are six things which seem more especially to threaten ruin and dissolution to the present States of Christendom.

[61] '1st. The great growth of atheism and infidelity, particularly amongst the governing parts of these States.

[62] '2nd. The open and abandoned lewdness to which great numbers of both sexes, especially in the high ranks of life, have given themselves up.

[63] '3rd. The sordid and avowed self-interest, which is almost the sole motive of action in those who are concerned in the administration of public affairs.

[64] '4th. The licentiousness and contempt of every kind of authority, divine or human, which is so notorious in inferiors of all ranks.

[65] '5th. The great worldly-mindedness of the clergy, and their gross neglect in the discharge of their proper functions.

[66] '6th. The carelessness and infatuation of parents and magistrates with respect to the education of youth, and the consequent early corruption of the rising generation.

[67] 'All these things have evident mutual connexions and influences; and as they all seem likely to increase from time to time, so it can scarce be doubted by a considerate man, whether he be a religious one or no, but that they will, sooner or later, bring on a total dissolution of all the forms of government that subsist at present in the Christian countries of Europe.'

[68] Though there is this entire unanimity as to the fact of the prevailing corruption, there is the greatest diversity of opinion as to its cause. Each party is found in turn attributing it to the neglect or disbelief of the abstract propositions in which its own particular creed is expressed. The Nonjurors and High-Churchmen attribute it to the Toleration Act and the latitudinarianism allowed in high places. One of the very popular pamphlets of the year 1721 was a fast sermon preached

before the Lord Mayor by Edmund Massey, in which he enumerates the evils of the time, and affirms that they 'are justly chargeable upon the corrupt explication of those words of our Saviour, "My kingdom is not of this world"—*i.e.*, upon Hoadley's celebrated sermon.[208] The latitudinarian clergy divide the blame between the Freethinkers and the Nonjurors. The Freethinkers point to the hypocrisy of the Clergy, who, they say, lost all credit with the people by having preached 'passive obedience' up to 1688, and then suddenly finding out that it was not a scriptural truth.[209] The Nonconformists lay it to the enforcement of conformity and unscriptural terms of communion; while the Catholics rejoice to see in it the Protestant Reformation at last bearing its natural fruit. Warburton characteristically attributes it to the bestowal of 'preferment' by the Walpole administration. (Dedication to Lord Mansfield, *Works*, ii. 268.) The power of preferment was not under-estimated then. George II. maintained to the last that the growth of Methodism was entirely owing to ministers not having listened to his advice, and 'made Whitefield a bishop.'[210] Lastly, that everyone may have his say, a professor of moral philosophy in our day is found attributing the same facts to the prevalence of 'that low view of morality which rests its rules upon consequences merely.'

9] 'The reverence which,' says Dr. Whewell, 'handed down by the traditions of ages of moral and religious teaching, had hitherto protected the accustomed forms of moral good, was gradually removed. Vice, and crime, and sin, ceased to be words that terrified the popular speculator. Virtue, and goodness, and purity were no longer things which he looked up to with mute respect. He ventured to lay a sacrilegious hand even upon these hallowed shapes. He saw that when this had been dared by audacious theorists, those objects, so long venerated, seemed to have no power of punishing the bold intruder. There was a scene like that which occurred when the barbarians broke into the Eternal City. At first, in spite of themselves, they were awed by the divine aspect of the ancient magistrates; but when once their leader had smitten one of these venerable figures with impunity, the coarse and violent mob rushed onwards, and exultingly mingled all in one common destruction.' (*Moral Philosophy in England*, p. 79.)[211]

] The actual sequence of cause and effect seems, if it be not presumptuous to say so, to be as nearly as possible inverted in this eloquent statement.[212] The licentiousness of talk and manners was not produced by the moral doctrines promulgated; but the doctrine of moral consequences was had recourse to by the divines and moralists as the most likely remedy of the prevailing licentiousness. It was an attempt, well-meant but not successful, to arrest the wanton proceedings of 'the coarse and violent mob.' Good men saw with alarm, almost with despair, that what they said in the obsolete language of religious teaching was not listened to, and tried to address the age in plain and unmistakeable terms. The new theory of consequences was not introduced by 'men of leisure' to supplant and overthrow a nobler and purer view of religion and morality, it was a plain fact of religion stated in plain language, in the hope of deterring the wicked from his wickedness. It was the address of the Old Testament prophet, 'Why will ye die, O house of Israel?' That there is a God and moral Governor, and that obedience to His commands is necessary to secure our interests in this world and the next—if any form of rational belief can control the actions of a rational being, it is surely this.[213] On the rationalist hypothesis, the morality of consequences ought to produce the most salutary effects on the general behaviour of mankind. This obligation of obedience, the appeal to our desire of our own welfare, was the substance of the practical teaching of the age. It was stated with great cogency of reasoning, and enforced with every variety of illustration. Put its proof at the lowest, let it be granted that they did not succeed in removing all the objections of the Deistical writers, it must, at least, be allowed that they showed, to the satisfaction of all prudent and thinking men, that it was *safer* to believe Christianity true than not. The obligation to practice in point of prudence was as perfect as though the proof had been demonstrative. And what was the surprising result? That the more they demonstrated the less people believed.[214] As the proof of morality was elaborated and strengthened, the more it was disregarded, the more ungodliness and profaneness flourished and grew. This is certainly not what we should antecedently expect. If, as Dr. Whewell assumes, and the whole *doctrinaire* school with him, the speculative belief of an age determines its moral character, that should be the purest epoch where the morality of consequences is placed in the strongest light—when it is most convincingly set before men that their present and future welfare depends on how they act; that 'all we enjoy, and great part of what we suffer, is placed in our own hands.'[215]

[71] Experience, however, the testimony of history, displays to us a result the very reverse. The experiment of the eighteenth century may surely be considered as a decisive one on this point. The failure of a prudential system of ethics as a restraining force upon society was perceived, or felt in the way of reaction, by the Evangelical and Methodist generation of teachers who succeeded the Hanoverian divines. So far their perception was just. They went on to infer that, because the circulation of one system of belief had been inefficacious, they should try the effect of inculcating a set of truths as widely remote from the former as possible. Because legal preaching, as they phrased it, had failed, they would essay Gospel preaching. The preaching of justification by works had not the power to check wickedness, therefore justification by faith, the doctrine of the Reformation, was the only saving truth. This is not meant as a complete account of the origin of the Evangelical school. It is only one point of view—that point which connects the school with the general line of thought this paper has been pursuing. Their doctrine of conversion by supernatural influence must on no account be forgotten. Yet it appears that they thought that the channel of this supernatural influence was, in some way or other, preaching. Preaching, too, not as rhetoric, but as the annunciation of a specific doctrine—the Gospel. They certainly insisted on 'the heart' being touched, and that the Spirit only had the power savingly to affect the heart; but they acted as though this were done by an appeal to the reason, and scornfully rejected the idea of religious education.[216]

72] It should also be remarked that even the divines of the Hanoverian school were not wholly blind to some flaw in their theory, and to the practical inefficacy of their doctrine. Not that they underrated the force of their demonstrations. As has been already said, the greater part of them over-estimated their convincingness, but they could not but see that they did not, in fact, convince. When this was forced upon their observation, when they perceived that all *a priori* demonstration of religion might be placed before a man, and that he did not see its force, then, inconsequent with their own theory, they had recourse to the notion of moral culpability. If a person refused to admit the evidence for revelation, it was because he did not examine it with a dispassionate mind. His understanding was biassed by his wishes; some illicit passion he was resolved on gratifying, but which prudence, forsooth, would not have allowed him to gratify so long as he continued to believe in a future judgment. The wish that there *were* no God suggested the thought that there *is* not. Speculative unbelief is thus asserted to be a consequence of a bad heart: it is the grounds upon which we endeavour to prove to ourselves and others that the indulgence of our passions is consistent with a rational prudence. As levelled against an individual opponent, this is a poor controversial shift. Many of the Deists were men of worth and probity; of none of them is anything known which would make them worse men than the average of their class in life. Mr. Chichester (*Deism compared with Christianity*, 1821, vol. iii. p. 220) says 'Tindal was infamous for vice in general;' but I have not been able to trace his authority for the assertion.[217] As an imputation, not against individual unbelievers, but against the competency of reason in general, it may be true, but is quite inconsistent with the general hypothesis of the school of reasoners who brought it. If reason be liable to an influence which warps it, then there is required some force which shall keep this influence under, and reason alone is no longer the all-sufficient judge of truth. In this way we should be forced back to the old orthodox doctrine of the chronic impotence of reason, superinduced upon it by the Fall; a doctrine which the reigning orthodoxy had tacitly renounced.

] In the Catholic theory the feebleness of Reason is met half-way and made good by the authority of the Church. When the Protestants threw off this authority, they did not assign to Reason what they took from the Church, but to Scripture. Calvin did not shrink from saying that Scripture 'shone sufficiently by its own light.'[218] As long as this could be kept to, the Protestant theory of belief was whole and sound. At least it was as sound as the Catholic. In both, Reason, aided by spiritual illumination, performs the subordinate function of recognising the supreme authority of the Church, and of the Bible, respectively. Time, learned controversy, and abatement of zeal drove the Protestants generally from the hardy but irrational assertion of Calvin. Every foot of ground that Scripture lost was gained by one or other of the three substitutes: Church-authority, the Spirit, or Reason. Church-authority was essayed by the Laudian divines, but was soon found untenable, for on that footing it was found impossible to justify the Reformation and the breach with Rome. The Spirit then came into favour along with Independency. But it was still more quickly discovered that on such a basis only discord and disunion could be reared. There remained to be tried Common Reason, carefully distinguished from recondite learning, and not based on metaphysical assumptions. To apply this instrument to the contents of Revelation was the occupation of the early half of the eighteenth century; with what success has been seen. In the latter part of the century the same Common Reason was applied to the external evidences. But here the method fails in a first requisite—universality; for even the shallowest array of historical proof requires some book-learning to apprehend. Further than this, the Lardner and Paley school could not complete their proof satisfactorily, inasmuch as the materials for the investigation of the first and second centuries of the Christian era were not at hand.[219]

[74] Such appears to be the past history of the Theory of Belief in the Church of England. Whoever would take the religious literature of the present day as a whole, and endeavour to make out clearly on what basis Revelation is supposed by it to rest, whether on Authority, on the Inward Light, on Reason, on self-evidencing Scripture, or on the combination of the four, or some of them, and in what proportions, would probably find that he had undertaken a perplexing but not altogether profitless inquiry.[220]

6 Notes to Mark Pattison

1. The Treaty of Utrecht (11 Apr. 1713) ended the War of the Spanish Succession between France and England and their continental allies and included the confirmation of the English political and religious settlement of the Revolution of 1688. This date is conventional for the transition from French to English domination of the European balance of power. George II reigned from 1727 to 1760. Henry Hallam published *The Constitutional History of England* (1827), written from a Whig perspective and stressing constitutionalism and notions of progress. Pattison makes an elision in his quotation: ". . . which has ensued. A distinguished writer has observed that the labourer's wages. . . ." Hallam documents his source: "Malthus, Principles of Political Economy (1820), p. 279" (Hallam [1827] 1842, 2:446).

See also the appendix on Bodley MS. Pattison 106, fols. 1–7.

2. For "rebuke and blasphemy" see 1 Kings 19:3 and Isa. 37:3. Blasphemy was of contemporary interest from 1857 to 1859 when the mentally unstable Thomas Pooley was convicted of blasphemy by Sir John Coleridge, with his son, John Duke Coleridge as prosecutor. The case was taken up by London secularists led by George Holyoake. See Toohey 1987.

The Jacobite clergy were adherents of the exiled James II or supporters of the Stuarts after the Revolution of 1688. This group included the Non-jurors, about 400 clergy including eight bishops, who refused to take the oath of allegiance to William and Mary in 1689, arguing that to do so would be to break the oath already taken to James II and his successors.

For "decay of religion" see the opening of Butler's *Durham Charge* (1751): "It is impossible for me, my brethren, upon our first meeting of this kind, to forbear lamenting with you the general decay of religion in this nation; which is now observed by everyone, and has been for some time the complaint of all serious persons" (Butler 1896, 2:397). The phrase "light without love" has not been located; for "of the earth, earthy" see 1 Cor. 15:47. The collocation Mill, Carlyle, and Newman aligns three intellectual positions, rationalism, Protestant mysticism, and Roman Catholicism.

See also the appendix on Bodley MS. Pattison 106, fol. 7.

3. Pattison refers to Seneca's *ad Lucilium epistulae morales* (*Moral Epistles Addressed to Lucilius*), to sec. 29 of Letter 66: *illa bona optabilia, haec mirabilia sunt*, in which Seneca comments that if all goods are equal, then the goods of the soul and material goods are also equal: "The goods of the first kind are desirable, while those of the second are worthy of admiration" (trans. Richard M. Gummere, *Loeb* 2:20–21). Stoic moral philosophy, named after the stoa, or colonnade, in Athens where Zeno of Citium taught from c. 300 B.C.E., lasted into second-century Rome. Leading Roman Stoics also included Epictetus and the emperor Marcus Aurelius. Stoicism holds that virtue, attained through knowledge and mastery over the passions, is the only good, and by the exercise of virtue, one's life is aligned with the rational order of the world.

See also the appendix on Bodley MS. Pattison 106, fol. 7[v].

4. "Modern economists" such as Adam Smith and David Ricardo discuss "luxury" as differentiated from necessity in matters of taxation rather than attributing to it any moral opprobrium; see, for instance, Smith's *The Wealth of Nations* (1776, bk. 5, chap. 2, art. 4) and Ricardo's *The Principles of Political Economy and Taxation* (1817, chap. 16). In a discussion "of the checks to population among the Romans," Thomas Malthus links population to food supply, not moral degeneracy: "It may be laid down as a position not to be controverted, that, . . . allowing some variation for the prevalence of luxury or of frugal habits, the population of these countries will always be in proportion to the food which the earth is made to produce. And no cause, physical or moral . . . will have any considerable and permanent effect on the population, except in as far as it influences the production and distribution of the means of subsistence" (Malthus [1798] 1973, 151). On "luxury" and its relation to "licentiousness of morals" see also ¶59.

5. *Catena Patrum* (Chain of the Fathers) refers to the *Catena Aurea* (the Golden Chain) of Thomas Aquinas, a collection of quotations drawn from the Church Fathers. In 1839 Pattison under the influence of Newman and Pusey helped translate Thomas Aquinas: "When Newman projected a translation of Thomas Aquinas' *Catena Aurea* on the Gospels, I undertook Matthew and Mark, but afterwards contented myself with Matthew, passing on Mark to another hand. Even Matthew took me nearly the whole of 1839. . . . I hunted up the whereabouts of all the quotations in each case in the best edition of the Fathers; I spent hours and days over the work in the Bodleian, and would not be beat" (Pattison 1885a, 181). Daniel Waterland was opposed to Latitudinarianism. Thomas Brett declined to take the oath on the accession of George I and resigned his parochial duties; he was consecrated a Non-Juring bishop in

1760. The *Tracts for the Times* included four tracts with the title *Catena Patrum* providing citations on specific doctrines (1836–37): LXXIV and LXXVI by J. H. Newman, LXXVIII by Manning and C. Marriott, and LXXXI by Pusey. Charles II dated his reign (1660–1685) from the death of his father, Charles I, executed in 1649, thus not recognizing the legitimacy of the Commonwealth and Protectorate.

6. For "eternal verities" see Thomas Cranmer's sermon "Of the True and Lively Faith" (pt. 2) in the first book of *Sermons or Homilies* (1547): "Christ himself, the eternal and infallible verity"; and in the second book of *Homilies* (1563), in the sermon "Of the Resurrection": "the everlasting Verity, God's Son, risen to life" (*Sermons* [1547, 1563] 1802, 33, 369).

See also the appendix on Bodley MS. Pattison 106, fol. 8.

7. See also the appendix on Bodley MS. Pattison 106, fol. 8^v^.

8. On the Edict of Toleration and the Act of Toleration see Wilson ¶27 and n. 51.

9. On 23 July 1858 legislation was passed to remove restrictions on Jews' entering Parliament.

10. Methodism is the religious revival, originally within the established church, inaugurated by John and Charles Wesley from their conversion experience in 1738. From 1795 Methodists gradually seceded to form independent congregations. The Evangelicals in England, to which Pattison refers (as distinguished from the German Evangelicals, a union of the Lutheran and Reformed churches in 1817), continued the teaching of the Wesleys and George Whitefield but remained within the Church of England. Their leaders included Charles Simeon and the members of the Clapham Sect. Evangelical theology stressed conforming one's life to the gospels (evangelists), advocating personal conversion, salvation through Christ's atonement, and the verbal inspiration of the Bible. See Overton 1886; Glover 1954; Davies and Rupp 1965–88; Armstrong 1973; Rupp 1986; and Clifford 1990.

11. Rationalism is the philosophical position in which reason rather than sensation is the ground of knowledge, as found in Descartes, Leibnitz, and Spinoza. In its theological sense rationalism, the explanation of religion and the Bible according to reason, referred in England to a group of German theologians and biblical critics from about 1740 to 1836, including Semler, Ernesti, Michaelis, and Eichhorn. For the relation of rationalism to intellectual movements in the eighteenth century see Stephen [1876] 1962; for the impact of these critics on English literature see Shaffer 1975.

See also the appendix on Bodley MS. Pattison 106, fol. 9.

12. In England the term *Kantian philosophy* refers to the theory of knowledge that depends upon a synthetic act of understanding combining the detached elements of sense experience, perceived in the forms of space and time, according to Kant's categories of cognition. Kantian philosophy was associated with rationalism in religious thought and with ethical conduct that conformed to an innate moral imperative of duty. Hence, it provided a basis both for the rational method in metaphysical speculation and for the emphasis on moral principles and ethical conduct that for Pattison characterize eighteenth-century religious thought. For Kant's conception of religion in relation to deism and English rationalism see Byrne 1989, 128–40.

See also the appendix on Bodley MS. Pattison 106, fol. 9^v^.

13. "Churchman" generally refers to a member of the Church of England who accepts the three historic creeds, the Book of Common Prayer, and the Bible as the record of divine revelation. More narrowly, a "Churchman" designates a member of the High Church party, one who holds orthodox views concerning the Trinity and the divinity of Christ, and the church as an exclusive sacramental community of believers. "Socinians" were followers of Lelio Francesco Sozzini (Socinus) and his nephew, Fausto Paolo Sozzini, Italian theologians who denied the divinity of Christ (and hence undermined the orthodox view of the Trinity, making Christ only a titular God). They also denied the immortality of the soul, and proclaimed toleration as a principle. In England a highly intolerant controversy on Socinianism arose in the 1690s. To High Churchmen, Socinianism was almost synonymous with deism, and both were first steps into atheism. The controversy involved attacks on clergy holding Socinian views of the Trinity, for instance on William Sherlock's *Vindication of the Doctrines of the Trinity and of the Incarnation* (1690) and *An Apology for Writing against the Socinians* (1693), answered by Robert South, *Tritheism Charged upon Dr. Sherlock's New Notion of the Trinity* (1695). John Edwards, Calvinist theologian, published *Some Brief Reflections upon Socinianism* (1695), *Some Thoughts concerning the Several Causes and Occasions of Atheism* (1695), and *The Socinians' Creed . . . Wherein . . . Is Shewn the Tendency Therein to Irreligion and Atheism* (1697). Locke, Toland, Whiston, Samuel Clarke, and even Archbishop Tillotson among others, were charged by John Wallis as having Socinian tendencies. Among the many pamphlets are Charles Leslie's *The Charge of Socinianism against Dr. Tillotson Considered* (1695) and *The Socinian Controversy Discuss'd, in 6 Parts* (1708); and Francis Fulwood's *The Socinian Controversy Touching the Son of God Reduced . . . with an Humble and Serious Caution to the Friends of the Church of England against the Approaches of Socinianism* (1693). Locke was attacked by John Milner in *An Account of Mr. Lock's Religion, Out of His Own Writings . . . a Brief Enquiry Whether Socinianism Be Justly Charged upon Mr. Lock* (1700). Sherlock summed up the debate in *Present State of the Socinian Controversy* (1698). In

Tract LXXIII, quoted below in ¶4, Newman repeatedly charges rationalist contemporaries with being Socinian (1836a, 35). On Socinianism in England see McLachlan 1951; Stromberg 1954, 34–51; Reedy 1977; Robert E. Sullivan 1982, 82–108; for Socinianism in the political and theological context of England 1660–1750 see Redwood 1976, 75, 88; 156–74.

14. John Toland in *Christianity Not Mysterious* (1696) asserts that revelation is not beyond the comprehension of human reason and that the mysteries of Christianity are pagan and Levitical interpolations. The book was presented to the grand jury of Middlesex soon after publication. Toland fled to Dublin where it was condemned by Irish Parliament in 1697, ordered to be burned, and Toland arrested and prosecuted, whereupon Toland fled back to England, living there and on the Continent. John Leland's *A View of the Principal Deistical Writers That Have Appeared in England during the Last and Present Century* (1754–56, 3 vols.) attacks Toland, Tindal, Hume, Bolingbroke and others. Leibniz published *Annotatiunculae subitaneae ad Librum de Christianismo Mysteriis Carente* (1701; Little spontaneous annotations to the book *Christianity Not Mysterious*); repr. Toland 1747, 2:60–76 [appendix]). Pattison translates the following Latin passage: "*ego mihi libenter persuadeo scopum Autoris, viri doctrina & ingenio non vulgari praediti, & ut arbitror bene animati, fuissi ut homines a Theologia theoretica ad practicam*" (2:60–61). For relations between Leibniz and Toland see Jolley 1978; and Robert E. Sullivan 1982, 19–20, 178–79, and 190–91.

15. David Hume's *Dialogues concerning Natural Religion*, published posthumously in 1779, introduces three interlocutors, Demea, Cleanthes, and Philo, who represent different theological opinions. Cleanthes, a deist, argues that the doctrine of the incomprehensibility of God's attributes, held by Demea (a believer who holds that the being of God can be proved), is in reality close to the atheism of Philo, the sceptic.

"Athanasianism" is named after St. Athanasius, who helped define the Trinity and the person of Christ against the Arian heresy at the Councils of Nicaea (325) and Alexandria (362). In the Trinitarian controversies of the 1690s, Athanasianism referred to the theological position of orthodox Christianity against the supposed atheism of the Socinians and deists. For instance, Athanasius and the creed were defended by George Bull in *Defensio Fidei Nicaenae* (1685; The defense of the faith of Nicaea) and William Sherlock in *A Vindication of the Doctrine of the Holy and Ever Blessed Trinity* (1690); they were attacked by William Frere in *Brief Notes on the Creed of Athanasius* (1694?), and answered by John Savage, *An Antidote against Poyson: or, an Answer to the Brief Notes upon the Creed of St. Athanasius* (1690). Other tracts on the subject include Stephen Nye's *Observations on the 4 Letters of Dr. J. Wallis, concerning the Trinity and the Creed of Athanasius* (1691), and *Considerations on the Explications of the Doctrine of the Trinity, by Dr Wallis, Dr Sherlock, Dr S—th, Dr Cudworth, and Mr Hooker; as Also on the Account Given by Those That Say, the Trinity Is an Unconceivable and Inexplicable Mystery* (1693); Matthew Tindal's defense of William Sherlock in which he attacks Wallis and South, *A Letter to the Reverend the Clergy of Both Universities concerning the Trinity and the Athanasian Creed* (1694); Edward Stillingfleet's *A Discourse in Vindication of the Doctrine of the Trinity* (1697); and Styan Thirlby's *A Defence of the Answer to Mr Whiston's Suspicions, and an Answer to His Charge of Forgery against Athanasius* (1713). Daniel Waterland published *A Critical History of the Athanasian Creed* (1724). For the Trinitarian controversy of the 1690s see Wilbur 1952, 2:185–270; on nineteenth-century controversy concerning the Athanasian Creed see Wilson ¶7 and n. 17.

Tract LXXIII by J. H. Newman is entitled "On the Introduction of Rationalistic Principles into Religion." For the cited passage, slightly misquoted, see 1836a, 14.

John Locke argues in the concluding paragraph of *The Reasonableness of Christianity*: "God . . . gave him [humankind] reason, and with it a law, that could not be otherwise than what reason should dictate, unless we should think, that a reasonable creature, should have an unreasonable law. . . . These are articles that the labouring and illiterate man may comprehend" ([1695] 1965). Locke's book was attacked by John Edwards (1695) and his tract provoked several responses.

16. John Hales published *Schism and Schismatics* (1642), attacking the High Church orthodoxy of Archbishop William Laud concerning ecclesiastical polity and advocating church union through individual moral reformation rather than on doctrinal grounds. On the Arminians see Wilson ¶51, n. 91. Laud and the clerical party at the court of Charles I, rejecting the Calvinist notion that Christ died only for the elect, emphasized the institutional church and its worship and sacraments, alienated the Puritans in Parliament and the Calvinistic clergy who accused the Laudians of Arminianism. See Peter White 1983, 1987; Tyacke 1987a, 1987b; on the historiography of Arminianism see the review of Tyacke in the *Times Literary Supplement* and subsequent correspondence (14 Aug. 1987; 21 Aug.–18 Sept. 1987). William Cave published *Antiquitates Apostolici [The antiquities of the Apostoles] . . . with Introductory Discourse concerning the Three Great Dispensations of the Church, Patriarchal, Mosaical, and Evangelical* (1677). The Latin phrase means "the rationalistic age."

17. *The Evidences of the Christian Religion* by Joseph Addison was published posthumously in 1721. Richard Bentley delivered two sets of Boyle Lectures (1692, 1694). In the first, "A Confutation of Atheism," he attempts to present Newtonian physics in a

popular form to prove the existence of an intelligent creator. *Four Letters to Dr. Bentley; Containing Some Arguments in Proof of a Deity* by Isaac Newton was published posthumously in 1756.

18. Anthony Collins's *A Discourse* (1724) attacks William Whiston's allegorical interpretation of Hebrew prophecy. More than thirty-five answers to Collins were published including those by Edward Chandler, Arthur Sykes, and Samuel Clarke. Collins responded to Chandler with *Scheme of Literal Prophecy Considered* (1727). For Collins's life and works see O'Higgins 1970.

"This refers to a list given in the Preface to Collins's later book, *Scheme of Literal Prophecy* (1727)" [Stephen's note].

19. Pattison refers here to the substitutionary view of the atonement that prevailed in evangelicalism. Atonement is the doctrine of reconciliation with God through "the death of Christ." To many Church Fathers, from Origen to Augustine, the death of Christ was the ransom paid to Satan who by the Fall had rights over sinful humans (the substitutionary theory). In the *Cur Deus Homo* (c. 1097; Why God became a man), Anselm of Canterbury developed the satisfaction, or juridical theory, whereby the infinite nature of sin required an infinite satisfaction owed to God which no finite human being could offer. In Anselm's theory only God, being infinite, could take the place of humans in Christ's sacrificial death to satisfy the demands of "Divine Justice." Protestant reformers, from Luther to Calvin, extended the Augustinian substitutionary theory, seeing Christ's voluntary submission to death of Christ as an act counted by God as substituting for the punishment due to human sin. Reacting against this view, the Socinians, following the theology of Peter Abelard, denied the objective efficacy of the death of Christ in favor of it as an example evoking the response of love in a Christian. This view was adopted by Jowett (thereby provoking controversy) in "On Atonement and Satisfaction" ([1855] 1859, 2:547–95), in which he surveys the history of theories of the atonement and the differences between English and German views in the nineteenth century. The atonement overshadowed all other Christological doctrines such as the Incarnation until the publication of *Lux Mundi* in 1890. Treatises included Joseph Gilbert's *The Christian Atonement: Its Basis, Nature, and Bearings; or, the Principle of Substitution Illustrated as Applied in the Redemption of Man* (1836); William Thomson's Bampton Lectures *The Atoning Work of Christ, Viewed in Relation to Some Current Theories* (1853); McLeod Campbell's *The Nature of Atonement* (1856); and Hastings Rashdall's Bampton Lectures, *The Idea of the Atonement in Christian Theology* (1919). On the atonement see Aulen 1951 and Hengel 1981.

See also the appendix on Bodley MS. Pattison 106, fol. 10ᵛ.

20. Old Bailey is the name of the Central Criminal Court in London; the *OED* notes a similar usage in 1865: "The phrase, 'Old Bailey style,' . . . [means] a certain license of vituperation which has been supposed, rightly or wrongly, to characterise its proceedings" (s.v. "Bailey"). The reference to Johnson has not been located. The Apostles and forgery alludes to *The Tryal of the Witnesses of the Resurrection of Jesus* (1729) by Thomas Sherlock and to Hume's extension of its argument concerning the reliability of human testimony in "Of Miracles," published in *Philosophical Essays concerning Human Understanding* (1748; renamed *An Enquiry concerning Human Understanding* in 1758).

21. "This evidential school" refers to the theologians who argued that the proof for the existence and attributes of God can be demonstrated through the analogy of nature, particularly in the works of Butler and Paley. Nathaniel Lardner's *The Credibility of the Gospel History* (1727–57, 14 vols.) defends the factual evidence of the biblical record against the deists by reconciling the discrepancies in the Bible.

22. Hexameters in classical poetry are twelve-syllable lines, composed of six dactylic feet, used primarily in epic poetry, such as Homer's *Iliad* and *Odyssey*, and Virgil's *Aeneid*. A common exercise for students in public schools and universities involved translating English verse into classical Greek and Latin meters, including hexameters. Thus Pattison ridicules the eighteenth- and nineteenth-century's slavish imitations of classical examples as appropriate models for poetry, literature, and education (see Brink 1986, 126–28).

23. The term "*Origines*" [Lat. origins] was used of works discussing the origins of Christianity, like *Origines Sacrae, or a Rational Account of the Christian Faith as to the Truth and Divine Authority of the Scriptures* (1662) and *Origines Britannicae, or Antiquities of the British Church* (1685), by Edward Stillingfleet; and *Origines Ecclesiasticae, or Antiquities of the Christian Church* (1708–22, 10 vols.) by Joseph Bingham.

Such searches were also directed toward the origins of language, literature, and civilizations in the eighteenth century in such works as Thomas Blackwell's *Enquiry into the Life and Writings of Homer* (1735), Robert Wood's *Essay on the Original Genius and Writings of Homer* (1769), Condillac's *Essai sur l'origine des connaissances humaines* (1746; Essay on the origin of human knowledge), Herder's *Über den Ursprung der Sprache* (1772; On the origin of language), and Rousseau's two studies, *Discours sur l'origine et les fondemens de l'inégualité parmi les hommes* (1755; Discourse on the origin and the foundations of inequality among men) and *Essai sur l'origine des langues* (1781, Essay on the origin of languages). F. A. Wolf's *Prolegomena to Homer* (1795) has, as its subtitle, *Concerning the Original and*

Genuine Form of the Homeric Works and Their Various Alterations and the Proper Method of Emendation.

Such studies continued into the nineteenth century, continuing to be applied to the study of the origins of language, and the search for both an "Adamic" original, and for the relations between languages in the new comparative philology that studied the associations between English and Sanskrit through the use of Indo-European grammars and dictionaries. For instance, F. W. Farrar published *Essay on the Origin of Language* (1860); and Darwin's *On the Origin of Species* (1859) redirects this theological convention to scientific and especially biological discourse (see Burrow 1967). Jowett places considerable emphasis on the task of the interpreter as one of recovering the "original" meaning of the Bible; see Jowett ¶s 10–15 and notes.

Various aspects of the metaphysical foundations of eighteenth-century theories of origins are discussed in Foucault 1973, 328–35. The epistemological problems in notions of the origins of natural language in speech are discussed extensively in recent deconstructive readings of Rousseau. According to Vincent Leitch, Derrida's reading of Rousseau's study of language in *Of Grammatology* "initiates the poststructuralist era" (Leitch 1983, 169; see Derrida [1967] 1976, 141–316).

24. Gibbon's *Autobiography* was published posthumously (1796), edited by Lord Sheffield. In the cited passage he comments on and lists "the Writers who wrote against the fifteenth and sixteenth Chapters" of *Decline and Fall.* He answered these opponents in *A Vindication of Some Passages in . . . the History of the Decline and Fall of the Roman Empire* (1779). See Gibbon [1796] 1962, 185–88.

25. Samuel Taylor Coleridge's *Aids to Reflection in the Formation of a Manly Character on the Several Grounds of Prudence, Morality and Religion* (1825) advocates Christianity as "personal revelation." Pattison cites the 1836 edition (401–2).

26. Herbert Marsh was appointed Lady Margaret Professor of Divinity at Cambridge in 1807 and was consecrated bp. of Llandaff (1816) and Peterborough (1819). He published a four-volume annotated translation of J. D. Michaelis's *Introduction to the New Testament* (1750), one of the first works to introduce German higher criticism into England (1796–1801). Marsh's Cambridge lectures on biblical criticism between 1809 and 1816 were based on German critical methods: *The History of Sacred Criticism* was the first of these courses.

27. J. S. Mill published "Coleridge" (1840); for the cited passage see Mill 1963–91, 10:139. The term *philosophes* refers to a group of eighteenth-century French rationalists, including d'Alembert, Diderot, Voltaire, Montesquieu, and others associated with the *Encyclopédie* (1751–72, 28 vols.).

"The historical sense was very feeble, but many important historical books were being written" [Stephen's note].

28. The letter Hume wrote in 1756 has not been located, but he wrote to Dr. Blair on 23 August 1765: "I have a reluctance to think of living among the factious barbarians of London" (Burton 1846, 2:290). Hume recounts the cited anecdote concerning the publication of *History of England* (1754–61, 6 vols.) in his autobiography: "The book seemed to sink into oblivion. Mr Millar told me, that in a twelvemonth he sold only forty-five copies of it. I scarcely, indeed, heard of one man in the three kingdoms, considerable for rank or letters, that could endure the book" ([1776] 1826, 5). Andrew Millar was Hume's London publisher. Despite Hume's gloom, the *History* did sell: "Within ten years, the completed *History of England* was to become the most popular and best-selling history published in Britain before Gibbon" (Mossner 1980, 305).

29. Pattison wrote "Life of Bishop Warburton" (1863b). Thomas Hearne was made assistant keeper of the Bodleian Library, Oxford, in 1699 and second keeper in 1712; in 1716 he was dismissed as a Non-juror. His chief project from 1716 was the editing of the English chroniclers, anticipating the Rolls Series of historical documents. Samuel Parr's *Tracts of Warburton, and a Warburtonian; Not Admitted into the Collections of Their Respective Works* (1789) included material that had been suppressed in the recently published *Works* of Warburton (1788–94, 7 vols.) edited by Richard Hurd. Warburton's tract, "A Critical and Philosophical Enquiry into the Causes of Prodigies and Miracles, as Related by Historians," introduces the citation as follows: "Every Monkish Tale, and Lye, and Miracle, and Ballad, are rescued from their Dust and Worms, to proclaim the Poverty of our Forefathers; whose Nakedness, it seems, their pious Posterity take great pleasure to pry into: For of all those Writings given us by the *Learned Oxford Antiquary* [Hearne], there is not one that is not a Disgrace to Letters; most of them are so to common Sense, and some even to human Nature. Yet how set out! how trick'd! how adorned! how extolled!" (Warburton 1789, 109).

30. The first and last quotation are from the Author's Preface to *Aids to Reflection in the Formation of a Manly Character* (1825). The second and third, Coleridge's comments on Taylor's *Liberty of Prophesying*, are from "Notes on Jeremy Taylor" in S. T. Coleridge 1836–39, 3:203–391.

31. See also the appendix on Bodley MS. Pattison 106, fol. 13.

32. See also the appendix on Bodley MS. Pattison 106, fol. 13.

33. The collocation of "genuineness and authenticity" is related specifically to "some writers, especially on the Christian evidences" (*OED*, s.v. "Authenticity"). For "genuineness and authenticity" see Paley, in the opening paragraph of *Horae Paulinae*: "By assuming the genuineness of the letters

[of Paul], we may prove the substantial truth of the history; or, by assuming the truth of the history, we may argue strongly in support of the genuineness of the letters. . . . But . . . [my argument shows] that a comparison of the different writings would, even under these circumstances, afford good reason to believe the persons and transactions to have been real, the letters authentic, and the narration in the main to be true" (Paley 1819, 2:129–30). For "undesigned coincidences" see Paley's comment on Romans: "If, therefore, coincidences of circumstances can be pointed out in this epistle, depending upon its date, or the place where it was written, when that date and place are only ascertained by other circumstances, such coincidences may fairly be stated as *undesigned*" (chap. 2, sect. 2; 1819, 2:147–48). Paley examined "undesigned coincidences" further in *Evidences of Christianity* (pt. 2, chap. 7; [1794] 1859, 295), pointing out that the agreements between the letters of Paul and the book of Acts are such coincidences.

34. Milton, *Paradise Lost* 1:24.

35. Alexander Campbell Fraser, editor of the works of George Berkeley and of John Locke, published *Essays in Philosophy* (1856), a collection written for the *North British Review* when he was editor from 1850.

36. All of the cited names, Robert South, John Tillotson, Isaac Barrow, and William Sherlock, were celebrated preachers of their day, from about 1650 to 1750; except for Barrow, they were also involved in the Jacobite controversy over the oath of allegiance to William and Mary.

37. All of the cited clerics, Jacques Bossuet, Louis Bourdaloue, and Jean-Baptiste Massillon, were leading preachers of their day in France, from about 1650 to 1740.

38. The Tractarians claimed the seventeenth-century divines from Lancelot Andrewes to Jeremy Taylor constituted an Anglican "classical theology," publishing their works in *Tracts for the Times* and elsewhere. The French quotation, "Whoever has no readers has no adversaries," has not been identified; however, Hume writes to the earl of Balcarres in 1754: "The misfortune of a book, says Boileau, is not being ill spoke of, but the not being spoken of at all" (Burton 1846, 1:412).

39. On the "Deistical Controversy" see the General Introduction. A latitudinarian in theology, Edward Stillingfleet published *Rational Account of the Grounds of the Protestant Religion* (1664) in which he attacked the Roman Catholic account of the disputation in 1622 before the countess of Buckingham between John Percy, known as "Fisher the Jesuit," and William Laud. The debate inaugurated a spate of pamphlets written against the Roman Catholics. Anti–Roman Catholic sentiments boiled over at the time of the "Popish Plot" (1678), were exacerbated by the Catholicism of James II's short reign (1685–88), and were enacted in legislation during the reign of William I. At the same time, the Non-jurors raised further questions about the loyalty of those who had sworn allegiance to James II and, since he still lived, refused to swear it to William and Mary. Debate on this "Romanist controversy" continued to the end of the century. In 1696–97 Stillingfleet published three pamphlets against Locke's *Essay concerning Human Understanding* (1690). For an account of this exchange see Cranston 1957, 412–16.

40. The Bangorian controversy began in 1717 when Benjamin Hoadly (often spelled Hoadley, as by Pattison in ¶68), preached (and subsequently published) a sermon before George I on "The Nature of the Kingdom or Church of Christ" (using John 18:36 as a text). He argues that there are no grounds in the gospels for a visible church authority. Hoadly was a prominent Erastian, advocating the subordination of the church to the state, and hence beloved by the Whigs and reprobated by the Non-jurors. Hoadly extended his views in *A Preservative against the Principles and Practices of the Non-Jurors Both in Church and State* (1716) provoking an attack from Thomas Sherlock. When Convocation, the governing body of the C. of E., was about to condemn Hoadly, the king prorogued it. It did not meet again for debate and the transaction of business until 1852. Then, as a result of the Hampden and Gorham cases, in the context of the "papal aggression" of the 1850s, and under the influence of Samuel Wilberforce, Thomas Hoare, and the Convocation Society, the prime minister, Derby, allowed Convocation to debate matters of current theological concern. Hence, the Bangorian controversy was linked to the restoration of the rights of Convocation after almost 150 years, eventually enabling clergy to debate the impact of *Essays and Reviews*. On the Bangorian controversy see Rack 1976; and Rupp 1986, 88–107.

41. For "fell dead-born from the press" see Hume [1776] 1826, 2; cf. Pope, "Epilogue to the *Satires*," (1738), Dialogue II, 226–27, 325. For "the only work of mine" see Hume [1776] 1826, 4.

42. Bolingbroke published *The Idea of a Patriot King* (1749); his two deistical tracts, *On the Rise and Progress of Monotheism* and *On Authority in Matters of Religion,* were first published in 1754 by David Mallet. On his deism see Merrill 1949, 11. Johnson remarked about Bolingbroke: "Sir, he was a scoundrel and a coward: a scoundrel for charging a blunderbuss against religion and morality; a coward, because he had not resolution to fire it off himself, but left half a crown to a beggarly Scotchman, to draw the trigger after his death" (Boswell [1791] 1936, 1:268). The "beggarly Scotchman" is the editor and publisher David Mallet.

See also the appendix on Bodley MS. Pattison 106, fol. 14^{v}.

43. In the diverse statements from late seventeenth- and early eighteenth-century preachers,

Pattison establishes their common ground in adopting philosophical rationalism to oppose deism.

44. Edmund Gibson wrote against Latitudinarians and deists in his pastoral letters, where he defends "gospel revelation" against their "lukewarmness" and against the "enthusiasm" of the Methodists (Edmund Gibson 1730, 4).

See also the appendix on Bodley MS. Pattison 106, fol. 15.

45. Humphrey Prideaux published *A Letter to the Deists, Shewing That the Gospel of Jesus Christ Is No Imposture, but the Sacred Truth of God* in 1696. The tract was republished in *The Life of Humphrey Prideaux, D.D., Dean of Norwich, with Several Tracts and Letters* (1748), the edition to which Pattison refers.

46. The *Sermons* of John Tillotson were published posthumously (1695–1704, 14 vols.). Pattison refers to sermon 86, "Honesty the Best Preservative against Dangerous Mistakes in Religion" (Tillotson 1820, 5:24–25). His being in Pattison's list in relation to deism and rationalism is ambiguous: "In trying to hold to the middle-of-the-road between High Church and Puritan and to defend his position by means of reason, the archbishop played into the hands of a new group of religious rationalists, the Deists or Naturalists" (Mossner 1936, 23).

47. John Rogers opposed Hoadly in the Bangorian controversy, publishing *A Discourse of the Visible and Invisible Church of Christ* (1719), arguing that the powers of the clergy were consistent with the supremacy of Christ and Christian liberty; for his role in the controversy, Oxford conferred the D.D. on him. Pattison refers to Rogers's Boyle Lectures, *The Necessity of Divine Revelation, and the Truth of the Christian Revelation Asserted in Eight Sermons* (1727, 58–59) that included an attack on Collins's *The Scheme of Literal Prophecy Consider'd* (1727).

48. Butler 1896, 1:209, 367 (bk. 2, chap. 1, sec. 35; bk. 2, chap. 8, secs. 23–24). Butler's biographer calls the *Analogy* "a late defence of religion against the Deistic charges" (Mossner 1936, 79).

See also the appendix on Bodley MS. Pattison 106, fol. 15[v].

49. Pattison cites James Foster's *The Usefulness, Truth, and Excellency of the Christian Revelation Defended against the Objections Contain'd in a Late Book, Intitled, "Christianity as Old as the Creation"* [by Matthew Tindal] (1731, 42–43), omitting one sentence before the last: "Their noble powers of thought and reflection, if they can enable them to find out the truth, must be sufficient, if they make a right use of them, to recover them from error."

50. Warburton published *The Divine Legation of Moses Demonstrated on the Principles of a Religious Deist, from the Omission of the Doctrine of a Future State of Rewards and Punishments in the Jewish Dispensation* (1737–41, 2 vols.). He argues against the deists by upholding the divine origin and typology of the Mosaic law. For the cited passage see Warburton 1811, 6:242–43.

51. After the series of quotations, Pattison cites Locke's "Of Enthusiasm" in *An Essay concerning Human Understanding* ([1690] 1975, 698), to establish the source of the "common character" of their "rationalism," (¶13). It is implicit in Pattison's listing of self-evident quotations that Locke sets the frame of reference for the eighteenth century concerning the role of reason in theological debate.

52. Matthew Tindal first published the work cited in 1730 (not 1732 as Pattison states). He argues that positive revelation is superfluous. *Christianity as Old as the Creation*, often called "the Bible of Deism," provoked at least 30 responses and "marked the culminating point of the controversy" (*DNB*). Other editions were published in 1730, 1731, and 1732.

"It was published in different editions in 1710, 1730, and 1732" [Stephen's note].

53. Butler 1896, 1:244 (bk. 2, chap. 4, sec. 2).

54. Warburton 1811, 6:223.

55. Butler 1896, 1:198 (bk. 2, chap. 1, sec. 19).

56. Robert Ferguson published *The Interest of Reason in Religion . . . with Reflections on a Discourse by Mr. Sherlock* (1675).

57. In *An Essay concerning Human Understanding* (bk. 4, chap. 18), for instance, Locke discusses "Faith and Reason, and their distinct Provinces": "we may come to lay down the Measures and *Boundaries between Faith and Reason*. . . . For whatsoever Truth we come to the clear discovery of, from the Knowledge and Contemplation of our own *Ideas*, will always be certainer to us, than those which are conveyed to us by *Traditional Revelation* (Locke [1690] 1975, 688, 690). Locke explains his view of the relations between reason and revelation in *The Reasonableness of Christianity as Delivered in the Scriptures* (1695): "The other parts of divine revelation are objects of faith, and are so to be received. They are truths, whereof no one can be rejected; none that is once known to be such, may or ought to be disbelieved; for to acknowledge any proposition to be of divine revelation and authority, and yet to deny or disbelieve it, is to offend against this fundamental article, and ground of faith, that God is true" (Locke [1695] 1965, 191; sec. 251).

58. "Social contract" refers generally to the political theory which sets out the mutual obligations and rights of rulers and ruled by tracing the origins of human society. It is associated primarily with Hobbes (*Leviathan* [1651]), Locke (*Two Treatises of Government* [1690]), and Rousseau (*Du Contrat Social* [1762; The social contract]). "'Original contract'" and "hypothesis necessary" refer specifically to Hume's critique of contract theory in "Of the Original Contract" in *Essays Moral and Political* (1748), in which he argues that the "original contract by which the subjects have tacitly reserved the power of resisting their sovereign" (Hume [1748] 1985, 466) has no

traceable historical origin. For both "social contract" and "original contract" see Riley 1982; Pateman 1985; and Lessnoff 1986.

59. Pattison raises the question of whether the deist position, that freethinkers or rationalists who followed the moral dictates of reason, were, like the Gentiles referred to in Rom. 2:14, justified by doing "by nature the things contained in the law." This paragraph differentiates between the "Protestant expositors" and their exclusivist position (following Augustine), and three Anglican positions: the first (Taylor), moderately tolerant, the second (Wilkins), justifying the morality of rationalists as salvific, the third (Burnet), as a compromise between the two. Augustine wrote *De Spiritu et littera* (c. 412; On the spirit and the letter); after quoting Rom. 2:14, Augustine argues: "They who do by nature the things contained in the law must not be regarded as yet in the number of those whom Christ's grace justifies, but rather as among those, some of whose actions . . . we not only cannot blame, but even justly and rightly praise, since they have been done . . . according to the rule of righteousness" (trans. Peter Holmes, *NPNCF*1 5:103).

60. Jeremy Taylor published *Ductor Dubitantium, or The Rule of Conscience in All Her Generall Measures; Serving as a Great Instrument for the Determination of Cases of Conscience* (1660), dedicated to Charles II, to help clergy with confessions. Taylor's *Unum Necessarium, or the Doctrine and Practice of Repentance* (1655), on sin and repentance, provoked accusations of Pelagianism. See Williams ¶32 and n. 133. Augustine was the chief theological opponent of Pelagius, especially in the treatise Pattison cites. John Wilkins published posthumously *Of the Principles and Duties of Natural Religion* (1675), anticipating Butler's *Analogy*. The cited passage in the final chapter, concerning the beliefs "of a rational man," argues for "the excellency of the Christian religion . . . according to the nature of the things to be proved" (bk. 2, chap. 9; Wilkins 1675, 408–9). Gilbert Burnet, a Whig in politics and a Latitudinarian in theology, published *Exposition of XXXIX Articles* (1699), a Latitudinarian interpretation of the articles, advocating the incorporation of Nonconformists into the C. of E. On the Eighteenth Article of Religion Burnet writes: "All that are saved, are saved through Christ; but whether all these shall be called to the explicit knowledge of him, is more than we have any good ground to affirm. Nor are we to go into that other question; whether any that are only in a state of nature, live fully up to its light? This is that about which we can have no certainty, no more than whether there may be a common grace given to them all, proportioned to their state, and to the obligations of it" (Burnet 1819, 243). On the implications of casuistry and cases of conscience in the early seventeenth century see Elliot Rose 1975.

61. The Shaftesbury passage, in a section entitled "An Inquiry concerning Virtue and Merit," claims that hope is "an Evidence of our loving it the more sincerely and *for its own sake*," and cannot "be justly call'd *selfish*; for if the Love of Virtue be not mere Self-Interest, the Love and Desire of Life for Virtue's sake cannot be esteem'd so. But if the Desire of Life be only thro the Violence of that natural Aversion to Death; if it be thro the Love of something else than virtuous Affection, or thro the Unwillingness of parting with something else than what is purely of this kind; then is it no longer any sign or token of real Virtue" (bk. 1, pt. 3, sec. 3; Shaftesbury [1711] 1714, 2:65–66).

See also the appendix on Bodley MS. Pattison 106, fol. 19[v].

62. This story about Anthony Collins is recounted in *Biographica Britannica* (1747–66] 1778–93, 1:626, note G).

63. Tillotson states in Sermon 3 that the "religion and virtue are the great causes of public happiness and prosperity. . . . Religion tends to make men peaceable one towards another. For it endeavours to plant all those qualities and dispositions in men which tend to peace and unity, and to fill men with a spirit of universal love and good-will" (Tillotson 1820, 1:410, 415–16).

64. The cited passage is in *Principles of Moral and Political Philosophy* (bk. 2, chap. 3), Mill's attack on Paley, that the motive for moral action derives from fear of damnation rather than from "loving and practising good from a pure love, simply because it is good" (Mill 1963–91, 10:145). Similarly, Berkeley's quarrel with Shaftesbury in *Alciphron* (1732) turns on Shaftesbury's location of virtue in "'independent' grounds." Berkeley grounds his position on "religious sanction." See Dialogue 3 on Shaftesbury and virtue; and Dialogue 4 on theism (Berkeley 1948–56, 3:112–73).

65. Laudian High Churchmen, adherents of Laud's theology, were accused of Arminianism for adopting anti-Calvinist theology respecting the doctrines of free will, faith, grace, and good works (such as religious observances and acts of charity). Arminians rejected the Calvinistic doctrine that Christ died only for the elect and that free will is totally subservient to divine predestination. To Laudians good works are a function of free will and are the result of faith. In Calvinistic theology justification, the state of being counted righteous, excludes any idea that sinful human beings can deserve justification through good works or merit, but only as a free gift of faith alone (as in Luther) or through a predestinating act of God (as in Calvin) through the freely imparted grace of God. Sanctification is the state of holiness once the sinner has been justified (Rom. 8:29–30). To Laudians, justification and sanctification are results of prevenient grace that prepares the sinner for the reception of sanctifying grace in the Bible and sacraments (a view derived

from Augustine). Commenting on Rom. 5:12–21 in *The Epistles of St. Paul,* Jowett relates these topics to Pelagian, Calvinist, Roman Catholic, and Anglican views ([1855] 1859, 2:170–87; see also Jowett ¶s 2, 3, and notes).

66. Ger. "Good works do not make a good man, but a good man does good works." Martin Luther, *Von der Freiheit eines Christenmenschen* (1520), in Luther 1883–1995, 7:32; trans. "The Freedom of a Christian," in Luther 1955–86, 31:361.

67. For "inner man" see Eph. 3:16.

68. For the ways that the sermon "accommodates" the "thought of any age," see Mitchell 1962, 3, 5. For "the powerful influence of the pulpit at the Reformation" see Hill and Dell 1949, 165; and Blench 1964). See also Jowett's comments on accommodation and the "thought of any age," ¶s 22, 25, 29, 40, and notes.

The Long Parliament sat from 3 November 1640 to 16 March 1660, throughout the time of the English Civil War (1642–49). The *Canons of 1640,* drawn up by the royalist supporters of Charles I, were passed before the Long Parliament was convened. They required that "every parson, vicar, curate, preacher, upon some one Sunday in every quarter of the year . . . shall in the place where he serves . . . audibly read these explanations of the regal power. . . . The most high and sacred order of kings is of divine right, being the ordinance of God himself, founded in the prime laws of nature" (Hill and Dell 1949, 167). Such reactionary defenses of monarchy were undercut by Puritan preaching: "The preachers . . . did most in the long run to prepare the temper of the Long Parliament and to spread among their countrymen the characteristic Puritan version of . . . spiritual striving" (Haller 1938, 18). Chandos also comments on the role of Protestant and patriotic preaching at the outbreak of the civil war, "a way of life . . . enlarged almost to obsession in the battle against threats, real or imaginary, from 'the enemy,' Satan's emissary on earth, the anti-christ enthroned in Rome" (Chandos 1971, xxii; see also Ethyn Kirby 1939; Maclure 1958; and Christianson 1978).

Methodist gatherings began in 1729 at Oxford when John and Charles Wesley, George Whitefield, and others held meetings for religious study, but the revival proper began in 1738 with their conversion. Writing of Whitefield, Downey comments on the location for Methodist sermons, and on the classes to whom he preached: "He preached from pulpits, balconies, windows, staircases, mountebank stands, coffins of executed criminals, on street corners, in church yards, and in open fields. . . . [Like the medieval friars, the Methodists] drew their congregations from the poorer social classes; both preached mainly in the open air" (Downey 1969, 156, 164). For a fictional account of Methodist preaching see George Eliot's *Adam Bede* (1859), bk. 1, chap. 2 ("The Preaching").

69. Francis Hare was a controversialist in theology and classical studies, engaging in disputes with Bentley, Swift (who ridiculed a sermon of Hare's of 1711 in "A Learned Comment Upon Dr. Hare's Excellent Sermon Preach'd before the Duke of Marlborough on the Surrender of Bouchain" [1711]) and Hoadly (on the Bangorian Controversy). He was praised by Warburton in the preface to the second volume of *The Divine Legation.* Pope groups him (in *The Dunciad* [1728] bk. 3, l. 204) with William Sherlock and Thomas Gibson as three bishops (in 1728 they were bishops of Bangor, St. Asaph, and London respectively); all three were famous preachers and controversialists who took part in the Bangorian controversy. They preached "in vain" because of the popularity of John Henley, the "orator" who charged admission to his sermons, attacking the abuses of the day, his contemporaries, and many of the doctrines of the church; he called himself the "Restorer of ancient eloquence" in the church, but was well known to be sympathetic to many of the teachings of the deists. Hence, Pope contrasts him to the orthodox bishops, referring scatologically to "his breeches rent," "imbrown'd with native Bronze," and declaring that he is a worthy successor to the deists, "In Toland's, Tindal's, and in Woolston's days" (*The Dunciad* [1728] bk. 3, ll. 193–208). Pope refers to Henley's "tub" at bk. 2, ll. 2, 425.

"Dunciad, III. 204" [Stephen's note, inserted after "preach in vain"].

70. George Whitefield's preaching tours eventually resulted in over 18,000 sermons, though he published only 78 of them (Downey 1969, 156). Methodism targeted those who were untouched by the parochial system of the C. of E., such as the mineworkers of Wales and the industrial workers in the midlands, unlike the upper-class audiences of the archbishop of Canterbury, John Tillotson, who had been chaplain to Charles II but whose sermons were models for eighteenth-century homilists, and the Baptist, John Foster, who had only very small congregations in Newcastle, Dublin, Chichester, and Bristol.

71. For the cited passage see Macaulay [1849–55] 1913, 2:826 (chap. 7). Pattison omits the sources Macaulay cites at the end of the quoted passage.

See also the appendix on Bodley MS. Pattison 106, fol. 20v.

72. "Whitefield never drew as much attention as a mountebank does; he did not draw attention by doing better than others, but by doing what was strange. Were Astley to preach a sermon standing upon his head on a horse's back, he would collect a multitude to hear him; but no wise man would say he had made a better sermon for that. I never treated Whitefield's ministry with contempt; I believe he did good. He had devoted himself to the lower classes of mankind, and among them he was of use. But when familiarity and noise claim the praise due to knowl-

edge, art, and elegance, we must beat down such pretensions" (Boswell [1791] 1936, 3:409).

73. John Mason Neale published *Mediaeval Preachers and Mediaeval Preaching* (1856). At the cited page he refers to John Newton, who came under the influence of Whitefield and who published *Sermons Preached in the Parish Church of Olney* (1767). Neale also published six sermons of Guarric, the abbot of Igniac in the mid-twelfth century (1856, 139–53).

74. Pattison refers not to John but to James Blair, who published *Our Saviour's Divine Sermon on the Mount* (1722, 5 vols.; 2d ed. 1740, 4 vols.).

75. John Selden represented Oxford in the Long Parliament. The cited quotation is from Whitelocke ([1682] 1853, 1:209). It is quoted (as Pattison indicates) in George William Johnson's *Memoirs of John Selden and Notices of the Political Contest during His Time* (1835).

76. The *DNB* confirms Pattison's claims about Isaac Barrow: "It is as a preacher that [he] is best known; though, curiously enough, his fame in this capacity was posthumous rather than contemporary. . . . The drawback to Barrow's sermons is their inordinate length—inordinate even for those days of long sermons" (s.v. "Barrow, Isaac"). The *DNB* also confirms Pattison's view of Robert South: "His use of humour in the pulpit suggested to Tillotson a want of seriousness in his character. Yet no preacher was more direct in his dealings with the vices of the age, no court preacher more homely in his appeals. His humour has a native breadth and freshness" (s.v. "South, Robert").

77. The cited passage is in the *Biographica Britannica* ([1747–66] 1778–93, 1:626, note G).

"*Biog. Brit.* Art. 'Barrington, John Shute'" [Stephen's note].

78. For the cited passage see Waterland 1843, 4:419. As in ¶26 Pattison refers not to John but James Blair and to the second edition of his sermons (1740), for which Waterland wrote a "recommendatory preface." Blair founded the College of William and Mary in Virginia in 1693. Hugh Blair, a Latitudinarian in theology, published *Lectures on Rhetoric* (1783).

79. Boswell [1791] 1936, 3:104. Hugh Blair's *Sermons* (1771–1801, 5 vols.) were highly popular: the nineteenth edition in four volumes was published by 1794. The "polished periods and flowery rhetoric" were described in Blair's equally popular *Lectures on Rhetoric* (1783; 14th ed. 1825).

80. Hugh James Rose was the Select Preacher at Cambridge on six occasions between 1828 and 1834. He published *The Commission and Consequent Duties of the Clergy in a Series of Discourses Preached before the University of Cambridge* (1828). Pattison refers to Rose's discussion of the polished style of eighteenth-century divines who "sneer and scoff" with "their cold hearts and decent lives" (Rose 1834, 56). For John Tillotson see ¶15 and note. John Sharp published *Fifteen Sermons on Several Occasions* that reached the seventh edition by 1738; his collected works (mostly sermons) were published in 7 vols. (1754) and in 5 vols. (1829). Edmund Calamy published *Thirteen Sermons concerning the Doctrine of the Trinity* (1722). Thomas Sprat published *The History of the Royal Society* (1667) and two collections of sermons (1697, 1710). Offspring Blackall (or "Blackhall") was involved in theological controversies with John Toland in 1699–1700 and with Benjamin Hoadly in 1709. Sir William Daws, in the posthumous edition of the *Sermons*, claimed Blackall had "universally acquired the reputation of being one of the best preachers of his time." He published *Fourteen Sermons* (1706) and his *Collected Works* were issued after his death (1723, 2 vols.). Benjamin Hoadly's *Works* (1773, 3 vols.) were published posthumously. For Robert South see ¶s 11, 27, and notes. William Claggett's sermons were published posthumously (1689–1720, 4 vols.). Francis Atterbury, "regarded as indisputably the best preacher of his day" (*DNB*), published *Fourteen Sermons on Several Occasions* (1708). Selected sermons of the time are reprinted in Chandos 1971 and Sisson 1976.

81. John Scott published *The Christian Life from Its Beginnings to Its Consummation in Glory . . . with Directions for Private Devotion and Forms of Prayer Fitted to the Several States of Christians* (1681, 2 pts.).

"John Scott, D.D. (1638–1694), best known as author of the *Christian Life*" [Stephen's note; the *DNB* gives his dates as 1639–95].

82. For "'Sharp's, Calamy's . . . in his style" and "they are the easiest . . . yet extant" see Waterland's tract of 1730, *Advice to a Young Student, with a Method of Study for the First Four Years* (Waterland 1843, 4:409, 404).

83. Butler 1896, 2:105 (Sermon 5, sec. 13). Shaftesbury in "The Moralists: A Philosophical Rhapsody" (1709) writes of bringing the philosophy of the cloister into the drawing room ([1711] 1728, 2:182–84). On Shaftesbury as a moralist in defining taste and civil society see Caygill 1989, 44–53.

84. Richard Baxter fought in the Civil War for the Parliamentary Army and published *The Saints' Everlasting Rest* (1650) and over 200 other books. On the restoration of Charles II he was offered the bishopric of Hereford but declined it. Edmund Calamy published Baxter's autobiography, *Reliquiae Baxterianae or Mr. Richard Baxter's Narrative of the Most Memorable Passages of His Life and Times* (1696), as well as the abridgement that Pattison cites (Calamy [1702] 1713, 1:220). Jowett delivered a sermon on Baxter in Westminster Abbey in 1892 (1899, 65–85).

85. For "the new court-jargon" see Pope, *Epistles of Horace Imitated* (1738), Epistle 1, l. 98.

86. John Shute inherited the estate of Tofts in Essex. Collins was a frequent visitor. For the cited passage see *Biographica Britannica* [1747–66]

1778–93, 1:626, note G.

87. Selina Hastings, countess of Huntingdon, supported Isaac Watts, John and Charles Wesley, and Whitefield, making the last one of her chaplains and employing him to preach in her London home to congregations that included Walpole, Chesterfield, and Bolingbroke. She established sixty-four Calvinistic Methodist chapels throughout England, known as the Countess of Huntingdon's Connexion, and a Methodist college in Wales. Her "sole purpose in life was to bring about a revival of religion among the upper classes" (Overton and Relton 1906, 87). A. C. H. Seymour published *The Life and Times of Selina Countess of Huntingdon by a Member of the Houses of Shirley and Hastings* (1839, 2 vols.).

88. Butler published *A Charge Delivered to the Clergy at the Primary Visitation of the Diocese of Durham* (1751). The cited passage is in sect. 4; see Butler 1896, 2:399.

See also the appendix on Bodley MS. Pattison 106, fol. 23[v].

89. Matthew Tindal was converted to Roman Catholicism in 1685 but reconverted to Anglicanism in 1688. Edmund Curll, a Grub Street publisher and the author of *Memoirs of the Life and Writings of Matthew Tindal, LL.D. with a History of the Controversies Wherein He Was Engaged* (1733), was the object of Pope's attack in *The Dunciad* (1728: see bk. 2, ll. 54 ff.).

90. Waterland published *A Critical History of the Athanasian Creed* (1723) to "inquire into the *age, author* and value of that celebrated Confession" that has become the subject of "common and ordinary conversation" (Waterland 1843, 3:105–6). See Kelly 1964, 5–7.

91. George Berkeley published *Alciphron, or the Minute Philosopher, Containing an Apology for the Christian Religion, against Those Who Are Called Free-Thinkers* (1732) where he defends Christianity particularly against freethinkers who espoused deism not out of philosophical conviction but for reasons of social prudence. In the first Dialogue, Euphranor, a scholar-farmer, is invited to the home of his friend, Crito, a parish priest, to discuss philosophical theology with two freethinkers who are staying with him, Alciphron, a forty-year-old lawyer, and his younger friend, Lysicles, who has imperiled his health and fortune with the hedonistic pleasures of polite society. Sec. 11 concerns what sorts of persons freethinkers are and how they are educated. Pattison has omitted two of Berkeley's arguments: first, Alciphron's attack on "a college education," with its stress on "ancient authors" in favor of "frequenting good company"; and, second, indicated by the ellipsis, Lysicles' assertion that the "method, or course of studies" for freethinking education is "easy free conversation without any rule or design" (Berkeley 1948–56, 3:47–49).

92. See Pope, "Epistles to Several Persons (Moral Essays): Epistle 1. To Richard Temple, Lord Viscount Cobham," l. 10.

93. See Origen, *Contra Celsum* (Against Celsus), Preface, sec. 4; trans. Frederick Crombie, *ANF* 4:396.

94. Thomas Reid published *An Inquiry into the Human Mind, on the Principles of Common Sense* (1764), an analysis of empirical sense perception in reaction to the scepticism of Hume and the reduction of reality to unconnected particular perceptions. Reid posits common sense as an aspect of reason as judging of things that are self-evident. By 1823 it had been published in 14 editions. For the cited passage see Reid [1764] 1970, 13.

See also the appendix on Bodley MS. Pattison 106, fol. 25[v].

95. Edmund Burke is mentioned by Samuel Rogers, who kept a notebook on his contemporaries, edited by William Sharpe as *Recollections by Samuel Rogers* (1856; 2d ed. 1859). The quotation is not on the cited page of either edition. For Rogers see Masson 1856.

96. Pattison refers to the synoptic problem, concerning the relations among the gospels of Matthew, Mark, and Luke that give a synopsis of the life of Jesus, often in identical or similar content, ordering, and wording, raising questions of difference and common sources. On the synoptic problem see Wilson ¶22, n. 40 and Jowett ¶13, n. 22; ¶37, nn. 72, 73; and ¶49.

97. 1 John 5:7–8a contains the crux known as the 'Johannine comma,' whereby the explicit mention of the Trinity (from "in heaven" on) are known in no Vulgate Latin MS. earlier than 800, and in no Greek MSS. before the fifteenth century. The earliest citation of the text is Priscillian (c. 380), and from the fifth century in Old Latin MSS., reflecting the Trinitarian orthodoxy of the period.

Gibbon denounces "the memorable text" as a "pious fraud" of editors' "prejudices" acclaimed equally at Rome and Geneva (Gibbon [1776–88] 1858, 3:556–57 [chap. 37]). Gibbon was challenged on this point by Archdeacon Travis, but Travis was silenced by Richard Porson's *Letters to Archdeacon Travis, on the Spurious Verse 1 John v. 7* (1788–89), a definitive scholarly rebuke that Gibbon described as "the most acute and accurate piece of criticism since the days of Bentley." In one of his "Notes on some Passages of Dogmatic Importance," Tregelles comments: "To enter into a formal discussion of the genuineness of . . . 1 John V. 7 is really superfluous" since the passage contains "words not known by the ancient authorities" (Tregelles 1854, 226). The text, nevertheless, continues to be reprinted in editions of the AV to this day.

98. For transubstantiation see Williams ¶31, and n. 130. The Twenty-eighth Article of Religion repudiates the term and its materialistic emphasis in late-medieval Roman Catholicism. This view made the scholastic distinction between substance and acci-

dents meaningless, a point raised in the controversy between Lancelot Andrewes and Cardinal Roberto Bellarmine from 1608 to 1610 on the subject of transubstantiation. John Tillotson, continuing this line, attacks the Roman Catholic doctrine of transubstantiation in his sermon entitled *A Discourse against Transubstantiation* (1684), to which Hume refers in the opening paragraph of his essay "Of Miracles." Two further controversies concerning transubstantiation occurred during Pattison's period of analysis. The first concerned the "Usages" question among the Non-jurors from 1716 to 1735 on revisions to the eucharistic prayer and the mixed chalice; the second concerned the Latitudinarian response to the devotionalism of Waterland's *The Nature, Obligation, and Efficacy of the Christian Sacraments Considered; in Reply to a Pamphlet Entitled, An Answer to the Remarks upon Dr. Clarke's Exposition of the Catechism* (1730) and especially Benjamin Hoadly's *Plain Account of the Nature and End of the Sacrament of the Lord's Supper* (1735) that initiated a prolonged controversy, in which he was supported by the deists and Latitudinarians and attacked by the orthodox (see Dugmore 1942, 23–29, 134–39, 159–83). On transubstantiation and nineteenth-century controversies to which Pattison makes indirect allusion, see Williams ¶31 and n. 130.

Hegel's *Lectures on the Philosophy of Religion* (delivered 1824, published 1832) discuss the "definition of God" extensively, in passages such as the following: "God is *spirit*—that which we call the Triune God, a purely *speculative* content, i.e., the *mystery* of God. God is spirit, absolute activity, *actus purus*, i. e. subjectivity, infinite personality, infinite distinction of himself from himself, as the term begetting suggests" (Hegel [1832] 1985, 3:78).

99. For "the extirpation of the Canaanites" see Num. 21:1–3; for "the eternity of hell-torments," Luke 16:23, and the anathemas in the Athanasian Creed (*BCP*).

100. For the cited passages see Butler 1896, 2:403 (sec. 11).

101. Abel François Villemain published an edition of Pascal's *Lettres écrites à un Provincial, . . . précédées d'une notice sur Pascal* (1829; trans. as *The Provincial Letters . . . with an Essay on Pascal Considered as a Writer and Moralist by M. Villemain*, 1847). Blaise Pascal came under the influence of the Jansenists at the convent of Port-Royal near Paris. They held that the following of any of God's commandments is impossible without the gift of grace and also that this grace, once conferred, was irresistible. Pascal supported these views, writing his *Lettres provinciales* (1656–57) against the Jesuits, who held that grace involves the divine foreknowledge of free human cooperation with the gifts of God. Pascal's *Pensées*, meditative and epigrammatic thoughts on religious and other topics, were first published in 1670. In his review of Pascal's *Provincial Letters* in the *Academy* Pattison compares them with the *Pensées*: "The extraordinary reputation which Pascal enjoyed in his own century was created for him by his *Lettres provinciales*, and not by his *Pensées*. In the nineteenth century the estimation of the two books is reversed; everyone reads the *Pensées*, and is content to have heard of the *Lettres provinciales*. The *Pensées* are for all time; the *Lettres provinciales* were an ephemeral pamphlet" (Pattison 1881, 1).

John Calvin writes extensively on the "depravity . . . of our fallen nature" in *The Institutes of the Christian Religion* (1536); see, for instance, bk. 2, chap. 3, sec. 5; Calvin [1536] 1957, 1:254. François de la Rochefoucauld published *Maxims* (1655) with the epigraph "Nos vertus ne sont le plus souvent que des vices déguisés" (Fr. Our virtues are most frequently but vices in disguise). For the spelling of Rochefoucauld see textual notes. For "not belonging to any age" see Ben Jonson's "To the Memory of My Beloved, the Author, Mr. William Shakespeare" that prefaced the First Folio of 1623: "He was not of an age, but for all time!" and Pattison's phrase about Pascal, "The *Pensées* are for all time," cited above.

102. For "consists in a long series . . . present time" see Butler 1896, 2:401 (sec. 8); for "compass of thought . . . rank," Butler 1896, 2:19 (sec. 26); for "justice must be done . . . considering it," Butler 1896, 2:90 (sec. 18).

See also the appendix on Bodley MS. Pattison 106, fol. 27.

103. Francis Bacon published *Of the Proficience and Advancement of Learning, Divine and Human* (1605). The cited passage is from bk. 2, chap. 14, sec. 9.

104. The Non-juror Robert Jenkin eventually took the oaths of allegiance to Queen Anne and was appointed Lady Margaret Professor of Divinity in 1711. He published *The Reasonableness and Certainty of the Christian Religion* (1696–97, 2 vols.). The fifth edition was published in 1721.

105. Butler 1896, 2:401 (sec. 8). In 1736 Butler was appointed "clerk of the closet" to Queen Caroline and as such took part in the two-hour philosophical discussions that the queen convened every evening (see Mossner 1936, 4–5).

106. James Mackintosh published *Dissertation on the Progress of Ethical Philosophy, Chiefly during the Seventeenth and Eighteenth Centuries*, originally for the seventh edition of the *Encyclopaedia Britannica* (1830–42). On Butler he writes: "No thinker so great was ever so bad a writer"; and on Berkeley: "Of the exquisite grace and beauty of his diction, no man accustomed to English composition can need to be informed. His works are, beyond dispute, the finest models of philosophical style since Cicero" (Mackintosh 1851, 58, 63).

107. Walter Bagehot published "Bishop Butler" in the *Prospective Review* 10 (Nov. 1854): 524–74; repr. in *Estimates of Some Englishmen and Scotchmen: A*

Series of Articles Reprinted by Permission Principally from the National Review (1858). For the cited passage see Bagehot 1965–86, 1:235. "Quaestiunculae" (Lat. little or trifling questions).

108. Thomas Hobbes published *Leviathan* (1651). William Wollaston published *The Religion of Nature Delineated* (1722). François Fénelon published *Traité de l'Education des filles* (1687; Treatise on the education of girls) and *Traité de l'Existence de Dieu* (1712; Treatise on the existence of God). Hobbes and Shaftesbury are cited three times in Butler's sermons, Woolston once; except for two Hobbes citations, all occur in the Preface. There are two indirect references to the controversy between Bossuet and Fénelon on the love of God (Preface, sec. 38; and the first paragraph of Sermon 13; Butler 1896, 28, 229). For "light reading" see Butler 1896, 2:2 (sec. 2).

109. Independency in mid-seventeenth-century England referred to a church polity in which each congregation was independent of any external authority, and of each other, except in a loose association. Hence, the term was applied in the Long Parliament to Congregationalists, the supporters of Cromwell against Charles I. For a contemporary account see, for instance, Clement Walker, *Relations and Observations Historicall and Politick, upon the Parliament Begun 1640; Divided into Two Books. I. The Mystery of the Two Juntos; II. The History of Independency* (1648).

Presbyterian church polity in the seventeenth century consisted of a congregation governed by a pastor (presbyter), with the congregations related to each other through synods. Presbyterians were active as a political party in the Long Parliament. On the political and theological background of Presbyterians in England see Peter Lake 1988.

Both Independents and Presbyterians were Calvinist in doctrine. William Hunt defines "Puritan" as "a body of opinion within English Protestantism characterized by an intense hostility to the Church of Rome as the incarnation of Antichrist; an emphasis on preaching and Bible study rather than ritual as the means of salvation; and a desire to impose a strict moral code . . . upon society as a whole" (1983, x). For a historiographical discussion of the definition of Puritanism, and its relation to Independency, Presbyterianism, and the C. of E. see Todd 1987, 1–21.

Matthew Tindal writes about the move of orthodox clergy into Presbyterianism in *New High Church Turn'd Old Presbyterian* (1709). Concerning the shifts in these political and doctrinal affiliations of Puritanism after the restoration of 1688 see Hill 1986, 2:314.

110. Ralph Cudworth published *The True Intellectual System of the Universe* (1678). The Cambridge Platonists argued for toleration and inclusiveness in the C. of E. on the basis of reason as the indwelling of God in the mind as "the candle of the Lord."

See also the appendix on Bodley MS. Pattison 106, fol. 29v.

111. The phrase "sectaries of the last age" has not been located. Sectaries were associations, sects or adherents of the religiously unorthodox in the late seventeenth and eighteenth centuries. For the cited passage see Locke [1690] 1975, 707–8. The passage (with two minor elisions) is from *An Essay concerning Human Understanding*, bk. 4, chap. 19 in the first to third editions, renumbered chap. 20 after the fourth, because Locke added a new chapter.

112. The Greek word μυστήριον (*mysterion*), translated 22 times in the NT as "mystery," originally referred to the secret initiation rituals of Hellenistic religions; Paul argues that with Christ the "mystery" is revealed (see especially Rom. 16:25–26), and so has become an object of knowledge. Richard Whately published *Essays (Second Series) on Some of the Difficulties in the Writings of St. Paul, and in Other Parts of the New Testament* (1828; 5th ed. rev. and enlarged, 1845). In the passage cited, Whately discusses "mystery" as denoting "those designs of God's providence, and those doctrinal truths, which had been kept concealed from mankind 'till the fulness of time' [Gal. 4:4] was come 'but now were *made manifest*' to believers [Col. 1:26]" (Whately [1828] 1845, 289).

113. For "'cast-off clothes' of the Deists" see Whately's Introduction to Paley's *Evidences:* "Modern infidelity. . . . may seem to present a terrible form in the obscurity which German metaphysics have thrown around it; but upon a nearer view, the spectre will resolve itself into the old worn-out clothes of Collins, and Toland, and Chubb, and Hume, which are now too soiled and threadbare to be exhibited openly in the daylight" (Paley [1794] 1859, 1–2). Whately quotes *Cautions for the Times* (1851, No. 28), an anonymous tract written by his friend William Fitzgerald (that Whately himself edited).

On the "argument of Toland" Reedy comments: "For Toland, as for the Socinians before him, mysteries in the New Testament are called so 'not from any present inconceivableness for Obscurity, but with respect to what they were before this *Revelation* . . .' [*Christianity Not Mysterious*, 2d ed. 1696, p. 89]. Toland's threefold division of mystery is . . . : mystery as God's general plan (95–99), mystery as special revelation to some individuals (100–104), and mystery as parable (104–5)" (Reedy 1977, 294).

The cited page from Thomas Balguy's *Discourses on Various Subjects* (1785) is "On the Distinct Provinces of Reason and Faith." After citing Rom. 16:25 and Eph. 3:4, Balguy writes "that it is no way essential to a mystery, to be ill understood: the word evidently refers to men's *past* ignorance, not their *present.* In this sense, the *revelation* of a mystery destroys the very *being* of it: the moment it becomes an article of belief, it is mysterious no longer" (Balguy 1785, 236–37).

114. Pattison alludes to titles and phrases from Butler's *Analogy* (bk. 1, chap. 2, "Of the Government of God by Rewards and Punishments; and Particularly of the Latter"; and bk. 1, chap. 3, "Of the Moral Government of God," Butler 1896, 1:47–63, 63–94). Throughout both chapters (and elsewhere, as at 1:190 [bk 2, chap. 1]) Butler repeatedly uses the phrase "moral governor of the world." In the *BCP* version of the Psalms (based on Coverdale's Great Bible version of 1539), Psalm 8:1 begins: "O Lord our governor, how excellent is thy name in all the earth." See also Warburton's *Divine Legation* (1811, 6:246) and William Van Mildert's life of Waterland: "the Divine Lawgiver himself, the Moral Governor of the universe" (Waterland 1843, 1:123).

115. Pattison refers to Robert Alfred Vaughan whose *Essays and Remains* were edited by his father, Robert Vaughan (1858, 2 vols.). On the cited page, Pattison quotes from Vaughan's review of Schleiermacher's *Der christliche Glaube* (1821–22; *The Christian Faith*; trans. 1828) that was first published as "Schleiermacher," in *British Quarterly Review* (May 1849).

116. Friedrich August Gottreu Tholuck published *Vermischte Schriften* (1839; Miscellaneous works).

117. For "proper study of man" see Pope, *An Essay on Man* (1733), Epistle 2, ll. 1–2.

118. Butler 1896, 2:271–73; secs. 14–15.

119. Francis Bacon published *Novum Organum* (1620). Pattison misquotes Bacon slightly: "Itaque hominum intellectui non plumae addendae, sed plumbum potius et pondera" (Lat. And so we must not add wings to human understanding, but rather lead and ballast). For the cited passage see Bacon 1858–74, 1:205.

120. For "constitution and course of *nature*" see Butler's subtitle to *The Analogy of Religion, Natural and Revealed, to the Constitution and Course of Nature* (1736); for "constitution of things" and "the writings of Solomon," Butler 1896, 2:259; sec. 1.

121. John Balguy used the pseudonym "Silvius" in supporting Hoadly against the High Church position in the Bangorian controversy. Balguy published *Divine Rectitude: or, a Brief Inquiry concerning the Moral Perfections of the Deity; Particularly in Respect of Creation and Providence* (1730).

122. Whewell published *Lectures on the History of Moral Philosophy in England* (1852). The cited passages, adapted slightly, are from Lecture 8, "Butler" (Whewell 1852, 108–9). In the Preface to the Second Edition, Whewell responds to Pattison's remarks: "Mr. Pattison also thinks that I am in error in saying that Butler shuns the use of technical terms, and is thus driven to indirect modes of expression. The matter is not of much consequence, but what I said was not lightly said, and I still believe that a careful examination of Butler's writings will prove its truth" (Whewell [1852] 1862, x).

123. Whewell writes: "Though he lays down his arguments in a clear and orderly manner, in good plain language, and with sufficient detail of steps and circumstances, he has always been found, by common readers, a difficult and obscure writer" (Whewell 1852, 109). For "Hort's remark" see Hort 1856.

See also the appendix on Bodley MS. Pattison 106, fol. 32.

124. The Greek Stoic philosopher Epictetus published nothing, but his lectures were taken down by his students as Ἐπικτήτου Διατριβαί (Discourses of Epictetus), and *Encheiridion* (Handbook). Antoninus Liberalis (2d century), Greek grammarian and mythographer, wrote Μεταμορφώσεων συναγωγή (A collection of metamorphoses). Plutarch wrote extensively on morals and issued a series of parallel lives of Greeks and Romans. Pattison contrasts the rhetorical style of philosophical writing in the early eighteenth century with the period from Bacon to Locke, setting it in parallel with the second-century writers of Greek in the rhetorical schools of the Roman Empire in contrast to the "metaphysical language" of Aristotle.

125. *Tract LXXXV*, "Lectures on the Scripture Proof of the Doctrines of the Church" (1838) by J. H. Newman was published anonymously. Newman writes: "If we will not go by evidence in which there are (so to say) three chances for revelation and only two against, we cannot be Christians" (J. H. Newman 1838, 112). The three chances for revelation are the canon of the Bible, the doctrine of the early church, and the apostolic ordinances and practices; the two against are doubt and difficulties, as adduced against all three.

126. For "cantare pares" (Lat. "ready in a match to sing, as well as to make reply"), see Virgil, Eclogue 7, l. 5 (trans. H. R. Fairclough, *Loeb*). The cited comment is in a passage on the Arcadian shepherds' responsive verse competitions, defined as "amoebaean" by Edward Phillips in *The New World of Words* (1658) (*OED* s.v. "Amoebaean").

127. The title of Sherlock's treatise to which Pattison makes reference in ¶45.

128. In *Theological Essays* (1853) F. D. Maurice denied eternal punishment and argued that the NT concept of eternity has nothing to do with time. Pattison's quoting of this "coarse and vulgar dictum of Mr. Maurice" was condemned by the *Christian Remembrancer* (Oct. 1860, 357) as "disingenuous" and full of "wilful misrepresentation," since it suggests that the probability of the truth of revelation is doubtful, or at most only slightly greater than that of its falsehood.

129. *Organon* (Gk. instrument) is the title of Aristotle's treatise on logic; Bacon uses it in his title *Novum Organum* (1620); to Pattison it refers to some new instrument or treatise of reasoning.

130. For "coram populo" see Horace, *Ars*

Poetica, l. 185: "before the people" (trans. H. R. Fairclough, *Loeb*). Horace's phrase warns the young dramatist not to allow an audience to see a murder on stage; more generally the phrase signifies public discussion in newspapers or speeches.

131. Charles François Marie Rémusat published on the history of English philosophy, including *L'Angleterre au dix-huitième siècle* (1856; England in the eighteenth century). The cited passage (Fr. Among us a religious man is all too often a man who believes himself surrounded by enemies, who look with suspicion or scandal at the events and institutions of the age, who is desolated for being born in a cursed time, and who needs a great foundation of innate goodness to prevent his pious aversions from becoming mortal hatreds [1:41]) is from the section on religion in the introduction.

132. For "Nullum numen" see Juvenal, Satire 10, ll. 365–66: "nullum numen habes, si sit prudentia: nos te, / nos facimus, Fortuna, deam caeloque locamus:" ("Thou wouldst have no divinity, O Fortune, if we had but wisdom; it is we that make a goddess of thee, and place thee in the skies" [*Juvenal and Perseus*, trans. G. G. Ramsay, *Loeb*]). Pattison argues that eighteenth-century pulpit oratory "has no divinity unless it be prudence," in which the transcendence of God is devalued in favor of God as the "moral governor" (see ¶36 and note).

133. A space occurs in the text at this point in all editions of *Essays and Reviews* before the beginning of the next paragraph; in Nettleship's reprinting of the essay there is no break.

134. Controversial theology was a recognized branch of academic study in the period Pattison is discussing. For instance, Cardinal Bellarmine was professor of controversial theology at the Collegium Romanum; Shaftesbury writes: "Among the many improvements daily made in the Arts of Writing, there is none perhaps which can be said to have attain'd a greater Height than that of *Controversy*, or the Method of *Answer* and *Refutation*" ([1711] 1728, 3:9). Two of the major controversies of the period are the Bangorian and the deist.

"Caroline divines" refers to the Anglican theologians of the seventeenth century, especially the Laudian advocates of High Church principles concerning church and state, and including theologians from Lancelot Andrewes to the secession of the Nonjurors about 1690, hence extending beyond the reigns of Charles I and Charles II. Pattison refers to the antipapal writings of the early seventeenth century, resulting from such crises as the Gunpowder Plot of 5 November 1605, described in "coarse scurrilities" in a sermon by William Barlow as "a cruell execution, an inhumane crueltie, a brutish immanitie, a divelish brutishnes, an Hyperbolicall, yea an hyperdiabolicall divelishnes" (*Sermon Preached at Paules Crosse*, 1605; cited in Horton Davies 1986, 313). Such anti-Romanist propaganda culminated in the Laud-Fisher controversy of 1622 (see ¶s 14, 15, and notes).

135. "Roaring blades" was a common collocation in the mid-seventeenth century for riotous youth; the exact phrase is used in Washington Irving's story about "Ready Money Jack" referring to the hero's exploits in the mid-eighteenth century: "When a youth, he was one of the most roaring blades of the neighbourhood" (Irving [1822] 1977, 37); similarly, "to ruffle it" was in common use in the period 1540–1650 for arrogant, swaggering, and hectoring behavior, often in a religious context (s.v. "ruffle" *OED*).

In the "Life of Bishop Warburton" (1863), Pattison discusses at length the controversy concerning biblical translation between Warburton and Robert Lowth (Pattison 1889, 2:134–44). In his lectures as Professor of Poetry at Oxford, Lowth attacked Warburton not only on biblical translation in general but also because of the notions of the word of God in the light of the originary theories of language. Pattison writes: "Castigation for this insolence could not be withheld without direct abdication. The next edition of the *Divine Legation*, 1765, accordingly, pilloried the offender." But, according to Pattison, "Lowth's victory had been won by the weapon of refined irony and sarcasm, against which the Warburtonian cudgel was a very poor defence" (2:138, 144). For the Warburton-Lowth exchange see Hepworth 1978, 99–105.

For the ways in which the disputatious "air of vulgarity . . . pervaded society" see Redwood 1976, 14, 25–26, 196.

136. For the cited passage see Henry Richards Luard's "Life of Porson" (*Cambridge Essays* [1857]: 147). Richard Porson's appointment to Trinity College, Cambridge (1792), was disputed because of his refusal to be ordained.

137. Robert Walpole was Whig prime minister of England from 1721 to 1742. His opposition included Henry St. John (Viscount Bolingbroke), George Grenville, and William Pitt (1st earl of Chatham). Frederick, Lord North, Tory prime minister of England from 1770 to 1782, was condemned by George III "with treachery and ingratitude of the blackest nature" (Buckingham, *Court and Cabinets of George III*, 1:303; cited in *DNB*). William Nathaniel Massey published *A History of England during the Reign of George III* (1855–63, 4 vols.).

138. For "every virtue under heaven" see Pope, "Epilogue to the Satires," Dial. 2, l. 73, a reference to Berkeley. Dr. Johnson in his "Life of Pope" (Johnson 1905, 3:151) refers to the "malignity of meaning" attributed to Pope for his treatment of the politician and writer George Ducket in *The Dunciad* (1728; bk. 3, l. 176). Johnson also comments on the design of Pope's poem as "moral" but containing "petulance and malignity enough" (Johnson 1905, 3:241). Pattison calls Warburton's attack on Lowth "malignant" (1889, 2:140).

139. The poet Anna Seward, known as the "Swan of Lichfield," was involved in a controversy with Boswell over her attacks on Johnson (Boswell [1791] 1936, 1:92; 2:467; 4:331). On Seward see Walter Scott 1827; E. V. Lucas 1907; and Ashmun 1931.

140. For Fraser see ¶11 and note.

141. A legal term asserting that a common error, repeated many times, makes law.

142. The editors have been unable to locate the author or the work (Ger. The task of Catholic apologetic). Stephen in a note changes the spelling to Hagemann in Pattison's *Collected Essays* (1889). Pattison is possibly referring to Hermann Hagemann, who later published *Die römische Kirche* (1864; The Roman Church).

"Hagemann, *Die Aufgabe der Catholischen Apologetik*" [Stephen's note].

143. According to the *DNB* George Jeffreys was one of the most partisan and arbitrary justices to serve as Lord Chief Justice of England. Jeffreys took a prominent part in the trial of those accused in the Popish Plot and "incited Lord-chief-justice Scroggs in his vindictive proceedings, and, while passing sentence after conviction, took every opportunity of insulting the prisoners and scoffing at the faith which they professed." For his actions Jeffreys was described by Henry Booth in the House of Commons as having "behaved himself more like a jack-pudding than with the gravity that beseems a judge." Charles II declared that Jeffreys had "no learning, no sense, no manners, and more impudence than ten carted street-walkers." He presided over the more than 300 executions of the Bloody Assizes of 1685: "Devoid of principle, of drunken and extravagant habits, he was reckless in everything save his own advancement. A master of scurrilous invective, he delighted in giving what he called 'a lick with the rough side of his tongue' to those from whom he had nothing to expect" (s.v. "Jeffreys, George").

144. Thomas Sherlock took part in the Bangorian controversy against Hoadly (see ¶12 and note), and published anonymously *The Tryal of the Witnesses of the Resurrection of Jesus* (1729), a fictional reply to Thomas Woolston's *Sixth Discourse on the Miracles of Our Saviour.* The cited passage is on the last page of the tract (11th ed. 1743, 109–10). Woolston is the prosecutor of the Apostles in Sherlock's *Tryal*: they are charged with giving false evidence about the resurrection of Jesus (Stephen [1876] 1962, 205).

145. John Locke's letter to Anthony Collins, 29 October 1703, in Locke 1976–89, 8:97. It was first published in *A Collection of Several Pieces of Mr. John Locke* (1739) and was republished in the fourth edition of Locke's *Works* (1740). Locke's concept of loving "Truth for Truth's sake" is discussed in "On Enthusiasm" in *An Essay concerning Human Understanding* (Locke [1690] 1975, 697).

146. Ger. How we save ourselves. Johann Joachim Spalding's autobiography was edited by his son as *J. J. Spalding's Lebensbeschreibung von ihm selbst aufgesetzt, und herausgegeben mit einem Zusatze von dessen Sohne G. L. Spalding* (1804; J. J. Spalding's life history composed by himself and edited with an addition by his son, G. L. Spalding).

147. Butler 1896, 2:179; sec. 13.

148. Isaac Casaubon "first visited" Paris in 1600, living there under the patronage of Henry IV. Pattison published a review of two books on Casaubon (1853), and a monograph (1875).

149. See Butler 1896, 356; bk. 2, chap. 8, sec. 5. Butler's entire chapter argues against a hypothetical opponent of the *Analogy*.

See also the appendix on Bodley MS. Pattison 106, fol. 38.

150. For the cited passage see Whately [1828] 1845, 22.

151. John Byrom was a friend of Bentley, Butler, Samuel Clarke, Collins, William Law, and Woolston and kept a diary over many years, published as *The Private Journal and Literary Remains of John Byrom Related by Richard Parkinson* (1854–57, 2 vols.).

152. See Butler 1853, 9.

153. For "is very little" see Warburton 1811, 1:199. Butler conducted a correspondence in 1713 with Samuel Clarke concerning Clarke's two sets of Boyle Lectures (1704–5): *A Discourse concerning the Being and Attributes of God, the Obligations of Natural Religion, and the Truth and Certainty of the Christian Revelation* (1705–6). The Butler-Clarke correspondence is published in *Correspondence with Dr. Clarke* (1716); Clarke's *Works*, ed. Hoadly (1738 vol. 2); and in Butler 1896, 1:413–35. The cited passage is at the end of Butler's fourth letter (16 Dec. 1713; Butler 1896, 1:430). For the cited passage from Sermon 7 see Butler 1896, 2:129; sec. 10.

154. Thomas Bartlett published *Memoirs of the Life, Character, and Writings, of Joseph Butler, D.C.L., Late Lord Bishop of Durham* (1839).

155. William Wilberforce records William Pitt's remark in 1785: "But amongst other things he declared to me, that Bishop Butler's work raised in his mind more doubts than it had answered" (Wilberforce and Wilberforce 1838, 1:95).

156. Robert Southey composed the epitaph for Butler's memorial in Bristol cathedral where he was bishop (1738–50): "Others had established the Historical and Prophetical grounds / of the Christian Religion, / And that sure Testimony of its Truth, / Which is found in its perfect adaptation to the heart of man. / It was reserved for him to develop / its analogy to the constitution and course of nature; / And laying his strong foundations / In the depth of that great argument, / There to construct another and irrefragable Proof; / Thus rendering Philosophy subservient to Faith; / And finding in outward and visible things / The type and evidence of those within the veil" (Mossner 1936, 204). For "a man may be . . ."

see Butler 1896, 2:401; sec. 7.

157. In 1710 Bentley published the literary fragments of Menander and Philemon under the pseudonym "Phileleutherus Lipsiensis." Three years later Bentley used the same pseudonym to attack Collins's *Discourse of Freethinking,* arguing that Collins's "freethinking" was really atheism. His main line of attack, however, was to expose Collins's gross blunders in scholarship, particularly in translating classical authors. For an account of the exchange see O'Higgins 1970, 77–96. Leslie Stephen writes that Collins's discourse "brought down upon him the sledge-hammer of Bentley's criticism. . . . The contempt . . . of a thoroughly trained and deeply learned critic for a mere dabbler in literature, and the hatred of a theologian for a man who holds a different opinion, are blended in every paragraph, and animate the terse manly Bentleian style" ([1876] 1962, 1:172–73). Jonathan Swift also published an attack on Collins, "Mr. C-ns's Discourse of Free-Thinking, Put into Plain English, by Way of Abstract, for the Use of the Poor" (1713).

158. At the end of his discourse, Collins publishes a long list of fragments from Socrates to Tillotson, establishing a lineage of "freethinkers." In this list he makes most of his mistakes in translation. The Roman poet Lucan was the author of *Pharsalia.* Tully was the name by which Cicero was known to English readers until the mid-nineteenth century, as in Browning's "The Bishop Orders His Tomb" (1845, l. 77). For Seneca see ¶3 and note.

159. For the cited passage see Macaulay [1843] 1850, 685. For Joseph Addison's essay "Of the Christian Religion" see Addison [1737] 1811. The "Cock-lane ghost" haunted 33 Cock Lane, Smithfield, London, in 1762. It was exposed as a fraud, in part by Samuel Johnson, who wrote "Account of the Detection of the Imposture in Cock-Lane" in the *Gentleman's Magazine* (Sept. 1762). William Henry Ireland attributed his *Vortigern and Rowena* (1795) to Shakespeare. The "thundering legion," the twelfth legion of the Roman army, bore on its standard the thunderbolt of Jupiter. A myth conferred the name on the legion during a campaign of Marcus Aurelius (c. 172) when Christian soldiers prayed for rain that not only saved them and the whole Roman army but also devastated their enemies. Addison refers to the emperor Tiberius' enrolling of Jesus among the Roman gods (Addison [1737] 1811, 258; see also Gibbon [1776–88] 1858, 2:46). Abgar V of Edessa was afflicted with leprosy and sent a letter to Jesus seeking his help. This letter is given in Eusebius, *Church History* (trans. Arthur Cushman McGiffert, Bk. 1, chap. 13. *NPNCF2*, 1:100–102). Gibbon, in denouncing the story of Abgar, includes Addison "among the herd of bigots who are forcibly driven from this convenient, but untenable, post" ([1776–88] 1858, 5:5).

160. For Bentley and Boyle see Brink 1986, 55–60; for the response of "the public" see Jebb [1882] 1889, 77–85. On the Battle of the Books see Temple ¶35 and note. In the second American edition (1861, 483–84) of *Essays and Reviews* the following note was added as "On the 'Phalaris Controversy'":

> The controversy here referred to was a learned dispute between Charles Boyle, afterward Earl of Orrery, and Richard Bentley, respecting the genuineness of the Epistles ascribed to Phalaris, the Agrigentine tyrant of Brazen-bull memory, but proved to be a forgery of comparatively recent date.
>
> The controversy originated in the following manner. In the year 1690, Sir William Temple published in his *Miscellanea* an "Essay upon Ancient and Modern Learning," in which he spoke in extravagant terms of the Epistles of Phalaris, as exemplifying the vast superiority of ancient over modern learning. This eulogy from a writer of such high authority suggested to Dr. Aldrich, then Dean of Christ Church, Oxford, the republication of the work in question, an undertaking which he assigned to the Hon. Charles Boyle, a student of that College. In 1697, the Rev. William Wotton published a second edition of his "Reflections on Ancient and Modern Learning," to which Bentley, at his request, contributed a "Dissertation" on the Epistles of Phalaris and other topics connected with Wotton's publication. This paper contained a severe attack on the Epistles, and on Boyle's edition, and was thought by the scholars of Christ Church to reflect injuriously on the credit of that College. A bitter reply was published during the following year, entitled "Dr. Bentley's Dissertations on the Epistles of Phalaris and the Fables of Aesop, examined by the Honorable Charles Boyle, Esq." Though bearing the name of Boyle, the work is supposed to have been the production of Francis Atterbury, his tutor, assisted by various contributors. This superficial but ingenious and amusing essay obtained great popularity, and passed at once to a second edition. It was deemed a complete success, and figures in Swift's "Battle of the Books" as a signal victory achieved by a gifted youth, with the aid of Apollo, over a rude and contemptuous adversary. Bentley was undisturbed, and uttered on this occasion the memorable saying, that "No man was ever written down by anybody but himself." In 1699 he published his "Dissertation upon the Epistles of Phalaris: with an Answer to the Objections of the Hon. Charles Boyle, Esq.,"—which set the matter forever at rest. The spuriousness of the Epistles, the ignorance and impudence of the author of Boyle's Examination, were triumphantly ex-

posed. An answer was threatened, but none was attempted, and none was possible.

See Dyce's Preface to Bentley's Works, Monk's Life of Bentley, and Macaulay's Life of Francis Atterbury (the latter in the Encyclopaedia Britannica, Am. ed.).

161. Henry Cornelius Agrippa von Nettesheim published *De Incertitudine et Vanitate Scientiarum et Artium atque Excellentia Verbi Dei Declamatio* (1531; Concerning the uncertainty and vanity of the sciences and arts and also the excellences of the word of God declaimed), a sarcastic attack on science and learning of his time.

162. For the cited passage see Bentley [1836] 1966, 3:473. The remark originally appeared in Monk 1830, 373.

163. See Bentley [1836] 1966, 3:297. The "Prophets" refers to the biblical books from Isaiah to Malachi; Solomon is the king of Israel (1 Kings), to whom is attributed the Song of Solomon; Plutarch, Greek biographer, historian, and moral philosopher; Zosimus is the author of an extant history in Greek of the Roman Empire from Augustus to the sack of Rome in 410; Cicero is the Roman orator and Lucan the author of an epic poem on the Roman civil war, usually called the *Pharsalia*: all are discussed extensively by Bentley in the passage cited.

164. Sydney Smith's "Letter to Archdeacon Thomas Singleton" (1837) argues against the decisions of the Ecclesiastical Commission (1836) to redistribute church endowments. According to Smith, the commission "was packed with bishops, who were busy appropriating power to themselves and robbing the inferior clergy of their few traditional privileges. A special grievance, which was incidently a personal one, was that patronage, the gift of offices and livings, was to be taken out of the hands of Deans and Chapters" (Bullet 1951, 79). The spelling "Sidney" is changed to "Sydney" in the 4th edition of *Essays and Reviews*. Bentley's *Remarks* is prefixed with a letter (containing the phrase "opinions . . . capable of"), addressed "To my very learned and honoured Friend F. H., D.D.," that is, to Francis Hare (Bentley [1836] 1966, 3:289–92). On the Ecclesiastical Commission see Wilson ¶7 and n. 15.

165. See Bentley [1836] 1966, 3:388–89.

166. Bentley attacks Collins in *Remarks upon a Late Discourse on Freethinking* for the distinctions between the Latin *ac* (the abbreviation of *atque*, meaning "and," used before consonants to link words or ideas that form a total concept, emphasizing the idea or word that follows the conjunction as a culmination) and *et* (which also means "and," used as a formal connective in a grammatical sequence). John Toland worked as an editor and ghostwriter for various Whig nobles and Dissenters from 1698 to 1705 (Robert E. Sullivan 1982, 141–73). Matthew Tindal, elected to a law fellowship at All Souls' College, Oxford, in 1678, wrote, like Toland, a number of political pamphlets advocating Whig positions; Thomas Chubb, apprentice to a Salisbury glover in 1694, received no formal education, but from 1715 until his death published a number of tracts on theological issues from a deist perspective.

167. Francis Hutcheson in the Preface to *Inquiry into the Original of Our Ideas of Beauty and Virtue* (1725) refers to Shaftesbury as "that ingenious nobleman"; Berkeley refers to him in the last sentence of the Advertisement to *Alciphron* as "a certain admired writer." An anonymous tract was published in 1734 entitled *A Vindication of the Reverend D—B—y from the Scandalous Imputation of Being the Author of a Late Book, Intitled, Alciphron, or the Minute Philosopher. To Which s Subjoined, the Predictions of the Late Earl of Shaftesbury concerning That Book.* On 10 August 1720 the *Independent Whig* referred to "a late noble and great Genius of our Age and Country"; Pattison cites the newspaper in ¶s 51 and 55.

168. See Shaftesbury [1711] 1714, 3:316; in "Miscellaneous Reflections," Miscellany 5, chap. 3.

169. John James Tayler published *A Retrospective of the Religious Life of England, or the Church, Puritanism, and Free Inquiry* (1845).

170. For "public opprobrium" see Beattie: "For the most part the pillory was a scene . . . of terror. With good reason prisoners spoke of their 'dread and apprehension' of their hour before the public, or 'begged for any chastisement rather than the pillory' [*London Evening Post*, 6 Apr. 1738]. For some indeed it proved to be fatal" (1986, 466–69). The pillory was not abolished until 1837.

See also the appendix on Bodley MS. Pattison 106, fol. 42.

171. Bernard de Mandeville published *The Grumbling Hive* (1705) in heroic couplets, revised and republished as *The Fable of the Bees, or Private Vices Public Benefits* (1714), a satire on England in 1705. Marlborough was accused by the Tories of urging war with France for personal reasons. This situation is generalized by Mandeville on the premise that the selfishness of human desires overdetermines all acts, even altruistic ones, and hence society, as a compromise with such desires, is established on vice, on which virtues depend. The work was declared "a nuisance" in June 1723 by the grand jury of Middlesex, and Mandeville was attacked for recommending "Luxury, Avarice, Pride, and all vices, as being necessary to *Public Welfare*" (*British Journal*, 3 July 1723). Mandeville then published "A Vindication of the Book from the Aspersions of the Grand-Jury of Middlesex" that he added to the 1724 edition of *Fables*. Mandeville was answered by a flurry of pamphlets, including William Law's *Remarks on a Late Book Entituled The Fable of the Bees* (1724) and John Dennis's *Vice and Luxury Publick Mischiefs* (1724). Mandeville's philosophical position was

answered by Archibald Campbell in *An Enquiry into the Original of Moral Virtue* (1734), supporting Shaftesbury's position that moral virtue is an inherent human quality. On Mandeville see Hundert 1994. For the reception of Bolingbroke's *Works* (1752) see Dickinson 1970, 297–99.

For Toland see Pattison ¶4 and n. 14. Collins went to Holland in 1713 following the publication of *Discourse of Freethinking*.

172. "The statement is a little too sweeping. In 1703, in Dublin, Thomas Emlyn was sentenced to a year's imprisonment, and a fine of £1000, for Arianism. In 1721 Joseph Hall was convicted and sentenced to the pillory, a fine of £200, and three months' imprisonment, for a blasphemous pamphlet; the pillory, however, was remitted, and the fine reduced to £50. Peter Annet, in 1763, was sentenced to a year's hard labour for blasphemous libel" [Stephen's note].

173. After publishing the fourth *Discourse on the Miracles of Our Saviour*, Thomas Woolston was tried on 4 March 1729 by Chief Justice Robert Raymond. He was found guilty on four counts and was sentenced to one year's imprisonment and a fine of £100. *An Account of the Trial* was published in 1729. Blackstone in his legal *Commentaries* refers to the offense of "apostasy," or "a total renunciation of Christianity," that "'has for a long time been' the object only of the ecclesiastical courts, which correct the offender *pro salute animae*" [Lat. for the health of his soul] (Blackstone [1765–69] 1876, 4:34–35). In a note appended to this passage in 1857, the adapter, Robert Malcolm Kerr, states: "It was enacted by statute 9 & 10 Will. III. c. 32, that if any person educated in the Christian religion, or professing the same, should deny the Christian religion to be true, or the Holy Scriptures to be of divine authority, he should upon the first offence be rendered incapable to hold any office or place of trust; and, for the second, be rendered incapable of bringing any action, or being guardian, executor, legatee, or purchaser of lands, and shall suffer three years' imprisonment without bail" (Blackstone [1765–69] 1876, 4:35). The statute is specifically addressed to those "who by speaking or writing should deny any of the persons in the Trinity to be God or assert that there are more Gods than one."

174. Under the pseudonym "John Search," Richard Whately published *Considerations on the Law of Libel as Relating to Publications on the Subject of Religion* (1833). Matthew Hale published *History of the Common Law of England, with an Analysis of the Law* (1713) and *Historia placitorum Coronae, or History of the Pleas of the Crown* (1736); his *Works, Moral and Religious* (1805, 2 vols.) were edited by Gilbert Burnet, who also wrote a biography. Robert Raymond published *Reports of Cases Argued and Adjudged in the Courts of King's Bench and Common Pleas in the Reigns of the Late King William, Queen Anne, King George the First and King George the Second* (1743, 2 vols.). "Part and parcel" is a legal term emphasizing an integral or essential portion of a larger entity, usually used in property law. The Latin phrase is from Virgil, *Aeneid* 10:396: "And the dying fingers twitch and clutch again at the sword" (trans. H. R. Fairclough, *Loeb*).

"See also James Paterson, *Liberty of the Press, Speech, and Public Worship* (Macmillan, 1880)" [Stephen's note].

Pattison refers to this work in his marginal notes in Bodley MS. Pattison 106, fol. 42.

175. William Beveridge was an expert in the canons and decrees of the early church. After his death, his literary executor published *Private Thoughts upon Religion* (1709), with a Preface attacking the age because "*Christianity* under the Notion of Enthusiasm, [is] expos'd to the Contempt of the meanest Capacities, and hooted out of the World by the very Dregs of the People. . . . But, however, the Doctrine and Discipline of our Church may be misrepresented, exploded, and despis'd, and our Holy Religion become only a *Name*, which is almost *every where spoken against*; This Good Bishop will nevertheless have the Honour . . . of having done all that he cou'd . . . to restrain and subdue it" (Beveridge 1709, xii–xiv).

See also the appendix on Bodley MS. Pattison 106, fol. 43.

176. Butler 1896, 1:1–2; sec. 2.

177. The *Independent Whig*, edited by John Trenchard and Thomas Gordon, was issued weekly from 20 January 1720 to 4 January 1721. See also ¶53 and n. 189.

178. Both John Balguy and Waterland wrote against deism from 1726 to 1732. Balguy attacked Shaftesbury in *A Letter to a Deist, concerning the Beauty and Excellency of Moral Virtue* (1726) and *A Second Letter to a Deist* (1731), where he defended Clarke against Tindal's *Christianity as Old as Creation* (1730). Waterland also attacked Tindal in *Scripture Vindicated* (1730–32). Waterland recommends Balguy's sermons in his tract of 1730, *Advice to a Young Student* (Waterland 1843, 4:415).

179. For the Catholic "calumnies against Luther" see Hazlitt's edition of Luther's *Table Talk* and Chalmers's "Life" (Luther 1856, lxxxviii–xcii).

180. William Van Mildert prefaced *The Works of Daniel Waterland* (1823, 10 vols.) with a study of his life and writings. Conyers Middleton wrote an anonymous *Letter to Waterland* (1731) in response to *Scripture Vindicated* (1730). Middleton's *Letter* is described by Van Mildert as "vehement, but unguarded" (Waterland 1843, 1:124); see also Rupp 1986, 275–77. Before ordination Thomas Rundle had also been a part of a society for the promotion of primitive Christianity which was grouped around William Whiston. William Talbot nominated Rundle for the see of Gloucester in 1733, but the nomination was

blocked by the bishop of London, Edmund Gibson, by accusations that Rundle was a deist. Rundle was made bishop of Derry after the Gloucester nomination failed.

181. "Too much seems here to be attributed to a mere repetition of a bit of scandal, which was, moreover, never published by Chesterfield, but only left among his papers" [Stephen's note].

182. Lord Chesterfield was a Whig politician in Walpole's administration involved in the condemnation of Atterbury in the House of Lords. Robert Carruthers published *The Life of Alexander Pope* (1857). For Pope's letter, sent after Atterbury was exiled to France for treason, in which Pope claims him to be a sceptic, see Carruthers 1857, 213–14. For Atterbury see Bennett 1975.

183. Lollard (from the middle Dutch verb meaning to murmur or mutter) was first applied in disapproval to members of religious fraternities, including associates of the Franciscan Third Order (about 1300), who murmured their prayers and were noted for their exaggerated piety, but also for their care for the sick and dying among the poor. In England the followers of John Wycliffe were called "Lollards" because of their stress on the Bible and pious concern for the reformation of manners and care for the poor. The term came to be applied more generally from 1382 to about 1520 to those critical of the church. On the Lollards see J. A. F. Thomson 1965).

184. Macaulay's "portrait" entitled "The Clergy," describing how their way of life, their class position, and their social function had changed since 1640, is in the third chapter of "The State of England in 1685" ([1849–55] 1913, 1:313–22). Churchill Babington published *Mr Macaulay's Character of the Clergy in the Seventeenth Century Considered* (1849), in which he defended the seventeenth-century clergy against Macaulay's disparaging portrayal.

Erasmus portrays the "begging friar" in *Praise of Folly* ([1511] 1971, 164–65). Ulrich von Hutten published *Epistolae Obscurorum Virorum ad Dominus Magistrum Ortvinum Gratium* (1515; Letters of obscure men to Master Ortwin Gratius), a satiric collection of fictional letters purporting to congratulate scholastics who attacked the humanist Johannes Reuchlin. See Hutten [1515] 1909.

185. Byron uses this phrase to describe Gibbon: "Sapping a solemn creed with solemn sneer" (*Childe Harold's Pilgrimage*, canto 3, st. 107).

186. John Wycliffe wrote over 100 works in Latin including many polemical tracts and sermons that combined an appeal to the Bible with a denunciation of clerical immorality and ecclesiastical abuses. His followers wrote and published popular treatises in Latin and English attacking the friars and other clergy. A collection of such songs dating from 1380 was edited by Thomas Wright, *Political Poems and Songs Relating to English History: Composed during the Period from the Accession of Edward III* (1859–61, 2 vols.).

187. For "poor persoun" and "Christe's Gospel" see Chaucer, *The Canterbury Tales*, General Prologue, ll. 477–82.

188. "By Thomas Gordon, also translator of Tacitus, in co-operation with Trenchard. It carried on the Whig opposition to the Church, previously shown in the Sacheverell and Bangorian controversies. It represents Hoadly as against Atterbury, but does not imply a general estimate of the clergy from an extra-political standpoint. It is really an imitation of Swift's *Examiner*, Defoe's *Review*, &c., not of the *Tatler*, which was outside politics" [Stephen's note].

189. The issues of the *Independent Whig* were collected into book form by Thomas Gordon in 1721, as *The Independent Whig: or, a Defence of Primitive Christianity, and of Our Ecclesiastical Establishment, against the Exorbitant Claims and Encroachments of Fanatical and Disaffected Clergymen*. See *Independent* 1753. See also ¶51 and n. 177.

190. In 1721 Thomas Wilson issued a bull banning the *Independent Whig* from entering his diocese, Sodor and Man. The bull was reprinted in subsequent editions of the volume with extensive discussion (*Independent* 1753, 1:xxix–xxxviii). Wilson held the bishopric from 1698, building churches and promoting education, imposing church discipline according to the Ecclesiastical Constitutions of 1704 that inflicted public penance for slander, perjury, and immorality, involving him in extensive legal disputes. *Sacra Privata*, his devotional writings, was published in *The Works of the Right Reverend Father in God, Thomas Wilson, D.D.*, ed. C. Cruttwell (1781, 2 vols.).

191. "The Honour therefore of the good Clergy is consulted and promoted by exposing the bad" (*Independent* 1753, 1:16; 3 Feb. 1720). This issue, entitled "Of the Contempt of the Clergy," attacks clerical abuses: "If Clergymen would avoid contempt, let them avoid the Cause of it: Let them not be starting and maintaining eternal Claims to worldly Power: Let them not be hunting after Honours, courting Preferments, and bustling for Riches" (1:15).

192. James Burgh published *Political Disquisitions: or, an Enquiry into Public Errors, Defects, and Abuses* (1774–75, 3 vols.).

"The French influence can hardly be perceived till after the middle of the century. Voltaire, in his sceptical writings, and Rousseau, introduced this influence, itself partly affected by English Deism" [Stephen's note].

193. "Above all, avoid zeal." The remark was made in the form "N'ayez pas de zèle" (Fr. Do not have zeal) by Charles Maurice de Talleyrand to Madame de Staël, according to Sainte-Beuve ([1845] 1869, 132). The term *zèle* connotes religious enthusiasm.

194. Although Pattison refers to attacks on enthusiasm in Methodism around 1750, these on-

slaughts are the culmination of 100 years of attack. For instance, in 1700 Locke added a new chapter "Of Enthusiasm" (bk. 4, chap. 19) to the fourth edition of *An Essay concerning Human Understanding*, where he defined enthusiasm: "It takes away both Reason and Revelation, and substitutes in the room of it, the ungrounded Fancies of a Man's own Brain, and assumes them for a Foundation both of Opinion and Conduct. . . . [It] is an Illumination from the Spirit of God, and presently of divine Authority" (Locke [1690] 1975, 698–99; bk. 4, chap. 19. secs. 3, 4). Other works on enthusiasm include Méric Casaubon, *A Treatise concerning Enthusiasme* (1655); Henry More, *Enthusiasmus Triumphatus, or a Discourse of the Nature, Causes, Kinds and Cure of Enthusiasme* (1662); Lord Shaftesbury, *A Letter concerning Enthusiasm* (1708); George Hickes, *The Spirit of Enthusiasm Exorcised, in a Sermon Preach'd before the University of Oxford* (1709); Archibald Campbell, *A Discourse Proving That the Apostles Were No Enthusiasts* (1730); and George Lavington, *The Enthusiasm of Methodists and Papists Compared* (1749). The subject continued to provoke interest at the time of the publication of *Essays and Reviews* as in Isaac Taylor, *Natural History of Enthusiasm* (1855, 9th ed.) and George Eliot, *Adam Bede* (1859).

195. Pattison draws a distinction, common from the period of the Civil War, between "Gospel preachers" and "dumb dogs," that is, between devout Puritans or Evangelicals and the clergy of the C. of E. who neglect their parishioners (see Hill [1961] 1969, 145). "Dumb dogs" (Isa. 56:10) is a slighting term for the conforming Laudians, with their empty or "dumb" popish ceremonials, who followed the letter of the *BCP* and read the *Book of Homilies* or catechized rather than preaching. Country clergy as "fox hunters" more addicted to blood sports than pastoral duties were attacked by Joseph Addison in the *Freeholder* (5 Mar. 1716). A "pluralist" was a clergyman who held more than one benefice simultaneously: for instance, the deanery of St. Paul's and the bishopric of Rochester were held conjointly throughout the eighteenth century. Such abuses were much reduced by the Pluralities Acts of 1838 and 1850.

"Hophni and Phinehas," the sons of Eli, were immoral priests at the sanctuary in Shiloh where they stole meat from the sacrifices and had sexual intercourse with the women assistants at the shrine. They died at the hands of the Philistines and became a byword for faithless priests (1 Sam. 1:3; 2:12–17; 22–25; 4:11). Thomas Arnold uses the phrase "Hophni and Phineas school" of "low worldly clergy, careless and grossly ignorant,—ministers not of the Gospel but of the aristocracy who belong to Christianity only from the accident of its being established by law" (1836, 235). The quotation "careless . . . a year" has not been identified.

196. William Cowper published the satiric poem "Truth" on the abuses of religious truth in *Poems* (1782). John Huss preached and wrote against the immorality of the clergy; Girolamo Savonarola preached against the abuses of the clergy and the Florentines and organized a theocratic state in opposition to the governing Medici family. Both were burned at the stake as heretics. For Huss see Spinka 1968; for Savonarola, Erlanger 1988 and Polizzotto 1994.

197. *Prelacy* was used by the Puritans as a hostile term for the episcopal government of the church; for example, *The Solemn League and Covenant* (1643) advocates "the extirpation of popery, prelacy . . . superstition, heresy, schism, [and] profaneness" (Gardiner 1906, 268–69).

See also the appendix on Bodley MS. Pattison 106, fol. 47.

198. The Reform Bill of 1832 was opposed by the bishops in the House of Lords who feared that a reformed Parliament would lead to a reformed church. Any redistribution of seats away from established Tory property interests to the new industrial towns would involve conferring the franchise on Dissenters and their elected representatives. Parliament's responsibility for the care of the established church might therefore pass from the hands of Anglicans into those of Nonconformists. At the same time the government was threatening to abolish ten out of twenty-two Irish bishoprics, and in the Church Temporalities Act (1833) did so. This act was the occasion for John Keble's Assize Sermon of 1833 that J. H. Newman took as the inaugural moment of the Tractarian Movement (see Owen Chadwick 1966–70, 1:24–47).

199. The cited passage is in the *Freeholder*, no. 22 (5 Mar. 1716). The *Freeholder*, edited by Joseph Addison, was published from 23 December 1715 to 29 June 1716. George Hickes was a Non-juring bishop. The posthumous publication of his *Constitution of the Catholic Church and the Nature and Consequences of Schism* (1716) was one of the causes of the Bangorian controversy.

200. For Butler's relation with Queen Caroline see ¶33 and n. 105. In 1724 she urged Thomas Wilson to accept the see of Exeter, but he declined.

201. The duke of Newcastle was a supporter of Walpole and held the post of secretary of state for thirty years (from 1724). From 1736 he was ecclesiastical minister and as such was officially responsible for conferring patronage positions, including the appointments of bishops and other church titles. The second Jacobite Rebellion of 1745–46 and the ongoing War of the Austrian Succession (1740–48) provoked a crisis in the cabinet in 1746 in which Newcastle and his brother, Henry Pelham, organized the collapse of the government, after which they assumed power. For the crisis of 1746 see Marshall 1962, 208–15. For Newcastle as a dispenser of ecclesiastical patronage see Sykes 1966.

202. Berkeley's "two peculiar metaphysical notions" are established in *Principles of Human Knowledge* (1710): first, that for anything to exist it must be perceived as a sensible thing or idea, and second, that the mind of God is the active agency of perception that holds ideas in existence (sec. 46). These notions, related to Plato's *Timaeus*, are alluded to by Alciphron's attack on Locke's empiricism and deism: "I was aware, indeed, of a certain metaphysical hypothesis of our seeing all things in God by the union of the human soul with the intelligible substance of the Deity, which neither I, nor any one else could make sense of" (Berkeley 1948–56, 3:159; Dial. 4, sec. 14).

See also the appendix on Bodley MS. Pattison 106, fol. 47ᵛ.

203. Nicolas Malebranche's *De la recherche de la verité* (1647; On the search for truth), influenced Berkeley's theory of vision and the role of perception in ontology (see Luce 1934).

204. Berkeley's interest in "practical science" includes *An Essay towards a New Theory of Vision* (1709), a study of motion, *De Motu* (written 1716–20), and *A Defence of Freethinking in Mathematics* (1735). His "practical schemes, social and philanthropic" include *An Essay towards Preventing the Ruin of Great Britain* (1721), advocating a recovery of "public spirit" through the construction of public monuments, the encouragement of industry, and a return to seriousness in public diversions like sport and entertainment (Berkeley 1948–56, vol. 6). He also published *A Proposal for the Better Supplying of Churches in Our Foreign Plantations* (1725) promoting interest in Bermuda, especially founding a university there under a charter granted in 1725. Berkeley also published *Siris: A Chain of Philosophical Reflexions and Inquiries concerning the Virtues of Tar Water* (1744), ostensibly on the efficacy of treating smallpox with tarwater, but actually on absolute space and the Trinity. "*Siris*" was added to the title in the second edition in 1744.

205. For "corruption of manners" see John Dennis, *The Usefulness of the Stage, to the Happiness of Mankind, to the Government, and to Religion* (1698), his reply to Jeremy Collier's *Short View of the Profaneness and Immorality of the English Stage* (1698). Dennis uses the phrase "corruption of manners" frequently in pt. 1, chap. 3. For "lying in wickedness" see 1 John 5:19.

William Law, author of *A Serious Call to a Devout and Holy Life* (1728), attacked the rationalism of Hoadly, Mandeville, and Tindal and also attacked the immorality of the theater in *The Absolute Unlawfulness of the Stage-Entertainment Fully Demonstrated* (1726), answered by John Dennis in *The Stage Defended, from Scripture, Reason, Experience, and Common Sense of Mankind, for Two Thousand Years. Occasioned by Mr. Law's Late Pamphlet against Stage-Entertainments* (1726). See also the use of the phrase in Pattison's essay on "Philanthropic Societies in the Reign of Queen Anne" in *Fraser's Magazine*, 1860: "All historians agree that the corruption of manners, as far as its external signs were concerned, was never greater in our country than about the middle of George II's reign" (Pattison 1885b, 2:315).

For qualification to Pattison's claim that all political and religious parties joined in condemning the moral license of the age and that "all historians agree" with them, see Spadafora 1990.

John Jewell published *Apologia Ecclesiae Anglicanae* (1562), trans. *An Apology, or Answer, in Defence of the Church of England* (1564), the first systematic treatment of the differences between the Church of England and Rome; for the morals of third-century Christians, see, for instance, pt. 3, chap. 7 to pt. 4, chap. 5.

See also the appendix on Bodley MS. Pattison 106, fol. 48.

206. For "decay of religion" see ¶2 and n. 2.

See also the appendix on Bodley MS. Pattison 106, fol. 48ᵛ.

207. David Hartley published *Observations on Man, His Frame, His Duty, and His Expectations* (1791, 3 vols.), where, in the first part, he explains associational psychology, and in the second, argues for the existence of God, defends the truth of Christianity, and sets out rules of conduct. The cited passage is on the specified page, in the Conclusion to the second part.

208. Edmund Massey published *The Signs of the Times. A Sermon Preached before the Right Honourable the Lord-mayor, and Court of Aldermen, at the Cathedral of St. Paul, on Friday the 8th of December, 1721. Being the Day Appointed for a General Fast for the Prevention of the Plague* (1722). "Hoadley" is spelled "Hoadly" in ¶27.

209. "Passive obedience" refers to the strategy adopted by many Non-Juring clergy and their associates concerning the requirements of church discipline and authority that came into conflict with the settlement of church-state relations after 1688. They conformed without resistance to the dictates of authority, while questioning their legal status: "All passive obedience doth properly consist in patient suffering such things as are enjoyned by lawfull authority" (Thomas Jackson 1613–40: bk. 8, chap. 12, sec. 7). On passive obedience see *The Whole Duty of Man* ([1658] 1842, 232–33); the tract attributed to Michael Maittaire, *The Doctrine of Passive Obedience, and Non-Resistance Stated* (1710); Berkeley, *Passive Obedience; or, the Christian Doctrine of Not Resisting the Supreme Power, Proved and Vindicated, upon the Principles of the Law of Nature in a Discourse Delivered at the College Chapel* (1712); and [Matthias Earbery], *Passive Obedience Prov'd to be the Doctrine of the Church of England, from the Reformation to These Times* (1717). Henry Sacheverell defended passive obedience in his anti-Whig sermon of 1709

attacking the bishop of Salisbury, Gilbert Burnet, and prominent Whigs, for which he was impeached and tried for sedition, provoking riots in London, Norwich, and elsewhere. On passive obedience see Dickinson 1979, 34; and J. C. D. Clark 1985, 119–61; on the Sacheverell riots see Nicholas Rogers 1989; Rupp 1986, 64–71; and Gilmour 1992.

210. In 1765 Warburton published a new edition of the second part (bks. 3–6) of the *Divine Legation,* dedicating it to William Murray, first earl of Mansfield. The dedication was republished as Pattison specifies. The phrase about Whitefield has not been located.

211. The "professor" in the previous paragraph is Whewell. The cited passages are from Lecture 6, "Mandeville. Warburton" (Whewell 1852, 79). In the Preface to the Second Edition, Whewell takes particular exception to Pattison's treatment of him (Whewell [1852] 1862, vii–viii).

212. In the Preface to the Second Edition of *Lectures on the History of Moral Philosophy in England,* Whewell writes: "I do not wish to revive here the discussion of this point. When licentiousness of talk and manners prevail at the same time as low moral doctrines, it must needs be very difficult to say in what degree each is cause and is effect" (Whewell [1852] 1862, viii–ix).

213. For "wicked from his wickedness" see Ezek. 3:18–19; 18:27; 33:19; "Why will ye die," Ezek. 18:31. For the phrase "moral Governor" see ¶36 and n. 114. The phrases "coarse and violent mob" and "men of leisure" have not been identified.

See also the appendix on Bodley MS. Pattison 106, fol. 50.

214. Assuming Butler's notion that the world is indeed controlled by a moral governor, the rational principle of prudential seeking of one's own interests by fulfilling moral obligations continues into the nineteenth century in references to Butler in positions as diverse as utilitarianism and evangelical Christianity. See J. S. Mill's account of Butler's influence on his father, James Mill (Mill 1963–91, 1:41). J. H. Newman had a very different reaction to reading Butler from whom he claimed "the underlying principles" of his teaching: "the very idea of an analogy between the separate works of God" that suggests the lesser system of this world "economically or sacramentally connected with the more momentous system" and, secondly, the "doctrine that Probability is the guide of life" (Newman [1864] 1967, 22–23).

215. Whewell discusses "the Springs of Human Action" and "the Supreme Rule of Human Action" extensively in the Introductory Lecture to *Lectures on the History of Moral Philosophy in England* (Whewell 1852, ix–xxvi). In the Preface to the Second Edition, regarding Pattison's reference to him, he writes: "I do not at all know who the *doctrinaire* school are, who, Mr Pattison says, agree with me in holding this; but I think we have with us the common voice of mankind. It seems to be a general opinion that Epicurean principles of morality are likely to be accompanied by licentious talk and licentious action. The morality which reasons from the consequences of action does not break this connexion" (Whewell [1852] 1862, ix–x). On "doctrinaire" see Raymond Williams 1976, citing Pattison's "Suggestions on Academical Organization" (1868) as a late usage in the neutral sense of "indoctrination."

See also the appendix on Bodley MS. Pattison 106, marginal entry following fol. 50^{v}.

216. On the heart "being touched" see, for instance, the hymn of Charles Wesley, "O for a heart to praise my God" (1742), in which "heart" occurs eight times in six stanzas (*Collection* [1780] 1875, no. 343). John Wesley records his own conversion on 24 May 1738 when he heard Luther's Preface to the *Epistle to the Romans* being read: "About a quarter before nine, while he was describing the change which God works in the heart through faith in Christ, I felt my heart strangely warmed" (Wesley 1909–16, 1:475–76). In his sermons he set all questions of religious disagreement aside in favor of only one issue: "Let all these things stand by: we will talk of them, if need be, at a more convenient season; my only question at present is this, 'Is thine heart right, as my heart is with thy heart?'" (Wesley 1961, 2:136).

See also the appendix on Bodley MS. Pattison 106, fols. 51^{v}–52^{v}.

217. Edward Chichester published *Deism Compared with Christianity; Being an Epistolary Correspondence, Containing All the Principal Objections against Revealed Religion, with the Answers Annexed* (1821, 3 vols.). The charges in the quoted passage are even more unsubstantiated and sweeping than Pattison claims: "The profligacy of Rochester and Wharton was notorious. Blount committed suicide because he was prevented an incestuous marriage. Tyndal was protestant, papist, and protestant again, according to the times, and was infamous for vice in general. When dying he said, 'If there be a God, let him have mercy on me'" (3:220).

218. For Calvin on the self-sufficiency of the Bible see for, instance, Calvin [1536] 1957, 1:68–83; 1:84–86: Bk. 1, chap. 7, sec. 1 to chap. 8, sec. 13; and bk. 1, chap. 9, secs. 1–3.

219. See also the appendix on Bodley MS. Pattison 106, fol. 52^{v}.

220. See also the appendix on Bodley MS. Pattison 106, fols. 55–58^{v}.

Appendix to Pattison's Essay

Bodley MS. Pattison 106

Bodley MS. Pattison 106 consists of a disbound copy of Pattison's essay from the printed text of the tenth edition of *Essays and Reviews* (1862). It is mounted in a MS. book and is interleaved with larger blank MS. pages, measuring 6¾ x 10¼ inches. Folios 1 and 5–6ᵛ, preceding p. 305, the opening page of Pattison's text in the tenth edition, are heavily annotated in ink. Other annotations occur throughout this interleaved copy, both on the pages of the printed text from the tenth edition, and on the interleaved blank folios. Pattison also annotates a number of folios at the end of the MS., after the printed text of the essay (fols. 53–58ᵛ). Throughout this printed text of the tenth edition Pattison underlined in pencil every internal reference and wrote "note" in the margin, an indication that in a future edition or revision such a reference is to be removed from the text and is to be printed as a footnote. The comments and references on the MS. pages were evidently added at different times, since they are written in several different colours of ink and in pencil; some are in a very shaky hand. Many annotations refer to late seventeenth- and eighteenth-century tracts, others to works by Pattison's contemporaries published before *Essays and Reviews.* Sixteen references refer to works published in the 1870s; the most recent are two references to works of the 1880s (fols. 8ᵛ and 42), indicating that Pattison was correcting the MS. until at least that date.

Most of these materials are of three kinds: bibliographic references to late seventeenth- and eighteenth-century English tracts on deism and religious rationalism, and on the controversies that Pattison refers to in the course of his essay. To several of them he has added shelf marks from the Bodleian library catalogue. A second group of materials concerns nineteenth-century French historians who were writing about eighteenth-century rationalism in France and England. The third group of materials concerns references to the major German philosophers, including Kant, Hegel, Fichte, and Schleiermacher, together with a few theologians and historians of philosophy. In most instances Pattison adds a phrase or sometimes a longer comment, linking the reference to his argument, or pointing out its general application. Occasionally he qualifies a comment he had written in his essay.

All of the entries from Bodley MS. Pattison 106 are given below. Each entry is identified with the appropriate folio number, and its location in reference to the text of Pattison's essay is indicated. In the endnotes to Pattison's essay reference is made to his annotations in MS. Pattison 106. Pattison was generally consistent in using quotation marks for cited material which he usually quotes accurately; at times he paraphrases or makes a comment on the passage he refers to without quoting. The present editors supply, in brackets after Pattison's entry, translations, bibliographic references, emendations, and occasionally brief identifications. By consulting Pattison's references we have been able to identify most of his sources in detail. To help the reader we have also referred to modern editions or published translations if they are available; other translations have been supplied by the editors. Occasionally it has not been possible to identify the edition Pattison used; in such cases we have supplied a reference to a standard edition. Citations conform generally to the editorial practices in this edition: full bibliographic information is given in the list of works cited, except for Pattison's references to eighteenth-century tracts, for which we give the author, the full title, date, and any other pertinent information. Abbreviations have been expanded in brackets by the editors; illegible words have been marked with a question mark in brackets, thus: [?].

[In his annotated copy of the text, Pattison adds the following comments and citations on fols. 1 to 6[v] before the first page of the printed text (Bodley MS. Pattison 106).]

[Fol. 1:]

"Je parle enquérant et ignorant, me rapportant de la résolution, purement & simplement, aux créances communes et légitimes. Je n'enseigne point, je raconte." Montaigne liv. 3. ess. 2. ["I speak as an ignorant enquirer, referring the decision purely and simply to the common and authorized beliefs. I do not teach, I tell" (Montaigne 1965, 612; bk. 3, essay 2, "Of Repentance"; trans. Donald M. Frame). Montaigne published *Essays* 1580 (bks. 1 and 2) and 1588 (bk. 3). Pattison's "Life of Montaigne" was published in the *Quarterly Review* (Apr. 1858); repr. Pattison 1889, 2:323–49.]

"The worthless & bankrupt century which ended by committing suicide," quoted by H. Kingsley *Silcote of Silcotes*. [Henry Kingsley, 1867. Henry Kingsley is the brother of the better-known Charles Kingsley.]

Ea quae vis, ut potero explicabo; nec tamen quasi Pythius Apollo, certa ut sint et fixa quae dixero, sed ut homunculus unus e multis, probabilia coniectura sequens. Ultra enim quo progrediar quam ut veri similia videam non habeo. Certa dicent ii, qui et percipi ea posse dicunt et se sapientes esse profitentur. Cic. Tusc. Disp. 1. 17. ["I shall humour you and explain what you wish as best I can, not however as if I were the Pythian Apollo making statements to be regarded as certain and unalterable, but following out a train of probabilities as one poor mortal out of many. For further than likelihood I cannot get. Certainty will be for those who say that such things can be known and who claim wisdom for themselves" (Cicero, *Tusculan Disputations*, bk. 1, chap. viii. sec. 17; trans. J. E. King, *Loeb* 20–22).]

On the high art of writing popular exposition with Gemütlichkeit [informality] which was attained by Hume & by Shaftesbury, see Kant *Logik* B. 1. 373. [The cited passage is "To learn true popularity, however, one must read the ancients, e.g. Cicero's philosophical writings, the poets *Horace*, *Virgil*, etc., and among the moderns Hume, Shaftesbury et al. Men who have had a good deal of intercourse with the refined world, without which one cannot be popular" (Kant 1992, 556). Immanuel Kant's lectures were edited and published by his pupil Gottlob Benjamin Jäsche, as *Immanuel Kants Logik* (1800).]

On the relation of Philosophy to the popular religions see Gieseler Kirchengeschichte. 1. i. §13 with references in note. [Gieseler 1827.]

On common-sense philosophy Gervinus Geschichte & national-literatur &c 5. 407. [Gervinus 1842.]

On the early deists see Jer. Taylor Works 9. 155. [Jeremy Taylor in *Ductor Dubitantium, or The Rule of Conscience* (1660) writes here on the role of probability in the moral demonstration of God, against "the gay impieties and bold wits of the world who are witty against none more than God and God's wisdom, (and who) have made it now to be but too seasonable" (Taylor 1847–54, 9:155).]

On the rationalism of the Platon[ic]-Aristot[elian] period contrasted with the mystical transcendental theosophy of the Alexandrian period, see Zeller. 5. 377. [Zeller (1844–52) 1856–68, 5:377.]

[Fols. 1^{v}--4^{v}: blank]

[Fol. 5:]

"Les honnêtes gens qui pensent ont à peu près les mêmes principes, et ne composent qu'une république." Voltaire. Ded. to Zaire. [The honest people who think they are a little nearer the same principles and who only make up a republic (Voltaire [1732] 1972, 46; dedication); Voltaire published his tragedy *Zaïre* in 1732.]

"Son époque inquiète et turbulente n'avait l'oreille qu'aux débats de la polémique religieuse, où la vérité de tous les temps n'a qu'une petit place." D. Nisard (Of the time of Erasmus). [Nisard 1855, 52; His epoch, restless and turbulent, only had ear for religious polemic, where the eternal verities occupy only a little place.]

The application of the idea of chronology and succession to philosophical thinking much later than to political events. Retrospective Rev[iew], Novemb. 1853.

On general laws deducible from the course of human history, see Kant, Werke. 4. 274. Man kann sich eines gewissen Unwillens &c. ["One cannot suppress a certain indignation when one sees men's actions on the great world-stage and finds, beside the wisdom that appears here and there among individuals, everything in the large woven together from folly, childish vanity, even from childish malice and destructiveness" (from *Idea for a Universal History* in Kant 1988, 415–16).]

[Fol. 5^v:]

Combat nat.[ural] science. "Les philosophes français sont les avant-gardes de la révolution. Ils devaient faire appel aux passions. S'ils s'étaient bornés, comme les Kant et les Fichte, à faire des leçons et à écrire des livres que les philosophes seuls lisent, l'Europe en serait encore aujourd'hui au régime des Pompadour et du Parc-aux-cerfs. Gloire à ces hardis lutteurs qui ont ouvert le combat! Nous souhaitons que ceux qui sont appelés à le poursuivre soient tous animés de sentiments aussi généreux, aussi désintéressés, que les philosophes du 18ième siècle." Laurent. Etudes 11. 613. [Laurent 1850–70, 11:613; The French philosophes are the fore-runners of the revolution. They had to make an appeal to the passions. If they had restricted themselves, like the Kants and the Fichtes, to teaching and writing books that philosophers alone read, Europe would still to-day be in the regime of the Pompadours and the Parc-aux-cerfs (deer park, a mansion at Versailles where girls were kept, with the help of Mme. de Pompadour, for the pleasure of Louis XV). Glory to those bold contenders who opened the battle! We hope that those who are moved to follow are all animated with sentiments as generous, as disinterested, as the philosophes of the 18th century.]

For characteristics of church of France tem [*tempus*, Lat. at the time of] Louis XIV see Carné. Monarchie française, chap 3, especially pp. 104–6. [Carné 1859, 1:104–6.]

The powers of a community or an assembly embrace the enactment of law or statute. They can never extend to determination of truth. Different fortunes of rationalism in France & in Britain. See de Carné. Mon. franç. p. 445. [Carné 1859, 1:445.]

Complete humiliation of the clergy in the controversy with the philosophes. ibid. p. 408. [Carné 1859, 1:408.]

"Le clergé recula sur tous les points n'abordant la lice qu'avec timidité, paraissant reconnaître lui-même la supériorité intellectuelle de ses ennemis, et semblant parfois demander grâce pour l'intégrité du dogme dont il gardait le dépôt." [Carné 1859, 1:408; The clergy retreat on all points approaching the lists only with timidity, having appeared to recognize themselves the intellectual superiority of their enemies, and seeming at times to beg for mercy for the integrity of the dogma which they hold in trust.]

Catholic reaction on Locke "dans l'étude de la philosophie le mépris de Locke est le commencement de la sagesse" De Maistre 1.442. [Maistre 1821, 1:442; In the study of philosophy contempt for Locke is the beginning of wisdom.]

[Fol. 6:]

"À tous ceux qui veulent suivre une longue filiation et acquérir ainsi le vrai sentiment de l'histoire je conseille d'étudier les enchaînements des opinions religieuses. Rien de fortuit; partout la succession y est nécessitée. Ces opinions forment une trame serrée de prémisses et de conséquences." Littré. *Littérature et histoire*, p. 371. [Littré 1875, 371; To all those who wish to follow a long line of descent and so to acquire the true feeling of history I advise studying the succession of religious opinions. Nothing is haphazard. Everywhere succession is by necessity. These opinions form a closely-woven web of premises and consequences.]

On the position of the men of letters in France—Louis XV—see Sainte-Beuve 2. 488. [Sainte-Beuve 1850, 2:488; from Sainte-Beuve's *Causerie de Lundi* (Monday chat) on "Madame de Pompadour" (16 Sept.), see 1850, 2:486–511.]

"C'est bien moins par les choses accomplies, que par les hommes et les idées qu'ils laissent après eux qu'il faut apprécier les diverses époques." de Carné. Monarchie franç. p. 41. [Carné 1859, 1:41; It is not so much by the things accomplished, as by the men and the ideas that they leave after them that it is necessary to understand different epochs.]

De Rancé poisoning Saint-Simon's mind by calumnies against certain Jansenists. Observe the words "il me demanda le secret jusqu'à sa mort." ap[*apud*, Lat. in the writings of] Chéruel, p. 30. [Chéruel 1864, 30; He kept asking me for the secret up to his death; Armand de Rancé (1626–1700), French cleric at the court of Louis XIV and founder of the Trappist Cistercians; Louis de Rouvroy, duc de Saint-Simon (1675–1755), French diplomat and writer of memoirs, wrote of Rancé and Jansenism in his *Mémoires*, ed. Chéruel (Saint-Simon 1856–58, 6:127–28).]

Louis XIV. "Comme Mad[elle] de Maintenon n'entendait rien aux affaires publiques et que cependant elle avait besoin pour le maintien de son influence d'agir incessamment sur l'esprit du roi, elle attira ou du moins elle retint Louis XIV dans la sphère des questions religieuses. Louis avait un fonds de religion sincère, mais étroit et sans aucune lumière. A cette extrême ignorance [le mot est . . . de Mme de Maintenon] se joignait une fâcheuse disposition à faire pénitence aux dépens des autres. 'Il croyait [. . . c'est encore elle que le dit] expier ses fautes quand il était inexorable sur celles des autres.'" Joubert in Biogr. Gen. "Maintenon." [Joubert 1860, 32:926; Just as Mademoiselle de Maintenon heard nothing of public affairs, so too she took care to maintain her influence to act incessantly on the spirit of the king; she drew, or at least she retained Louis XIV in the sphere of religious questions. Louis was sincerely religious, but strict and unenlightened. To this extreme ignorance (the word is . . . from Madame de Maintenon) was united an annoying disposition to do penance at the expense of others. "He believed (. . . it is still she who says it) to expiate his faults when he was unrelenting over the faults of others".]

18th cent. has its roots in the 17th. "Quand il sera bien reconnu que la philosophie du dernier siècle a ses racines dans les siècles qui précèdent, les plus aveugles partisans du passé devront cesser de la maudire, ou il faut qu'ils reportent leur malédiction dans des temps plus éloignés." Laurent. Etudes, 11, 462. [Laurent 1850–70, 11:462; When it will be fully recognized that the philosophy of the last century has its roots in the centuries that precede, the most blind partisans of the past must either cease from cursing, or must focus their curses on a more distant time.]

[Fol. 6v:]

The contrasts between the "rationalistic" and the "scientific" ages, is nowhere more clearly developed than by Fichte: "Die Grundzüge des gegenwärtigen Zeitalters" See *Werke* b[and, Ger. volume] 7. pp. 21, 22. [Fichte [1804] 1845–46, 7:21–22; The Characteristics of the present age.]

Zeller. Gr. Phil. 5. 295. "Was uns von der alexandrinischen Spekulation vor Philo überliefert ist, zeigt uns mehr nur einen unbewussten und vereinzelten Einfluss grieschicher Philosopheme; bei Philo zuerst begegnet uns die klar ausgesprochene Ueberzeugung, dass die wahre Theologie durch ein umfassendes gelehrtes und philosophisches Wissen bedingt sei, hier zuerst der Versuch, mit diesen Hülfsmitteln den ganzen Inhalt des religiösen Glaubens denkend zu durchdringen, und ihn unter Ergänzung der hiefür nöthigen Mittelglieder mit gewissen philosophischen und theologischen Grundanschauungen innerlich zu verknüpfen." [Zeller (1844–52) 1856–68, 5:295; That which is transmitted to us in the way of Alexandrian speculation before Plato shows to us rather only the unconscious and sporadic influence of Greek philosophical doctrines. In Philo we first encounter the clearly expressed conviction that true theology depends on comprehensive, learned, and philosophical knowledge. This is the first attempt to penetrate rationally the whole content of religious belief with these ancillary means, and, through supplementing the necessary and intermediate states, to link this content to certain fundamental philosophical and theological points of view.]

The whole section on Leibnitz in *Hettner* (Deutsch Litteratur B. 3. p. 115 seq.) is excellent, & to the point. [Hettner 1856–70, 3:115 ff.]

On the transplantation of English Deism into N. Germany, see Mahne, Vita Wyttenbachii, p. 54 (ed. Gul[ielmus] Mahne). [Wyttenbach 1823, 54.]

The custom of having libraries for the use of the clergy. So Harsnet at Colchester. [Samuel Harsnett (1561–1631), abp. of York, bequeathed a library to his birth-town for the use of the clergy; it was catalogued as *A Catalogue of the Harsnett Library at Colchester* (1888).]

For general comparison of the 18th with those of the 17th cent. in France, in respect of political intelligence, see Sainte-Beuve. *Nouveaux Lundis* 3. 230.

seq. [The article for Lundi, 22 Sept. 1862, "Connaissait-on mieux la nature humaine au XVIIe siècle après la Fronde qu'au XVIIIe siècle avant et après '89?" (Did we know human nature in the 17th century after the Fronde better than in the 18th century before and after 1789?); see Sainte-Beuve 1863–70, 3:220–42.]

"Lumières": le propre de ce qu'on appelle *lumières* est d'être répandu et de circuler. Ibid. p. 239. [Sainte-Beuve 1863–70, 3:239; Lights: The attribute of those we call *lights* is to be diffused and to circulate.]

On the "bon sens" of the 18th cent. see Vinet, L'éducation. p. 161. [Vinet 1855, 161.]

Best words on Voltaire's religion in Martin. Histoire de France. tome 15, pp. 361 ff. [Martin, 1837–65, 15:361 ff.]

[On the first page of his printed text Pattison adds in the margin, beside the first paragraph and opposite fol. 7:]

"On inventait la théorie du crédit, tout en faisant banqueroute on travaillait au progrès de la raison, au milieu de la ruine des moeurs." Villemain. Tableau, 1. 12. [Villemain 1829, 1:12; We invented the theory of credit, while going bankrupt we were working for the progress of reason in the midst of the ruin of morals.]

[Opposite ¶2 Pattison adds on fol. 7:]

"Là se manifeste tout ce qu'il y a de puissance conservatrice dans la liberté quand elle est un droit reconnu, constamment exercé. En Angleterre, où tous les dogmes religieux, tous les principes politiques pouvaient être attaqués, sans autre répression que la loi & le jury, les doctrines sceptiques proclamées avec tant de hardiesse par Thomas Chubb, Woolston, Tindal, Bolingbroke, Shaftesbury, trouvèrent dès l'origine une forte résistance, et n'eurent jamais l'empire. Il y eut combat égal entre les opinions avec ce suffrage de faveur que trouvent dans les âmes des traditions antiques et consolantes." Villemain. Tableau de la littérature. 1. 10. [Villemain 1829, 1:10; There is manifested the full conservative power of liberty, when it is a recognized right, constantly exercised. In England, where all religious dogmas, all political principles were open to attack, without any repression except the law and the jury, the sceptical doctrines proclaimed so boldly by Thomas Chubb, Woolston, Tindal, Bolingbroke, Shaftesbury, from the outset met strong resistance, and never gained ascendency. There was an equal battle between opinions with the approval being given to the ancient and consoling traditions in the soul.]

On the rationalism of 18th cent. in general see Strauss, Reimarus &c Le compte rendu 1869, p. 481, art. by Ch. Ritter. [Reimarus (1694–1768) was a German deist; David Friedrich Strauss published *Hermann Samuel Reimarus und seine Schutzschrift für die vernünftigen Verehrer Gottes* (1861; Hermann Samuel Reimarus and his tract in defense of the reasonable worshippers of God); Strauss's life is translated by Charles Voysey,

Fragments from Reimarus (1879). The article by Christian (?) Ritter in *Le comte rendu* has not been located.]

On the unity of the esprit moderne from the 12th to the 19th cent. see Renan, Etudes morales, p. 215. [Renan 1859, 215.]

On the comparative "lumières" of the latter half of the 17th and of the 18th cent. see an interesting art in "Nouveaux Lundis" tome 3, p. 225. [Sainte-Beuve 1863–70, 3:225.]

The optimism which is characteristic of the 18th cent. is a mixture of speculative dreaming on social problems, and want of practical experience of human nature. Philosophy is not this or that system, but the maintenance of the rights of truth of fact against power and tradition.

Organisation for a practical and useful—organisation for opinion = a church—destruction of truth. The 39 arts. [articles of religion are] articles of practical consensus—not declarations of truth—therefore scientifically worthless. See Arnold. St. Paul, p. 16. [Matthew Arnold 1960–77, 6:80. The citation is from *St. Paul and Protestantism* (1869–70).]

"God creation, will, e[t] c[etera],—these terms [. . .] however much they might in the bible be used in a concrete and practical manner, yet had in themselves a provocation to abstract thought, carried with them the occasions of a criticism and a philosophy which sooner or later must make its appearance in the church." Ibid, p. 31. [Matthew Arnold 1960–77, 6:89.]

[Opposite ¶3, at the reference to Seneca, Pattison adds on fol. 7v:]

The idea of the Church as a source of truth had overlaid and extinguished the idea of the teachers—quote seq.—who have not to enact a law, or to guard a sacred tradition but to teach and edify. Such a class of men essential in every society. See. Plato. R[es] P[ublica; The Republic] Ueberweg 1. 138. [Ueberweg 1863–66, 1:138.]

"English philosophy became tainted at the Revolution with a certain political bias, and it may be a question how far it is yet emancipated from it." Tulloch, Rat. Theol. p. xi. [Tulloch 1872, 1:xi.]

See Tulloch for view that religious thought [that] preceded the Reformation, was extinguished for a time by the violence of the religious leaders, then chained up by the dogmatic confessionalism of the churches & broke out again in the form of Arminianism.

"The Puritans had an advantage with the populace and even the ordinary theological mind in the very narrowness of their theory." Tulloch 1. 57. [Tulloch 1872, 1:57.]

The Jansenist party discredited by their own miracles. Martin. Hist. de Fr. 15.346. [Martin 1837–65, 15:346.]

Contempt of the clergy by society its commencement—égalité négative. Ibid. p. 348. [Martin 1837–65, 15:348.]

d'Argenson: "aimer dieu se méfier des prêtres." Ibid. p. 359. [Love God, distrust the priests. This statement is attributed to René Louis de Voyer de Paulmy, marquis d'Argenson (1694–1737), minister of state under Louis XIV, man of letters, and friend of Voltaire (Martin 1837–65, 15:359).]

Voltaire. "Dieu est pour lui [. . .] plutôt une vérité qu'un être; il en comprend la nécessité; il ne semble pas en sentir la presence. Ibid. 362. [Martin 1837–65, 15:362; God is for him rather a truth than a being; he understands the need for him; he does not seem to feel his presence.]

Voltaire contrasted w[ith] Descartes. Ibid. p. 362. [Martin 1837–65, 15:362.]

Men must not be judged by the event, which is the only key to *facts*. 362. [Martin 1837–65, 15:362.]

The philosophical movement of the 18th cent. "n'était pas une philosophie d'école, c'était une explosion des sentiments, et des besoins de l'humanité." Laurent. Etudes. 11. 160. [Laurent 1850–70, 11:160; Was not an academic philosophy but an explosion of feelings and of human needs.]

[Opposite ¶3, at "religious truth," Pattison adds on fol. 8:]

Ideas of the siècle. Right divine. Laurent 11. 138 seq. [Laurent 1850–70, 11:138 ff.]

Louis XIV. "La grandeur de L. XIV [dit Frédéric II,] était l'ouvrage de ses ministres et de ses généraux." Ibid. 11. [Laurent 1850–70, 11:139; The greatness of Louis XIV (said Frederick II), was the work of his ministers and of his generals.]

"Il faut aller plus loin." The mediocrity of those ministers formed under his reign. See Laurent 11. 139. [Laurent 1850–70, 11:139; It is necessary to go further.]

[Opposite the final two sentences of ¶3 Pattison adds on fol. 8[v]:]

Diffusion of Infidelity. Jer. Taylor. Sermons. 4. 570. "There is a sort of men who, because they will be vicious & atheistical in their lives, have no way to go on with any plaisance . . . but by being also atheistical in their opinions." (date 1653). [Taylor 1847–54, 4:570; from Sermon 18, "The Foolish Exchange".]

Commonsense—Selon Grimm "il n'y a que deux manières de s'y prendre; ou bien s'appliquer à faire concevoir le plus clairement possible le petit nombre de vérités qu'on peut savoir; c'est ce qui a fait Locke—ou bien joindre vivement l'impression particulière qu'on reçoit de ces mêmes vérités; c'est ce qu'a fait Montaigne." Grimm ap[*apud*, Lat. in the writing on] Catherine p. 250. [Grimm 1880, 250; According to Grimm there are two ways of going about it (common sense); either one should apply oneself to formulating as clearly as possible the small number of truths that one is able to know; that is what Locke did —or engage actively in the particular impression that one receives from these same truths; that is what Montaigne did.]

[Opposite ¶4, at "the present century," Pattison adds on fol. 9:]

Modern use of Rationalism: "En France, dès qu'un homme ne soit plus à la parole de son curé, n'accepte plus la force probante du farceux mot 'credo quia absurdam,' on l'appelle *rationaliste.* A ne consulter que l'etymologie du mot, chacun devrait être fier de cette qualification. Si le nom de rationaliste désigne celui qui fait usage de sa raison, qui réfléchit et cherche à se rendre compte des motifs de sa foi, personne ne voudra consentir à laisser à d'autre ce beau titre. Pour le vulgaire un rationaliste est un homme qui [?] ce qu'il comprend et les apologètes contemporains du christianisme se donnent le facile plaisir de triompher d'une manière de voir qui n'est guère représentée que par ses conradicteurs, et qui repent être sentencer [?] que par les ignorants. A cette motive générale inexacte du rationalisme, ceux qui ont quelque connaissance de l'histoire de la théologie ajoutent l'affirmation suspecte que c'est un point des [?] vieille, et qui vraiment n'est plus de mode. Pour des hommes cependant qui font état de savoir et de raisonner, il ne devrait pas être permis d'employer des termes qui ont une signification historique bien determinée et de les transporter dans les opinions contemporaines en leur donnant un sens qui en fait bientôt une calomnie. Laissons au passé ses étiquettes et ses noms de guerre, et cherchons à serrer de près la pensée de nos adversaires sans les affublements d'un costume de mode." Revue Moderne (Fontane) Tome 37, p. 95. See also the continuation of the passage pp. [9]6, [9]7. [This citation has not been located; In France, as soon as a man no longer talks to his priest, as soon as he no longer accepts the self-evident farce of the stupid word "I believe because it is absurd," then he is called a *rationalist.* If you only look at the etymology of the word everyone ought to be proud to be called a rationalist. If a rationalist means one who uses his reason, who reflects upon and who tries to understand the grounds of his faith, nobody would want to leave to another this fine title. For the man in the street, a rationalist is a man who (acts according to?) what he understands, and the contemporary apologists for Christianity give themselves the easy pleasure of a triumph over a way of seeing which is scarcely represented by those who attack it. To this generally inexact characterization of rationalism those who have some general knowledge of history add this dubious affirmation that it is an old (belief?) which is no longer fashionable. Those people, however, who claim to know and to reason should not be allowed to use terms which have a clear, determined, historical meaning, and to transport them into a contemporary context, giving them an incorrect meaning which makes them into a lie. Let us leave to the past its labels and its battle cries, and let us try to come to grip with the thought of our adversaries without the foolish costume of a modern style. The Latin phrase, *credo quia absurdam,* is a variant of Tertullian's *certum est quia impossibile est* (the fact is certain because it is impossible) from *De Carne Christi* (On the Flesh of Christ), chap. 5, trans. Peter Holmes *ANF* 3:525.]

On the contrast between the "ordinary consciousness" and "thought in the native medium" —see Wallace. Prolegomena to Hegel's Logic. passim, especially pp. . . . [The cited phrases are in chap. 7 ("Kant and His Problem") of William Wallace's "Prolegomena": The philosopher of science "has dealt with thought as if it were a finer sort of material product, a fixed and assailable point: and this is perhaps the character of the generalised images, or material thoughts of ordinary consciousness. But thoughts in their native medium are not solid, but, as it were, fluid and transparent, and can easily escape the divisions and lines which the analytical intellect would impose" (Hegel 1874, lvi).]

Because this principle viz. the identity of faith and reason—had been made the ground of Théodicée by Leibniz. [Leibniz 1710; Leibniz is responding to the Calvinist Pierre Bayle's separation of faith and reason.]

"La loi, en général, est la raison humaine: [en tant qu'elle gouverne tous les peoples de la terre] les lois politiques et civiles de chaque nation ne doivent être que les cas particuliers où s'applique cette raison humaine." Montesquieu. [Montesquieu (1748) 1973, 1:12; Law in general is human reason: (inasmuch as it governs all the peoples of the earth), the political and civil laws of each nation ought to be only the particular cases where this human reason is applied.]

[Opposite ¶4, at "and in England," Pattison adds on fol. 9v:]

On the reaction against the Aufklärung [enlightenment] in Prussia, a good account in Kuno Fischer, Geschichte d. n. Philosophie 3. 75. seq. & from Hegel Phenomenologie des Geistes. 393 has a section on the struggle between the Aufklärung and Faith. [Fischer (1852–72) 1872–82, 3:75 ff. and Hegel (1807) 1834–44, 2:393 ff.; see also Hegel (1807) 1977, 328–55.]

Lessing. Sammtl. Schr. 11.2 seq. for sketch of struggle between the Aufklärung & Faith." [Lessing 1853–57, 11:2 ff.]

[Fol. 10: blank]

[Opposite ¶5, at "its substitute," Pattison adds on fol. 10v:]

On the *Aufklärung*, or the assertion of the subjective consciousness, i.e. that all that is to be acknowledged by one shall establish itself as reasonable to my consciousness, see Schwegler, Handbuch der Geschichte d. Phil. p. 19 &c. On the Sophists & die aufklärerische Reflektion; sie ist daher auch kein philosophisches System. &c. ["The illuminated reflection; they have no philosophical system" (Schwegler [1848] 1868, 31). In the passage on the Sophists that Pattison refers to Schwegler writes: "The preceding philosophers all tacitly assume that our subjective consciousness is in subordination and subjection to objective actuality, or that the objectivity of things is the source of our knowledge. . . . In the Sophists a new principle appears, the principle of subjectivity; the view, namely, that things are as they seem to us and that any universal truth exists not" (30).]

"Nicht die Sicherheit eines in sich beruhenden Selbstbewusstseins, sondern die Sehnsucht nach einer höheren Mittheilung der Wahrheit, welche der

Mensch in sich selbst nicht findet, ist die Wurzel des Neuplatonismus." Zeller. Phil d. G. 5. 381. [Zeller (1844–52) 1856–68, 5:381; The root of neo-Platonism is not the surety of a self-consciousness which reposes in itself, but the yearning for a higher communication of truth which human beings do not find in themselves.]

On science & reason as being addressed to distinct classes, see Hartmann reviewed by Sully in Fortnightly Aug. 1876. [Sully 1876.]

"Persons & personal interests hold the second place, being no more than instruments or convenient names for critical turning points in the large movements of peoples." Morley. Voltaire. p. 291. [Morley 1872, 291.]

[Fols. 11–12v: blank]

[Opposite the end of ¶8, at "century before," Pattison adds on fol. 13:]

"In Coleridge there was a resumption & reissue of the elements of a rich & free native Anglicanism, the tradition of which had been long moribund & frittered away." Masson, Recent British Philosophy, p. 240. [Masson 1865, 240.]

[Opposite ¶9, at "period 1688–1750," Pattison adds on fol. 13:]

In this period Christianity was stripped of its incidental, historical, & miraculous envelope, and reappeared with the original nucleus of Stoicism, rational morality, all in it that was eternal and immutable.

[in a shaky hand:] Religion & philosophy differing in form, but identical in substance. See Zeller, Life of Strauss, p. 77. ["He (Strauss) disputes indeed Hegel's assertion that religion and philosophy are identical in their substance and only different in form, but he acknowledges that it is one and the same reason which finds its purest expression in philosophy, but which also governs the activity of the imagination and through the successive series of religions leads to ever greater approximation to the truth" (Zeller 1874, 77).]

Kant vindicates Hume for thorny questions[?.] Kant, Werke, 2, 561. [Pattison is referring to Kant's long discussion of David Hume in the Preface to the *Prolegomena to any Future Metaphysics* (1783); see Kant 1903–80, 4:260. Kant praises Hume as the one who "first interrupted my dogmatic slumber" and gave his "speculative philosophy a quite new direction" because of the questions he posed (from *Prolegomena* in Kant 1988, 159).]

Common sense Barni, Kant, p. 147. [Barni 1850, 147.]

[In different ink:] Fichte contrasts the period of ready made commonsense with the age of science. So, e.g. the age of commonsense has this great advantage over the age of science that it knows all things without having learned anything &c &c. Characteristics. Engl. translation, p. 20. ["The Age of Freedom—does not know that man must first through labour, industry, and art learn *how to know*; but it has certain fixed standards for all conceptions, and an established *Common Sense of Mankind* always ready and at hand, innate, and ever present. . . . It has this advantage over the Age of Knowledge, that it knows all things without having learned anything" (Fichte [1804] 1977, 21).]

[Fols. 13^{v}–14: blank]

[Opposite the end of ¶12 Pattison adds on fol. 14^{v}:]

Bolingbroke. See Coleridge's judgment in Conversations at Cambridge. p. 19. [S. T. Coleridge is quoted in Willmott 1836, 18–20.]

[Between ¶s 13 and 14 Pattison adds on fol. 15:]

Laud. Conf. w[ith] Fisher. p. 47 (ed. Oxf. 1839) "All that have not imbrutished themselves, and sunk below their species and order of nature, give even natural reason leave to come in, and make some proof, and give some approbation upon the weighing and the consideration of other arguments." cf. also p. 61 "The last way, which gives reason leave to come in and prove what it can, may not justly be denied by any reasonable man. &c." But e contrario [Lat. on the contrary] p. 85. "The principles of divinity resolve not into the grounds of natural reason,—for then there would be no room for faith, but, all would be either knowledge or vision,—but into the maxims of divine knowledge supernatural." [Laud (1639) 1849, 71, 87, 118.]

[Opposite ¶17 Pattison adds on fol. 15^{v}:]

Analogy pt. 2 ch. 3 "I express myself with caution, lest I should be mistaken to vilify reason, which is indeed the only faculty we have wherewith to judge concerning anything, even revelation itself." [Butler 1896, 1:222 (bk. 2, chap. 3, sec. 3).]

[Fols. 16–19: blank]

[Opposite ¶24, at "For we find Shaftesbury," Pattison adds on fol. 19^{v}:]

Cf. Dean of Exeter. Dogmatic Teaching from the Pulpit, 20th Congress p. 92 [Very likely a reference to Archibald Boyd (1803–1883), who was dean of Exeter from 1867 to 1883. He had earlier published *Sermons on the Church* (1838) and in the 1850s and 1860s preached frequently at St. Paul's Cathedral, London. The work cited has not been identified.]

[Fol. 20: blank]

[Opposite ¶25, at "Nor did they preach to empty pews," Pattison adds on fol. 20^{v}:]

Of Preaching in 1572 ". . . the licentious & [?] of preaching used nowadays at Cambridge by divers groups of preachers, who are not afraide to attack [?] openly in pulpett, not only the booke of common prayer, but allso particular doctrines [?] of all people [?] both honourable that be about, and other that be present according to the licence of the old poetes." Whitgift to Abp. of Cant. Heywoods Puritan Transactions. 1. p. 59. [This quotation has not been located.]

Of Jeremy Taylor's Sermons a writer in the "Eclectic" suggests that he is aimed at in the following passage. South, Sermons. vol. [blank] p. [blank.] "I speak the words of soberness said St. Paul, and I preach the Gospel not with the enticing words of man's wisdom. This was the way of the

Apostle's discussing of things sacred. Nothing here of the fringes of the north star." &c. &c. [Robert South, *Sermons Preached Upon Several Occasions*, 1679; 1697–98, 3 vols.; 1823, 7 vols.; this reference has not been located.]

[Fols. 21–23: blank]

[Opposite ¶28, at "Bishop Butler gives his clergy hints," Pattison adds on fol. 23v:]

Morley, Rousseau, i. 199: "The highest things were thus brought down to the level of the banalities of discourse, and subjects which the wise take care only to discuss with the wise, were here everyday topics for all comers." [Morley 1873, 1:199.]

[Fols. 24–25: blank]

[Opposite ¶30, at "The philosophy of the age," Pattison adds on fol. 25v:]

On the philosophy of Common Sense and of erudition, see Véra, L'Hégelianisme & la Philosophie p. 17. [Vera 1861, 17.]

"Il y a entre l'érudition et le bon sens une affinité plus intime qu'on le croit" &c. &c. [Vera 1861, 17; There is between erudition and good sense an affinity more intimate than one might believe.]

[Fols. 26–26v: blank]

[Opposite ¶33, at "He will never forget," Pattison adds on fol. 27:]

On Butler see Tyndall "Belfast Address" Academy. vol 6 p. 209 Matth. Arnold. Cont. Rev." [John Tyndall (1820–93), British physicist, delivered the Presidential Address to the British Association for the Advancement of Science, meeting in Belfast in 1874. He traces the development of scientific thought from the pre-Socratics to his own time, discussing Butler's use of analogy before proceeding to discuss Lamarck, Chambers, and Darwin (Tyndall 1874, 209–17). Matthew Arnold's "Bishop Butler and the *Zeit-Geist*" was published in *Contemporary Review* 27 (Feb. 1876: 377–95); (Mar. 1876: 571–92); repr. in *Last Essays on Church and Religion* (1877; see Arnold 1960–77, 8:11–62). The second section of Arnold's article is followed by Pattison's essay "The Religion of Positivism, by a Theosophist," *Contemporary Review* 27 (Mar. 1876): 593–614.]

[Fols. 27v–29: blank]

[Opposite ¶35, at "The inner light," Pattison adds on fol. 29v:]

Enthusiasm. See Green, Thos. Bp. of Lincoln. A Dissertation on Enthusiasm. Lond. 1755. [Green 1755; John Green was bp. of Lincoln]

[Fols. 30–31v: blank]

[Pattison wrote an 'x' in the margin of ¶37, at "Mr. Hort's remark"; opposite this passage he adds on fol. 32:]

The comparison between the 2d and the 18th century to be worked out as a separate topic . . . vid.[*videte*, Lat. see] serm[on] before University. 24 Feb. 1867. [Pattison preached on 1 Cor. 1:26–27 and 21, on the notion of wisdom, taking up the relationship between Christianity and philosophy, especially in the Hellenistic period. See Pattison 1885b, 137–67.]

[Fols. 32v–37v: blank]

[Opposite ¶46, at "Butler does not," Pattison adds on fol. 38:]

"If Shaftesbury (said the great Bp. Butler) had lived to see the candour and moderation of the present times in discussing religious subjects he would have been a good Christian." Js. Warton, Life & Writings of Pope 2.97." [Warton (1757–82) 1806, 2:97.]

[Fols. 38v–41v: blank]

[Opposite ¶50, at "In days when the pillory," Pattison adds on fol. 42:]

6 March 1721 Joseph Hall was convicted of publishing a blasphemous pamphlet entitled "A sober reply to Mr. Higgs's merry arguments for the tritheistical doctrine of the Trinity." [Joseph Hall, *A Sober Reply to Mr. Higgs's Merry Arguments, from the Light of Nature, for the Tritheistick Doctrine of the Trinity, with a Postscript Relating to the Reverend Dr. Waterland*, 1720.]

28 Ap[ril] An Order in Council was issued for suppressing of blasphemous clubs consciously called "Hell Fire Clubs," wh[ich] abounded at that time. [Three such clubs were suppressed in 1721; see *Notes and Queries*, 12 May 1860 and *Haydn's Dictionary of Dates*, 1881.]

15 June Joseph Hall was sentenced to stand in the Pillory, to pay a fine of £200, be imprisoned for 3 months, and to give security for his good behaviour for 7 years. The pillory was afterwards remitted, & the fine reduced ~~by half~~ to £5. [See Pattison ¶50 and note.]

On the law of religious libel, see Paterson, James, Liberty of the Press, Speech, & Public Worship. Macmillan & Co. 1880. [See Pattison ¶50 and note.]

[Fol 42v: blank]

[Pattison writes "+" in the margin of ¶51 at "only a name," and adds on fol. 43:]

+ cf. with this Schleiermacher's complaint that "[?] vernachlässigt und verachtet" Dilthey. I. 65. [Dilthey 1870, 1:65; neglected and despised.]

[Fols. 43v–46v: blank]

[Opposite ¶57, at "something too of the old," Pattison adds on fol. 47:]

"Eusebius in his Evangelical Preparation draws a long parallel between the Ox & the Christian priesthood. Hence the dignified clergy, out of mere humility, have ever since called their thrones by the name of stalls. To which a [. . .] Prelate of Winchester (one W. Edinton), modestly alluding, has rendered his name immortal by this ecclesiastical aphorism [. . .] 'Canterbury is the higher rock, but Winchester is the better manger.'" Scriblerus Pope's Works IV. 329 (ed. 1766). [Pope 1766, 4:329, note. The reference is to the fact that the episcopal income at Winchester was the greatest in England; when Wilberforce was transferred there from Oxford in 1869, his income was £7,000 per annum.]

[Opposite ¶58, at "a general relaxation of manners," Pattison adds on fol. 47v:]

The common creed of the French illuminati was the progress of reason. On the Abbé Galiani's freedom from this illusion of his friends, see Sainte-

Beuve 2. 436. [Sainte-Beuve 1850, 2:436; on "L'abbé Galiani," 26 Aug. 1850.]

[Opposite ¶59, at "Where the 'corruption of manners,'" Pattison adds on fol. 48:]

"Depravity of manners," a cant phrase of the age common to all parties: "to enter in the most plain and solemn manner he could, a sort of protest against that insuperable corruption and depravity of manners which he had been so unhappy as to live to see" Pope—note to Epilogue to the Satires. Works 4. 222 (Carruth.). [Pope 1853, 4:222. This citation occurs in Carruthers's last notation on Pope's "Epilogue to the Satires" (1738).]

Locke seems to countenance the notion "if we look into the common management of children, we shall have reason to wonder, in the great dissoluteness of manners, which the world complains of, that there are any footsteps at all left to virtue." Of Education, p. 29 & cf. p. 58. [Locke (1693) 1989, 105.]

[In a shaky hand:] Kant. 1798. "Auch Geistliche weissagen gelegentlich den gänzlichen Verfall der Religion und die nahe Erscheinung des Antichrists, während dessen sie gerade das thun, was erforderlich ist, ihn einzuführen: indem sie nämlich ihrer Gemeine nicht sittliche Grundsätze ans Herz zu legen bedacht sind, die geradezu aufs Bessern führen, sondern Observanzen und historischen Glauben zur wesentlichen Pflicht machen, die es indirect bewirken sollen, woraus zwar mechanische Einhelligkeit als in einer bürgerlichen Verfassung, aber keine in der moralischen Gesinnung erwachsen kann." Streit der Facultäten, *Werke* 1. 282. [The cited passage is from the second part of Kant's *Conflict of the Faculties* on "The Conflict of the Philosophy Faculty with the Faculty of Law, and particularly concerns the progress of the human race": "Ecclesiastics, too, occasionally prophesy the complete destruction of religion and the imminent appearance of Antichrist; and in doing so they are performing precisely what is requisite to call him up. This happens because they have not seen to impressing on their parishes moral principles which lead directly to the better, but rather fabricate into essential duty observances and historical beliefs which are supposed to effect it indirectly; from this, of course, can grow the mechanical unanimity as in a civil constitution, but none in moral disposition" (Kant [1798] 1979, 143).]

"When we examine into what his (G. Wither's) title to the prophetic character consisted, we find that it was chiefly in an unusually strong degree of the conviction (pretty sure to be right at any time) that the cup 'of social iniquity was full.'" Masson, Life of Milton, 1, 369." [Masson 1859–80, 1:369.]

[Opposite ¶59, at "after making every allowance," Pattison adds on fol. 48v:]

So Fichte's denunciation of this age as the "Zeitalter der absoluten Gleichgültigkeit" [gegen alle Wahrheit, und der völligen Ungebundenheit ohne einigen Leitfaden.] [Pattison cites only the first part of Fichte's phrase, "The Age of absolute indifference," that continues: "towards all truth, and of entire and unrestrained licentiousness" (Fichte [1804] 1845–46, 7:16; for our translation see Fichte [1804] 1977, 17).]

[Fols. 49–49v: blank]

[Opposite ¶70, at "The licentiousness of talk," Pattison adds on fol. 50:]

1. Want of public system of schools. Education proposed as the remedy for this "licentiousness" by Dr. John Brown, author of the "Estimate &c." vid[*videte*, Lat. see] passage quoted from his *Thoughts on Civil Liberty, Licentiousness & Faction.* op[*opus*, Lat. the work] D. Stewart. Pol. Econ. Works, vol. 8 p. 53. [Stewart 1854–60, 8:53. Brown's treatise was published in 1765.]

2. "During the greater part of the 18th cent. the received opinions in religion & ethics were chiefly attacked as by Shaftesbury and [even by] Hume on the ground of instinctive feelings of virtue, and the theory of a moral taste or sense. As a consequence of this, the defenders of established opinions, both lay & clerical, commonly professed utilitarianism. To the many writers on the side of orthodoxy of the utilitarian school, mentioned by Dr Whewell, might be added several, of at least equal note whom he has omitted" (John Brown, Soame Jenyns, Johnson, Paley). Mill, *Dissertations* 2. 445. [J. S. Mill, "Whewell on Moral Philosophy" (*Westminster Review*, [Oct. 1852]) in *Dissertations and Discussions Political, Philosophical, and Historical, Reprinted Chiefly from the Edinburgh And Westminster Reviews*, 1859–75, 3:349–85; for the cited passage see Mill 1963–91, 10:170.]

[In a shaky hand:] "That ideas do not govern and overthrow the world . . . social mechanism rests upon character." See this in Herbert Spencer Essays 3. 69. [Spencer 1858–63, 3:69.]

[In a steady hand:] "La legislation de la raison humaine." See Barni. Kant. p. 141.[Barni 1850, 141; The legislation of human reason.]

The reaction towards spiritualism was not brought about by the vindications of the clergy, but in France by Rousseau. See on his influence Morley, Rousseau i. 313. ["It was Rousseau, and not the feeble controversialists put up from time to time by the Jesuits and other ecclesiastical bodies, who proved the effective champion of religion, and the only power who could make head against the triumphant onslaught of the Voltaireans" (Morley 1873, 1:312–13).]

[Fol. 50v: blank]

[In the margin of ¶70, after the words "as Dr. Whewell assumes," Pattison adds in pencil the name:]

Harris. [This name is very likely a reference to John Harris (1666–1719), English writer and divine, who delivered and published his Boyle Lectures, *Atheistical Objections Against the Being of God and his Attributes Fairly Considered and Fully Refuted*, 1698 in which he writes concerning the "doctrine" of both the deists and their orthodox attackers: "And now upon the whole, there being thus plainly proved an essential and natural difference between *moral Good* and *Evil*: that Men agree in this Point; that *Morality* conduces to our Happiness, and Immorality to our Misery; we may justly conclude, that all other rational Agents must judge of *Good* and *Evil* after the same Manner: And they must also know, that their Perfection and Happiness consists in acting according to the eternal Rules of right Reason, and moral Virtue" (Burnet 1737, 1:284–85).]

[Fol. 51: blank]

[Opposite ¶71, at "The certainly insisted," Pattison adds on fol. 51ᵛ:]

On the morality of atheism see the code of virtue in the Système de la nature. ap.[*apud*, Lat. In the writing of] Robinson's D'Holbach p. 81. [Holbach [1770] 1970, 81; see also chap. 10: "Is Atheism Compatible with Morality," 306–14.]

[Opposite ¶71, at "If reason be liable," Pattison adds on fol. 52 and 52ᵛ:]

An account of the growth of Deism in England. London. Printed for the author 1696. Assigned in the Bodleian new cat. to William Treke. Treke acc. to [Anthony à] Wood was born in 1663. See Dialogue between Timotheus and Judas. Lond. 1696 24° (Bodl. pamph. 222) in which it is said of the author of "An Account &c" that "now he is above three score" p. 6. [The anonymous tract, *An Account of the Growth of Deism in England*, 1696, is now assigned to William Stephens; Henry Hill, *A Dialogue Between Timotheus and Judas*, 1696.]

"Reflections upon a pamphlet intituled 'An account of the growth of deism in England.'" 4° Lond. 1696. This anonymous pamphlet gives a summary of the reasons usually assigned for the growth of deism. It is sober & sensible, and has something of the spirit of Butler. [Richard Willis, *Reflections upon a Pamphlet, Intituled, An Account of the Growth of Deism in England, Together with Some Considerations About the Christian Religion*, 1696.]

Favour shown to the Jacobite clergy. Growth of deism p. 9 "Though turned out of their livings by law for professing allegiance, yet . . . if the livings they lose are in the bishop's gift, he shall present any friend which the dispossessed Jacobite shall recommend; now what can be more by them deriv'd, then to enjoy the profits of their livings, and put in what curate they please?" [William Stephens, *An Account of the Growth of Deism in England*, 1696.]

An appeal to honest people against wicked priests . . . publish'd on occasion of Dr Sacheverell's last sermon (attributed in Bodl. cat. to Toland) 8° Lond. 1712. ["Hierophilus" (pseudonym for John Toland?), *An Appeal to Honest People Against Wicked Priests: or, The Very Heathen Laity's Declarations for Civil Obedience and Liberty of Conscience, Contrary to the Rebellious and Persecuting Principles of Some of the Old Christian Clergy . . . Published on the Occasion of Dr. Sacheverell's Last Sermon*, 1712. Sacheverell's sermon was entitled "False Notions of Liberty".]

Against clerical aggression arguments drawn from church history. The church's preaching itself independent of the state the cause of most of the 10 persecutions: the clergy had exerted an imperium in imperio. Julian's apostasy was occasioned by the hypocrisy of the Christian bishops &c. of which he had been witness in the court of Constantius. [The Latin phrase means literally the rule within a rule, a government, in this case of the church as a separate constituency, independent of the authorized government of the state.]

Praises Sir W. Temple's remark that "religion may perhaps do more good elsewhere, but that it does less hurt in Holland than anywhere in the world." Hickes' "Prefaces-general." [Possibly a reference to George Hickes (1642–1715), Non-juror and dean of Worcester; this reference, together with the following references to the same document, has not been located.]

Popery is nothing else but the clergy assuming a right to think for the laity.

p. 39. quot. from Donne "Letters."

p. 43. "How far the fashion of our country may justify their haunting of taverns & coffee houses, a thing highly scan-

[fol. 52ᵛ:]

dalous among the reformed abroad, I shall not take upon me to determine."

p. 44. "parsons clubs."

45. Keeping of domestic chaplains out of fashion.

54. "unless with a certain prelate at the Dr's tryal, we acknowledge these things to be true, but yet keep 'em as grand secrets from the people."

[Opposite ¶73, at "There remained to be tried Common Reason," Pattison adds on fol. 52ᵛ:]

Society for Promoting Christian Knowledge . . . An Account of its origin is appended to a sermon of John Heylin 4° Lond. 1734 (Bodl. pamph. 401 4°). [John Heylin, *A Sermon Preached April the 25th, 1734. To Which is Annexed An Account of the Origin and Designs of the Society for Promoting Christian Knowledge*, 1734.]

In 1719 Mangey published a sermon preached at the Bishop's visitation at Chertsey which is said to be "published at the request of the clergy there present." Who was the bishop? The subject is "The eternal existence of Christ." [Thomas Mangey, *The Eternal Existence of our Lord Jesus Christ: Set Forth in a Sermon*, 1719; Chertsey is in north Surrey on the Thames, in the Diocese of London in the eighteenth century. In 1719 Mangey (1688–1755) was Chaplain to the bishop of London, John Robinson. Mangey upheld orthodox Christianity against the deists.]

See John Bull, 30 Jany 1875 for art on J. H. Newman. ["The Divine *versus* the Politician." *John Bull.* 55 (30 Jan. 1875): 73–74.]

Abp Sharp saying the bible and Shakespeare had made him Abp. of York; &

he recommended the same course of reading to his clergy! [John Sharp (1645–1714); the saying is attributed to Sharp by Arthur Onslow in Gilbert Burnet's *History of His Own Time* (1724–33) 1823–33, 3:100. For Onslow see Pattison ¶26 and note.]

[After the last page of his interleaved text, fols. 53–54ᵛ are blank]

[On fol. 55 Pattison adds:]

France. D'Aguesseau Oeuvres. tome 13. Contains Mémoires historiques sur les affaires de l'église de France 1647–1700. [Historical memoirs on the affairs of the church in France. Henri François D'Aguesseau, *Oeuvres complètes* (1819, 16 vols.)]

[Fols. 55ᵛ–57ᵛ: blank]

[On fol. 58 Pattison adds:]

S. Richardson. Of the Torments of Hell. 12° Lond 1660 (1658) This is the book to which Brandon's "Everlasting fire no fancy" 1678 is an answer. [Samuel Richardson, *A Discourse of the Torments of Hell: the Foundation and Pillars Thereof Discovered, Searched, Shaken, and Removed.* 1658; on John Brandon, see below fol. 58ᵛ.]

Anabaptisticum et enthusiasticum Pantheon 1702. [*Anabaptisticum et enthusiasticum pantheon und geistliches Rüst-Hauss, wider die alten Quacker und neuen Frey-Geister* (1702; Pantheon of Anabaptists and Enthusiasts and spiritual arsenal against the old Quakers and the new Freethinkers).]

Rubichon Influence du clergé dans les sociétés modernes. [Maurice Rubichon, *De l'Action du clergé dans les sociétés modernes* (1829; On the action of clergy in modern society).]

On the deists Morley. Voltaire. especially pp. 90, 91. [Morley 1872, 90–91.]

Capel Berrow, Rector of Rossington *Theological Dissertation.* 4° Lond. (Dodsley) 1772. [Printed entry clipped from bookseller's catalogue, pasted in:] 643 Sacheverell (Dr. Henry) An impartial account of what passed . . . 8° 1710. [(Henry Sacheverell [?]), *An Impartial Account of What Pass'd Most Remarkable in the Last Session of Parliament Relating to the Case of Dr. Henry Sacheverell,* 1710.] [The hand-written list continues:]

Lay-craft exemplified in a discovery of the weakness of the late attempts of the author of Priest-craft in perfection &c. 1710 Bodley Pamph. 292 8°. [Anon. *Lay-craft Exemplified in a Discovery of the Weakness of the Late Attempts of the Author of Priest-craft in Perfection* (by Anthony Collins) *and Mr. Benjamin Robinson, Minister of the Gospel, to Prove the English Clergy Guilty of Forgery,* 1710; Collins's tract, sometimes wrongly attributed to Matthew Tindal, was *Priest-Craft in Perfection; or, A Detection of the Fraud of Inserting and Continuing this Clause,—The Church Hath the Power to Decree Rites and Ceremonys, and Authority in Controversys of Faith, in the Twentieth Article of the Articles of the Church of England,* 1710.]

[On fol. 58ᵛ Pattison adds:]

Clendon (John) Tractatus Philosophico-theologicus de Persona. Lond. 1710.

[John Clendon, *Tractatus Philosophico-theologicus de Persona, or, A Treatise of the Word Person*, 1710.]

Murray Rev. Jas. *History of Religion*, 2nd ed. Lond. 1765. [James Murray, *The History of Religion: Particularly of the Principle Denominations of Christians, by an Impartial Hand* (1765, 4 vols., 2d ed.). The first edition was published in 1764.]

Murray Rev. Jas. Sermons to Asses, Doctors of Divinity &c reprint in 1 vol by Hone 1819. [James Murray, *Sermons to Asses, to Doctors in Divinity, to Lords Spiritual, and to Ministers of the State*, ed. W. Hone, 1819.]

Lindsey, Th. Vindiciae Priestleianae Lond. 1788–92. [Theophilus Lindsey, *Vindiciae Priestleianae, an Address to the Students of Oxford and Cambridge, Occasioned by a Letter to Dr. Priestley from an Undergraduate, Ascribed to Dr. Horne*, 1788.]

Brandon John Everlasting fire no fancy being an answer to The foundations of hell torments shaken. 4° London 1678. [John Brandon, Τὸ πύρ τό αἰῶνιον*: or Everlasting Fire No Fancy, Being an Answer to a Late Pestilent Pamphlet Entituled "The Foundations of Hell-Torments Shaken and Removed,"* 1678. Brandon was addressing a pamphlet by Samuel Richardson; see above fol. 58.]

Dodwell, W. A free answer to Dr. Middleton's Free Inquiry. 1749. [William Dodwell, *A Free Answer to Dr. Middleton's Free Inquiry into the Miraculous Powers of the Primitive Church, in a Letter to a Friend*, 1749.]

Groome, John. Historical collections shewing how useful the clergy have been to this nation. Lond. 1710. [John Groome, *The Dignity and Honour of the Clergy, Represented in an Historical Collection: Shewing How Useful and Serviceable the Clergy Have Been to This Nation*, 1710.]

Assheton, W. Seasonable vindication of the clergy . . . answer to the Rights of the Christian Church asserted 1709. [William Assheton, *Seasonable Vindication of the Clergy, Being an Answer to Some Reflections, in a Late Book Entituled, The Rights of the Christian Church Asserted*, 1709. Assheton was answering a book by the deist Matthew Tindal; see Pattison ¶21 and note.]

Le rituel des esprits forts. 2nd ed. Paris. 1762. [Joseph-Marie Gros de Besplas, *Le rituel des esprits-forts, ou Le voyage d'outre-monde. En forme de dialogues* (1759; The ritual of the free-thinkers, or the voyage of the world beyond. In the form of dialogues). The title was changed for the second edition to: *Le rituel des esprits-forts, ou le Tableau des incrédules modernes au lit de la mort avec l'oraison funèbre d'un philosophe et un discours aux incrédules* (1762; The ritual of the free-thinkers, or the picture of modern unbelievers on their death-bed with the funeral sermon of a philosophe and a discourse on the unbelievers).]

For history of Humanism: Lettres d'un voyageur à l'Abbé Barruel 8° Lond. 1800 (Bodl. G. P. 2106). [Anon. *Lettres d'un voyageur à l'abbé Barruel, ou*

Nouveaux documens pour ses mémoires (1800; Letters from a traveler to the Abbé Barruel, or new documents for his memoirs): Augustin Barruel (1741–1820) was a French philosopher.]

Donaldson, Christian Orthodoxy. [John William Donaldson, *Christian Orthodoxy Reconciled with the Conclusions of Modern Biblical Learning*, 1857.]

Vignié Histoire de l'Apologie chrétienne. [Possibly a reference to Nicolas Vignier. *Apologie catholique de la doctrine des églises réformées contre un écrit du P. Cotin* (1617; Catholic apology concerning the doctrine of the reformed churches against a writing of P. Cotin).]

Nicolas Du Protestantisme. Paris 1852. [Jean Jacques Auguste Nicolas. *Du Protestantisme et de toutes les hérésies dans leur rapport avec le socialisme, précédé de l'examen d'un écrit de M. Guizot* (1852; On Protestantism and all the heresies in their relation with socialism, preceded by an examination of a writing by M. Guizot).]

Vinet L'education, la famille. 1855. [Alexandre Rodolphe Vinet, *L'Éducation, la famille et la société* (1855; Education, family and society).]

On Dissenters in country places see Pall Mall Gazette, 17 Dec. 1872.

Erdmann, Geschichte der Philosophie Band 2, especially p. 77 seq. [Johann Eduard Erdmann, *Grundriss der Geschichte der Philosophie* (1866, 2 vols.; Outline of the history of philosophy).]

Bonnet, Charles. Recherches philosophiques. Genève 1769. contains a treatment of the essential points of natural theology & Christian evidences. [Charles Bonnet, *Recherches philosophiques sur les preuves du christianisme* (1769; Philosophical researches on the proofs for Christianity).]

Rolleston Philosophical dialogue concerning decency 1751. [Samuel Rolleston, *A Philosophical Dialogue concerning Decency, to Which is Added a Critical and Historical Dissertation on Places of Retirement for Necessary Occasions*, 1751.]

Schmidt. W. A. Geschichte der Denk u. Glaubensfreiheit. [Wilhelm Adolf Schmidt, *Geschichte der Denk-und Glaubensfreiheit im ersten Jahrhundert der Kaiserherrschaft und des Christenthums* (1847; The history of freedom of thought and belief in the first century of the imperial rule and Christianity).]

Barruel Les Helviennes, ou lettres provinciales philosophiques. 5 vols. 12° Par. 1788. [Augustin Barruel, *Les Helviennes, ou, Lettres provinciales philosophiques* (1788, 5 vols.; The Helviennes, or provincial philosophical letters). Augustin Barruel used the name "Helviennes" for the ancient inhabitants (Helvii) of the Vivarais region of the south of France, now the Ardèche, west of the Rhône, his own birthplace.]

7 *Benjamin Jowett*

On the Interpretation of Scripture

It is a strange, though familiar fact, that great differences of opinion exist respecting the Interpretation of Scripture. All Christians receive the Old and New Testament as sacred writings, but they are not agreed about the meaning which they attribute to them. The book itself remains as at the first; the commentators seem rather to reflect the changing atmosphere of the world or of the Church. Different individuals or bodies of Christians have a different point of view, to which their interpretation is narrowed or made to conform.[1] It is assumed, as natural and necessary, that the same words will present one idea to the mind of the Protestant, another to the Roman Catholic; one meaning to the German, another to the English interpreter. The Ultramontane or Anglican divine is not supposed to be impartial in his treatment of passages which afford an apparent foundation for the doctrine of purgatory or the primacy of St. Peter on the one hand, or the three orders of clergy and the divine origin of episcopacy on the other.[2] It is a received view with many, that the meaning of the Bible is to be defined by that of the Prayer-book; while there are others who interpret 'the Bible and the Bible only' with a silent reference to the traditions of the Reformation. Philosophical differences are in the background, into which the differences about Scripture also resolve themselves. They seem to run up at last into a difference of opinion respecting Revelation itself—whether given beside the human faculties or through them, whether an interruption of the laws of nature or their perfection and fulfilment.[3]

This effort to pull the authority of Scripture in different directions is not peculiar to our own day; the same phenomenon appears in the past history of Church. At the Reformation, in the Nicene or Pelagian times, the New Testament was the ground over which men fought; it might also be compared to the armoury which furnished them with weapons.[4] Opposite aspects of the truth which it contains were appropriated by different sides. 'Justified by faith without works' and 'justified by faith as well as works' are equally Scriptural expressions; the one has become the formula of Protestants, the other of Roman Catholics.[5] The fifth and ninth chapters of the Romans, single verses such as 1 Corinthians iii. 15, John iii. 3, still bear traces of many a life-long strife in the pages of commentators. The difference of interpretation which prevails among ourselves is partly traditional, that is to say, inherited from the controversies of former ages. The use made of Scripture by Fathers of the Church, as well as by Luther and Calvin, affects our idea of its meaning at the present hour.[6]

[3] Another cause of the multitude of interpretations is the growth or progress of the human mind itself. Modes of interpreting vary as time goes on; they partake of the general state of literature or knowledge. It has not been easily or at once that mankind have learned to realize the character of sacred writings—they seem almost necessarily to veil themselves from human eyes as circumstances change; it is the old age of the world only that has at length understood its childhood.[7] (Or rather perhaps is beginning to understand it, and learning to make allowance for its own deficiency of knowledge; for the infancy of the human race, as of the individual, affords but few indications of the workings of the mind within.) More often than we suppose the great sayings and doings upon the earth, 'thoughts that breathe and words that burn,' are lost in a sort of chaos to the apprehension of those that come after. Much of past history is dimly seen and receives only a conventional interpretation, even when the memorials of it remain. There is a time at which the freshness of early literature is lost; mankind have turned rhetoricians, and no longer write or feel in the spirit which created it. In this unimaginative period in which sacred or ancient writings are partially unintelligible, many methods have been taken at different times to adapt the ideas of the past to the wants of the present. One age has wandered into the flowery paths of allegory,

> 'In pious meditation fancy fed.'

Another has straitened the liberty of the Gospel by a rigid application of logic, the former being a method which was at first more naturally applied to the Old Testament, the latter to the New.[8] Both methods of interpretation, the mystical and logical, as they may be termed, have been practised on the Vedas and the Koran, as well as on the Jewish and Christian Scriptures, the true glory and note of divinity in these latter being not that they have hidden mysterious or double meanings, but a simple and universal one, which is beyond them and will survive them.[9] Since the revival of literature, interpreters have not unfrequently fallen into error of another kind from a pedantic and misplaced use of classical learning; the minute examination of words often withdrawing the mind from more important matters. A tendency may be observed within the last century to clothe systems of philosophy in the phraseology of Scripture. But new wine cannot thus be put 'into old bottles.' Though roughly distinguishable by different ages, these modes or tendencies also exist together; the remains of all of them may be remarked in some of the popular commentaries of our own day.[10]

[4] More common than any of these methods, and not peculiar to any age, is that which may be called by way of distinction the rhetorical one. The tendency to exaggerate or amplify the meaning of simple words for the sake of edification may indeed have a practical use in sermons, the object of which is to awaken not so much the intellect as the heart and conscience. Spiritual food, like natural, may require to be of a certain bulk to nourish the human mind. But this 'tendency to edification'

has had an unfortunate influence on the interpretation of Scripture. For the preacher almost necessarily oversteps the limits of actual knowledge, his feelings overflow with the subject; even if he have the power, he has seldom the time for accurate thought or inquiry. And in the course of years spent in writing, perhaps, without study, he is apt to persuade himself, if not others, of the truth of his own repetitions. The trivial consideration of making a discourse of sufficient length is often a reason why he overlays the words of Christ and his Apostles with commonplaces. The meaning of the text is not always the object which he has in view, but some moral or religious lesson which he has found it necessary to append to it; some cause which he is pleading, some error of the day which he has to combat. And while in some passages he hardly dares to trust himself with the full force of Scripture (Matthew v. 34; ix. 13; xix. 21; Acts v. 29), in others he extracts more from words than they really imply (Matthew xxii. 21; xxviii. 20; Romans xiii. 1; &c.), being more eager to guard against the abuse of some precept than to enforce it, attenuating or adapting the utterance of prophecy to the requirements or to the measure of modern times. Any one who has ever written sermons is aware how hard it is to apply Scripture to the wants of his hearers and at the same time to preserve its meaning.[11]

The phenomenon which has been described in the preceding pages is so familiar, and yet so extraordinary, that it requires an effort of thought to appreciate its true nature. We do not at once see the absurdity of the same words having many senses, or free our minds from the illusion that the Apostle or Evangelist must have written with a reference to the creeds or controversies or circumstances of other times. Let it be considered, then, that this extreme variety of interpretation is found to exist in the case of no other book, but of the Scriptures only. Other writings are preserved to us in dead languages—Greek, Latin, Oriental, some of them in fragments, all of them originally in manuscript. It is true that difficulties arise in the explanation of these writings, especially in the most ancient, from our imperfect acquaintance with the meaning of words, or the defectiveness of copies, or the want of some historical or geographical information which is required to present an event or character in its true bearing. In comparison with the wealth and light of modern literature, our knowledge of Greek classical authors, for example, may be called imperfect and shadowy. Some of them have another sort of difficulty arising from subtlety or abruptness in the use of language; in lyric poetry especially, and some of the earlier prose, the greatness of the thought struggles with the stammering lips. It may be observed that all these difficulties occur also in Scripture; they are found equally in sacred and profane literature.[12] But the meaning of classical authors is known with comparative certainty; and the interpretation of them seems to rest on a scientific basis. It is not, therefore, to philological or historical difficulties that the greater part of the uncertainty in the interpretation of Scripture is to be attributed. No ignorance of Hebrew or Greek is sufficient to account for it. Even the Vedas and the Zendavesta, though beset by obscurities of language probably greater than are found in any portion of the Bible, are interpreted, at least by European scholars, according to fixed rules, and beginning to be clearly understood.[13]

[6] To bring the parallel home, let us imagine the remains of some well-known Greek author, as Plato or Sophocles, receiving the same treatment at the hands of the world which the Scriptures have experienced. The text of such an author, when first printed by Aldus or Stephens, would be gathered from the imperfect or miswritten copies which fell in the way of the editors; after awhile older and better manuscripts come to light, and the power of using and estimating the value of manuscripts is greatly improved. We may suppose, further, that the readings of these older copies do not always conform to some received canons of criticism. Up to the year 1550, or 1624, alterations, often proceeding on no principle, have been introduced into the text; but now a stand is made—an edition which appeared at the latter of the two dates just mentioned is invested with authority; this authorized text is a *pièce de resistance* against innovation. Many reasons are given why it is better to have bad readings to which the world is accustomed than good ones which are novel and strange—why the later manuscripts of Plato or Sophocles are often to be preferred to earlier ones—why it is useless to remove imperfections where perfect accuracy is not to be attained. A fear of disturbing the critical canons which have come down from former ages is, however, suspected to be one reason for the opposition. And custom and prejudice, and the nicety of the subject, and all the arguments which are intelligible to the many against the truth, which is intelligible only to the few, are thrown into the scale to preserve the works of Plato or Sophocles as nearly as possible in the received text.[14]

[7] Leaving the text we proceed to interpret and translate. The meaning of Greek words is known with tolerable certainty; and the grammar of the Greek language has been minutely analyzed both in ancient and modern times. Yet the interpretation of Sophocles is tentative and uncertain; it seems to vary from age to age: to some the great tragedian has appeared to embody in his choruses certain theological or moral ideas of his own age or country; there are others who find there an allegory of the Christian religion or of the history of modern Europe. Several schools of critics have commented on his works; to the Englishman he has presented one meaning, to the Frenchman another, to the German a third; the interpretations have also differed with the philosophical systems which the interpreters espoused. To one the same words have appeared to bear a moral, to another a symbolical meaning; a third is determined wholly by the authority of old commentators; while there is a disposition to condemn the scholar who seeks to interpret Sophocles from himself only and with reference to the ideas and beliefs of the age in which he lived. And the error of such an one is attributed not only to some intellectual but even to a moral obliquity which prevents his seeing the true meaning.[15]

[8] It would be tedious to follow into details the absurdity which has been supposed. By such methods it would be truly said that Sophocles or Plato may be made to mean anything. It would seem as if some *Novum Organum* were needed to lay down rules of interpretation for ancient literature. Still one other supposition has to be introduced which will appear, perhaps, more extravagant than any which

have preceded. Conceive then that these modes of interpreting Sophocles had existed for ages; that great institutions and interests had become interwoven with them, and in some degree even the honour of nations and churches—is it too much to say that in such a case they would be changed with difficulty, and that they would continue to be maintained long after critics and philosophers had seen that they were indefensible?[16]

9] No one who has a Christian feeling would place classical on a level with sacred literature; and there are other particulars in which the preceding comparison fails, as, for example, the style and subject. But, however different the subject, although the interpretation of Scripture requires 'a vision and faculty divine,' or at least a moral and religious interest which is not needed in the study of a Greek poet or philosopher, yet in what may be termed the externals of interpretation, that is to say, the meaning of words, the connexion of sentences, the settlement of the text, the evidence of facts, the same rules apply to the Old and New Testaments as to other books. And the figure is no exaggeration of the erring fancy of men in the use of Scripture, or of the tenacity with which they cling to the interpretations of other times, or of the arguments by which they maintain them. All the resources of knowledge may be turned into a means not of discovering the true rendering, but of upholding a received one. Grammar appears to start from an independent point of view, yet inquiries into the use of the article or the preposition have been observed to wind round into a defence of some doctrine. Rhetoric often magnifies its own want of taste into the design of inspiration. Logic (that other mode of rhetoric) is apt to lend itself to the illusion, by stating erroneous explanations with a clearness which is mistaken for truth. 'Metaphysical aid' carries away the common understanding into a region where it must blindly follow. Learning obscures as well as illustrates; it heaps up chaff when there is no more wheat. These are some of the ways in which the sense of Scripture has become confused, by the help of tradition, in the course of ages, under a load of commentators.[17]

0] The book itself remains as at the first unchanged amid the changing interpretations of it. The office of the interpreter is not to add another, but to recover the original one; the meaning, that is, of the words as they first struck on the ears or flashed before the eyes of those who heard and read them. He has to transfer himself to another age; to imagine that he is a disciple of Christ or Paul; to disengage himself from all that follows. The history of Christendom is nothing to him; but only the scene at Galilee or Jerusalem, the handful of believers who gathered themselves together at Ephesus, or Corinth, or Rome. His eye is fixed on the form of one like the Son of man, or of the prophet who was girded with a garment of camel's hair, or of the Apostle who had a thorn in the flesh. The greatness of the Roman Empire is nothing to him; it is an inner not an outer world that he is striving to restore. All the after-thoughts of theology are nothing to him; they are not the true lights which light him in difficult places. His concern is with a book in which as in other ancient writings are some things of which we are ignorant; which defect of our knowledge cannot however be supplied by the conjectures of fathers or divines. The simple words of that book he tries to preserve absolutely pure from the refinements or distinctions of later times. He acknowledges that they are fragmentary, and would suspect himself, if out of fragments he were able to create a well-rounded system or a continuous history. The greater part of his learning is a knowledge of the text itself; he has no delight in the voluminous literature which has overgrown it. He has no theory of interpretation; a few rules guarding against common errors are enough for him. His object is to read Scripture like any other book, with a real interest and not merely a conventional one. He wants to be able to open his eyes and see or imagine things as they truly are.[18]

[11] Nothing would be more likely to restore a natural feeling on this subject than a history of the Interpretation of Scripture. It would take us back to the beginning; it would present in one view the causes which have darkened the meaning of words in the course of ages; it would clear away the remains of dogmas, systems, controversies, which are encrusted upon them. It would show us the 'erring fancy' of interpreters assuming sometimes to have the Spirit of God Himself, yet unable to pass beyond the limits of their own age, and with a judgment often biassed by party. Great names there have been among them, names of men who may be reckoned also among the benefactors of the human race, yet comparatively few who have understood the thoughts of other times, or who have bent their minds to 'interrogate' the meaning of words. Such a work would enable us to separate the elements of doctrine and tradition with which the meaning of Scripture is encumbered in our own day. It would mark the different epochs of interpretation from the time when the living word was in process of becoming a book to Origen and Tertullian, from Origen to Jerome and Augustine, from Jerome and Augustine to Abelard and Aquinas; again making a new beginning with the revival of literature, from Erasmus, the father of Biblical criticism in more recent times, with Calvin and Beza for his immediate successors, through Grotius and Hammond, down to De Wette and Meier, our own contemporaries. We should see how the mystical interpretation of Scripture originated in the Alexandrian age; how it blended with the logical and rhetorical; how both received weight and currency from their use in support of the claims and teaching of the Church. We should notice how the 'new learning' of the fifteenth and sixteenth centuries gradually awakened the critical faculty in the study of the sacred writings; how Biblical criticism has slowly but surely followed in the track of philological and historical (not without a remoter influence exercised upon it also by natural science); how, too, the form of the scholastic literature, and even of notes on the classics, insensibly communicated itself to commentaries on Scripture. We should see how the word inspiration, from being used in a general way to express what may be called the prophetic spirit of Scripture, has passed, within the last two centuries, into a sort of technical term; how, in other instances, the practice or feeling of earlier ages has been hollowed out into the theory or system of later ones. We should observe how the popular explanations of prophecy as in heathen (Thucyd. ii. 54), so also in Christian times, had adapted themselves to the circumstances of

mankind. We might remark that in our own country, and in the present generation especially, the interpretation of Scripture had assumed an apologetic character, as though making an effort to defend itself against some supposed inroad of science and criticism; while among German commentators there is, for the first time in the history of the world, an approach to agreement and certainty. For example, the diversity among German writers on prophecy is far less than among English ones. That is a new phenomenon which has to be acknowledged. More than any other subject of human knowledge, Biblical criticism has hung to the past; it has been hitherto found truer to the traditions of the Church than to the words of Christ. It has made, however, two great steps onward—at the time of the Reformation and in our day. The diffusion of a critical spirit in history and literature is affecting the criticism of the Bible in our own day in a manner not unlike the burst of intellectual life in the fifteenth or sixteenth centuries. Educated persons are beginning to ask, not what Scripture may be made to mean, but what it does. And it is no exaggeration to say that he who in the present state of knowledge will confine himself to the plain meaning of words and the study of their context may know more of the original spirit and intention of the authors of the New Testament than all the controversial writers of former ages put together.[19]

Such a history would be of great value to philosophy as well as to theology. It would be the history of the human mind in one of its most remarkable manifestations. For ages which are not original show their character in the interpretation of ancient writings. Creating nothing, and incapable of that effort of imagination which is required in a true criticism of the past, they read and explain the thoughts of former times by the conventional modes of their own. Such a history would form a kind of preface or prolegomena to the study of Scripture. Like the history of science, it would save many a useless toil; it would indicate the uncertainties on which it is not worth while to speculate further; the byepaths or labyrinths in which men lose themselves; the mines that are already worked out. He who reflects on the multitude of explanations which already exist of the 'number of the beast,' 'the two witnesses,' 'the little horn,' 'the man of sin,' who observes the manner in which these explanations have varied with the political movements of our own time, will be unwilling to devote himself to a method of inquiry in which there is so little appearance of certainty or progress. These interpretations would destroy one another if they were all placed side by side in a tabular analysis. It is an instructive fact, which may be mentioned in passing, that Joseph Mede, the greatest authority on this subject, twice fixed the end of the world in the last century and once during his own lifetime. In like manner, he who notices the circumstance that the explanations of the first chapter of Genesis have slowly changed, and, as it were, retreated before the advance of geology, will be unwilling to add another to the spurious reconcilements of science and revelation. Or to take an example of another kind, the Protestant divine who perceives that the types and figures of the Old Testament are employed by Roman Catholics in support of the tenets of their church, will be careful not to use weapons which it is impossible to guide, and which may with equal force be turned against himself. Those who have handled them on the Protestant side have before now fallen victims to them, not observing as they fell that it was by their own hand.[20]

[13] Much of the uncertainty which prevails in the interpretation of Scripture arises out of party efforts to wrest its meaning to different sides. There are, however, deeper reasons which have hindered the natural meaning of the text from immediately and universally prevailing. One of these is the unsettlement of many questions which have an important but indirect bearing on this subject. Some of these questions veil themselves in ambiguous terms; and no one likes to draw them out of their hiding-place into the light of day. In natural science it is felt to be useless to build on assumptions; in history we look with suspicion on *a priori* ideas of what ought to have been; in mathematics, when a step is wrong, we pull the house down until we reach the point at which the error is discovered. But in theology it is otherwise; there the tendency has been to conceal the unsoundness of the foundation under the fairness and loftiness of the superstructure. It has been thought safer to allow arguments to stand which, although fallacious, have been on the right side, than to point out their defect. And thus many principles have imperceptibly grown up which have overridden facts. No one would interpret Scripture, as many do, but for certain previous suppositions with which we come to the perusal of it. 'There can be no error in the Word of God,' therefore the discrepancies in the books of Kings and Chronicles are only apparent, or may be attributed to differences in the copies. 'It is a thousand times more likely that the interpreter should err than the inspired writer.' For a like reason the failure of a prophecy is never admitted, in spite of Scripture and of history (Jer. xxxvi. 30; Isai. xxiii.; Amos vii. 10–17); the mention of a name later than the supposed age of the prophet is not allowed, as in other writings, to be taken in evidence of the date (Isaiah xlv. 1). The accuracy of the Old Testament is measured not by the standard of primeval history, but of a modern critical one, which, contrary to all probability, is supposed to be attained; this arbitrary standard once assumed, it becomes a point of honour or of faith to defend every name, date, place, which occurs. Or to take another class of questions, it is said that 'the various theories of the origin of the three first Gospels are all equally unknown to the Holy Catholic Church,' or as another writer of a different school expresses himself, 'they tend to sap the inspiration of the New Testament.' Again, the language in which our Saviour speaks of his own union with the Father is interpreted by the language of the creeds. Those who remonstrate against double senses, allegorical interpretations, forced reconcilements, find themselves met by a sort of presupposition that 'God speaks not as man speaks.' The limitation of the human faculties is confusedly appealed to as a reason for abstaining from investigations which are quite within their limits. The suspicion of Deism, or perhaps of Atheism, awaits inquiry. By such fears a good man refuses to be influenced, a philosophical mind is apt to cast them aside with too much bitterness. It is better to close the book than to read it under conditions of thought which are imposed from without. Whether those

conditions of thought are the traditions of the Church, or the opinions of the religious world—Catholic or Protestant—makes no difference. They are inconsistent with the freedom of the truth and the moral character of the Gospel. It becomes necessary, therefore, to examine briefly some of these prior questions which lie in the way of a reasonable criticism.[21]

§ 2.

4] Among these previous questions, that which first presents itself is the one already alluded to—the question of inspiration. Almost all Christians agree in the word, which use and tradition have consecrated to express the reverence which they truly feel for the Old and New Testaments. But here the agreement of opinion ends; the meaning of inspiration has been variously explained, or more often passed over in silence from a fear of stirring the difficulties that would arise about it. It is one of those theological terms which may be regarded as 'great peacemakers,' but which are also sources of distrust and misunderstanding. For while we are ready to shake hands with any one who uses the same language as ourselves, a doubt is apt to insinuate itself whether he takes language in the same senses—whether a particular term conveys all the associations to another which it does to ourselves—whether it is not possible that one who disagrees about the word may not be more nearly agreed about the thing.[22] The advice has, indeed, been given to the theologian that he 'should take care of words and leave things to themselves;' the authority, however, who gives the advice is not good—it is placed by Goethe in the mouth of Mephistopheles. Pascal seriously charges the Jesuits with acting on a similar maxim—excommunicating those who meant the same thing and said another, holding communion with those who said the same thing and meant another. But this is not the way to heal the wounds of the Church of Christ; we cannot thus 'skin and film' the weak places of theology. Errors about words, and the attribution to words themselves of an excessive importance, lie at the root of theological as of other confusions. In theology they are more dangerous than in other sciences, because they cannot so readily be brought to the test of facts.[23]

The word inspiration has received more numerous gradations and distinctions of meaning than perhaps any other in the whole of theology. There is an inspiration of superintendence and an inspiration of suggestion; an inspiration which would have been consistent with the Apostle or Evangelist falling into error, and an inspiration which would have prevented him from erring; verbal organic inspiration by which the inspired person is the passive utterer of a Divine Word, and an inspiration which acts through the character of the sacred writer; there is an inspiration which absolutely communicates the fact to be revealed or statement to be made, and an inspiration which does not supersede the ordinary knowledge of human events; there is an inspiration which demands infallibility in matters of doctrine, but allows for mistakes in fact. Lastly, there is a view of inspiration which recognises only its supernatural and prophetic character, and a view of inspiration which regards the Apostles and Evangelists as equally inspired in their writings and in their lives, and in both receiving the guidance of the Spirit of truth in a manner not different in kind but only in degree from ordinary Christians.[24] Many of these explanations lose sight of the original meaning and derivation of the word; some of them are framed with the view of meeting difficulties; all perhaps err in attempting to define what, though real, is incapable of being defined in an exact manner. Nor for any of the higher or supernatural views of inspiration is there any foundation in the Gospels or Epistles. There is no appearance in their writings that the Evangelists or Apostles had any inward gift, or were subject to a power external to them different from that of preaching or teaching which they daily exercised; nor do they anywhere lead us to suppose that they were free from error or infirmity.[25] St. Paul writes like a Christian teacher, exhibiting all the emotions and vicissitudes of human feeling, speaking, indeed, with authority, but hesitating in difficult cases and more than once correcting himself, corrected, too, by the course of events in his expectation of the coming of Christ.[26] The Evangelist 'who saw it, bare record, and his record is true: and he knoweth that he saith true' (John xix. 35). Another Evangelist does not profess to be an original narrator, but only 'to set forth in order a declaration of what eye-witnesses had delivered,' like many others whose writings have not been preserved to us (Luke i. 1, 2). And the result is in accordance with the simple profession and style in which they describe themselves; there is no appearance, that is to say, of insincerity or want of faith; but neither is there perfect accuracy or agreement. One supposes the original dwelling place of our Lord's parents to have been Bethlehem (Matthew ii. 1, 22), another Nazareth (Luke ii. 4); they trace his genealogy in different ways; one mentions the thieves blaspheming, another has preserved to after-ages the record of the penitent thief; they appear to differ about the day and hour of the Crucifixion; the narrative of the woman who anointed our Lord's feet with ointment is told in all four, each narrative having more or less considerable variations. These are a few instances of the differences which arose in the traditions of the earliest ages respecting the history of our Lord.[27] But he who wishes to investigate the character of the sacred writings should not be afraid to make a catalogue of them all with the view of estimating their cumulative weight. (For it is obvious that the answer which would be admitted in the case of a single discrepancy, will not be the true answer when there are many.) We should further consider that the narratives in which these discrepancies occur are short and partly identical—a cycle of tradition beyond which the knowledge of the early fathers never travels, though if all the things that Jesus said and did had been written down, 'the world itself could not have contained the books that would have been written' (John xx. 30; xxi. 25). For the proportion which these narratives bear to the whole subject, as well as their relation to one another, is an important element in the estimation of differences. In the same way, he who would understand the nature of prophecy in the Old Testament, should have the courage to examine how far its details were minutely fulfilled. The absence of such a fulfilment may further lead him to discover that he took the letter for the spirit in expecting it.[28]

6] The subject will clear of itself if we bear in mind two considerations:— First, that the nature of inspiration can only be known from the examination of Scripture. There is no other source to which we can turn for information; and we have no right to assume some imaginary doctrine of inspiration like the infallibility of the Roman Catholic Church. To the question, 'What is inspiration?' the first answer therefore is, 'That idea of Scripture which we gather from the knowledge of it.' It is no mere *a priori* notion, but one to which the book is itself a witness. It is a fact which we infer from the study of Scripture—not of one portion only, but of the whole.[29] Obviously then it embraces writings of very different kinds—the book of Esther, for example, or the Song of Solomon, as well as the Gospel of St. John. It is reconcileable with the mixed good and evil of the characters of the Old Testament, which nevertheless does not exclude them from the favour of God, with the attribution to the Divine Being of actions at variance with that higher revelation, which he has given of himself in the Gospel; it is not inconsistent with imperfect or opposite aspects of the truth as in the book of Job or Ecclesiastes, with variations of fact in the Gospels or the books of Kings and Chronicles, with inaccuracies of language in the Epistles of St. Paul. For these are all found in Scripture; neither is there any reason why they should not be, except a general impression that Scripture ought to have been written in a way different from what it has. A principle of progressive revelation admits them all; and this is already contained in the words of our Saviour, 'Moses because of the hardness of your hearts;' or even in the Old Testament, 'Henceforth there shall be no more this proverb in the house of Israel.' For what is progressive is necessarily imperfect in its earlier stages, and even erring to those who come after, whether it be the maxims of a half-civilized world which are compared with those of a civilized one, or the law with the Gospel. Scripture itself points the way to answer the moral objections to Scripture. Lesser difficulties remain, but only such as would be found commonly in writings of the same age or country. There is no more reason why imperfect narratives should be excluded from Scripture than imperfect grammar; no more ground for expecting that the New Testament would be logical or Aristotelian in form, than that it would be written in Attic Greek.[30]

The other consideration is one which has been neglected by writers on this subject. It is this—that any true doctrine of inspiration must conform to all well-ascertained facts of history or of science. The same fact cannot be true and untrue, any more than the same words can have two opposite meanings. The same fact cannot be true in religion when seen by the light of faith, and untrue in science when looked at through the medium of evidence or experiment. It is ridiculous to suppose that the sun goes round the earth in the same sense in which the earth goes round the sun; or that the world appears to have existed, but has not existed during the vast epochs of which geology speaks to us. But if so, there is no need of elaborate reconcilements of revelation and science; they reconcile themselves the moment any scientific truth is distinctly ascertained. As the idea of nature enlarges, the idea of revelation also enlarges; it was a temporary misunderstanding which severed them. And as the knowledge of nature which is possessed by the few is communicated in its leading features at least to the many, they will receive with it a higher conception of the ways of God to man. It may hereafter appear as natural to the majority of mankind to see the providence of God in the order of the world, as it once was to appeal to interruptions of it.[31]

[18] It is true that there are a class of scientific facts with which popular opinions on theology often conflict which do not seem to conform in all respects to the severer conditions of inductive science: such especially are the facts relating to the formation of the earth and the beginnings of the human race. But it is not worth while to fight on this debateable ground a losing battle in the hope that a generation will pass away before we sound a last retreat. Almost all intelligent persons are agreed that the earth has existed for myriads of ages; the best informed are of opinion that the history of nations extends back some thousand years before the Mosaic chronology; recent discoveries in geology may perhaps open a further vista of existence for the human species, while it is possible, and may one day be known, that mankind spread not from one but from many centres over the globe; or as others say, that the supply of links which are at present wanting in the chain of animal life may lead to new conclusions respecting the origin of man. Now let it be granted that these facts, being with the past, cannot be shown in the same palpable and evident manner as the facts of chemistry or physiology; and that the proof of some of them, especially of those last mentioned, is wanting; still it is a false policy to set up inspiration or revelation in opposition to them, a principle which can have no influence on them and should be rather kept out of their way. The sciences of geology and comparative philology are steadily gaining ground (many of the guesses of twenty years ago have become certainties, and the guesses of to-day may hereafter become so). Shall we peril religion on the possibility of their untruth? on such a cast to stake the life of man implies not only a recklessness of facts but a misunderstanding of the nature of the Gospel. If it is fortunate for science, it is perhaps more fortunate for Christian truth, that the admission of Galileo's discovery has for ever settled the principle of the relations between them.[32]

[19] A similar train of thought may be extended to the results of historical inquiries. These results cannot be barred by the dates or narrative of Scripture; neither should they be made to wind round into agreement with them. Again, the idea of inspiration must expand and take them in. Their importance in a religious point of view is not that they impugn or confirm the Jewish history, but that they show more clearly the purposes of God towards the whole human race. The recent chronological discoveries from Egyptian monuments do not tend to overthrow revelation, nor the Ninevite inscriptions to support it. The use of them on either side may indeed arouse a popular interest in them; it is apt to turn a scientific inquiry into a semi-religious controversy. And to religion either use is almost equally injurious, because seeming to rest truths important to human life on the mere accident of an archaeological discovery. Is it to be thought that Christianity

gains anything from the deciphering of the names of some Assyrian and Babylonian kings, contemporaries chiefly with the later Jewish history? As little as it ought to lose from the appearance of a contradictory narrative of the Exodus in the chamber of an Egyptian temple of the year B.C. 1500. This latter supposition may not be very probable. But it is worth while to ask ourselves the question whether we can be right in maintaining any view of religion which can be affected by such a probability.[33]

[20] It will be a further assistance in the consideration of this subject, to observe that the interpretation of Scripture has nothing to do with any opinion respecting its origin. The meaning of Scripture is one thing; the inspiration of Scripture is another. It is conceivable that those who hold the most different views about the one, may be able to agree about the other. Rigid upholders of the verbal inspiration of Scripture, and those who deny inspiration altogether, may nevertheless meet on the common ground of the meaning of words. If the term inspiration were to fall into disuse, no fact of nature, or history, or language, no event in the life of man, or dealings of God with him, would be in any degree altered. The word itself is but of yesterday, not found in the earlier confessions of the reformed faith; the difficulties that have arisen about it are only two or three centuries old. Therefore the question of inspiration, though in one sense important, is to the interpreter as though it were not important; he is in no way called upon to determine a matter with which he has nothing to do, and which was not determined by fathers of the Church. And he had better go on his way and leave the more precise definition of the word to the progress of knowledge and the results of the study of Scripture, instead of entangling himself with a theory about it.

[21] It is one evil of conditions or previous suppositions in the study of Scripture that the assumption of them has led to an apologetic temper in the interpreters of Scripture. The tone of apology is always a tone of weakness and does injury to a good cause. It is the reverse of 'ye shall know the truth, and the truth shall make you free.' It is hampered with the necessity of making a defence, and also with previous defences of the same side; it accepts, with an excess of reserve and caution, the truth itself, when it comes from an opposite quarter. Commentators are often more occupied with the proof of miracles than with the declaration of life and immortality; with the fulfilment of the details of prophecy than with its life and power; with the reconcilement of the discrepancies in the narrative of the infancy, pointed out by Schleiermacher, than with the importance of the great event of the appearance of the Saviour. '*To that end was I born and for this cause came I into the world that I should bear witness unto the truth.*'[34] The same tendency is observable also in reference to the Acts of the Apostles and the Epistles, which are not only brought into harmony with each other, but interpreted with a reference to the traditions of existing communions. The natural meaning of particular expressions, as for example: 'Why are they then baptized for the dead' (1 Corinthians xv. 29)? or the words 'because of the angels' (1 Corinthians xi. 10); or, 'this generation shall not pass away until all these things be fulfilled' (Matthew xxiv. 34); or, 'upon this rock

will I build my Church' (Matthew xvi. 18), is set aside in favour of others, which, however improbable, are more in accordance with preconceived opinions, or seem to be more worthy of the Sacred writers. The language, and also the text, are treated on the same defensive and conservative principles.[35] The received translations of Philippians ii. 6 ('Who, being in the form of God, thought it not robbery to be equal with God'), or of Romans iii. 25 ('Whom God hath set forth to be a propitiation through faith in his blood'), or Romans xv. 6 ('God, even the Father of our Lord Jesus Christ'), though erroneous, are not given up without a struggle; the 1 Timothy iii. 16, and 1 John v. 7, (the three witnesses), though the first (God manifest in the flesh, ΘΣ for ΟΣ) is not found in the best manuscripts, and the second in no Greek manuscript worth speaking of, have not yet disappeared from the editions of the Greek Testament commonly in use in England, and still less from the English translation.[36] An English commentator who, with Lachman and Tischendorf, supported also by the authority of Erasmus, ventures to alter the punctuation of the doxology in Romans ix. 5 ('Who is over all God blessed for ever') hardly escapes the charge of heresy. That in most of these cases the words referred to have a direct bearing on important controversies is a reason not for retaining, but for correcting them.[37]

[22] The temper of accommodation shows itself especially in two ways: first, in the attempt to adapt the truths of Scripture to the doctrines of the creeds; secondly, in the adaptation of the precepts and maxims of Scripture to the language or practice of our own age.[38] Now the creeds are acknowledged to be a part of Christianity; they stand in a close relation to the words of Christ and his Apostles; nor can it be said that any heterodox formula makes a nearer approach to a simple and scriptural rule of faith. Neither is anything gained by contrasting them with Scripture, in which the germs of the expressions used in them are sufficiently apparent. Yet it does not follow that they should be pressed into the service of the interpreter. The growth of ideas in the interval which separated the first century from the fourth or sixth makes it impossible to apply the language of the one to the explanation of the other. Between Scripture and the Nicene or Athanasian Creed, a world of the understanding comes in—that world of abstractions and second notions; and mankind are no longer at the same point as when the whole of Christianity was contained in the words, 'Believe on the Lord Jesus Christ and thou mayest be saved,' when the Gospel centred in the attachment to a living or recently departed friend and Lord. The language of the New Testament is the first utterance and consciousness of the mind of Christ; or the immediate vision of the Word of life (1 John i. 1) as it presented itself before the eyes of his first followers, or as the sense of his truth and power grew upon them (Romans i. 3, 4); the other is the result of three or four centuries of reflection and controversy. And although this last had a truth suited to its age, and its technical expressions have sunk deep into the heart of the human race, it is not the less unfitted to be the medium by the help of which Scripture is to be explained. If the occurrence of the phraseology of the Nicene age in a verse of the Epistles would detect the spuriousness of the verse in which it was

found, how can the Nicene or Athanasian Creed be a suitable instrument for the interpretation of Scripture? That advantage which the New Testament has over the teaching of the Church, as representing what may be termed the childhood of the Gospel, would be lost if its language were required to conform to that of the Creeds.[39]

3] To attribute to St. Paul or the Twelve the abstract notion of Christian truth which afterwards sprang up in the Catholic Church, is the same sort of anachronism as to attribute to them a system of philosophy. It is the same error as to attribute to Homer the ideas of Thales or Heraclitus, or to Thales the more developed principles of Aristotle and Plato.[40] Many persons who have no difficulty in tracing the growth of institutions, yet seem to fail in recognising the more subtle progress of an idea. It is hard to imagine the absence of conceptions with which we are familiar; to go back to the germ of what we know only in maturity; to give up what has grown to us, and become a part of our minds. In the present case however the development is not difficult to prove. The statements of Scripture are unaccountable if we deny it; the silence of Scripture is equally unaccountable. Absorbed as St. Paul was in the person of Christ with an intensity of faith and love of which in modern days and at this distance of time we can scarcely form a conception—high as he raised the dignity of his Lord above all things in heaven and earth—looking to him as the Creator of all things, and the head of quick and dead, he does not speak of him as 'equal to the Father,' or 'of one substance with the Father.' Much of the language of the Epistles (passages for example such as Romans i. 2; Philippians ii. 6) would lose their meaning if distributed in alternate clauses between our Lord's humanity and divinity. Still greater difficulties would be introduced into the Gospels by the attempt to identify them with the Creeds. We should have to suppose that He was and was not tempted; that when he prayed to his Father he prayed also to Himself; that He knew and did not know 'of that hour' of which He as well as the angels were ignorant. How could He have said 'My God, my God, why hast thou forsaken me?' or 'Father, if it be possible let this cup pass from me.' How could He have doubted whether 'when the Son cometh he shall find faith upon the earth?' These simple and touching words have to be taken out of their natural meaning and connexion to be made the theme of apologetic discourses if we insist on reconciling them with the distinctions of later ages.[41]

Neither, as has been already remarked, would the substitution of any other precise or definite rule of faith, as for example the Unitarian, be more favourable to the interpretation of Scripture. How could the Evangelist St. John have said 'the Word was God,' or 'God was the Word' (according to either mode of translating), or how would our Lord Himself have said, 'I and the Father are one,' if either had meant that Christ was a mere man, 'a prophet or as one of the prophets?'[42] No one who takes words in their natural sense can suppose that 'in the beginning' (John i. 1) means 'at the commencement of the ministry of Christ,' or that 'the Word was with God,' only relates 'to the withdrawal of Christ to commune with God,' or that 'the Word is said to be God,' in the ironical sense of John x. 35. But while venturing to turn one eye on these (perhaps obsolete) perversions of the meanings of words in old opponents, we must not forget also to keep the other open to our own. The object of the preceding remark is not to enter into controversy with them, or to balance the statements of one side with those of the other, but only to point out the error of introducing into the interpretation of Scripture the notions of a later age which is common alike to us and them.[43]

[25] The other kind of accommodation which was alluded to above arises out of the difference between the social and ecclesiastical state of the world, as it exists in actual fact, and the ideal which the Gospel presents to us. An ideal is, by its very nature, far removed from actual life. It is enshrined not in the material things of the external world, but in the heart and conscience. Mankind are dissatisfied at this separation; they fancy that they can make the inward kingdom an outward one also. But this is not possible. The frame of civilization, that is to say, institutions and laws, the usages of business, the customs of society, these are for the most part mechanical, capable only in a certain degree of a higher and spiritual life. Christian motives have never existed in such strength, as to make it safe or possible to entrust them with the preservation of social order. Other interests are therefore provided and other principles, often independent of the teaching of the Gospel, or even apparently at variance with it. 'If a man smite thee on the right cheek turn to him the other also,' is not a regulation of police but an ideal rule of conduct, not to be explained away, but rarely if ever to be literally acted upon in a civilized country; or rather to be acted upon always in spirit, yet not without a reference to the interests of the community. If a missionary were to endanger the public peace and come like the Apostles saying, 'I ought to obey God rather than man,' it is obvious that the most Christian of magistrates could not allow him (say in India or New Zealand) to shield himself under the authority of these words.[44] For in religion as in philosophy there are two opposite poles; of truth and action, of doctrine and practice, of idea and fact. The image of God in Christ is over against the necessities of human nature and the state of man on earth. Our Lord himself recognises this distinction, when he says, 'Of whom do the kings of the earth gather tribute?' and 'then are the children free.' (Matth. xvii. 26.) And again, 'Notwithstanding lest we should offend them,' &c. Here are contrasted what may be termed the two poles of idea and fact.[45]

[26] All men appeal to Scripture, and desire to draw the authority of Scripture to their side; its voice may be heard in the turmoil of political strife; a merely verbal similarity, the echo of a word, has weight in the determination of a controversy. Such appeals are not to be met always by counter-appeals; they rather lead to the consideration of deeper questions as to the manner in which Scripture is to be applied. In what relation does it stand to actual life? Is it a law, or only a spirit? for nations, or for individuals? to be enforced generally, or in details also? Are its maxims to be modified by experience, or acted upon in defiance of experience? Are the accidental circumstances of the first believers to become a rule for us? Is everything, in short, done or said by our Saviour and His Apostles, to be regarded

as a precept or example which is to be followed on all occasions and to last for all time?[46] That can hardly be, consistently with the changes of human things. It would be a rigid skeleton of Christianity (not the image of Christ), to which society and politics, as well as the lives of individuals, would be conformed. It would be the oldness of the letter, on which the world would be stretched; not 'the law of the spirit of life' which St. Paul teaches. The attempt to force politics and law into the framework of religion is apt to drive us up into a corner, in which the great principles of truth and justice have no longer room to make themselves felt. It is better, as well as safer, to take the liberty with which Christ has made us free. For our Lord himself has left behind Him words, which contain a principle large enough to admit all the forms of society or of life; 'My kingdom is not of this world.' (John xviii. 36.) It does not come into collision with politics or knowledge; it has nothing to do with the Roman government or the Jewish priesthood, or with corresponding institutions in the present day; it is a counsel of perfection, and has its dwelling-place in the heart of man. That is the real solution of questions of Church and State; all else is relative to the history or circumstances of particular nations. That is the answer to a doubt which is also raised respecting the obligation of the letter of the Gospel on individual Christians. But this inwardness of the words of Christ is what few are able to receive; it is easier to apply them superficially to things without, than to be a partaker of them from within. And false and miserable applications of them are often made, and the kingdom of God becomes the tool of the kingdoms of the world.[47]

7] The neglect of this necessary contrast between the ideal and the actual has had a twofold effect on the Interpretation of Scripture. It has led to an unfair appropriation of some portions of Scripture and an undue neglect of others. The letter is in many cases really or apparently in harmony with existing practices, or opinions, or institutions. In other cases it is far removed from them; it often seems as if the world would come to an end before the words of Scripture could be realized. The twofold effect just now mentioned, corresponds to these two classes. Some texts of Scripture have been eagerly appealed to and made (in one sense) too much of; they have been taken by force into the service of received opinions and beliefs; texts of the other class have been either unnoticed or explained away. Consider, for example, the extraordinary and unreasonable importance attached to single words, sometimes of doubtful meaning, in reference to any of the following subjects:—1, Divorce; 2, Marriage with a Wife's Sister; 3, Inspiration; 4, the Personality of the Holy Spirit; 5, Infant Baptism; 6, Episcopacy; 7, Divine Right of Kings; 8, Original Sin. There is, indeed, a kind of mystery in the way in which the chance words of a simple narrative, the occurrence of some accidental event, the use even of a figure of speech, or a mis-translation of a word in Latin or English, have affected the thoughts of future ages and distant countries. Nothing so slight that it has not been caught at; nothing so plain that it may not be explained away. What men have brought to the text they have also found there; what has received no interpretation or witness, either in the customs of the Church or in 'the thoughts of many hearts,' is still 'an unknown tongue' to them. It is with Scripture as with oratory, its effect partly depends on the preparation in the mind or in circumstances for the reception of it. There is no use of Scripture, no quotation or even misquotation of a word which is not a power in the world, when it embodies the spirit of a great movement or is echoed by the voice of a large party.[48]

[28] On the first of the subjects referred to above, it is argued from Scripture that adulterers should not be allowed to marry again; and the point of the argument turns on the question whether the words (ἐκτὸς λόγου πορνείας) saving for the cause of fornication, which occur in the first clause of an important text on marriage, were designedly or accidentally omitted in the second (Matth. v. 32.) 'Whosoever shall put away his wife, saving for the cause of fornication, causeth her to commit adultery, and whosoever shall marry her that is divorced committeth adultery' (compare also Mark x. 11, 12).[49] 2. The Scripture argument in the second instance is almost invisible, being drawn from a passage the meaning of which is irrelevant (Lev. xviii. 18. 'Neither shalt thou take a wife to her sister to vex her, to uncover her nakedness beside the other in her lifetime'); and transferred from the Polygamy allowed which prevailed in Eastern countries 3000 years ago to the Monogamy of the nineteenth century and the Christian Church, in spite of the custom and tradition of the Jews and the analogy of the brother's widow.[50] 3. In the third case the word (Θεόπνευστος) 'given by inspiration of God' is spoken of the Old Testament, and is assumed to apply to the New, including that Epistle in which the expression occurs (2 Tim. iii. 16.)[51] 4. In the fourth example the words used are mysterious (John xiv. 26; xvi. 15), and seem to come out of the depths of a divine consciousness; they have sometimes, however, received a more exact meaning than they would truly bear; what is spoken in a figure is construed with the severity of a logical statement, while passages of an opposite tenour are overlooked or set aside.[52] 5. In the fifth instance, the mere mention of a family of a jailer at Philippi who was baptized ('he and all his,' Acts xvi. 33), has led to the inference that in this family there were probably young children, and hence that infant baptism is, first, permissive, secondly, obligatory.[53] 6. In the sixth case the chief stress of the argument from Scripture turns on the occurrence of the word (ἐπίσκοπος) bishop in the Epistles to Timothy and Titus, which is assisted by a supposed analogy between the position of the Apostles and of their successors; although the term bishop is clearly used in the passages referred to as well as in other parts of the New Testament indistinguishably from Presbyter, and the magisterial authority of bishops in after ages is unlike rather than like the personal authority of the Apostles in the beginning of the Gospel. The further development of Episcopacy into Apostolical succession has often been rested on the promise, 'Lo, I am with you alway, even to the end of the world.'[54] 7. In the seventh case the precepts of order which are addressed in the Epistle to the 'fifth monarchy men of those days,' are transferred to a duty of obedience to hereditary princes; the fact of the house of David, 'the Lord's anointed' sitting on the throne of Israel is converted into a principle for all times and countries. And the higher lesson which our

Saviour teaches: 'Render unto Caesar the things which are Caesar's,' that is to say, 'Render unto all their due, and to God above all,' is spoiled by being made into a precept of political subjection.[55] 8. Lastly, the justice of God 'who rewardeth every man according to his works,' and the Christian scheme of redemption has been staked on two figurative expressions of St. Paul to which there is no parallel in any other part of Scripture (1 Corinthians xv. 22. 'For as in Adam all die, even so in Christ shall all be made alive,' and the corresponding passage in Romans v. 12); notwithstanding the declaration of the Old Testament as also of the New, 'Every soul shall bear its own iniquity,' and 'neither this man sinned nor his parents.' It is not necessary for our purpose to engage further in the matters of dispute which have arisen by the way in attempting to illustrate the general argument.[56] Yet to avoid misconception it may be remarked that many of the principles, rules, or truths mentioned, as for example, Infant Baptism, or the Episcopal Form of Church Government, have sufficient grounds; the weakness is the attempt to derive them from Scripture.[57]

[29] With this minute and rigid enforcement of the words of Scripture in passages where the ideas expressed in them either really or apparently agree with received opinions or institutions, there remains to be contrasted the neglect, or in some instances the misinterpretation of other words which are not equally in harmony with the spirit of the age. In many of our Lord's discourses he speaks of the 'blessedness of poverty:' of the hardness which they that have riches will experience 'in attaining eternal life.' 'It is easier for a camel to go through a needle's eye,' and 'Son, thou in thy lifetime receivedst thy good things,' and again, 'one thing thou lackest, go sell all that thou hast.' Precepts like these do not appeal to our own experience of life; they are unlike anything that we see around us at the present day, even among good men; to some among us they will recall the remarkable saying of Lessing, 'that the Christian religion had been tried for eighteen centuries; the religion of Christ remained to be tried.'[58] To take them literally would be injurious to ourselves and to society (at least, so we think). Religious sects or orders who have seized this aspect of Christianity have come to no good, and have often ended in extravagance. It will not do to go into the world saying 'Woe unto you, ye rich men,' or on entering a noble mansion to repeat the denunciations of the prophet about 'Cedar and vermillion,' or on being shown the prospect of a magnificent estate to cry out 'Woe unto them that lay field to field that they may be placed alone in the midst of the earth.' Times have altered, we say, since these denunciations were uttered; what appeared to the Prophet or Apostle a violation of Providence has now become a part of it. It will not do to make a great supper, and mingle at the same board the two ends of society, as modern phraseology calls them, fetching in 'the poor, the maimed, the lame, the blind,' to fill the vacant places of noble guests. That would be eccentric in modern times, and even hurtful. Neither is it suitable for us to wash one another's feet, or to perform any other menial office, because our Lord set us the example. The customs of society do not admit it; no good would be done by it, and singularity is of itself an evil. Well, then,

are the precepts of Christ not to be obeyed? Perhaps in their fullest sense they cannot be obeyed. But at any rate they are not to be explained away; the standard of Christ is not to be lowered to ordinary Christian life, because ordinary Christian life cannot rise, even in good men, to the standard of Christ.[59] And there may be 'standing among us' some one in ten thousand 'whom we know not,' in whom there is such a divine union of charity and prudence that he is most blest in the entire fulfilment of the precept—'Go sell all that thou hast,'—which to obey literally in other cases would be evil, and not good. Many there have been, doubtless (not one or two only), who have given all that they had on earth to their family or friends—the poor servant 'casting her two mites into the treasury,' denying herself the ordinary comforts of life for the sake of an erring parent or brother; that is not probably an uncommon case, and as near an approach as in this life we make to heaven. And there may be some one or two rare natures in the world in whom there is such a divine courtesy, such a gentleness and dignity of soul, that differences of rank seem to vanish before them, and they look upon the face of others, even of their own servants and dependents, only as they are in the sight of God and will be in His kingdom. And there may be some tender and delicate woman among us, who feels that she has a divine vocation to fulfil the most repulsive offices towards the dying inmates of a hospital, or the soldier perishing in a foreign land. Whether such examples of self-sacrifice are good or evil, must depend, not altogether on social or economical principles, but on the spirit of those who offer them, and the power which they have in themselves of 'making all things kin.'[60] And even if the ideal itself were not carried out by us in practice, it has nevertheless what may be termed a truth of feeling. 'Let them that have riches be as though they had them not.' 'Let the rich man wear the load lightly; he will one day fold them up as a vesture.' Let not the refinement of society make us forget that it is not the refined only who are received into the kingdom of God; nor the daintiness of life hide from us the bodily evils of which the rich man and Lazarus are alike heirs. Thoughts such as these have the power to reunite us to our fellow-creatures from whom the accidents of birth, position, wealth have separated us; they soften our hearts towards them, when divided not only by vice and ignorance, but what is even a greater barrier, difference of manners and associations. For if there be anything in our own fortune superior to that of others, instead of idolizing or cherishing it in the blood, the Gospel would have us cast it from us; and if there be anything mean or despised in those with whom we have to do, the Gospel would have us regard such as friends and brethren, yea, even as having the person of Christ.[61]

[30] Another instance of apparent, if not real neglect of the precepts of Scripture, is furnished by the commandment against swearing. No precept about divorce is so plain, so universal, so exclusive as this; 'Swear not at all.' Yet we all know how the custom of Christian countries has modified this 'counsel of perfection' which was uttered by the Saviour. This is the more remarkable because in this case the precept is not, as in the former, practically impossible of fulfilment or even difficult. And yet in this instance again, the body who have endeavoured to follow more

nearly the letter of our Lord's commandment, seem to have gone against the common sense of the Christian world. Or to add one more example: Who, that hears of the Sabbatarianism, as it is called, of some Protestant countries, would imagine that the Author of our religion had cautioned his disciples, not against the violation of the Sabbath, but only against its formal and Pharisaical observance; or that the chiefest of the Apostles had warned the Colossians to 'Let no man judge them in respect of the new moon, or of the sabbath-days.' (ii. 16.)[62]

31] The neglect of another class of passages is even more surprising, the precepts contained in them being quite practicable and in harmony with the existing state of the world. In this instance it seems as if religious teachers had failed to gather those principles of which they stood most in need. 'Think ye that those eighteen upon whom the tower of Siloam fell?' is the characteristic lesson of the Gospel on the occasion of any sudden visitation. Yet it is another reading of such calamities that is commonly insisted upon. The observation is seldom made respecting the parable of the good Samaritan, that the true neighbour is also a person of a different religion. The words, 'Forbid him not: for there is no man which shall do a miracle in my name, that can lightly speak evil of me,' are often said to have no application to sectarian differences in the present day, when the Church is established and miracles have ceased. The conduct of our Lord to the woman taken in adultery, though not intended for our imitation always, yet affords a painful contrast to the excessive severity with which even a Christian society punishes the errors of women. The boldness with which St. Paul applies the principle of individual judgment, 'Let every man be fully persuaded in his mind,' as exhibited also in the words quoted above, 'Let no man judge you in respect of the new moon, or of the sabbath-days,' is far greater than would be allowed in the present age. Lastly, that the tenet of the damnation of the heathen should ever have prevailed in the Christian world, or that the damnation of Catholics should have been a received opinion among Protestants, implies a strange forgetfulness of such passages as Romans ii. 1–16. 'Who rewardeth every man according to his work,' and 'When the Gentiles, which know not the law, do by nature the things contained in the law,' &c. What a difference between the simple statement which the Apostle makes of the justice of God and the 'uncovenanted mercies' or 'invincible ignorance' of theologians half reluctant to give up, yet afraid to maintain the advantage of denying salvation to those who are '*extra palum Ecclesiae!*'[63]

2] The same habit of silence or misinterpretation extends to words or statements of Scripture in which doctrines are thought to be interested. When maintaining the Athanasian doctrine of the Trinity, we do not readily recall the verse, 'of that hour knoweth no man, no not the Angels of God, *neither the Son,* but the Father.' (Mark xiii. 32.) The temper or feeling which led St. Ambrose to doubt the genuineness of the words marked in italics, leads Christians in our own day to pass them over. We are scarcely just to the Millenarians or to those who maintain the continuance of miracles or spiritual gifts in the Christian Church, in not admitting the degree of support which is afforded to their views by many passages of Scripture. The same remark applies to the Predestinarian controversy; the Calvinist is often hardly dealt with, in being deprived of his real standing ground in the third and ninth chapters of the Epistle to the Romans. And the Protestant who thinks himself bound to prove from Scripture the very details of doctrine or discipline which are maintained in his Church, is often obliged to have recourse to harsh methods, and sometimes to deny appearances which seem to favour some particular tenet of Roman Catholicism. (Matthew xvi. 18, 19; xviii. 18; 1 Cor. iii. 15.) The Roman Catholic, on the other hand, scarcely observes that nearly all the distinctive articles of his creed are wanting in the New Testament; the Calvinist in fact ignores almost the whole of the sacred volume for the sake of a few verses. The truth is, that in seeking to prove our own opinions out of Scripture, we are constantly falling into the common fallacy of opening our eyes to one class of facts and closing them to another. The favourite verses shine like stars, while the rest of the page is thrown into the shade.[64]

[33] Nor indeed is it easy to say what is the meaning of 'proving a doctrine from Scripture.' For when we demand logical equivalents and similarity of circumstances, when we balance adverse statements, St. James and St. Paul, the New Testament with the Old, it will be hard to demonstrate from Scripture any complex system either of doctrine or practice. The Bible is not a book of statutes in which words have been chosen to cover the multitude of cases, but in the greater portion of it, especially the Gospels and Epistles, 'like a man talking to his friend.' Nay, more, it is a book written in the East, which is in some degree liable to be misunderstood, because it speaks the language and has the feeling of Eastern lands. Nor can we readily determine in explaining the words of our Lord or of St. Paul, how much (even of some of the passages just quoted) is to be attributed to Oriental modes of speech. Expressions which would be regarded as rhetorical exaggerations in the Western world are the natural vehicles of thought to an Eastern people. How great then must be the confusion where an attempt is made to draw out these Oriental modes with the severity of a philosophical or legal argument! Is it not such a use of the words of Christ which he himself rebukes when he says, 'It is the spirit that quickeneth, the flesh profiteth nothing.' (John vi. 52, 63.)[65]

[34] There is a further way in which the language of creeds and liturgies as well as the ordinary theological use of terms exercises a disturbing influence on the interpretation of Scripture. Words which occur in Scripture are singled out and incorporated in systems like stones taken out of an old building and put into a new one. They acquire a technical meaning more or less divergent from the original one. It is obvious that their use in Scripture, and not their later and technical sense, must furnish the rule of interpretation. We should not have recourse to the meaning of a word in Polybius, for the explanation of its use in Plato, or to the turn of a sentence in Lycophron, to illustrate a construction of Aeschylus. It is the same kind of anachronism which would interpret Scripture by the scholastic or theological use of the language of Scripture.[66] It is remarkable that this use is indeed partial, that is to say it affects one class of words and not another. Love and truth, for example,

have never been theological terms; grace and faith, on the other hand, always retain an association with the Pelagian or Lutheran controversies. Justification and inspiration are derived from verbs which occur in Scripture, and the later substantive has clearly affected the meaning of the original verb or verbal in the places where they occur.[67] The remark might be further illustrated by the use of Scriptural language respecting the Sacraments, which has also had a reflex influence on its interpretation in many passages of Scripture, especially in the Gospel of St. John. (John iii. 5; vi. 56, &c.) Minds which are familiar with the mystical doctrine of the Sacraments seem to see a reference to them in almost every place in the Old Testament as well as in the New, in which the words 'water,' or 'bread and wine' may happen to occur.[68]

35] Other questions meet us on the threshold of a different kind, which also affect therefore the interpretation of Scripture, and demand an answer. Is it admitted that the Scripture has one and only one true meaning? Or are we to follow the fathers into mystical and allegorical explanations? or with the majority of modern interpreters to confine ourselves to the double senses of prophecy, and the symbolism of the Gospel in the law?[69] In either case, we assume what can never be proved, and an instrument is introduced of such subtlety and pliability as to make the Scriptures mean anything—'*Gallus in campanili*,' as the Waldenses described it; 'the weathercock on the church tower,' which is turned hither and thither by every wind of doctrine. That the present age has grown out of the mystical methods of the early fathers is a part of its intellectual state. No one will now seek to find hidden meanings in the scarlet thread of Rahab, or the number of Abraham's followers, or in the little circumstance mentioned after the resurrection of the Saviour that St. Peter was the first to enter the sepulchre.[70] To most educated persons in the nineteenth century, these applications of Scripture appear foolish. Yet it is rather the excess of the method which provokes a smile than the method itself. For many remains of the mystical interpretation exist among ourselves; it is not the early fathers only who have read the Bible crosswise, or deciphered it as a book of symbols. And the uncertainty is the same in any part of Scripture if there is a departure from the plain and obvious meaning. If, for example, we alternate the verses in which our Lord speaks of the last things between the day of judgment and the destruction of Jerusalem; or, in the elder prophecies, which are the counterparts of these, make a corresponding division between the temporal and the spiritual Israel; or again if we attribute to the details of the Mosaical ritual a reference to the New Testament; or, once more, supposing the passage of the Red Sea to be regarded not merely as a figure of baptism, but as a preordained type, the principle is conceded; there is no good reason why the scarlet thread of Rahab should not receive the explanation given to it by Clement. A little more or a little less of the method does not make the difference between certainty and uncertainty in the interpretation of Scripture. In whatever degree it is practised it is equally incapable of being reduced to any rule; it is the interpreter's fancy, and is likely to be not less but more dangerous and extravagant when it adds the charm of authority from its use in past ages.[71]

[36] The question which has been suggested runs up into a more general one, 'the relation between the Old and New Testaments.' For the Old Testament will receive a different meaning accordingly as it is explained from itself or from the New. In the first case a careful and conscientious study of each one for itself is all that is required; in the second case the types and ceremonies of the law, perhaps the very facts and persons of the history, will be assumed to be predestined or made after a pattern corresponding to the things that were to be in the latter days. And this question of itself stirs another question respecting the interpretation of the Old Testament in the New. Is such interpretation to be regarded as the meaning of the original text, or an accommodation of it to the thoughts of other times?

[37] Our object is not to attempt here the determination of these questions but to point out that they must be determined before any real progress can be made or any agreement arrived at in the interpretation of Scripture. With one more example of another kind we may close this part of the subject. The origin of the three first Gospels is an inquiry which has not been much considered by English theologians since the days of Bishop Marsh. The difficulty of the question has been sometimes misunderstood; the point being how there can be so much agreement in words, and so much disagreement both in words and facts; the double phenomenon is the real perplexity—how in short there can be all degrees of similarity and dissimilarity, the kind and degree of similarity being such as to make it necessary to suppose that large portions are copied from each other or from common documents; the dissimilarities being of a kind which seem to render impossible any knowledge in the authors of one another's writings. The most probable solution of this difficulty is that the tradition on which the three first Gospels are based was at first preserved orally, and slowly put together and written in the three forms which it assumed at a very early period, those forms being in some places, perhaps, modified by translation.[72] It is not necessary to develope this hypothesis farther. The point to be noticed is, that whether this or some other theory be the true account (and some such account is demonstrably necessary), the assumption of such a theory, or rather the observation of the facts on which it rests, cannot but exercise an influence on interpretation. We can no longer speak of three independent witnesses of the Gospel narrative. Hence there follow some other consequences. (1.) There is no longer the same necessity as heretofore to reconcile inconsistent narratives; the harmony of the Gospels only means the parallelism of similar words. (2.) There is no longer any need to enforce everywhere the connexion of successive verses, for the same words will be found to occur in different connexions in the different Gospels. (3.) Nor can the designs attributed to their authors be regarded as the free handling of the same subject on different plans; the difference consisting chiefly in the occurrence or absence of local or verbal explanations or the addition or omission of certain passages. Lastly, it is evident that no weight can be given to traditional statements of facts about the authorship, as, for example, that respecting St. Mark being the interpreter of St. Peter, because the Fathers who have handed down these

statements were ignorant or unobservant of the great fact, which is proved by internal evidence, that they are for the most part of common origin.[73]

[38] Until these and the like questions are determined by interpreters, it is not possible that there should be agreement in the interpretation of Scripture. The Protestant and Catholic, the Unitarian and Trinitarian will continue to fight their battle on the ground of the New Testament. The Preterists and Futurists, those who maintain that the roll of prophecies is completed in past history, or in the apostolical age; those who look forward to a long series of events which are yet to come [εἰς ἀφανὲς τὸν μῦθον ἀνενεγκὼν οὐκ ἔχει ἔλεγχον], may alike claim the authority of the Book of Daniel, or the Revelation.[74] Apparent coincidences will always be discovered by those who want to find them. Where there is no critical interpretation of Scripture, there will be a mystical or rhetorical one. If words have more than one meaning, they may have any meaning. Instead of being a rule of life or faith, Scripture becomes the expression of the ever-changing aspect of religious opinions. The unchangeable word of God, in the name of which we repose, is changed by each age and each generation in accordance with its passing fancy. The book in which we believe all religious truth to be contained, is the most uncertain of all books, because interpreted by arbitrary and uncertain methods.

§ 3.

[39] It is probable that some of the preceding statements may be censured as a wanton exposure of the difficulties of Scripture. It will be said that such inquiries are for the few, while the printed page lies open to the many, and that the obtrusion of them may offend some weaker brother, some half-educated or prejudiced soul, 'for whom,' nevertheless, in the touching language of St. Paul, 'Christ died.' A confusion of the heart and head may lead sensitive minds into a desertion of the principles of the Christian life, which are their own witness, because they are in doubt about facts which are really external to them. Great evil to character may sometimes ensue from such causes. 'No man can serve two' opinions without a sensible harm to his nature. The consciousness of this responsibility should be always present to writers on theology. But the responsibility is really two-fold; for there is a duty to speak the truth as well as a duty to withhold it. The voice of a majority of the clergy throughout the world, the half sceptical, half conservative instincts of many laymen, perhaps, also, individual interest, are in favour of the latter course; while a higher expediency pleads that 'honesty is the best policy,' and that truth alone 'makes free.' To this, it may be replied that truth is not truth to those who are unable to use it; no reasonable man would attempt to lay before the illiterate such a question as that concerning the origin of the Gospels. And yet it may be rejoined once more, the healthy tone of religion among the poor depends upon freedom of thought and inquiry among the educated. In this conflict of reasons, individual judgment must at last decide.[75] That there has been no rude, or improper unveiling of the difficulties of Scripture

in the preceding pages, is thought to be shown by the following considerations:

[40] First, that the difficulties referred to are very well known; they force themselves on the attention, not only of the student, but of every intelligent reader of the New Testament, whether in Greek or English. The treatment of such difficulties in theological works is no measure of public opinion respecting them. Thoughtful persons, whose minds have turned towards theology, are continually discovering that the critical observations which they make themselves have been made also by others apparently without concert. The truth is that they have been led to them by the same causes, and these again lie deep in the tendencies of education and literature in the present age. But no one is willing to break through the reticence which is observed on these subjects; hence a sort of smouldering scepticism. It is probable that the distrust is greatest at the time when the greatest efforts are made to conceal it. Doubt comes in at the window, when Inquiry is denied at the door. The thoughts of able and highly educated young men almost always stray towards the first principles of things; it is a great injury to them, and tends to raise in their minds a sort of incurable suspicion, to find that there is one book of the fruit of the knowledge of which they are forbidden freely to taste, that is, the Bible. The same spirit renders the Christian minister almost powerless in the hands of his opponents. He can give no true answer to the mechanic or artizan who has either discovered by his mother-wit or who retails at second-hand the objections of critics; for he is unable to look at things as they truly are.[76]

[41] Secondly, as the time has come when it is no longer possible to ignore the results of criticism, it is of importance that Christianity should be seen to be in harmony with them. That objections to some received views should be valid, and yet that they should be always held up as the objections of infidels, is a mischief to the Christian cause. It is a mischief that critical observations which any intelligent man can make for himself, should be ascribed to atheism or unbelief. It would be a strange and almost incredible thing that the Gospel, which at first made war only on the vices of mankind, should now be opposed to one of the highest and rarest of human virtues—the love of truth. And that in the present day the great object of Christianity should be, not to change the lives of men, but to prevent them from changing their opinions; that would be a singular inversion of the purposes for which Christ came into the world. The Christian religion is in a false position when all the tendencies of knowledge are opposed to it. Such a position cannot be long maintained, or can only end in the withdrawal of the educated classes from the influences of religion. It is a grave consideration whether we ourselves may not be in an earlier stage of the same religious dissolution, which seems to have gone further in Italy and France. The reason for thinking so is not to be sought in the external circumstances of our own or any other religious communion, but in the progress of ideas with which Christian teachers seem to be ill at ease. Time was when the Gospel was before the age; when it breathed a new life into a decaying world—when the difficulties of Christianity were difficulties of the heart only, and the highest minds found in its truths not only the rule of their lives, but a well-

spring of intellectual delight. Is it to be held a thing impossible that the Christian religion, instead of shrinking into itself, may again embrace the thoughts of men upon the earth? Or is it true that since the Reformation 'all intellect has gone the other way?' and that in Protestant countries reconciliation is as hopeless as Protestants commonly believe to be the case in Catholic.[77]

42] Those who hold the possibility of such a reconcilement or restoration of belief, are anxious to disengage Christianity from all suspicion of disguise or unfairness. They wish to preserve the historical use of Scripture as the continuous witness in all ages of the higher things in the heart of man, as the inspired source of truth and the way to the better life. They are willing to take away some of the external supports, because they are not needed and do harm; also, because they interfere with the meaning. They have a faith, not that after a period of transition all things will remain just as they were before, but that they will all come round again to the use of man and to the glory of God. When interpreted like any other book, by the same rules of evidence and the same canons of criticism, the Bible will still remain unlike any other book; its beauty will be freshly seen, as of a picture which is restored after many ages to its original state; it will create a new interest and make for itself a new kind of authority by the life which is in it. It will be a spirit and not a letter; as it was in the beginning, having an influence like that of the spoken word, or the book newly found. The purer the light in the human heart, the more it will have an expression of itself in the mind of Christ; the greater the knowledge of the development of man, the truer will be the insight gained into the 'increasing purpose' of revelation. In which also the individual soul has a practical part, finding a sympathy with its own imperfect feelings, in the broken utterance of the Psalmist or the Prophet as well as in the fulness of Christ. The harmony between Scripture and the life of man, in all its stages, may be far greater than appears at present. No one can form any notion from what we see around us, of the power which Christianity might have if it were at one with the conscience of man and not at variance with his intellectual convictions. There, a world weary of the heat and dust of controversy—of speculations about God and man—weary too of the rapidity of its own motion, would return home and find rest.[78]

3] But for the faith that the Gospel might win again the minds of intellectual men, it would be better to leave religion to itself, instead of attempting to draw them together. Other walks in literature have peace and pleasure and profit; the path of the critical Interpreter of Scripture is almost always a thorny one in England. It is not worth while for any one to enter upon it who is not supported by a sense that he has a Christian and moral object. For although an Interpreter of Scripture in modern times will hardly say with the emphasis of the Apostle, 'Woe is me, if I speak not the truth without regard to consequences,' yet he too may feel it a matter of duty not to conceal the things which he knows. He does not hide the discrepancies of Scripture, because the acknowledgment of them is the first step towards agreement among interpreters. He would restore the original meaning, because 'seven other' meanings take the place of it: the book is made the sport of opinion and the instrument of perversion of life. He would take the excuses of the head out of the way of the heart; there is hope too that by drawing Christians together on the ground of Scripture, he may also draw them nearer to one another. He is not afraid that inquiries, which have for their object the truth, can ever be displeasing to the God of truth; or that the Word of God is in any such sense a word as to be hurt by investigations into its human origin and conception.[79]

[44] It may be thought another ungracious aspect of the preceding remarks, that they cast a slight upon the interpreters of Scripture in former ages. The early Fathers, the Roman Catholic mystical writers, the Swiss and German Reformers, the Nonconformist divines, have qualities for which we look in vain among ourselves; they throw an intensity of light upon the page of Scripture which we nowhere find in modern commentaries. But it is not the light of interpretation. They have a faith which seems indeed to have grown dim now-a-days, but that faith is not drawn from the study of Scripture; it is the element in which their own mind moves which overflows on the meaning of the text. The words of Scripture suggest to them their own thoughts or feelings. They are preachers, or in the New Testament sense of the word, prophets rather than interpreters. There is nothing in such a view derogatory to the saints and doctors of former ages. That Aquinas or Bernard did not shake themselves free from the mystical method of the Patristic times, or the Scholastic one which was more peculiarly their own; that Luther and Calvin read the Scriptures in connexion with the ideas which were kindling in the mind of their age, and the events which were passing before their eyes, these and similar remarks are not to be construed as depreciatory of the genius or learning of famous men of old; they relate only to their interpretation of Scripture, in which it is no slight upon them to maintain that they were not before their day.[80]

[45] What remains may be comprised in a few precepts, or rather is the expansion of a single one. *Interpret the Scripture like any other book.* There are many respects in which Scripture is unlike any other book; these will appear in the results of such an interpretation. The first step is to know the meaning, and this can only be done in the same careful and impartial way that we ascertain the meaning of Sophocles or of Plato. The subordinate principles which flow out of this general one will also be gathered from the observation of Scripture. No other science of Hermeneutics is possible but an inductive one, that is to say, one based on the language and thoughts and narrations of the sacred writers. And it would be well to carry the theory of interpretation no further than in the case of other works. Excessive system tends to create an impression that the meaning of Scripture is out of our reach, or is to be attained in some other way than by the exercise of manly sense and industry. Who would write a bulky treatise about the method to be pursued in interpreting Plato or Sophocles? Let us not set out on our journey so heavily equipped that there is little chance of our arriving at the end of it. The method creates itself as we go on, beginning only with a few reflections directed against plain errors. Such reflections are the rules of common sense, which we acknowledge with respect to other works written in dead languages: without pretending to

novelty they may help us to 'return to nature' in the study of the sacred writings.[81]

46] First, it may be laid down that Scripture has one meaning—the meaning which it had to the mind of the prophet or evangelist who first uttered or wrote, to the hearers or readers who first received it. Another view may be easier or more familiar to us, seeming to receive a light and interest from the circumstances of our own age. But such accommodation of the text must be laid aside by the interpreter, whose business is to place himself as nearly as possible in the position of the sacred writer. That is no easy task—to call up the inner and outer life of the contemporaries of our Saviour; to follow the abrupt and involved utterance of St. Paul or one of the old Prophets; to trace the meaning of words when language first became Christian. He will often have to choose the more difficult interpretation (Galatians ii. 20; Romans iii. 15, &c.), and to refuse one more in agreement with received opinions, because the latter is less true to the style and time of the author. He may incur the charge of singularity, or confusion of ideas, or ignorance of Greek, from a misunderstanding of the peculiarity of the subject in the person who makes the charge. For if it be said that the translation of some Greek words is contrary to the usages of grammar (Galatians iv. 13), that is not in every instance to be denied; the point is whether the usages of grammar are always observed. Or if it be objected to some interpretation of Scripture that it is difficult and perplexing, the answer is—'that may very well be—it is the fact,' arising out of differences in the modes of thought of other times, or irregularities in the use of language which no art of the interpreter can evade. One consideration should be borne in mind, that the Bible is the only book in the world written in different styles and at many different times, which is in the hands of persons of all degrees of knowledge and education. The benefit of this outweighs the evil, yet the evil should be admitted—namely, that it leads to a hasty and partial interpretation of Scripture, which often obscures the true one. A sort of conflict arises between scientific criticism and popular opinion. The indiscriminate use of Scripture has a further tendency to maintain erroneous readings or translations; some which are allowed to be such by scholars have been stereotyped in the mind of the English reader; and it becomes almost a political question how far we can venture to disturb them.[82]

7] There are difficulties of another kind in many parts of Scripture, the depth and inwardness of which require a measure of the same qualities in the interpreter himself. There are notes struck in places, which like some discoveries of science have sounded before their time; and only after many days have been caught up and found a response on the earth. There are germs of truth which after thousands of years have never yet taken root in the world. There are lessons in the Prophets which, however simple, mankind have not yet learned even in theory; and which the complexity of society rather tends to hide; aspects of human life in Job and Ecclesiastes which have a truth of desolation about them which we faintly realize in ordinary circumstances. It is, perhaps, the greatest difficulty of all to enter into the meaning of the words of Christ—so gentle, so human, so divine, neither adding to them nor marring their simplicity. The attempt to illustrate or draw them out in detail, even to guard against their abuse, is apt to disturb the balance of truth. The interpreter needs nothing short of 'fashioning' in himself the image of the mind of Christ. He has to be born again into a new spiritual or intellectual world, from which the thoughts of this world are shut out. It is one of the highest tasks on which the labour of a life can be spent, to bring the words of Christ a little nearer the heart of man.[83]

[48] But while acknowledging this inexhaustible or infinite character of the sacred writings, it does not, therefore, follow that we are willing to admit of hidden or mysterious meanings in them (in the same way we recognise the wonders and complexity of the laws of nature to be far beyond what eye has seen or knowledge reached, yet it is not therefore to be supposed that we acknowledge the existence of some other laws different in kind from those we know which are incapable of philosophical analysis). In like manner we have no reason to attribute to the Prophet or Evangelist any second or hidden sense different from that which appears on the surface. All that the Prophet meant may not have been consciously present to his mind; there were depths which to himself also were but half revealed. He beheld the fortunes of Israel passing into the heavens; the temporal kingdom was fading into an eternal one. It is not to be supposed that what he saw at a distance only was clearly defined to him; or that the universal truth which was appearing and reappearing in the history of the surrounding world took a purely spiritual or abstract form in his mind. There is a sense in which we may still say with Lord Bacon, that the words of prophecy are to be interpreted as the words of one 'with whom a thousand years are as one day, and one day as a thousand years.' But that is no reason for turning days into years, or for interpreting the things 'that must shortly come to pass' in the book of Revelation, as the events of modern history, or for separating the day of judgment from the destruction of Jerusalem in the Gospels. The double meaning which is given to our Saviour's discourse respecting the last things is not that 'form of eternity' of which Lord Bacon speaks; it resembles rather the doubling of an object when seen through glasses placed at different angles.[84] It is true also that there are types in Scripture which were regarded as such by the Jews themselves, as for example, the scapegoat, or the paschal lamb. But that is no proof of all outward ceremonies being types when Scripture is silent;—(if we assume the New Testament as a tradition running parallel with the Old, may not the Roman Catholic assume with equal reason a tradition running parallel with the New?) Prophetic symbols, again, have often the same meaning in different places (*e.g.*, the four beasts or living creatures, the colours white or red); the reason is that this meaning is derived from some natural association (as of fruitfulness, purity, or the like); or again, they are borrowed in some of the later prophecies from earlier ones; we are not, therefore, justified in supposing any hidden connexion in the prophecies where they occur.[85] Neither is there any ground for assuming design of any other kind in Scripture any more than in Plato or Homer. Wherever there is beauty and order, there is design; but there is no proof of any artificial design, such as is often traced by the Fathers, in the

relation of the several parts of a book, or of the several books to each other. That is one of those mischievous notions which enables us, under the disguise of reverence, to make Scripture mean what we please. Nothing that can be said of the greatness or sublimity, or truth, or depth, or tenderness, of many passages, is too much. But that greatness is of a simple kind; it is not increased by double senses, or systems of types, or elaborate structure, or design. If every sentence was a mystery, every word a riddle, every letter a symbol, that would not make the Scriptures more worthy of a Divine author; it is a heathenish or Rabbinical fancy which reads them in this way. Such complexity would not place them above but below human compositions in general; for it would deprive them of the ordinary intelligibleness of human language. It is not for a Christian theologian to say that words were given to mankind to conceal their thoughts, neither was revelation given them to conceal the Divine.[86]

[49] The second rule is an application of the general principle; 'interpret Scripture from itself' as in other respects, like any other book written in an age and country of which little or no other literature survives, and about which we know almost nothing except what is derived from its pages. Not that all the parts of Scripture are to be regarded as an indistinguishable mass. The Old Testament is not to be identified with the New, nor the Law with the Prophets, nor the Gospels with the Epistles, nor the Epistles of St. Paul to be violently harmonized with the Epistle of St. James. Each writer, each successive age, has characteristics of its own, as strongly marked, or more strongly, than those which are found in the authors or periods of classical literature. These differences are not to be lost in the idea of a Spirit from whom they proceed or by which they were overruled.[87] And therefore, illustration of one part of Scripture by another should be confined to writings of the same age and the same authors, except where the writings of different ages or persons offer obvious similarities. It may be said further that illustration should be chiefly derived, not only from the same author, but from the same writing, or from one of the same period of his life. For example, the comparison of St. John and the 'synoptic' Gospels, or of the Gospel of St. John with the Revelation of St. John, will tend rather to confuse than to elucidate the meaning of either; while, on the other hand, the comparison of the Prophets with one another, and with the Psalms, offers many valuable helps and lights to the interpreter. Again, the connexion between the Epistles written by the Apostle St. Paul about the same time (*e. g.* Romans, 1 and 2 Corinthians, Galatians,—Colossians, Philippians, Ephesians,—compared with Romans, Colossians,—Ephesians, Galatians, &c.,) is far closer than of Epistles which are separated by an interval of only a few years.[88]

[50] But supposing all this to be understood, and that by the interpretation of Scripture from itself is meant a real interpretation of like by like, it may be asked, what is it that we gain from a minute comparison of a particular author or writing? The indiscriminate use of parallel passages taken from one end of Scripture and applied to the other (except so far as earlier compositions may have afforded the material or the form of later ones) is useless and uncritical. The uneducated, or

imperfectly educated person who looks out the marginal references of the English Bible, imagining himself in this way to gain a clearer insight into the Divine meaning, is really following the religious associations of his own mind. Even the critical use of parallel passages is not without danger. For are we to conclude that an author meant in one place what he says in another? Shall we venture to mend a corrupt phrase on the model of some other phrase, which memory, prevailing over judgment, calls up and thrusts into the text? It is this fallacy which has filled the pages of classical writers with useless and unfounded emendations.[89]

[51] The meaning of the Canon '*Non nisi ex Scripturâ Scripturam potes interpretari*,' is only this, 'That we cannot understand Scripture without becoming familiar with it.' Scripture is a world by itself, from which we must exclude foreign influences, whether theological or classical. To get inside that world is an effort of thought and imagination, requiring the sense of a poet as well as a critic—demanding much more than learning a degree of original power and intensity of mind. Any one who, instead of burying himself in the pages of the commentators, would learn the sacred writings by heart, and paraphrase them in English, will probably make a nearer approach to their true meaning than he would gather from any commentary. The intelligent mind will ask its own questions, and find for the most part its own answers. The true use of interpretation is to get rid of interpretation, and leave us alone in company with the author. When the meaning of Greek words is once known, the young student has almost all the real materials which are possessed by the greatest Biblical scholar, in the book itself. For almost our whole knowledge of the history of the Jews is derived from the Old Testament and the Apocryphal books, and almost our whole knowledge of the life of Christ and of the Apostolical age is derived from the New; whatever is added to them is either conjecture, or very slight topographical or chronological illustration. For this reason the rule given above, which is applicable to all books, is applicable to the New Testament more than any other.[90]

[52] Yet in this consideration of the separate books of Scripture it is not to be forgotten that they have also a sort of continuity. We make a separate study of the subject, the mode of thought, in some degree also of the language of each book. And at length the idea arises in our minds of a common literature, a pervading life, an overruling law. It may be compared to the effect of some natural scene in which we suddenly perceive a harmony or picture, or to the imperfect appearance of design which suggests itself in looking at the surface of the globe. That is to say, there is nothing miraculous or artificial in the arrangement of the books of Scripture; it is the result, not the design, which appears in them when bound in the same volume. Or if we like so to say, there *is* design, but a natural design which is revealed to after ages. Such continuity or design is best expressed under some notion of progress or growth, not regular, however, but with broken and imperfect stages, which the want of knowledge prevents our minutely defining. The great truth of the unity of God was there from the first; slowly as the morning broke in the heavens, like some central light, it filled and afterwards dispersed the mists of

human passion in which it was itself enveloped. A change passes over the Jewish religion from fear to love, from power to wisdom, from the justice of God to the mercy of God, from the nation to the individual, from this world to another; from the visitation of the sins of the fathers upon the children, to 'every soul shall bear its own iniquity;' from the fire, the earthquake, and the storm, to the still small voice. There never was a time after the deliverance from Egypt, in which the Jewish people did not bear a kind of witness against the cruelty and licentiousness of the surrounding tribes. In the decline of the monarchy, as the kingdom itself was sinking under foreign conquerors, whether springing from contact with the outer world, or from some reaction within, the undergrowth of morality gathers strength; first, in the anticipation of prophecy, secondly, like a green plant in the hollow rind of Pharisaism,—and individuals pray and commune with God each one for himself. At length the tree of life blossoms; the faith in immortality which had hitherto slumbered in the heart of man, intimated only in doubtful words (2 Sam. xii. 23; Psalm xvii. 15), or beaming for an instant in dark places (Job xix. 25), has become the prevailing belief.[91]

3] There is an interval in the Jewish annals which we often exclude from our thoughts, because it has no record in the canonical writings—extending over about four hundred years, from the last of the prophets of the Old Testament to the forerunner of Christ in the New. This interval, about which we know so little, which is regarded by many as a portion of secular rather than of sacred history, was nevertheless as fruitful in religious changes as any similar period which preceded. The establishment of the Jewish sects, and the wars of the Maccabees, probably exercised as great an influence on Judaism as the captivity itself. A third influence was that of the Alexandrian literature, which was attracting the Jewish intellect, at the same time that the Galilaean zealot was tearing the nation in pieces with the doctrine that it was lawful to call 'no man master but God.' In contrast with that wild fanaticism as well as with the proud Pharisee, came One most unlike all that had been before, as the kings or rulers of mankind. In an age which was the victim of its own passions, the creature of its own circumstances, the slave of its own degenerate religion, our Saviour taught a lesson absolutely free from all the influences of a surrounding world. He made the last perfect revelation of God to man; a revelation not indeed immediately applicable to the state of society or the world, but in its truth and purity inexhaustible by the after generations of men. And of the first application of the truth which he taught as a counsel of perfection to the actual circumstances of mankind, we have the example in the Epistles.[92]

Such a general conception of growth or development in Scripture, beginning with the truth of the Unity of God in the earliest books and ending with the perfection of Christ, naturally springs up in our minds in the perusal of the sacred writings. It is a notion of value to the interpreter, for it enables him at the same time to grasp the whole and distinguish the parts. It saves him from the necessity of maintaining that the Old Testament is one and the same everywhere; that the books of Moses contain truths or precepts, such as the duty of prayer or the faith in immortality, or the spiritual interpretation of sacrifice, which no one has ever seen there. It leaves him room enough to admit all the facts of the case. No longer is he required to defend or to explain away David's imprecations against his enemies, or his injunctions to Solomon, any more than his sin in the matter of Uriah. Nor is he hampered with a theory of accommodation. Still the sense of 'the increasing purpose which through the ages ran' is present to him, nowhere else continuously discernible or ending in a divine perfection. Nowhere else is there found the same interpenetration of the political and religious element—a whole nation, 'though never good for much at any time,' possessed with the conviction that it was living in the face of God—in whom the Sun of righteousness shone upon the corruption of an Eastern nature—the 'fewest of all people,' yet bearing the greatest part in the education of the world. Nowhere else among the teachers and benefactors of mankind is there any form like His, in whom the desire of the nation is fulfilled, and 'not of that nation only,' but of all mankind, whom He restores to His Father and their Father, to His God and their God.[93]

[55] Such a growth or development may be regarded as a kind of progress from childhood to manhood. In the child there is an anticipation of truth; his reason is latent in the form of feeling; many words are used by him which he imperfectly understands; he is led by temporal promises, believing that to be good is to be happy always; he is pleased by marvels and has vague terrors. He is confined to a spot of earth, and lives in a sort of prison of sense, yet is bursting also with a fullness of childish life: he imagines God to be like a human father, only greater and more awful; he is easily impressed with solemn thoughts, but soon 'rises up to play' with other children. It is observable that his ideas of right and wrong are very simple, hardly extending to another life; they consist chiefly in obedience to his parents, whose word is his law. As he grows older he mixes more and more with others; first with one or two who have a great influence in the direction of his mind. At length the world opens upon him; another work of education begins; and he learns to discern more truly the meaning of things and his relation to men in general. (You may complete the image, by supposing that there was a time in his early days when he was a helpless outcast 'in the land of Egypt and the house of bondage'). And as he arrives at manhood he reflects on his former years, the progress of his education, the hardships of his infancy, the home of his youth (the thought of which is ineffaceable in after life), and he now understands that all this was but a preparation for another state of being, in which he is to play a part for himself. And once more in age you may imagine him like the patriarch looking back on the entire past, which he reads anew, perceiving that the events of life had a purpose or result which was not seen at the time; they seem to him bound 'each to each by natural piety.'[94]

[56] 'Which things are an allegory,' the particulars of which any one may interpret for himself. For the child born after the flesh is the symbol of the child born after the spirit. 'The law was a schoolmaster to bring men to Christ,' and now 'we are under a schoolmaster' no longer. The anticipation of truth which came from without to the childhood or youth of the human race is witnessed to within; the

revelation of God is not lost but renewed in the heart and understanding of the man. Experience has taught us the application of the lesson in a wider sphere. And many influences have combined to form the 'after life' of the world. When at the close (shall we say) of a great period in the history of man, we cast our eyes back on the course of events, from the 'angel of his presence in the wilderness' to the multitude of peoples, nations, languages, who are being drawn together by His Providence—from the simplicity of the pastoral state in the dawn of the world's day, to all the elements of civilization and knowledge which are beginning to meet and mingle in a common life, we also understand that we are no longer in our early home, to which, nevertheless, we fondly look; and that the end is yet unseen, and the purposes of God towards the human race only half revealed. And to turn once more to the Interpreter of Scripture, he too feels that the continuous growth of revelation which he traces in the Old and New Testament, is a part of a larger whole extending over the earth and reaching to another world.[95]

§ 4.

7] Scripture has an inner life or soul; it has also an outward body or form. That form is language, which imperfectly expresses our common notions, much more those higher truths which religion teaches. At the time when our Saviour came into the world the Greek language was itself in a state of degeneracy and decay. It had lost its poetic force, and was ceasing to have the sway over the mind which classical Greek once held. That is a more important revolution in the mental history of mankind, than we easily conceive in modern times, when all languages sit loosely on thought, and the peculiarities, or idiosyncrasies of one are corrected by our knowledge of another. It may be numbered among the causes which favoured the growth of Christianity. That degeneracy was a preparation for the Gospel—the decaying soil in which the new elements of life were to come forth—the beginning of another state of man, in which language and mythology and philosophy were no longer to exert the same constraining power as in the ancient world. The civilized portion of mankind were becoming of one speech, the diffusion of which along the shores of the Mediterranean sea made a way for the entrance of Christianity into the human understanding, just as the Roman empire prepared the framework of its outward history. The first of all languages, 'for glory and for beauty,' had become the 'common' dialect of the Macedonian kingdoms; it had been moulded in the schools of Alexandria to the ideas of the East and the religious wants of Jews. Neither was it any violence to its nature to be made the vehicle of the new truths which were springing up in the heart of man. The definiteness and absence of reflectiveness in the earlier forms of human speech, would have imposed a sort of limit on the freedom and spirituality of the Gospel; even the Greek of Plato would have 'coldly furnished forth' the words of 'eternal life.' A religion which was to be universal required the divisions of languages, as of nations, to be in some degree broken down. ['*Pœna linguarum dispersit homines, donum linguarum in unum collegit.*'] But this community or freedom of language was accompanied by corresponding defects; it had lost its logical precision; it was less coherent; and more under the influence of association. It might be compared to a garment which allowed and yet impeded the exercise of the mind by being too large and loose for it.[96]

[58] From the inner life of Scripture it is time to pass on to the consideration of this outward form, including that other framework of modes of thought and figures of speech which is between the two. A knowledge of the original language is a necessary qualification of the Interpreter of Scripture. It takes away at least one chance of error in the explanation of a passage; it removes one of the films which have gathered over the page; it brings the meaning home in a more intimate and subtle way than a translation could do. To this, however, another qualification should be added, which is, the logical power to perceive the meaning of words in reference to their context. And there is a worse fault than ignorance of Greek in the interpretation of the New Testament, that is, ignorance of any language. The Greek Fathers, for example, are far from being the best verbal commentators, because their knowledge of Greek often leads them away from the drift of the passage. The minuteness of the study in our own day has also a tendency to introduce into the text associations which are not really found there. There is a danger of making words mean too much; refinements of signification are drawn out of them, perhaps contained in their etymology, which are lost in common use and parlance. There is the error of interpreting every particle, as though it were a link in the argument, instead of being, as is often the case, an excrescence of style.[97] The verbal critic magnifies his art, which is really great in Aeschylus or Pindar, but not of equal importance in the interpretation of the simpler language of the New Testament. His love of scholarship will sometimes lead him to impress a false system on words and constructions. A great critic[98] who has commented on the three first chapters of the Epistle to the Galatians, has certainly afforded a proof that it is possible to read the New Testament under a distorting influence from classical Greek. The tendency gains support from the undefined feeling that Scripture does not come behind in excellence of language any more than of thought. And if not as in former days, the classic purity of the Greek of the New Testament, yet its certainty and accuracy, the assumption of which, as any other assumption, is only the parent of inaccuracy, is still maintained.

[59] The study of the language of the New Testament has suffered in another way by following too much in the track of classical scholarship. All dead languages which have passed into the hands of grammarians, have given rise to questions which have either no result or in which the certainty; or if certain, the importance of the result, is out of proportion to the labour spent in attaining it. The field is exhausted by great critics, and then subdivided among lesser ones. The subject, unlike that of physical science, has a limit, and unless new ground is broken up, as for example in mythology, or comparative philology, is apt to grow barren. Though it is not true to say that 'we know as much about the Greeks and Romans as we ever

shall,' it is certain that we run a danger from the deficiency of material, of wasting time in questions which do not add anything to real knowledge, or in conjectures which must always remain uncertain, and may in turn give way to other conjectures in the next generation. Little points may be of great importance when rightly determined, because the observation of them tends to quicken the instinct of langauge; but conjectures about little things or rules respecting them which were not in the mind of Greek authors themselves, are not of equal value. There is the scholasticism of philology, not only in the Alexandrian, but in our own times; as in the middle ages, there was the scholasticism of philosophy. Questions of mere orthography, about which there cannot be said to have been a right or wrong, have been pursued almost with a Rabbinical minuteness. The story of the scholar who regretted 'that he had not concentrated his life on the dative case,' is hardly a caricature of the spirit of such inquiries. The form of notes to the classics often seems to arise out of a necessity for observing a certain proportion between the commentary and the text. And the same tendency is noticeable in many of the critical and philological observations which are made on the New Testament. The field of Biblical criticism is narrower, and its materials more fragmentary; so too the minuteness and uncertainty of the questions raised has been greater. For example, the discussions respecting the chronology of St. Paul's life and his second imprisonment: or about the identity of James, the brother of the Lord, or in another department, respecting the use of the Greek article, have gone far beyond the line of utility.[99]

o] There seem to be reasons for doubting whether any considerable light can be thrown on the New Testament from inquiry into the language. Such inquiries are popular, because they are safe; but their popularity is not the measure of their use. It has not been sufficiently considered that the difficulties of the New Testament are for the most part common to the Greek and the English. The noblest translation in the world has a few great errors, more than half of them in the text; but 'we do it violence' to haggle over the words. Minute corrections of tenses or particles are no good; they spoil the English without being nearer the Greek. Apparent mistranslations are often due to a better knowledge of English rather than a worse knowledge of Greek. It is true that the signification of a few uncommon expressions, *e.g.*, ἐξουσία, ἐπιβαλών, συναπαγόμενοι, κ. τ. λ., is yet uncertain.[100] But no result of consequence would follow from the attainment of absolute certainty respecting the meaning of any of these. A more promising field opens to the interpreter in the examination of theological terms, such as faith (πίστις), grace (χάρισ), righteousness (δικαιοσύνη), sanctification (ἁγιασμός), the law (νόμος), the spirit (πνεῦμα), the comforter (παράκλητος), &c., provided always that the use of such terms in the New Testament is clearly separated (1) from their derivation or previous use in Classical or Alexandrian Greek, (2) from their after use in the Fathers and in systems of theology. To which may be added another select class of words descriptive of the offices or customs of the Apostolic Church, such as Apostle (ἀπόστολος), Bishop (ἐπίσκοπος), Elder (πρεσβύτερος), Deacon and Deaconess (ὁ καὶ ἡ διάκονος), love-feast (ἀγάπαι), the Lord's day (ἡ κυριακὴ ἡμέρα), &c. It is a lexicon of these and similar terms, rather than a lexicon of the entire Greek Testament that is required. Interesting subjects of real inquiry are also the comparison of the Greek of the New Testament with modern Greek on the one hand, and the Greek of the LXX. on the other. It is not likely, however, that they will afford much more help than they have already done in the elucidation of the Greek of the New Testament.[101]

[61] It is for others to investigate the language of the Old Testament, to which the preceding remarks are only in part applicable. [It may be observed in passing of this, as of any other old language, that not the later form of the language, but the cognate dialects, must ever be the chief source of its illustration. For in every ancient language, antecedent or contemporary forms, not the subsequent ones, afford the real insight into its nature and structure. It must also be admitted that very great and real obscurities exist in the English translation of the Old Testament, which even a superficial acquaintance with the original has a tendency to remove.] Leaving, however, to others the consideration of the Semitic languages which raise questions of a different kind from the Hellenistic Greek, we will offer a few remarks on the latter. Much has been said of the increasing accuracy of our knowledge of the language of the New Testament; the old Hebraistic method of explaining difficulties of language or construction, has retired within very narrow limits; it might probably with advantage be confined to still narrower ones—[if it have any place at all except in the Apocalypse or the Gospel of St. Matthew]. There is, perhaps, some confusion between accuracy of our knowledge of language, and the accuracy of language itself; which is also strongly maintained. It is observed that the usages of barbarous as well as civilized nations conform perfectly to grammatical rules; that the uneducated in all countries have certain laws of speech as much as Shakespear or Bacon; the usages of Lucian, it may be said, are as regular as those of Plato, even when they are different. The decay of language seems rather to witness to the permanence than to the changeableness of its structure; it is the flesh, not the bones, that begins to drop off. But such general remarks, although just, afford but little help in determining the character of the Greek of the New Testament, which has of course a certain system, failing in which it would cease to be a language. One further illustration is needed of the change which has passed upon it. All languages do not decay in the same manner; and the influence of decay in the same language may be different in different countries; when used in writing and in speaking—when applied to the matters of ordinary life and to the higher truths of philosophy or religion. And the degeneracy of language itself is not a mere principle of dissolution, but creative also; while dead and rigid in some of its uses, it is elastic and expansive in others. The decay of an ancient language is the beginning of the construction of a modern one. The loss of some usages gives a greater precision and freedom to others. The logical element, as for example in the Mediaeval Latin, will probably be strongest when the poetical has vanished. A great movement, like the Reformation

in Germany, passing over a nation, may give a new birth also to its language.[102]

62] These remarks may be applied to the Greek of the New Testament, which although classed vaguely under the 'common dialect,' has, nevertheless, many features which are altogether peculiar to itself, and such as are found in no other remains of ancient literature. 1. It is more unequal in style even in the same books, that is to say, more original and plastic in one part, more rigid and unpliable in another. There is a want of the continuous power to frame a paragraph or to arrange clauses in subordination to each other, even to the extent to which it was possessed by a Greek scholiast or rhetorician. On the other hand there is a fullness of life, 'a new birth,' in the use of abstract terms which is not found elsewhere, after the golden age of Greek philosophy. Almost the only passage in the New Testament which reads like a Greek period of the time, is the first paragraph of the Gospel according to St. Luke, and the corresponding words of the Acts. But the power and meaning of the characteristic words of the New Testament is in remarkable contrast with the vapid and general use of the same words in Philo about the same time. There is also a sort of lyrical passion in some passages (1 Cor. xiii.; 2 Cor. vi. 6–10; xi. 21–23) which is a new thing in the literature of the world; to which, at any rate, no Greek author of a later age furnishes any parallel.[103] 2. Though written, the Greek of the New Testament partakes of the character of a spoken language; it is more lively and simple, and less structural than ordinary writing—peculiarity of style which further agrees with the circumstance that the Epistles of St. Paul were not written with his own hand, but probably dictated to an amanuensis, and that the Gospels also probably originate in an oral narrative.[104] 3. The ground colours of the language may be said to be two; first, the LXX. which is modified, secondly, by the spoken Greek of eastern countries, and the differences which might be expected to arise between a translation and an original; many Hebraisms would occur in the Greek of a translator, which would never have come to his pen but for the influence of the work which he was translating.[105] 4. To which may be added a few Latin and Chaldee words, and a few Rabbinical formulae. The influence of Hebrew or Chaldee in the New Testament is for the most part at a distance, in the background, acting not directly, but mediately, through the LXX. It has much to do with the clausular structure and general form, but hardly anything with the grammatical usage. Philo too, did not know Hebrew, or at least the Hebrew Scriptures, yet there is also a 'mediate' influence of Hebrew traceable in his writings.[106] 5. There is an element of constraint in the style of the New Testament, arising from the circumstance of its authors writing in a language which was not their own. This constraint shows itself in the repetition of words and phrases; in the verbal oppositions and anacolutha of St. Paul; in the short sentences of St. John. This is further increased by the fact that the writers of the New Testament were 'unlearned men,' who had not the same power of writing as of speech. Moreover, as has been often remarked, the difficulty of composition increases in proportion to the greatness of the subject; *e.g.*, the narrative of Thucydides is easy and intelligible, while his reflections and speeches are full of confusion; the effort to concentrate seems to interfere with the consecutiveness and fluency of ideas. Something of this kind is discernible in those passages of the Epistles in which the Apostle St. Paul is seeking to set forth the opposite sides of God's dealing with man, *e.g.*, Romans iii. 1–9; ix., x.; or in which the sequence of the thought is interrupted by the conflict of emotions, 1 Cor. ix. 20; Gal. iv. 11–20.[107] 6. The power of the Gospel over language must be recognised, showing itself, first of all, in the original and consequently variable signification of words (πίστις, χάρις, σωτηρία) which is also more comprehensive and human than the heretical usage of many of the same terms, *e.g.*, γνῶσις (knowledge), σοφία (wisdom), κτίσις (creature, creation); secondly, in a peculiar use of some constructions, such as—δικαιοσύνη Θεοῦ (righteousness of God), πίστις 'Ιησοῦ Χριστοῦ (faith of Jesus Christ), ἐν Χριστῷ (in Christ), ἐν Θεῷ (in God), ὑπὲρ ἡμῶν (for us), in which the meaning of the genitive case or of the preposition almost escapes our notice, from familiarity with the sound of it.[108] Lastly, the degeneracy of the Greek language is traceable in the failure of syntactical power; in the insertion of prepositions to denote relations of thought, which classical Greek would have expressed by the case only; in the omission of them when classical Greek would have required them; in the incipient use of ἰνὰ with the subjunctive for the infinitive; in the confusion of ideas of cause and effect; in the absence of the article in the case of an increasing number of words which are passing into proper names; in the loss of the finer shades of difference in the negative particles; in the occasional confusion of the aorist and perfect; in excessive fondness for particles of reasoning or inference; in various forms of apposition, especially that of the word to the sentence; in the use, sometimes emphatic, sometimes only pleonastic, of the personal and demonstrative pronouns. These are some of the signs that the language is breaking-up and losing its structure.[109]

[63] Our knowledge of the New Testament is derived almost exclusively from itself. Of the language, as well as of the subject, it may be truly said that what other writers contribute is nothing in comparison of that which is gained from observation of the text. Some inferences which may be gathered from this general fact, are the following: First, that less weight should be given to lexicons, that is, to the authority of other Greek writers, and more to the context. The use of a word in a new sense, the attribution of a neuter meaning to a verb elsewhere passive, (Romans iii. 9, προεχόμεθα), the resolution of the compound into two simple notions, (Galatians iii. 1, προεγράφη), these, when the context requires it, are not to be set aside by the scholar because sanctioned by no known examples.[110] The same remark applies to grammars as well as lexicons. We cannot be certain that διὰ with the accusative never has the same meaning as διὰ with the genitive, (Gal. iv. 13; Phil. i. 15), or that the article always retains its defining power (2 Cor. i. 17; Acts xvii. 1), or that the perfect is never used in place of the aorist (1 Cor. xv. 4; Rev. v. 7, &c.); still less can we affirm that the latter end of a sentence never forgets the beginning (Rom. ii. 17–21; v. 12–28; ix. 22; xvi. 25–27; &c. &c.).[111] Foreign influences tend to derange the strong natural perception or remembrance of the

analogy of our own language. That is very likely to have occurred in the case of some of the writers of the New Testament; that there is such a derangement, is a fact. There is no probability in favour of St. Paul writing in broken sentences, but there is no improbability which should lead us to assume in such sentences, continuous grammar and thought, as appears to have been the feeling of the copyists who have corrected the anacolutha. The occurrence of them further justifies the interpreter in using some freedom with other passages in which the syntax does not absolutely break down. When 'confusion of two constructions,' 'meaning to say one thing and finishing with another;' 'saying two things in one instead of disposing them in their logical sequence,' are attributed to the Apostle; the use of these and similar expressions is defended by the fact that more numerous anacolutha occur in St. Paul's writings than in any equal portion of the New Testament, and far more than in the writings of any other Greek author of equal length.[112]

54] Passing from the grammatical structure, we may briefly consider the logical character of the language of the New Testament. Two things should be here distinguished, the logical form and the logical sequence of thought. Some ages have been remarkable for the former of these two characteristics; they have dealt in opposition, contradiction, climax, pleonasm, reason within reason, and the like; mere statements taking the form of arguments—each sentence seeming to be a link in a chain. In such periods of literature, the appearance of logic is rhetorical, and is to be set down to the style. That is the case with many passages in the New Testament which are studded with logical or rhetorical formulae, especially in the Epistles of St. Paul. Nothing can be more simple or natural than the object of the writer. Yet 'forms of the schools' appear (whether learnt at the feet of Gamaliel, that reputed master of Greek learning, or not,) which imply a degree of logical or rhetorical training.[113]

5] The observation of this rhetorical or logical element has a bearing on the Interpretation of Scripture. For it leads us to distinguish between the superficial connexion of words and the real connexion of thoughts. Otherwise injustice is done to the argument of the sacred writer, who may be supposed to violate logical rules, of which he is unconscious. For example, the argument of Rom. iii. 19, may be classed by the logicians under some head of fallacy ('Ex aliquo non sequitur omnis'); the series of inferences which follow one another in Rom. i. 16–18, are for the most part different aspects or statements of the same truth. So in Rom i. 32 the climax rather appears to be an anticlimax. But to dwell on these things interferes with the true perception of the Apostle's meaning which is not contained in the repetitions of γάρ by which it is hooked together; nor are we accurately to weigh the proportions expressed by his οὐ μόνον—ἀλλὰ καὶ; or πολλῷ μᾶλλον; neither need we suppose that where μὲν is found alone, there was a reason for the omission of δὲ, (Rom. i. 8; iii. 2); or that the opposition of words and sentences is always the opposition of ideas (Rom. v. 7; x. 10).[114] It is true that these and similar forms or distinctions of language, admit of translation into English; and in every case the interpreter may find some point of view in which the simplest truth of feeling may be drawn out in an antithetical or argumentative form. But whether these points of view were in the Apostle's mind at the time of writing may be doubted; the real meaning, or kernel, seems to lie deeper and to be more within. When we pass from the study of each verse to survey the whole at a greater distance, the form of thought is again seen to be unimportant in comparison of the truth which is contained in it. The same remark may be extended to the opposition, not only of words, but of ideas, which is found in the Scriptures generally, and almost seems to be inherent in human language itself. The law is opposed to faith, good to evil, the spirit to the flesh, light to darkness, the world to the believer, the sheep are set 'on his right hand, but the goats on the left.' The influence of this logical opposition has been great and not always without abuse in practice. For the opposition is one of ideas only which is not realized in fact. Experience shows us not that there are two classes of men animated by two opposing principles, but an infinite number of classes or individuals from the lowest depth of misery and sin to the highest perfection of which human nature is capable, the best not wholly good, the worst not entirely evil. But the figure or mode of representation changes these differences of degree into differences of kind. And we often think and speak and act in reference both to ourselves and others, as though the figure were altogether a reality.[115]

[66] Other questions arise out of the analysis of the modes of thought of Scripture. Unless we are willing to use words without inquiring into their meaning, it is necessary for us to arrange them in some relation to our own minds. The modes of thought of the Old Testament are not the same with those of the New, and those of the New are only partially the same with those in use among ourselves at the present day. The education of the human mind may be traced as clearly from the Book of Genesis to the Epistles of St. Paul, as from Homer to Plato and Aristotle. When we hear St. Paul speaking of 'body and soul and spirit,' we know that such language as this would not occur in the Books of Moses or in the Prophet Isaiah. It has the colour of a later age, in which abstract terms have taken the place of expressions derived from material objects. When we proceed further to compare these or other words or expressions of St. Paul with 'the body and mind,' or 'mind' and 'matter,' which is a distinction, not only of philosophy, but of common language among ourselves, it is not easy at once to determine the relation between them. Familiar as is the sound of both expressions, many questions arise when we begin to compare them.[116]

[67] This is the metaphysical difficulty in the Interpretation of Scripture, which it is better not to ignore, because the consideration of it is necessary to the understanding of many passages, and also because it may return upon us in the form of materialism or scepticism. For some who are not aware how little words affect the nature of things it may seem to raise speculations of a very serious kind. Their doubts would, perhaps, find expression in some such exclamations as the following:—'How is religion possible when modes of thought are shifting? and words changing their meaning, and statements of doctrine though 'starched' with

philosophy, are in perpetual danger of dissolution from metaphysical analysis?'

[58] The answer seems to be, that Christian truth is not dependent on the fixedness of modes of thought. The metaphysician may analyse the ideas of the mind just as the physiologist may analyse the powers or parts of the bodily frame, yet morality and social life still go on, as in the body digestion is uninterrupted. That is not an illustration only; it represents the fact. Though we had no words for mind, matter, soul, body, and the like, Christianity would remain the same. This is obvious, whether we think of the case of the poor, who understand such distinctions very imperfectly, or of those nations of the earth, who have no precisely corresponding division of ideas. It is not of that subtle or evanescent character which is liable to be lost in shifting the use of terms. Indeed it is an advantage at times to discard these terms with the view of getting rid of the oppositions to which they give rise. No metaphysical analysis can prevent 'our taking up the cross and following Christ,' or receiving the kingdom of heaven as little children. To analyse the 'trichotomy' of St. Paul is interesting as a chapter in the history of the human mind and necessary as a part of Biblical exegesis, but it has nothing to do with the religion of Christ. Christian duties may be enforced, and the life of Christ may be the centre of our thoughts, whether we speak of reason and faith, of soul and body, or of mind and matter, or adopt a mode of speech which dispenses with any of these divisions.[117]

[59] Connected with the modes of thought or representation in Scripture, are the figures of speech of Scripture, about which the same question may be asked: 'What division can we make between the figure and the reality?' And the answer seems to be of the same kind, that 'We cannot precisely draw the line between them.' Language, and especially the language of Scripture, does not admit of any sharp distinction. The simple expressions of one age become the allegories or figures of another; many of those in the New Testament are taken from the Old. But neither is there anything really essential in the form of these figures; nay, the literal application of many of them has been a great stumblingblock to the reception of Christianity. A recent commentator on Scripture appears willing to peril religion on the literal truth of such an expression as 'We shall be caught up to meet the Lord in the air.' Would he be equally ready to stake Christianity on the literal meaning of the words, 'Where their worm dieth not, and the fire is not quenched?'[118]

[60] Of what has been said, this is the sum;—'That Scripture, like other books, has one meaning, which is to be gathered from itself without reference to the adaptations of Fathers or Divines; and without regard to *a priori* notions about its nature and origin. It is to be interpreted like other books, with attention to the character of its authors, and the prevailing state of civilization and knowledge, with allowance for peculiarities of style and language, and modes of thought and figures of speech. Yet not without a sense that as we read there grows upon us the witness of God in the world, anticipating in a rude and primitive age the truth that was to be, shining more and more unto the perfect day in the life of Christ, which again

is reflected from different points of view in the teaching of His Apostles.'[119]

§ 5.

[71] It has been a principal aim of the preceding pages to distinguish the interpretation from the application of Scripture. Many of the errors alluded to, arise out of a confusion of the two. The present is nearer to us than the past, the circumstances which surround us pre-occupy our thoughts; it is only by an effort that we reproduce the ideas, or events, or persons of other ages. And thus, quite naturally, almost by a law of the human mind, the application of Scripture takes the place of its original meaning. And the question is, not how to get rid of this natural tendency, but how we may have the true use of it. For it cannot be got rid of, or rather is one of the chief instruments of religious usefulness in the world: 'Ideas must be given through something;' those of religion find their natural expression in the words of Scripture, in the adaptation of which to another state of life it is hardly possible that the first intention of the writers should be always preserved. Interpretation is the province of few; it requires a finer perception of language, and a higher degree of cultivation than is attained by the majority of mankind. But applications are made by all, from the philosopher reading 'God in History,' to the poor woman who finds in them a response to her prayers, and the solace of her daily life. In the hour of death we do not want critical explanations; in most cases, those to whom they would be offered are incapable of understanding them. A few words, breathing the sense of the whole Christian world, such as 'I know that my Redeemer liveth' (though the exact meaning of them may be doubtful to the Hebrew scholar); 'I shall go to him, but he shall not return to me;' touch a chord which would never be reached by the most skilful exposition of the argument of one of St. Paul's Epistles.[120]

[72] There is also a use of Scripture in education and literature. This literary use, though secondary to the religious one, is not unimportant. It supplies a common language to the educated and uneducated, in which the best and highest thoughts of both are expressed; it is a medium between the abstract notions of the one and the simple feelings of the other. To the poor especially, it conveys in the form which they are most capable of receiving, the lesson of history and life. The beauty and power of speech and writing would be greatly impaired, if the Scripture ceased to be known or used among us. The orator seems to catch from them a sort of inspiration; in the simple words of Scripture which he stamps anew, the philosopher often finds his most pregnant expressions. If modern times have been richer in the wealth of abstract thought, the contribution of earlier ages to the mind of the world has not been less, but, perhaps greater, in supplying the poetry of language. There is no such treasury of instruments and materials as Scripture. The loss of Homer, or the loss of Shakespear, would have affected the whole series of Greek or English authors who follow. But the disappearance of the Bible from the books which the world contains, would produce results far greater; we can scarcely

conceive the degree in which it would alter literature and language—the ideas of the educated and philosophical, as well as the feelings and habits of mind of the poor. If it has been said, with an allowable hyperbole, that 'Homer is Greece,' with much more truth may it be said, that 'the Bible is Christendom.'[121]

73] Many by whom considerations of this sort will be little understood, may, nevertheless, recognise the use made of the Old Testament in the New. The religion of Christ was first taught by an application of the words of the Psalms and the Prophets. Our Lord Himself sanctions this application. 'Can there be a better use of Scripture than that which is made by Scripture?' 'Or any more likely method of teaching the truths of Christianity than that by which they were first taught?' For it may be argued that the critical interpretation of Scripture is a device almost of yesterday; it is the vocation of the scholar or philosopher, not of the Apostle or Prophet. The new truth which was introduced into the Old Testament, rather than the old truth which was found there, was the salvation and the conversion of the world. There are many quotations from the Psalms and the Prophets in the Epistles, in which the meaning is quickened or spiritualized, but hardly any, probably none, which is based on the original sense or context. That is not so single a phenomenon as may at first sight be imagined. It may appear strange to us that Scripture should be interpreted in Scripture, in a manner not altogether in agreement with modern criticism; but would it not be more strange that it should be interpreted otherwise, than in agreement with the ideas of the age or country in which it was written? The observation that there is such an agreement, leads to two conclusions which have a bearing on our present subject. First, it is a reason for not insisting on the applications which the New Testament makes of passages in the Old, as their original meaning. Secondly, it gives authority and precedent for the use of similar applications in our own day.[122]

4] But, on the other hand, though interwoven with literature, though common to all ages of the Church, though sanctioned by our Lord and His Apostles, it is easy to see that such an employment of Scripture is liable to error and perversion. For it may not only receive a new meaning; it may be applied in a spirit alien to itself. It may become the symbol of fanaticism, the cloke of malice, the disguise of policy. Cromwell at Drogheda, quoting Scripture to his soldiers; the well-known attack on the Puritans in the State Service for the Restoration, 'Not every one that saith unto me, Lord, Lord;' the reply of the Venetian Ambassador to the suggestion of Wolsey, that Venice should take a lead in Italy '*which was only* the Earth is the Lord's and the fullness thereof,' are examples of such uses. In former times, it was a real and not an imaginary fear, that the wars of the Lord in the Old Testament might arouse a fire in the bosom of Franks and Huns.[123] In our own day such dangers have passed away; it is only a figure of speech when the preacher says, 'Gird on thy sword, O thou most mighty.' The warlike passions of men are not roused by quotations from Scripture, nor can states of life such as slavery or polygamy which belong to a past age, be defended, at least in England, by the example of the Old Testament. The danger or error is of another kind; more subtle, but hardly less real. For if we are permitted to apply Scripture under the pretence of interpreting it, the language of Scripture becomes only a mode of expressing the public feeling or opinion of our own day. Any passing phase of politics or art, or spurious philanthropy, may have a kind of Scriptural authority. The words that are used are the words of the Prophet or Evangelist, but we stand behind and adapt them to our purpose. Hence it is necessary to consider the limits and manner of a just adaptation; how much may be allowed for the sake of ornament; how far the Scripture, in all its details, may be regarded as an allegory of human life—where the true analogy begins—how far the interpretation of Scripture will serve as a corrective to its practical abuse.[124]

[75] Truth seems to require that we should separate mere adaptations, from the original meaning of Scripture. It is not honest or reasonable to confound illustration with argument, in theology, any more than in other subjects. For example, if a preacher chooses to represent the condition of a church or of an individual in the present day, under the figure of Elijah left alone among the idolatrous tribes of Israel, such an allusion is natural enough; but if he goes on to argue that individuals are therefore justified in remaining in what they believe to be an erroneous communion—that is a mere appearance of argument which ought not to have the slightest weight with a man of sense. Such a course may indeed be perfectly justifiable, but not on the ground that a prophet of the Lord once did so, two thousand five hundred years ago. Not in this sense were the lives of the Prophets written for our instruction. There are many important morals conveyed by them, but only so far as they themselves represent universal principles of justice and love. These universal principles they clothe with flesh and blood; they show them to us written on the hearts of men of like passions with ourselves. The prophecies, again, admit of many applications to the Christian Church or to the Christian life. There is no harm in speaking of the Church as the Spiritual Israel, or in using the imagery of Isaiah respecting Messiah's kingdom, as the type of good things to come. But when it is gravely urged, that from such passages as 'Kings shall be thy nursing fathers,' we are to collect the relations of Church and State, or from the pictorial description of Isaiah, that it is to be inferred there will be a reign of Christ on earth—that is a mere assumption of the forms of reasoning by the imagination. Nor is it a healthful or manly tone of feeling which depicts the political opposition to the Church in our own day, under imagery which is borrowed from the desolate Sion of the captivity. Scripture is apt to come too readily to the lips, when we are pouring out our own weaknesses, or enlarging on some favourite theme—perhaps idealizing in the language of prophecy the feebleness of preaching or missions in the present day, or from the want of something else to say. In many discussions on these and similar subjects, the position of the Jewish King, Church, Priest, has led to a confusion, partly caused by the use of similar words in modern senses among ourselves. The King or Queen of England may be called the Anointed of the Lord, but we should not therefore imply that the attributes of sovereignty are the same as those which belonged to

King David. All these are figures of speech, the employment of which is too common, and has been injurious to religion, because it prevents our looking at the facts of history or life as they truly are.[125]

76] This is the first step towards a more truthful use of Scripture in practice—the separation of adaptation from interpretation. No one who is engaged in preaching or in religious instruction can be required to give up Scripture language; it is the common element in which his thoughts and those of his hearers move. But he may be asked to distinguish the words of Scripture from the truths of Scripture—the means from the end. The least expression of Scripture is weighty; it affects the minds of the hearers in a way that no other language can. Whatever responsibility attaches to idle words, attaches in still greater degree to the idle or fallacious use of Scripture terms. And there is surely a want of proper reverence for Scripture, when we confound the weakest and feeblest applications of its words with their true meaning—when we avail ourselves of their natural power to point them against some enemy—when we divert the eternal words of charity and truth into a defence of some passing opinion. For not only in the days of the Pharisees, but in our own, the letter has been taking the place of the spirit; the least matters, of the greatest, and the primary meaning has been lost in the secondary use.[126]

7] Other simple cautions may also be added. The applications of Scripture should be harmonized and, as it were, interpenetrated with the spirit of the Gospel, the whole of which should be in every part; though the words may receive a new sense, the new sense ought to be in agreement with the general truth. They should be used to bring home practical precepts, not to send the imagination on a voyage of discovery; they are not the real foundation of our faith in another world, nor can they, by pleasant pictures, add to our knowledge of it. They should not confound the accidents with the essence of religion—the restrictions and burdens of the Jewish law with the freedom of the Gospel—the things which Moses allowed for the hardness of the heart, with the perfection of the teaching of Christ. They should avoid the form of arguments, or they will insensibly be used, or understood to mean more than they really do. They should be subjected to an overruling principle, which is the heart and conscience of the Christian teacher, who indeed 'stands behind them,' not to make them the vehicles of his own opinions, but as the expressions of justice, and truth, and love.[127]

8] And here the critical interpretation of Scripture comes in and exercises a corrective influence on its popular use. We have already admitted that criticism is not for the multitude; it is not what the Scripture terms the Gospel preached for the poor. Yet, indirectly passing from the few to the many, it has borne a great part in the Reformation of religion. It has cleared the eye of the mind to understand the original meaning. It was a sort of criticism which supported the struggle of the sixteenth century against the Roman Catholic Church; it is criticism that is leading Protestants to doubt whether the doctrine that the Pope is Antichrist, which has descended from the same period, is really discoverable in Scripture. Even the isolated thinker, against whom the religious world is taking up arms, has an influence on his opponents. The force of observations, which are based on reason and fact, remains when the tide of religious or party feeling is gone down. Criticism has also a healing influence in clearing away what may be termed the Sectarianism of knowledge. Without criticism it would be impossible to reconcile History and Science with Revealed Religion; they must remain for ever in a hostile and defiant attitude. Instead of being like other records, subject to the conditions of knowledge which existed in an early stage of the world, Scripture would be regarded on the one side as the work of organic Inspiration, and as a lying imposition on the other.[128]

[79] The real unity of Scripture, as of man, has also a relation to our present subject. Amid all the differences of modes of thought and speech which have existed in different ages, of which much is said in our own day, there is a common element in human nature which bursts through these differences and remains unchanged, because akin to the first instincts of our being. The simple feeling of truth and right is the same to the Greek or Hindoo as to ourselves. However great may be the diversities of human character, there is a point at which these diversities end, and unity begins to appear. Now, this admits of an application to the books of Scripture, as well as to the world generally. Written at many different times, in more than one language, some of them in fragments, they, too, have a common element of which the preacher may avail himself. This element is two-fold, partly divine and partly human; the revelation of the truth and righteousness of God, and the cry of the human heart towards Him. Every part of Scripture tends to raise us above ourselves to give us—a deeper sense of the feebleness of man, and of the wisdom and power of God. It has a sort of kindred, as Plato would say, with religious truth everywhere in the world. It agrees also with the imperfect stages of knowledge and faith in human nature, and answers to its inarticulate cries. The universal truth easily breaks through the accidents of time and place in which it is involved. Although we cannot apply Jewish institutions to the Christian world, or venture in reliance on some text to resist the tide of civilization on which we are borne, yet it remains, nevertheless, to us, as well as to the Jews and first Christians, that 'Righteousness exalteth a nation,' and that 'love is the fulfilling not of the Jewish law only, but of all law.'[129]

[80] In some cases, we have only to enlarge the meaning of Scripture to apply it even to the novelties and peculiarities of our own times. The world changes, but the human heart remains the same; events and details are different, but the principle by which they are governed, or the rule by which we are to act, is not different. When, for example, our Saviour says, 'Ye shall know the truth, and the truth shall make you free,' it is not likely that these words would have conveyed to the minds of the Jews who heard Him any notion of the perplexities of doubt or inquiry. Yet we cannot suppose that our Saviour, were He to come again upon earth, would refuse thus to extend them. The Apostle St. Paul, when describing the Gospel, which is to the Greek foolishness, speaks also of a higher wisdom which is known to those who are perfect. Neither is it unfair for us to apply this passage to that reconcilement of faith and knowledge, which may be termed Christian philosophy,

as the nearest equivalent to its language in our own day. Such words, again, as 'Why seek ye the living among the dead?' admit of a great variety of adaptations to the circumstances of our own time. Many of these adaptations have a real germ in the meaning of the words. The precept, 'Render unto Caesar the things that are Caesar's, and to God the things that are God's,' may be taken generally as expressing the necessity of distinguishing the divine and human—the things that belong to faith and the things that belong to experience. It is worth remarking in the application made of these words by Lord Bacon, 'Da fidei quae fidei sunt;' that, although the terms are altered, yet the circumstance that the form of the sentence is borrowed from Scripture gives them point and weight.[130]

31] The portion of Scripture which more than any other is immediately and universally applicable to our own times is, doubtless, that which is contained in the words of Christ Himself. The reason is that they are words of the most universal import. They do not relate to the circumstances of the time, but to the common life of all mankind. You cannot extract from them a political creed; only, 'Render unto Caesar the things that are Caesar's,' and 'The Scribes and Pharisees sit in Moses' seat; whatsoever, therefore, they say unto you do, but after their works do not.' They present to us a standard of truth and duty, such as no one can at once and immediately practise—such as, in its perfection, no one has fulfilled in this world. But this idealism does not interfere with their influence as a religious lesson. Ideals, even though unrealized, have effect on our daily life. The preacher of the Gospel is, or ought to be, aware that His calls to repentance, his standard of obligations, his lamentations over his own shortcomings or those of others, do not at once convert hundreds or thousands, as on the day of Pentecost. Yet it does not follow that they are thrown away, or that it would be well to substitute for them mere prudential or economical lessons, lectures on health or sanitary improvement. For they tend to raise men above themselves, providing them with Sabbaths as well as working days, giving them a taste of 'the good word of God' and of 'the powers of the world to come.' Human nature needs to be idealized; it seems as if it took a dislike to itself when presented always in its ordinary attire; it lives on in the hope of becoming better. And the image or hope of a better life—the vision of Christ crucified—which is held up to it, doubtless has an influence; not like the rushing mighty wind of the day of Pentecost; it may rather be compared to the leaven 'which a woman took and hid in three measures of meal, till the whole was leavened.'[131]

] The Parables of our Lord are a portion of the New Testament, which we may apply in the most easy and literal manner. The persons in them are the persons among whom we live and move; there are times and occasions at which the truths symbolized by them come home to the hearts of all who have ever been impressed by religion. We have been prodigal sons returning to our Father; servants to whom talents have been entrusted; labourers in the vineyard inclined to murmur at our lot, when compared with that of others, yet receiving every man his due; well satisfied Pharisees; repentant Publicans:—we have received the seed, and the cares of the world have choked it—we hope also at times that we have found the pearl of great price after sweeping the house—we are ready like the Good Samaritan to show kindness to all mankind. Of these circumstances of life or phases of mind, which are typified by the parables, most Christians have experience. We may go on to apply many of them further to the condition of nations and churches. Such a treasury has Christ provided us of things new and old, which refer to all time and all mankind—may we not say in His own words—'Because He is the Son of Man?'[132]

[83] There is no language of Scripture which penetrates the individual soul, and embraces all the world in the arms of its love, in the same manner as that of Christ Himself. Yet the Epistles contain lessons which are not found in the Gospels, or, at least, not expressed with the same degree of clearness. For the Epistles are nearer to actual life—they relate to the circumstances of the first believers, to their struggles with the world without, to their temptations and divisions from within—their subject is not only the doctrine of the Christian religion, but the business of the early Church. And although their circumstances are not our circumstances—we are not afflicted or persecuted, or driven out of the world, but in possession of the blessings, and security, and property of an established religion—yet there is a Christian spirit which infuses itself into all circumstances, of which they are a pure and living source. It is impossible to gather from a few fragmentary and apparently not always consistent expressions, how the Communion was celebrated, or the Church ordered, what was the relative position of Presbyters and Deacons, or the nature of the gift of tongues, as a rule for the Church in after ages;— such inquiries have no certain answer, and at the best, are only the subject of honest curiosity.[133] But the words, 'Charity never faileth,' and 'Though I speak with the tongues of men and of angels, and have not charity, I am nothing,'—these have a voice which reaches to the end of time. There are no questions of meats and drinks now-a-days, yet the noble words of the Apostle remain: 'If meat make my brother to offend, I will eat no flesh while the world standeth, lest I make my brother to offend.' Moderation in controversy, toleration towards opponents or erring members, is a virtue which has been thought by many to belong to the development of Christianity, and which is rarely found in the commencement of a religion. But lessons of toleration may be gathered from the Apostle, which have not yet been learned either by theologians or by mankind in general. The persecutions and troubles which awaited the Apostle, no longer await us; we cannot, therefore, without unreality, except, perhaps, in a very few cases, appropriate his words, 'I have fought the good fight, I have finished my course, I have kept the faith.' But that other text still sounds gently in our ears: 'My strength is perfected in weakness,' and 'when I am weak, then am I strong.' We cannot apply to ourselves the language of authority in which the Apostle speaks of himself as an ambassador for Christ, without something like bad taste. But it is not altogether an imaginary hope that those of us who are ministers of Christ, may attain to a real imitation of his great diligence, of his sympathy with others, and consideration for them—of his willingness to spend and be spent in his Master's service.[134]

84] Such are a few instances of the manner in which the analogy of faith enables us to apply the words of Christ and His Apostles, with a strict regard to their original meaning. But the Old Testament has also its peculiar lessons which are not conveyed with equal point or force in the New. The beginnings of human history are themselves a lesson having a freshness as of the early dawn. There are forms of evil against which the Prophets and the prophetical spirit of the Law carry on a warfare, in terms almost too bold for the way of life of modern times. There, more plainly than in any other portion of Scripture, is expressed the antagonism of outward and inward, of ceremonial and moral, of mercy and sacrifice. There all the masks of hypocrisy are rudely torn asunder, in which an unthinking world allows itself to be disguised. There the relations of rich and poor in the sight of God, and their duties towards one another, are most clearly enunciated. There the religion of suffering first appears—'adversity, the blessing' of the Old Testament, as well as of the New. There the sorrows and aspirations of the soul find their deepest expression, and also their consolation. The feeble person has an image of himself in the 'bruised reed;' the suffering servant of God passes into the 'beloved one, in whom my soul delighteth.' Even the latest and most desolate phases of the human mind are reflected in Job and Ecclesiastes; yet not without the solemn assertion that 'to fear God and keep his commandments' is the beginning and end of all things.[135]

5] It is true that there are examples in the Old Testament which were not written for our instruction, and that, in some instances, precepts or commands are attributed to God Himself, which must be regarded as relative to the state of knowledge which then existed of the Divine nature, or given 'for the hardness of men's hearts.' It cannot be denied that such passages of Scripture are liable to misunderstanding; the spirit of the Old Covenanters, although no longer appealing to the action of Samuel, 'hewing Agag in pieces before the Lord in Gilgal,' is not altogether extinguished. And a community of recent origin in America found their doctrine of polygamy on the Old Testament. But the poor generally read the Bible unconsciously; they take the good, and catch the prevailing spirit, without stopping to reason whether this or that practice is sanctioned by the custom or example of Scripture. The child is only struck by the impiety of the children who mocked the prophet; he does not think of the severity of the punishment which is inflicted on them. And the poor, in this respect, are much like children; their reflection on the morality or immorality of characters or events is suppressed by reverence for Scripture. The Christian teacher has a sort of tact by which he guides them to perceive only the spirit of the Gospel everywhere; they read in the Psalms, of David's sin and repentance; of the never-failing goodness of God to him, and his never-failing trust in Him, not of his imprecations against his enemies. Such difficulties are greater in theory and on paper, than in the management of a school or parish. They are found to affect the half-educated, rather than either the poor, or those who are educated in a higher sense. To be above such difficulties is the happiest condition of human life and knowledge, or to be below them; to see, or think we see, how they may be reconciled with Divine power and wisdom, or not to see how they are apparently at variance with them.[136]

§ 6.

[86] Some application of the preceding subject may be further made to theology and life.

[87] Let us introduce this concluding inquiry with two remarks.

[88] First, it may be observed, that a change in some of the prevailing modes of interpretation is not so much a matter of expediency as of necessity. The original meaning of Scripture is beginning to be clearly understood. But the apprehension of the original meaning is inconsistent with the reception of a typical or conventional one. The time will come when educated men will be no more able to believe that the words, "Out of Egypt have I called my son" (Matth. ii. 15; Hosea xi. 1), were *intended* by the prophet to refer to the return of Joseph and Mary from Egypt, than they are now able to believe the Roman Catholic explanation of Gen. iii. 15, 'Ipsa conteret caput tuum.' They will no more think that the first chapters of Genesis relate the same tale which Geology and Ethnology unfold than they now think the meaning of Joshua x. 12, 13, to be in accordance with Galileo's discovery.[137]

[89] From the circumstance that in former ages there has been a four-fold or a seven-fold Interpretation of Scripture, we cannot argue to the possibility of upholding any other than the original one in our own. The mystical explanations of Origen or Philo were not seen to be mystical; the reasonings of Aquinas and Calvin were not supposed to go beyond the letter of the text. They have now become the subject of apology; it is justly said that we should not judge the greatness of the Fathers or Reformers by their suitableness to our own day. But this defence of them shows that their explanations of Scripture are no longer tenable; they belong to a way of thinking and speaking which was once diffused over the world, but is now passed away. And what we give up as a general principle we shall find it impossible to maintain partially, *e.g.*, in the types of the Mosaic Law and the double meanings of prophecy, at least, in any sense in which it is not equally applicable to all deep and suggestive writings.[138]

[90] The same observation may be applied to the historical criticism of Scripture. From the fact that Paley or Butler were regarded in their generation as supplying a triumphant answer to the enemies of Scripture, we cannot argue that their answer will be satisfactory to those who inquire into such subjects in our own. Criticism has far more power than it formerly had; it has spread itself over ancient, and even modern, history; it extends to the thoughts and ideas of men as well as to words and facts; it has also a great place in education. Whether the habit of mind which has been formed in classical studies will not go on to Scripture; whether Scripture can be made an exception to other ancient writings, now that the nature of both is more understood; whether in the fuller light of history and science the views of the last century will hold out—these are questions respecting which the course of religious opinion in the past does not afford the means of truly judging.[139]

91] II. It has to be considered whether the intellectual forms under which Christianity has been described may not also be in a state of transition and resolution, in this respect contrasting with the never-changing truth of the Christian life. (1 Cor. xiii. 8.) Looking backwards at past ages, we experience a kind of amazement at the minuteness of theological distinctions, and also at their permanence. They seem to have borne a part in the education of the Christian world, in an age when language itself had also a greater influence than now-a-days. It is admitted that these distinctions are not observed in the New Testament, and are for the most part of a later growth. But little is gained by setting up theology against Scripture, or Scripture against theology; the Bible against the Church, or the Church against the Bible. At different periods either has been a bulwark against some form of error: either has tended to correct the abuse of the other. A true inspiration guarded the writers of the New Testament from Gnostic or Manichean tenets; at a later stage, a sound instinct prevented the Church from dividing the humanity and Divinity of Christ. It may be said that the spirit of Christ forbids us to determine beyond what is written; and the decision of the council of Nicaea has been described by an eminent English prelate as 'the greatest misfortune that ever befel the Christian world.' That is, perhaps, true; yet a different decision would have been a greater misfortune. Nor does there seem any reason to suppose that the human mind could have been arrested in its theological course. It is a mistake to imagine that the dividing and splitting of words is owing to the depravity of the human heart; was it not rather an intellectual movement (the only phenomenon of progress then going on among men) which led, by a sort of necessity, some to go forward to the completion of the system, while it left others to stand aside? A veil was on the human understanding in the great controversies which absorbed the Church in earlier ages; the cloud which the combatants themselves raised intercepted the view. They did not see—they could not have imagined—that there was a world which lay beyond the range of the controversy.[140]

92] And now, as the Interpretation of Scripture is receiving another character, it seems that distinctions of theology, which were in great measure based on old Interpretations, are beginning to fade away. A change is observable in the manner in which doctrines are stated and defended; it is no longer held sufficient to rest them on texts of Scripture, one, two, or more, which contain, or appear to contain, similar words or ideas. They are connected more closely with our moral nature; extreme consequences are shunned; large allowances are made for the ignorance of mankind. It is held that there is truth on both sides; about many questions there is a kind of union of opposites; others are admitted to have been verbal only; all are regarded in the light which is thrown upon them by church history and religious experience. A theory has lately been put forward, apparently as a defence of the Christian faith, which denies the objective character of any of them. And there are other signs that times are changing, and we are changing too. It would be scarcely possible at present to revive the interest which was felt less than twenty years ago in the doctrine of Baptismal Regeneration; nor would the arguments by which it was supported or impugned have the meaning which they once had. The communion of the Lord's Supper is also ceasing, at least in the Church of England, to be a focus or centre of disunion—

'Our greatest love turned to our greatest hate.'[141]

A silence is observable on some other points of doctrine around which controversies swarmed a generation ago. Persons begin to ask what was the real difference which divided the two parties. They are no longer within the magic circle, but are taking up a position external to it. They have arrived at an age of reflection, and begin to speculate on the action and reaction, the irritation and counter-irritation, of religious forces; it is a common observation that 'revivals are not permanent;' the movement is criticised even by those who are subject to its influence. In the present state of the human mind, any consideration of these subjects, whether from the highest or lowest or most moderate point of view, is unfavourable to the stability of dogmatical systems, because it rouses inquiry into the meaning of words. To the sense of this is probably to be attributed the reserve on matters of doctrine and controversy which characterizes the present day, compared with the theological activity of twenty years ago.[142]

[93] These reflections bring us back to the question with which we began—'What effect will the critical interpretation of Scripture have on theology and on life?' Their tendency is to show that the result is beyond our control, and that the world is not unprepared for it. More things than at first sight appear are moving towards the same end. Religion often bids us think of ourselves, especially in later life, as each one in his appointed place, carrying on a work which is fashioned within by unseen hands. The theologian, too, may have peace in the thought that he is subject to the conditions of his age rather than one of its moving powers. When he hears theological inquiry censured as tending to create doubt and confusion, he knows very well that the cause of this is not to be sought in the writings of so-called rationalists or critics who are disliked partly because they unveil the age to itself; but in the opposition of reason and feeling, of the past and the present, in the conflict between the Calvinistic tendencies of an elder generation, and the influences which even in the same family naturally affect the young.[143]

[94] This distraction of the human mind between adverse influences and associations, is a fact which we should have to accept and make the best of, whatever consequences might seem to follow to individuals or Churches. It is not to be regarded as a merely heathen notion that 'truth is to be desired for its own sake even though no "good" result from it.' As a Christian paradox it may be said, 'What hast thou to do with "good;" follow thou me.' But the Christian revelation does not require of us this Stoicism in most cases; it rather shows how good and truth are generally coincident. Even in this life, there are nevertheless links which unite moral good with intellectual truth. It is hardly too much to say that the one is but a narrower form of the other. Truth is to the world what holiness of life is to the individual—to man collectively the source of justice and peace and good.[144]

95] There are many ways in which the connexion between truth and good may be traced in the interpretation of Scripture. Is it a mere chimera that the different sections of Christendom may meet on the common ground of the New Testament? Or that the individual may be urged by the vacancy and unprofitableness of old traditions to make the Gospel his own—a life of Christ in the soul, instead of a theory of Christ which is in a book or written down? Or that in missions to the heathen Scripture may become the expression of universal truths rather than of the tenets of particular men or churches? That would remove many obstacles to the reception of Christianity. Or that the study of Scripture may have a more important place in a liberal education than hitherto? Or that the 'rational service' of interpreting Scripture may dry up the crude and dreamy vapours of religious excitement? Or, that in preaching, new sources of spiritual health may flow from a more natural use of Scripture? Or that the lessons of Scripture may have a nearer way to the hearts of the poor when disengaged from theological formulas? Let us consider more at length some of these topics.[145]

96] I. No one casting his eye over the map of the Christian world can desire that the present lines of demarcation should always remain, any more than he will be inclined to regard the division of Christians to which he belongs himself, as in a pre-eminent or exclusive sense the Church of Christ. Those lines of demarcation seem to be political rather than religious; they are differences of nations, or governments, or ranks of society, more than of creeds or forms of faith. The feeling which gave rise to them has, in a great measure, passed away; no intelligent man seriously inclines to believe that salvation is to be found only in his own denomination. Examples of this 'sturdy orthodoxy,' in our own generation, rather provoke a smile than arouse serious disapproval. Yet many experiments show that these differences cannot be made up by any formal concordat or scheme of union; the parties cannot be brought to terms, and if they could, would cease to take an interest in the question at issue. The friction is too great when persons are invited to meet for a discussion of differences; such a process is like opening the doors and windows to put out a slumbering flame. But that is no reason for doubting that the divisions of the Christian world are beginning to pass away. The progress of politics, acquaintance with other countries, the growth of knowledge and of material greatness, changes of opinion in the Church of England, the present position of the Roman Communion—all these phenomena show that the ecclesiastical state of the world is not destined to be perpetual. Within the envious barriers which 'divide human nature into very little pieces' (Plato, *Rep.* iii. 395), a common sentiment is springing up of religious truth; the essentials of Christianity are contrasted with the details and definitions of it; good men of all religions find that they are more nearly agreed than heretofore. Neither is it impossible that this common feeling may so prevail over the accidental circumstances of Christian communities, that their political or ecclesiastical separation may be little felt. The walls which no adversary has scaled may fall down of themselves. We may perhaps figure to ourselves the battle against error and moral evil taking the place of one of sects and parties.[146]

[97] In this movement, which we should see more clearly but for the divisions of the Christian world which partly conceal it, the critical interpretation of Scripture will have a great influence. The Bible will be no longer appealed to as the witness of the opinions of particular sects, or of our own age; it will cease to be the battle field of controversies. But as its true meaning is more clearly seen, its moral power will also be greater. If the outward and inward witness, instead of parting into two, as they once did, seem rather to blend and coincide in the Christian consciousness, that is not a source of weakness but of strength. The Book itself, which links together the beginning and end of the human race, will not have a less inestimable value because the Spirit has taken the place of the letter. Its discrepancies of fact, when we become familiar with them, will seem of little consequence in comparison with the truths which it unfolds. That these truths, instead of floating down the stream of tradition, or being lost in ritual observances, have been preserved for ever in a book, is one of the many blessings which the Jewish and Christian revelations have conferred on the world—a blessing not the less real, because it is not necessary to attribute it to miraculous causes.

[98] Again, the Scriptures are a bond of union to the whole Christian world. No one denies their authority, and could all be brought to an intelligence of their true meaning, all might come to agree in matters of religion. That may seem to be a hope deferred, yet not altogether chimerical. If it is not held to be a thing impossible, that there should be agreement in the meaning of Plato or Sophocles, neither is it to be regarded as absurd, that there should be a like agreement in the interpretation of Scripture. The disappearance of artificial notions and systems will pave the way to such an agreement. The recognition of the fact, that many aspects and stages of religion are found in Scripture; that different, or even opposite parties existed in the Apostolic Church; that the first teachers of Christianity had a separate and individual mode of regarding the Gospel of Christ; that any existing communion is necessarily much more unlike the brotherhood of love in the New Testament than we are willing to suppose—Protestants in some respects, as much so as Catholics—that rival sects in our own day—Calvinists and Arminians—those who maintain and those who deny the final restoration of man—may equally find texts which seem to favour their respective tenets (Mark ix. 44–48; Romans xi. 32)—the recognition of these and similar facts will make us unwilling to impose any narrow rule of religious opinion on the ever-varying conditions; of the human mind and Christian society.[147]

[99] II. Christian missions suggest another sphere in which a more enlightened use of Scripture might offer a great advantage to the teacher. The more he is himself penetrated with the universal spirit of Scripture, the more he will be able to resist the literal and servile habits of mind of Oriental nations. You cannot transfer English ways of belief, and almost the history of the Church of England itself, as the attempt is sometimes made—not to an uncivilized people, ready like children to receive new impressions, but to an ancient and decaying one, furrowed with the

lines of thought, incapable of the principle of growth. But you may take the purer light or element of religion, of which Christianity is the expression, and make it shine on some principle in human nature which is the fallen image of it. You cannot give a people who have no history of their own, a sense of the importance of Christianity, as an historical fact: but, perhaps, that very peculiarity of their character may make them more impressible by the truths or ideas of Christianity. Neither is it easy to make them understand the growth of Revelation in successive ages—that there are precepts of the Old Testament which are reversed in the New—or that Moses allowed many things for the hardness of men's hearts. They are in one state of the world, and the missionary who teaches them is in another, and the Book through which they are taught, does not altogether coincide with either. Many difficulties thus arise which we are most likely to be successful in meeting, when we look them in the face. To one inference they clearly point, which is this: that it is not the Book of Scripture which we should seek to give them, to be reverenced like the Vedas or the Koran, and consecrated in its words and letters, but the truth of the Book, the mind of Christ and His Apostles, in which all lesser details and differences should be lost and absorbed. We want to awaken in them the sense that God is their Father, and they His children;—that is of more importance than any theory about the inspiration of Scripture. But to teach in this spirit, the missionary should himself be able to separate the accidents from the essence of religion; he should be conscious that the power of the Gospel resides not in the particulars of theology, but in the Christian life.[148]

00] III. It may be doubted whether Scripture has ever been sufficiently regarded as an element of liberal education. Few deem it worth while to spend in the study of it the same honest thought or pains which are bestowed on a classical author. Nor as at present studied, can it be said always to have an elevating effect. It is not a useful lesson for the young student to apply to Scripture, principles which he would hesitate to apply to other books; to make formal reconcilements of discrepancies which he would not think of reconciling in ordinary history; to divide simple words into double meanings; to adopt the fancies or conjectures of Fathers and Commentators as real knowledge. This laxity of knowledge is apt to infect the judgment when transferred to other subjects. It not easy to say how much of the unsettlement of mind which prevails among intellectual young men is attributable to these causes; the mixture of truth and falsehood in religious education, certainly tends to impair, at the age when it is most needed, the early influence of a religious home.

01] Yet Scripture studied in a more liberal spirit might supply a part of education which classical literature fails to provide. 'The best book for the heart might be made the best book for the intellect.' The noblest study of history and antiquity is contained in it; a poetry which is also the highest form of moral teaching; there, too, are lives of heroes and prophets, and especially of One whom we do not name with them, because He is above them. This history, or poetry, or biography is distinguished from all classical secular writings by the contemplation of man as he appears in the sight of God. That is a sense of things into which we must grow as well as reason ourselves, without which human nature is but a truncated, half-educated sort of being. But this sense or consciousness of a Divine presence in the world, which seems to be natural to the beginnings of the human race, but fades away and requires to be renewed in its after history, is not to be gathered from Greek or Roman literature, but from the Old and New Testament. And before we can make the Old and New Testament a real part of education, we must read them not by the help of custom or tradition, in the spirit of apology or controversy, but in accordance with the ordinary laws of human knowledge.[149]

[102] IV. Another use of Scripture is that in sermons, which seems to be among the tritest, and yet is far from being exhausted. If we could only be natural and speak of things as they truly are with a real interest and not merely a conventional one! The words of Scripture come readily to hand, and the repetition of them requires no effort of thought in the writer or speaker. But, neither does it produce any effect on the hearer, which will always be in proportion to the degree of feeling or consciousness in ourselves. It may be said that originality is the gift of few; no Church can expect to have, not a hundred, but ten such preachers as Robertson or Newman. But, without originality, it seems possible to make use of Scripture in sermons in a much more living way than at present. Let the preacher make it a sort of religion, and proof of his reverence for Scripture, that he never uses its words without a distinct meaning; let him avoid the form of argument from Scripture, and catch the feeling and spirit. Scripture is itself a kind of poetry, when not overlaid with rhetoric. The scene and country has a freshness which may always be renewed; there is the interest of antiquity and the interest of home or common life as well. The facts and characters of Scripture might receive a new reading by being described simply as they are. The truths of Scripture again would have greater reality if divested of the scholastic form in which theology has cast them. The universal and spiritual aspects of Scripture might be more brought forward to the exclusion of questions of the Jewish law, or controversies about the sacraments, or exaggerated statements of doctrines which seem to be at variance with morality. The life of Christ, regarded quite naturally as of one 'who was in all points tempted like as we are, yet without sin,' is also the life and centre of Christian teaching. There is no higher aim which the preacher can propose to himself than to awaken what may be termed the feeling of the presence of God and the mind of Christ in Scripture; not to collect evidences about dates and books, or to familiarize metaphysical distinctions; but to make the heart and conscience of his hearers bear him witness that the lessons which are contained in Scripture—lessons of justice and truth—lessons of mercy and peace—of the need of man and the goodness of God to him, are indeed not human but divine.[150]

[103] V. It is time to make an end of this long disquisition—let the end be a few more words of application to the circumstances of a particular class in the present age. If any one who is about to become a clergyman feels or thinks that he feels that some of the preceding statements cast a shade of trouble or suspicion on his future walk of life, who, either from the influence of a stronger mind than his own, or

from some natural tendency in himself, has been led to examine those great questions which lie on the threshold of the higher study of theology, and experiences a sort of shrinking or dizziness at the prospect which is opening upon him; let him lay to heart the following considerations:— First, that he may possibly not be the person who is called upon to pursue such inquiries. No man should busy himself with them who has not clearness of mind enough to see things as they are, and a faith strong enough to rest in that degree of knowledge which God has really given; or who is unable to separate the truth from his own religious wants and experiences. For the theologian as well as the philosopher has need of 'dry light,' 'unmingled with any tincture of the affections,' the more so as his conclusions are oftener liable to be disordered by them. He who is of another temperament may find another work to do, which is in some respects a higher one. Unlike philosophy, the Gospel has an ideal life to offer, not to a few only, but to all. There is one word of caution, however, to be given to those who renounce inquiry; it is that they cannot retain the right to condemn inquirers. Their duty is to say with Nicodemus, 'Doth the Gospel condemn any man before it hear him?' although the answer may be only 'Art thou also of Galilee?' They have chosen the path of practical usefulness, and they should acknowledge that it is a narrow path. For any but a 'strong swimmer' will be insensibly drawn out of it by the tide of public opinion or the current of party.[151]

04] Secondly, let him consider that the difficulty is not so great as imagination sometimes paints it. It is a difficulty which arises chiefly out of differences of education in different classes of society. It is a difficulty which tact, and prudence, and, much more, the power of a Christian life may hope to surmount. Much depends on the manner in which things are said; on the evidence in the writer or preacher of a real good will to his opponents, and a desire for the moral improvement of men. There is an aspect of truth which may always be put forward so as to find a way to the hearts of men. If there is danger and shrinking from one point of view, from another, there is freedom and sense of relief. The wider contemplation of the religious world may enable us to adjust our own place in it. The acknowledgment of churches as political and national institutions is the basis of a sound government of them. Criticism itself is not only negative; if it creates some difficulties, it does away others. It may put us at variance with a party or section of Christians in our own neighbourhood. But on the other hand, it enables us to look at all men as they are in the sight of God, not as they appear to human eye, separated and often interdicted from each other by lines of religious demarcation; it divides us from the parts to unite us to the whole. That is a great help to religious communion. It does away with the supposed opposition of reason and faith. It throws us back on the conviction that religion is a personal thing, in which certainty is to be slowly won and not assumed as the result of evidence or testimony. It places us, in some respects (though it be deemed a paradox to say so), more nearly in the position of the first Christians to whom the New Testament was not yet given, in whom the Gospel was a living word, not yet embodied in forms or supported by ancient institutions.[152]

[105] Thirdly, the suspicion or difficulty which attends critical inquiries is no reason for doubting their value. The Scripture nowhere leads us to suppose that the circumstance of all men speaking well of us is any ground for supposing that we are acceptable in the sight of God. And there is no reason why the condemnation of others should be witnessed to by our own conscience. Perhaps it may be true that, owing to the jealousy or fear of some, the reticence of others, the terrorism of a few, we may not always find it easy to regard these subjects with calmness and judgment. But, on the other hand, these accidental circumstances have nothing to do with the question at issue; they cannot have the slightest influence on the meaning of words, or on the truth of facts. No one can carry out the principle that public opinion or church authority is the guide to truth, when he goes beyond the limits of his own church or country. That is a consideration which may well make him pause before he accepts of such a guide in the journey to another world. All the arguments for repressing inquiries into Scripture in Protestant countries hold equally in Italy and Spain for repressing inquiries into matters of fact or doctrine, and so for denying the Scriptures to the common people.[153]

[106] Lastly, let him be assured that there is some nobler idea of truth than is supplied by the opinion of mankind in general, or the voice of parties in a church. Every one, whether a student of theology or not, has need to make war against his prejudices no less than against his passions; and, in the religious teacher, the first is even more necessary than the last. For, while the vices of mankind are in a great degree isolated, and are, at any rate, reprobated by public opinion, their prejudices have a sort of communion or kindred with the world without. They are a collective evil, and have their being in the interest, classes, states of society, and other influences amid which we live. He who takes the prevailing opinions of Christians and decks them out in their gayest colours—who reflects the better mind of the world to itself—is likely to be its favourite teacher.[154] In that ministry of the Gospel, even when assuming forms repulsive to persons of education, no doubt the good is far greater than the error or harm. But there is also a deeper work which is not dependent on the opinions of men in which many elements combine, some alien to religion, or accidentally at variance with it. That work can hardly expect to win much popular favour, so far as it runs counter to the feelings of religious parties. But he who bears a part in it may feel a confidence, which no popular caresses or religious sympathy could inspire, that he has by a Divine help been enabled to plant his foot somewhere beyond the waves of time. He may depart hence before the natural term, worn out with intellectual toil; regarded with suspicion by many of his contemporaries; yet not without a sure hope that the love of truth, which men of saintly lives often seem to slight, is, nevertheless, accepted before God.[155]

7 Notes to Benjamin Jowett

1. Jowett sets up the first of many oppositions in his essay, between the acceptance by "all Christians" of the canonical "sacred writings" and the differences among individuals and Christian bodies about interpretation; between a static "book itself" and commentators whose interpretations reflect the "changing atmosphere" of the world or the church. One standard account of three differing senses of interpretation (which Jowett generally opposes) is in Horne's *Introduction to the Study of the Holy Scriptures*: the literal sense (that encompasses the grammatico-historical sense), the mediate, spiritual, or mystical sense (with its subcategories: allegorical, typical, and parabolical senses), and the moral sense ([1818] 1828, 2:281–86).

2. Jowett's series of supposed "foundations" for interpretation, dismissed as false examples, include ultramontanism. "Ultramontane" refers to the movement in nineteenth-century Roman Catholicism that advocated the consolidation of pedagogical, doctrinal, and moral authority in the papacy and papal court, rather than delegating it to national churches or individual bishops; it opposed liberalism, as in Pius IX's *Syllabus of Errors* (1864) that explicitly condemned latitudinarianism, socialism, communism, Bible societies, and liberalism. English Ultramontanes included William George Ward and Henry Edward Manning, both converts from Anglicanism to Roman Catholicism. Ultramontanists and Anglicans disputed the doctrine of purgatory (as in 2 Macab. 12:39–43 and 2 Tim. 1:18) and the "primacy of St. Peter" (Matt. 16:18) but agreed on the three orders of clergy (bishops, priests, and deacons; 1 Tim. 3; Acts 6:1–7, 14:21–23; Eph. 4:11–13) and on the "divine origin" of episcopacy (John 20:19–23; Acts 20:28), since the same passages of the Bible are read at ordination services for each.

3. Jowett contrasts the "many" Anglicans who interpret the Bible as containing "all things necessary to salvation" (Sixth Article of Religion) to the "others," especially Nonconformists who adhere to William Chillingworth's phrase in *The Religion of Protestants a Safe Way to Salvation*: "The Bible, I say, the Bible only is the religion of Protestants" (1638; chap. 6). This phrase was widely misread by Protestants as advocating a kind of biblicism that rejects the historical-critical method, stresses individual words taken literally, and by free association uses them out of context as proof texts for a theological point. Chillingworth was echoed in the title of Thomas Burgess's *The Bible, and Nothing but the Bible: The Religion of the Church of England* (1815). The phrase was also referred to by S. T. Coleridge in letter 6 of his epistolary commentary on the inspiration of the Bible, *Confessions of an Inquiring Spirit* (1825). The "silent reference to . . . the Reformation" is to the doctrine of *sola scriptura* (scripture only), "the watchword of the Reformation" in Lutheran and Calvinist doctrine (Muller 1985, 284). Such differences in interpretation are grounded on whether revelation is outside reason as a break with natural law ("special revelation" [*revelatio specialis*] to the Reformation theologians, referring to the special interventions of God in theophanies, visions, words, and actions, recorded in the Hebrew and Christian Bibles) or as functioning through human reason as the perfecting of the natural order ("general revelation" [*revelatio generalis*], referring to divine revelation known through human reason in interpreting the two books, the Bible and nature).

4. In the Reformation, Luther accepted the canon of the Bible as a given, but argued that parts of the NT were of greater worth than other parts. In his Preface to the New Testament (1522) the gospel of John is the "true chief Gospel, far, far to be preferred to the other three. . . . So, too, the Epistles of St. Paul and St. Peter far surpass the other three Gospels. . . . St. James' Epistle is really an epistle of straw . . . it has nothing of the nature of the Gospel about it" (1932, 6:444). At the Council of Nicaea (325), the condemnation of Arianism, denying the divinity of Christ, hinged upon the support the NT gave for the formulation that Christ was "of one substance with the Father . . . according to the scriptures." On Pelagius see Williams ¶32 and n. 133. In *The Epistles of St. Paul* Jowett writes on Rom. 5:12: "The hinge of the Pelagian controversy is the free agency of man. . . . Can the will, by its unaided power, accept and appropriate the work of salvation?" ([1855] 1859, 2:170).

5. For "justified by faith without works" see Rom. 3:28–4:2; for "justified by faith as well as works," 2 Jas. 20, 26. The former is the Lutheran position based on "faith alone," the latter the Roman Catholic stress on faith and works. Luther's translation of Rom. 3:28 added the word "alone"—"man is justified by faith [alone] apart from works of the Law"—a translation repudiated by the Council of Trent: "If anyone saith that justifying faith is nothing else than confidence in the divine mercy which remits sin for Christ's sake, or that his confidence alone is that whereby we are justified, let him be anathema" (Session 6, Canon 12).

In *The Epistles of St. Paul* Jowett points out that

questions raised by Rom. 3:28 involve "the fates of nations and of Churches." According to Jowett, Paul "meant only that men were justified from within, not from without; from above, not from below; by the grace of God, and not of themselves; by Christ, not by the law; not by the burden of ordinances; but by the power of an endless life" ([1855] 1859, 2:136). On Pelagian, Calvinist, Roman Catholic, and other views of the relation between sin, grace, and justification see Jowett on Rom. 5:12–21 ([1855] 1859, 2:170–73). In "On Righteousness of Faith" appended to *The Epistles of St. Paul* Jowett discusses the same doctrinal battles: "What Luther sought for was to find a formula which expressed most fully the entire, unreserved, immediate dependence of the believer on Christ. What the Catholic sought for was to modify this formula as not to throw dishonour on the Church by making religion a merely personal or individual matter" ([1855] 1859, 2:525).

6. Rom. 5 and 9 are on justification by faith. Jowett comments on Rom. 5:12–21: "The threads of later controversy are too fine for the Apostolical age; they belong to another stage of human thought and culture. . . . The living elements of [Paul's] thoughts can only be traced in the writings of himself and his contemporaries" ([1855] 1859, 2:171). Jowett's reference to Rom. 9, on the elect in Israel and the church, alludes to the new emphasis given to Romans in F. C. Baur's *Paul, the Apostle of Jesus Christ* (1845) in redirecting emphasis from the doctrinal sections (chapters 1–8) to the historical context of an attack on Jewish exclusivism in the matter of election. Jowett acknowledged his debt to Baur in his introduction to *The Epistles of St. Paul,* and in his comments on chaps. 8 and 9 ([1855] 1859, 2:268–69).

Historical and contemporaneous controversy over 1 Cor. 3:15 concerned whether the passage referred to the purification of the individual soul by grace or by the atonement; the correcting of the Christian community; or the damned burning in hell or the purification of the soul by fire in purgatory. Calvin comments extensively on these positions (Calvin [1546] 1976, 77–78). In his commentary Stanley cites historical references for the "two interpretations" of the "famous" passage, the first burning forever, the second, purgatory. (1855, 1:79).

Controversy over Jesus' words to Nicodemus about being born again (John 3:3) concerned whether they referred to spiritual rebirth through the conversion of the soul or to sacramental rebirth and regeneration in baptism. Until Calvin all Christian writers (the "Fathers of the Church" to whom Jowett refers) argue that the passage refers to baptism (Nias 1951, 11). The passage is prescribed as the reading for the public baptism of adults in the *BCP.* The Gorham case of 1850 on baptismal regeneration brought the passage into contemporary conflict between the Tractarians and the Evangelicals about the efficacy of the sacrament (see Pusey's three *Tracts for the Times,* nos. LXVII–LXIX). Gorham cites this passage as asserting justification by faith, not by sacramental efficacy (Nias 1951, 11–44). Nias lists 105 pamphlets concerning the baptismal controversy. In the midst of the legal disputes around *Essays and Reviews,* J. B. Mozley's *The Baptismal Controversy* (1862) summarized contemporary positions; see Wilson ¶76 and n. 124.

7. Jowett places differences to the "growth or progress of the human mind itself" in the context of human development from childhood to old age (see Temple, especially ¶s 6–8 and notes). On Jowett's possible indebtedness to Vico's *The New Science* (1725), that all nations develop according to the rate at which specific fundamental concepts, chiefly truth and justice, emerge as human beings interact in society, see Frank M. Turner 1981, 418–19.

In the preface to his translation of Plato's *Theaetetus* (1871) Jowett argues that "human intellect" is "the joint work of many who are of all ages and countries," traceable "in history, and more especially in the history of philosophy" (Jowett 1902a, 191); he argues similarly in his preface to Plato's *Republic* (Jowett 1902a, 149).

8. Jowett argues that both the allegorical or mystical methods and logical methods of interpretation are defective.

Allegorical methods of interpretation (often called the "mystical") derive from Gal. 4:24–31 and 2 Cor. 3:6. Clement of Rome, Irenaeus, and Tertullian used the allegorical method of reading the OT, but it was associated especially with the exegetical school of Alexandria, where Origen used a tripartite method of interpretation, literal, moral, and allegorical, preferring the last in his commentaries on the OT (see his *On First Principles,* bk. 4) so that the Bible as a whole is read as the journey of the soul from body to spirit, so that Israel (the soul) leaves Egypt (the flesh) for the promised land (grace). This method continued at Alexandria to the fourth century in the works of Athanasius and Cyril. On the other hand, the Antiochene tradition, as in the commentaries of John Chrysostom, stressed the historical and rhetorical context of biblical interpretation. Allegory was later combined with other methods leading to the fourfold interpretation used in the Middle Ages and continuing to Jowett's time. Fourfold interpretation (semantic applications of the four causes of Aristotle: material, formal, efficient, and final) stresses the literal or historical meaning of a passage first, then the allegorical meaning in relation to the life of Christ and its extension in the life of the Christian church on earth, then the moral (or tropological) in which passages are related to the nurture of the soul in the Christian virtues, and finally the anagogical level, reading a passage in the light of the last judgment, the final destiny of the soul, and the church triumphant in heaven. See John Cassian (*Collations* c. 420; 14:8, with the example of Jerusalem as the historic city in Palestine, the Christian church, the soul, and the heavenly realm; Augustine uses the same instance to organize *The City of God*); Thomas Aquinas (*Summa Theologiae* bk. 1, chap. 1, quest. 10, *sed contra* [c. 1265]); Bernard of Clairvaux (commentary on the Song of Songs); and Dante ("Letter to Can Grande della Scala" [c. 1318]). For allegory see Lubac 1959; D. W. Robertson 1963, 286–390; Fletcher 1974; and Rollinson 1981.

Luther and Calvin rejected the allegorical method (see also Jowett ¶44 and n. 80). In the nineteenth century, allegory was distinguished from typology in that the former "is a narrative, either expressly feigned for the purpose, or . . . describing . . . for the purpose of representing certain higher truths or principles than the narrative, in its literal aspect, whether real or fictitious, could possibly have taught" (Fairbairn [1845–47] 1882, 1:18); typology, on the other hand, "is not properly a different or higher sense, but a different or higher application of the same sense" (1:19). Thomas Hartwell Horne defines a type as "a symbol of something future and distant, or an example prepared and evidently designed by God to prefigure that future thing. What is prefigured is called the *antitype*" ([1818] 1828, 2:455). Jowett argues that Paul links "the interpretation of the allegory with the narrative itself" ([1855] 1859, 1:344–45). For allegory and typology in nineteenth-century religious and literary discourse see Landow 1980 and Shaw 1987, 174–88; for allegory as rhetoric see Kennedy 1983; for allegory and mythology in religion and literary study see Shaffer 1975.

The "application of logic" refers to contemporary German higher criticism especially at Tübingen and Göttingen and is associated with Hegel, whose philosophy and logic were the foundation of thought there. The most notorious example was Strauss's *Leben Jesu* ([1835] 1846) (see Willis 1988).

The "freshness of early literature" and the questions about "ancient writings" refer to contemporary debates on Homer prompted by Francis Newman's Preface and translation of 1856, the debates concerning the dating of Homer and his language in the writings of Gladstone, and Matthew Arnold's lectures on Homer of 1861.

For "Thoughts that breathe" see Thomas Gray, *The Progress of Poetry*, (1757; pt. 3, st. 3). For "In pious meditation," compare Shakespeare, *A Midsummer Night's Dream*: "In maiden meditation fancy-free," 2.1.164.

9. For the Vedas see Wilson ¶13 and n. 29. The Vedas, together with the *Bhagavad-Gita*, and the national and sacred epics (*Mahabharata* and *Ramayana*), comprise a part of the sacred texts of Hinduism (which does not have a fixed canon). They were the product and care of the educated classes, particularly the Brahmins, who also produced devotional commentaries in the Brahmanas (900–700 B.C.E.); hence, Jowett's claim in ¶46 that the Bible differs in being the product and care of people of diverse education.

The Koran (or Qur'an) is the sacred book of Islam, believed to be the words of Allah spoken to the Prophet Mohammed (c. 570–632) through the mediation of the Angel Gabriel. It consists of 114 suras or chapters and was collated into canonic form under Caliph 'Uthmân (d. 656). The mystical interpretations of the Koran are grounded in Sufism, or Islamic mysticism, and can be found especially in writings attributed to Ibn al-'Arab.

Interpretations of the Vedas and the Koran in the nineteenth century depended upon translations; both religious traditions were viewed with suspicion and were objects of missionary zeal; such comments on Hinduism, Buddhism, and Islam by Williams, Wilson, and Jowett were anathema to most readers of *Essays and Reviews*. Horace Hayman Wilson published the first Sanskrit-English dictionary (1819) and in 1832 was appointed to the chair of Sanskrit at Oxford. His translation of the Vedas in 6 volumes was published (1850–62). J. Muir also translated the *Original Sanskrit Texts on the Origin and History of the People of India, their Religion and Institutions* in 5 volumes (1860–72); and Max Müller, H. H. Wilson's student, published his *History of Ancient Sanskrit Literature So Far as It Illustrates the Primitive Religion of the Brahmans* (1859), and contested the Sanskrit chair on Wilson's death (1860) but was defeated because of his theological liberalism. Theodor Nöldeke's *Geschichte des Qorans* (1859–60; History of the Koran); a collection of writings from the Sufi tradition was published by the German Protestant theologian Friedrich August Tholuck in his *Sufismus sive theosophia Persarum pantheistica* (1821; Sufism according to the pantheistic theosophy of the Persians). In his Boyle Lectures, *The Religions of the World and their Relations to Christianity*, F. D. Maurice comments on "the primary idea of an Inconceivable, Absolute, Unseen Being" of Hinduism (1847, 51).

10. "Revival of literature" refers to the renaissance of study of the classical and vernacular literatures, beginning in Italy in the fifteenth century. The phrase is used, for instance, by J. A. Symonds in his *Renaissance in England: The Revival of Learning* (1877).

For the relationship between Homeric and biblical criticism see Frank M. Turner 1981, 140–54). As examples of "pedantic and misplaced" classical learning, Horne relates Hebrew and Greek terms in his commentary on the Hebraisms in the NT ([1818] 1828, 2:23–27), and Herder used comparative philology and religion to propose that Hebrew thought is characteristic in the verb, Greek in the noun (Herder 1833, 1:29–30); see Barr 1961, 14–15, 85.

Many romantic "systems of philosophy" used biblical language, as in S. T. Coleridge's *Aids to Reflection* (1825), Schleiermacher's *Discourses on Religion* (1799), and Carlyle's representation in *Sartor*

Resartus (1833–34) of Johann Paul ("Jean Paul") Richter's *Introduction to Aesthetics* (1804).

For "new wine" and "old bottles" see Matt. 9:17; Mark 2:22; Luke 5:27. "Popular commentaries" of Jowett's day include the edition of the Bible with notes by C. of E. clergy, ed. G. D'Oyly and Richard Mant (1817, 3 vols.) published by Oxford under the auspices of the SPCK. Another edited by Thomas Scott (1822) sold over 12,000 copies in England and 22,000 in the U.S.A., with a new edition in 6 volumes published in 1861. Among other "popular commentaries" were Charles Girdlestone's *Commentary* (1843, 6 vols); and the *Commentary* by Patrick, Lowth, Whitby, and Arnald (various dates 1848, 3 vols.).

11. For "spiritual food" see 1 Cor. 10:3–4; "tendency to edification," 1 Cor. 14:2–12.

The first four passages deal with injunctions of the Christian life that are hard to follow: the prohibitions against swearing (Matt. 5:34); the calling of sinners not the righteous to repentance (Matt. 9:13); true discipleship in selling all one has to give to the poor (Matt. 19:21); and obeying God rather than men (Acts 5:29). Jowett alleges that such passages are trivialized with inappropriate moralizing by edifying sermonizers, whether Tractarian or evangelical, carried away by feelings or the repetition of their own commonplaces, and without a grounding in thorough study.

The final three passages are often heaped with unwarranted implications. Hence, Matt 22:21 (rendering to Caesar and to God), is often read as separating secular from sacred duties and giving each what is appropriate, as Alford comments: "These weighty words, so much misunderstood, bind together instead of separating the political and religious duties of the followers of Christ" ([1849] 1863, 1:221). Matt. 28:20 is often taken as justification for apostolical succession (see Jowett ¶28 and n. 55; also Jowett ¶s 80, 81). Rom. 13:1 is used in the prayers after communion in the *BCP*, identifying presenting one's body and "reasonable service" with eucharistic worship. In *The Epistles of St. Paul* Jowett argues: "The translation 'reasonable service,' in the English version [AV], is not an accurate explanation of λογικὴ λατρεία [*logike latreia*], which is an oxymoron or paradoxical expression, meaning 'an ideal service, a ceremonial of thought and mind'" ([1855] 1859, 2:341–42).

12. On the comparison between the transmission of the classical authors and the NT, Kenneth W. Clark writes: "The New Testament is found to have the advantage. Most of the classics survive in manuscripts no earlier than twelve to sixteen centuries later than the authors. The interval is shorter for Lucretius, Horace, and Terence, and shortest of all for Vergil, for whom there is a gap of just less than four hundred years (but for one fragment a gap of less than three centuries)" (1957, 617). For nineteenth-century Greek and Latin scholarship see Sandys 1908, 3:448–70; on Oriental languages and literature see Aarsleff [1966] 1983, 115–62.

For "stammering lips" see Isa. 28:11. In *The Epistles of St. Paul* Jowett also uses the passage: "With 'stammering lips and another tongue' the Gospel spoke to the child and to the simple" ([1855] 1859, 1:43).

The "lyric poetry" (or poetry sung to a lyre) of the early Greeks flourished from 670 to 440 B.C.E. The Aeolian tradition is associated particularly with Alcaeus (7th cent. B.C.E.) and Sappho (7th cent. B.C.E.); the Dorian, with Alcman (7th cent. B.C.E.) and Stesichorus (6th cent. B.C.E.). The "difficulty" in interpretation to which Jowett alludes includes the loss of the accompanying music, as well as the fragmentary survival of the poetry (see K. O. Müller 1847, 164–216).

Early Greek prose writers were philosophers and chroniclers. These include the philosophers Pherecydes of Syros (fl. 550 B.C.E.), Anaximander (c. 610–545 B.C.E.) and Anaximenes (fl. 550 B.C.E.) of Miletus. The "difficulty" to which Jowett alludes concerns the separation of philosophic prose from the ornaments of poetry as K. O. Müller argues (1847:238–55).

13. The rules for interpretation of the Vedas (see Jowett ¶3 and n. 9), using the materials and methods of comparative philology (meter, literary form, etymology, philology, social and anthropological context, comparative mythology, etc.), are set out by Max Müller, along with the factors that had retarded the study of Sanskrit philology and literature (Müller 1859, 7).

The Zendavesta is the sacred book of Zoroastrianism, the religion of pre-Islamic Iran, and of the Parsees in India. It is the only document written in this language, Avestan (extinct about 400 B.C.E.), dates from c. 600 B.C.E., and survives as an extensive fragment in late medieval MSS. It was edited by the Dutch scholar N. L. Westergaard in 1852–54 and was analyzed by Martin Haug, *Essays on the Sacred Language, Writings, and Religion of the Parsis* (1862).

14. The "authorized version" is the translation of the Bible published in 1611 as "Approved to be read in Churches"; it is also known as the King James version, after James I, who ordered it to be undertaken. "The received text" is a translation of the Latin *textus receptus*, referring to the Greek text of the NT that followed closely that of Erasmus (1516), Beza (1565), and Stephanus (1550). Although "the received text" was abandoned by Karl Lachmann in his edition of the NT (1831) in favor of the oldest Greek manuscript, it was the one ordinarily translated until the end of the nineteenth century. In *The Epistles of St. Paul* Jowett defends his choice of Lachmann's edition instead of the *textus receptus*: "No one who is acquainted with Sophocles or Thucydides and the

volumes of Dindorf or Bekker, would be willing to reprint the texts of those authors as it is to be found in editions of two centuries ago. No apology is therefore needed for laying aside the "Textus Receptus" of the NT. The text of Lachmann, which has been adopted instead, has many claims to be considered as the most perfect that has hitherto appeared" ([1855] 1859, 1:vii–viii).

Jowett also refers to the "authorised English translation": "The various readings of the third edition of Robert Stephens [Stephanus], 1550, are placed under the text; they will be found to agree very nearly with the Textus Receptus and the authorised English translation. The latter is added on the opposite page with slight corrections; which, where they are occasioned by variation of reading, are marked by numbers referring to the authorised text, which is retained underneath" ([1855] 1859, 1:xii). As with "1550," "1624" refers to a specific edition, the Greek NT first published by the Elzevir press at Leyden, using Beza's 1565 text.

In his translation of Plato, Jowett is extremely brief about textual matters: "The text which has been mostly followed in this Translation of Plato is the latest 8vo. edition of Stallbaum" ([1871] 1875, 1:vii). Johann Gottfried Stallbaum edited Plato in two complete editions (1821–25 and 1827–60). Lewis Campbell, Jowett's colleague, friend, and biographer, edited Sophocles in two volumes (1871, 1881). The Preface to the second vol. has a lengthy discussion of interpolations and anomalies in the textual history (1881, 2:vi–xi). On the still-unresolved problems of the text of Sophocles see Hogan 1991, 16.

15. Jowett implies that just as biblical scholarship can be differentiated into national schools (Jowett ¶1), so too can classical scholarship.

Matthew Arnold in "On the Modern Element in Literature" (a lecture read at Oxford on 4 Nov. 1858) argues for the universal role of Sophocles: "The peculiar characteristic of the highest literature—the poetry—of the fifth century in Greece before the Christian era is its *adequacy*; the peculiar characteristic of the poetry of Sophocles is its consummate, its unrivalled *adequacy*; that it represents the highly developed human nature of that age" (1965–77, 1:28). In *The Idea of a University* J. H. Newman writes: "The majestic lessons concerning duty and religion, justice and providence, which occur in Aeschylus and Sophocles, belong to a higher school than that of Homer"; and "[Shakespeare] upholds the broad laws of moral and divine truth with the consistency of an Aeschylus, Sophocles, or Pindar" ([1852] 1976, 218, 262).

Most contemporary scholarship on Sophocles, both textual and critical, was being done in Germany. Among the more important of Jowett's contemporaries were G. E. Lessing, *Leben des Sophokles* (1790; Life of Sophocles); K. W. Dindorf, *Ad Sophoclis tragoedias annotationes* (1836; Annotations on Sophocles' tragedies); F. Schultz, *De Vita Sophoclis poetae* (1836; On the life of Sophocles the poet); A. Schöll, *Sophokles. Sein Leben und Wirken* (1842; Sophocles, his life and works); A. Capellmann, *Die weiblichen Charaktere bei Sophokles* (1843; The female characters of Sophocles); J. P. Behaghel, *Das Familienleben nach Sophokles* (1844; The family life of Sophocles); F. Lübker, *Die sophokleische Theologie und Ethik* (1851; Sophoclean theology and ethics); C. J. Ehlinger, *De fati apud Sophoclem notione* (1852; The notion of fate according to Sophocles); A. Hagemann, *De fato Sophocleo* (1853; On Sophoclean fate); F. W. Ullrich, *Über die religiöse und sittliche Bedeutung der Antigone* (1853; On the religious and moral significance of Antigone); and W. H. Kolster, *Sophokleische Studien* (1859; Sophoclean studies). On Sophocles in Victorian Britain see Jenkyns 1980, 87–111.

16. *Novum Organum* (1620; New method) is a Latin treatise by Francis Bacon, the second part, with *The Advancement of Learning* (1605), of a program for intellectual and scientific reform. In *The Epistles of St. Paul,* Jowett extended the comparison between the scientific interpretation of language and that of nature: "The author of the 'Novum Organum' has put men upon their guard against the illusions of words in the study of natural sciences. . . . But is it therefore to be supposed that language, which is the source of half the exploded fallacies of chemistry and physiology, is an adequate or exact expression of moral and spiritual truth?" ([1855] 1859, 2:622).

17. Grammar, rhetoric, and logic constitute the medieval *trivium,* the first three subjects taught in the medieval university as the arts of language.

Jowett is concerned to show how classical and biblical texts use the same methods: in lower criticism textual methods establish the most reliable text on the basis of manuscript evidence, accounting for the historical process of variants or changes in the documents; higher criticism uses literary and historical methods to study the forms and sources of texts; both were used in the study of classical and biblical texts, a point that was widely accepted in scholarly circles (see *EB* 3:859; s.v. "Bible"). Similarly, while Gladstone argues that "the poems of Homer never can be put in competition with the Sacred Writings of the Old Testament," he also devotes a section of his second volume to an explicit comparison of the Homeric epics and the Bible (1858, 2:521–33).

For "a vision and faculty divine" see W. Wordsworth, *The Excursion* (1814, bk. 1, l. 77); for "metaphysical aid," Pope, *The Dunciad* (1742, bk. 4, l. 646); for "chaff" and "wheat," Matt. 3:12 and Luke 3:17.

18. This paragraph contains three of the essay's central ideas, the unchanging nature of "the book itself," and the double task of the interpreter of "the book": "to recover the original meaning," and also "to read Scripture like any other book."

For the night vision in Daniel, often interpreted messianically, see Dan. 7:13; Christ adopted the cognomen "Son of man" (as in Matt. 8:20) from Ezekiel (as in Ezek. 2:1 and frequently elsewhere); for John the Baptist, "girded with a garment of camel's hair," Matt. 3:4; Mark 1:6; for Paul with a "thorn in the flesh," 2 Cor. 12:7; for "true lights which light him," John 1:9; and for "open his eyes that he may see," 2 Kings 6:17.

Direct visual perception of "things as they truly are" became a cliché in the aesthetics of critical perception. Within 10 months of the publication of *Essays and Reviews,* Matthew Arnold in his second lecture "On Translating Homer" (8 Dec. 1860) claimed: "Of these two literatures [of France and Germany] . . . the main effort . . . has been a *critical* effort; the endeavour, in all branches of knowledge,—theology, philosophy, history, art, science,—to see the object as in itself it really is" (Arnold 1960–77, 1:140). The same phrase is repeated in the opening paragraph of "The Function of Criticism at the Present Time" (1864), is alluded to by Walter Pater in the Preface to *Studies in the Renaissance* (1873) and by Joseph Conrad in the Preface to *The Nigger of the Narcissus* (Conrad [1897] 1979, 147). Jowett repeats the phrase in ¶s 39 and 102–3.

19. Although Herbert Marsh devoted two lectures to the "History of Biblical Interpretation" in *Lectures on the Criticism and Interpretation of the Bible* (1828), there was no comprehensive history in English until F. W. Farrar's Bampton Lectures, *The History of the Interpretation of the Bible* (1886). The important German study was Gottlob Wilhelm Meyer's *Geschichte der Schrifterklärung* (1802–9, 5 vols.; The history of the interpretation of the scriptures). Jowett divides the stages of interpretation according to traditional periods of ecclesiastical history, still a conventional method (Coggins and Houlden 1990, 318). For similar periodization and biblical critics identified with each period of ecclesiastical history see, for instance, Neander 1858; and Rogerson, Rowland, and Lindars, 1988.

First Jowett identifies the apostolic period of canon-formation from the end of the first century to the time of the Alexandrian allegorizing biblical critic Origen (who edited the *Hexapla,* a Hebrew and five variant Greek texts of the OT) and the Latin theologian, Tertullian, who argues that the church alone has the right to interpret the Bible (*De Praescriptione Haereticorum* [c. 200; Concerning the prescription of heretics]). The patristic period from Origen to the fall of the Roman Empire in the West, includes Jerome's translation of the Bible from Hebrew and Greek into Latin (the Vulgate) and commentaries using philological and topographical methods. Augustine concluded the *Confessions* (c. 400) with an allegorical commentary on the first eight verses of Genesis (trans. J. G. Pilkington, *NPNCF*1 1:163–207, bks. 11–13) and wrote other commentaries on Genesis, Psalms, Galatians, Romans, and John. Jowett's third period, the medieval, continues to the triumph of scholasticism from Peter Abelard (a commentary on Romans) to Thomas Aquinas (an exegetical commentary on the gospels, *Catena Aurea* [Golden chain], and commentaries on Isaiah, Jeremiah, Psalms, Job, and Paul's Epistles).

For the fourth period, the Renaissance and Reformation, Jowett mentions Erasmus (an edition of the NT, with a translation into classical Latin (1516), John Calvin (commentaries on the whole of the Bible), and his biographer Theodore Beza (an annotated Latin translation of the Greek NT and an important critical edition [1565]). In the fifth period, the seventeenth-century, Hugo Grotius published *Annotatione in Vetus et Novum Testamentum* (1642; Annotations on the Old and New Testaments), for the first time stressing philological criticism with ecclesiastical tradition; in England, Henry Hammond published *A Paraphrase and Annotations upon All the Books of the New Testament* (1653). In the sixth period, the eighteenth and nineteenth centuries, Jowett mentions the controversial rationalist exegete Wilhelm Martin Leberecht De Wette, whose *Die biblische Dogmatik* (1813; The Bible dogmatics) and *Einleitung ins Neue Testament* (1826; Introduction to the New Testament; translated into English in 1858) popularized higher criticism. By "Meier" Jowett refers to Heinrich August Wilhelm Meyer, who edited *Kritische-exegetischer Kommentar zum Neuen Testament* (1832–52, 16 vols.; trans. *Critical and Exegetical Commentary on the New Testament* [1873–95], 20 vols.). To Meyer, Jowett owes "great obligations" in the Preface to *The Epistles of St. Paul,* as well as to "Usteri, F. Baur, Ewald, Neander, Winer, Tholuck, Olshausen, Fritsche . . . and in the essay on Philo, to Gfrörer" ([1855] 1859, 1:xii).

Thucydides concludes his discussion of the plague in Athens (430 B.C.E.) with the Athenians' recollection of an old prophecy concerning either a plague (*loimos*) or a famine (*limos*), the oracle being interpreted according to the circumstances of the time. In his note to this passage in his translation of Thucydides, Jowett comments: "But Thucydides, not wishing to commit himself to the fulfilment of the oracle, is content to lay the two statements side by side, leaving the reader to draw his own inference" (1881, 2:121).

Jowett's assertion that there is far less diversity concerning prophecy in Germany than in England (because in Germany it was treated historically using the methods of higher criticism; see Jowett ¶13 and n. 21) is based on the supposition that the German higher critics generally dominated the German universities; however, his assertion needs to be qualified in that a number of conservative biblical scholars, such as E. W. Hengstenberg, C. F. Keil, and Franz Delitzsch, were hostile to many of the views of the higher critics. Christopher Wordsworth attacked

Jowett's claim for German "agreement and certainty," arguing: "No one now ever reads their [the higher critics'] writings, or cares one jot for their theories. They are exploded. . . . The pantheistic speculations of Strauss and others who followed them have fared little better, and a struggle has ensued between more orthodox interpreters, such as Hengstenberg, Hävernick, Delitzsch, Oehler, Stier, on the one side, and a sceptical and destructive school of expositors on the other" (1862, 427–28).

Specific schools of "interpretation" had developed in the twenty Protestant university faculties of theology in Germany, identified with such scholars as J. D. Michaelis and J. G. Eichhorn at Göttingen, J. P. Gabler at Jena, and F. C. Baur at Tübingen, all using historical and higher-critical methods, but they were not in agreement among themselves. For instance, De Wette's *Contributions to Old Testament Introduction* (1806–7) attacked the mythical interpretations of Eichhorn and Gabler, while De Wette (at Basel in Switzerland) in turn was reviled for having given rise to methods of interpreting the Pentateuch that were applied with scepticism to the NT by D. F. Strauss in *Leben Jesu* ([1835] 1846). Lutheran orthodoxy was defended against these revisionary interpretations by such scholars as E. W. Hengstenberg at Berlin, while they were made use of and disseminated by many writers, including C. C. J. Bunsen, the subject of Williams's essay. Bunsen popularized the views of G. H. A. von Ewald of Göttingen concerning historical providence and the use God made in first educating the Jews and through them the whole of the human race. Ewald developed his views in *Geschichte des Volkes Israël* (1843–59, 7 vols.; trans. R. Martineau and J. E. Carpenter, *History of Israel* [1867–74, 5 vols.]).

Scholars in England reacted against the new biblical scholarship, even those who, like E. B. Pusey, had studied there: "From the 1830s there was a determined attempt to keep German criticism out of Britain at all costs, and the barriers that were created did not begin to crumble until the 1880s, although they were quite badly shaken in the 1860s" (Rogerson, Rowland, and Lindars 1988, 119). Substantial British biblical commentaries and handbooks, such as the volumes by T. H. Horne ([1818] 1828) and the three-volume *Dictionary of the Bible* (1863) to which most of the leading scholars of the day contributed (including A. P. Stanley, but none of the Essayists and Reviewers), maintained a measured distance from German critical methods of interpretation. For the interpretation of the Bible in the nineteenth century see Kümmel 1972; Grant and Tracy 1984; Robert Morgan and Barton 1988; Rogerson, Rowland and Lindars 1988; and W. R. Ward in Helmstadter and Lightman 1990.

Jowett's reference to interpreting according to the "plain meaning" and "context" of words is an appeal to the Enlightenment grammatical-historical hermeneutics advocated by Ernesti and others. This point was also advocated by Schleiermacher, provided it was supported by the "technical-psychological" method, that interpretation is a technique or art, and involves understanding the author of the text as a writer and as a person. The historical antecedent of the relation of the literal sense to authorial intention was located by one of Jowett's critics, John Cazenove: "It was not left to the nineteenth century to make such a discovery as this. It might be supposed that the Professor had borrowed from the language of the chief among the schoolmen, '*sensus literalis est quem auctor intendit*' [the literal sense is that which the author intended]. And Aquinas here is only laying down what his great master Augustine had evidently taught before him" (1861, 31). See also Jowett ¶71.

20. For "number of the beast" see Rev. 13:17–18; "the two witnesses," Rev. 11:3; "the little horn," Dan. 7:8, 8:9; "the man of sin," 2 Thess. 2:3. These passages were key texts in anti–Roman Catholic polemic. For instance, Christopher Wordsworth's Hulsean *Lectures on the Apocalypse* (1848) identify the beast with the "man of sin," referring prophetically to the pope as Antichrist as well as to the religious orders (1849a, 274, n. 3), while the "two witnesses" are the law and the gospel (242–43); all are greatly expanded in the second edition and use Dan. 7 (1849a, 505–35). In his edition of *The Apocalypse* (1849) Wordsworth includes an appendix "on the name and number of the beast" equating it with "the supremacy of Papal Rome" (1849b 151–62); he also includes a long series of Latin quotations from Lancelot Andrewes's controversy with Cardinal Bellarmine, on the "two witnesses" and the connection of Antichrist with the "man of sin" and the papacy (1849b, 166–203). Wordsworth expanded his views on the papacy as the Antichrist in *Is the Church of Rome the Babylon of the Book of Revelation?* (1850). In *The Epistles of St. Paul* Jowett explicitly rejects such identifications ([1855] 1859, 1:163).

For "labyrinths in which men lose themselves" see the labyrinth of Daedalus in Ovid, *Metamorphoses* (bk. 8, ll. 152–259). The type of the dry-as-dust philosopher lost in fruitless research is a cliché in nineteenth-century literature, as in Walter Scott's preface to *Ivanhoe* (1819) in the person of the Rev. Dr. Jonas Dryasdust, through Carlyle's pedantic, antiquarian annotator in *Past and Present* (1843; bk. 2, chap. 3) and the Prussian historians, classical scholars, and philosophers summed up as "Dryasdust" in *Frederick the Great* (1858; bk. 1, chap. 3), to George Eliot's Mr. Casaubon searching for the "Key to All Mythologies" in *Middlemarch* (1871–72).

Joseph Mead or Mede, the most learned millenarianist of his age, published *Clavis Apocalyptica* (1627; trans. Richard More, *The Key of the Revelation* 1643) and *The Apostasy of the Latter Times* (1641). Mede's analysis of the book of Revelation used numerology, and a wide range of biblical and scholarly knowledge, to relate the images of the opening of the seals with history from the time of the death of Christ to the present and into future predictions of the millennial rule of the saints. According to his chronology the fall of the Antichrist would take place during his lifetime and would conclude in 1655 (1677, 558–602). Mede identified the killing of the "two witnesses" as a time of trial for the reformed churches in his own day. Other contemporaries, such as John Mayer, predicted that the world would end in 1860, the year of the publication of *Essays and Reviews* (in his *Ecclesiastica interpretatio*, 1627). Mede was the tutor of John Milton at Christ's College, Cambridge (see Christianson 1978, 124–31).

The major study of typology by "a Protestant divine" was *The Typology of Scripture Viewed in Connection with the Whole Series of the Divine Dispensations* (1844–47; 3d ed. 1858) by Patrick Fairbairn. The more extremist typologists combined typology with aspects of prophetic millenarianism and anti–Roman Catholic polemic. One such group was the Hutchinsonians, the followers of John Hutchinson, whose *Moses's Principia* (1724) was an attack on Isaac Newton's *Principia mathematica*, arguing that the Bible contains the key to all knowledge. His followers included George Horne, whose *Commentary on the Psalms* (1771) read the psalms typologically as predictive of Christ, and Samuel Eyles Pierce, who published *The Book of Psalms, an Epitome of the Old Testament Scripture, Opened* (1817). Roman Catholic typologists included J. H. Newman both before and after his conversion to Rome in 1845. In the introduction to the response of Newman to Jowett's essay, the editor comments: "During the whole of his Anglican period and even during a great part of his Catholic career, Newman preferred by far the 'mystical,' 'allegorical,' 'sacramental,' 'figurative,' or 'spiritual' method of Bible interpretation to the 'critical and literal' (Seynaeve 1953, 311). For other instances of typological readings see Newman 1833e and 1850; see also Burtchaell 1969.

The fall of a "Protestant divine" refers to Samuel Davidson. In 1843 Davidson published *Sacred Hermeneutics Developed and Applied* in which he set out various methods of biblical interpretation, including an attack on pietist reliance on the inner light of faith, with an implied attack on plenary inspiration and typological interpretation. Then, in 1856, Davidson published a revision of the tenth edition of a leading typologist, T. H. Horne's *Introduction to the Critical Study . . . of the Holy Scriptures.* In fact, however, Davidson only completed a revision of the second volume, *The Text of the Old Testament,* which a recent critic calls "the most detailed information yet available in England about critical studies in Germany" (Rogerson 1984, 197; for Davidson see also Goodwin ¶6 and note). Davidson had been teaching at the Lancashire Independent College, but when questions were raised about his views on biblical inspiration he was forced to resign in an atmosphere of public controversy (see Rogerson 1984, 197–208). Davidson stayed with Jowett in 1866, and was considered by him and H. B. Wilson as a potential contributor to another volume of *Essays and Reviews* in 1870 (Letter 348). Jowett also defended Davidson in testimony to the Select Committee of the House of Lords on University Tests (1871) (see Abbott and Campbell 1899, 32).

21. The traditional seven liberal arts were divided into the *trivium* or three ways to knowledge in the medieval schools (the language arts of grammar, logic, and rhetoric) and the *quadrivium* (the mathematical arts of arithmetic, geometry, astronomy, and music). This organization of knowledge was under much revision since the Renaissance as Jowett's summary demonstrates (natural science, history, mathematics, and theology). On the trivium see ¶9.

The four unattributed quotations in this paragraph, "no error," "thousand times," "various theories," and "tend to sap," are conventional statements concerning biblical inerrancy, the hermeneut's limitations, the synoptic problem, and the erosion (particularly by higher-critical arguments) of the idea of inspiration in the NT. All derive from conservative interpretation of the Bible common to both the evangelical and the High Church parties in the C. of E. and among Nonconformists. Such comments are widespread, as in Christopher Wordsworth's *On the Inspiration of Holy Scripture* (1851), or William Lee's *The Inspiration of Holy Scripture* (1857), and in the periodical press: "'But no man will ever prove that they [the writers of the Gospels] have committed one positive and essential error even to a day or an hour" (Cairns 1852, 169). Inspiration was of major concern in the 1850s (see Jowett ¶s 14–15 and notes). Such views have a long history, as in Augustine's well-known letter to Jerome, attributing biblical contradictions to MS. errors, bad translations, or failure of the interpreter's understanding: "I have learned to yield this respect and honour only to the canonical books of Scripture; of these alone do I most firmly believe that the authors were completely free from error" (trans. J. G. Cunningham, *NPNF*1, 1:350 [Letter 82]).

The parallels and discrepancies between Kings and Chronicles were a commonplace in higher-critical commentaries, and included such passages as 2 Chron. 1:14–17 and 1 Kings 10:26–29; 2 Chron. 8:18 and 1 Kings 9:28; 2 Chron. 14:1–4 and 1 Kings 15:11–12, and so on. They were outlined in considerable detail by De Wette ([1817] 1843, 266–305). J. H. Newman attempted to reconcile them in *Tract LXXXV* (1838, 40–45); Harvey Goodwin commented on them in his Hulsean Lectures, *The Doctrines and Difficulties of the Christian Faith* (1856): "Of some alleged discrepancies. . . . we reply, that the text is corrupt" (247). These contradictions were also commented on extensively in Rawlinson's Bampton Lectures in 1859: "The discrepancies . . . have been largely . . . stated by De Wette. . . . Some, however, as the difference of numbers and names, cannot but remain discrepancies; in these we may be allowed to suspect corruptions of the original text, by carelessness in transcription, or by the insertion of marginal addenda" ([1859] 1860, 319–20).

The "failure of a prophecy" that is "never admitted" had been argued by the German higher critics and was repeated in W. R. Greg's *Creed of Christendom,* mentioning the Jeremiah and Amos passages cited by Jowett ([1848] 1875, 1:76). Jeremiah's prophecy of the death of Jehoiakim (36:30) agrees with Jer. 22:18–19, but not with 2 Kings 24:1–7, without arguing, as the harmonizers did, that his "sleeping with his fathers" implied his death, and not his burial since he was "cast out" and not regarded as part of the Davidic line. Isa. 23 is a collection of prophetic oracles concerning the destruction of Phoenicia, otherwise unattested. The Amos passage concerns a controversy between Amos and Amaziah, the priest of Bethel, concerning prophesying and relates to the allegation that Amos prophesied that King Jeroboam would die by the sword, while in 2 Kings 14:24–29 there is no mention of this form of his death. These discrepancies between prophecy and fulfilment were noted in Christopher Wordsworth's attack on Jowett (1862, 431–32). Samuel Wilberforce points out that in the Amos passage the allegation is put into the mouth of the false priest, and is not specified as a true prophecy of Amos (1861, 229; see also C. Wordsworth 1862, 435–36). The reference in Isa. 45:1 to Cyrus II, who began to rule after deposing Astyages of Media in 550 B.C.E., is anachronistic if it be assumed that the whole of Isa. was written by Isaiah of Jerusalem in the second half of the eighth century B.C.E.; otherwise it is prophetic of Cyrus's rule. On the controversy over the unity of Isaiah see Williams ¶14 and n. 57.

"The standard of primeval history" refers to the historical investigation of ancient peoples initiated by Barthold Georg Niebuhr. His *Römische Geschichte* (1812–31, 3 vols.; trans. Julius Hare and Connop Thirlwall, *History of Rome* [1828–32]) rejects the notion of the uniformity of human nature through time, and, by looking at the history of the ancient Roman peoples, especially at their institutions and customs rather than their lawgivers and military leaders as individuals, perceived history as analogous to stages of human development and growth. Niebuhr's views were influential on his friend Bunsen and were extended to the study of ancient Israel by Ewald, *Geschichte des Volkes Israël* (1843–59, 7 vols.; trans. R. Martineau and J. E. Carpenter, *History of the Israel* [1867–74, 5 vols.]), and were incorporated in England in the works of the liberal theologians and historians, Henry Hart Milman's *History of the Jews* (1829), Thomas Arnold's *The History of Rome* (1842, 3 vols.), and Connop Thirlwall's *History of Greece* (1835–44, 8 vols.). Jowett's negative reference to a "modern critical" standard of historical explanation is not to the German critical-historical method but to the "arbitrary standard" of the biblical harmonizers who rationalize discrepancies on the basis of biblical inerrancy rather than the historical investigation promoted by Niebuhr, Ewald, and Arnold.

Jowett also alludes to the "synoptic problem" concerning the first three gospels as synopsis of the life of Jesus. The problem is how to account for the close similarities in subject matter and phrasing as well as the striking differences among these three gospels. See Wilson ¶22 and n. 40 and Jowett ¶s 37 and 49.

The passages where Jesus speaks in John's gospel concerning his identity with God as "father" (e.g. John 16:28; 17:21) were used in the Ecumenical Councils to defend the notion of Christ united "as one substance" (*homoousios*) with the Father, as in the definition of Nicaea (325). For "God speaks not as man speaks" see Exod. 33:11; 1 Sam. 16:7.

Deist and atheistic accusations were often incurred by the Essayists and Reviewers for rejecting biblical inerrancy and for promoting German higher criticism, or "German infidelity," as Jowett already knew from attacks on *The Epistles of St. Paul.* These attacks were renewed after the publication of *Essays and Reviews* and during his trial in the Chancellor's Court at Oxford. Pattison was also charged with espousing the deist views he discussed in his essay.

22. For "great peacemaker" see Matt. 5:9.

Both evangelical and High Church parties in the C. of E. generally accepted some notion of verbal inspiration (see Jowett ¶15 and notes), and with it several related concepts: the "authority" of the Bible in matters of belief and action, the inerrancy of the Bible, and its infallibility. However, Broad Church biblical critics, following some of the Reformation leaders like Martin Luther, and German higher criticism of the previous 100 years, qualified these concepts in various ways. Nonconformists' views of the Bible were very close to the orthodoxy of the C. of E. Similarly, the Roman Catholic Church held, dogmatically since the Council of Trent (Session 4, 8 Apr. 1546, "Decree concerning the Canonical Scriptures"; see Schaff [1877] 1983, 2:79–83), that the Bible was inspired, although with the condition that it was the "possession" of the church, its only valid interpreter.

In literary history, inspiration has a venerable but troubled ancestry. Inspiration is a gift from the gods (*Odyssey* 23:347–48), and Homer, Hesiod, Pindar, and other poets invoke divine inspiration for the poet and the poem. Plato, however, says that poetic inspiration is a divine possession or madness, and so poets are a threat to the education and stability of the ideal republic (*Laws* 719c; *Symposium* 197a; *Phaedrus* 244–45; *Republic* 398a; and the whole of the *Ion*). In the Introduction to his translation of Plato's *Ion*, Jowett connects the poet to divine inspiration and to genius and madness: "The poet is the inspired interpreter of the God. . . . The elements of a true theory of poetry are contained in the notion that the poet is inspired. Genius is often said to be unconscious, or spontaneous, or a gift of nature: that genius is akin to madness is a popular aphorism of modern times [John Dryden, *Absalom and Achitophel* (1681) 1:163–64] (Jowett [1871] 1875, 1:239–41). Divine inspiration for the Hebrew poets, especially David, and the prophets (see Joel 2:28–30; Ezek. 2:1–10) is alluded to by Jerome and Augustine. Divine inspiration in oracular poetry recurs from Bede's account of Caedmon (1969, 414–20; bk. 4, chap. 24) through Milton to S. T. Coleridge ("The Aeolian Harp") and W. Wordsworth (the conclusion to *The Recluse*).

The notion that inspiration arises from innate talent or "genius" rather than from a divine effect is a rival theory. In the neo-classical period, "genius" was often appealed to as a ground for poetic authority, as in Edward Young's *Conjectures upon Original Composition* (1759), and in the romantic period Coleridge discusses the concept of "genius" in *Biographia Literaria* ([1817] 1983, 7:30–47; chap. 2). For the roles of imagination and genius in romantic literary theory see Abrams 1953, 188–93; and Harding 1985.

23. For "take care of words" see Goethe's *Faust* (1808; pt. 1, line 1990), where Mephistopheles' advice to the student who wishes to study theology is "*haltet Euch an Worte!*" (Stick to the word). Blaise Pascal attacked the Jesuits in his series of anonymously published letters, *Les Lettres provinciales* (1656–57; The provincial letters) in defense of the leader of the Jansenists at Port-Royal, Antoine Arnauld. Arnauld was attacked by the Jesuits and was eventually condemned as a heretic, though he was defended by the Dominicans. In the first of the letters, Pascal defends Arnauld, showing how he, the Jesuits, and the Dominicans agree and differ concerning words, meanings, misinterpretations, and condemnations. Jowett made MS. notes on Pascal's *Provincial Letters* (Balliol MS. Jowett H21 fols. 6^v–19^v). Jowett's phrase anticipates the March Hare's advice to Alice: "You should say what you mean," and Alice's reply, "I mean what I say—that's the same thing, you know" ([1865] 1992, 55); and the Duchess's moral "'Take care of the sense and the sounds will take care of themselves'" (70). For "heal the wounds" see Jer. 30:17; for "skin and film," Shakespeare, *Hamlet* 3.4.147.

24. Jowett's "distinctions of meaning" concerning inspiration set out "gradations" in contemporary debate. They depend upon whether the divine or the human aspects in the writing of the Bible received the greater emphasis. In general Jowett contrasts the notion of plenary inspiration (allowing for some degrees of modification in the light of recent biblical scholarship, but usually extended to include verbal inspiration) with a more radical view of inspiration (resulting from the effects of the critical-historical approach to the Bible). Plenary inspiration is the doctrine that there is a full, complete, and equal inspiration of the Bible in all of its parts, that the one author of the Bible is God, that the focus of inspiration is the writing of the Bible by the prophets, evangelists, and apostles, and other writers, and that these writers are inspired in their writing. This view was widely held at Jowett's time by Anglicans both High Church and Evangelical), Nonconformists, Calvinists, Lutherans, and Roman Catholics (see Burtchaell 1969). Plenary inspiration was usually assumed to include biblical infallibility.

The unqualified equation of infallibility with verbal inspiration, however, was denied as the exclusive view of the C. of E. during the Arches trial by Phillimore and John Duke Coleridge, two of the lawyers acting against Rowland Williams. Those acting for Williams, Deane and Stephen, drew on much more liberal views of inspiration, asserting that the C. of E. had avoided giving any precise definition of the doctrine. Thirty years later, Jowett's student William Sanday identified plenary inspiration narrowly in what was then called a "high" mode, as the traditional theory: "The Bible as a whole and in all its parts was the Word of God and as such . . . was endowed with all the perfections of that Word. . . . All parts of it were equally authoritative and in history as well as in doctrine it was exempt from error" ([1893] 1896, 392). "Exempt from error" allowed for taking into account some forms of critical reading of the Bible while still arguing for plenary inspiration. Pusey had declared in favor of plenary inspiration in *An Historical Enquiry into the Probable Causes of the Rationalist Character Lately Predominant in the Theology of Germany*, distinguishing between what, on the one hand, was necessary to be revealed in which the writers were free from error and what, on the other hand, consisted of matters of customs, earlier religious traditions, and dates in which the writers' "former knowledge" was neither "obliterated" nor made "perfect" (1828, 66–87). J. H. Newman, in response to Jowett's essay, sets out the Roman Catholic position on plenary inspiration and inerrancy in detail, quoting from the major patristic and dogmatic authorities ([1861] 1979).

The first five of Jowett's eleven theories may be included within the category of plenary inspiration; the final six allude to more radical theories; however, his criteria for the designation of these theories are often overlapping, and different writers on inspiration can be identified with more than one of them. Jowett's contemporaries also disagreed about the classification of the various kinds of inspiration. At times Jowett opposes some aspect of a theory of inspiration to juxtapose different views (theories three and four, eight and nine). Some (one, two, four, and eleven) draw on the distinctions of late medieval controversy; all can be sanctioned with some reference to patristic, medieval, and Reformation precedents (set out elaborately in William Lee 1857, 395–409). Popular handbooks of theology of Jowett's day trace some of the same connections, but are far from consistent or systematic. See, for instance, Buck 1851, 382–86; Hook 1852, 578–80; and Kitto 1864, 2:388–95. The replies to Jowett on this topic are no more systematic, reiterating the notion of plenary inspiration, deriving it from scriptural evidence, patristic precedent, and Reformation principles (Browne 1862, 287–321; C. Wordsworth 1862, 409–98). The topic was one of contemporary interest, and is variously described as having "ceased to be a controversy among the orthodox" (Cairns 1852, 140) or the subject of "controversy among orthodox divines" (Kitto 1864, 391). As well as William Lee's book (1857), other treatments include S. T. Coleridge [1840] 1988; Gaussen [1842] 1888; Shirley 1847; Christopher Wordsworth [1848] 1851; Cairns 1852, citing 20 contemporary studies; Macnaught 1856; Rawlinson [1859] 1860; J. H. Newman [1861] 1979; Hannah 1863; Row 1864; J. H. Newman [1884] 1967; and Sanday [1893] 1896. In 1893 Leo XIII issued his encyclical *Providentissimus Deus* (The most provident God) on biblical inspiration. Recent treatments of inspiration include Vawter 1972; Achtemeier 1980; Abraham 1981; and Trembath 1987; for the debates concerning inspiration and biblical veracity in nineteenth-century Britain see Cameron 1987.

Jowett's theories can be set out in his order:

(1) "Inspiration of superintendence." The phrase refers in theological use to the explicit guidance conferred by the Holy Spirit on the minds of the writers of the Bible. Hence, John Goodwin, Nonconformist divine, in Πλήρωμα τό πσευματικως, *or Being Filled with the Spirit* (1670), maintains that the apostles and evangelists write "by virtue of a certain superintendence and instigation of the Spirit of God" ([1670] 1867, 83). Abraham Rees's *Cyclopaedia* (1819) defines "the "inspiration of *superintendency*" as that in which "God does so influence and direct the mind of any person, as to keep him more secure from error in some various and complex discourse, than he would have been merely by the use of his natural faculties. . . . The New Testament was written by a superintendent inspiration: for without this the discourses and doctrines of Christ could not have been faithfully recorded by the evangelists and apostles" (s.v. "Inspiration"). Daniel Wilson, noting that the biblical writers were preserved from positive error, defines inspiration of superintendence as "that watchful care which preserved generally from anything being put down derogatory to the revelation with which it was connected" (1828, 1:508). A variant of this notion was advanced by H. P. Liddon in a sermon on "The Inspiration of Selection" who argues that the biblical writers were enabled to select at the prompting of the Holy Spirit such materials from earlier documents or traditions as were appropriate to the composition before them (in Sanday ([1893] 1896, 420–23).

(2) "Inspiration of suggestion." To Reformation theologians, the theory of "suggestion" clarified the doctrine plenary inspiration. Hence, two related aspects of the "inspiration of suggestion" are implied, an inspiration of the writers according to the "suggestion" of the Holy Spirit with respect to things, concepts, or events (*suggestio rerum*) and a "suggestion" of words (*suggestio verborum*) whereby not only the minds of the writers and the ideas in the text are so inspired, but also the words of the text. Philo and Justin Martyr attributed inspiration to a similar kind of Platonic possession (for Philo see William Lee 1857, 64–67, 418–23; for Justin, see *Dialogue with Trypho*, trans. G. Reith; chap. 7, *ANF* 1:198; and *Hortatory Address*, trans. Marcus Dods; chaps. 2–8, *ANF* 1:273–76), points made by Ellicott in his attack on Jowett (1861, 408); Luther refers to the biblical writers as the "channels" of the Spirit. Similarly, the First Vatican Council maintained that God was the author of the Bible, and that the writers wrote "by the inspiration of the Holy Ghost" (Decree of the Council of Trent, 8 Apr. 1546 and the First Vatican Council, 1870; see Schaff [1877] 1983, 2:79–80, 241–42). Rees maintains that there is an inspiration of suggestion "when the use of the faculties is superseded, and God does, as it were, speak directly to the mind, making fresh discoveries to it as it could not otherwise have obtained, and dictating the very words in which such discoveries are to be communicated, as if they are designed as a message to others" (1819, s.v. "Inspiration"). In this context Daniel Wilson gives his definition: "By the Inspiration of *Suggestion* is meant, such communications of the Holy Spirit as suggested and dictated minutely every part of the truths delivered" (1828, 1:508). This view, a variant of verbal inspiration (theory five), was elaborated by the Lutheran dogmaticians of the seventeenth century in their debates with the Jesuits (see Preus [1953] 1957).

(3) "Consistent . . . with falling into error." This theory, sometimes called the accommodation theory, while asserting the efficacy of plenary inspiration, places emphasis upon the positive illumination of the biblical writers but still makes allowances for human frailty, tolerating human lapses, infelicities of expression, or inexact wording. In particular, it argues for the historicity of revelation, that since the Bible is a document to be understood by different peoples at different times, with particular intellectual and spiritual accomplishments and predispositions, the Bible is accommodated to those thought forms, modes of expression, and human limitations to enable comprehension. This notion dates from

Origen and John Chrysostom (see Jack B. Rogers and McKim 1979, 9–11, 98–100). At the beginning of the period of historical criticism it was revived, as in J. S. Semler: "That teachers, after the undeniable example of Jesus and the apostles, condescended to their listeners' mode of thought, or accommodated themselves to their own circumstances, is historically certain" (cited in Baird 1992, 124); Semler did not hold, however, that all of the Bible was wholly or equally inspired, and so his view overlaps with Jowett's theory ten. In England accommodation was advocated by Thomas Arnold ([1832] 1844, 2:382–405), overlapping with theory six.

(4) "Inspiration which would have prevented him from erring." This inspiration of direction indicates what the writer is to insert or what to omit and is defined by Daniel Wilson: "[By] the Inspiration of *Direction* is meant of such assistance as left the writers to describe the matter revealed in their own way, directing only the mind in the exercise of its powers" (1828, 1:508). Stressing the opposite of Jowett's third theory, this view asserts that the writers of the Bible were restrained negatively, so that they were prevented from error, but otherwise acted as free agents. Thomas Aquinas, for instance, distinguishes between "*direct* [inspiration], which is to be found where doctrinal and moral truths are directly taught, and the *indirect,* which appears in historical passages, whence the doctrinal and moral can only be indirectly evolved by the use of allegorical interpretation" (*EB,* 14:647). Thomas writes: "Many of the [writers of the sacred books] wrote more often of those things which can be known by human reason, not as it were from the mouth of God, but out of their own mouths, and yet with the help of a divine light" ([1265] 1962–64, 45:77). According to the *EB,* "This view has the support of such names as Erasmus, Hugo Grotius, Richard Baxter, W. Paley and J. J. I. von Döllinger" (14:647).

(5) "Verbal organic inspiration." This theory of verbal inspiration, or "mechanical" dictation (*OED,* "organic," meaning 2b), asserts that the words and letters ("literal" inspiration) of the texts in their original languages and forms were divinely inspired in their totality and parts and that the writers were the passive agents of divine communication or dictation: "The writers of the books of the Bible were God's pens rather than His penmen; every word was given them by God" (*EB,* 14:646; s.v. "Inspiration"). Verbal inspiration is closely linked to two related concepts, inerrancy and infallibility: inerrancy, in the Calvinist tradition and its successors, refers to the notion that the "original" autographs (papyri, skins, clay tablets) were without error in any respect (Geisler 1979, 267–304); "infallibility" refers to the unfailing certainty that the Bible does not err in matters concerning revelation. However, the use of these two terms remains controversial in the late twentieth century (see S. T. Davis 1977 and the 1978 "Chicago Statement on Biblical Inerrancy," drawn up by largely American fundamentalists maintaining verbal organic inspiration, repr. in Geisler 1979, 493–502). "Inerrancy" is used in Roman Catholic documents to define the truth claims of the Bible, while "infallibility" is reserved for the teaching authority of the church expressed through the pope (see Mangenot 1923; Courtade 1945, 520–58; Burtchaell 1969, especially 121–229). As Jowett points out below (¶20), the "earlier confessions of the reformed faith," such as the Augsburg Confession (1530), Zwingli's Sixty-Seven Articles (1523), the Lutheran Formula of Concord (1580, which refers to the Bible as a "rule and norm" in the first clause of the opening epitome), the Anglican Thirty-Nine Articles of Religion (1562), and the Reformed Canons of Dort (1619) do not contain clauses explicitly referring to the inspiration of the Bible, though they usually refer to the canonicity of the received books and to the Bible in general as the word of God. The later confessional statements of belief from the Evangelical Reformed churches usually begin with clauses concerning the inspiration of the Bible. The earliest to do so, the Belgic Confession of the Dutch Reformed Church (1561), for instance, refers to the Bible as "written with his [God's] own finger" (Exod. 31:18) as "this infallible rule" (articles 3 and 7); the Second Helvetic Confession (1566) contains statements on biblical inspiration in its first chapter. By the mid-seventeenth century the controversy with the deists ensured that doctrinal formulations contained explicit references to the inspiration of the Bible. Hence, the Presbyterian Westminster Confession (1647) asserts "the infallible truth, and divine authority" of the Bible (chap. 1, sec. 7). The Swiss Calvinist Helvetic Consensus Formula (1675) goes so far as to assert that even the vowel-pointings of the Hebrew Bible, introduced into the Masoretic text by Jewish scribes of the 5th to 10th centuries, centuries after the first manuscripts were produced, were part of the verbal inspiration (articles 1–3). See Schaff [1877] 1983, 3:385, 388, 603; 1:487; Vawter 1972, 81. Among the German conservative biblical critics, E. W. Hengstenberg maintained both verbal inspiration and inerrancy, and his position was frequently appealed to by both evangelical and High Church critics in England (see Baird 1992, 279–82).

(6) "Inspiration which acts through the character of the sacred writer." This theory, a variant of theory eleven, is usually referred to as the dynamic theory: "The writers of the Bible had their spiritual faculties quickened and enlarged by the Holy Ghost, without losing their literary freedom or the peculiarities of their style" (Francis J. Hall 1933, 30). The theory is based on a comment of St. Augustine in *City of God*: "The wisdom of God . . . insinuates itself into holy souls, and makes them the friends of God and His prophets, and noiselessly informs them of his works. They are taught also by the angels of God"

(trans. Marcus Dods *NPNF*1 2:206, [bk. 14, chap. 4]). This view also overlaps with the notion of accommodation, and is sometimes linked to theory three. Hence, Thomas Arnold writes: "When God chooses a being of finite knowledge to be the medium of his revelations, it is at once understood that the faculties of this being are left in their natural state, except so far as regards the especial message with which he is entrusted. But, perhaps, we do not enough consider how in the very message itself, there must be a mixture of accommodation to our ignorance" ([1832] 1844, 2:383).

(7) "Inspiration which absolutely communicates the fact to be revealed or statement to be made." This theory stresses the act and fact of communication, a kind of reception theory, whereby the Bible communicates revelation to an inspired reader or hearer of the text: hence the inspiration of the text is ratified in the reader. This theory received a good deal of attention from Reformation thinkers. For instance, Calvin in the *Institutes of the Christian Religion* discusses the notion of the inward testimony of the Holy Spirit ([1536] 1957, 1:171) that makes the Bible into an instrument for the salvation of an individual. S. T. Coleridge too refers to the fact that the "words of the Bible find me at greater depths of my being" ([1840] 1988, 27). But such a view remains relatively silent concerning the means by which the text itself is inspired and allows for a good deal of latitude in relating it to historical and critical data. It is sometimes called the "vital" theory (*EB*, 14:647).

(8) "Inspiration which does not supersede the ordinary knowledge of human events." This "limited inspiration," or partial inspiration, was first elaborated in the doctrinal controversies between the Jesuits and Lutherans in the seventeenth century. It was advocated by the Spanish Jesuit Francisco de Suarez, who argued that the writers were inspired concerning doctrine but were not specially inspired concerning general human knowledge, though they were preserved from error. Such a view had the polemical purpose of relating the notion of the inspiration of the Bible as the possession of the church to its unwritten tradition that interpreted the Bible authoritatively. The conservative Lutherans opposed the Jesuit arguments with the notion of *sola scriptura* (scripture alone as the guide to salvation), linked to the theory of suggestion, Jowett's theory two (see Preus [1953] 1957, 35–36; Geisler 1979, 279–81). Incorporating the notion of the development of doctrine and tradition into his theory of inspiration, J. H. Newman advocates similar distinctions between divine inspiration in terms of its relation to matters of faith and morals, rather than to its means of using human knowledge. Newman argues: "By *obiter dicta* [Lat. things said by the way] [are] meant phrases, clauses, or sentences in Scripture about matters of mere fact, which, as not relating to faith and morals, may without violence be referred to the human element in composition" ([1884] 1967, 141). This view overlaps with theory four to some extent.

(9) "Inspiration which demands infallibility in matters of doctrine, but allows for mistakes in fact." This essential, or doctrinal, theory argues that there are differences in the Bible between levels and purposes of discourse and that the writers were inspired to write infallible doctrine and morality, while those matters and passages concerned with other matters are not inspired; similarly, the particular form of their writings is attributable to human choice. The problem with this theory, of course, is how to distinguish the essential doctrine and morality from the rest. One form of this argument was to relate the biblical writings to their cultures and to seek the reconciliation of discrepancies in cultural factors, locating inspiration in the integrity of the theological perspective.

(10) "Inspiration which recognizes only its supernatural and prophetic character." This view, like theory nine, emphasizes the divine, rather than the human, side of inspiration, stressing the divine function in revelation and in prophecy but says nothing concerning human agency or instrumentality. Hence, some kinds of biblical writings can be referred to as inspired, for which the term is reserved, while others are not inspired. Michaelis held this view, following some remarks of Eusebius that distinguished between the undoubted authority of some books of the Bible, the doubtful ones, and the spurious. He only discusses the first category in his commentary, applying it to the four gospels, Acts, all the epistles of Paul, the first epistle of Peter and the first of John ([1750] 1793–1801, 1:23–30). Sanday differentiates different kinds of inspiration in the various books of the OT: "There are some books in which the Divine element is at the *maximum* and others in which it is at the *minimum*" ([1893] 1896, 398).

(11) "Inspiration which regards [the writers of the NT] as equally inspired in their writings and in their lives." This theory is the inspiration of elevation. Daniel Wilson defines it: "The inspiration of *Elevation* added a greater strength and vigour to the efforts of the mind, than the writers could otherwise have attained" (1828, 1:508). This view is sometimes identified as one of the subcategories of plenary inspiration.

Jowett omits two significant theories of inspiration: first, that the writers of the Bible have an inspiration that is not different in kind from other writers but only in degree; and second, that the biblical writers had no divine inspiration whatsoever. On the first, he comments on Gal. 4:20 in *The Epistles of St. Paul*: "Whatever difference there is between him [St. Paul] and them [the Christian Alexandrian writers], or between Philo and the Christian fathers as interpreters of Scripture, is not one of kind but of degree. A truer difference is made by the noble spirit of the Apostle shining through the elements of the law in which he clothes his meaning" ([1855] 1859, 1:345). As an example of the second position, Schleiermacher held that the Holy Spirit was the common spirit active in the early Christian community and that the Bible is an instance of the spirit's work in expressing the psychological life and experience of that community ([1821–22] 1928, 597–603).

Preaching at St. Mary-the-Virgin University Church in Oxford, John William Burgon attacked Jowett's essay for a defective view of plenary inspiration: "The Bible is none other than the voice of Him that sitteth upon the throne. Every book of it, every chapter of it, every verse of it, every word of it, every syllable of it, (where are we to stop?) every letter of it, is the direct utterance of the Most High. The Bible is none other than the Word of God, not some part of it more, some part of it less, but all alike the utterance of Him who sitteth upon the throne, faultless, unerring, supreme" (1861, 89). His statement was described by contemporaries as smiting the Philistines "with the jawbone of an ass" (Neil 1963, 283). The same passage from Burgon was quoted by Colenso in *The Pentateuch and the Book of Joshua Critically Examined* to explain the doctrinal position he was reared in and against which he was rebelling: "Petty contradictions met me, which seemed to my reason to conflict with the notion of the absolute historical veracity of every part of Scripture, and which, as I felt, *in the study of any other book*, we should honestly treat as errors or misstatements" (1862–79, 1:6).

In his defense of Rowland Williams in the Court of Arches, James Fitzjames Stephen outlined three views of inspiration that simplify Jowett's eleven, focusing on the major positions. The first is "that the Bible is absolutely true all through, the consonants as well as the vowels, and the force of the vowel points as well as the consonants" (James Fitzjames Stephen 1862, 182). This view is that of the Helvetic Confession, John William Burgon, and Jowett's theories one, two, and five. The second view is "that if they do not believe in the absolute inspiration of a specific book; then they believe in the total infallibility of a particular book and its partial inspiration. That is to say, a part of the Bible is inspired, a part of the Bible is not inspired; and that part of the Bible which is not inspired is infallible, because it has got mixed up with that part which is inspired" (James Fitzjames Stephen 1862, 183). The view is, according to Stephen, that of Daniel Wilson, Reginald Heber, Thomas Hartwell Horne, as well as Jowett's theories four, six, and eight. The third view is "the theory of partial inspiration without infallibility as to the rest. . . . Inspired men are not of necessity infallible because of their inspiration." Stephen argues that this is the view of Warburton, Whewell, and Sumner, as well as Tillotson, Whately, and Alford: "They say that the language of Scripture upon scientific subjects is to be interpreted not by its plain and literal meaning, but by the aid of science; that you are to arrive at what the Bible means by finding out what science says" (James Fitzjames Stephen 1862, 184). This theory includes the accommodation theory (Jowett's theory three) and also approximates Jowett's theories nine and ten.

25. The word "inspiration" occurs only once in the AV, a translation of the single Greek usage in the NT at 2 Tim. 3:16. "Inspiration" derives from the Latin verb *inspiro* used to translate various Hebrew and Greek terms in the Vulgate (Gen. 2:7; Wisd. 15:11; Sirach 4:12; 2 Tim. 3:16; 2 Pet. 1:21) and the noun *inspiratio* (2 Sam. 22:16; Job 32:8; Ps. 18:15; Acts 17:25). The Greek term, Θεόπνευστος (*Theopneustos*), derives from Θεός (*Theos*, God) and πνέω (*pneo*, to breathe). Warfield, like Jowett, alludes to the problems of translation in the AV:

> This phrase [inspired by God] is the rendering of the Latin *divinitas inspirata*, restored from the Wyclif ("Al Scripture of God ynspyrid is . . . ") and Rhemish ("All Scripture inspired of God is . . .") versions of the Vulg[ate].The Greek word does not even mean, as [AV] translated it, "given by inspiration of God," although that rendering (inherited from Tyndale "All Scripture given by inspiration of God is . . .") is a somewhat clumsy, perhaps, but not misleading, paraphrase of the Greek term in the theological language of the day. The Greek term has, however, nothing to say of *in*spiring or of *in*spiration: it speaks only of "aspiring" or "aspiration." What it says of Scripture is, not that it is "breathed into by God" or is the product of the divine "inbreathing" into its human authors, but that it is breathed out by God, "God-breathed," the product of the creative breath of God. In a word, what is declared by this fundamental passage is simply that the Scriptures are a divine product, without any indication of how God has operated in producing them (1982, 840).

S. T. Coleridge also points to the lack of foundation for higher views of inspiration in the biblical writers: "I cannot find any such claim [to authority], as the Doctrine in question [inspiration] supposes. . . . [They] in all points express themselves as sober minded and veracious writers under ordinary circumstances are known to do" ([1840] 1988, 29). While Jowett's critics agree with him that the writers of the NT declare themselves liable to human frailty (as in Acts 14:15, James 3:2), they "flatly deny" his claim that there is no supernatural view of inspiration in the NT. Among the test passages cited against Jowett to support traditionalist views of inspiration and inerrancy were John 21:24–25; 1 Cor. 2:13; and 2 Pet. 1:19–21 (see C. Wordsworth 1862, 437–40).

The passage from ¶15, "Nor for any of the higher.... error or infirmity," was cited as "false and dangerous" in the Synodical Condemnation of *Essays and Reviews* on 21 June 1864 for rejecting the plenary inspiration of the Bible (*Chronicle* 1859–64:1864, Session 66, 1659).

Opposite this passage on inspiration, Gladstone comments in the margin of his copy of *Essays and Reviews* in St. Deiniol's Library: "Surely there is necessity to examine into a deduction from Inspiration when it may be lawful to question Inspiration itself."

26. Paul frequently refers to his infirmities (Rom. 8:26; 2 Cor. 1:9; 2:13; 11:30; 12:5; Gal. 4:13). In *The Epistles of St. Paul* Jowett discusses these frailties in a separate section "On the Character of Paul" ([1855] 1859, 1:351–69). On the second coming of Christ, see Jowett "The Belief in the Coming of Christ in the Apostolical Age" ([1855] 1859, 1:108–24), where he quotes a number of Pauline passages on the immediacy of the parousia, and on its delay, discrepancies which challenge the alleged "infallibility of the Apostle . . . respecting the end of the world" (120). For "with authority" see Acts 26:12.

Christopher Wordsworth attacks Jowett for his view that "St. Paul therefore, was in error when he wrote . . . '*we*, who are alive and remain till the Coming of the Lord, shall not prevent [that is, go before] them that are asleep' [1 Thess, 4:15]. This also is no new objection: it has been urged by the same sceptical writer already cited [W. R. Greg], and unhappily it has derived undue importance from the name of a celebrated person [Thomas Arnold] who, if his life had been spared would probably have regretted and retracted some of his rash and unsound assertions on such matters as these" (1862, 441).

27. Jowett specifies well-known differences in the synoptic gospels, giving references for some of them. In Matt. 1:1–17 the genealogy of Jesus is traced as a royal succession through Joseph, but in Luke 3:23–38, where the much longer genealogy of the "supposed" son of Joseph is interpreted by the early church as a personal connection through Mary. It was argued that Joseph was the legal son of Heli (Luke 3:23) because he married Heli's daughter, Mary. Matt. 27:44 tells of the "thieves blaspheming" while Luke 23:39–43 tells of the "penitent thief." Differences concerning the day and time of the crucifixion (in Matthew 26:17–19; 27:45; Mark 14:12–16; 15:33; and Luke 22:7–13; 23:44, as opposed to John 19:19–37) point to the fact that "the time-note is inexact, in that the day on which they sacrificed the Paschal lamb was not the first day of the Feast of Unleavened Bread, but the day preceding. . . . Apart from [these passages], nothing in Mark or Matthew would lead us to think that the Last Supper was a Passover meal; and in the Fourth Gospel it is explicitly laid on the evening before the Passover" (Beare 1962, 223). Responding in detail to Jowett's argument, Christopher Wordsworth attempts to harmonize each of Jowett's points of difference arguing that "Schleiermacher, De Wette, Strauss, Bruno Bauer, and others . . . have made the same objections before him" (1862, 446). For a contemporary account of some of these problems see *JBC*, 451 (on John 13:1). For the anointing at Bethany see Matt. 26:6–13; Mark 14:3–9; Luke 7:36–50; and John 12:1–8, where the episode is set six days before the passover.

28. Discrepancies in the gospel accounts have been variously reconciled, from the construction of a continuous narrative in the *Diatesseron* of Tatian (c. 150) to D. F. Strauss's exploitation of the differences in *Leben Jesu* ([1835] 1846) and the efforts of scholars to harmonize discrepancies. In 1776 J. J. Griesbach first set out the synoptic gospels in parallel without reconciling their differences. The "gospel parallels" set out the synoptics in parallel columns to show parallel passages while allowing the differences to become immediately visible. The standard edition of the Gospel parallels (in Greek) is Huck 1892; the RSV parallel of the synoptics is Throckmorton 1979. For "letter and spirit" see 2 Cor. 3:6. The fulfilling of the OT in the NT is mentioned 16 times in Matthew, 4 in Mark, 8 in Luke, and 10 in John.

29. According to the *New Catholic Encyclopedia*, "Infallibility . . . is a positive perfection, ruling out the possibility of error and entailing necessarily a central fidelity to the Christian revelation in the doctrine taught and accepted by the Church. Infallibility is always primordially a gift of the Holy Spirit; although it is not to be confused with prophetic or Biblical inspiration" (s.v. "Infallibility").

Jowett's self-referential definition of inspiration as "the idea of Scripture" that "must be gathered from the knowledge of it" is based on such passages as 2 Tim. 3:16, 17 and Rom. 15:4, a view elaborated by Augustine in *On Christian Doctrine* (trans. J. F. Shaw, *NPNF1* 2:539; bk. 2, chap. 9). Compare Thomas à Kempis in *The Imitation of Christ*: "All [sacred] scripture ought to be read in the same spirit in which it was written" ([1471] 1874, 15). As a principle of biblical interpretation, the same rule was set out by Spinoza: "Scriptural interpretation proceeds by the examination of Scripture, and inferring the intention of its authors as a legitimate conclusion from its fundamental principles. By working in this manner everyone will always advance without danger of error—that is, if they admit no principles for interpreting Scripture, and discussing its contents save such as they find in Scripture itself. . . . Therefore the knowledge of all these—that is, of nearly the whole contents of Scripture, must be sought from Scripture alone. . . . Our knowledge of Scripture must then be looked for in Scripture only" ([1670] 1951, 99–100). Among Jowett's contemporaries, R. C. Trench argued that Augustine's view of inspiration functions "according to the analogy of faith; in other words, that no single Scripture there shall receive such an explanation as shall put them in contradiction with the whole body and complex of doctrinal truth drawn from other Scriptures" (Trench 1851, 31). See also Jowett ¶84 and note.

30. The Book of Esther is in the form of a novella; the Song of Solomon, a series of songs. The Gospel of St. John differs radically from the other three gospels: there is no sermon on the mount, nor does he tell his parables, or give moral or religious teaching, but delivers discourses on his messianic claims or debates with his opponents. The "mixed . . . characters" of the OT include David, King of Israel from c. 1010 to 970 B.C.E., whose story is recounted in 1 Sam. 16:13–1 Kings 2:12. Although he was the anointed king, he ordered the death of Uriah the Hittite in order to commit adultery with Bathsheba. The "actions at variance" include the apparently arbitrary and malevolent orders of God in the OT, such as the command that Abraham slay his son Isaac (Gen. 22) or the slaughter of entire peoples adjacent to the Israelites, such as the Canaanites (Num. 21:1–3) and the Midianites (Num. 31:1–20). Both Job and Ecclesiastes are forms of wisdom literature which present complex questions to which only partial answers are given. The Book of Job addresses the problem of human suffering by means of the story of undeserved sufferings of Job before a silent and inactive God. Ecclesiastes presents the wise "Preacher, son of David" (Eccles. 1:1) who questions the meaning of life and finds it "vanity." Kings and Chronicles give accounts of the Kingdom of Israel which contradict each other on certain matters of "fact"; similar contradictions are also inscribed in the Gospels (for citations see ¶13 and note).

To maintain the inerrancy of the Bible, many scholars have reconciled such contradictions. For instance, Horne reconciles 2 Kings 24:8 and 2 Chron. 36:9 by positing a joint rule succeeded by sole rule for Jehoiachim ([1818] 1828, 2:509–10).

Jowett alludes to various scholars' resolution of Paul's apparent incongruities of grammar, syntax, and contradictions in meaning by means of their emendations, alternative readings, or glossings. See, for instance, his lengthy discussion of the Greek article as a part of speech in relation to Lachmann's emendations for Rom. 6:16–20 ([1855] 1859, 2:199–201); or, on "those who refer the ambiguous clause to God and not to Christ it is argued . . . that the grammar is awkward and defective" in Rom. 9:6 ([1855] 1859, 2:276–78).

Critical-historical discussions of the authorship, authenticity, and theology of Paul's epistles began with Johann Salomo Semler's commentary on Corinthians (1776) that "swept scholars of all persuasions and schools into the debate on . . . Pauline letters for the next two hundred years" (Betz 1985, 4). In these debates the commentaries of Stanley and Jowett took a more liberal stance, but even the conservative C. J. Ellicott notes Paul's "many peculiarities of language, and many singularities of expression, and . . . an inter-dependence of thought that is noticeable and characteristic" (1856, xvi–xvii).

H. Richard Niebuhr defines "progressive revelation," demonstrating the internalization of the process as guaranteed by the "heart": "A revelation which furnishes the practical reason with a starting point for the interpretation of past, present and future is subject to progressive validation. The more apparent it becomes that the past can be understood, recovered and integrated by means of a reasoning starting with revelation, the more contemporary experience is enlightened and response to new situations aptly guided by this imagination of the heart, the more a prophecy based on this truth is fulfilled, the surer our conviction of its reality becomes" (1941, 132; see 132–37). On progressive revelation and Thomas Arnold's doctrine of accommodation, see ¶22 and note.

For "Moses because . . ." see Matt. 19:8; for "proverb in the house of Israel," Ezek. 12:23; 18:3.

For a contemporaneous discussion of "moral objections" to scriptural injunctions see Horne [1818] 1828, 2:519–34, wherein are listed a number of "seeming contradictions to morality" in the Bible and their resolutions. In each case, Horne tries to demonstrate "the wide difference which subsists between antient and modern manners," or he argues that the immoral actions and characters of the Bible are "by no means proposed for our imitation" (2:519). For "imperfect narratives" see Horne [1828] 1828, 507–12; for "imperfect grammar," Horne [1818] 1828, 181–82.

Aristotelian logic takes the form of the syllogism, consisting of a major and minor premise, and a conclusion. The logic is found in six extant treatises, known primarily by their Latin titles: *Categoriae* (Predicates), *De interpretatione* (On interpretation), *Analytica priora* and *posteriora* (Prior and posterior analytics), *Topica* (Topics), and *De sophisticis elenchis* (Refutations in the manner of the sophists). "Attic Greek" is the dialect of ancient Athens, the literary language of classical Greece.

31. Jowett raises a second problem concerning inspiration, that it must also conform to history and science. He alludes to the geocentric/heliocentric controversies at the time of Galileo and to the controversies between Genesis and geology in his own day (the main topic of Goodwin).

On the general point of the relations between theology and science, William Whewell argues that "the phrases which are employed in Scripture respecting astronomical facts, are not to be made use of to guide our scientific opinions" (1837, 1:401–2). Whewell also refers to the two instances mentioned by Jowett, the heliocentric demonstrations of Copernicus and Galileo (1837, 1:392–95) and the relation of the record of geology, the "vast epochs" of the age of the earth, and a literalist Mosaic cosmogony to Ussher's conventional date of creation (1837,

3:passim).

For "ways of God to man" see Milton, *Paradise Lost* 1.26.

32. Jowett's advocacy of the inductive method in science and theology is based on Francis Bacon (whom Jowett mentions four times) and was a matter of contemporary discussion in the writings of such theologians and scientists as William Whewell.

Bacon discusses the relations between philosophy and theology in *Novum Organum* (1620), especially in Aphorism 65 ([1620] 1855, 36–37). In *The Philosophy of the Inductive Sciences* (1840) Whewell's task is to be "an application of the plan of Bacon's *Novum Organon* to the present condition of Physical Science": "Of the doctrines promulgated by Bacon, none has more completely remained with us, as a stable and valuable truth, than his declaration that true knowledge is to be obtained from Facts by *Induction* . . . [in] the Physical Sciences alone, in which the truths established are universally assented to and regarded with comparative calmness" ([1840] 1857, 1:v–vii).

For "a generation will pass away" see Luke 21:32.

Whewell also deals with the inductive "facts" of chemistry and physiology in *The History of the Inductive Sciences* (1837, 3:passim). In *On the Plurality of Worlds: An Essay* (1853), he discusses the relations among geology, astronomy, the plurality of worlds like earth (which he attacks as religiously suspect and scientifically indefensible), and religion. His attack provoked 20 books in reply (including Powell's *Essays on the Spirit of the Inductive Philosophy, the Unity of Worlds, and the Philosophy of Creation* [1855]), many reviews, and renewed controversy in the popular and scientific press (see Crowe 1986, 265–355). On human physiology and ethnography see Williams ¶7 and n. 15; Powell ¶122; and Wilson ¶74 and n. 120.

On "the admission of Galileo's discovery" Whewell comments: "Admiral [William Henry] Smyth in his *Cycle of Celestial Objects* [1844], vol. i. p. 65, says—'At length, in 1818, the voice of truth was so prevailing, that Pius VII. repealed the edicts against the Copernican system, and thus, in the emphatic words of Cardinal Toriozzi, "wiped off this scandal from the Church."' . . . I have not been able to learn that there is any further foundation for these statements than this: In 1818, on the revisal of the *Index Expurgatorius*, Galileo's writings were, after some opposition, expunged from that Catalogue" (1857, 57).

33. Jowett's phrase "the purposes of God towards the whole human race" refers to the Final Cause in his theology which underlies his discussion of progressive revelation and the proofs of different systems of knowledge, especially in physiology and comparative anatomy (relevant to Jowett's discussion in ¶18). In a *Supplementary Volume* to *The History of the Inductive Sciences* Whewell adds a long note on "Final Causes" in "Physiology and Comparative Anatomy," asserting: "If there be advocates of Final Causes in Physiology who would push their doctrine so far as to assert that every feature and every relation in the structure of animals have a purpose discoverable by man, such reasoners are liable to be perpetually thwarted and embarrassed by the progress of anatomical knowledge; for this progress often shows that an arrangement which had been explained and admired with reference to some purpose, exists also in cases where the purpose disappears; and again, that what had been noted as a special teleological arrangement is the result of a general morphological law. . . . There are, in such speculations, two elements; one given, the other to be worked out from our examination of the case; the *datum* and the *problem*; the homology and the teleology" (1857, 147–48). Whewell refers to the morphological structures of animals and their homologies as recently discussed in the theories of the comparative anatomist Richard Owen, particularly in *Archetype and Homologies of the Vertebrate Skeleton* (1848) and in *On the Nature of Limbs* (1849). Darwin, with his analysis of the modification of finches, addressed the fixity of such morphologies and homologies in *The Origin of Species* (1859).

For the "recent chronological discoveries" in Egypt under Napoleon's archaeologists see Williams ¶6 and notes 10–12. On J. F. Champollion's identification of "Hebrews" in the Egyptian records in Shishak's lists at Thebes, dating from the 10th century B.C.E., suggesting a possible revision in the date of the exodus, see Williams ¶7 and n. 22. Samuel Birch writes: "So important have been those studies of the synchronistic history of the two nations [Israel and Egypt], that it will be impossible hereafter to adequately illustrate the history of the Old Testament without referring to the contemporaneous monuments of Egypt" (1872, 3).

The French archaeologist Paul Émile Botta excavated monuments and inscriptions from Khorsabad in Assyria and brought them back to Paris where for the first time the name of an Assyrian king, Sargon II (c. 721–705 B.C.E.), was deciphered by A. de Longperrier. The results were published in *Revue Archéologique* (1848), linking Sargon to Isa. 20:1. Henry Layard also excavated Assyrian remains and shipped to England the winged bulls that are in the British Museum, publishing accounts of their discovery and exhumation in *Nineveh and Its Remains* (1849, 2 vols.). To literalists the ruin of Assyrian Nineveh proved that the prophecies of Jonah 3:1–10 and all three chapters of Nahum are fulfilled. Hence, Pusey in *The Minor Prophets with a Commentary* includes a long account of "the fulfilment of prophecy" (1860, 359) in the destruction of Assyria and Nineveh: "The recent excavations have shown that fire was a great instrument in the destruction of the Nineveh palaces" (1860, 368). Pusey traces the accounts of the site from Xenophon to Layard, concluding that "humanly speaking, even if destroyed, it was probable before-hand that it would not altogether perish" (369), for it was in the ground to be unearthed to confirm the prophet's words.

34. Jowett's sense of "apology" here combines two notions, a self-justification and a defense. For apology see Powell ¶18 and n. 6; for Jowett's comments on apologetics see [1855] 1859, 2:580. Among Jowett's contemporaries "apology" often signals an opposition to High Church and Roman Catholic dogmatism.

For "Ye shall know . . . free" see John 8:32; for "To that end . . . the truth," John 18:37.

Many commentators had pointed out inconsistencies in the infancy narratives. For instance, Friedrich Schleiermacher writes that Matthew and Luke "have no single point . . . no entire fact, in common, and also . . . they are not at all supplemental to each other, but, on the contrary, the corresponding members of the two successions almost entirely exclude each other" ([1817] 1825, 44–45). Thirlwall, Schleiermacher's translator, adds a long note on attempts to reconcile these discrepancies but ends agreeing with Schleiermacher (315–17).

35. The four biblical passages cited by Jowett are often used to justify sectarian religious practices or beliefs. First, concerning baptism for the dead (1 Cor. 15:29), Stanley gives a five-page commentary on the verse referring first to its difficulty and to its use in baptizing the living "vicariously for the dead" in "some sects in the first three centuries, one at least which extends back to the Apostolical age, who had this practice," citing Tertullian and Chrysostom (1855, 1:372). The Mormons (Church of Jesus Christ of Latter-Day Saints), founded in 1840, continued this practice, baptized a living person vicariously for someone who had died.

On 1 Cor. 11:10 Stanley comments that "the subordination of the woman to the man" is "happily of no practical importance" (1855, 1:222). Despite Stanley's claims the passage as a whole was often used to justify patriarchy and the subordination of women, especially in the controversy from the 1850s leading to the Divorce Act of 1857 and the Married Women's Property Bill of 1870 (see Shanley 1989). An unmarried woman was referred to in Norman-French legal parlance as a "*feme sole*" (single woman), while a married woman was a "*feme covert*" (covered woman), under the "wing, protection, and *cover*" of her husband" (Blackstone [1764–70] 1979, 1:430). The *feme covert,* deriving from the same passage (especially 1 Cor. 11:10–15), refers to a woman's covering her head with the veil of marriage, a custom also required by the *Book of Sermons or Homilies* ([1547, 1563] 1802, 430). In an anonymous pamphlet prepared as part of the agitation for the Married Women's Property Bill, the link with the same Corinthians passage is again made explicit: "'In short,' says Judge Hurlbut, 'a woman is courted and wedded as an angel, and yet denied the dignity of a rational and moral being ever after'" (*A Brief Summary* 1854, 13). The passage was the basis of requiring that women wear hats in church. Stanley's seven-page commentary and five-page note call into question his estimate of their lack of "practical importance" and also show how the "customs of Christendom," that no man enters a church "with his head covered; no female with hers bare," can be built on "two obscure expressions (in verse 10)" that are "an occasion for the diligence and ingenuity of scholar after scholar in the whole field of philological and antiquarian learning" (1855, 1:230–31).

The imminence of the parousia (coming), or day of judgment, referred to in Matt. 24:34 and frequently in Paul's letters was a belief of early Christianity. In 1854 Samuel Waldegrave delivered and published the Bampton Lectures on *New Testament Millenarianism; or, the Kingdom and Coming of Christ as Taught by Himself and His Apostles.* Alford refers to Matt. 24:34 as "one of the points on which the rationalizing interpreters (De Wette &c.) lay most stress to show that prophecy has *failed*" ([1849] 1863, 1:243). On the other hand, the verses were appealed to by millenarianists such as Edward Irving who translated the work of the Spanish Jesuit Lacunza as *The Coming of the Messiah in Glory and Majesty* (1827), and William Miller, the founder of the Adventist Church (1831), who predicted that the Second Coming of Christ would occur in 1843–44. When the date passed, the Seventh-Day Adventist group broke away and were established as a separate church also holding millenarian views. Alford points out that the word for generation (γενεά, *genea*) has "in Hellenistic Greek the meaning of *a race or family of people*" so that the passage "symbolizes the *future reviviscence* of [the Jewish people as] that race which the Lord declares shall not pass away till all be fulfilled . . . the true meaning of that verse" ([1849] 1863, 1:243). See also Wilson ¶17 and note.

On the Petrine claims of the Roman Catholic church, often based on Matt. 16:18–19, see Temple ¶49 and n. 75. While Alford agrees that the verses show the pre-eminence of Peter among the apostles, he adds: "Nothing can be further from any legitimate interpretation of this promise, than the idea of a perpetual primacy in the successors of Peter" ([1849] 1863, 1:172).

36. Jowett gives three examples of mistranslations. Phil. 2:6 in the AV translates ὑπάρχων (*huparchon*) as "being," the present participle (ὤν, *on*) of the verb to be (εἰμί, *eimi*), when in fact it means "to be in existence," or "to subsist." Alford comments: "The participle is hardly equivalent to 'although he subsisted' . . . still less 'inasmuch as he subsisted;' but simply states its fact as a link in the logical chain, 'subsisting as He did;' without fixing that link as causal or concessive" ([1849] 1863, 3:166).

Jowett comments in *The Epistles of St. Paul* on Rom. 3:25: "No such expression occurs in Scripture as faith in the blood, or even in the death of Christ. Nor is πίστις [faith] followed by ἐν [in] in the New Testament, though faith, like all other Christian states, is often spoken of as existing in Christ (Gal. iii. 26). The two clauses should therefore be separated, 'through faith—by his blood'" ([1855] 1859, 2:134). On Rom. 15:6, Jowett writes: "Not God, even the Father of our Lord Jesus Christ, as in the English Version; a translation which apparently arises out of a fear of calling God, the God of our Lord Jesus Christ; but 'the God and Father of our Lord Jesus Christ," as in Gal. i. 4. God is called, 'our God and Father'" ([1855] 1859, 2:411).

Jowett then gives two examples from the AV with no textual authority. The AV translation "God was manifest in the flesh" at 1 Tim. 3:16 with important theological implications concerning the nature of Christ, depends upon the abbreviation ΘΣ for God (θεός, *theos*) in the *textus receptus*, or received text (published by Stephanus in 1550), on which the translation "God was manifest in the flesh" depends. It occurs in the codices Bezae (Alford: "in critical weight it ranks the lowest of the leading MSS" [(1849), 1863, 1:109], but was very likely a later emendation), Cyprius, and Regius Parisiensis, all late; it does not occur in the oldest MSS., Alexandrinus and Ephraemi. These last MSS., written in uncials or capital letters, read ΟΣ (= ὃς, *hos*, the relative pronoun "who" or "which"). In a long textual note Alford writes of his examination of the Alexandrinus (fifth century in the BL), the oldest authority then available (the Codex Sinaiticus, from the fourth century, discovered in 1859, was not published until 1863; it reads ΟΣ). Alford declares that the reading ΟΣ "is now *matter of certainty*" ([1849] 1863, 3:332). θεός was still being reprinted in the *textus receptus* version in the Oxford edition of Mill's Greek text of 1833; Westcott and Hort rejected the *textus receptus* reading in their edition of 1881; the Revised Version of 1880 first changed the translation to "He who," noting that the reading "God" was not in the ancient MSS.

Similarly, the *textus receptus* for 1 John 5:7 supports the Trinitarian reading of the AV: "For there are three that bear record in heaven, the Father, the Word, and the Holy Ghost: and these three are one." However, as Alford points out, all of the Greek words after "bear record" are "omitted in all Greek MSS. previous to the beginning of the 16th century; all the Greek Fathers (even when producing texts in support of the doctrine of the Holy Trinity). . . ; all the ancient versions (including the Vulgate as it came from Jerome . . . and . . . the Syriac); and many Latin Fathers . . . . The Greek words were first inserted in the Complutensian edition of 1514. . . . Erasmus enquired whether the editors really had mss so different from any he had seen. . . . Erasmus unfortunately pledged himself to insert the words if they existed in any one Greek ms. A Codex Britannicus was at length found [Codex Montfortianus, Trinity College, Dublin, fifteenth century] which contained them. Erasmus, in his 3rd edition (1522), fulfilled his promise" (Alford [1849] 1863, 4:502–5). The verse had been the subject of a prolonged controversy in England when the classical scholar Richard Porson published in the *Gentleman's Magazine* in 1788–89 a series of *Letters to Archdeacon Travis, on the Spurious Verse 1 John v. 7* (published as a book, 1790). The controversy continued for the next forty years. He was attacked by Thomas Burgess and was defended by Thomas Turton in *A Vindication of the Literary Character of the Late Professor Porson, from the Animadversions of the Right Reverend Thomas Burgess* (1827).

37. The disputed passage at Rom. 9:5 reads as follows in the AV: "Whose are the fathers, and of whom as concerning the flesh Christ came, who is over all, God blessed for ever. Amen." The issue is whether the doxology in the final phrase is to be accorded to Christ as God, or whether, by altering the punctuation according to the NT editions of Erasmus, Lachmann, and Tischendorf, the passage is to be read as Jowett, the "English translator," translates it in *The Epistles of St. Paul*: "Whose are the fathers, and of whom as concerning the flesh Christ came. God, who is over all, is blessed for ever. Amen" ([1855] 1859, 2:276–78). Jowett cites a number of third- and fourth-century authorities. Alford too mentions the disputes over the passage and ties them to the Christological debates of the early church: "The punctuation and application of this doxology have been much disputed" ([1849] 1863, 2:404–5).

38. Accommodation is one of the principles in the interpretive method of Thomas Arnold from which Jowett distances himself with the notion of progressive revelation (see ¶16). To Arnold "the revelations of God to man were gradual and adapted to his state at the several periods when they were successively made. And, on the same principle, commands were given at one time which were not given at another. . . . This brings us to the famous doctrine of *accommodation*. . . . In any communication between a Being of infinite knowledge and one of finite, it is obvious that the former must speak sometimes according to the views of the latter. . . . In short, unless revelation be universal; that is, unless it extend to the removal of all error, and the communication of all truth, there must be an accommodation in it to the opinions of mankind" ([1832] 1844, 2:382–83). Arnold also stresses accommodation in the development of moral education (2:386–91). Jowett returns to the notion of accommodation in ¶s 25, 29, and 40; see also Pattison ¶25 and note.

39. Christianity has three major creeds (Latin, *credo*, I believe): (1) The Apostles' Creed, dating from fourth century, referred to in Ambrose's Epistle 42 (c.

490), had evolved from the Old Roman Creed, and was the baptismal creed of the Western church; (2) the Nicene Creed was established as a profession of faith at the Council of Nicaea (325) against the Arian heresy. It was expanded later, perhaps at the Council of Constantinople (381), and was ratified at the Council of Chalcedon (451). It is the baptismal creed of the Eastern church and is used in the eucharist in both the East and the West; and (3) the Athanasian Creed, dating from the early fourth century, was also a construction of the Western church, from southern Gaul, shaped to combat various Christological heresies. It was not a baptismal creed but was used in the Roman Catholic breviary at the monastic office of Prime, was accepted by the Lutherans as a statement of faith, and was used in the Anglican Church on thirteen specified days during the year. Because of its anathemas or cursing clauses, there was a movement in the C. of E. from 1867 to have it removed from formal worship. See Williams ¶32 and note; Wilson ¶7 and note; see also Kelly 1964.

On the "germs of the expressions" in the creeds as found in the "words of . . . the Apostles," Stanley comments on the credal format, phrasing, and relation to the Apostles' Creed of 1 Cor. 15:3–8 (1855, 1:345–53). In an appended "dissertation" he elaborates further: "Amongst all the forms, some of them of considerable length, which are preserved, of the creeds of the first four centuries, there are only two (that of Tertullian and of Epiphanius; from whom, probably, it was derived in the Nicene Creed), which contain the expressions here twice repeated, 'according to the Scriptures,' and in those two probably imitated from this place [in Corinthians]" (1855, 1:358–59). Stanley refers to Tertullian's *Against Praxeas* (c. 213; chap. 2) and the *Ancoratus* of Epiphanius, in the MSS. of which the Nicene-Constantinopolitan Creed first appears.

While the three formal creeds refer to biblical events and doctrines, echo biblical language, and have a tripartite structure following Matt. 28:19, their theological elaboration reflects doctrinal controversy rather than biblical narrative. Efforts to relate the creeds to the Bible included J. H. Newman's *Lectures on the Scripture Proof of the Doctrines of the Church* (1838; Tract 85) dealing with credal doctrines in general and also including an attack on latitudinarianism. The major Anglican document is George Bull's *Defensio Fidei Nicaenae* (1685; Defence of the Nicene Creed), republished by Newman in the Library of Anglo-Catholic Theology series in 1851.

For "Believe . . . saved" see Acts 16:31; for "the mind of Christ," 1 Cor. 2:16. On Rom. 1:3–4 Jowett comments in *The Epistles of St. Paul*: "The verses that follow are some of the most difficult in the Epistles of St. Paul. . . . This difficulty arises partly from the dimness of the thought as it presents itself to our minds compared with its intensity to St. Paul; partly from the inversion of modes of thought, so that what is with us the effect is to the Apostle the cause, or conversely; and also from the imperfect and fragmentary character of the antithesis, which is begun, but not carried out fully, and in which it is in vain to look for the correspondence of the different members, as it breaks off almost as soon as we observe it" ([1855] 1859, 2:44).

40. In *The Epistles of St. Paul* Jowett denies as anachronistic an "abstract notion of Christian truth" or "system of philosophy" in Paul: "There is no system which is presupposed in them; nor can any be constructed out of them without marring their simplicity. They have almost wholly a practical aim, and are fragmentary and occasional. . . . There is a growth in the Epistles of St. Paul, it is true; but it is growth not of reflection, but of spiritual experience, enlarging as the world widens before the Apostle's eyes, passing from life to death, or from strife to peace, with the changes in the Apostle's own life, or the circumstances of his converts" ([1855] 1859, 1:3–4).

The "notion . . . in the Catholic Church" refers to appeals to Paul for support in later and different doctrinal controversies, such as those involving Chrysostom and Christological heresies (see Francis M. Young 1983, 156–57) and disputes over the eucharistic sacrifice in Jowett's day (see J. H. Newman, quoted in Norris 1977, 139).

Most scholars now place Homer in the eighth century B.C.E., but there was disagreement in Jowett's day over the date and authorship of Homer (the "Homeric Question"). Gladstone and F. W. Newman locate Homer in the Bronze Age (c. 2800–1050 B.C.E.), while Matthew Arnold collapses Homer and his poems onto the ideals of fifth-century Periclean Athens. Nevertheless, to attribute the views of later writers to Homer would be anachronistic (as Arnold tended to be). Thales is said to be the founder of Greek philosophy, and one of the Seven Sages. No writing of his survives: he is known only through references to him in other writings. For instance, Aristotle refers to him in *Metaphysics* (bk. 1, sec. 2, l. 7). Heraclitus is best known for *On Nature* (surviving only in fragments), and the reference to him in Plato's *Cratylus*: "Heracleitus says, you know, that all things move and nothing remains still, and he likens the universe to the current of a river, saying that you cannot step twice into the same stream" (402A trans. H. N. Fowler *Loeb* 67). Jowett inverts the chronological order of Aristotle and Plato. He also alludes to classical authors to argue against "anachronism" in ¶34.

41. The phrase "silence of scripture" is a technical term concerning matters not covered in the Bible, as, for example, the youth and early manhood of Jesus. Such materials are dealt with contemporaneously in a chapter on "The Silence of the Gospels Proofs of their Inspiration" in Row 1864, 285–97.

Jowett contrasts Paul's "intensity of faith" to "modern days" in *The Epistles of St. Paul* by means of

Greek philosophy: "The Greek philosophers spoke of a world of phenomena, of true being, of knowledge and opinion; and we know that what they meant by these distinctions is something different from the tenets of any philosophical school of the present day. But not less different is what St. Paul meant by the life hidden with Christ and God, the communion of the Spirit, the possession of the mind of Christ; only that this was not a mere difference of speculation, but of practice also" ([1855] 1859, 1:360–61).

For "raised . . . above all things" see Eph. 1:20–22; for "Creator of all things," Col. 1:16; for "quick and dead," 2 Tim. 4:1; and 1 Peter 4:5; for "equal to God," Phil. 2:6. For "one substance" (*homoousios*) see the Nicene Creed; the phrase was designed to exclude Arianism (see Williams ¶27 and n. 110).

In the two examples (Rom. 1:2–4 and Phil. 2:6) Paul describes the nature of Christ's person by means of a series of antitheses (see Jowett [1855] 1859, 1:42 and Jowett ¶22 and n. 39). Alford argues that Paul's phrases distribute meaning "in alternate clauses between our Lord's humanity and divinity." Similarly Alford interprets the Phil. 2:6 Christologically ([1849] 1863, 2:313; 3:166). Jowett criticizes such views because they are predetermined not by analogous passages in the Bible but by later credal distinctions.

For "He was . . . tempted" see Matt. 4:1; Mark 1:13; Luke 4:2; and Heb. 4:15; for "when he prayed," Matt. 6:9, 26:39, 26:42, and 26:53; for "of that hour," Mark 13:32; for "why hast thou," Mark 15:34; and Matt. 27:46; for "if it be possible," Luke 22:42; and Matt. 26:39; and for "when the son cometh," Luke 18:8.

42. Unitarians, denying Christian dogmatic definitions concerning the Trinity, held that God was a single person, and so rejected the divinity of Christ. A leading Victorian Unitarian, James Martineau, in a lecture on "The Divinity of Christ" published in *Unitarianism Defended* (1839), claimed that Christ was a human manifestation of the Platonic form or idea of God. His argument is based partly on a reading of the prologue to John's Gospel in the context of Hellenistic Platonism.

For "the Word was God" see John 1:1; "God was the word" is the order of the words in Greek; for "I and my Father are one," John 10:30; for "a prophet or one of the prophets," Mark 6:15.

43. For "In the beginning" see John 1:1, an echo of the Septuagint version of Gen. 1:1 (made explicit in John 1:3, "without him was not anything made that was made." This passage very likely also refers to Prov. 8:22, identifying "Word" (*logos*) with wisdom (*sophia*). Hence, this appeal to the cosmic origins of creation is quite different from the use of "beginning" (*arche*) at Mark 1:1. The preposition *pros* with the accusative case means "in the presence of" in classical Greek, but "toward" or "with" in NT Greek (as at Mark 6:3); hence, the *logos* is said to be co-present "with God" in the sense of Wisdom's being "with God" in Prov. 8:30. The glossing of the third clause of John 1:1 ("the Word was God") in an ironic sense as "the Word is said to be God" is contrasted with Jesus' rebuke to his attackers at John 10:34–36. Jowett echoes Plato's second paragraph of the *Symposium* concerning the false words and slanders of "old opponents."

44. For "inward kingdom" and "external world" see John 18:36; for "If a man smite," Matt. 5:39; for "I ought to obey God," Acts 5:29.

Jowett makes a similar argument that the civil or social order is both an external frame and "mechanical" in *The Epistles of St. Paul,* in which he foregrounds the function of language and the constructedness of such concepts: "Now the world may be imagined as a vast machine, as an animal or living being, as a body endowed with a rational or divine soul. All these are figures of speech, and the associations to which they give rise, have an insensible influence on our ideas. The representation of the world as a machine is a more favourite one, in modern times, than the representation of it as a living being; and with mechanism is associated the notion of necessity" ([1855] 1859, 2:625). For other uses of the "mechanical" to represent the external or outer world see Temple ¶3 and note. Matthew Arnold uses the same device throughout *Culture and Anarchy* to dismiss arguments which, he claims, mistake means for ends (see, for instance, 1960–77, 5:95–114).

In discussing Rom. 3:30, Jowett makes a similar comparison between "India" and a "civilized country," establishing relations of identity rather than difference: "Even to us it is hard to imagine that the islander of the South Seas, the pariah of India, the African in his worst estate, is equally with ourselves God's creature. . . . No one can interpose impediments of rank or fortune, or colour or religious opinion, between those who are one in Christ" ([1855] 1859, 2:140–41). On class and race as impediments to universal salvation see Wilson ¶s 2–27, 43, 77–81.

Missionaries were required to conform to both British law and local codes and customs according to the notion of "sanction." According to T. E. Holland in *The Elements of Jurisprudence* (1906), "the real meaning of all law is that, unless acts conform to the course prescribed by it, the state will not only ignore and render no aid to them, but will also, either of its own accord or if called upon, intervene to cancel their effects. This intervention of the state is what is called the 'sanction' of law" (cited in *EB*, s.v. "sanction"). This notion dates from the legal codification of Justinian. The appeal to a divine sanction above the civil law to permit breaking it is argued on the basis of Acts 5:29 ("Peter and the other apostles answered and said, 'We ought to obey God rather than men'"), and is argued against on the basis of Jesus' words, "Render to Caesar the things that are

Caesar's and to God the things that are God's" (Matt. 22:21); and Tit. 3:1 ("Put them in mind . . . to obey magistrates"). The establishment role of the missionaries was controversial: "They were . . . attacked by believers in a native culture entitled to respect as well as by devotees of the divine right of the white man to do whatever he liked" (Kiernan [1969] 1972, 268); see also Wilson ¶12 and note.

The Indian Rebellion, or Mutiny, of 1857 was succeeded by the termination of the East India Company and the assumption of administrative authority and colonial power over India by Britain in the India Act of 1858 that included the establishment of Indian magistrates and, in 1860, by the reform of the penal code. In the proclamation of the Act of 1858 Queen Victoria added in her own hand the first phrases: "*Firmly relying ourselves on the truth of Christianity, and acknowledging with gratitude the solace of religion,* We disclaim alike the right and the desire to impose Our convictions on any of Our subjects. We declare it to be Our royal will and pleasure that none be in any-wise favoured, none molested or disquieted by reason of their religious faith or observance, but that all alike shall enjoy the equal and impartial protection of the law" (Neill 1964a, 323). Jowett's co-Essayist C. W. Goodwin was appointed one of the imperial magistrates, as an assistant judge in the Supreme Court of China and Japan located in Shanghai, one of the "treaty" ports guaranteed under the treaty of Nanking (1842) where according to the principle of "extra-territoriality" foreigners were "guaranteed the right of trial under their own laws, and by the officials of their own country" (Neill 1964a, 282).

45. For "Of whom . . . free" see Matt 17:25–26.

The oppositions drawn by are commonplaces from Plato and Hegel ([1807] 1977, 325–26; 453–78). Coleridge in *The Constitution of Church and State* (1829) has a long note on distinctions between the ideal and the actual which are foundational to Broad Church theology ([1829] 1976, 47). See Willis 1988.

46. Jowett refers to the rhetorical use of biblical tags to lend "weight" to arguments in ordinary speech or in "political strife" or "controversy." Two notable instances among many in the Victorian period, both related to Wilberforce and to the reception of *Essays and Reviews,* were uttered by Thomas Henry Huxley and Lord Westbury. During the Oxford Debate on Darwin's theory of evolution on 30 June 1860, when Wilberforce broke the bounds of decorum and asked Huxley whether he was descended from an ape on the side of his grandfather or his grandmother, Huxley exclaimed: "The Lord has delivered him into mine hand" (1 Sam. 23:7, Saul's comment on preparing to capture David). See Powell ¶126 and n. 87; J. R. Lucas 1979; and Gilley 1981. Lord Westbury, speaking as Lord Chancellor in the House of Lords in 1864 after he had acquitted *Essays and Reviews* in the Judicial Committee, and while attacking the C. of E. Convocation for having synodically condemned the whole of the book rather than specific passages or specific authors, threatens the bishops with *praemunire* [Lat. Let so-and-so be warned; used of an ecclesiastical offence] and having to come before the House of Lords "as penitents in sackcloth and ashes," an echo of several passages in the Bible, such as Esth. 4:3; Dan 9:3; and Matt. 11:21 (*Times,* 16 July 1864, 8). Jowett returns to the use of proof texts in biblical interpretation and doctrinal controversy in ¶s 32–33.

Jowett's series of rhetorical questions extend the argument on the ideal and the actual into further contradictions. Literalists from both the High and Low Church agreed that the precepts of the Bible are to apply as both law and spirit to actual life, to both nations and individuals, to be enforced generally and in detail. But this "ideal" notion was not followed in practice in Victorian society concerning, for example, Levitical instructions, dietary laws, prescriptions concerning worship and animal sacrifice, as well as Jesus' injunctions on loving one's neighbor or the other precepts of the sermon on the mount. On the attempt of the Calvinist church in Geneva to follow biblical precepts see Wilson ¶s 1–5.

47. For "the law . . . of life" see Rom. 8:2; for "liberty . . . free," Gal. 5:1; see Jowett [1855] 1859, 1:374. In *The Freedom of a Christian Man* (1520) Luther maintains the freedom of social relations, politics, and law from religious compulsion. Jowett's citation of John 18:36 may be glossed by Jesus' claim that the "kingdom of God is within you" (Luke 17:20).

In the NT the "counsels of perfection," or "the evangelical counsels," are often located in the sermon on the mount (Matt. 5–7), or in achieving perfection by selling all that one has to give to the poor and to follow Christ (Matt. 19:21), or in the injunction to love God with all the heart and soul and mind, and one's neighbor as one's self (Matt. 22:37–39). Traditionally they are identified as three monastic virtues of poverty, chastity, and obedience (Thomas Aquinas, *Summa,* bk. 1, pt. 2, quest. 108, art. 4). The medieval *Speculum perfectionis* (The mirror of perfection, 13th century) is the story of the life of St. Francis of Assisi as modeled on the precepts of the gospels and the life of Christ. It gave rise to a body of "perfection" literature that included Thomas à Kempis's *Imitation of Christ* (1418), *The Ladder of Perfection* (printed 1494) by the English mystic Walter Hilton (d. 1396), and William Law's *A Practical Treatise upon Christian Perfection* (1726) that influenced John and Charles Wesley and the Methodist revival, bringing the concept into nineteenth-century discussions of personal religion. The doctrine of perfection became "a widely discussed topic in 18th- and 19th-cent. theology and literature" (Rudolph 1992, 603). For instance, in *Culture and Anarchy* Matthew Arnold discusses the role of "beauty and sweetness" as "essential characters of a complete human perfection" in extended passages (1960–77, 5:106).

For "dwelling-place in the heart of man" compare W. Wordsworth, "And I have felt a presence . . . whose dwelling is . . . in the mind of man" ("Tintern Abbey," ll. 93–98).

For the role of the national church in nation building and the nurture of individuals see Wilson ¶35. Matthew Arnold's comments in *Culture and Anarchy* demonstrate the adaptability of this Broad Church theological point to secular ends: "The idea of perfection as an *inward* condition of the mind and spirit is at variance with the mechanical and material civilisation in esteem with us" (1960–77, 5:95); "Culture, which is the study of perfection, leads us . . . to conceive of true human perfection as a *harmonious* perfection, developing all sides of our humanity; and as a *general* perfection, developing all parts of our society" (1960–77, 5:235).

For "the kingdom of God . . . world" Jowett reverses the apocalyptic phrases of Rev. 11:15.

48. Each of the eight subjects Jowett mentions is a recent theological or social issue, and each is returned to for detailed comment by Jowett in ¶28 and is discussed in notes there. Each case involves the intersection of church and state as complementary or rival institutions and authorities; and each depends upon classical or biblical languages or historical contexts that have also been subject to accusations of mistranslation and misinterpretation.

For "the thoughts of many hearts" see Luke 2:35; for "unknown tongue," 1 Cor. 14: 2–27. The terms *great movement* and *large party* refer to such contemporary phenomena as the alignments between the Oxford Movement and the Tory party or the Nonconformists with the Liberals.

49. On the issue of divorce and the remarriage of divorced partners, Jowett cites two parallel texts from the gospels. The first, part of the discussion of the law on adultery from the sermon on the mount, glosses the seventh commandment (Exod. 20:14) and specifies an exception (given in Greek and translated). "Fornication" in this passage was widely understood not in its usual sense, the sexual intercourse of unmarried persons, but as adultery involving the female partner, the sexual intercourse of a married woman with a person other than the spouse. Further, divorce for any reason other than fornication was not allowed since it would also lead to adultery. The marrying of a divorced person is also adulterous. The second text, however, the parallel passage in Mark 10:11–12 (Jowett does not mention the other parallel in Luke 16:18), does not specify the exception. The action of the woman in divorcing the man was allowed in Greek and Roman but not in Jewish law. See Jowett's further discussion in ¶31 and note.

Before 1857 divorce in England was only possible by an elaborate and costly process, the plaintiff carrying it first through the ecclesiastical courts, and then through the House of Lords according to a procedure established in 1697 (the Private Act Procedure). The ecclesiastical courts allowed only two processes for divorce: the first, divorce *a mensa et toro* (from table and bed) for adultery, extreme cruelty, or desertion, was in fact only a separation since neither party could remarry; the second, divorce *a vinculo* (from the marriage bonds), was in fact an annulment when the marriage was stated to be invalid for such reasons as impotence, fraud, or age. To proceed to a civil divorce one had to have secured the formal writ from the ecclesiastical court and then win in a private civil suit in Parliament against the lover for "criminal conversation."

Such procedures were very costly, upwards of £700, the income of a modest middle-class family for a year (it was the sum that Dorothea Brooke managed her household with after her marriage to Casaubon in George Eliot's *Middlemarch* [1871–72]). In Dickens's *Hard Times* (1854) Josiah Bounderby tells his weaver, Stephen Blackpool, how to be rid of his drunken wife who has ruined him: "Why, you'd have to go to Doctors' Commons with a suit, and you'd have to go to a court of Common Law with a suit, and you'd have to go to the House of Lords with a suit, and you'd have to get an Act of Parliament to enable you to marry again, and it would cost you (if it was a case of very plain sailing), I suppose from a thousand to fifteen hundred pound. . . . Perhaps twice the money" (bk. 1, chap. 11; [1854] 1975, 113).

The Divorce and Matrimonial Causes Act of 1857 (20 and 21 Victoria, chap. 85) created a civil divorce court in London. Simple adultery by the wife was grounds for the husband to divorce her; for the husband to be the guilty party, adultery had to be either incestuous or bigamous, or compounded by cruelty toward the wife, bestiality, or desertion for more than two years. The notion of the double standard, more vicious conduct being required of the husband than for the wife to have grounds for divorce, was preserved. Throughout the whole of the previous decade there was a flurry of articles and pamphlets, including Barbara Bodichon's *A Brief Summary in Plain Language of the Most Important Laws of England concerning Women* (1856) and John Keble's *An Argument for Not Proceeding Immediately Repealing the Laws Which Treat the Nuptial Bonds as Indissoluble* (1857). The subplot of Thackeray's novel *The Newcomes* (1853–55) concerns the divorce through the ecclesiastical court and the House of Lords of the villain, Sir Barnes Newcome, from his wife, Lady Clara.

Discussion in and out of Parliament focused on the texts Jowett cites, summarized in the article by Gladstone (published anonymously) in the *Quarterly Review* in the month that the act was passed (Gladstone 1857). Keble was referred to and Gladstone's article was misquoted on the meaning of the Greek word for fornication by the attorney general, Sir Richard Bethell, later Lord Westbury (who was to preside over the *Essays and Reviews* appeal in 1864), only to be corrected in debate by Gladstone himself (referring to without acknowledging the authorship of his own article and other texts). Again Gladstone explicates the meanings then current concerning whether "fornication" refers to adultery, whether it is an exception to the laws for divorce (in fact it was punishable by execution), and how these texts bear on the amendment of the law (Jowett's point), stating that "a very great diversity prevails with respect to the true construction to be put on Scripture in this matter" (*Hansard* 147, 836–39). For adultery in the nineteenth century see Lawson 1988; and E. A. Smith 1993; on divorce see Horstman 1985; and Phillips 1988, 227–41, 412–22.

50. Leviticus 18:17 is part of the so-called "holiness code" (Lev. 17:1–26:46). Lev. 18:1–30 deals with unlawful sexual relations and presumes both the conditions of polygamy as practiced by the Israelites (for example, by Lamech, Gen. 4:19; Abraham, Gen. 16:1–2; and Jacob, Gen 29:15–30) and the fact that extended families lived in close proximity or together. The cited text does not refer to marriage with the sister of a deceased wife, but prohibits taking, as a second wife, the sister of a woman who is already a wife. Hence, the polygamy that Jowett refers to is assumed in the text. The custom and tradition of the Jews relates particularly to the "brother's widow," the custom sanctioned in Deut. 25:5–10 concerning levirate marriage (Lat. *levir*, brother-in-law), whereby the brother of a deceased man was required to marry the widow, and the first male child of the new union would bear the name of the deceased husband. See Millar Burrows 1940; and Neufeld 1944.

The passage, however, was cited as biblical justification for proscribing the marriage by a widower with the sister of his deceased wife, as in the Table of Kindred and Affinity in the *BCP*. This table, setting out relationships in the family by blood relationships (consanguinity) and marriage (affinity) within which one was not allowed to marry, was published by Archbishop Matthew Parker in 1563, and is based on the prohibitions in Lev. 18. It became part of the canon law of the C. of E. in 1603 (canon 99), was incorporated in the civil code in the Marriage Act of 1835, and included marriage with deceased wife's sister, on the understanding that such a relationship was incestuous. The Act of 1835 made such a marriage absolutely null and void, instead of voidable—and so contentious—as had been the case for such marriages since the Reformation. A bill to make such a marriage valid passed the Commons in 1850 but was defeated in the Lords in 1851. Immediately before the publication of *Essays and Reviews*, similar bills came forward but were defeated in 1855, 1856, 1858, and 1859. A further twenty-six proposals were lost until it was finally legalized in 1906–7. There was widespread discussion of the issue in the press, in such articles as Henry Rogers's "Marriage with a Deceased Wife's Sister" (1853) and William Stirling Maxwell's "The Law of Marriage and Divorce" (1855). Henry Phillpotts, bp. of Exeter and one of the prosecutors in the *Essays and Reviews* trial, published his House of Lords speech attacking the proposal (*Speech Delivered in the House of Lords on Tuesday Feb. 25, 1851* [1851]). In the same year the Marital Law Reform Association was formed to promote the legalizing of such marriages.

In *Culture and Anarchy* Matthew Arnold satirizes the 2 May 1866 speech supporting marriage reform (and especially marriage with one's deceased wife's sister) by Thomas Chambers in Parliament which Arnold had heard (Arnold 1960–77, 5:205–6). The cause came forward so often that Gilbert and Sullivan referred to it in *Iolanthe* (1882): "He shall prick that annual blister / Marriage with deceased wife's sister" (Act 1).

51. For the Greek term for "inspired by God" from 2 Tim. 3:16 see Jowett ¶s 14–15 and notes.

52. Jowett specifies two passages from Jesus' farewell discourses to the disciples concerning "the personality of the Holy Spirit." The word translated "Comforter" in the AV in John 14:26 is παράκλητος (*paracletos*), which means "called to one's aid" in classical Greek, as in a legal court. Hence, a paraclete is a legal advisor or helper, the "figure" to which Jowett refers. In 1 John 2:1 the same Greek term is translated "Advocate" in the AV, following the Vulgate Latin "*advocatus*" and drawing on the classical Greek legal connotation. Elsewhere the term is used only at John 14:16; 15:26; and 16:7. In the Rabbinical writings the Messiah is often referred to as *M^enahem* (Heb. comforter) (see Lightfoot 1822–25, 12:384). The English "Holy Ghost" is a translation of τὸ πνεῦμα τὸ ἅγιον (Gk. *to pneuma to hagion*, "the spirit the holy"), the only occurrence in John's gospel (John 14:26) where the two definite articles are used. The phrase without the articles occurs fifty-two times in the NT, and was customarily identified by biblical commentators as referring to the gift of the spirit; on the other hand its use with the articles (28 times) denotes the giver or agent, the "more exact meaning that they [the words] would truly bear." Jowett's references to the "mysterious" and "depths of a divine consciousness" explicate the idea that the Holy Spirit will "bring all things to your remembrance" that Jesus taught the disciples. The second of the passages was interpreted in the nineteenth century as a reference to, or proof for, the Trinity: "Here we have given us a glimpse into the essential relationships of the Blessed Trinity. . . . And this Revelation, the Revelation of the Father by Christ—is carried on by the blessed Spirit in the hearts of the disciples of Christ. . . . This verse contains the plainest proof by inference of the ortho-

dox doctrine of the Holy Trinity" (Alford [1849] 1863, 1:862).

"Passages of an opposite tenour" include Acts 1:7–8, where the prediction of the coming of the spirit is accompanied by the saying that the disciples will not know the times and the places, in apparent contradiction to being taught all things, and the controverted meanings of inspiration (see ¶14 and notes).

53. The phrase "he and all his" (καὶ οἱ αὐτοῦ πάντες, *kai hoi auto pantes*, Acts 16:33) is anticipated in the two previous verses in reference to "all that were in his house." Jowett alludes to a presumption that the phrase indicates the baptism of the jailor and his family, including children within the designation "house." But if there were no children in his household (here the text is silent), this text cannot even be used for a permissive condition, quite apart from an obligatory one.

Pusey in his tracts on baptism (1835, 215) refers to the passage, without mentioning infant baptism. Alford comments on a similar phrase in Acts 16:15 about the baptism of Lydia "and all her house": "It *may be* . . . that no inference for infant-baptism is hence deducible. The practice, however, does not rest on *inference*, but on the *continuity and identity of the covenant of grace to Jew and Christian*, the *sign only* of admission being altered. . . . The practice thus by universal consent, tacitly (because at first unquestioned) pervaded the universal church, can hardly with any reason be doubted" ([1849] 1863, 2:179). W. Denton, referring to Alford, comments on the phrase Jowett cites from Acts 16:33: "*With all his house*—therefore infants, for *all* needed baptism, *all* needed spiritual enlightenment and deliverance, and to *all* was the message of salvation sent" (Denton 1876, 2:104). The lesson read at the baptism of infants in the *BCP* (Mark 10:13–16) includes Jesus' remarks welcoming children, and receiving the kingdom of heaven as a child, interpreted as a dominical injunction concerning infant baptism (see Mozley 1862).

Modern debate on infant baptism and its biblical sources (Acts 16:15 and 1 Cor. 1:16) points to the "*oikos* formula," the reference to the baptism of a "household," as indicative of the probable practice of baptizing all children and adults into the Christian faith upon the conversion of the father of the house. For the evidence from apostolic times to the beginning of the third century when infant baptism was customary, as in Tertullian's *De Baptismo* (c. 200, On Baptism), see Jeremias 1960.

54. The Greek term, ἐπίσκοπος, meaning a bishop or "overseer," is found at 2 Tim. 3:2 and Tit. 1:7. The term is used elsewhere at Acts 20:28; Phil. 1:1; and 1 Pet. 2:25. Presbyter (priest, elder) is synonymous with *episcopos* at Acts 20:17, 28. The "supposed analogy" depends upon the fact that the apostles chose replacements to fill up their number or succeed them, such as Matthias to replace Judas ("his bishoprick let another take," see Acts 1:20–26). For "Lo I am with you" see Matt. 28:20, the so-called apostolical or ministerial commission. The commission to "teach" all nations was claimed as authority for the apostolical succession of bishops as the chief teachers of the church, and Jesus' declaration that he was "with you" (that is, with the apostles and, by implication, with their successors) to the end of the world was claimed as a dominical sanction for the succession of bishops as continuously having Christ's presence. The passage was so referred to by John Keble in the *Tracts for the Times* (1833), and by J. H. Newman in the *Tracts* (1833a; 1833b; 1833c; and 1833d). Such views were questioned or repudiated by some commentators: "To understand ["with you"] only of the Apostles and their (?) successors, is to destroy the whole force of these most weighty words" (Alford [1849] 1863, 1:307).

55. The seventh issue is the "Divine Right of Kings." The "precepts of order" are the relations of civil order to divine law in Rom. 13:1. In *The Epistles of St. Paul* Jowett translates the passage: "Let every-one be in his place under the powers above him, for they have their place from God himself" ([1855] 1859, 2:361). By some commentators this passage was taken to sanction the divine right of kings. In the homily "Against Disobedience and Wilful Rebellion" (1569), Rom. 13:1 is related to the divine right of kings (*Book of Sermons or Homilies* [1547, 1563] 1802, 470). The doctrine was opposed by the Puritans (who challenged it directly with the execution of Charles I) and was supported by most of the Caroline divines of the C. of E. during the reign of Charles II.

The "Fifth Monarchy men" were a sect of Puritans at the time of the Protectorate (c. 1650) who argued for the immanence of Christ's second coming to establish the fifth universal monarchy, succeeding those of the Assyrians, Persians, Macedonians, and Romans (Dan. 2:44, read prophetically and apocalyptically). The immanence of the parousia is expected in various parts of the NT such as Jas. 5:1–8.

For the anointing of David see 1 Sam. 16:6–16; for "sitting on the throne of Israel," 1 Kings 8:20; and 2 Chron 6:16; for "Render unto Caesar," Matt. 22:21; and Luke 20:25; for "Render to all," compare Deut. 10:12; Matt. 22:37; Mark 12:30; and Luke 10:27. The notion of using Matt. 22:21 as a sanctioning of political subjection of the colonized is on the analogy of the subjection of Palestine as a Roman province to the authority of Caesar. Alford comes close to making this argument: "The Lord's answer convicts them [the Pharisees] . . . of subjection to (Tiberius) Caesar, and recognition of that subjection. . . . The answer also *gives them the real reason why they were now under subjection to Caesar:* viz. *because they had fallen from their allegiance to God*. . . . They had again and again rejected their theocratic inheritance;—they refused it in the wilderness;—they would not have God to reign over them, but a king;—therefore were they subjected to foreigners" ([1849] 1863, 1:220–21). For other discussions of this passage see Jowett ¶s 4, 80, and 81).

On the relation of the theory of the divine right of kings to the common law and theology as part of the background of the English leaders of the Reformation, see Kantorowicz 1957; on the relation of the king and the nation see Coleridge [1829] 1976, 82–94.

56. Jowett's eighth controversial topic, "Original Sin," involves the theology of baptism (especially baptismal regeneration) and the carrying out of the justice of God against sin. Original sin is defined in the Ninth Article of Religion as "the fault and corruption of the Nature of every man, that naturally is engendered of the offspring of *Adam*; whereby man is very far gone from original righteousness, and is of his own nature inclined to evil, so that the flesh lusteth always contrary to the spirit; and therefore in every person born into this world, it deserveth God's wrath and damnation." The fall of Adam and Eve from original righteousness or grace (Gen. 3) was regarded as a historical account from the early church through to the nineteenth century. According to Augustine in his writings against Pelagius, this original sin was transmitted biologically to succeeding generations through sexual procreation. To Calvin, Luther, and the theologians of the Westminster Confession, Adam is not only the type of succeeding generations but acted on behalf of them.

The relation of Adam and Christ to the doctrine of original sin is set out in Rom. 5:12–21 and 1 Cor. 15. Commenting on the former, Jowett writes that "every verse and almost every particle . . . bears the traces of theological warfare in the pages of commentators" ([1855] 1859, 2:170). He then discusses the Pelagian controversy, particularly its attacks on original sin, by asserting that human beings are free moral agents who do not require divine grace to act righteously. To Jowett the use of the word ἁμαρτία (*hamartia*, sin) is the figure of speech of personification (death by the agency of sin): the word means "neither original sin nor actual, nor the guilt of sin as distinguished from sin itself, . . . nor . . . confined to the act of sin. . . . [It] describes sin rather as a mental state or in relation to the mind. . . . It is often the power of sin, or sin collectively, sometimes, as here, the personification of it" (2:173). Jowett follows his detailed discussion of the Greek text of Romans with a longer note on the same topic, on "The Imputation of the Sin of Adam" (2:180–88). For other discussions see Wilson ¶s 51, 76, and notes; and Williams ¶s 26, 31, 32, and notes.

On 1 Cor. 15:20 Stanley comments: "The reason of this connexion between His resurrection and ours is, that He is the representative of the whole human race in its second creation. . . . The second part of the argument where 'man' is individualised in Adam and Christ, explains the first part. 'As in the Adam . . . so in the Messiah . . . or Second Man'" (1855, 1:367–68).

For "rewardeth every man . . . works" see Matt. 16:27; for "every soul . . . iniquity," Jer. 31:30 and compare Gal. 6:5; for "neither this man . . . parents," John 9:3.

57. Jowett implies that there are sufficient historical but not biblical grounds for the institutional practices he has outlined, specifying among his eight topics as examples infant baptism and the episcopal system. In an unpublished fragment on the latter Jowett writes: "There are few or rather no traces of Episcopacy in the New Testament, but at the end of the second century the Episcopal fabric is complete. . . . How the simple words of Christ, 'Believe on Me,' grew into a vast system set forth in hard and technical terms which the first teachers of the word could not even have understood, is a strange reflection which, living eighteen centuries afterwards, we are unable adequately to realize" (Jowett 1902b, 54–55; see also Jowett [1855] 1859, 2:341–42). Christopher Wordsworth in his essay in *Replies to Essays and Reviews* (1862) agrees with Jowett that there is no literal injunction in the Bible concerning infant baptism and the episcopal form of ecclesiastical polity, but he devotes two pages to argue that they "ought to be *derived* by *logical inference* from Holy Scripture" (1862, 424–25).

58. Jowett refers to the principle of accommodation as it was used in three senses: first, the giving of a new meaning to a text that differs from its literal meaning or conditions, as in the application to Christ of texts from the prophets in the context of typology or Messianic prophecy; second, to designate in German liberal biblical criticism the tempering of the revelation of God to allow for the limitations of human understanding at any given period: hence, Jesus' words about the authorship of books of the Hebrew scriptures follows the conventions of the day (see Jowett ¶15 and n 29 and ¶22 and n. 38); and third, the modifying of troubling, unpopular, or difficult precepts in the NT to bring them into line with current social, moral, or doctrinal practices or to allow other, perhaps more fundamental faith positions, to be more easily accepted. Isaac Williams published a version of this third sense in *Tract LXXX, On Reserve in Communicating Religious Knowledge* (1837). Hence, in an age of material prosperity for the middle classes, as in mid-Victorian England, gospel precepts concerning the virtues of poverty are accommodated in the burgeoning of Victorian charities and good works which do not challenge the system that produces poverty and that mollify the do-gooder. Attacks on such practices, especially those institutionalized in the poorhouses, workhouses, and in the New Poor Law Act (1834) can be found in Dickens's *Oliver Twist* (1837–38).

The "spirit of the age," a phrase also used by Pattison in ¶28, is a translation of the term *Zeitgeist* (time spirit, itself a translation of the Lat. *genius saeculi*), common in the German enlightenment and romantic philosophy and literature to refer to the intellectual, social, moral, and religious trends of a historical period as particularly characteristic of that period and also of the perceived conformity of individuals and generalized culture to those dominant trends. The concept was discussed in Hegel's *Lectures on the Philosophy of History* ([1834] 1881), first published in an English translation in 1857. Many works were published using this phrase in their titles: Hazlitt's *The Spirit of the Age* (1825); J. S. Mill's series of articles in the *Examiner* (1831); and R. H. Horne's *The New Spirit of the Age* (1844).

For "blessedness of poverty" see, for example, Matt. 5:3, 11:5; Luke 6:20, 7:22; for "riches . . . 'in attaining eternal life,'" Matt 19:16–23; Mark 10:17–24; Luke 18:18–24; for "It is easier for a camel," Matt. 19:24; Mark 10:25; Luke 18:25; for "Son, thou . . . good things," Luke 16:25; for "one thing . . . hast," Mark 10:21.

59. The wealth of some of the medieval religious orders was legendary, and their abandonment of the gospel precept of poverty inspired many reform movements, such as that led by Bernard of Clairvaux. Chaucer satirizes the abuses of the gospel precepts in his portrayal of the Monk, the Friar, and the Prioress in the *Canterbury Tales* (1400). The dissolution of the English monasteries to obtain their wealth (detailed in the *Valor Ecclesiasticus*, the official evaluation in 1535 of monastic revenues in England, published in six volumes for the Record Commission, from 1810 to 1834) was effected by Henry VIII between 1536 and 1539. Such materials provided contexts for a number of Victorian historical novels, beginning with Sir Walter Scott's two novels of 1820, *The Monastery* and *The Abbot*. In *Past and Present* (1843) Carlyle appeals for solutions to the problems of the "condition of England" (scepticism, poverty, and lack of leadership because of the failures of democracy, and materialism) to Abbot Samson, the reformer of the wealthy abbey of St. Edmundsbury, the medieval model by which he hoped to inspire nineteenth-century captains of industry. The idealized and romanticized medieval aspect of the wealth and culture of the monasteries is set out in Charles Reade's *The Cloister and the Hearth* (1861). The double motif of the monasteries as ideals and abuses continued throughout the impact of the Oxford Movement, especially in the establishment of sisterhoods devoted to acts of charity, such as the Sisters of All Saints (1851) that included Maria Francesca Rossetti, and the Christ Church Sisterhood at Coatham in Yorkshire (later the Community of the Holy Rood) that included both Dorothy Wyndlow Pattison and Frances Pattison (who became the superior of the order in 1885), sisters of Mark Pattison, whose task was nursing (with which Jowett was thoroughly familiar through his long friendship with Florence Nightingale).

Jowett lists a number of biblical imprecations against ostentatious wealth and instructions on humility: for "Woe unto you" see Luke 6:24; and James 5:1; for "cedar and vermillion," Jer. 22:14; for "Woe unto them . . . earth," Isa. 5:8; for "great supper . . . the blind," Luke 14:16–24; for "wash one another's feet," John 13:14.

The "standard of Christ" (compare Gal. 6:2) is represented in such passages as the following: Matt. 16:24; Mark 8:34; Luke 9:23; to give to the poor and to follow, Mark 10:21; and to be a servant of all, John 12:26.

60. For "standing among us . . . know not" see John 1:26; for "Go sell all that thou hast," Luke 18:22; for "casting her two mites into the treasury," Mark 12:42–44; and Luke 21:1–4; for "making all things kin," Shakespeare, *Troilus and Cressida* 3.3.175.

The "tender and delicate woman among us" who nursed "the dying inmates" and "the soldier" is Florence Nightingale. She had gone to Scutari in Turkey from 1854 to 1856 to care for the wounded in the Crimean War. On her return she set about reforming the sanitary conditions in the army, instigating a royal commission in 1857, and a second one concerning the Indian army in 1859, for both of which she wrote most of the reports. She published *Notes on Nursing: What It Is and What It Is Not* (1859) that had an enormous success exactly contemporaneously with *Essays and Reviews*, and a theological treatise, *Suggestions for Thought to the Searchers after Truth among the Artizans of England* (privately printed, 1860), that her secretary, Arthur Hugh Clough, sent to Jowett for comment, thereby inaugurating an intimate friendship with Nightingale that lasted until Jowett's death. They conducted a long correspondence in which Jowett's part (hers was largely destroyed by her executors) has been published (Quinn and Prest 1987). On the last day of 1879 Jowett wrote to her: "There was a great deal of romantic feeling about you 23 years ago when you came home from the Crimea. . . . And now you work on in silence, & nobody knows how many lives are saved by your nurses in hospitals. . . . But I know it & often think about it. . . . Like Dr. Pusey you are a Myth in your own life time. Do you know that there are thousands of girls about the ages of 18 to 23 named after you? . . . every body has heard of you, & has a sweet association connected with your name" (Quinn and Prest 1987, 280–81).

61. For "Let them that have riches" see Mark 10:23; and 1 Cor. 7:29; for "Let the rich man" and "fold them up as a vesture," Jer. 9:23; and Heb. 1:12; for the rich man "who fared sumptuously," Luke 16:19–31; for "cast it from us," Matt. 5:29–30.

Jesus in the parable of the last judgment (Matt 25:31–46) tells of the kingdom prepared for those who feed the hungry and thirsty, welcome the strangers, clothe the naked, and visit the sick and imprisoned. Instead of "accidents *of* birth" the device of "accidents *at* birth" was the trigger to recognition scenes in Victorian novels when the "barrier" of social class is overcome by the discovery of a long-lost relative or inheritance (as in Charlotte Brontë's *Jane Eyre* [1847] or Dickens's *Great Expectations* [1860–61]) or by the loss of all wealth, property, and social position, and the reduction to poverty or imprisonment for debt (as in Dickens's *Dombey and Son* [1846–48] and *Little Dorrit* [1855–57]). The ideals of service in aid of others, or the sympathetic treatment of the outcasts of society, such as prostitutes, is set out in Elizabeth Gaskell's *Ruth* (1853), the moral improvement novels of Charlotte Mary Yonge, such as *The Daisy Chain* (1856), or the social problem novels of the 1840s and 1850s, such as Charles Kingsley's *Yeast* (1848) and Elizabeth Gaskell's *North and South* (1855). Social philanthropy was a large-scale movement, chiefly motivated by the women in evangelical Christianity, to ameliorate the lot of the poor for humanitarian and religious reasons, but it often resisted the wholehearted acceptance of Victorian outcasts as "friends and brethren" in the interest of exercising social controls to reduce the threat of public unrest (see Prochaska 1980).

62. For "Swear not at all" see Matt. 5:33–38, where Jesus reinterprets the fourth commandment (Exod. 20:7). Directly prior to this statement, Jesus reinterprets the OT precepts on "divorce" (Matt. 5:31–32). Section 8 of the Town Police Clauses Act (1847) made the use of profane or obscene language an offense punishable by summary conviction by a fine not exceeding 40s. or a jail term not exceeding 14 days. The offense had to be committed on the street. For a history of swearing see Hughes 1991.

"Swearing" also included the taking of oaths, by the sovereign, members of Parliament, the judiciary, witnesses in law courts, and clergy before ordination (swearing obedience to the bishop and signing the Articles of Religion). Article Thirty-Nine is on the subject of "A Christian Man's Oath." In the seventeenth century the controversy over swearing oaths involved the Non-jurors who refused the oath of allegiance to William and Mary in 1689 because they had previously sworn allegiance to James II and his heirs and successors (see Pattison ¶2 and note). Three groups questioned swearing an oath in nineteenth-century Britain: religious people such as the Quakers, who refused to swear oaths on the grounds of Matt. 5:33–38; the clergy were increasingly restive about subscription to the Articles of Religion and some formed an association to resist subscription (see Williams ¶4 and n. 8); and finally atheists and freethinkers could not make a legal oath at all in England since to do so required a religious profession. The most notable figure in the last category was the atheist Charles Bradlaugh who frequently refused the judicial oath and was punished (see Wilson ¶57 and n. 96; see also Wilson ¶s 9, 43–47, and 51, and notes).

For "counsel of perfection" see Jowett ¶26 and note.

The "body who have endeavoured to follow" Jesus' "commandment" (to love one's neighbour) very likely refers to the Society of Friends. The Quakers, known for adhering to the "counsels" of the gospels, refused to take the oath as a matter of religious scruple and so in the nineteenth century began to be allowed to make a "solemn affirmation."

"Sabbatarianism" refers to the strict observance of Sunday (and for some Christians, such as the Seventh Day Adventists, Saturday) as a day of rest. For a discussion of its nineteenth-century context see Temple ¶54 and notes. Jowett refers to Matt. 12:1–8, where Jesus is attacked by the Pharisees for not observing the Sabbath. This reference, along with that to Paul, continues Jowett's list of biblical citations which call for toleration against restrictions and prohibitions based on a literal reading of the Bible.

63. This "class of passages" is cited as instances of toleration for differences. The "tower of Siloam" is part of a rhetorical question asked by Jesus in order to reject the notion that suffering was the consequence of sin (Luke 13:1–5). The location of this tower is unknown: presumably it was in the fortification of Jerusalem around the area of Siloam, part of the complex system of carrying water from the spring of Gihon to the pool of Siloam or Shiloah during the reign of King Hezekiah (727–698 B.C.E.). As the rest of the passage demonstrates, the point is that those who died did so not because "they were sinners above all men that dwelt in Jerusalem" but because of their presence there at the time of the accident. The "good Samaritan," who despite the mutual hatred of Samaritans and Jews helps a Jew that has been wounded by thieves, is the basis of Jesus' parable about the "true neighbor" (Luke 10:29–37). "Forbid him not" is spoken by Jesus in reference to the thrusting out of an exorcist by the apostles (Mark 9:39). The passage undercuts any exclusivist claims by the apostles as the only followers of Christ.

In the OT adultery is defined as sexual relations between a married or betrothed woman and any man not her husband: it was committed only against a husband, never against a wife. The punishment was death (see, for instance, Exod. 20:14; Deut. 5:18, 22:22–24; and Lev. 18:20). In the NT Jesus places the guilt equally on the man (Matt. 5:27–32; Mark 10:2–12; and Luke 16:18). On adultery and divorce in their biblical and nineteenth-century contexts see Jowett ¶28 and notes.

For "Let every man" see Rom. 14:5; for "Let no man," Col. 2:16. In *The Epistles of St. Paul,* Jowett comments on the former text: "Let each be satisfied in his own mind, not compelled by some external rule. This individual liberty of conscience is with the Apostle an essential part of the Gospel, a law for ourselves, and to be respected in others" ([1855] 1859, 2:374). The latter text applies to the "present day" in the Sabbatarian movement, as discussed in Jowett ¶30 and n. 62.

Human restraint from judging others, and God's justice in judging all by their deeds (Rom. 2:1–16), suggest to Jowett that facile damnation of the "heathen" by Christians or Catholics by Protestants is not supported by the NT ([1855] 1859, 2:117–18). For "good men had lived among the heathen" and "the damnation of the heathen" see also Temple ¶33; and Wilson ¶s 15–16, 66, and especially ¶81 and notes.

For "rewardeth every man" see Matt. 16:27; for "When the Gentiles," Rom. 2:14. "Uncovenanted mercies" and "invincible ignorance" are phrases used in British religious controversies of the seventeenth and eighteenth centuries. The former refers to grace that is not promised or secured by God: see, for instance, William Sherlock: "They must be saved by uncovenanted Grace and Mercy" ([1689] 1703, bk. 3, sec. 7); or Samuel Horsley: "I will cast on his free uncovenanted mercy" (1810–22, 3:38). The latter refers to an "ignorance" of the means for salvation, the possessor of which has no way of overcoming or removing. Thomas Aquinas's phrase "*ignorantia invinciblis*" in *Summa Theologica* (quest. 76, art. 2; [1265–] 1962–64, 25:147–49) is used by Gilbert Burnet in *An Exposition on the Thirty-Nine Articles of the Church of England*: "God only knows . . . how far our ignorance is affected or invincible" ([1699] 1819, 8).

"*Extra palum Ecclesiae!*" (Lat. outside, or beyond, the pale of the church) is a variant of *Salus extra ecclesiam non est* (Lat. outside of the church there is no salvation) from Cyprian, who was demanding that schismatics be rebaptised in order to achieve salvation (trans. Robert Ernest Wallis, *Epistles*, letter 72, sect. 21; *ANF* 5:384). The phrase is cited by Augustine in *De Baptismo contra Donatistas* (400; Concerning baptism against the Donatists, trans. J. R. King, *NPNCF*1 4:458, bk. 4, chap. 17). The phrase was common among scholastic theologians, as, for example, in Thomas Aquinas [1265–] 1962–64, 31:193). The *Tracts for the Times* included a series of "Records of the Church," translations of early Christian documents. Records 19–21 comprised Cyprian's treatise on the unity of the church. The cited passage is translated in Record 19, chapter 4 (*Tracts* 1833–41, 2:6).

64. The Athanasian "doctrine of the Trinity," expounded by St. Athanasius at Nicaea against the Arians (325), maintained that Christ was of one "substance" with God the Father. Nicene theology is summarized also in the "Athanasian Creed" (see Williams ¶32 and n. 138; Jowett ¶22 and notes; see also Melton 1987, 2–3). The assumption that Jesus shared divine foreknowledge is questioned by the limited knowledge disclosed in Mark 13:32. On this "embarrassing theological problem for the Church" see Hugh Anderson 1976, 301 and Gundry 1993, 793–800.

The "words marked in italics" were omitted by Codex Montanensis (983) and some Vulgate MSS. The parallel passage is Matt. 24:36; there is no parallel in Luke. For a discussion of its authenticity see A. L. Moore 1966, 191 ff. Ambrose discusses the passage in *De Spiritu Sancto* (381; On the Holy Spirit; bk. 2, chap. 11; Ambrose 1963, 136–37).

The "Millenarians" and "those who maintain the continuance of miracles" refer to forms of fundamentalism, Evangelical and Roman Catholic, respectively. Millenarians believe in the nearness of Christ's second advent, a belief based upon particular passages of the Bible such as Dan. 7:15–28 and Rev. 20. See also Williams ¶22; Wilson ¶17; and Jowett ¶21 and notes. For millenarianism see Barr 1977, 190–206; for millenarianism in Britain from 1845 to 1878, Sandeen 1970, 81–102.

"Miracles" are extended beyond the accounts of the life of Jesus and the apostles in the NT particularly in the lives of the saints. Citing Jowett, J. A. Froude writes: "The lives of the saints of the Catholic Church, from the time of the Apostles to the present day, are a complete tissue of miracles resembling those of the Gospels. . . . The Bible is equally a record of miracles; but as in other histories we reject miracles without hesitation, so of those in the Bible we insist on the universal acceptance: the former are all false, the latter are all true. . . . If with Professor Jowett 'we interpret the Bible as any other book,' the element of miracle which has evaporated from the entire surface of human history will not maintain itself in the sacred ground of the Gospels, and the facts of Christianity will melt in our hands like a snow-ball" ([1863] 1877, 1:184–85, 191–92).

The "Predestinarian controversy" refers both to Pelagianism and to Calvinism. For the relations between them concerning grace, justification, free will, and predestination see Jowett ¶s 2–3 and notes, as well as Jowett's lengthy commentary on Rom. 5:12–21 in *The Epistles of St. Paul* ([1855] 1859, 2:170–87). For Calvin's views on predestination see his commentary on Romans, particularly on Rom. 3 and 10 ([1539] 1973, 58–81, and 220–37). Jowett also wrote an appendix, "On Predestination and Free Will," in *The Epistles of St. Paul* ([1855] 1859, 2:596–632). in which he argues: "If any doctrine could be established by particular passages of Scripture, Calvinism would rest immoveable on the ninth chapter of the Romans. . . . It is answered by the opponents of Calvinism, that the Apostle is here speaking not of individual but of national predestination" ([1855] 1859, 2:606–7). Jowett makes another elaborate comparison of Calvinists, Lutherans, Arminians, and Roman Catholics in commenting on Rom. 9:8 (2:278–79). For an example of an opponent of Calvin who deprives him of "his real standing ground," see George Stanley Faber, who in an extended attack touches only briefly on Rom. 9 (1842,

348–54).

Matt. 16:18–19 refers to the "rock" upon which the church is to be built, and the "keys" to heaven; Matt. 18:18 refers to matters of church discipline: Roman Catholic theology bases the authority of the church partly upon these verses. In 1 Cor. 3:15 Paul refers to the "fire" by which a "man . . . shall be saved": Roman Catholic theologians use it to discuss purgatory (see Jowett ¶2 and note). The "distinctive articles" of the Roman Catholic "creed" absent from the NT refer not to a specific creed but to the general system of beliefs that are not, according to Jowett, justified on the basis of the scriptural passages he refers to directly above. Such arguments are commonplace among Anglican theologians: for instance, referring to Matt. 16:18–19, Richard Whately rejects the possibility that the verses justify Rome's claims to pre-eminence through Petrine succession, or as the sole possessor of the power of the keys of heaven and earth (1830, 169–70). Charles Hastings Collette published a refutation of a lecture on purgatory by Nicholas Wiseman, showing that "five out of the eight Fathers cited by Dr. Wiseman refer to the text, 1 Cor. iii. 15, a text which bears an admittedly different interpretation, and all these writers, it is pretended, quote the text as referring *exclusively* to the Popish doctrine of Purgatory. Such a notion is a pure invention—a fiction" (1860, 258–59).

65. An important attack against "proving a doctrine from Scripture" and ignoring the rest (as criticized at the end of Jowett ¶32) is in Hooker's *The Laws of Ecclesiastical Polity*. In the preface to the second book Hooker says that he will address "the very main pillar of your [the Calvinists'] cause, 'That Scripture ought to be the only rule of all our actions'" ([1594–1662] 1954, 1:122). He addresses the question of proof texts as exclusive in the face of often contradictory arguments that are silently set aside: "Might they [the Calvinists] not hereby even as well prove, that one commandment of Scripture is the only rule of all things, and so exclude the rest of the Scripture, as now they do all means beside Scripture?" (1:249).

The "adverse statements" between "St. James and St. Paul" are commented upon by Horne: "The venerable Martin Luther . . . excluded [James] from the sacred canon on account of its supposed contradiction of Saint Paul concerning the doctrine of justification by faith; but more mature experience and deeper research induced him subsequently to retract his opinion" ([1818] 1828, 4:442). The "adverse statements" between the NT and OT are summarized by Horne: "Some of the differences between the Old and New Testaments arise from numbers and dates . . . and others arise from the variances occurring in the quotations from the Old in the New Testament" ([1818] 1828, 2:547). Unlike Jowett, Horne devises elaborate explanations to reconcile these "apparent contradictions between the sacred writers" ([1818] 1828, 2:535). Jowett explicitly opposed such attempts, as he states in a college sermon of 1882: "Ingenious persons have attempted to harmonize these and similar discrepancies in the Gospels [concerning Jesus' last words]. But there is little wisdom in applying to Scripture a mode of reconciliation which we should not apply to an ordinary history" (1895, 327). See also Alford's discussion of the "discrepancies, apparent and real" among the Gospels ([1848] 1863, 1:12–14).

Jowett relies upon contemporary comparative linguistics that used the "new philology" to move away from etymological connections between language groups, instead finding their connectedness primarily in grammatical similarities. The term *oriental* rather than *semitic* had been used by the Danish philologist Rasmus Christian Rask in *Essay on the Origin of the Ancient Scandinavian and Icelandic Tongue* (1818). See Pedersen [1931] 1967, 11, 118. Renan developed comparative study of the semitic languages (*Histoire générale et système comparé des langues sémitiques* [1858; General history and comparative system of the Semitic languages]) and with Rask, Franz Bopp, and the other founders of the schools of "oriental languages" (referring to both semitic and indic language groups) established the philological basis for "orientalism" as the culturally, racially, and linguistically "other" (as in Jowett's comment; see Said [1978] 1979, 98–100; 130–43).

Jowett distinguishes between the languages the Bible is written in and the linguistic cultures of the people described in the Bible. One language spoken by the people of the OT was Aramaic, the language of the Aramean descendants of Abraham. Scribes used it in the bureaucracy of the Assyrian Empire which dominated the eastern Mediterranean from the eighth to the fourth centuries B.C.E. It was also used in dialects (as by Jesus and the disciples) up to the Roman occupation. Another language was ancient Hebrew, closely related to Aramaic. Most of the OT is written in Hebrew. The "language" of the NT is Hellenistic, or "koine" (common), Greek, dispersed throughout the Mediterranean through the conquests of Alexander the Great. Alford summarizes the widespread nineteenth-century assumptions that there were one or more sources for the gospels written in Aramaic ([1848] 1863, 1:6–12, 25–29). In his first edition he had proposed an Aramaic or Hebrew origin for Matthew; in the fifth edition, he opts for Greek as the original language of the gospel (see Metzger 1992; and Metzger and Coogan 1993, 45–46, 262–63, 271–73). For racialism directed against "Eastern lands. . . Eastern people" see Temple ¶27 and notes. On the relations between theology, ethnology, and philology in mid-nineteenth-century Oxford see Burrow 1967 and Dowling 1982.

There is a discrepancy between John 6:52 and 6:63 in what Jesus says regarding the flesh and blood of "the Son of Man" if his words are interpreted literally: in the first instance, he tells his followers to eat his flesh and drink his blood; in the second, he discounts the importance of the flesh, emphasizing "the spirit."

66. Jowett's views qualify and contradict Horne on the prevalence of doctrine in the Bible. Horne maintains: "As the Holy Scriptures contain the revealed will of God to man, they . . . present to our serious study, *doctrinal truths* of the utmost importance. . . . They are chiefly to be found in the apostolic epistles which, though originally designed for the edification of particular Christian churches or individuals, are nevertheless of *general application, and designed for the guidance of the universal church in every age.*" In his rules for "doctrinal interpretation," however, Horne is very close to Jowett's position: for instance, "The meaning of the Sacred Writings is not to be determined by modern notions and systems: but we must endeavour to carry ourselves back to the very times in which they were written, and realise the ideas and modes of thinking of the sacred writers" ([1818] 1828, 2:475–76). For a view opposite to that of Jowett's regarding the dogmatic interpretation of the Bible see J. H. Newman, *Tract LXXXV*, "Lectures on the Scripture Proof of the Doctrines of the Church" (1838); especially Lecture 2, "The Difficulties of Latitudinarianism" (1838, 14–26) and *Apolgia Pro Vita Sua*: "My battle was with liberalism; by liberalism I mean the anti-dogmatic principle and its developments. . . . From the age of fifteen, dogma has been the fundamental principle of my religion. . . . I thought that this was the doctrine of Scripture, of the early Church, and of the Anglican Church" ([1864] 1967, 54–55).

As in ¶34, Jowett's chronology of classical authors argues against "anachronism." Polybius was born over 150 years after the death of Plato; Lycophron (b. c. 320 B.C.E.) wrote a gloss on the tragedies of Aeschylus (525–56 B.C.E.) in his obscure poem *Alexandra.*

67. Jowett's three pairs of terms have very different theological histories. The first pair, *love* and *truth,* have prompted substantial devotional commentary but not controversy, largely because in the pastoral application of the NT in the Christian church love is widely agreed upon as the basis for spiritual formation and moral action; at the same time the philosophical distinctions in the categories of truth in Greek philosophy have not been part of the history of "truth" as a theological term. The chief noun for "love" in the NT, ἀγάπη (Gk. *agape* from ἀγαπάω, *agapao*), occurs almost 120 times, and the verb more than 130. In the Vulgate it is translated "*caritas*"; in the AV, "charity." It signifies the divine nature (1 John 4:8, 16) and is what characterizes the frequent injunctions to "love thy neighbor" (Mark 12:31); it is distinguished from the classical term, ἔρος (Gk. *eros*; Lat. *amor*), which is love attracted by qualities in the loved one, a word used in classical Greek for love between the sexes (it does not occur in the NT). The other term for love, φιλία (Gk. *philia*; Lat. *amicitia*) means friendship (so translated in the AV at the only occurrence, James 4:4), the relationship based on closeness and affection as in family relationships (Matt. 10:27); the verbal form (Gk. φιλέω, *phileo,* to love with the emotion of love and friendship; Lat. *amare*) is more frequent. This distinction is made clear at John 21:15–17 when Jesus asks Simon Peter three times if he loves him, to which Peter responds that he does. The first two times Jesus uses the verb ἀγαπᾷς (Gk. *agapas*) and Peter responds with φιλῶ (Gk. *philo*); then Jesus adopts the same verb, φιλεῖς (Gk. *phileis*). Alford comments in detail on the former as "that reverential love, grounded on high graces of character, which is borne towards God and man by the child of God," while the latter is "more the personal love of human affection" ([1849] 1863, 1:911). Augustine deals with the nature of love in detail in the *Enchiridion of Faith, Hope, and Love,* and in *The City of God* distinguishes between the "two loves," the love of God (Lat. *amor Dei*), which leads to the spiritual Jerusalem, the City of God, and the love of this world (Lat. *amor mundi*), which leads to the city of destruction, that Augustine names allegorically "Babylon." For discussions of love see Nygren 1932; C. S. Lewis 1960.

Truth (Gk. ἀλήθεια, *aletheia*) signifies the reality underlying appearance and is so used at Rom. 9:1 and 2 Cor. 11:10. Jesus is claimed by his followers as being "true" and as speaking "truth" at Matt. 22:16, and claims himself to be the truth at John 14:6. Such uses are frequent in the NT.

The second pair of terms, *grace* (Gk. χάρις, *charis*) and *faith* (Gk. πίστις, *pistis*), like love and truth, occur frequently in the NT, but unlike them they are terms that are associated with specific doctrinal controversies. Grace signifies favor that is freely bestowed, especially from a superior power to an inferior, and is often described as the power of God's love in redemption. Augustine played on the meaning of the Latin term, *gratia,* and the notion of it as the gift of God given freely (*gratis*), without merit or deserving, and without restriction (Rom. 5:15). Grace became a topic of theological controversy in the writing of Augustine against Pelagius, concerning the relation of grace to free will (*De natura et gratia,* 415; On nature and grace). For Pelagian views of grace see Jowett ¶s 2–3, 32, and notes. Commenting on Rom. 5:12 Jowett writes in *The Epistles of St. Paul*: "Pelagius would have said that man was free, independent, isolated, needing nothing for his salvation but his own free will and better mind, requiring neither grace preventive nor grace cooperative, but relying on himself for acceptance with God, according to the terms of the Gospel" ([1855] 1859, 2:170). The term was also crucial in Calvin's elaboration of the notion of predestination; see Wilson ¶s 26, 51, and notes; and Pattison ¶24 and note. Faith as a controversial term came into prominence in the debate between Luther and the Roman Catholic Church concerning the role and efficacy of good works, or the reliance of the Christian upon faith, or even "faith alone"; see also Jowett ¶2 and note; and Wilson ¶20 and note.

The third pair of terms, *justification* and *inspiration,* also the subject of much controversy at the Reformation and subsequently, are, as Jowett asserts, heavily dependant upon their verb forms for their meaning. This later history of theological controversy is read back into the terms in the NT. Justification (Gk. δικαίωσις, *dikaiosis*), the act of pronouncing justification or acquittal, is a legal term used only twice in the NT (Rom. 4:25 and 5:18), derived from frequent uses of the verb, δικαιόω (Gk. *dikaioo*), to pronounce righteous. Its use by Luther and Calvin, and its place in the history of Anglican debates with continental theologians (as, for instance, in Hooker's "Learned Discourse of Justification," 1585) became part of the doctrinal positions and interpretive strategies of later exegetes according to their theological affiliations. Inspiration (Gk. Θεόπνευστος, *theopneustos*) occurs only once in the NT (2 Tim. 3:16), and derives from Θέος (Gk. *theos*, God) and πνέω (Gk. *pneo*, to blow). The relation of this concept to the later doctrine of inspiration is discussed earlier in Jowett ¶s 11 and 14 ff. See also Wilson ¶20 and Pattison ¶24.

For each of these six terms with references to classical, NT, and subsequent usage see Kittel and Friedrich 1964–76.

68. John 3:5 refers to birth by "water" and "spirit" and is therefore interpreted as central to the sacrament of baptism; John 6:56 refers to "bread" and "flesh" and is therefore interpreted as central to the eucharist. Among the "minds" that Jowett refers to is E. B. Pusey, who wrote on both topics in three *Tracts for the Times* (numbers LXVII–LXIX), "Scriptural Views of Holy Baptism" (1835) and in his monograph *The Doctrine of the Real Presence* (1855). In the former, Pusey discusses "water" in John 3:5 at length (Pusey 1835, 28–68); in the latter, he discusses "bread and wine" in relation to "the Fathers" as well as the Bible (Pusey [1855] 1883, 131–34). For the contemporary controversy over baptism see Williams ¶s 27, 31, and notes; for the eucharist see Williams ¶31 and note; and Wilson ¶76 and note.

69. Jowett proposes four interpretive options: (1) the idea of a single "true" meaning, a notion related to plenary inspiration of the Bible as *the* word of God, and hence identified contemporaneously with a literalist reading. Jowett advocates "one meaning" though not on literalist grounds (see Jowett ¶s 15, 46, and notes); (2) the mystical/ allegorical method of the Alexandrian interpreters like Origen and his followers (see Jowett ¶s 3 and 11 and notes); (3) the double senses of prophecy, that the events prophesied in the Bible are fulfilled both in later events narrated in the Bible as well as in later secular history (Jowett ¶s 13, 19, and notes); and (4) the symbolical or typological method of reading the antitypes of the "Gospel" (or NT) in the "Law" (or OT) (Jowett ¶12 and note). For somewhat similar Jewish methods of interpretation see Alexander 1993.

70. The Latin phrase "the cock on the bell-tower" refers to the turning of the weather-cock to indicate the direction of the wind. The phrase "carried about with every wind of doctrine" (Eph. 4:14), is proverbial for changeableness in opinion. The use of a cock on the weathervane on the steeple of a church was enacted by a papal decree in the ninth century for every church in honor of St. Peter; see Rowland 1978, 20–28. The Waldensians, or "Vaudois," are a small anti–Roman Catholic sect still surviving in Piedmont, established by Peter Waldo of Lyons about 1170. They attacked ecclesiastical power and corruption and appointed their own clergy to oversee their rule of life based on the gospel precepts of simplicity, poverty, and piety. They were persecuted in a crusade against them by Pope Innocent III in 1209. Eventually they aligned themselves with the Reformation churches but were again persecuted in 1655 under Charles Emmanuel II, duke of Savoy, the occasion of Milton's sonnet on their behalf, "On the Late Massacre in Piedmont" (1673). The pun in the Latin tag *Gallus in campanili* is that the Gauls or the French are taking over the churches (see also W. Wordsworth's sonnet "The Vaudois" in the *Ecclesiastical Sonnets* [1822]).

For "the scarlet thread of Rahab" see Josh. 2:1–18; 6:17–25. Rahab is cited as an example of faith in Heb. 11:31, and as faith issuing in good works in James 2:25.

For "the number of Abraham's followers" see Gen. 14:14, where he has 318 servants. This passage (together with Gen 17:23) is commented on in the anonymous "Letter of Barnabas" (70–150): "Abraham, who first instituted circumcision, did it looking forward in spirit to Jesus. . . . Notice that he first mentions eighteen, and, after a pause, three hundred. Eighteen is I, and H—you have Jesus (IH)—and, because the cross in the T was to have grace, he says 'and three hundred' (T). So he indicates Jesus in the two letters and the cross in the other" (*The Apostolic Fathers* 1947, 205 [Barnabas 9:7–8]). The rabbis at Alexandria used a method of interpretation called "gematria" to reveal the hidden meaning of Hebrew words whereby each letter had a numerical value; the same method was used in Christian interpretation from Alexandria, with which the letter of Barnabas is associated. Hence, in the LXX the Greek letters have numerical values, and so 318 can be represented in letters as TIH (300 is represented by the Greek letter tau, 10 by iota, and 8 by eta, standing for the cross, and the first two letters of Jesus' name in Greek).

Peter is the first to enter the sepulchre after Jesus' crucifixion at John 20:6. In Luke 24:12 Peter runs to the sepulchre after the women have already entered it and have returned with the news that the body of Jesus is not there.

71. Jowett had earlier discussed the ways in which later doctrinal or sectarian positions were read back into biblical passages (Jowett ¶13), or were used as proof texts for such doctrines (¶s 26, 23, and 33), or were accommodated to present beliefs and practices (¶s 33 and 34). Jowett uses the conventional distinction between *exegesis* (a reading out of the meaning from the text, an explication of the meaning of the text in its day and for its first audiences) and *eisegesis* (a reading of later meanings back into the biblical passages). The latter is defined by William Fitzgerald in *Aids to Faith*: "A certain system of doctrine is first accepted . . . for the sake of the doctrine itself: the Scripture becomes valuable only as the vehicle of this doctrine . . . and the means of exciting a certain class of pious sentiments" (William Thomson 1861, 55). Fitzgerald was attacking Jowett for reading back his doubts into the NT texts. To Jowett, the early fathers of the church read eisegetically (see Jowett ¶48 and n. 86), for prophecy fulfilled, for typological correspondences between the Hebrew and Christian scriptures, and for allegories between the earthly and heavenly orders, as in the Epistle of Barnabas (early second century) and Justin Martyr's *Dialogue with Trypho* (mid-second century). See Kugel and Greer 1986, 137–42.

Jowett uses four examples of figurative readings to show how the methods of the early and medieval church were still active in biblical interpretation. First he refers to Jesus' prophecies of the last judgment (Matt. 24:4–36 and parallels, Mark 13:5–37; Luke 21:8–36) and the passages on the destruction of Jerusalem in 70 under Titus (Matt. 23:37–39; 24:1–3). They prophesy both the end of the ages and the destruction of the temple as events beyond time and as immanent shortly after Jesus' lifetime.

The second example distinguishes between a historical Israel and Israel as a spiritual community. The latter is a vehicle for the other nations to acknowledge God and by which God will demonstrate justice and power (Ezek. 36:22–23; 38:23; and Isa. 43:10–12). The constitution of the new or spiritual Israel is elaborated typologically as old covenant/new covenant, law/gospel, and Moses/Christ in Heb. 8:5–10, where the word *pattern* or *type* is used of Moses. J. H. Newman in his 1832 sermon on "Moses the Type of Christ" extended the typology of the two Israels, the historic nation with a spiritual destiny. Israel therefore "prefigures the condition of the Christian Church" ([1834–43] 1891, 7:118–19). In 1836 Newman preached on "Elisha a Type of Christ and His Followers" and in 1841 on "Joshua a Type of Christ and His Followers" (Newman 1991, 368–71).

The third example is the application of Mosaic ritual in Leviticus to events in the NT. Here Jowett refers to what Horne calls "*Legal types*, or those contained in the Mosaic law" ([1818] 1828, 2:528). One of the ceremonies for the day of atonement was the sending out of the scapegoat, laden with the sins of Israel, and wearing strands of scarlet wool (Lev. 16:1–34). William Holman Hunt, one of the Pre-Raphaelite Brotherhood of painters, went to Palestine (1854–55) and painted *The Scapegoat*, which was exhibited in the Royal Academy exhibition in February, 1856 with a substantial commentary in the Catalogue referring to the ceremonies for the day of atonement and the scarlet wool that Hunt says he placed "to suggest the crown of thorns" (Hunt 1969, 42; see also Landow 1979). In *Maud* (1855) Tennyson's hero attacks Maud's brother: "Some peculiar mystic grace / . . . heaped the whole inherited sin / On the huge scapegoat of the race, / All, all upon the brother" (ll. 483–85). See also Jowett ¶48 and note.

In the fourth example Jowett refers to the crossing of the Red Sea not only as a metaphorical figure for baptism that subsequent readers can interpret by eisegesis in the passages from Exodus but as a "preordained type," a meaning that is "given" in the text as part of its inspired utterance and that can be derived by exegesis, whereby the typological implications for the crossing of the Red Sea is a type of the baptism of Jesus and also of the resurrection. Such references to the typological readings are common in liturgy, for instance, in blessing the Easter candle on Holy Saturday. In the *BCP* the order for the "public Baptism of Infants" begins with a prayer addressed to God who "didst safely lead the children of Israel thy people through the Red Sea, figuring thereby thy holy baptism." The same typology is invoked in Easter hymns, such as "Come ye faithful, raise the strain" by John Damascene (c. 750), trans. by John Mason Neale.

Clement of Rome wrote two epistles to the Corinthians. The second is a homily. In the first he retells the story of Rahab as an instance of faith and hospitality who, though a harlot in Jericho, accepted the spies of Joshua, lodged them in her house, concealed them from a search, and accepted the judgment of God against Jericho. She enabled them to escape by means of a scarlet rope from the window of her house, a sign that eventually results in her being preserved from death when Jericho is taken. To Clement the scarlet rope prefigures the blood of Christ whereby redemption will come to all who believe and hope in God.

72. For a discussion of the "origin of the first three Gospels," the synoptic problem, see Wilson ¶22 and n. 40; and Jowett ¶13 and note. Herbert Marsh studied in Germany, at Leipzig and at Göttingen, under Johann David Michaelis. After his return to England he translated Michaelis's *Einleitung in die göttlichen Schriften des Neue Bandes* (1750) as *Introduction to the New Testament* (1793–1801, 4 vols.), embroiling himself in controversy concerning the literary relations among the gospels and their sources

in his essay on the synoptics (Marsh 1823, 3:167–409) and on German critical methods in *Lectures on the Criticism and Interpretation of the Bible* (1828). For the relation between the gospels and oral narratives see Jowett ¶62 and note.

73. Jowett's four points concern the failure of the three synoptic gospels to be "independent witnesses" because of their reliance upon common sources, written and oral. His "consequences" significantly separate his view of the synoptic gospels from those of many of his contemporaries who struggled to "harmonize" the gospels, concealing or ignoring differences among them in favor of a universalizing narrative. Alford points out the "impracticability of constructing a formal harmony of the three Gospels" ([1849] 1863, 1: 22]–24]). On gospel parallels see Jowett ¶15 and n. 28.

Second, the connection of verse to verse in a continuous sequence in each of the synoptic gospels cannot be sustained textually; only in those pericopes (or sections) that are in parallel can the continuity be sustained. Jowett is not repudiating all connections among verses, but only the need to "enforce [it] everywhere." The initial impact of this argument is to make sustained commentary on each of the Gospels independently more difficult; but for his contemporaries it turned the first three gospels into an assemblage of fragments, positing only a context in the parallel congruities where previously separate and individual contexts and sequences had been of primary importance.

Third, the attribution of overall design as deriving from intentionality on the part of the authors of the first three gospels, "the same subject on different plans," is rejected; or at least it is rejected as a "free handling" on the part of the author, since the author and his "plan" were implicated in the use of common sources. This rejection of some of the aspects of intentionality distances the traditional "authors" of the gospels from widely accepted contemporary doctrines of inspiration and destabilizes the authority of the text that derives in part from the magisterial and infallible authorial presence of the evangelists.

Fourth, the authorship of the synoptic gospels was traditionally assigned to persons mentioned in the NT. The author of Matthew was "universally believed to be the Apostle Matthew. With this belief the contents of the Gospel are not inconsistent" (Alford [1849] 1863, 1:24]); Mark is ascribed to the person referred to in various NT writings (e.g., Acts 12:12, 25) who was, as Jowett says, "the interpreter of St. Peter." According to Alford, "An unanimous tradition of the ancient Christian writers represents him as the 'interpres' of Peter: i. e. the secretary or amanuensis, whose office it was to commit to writing the orally-delivered instructions and narrations of the Apostle. . . . He is said to have become first bishop of the Church in that city [Alexandria], and to have suffered martyrdom there. All this [latter detail] however is exceedingly uncertain" (Alford [1849] 1863, 1:33]; citing Eusebius, *Ecclesiastical History*, bk. 2, chap. 15). To Alford, Luke and Acts are "universally" attributed to Luke the companion of Paul (Acts 16:10; Col. 4:14) and "here . . . there seems to be no reasonable ground of doubt" (Alford [1849] 1863, 1:40]–41]).

Modern scholars hold the two-document hypothesis with various modifications, that Mark was the first gospel written in point of time, and was followed by Matthew and Luke along with another source common to the latter two, "Q" (Ger. *Quelle*, "source"), now lost (a collection of sayings of Jesus, the source of some two hundred verses that are common to Matthew and Luke, but that are not found in Mark), and possibly some materials on which Matthew alone drew, with another for Luke. But this view is challenged by those who argue that Matthew is the earliest document, particularly the Roman Catholic Biblical Commission who decided (1907) in favor of the priority of Matthew, following Augustine, who argues that Mark abbreviated Matthew. For current scholarship on the synoptic problem see Farmer 1964, 1–30; Longstaff 1988; E. P. Sanders and Margaret Davies 1989; Koester 1990; Catchpole 1993; Meyboom 1993; and Tuckett 1993.

74. The "Preterists and Futurists," derived from Lat. *praeter* (past), are those who "hold that the prophecies of the Apocalypse have been already . . . fulfilled" (*OED*, s.v. "preterist"; citing this passage). The full phrase is used by Philip Charles Despres in *Apocalypse Fulfilled* (1854): "We have Praeterists and Futurists—one class of interpreters believing that the Apocalypse was fulfilled in the first three or four centuries of the Christian aera, another class maintaining that, with the exception of the first three chapters, none of it is fulfilled" (2).

Jowett applies to biblical prophecy a saying of Herodotus: "The opinion . . . is grounded in obscurity and needs no disproof" (*History of the Persian Wars*, bk. 2 chap. 23; trans. A. D. Godley, *Loeb* 1:301). Herodotus rejects the arcane view that the Nile floods because it flows from the river Oceanos that encircles the disc of the earth.

Daniel and Revelation were both appealed to by Jowett's contemporaries as prophesies of recent or future apocalyptic events, as in Karl August Auberlen's *The Prophecies of Daniel and the Revelations of St. John* (1854; trans. Adolph Sapir, 1858) and Samuel Sparkes's *A Historical Commentary on the Eleventh Chapter of Daniel, Extending from the Days of Cyrus to the Crimean War, Receiving Its Ultimate Accomplishment in the Fall of the Turkish Ottoman Empire* (1858). To Jowett such predictive readings are a misuse of prophecy: "The fulfilment of prophecy has been sought for in a series of events which have been sometimes bent to make them fit" even extending to "the passing circumstances of to-day or yesterday, at the distance of about two thousand years, and as many miles" (Jowett [1855] 1859, 2:135). To combat Williams's and Jowett's assertions on the traditional dating of Daniel, as well as to stress its predictive aspect, Pusey's undergraduate lectures were published in *Daniel the Prophet* (1864) (see Williams ¶s 13 and 22 and n. 95). Similarly, Christopher Wordsworth attacked Jowett's limiting of prophecy to the biblical events and his restriction of it to the disclosure of the holiness and the moral purposes of God (1862, 428–37).

75. For the "weak brother . . . for whom Christ died" see 1 Cor. 8:11; for "no man can serve two masters," Matt. 6:24; for "truth shall make you free," John 8:32.

In *The Epistles of St. Paul* Jowett discussed the same two audiences: "The poor and uneducated" should "read the Bible humbly with prayer," while "the critical and metaphysical student" should "throw himself back into the times, the modes of thought, the language of the Apostolic age" and "conceive the religion of Christ in its relation to the religions of other ages and distant countries, to the philosophy of our own or other times" ([1855] 1859, 1:366). Jowett also discusses the impact of critical study of the Bible and of doubt and scepticism on unexamined faith ([1855] 1859, 2:298–300).

76. For "to look at things as they truly are" see Jowett ¶10 and note; Jowett repeats the phrase again in ¶102.

Jowett's reference to "the mechanic or artizan" echoes Florence Nightingale's *Suggestions on Thought to the Searchers after Truth among the Artizans of England* (1860), that Jowett had been reading and commenting on from early in 1860 when Arthur Hugh Clough first sent him a copy (see Quinn and Prest 1987, xii–xiii and 5–14). On 17 November 1861 he wrote to Nightingale: "A book cannot be written for the Artizans separating them from the educated classes. It must embrace them both. There is one intellectual world with common ideas, & the more permanent part of that is the world of the higher classes. Therefore I would urge you not to write for the Artizans, but to write for everybody" (Quinn and Prest 1987, 13). Programs for the "mechanic and artizan" included the Mechanics' Institutes (founded in London, 1824), the London Working Men's Association (1836) chiefly to promote political reform and the extension of the franchise, and the Working Men's College (founded by F. D. Maurice in 1854), to promote literacy and liberal education, including biblical and theological study, among the workers of London. Compare also Matthew Arnold's program for educating the working classes (see McCarthy 1964).

77. Among reactionary efforts to protect the established church Jowett included the university tests, consisting of subscription to the Thirty-Nine Articles of Religion. In 1846 he wrote to A. P. Stanley attacking subscription (Abbott and Campbell 1899, 1–2). In 1871 he gave lengthy testimony before the Select Committee of the House of Lords against the University Tests (Abbott and Campbell 1899, 19–39).

"Religious dissolution" in Italy and France refers to the anticlerical movements that disestablished Roman Catholicism in France in 1792–93 in favor first of the worship of reason and then of nondenominational Christianity. Though Roman Catholic rights were restored after the fall of Napoleon in 1815, a strong anticlerical party continued to advocate the separation of church and state, succeeding in 1905. Anticlericalism in Italy developed with Italian nationalism and unification after 1840, in an effort to limit the political power and territorial extent of the Papal States. By 1861 the Papacy, though continuing to claim vast estates in Italy and France as the Patrimony of St. Peter, was territorially limited to the Vatican and the Lateran in Rome and the summer palace of Castel Gandolfo, a settlement confirmed in the Lateran Treaty of 1929.

For "breathe a new life into a decaying world" see Ezek. 37:9.

78. The "rules of evidence" and the "canons of criticism" are the principles of textual and literary interpretation that have been formulated to establish the texts of the classics and the Bible. Rules of evidence concern evaluating the reliability and context of a specific biblical text, including the history and readings of available biblical manuscripts in Hebrew and Greek, ancient translations into other languages, and quotations made by rabbis and Church Fathers. The evidence can be external regarding the date, sources, geographical distribution of the manuscripts or other documents, and the family relationships of such materials. Internal evidence includes the study of the transcription of the texts, its writing or palaeography, scribal habits, peculiarities, possible errors in transcription and the evaluation of them, dealing with such matters as reversing words or letters (metathesis), confusing successive or closely related lines that begin with the same words or letters (homoeoarchton), or that end with the same words or letters (homoeoteleuton), or skipping lines (parablepsis), or other kinds of omission of text (haplography). Analyzing such errors, noting their frequency and range, and comparing different readings can often restore readings, again following such principles as the more difficult reading is the one to be preferred, or the less harmonious reading is to be preferred (see Jowett ¶s 10, 48, and notes).

For "the letter . . . spirit" see 2 Cor. 3:6; for "mind of Christ," 1 Cor. 2:16; for "fulness of Christ," Eph. 4:13; for "increasing purpose," Tennyson, "Locksley Hall" (1842, l. 137); for "heat and dust of controversy" see Milton's *Areopagitica* (1931–38, 4:311); for examples from Homer of dust clouding the vision of combatants see Jowett ¶91 and note.

The restoration of old master paintings was a

lucrative profession in the Victorian period. Until the appointment of Richard Redgrave in 1856, the surveyor of the queen's pictures was also the royal cleaner and repairer; Redgrave, however, chose a series of restorers, including "Buttery, Pinti, Merritt, and Haines" (Millar 1977, 189–90). A number of their restored paintings from the royal collections, including three by Peter-Paul Rubens from Windsor Castle, and Tintoretto paintings from Hampton Court, were shown at the first major exhibition of old master paintings in Britain, the Art Treasures Exhibition at Manchester in 1857. The subject of restoration aroused controversy, particularly with respect to architecture. In *Seven Lamps of Architecture* (1849), John Ruskin inveighed against restoration as causing the most serious destruction which a building can undergo and William Morris helped establish the Society for the Protection of Ancient Buildings. Both campaigned against the destructive restoration of St. Mark's Cathedral in Venice which went on through the 1850s into the 1880s.

79. The path of the "critical Interpreter of Scripture" is thorny in England because of the entrenched hostility against German higher criticism in the theological establishment, from Oxford and Cambridge professors, the university presses, and the bishops. Christopher Wordsworth's invective against "all the critics of Germany" is typical (1862, 426–29); see Jowett ¶11 and note.

For "woe is me" see 1 Cor 9:16; for "seven other," Matt. 12:45; and Luke 12:26; that is, seven other" meanings have obscured and dispossessed the "original meaning."

Jowett's distinction between the "word of God" and its "human origin and conception" was attacked vehemently by Christopher Wordsworth (1862, 452–60).

80. Jowett's sequence of Christian biblical commentators (he ignores the Jewish tradition of interpretation altogether here) is chiefly composed not of interpreters but of theologians who use the Bible for mystical reflection or homily: from "the early Fathers" such as Origen, John Chrysostom, Augustine, the "Roman Catholic mystical writers," specifically Thomas Aquinas and Bernard of Clairvaux, "the Swiss and German Reformers," that is, Calvin and Luther, also mentioned, and "the Nonconformist divines," such as Doddridge or Guthrie. For the allegorical and historical methods of the "early Fathers," as well as Thomas Aquinas and Bernard, see Jowett ¶3 and n. 8. The "mystical" approach of Calvin and Luther was to read the Bible for support for their theological arguments concerning grace, justification, predestination, and so on: "Luther's commentaries read like sermons. John Calvin's works, though no less theological, were more pedagogical . . . less given to imaginative soarings, and more systematic in developing the theological sense of the text" (Wilken 1988, 62). Nonconformists divines include Philip Doddridge, whose biblical commentaries stress the moral application of the Bible to individual human life, as in *The Family Expositor* (1739–56, 6 vols.). Thomas Guthrie's *The Gospel in Ezekiel* (1856) reads Ezekiel as containing the antitypes of Christ and the Gospels. See Gilson 1940; Pelikan 1959; Smalley 1964; Longenecker 1975; Korshin 1982; and Kugel and Greer 1986.

Newman and Pusey in the *Library of the Fathers* (1838–85) included the biblical commentaries of John Chrysostom (15 vols.) and Augustine (11 vols. and the commentary on part of Genesis in *Confessions*), many of them commentaries in the form of "homilies" on those books; hence, Jowett's comment on their work as "preachers." Calvin's commentaries on Galatians and Ephesians were published as vol. 30 in *The Biblical Cabinet; or, Hermeneutical, Exegetical, and Philosophical Library*, trans. William Pringle (1841), as well as the 53 volumes of the "Calvin Translation Society" (1843–55) that included his biblical commentaries. Luther's *Selected Works* were published in 1826 in four volumes.

The word "prophet" (Gk. προφήτης, from *pro*, forth, *phemi*, to speak) in classical Greek refers to the one who speaks forth or interprets oracles in Aeschylus, Herodotus, Plato, and so on; in the NT it is used to mean the interpreter of the divine will in reference to the prophets of the OT (as Luke 4:27), prophets in general (Matt. 10:41), John the Baptist (Mark 6:15), Christ (Matt. 21:11), and other apostolic leaders (Acts 15:32). For instance, when Jesus read from the scroll of Isaiah and interpreted it, he described his role as "prophet" (Luke 4:24). Hence, Jowett in *The Epistles of St. Paul* defines a prophet in relation to interpretation and preaching: "The Son of God himself is 'that Prophet'—the Prophet, not of one nation only, but of all mankind, in whom the particularity of the old prophets is finally done away" ([1855] 1859, 2:140).

81. For "like any other book" see Jowett ¶10 and note. and ¶46 and n. 82.

"Inductive" hermeneutics deals both with the role of language, grammar, and form criticism in interpretation and also with its subjective aspects, the "thoughts . . . of the sacred writers." Friedrich Schleiermacher is usually credited with introducing the latter into the study of the Bible (see Jowett ¶10 and note): "For Schleiermacher, understanding as an art is the reexperiencing of the mental processes of the text's author. It is the reverse of composition, for it starts with the fixed and finished expression and goes back to the mental life from which it arose. The speaker or author constructed a sentence; the hearer penetrates into the structures of the sentence and the thought. Thus interpretation consists of two interacting moments: the 'grammatical' and the 'psychological.' . . . The principle . . . is that of the hermeneutical circle" (Burtchaell 1969, 86). See also

Sanday [1893] 1896, 392–402.

For the affinities of "inductive" hermeneutics with Jowett's Platonism, see, for instance, his Introduction to *The Republic* ([1871] 1875, 3:80–81). For "excessive system" in Plato and Sophocles see Jowett ¶7 and note and his Introduction to *Phaedo* ([1871] 1875, 1:426).

The appeal to "common sense" here contrasts with Jowett's earlier stress on historical matters such as archaeology and comparative religion or his later emphasis on interpreting the Bible from itself (¶s 49–51), or using the resources of philology and linguistics (¶s 57–61), or rhetoric and logic (¶s 64–65). Jowett's "rules of common sense" may be compared with the philosophical use in Williams ¶s 55 and n. 95 and Pattison ¶s 30 and 35.

For "return to nature" see Seneca, *Epistulae Morales* (Epistle 25; trans. R. M. Gummere, *Loeb* 1:184–85).

82. To interpret the Bible "like any other book," Jowett's first axiom is that there is only "one meaning" based on the kinds of linguistic, historical, contextual, and psychological study he has just introduced. That is, he rejects the notion of the polyvalency of the Bible in favor of what the passage meant at the moment of its first utterance or reception. The terms *one meaning* and *true meaning* are used 11 times in Jowett's essay. Christopher Wordsworth attacked Jowett for this argument concerning "one meaning," arguing that Isa. 53:4 is fulfilled or "means" differently at Matt. 8:17 and 1 Pet. 2:24 (1862, 457–58). Most critics, however, agree that Matthew uses Isaiah as a messianic prophecy that is fulfilled while 1 Pet. 2:24 echoes phrases of the Isaiah passage concerning the suffering servant (e.g., Alford [1849] 1863, 1:210–11; 4:355). A recent hermeneut continues Wordsworth's attack on Jowett's "one meaning": "The language of the Bible opens up a field of possible meanings. . . . The notion that Scripture has only one meaning is a fantastic idea and is certainly not advocated by the biblical writers themselves" (Steinmetz 1986, 70). Jowett first recorded the phrase in pencil and later circled it in ink in his small notebook of jottings and other notes on a variety of topics, including "The Interpretation of Scripture," that can be dated about 1855–56 (Balliol MS. Jowett H16, fol. 4v).

The discovery of the valid "one meaning," according to Jowett, may be determined by extending a principle of textual criticism to hermeneutics whereby "the more difficult interpretation" is chosen. That is, in a textual crux the more difficult reading is to be preferred (Lat. *lectio difficilior lectio potior*) over alternate readings of otherwise equal textual authority. This principle was first articulated by the classical editor Jean Le Clerc, who published a series of rules in 1697, in which the principle of the more difficult reading was "for the first time explicitly formulated" (Kenney 1974, 43). The rule was used to edit both classical and biblical texts in the eighteenth century, for example in John Mill's edition of the Greek NT (1707); J. A. Bengel's (1734); and Westcott and Hort's (1881) in which they write that the "precept to 'choose the harder reading' [is] the most famous of all 'canons of criticism'" (1881, 2:27–28). This precept is still invoked, as in Metzger and Coogan 1993, 739.

Commenting on Gal. 2:19–20, Jowett writes concerning the different meanings of the word "law" through which Paul claims to be dead to the law and to be crucified with Christ. In other words Jowett takes the more difficult reading, that being "dead" to the "law" means "the paralysis of our moral nature" and hence the moral law, not only that written in the law of Moses, which has no more power over a dead man who is now reborn to God ([1855] 1859, 1:303).

Rom. 3:15 is part of a series of quotations from the LXX or from other texts of the psalms or prophets, as Jowett makes clear in his annotations; however, one word, σύντριμμα (*suntrimma*, a fracture, a breaking in pieces), the first word in verse 16 and translated "destruction" in the AV, is translated by Jowett as "affliction," placing the distress in the moral sphere ([1855] 1859, 2:127).

At issue in Gal. 4:13 is the preposition διά (*dia*) which with the dative case means "through," but with the accusative, as here, means "on account of." To Jowett the AV translates the passage ungrammatically: "Ye know how *through* infirmity of the flesh I preached the gospel unto you at the first." Jowett translates "amid infirmity of the flesh" and he comments on the grammatical difficulties in *The Epistles of St. Paul* ([1855] 1859, 1:341–42).

83. Jowett does not specify the biblical passages that "have sounded before their time" or the "lessons in the prophets." The testing of Job's faith through undeserved suffering involved the loss of wife, children, flocks, and goods, and his reduction to a life of despair, disease, and rejection, yet without succumbing to the advice of his counsellors to "curse God and die." Ecclesiastes represents human life as a series of fragmented aspects of a larger cycle whose meaning is not clear, for all is futile or a "vanity."

For "has to be born again" see John 3:3–7. "Fashioning" is used in the sense of "transforming," as in the service for the ordination of deacons and of priests in the *BCP*: "to frame and fashion your own life . . . according to the doctrine of Christ" (echoing Phil. 3:21). For "mind of Christ" see 1 Cor. 2:16.

84. For "what eye has seen" see 1 Cor. 2:9. Jowett uses the distinction between literal and hidden meaning to indicate the limitations on authorial intention. He accords to God the lordship over time, but resists collapsing years into a sequence of days or days into years, a tactic that enabled some contemporary interpreters to read modern events as fulfilment of biblical prophecy or to read the accounts of the destruction of Jerusalem (66–71) in the gospels as a decontextualized prophecy of the last judgment

(Luke 21:20–28).

For "with whom a thousand . . . years" see 2 Peter 3:8. The same passage is quoted by Bacon in *The Advancement of Learning* ([1605] 1973; II.13.iii.2). For "things . . . come to pass" see Rev. 1:1. "Form of eternity" has not been located. Plato in *Timaeus* (c. 421 B.C.E.) discusses time as the form or image of eternity (37d, trans. R. G. Bury, *Loeb* 9:75–77), a notion taken up in detail in Plotinus, *Enneads* (c. 250), in the section on time and eternity (bk. 3, tractate 7). In *The Advancement of Learning* the term *form* is a modification of the scholastic use (the "essential determinant principle of a thing") as the "real or objective conditions on which a sensible quality or body depends for its existence" ([1605] 1973; II.8.iv.5). Jowett draws a parallel between the dual methods of historical and apocalyptic readings of Like 21:20–28, comparing it to the double vision induced by the reverse of stereoscopic lenses (that enable two images to be seen as one, as in the parlor stereoscope invented by Oliver Wendell Holmes), whereby one image is seen as two, the aberration of vision reproduced by having lenses set at different angles to see the same object doubled (compare 1 Cor. 13:12).

85. On the scapegoat and the paschal lamb see Lev. 16 and Heb. 9 and 10:1–22; and Jowett ¶35.

The Roman Catholic emphasis upon the Bible and tradition as sources of doctrinal authority was a matter of contemporary controversy, but it dates back to sixteenth-century debates. Reacting against the Reformation principle of the self-sufficiency of the Bible as interpreted by the individual believer (Luther's *sola scriptura*), the Council of Trent in the fourth session (8 Apr. 1546) declared the Bible and the tradition of the church to be held as of equal authority. The Sixth Article of Religion asserts the self-sufficiency of the Bible in opposition to the Tridentine position, and the Thirty-fourth Article states the contingency and diversity of the traditions of the church. The leaders of the Oxford Movement, when challenged over the issue of apostolic succession in 1833, had consistently appealed to the apostolic tradition as a ground of their position, as, for instance, in J. H. Newman's article on "Apostolical Tradition" in the *British Critic* (1836b) and Keble's sermon on 27 September 1836 in Winchester Cathedral on "Primitive Tradition" (Keble 1848, 341–421). Newman also challenged the Sixth and Thirty-fourth Articles of Religion in *Tract XC*: "The ancient Church made the Apostolic Tradition, as summed up in the Creed, and not the Bible, the *Regula Fidei* [Lat. rule of faith]" ([1841] 1865, 8). He addressed the matter of the Bible and tradition again in his *Essay on the Development of Christian Doctrine* (1845).

For "living creatures" and "four beasts" see Ezek. 1:5–15 and Rev. 4:6–8; for the "colours white or red" there are a number of parallels, including Rahab's scarlet thread that saves her family from destruction (Josh. 2:18; Heb. 11:31; James 2:25) or the washing of robes to make them white (Isa 1:18; Rev. 1:14; 7:9–14). The images drawn from nature include the comparisons of white with snow and wool (Isa. 1:14), red with blood (2 Kings 3:22).

86. The argument from design has a particular significance in Christian apologetics from the time of Thomas Aquinas on, particularly in the works of Paley (see Powell ¶24 and note). Here it is applied to the order, unity, and harmony of the Bible, also a topic of controversy in classical studies concerning the Homeric epics. If the Bible is to be read like any other book, its design (its internal ordering, patternings and structures, narrative prolepses and analepses, anticipations, echoes, parallelisms, contrasts, ellipses, climaxes, interpolations, catalogues, and all other manipulations of time, place, character, or ideas) is only to be attributed to human design. Whether the manipulation of these elements is intentional or not is not a matter Jowett raises.

Gladstone in *Studies on Homer and the Homeric Age* (1858, 3 vols.) argued on the basis of design for the literary unity, and unitary authorship of both of Homer's epics, against Grote's theory in *History of Greece* of an intermingling of two epics in the *Iliad*, one the story of Achilles, the other of the Trojan war (1848, 2:178–269). It is a position Gladstone returns to in the more popular *Landmarks of Homeric Study*: "The work of Homer, as an Epic poet, is to incorporate Beauty and Grandeur, and whatever most harmonises with them, in living action. . . . I further submit that the plot of the *Iliad* is a product of the nicest and most consummate constructive art" (1890, 106). Jowett's introductions to his translations of Plato also stress the role of literary design in representing religious and moral precepts: the *Euthyphro* "is manifestly designed to contrast the real nature of piety and impiety with the popular conceptions of them"; and in the *Cratylus*: "Neither is Plato wrong in supposing that an element of design and art enters into language. The creative power abating is supplemented by a mechanical process."

"Artificial design" imposes onto the Bible a theological doctrine of divinely implanted design, the reading practice, according to Jowett, of the early fathers of the church (see *eisegesis*, Jowett ¶35 and n. 71). For examples of "heathenish or Rabbinical fancy" see Jowett ¶35 and notes. The argument concerning concealment is a variant of the theories of reserve in communicating religious knowledge and of accommodation; see Jowett ¶s 22, 25, 29, 40, 54, and notes.

87. Jowett's second axiom in interpreting the Bible "like any other book" is to "interpret Scripture from itself" (see Jowett ¶46 and n. 82). This idea had been current in biblical and Homeric criticism from the end of the eighteenth century, but its roots lie in the Lutheran and Reformed doctrine that the Bible is its own self-authenticating authority. Hence, scripture is the interpreter of scripture (*scriptura*

interpres scripturae), or, in Luther's phrase, *scriptura . . . sui ipsius interpres* (Scripture is its own interpreter; Luther 1883–95, 7:97; see Bruns 1992, 139–58). Eichhorn had argued that the text of the Hebrew scriptures was written in different language conventions from those of the later Hebrews, preceding the work of the Masoretes from the fifth to tenth centuries with their vowel pointings, just as Bentley had demonstrated that the Aeolic digamma, a letter not known in the written Greek alphabet of classical times, was used earlier in Homer's text. Further, while both the Hebrew scriptures and the epics of Homer derive from historical times, few other sustained literary or historical works survive from the same periods. Archaeology had not yet unearthed the walls of Troy (by Heinrich Schliemann in 1871–79) or Jericho (by C. Warren in 1867 to Kathleen Kenyon in 1952–58) as evidence. On language and archaeology see Cardona, Hoenigswald, and Senn 1970; Crystal 1987; and Stern 1993; on archaeology and the popularization of OT criticism in the nineteenth century see MacHaffie 1981.

88. On the "synoptic" problem see Jowett ¶13 and note.

In Jowett's day scholars were not in agreement about the dating of the gospels. Alford gives the dates Matthew c. 50; Luke c. 50–58; Mark c. 60–70; and John c. 70–85. He dates the Revelation of St. John as c. 95–96 (Alford [1849] 1863, 1:24]–65]). Modern scholars generally date John (c. 100) later than the synoptics (Mark c. 70–75; Luke c. 80–85; Matthew c. 90). Jowett here presupposes, along with modern scholars, that the disciple John was not the author of either the gospel and Revelation.

The prophetic books date from the eighth and seventh centuries B.C.E., and include the three major prophets (Isaiah, Jeremiah, and Ezekiel) and the twelve minor prophets. Horne related many of the psalms to the events of the Babylonian captivity ([1818] 1828, 4:101–24; 147–242); so also did Franz Delitzsch in *The Psalms* ([1871] 1988). Modern scholars note the structure of Psalms as an anthology and recognize the great diversity of the psalms' dating and literary materials; see Gunkel [1926] 1967 and Kraus 1987–89.

Paul's letters to Romans, Corinthians, and Galatians are usually dated about 55, while Colossians, Philippians, and Ephesians are dated, respectively, roughly 65, early 60s, and from 80 to 90. In his essay "On the Probability that Many of St. Paul's Epistles Have Been Lost" Jowett writes: "It has been observed that within a single year of his life the Apostle wrote the Epistle to the Romans and the two Epistles to the Corinthians" ([1855] 1859, 1:195).

89. Parallel passages, as well as variants, notes of the translators, and alternative readings, some with doctrinal significance, were included in the "marginal references" of the Geneva Bible (1560). The margins of the AV (1611), however, included the literal meaning of some Hebrew and Greek words or phrases, alternate readings, and parallel passages. For instance, the marginal references give parallel passages for Gen. 1:1 as Psalm 33:6; Acts 14:15; and Heb. 11:3. The parallel passages for the first verse of the NT, Matt. 1:1 are Luke 3:23–28, Psalm 132:11; Isa. 11:1; Gen. 12:3, Gal. 3:16. All are verbal similarities or thematic associations, but have no critical authority as allusions to sources, derivations, or manuscript interdependence. Parallel passages where the text of the Bible repeats itself are termed "deuterographs" and vary from short phrases to extended passages (Gen. 49:26 is repeated in Deut. 33:15; Isa. 2:2–4 is repeated in Micah 4:2–3; Ezra 2 is parallel to Neh. 7:6–73; the four chapters of Isa. 36–39 are largely parallel to 2 Kings 18:13–20:19).

Emendation of the biblical text under the Masoretes (see Williams ¶16 and note and Goodwin ¶62 and note) continued into the Renaissance and to the present, sometimes incorporating into the text a marginal Masoretic variant or gloss. Editors such as Erasmus and Lightfoot introduced emendations: Erasmus at James 4:2 replaced the Greek for "ye kill" with "ye envy"; Lightfoot at Col. 2:18 emended the Greek for "intruding into those things which he hath not seen" to "to indulge in vain speculation." Contemporary emendations had been noted for both passages in J. J. Wettstein's edition of the Greek NT (1751–52).

An example of "useless and unfounded emendations" is Jean Le Clerc's edition of the fragments of Menander and Philemon (1709) that was ridiculed and corrected by Richard Bentley in his *Emendationes in Menandri et Philemonis Reliquias* (1710). Jowett disliked Bentley and was critical of "the baneful influence which a great philologer . . . may have on a whole generation of his followers—for how many wasted lives he may be responsible." He acknowledged him to be "a great interpreter" but argued that he lacked judgment and "never tried his art upon the more difficult authors" (Abbott and Campbell 1897, 2:186). On emendation in classical texts see F. W. Hall [1913] 1970, 150–98; and Brink 1986, 61–83.

90. The Latin canon, a variant on Luther's statement in ¶49 and n. 87, means "you are not able to interpret scripture except out of scripture"; another variant is *scripturam ex scriptura explicandam esse* (Scripture is to be explained from scripture).

The emphasis on paraphrase and especially memorization is an Augustinian precept; see Jowett ¶16 and note; see also Bacon's praise of memory in *The Advancement of Learning* [1605] 1973; II.15.i.3.

91. "Continuity" as a hermeneutical principle establishes the notion of the unity of the Bible. After commenting on the Bible as a "miscellaneous book," a collection or assemblage of texts of differing kinds of textual reliability, Northrop Frye makes an argument similar to Jowett's concerning biblical continuity and unity based on its structure, treatment of time

and history, and its pattern of images "which recur so often that they clearly indicate some kind of unifying principle. That unifying principle, for a critic, would have to be one of shape rather than meaning; or, more accurately, no book can have a coherent meaning unless there is some coherence in its shape" (1982, xii–xiii).

For progressive revelation see Jowett ¶16 and note. For "visitation of the sins . . . children" see Exod. 20:5; for "every soul . . . iniquity," Jer. 31:30; for "fire . . . voice," 1 Kings 19:12.

92. The "interval" of "over about four hundred years" is the intertestamental period, stretching from the last of the minor prophets, Haggai and Zechariah, writing after the return from Exile and the rebuilding of the Temple about 520 B.C.E. through to John the Baptist, the "forerunner" (Matt. 17:10–14). It includes the Persian period (539–333 B.C.E., from Cyrus II to Darius III), the Hellenistic period (333–63 B.C.E., from Alexander of Macedon to Aristobulus II) and the first decades of the Roman period (63 B.C.E.–135, from Pompey's defeat of Aristobulus and seizure of Jerusalem to the suppression of the Simon Bar Kochba revolt). It is treated in "secular" history by Flavius Josephus in the *Antiquities* (c. 94) and the *Jewish War* (c. 77–78), making use of the *Roman Antiquities* (c. 7 B.C.E.) of Dionysius of Halicarnassus and the *Universal History* written by Nicolaus of Damascus, court historian to Herod the Great from about 20 B.C.E. The "interval" is not covered by the biblical canon of the OT and NT, though the Apocrypha includes some books purporting to deal with the Persian period, but in fact dating from the second century B.C.E. (see Wilson ¶37 and n. 70). The Pseudepigrapha, sixty-five noncanonical documents attributed to various OT figures, date largely from the last three centuries B.C.E. The Dead Sea Scrolls from Qumran include many other texts unknown to Jowett. For this history and literature see Jagersma 1986 and Bickerman 1988.

For the distinction between sacred and secular history, drawing on the historiography of Thomas Arnold, see Temple ¶s 14–24 and notes.

The "Jewish sects" discussed by Josephus include the Pharisees, the Sadducees, and the Essenes, all dating from the second century B.C.E. (see Temple ¶17 and n. 22). The Maccabean wars involved the Hasmonean family in a series of revolts during the second and first centuries B.C.E., culminating in the seizure of Jerusalem from the Syrians and the rededication of the Temple in 164 B.C.E., commemorated in the festival of Hanukkah (see 1 and 2 Maccabees in the Apocrypha and Josephus' *Jewish War*). Alexandrian literature dominated the Hellenistic world from about 300 B.C.E. chiefly because of the city's library and museum built by Alexander the Great. The chief exemplars were Callimachus, author of the *Aetia*, on the legendary history and customs of Greece, and Apollonius of Rhodes, the author of the *Argonautica*, the epic poem about Jason, Medea, and the golden fleece. The Jewish population of Alexandria, the largest in the Diaspora, was involved in its literary and scholarly flowering , completing the translation of the Hebrew Bible into Greek (the Septuagint; see Williams ¶7 and n. 21), as well as the possible compilation of the Wisdom of Solomon, and, in the Alexandrian Christian community, the Letter to the Hebrews. Philo of Alexandria combined an interest in Hebrew literature, especially the law, with Greek philosophy.

The "Galilaean zealot" is Judas of Galilee, a zealot (Acts 5:37), whose revolt against the taxation of Quirinus (C.E. 6) is recorded in Josephus (*Antiquities* 18.1.1); for "no man . . . God" see Matt. 23:9; for the "counsel of perfection," Jowett ¶26 and note.

93. David ruled Israel from c. 1010 to 970 B.C.E., according to the account in 1 Sam. 16:13–1 Kings 2:12. That is, his narrative occupies the whole of 2 Sam. For his imprecations against his enemies see 2 Sam. 22, especially 2 Sam. 22:36–47; for his injunctions to Solomon, 2 Kings 2:1–9. David had sexual intercourse with Bathsheba, wife of Uriah the Hittite, and when she became pregnant, David had Uriah killed by placing him in the midst of battle and having him abandoned. He then took Bathsheba into his own house; she bore his son and successor, Solomon. But for his sin Nathan the prophet announced the judgment of God that his house would be riven with discord, rebellion, and fighting, and he would be bereaved of his children (2 Sam. 11–12).

For "theory of accommodation" see Jowett ¶22, 25, 29, and 40 and notes.

For "the increasing purpose . . . ran" see Tennyson, "Locksley Hall" (1842, l. 137); for "Sun of righteousness," Mal. 4:2; for "fewest of all people," Deut. 7:7; for "any form like His," Isa. 53:2; Phil 2:6–7; for "the education of the world" see Temple ¶1 and note; for "desire of the nations," Hag. 2:7; for "not of that nation only," John 11:52; for "His Father and their Father . . . God," John 20:17.

94. This paragraph, almost a summary of Temple's essay, draws on the same metaphor of the education of the child and the growth of the Christian in Gal. 3:23–4:9. It also echoes other accounts of the sequence of human life, as in Shakespeare's *As You Like It* 2.7.139–66 and William Wordsworth's "Ode: Intimations of Immortality" (1807).

For "rises up to play" see Exod. 32:6; 1 Cor. 10:7; for "in the land of Egypt and the house of bondage," Exod. 20:2; for "each to each by natural piety," William Wordsworth, "My Heart Leaps Up" (1807, l. 9).

95. For "Which things . . . allegory" see Gal. 4:24; for "child born . . . spirit," Gal. 4:22–31; for "law was a schoolmaster," Gal. 4:12; for "angel of his presence," Isa. 63:9; for "in the wilderness," Matt. 4:11; for "multitude of peoples, nations, languages," Rev. 7:9; 10:11.

96. For "glory and for beauty" see Exod. 28:2; for "coldly furnished forth," Shakespeare, *Hamlet* 1.2.181; for "words of 'eternal life,'" John 6:68; The source for "*Poena linguarum*" (Lat. The sin of tongues has scattered people; the gift of tongues has collected them into one), a reference to the Tower of Babel and Pentecost, has not been identified.

The Greek NT and LXX were written in Koine, or the common language. This common language absorbed Attic (the "Greek of Plato"; see Jowett ¶16 and note) and other forms of Greek after the liquidation of independent city-states and the unification of Greece under Alexander by 334 B.C.E. A recent scholar comments on the varieties of spoken dialects in the Greek-speaking Hellenistic world: "At the present time 'NT Greek' must be understood as a *Sammelbegriff* ('collective term'), not as a single linguistic system, and still less as a 'dialect' of Koine Greek" (Schuyler Brown 1989, 133). In *The Epistles of St. Paul* Jowett writes: "The indefiniteness of the language of the New Testament harmonises with the infinity of the subject. It has not the precision of Attic Greek; but could the precision of Attic Greek have expressed the truths of the Gospel?" ([1855] 1859, 1:43).

Jowett's assertion that the Greek language was in "a state of degeneracy and decay" involves linguistic, philological, stylistic, and aesthetic considerations. It is a nineteenth-century commonplace to contrast NT Greek to both Homeric and classical Greek. One of Nietzsche's aphorisms in *Beyond Good and Evil* (1886) makes a similar disparaging remark on biblical Greek: "It was subtle of God to learn Greek when he wished to become an author—and not to learn it better" (Nietzsche 1968, 276; Aphorism 121). Such views are rejected by modern linguists and textual critics: "The frequent practice of referring to the Greek of a particular NT author as 'good' or 'bad' is quite meaningless. . . . The comparison of a NT book with works of classical or modern Greek is methodologically invalid" (Schuyler Brown 1989, 130–31).

The study of NT Greek was revolutionized first in 1877 and again in the first decades of the twentieth century by the discovery of large numbers of papyrus manuscripts in Egypt which demonstrated that the biblical form of Greek was a vernacular language (see Schuyler Brown 1989, 130). In discussing these discoveries, C. F. D. Moule usefully contextualizes Jowett's argument. Moule argues that the "new" language "is not simply Classical Greek growing senile and going into a decline." Such a view was dominated "by two misleading ideas: one was that Classical standards could be applied to the language; and the other was that, if Biblical Greek differed from Classical Greek, it was also quite distinct from contemporary 'secular' Greek" (1953, 1–3). For Greek as a "common" language see Hatch 1889, 3–35; Moulton 1909, 1:1–42; and Moule 1953, 1–5. Tischendorf's edition of the NT (1869–72) made use of 64 uncial manuscripts of the NT and a single papyrus fragment, and he knew of only a few minuscules. Today editors have at their disposal 257 uncials, 2,795 minuscules, and some 88 papyri, a total of about 5,000 manuscripts. Some papyri (designated by the symbol 𝔓 and a number) are of primary significance, including those that contain the Gospels and Acts from the third century (Chester Beatty MS. 𝔓45), the letters of Paul (lacking 2 Thess., Phil., and the pastoral epistles; in Chester Beatty 𝔓46, dating from about 200), Revelation (in Chester Beatty 𝔓47, third century), John (Bodmer MS. 𝔓66, about 200); see Aland and Aland 1987, especially 56–59 and 79–95.

For "language . . . compared to a garment" compare Carlyle in *Sartor Resartus*: "Language is called the Garment of Thought: however, it should rather be, Language is the Flesh-Garment, the Body of Thought" ([1833–34] 1937, 73); compare Bacon's *The Advancement of Learning* [1605] 1973; II.23.iii.

97. The qualifications of an interpreter include a knowledge of the original language and a knowledge of the context of words, both denotation and connotation. The idea of an original language (see Pattison ¶7 and n. 23) is assumed to be a direct route to the original meaning that the interpreter seeks to elucidate. Translations, then, offer obscured meanings, distanced from what the Preface to the AV calls "the Originall": "The translation of the *Seventie* [the Septuagint] dissenteth from the Originall in many places, neither doth it come neer it, for perspecuitie, gravitie, majestie, yet which of the Apostles did condemn it? (Opfell 1982, 155–58). Jowett advocates a sense-to-sense translation, rather than a word-for-word literalism, but while the translators of the AV desired "that the Scripture may speak like it self, as in the language of *Canaan*, that it may be understood even of the very vulgar" (161), Jowett follows Mathew Arnold on translators of Homer in wanting the reader to accord complete trust to the translator: "These are scholars; who possess, at the same time with knowledge of Greek, adequate poetical taste and feeling. No translation will seem to them of much worth compared with the original; but they alone can say whether the translation produces more or less the same effect upon them as the original" (Arnold 1960–77, 1:99).

The Alexandrian "Greek Fathers" of the fourth century, such as Eusebius, Basil the Great, Gregory of Nyssa, Gregory Nazianzen, and Cyril of Alexandria use verbal, grammatical, and philological methods to provide the key to the divinely inspired meaning, an anagogical reading about the soul's ascent to God, continuing the methods of Origen. The "minuteness" of exegetical methods among both High Church and evangelical commentators of Jowett's "own day" continued typological, mystical, and moral interpretations, as in the works of J. H.

Newman, T. H. Horne, and Patrick Fairbairn; see Jowett ¶s 3, 11, 12, 35, and notes. An etymological basis for this typology was elaborated, for example, in the sermons of the popular Baptist preacher Charles Haddon Spurgeon (1834–1892) at London's Metropolitan Tabernacle. He argued that the rock in Horeb that Moses smote to bring forth water (Exod. 17:6) refers to Christ on the basis that "Horeb" means "barrenness" and its other name, "Rephidim" means "bed of rest"; Christ is "a rock in a barren and dry land" and also a bed of rest (Spurgeon 1856, 2:314). John Keble also used such methods in his interpretations of the name of Christ, as in his sermon on "The Saving Name" (Keble 1879–80, 2:183).

The problem of interpreting every particle (an indeclinable word: a preposition, conjunction, or interjection) as redolent with meaning is referred to by Jowett in *The Epistles of St. Paul*, commenting on Rom. 5:12–21: "As a preface to the following passage, every verse and almost every particle of which bears the traces of theological warfare in the pages of commentators, it will be convenient to state very briefly the chief points in dispute in the Pelagian controversy" ([1855] 1859, 2:170). Alford discusses the "acknowledged difficulty" in the same verse for almost three columns ([1849] 1863, 2:359–61).

98. Herman [Jowett's note]; Jowett's only footnote is marked by an asterisk in the first edition.

Johann Gottfried Jakob Hermann, professor of poetry at Leipzig, published *De Pauli Epistolae as Galatas tribus primus capitibus* (1832; On the first three chapters of Paul's Epistle to the Galatians). A distinguished classicist and grammarian, Hermann edited Sophocles, Euripides, Aristophanes, Aeschylus, Aristotle, and Homer. His grammatico-critical method (as in *De Emendanda Ratione Graecae Grammaticae* [1801; On the logic for emending Greek grammar]) was opposed by Karl Otfried Müller, who defended a historical and antiquarian basis for interpreting the classics.

The texts of Aeschylus and Pindar have demanded considerable editorial intervention because of late manuscripts, gaps, and corruptions (see F. W. Hall [1913] 1970, 46–48).

99. Jowett alludes to scholarly concerns that he regards as minutiae interfering with the task of the interpreter: obsessive attention to the details of grammar; over interpretation of the paucity of documentary materials; excessive attention to philology and orthography; and the elaboration of conjectural positions. Each of these points is a current issue in NT study.

Grammarians of the classical languages include Joseph Justus Scaliger and Isaac Casaubon in the sixteenth century, of whom Mark Pattison wrote biographies. Among Jowett's contemporaries, the leading Greek grammarian was the Dutch scholar Carel Gabriel Cobet and the leading Latin grammarian was the Danish philologist Johan Nicolai Madvig. The role of the grammarian in relation to knowledge and truth is set out ambiguously in Browning's "A Grammarian's Funeral" (1855). Attempts to extend the range of Greek and Latin in the context of comparative philology were advocated by J. W. Donaldson in *The New Cratylus* (1839) and F. W. Farrar's *Essay on the Origin of Language* (1860) and *Greek Syntax* (1867). See Burrow 1967 and Dowling 1982. According to Schuyler Brown, "A comprehensive grammar of Hellenistic Greek has yet to be written" (1989, 132).

The study of mythology as a "new ground," or field of knowledge, was set out by Karl Otfried Müller in *Prolegomena zu einer wissenschafftlichen Mythologie* (1825; trans. J. Leitch, *Introduction to a Scientific Study of Mythology*, 1844) and was applied by B. G. Niebuhr in denying historical validity to myths of early Roman origins in Livy (in his *History of Rome*, 1828–32) and by George Grote in *A History of Greece* (1846) in relating the Greek myths to their cultural function. Similar applications of historicist principles to biblical mythology were undertaken by D. F. Strauss in *Leben Jesu* ([1835] 1846). For Victorian attitudes to mythology see Yoder 1971 and Frank M. Turner 1981, 77–134. Comparative philology was the special field of study undertaken at Oxford by Jowett's friend Max Müller, who presented his views in a series of *Lectures on the Science of Language* (1861). See Shaffer 1975 and Dowling 1982 and 1986.

For the "scholasticism of philology" from Alexandrian to "our times" see Jowett ¶2 and note; such scholasticism was also applied to the classics, as in the work of the Alexandrian scholiasts on Homer: see Williams ¶30 and note; and Aarsleff [1966] 1983.

Orthography, that is, correct or conventionally accepted spelling, is often a problem in transliteration of Hebrew or Greek. Scribal errors or variants were introduced into manuscripts of the Bible through various omissions, additions, or substitutions of letters, or the changing of words for doctrinal reasons. For instance, the Hebrew text of the OT includes only the consonants, vowels being added from the sixth century, though not in the Torah scroll used for reading in the synagogue; further, some consonants look much like others (only a small mark, the tittle, distinguishes the *beth* ב from the *kaph* כ). Hence, as Rypins comments, "As students of Biblical palaeography are constantly aware, textual variants which are the result merely of mistaking one Hebrew consonant for another of nearly identical form occur more frequently in Hebrew manuscripts than in those written in Latin or Greek. . . . The most accurate transcription of a purely consonantal text cannot relieve it of obscurities. . . . There occur numerous differences whose explanation is found only in the uncertainties of the ancient consonantal orthography" (1951, 30–32). For instance, the word given as "the bed" in the AV at Gen. 47:31 becomes "the staff" with a vowel change as in the Peshitta (the Syriac translation of the second century), and is translated "staff" in Heb. 11:21, following the Septuagint. Similarly, in the Greek versions there are also errors in orthography with concomitant shifts in meaning: "omissions and additions, whether through haplography, dittography, assimilation, conflation, incorporation of marginalia, or other cause, occur again and again" (Rypins 1951, 128). For instance, in uncial script the Greek word for God (θέος, *theos*) was contracted to ΘC, but was confused with OC (ός, *os*, who or which) at 1 Tim. 3:16 (see Jowett ¶21 and n. 36 and Alford [1849] 1863, 3:332). Transliteration from Latin into English was also a problem. Hence, the Thirty-nine Articles of Religion refer to the Book of Esdras (Ezra); other variants in spelling derive from the Latin Vulgate versions of proper names in the Bible. For instance, "Jesus" was usually rendered "Iesu" or "Ihesu" in the Middle English period, derived from the objective case of Old French, with the usual printer's substitution of "J" by "I." The Vulgate nominative case ("Iesus") was replaced by the Vulgate's vocative ("Iesu") in Tyndale's NT (1525–34), Coverdale's Bible (1535), the Great Bible (1539) and in vocative instances in the Bishop's Bible (1568). The reform of the spelling of Greek classical names to avoid their Latinate versions resulted in versions of common Greek names that were hardly familiar and scarcely acceptable to Victorian readers. Browning, for instance, was one of the proponents of a reformed orthography, using such spellings as Sophokles, Alkestis, Plouton, Kokutos (Cocytus) and so on in *Balaustion's Adventure* (1871). For orthography in relation to Greek texts in the nineteenth century see Jenkyns 1980, 160–61.

The story of the scholar who wished to devote himself to the dative case has not been located.

Jowett's uncertain questions concern first the disputed issue of the second imprisonment of Paul (after that in Rome recorded in Acts 28), before and during which Paul is alleged to have written epistles to Timothy and Titus (Alford [1849] 1863, 3:87]–97]), now widely accepted as pseudonymous documents of the Pauline circle (Meeks 1972, 132–34); the chronology of Paul has "taken on a new importance in the last several decades" (Epp and MacRae 1989, 329). The second question concerns the identity of James, the brother of Jesus (Gal. 1:19; Matt. 13:55), and whether he was the author of the epistle of James, and bishop of Jerusalem or whether the epistle is attributable to James, the son of Alphaeus, one of the disciples (Matt. 10:3); Alford settles on the former after a lengthy discussion ([1849] 1863, 4:87]–99]). Among recent scholars, Sevenster (1968) and J. A. T. Robinson (1976) agree with Alford, while many regard it as pseudonymous (Epp and MacRea 1989, 373–74). The third question, concerning the disputed use and translation of the Greek article, occurs, for example, in the Septuagint Greek of Isa. 7:14 (AV: "Behold, a virgin shall conceive and bear a son"), quoted at Matt. 1:23, where in both instances the translators give the Greek definite article (in both the LXX and the NT Greek) as an indefinite article.

100. There are many errors in the "noblest translation," that is, the AV. These include such matters as printers' errors in the 1611 text: "then cometh Judas" instead of "then cometh Jesus" at Matt. 26:36; in the 1631 edition of the AV (the "Wicked Bible") "not" is omitted from the seventh commandment to read "Thou shalt commit adultery" (Exod. 20:14). Among the important MSS. available to the translators of the AV, only the Codex Bezae (at Cambridge from 1581) was near at hand to consult for the NT, but there is no evidence that it was studied. They followed the revised NT texts of Desiderius Erasmus (1516) and of Theodore Beza (1565), and for the Hebrew writings had the Complutensian Polyglot (1517), the Antwerp Polyglot (1572), a single text for the Septuagint, and the Clementine edition of the Vulgate (1592) including accumulated corruptions. By following these defective sources, then, the AV repeated previous errors and introduced new ones, such as duplicating several words in 2 Kings 7:13 and elsewhere. Currently there are about 800 Hebrew MSS., 1,500 versions and fragments of the LXX, 525 identified texts from the Dead Sea Scrolls, and many early translations into other languages, such as an early version of Jerome's vulgate Latin in the Codex Amiatinus, dating from 541 (see Jowett ¶57 and n. 96; and Tov 1992).

Among the "few great errors" are the inclusion of the marginal readings into the text, on no manuscript evidence before the sixteenth century at 1 John 5:7 and the translation at 1 Tim. 3:16, both of which, along with other mistranslations, Jowett commented on earlier (see Jowett ¶21 and notes), as well as the addition of the doxology to the Lord's Prayer in Matt. 6:13b ("For Thine is the kingdom, and the power, and the glory, for ever. Amen"), attributing it to the direct words of Jesus on no early manuscript authority. On the latter Alford comments: "The *doxology* must on every ground of sound criticism be omitted" ([1849] 1863, 1:62).

Other mistranslations occur because of paraphrase ("give up the ghost" for "expire" at Gen. 25:8); faulty renderings ("observed him" for "preserved him" at Mark 6:20); changes in English meaning ("charity" for "love" in 1 Cor. 13, although *agape* is translated "love" in 286 of 312 occurrences); lack of archaeological knowledge ("Que" is a location in Cilicia not "linen yarn" in 1 Kings 10:28); inconsistencies in spelling (Sheth and Seth, Marcus and Mark, Sina and Sinai, Jewry and Judea); inconsistencies in translating the same word in the source language (*semeion*, "sign," is sometimes translated "sign," but more often "miracle"; in Matt. 25:46 the same word, "*aionion*" is translated as everlasting and eternal, with theological and philosophical implications: "everlasting punishment . . . life eternal"); and because of doctrinal or ecclesiological predispositions or bias (for instance, the use of "be converted" rather than "convert" as a translation of *metanoein* or *strephein* as at Matt. 18:3 and Acts 3:19, suggests human passivity, and perhaps predestination; or translating *ecclesia* as "church" rather than "congregation," which is used only once at Acts 13:43). Such examples and many others were well known to Jowett's contemporaries, as in, for example, R. C. Trench, *On the Authorized Version of the New Testament* (1859). Detailed lists and further references are given in Jack Lewis 1991.

Jowett was criticized for minor mistakes in translating the Greek of his Plato, and responded: "It is not that I do not *know* these elementary things; but the effort of making the English harmonious is so great, that one's mind is insensibly drawn away from the details of the Greek" (Sandys 1908, 3:419).

For "we do it violence" see Jer. 22:17.

Jowett's "uncommon expressions" in Greek are as follows: ἐξουσία (*exousia*: liberty or power to act, as at 1 Cor. 9:12 or messianic authority at Matt. 9:6); ἐπιβαλών (*epibalon*: to put one's mind to, to think about, as at Mark 14:72, "he thought thereon"); and συναπαγόμενοι (*sunapagomenoi*: to be carried away with, as at Rom. 12:16, "condescend"). Alford begins his discussion of Mark 14:72 by stating that "no entirely satisfactory meaning has yet been given for this word" ([1849] 1863, 1:420). All these terms have now been studied in relation to usage in earlier and noncanonical texts (Kittel and Friedrich 1964–76).

101. The seven "theological terms" are more "promising fields" for the interpreter than rare or unusual usages because clarification of them may help to dispel potential doctrinal disagreements. Except for the last, all are used in Romans, faith at least 35 times, grace 23 times, righteousness 38 times, sanctification (translated as "holiness") twice, law 77 times, and spirit 29 times, often in opposition to law. The last term, comforter, is used of the Holy Spirit 4 times in John and once in 1 John: see ¶28 and note on Jowett's fourth example there. The first six terms are used by Paul to structure his theological argument in Romans on the economy of salvation, and all are discussed by Jowett in detail in *The Epistles of St. Paul*, making comparisons with classical and Alexandrine Greek (for example [1855] 1859, 2:96–110). Each term took on enormous significance and elaboration in the theology of the Church Fathers, especially in Augustine, as well as in later "systems" like Calvin's theology. All incited theological controversies concerning Pauline theology or the person of God.

The second seven are all ecclesiological and represent disputes in ecumenical theology, the differences between the churches on the basis of institutional officers and their administrative roles, as well as congregational worship: see ¶28 and note on Jowett's sixth example there. Jowett wants a theological lexicon for terms that have been historical focal points in religious controversy. Augustus Hermann Cremer published his *Biblisch-theologisches Wörterbuch der Neutestament-lichen Gräcität* (1867; trans. D. W. Simon and W. Urwick, *Biblico-Theological Lexicon of New Testament Greek Idioms*, 1872), in which he compared the Greek of the NT with classical and Hellenistic Greek, and with that used in rabbinical Judaism. Cremer's work was succeeded by Walter Bauer's *Griechisch-Deutsches Wörterbuch zu den Schriften des Neuen Testaments und der übrigen urchristlichen Literatur* (1928; trans. William F. Arndt and F. Wilbur Gingrich, *Greek-English Lexicon of the New Testament and Other Early Christian Literature*, 1957) and Kittel and Friedrich (1964–76).

102. Jowett here qualifies his remarks in ¶57 on the "decay" of language. He continues to stress the diachrony of linguistic development, emphasizing etymological sources for current usage and contemporary variation. He also notes the synchrony of a language at a particular moment, and accords to both "barbarous as well as civilized nations" the complexities of linguistic systems. His general theory of language is set within the rhetoric of national identity, with examples drawn from English and Greek canonical authors. Plato represents classical Greek, and Lucian, Hellenistic. In Reformation Germany, Luther's translation of the Bible into German (NT in 1522; complete, 1534) was an instrumental linguistic and political factor in German nationalism. In his Introduction to *Cratylus* Jowett discusses language in terms of nation and cycles of development: "Language is an aspect of man, of nature, and of nations, the transfiguration of the world in thought. . . . There is no abstract language '*in rerum natura*' [in the state of nature] any more than there is an abstract tree, but only languages in various stages of growth, maturity, and decay" ([1871] 1875, 2:200–201).

103. Alford also comments on the "peculiar" Greek style of the opening paragraph of Luke ([1849] 1863, 1:436); and on the opening of Acts (Acts 1:1), accepting the conventional and still current view that they form a continuous narrative, Acts being "introduced without preface, as a *second part* following on the former treatise: a δεύτερος λόγος [second word] to the Gospel" ([1849] 1863, 2:15]).

Stanley also comments, like Jowett, on the "lyrical passion" of the language of 1 Cor. 13:2, the so-called hymn to love (1855, 1:275–76). Stanley refers to 2 Cor. 6:6–10 as "the impassioned description of his own [Paul's] sufferings" and says the passage "is the climax of the first part of the Epistle," parallel to the climactic position of 1 Cor. 13 (1855, 2:126, 100).

Jowett rejects the "vapid and general use" of theological terms by the Jewish exegete Philo of Alexandria, whose reading of Genesis (in *Allegories of the Sacred Laws*) allegorizes the characters as states of the soul, and their actions as general types of moral and immoral conduct. In *The Epistles of St. Paul* Jowett gives a more detailed commentary on "St.

Paul and Philo" [1855] 1859, 1:448 ff. The reviewer of *Essays and Reviews* in the *Literary Gazette* (14 Apr. 1860) attacks Jowett as "so untrustworthy. He makes some astonishing mistakes. The Dean of Ely [Harvey Goodwin] has pointed out that in his great work he rarely deals fairly with Philo" (460).

104. The precedence accorded to speech over writing in this passage accords with recent linguistic and literary analysis of the oral components of the NT documents, especially the parables (see Epp and MacRae 1989, 175–83; on the Bible and post-structuralism see Detweiler 1982; and Stephen Moore 1989 and 1992).

Paul's letter to the Romans refers to his amanuensis (Rom. 16:22). Alford comments on the transitions in pronouns that indicate oral composition ([1849] 1863, 2:469). Other evidence of oral composition is often identified (for example, Rom. 2:17–21). Paul's use of rhetorical and oral-formulaic literary forms in the epistolary conventions of the Hellenistic world is surveyed in Epp and MacRae 1989, 322–26.

Some of Jowett's contemporaries, such as Alford, argue for diverse oral sources, modified, revised, and eventually coalescing as a "common substratum of apostolic teaching . . . [as] the original source of the common part of our three Gospels" ([1849] 1863, 1:9]). It is now widely agreed that oral sources lie behind the synoptics, particularly the "sayings" of Jesus contained in "Q," the source of some 200 verses common to Matthew and Luke alone (see Jowett ¶13 and n. 21). Form criticism draws attention to individual units of oral tradition behind the synoptics: see Kelber 1982 and Henaut 1993.

105. "Ground colours" refers to the base, background, or underlayer of color applied to a painting; in linguistics, "colours" refers to figures of speech, as in Chaucer's "Clerk's Prologue" (l. 16) or the "colours of rethoryk" in the "Franklin's Prologue" (l. 18). Such "colours" here refer to the particular stylistic traits and localized contexts that characterize the language of the NT, particularly the influence of the LXX and the spoken Greek of the Eastern Empire from Alexander the Great to Augustus. The influence of "the Greek Bible [LXX] . . . is seen not only in 'Septuagintisms' (constructions which, because they use elements of Hebrew grammar incorrectly, cannot be Hebraisms) but also in the use of Greek vocabulary to express religious conceptions of the OT" (Schuyler Brown 1989, 134). For examples of such Septuagint studies see Gehman 1951; and Katz 1973; on Hebraisms and Semiticisms see Millar Burrows 1951; for "spoken Greek of eastern countries" see ¶57 and note.

106. Latin is one of the languages used to identify Jesus on the cross at John 19:20; specific Latin terms used in the NT include the coin "*denarius*" (Matt. 18:28; 20:2–13), "*Caesar*" (Mark 12:15), "*census*" (Mark 12:14), "*centurion*" (Mark 15:39–45), "*legion*" (Mark 5:9), and "*speculator* [executioner]" (Mark 6:27). The Greek transliteration of the Aramaic "Golgotha" ("skull," Luke 23:33), the site of Jesus' crucifixion, is translated as *calvaria* in the Latin vulgate, the source for the AV's "Calvary."

Chaldee was the term used in the nineteenth century to refer to the Aramaic portions of Ezra and Daniel; the Targums or vernacular translations and paraphrases of the Hebrew scriptures were also written in Aramaic (see Williams ¶14 and n. 57). In the NT there are a number of Aramaic words, including *bar* for son (instead of the Hebrew *ben*) in a number of proper names, Barabbas, Bartholomew, Bartimaeus, and Simon Bar-Jonah (Matt. 16:17); in such place names as Golgotha, Gabbatha (John 19:13), and Aceldama (Acts 1:19); and in such quoted phrases of Jesus as *Talitha cumi* (Mark 5:41, "Damsel, I say unto thee arise") and *Eloi, Eloi, lama sabachthani* (Mark 15:34; "My God, my God, why hast thou forsaken me" and parallels).

For Semitic clausular structure in the NT and general forms of the Aramaic and Hebrew languages (rather than grammar, with its stress on morphology and lexical classes) see Beyer 1968 and Maloney 1981. For "Rabbinical formulae," such as the relation between the questions of the four types of sons in the Passover Haggadah and the questions in Mark 12, see W. D. Davies 1955, Daube 1956; and the survey of scholarship in Epp and MacRae 1989, 27–54. On Philo see Jowett ¶62 and n. 103.

107. Jowett assumes that the Koine Greek of the NT is "a language not their own" because it was the formal literary language of the Hellenistic world, while the "authors" of the NT books very likely spoke a vernacular Aramaic. He refers to four figures of speech, repetition (*repititio*, as at Rom 2:21–23), opposition (or contraries, *etantiosis*; or contrast, *antithesis*, as at Rom. 5:18–19; 8:15), *anacoluthon* (or fragmentary sequences of thought, as at Rom. 8:3) and short sentences (usually arranged in the form of a *climax*, as at John 1:4–5). Jowett remarks in *The Epistles of St. Paul* on the proclivity of Paul to think in binary oppositions: "Antithesis is a favorite figure in the writings of St. Paul; almost (may we not say?) the very form in which he conceives the Gospel itself. . . . It is the dialectical frame in which the ideas of the Apostle are arranged; it is the grammatical frame in which his sentences are cast" ([1855] 1859, 2:45). So too Alford comments on Paul's "frequent and complicated antitheses, requiring great caution and discrimination in exegesis" ([1849] 1863, 2:43]). For "unlearned men" see Acts 4:13, and compare Origen's *Against Celsus* (trans. Frederick Crombie, *ANF* 4:423–24, bk. 1, chap. 62).

Jowett hoped to add a third volume to his translation of *Thucydides* (1881, 2 vols.), to consist of a series of essays, among them one on the "simplicity and complexity of the language" and another on "the structure of the speeches," but these essays were never completed, and the volume never issued (Abbott and

Campbell 1897, 2:183).

Jowett's discussion of Rom. 3:1–9 draws out the implications of oppositional argument as Paul presents his own view and an opposing one ([1855] 1859, 2:120–22). He also refers to Rom. 9 and 10 as raising opposing "sides of a question" ([1855] 1859, 2:269–70). On 1 Cor. 9:19–20 Stanley points out that the transitions in argument, with their interruptions of personal biographical details, are governed by Paul's "endeavour to accommodate himself to the various feelings of all his converts in the hope that of this mass he might gain the greater part . . . to the cause of Christ" (1855, 12:179). On Gal. 4:11–20 Jowett argues that Paul is explaining how he labored, despite his afflictions, on their behalf and how they welcomed him and his message, but "the difficulties of this passage" lead to problems in interpreting it. Paul's affection for the Galatians seems to Jowett to underlie the confusion ([1855] 1859, 1:342–45).

108. The first set of three Greek words is rendered by various English equivalents in the AV to account for their "variable signification" in Greek. Hence, πίστις (*pistis*) is usually rendered faith in the NT, but it is also translated as assurance (Acts 17:31), belief (2 Thess. 2:13), confidence (6 cognates), fidelity (Tit. 2:10), persuasion (Gal. 5:8, a cognate), and trust (9 cognates). The term χάρις (*charis*) is usually translated as grace, but other equivalents are gracious (Luke 4:22), benefit (2 Cor. 1:15), favor (Luke 1:30 and 6 other instances), gift (2 Cor. 8:4 and 10 cognates), joy (Phil. 1:7 and many cognate usages), liberality (1 Cor. 16:3), pleasure (Acts 24:27; 25:9), and thanks (1 Cor. 14:57 and three other uses). Σωτηρία (*soteria*) is translated salvation in the AV.

γνῶσις (*gnosis*, knowledge), σοφία (*sophia*, wisdom), κτίσις (*ktisis*, creature, creation) are terms that are associated with the heretical sect of Gnosticism in the Hellenistic world; see Jowett's discussion of Gnosticism and related sects in ¶91 and note.

The constructions Jowett cites all make use of the genitive case: δικαιοσύνη Θεοῦ (*dikaiosune Theou*, righteousness of God) occurs 7 times in the NT, 4 of those in Romans, as at Rom. 1:17. On this passage Alford cites De Wette in a long note concerning the theology of righteousness and concludes with a rejection of Jowett's view that he added after Jowett published *The Epistles of St. Paul*: "To say, with Jowett, that all attempts to define δικαιοσ[ύνη] Θεοῦ are 'the afterthoughts of theology, which have no real place in the interpretation of Scripture,' is in fact to shut our eyes to the great doctrinal facts of Christianity, and to float off at once into uncertainty about the very foundations of the Apostle's argument and our own faith: of which uncertainty his note here is an eminent example" ([1849] 1863, 2:320). πίστις 'Ιησοῦ Χριστοῦ (*pistis Iesou Christou*, faith of Jesus Christ) occurs 3 times, as at Rom. 3:22; ἐν Χριστῷ (*en Christo*, in Christ) occurs 64 times; ἐν Θεῷ (*en Theo*, in God) 16 times, and ὑπὲρ ἡμῶν (*huper hymon*, for us) 39 times. Such phrases, all highly popular in pietistic religion and sermons, tend to devalue the force of the preposition in order to stress a religious state of identification between the believer and the object of the preposition. Nigel Turner, in his completion of the third volume of Moulton's *Grammar of New Testament Greek*, comments: "The translator will look askance at the 'theology of prepositions' and will remember that Hellenistic writers much prefer to add prepositions, especially composite prepositions and between the cases so that the exegete must always look at the context" (1963, 3).

109. On the general question of the "degeneracy of the Greek language" see ¶57 and note. Jowett's position on these points concerning syntax is supported by his contemporaries and by recent scholarship.

Jowett specifies eleven kinds of so-called decay when contrasted with classical Greek, the first being a general syntactical failure that the other points elaborate. On the insertion of prepositions, Alford refers to the "accumulation of prepositions often with the same or very slightly different meanings" ([1849] 1863, 2:44]). On this adding and omitting of prepositions see Nigel Turner (1963, 249–50). On the use of ἰνὰ (*hina* that, in order that) as a conjunction Turner writes: "One must at least underline the difficulty of finding anywhere but in Biblical books such a wide variety in the use of ἵνα, imperatival, causal, consecutive, epexegetical, within so small a space" (Nigel Turner 1963, 8–9). On the article with proper names, Turner again: "In class.[ical] Greek, names of persons without attribute or apposition have no art.[icle] at their first mention. . . . The final development of the popular tendency to use the art. is seen in M[odern] Greek where proper names almost always have it" (1963, 165–66). On negative particles: "in post-classical prose, appreciation of the nice differences between οὐ [*ou*, not] and μή [*me*, not], which broadly speaking are like those between *non* and *ne*, has partially disappeared. . . . The same observations apply to the NT. There is sometimes no valid reason in favour of one particle against another" (Nigel Turner 1963, 281). On the confusion of the Greek aorist or indefinite past tense and the perfect, as at Matt 14:3 or John 18:24, Alford comments: "The distinction between the aorist and perfect tenses is in our authorized version very commonly disregarded, and thereby the point of the sentence altogether missed. Instances are continually occurring in the Epistles" ([1849] 1863, 2:45]); and Turner: "In the Hellenistic period . . . the perfect increasingly trespassed on the sphere of the aorist" (Nigel Turner 1963, 68). Similarly on particles, apposition, and pleonasms (repetitions of a similar meaning using different words): "The Koine and NT are more careless than the older Greek regarding the position of the particle and, as in syntax generally, display the popular love of over emphasis"; "The Semiticism derived through the LXX involves the 'pleonastic' insertion of personal pronouns" as at Matt. 3:12, John 1:33, and Acts 15:17 (Nigel Turner 1963, 329, 325).

110. "Lexicon," the Latinized form of the Greek λεξικόν, derived from λέξις (*lexis*, word) and from λέγειν (*legein*, to speak), is used for a dictionary of the Greek language and sometimes for Hebrew or Aramaic. Meaning in a lexicon is derived from a comparison of usages in different authors, often with citations. Hence, meanings in the NT are often derived from contexts in other texts, from classical and Hellenistic writers. Jowett argues that since the NT is one of the primary documents of Koine Greek, it should be used as the chief evidence for usage.

In *The Epistles of St. Paul* Jowett comments on the verb in Rom. 3:9, a unique occurrence in the NT: "'What then? are we better than they? No, by no means.' This way of taking the passage gives the best sense, and does the least violence to the language. The objection to it is that the middle [voice], which would ordinarily have the significance of 'to hold before,' 'put forward as a pretext,' is here used like the active in the sense of 'surpass,' 'excel.' . . . The emphatic use of προεχόμεθα [*proechometha*] in the sense of 'have we a pretext?' is still more contrary to analogy than the confusion of the middle and active voice" ([1855] 1859, 2:126). In Greek the middle voice suggests that the subject of the verb is acting for itself, or acting upon something that pertains to itself; this verb means literally "to hold above" and in the middle voice something like "to hold ourselves superior for our own sakes." But the AV translation, "Are we better than they?" puts it into the active voice, the point that Jowett is making. A long note on the verse by Alford draws on the lexicon tradition, calling attention to usage from other Greek writers ([1849] 1863, 2:339–40).

Jowett also comments on Gal. 3:1 and the verb προεγράφη (*proegraphe*): "not 'written down beforehand,' or 'written down openly' (which, whether referred to the prophecies or to the Epistles of St. Paul, is wanting in point), but 'pictured openly;' πρό [*pro*] being used of place, and not of time, and γράφειν [*graphein*] in the sense of 'to paint.'. . . It is a sound canon of criticism that where the style and use of words are irregular, as in the NT, more weight should be given to the context, and less to precedent and authority" ([1855] 1859, 1:313). Jowett's reading is attacked, despite its agreement with other eminent translators, by Alford ([1849] 1863, 3:23).

111. For the grammatical case in Gal. 4:13 see ¶46 and note.

With the genitive case διὰ (*dia*) means "through"; with the accusative, "on account of." In Phil. 1:15 the accusative is used, though the AV translates with a genitive: "Some indeed preach Christ even *of* envy and strife."

Three definite articles in the Greek text of 2 Cor. 1:17 are omitted in the AV: " [the] lightness . . . [the] yea yea, and [the] nay nay." Stanley comments on the article in the Greek text and also draws attention to the other similar use of the article with "the reduplication being understood only as adding strength" at James 5:12 (1855, 2:29–30).

Acts 17:1 in the AV refers to "a synagogue" in Thessalonica though there is a definite article (*the* synagogue) in Greek. Alford argues that the definite article implies "that there was no other synagogue for the towns lately traversed: and shewing the same minute acquaintance with the peculiarities of the district as our narrative has shown since the arrival at Neapolis" ([1849] 1863, 2:187).

In 1 Cor. 15:4 the perfect tense of the verb ἐγείρω (*egeiro*, to raise), ἐγήγερται (*egegertai*) means "he has been raised." The Greek aorist tense (used elsewhere in the sentence) refers to a simple past ("he was raised") while the perfect, in Stanley's words, implies the consequences of the verb; its force "seems to be 'has been raised and is alive'" (1855, 1:348).

In Rev. 5:7 the phrase "And he came and took the book" is made up of conjunctions and two verbs in Greek, the first in the aorist tense (simple past: "he came"), and the second in the perfect (he has taken). To Alford the second verb is the perfect as aorist: "The perfect . . . apparently cannot be pressed" ([1849] 1863, 4:607–8).

In each of the passages cited from Romans, Jowett is concerned with the figure of anacoluthon, beginning a sentence in one way, and concluding it in another. In *The Epistles of St. Paul* Jowett translates Rom. 2:17–21 as one sentence, at the end of which in the "apodosis" or concluding clause, according to Jowett, Paul turns against himself, "though the length of the sentence and the rhetorical accumulation of clauses have prevented the Apostle from resuming the thread of the grammar" ([1855] 1859, 2:89). On Rom. 5:12–18 Jowett discusses alternative constructions and proposed solutions for three columns ([1855] 1859, 2:171–72). On Rom. 9:22 he writes: "There is no apodosis. . . . The thread of the sentence is lost in the digression of verses 23, 24, 25. The corresponding clause should have been, What is that to thee?" (2:283). On Rom. 16:25–27 he writes: "Owing to the length of the sentence, the latter end has forgotten the beginning" (2:427).

112. On anacoluthon as a figure of speech see ¶62 and notes. The three quotations are textbook definitions of the figure of anacoluthon; see Bullinger [1898] 1968, 720–24.

113. Jowett's distinction between "logical form" and "logical sequence of thought" is based on the rhetorical distinction between figures of speech and figures of thought. This often arbitrary distinction derives from classical rhetorical and logical analysis,

a problematic differentiation between speech as the external form of thought that obscures the relations between linguistics and the social construction of discourse. It is set out by Quintilian (*Institutes* 9. 1. 17), following earlier distinctions in Ciceronian rhetoric. Jowett draws on this distinction in his discussion of Rom. 5:13–18 (see Jowett ¶63 and note) and concludes by abandoning the problems in the "irregular . . . syntax" to stress the "logical sequence of thought" ([1855] 1859, 2:172). His examples of figures of thought include opposition (antithesis), contradiction (enantiosis), climax (anabasis), pleonasm (or redundancy, using more words than needed), reason within reason (epidiegesis, repetition to restate; or paradiegesis, reasoning by the introduction of outside facts); all are discussed with biblical examples in Bullinger [1898] 1968.

"Forms of the schools" refers to the rhetorical figures and logical constructions taught in the schools of Greek rhetoric, such as those at Alexandria and Rome; the latter are described in book 2 of Quintilian's *Institutes of Oratory*.

Gamaliel I (the Elder), one of the leaders of the Sanhedrin, taught the Jewish law to Paul (Acts 22:3). He is listed in the Mishnah (the collection of Palestinian rabbinic laws dating from about 200) after Hillel, and may have been his grandson.

114. The Latin description of the "fallacy of composition" means "it does not follow that [what is claimed] concerning one thing [applies] to all things," or what is true of the parts is necessarily true of the whole (the parts of the machine are light in weight; therefore the whole machine is light in weight). In *The Epistles of St. Paul* Jowett comments on the alleged fallacy in Rom. 3:19, asking: "Is St. Paul referring here to the Jews or to mankind in general? If the former, there arises a difficulty respecting the meaning of the words, 'every mouth,' 'all the world,' which seem coextensive with 'those under the law' ([1855] 1859, 2:128).

On Rom. 1:16–18 Jowett comments in *The Epistles of St. Paul*: "Passing onward to the height of his great argument, the Apostle involves reason within reason, four times in three successive verses. Such is the over-logical form of Hellenistic Greek" ([1855] 1859, 2:53).

On Rom. 1:32 Jowett argues that : "The climax breaks down if we translate the words in their legitimate sense, 'who not only do, but assent to those who do them.' . . . The opposition is really one of particles, not of ideas" ([1855] 1859, 2:67–69).

Each part of the "series of inferences" in Rom. 1:16–18 is linked by the preposition: "The repetition of γὰρ [*gar*, for] does but represent the different stages and aspects of the Apostle's thought" ([1855] 1859, 2:53). The Greek phrases are from Rom. 1:32: οὐ μόνον—ἀλλὰ καὶ (*ou monon—alla kai*, not only . . . but also) that set up the concluding oppositions in Paul's argument. The phrase πολλῷ μᾶλλον (*pollo mallon*, much more) occurs, for example, in successive verses to structure Paul's argument at Rom. 5:9, 10, 15, 17. In *The Epistles of St. Paul* Jowett comments on "the Apostle's tendency to reduplication of his thoughts" in this passage based on the "common antithesis . . . between the law and the promise, faith and works," in that what was once true of one side of the antithesis is "much more" true of the other, repeated four times ([1855] 1859, 2:169, 177).

The conjunctive particle μὲν (*men*) is usually related to the contrasting conjunction δὲ (*de*) that follows it (on the one hand . . . on the other; indeed . . . but). At Rom. 1:8 and 3:2, however, μὲν "is found alone." Hence, the AV translation "first" has no "second" to follow in the argument (Jowett [1855] 1859, 2:49). In Rom. 5:7 two different words, a *righteous* person and a *good* person have provoked unnecessary elaboration, according to Jowett: "It is not necessary to suppose any opposition between" the words, but to see the clauses as parallel ([1855] 1859, 2:168). On Rom. 10:10 Jowett comments on efforts to explain the verbal opposition in terms of inner disposition and outward confession: "Instead of adopting explanations so forced, it is better to acknowledge that the antithesis is one of style . . . which need not be insisted upon" ([1855] 1859, 2:292–93).

115. The "oppositions" Jowett elaborates culminate in Jesus' parable of the final judgment, and the separation of the sheep from the goats, the right hand from the left (Matt. 25:33). The series of theological oppositions occurs throughout the NT but is particularly important in Romans: law and faith (Rom. 3:21–31); good and evil (Rom. 7:19–21; 12:17–21); spirit and flesh (Rom. 7:25–8:13); light and darkness (Rom. 2:19, and also John 1:5–9); and world and believer (Rom. 12:2). Jowett's view, that such oppositions are not the absolutes they appear to be when mixed in individual persons, led his critics to charge him here with relativism.

The passage from ¶65, "When we pass. . . . altogether a reality," was cited as "false and dangerous" in the Synodical Condemnation of *Essays and Reviews* on 21 June 1864. Jowett was condemned for rejecting a plenary view of the inspiration of the Bible (*Chronicle* 1859–64:1864, Session 66, 1658).

116. For "body and soul and spirit" see 1 Thess. 5:23.

Tripartite views of human nature (the Hellenistic body, mind, and spirit categories) or Plato's rational, spirited, and appetitive souls (*The Republic*, especially bk. 9) were difficult to harmonize with the use in the Pentateuch of *ruach* (breath, spirit; LXX *pneuma*) and *nephesh* (soul, life; LXX *psuche*). To Alford *pneuma* is "the spirit, the highest and distinctive part of man, the immortal and responsible *soul*," while *psuche* "is the lower or animated soul, containing the passions and desires . . . That St. Paul had these distinctions in mind, is plain (against Jowett) from such places as 1 Cor. ii. 14" ([1849] 1863, 3:282).

The body-mind or mind-matter dualism of philosophers includes those of Plato (bodies known to the senses and ideas), Descartes (the thinking subject and the physical world), and Kant (the noumenal and the phemonenal worlds); the dualism of common language and logic includes the binary oppositions by which dialectical argument is constructed.

117. For "take up . . . Christ" see Matt. 9:6; Mark 8:34, 10:21; Luke 9:23; for "receiving the kingdom . . . children," Matt. 18:4; Mark 10:15; Luke 18:17.

The "trichotomy" of Paul is his classification of human nature into its three constituent parts, body, soul, and spirit discussed in Jowett ¶66. Making a similar point, the reviewer of contemporary books of theology in 1868 in the *Contemporary Review* comments: "Popular theology is rather founded on the dichotomy of man into body and soul, than on the Christian trichotomy of body, soul, and spirit (7:598).

118. For "stumblingblock" see Rom. 14:13; for "We shall . . . the air," 1 Thess. 4:17; for "Where their worm dieth . . . quenched," see Mark 9:44, 46, 48, echoing the last verse of Isaiah (66:24). The "commentator" is very likely Henry Alford, who takes the account of the resurrection in 1 Thess. 4:14–17 as literal and in his revised edition attacks Jowett: "Attempts like that of Mr. Jowett, to interpret such a passage as this by the rules of mere figurative language, are entirely beside the purpose. The Apostle's declarations here are made in the practical tone of strict matter of fact, and are given as literal details. . . . It is a fair opportunity for an experimentum crucis [a crucial experiment]: and such test cannot be evaded by Mr. Jowett's intermediate expedient of figurative language" ([1849] 1863, 3:276).

The identical verses at Mark 9:44 and 46 (quoting Isa. 66:24) do not occur in the earliest manuscripts, such as Sinaiticus, Vaticanus, and Ephraemi. The verses anticipate verse 48 where all of the manuscripts agree. Alford, however, defends verses 44 and 46 despite their lack of early MS. authority; to him they are not "to be regarded as arbitrary insertions by this or that Evangelist, but as the truth of what was uttered by our Lord. . . . This triple repetition gives sublimity, and leaves no doubt of the discourse having been *verbatim* thus uttered" ([1849] 1863, 1:377–78).

The summary paragraph (¶70) that follows was separated from the rest of §4 by a double space in the first and subsequent editions.

119. For shining . . . perfect day" see Prov. 4:18.

120. For "Ideas must be given through something" see the conclusion to Plato's *Cratylus* for the discussion of the relation of language to things. In *The Epistles of St. Paul* Jowett discusses at length the mediation of language in representing abstract ideas: "One of the points in which theology and philosophy are brought into connexion by language, is their common usage of abstract words, and of . . . ideas not yet freed from associations of time or sense" ([1855] 1859, 2:96).

The "philosopher" is very likely G. W. F. Hegel, whose *Der Philosophie der Geschichte* (1832; The philosophy of history) was an important influence on Jowett, who with Stanley had read Hegel in 1844 and was one of Hegel's advocates in Oxford (see Willis 1988, 96). More particularly, the German Hegelian C. K. Bunsen published the title Jowett cites, *Gott in der Geschichte* (1857; trans. Susanna Winkworth, *God in History*, 1868–70, 3 vols., with an introduction by A. P. Stanley). For a discussion of Bunsen's volumes see Williams ¶10–24. The contrast between the philosopher and the poor woman (compare the poor widow at Mark 12:42) elaborates a consistent theme in Jowett, the contrast between the interpretation of the Bible by the elite and the application of it to the poor, based on Matt. 11:5; see Jowett ¶s 29, 72, 78, 84–85, and 95.

For "hour of death" see the Litany in *BCP*; for "I know that my Redeemer liveth," Job 19:25; for "I shall go . . . return to me," 2 Sam. 12:23. The "doubtful" meaning in Job relates to the translation of the Hebrew *go'ali* variously translated as "avenger," "revenger" or "redeemer," capitalized in the AV to stress messianic implications under Christian influence.

121. The close relation of education and literature to religion (and especially Homer to the Bible) was a commonplace in the nineteenth century. Hence, to Henry Nelson Coleridge, a reader should "approach it [the *Iliad*] with something of the kind of reverence which we yield to the Hebrew Genesis, and be perpetually familiar with its contents, as with the secular Bible of mankind. . . . and almost believe that the Iliad, like the Bible, is collateral with all time, is for now and for ever" ([1830] 1834, 176–77). Matthew Arnold in *On Translating Homer* (1861) makes a point similar to Jowett's comparison of Homer to the Bible: "He will find one English book and one only, where, as in the *Iliad* itself, perfect plainness of speech is allied with perfect nobleness; and that book is the Bible" (1960–77, 1:155–56). Both Gladstone and Matthew Arnold conflated literature and religion in their studies of ancient Greece and both connected Homer, Greece, and the Bible (for Gladstone and Homer see Jowett ¶9 and note). Arnold wrote in 1864 that fifth-century Greece is "the Greece we mean when we speak of Greece,—a country hardly less important to mankind than Judaea" (1960–77, 3:230); and in *Culture and Anarchy* (1869) he identifies culture and religion (1960–77, 5:93–94). R. C. Jebb, following another of Arnold's themes (Hellenism and Hebraism in chap. 5 of *Culture and Anarchy*), discerned "no inherent conflict between true Hellenism and spiritualized Hebraism,

such as is contained in Christianity" (1907, 569). For the relations between classical Greece and Victorian England see Jenkyns 1980 and Frank M. Turner 1981; for the replacement of religion by literature as ideologies throughout the nineteenth century see Eagleton 1982, 22–27.

122. An example of Jowett's "new truth" introduced into the Hebrew Bible is the sermon of Acts 2:14–36, where Peter speaks of the death and resurrection of Jesus as the fulfillment of Hebrew prophecies, quoting Joel 2:28–31, Ps.16:8–11, and Ps. 110:1. Jesus' "sanction" for such usage is borne out in his reading from the scroll of Isaiah in the synagogue at Nazareth (Luke 4:16–30).

For the first rhetorical question, "Can there be . . . Scripture?," compare Luke 4:21; John frequently uses the phrase "that the scripture might be fulfilled" as at John 19:28. The second rhetorical question "Or any more likely . . . taught?" refers to Peter's sermon in Acts.

The passage from ¶73, "There are many quotations from the Psalms . . . in our own day," was cited as "false and dangerous" in the Synodical Condemnation of *Essays and Reviews* on 21 June 1864. Jowett was condemned for rejecting the idea that "the Prophesies of the Old Testament" can offer "the direct prediction of future events" (*Chronicle* 1859–64:1864, Session 66, 1657–58).

123. Oliver Cromwell was appointed lord-lieutenant of Ireland and invaded to put down rebellion there; the use of the Bible as a "symbol of fanaticism" occurred on 10 September 1649 when he stormed the fortress at Drogheda, executing most of the 2,200 of its defenders, sending the rest to the Barbados in slavery.

The Form of Prayer with Thanksgiving prescribed for 29 May celebrates the Restoration of Charles II. It was added to the *BCP* in 1662, was expanded with stronger language in 1685, and added the offertory sentence that Jowett cites (Matt. 7:21), a "cloke of malice" in quoting the Bible to attack the politics and piety of the Puritans.

Thomas Wolsey suggested to Sebastian Giustiniani, the Venetian ambassador to England, that Venice should take a more dominant role in Italy, to which Giustiniani replied by quoting 1 Cor. 10:26 (echoing Ps. 24:1) as "the disguise of policy."

Gibbon records that Bishop Ulphilas first translated the Bible into Gothic for the Franks, but "he prudently suppressed the four books of Kings [1 and 2 Samuel; 1 and 2 Kings], as they might tend to irritate the fierce and sanguinary spirit of the Barbarians" ([1776–88] 1858, 3:541).

124. For "Gird on . . . mighty" see Ps. 45:3.

Jowett's qualification of "slavery or polygamy which belong to a past age . . . at least in England" opposes the contemporaneous situation in the United Slates. Abraham Lincoln was elected on an antislavery ticket in 1860, a signal to the South, resulting in the Civil War (1861–65) and the Act of Emancipation in 1863. An act to abolish slavery in all British colonies had been passed in 1833 at the instigation of William Wilberforce. At the time that Jowett was writing, polygamy was practiced in various British colonies, including India. In America it was a precept of the Church of Jesus Christ of Latter-Day Saints (Mormons); see Jowett ¶85 and n. 136). Both slavery and polygamy were practices sanctioned by the Hebrew scriptures and practiced in Ancient Israel.

For the use of biblical quotations to lend weight or authority to politics and "public feeling or opinion" see Jowett ¶26 and note. Ruskin used biblical phraseology and typology throughout his writings, but especially in his art criticism on, for example, J. M. W. Turner in *Modern Painters* (1841–60); see Landow 1971, 321–457.

On the "true analogy" with the moral impulse and in relation to the analogy of faith see Jowett ¶84 and notes.

125. Jowett argues (¶s 75–77) that an application of a biblical phrase or example should be "harmonized" (¶77) with the theological and moral point that is being alluded to while an interpretation needs to be accommodated to both the historical, social, literary, and linguistic conditions in which it first occurred, as well as to the human knowledge and comprehension witnessing, recording, and subsequently reading such an allusion.

Typological readings usually parallel Elijah with John the Baptist, or Elijah's being caught up in the chariot with Christ's ascension, as in the stained-glass windows of Keble College, Oxford (1852); see Landow 1980, 138–39. Jowett refers, however, to Elijah's conflict with the prophets of Baal during the reign of King Ahab in the first half of the ninth century B.C.E. (1 Kings 16:29–19:18). To read this narrative typologically as a justification for Tractarians' or Calvinists' remaining in the C. of E. as an erroneous communion as a means of confronting its errors, would, in Jowett's view, be a fallacy of accident and "*secundum quid*" (the fallacy of the concealed qualification); that is, the circumstances of the original condition that demanded Elijah's remaining isolated in Israel to confront idolatry cannot be generalized into a universal mandate; and, secondly, Elijah's prophetic message cannot be applied to other circumstances when the occasion of the error or idolatry is concealed, or the implications of remaining in the erroneous communion against conscience are suppressed. Luther, for instance, compares Elijah to the leaders of the German Reformation and the leaders of the Roman Catholic Church as the prophets of Baal (1955–86, 35:200–201).

For "written on the hearts" see Rom. 2:15 and 2 Cor. 3:2–3; for "type of good things to come," Heb. 10:1; for "Kings . . . fathers," Isa. 49:23; for "desolate Sion of the captivity," Ps. 121:1. Sion, or Zion, is one of the hills on which Jerusalem was built. Jowett refers to the agnostic movements and those advocating freethought, disestablishment of the C. of E. and the abolition of all religious affiliations of church and state, such as the National Secular Society and the work of Charles Bradlaugh; see Royle 1974 and Lightman 1987; see also Williams ¶4 and n. 8; Wilson ¶s 43–47 and notes; and Jowett ¶30 and n. 62.

For the relation of the Jewish concepts of king, church, and priest, see Wilson ¶s 31 and 75 and notes.

For "the anointed of the Lord" see 1 Sam. 24:6 as used by David concerning Saul. For the anointing of David by the men of Judah see 2 Sam. 2–7. The anointing of Solomon is recorded at 1 Kings 1:39. "Anointed" here means a confirmation by divine sanction and approval; the Hebrew term *mashiach* eventually becomes "messiah," the one anointed by God. It is translated by the Greek *Christos*, the honorific term applied to Jesus of Nazareth in the early Christian writings, as when Peter makes such a claim in a sermon (Acts 10:38). In the coronation service the British sovereign has been anointed with oil since the eighth century, while part of 1 Kings 1:38–45 is sung, and the archbishop of Canterbury says "Be thy head anointed with holy oil: as kings, priest, and prophets were anointed. And as Solomon was anointed king by Zadok the priest and Nathan the prophet, so be you anointed, blessed, and consecrated Queen over the peoples, whom the Lord your God hath given you to rule and govern."

126. For Pharisees see Wilson ¶23 and note; and Jowett ¶53 and note. The Pharisees' literalist interpretations of the Mosaic law were challenged by Jesus at Matt. 19:3–12 and Mark 2:23–28. For "letter . . . spirit" see 2 Cor. 3:6. Jowett's elision omits the verbal form from the previous clause: "the least matters [have been taking the place] of the greatest"; he has already given examples of such practices, for example, in ¶s 21 and 27–31.

127. On the harmonization of scriptural applications see ¶74 and note. For "hardness of the heart" see Matt. 19:8. The pedagogue, or "schoolmaster," at Gal. 3:24 had as a duty to take the child to school and to stand behind him to ensure that he devoted himself to his lessons. See Temple ¶8 and note.

128. For "the Gospel preached to the poor" see Matt. 11:5; for "cleared the eye of the mind," Shakespeare, *Hamlet* 1.1.112 and 1.2.85 ("mind's eye").

For Reformation and later attacks of Protestantism on the pope as Antichrist, including those of Christopher Wordsworth among Jowett's contemporaries, see Jowett ¶12 and note. Isolated thinkers under attack by "the religious world" include D. F. Strauss for *Leben Jesu* ([1835] 1846), F. D. Maurice, for both *The Kingdom of Christ* (1835) and *Theological Essays* (1853); see Williams ¶27 and n. 110. But it was the controversy concerning the theory of evolution as promulgated by Darwin in *The Origin of Species* in the year before *Essays and Reviews* that was beginning to arouse theological controversy. For religious controversy at the midpoint of the nineteenth century see Crowther 1970. Powell makes direct reference to Darwin in his efforts to reconcile science and religion (see Powell ¶126 and note); Goodwin too makes use of geologists who have relied upon "the force of observation" in empirical science to draw connections with theological arguments.

129. Jowett's appeal to a universalist morality as a common and "simple feeling of truth and right" shared amongst all people and times, as instanced between the Hellenistic Greeks and the "Hindoo" of his own time, was a common, but also a contested, trope. It was developed by Rowland Williams in his essay on *Christianity and Hinduism* (1855), and Wilson in "Vedic Religion" in the *Westminster Review* (1860), but was attacked implicitly in Macaulay's "Minute on Indian Education" (1835; in Macaulay 1972, 235–52); see also Wilson ¶13 and note.

For "wisdom and power of God" see the eight Bridgewater Treatises "On the Power, Wisdom, and Goodness of God, as Manifested in the Creation" (1833–40). Jowett is most likely alluding to the soul's love of wisdom in his translation of *The Republic* (10:618c).

For "righteousness . . . nation" see Prov. 13:34; for "love . . . law," Rom. 13:10.

130. Jowett gives four examples of possible contemporary applications of passages that have in their biblical contexts rather narrow meanings; such a practice is the opposite to that in Jowett ¶28 where he was concerned with terms and passages separated from their biblical contexts to be applied in later theological disputes. For "Ye shall know . . . free" see John 8:32, a dispute with believing Jews concerning freedom under the law and freedom from bondage to sin, as applied widely to broad notions of truth, doubt, and questioning as facilitating human freedom in a liberal and Broad Church interpretation of democratic history. For "Gospel which is to the Greek foolishness" see 1 Cor. 1:23. To the Greeks the cross of Jesus (about which Paul is writing) is foolishness because they seek wisdom (1 Cor. 1:22) and the cross does not signify wisdom. For "higher wisdom . . . perfect" see 1 Cor. 2:5–7 and Eph. 4:13, passages that support the suggestion such a reading of the relation of "higher wisdom" to the reconciling of faith and knowledge as a contemporary issue in "Christian philosophy." For "why seek ye the living among the dead?" see Luke 24:25; in Jowett's day the angel's question at the resurrection was posed concerning classical languages and education, political and religious issues like prayer-book revision and subscription, and literary fashions. The phrase "render unto Caesar . . . God's" (Matt. 22:21; Mark 12:17; Luke 20:25) occurs in the context of a dispute concerning the propriety of religious Jews paying tributary taxes to Roman governors and paying to God what belongs to God. While the latter is not

defined, it is often, perhaps wrongly, taken to separate the moral autonomy of the spiritual and secular realms, a position that Jowett comes close to condoning (see Jowett ¶s 4, 28, and 81). The phrase of Bacon's, "Give to the faith those things which belong to the faith," has not been located.

131. The "words of Christ Himself" began to be printed in "red letter" editions of the Bible in the late nineteenth century under the influence of Louis Klopsch, publisher of *The Christian Herald.* For reconstructions of the authentic words of Jesus as determined on historical-critical grounds see Breech 1983; Funk 1991; and Funk, Hoover, and the Jesus Seminar 1993.

For "render unto Caesar" see Matt. 22:21; Mark 12:17; Luke 20:25; for "the Scribes . . . do not," Matt. 23:2; for conversions on the day of Pentecost, see Acts 2:1–41. For an account of the popular religious revival that peaked in 1859–60 in what J. E. Orr called "the second evangelical awakening" see Orr 1949; and Gilbert 1976, 187–96. Isabella Bird published "Religious Revivals" in the *Quarterly Review* in January, 1860 (107:148–68), just before *Essays and Reviews* was published.

Lessons and lectures were a popular form of adult education, both as occasional events for the middle class and to promote literacy and education among the working class (see Jowett ¶40 and n. 76). The relation between public health and sanitary reform was brought to public attention in Edwin Chadwick's *Report on the Sanitary Condition of the Labouring Population of Great Britain* (1842). Chadwick was a strong supporter of the work for sanitary reform promoted in *A Contribution to the Sanitary History of the British Army* (1859) and *Notes on Hospitals* (1859) by Florence Nightingale, a friend and correspondent of Jowett's. For her work on health reform see Nightingale 1989, 159–234; and for sanitation in general in relation to Victorian ideas of the natural theology of disease see Hamlin 1985.

For "Sabbaths as well as working days" see Ezek. 46:1; for "good word of God . . . to come," Heb. 6:5; for "rushing mighty wind" on the day of Pentecost, Acts 2:1–2; for the leaven "which a woman . . . leavened," Matt. 13:33 and Luke 13:21.

132. The parables of Jesus are brief narratives that have a double meaning. On the surface they make a literal and realistic reference, and on a metaphorical level a religious or moral precept, occasionally explained but more often only implied. A number of the parables in Matthew begin with the phrase "The kingdom of heaven is like. . . ." Jowett refers to seven parables as typifying Christian experience: the prodigal son (Luke 15:11–32); the talents (Matt. 25:14–30; Luke 19:11–27); the laborers in the vineyard (Matt. 20:1–15); the Pharisee and publican (Luke 18:10–13); the sower and the seed (Matt. 13:3–8; Mark 4:3–8; Luke 8:5–8); the pearl of great price (Matt. 13:45–46); and the good Samaritan (Luke 10:30–35). For the parables see the survey of the scholarship in Epp and MacRae 1989, 177–98.

For "live and move" see Acts 17:28; for "treasury . . . old," Matt. 13:52; for "because He is the Son of Man," John 5:27.

133. Some of the Epistles are directed to specific problems in each congregation to whom the letter is addressed, as Robert Jewett comments: "All of the evidence points to the conclusion that these occasional letters were intended for the use of specific local congregations facing particular issues that were not necessarily present in other congregations" (*Harper's Bible Commentary* 1988, 1126). The "business of the early Church" included such matters as whether Gentile converts should undergo circumcision—a position rejected at the Jerusalem council (Acts 15:1–35), and one of the points of the letter to the Galatians. Another matter of "business" concerned Paul's collecting of money for the church in Jerusalem, mentioned in various Epistles, including 1 Cor. 16:1–4.

For "afflicted" see 2 Cor. 1:6; for "persecuted," 2 Cor. 4:9; for "driven out of the world," 1 Cor. 5:10.

References to the celebration of holy communion (1 Cor. 10:16; 11:20–29; Matt. 26:26–28; Mark 14:22–24; Luke 22:19–20; 24:35; Acts 2:42) echo the words of institution of the eucharist at the last supper; passages on church order or government and the role of presbyters and deacons in the government of the church are discussed in Jowett ¶28 and note and in Wilson passim; the "gift of tongues," or speaking in tongues, is referred to in various places in the NT, particularly after outpourings of Holy Spirit, as in Acts 2:4; 10:46; 19:6; 1 Cor. 12:10, 30; 14:18–23; 1 Thess. 5:19; and Eph. 5:18. The words of those so speaking are sometimes understood clearly and at other times apparently require interpretation; Paul's correspondence with the Corinthians indicates that he viewed the phenomenon with some suspicion. Each of these topics was a contemporary matter of dispute. For instance, the mode of celebrating holy communion was a point of controversy between the Evangelicals and the Tractarians, the latter advocating the revival of medieval English and Roman Catholic ritual and ceremonial practice, such as the so-called "six points" (so named by the English Church Union in a resolution of 1875): the eastward position of the celebrant of the eucharist, the use of eucharistic vestments, the mixed chalice (with wine and a little water), candles on the altar, unleavened bread, and incense; the Ritual Commission was set up by the Convocation of Canterbury to inquire into such practices (1867); it included in its membership a number of the participants in the *Essays and Reviews* controversy, Archbishop Longley, Bishops Tait and Wilberforce, A. P. Stanley, and Sir Robert Phillimore. Similarly, church order and government, and the roles of the orders of ministry (bishops, priests, and deacons) were linked to issues of church authority and apostolical succession by the Tractarians, as in Newman's first tract, "Thoughts on the Ministerial Commission" (1833). Speaking with tongues was termed "glossolalia" in the nineteenth century. Such ecstatic outbursts were variously interpreted—as evidence of possession by demons, as a mark of mental instability or insanity, or as a sign of religious favor. Speaking with tongues as part of a religious revival was often identified with Edward Irving (see Powell ¶33 and n. 16) and the Assemblies of God or Pentecostal Churches from their inception in 1907. On the relation to some of these issues with the theology and practice of the eucharist see Jowett ¶s 34 and 92.

134. For "charity never faileth" see 1 Cor. 13:8; for "though I speak . . . nothing," 1 Cor. 13:1–2; for "if meat . . . offend," 1 Cor. 8:13; for "I have fought the good fight . . . faith," 2 Tim. 4:7; for "my strength . . . weakness," 2 Cor. 12:9; for "when I am weak, then I am strong," 2 Cor. 12:10; for "ambassador of Christ," Eph. 6:20; for "spend and be spent," 2 Cor. 12:15. Jowett alludes to the persecutions and imprisonments of Paul: he was beaten at Philippi (Acts 16:22) and imprisoned there (Acts 16:23–39). He was probably imprisoned at Ephesus (2 Cor. 1:8–11) and was certainly imprisoned in Jerusalem (Acts 21:27–23:30) and, on appealing for justice to Caesar, in Rome (Acts 27:1–28:31). Paul's work as an "ambassador" on a diplomatic or doctrinal "mission" to the churches he established is compared with the work of the clergy who, while not imitating Paul's persecutions, may imitate his other virtues. Ironically, the term *persecution* is used by both the Essayists and their opponents in the trials that ensued on the publication of *Essays and Reviews*; for instance, in 1862 Rowland Williams published *Persecution for the Word* on the interlocutory judgment against him in the Court of Arches trial; and in the trial of Jowett before the Chancellor's Court in Oxford, Pusey protested that "prosecution is not persecution" (Letter to the *Times* 19 Feb. 1863; Letter 175).

135. The term *analogy of faith* (Rom. 12:6) was elaborated from Paul by the Caroline divines, such as Launcelot Andrewes, and was widely used in nineteenth-century hermeneutics to argue that there is a similitude or analogy between the Bible and the doctrines of faith, the former issuing in the latter, and the doctrines established by proofs in the Bible. For instance, Horne defines it as "the constant and perpetual harmony of Scripture in the fundamental points of faith and practice . . . or . . . that proportion which the doctrines of the Gospel bear to each other, or the close connection between the truths of Revealed Religion" ([1818] 1828, 2:335).

Jowett's oppositions have biblical references: outward and inward (1 Sam. 16:7), ceremonial and moral law (the priestly and holiness codes in Exodus and Leviticus that set out ritual observances and the moral precepts of the covenant code, as in Exod. 21–23), and mercy and sacrifice (Prov. 21:3; Hosea 6:6; and Amos 5:21). For the duties of the rich to the poor see 2 Sam. 12:1–5; for the religion of suffering exemplified in the role of the suffering servant see Isa. 52:13–53:12. For "adversity, the blessing" see Bacon's essay "Of Adversity": "Prosperity is the blessing of the Old Testament; adversity is the blessing of the New" (Bacon 1858–74, 12:94). For "bruised reed" see Isa. 42:3; for "beloved one . . . delighteth," Isa. 42:1; for "to fear God . . . commandments," Eccles. 12:13; for "beginning and end of all things," 1 Pet. 4:7 and Rev. 21:6.

136. Jowett contradicts 2 Tim. 3:16 that "all scripture is given by inspiration of God, and is profitable for doctrine, for reproof, for correction, for instruction in righteousness." The phrase "hardness of your hearts" occurs five times in the NT, two of them in relation to the law of Moses on divorce (see Jowett ¶28 and notes). Other problems concern the occasional references to the divine origin of human sin and of human obtuseness, stubbornness, and persistence in sin (Deut. 2:30; 1 Sam. 2:25; 1 Kings 12:15; Ps. 81:12; and Isa. 6:9–10). Such objections with rebuttals were common: Horne had included discussions of "objections of unbelievers to the doctrine and morality of the Bible" ([1818] 1828, 1:411–37) and of "seeming contradictions to morality (2:519–34). Jowett refers in a sermon to similar moral difficulties in accepting all biblical texts as "instruction": "We are not bound to give our assent either to the conception of God, or the acts or words of inspired men, if our conscience revolts at them, merely because they are found in Scripture or read in churches" (Jowett 1895, 289–91). Recent commentators summarize the scholarship on the moral theology of the Hebrew Bible since 1945 in similar terms: "There is no way that twentieth-century theologians can say that their contemporaries should follow the ethical principles of the Bible just because they are in the Bible" (Knight and Tucker 1985, 254).

The "Old Covenanters" were Scottish Presbyterians of the sixteenth and seventeenth centuries who signed covenants to protect their religious beliefs: signatories to the King's Confession (1581) included James VI and his family; a National Covenant (1638) was signed to protest the introduction of a Scottish *BCP*; and in 1643 the English Parliament drew up an alliance with rebels in Scotland in the Solemn League and Covenant. For "hewing Agag . . . in Gilgal" see 1 Sam. 15:33; modern examples of regicide for religio-political motives include the execution of Charles I (1649); see also Jowett ¶74 and n. 123. Walter Scott presented the Covenanters critically in *Old Mortality* (1816) and more sympathetically in *The Heart of Midlothian* (1818). The Covenanters' relating of democratic parliamentarianism to imperial monarchy was a popular motif in the visual arts in the nineteenth century: between 1820 and 1900 about 175 paintings were exhibited at the Royal Academy connected with Charles I, Cromwell, and the Civil War (Strong 1978, 136–45).

"Polygamy" in America refers to the Mormons or Church of Jesus Christ of Latter-Day Saints, established in 1830 by Joseph Smith on the basis of a series of revelations, including one in 1843 that sanctioned polygamy which continued to be practisced by them until 1890 when it was abandoned under legal negotiations to have the state of Utah (where their headquarters were located) enter into the Union. See Jowett ¶74 and n. 124.

For the forty-two children who were savaged for mocking the prophet Elisha see 2 Kings 2:23–24.

137. Jowett distinguishes between the "*intention*" of Hosea to prophesy the specifics of Joseph and Mary's life and the typological interpretation of the passage as in Matthew or Alford: "This citation [from Hosea] shows the almost universal application in the N.T. of the prophetic writings to the expected Messiah, as the general anti-type of all the events of the typical dispensation. . . . It seems to have been a received axiom of interpretation (which has, by its adoption in the N.T., received the sanction of the Holy Spirit Himself, and now stands for our guidance,) that the subject of all allusions, the represented in all parables and dark sayings, was He who was to come, or the circumstances attendant on His advent and reign" (Alford [1849] 1863, 1:15).

The feminine pronoun in the Vulgate reading of Gen 3:15 which Jowett quotes ("*she* shall bruise thy head") is masculine in the Hebrew and the Septuagint; the Vulgate version was cited as typological evidence by Roman Catholics to justify the doctrine of the Immaculate Conception of the Virgin Mary, promulgated by Pius IX in 1854.

On the relation of Genesis and geology and ethnology see Goodwin passim and Wilson ¶74 and note.

Joshua's commanding of the sun to stand still was discussed by Galileo in his *Letter to the Grand Duchess Christina* (1632; in Galileo 1957, 211–15). For Galileo see also Temple ¶53 and Goodwin ¶s 1–9 and notes.

138. For the fourfold method of interpretation, and the methods of Philo, Origen, Calvin, and Thomas Aquinas, see Jowett ¶3 and notes. Sevenfold methods use the four terms and three close equivalents: literal (and historical), allegorical, moral (tropological) and anagogical (mystical). Another sevenfold method of interpretation is that of Rabbi Hillel of Jerusalem (see Williams, ¶16, n. 72). In the nineteenth century Ruskin in *Seven Lamps of Architecture* (1849) uses the seven "lamps" of interpretation: sacrifice, truth, power, beauty, life, memory, and obedience.

The typology of the Mosaic law, contrasted elaborately with the gospel by Paul in Romans, concerned both patristic and medieval thinkers. In the *Apostolic Constitutions* (4th century) the laws given after the worship of the Golden Calf (Exod. 32) are given to Israel in apostasy and are presumed not to apply to Christians, who have a "dispensation" from following them. To Thomas Aquinas the Mosaic Law is divided into three: the moral that applies to all (as in the Ten Commandments which contain the natural law), the ceremonial, and the judicial (both of which are specific to ancient Israel, but which, nevertheless, have a spiritual or typological purpose in alluding to Christ (Thomas Aquinas [1265–] 1962–64, 29:114–15). The double meaning of prophecy is explained by Jowett in *The Epistles of St. Paul*: "In these 'terrors of the day of the Lord,' of which the Prophets speak, the fortunes of the Jewish people mingle with another vision of a more universal judgement, and it has been usual to have recourse to the double senses of prophecy to separate the one from the other, an instrument of interpretation which has also been applied to the New Testament for the same purpose. Not in this way could the Prophet or Apostle themselves have conceived them. To them they were not two, but one; not 'double one against the other,' or separable into the figure and the thing signified. . . . If a separation is made at all, let us rather separate the accidents of time and place . . . [into] this twofold lesson of goodness and severity" ([1855] 1859, 2:141).

139. "Historical criticism" refers here to interpretations that answered attacks specific to their own historical periods, as in the works of Paley and Butler. Such arguments, according to Jowett, do not necessarily have currency in the present age. For the role of Paley and Butler in Oxford and Cambridge examinations in the nineteenth century, see Powell ¶105 and note. The reform of the curriculum and the structure of the university at Oxford in 1853, in which both Jowett and Stanley were active supporters, resulted in a much greater emphasis upon literary and historical study of the classics and tended to move biblical study in the same direction (see W. R. Ward 1965, 20–39; 80–103; 128–234).

140. This paragraph begins "Secondly, it has to be considered . . ." in Lewis Campbell's reprinting of the essay in his edition of Jowett, *The Epistles of St. Paul* (1894, 2:88).

Paul's panegyric on love (1 Cor. 13) asserts in v. 8 that while other forms of inspired discourse, such as prophecy and speaking in tongues, and knowledge, will "vanish away," love "never faileth," and hence, is a "never-changing truth of the Christian life." Stanley comments on this verse: "This is the last and crowning glory of Love, that it is imperishable; everything else may be changed in the great change of death, but the affections may still be regarded as surviving" (1855, 1:281).

For the opposition between theology and the Bible or between the church and the Bible, especially as polarized at the Reformation and revived in the rivalry between both Evangelicals and Tractarians in the C. of E. and the Church of Rome, see Jowett ¶s 11, 14, 28, and notes.

On the role of inspiration and theological orthodoxy see especially Jowett ¶s 1–3, 14–15, and notes. The Gnostic sects (Gk. *gnosis*, knowledge) of the second century held that a special knowledge was communicated by Jesus to the apostles, or by the apostles to Gnostic adherents, or by direct revelation to the founder of the sect. Such teaching (like the apostolic tradition in orthodox Christianity based on Matt. 28:20; John 14:26; and Acts 2:42) was cautioned against as "false teaching" in such passages as 2 Peter 2:1 and 1 John 4:1. Gnostics believed in an unknowable Divine Being and the lesser deity, or Demiurge, who as creator made the world as imperfect. Hence, earthly or fleshly knowledge is hostile to true spiritual knowledge that was divinely implanted in some persons, those who are spiritual or knowing. By *gnosis*, or spiritual knowledge, and religious rites, the spirit is freed from corrupting matter to return to the Divine Being. Jesus is the prime exemplar of those with such spiritual knowledge, only temporarily assuming a human being, or appearing to do so. Among these Gnostic sects were the Marcionites, the followers of Marcion. He argued that the particular kind of knowledge imparted by Jesus and Christianity was love, to the exclusion of law; hence, he rejected all of the Hebrew scriptures and much of the NT, except for the epistles of St. Paul and Luke. His views were attacked by Tertullian in his treatise *Against Marcion* (c. 207). Another group associated with the Gnostics was the Manichees, the followers of Manes, who held that religious practice had as its goal the release of particles of light trapped in the human brain by Satan when he stole light from heaven in the primary cosmic conflict between light and darkness, good and evil. Victory over this dualism is accomplished with the help of ascetical religious leaders (Jesus, Buddha) and practices (including vegetarianism). Augustine was a Manichee for the nine years before his conversion to Christianity and tells of their teachings and practices in *Confessions* (c. 400).

The relation of the divinity and humanity of Christ was debated in the ecumenical councils of the church, from the first at Nicaea (325) to Chalcedon (451) and the second council of Constantinople (553). The Nicene creed sets out the distinction by asserting in technical theological language of the time that on the one hand he "was made man" and on the other that he was "of one substance with the Father." The "eminent English prelate" has not been identified.

The "dividing and splitting of words" is very likely a reference to the most controversial word of the Nicene creed, whether the compound adjective describing Christ's relationship with the Father would read "*homoousios*" (of the same substance) as the orthodox held, or "*homoiousios*" (of like substance) as the Arians and semi-Arians held; for a discussion of the theological implications of this distinction see Kelly 1950, 205–62; and Williams ¶27 and n. 110.

The image of the veil on the understanding and the cloud that the combatants raised to envelop their fighting has been used earlier (Jowett ¶42 and note) and here may be paralleled to such Homeric examples as the dust cloud that was sent over the fighters at the battle at the ships to cloud their minds and vision (*Iliad*, 12.251 ff.), the mist that enshrouded Patroklos just before his death (*Iliad*, 16.790), or the cloud of mist enveloping the Greeks and Trojans at the beginning of *Iliad*, 21. Tennyson uses a similar device to confuse the combatants in King Arthur's last battle in the West with Modred ("The Passing of Arthur" [1869] 95–117).

141. Jowett describes the changes in interpretation imported from Germany and adopted by such Broad Church theologians as Thomas Arnold, F. D. Maurice, A. P. Stanley, and Frederick Temple. Interpretation that formally depended upon similar biblical phrases (see Jowett ¶50 and note), word associations, or thematic links perceived by the translators of the AV is, in Jowett's day, applied as of universal validity to "our moral nature." In *The Epistles of St. Paul* Jowett counters this view with a long essay on the role of conscience in determining right and wrong ("Casuistry"), an interpretation of Rom. 14 ([1855] 1859, 2:384).

For the "Baptismal Regeneration" controversy associated with the Gorham case of 1850 see Jowett ¶s 2, 28, and notes. Controversy concerning the eucharist included the case of George Anthony Denison, a High Churchman (and voluminous opponent of *Essays and Reviews*) whose teaching on the real presence of Christ in the eucharist led to prosecution before the church and civil courts from 1854 to 1858, charges supported by the Evangelical Alliance (established 1846 "against Popery and Puseyism, and to promote the interests of a Scriptural Christianity"). In this controversy Robert Isaac Wilberforce published *The Doctrine of the Holy Eucharist* (1853), Pusey, *The Doctrine of the Real Presence* (1855), and Keble, *On Eucharistical Adoration* (1858), all supporting Denison's views. A subsequent controversy, concerning ceremonial at the eucharist that was supported by the Tractarians and attacked by the Evangelicals at the parish of St. George's-in-the-East, London, was exactly contemporaneous with the publication of *Essays and Reviews*. On Denison's case see Owen Chadwick 1966–70, 1:491–95; on St. George's, 1:495–501; see also Jowett ¶s 34, 83, and notes. Jowett, however, was wrong in thinking that such controversies were dead: baptism continues to be an issue in church discipline when nonpracticing parents bring children for baptism according to conventional family custom. The establishment of the Ritual Commission in 1867 had to deal with continued controversy concerning ritual associated with the eucharist; the report of the commission left matters unresolved until the Public Worship Regulation Act of 1874 led to imprisonments for High Church transgressors as the act fell into disuetude. See Owen Chadwick 1966–70, 2:347–58.

For "Our greatest love . . . hate" compare *Romeo and Juliet* 1.5.142.

142. The controversies of the previous generation included those surrounding the Oxford Movement (1833–45) and its defense of the C. of E. as both catholic and apostolic in the ninety numbers of *Tracts for the Times*, with John Keble, J. H. Newman, and E. B. Pusey as the primary instigators. Opposition came from Broad Church theologians like Thomas Arnold, Richard Whately, and R. D. Hampden. H. B. Wilson had been involved in the "Protest of the Four Tutors" (along with A. C. Tait) over J. H. Newman's *Tract XC* (1841); another agitator, from the evangelical wing, was C. P. Golightly. While the immediate controversies concerning the *Tracts* had subsided, the issues they raised were still debated, as is clear from Jowett's allusions to them and from continuing concerns over secessions to the Roman Catholic Church with the no-popery riots of the 1850s (see Wilson ¶55 and 76 and notes 94 and 124).

The magic circle of necromancy is used by Shakespeare in *Henry V* (5.2.320), throughout *The Tempest*, and by Marlowe in *Dr. Faustus* in the conjuring scene (sc. 3). Jowett most likely refers to the protection of the magic circle of romantic inspiration in the last four lines of Coleridge's "Kubla Khan" (1816), suggesting that both the High Church and evangelical parties are less committed to protectionist institutional attitudes concerning biblical inspiration than previously. Jowett is premature in declaring a truce between the parties, both of whom attacked *Essays and Reviews* on the topic of inspiration, though it is true that they buried their differences in opposition to the appointment of Frederick Temple to the bishopric of Exeter in 1869.

For "revivals are not permanent" compare Jowett's edition of Plato's *Phaedo*: "And revival, if there be such a thing, is the birth of the dead into the world of the living" ([1871] 1875, 1:446).

143. For Jowett's earlier discussion of the effect of critical interpretation on theology and life see Jowett ¶s 38, 73, and 78.

144. For "What has thou . . . follow thou me" see, for example, 2 Kings 9:18–19; Matt. 4:19; 8:22 and many other locations where Jesus calls the disciples.

About 300 B.C.E. Zeno of Citium established the Greek school of philosophers known as the stoics, named after the public hall, or stoa, in Athens where they met. They continued there for about 600 years, until the third century, with an important following in Rome, including Seneca, Epictetus, and the emperor Marcus Aurelius. Their views included a reliance upon reason (*logos*) as the overriding law of nature, life, and public duty; hence, the wise person was indifferent to emotions, and endured pain with fortitude.

145. For "rational service" see Rom. 12:1.

146. An example of a "formal concordat" is the Concordat of 1801 between Pius VII and Napoléon Bonaparte concerning the restoration of the Roman Catholic church in France with new diocesan boundaries, provisions for the appointments of bishops, and arrangements concerning church property and income.

The citation from Plato's *Republic* occurs in a discussion of the limitations on mimesis, or imitation, in literature, tragic drama, and the education of the guardians.

The image of the walls that fall down is an extension of the attack of Joshua on Jericho (Josh. 6:5, 20; and Heb. 11:30).

147. Wilson's essay deals extensively with the substance of Jowett's ¶s 97 and 98; Jowett's concern, however, is less with the requirements for a "national church" than for a broader ecumenical movement involving "the whole Christian world" in which differences in political position, as well as in theological doctrine and institutional affiliation, will be recognized as characterizing even the earliest Christian communities (as in the conflicts described in 1 Cor. 1:11–3:23).

In *The Epistles of St. Paul* Jowett comments on Rom. 11:26 on the admission of Gentiles to the church and the related question of the fate of the faithful Jews: "Modern criticism detaches the meaning of the Apostle from the event of the prophecy ['And so all Israel shall be saved']. It has no need to pervert his words, from a determination as it may be called, such as Luther expresses, that the Jews shall not be saved, or with Calvin to transfer them to the Israel of God, because the time seems to have passed for their literal fulfilment. Happy would it have been for the fortunes of the Jewish race and the honour of the Christian name had they never been so wrongly applied." Jowett then refers to Rom. 11:32 and on that verse comments: "The very rejection of the Jews is a kind of argument from analogy for their acceptance: what they were, the Gentiles are [sinners under the law, but people of faith]; therefore, what the Gentiles are, they will become" ([1855] 1859, 2:313–14; 315–16).

148. The sectarian divisions of European and North American Christianity were imposed on the rest of the world through the activities of the various denominational and interdenominational missionary societies. As an important part of nineteenth-century colonization they often tended to designate the colonized as children in the ethnographical development of the human race, explained by the notion of different rates of progress or even of evolution for different races and regions of the world. The spiritual, economic, and cultural "poverty" of the colo-

nized, according to such views, made them the appropriate subjects, when defined as the "poor" who must have the gospel preached to them (Matt. 11:5), for the concomitant interests of an expansionist Christianity, commerce, and Western civilization.

On the growth of such missionary activity, see Jowett ¶s 25, 79, and notes; on Christian missions and on the Vedas and Koran see Wilson ¶s 10–12 and notes. On the Eurocentric and racialist notion of an "ancient and decaying culture" in India, and the notion of "servile habits of mind" and "no history" in the "orient" see Wilson ¶s 13–14 and notes; and especially on Macaulay's views in his "Minute on Indian Education" (1835) see Temple ¶27 and notes.

For "hardness of men's hearts" see Matt. 19:8; Mark 3:5; 10:5. For the references to Moses in these passages, concerning divorce, see Deut. 24:1. For "mind of Christ" see 1 Cor. 2:16.

149. Jowett claims again that the Bible should be read or studied like any other book, here using terms of liberal education, applying the methods of classical textual and historical scholarship to the Bible. Liberal education, and especially the study of literature (and the Bible as literature) as a humanizing activity that can replace religion, as Matthew Arnold comes close to suggesting, can therefore assume the role of salvation: "to save our souls and heal the State" (George Gordon cited in Eagleton 1983, 23).

150. For "things as they truly are" see Jowett ¶10 and 39 and notes.

Jowett refers to two notable preachers of his day: Frederick William Robertson, whose sermons were published posthumously (1855–63), and J. H. Newman, whose sermons preached at St. Mary's Church, Oxford, were published as *Parochial and Plain Sermons* (1834–43).

For "who was in all points . . . without sin" see Heb. 4:15.

151. For "see things as they are" see Jowett ¶10 and 39 and notes.

For "dry light" see Bacon's essay "On Friendship."

Nicodemus was a Pharisee who came under the influence of Jesus (John 3), and later defended him (John 7:50–52) and prepared his body for burial (John 19:39). For the cited passages see John 7:51–52.

For "strong swimmer" see Byron, *Don Juan* (1819–24; canto 2, st. 53).

152. On the class position of the clergy and the proprieties that govern their conduct and admonitions see Pattison passim; see also Reader 1966; Heeney 1976; and Haig 1984.

Gladstone's annotation on this passage in his copy of *Essays and Reviews* in St. Deiniol's Library notes that Jowett has valued "the Old above the New Dispensations."

153. For "all men speaking well of us" see Luke 6:26; for "acceptable in the sight of God," 1 Tim. 2:3.

Free inquiry into questions of religious doctrine and the meaning of the Bible in Italy and Spain in 1860 was severely limited by the force of papal censorship, the proscription of books in the *Index librorum prohibitorum* (List of prohibited books), and the role of the inquisition in maintaining a prescribed orthodoxy. The Spanish Inquisition was instituted with papal approval by Ferdinand V and Isabella in 1479, particularly directed against converts from Judaism and Islam, but eventually against Protestants and all dissidents. The first Grand Inquisitor was Tomás de Torquemada, who was also responsible for the expulsion of Jews who resisted baptism from Spain in 1492. The Spanish Inquisition was finally abolished in 1820. In Italy the same role was taken by the Holy Office as the final court of appeal in heresy trials. It still renders final decisions on controversies and particular charges concerning alleged infringements on faith and morals. George Borrow worked as an agent of the British and Foreign Bible Society in Spain, publishing an account of his efforts in *The Bible in Spain* (1843, 3 vols.).

154. Gladstone annotates his copy of *Essays and Reviews* in St. Deiniol's Library; at the phrase concerning the need for each to "make war against his prejudices" Gladstone adds "none more than the writer of this essay"; at "mind of the world" Gladstone asks: "What is the better mind of the World? There is none that doeth good" [Rom. 3:12].

155. The composite image of the ideal teacher is embodied in Thomas Arnold. At the same time, it anticipates two ideas of Matthew Arnold, one in the phrase from "The Function of Criticism at the Present Time" (1864): "reflects the better mind of the world to itself," suggesting the notion that criticism is to know "the best that has been known and thought in the world" (1960–77, 3:283); and second, in *Culture and Anarchy* the notion that "aliens" or persons "mainly led, not by their class spirit, but by a general *humane* spirit, by the love of human perfection" still accomplish a "deeper work" (1960–77, 5:146).

Opposite this passage on the "love of truth," Gladstone comments in the margin of his copy of *Essays and Reviews* in St. Deiniol's Library: "How can a man Love the truth who loves not the Lord Jesus Christ." At the end of ¶106 Gladstone adds: "a cold vain barren Philosophy, ending with the Grave here. The sport and Triumph of devils hereafter."

Textual Notes

English Editions

Each variant in the English editions is keyed to the present edition by page and line number, counting from the top of the text, and excluding from the numbering the running chapter heading. Variants in the Essayists' notes are keyed to the note number in the present edition and the line number in the note (not on the page). Variants in the notes are listed in the page sequence of the text. The cue-phrase reference is printed in italics, followed by a slash / and the variant in Roman face; any words in italics in the copytext are in underlined italics in the cue-phrase; words in italics in the variant are given in italics. Following the variant, the edition that introduces it is noted in brackets together with any other relevant information. The three issues of the tenth edition are not distinguished in the list of variants; the edition of 1869, designated as "The Twelfth Edition" on the title page, is actually the thirteenth, and is so designated in the list of variants. The sign→ indicates that the specified change continued until the next edition noted, or until the thirteenth edition if no other edition is mentioned. If there is no reference to an American edition in annotation to variants in the English edition, the American editions do not include further variants. However, numerous additional variants in the pirated American editions have not been included. Both the English and American editions used chapter titles as running heads or page heads; they are replaced in the present edition by the title *Essays and Reviews* and each Essayists' name.

Variants in typographical conventions in the English editions have not been included in the Textual Notes, though in each case they indicate ways in which the text was reset. These variants include the addition of blank pages in the prelims (only noted on the collation chart, p. 598); broken or omitted type (corrected in subsequent editions, as, for example, the sixth edition's misnumbering of its p. 261 as 61, and the first edition's p. 403 with no number at all until the third edition); changes in line breaks, usually but not always resulting from re-composition to accommodate added text; and different number of lines to the page in some editions (for example, the tenth and eleventh editions set their p. 401 with 33 lines to the page instead of the customary 32; in the twelfth and thirteenth editions it is set with 32 lines to the page).

Publishers' catalogues are bound into the first to ninth editions as shown on the collation chart. The publisher's advertisements bound after the last page of text in perfect copies of the first edition consist of six pages to complete the gathering FF beginning on p. 433 (Publisher's Catalogue 1 on the page of collations). The advertisements consist of John Parker's undated publisher's catalogue of six pages: one unnumbered page for *Oxford Essays* and *Cambridge Essays* (1855–58) and one for

Fraser's Magazine, announcing "*The Number for MARCH, 1860 contains. . . . The APRIL Number will contain. . . .*" Then follows Parker's list of "New Books and New Editions" in four numbered pages. Similar advertisements are used in the second and third editions, listing current content for *Fraser's Magazine* and an almost identical four-page list of "new books." In the fourth edition, published by Longman, there are two catalogues. The first consists of six unnumbered pages to complete the gathering: a page on Macaulay; one on Sydney Smith; one on Horne's *Introduction to . . . Holy Scriptures*; one on *My Life . . . by an Old Maid*; one on "Books of Instruction" by "the author of *Amy Herbert*; and one on W. Walter Wilkins's edition of *Political Ballads* (Publisher's Catalogue 2). This list is followed by Longman's current "List of Works in General Literature," twenty-four numbered pages on thinner paper and in smaller type, dated "*October* 1860" (Publisher's Catalogue 3). It continued to be published unchanged at the end of *Essays and Reviews* until the ninth edition. From the tenth to the thirteenth there are no publisher's catalogues bound in; instead, the endpapers are used for the publisher's advertisements. The thirteenth edition also includes Longman's "General List of Works," thirty-two numbered pages, twenty-eight pages of catalogue, and four pages of index, dated January, 1870 (Publisher's Catalogue 4).

American Editions

ALTHOUGH THE TITLE PAGE of the first American edition states: "Reprinted from the Second London Edition," this claim cannot be substantiated. For instance, none of the substantive changes made in the second English edition resulting from Powell's emendation was incorporated in the first American edition. In every case the reading in the American text follows that of the English first edition, the one possible exception being p. 260, l. 10, where "To conclude," is changed to "To conclude:" in the second edition; and the first American edition accords here, but also follows the general editorial convention of the American editions. The American editor introduced a large number of fresh variants, however. These consist largely of changes in accidentals: spellings, typographical conventions, variations in capitalization, the omission and addition of punctuation, and the use of double quotation marks for single quotation marks; brackets are replaced by parentheses. Foot-note numbers are changed to typographical symbols and the typesetting of long passages of quoted material is indented and in smaller type; signature numbers are not letters (as in the English editions), but arabic numbers. American conventions in spellings include the changing of many words ending in "-our" to "-or": hence, "color" and "colored" replace "colour" and "coloured" [Temple ¶s 29, 31]; "colors" replaces "colours" [Pattison ¶58]; "labor" and "labors" replace "labour" and "labours" [Temple ¶s 28, 58]; and "honor" replaces "honour" in this word and its cognates [Pattison ¶s 30, 36, 45]. Some typographical errors in the first English edition were corrected in the American editions before the English, such as p. 192, n. 81. Other errors were introduced, such as the spelling of "rereward" as "rearward" at p. 191, l. 22.

Examination of copies of each of the American editions from 1861 to 1874 indicates that a significant number of variants was introduced from the first to the second American editions. For instance, the Preface entitled "To the Reader" has been set with different line breaks. In the dedicatory poem to Bunsen that concludes Williams's essay, the seventh line concludes in all copies of the English editions with the word "Tongue" followed by a semicolon; in the first American the word is "tongue" with a semicolon; in the second and following American editions the word is "tongues" followed by a comma. Numerous other changes in accidentals indicate that there were many interventions in the text between the first and second American editions. For instance, pp. 514, ll. 30–43 and 515, ll. 1–3 in the present edition are set with different line-endings from the first to the second and subsequent American editions, accommodating different spacing for Jowett's numbering of items in these passages. For a discussion of the significance of these variants, see Part 1, section 2. The two prefaces to the American Editions are included in Part 3: Documentation.

Collations

Editions	1	2	3	4	5	6	7	8	9	10	11	12	13
Endpapers	buff	buff	brown	brown	brown	brown	marbled	brown	printed	printed	printed	printed	printed
Endpaper v°	blank	blank	blank	printed	blank	blank	blank	blank	blank	blank	blank	blank	blank
Half title r°	i	i	i	i	i	i	i	i	i	i	i	—	—
[Blank] v°	ii	ii	ii	ii	ii	ii	ii	ii	ii	ii	ii	—	—
Title page r°	iii	iii	iii	iii	iii	iii	iii	iii	iii	iii	iii	i	i
Imprint v°	iv	iv	iv	iv	iv	iv	iv	iv	iv	iv	iv	ii	ii
Preface to the Twelfth Edition r°												iii*	iii*
[Blank] v°												iv*	iv*
To the Reader r°	v	v	v	v	v	v	v	v	v	v	v	v	v
[Blank] v°	vi	vi	vi	vi	vi	vi	vi	vi	vi	vi	vi	vi	vi
Contents r°	vii	vii	vii	vii	vii	vii	vii	vii	vii	vii	vii	vii	vii
[Blank] v°	viii	viii	viii	viii	viii	viii	viii	viii	viii	viii	viii	viii	viii
Text	1[B]–433[FF]	1–433	1–433	1–433	1–433	1–433	1–433	1–433	1–433	1–527	1–527	1–527	1–527
Note on Bunsen	[434]	[434]	[434]	[434]	[434]	[434]	[434]	[434]	[434]	[528]	[528]	[528]	[528]
Publisher's Catalogue 1	yes	yes	yes	—	—	—	—	—	—	—	—	—	—
Publisher's Catalogue 2	—	—	—	yes	yes	yes	yes	yes	yes	no	no	no	no
Publisher's Catalogue 3	—	—	—	yes	yes	yes	yes	yes	yes	no	no	no	no
Publisher's Catalogue 4	—	—	—	—	—	—	—	—	—	—	—	—	yes
Adverts on Endpapers	—	—	—	—	—	—	—	—	—	yes	yes	yes	yes

List of Variants

[Preliminaries: the pagination of the preliminary pages varies from edition to edition and even within editions. Some copies examined are missing the half title; in some copies an extra blank sheet has been inserted before the half title, perhaps in rebinding.]

[i] [Half title] ESSAYS AND REVIEWS. [In some copies there is no half title (Oxford: Bodley, Baden Powell, 122); in the 12th and 13th editions, the half title and verso (i–ii) are replaced with the title page and imprint, followed by the new "Preface to the Twelfth Edition" and the rest of the preliminaries to make 8 pages for the gathering. The half title is not included in this edition]

133 [Title page] ESSAYS AND REVIEWS. / [Printer's device of wood-engraved monogram] / LONDON: /JOHN W. PARKER AND SON, WEST STRAND / 1860. / [*The Authors reserve the right of Translation.*]

[See fig. 11, p. 133. In the 2d and 3d Parker editions the number of the edition is stated in italic capitals below the ornament in small italic capitals: *THE SECOND EDITION.* The printer's device is replaced by pair of ornaments above and below the number of the edition in all Longman publications from the 4th→. The (thirteenth edition) of 1869 continues to be printed as *THE TWELFTH EDITION.* From the 10th→, the ornament below the edition number is inverted]

JOHN W. PARKER AND SON, WEST STRAND / LONGMAN, GREEN, LONGMAN, AND ROBERTS. [4th→10th] / LONGMAN, GREEN, LONGMAN, ROBERTS, AND GREEN. [11th] / LONGMAN, GREEN, LONGMAN, ROBERTS, & GREEN. [12th] / LONGMANS, GREEN, AND CO. [13th]

[date: changes according to published date of each edition]

[The Authors reserve the right of Translation.] / [*The Author reserves the right of Translation.*] [2d] / [*The Authors reserve the right of Translation.*] [3d→9th; omitted 10th→]

[The 2d American prints a "Publishers' Note" opposite the title page (vi):]

The first edition of "Recent Inquiries" was absorbed almost immediately after publication. To this present edition is added an *Appendix*, containing a valuable note by the American Editor, and Dr. Temple's admirable Sermon delivered before the University of Oxford, during the meeting of the British Association.

BOSTON, January, 1861.

[iv] [Imprint page] LONDON: / SAVILL AND EDWARDS, PRINTERS, CHANDOS STREET, / COVENT GARDEN. *SAVILL . . . GARDEN.* / LONDON: PRINTED BY / SPOTTISWOODE AND CO., NEW-STREET SQUARE / AND PARLIAMENT STREET [13th; not included in the present edition]

134 [A new "Preface to the Twelfth Edition" was added on p. iii* before p. v "To the Reader" 12th→]

THE opportunity / THE OPPORTUNITY [13th. To accommodate the insertion of this new preface with 8 pages in the first gathering of preliminary materials, the half title page was dropped, and the title page is p. [i], the imprint page is p. [ii], and the new preface is p. [iii*] with its blank verso, p. [iv*]. Then follows the Preface, "To the Reader." In the 13th the whole of this preface, still entitled "Preface to the Twelfth Edition." is set with different line breaks. See collation chart]

135 [The Preface entitled "To the Reader" was marked in the 12th→ by single and double quotation marks to indicate it was cited in the Court of Arches and Judicial Committee of the Privy Council proceedings; it is indicated in this edition by double underlining. For passages cited for heresy, see pp. 611–13]

l. 8 [*March*, 1860.] [12th after a two-line space] / *March* 1860. [13th]

136 [Contents-page]

ll. 5–7 *WILLIAMS, D.D., Vice-Principal and Professor of Hebrew, St. David's College, Lampeter; Vicar of Broad Chalke, Wilts* / WILLIAMS, D.D., Vicar of Broad Chalke, Wilts; late Vice-Principal and Professor of Hebrew, St. David's College, Lampeter [12th→]

l. 8 *Note on Bunsen's Biblical Researches* [1st→ followed Jowett's essay; in this edition it is relocated to follow William's essay to which it is an appendage]

l. 9 *POWELL, M.A., F.R.S., &c. &c., Savilian* / POWELL, M.A., F.R.S., Savilian [2d→11th] / late Savilian [12th→]

l. 16 *PATTISON, B.D.* / PATTISON, B.D., Rector of Lincoln College, Oxford [5th→]

137 [byline] [A byline is added to the title of each essay in the 1st American→ giving the author's name in small caps: BY FREDERICK TEMPLE, D.D. In this edition each Essayist's name is added to the title]

142 l. 22 *not be found* / not to be found [2d→ , and 1st American→]

144 l. 5 *church* / Church [4th→]

145 ll. 12, 18 *Judea* / Judaea [1st American→]

147 l. 18 *church* / Church [4th→]

152–54 (¶36) *Early Church* [After two usages of caps there are five with lower case, and a final one with caps. That is, the phrase is used eight times in this essay; it is capitalized three times only. There is an inconsistency in capitalizing the phrase in the 1st edition. It has capitals in the first and third sentences of this paragraph, but no capitals in the sixth sentence. From edition to edition there is considerable variation in the capitalization throughout this passage. See the accompanying chart]

Selected Variants in Capitalization

pp 152–54 line	present Edition	pp. 28–31. line 1st–3d Editions	4th Edition	5th Edition	6th Edition	pp. 33–34 line 10th Edition	11th Edition→	pp. 32–35 line 1st American Ed.→
152: 38	Early Church	18 Early Church	Early Church	Early Church	Early Church	29 Early Church	Early Church	15 Early Church
41	church government	23 church government	church government	church government	church government	2 church government	church government	20 church-government
153: 1	Early Church	28 Early Church	Early Church	Early Church	Early Church	7 Early Church	Early Church	25 Early Church
5	early church	34 early church	early Church	early Church	early Church	13 early Church	Early Church	31 Early Church
10	church government	3 church government	church government	church government	church government	20 church government	church government	4 church-government
13	early church	9 early church	early Church	early Church	early Church	26 early Church	Early Church	10 Early Church
26	the church	29 the church	the Church	the Church	the Church	14 the Church	the Church	30 the Church
29	early church	34 early church	early Church	early Church	early Church	19 early Church	Early Church	1 Early Church
30	church of Jerusalem	36 church of Jerusalem	church of Jerusalem	Church of Jerusalem	Church of Jerusalem	21 Church of Jerusalem	Church of Jerusalem	3 church of Jerusalem
32	church of Jerusalem	1 early church	early Church	early Church	early Church	24 early Church	Early Church	6 Early Church
33	church has over	3 church has over	Church has over	Church has over	Church has over	26 Church has over	Church has over	8 Church has over
154: 1	whole church	20 whole church	whole Church	whole Church	whole Church	11 whole Church	whole Church	25 whole church
9	early church	33–4 early church	early Church	early Church	early Church	24–5 early Church	Early Church	4 Early Church

[Hence, there is textual agreement from the first to the third editions, but there are variations between the third and fourth, and further variants between the fourth and sixth editions (only: "church of Jerusalem" to "Church of Jerusalem"). The sixth to tenth editions are identical. Further variants show between the tenth and the eleventh editions (all concerning the capitalizing of "Early" when used as an adjective with "Church"). The twelfth and thirteenth editions are identical to the 11th. After two usages of upper case letters there are five with lower case, and a final upper case. That is, the phrase "early church" is used eight times in this essay, it is capitalized three times only. There is an inconsistency in the capitalizing the phrase in the first edition. It has capitals in the first and third sentences of this paragraph, but no capitals in the sixth sentence. From edition to edition there is considerable variation in the capitalization throughout this passage. The first and second American editions are identical to each other, but introduce a hyphen into "church-government," and regularize the spelling of "Early Church" throughout. However, the American editions are inconsistent in the use of "church" or "Church," and do not follow the English first edition—or the second which it claims as copytext.]

183 l. 32 *primaeval* / primeval [4th→]
184 l. 5 *primaeval* / primeval [4th→]
l. 17 *primaeval* / primeval [4th→]
185 l. 35 *'high hand'* / "high hand" [12th→]
188 l. 16 *freedom.* / freedom.[1] [12th→]
l. 16 n.39 [1] [See Note at the end of the volume.] [footnote in brackets added in 12th→]
189 l. 6 *Messianic;* / Messianic[1]; [12th→]
l. 6 n. 49 [1] [He is stated by Hey to have alleged as many as twelve passages from the Old Testament as directly Messianic; it seems, he said he could have alleged more.] [footnote in brackets added in 12th→]
l. 7 n. 50 [2] *Collected in the Boyle Lectures.* / [2]'Collected in the *Boyle Lectures.*' [12th→]
n. 54 ll. 7–8 *apply to the Psalms, and Prophets, and Epistles.* /apply to the sacred volume at large. [12th→]
n. 54 ll. 25–26 *received in the New* / received from the New [10th→]
n. 54 ll. 30 ff. *As to his main argument (surely a strange parody of Butler), the sentence from Sir W. Hamilton* / As to his main argument (surely a strange parody of Butler), the sentence of Sir. W. Hamilton [10th, 11th] /As to his main argument (which differs from Butler by as much as analogy with false systems is a less recommendation than analogy with acknowledged Truth), the sentence of Sir W. Hamilton [12th→]
n. 54 ll. 40–52 *We are promised . . . and undefiled!* / In the *Catena Aurea*, published under high auspices in the University of Oxford, the narrative of Uriah . . . and undefiled! [12th→]
n. 54 l. 52 This comes from Anselm on St. Matthew, ch. i [added 10th→]
191 n. 65 l. 10 *Jahrhunderts . . . id.* / Jahrhunderts' . . . *Id.* [3d] / Jahrhunderts' . . . *id.* [4th] / Jahrhunderts' . . . *Id.* [5th→] / Jahrhunderts." — Id., p. 151. [1st American] / Jahrhunderts." — Id. p. 151. [2d American→]
191 l. 22 *rereward* / rearward [1st American→; "rereward" is the AV reading at Isa. 52:12]
192 n. 81 *Jer. xviii. 20; xiv. 11; xv, i* / Jer. xviii. 20; xiv. 11; xv, 1 [12th→; 1st American→]
200 l. 40 *church* / Church [4th→; 1st American→]
202 l. 42 *Tongue;* / tongue; [1st American] / tongues, [2d American→]
204 l. 1 [The "Note on *Bunsen's Biblical Researches*" is printed on the unnumbered page after Jowett's essay, 1st→; the first line of the "Note on *Bunsen's Biblical Researches*" is indented 1st American→; it follows Williams's article, on p. 105, as in the present edition]
l. 12 *author's tone* / author's tone, [10th→11th] / author's tone [12th→13th; 1st American→]

ll. 16 ff.	. . . *of his researches,* / . . . of his researches. [12th→; the following passage is added at this point in the 12th→ in brackets:] [The prayer expressed at page 75, which a higher Wisdom saw not fit to grant, was the offspring of a presentiment destined too soon to be fulfilled. Baron de Bunsen died at Bonn in the morning of Nov. 28th, 1860. His end was full of trust and peace. It will, of course, be understood that subsequent continuations of his Commentary, left by him in I know not how prepared a state, could form no part of the subject-matter of the Review contained in this volume.] R. W.
234 l. 7	*or to regard this* / and to regard this [emended by Powell in ink in his copy of 1st (Bodley: Baden Powell 122), and incorporated in 2d→]
237 l. 35	*mediaeval church* / medieval church [4th→] Mediaeval Church [1st American→]
239 l. 3	*confessedly* / [deleted in 2d→ ; emended by Powell in ink in his copy of 1st (Bodley: Baden Powell 122)]
240 l. 14	*of surprise* / by the surprise [emended by Powell in ink in his copy of 1st (Bodley: Baden Powell 122), and incorporated in 2d→]
241 l. 34	*can hardly even conceive* /cannot even conceive [emended by Powell in ink in his copy of 1st (Bodley: Baden Powell 122), and incorporated in 2d→]
244 ll. 31–32	*But all such Theistic reasonings are but one sided, and if pushed further must lead* / All such Theistic reasonings, in fact, if pushed to their consequences, must lead [emended by Powell in ink in his copy of 1st (Bodley: Baden Powell 122), and incorporated in 2d→]
244 n. 25	*Persuasio* / 'Persuasio [2d→, but not one of Powell's emendations (Bodley: Baden Powell 122); missing quotation mark added by editors on authority of 2d→] / "Persuasio [1st American→]
245 n. 31	*Letter and Spirit by Rev. J. Wilson* / *The Letter and Spirit of Scripture*, by the Rev. Thomas Wilson, M.A. [6th→] / Letter and Spirit, by Rev. J. Wilson [1st American→]
246 l. 9	*cotemporaries* / contemporaries [4th→; 2d American→; the 2d American then has not changed on the basis of the English where this emendation was not introduced until the 4th]
249 l. 12	*moral and spiritual tribunal* / moral and spiritual judgement [emended by Powell in ink in his copy of 1st (Bodley: Baden Powell 122); / judgment [2d→]
253 l. 16	*objections honestly felt* / objections *generally* felt [emended by Powell in ink in his copy of 1st (Bodley: Baden Powell 122), and incorporated in 2d→]

258 l. 20	*alleged production* / asserted production [emended by Powell in ink in his copy of 1st (Bodley: Baden Powell 122), and incorporated in 2d→]
260 l. 5	*beyond reason* / beyond science [emended by Powell in ink in his copy of 1st (Bodley: Baden Powell 122), and incorporated in 2d→]
l. 10	*To conclude,* / To conclude: [emended by Powell in ink in his copy of 1st (Bodley: Baden Powell 122), and incorporated in 2d→; 1st American→]
l. 19	*influence of faith.* [paragraph] / influence of faith. [no paragraph break, to accommodate Powell's emendation in l 28 in 2d→]
l. 21	*light, or perhaps* / light, as requiring some suspension of judgement as to their nature & circumstances, or perhaps [emended by Powell in ink in his copy of 1st (Bodley: Baden Powell 122)] / light, as requiring some suspension of judgment as to their nature and circumstances, or perhaps [incorporated in this form in 2d→]
l. 23	*sake of the doctrine* / sake of, the doctrine [11th→]
261 l. 3	*cotemporaries* / contemporaries [4th→ and 2d American→]
275	[title] *SEANCES* /SÉANCES [2d→; 1st American→]
276–77	[page-head] *Séances Historiques de Geneve.* / *Séances Historiques de Genève.* [2d→] / SEANCES HISTORIQUES DE GENEVE [1st American→; the page-head omits the dash from the title of the essay throughout 1st→; 1st American→]
284 l. 1	*develope* / develop [1st American→]
n. 39 l. 15	*imagine, that* / imagine that [10th→]
l. 35	*to be and do* / to be and to do [10th→]
l. 36	*His life* / His Life [10th→]
285 l. 3	*Jewish church* / Jewish Church [10th→; 1st American→]
l. 4	*Sadducees:* / Sadducees; [5th→]
l. 30	*indicated,* /indicated [10th→]
l. 33	*future recompense.* /future reward. [4th→]
n. 44 l. 2	*Hymenaeus,* / Hymenaeus [4th→; 2d American→]
286 l. 6	*and, secondly* / and secondly [5th→]
l. 10	*enjoined, no not to eat with him* / enjoined no not to eat with him [5th→9th] / enjoined 'no not to eat' with him [10th→; the phrase from 1 Cor. 5:11 is put in quotes] / enjoined, no, not to eat with him [1st American→]
l. 15	*comprised,* / comprised [10th→]
ll. 26–27	*The Apostolic Churches were thus multitudinist, and they early tended to become National Churches* / The apostolic churches were thus Multitudinist, and they early tended to become national churches [1st American→]
l. 36	*commonplace to speak* / commonplace, to speak [4th→]
287 l. 16	*Churches* / churches [5th→; 1st American→]

	l. 26	*matter,* / mater [2d, 3d] / matter, [4th→]
	l. 33	*from the traditional* / from traditional [10th→]
288	l. 1	*balance* / balancing [4th→]
	ll. 10–11	*period to look upon the heathen State* / period, to look upon the heathen state [4th→] / period to look upon the Heathen State [1st American→]
289		[page-head] [The page-head in 1st reads *Séances Historiques de Genève.* on the verso, and *The National Church.* on the recto up to p. 169 of the 1st (289 of the present edition). On p. 290 the same page-head, *The National Church.*, is used on both recto and verso, 1st→; 1st American→]
	ll. 7–9	*framework, and a spiritual organization, re-constituting governors, laws, and magistrates, educators, and ministers of religion* / framework and a spiritual organization, re-constituting governors, laws and magistrates, educators and ministers of religion [4th→] / framework and a spiritual organization; re-constituting governors, laws, and magistrates, educators, and ministers of religion [1st American→]
	l. 17	*customs; their worship* / customs; whose worship [4th→] / customs. Their worship [1st American→]
	n. 62 l. 22	*theocracy,* / theocracy [4th→; 1st American→]
	l. 39	*breaking in* / breaking-in [5th→; 1st American→]
	ll.41–42	*St. Paul and the Lord Jesus himself* / St. Paul, and the Lord Jesus himself, [4th→]
290	l. 11	*Nationalism* / Nationalism, [5th→; 1st American→]
	l. 17	*first,* / first [4th→]
	l. 31	*breaking up of the Roman empire* / breaking-up of the Roman empire [5th] / breaking up of the Roman empire [6th→] / breaking-up of the Roman Empire [1st American→]
	l. 43	*nor, if it be* / much less, if it be [4th→]
291	ll. 6–7	*for a reaction* / for reactions [4th→] / for a re-action [1st American] / for a reaction [2d American→]
	l. 36	*applied to the canonical books* / applied collectively to the books [4th→]
	l. 37	*never applied* / never so applied [4th→]
292	l. 2	*overruling* /overruling, [10th→]
	l. 15–16	*declarations,* / declaration, [10th→]
	n. 71 l. 11	*Doctrina* / *Doctrinâ* [4th→]
293	l. 14	*note and* / note or [10th→; 1st American→]
	n. 79 l. 24	*before the K. B.* / before the King's Bench [1st American→]
	n. 79 l. 26	*delivered,* / delivered [10th→; 1st American→]
	n. 79 l. 28	*breach of a penal* / breach of penal [4th→]
	n. 79 l. 35	*ex-officio* / *ex officio* [10th→; 1st American; the phrase *ex officio* is

used twice in this note in the 1st→9th together with the inconsistent *ex-officio*]

295 l. 20 *Article* / article [2d→]

l. 30 *explanatory* / explanatory, [10th→; 1st American]

296 l. 7 *opinion,* / opinion [10th→]

l. 14 *old* / old, [10th→; 1st American]

297 l. 1 *be an erroneousness* / be erroneousness [10th→]

298 l. 11 *develope* / develop [1st American→]

302 l. 16 *develop* / develope [3d→]

l. 43 *develop* / develope [3d→]

309 l. 39 *his Will.* / His Will. [4th→] / his will. [1st American→] / His Will."[1] [12th; there is a double quotation mark at the beginning of the last line and at the end, indicating the conclusion of a passage cited in the Privy Council] / Will.'[1] [13th; the double quotation mark is changed to a single quotation mark, despite the fact that there is a double mark at the beginning of the line and throughout this paragraph]

Will. / Will.[1] [footnote number and footnote in brackets added in 12th→:] [1] [1 Cor. xv. 28]

351 n. 25 l. 1 *Chap. iv. 33.* / Chap. iv. 23. [5th→]

l. 37 *primaeval* / primeval [4th→]

354 ll. 35–36 *'in the beginning . . . earth.'* / [Internal single quotation marks have been replaced by the editors with double quotation marks]

l. 43 [1st American→ prints this passage, and all of the subsequent cited passages, in smaller type, introducing each paragraph with double quotation marks, with internal quotations enclosed in single quotation marks]

355 l. 30–32 *'to give light . . . for years.'* / [Internal single quotation marks have been replaced by the editors with double quotation marks]

356 l. 19 *primaeval* / primeval [4th→; 1st American→]

359 ll. 41–42 *'without form and void,'; 'and darkness . . . deep,'* [Internal single quotation marks have been replaced by the editors with double quotation marks]

360 ll. 20–21 *'In the beginning . . . earth.'* [Internal single quotation marks have been replaced by the editors with double quotation marks]

l. 29 *primaeval* / primeval [1st American→]

361 l. 38 *'day'* [Internal single quotation marks have been replaced by the editors with double quotation marks]

362 l. 17 *'days'* [Internal single quotation marks have been replaced by the editors with double quotation marks]

365 l. 27 *'of herbs . . . their kind.'* [Internal single quotation marks have been replaced by the editors with double quotation marks]

ll. 38–39 *'yielding . . . kind.'* [Internal single quotation marks have been

	replaced by the editors with double quotation marks]
366 l. 28	*'Grand, indeed,'* [Internal single quotation marks have been replaced by the editors with double quotation marks]
ll. 29–34	*'was the fauna . . . of Africa'* [Internal single quotation marks have been replaced by the editors with double quotation marks]
l. 33	*primaeval* / primeval [1st American→]
l. 39	*'beasts . . . kind.'* [Internal single quotation marks have been replaced by the editors with double quotation marks]
394 ll. 9 ff.	*Deistical Controversy . . .Romanist Controversy . . . Bangorian controversy* / Deistical controversy . . . Romanist controversy . . . Bangorian controversy [1st American→; "controversy" is not capitalized consistently throughout this essay]
l. 43–396 l. 3	[1st American→ prints these citations in smaller type introducing each paragraph with double quotation marks, with internal quotations enclosed in single quotation marks]
397 l. 9	*informed of them. (<u>Analogy</u>, pt. 2, ch. 1.)* / informed of them.' (*Analogy*, pt. 2, ch. 1.) [3d→; missing quotation mark added by editors on authority of the 3d→] / informed of them" (*Analogy*, part 2, chap. 1) [1st American] / informed of them." (*Analogy*, part 2, chap. 1.) [2d American→]
l. 12	*<u>Ferguson,</u>* [1st→] / Ferguson, [1st American→; typographical error of italics for author's name removed by editors as corrected in American editions]
400 l. 35	*mediaeval* / medieval [4th→]
403 ll. 20 ff.	[1st American→ prints this citation in smaller type introducing each speaker with double quotation marks, with internal quotations enclosed in single quotation marks]
405 l. 41	*Rochefoucault* / Rochefoucauld [1st American→]
407 l. 2	*whole. (<u>Reasonableness, &c</u>. Pt. ii. Pref. 1721.)* / whole.' (*Reasonableness, &c*. Pt. ii. Pref. 1721.) [10th→; missing quotation mark added by editors on authority of the 10th→] / whole" (*Reasonableness, &c.*, part ii. Pref. 1721). [1st American] / whole." (*Reasonableness*, &c., part ii. Pref. 1721.) [2d American→]
l. 35	*Rochefoucauld* / Rochefoucault [10th→] / Rouchefoucauld [1st American→]
411 l. 36	*ended* / ended. [2d→; 1st American→; missing period added by editors on authority of the 2d→]
413 l. 7	[A space occurs in the text here in all eds. before the beginning of the next paragraph]
415 ll. 25–36	[1st American→ prints this citation in smaller type introducing each paragraph with double quotation marks, with internal quotations enclosed in single quotation marks]
ll. 31–36	*'What is this?'*; *'A fee, Sir'*; *'A fee . . . bribe'*; *'True, Sir'*; *'but you*

have resigned . . . . on his side' [Internal single quotation marks have been replaced by the editors with double quotation marks]

l. 36 *side."'* / side.'[1st→] / side.'" [1st American→]

416 l. 4 *virtues.* /virtues.' [3d→; missing quotation mark added by editors on authority of the 3d→] / virtues" [1st American] virtues." [2d American→]

418 l. 33 *Sidney* / Sydney [4th→]

418 l. 37–419 l. 25 [1st American→ prints this citation in ¶ 48 in smaller type introducing the paragraph with double quotation marks, with internal quotations enclosed in single quotation marks]

420 ll. 39–40 *'part and parcel;' 'semianimesque . . . retractant.'* [Internal single quotation marks have been replaced by the editors with double quotation marks; the final quotation mark is added by the editors]

421 l. 22 *pannic* / panic [4th→; 1st American→]

426 ll. 18–37 [1st American→ prints this citation in smaller type introducing each paragraph with double quotation marks, with internal quotations enclosed in single quotation marks]

427 l. 3 *'My kingdom . . . world'* [The internal quotation marks have been changed by the editors to double quotation marks]

ll. 18–30 [1st American→ prints this citation in smaller type introducing this paragraph with double quotation marks, with internal quotations enclosed in single quotation marks]

477 l. 2 *Interpretation* [Jowett capitalizes the term 10 times, and spells it with a lower case "i" 78 times in his essay] / interpretation [1st American→]

485 l. 7 *§ 2.* [Section 1 is not marked in Jowett's text]

490 l. 1 *my Church (Matthew xvi. 18),* / my Church, (Matthew xvi. 18), [2d→10th] / my Church' (Matthew xvi. 18), [11th→; corrected by the editors on the basis of the 11th→] / my Church" (Matt. xvi. 18)—[1st American→]

492 l. 31 *free.' (Matth. xvii. 26.)* / free" (Matt. xvii. 26). [1st American] / free." (Matt. xvii. 26.) [2d American→]

494 ll. 10–13 *(Matth. v. 32.) 'Whosoever . . . adultery;' compare also Mark x. 11, 12).* / (Matth. v. 32; 'Whosoever . . . adultery;' compare also Mark x. 11, 12). [4th→] / (Matt. v. 32). "Whosoever . . . adultery" (compare also Mark x, 11, 12). [1st American→; missing parenthesis added and semicolon removed by the editors as in the 1st American→] / (Matt. v. 32.) "Whosoever . . . adultery." (Compare also Mark x. 11, 12.) [2d American→]

495 l. 21 *poverty:'* / poverty;' [1st American→]

501 l. 9 *[εἰς . . . ἔλεγχον]* / (εἰς . . . ἔλεγχον) [1st American→]

l. 20 *§ 2.* / § 3. [2d→; 1st American→; in the 1st this section was erroneously marked § 2 so that there were two sections marked § 2; corrected in 2d and 1st American. All subsequent sections followed the revised numerical sequence. The editors have renumbered this and all subsequent sections correctly]

508 l. 17 *that* / than [4th→; 1st American→; corrected by the editors on the basis of the 4th→]

511 l. 16 *§ 3.* / §4. [3d→; 1st American→]

l. 43–512 l. 1 *['Poena linguarum . . . collegit.']* / (*'Poena linguarum . . . collegit.'*) [12th→] / ("Poena linguarum . . . collegit.") [1st American→]

512 l. 27 *critic** / critic[1] [5th→; footnote numbered in text and note]

l. 38 *certainty;* /certainty, [2d→; 1st American→]

ll. 38–39 *or in which the certainty; or if certain, the importance of the result, is out of proportion* / or in which the importance of the result, or the certainty, if certain, is out of proportion [4th→] / or in which certainty, or, if certain, the importance of the result, is out of proportion [1st American→]

514 ll. 10–16 *applicable.* [*It may be . . . remove.*] / applicable. And it may be . . . remove. [4th→] / applicable. (And it may be . . . remove.) [1st American→]

ll. 22–23 —[*if it have . . . Matthew*]. /—(if it have . . . Matthew). [12th→; 1st American→]

l. 28 *Shakespear* / Shakspeare [1st American] / Shakespeare [2d American→]

l. 42 *Mediaeval* / Medieval [4th→] / mediaeval [1st American→]

515 ll. 16–17 *6—10 . . . 21—33* / 6–10 . . . 21–33 [1st American→]

516 ll. 4–5 *1—9 . . . 11—20* / 1–9 . . . 11–20 [1st American→]

ll. 35, 38 *Galatians . . . Gal.* / Gal. . . . Gal. [1st American→]

l. 42 *17—21; v. 12—18 . . . 25—27* / 17–21; v. 12–18 . . . 25–27 [1st American→]

517 l. 34 *16—18* / 16–18 [1st American→]

519 l. 34 [double space in the text in 1st→; 1st American→]

520 l. 1 *Apostles.'* / Apostles. [10th→11th] Apostles.' [12th→]

l. 3 *§ 4.* / § 5. [3d→; 1st American→]

521 l. 31 *cloke* / cloak [1st American→]

528 l. 1 *§ 5.* /§ 6. [3d→; 1st American→]

l. 6 *First, it may* / I. It may [1st American→]

l. 11 " . . ." [use of double quotation marks in 1st is inconsistent: usually single quotation marks are used]

529 l. 1 *II. It has* / Secondly, it has [4th→]

530 ll. 37–38 *'good' . . . 'good'* [Internal single quotation marks have been replaced by the editors with double quotation marks]

532 l. 33 *44—48* / 44–48 [1st American→]

l. 37 *II.* / 2. [12th→]

533 l. 23 — *III.* / 3. [12th→]

534 l. 9 — *IV.* / 4. [12th→]

l. 39 — *V.* / 5. [12th→]

535 l. 36 — *demarcation,* / demarcation; [4th→; comma changed to a semicolon by the editors on the authority of the 4th→] / demarcation: [1st American→]

[after 536] — [page containing Williams's Note on Bunsen's Biblical Researches" is unnumbered 1st→ (actually 434); moved to follow Williams's essay in the present edition, as in the 1st American]

[rule]

Spottiswoode & Co., Printers, London and Westminster. [13th adds this printer's name and address to the revised note as in the 12th]

l. 43 — THE END [1st→; omitted in this edition]

[The second American edition includes two items in appendices: a "Note on the 'Phalaris Controversy'" (pp. 483–84), and Temple's sermon of 1860, "The Present Relations of Science to Religion" (pp. 485–98). Both items are published from the stereoplates, unchanged from the 2d→ American editions. The "Note on the 'Phalaris Controversy'" has been included in the annotations to Pattison, n. 160.]

Passages Cited in the Heresy Trials of *Essays and Reviews*

[The first group of passages that follow was originally cited in the proceedings of the Court of Arches against Williams and Wilson. Later in the legal process these passages were either withdrawn, or were rejected by Dr. Lushington in the interlocutory judgment. They were marked in the twelfth edition of 1865 by single quotation marks at the beginning of each cited line, and with a terminal quotation mark at the end of the cited passage, as the preface to that edition indicates. They were reprinted with the same quotation marks (the exception on p. 296 is noted below) in the thirteenth edition of 1869.]

WILLIAMS

184 ll. 15–23 'Our deluge. . . . genealogies.'

185 l. 35–186 l. 5 'Baron Bunsen. . . . accounts.'

187 ll. 3–11 'When the fierce. . . . themselves.'

188 l. 42–189 l. 30 'In our own country. . . . has been lowered.' [Notes 50 and 51 on p. 189 are cited; no terminal quotation mark is given in the 12th ed. after the conclusion of note 50. Note 52 already carried single quotation marks, and so additional double quotation marks were added by the printer to all of note 52, except for the part not included in single quotation marks, the reference at the end of the note to *Memoir of Cary*. Hence, note 52 is marked in the 12th ed. as though it were sustained by Lushington and passed on for consideration to the Privy Council. In fact, along with all of the cited passage on pp. 188-89 the note was rejected by Lushington in the interlocutory judgment. Its misleading marking occurs because of the typographical convention of raising the quotation marks from single to double for internal quotations. Note 54 on p. 189 was not cited before the Court of Arches]

189 l. 7 n. 50 [2]'Collected in the *Boyle Lectures*.'

l. 7 n. 51 '*A Literal Translation* . . . our Biblical scholars.'

l. 12 n. 52 'Of prophecies . . . vo. ii. p. 180.'

ll. 34–36 'To this inheritance. . . . ignorance.'

190 l. 12–192 l. 38 'He may read. . . .prophecy.'

193 ll. 27–29 'In distinguishing . . . the case.'

l. 40–194 l. 21 'The truth seems. . . . mythical theories.'

197 ll. 1–3 'Thus the incarnation . . . holiness.'

l. 5–198 l. 14 'If we would estimate. . . . St. Peter.'

198 l. 8 n. 121 'In my own judgment . . . 25–32.'

199 ll. 7–12 'The first Christians. . . . connexion with it.'

ll. 28–31 'Salvation. . . . ritual.'

WILSON

280 ll. 2–7 'But with respect. . . . dealt with.'
ll. 12–20 'First, if our traditions. . . . man a liar.'
282 ll. 12–16 'Moreover, to our great . . . same result.'
284 ll. 3–39 'But although the primitive. . . . of the universe.'
292 l. 30–293 l. 12 'Under the terms. . . . truth within.'
294 l. 38–296 l. 25 'As far as opinion. . . . the greater.' [All of this text is marked with single quotation marks in the 12th. In the 13th single quotation marks are omitted by a typographical error at p. 296, ll. 6–9 to indicate that the passage was cited in the Court of Arches, from "He does not maintain" to "and design" (bottom of p. 219). The quotation marks resume at "explained together" (top of p. 220)]
297 ll. 16–33 'We have spoken. . . . Divine Personalities.'
303 ll. 2–7 'Speculative doctrines. . . . in man.'
305 l. 9–307 l. 38 'It is sometimes said. . . . the literalist.'
308 ll. 31–39 'Jesus Christ has not revealed. . . . him life. [In the Court of Arches the passage cited in the 7th original Article of Charge ends with the words "committed to the Church" (308, l. 36). In the 12th, however, the whole of ¶78 is erroneously marked as cited in the Court of Arches]

[The following passages were cited and subsequently admitted in the judgment in the Court of Arches against Williams and Wilson. They were either withdrawn in the Judicial Committee of the Privy Council, or were rejected in the judgment of Lord Westbury. In each case the cited passage is marked with double quotation marks in the 12th and 13th editions at the beginning of each of the cited lines, and once at the end of the passage, except where indicated.]

134 "TO THE READER . . . treatment."

WILLIAMS

180 ll. 26–36 "As in his *Egypt*. . . . we breathe."
194 l. 22–195 l. 2 "But, if such a notion. . . . triumphantly confirmed."
196 ll. 2–14 "For, though he embraces. . . . offering of our hearts."
196 ll. 29–36 "Propitiation would be . . . Searcher of hearts." [Withdrawn without argument in the Judicial Committee]
202 l. 13–203 l. 33 "So, when he asks. . . . thank I GOD." [This passage was admitted as part of the 16th Article of Charge, but was only dealt with

generally by the Judicial Committee, without making specific reference to it; no specific breach of the Articles of Religion or of the Formularies was alleged concerning it. It was used only to assert that there was an identification of viewpoints between Williams and Bunsen]

WILSON

280 ll. 7–12 "And when we hear. . . . non-christian races." [Withdrawn without argument in the Judicial Committee]

291 l. 34–292 l. 30 "It has been a matter. . . . their own offence."

309 ll. 18–39 "The Christian Church . . . his Will." [In the 12th this passage ends with a single quotation mark and a footnote number, both added to the present edition with the note. Double quotation marks occur at the beginning of all the lines of this paragraph]

Part Three

Documentation

1 Chronology of *Essays and Reviews*

1796	Birth of Baden Powell at Stamford Hill, Kent.
1803	Birth of Henry Bristow Wilson in London.
1813	Birth of Mark Pattison at Hornby, in the North Riding of Yorkshire.
1817	Birth of Charles Wycliffe Goodwin at King's Lynn, Norfolk.
	Birth of Benjamin Jowett at Camberwell, south London.
	Birth of Rowland Williams at Hacklyn, Flintshire, Wales.
1821	Birth of Frederick Temple in the Ionian Islands.
1830	S. T. Coleridge publishes *On the Constitution of Church and State*.
1833	John Keble preaches the Assize Sermon in Oxford on "National Apostasy," inaugurating the Oxford or Tractarian Movement.
1837	Death of William IV. Accession of Queen Victoria.
1841	Wilson is a signatory of the "Protest of the Four Tutors" (with A. C. Tait) against Newman's *Tract XC*.
	The Jerusalem Bishopric is established by Britain and Prussia with the diplomatic assistance of Christian Bunsen, to the delight of the Broad Church, but the dismay of the Tractarians.
1842	Death of Thomas Arnold, founding headmaster of Rugby and Regius Professor of History at Oxford.
1843	Edward Bouverie Pusey is condemned and suspended by Oxford University for his sermon on the "Holy Eucharist."
1845	John Henry Newman secedes from the Church of England and joins the Church of Rome.
1846	David Friedrich Strauss's *Life of Jesus* (1835) is translated by George Eliot amidst controversy in Germany and England over rationalism.
1847–50	Gorham Controversy: Henry Phillpotts, bp. of Exeter, refuses to institute the Rev. G. C. Gorham into a parish because of Gorham's belief that baptismal regeneration is conditional upon worthy reception of the sacrament.
1850–51	Popular agitation erupts in England against "Papal Aggression" when Pius IX makes England an ecclesiastical province of the Roman Catholic Church, appointing Nicholas Wiseman a cardinal and abp. of Westminster. He arouses further concern with his pastoral, "From the Flaminian Gate" (7 Oct. 1850).

1851 Wilson delivers the Bampton Lectures on *The Communion of Saints: An Attempt to Illustrate the True Principles of Christian Union*, containing a demand for freedom of theological inquiry.

1855 Williams publishes *Rational Godliness after the Mind of Christ and the Written Voice of the Church*, resulting in his being charged with heterodoxy by Alfred Ollivant, bp. of Llandaff, and having to resign his chaplaincy at St. David's College, Lampeter. Powell publishes *Essays on the Spirit of Inductive Philosophy, the Unity of Worlds, and the Philosophy of Creation*. Jowett publishes *The Epistles of St. Paul to the Thessalonians, Galatians, and Romans*. On the same day, and in the same series, A. P. Stanley publishes *The Epistles of St. Paul to the Corinthians*.

1856 Williams publishes *Christianity and Hinduism*. Powell publishes *Christianity without Judaism*.

1857 Hugh Miller publishes *Testimony of the Rocks* to harmonize Genesis and geology. In *Oxford Essays* Wilson publishes "Schemes for Christian Comprehension."

1858 H. L. Mansell delivers the Bampton Lectures on *The Limits of Religious Thought Examined*.

1859 Publications of 1859 include Dickens, *A Tale of Two Cities*; FitzGerald, *The Rubáiyát of Omar Khayyám*; Eliot, *Adam Bede* (16,000 copies sold in first year); Meredith, *The Ordeal of Richard Feverel*; J. S. Mill, *On Liberty*; Smiles, *Self-Help*; Tennyson, *The Idylls of the King*. Powell publishes *The Order of Nature Considered in Reference to the Claims of Revelation*.

Feb. 10 Powell sends his MS. of "On the Evidences of Christianity" to Wilson for *Essays and Reviews*.

Oct. Quarterly Review publishes a scathing review of Powell's *The Order of Nature* by Richard Whately, abp. of Dublin, his former teacher, William Fitzgerald, bp. of Cork, Cloyne, and Ross, and his former pupil, and Whitwell Elwin, the editor of the *Quarterly Review*.

Oct. 15 *Saturday Review* first announces the publication of Charles Darwin's *On The Origin of Species*. Published by John Murray in an edition of 1,250 copies at 15 shillings a copy, it is disposed of to the booksellers completely before the official publication date of 24 November. By 1876, it sold 16,000 copies.

1860 Jan. 7 Publication of the second (slightly revised) edition of Darwin's *Origin* in a run of 3,000 copies.

Feb. The Court of Arches hears the case of Dunbar Isidore Heath, arraigned by Charles Sumner, bp. of Winchester, for unorthodox teaching about justification.

Mar. 21 1st edition, *Essays and Reviews*, 1,000 copies, at 10s 6d., is published by John W. Parker of London. The *Guardian* prints Parker's advertisement as published "This Day" (271) and lists the essays and Essayists.

Apr. 4 "Table-Talk" in the *Guardian* remarks that *Essays and Reviews* is "likely to create a sensation" (1).

Apr. 7 First review of *Essays and Reviews* appears in the *Spectator*, generally favorable.

Apr. 14 Unfavorable review in the *Literary Gazette.*

May Hostile review in *Christian Observer.*

May 23 Review in High Church weekly, the *Guardian*, is favorable to Temple, Pattison, and Jowett, critical of the other four.

June 1 The *Record*, an evangelical newspaper, begins a series of attacks on the volume.

June 6 2d edition, *Essays and Reviews*, is published, 1,000 copies. The *Guardian* prints Parker's advertisement as published "This Day, Second Edition, 8vo 10s. 6d." (512).

June 11 Death of Powell.

June 30 Huxley–Wilberforce debate on Darwin at Oxford, during the meeting of the British Association.

National Reformer, an openly atheistic publication under the editorship of Charles Bradlaugh, publishes a favorable review.

July Review in the *London Review*, a Methodist journal.

July 1 Temple preaches the Act Sunday Sermon on "The Present Relations of Science to Religion" before the University of Oxford, during the meeting of the British Association.

Aug. Favorable review in *Fraser's Magazine*, published by Parker.

Review in *North British Review*, denounces the volume from the position of the Scottish Free Kirk.

Aug. 27 The *Record* in a leading article discusses the quarrel between Williams and Thirlwall and notes *Essays and Reviews* is known as the "Oxford Revolver" (2).

Oct. Frederic Harrison's Review "Neo-Christianity" in *Westminster Review.*

Oct.–Nov. 1st American edition of *Essays and Reviews* is published as *Recent Inquiries in Theology.*

Nov. 7 Samuel Wilberforce, bp. of Oxford, delivers a pastoral charge to clergy at Woodstock, near Oxford, attacking *Essays and Reviews.*

Nov. 9 Death of John William Parker Jr., publisher of *Essays and Reviews.*

Nov. 14 The *Guardian* notes that the revision of the *BCP*, currently under discussion in Convocation of the Province of Canterbury, would be "practically impossible, especially now, when, by such writers as Dr. Temple and others, the very foundations of the faith were assailed" (990). The same issue prints the first letter to the editor concerning *Essays and Reviews,* from "A. R. A." of Culham, Oxfordshire, who describes the volume as "the Common Sense Heresy" and "semi-Socinian teaching" (987).

Nov. 15 Wilberforce publishes his charge.

Nov. 21 The *Guardian* publishes the full text of Wilberforce's Charge with the section on *Essays and Reviews* captioned "*Conclusion—Rationalism*" ("Supplement," 1017–20).

Nov. / Dec. 3d edition of *Essays and Reviews* is published in a run of 750 copies.

Dec. 7 Max Müller is rejected by electors at Oxford Convocation for the Chair in Sanskrit because of his association with the Essayists.

Dec. 27 The Ven. Archdeacon Coxe in Durham Cathedral preaches a sermon against *Essays and Reviews.* Charles Sumner, bp. of Winchester, attacks *Essays and Reviews* under the heading of the "Neologian School"in his Ordination Sermon.

1861 Jan. The 2d American edition of *Recent Inquiries in Theology* is published.

Jan. 23 Wilberforce publishes his anonymous review in *Quarterly Review.*

Jan. 25 Pattison is elected rector of Lincoln College.

Jan. 29 4th edition of *Essays and Reviews* is published in a run of 1,000 copies by Longman of London, who acquired publication rights from John W. Parker.

Late Jan. Temple first and then Jowett visit A. C. Tait, bp. of London, to discuss the impact of *Essays and Reviews.*

Feb. 1 A meeting of the bishops at Lambeth deals with the memorials addressed to them urging an episcopal response to *Essays and Reviews,* resulting in the "Episcopal Manifesto."

Feb. 6 Wilberforce and Charles Thomas Baring, bp. of Gloucester and Bristol, read charges attacking *Essays and Reviews.*

Feb. 13 In the *Guardian* a letter from "G. H. C." (123) gets four responses (143).

Feb. 16 The "Episcopal Manifesto" is published in the *Times.*

Feb. 19 5th edition of *Essays and Reviews* is published in a run of 2,000 copies.

Feb. 20 The *Guardian* moves the discussion to the first page with the account of the "Episcopal Manifesto" (161). The same issue prints the "Oxford Manifesto," or "Protest of the Clergy." An advertisement from Longman says that the 5th edition is "now ready" (175).

Feb. 26 First debate in Convocation of the Province of Canterbury on condemning *Essays and Reviews.*

Mar. 8 6th edition, *Essays and Reviews* is published in a run of 3,000 copies.

7th edition, *Essays and Reviews* is published in a run of 3,000 copies.

Mar. 12 8,500 signatures to the "Oxford Manifesto" are presented to the abp. of Canterbury at Lambeth.

Mar. 13 Kennard publishes the first two letters in the *Guardian* (245) in support of the Essayists, one to Walter Kerr Hamilton, bp. of Salisbury, and the other to Williams.

Mar. 21 Convocation of the Province of York concurs in the condemnation of *Essays and Reviews* in the "Episcopal Manifesto."

Mar. 22 8th edition, *Essays and Reviews* is published in a run of 3,000 copies.

Mar. 27 *Seven Answers to the Seven Essays and Reviews, with the London Review and Seven Special Supplements* is advertised in the *Guardian*. It is later issued (8 Jan. 1862) as a book, edited by John Nash Griffin, published by Longman.

Apr. 3 The 8th edition is advertised as "now ready." On the same page of the *Guardian* (328) is an advertisement for the 5th edition of the January issue of the *Quarterly Review* with Wilberforce's article. In addition, on the same page are advertisements for the following: *Essays and Reviews Anticipated,* extracts from a work published in 1825 and attributed to the bp. of St. David's (extracts from Schleiermacher, which Thirlwall later acknowledged he published as a young law student); George Wild, *Defence of the Essays and Reviews*, described as appearing "this day"; John H. Pratt, *Scripture and Science Not at Variance*, described in the advertisement as the 4th edition just published, "with additional illustrations from Darwin, Bunsen, and Goodwin on Mosaic Cosmogony: The Essays and Reviews refuted"; Samuel Wilberforce, *God's Revelation and Man's Trial*, 2 sermons preached on 27 Jan. and 3 Feb. 1861; the *Literary Churchman,* with the April issue as having an essay on *Essays and Reviews*, the 6th notice given by the journal; and R. W. Jelf, *Evidences of Unsoundness*, "2d edition, now ready," an attack on *Essays and Reviews*.

Apr. 5 9th edition of *Essays and Reviews* is published in a run of 3,000 copies.

Apr. 13 A. P. Stanley's review is published in the *Edinburgh Review*.

May 20 The *Guardian* carries news of the suit of Walter Kerr Hamilton, bp. of Salisbury, against Williams; it also quotes the *Standard* on the action.

May 23 Hamilton announces his suit against Williams in the *Times*.

June 1 Letter of Request from Hamilton to the Dean of the Court of Arches under the Church Discipline Act, requesting the convening of the Court against Williams.

June 19 Report of the Lower House of Convocation attacking *Essays and Reviews* is presented by George Anthony Denison, recommending synodical censure.

July 9 The bishops in the Upper House decide not to act on the recommendation for censure while the legal proceedings against Williams and Wilson are still before the courts.

Oct. [?] John William Colenso, bp. of Natal, publishes *St. Paul's Epistle to the Romans: Newly Translated, and Explained from a Missionary Point of View.*

Nov. 2 Lushington's judgment against Heath in the Court of Arches.

Dec. 16 Letter of Request from Thomas Turton, bp. of Ely, to Stephen Lushington, dean of the Court of Arches, in the case of Fendall *v.* H. B. Wilson.

Dec. 19 Trial of Williams and Wilson begins in the Court of Arches; reports of the proceedings continue to appear throughout December and January.

Dec. 20, 21 Hearing of the case of Williams in the Court of Arches.

1862 Jan. 10th edition of *Essays and Reviews*, 1st issue, is published in a smaller format and a run of 1,000 copies at 5s.

Jan. 7–13 Hearing of the case of Williams in the Court of Arches continues.

Jan. 29 James Fitzjames Stephen's *Defence of Dr. Williams* is announced in the *Guardian* as being ready "in a few days."

Feb. 22, 24, 25 Hearing of the case of Wilson in the Court of Arches.

Mar. 13 10th edition of *Essays and Reviews*, 2d issue, is published in a run of 1,000 copies.

Goodwin is appointed assistant judge in the Supreme Court for China and Japan.

Apr.–May [?] Colenso's *The Pentateuch and the Book of Joshua, Critically Examined*, pt. 1, is published in South Africa.

May Convocation of Canterbury meets and plans attack against Colenso for his views in *Romans* on the atonement.

May 6 10th edition of *Essays and Reviews*, 3d issue, is published in a run of 1,000 copies.

June Williams leaves St. David's College, Lampeter, for residence at Broad Chalke, near Salisbury. In August he severs his connection with St. David's.

June 6 Judicial Committee of the Privy Council confirms on appeal Lushington's judgment against Heath.

June 25 Lushington delivers the interlocutory decision of the Court of Arches against Williams and Wilson.

Sept. 6 Death of abp. of Canterbury, John Bird Sumner.

Sept. 12 The reformed articles against Williams and Wilson are brought before the Court of Arches, with defense arguments from Williams and Wilson. The hearing is deferred until 15 Dec.

Sept. 27 Announcement of the translation of Charles Thomas Longley from abp. of York to abp. of Canterbury. William Thomson appointed to York.

Oct. 29 Colenso's *The Pentateuch and Book of Joshua, Critically Examined* is published in England by Longman. In three weeks 8,000 copies are sold, amounting to four editions. In the preface Colenso mentions Lushington's judgment on *Essays and Reviews* and argues that it gives him freedom for a more liberal reading of the Bible.

Dec. 15 Lushington delivers the definitive sentence of the Court of Arches, condemning Williams and Wilson.

1863 Renan publishes *La Vie de Jésus*.

Sir Charles Lyell publishes *Evidences of the Antiquity of Man*.

Feb. 9 A letter is sent to Colenso, signed by forty-one English bishops, with Thirlwall alone not signing, advising him to resign his office.

Feb. 13 Proceedings against Benjamin Jowett are launched in the Chancellor's Court of the University of Oxford.

Feb. 14 An editorial in the *Times* attacks Pusey, Ogilvie, and Heurtley for using the outmoded legal procedure of the Chancellor's Court to secure a theological condemnation of Jowett.

Feb. 16 An editorial in the *Daily News* attacks the prosecutors of Jowett.

Feb. 19 Pusey attacks Jowett in a long letter to the *Times*.

Feb. 20 Chancellor's Court refuses to admit the articles against Jowett, thereby stalling the case and in effect ending it.

Mar. 11th edition of *Essays and Reviews* is published in a run of 500 copies.

Apr. 15 The appeals of Williams and Wilson are assigned by the Court of Appeals to be heard at the Privy Council Chambers, Whitehall.

May A report condemning Colenso's *Pentateuch* is presented to the May meeting of Convocation of Canterbury.

May 8 The co-prosecutors of Jowett at Oxford notify the vice-chancellor that they will not appeal decision of 20 Feb.

May 11 An editorial in the *Times* castigates Pusey, Ogilvie, and Heurtley for the malicious prosecution of Jowett that was "hopeless from the first." The *Times* advocates his "justly entitled" salary as Greek Professor.

May 18 Colenso is cited in Cape Town to appear before Archbishop Robert Gray.

June 19–26 The appeal of Williams and Wilson is presented before the Judicial Committee of the Privy Council.

June 24 Lord Kingsdown (who was also sitting on the Williams and Wilson cases) delivers the judgment of the Judicial Committee of the Privy Council in the case of Long vs. Archbishop Gray of Cape Town, an aspect of the Colenso affair.

Oct. Thirlwall delivers his long-awaited charge on *Essays and Reviews* and Bishop Colenso.

Nov. 16–21 Trial of Bishop Colenso begins at the Synod of South African bishops in his absence.

Dec. 16 Gray pronounces judgment against Colenso.

1864 Jan. 9 Stanley is installed as dean of Westminster.

Feb.–June Debates in Convocation on *Essays and Reviews.*

Feb. 8 Westbury delivers the Judgment of the Judicial Committee of the Privy Council, exonerating Williams and Wilson from all charges, dismissing costs against them and assigning them to W. K. Hamilton, bp. of Salisbury, and James Fendall.

Feb. 12 The Kingsley-Newman debate, which had been conducted by private letter from 30 Dec. 1863, appears in print in a pamphlet, *Mr. Kingsley and Dr. Newman: A Correspondence,* issued by Newman.

Feb. 25 Meeting at Oxford to prepare the "Oxford Declaration" of the Clergy (eventually signed by 11,000 clergy).

Mar. 4 Longley issues a "private assurance" published in the *Guardian* to allay clerical feeling that the abp. of Canterbury had surrendered in the decision of the Judicial Committee every Englishman's right to eternal damnation too easily.

Mar. 8 Proposed Oxford statute to endow the Greek Chair fails by 72 votes in the Convocation of the University of Oxford, 467 to 395.

Mar. 20 Kingsley issues *What, Then, Does Dr. Newman Mean?*, his attack on Newman.

Apr. 19, 20 Wilberforce presents a petition to the Upper House of Convocation asking that Convocation proceed to a synodical condemnation after a committee was appointed to report. The ten bishops present divide evenly, and Longley, abp. of Canterbury, casts the deciding vote in favor of condemnation.

Apr. 21 Canon Christopher Wordsworth presents the Declaration of the Students of the Natural and Physical Sciences to the Lower House of Convocation, signed by 28 names.

Apr. 21–June 2 On successive Thursdays, Newman issues the seven pamphlets, with an eighth as an appendix, issued on 16 June, of his *Apologia Pro Vita Sua.*

Apr. 30 Sentence of deposition is proclaimed against Colenso in Cape Town.

May Circulation of the Declaration of the Students of the Natural and

Physical Sciences for signatures. It was finally published in May 1865.

June 24 Synodical Condemnation of *Essays and Reviews* as a whole in Convocation of the Province of Canterbury.

June 27 Colenso's petition to the Privy Council is first considered, and is held over for six months.

July Exchange of letters between Pusey and Maurice is published in the *Times* on the eternal damnation of the reprobate.

July 12 Oxford Declaration of the Clergy is presented to the abp. of Canterbury.

July 15 Debate in the House of Lords on *Essays and Reviews* and the decision of the Judicial Committee of the Privy Council.

Sept. 2 Editorial in the *Times* criticizes Pusey's attack on the judgment of the Privy Council for allowing credence to the "fifteen different heresies, each worse than the preceding" of Wilson and Williams, and for the impropriety of the Committee's taking on theological matters.

Sept. 17 Editorial in the *Times* reproves Pusey for his tone and arguments.

Sept. 22 Editorial in the *Times* continues to attack Pusey for his "most odious charges against the probity of a Court which had failed to condemn a theological opponent," for indulging in personality attacks, for pushing issues to extremes, for reckless and intemperate language, and for faulty argument.

Dec. 14 Colenso's case is heard before the Judicial Committee of the Privy Council.

1865 A number of those who signed the Declaration of the Students of the Natural and Physical Sciences establish the "Victoria Institute, or Philosophical Society of Great Britain" to reconcile science with revelation.

J. R. Seeley publishes *Ecce Homo* anonymously, with seven editions in seven months.

Feb. 14 The Chapter of Christ Church finally agrees to pay Jowett £500 as the endowment for the Greek Professorship.

Feb. 28 12th edition of *Essays and Reviews* is published in a run of 1,000 copies at 5s.

Mar. 20 Westbury delivers the judgment of the Judicial Committee of the Privy Council in favor of Colenso.

Apr. 29 Goodwin is appointed by Queen's Warrant to the court in Shanghai, to which he departs.

May Publication of the signed list and the Declaration of the Students of the Natural and Physical Sciences.

June At the meetings of Convocation, Stanley defends the theological position of Colenso.

July — Colenso publishes *The Pentateuch and Book of Joshua* pt. 5.

Nov. 4 — Colenso arrives in Durban and on 10 Nov. obtains an interdict to allow him to take possession of his cathedral.

1866 Jan. 5 — Gray excommunicates Colenso.

June — During the meetings of Convocation, Wilberforce proposes a formal motion in support of Gray of South Africa.

1867 Sept. — First Lambeth Conference of Anglican bishops from around the world meets to discuss theological and administrative issues raised by *Essays and Reviews*, the Colenso affair, and other matters. Gray tries to secure a general condemnation of Colenso, but only secures a private condemnation.

1868 Nov. 12 — Disraeli writes to A. C. Tait, bp. of London, asking him to accept nomination as abp. of Canterbury to succeed Abp. C. T. Longley, who died on 28 Oct.

1869 Jan. — W. K. Macrorie is consecrated bp. of Natal in Cape Town, in opposition to Colenso. At this point a schism begins in the diocese of Natal, which lasts until 1911.

Sept. — Temple is offered the See of Exeter by Gladstone.

Oct. 8 — The *Times* reports unofficially that Temple has been offered Exeter.

Oct. 22 — An editorial in the *Times* reports on the requisite but reluctant election of Temple by the Cathedral Chapter at Exeter, comparing it to the controversial election of Hampden to Hereford in 1848.

Nov. 4 — An editorial in the *Times* castigates Pusey for his continued attacks on Temple and for his lack of toleration for theological difference.

Nov. 13 — An editorial in the *Times* comments on the election of Temple by the Chapter of the Diocese of Exeter and on party spirit in the church.

Nov. 16 — 13th edition of *Essays and Reviews* is published in a run of 2,000 copies, making a total run of 22,250 copies.

Dec. 8 — Temple's election as bp. of Exeter is formally confirmed at St. Mary-le-Bow Church, London.

Dec. 9 — An article in the *Times* reports on the confirmation of Temple's election and on the opposition to his election voiced at the ceremony.

Dec. 21 — Temple is consecrated bp. of Exeter in Westminster Abbey.

Dec. 22 — An article in the *Times* reports on the consecration of Temple and on further controversy and protests at the event.

Dec. 29 — Temple is enthroned as bp. of Exeter.

1870 Jan. 18 — Death of Rowland Williams at Broad Chalke.

Feb. 9 — At the Convocation of the Province of Canterbury, the archdea-

		con of Exeter announces that Temple would not publish his essay in *Essays and Reviews* again.
	Sept. 7	Jowett is elected master of Balliol College.
1871		Darwin publishes *The Descent of Man.*
1873	July 19	Death of Samuel Wilberforce.
1874		4th American edition of *Essays and Reviews*, retitled *Essays and Reviews by Eminent English Churchmen*, is published in New York.
1878	Jan.	Death of Charles Wycliffe Goodwin in Shanghai, where he was a judge in the Supreme Court.
1881	July 18	Death of Arthur Penrhyn Stanley.
1884	July 30	Death of Mark Pattison.
1885	Feb. 25	Temple is appointed bp. of London.
1888	Aug. 10	Death of Henry Bristow Wilson.
1889	Sept.–Oct.	*Lux Mundi* is published, edited by Charles Gore.
1893	Oct. 1	Death of Benjamin Jowett.
1896	Oct.	Temple is nominated abp. of Canterbury, and is consecrated in 1897.
1901	Jan. 22	Death of Queen Victoria; accession of Edward VII.
1902	Dec. 22	Death of Frederick Temple.

2 Prefaces to the American Editions

[The first American edition was published in the autumn of 1860 in Boston, with the title *Recent Inquiries in Theology, by Eminent English Churchmen; being "Essays and Reviews."* The editor of the volume, the Rev. Frederic Henry Hedge, wrote and signed an "Introduction to the American Edition," dated 14 August 1860. This same introduction continued to be printed through to the fifth edition of 1874, where it is retitled "Introduction to the First American Edition." For an account of the printing history of these editions, see Part 1, section 2.]

Introduction to the American Edition

THE favor with which "Essays and Reviews"—a very significant volume with a very insignificant title—has been received on this side of the water, suggested the following reprint, with altered name, for American use.

The seven dissertations, on as many distinct topics of theology, which compose this volume, are severally the productions of English Churchmen, writing independently each of each, and unconnected, save by the fellowship of a liberal faith. Some of the writers occupy conspicuous stations, and are men of distinguished repute. Two are professors in the University of Oxford; one is professor in St. David's College, in Wales; and one is successor to the late Dr. Arnold, in the headship of the Rugby School. The names of Jowett and of Rowland Williams are favorably known to American readers in connection with a volume of "Theological Essays," edited four years since by Professor Noyes.[1] That of Baden Powell[2] is no less eminent in physical science than in sacred learning.

These Essays have a value distinct from, and transcending, that of the speculations or conclusions they embody. They represent a new era in Anglican theology. The topics here discussed are handled with a frankness, a breadth, and a spiritual heroism, long unknown to ecclesiastical England. The sincerity which speaks in them recalls the better days of a church, which in Catholic ages, and as a branch of Catholic Christendom, could boast such names as John Scotus, Anselm, Duns, Alexander of Hales, and Roger Bacon, and which numbers a More and a Cudworth among her Protestant divines.[3]

The apathy into which the Church of England had fallen toward the close of the last century, her indifference to all theological inquiry, her barrenness of all theological learning, up to the time of the late Tractarian movement about a quarter of a century ago, are notorious and disgraceful alike to church and nation. It was during this period, precisely,—from the middle of the eighteenth century to the third decade of the nineteenth,—that German theology, ranging through an illustrious pedigree of profound scholars, from Semler and Griesbach to De Wette and Ewald, explored every field of biblical, ecclesiastical, dogmatic inquiry, and accomplished its great revolution.[4]

In these investigations and their results, the Church of England had no part or interest, and no faith; regarding in her supineness every inquiry which did not presume the inviolable truth of her own prepossessions, and confirm the *status quo* of the canon and the text, as made in the interest of infidelity. The period immediately preceding this (1700–1750) was, notwithstanding the condemnation in which the author of the sixth of these Essays concludes the entire century, an era of wide and beneficent activity. It embraced the works of Samuel Clarke, the worthy compeer of Newton and Leibnitz and Locke; it embraced the latter and liberal writings of Whitby; it embraced the labors of Waterland and Hoadly, of Bingham and Bishop Butler, of Lowth and Lardner and Prideaux and Middleton; it embraced the earnest philosophy of Berkeley, and the mystic piety of Law.[5]

A marked difference in the character and aims of leading Churchmen, divides, as Mr. Pattison admits, the second half of the century from the first. To the writers above named succeeded a generation of men who brought quite other powers to quite other tasks. With one or two honorable exceptions, like that of Herbert Marsh, whatever of learning or of insight English theology then could boast was outside of the Anglican Church.[6] The problem which mainly occupied the theological mind of the time was the attempt to prove the truth of the gospel by demonstrating an *external* relation between it and God. Christianity, whose fundamental postulate is the inner light by which it manifests itself as the truth of God, was advocated on the ground of certain facts, which, if true, would prove God to be its Author, and belief in it obligatory on pain of damnation. The student of the history of opinions might trace here a legitimate result of the then prevailing philosophy of Locke. A germ of mischief lurked in the immortal "Essay," whose fructification had so infected the intellectual atmosphere of the time, so vitiated its conceptions, so dimmed and confused the consciousness of God, that, instead of the divine Inpresence and informing Word of the old theologians, a prodigy in nature was held to be the only possible mediator between God and man, the only possible voucher and vehicle of revelation. Christianity was to be received on account of its miracles, not the miracles on account of the more commanding truth of Christianity.

Nor did the decline of faith stop here. The very being of God was no longer a self-evident truth, but a question of logic, to be tried and settled by the understanding. The living God was become a probable being; belief in God, the result of induction. To crown all, morality itself, the absolute right, was virtually denied, and moral obligation reduced to the expediency of obeying a being who possesses the power to harm us "in another world." And since the existence of such a being, for the human subject, was supposed to depend on a demonstration, moral obligation ceased, according to this view, for all whom that demonstration should fail to convince. The religious philosophy of unbelief reached its climax in Paley, exhibiting in him the strange phenomenon of a right-minded, Christian man, a preacher of the gospel, endeavoring to rear a system of ethics on a virtual negation of the fundamental distinction of right and wrong; a result commensurable only with the recent attempt of Mr. Mansel to base religion on Pyrrhonism.[7]

The practical evil attending this degraded theology, the apathy and irreligion of the "Georgian era," found a corrective in the rise of Methodism. That new dispensation of the gospel re-acted with healing power on the Church. Its intellectual aberrations encountered a check in the new turn of religious thought which dates with Coleridge. The "Aids to Reflection," fragmentary and unsatisfactory as a system, contained in its fruitful suggestions the germ of a new life, whose development is now in progress.[8]

Another contemporary re-action, of a more demonstrative kind, is that represented by Dr. Pusey, and popularly known by his name. But this movement, whose tendency is rather liturgical than theological, diverges too widely from the providential current of the time, and the genius of the people, to be any thing more than an episode in the history of the Church whose theoretical contradictions it has served to illustrate, and whose order it has so profoundly agitated. The full development and thorough application of the principles involved in it, necessitate, as recent defections from the national communion in favor of Romanism have shown, the entire abandonment of the Protestant ground.

The future of the Church is committed to another interest, and a different order of minds. The life of Anglican theology is now represented by such men as Powell and Williams and Maurice and Jowett and Stanley. Its strain and promise are apparent in these Essays.

The term "Broad Church" has been used to designate the new phase of ecclesiastical life, whose characteristics are breadth and freedom of view, and earnest spirit of inquiry and resolute criticism, joined to a reverent regard for ecclesiastical tradition and the common faith of mankind. The spirit of this theology is at once progressive and conservative; careful of all essential sanctities, careful also of the rights of the mind, of the interests of science, and the "liberty of prophesying;" carefully adjusting old views with new discoveries, transient forms with everlasting verities; regarding symbols and "Articles" as servants of thought, not as laws of thought; as imperfect attempts to articulate truth, not as the measure and gauge of truth.

Rationalistic it is, inasmuch as it is Protestant; for, of Rationalism, the only alternative is Romanism. Yet assuming in Christianity itself the perfection of reason, and believing that the truest insight in spiritual things is where the human intellect, freely inquiring, encounters the Holy Ghost, and that such encounter is afforded by the gospel, it goes about to analyze and interpret, not to gainsay or destroy; reverently listening, if here and there it may catch some accents of the

Eternal Voice amid the confused dialects of Scripture, yet not confounding the latter with the former; expecting to find in criticism, guided by a true philosophy, the key to revelation; in revelation, the sanction and condign expression of philosophic truth.

May this spirit, which is now leavening the Church of England, find abundant entrance into all the churches of our own land! and may this volume, its genuine product, though very imperfect exponent, contribute somewhat thereto!

F. H. HEDGE.

BROOKLINE, Aug. 14, 1860.

Preface to the Third American Edition

[This Preface was added not to the third American edition but to the fifth, published in New York in 1874. For an account of the printing history see Part 1, section 2. The Preface is dated 26 October 1874.]

FOURTEEN years have elapsed since the second American reprint of "Essays and Reviews," like the first, was published in Boston, with the title, "Recent Inquiries in Theology."

During that period some changes have occurred in the theological and ecclesiastical world of England, but none which have tended to discredit the views represented in this volume, or to check the progress of liberal theology. The author of the first Essay, formerly Head Master of Rugby, has been transferred to the Bishopric of Exeter; I will not say *promoted*, for I hold the former position to be quite as honorable as the latter. He has seen fit to withdraw his portion of the work from the later English editions of "Essays and Reviews" in England. The alleged cause of this secession—disagreement in some particulars with his associates—seems hardly a sufficient reason for refusing to appear in such company, where the general intent of all the co-workers was the same. And certainly the dissertation entitled "The Education of the World" contains nothing that can compromise the bishop's orthodoxy, or that need alarm the most conservative prelatical mind. That the views expressed in the other essays continue to find favor with a portion at least of the British public, may be inferred from their republication during the present year.[9]

Meanwhile, other agencies have combined to reinforce the cause of liberal thought within the pale of the Church.

Dr. Stanley, the frank and consistent advocate of toleration and free inquiry, from the vantage-ground of his position as Dean of Westminster, has contributed not a little to this end by the weight of his character and his brilliant gifts.

In humbler station, Mr. Stopford Brooke, who seems to have inherited the spirit, together with much of the peculiar talent of the late beloved Robertson, of Brighton, preaches and publishes discourses which show how piety and liberality, fervor of sentiment and mental emancipation, practical religion and independent thought, may unite in the service of truth.

Matthew Arnold's "Literature and Dogma," notwithstanding its weary iterations and its unaccountable misconception of Hebrew theism, has struck at the root of orthodox bigotry with its fundamental position that the Bible must be interpreted by literary, not by ecclesiastical canons.

Max Müller, the learned and philosophical interpreter of Oriental faiths, though not a theologian by profession, has extended the horizon of theological vision by his lectures on the "Science of Religion," and, like his compatriot, Bunsen, whose researches Dr. Williams discusses in this volume, has exercised a liberalizing influence on the English mind, whose power is felt in ecclesiastical circles no less than in the realm of science.[10]

In a different spirit and with different aims, the "Examination of Canon Liddon's Bampton Lectures," by a "Clergyman of the Church of England," and the Duke of Somerset's little treatise on "Christian Theology and Modern Scepticism," with the very significant motto inscribed on its title-page, have exposed, in the one case, the weakness of the Scriptural proof of a cherished dogma which Tradition has fastened on the creed of Christendom; in the other, the doubtful tenure of the whole system of Christian dogmatics, when viewed in the light of critical discoveries of recent time.[11]

The Revision of the English version of the Bible, authorized by the Convocation of Canterbury in 1870, and now in progress under supervision of English and American scholars of established repute, although mostly committed to men who are interested in maintaining the *status quo* of Christian theology, avails itself also, to some extent, of the counsel of critics of the liberal communion. Whatever its treatment of doubtful and disputed passages of Scripture, it can hardly fail to shake the superstition which idolizes the letter of the English text as the very identical, infallible word of God.

The frequent desertions from the Church of England to that of Rome which have come to our knowledge within the limits of the present generation, have been thought to indicate that the tendency of Anglicanism is retrogressive, instead of progressive; that it lies in the direction of external authority and materialism, rather than of growing illumination and generous trust. But these apostasies, so industriously bruited, seem to be not so much the result of intellectual conviction as of false sentiment—a romanticism in religion, like that which impelled a Christian emperor of the fourth century to secede from the Church and turn polytheist. It is hardly conceivable that any considerable portion of the laity of England should follow in a path which involves the renunciation of what in time past was so dearly won, that the sturdy sense of the English mind should accept the dictation of a foreign power, and consent to be "entangled again with the yoke of bondage."[12]

The Essays which, with this introduction, are once more spread before the American public, written independently of each other, were originally collected in one volume as agreeing in spirit and aiming in one direction—that of a larger and more philosophic interpretation of the ground-truths of Christianity than the writers found in the current theology of the English Church. The reader will find in them nothing destructive, nothing startling. The spirit of the "Broad Church," which these writers are supposed to represent, is not revolutionary, is not polemic. It aims neither to erect a new standard of doctrine nor to war against existing beliefs, but to open a door of toleration for different opinions, within the limits of one confession, for different interpretations of a common faith; to absolve from the yoke of dogmatism, to make worship, so far as may be, independent of creed. It aims to instaurate a religion which shall know how to separate what is essential in old traditions from what is incidental and obsolete; and while it maintains the eternal verities witnessed by the Past, shall adjust itself with the altered views and riper knowledge of the time; a religion which shall satisfy reverence, without doing violence to the understanding; a religion which shall reconcile science and faith.

Notes to American Editions

1. George Rapall Noyes published *A Collection of Theological Essays from Various Authors; with an Introduction* (1856). The volume included "The Law and the Gospel" by Powell; three essays by Rowland Williams from *Rational Godliness* (1855); twelve by Jowett from *The Epistles of St. Paul* (1855); and eight from Stanley's *The Epistles of St. Paul to the Corinthians* (1855).

2. The news has just reached us of the recent death of this eminent scholar. The University of Oxford loses in him one of its brightest ornaments, and the cause of liberal theology in the Church of England its ablest advocate [Hedge's note].

Powell died on 11 June 1860.

3. All of the theologians mentioned by Hedge were associated with England and were involved in theological controversy. John Scotus Erigena adapted Neoplatonic notions of emanations from the Godhead to Christian concepts of creation in *De Divisione Naturae* (Concerning the divisions of nature). His treatise, suspected of pantheism, was condemned by Pope Honorius III at a Council in Sens (1225), as "swarming with worms of heretical perversity." He was also involved in controversy concerning the freedom of the will. Unreliable accounts state that he was invited to Oxford by Alfred the Great and died as abbot of Malmesbury (*EB*, s.v. "Erigena"). Anselm of Canterbury published *Monologion* and *Proslogion*, both concerned with demonstrating the existence of God, the latter setting out the "ontological argument" that if God is that than which nothing greater can be thought, that existence is part of the condition of such a conception. He also wrote *Cur Deus Homo* (Why God became man) on the doctrine of the atonement. Duns Scotus defended the freedom of the human will, arguing that it was independent of the understanding, and that it was conditioned at the time of its creation in an individual by divine foreknowledge, and hence was subject to predestination. His most important writing is his *Commentary on the Sentences of Peter Lombard.* Alexander of Hales taught at Paris and published a *Commentary on the Sentences of Peter Lombard.* Roger Bacon published a large number of writings collected into the *Opus Maius* [Major work], *Opus Minus* [Minor work], and *Opus Tertium* [The third work], the first two of which were compiled at the request of Pope Clement IV for interrogation and possible commendation. They relate theology to philosophy, science, mathematics, grammar, and other fields of knowledge. Henry More and Ralph Cudworth were both associated with the theologians known as the "Cambridge Platonists." More published *Antidote against Atheism* (1653) and *Divine Dialogues* (1668), defending theism against the attacks of such rationalists as Thomas Hobbes. Cudworth also attacked Hobbes in *The True Intellectual System of the Universe* (1678).

4. Hedge refers to a succession of German theologians who pioneered with the new critical-historical approach to the NT concerning the text, interpretation, and the history of Israel and the early church. Each had a considerable influence in Germany and England, especially on the contributors to *Essays and Reviews* whose texts either cite them or allude to controversies in which they were involved.

5. Samuel Clarke studied at Cambridge under the influence of Isaac Newton, published two Boyle Lectures (*A Discourse concerning the Being and Attributes of God*, 1705–6) attacking John Locke's empiricism, and published his correspondence with G. W. Leibniz on the nature of time and space (1717). Of importance to Hedge's theological position was Clarke's *Scripture-Doctrine of the Trinity* (1712) that was attacked in Convocation for its Unitarianism. Daniel Whitby urged reconciliation between the Anglicans and Nonconformists and late in his life published *Last Thoughts* (1727), which aligned him with the Unitarians. Daniel Waterland was involved in the theological controversies with the deists concerning the divinity of Christ and the doctrine of the eucharist. Benjamin Hoadly was the central figure in the Bangorian Controversy concerning the question of the Non-jurors and their oaths of allegiance to George I. Joseph Bigham defended the tritheism of William Sherlock and also published *Origines Ecclesiasticae, or Antiquities of the Christian Church* (1708–22, 10 vols.). Pattison refers through his Essay to Bishops Butler and Berkeley but also alludes to Lowth, Lardner, Prideaux, and Middleton. William Law was also involved in the Bangorian controversy and published a popular book of devotional piety, *A Serious Call to a Devout and Holy Life* (1728).

6. Herbert Marsh studied in Germany under J. D. Michaelis and brought back to England the critical-historical methods of biblical interpretation. He translated Michaelis's *Introduction to the New Testament* (1793–1801, 4 vols.). As Lady Margaret professor of divinity at Cambridge he popularized such methods in his lectures, published as *The History of Sacred Criticism* (1809).

7. Henry Longueville Mansel's Bampton lectures, *The Limits of Religious Thought* (1858), argued that it was only through supernatural revelation that the human mind had any knowledge of

God, a view that provoked widespread controversy and attacks by F. D. Maurice and J. S. Mill.

Pyrrhonism is a general term designating sceptical thought, based on the system of sceptical philosophy associated with the Greek philosopher Pyrrho of Elis a view that certain knowledge about anything is impossible.

8. S. T. Coleridge published *Aids to Reflection* in 1825.

9. Temple agreed to withhold republication of his essay from editions of *Essays and Reviews* after 1869 (Letters 314–16, and 322), but no further edition was published in England during the nineteenth century; none was ever published with only his essay omitted.

Hedge's reference to the book's continuing "to find favor with a portion at least of the British public" alludes to his own republication in the fifth American edition (numbered the third) in 1874.

10. Stanley was appointed dean of Westminster in 1864 and sought to bring preachers there from all schools of Anglicanism, as well as Roman Catholics and Nonconformists. Pusey, Keble, and Liddon were reluctant or refused to preach there when the pulpit had been given to Jowett (Letters 220, 227, and 230).

Stopford Augustus Brooke came into conflict with the authorities in 1863 for his liberal views in his sermons, conflicts that continued with the publication of his *Life and Letters of the Late Frederick W. Robertson* (1865). Another Broad Church theologian and popular preacher, Frederick William Robertson, encountered opposition not only for his theology but also for his support of the ideas of the revolutions of 1848. In 1880 Stopford Brooke left the C. of E. to become a Unitarian clergyman.

Matthew Arnold published *Literature and Dogma* in 1873.

The philologist Friedrich Max Müller was introduced to Queen Victoria by Baron Bunsen, who also made him familiar with liberal thinkers, including Jowett, in Oxford. He spent most of his professional life in Oxford, where he was Taylorian professor of modern European languages and later professor of comparative philology. He was perhaps best known for his work on Sanskrit language and literature, publishing *History of Ancient Sanskrit Literature* (1859). In 1873 he published *Introduction to the Science of Religion*, lecturing on the same topic at Stanley's invitation in Westminster Abbey.

11. Henry Parry Liddon delivered the Bampton lectures on *The Divinity of Christ* (1867). The lectures were attacked in the anonymous *Examination of Canon Liddon's Bampton Lectures, by Clergyman of the Church of England* (1870).

Edward Adolphus Seymour Seymour, 12th duke of Somerset, published *Christian Theology and Modern Scepticism* (1872).

12. Flavius Claudius Julianus, known as Julian the Apostate, was Roman emperor from 361 to 363. He had early come under Christian influence and was a fellow student in Athens with Gregory Nazianzen. But he was influenced by Neoplatonism and repudiated Christianity, removing the privileges that had been granted to Christians under Constantine from 312. Julian actively persecuted Christians, seeking to revive the worship of the traditional Roman pantheon.

For "entangled again with the yoke of bondage" see Gal. 5:1.

3 Charges, Manifestos, Declarations, and Testimonials, 1860 to 1870

DURING THE FIRST YEARS of the notoriety of *Essays and Reviews* many public manifestos and declarations published, most antagonistic, while a few testimonials offered support. Each caused some kind of further controversy, provoked disagreements, and prompted incensed letters to the press. Some, such as the Episcopal Charges and Pastoral Letters, were the work of individual bishops; others, such as the Episcopal Manifesto and the Synodical Condemnation, were issued by the House of Bishops or were the joint efforts of the Upper and Lower Houses of Convocation. All necessarily carried great weight as authoritative statements from the bishops and from the synod in their teaching roles defining matters of faith. However, they fell far short of having a binding authority on the consciences of either the clergy or laity.

Reprinted here is a selection from such manifestos, including extracts from three episcopal charges and other pronouncements of the bishops spanning four years; various protests from the clergy, including those nationwide petitions to the archbishop of Canterbury and to the queen that garnered thousands of signatures; statements from groups of scientists, both for and against the volume, the most distinguished proffering the support of the leading scientists of the nineteenth century; and finally a number of petitions to the queen at the time of Temple's appointment to the See of Exeter in 1869. Two testimonials sponsored by friends of Jowett and Wilson are also reprinted, along with the Rugby Testimonial for Temple in 1869 and Temple's statement to the House of Bishops in 1870 that terminated public controversy.

Episcopal Charges

Samuel Wilberforce, Bishop of Oxford: the Charge of November 1860

[An episcopal "charge" is the address delivered by a bishop at a visitation to clergy of his diocese, in which the clergy are exhorted to their duties, and recent events and theological issues are summarized as a programme for action over the next

Dangers from Rationalism

For surely this is not a time when any of us would do anything which by ever so remote a consequence might tend to weaken our Church's hold or obscure its statement of fundamental truth. Are there not rather, Brethren, signs enough abroad amongst us of special danger from this side to make us drop all lesser differences, and combine together as one man in striving earnestly for the faith once delivered to the saints; when from within our own encampment are heard voices declaring that our old belief in the atonement wrought out for us by the sacrifice of the Cross is nothing better than an ignorant misconception, injurious to the character of God; that the miracles and prophecies of Scripture are parts of "an irrational supernaturalism," which it is the duty of a "remorseless criticism" to expose and account for by the notable discovery that "the imagination has allied itself with affection" to produce them [Williams ¶s 4 and note; and 2]; and that they may be safely brought down to a rational naturalism by such suggestions as that "the description of the passage of the Red Sea is the latitude of poetry," and that the "avenger who slew the first-born" was "the Bedouin host, akin nearly to Jethro and more remotely to Israel?" [Williams ¶s 7–8]—when the history of the Bible is explained away by being treated as legend, and its prophecy deprived of all supernatural character by being turned into a history of present or past events;—when we are taught that had our Lord come to us instead of to the youth of the world, "the truth of His divine nature would not have been recognised" [Temple ¶33], that is, that it was, after all, the peculiar state in which flesh and blood were, and not the revelation of "His Father which was in heaven," which enabled the apostles to believe on Him;—when, in the words "as far as opinion privately entertained is concerned, the liberty of the English Clergyman appears already to be complete" [Wilson ¶44], we are taught that men may sign any articles if it is only their own *opinions* which are at variance with them; that when required in one of the most solemn moments of their life to declare that they "ALLOW the Book of Articles, &c.," and "acknowledge the same to be agreeable to the Word of God," they may consider that "we 'allow' many things which we do not think wise or practically useful as the less of two evils, or an evil which cannot be remedied," &c., and that "many acquiesce in, submit to, 'allow' a law as it operates upon themselves which they would be horror-struck to have enacted;" and that "when he acknowledgeth the same to be agreeable to the Word of God, he does not maintain . . . it as his own feeling . . . or conviction" [Wilson ¶47];—when we are told that under the terms of the sixth Article one may accept literally, or allegorically, or as parable, or poetry, *or legend*, the story of a serpent-tempter, of an ass speaking with man's voice, of an arresting of the earth's motion, of a reversal of its motion, of waters standing in a solid heap, of witches, and a variety of apparitions; so, under the terms of the sixth Article, every one is free in judgment as to the primeval institution of the Sabbath, the universality of the deluge, the confusion of tongues, the corporeal taking up of Elijah into heaven, the nature of angels, the reality of demoniacal possession, the personality of Satan, and the miraculous particulars of many events [Wilson ¶38];—when Abraham's great act of obedience and faith in not withholding his son, even his only son, when called to offer him up by the express command of God, is transmuted into "the fierce ritual of Syria" as a "traditional revelation," "with the awe of a divine voice bidding him to slay his son," and his being stayed by the angel is watered down into "his trusting that the Father, whose voice from heaven he heard *at heart*, was better pleased with mercy than sacrifice" [Williams ¶10];—when it is maintained that St. Stephen, "full of the Holy Ghost" in the utterances of his martyrdom, or St. Paul, "sent forth by the Holy Ghost," [Acts 13:4] in proving, from the history of his people, that Jesus was the Christ, "would naturally speak," not the truth, but "after received accounts" [Williams ¶8]; when, I say, such words as these are deliberately uttered by our ordained brethren, whilst those who maintain the old truth are branded as the "400 priests who cry out for falsehood" [Williams ¶10]; and the slowness of even free English theologians to accept such a treatment of God's written revelation is scoffed at in such words as these, "Even with those in our Universities, who no longer repeat fully the required shibboleths, the explicitness of truth is rare; he who assents most, committing himself least to baseness, is reckoned wisest" [Williams ¶4];—when these things are thus spoken, is it not time for us, if we do hold simply by the Holy Scriptures as the one inspired voice of God's written revelation,—if we do hold to the ancient Creeds as the summary of the good deposit,—if we believe in the Lord Jesus Christ as Very God and Very Man,—if we believe in His offering of Himself upon the Cross as the "one only true and sufficient sacrifice, oblation, and satisfaction for the sins of the whole world," [*BCP*, prayer of consecration]—is it not time for us, laying aside suspicions and division about smaller matters, to combine together in prayer, and trust, and labour, and love, and watching, lest whilst we dispute endlessly about the lesser matters of the law, we be robbed unawares of the very foundations of the faith?

(Samuel Wilberforce, *A Charge Delivered at the Triennial Visitation of the Diocese, November, 1860*, 1860, 67–70)

Walter Kerr Hamilton, Bishop of Salisbury: The Charge of 8 August 1861

[Hamilton's charge was delivered midway between the beginning of the suit in the Court of Arches that he initiated against Williams on 23 May 1861 and the first hearings for the trial in December. Hence, Williams had already been arraigned and was under great suspicion. He was also subject to public attack in sermons, pamphlets, and books, but could say little publicly on matters under legal consideration. Hamilton was not, however, limited in the same way, and could speak out far more freely and powerfully; furthermore, his motives as the prosecutor were a subject of great interest in his diocese. This opportunity for clarification of motive on his part, therefore, was both opportune and delicate. In the charge Hamilton makes his position in condemning Williams's views perfectly clear; and Williams, though present, could not respond. As well, Hamilton submitted his charge to the *Times* (12 Aug. 1861, 5) thereby ensuring a widespread readership. This address to the clergy included the legal "Articles of Charge" submitted by Hamilton as his accusation of Williams in the Court of Arches (omitted here). They were printed following the bishop's charge, some citing passages from Williams, some alluding to his views in summary form; for many readers of the *Times* this was the first opportunity they had to read the details of the case against Williams.]

THIS MORNING the Bishop of Salisbury commenced the triennial visitation of his diocese. In consequence of the prosecution which his Lordship has commenced against the Rev. Dr. Rowland Williams, Vicar of Broad Chalk on account of his article "Bunsen's Biblical Researches," in *Essays and Reviews*, there was a very large attendance of both clergy and laity, an expectation having been formed that the subject would be adverted to in the charge. . . .

At the close of the service the bishop and clergy repaired to the nave, where the names of the clergy were called over. There were present the Rev. Dr. Rowland Williams, vicar of Broad Chalk; the Ven. Archdeacon Hony, the Rev. Prebendary Fowle, the Rev. Chancellor Lear, the Rev. J. N. Hensman, M.A., vicar of Durnford . . . and others.

The Bishop then proceeded to the delivery of his charge. He said he had looked forward to this visitation with more anxiety than to either of the two former which he had held. . . . His Lordship . . . said there were many other subjects of interest which he had intentionally passed over rather than weary the patience of the clergy. But there was one matter which he had passed over from very different considerations. He had felt precluded by the legal proceedings in which he was then engaged from enlarging on a subject which would be closer to all their hearts than any of those upon which he had touched, and one far more worthy of their deepest attention. They would all understand that he was alluding to a book, professing to be the work of six clergymen and one layman, called *Essays and Reviews*, and though he was not going, however much he might be tempted to do so, to break the rule of silence which circumstances had imposed upon him, still he felt he owed it to the diocese—both to the clergy and laity—to explain to them in not many words the reasons which had led him to adopt the course upon which he had now entered. He had instituted proceedings against the reputed writer of one of those Essays. There was much to dissuade him from acting as he had done. His belief was that there was not sufficient power in either of the Essays to exercise any permanent influence over the minds of men. This was one cause of hesitation. Again, he was not free from fear that legal proceedings would extend and intensify the influence, whatever it might be, and, further, he did not think that the constitution of our courts of judicature was as well fitted as one could desire to weigh the balance of truth on many of the questions which must necessarily be submitted to them. Then there was another cause for hesitation—the dictates of a righteous caution lest indignation against a reckless and ruthless attempt to pull down the fabric of Christianity to its foundation might make him forget the claims of charity and justice. There were these difficulties in the way of instituting legal proceedings; but on the other side there were preponderating reasons for formally submitting the essay to the Archbishop's Court, and to show that the Church disapproved it. The Church allowed great latitude, but there must be a limit somewhere. At the time of his consecration he (the Bishop) accepted the responsibility of keeping the teaching of his clergy within these wide limits. Again, the Archbishops and Bishops of the Church of England had testified by a public record that in this case the limits allowed by the Church had been transgressed, while the Lower House of Convocation and his own clergy had given in their adhesion to that testimony. Such testimony had helped to force the conclusion upon his mind that the case was beyond the bounds of toleration, and had quickened his sensibilities upon it. Upon the writers of the *Essays and Reviews* this record had had no effect. On the contrary, by frequent publications they had challenged the Bishops to show that their views were inconsistent with the law of the Church of England and her ministry. He might almost say that the writers had protested against informal acts, and had demanded in the name of justice a decision from those Courts to which decision on such points belonged. The matter had cast a heavy burden upon him, but loyalty to his Church compelled him to adopt the courses he had taken—any other course would have shown him to be cowardly and unfaithful to his trust. His Lordship proceeded to speak at some length on the incarnation, justification by faith, and the other doctrines assailed in *Essays and Reviews*, contending that upon them hinged the whole Christian system, and concluded by pronouncing the benediction.

The proceedings against Dr. Rowland Williams, to which the Bishop adverted in his charge, have so far progressed that the case will be ready for hearing early next term. The articles have been filed. In the preamble it is stated that Dr. Williams is charged with having, within the last two years, written, printed, published, dispersed, and set forth, in a book entitled *Essays and Reviews*, a certain article, or essay or review, with divers notes thereto, entitled *Bunsen's Biblical Researches*; and by having, in such article, or essay, or review, and in the notes thereto, advisedly affirmed and maintained certain erroneous, strange, and heretical doctrines, positions, and opinions, contrary and repugnant to the doctrine and teaching of the said united Church of England and Ireland. The following is a summary of the articles upon which Dr. Rowland Williams will be put on his defence:—[a summary of the Articles of Charge follows; Articles 7–17 are cited in full, and for some, such as Articles 7–9, passages from Williams cited in the charge are quoted at length. For a citation and discussion see "Trials and Appeals."]

(*Times*, 12 Aug. 1861, 5)

Connop Thirlwall, Bishop of St. David's: the Charge of October 1863

[Much was expected of Thirlwall as perhaps the most learned of the bench of Bishops, formerly a Fellow of Trinity College, Cambridge, and trained as a lawyer. He had collaborated with J. C. Hare in a translation of Niebuhr's *History of Rome* (1828–42) and published his own *History of Greece* in 8 volumes (1835–44), in recognition of which he was buried in the same grave as George Grote in Westminster Abbey. His early work, a translation of Schleiermacher's *Critical Essay on the Gospel of St. Luke* (1825), had been republished in 1861 without his consent, possibly to try to align him with the Essayists as advocates of the new German criticism of the Bible. But Thirlwall had already taken part in a published disagreement with Rowland Williams in 1860. Thirlwall's charge of 132 pages was delivered at a critical juncture in the appeal process, after Williams and Wilson had appeared before the Privy Council but before Westbury's judgment, and on the eve of the trial of Colenso before the Synod in South Africa; he dealt with both issues. During the charge he takes issue with, and sometimes quotes approvingly, the anonymous article by A. P. Stanley in the *Edinburgh*, stating that it was written by one of the same party in support of his friends. At this time Thirlwall was conducting an intense correspondence with Stanley, who also congratulated him on his charge (Thirlwall 1936, 233–34). The charge was published shortly after it was delivered, and was republished as part of his *Remains Literary and Theological* (1877) with added marginal subject captions, from which the present extract is reprinted.]

When men have been startled by a new phenomenon, it is natural that they should inquire after its cause, and so attempts have been not been wanting to trace the neology of our day to its source. . . . The real state of the case seems to be disclosed plainly enough by the writings [*Essays and Reviews*] which have suggested the question. They exhibit opinions which had been long floating in the public mind; some as old as the earliest attacks on the Christian faith, revived in the last century by our own deistical writers, since reproduced in various forms; in a few points perhaps of foreign origin, but on the whole of native growth. . . .

One thing is certain. It was not either the novelty of the opinions themselves, or the originality of the arguments by which they were maintained, that attracted public attention to the writings of which I am about to speak. The really new feature in the aspect which they were presented, was the character of the authors. . . . They were ministers of a Church which aims at a definite teaching, and exacts conformity to that teaching from those whom she admits into her ministry. . . . They were all men of literary eminence, some filling very important places in the rearing of the rising generation (4–7). . . . We cannot avoid noticing the peculiar form of the publication, as a collection of the independent contributions of different authors, writing wholly without concert with one another (9). . . . But before I proceed to consider what appears to me most important and characteristic in them, I think it may not be useless to make a few remarks on the public history of the book. Its private history will probably remain a secret confined to a few (9–10). . . . [Thirlwall then defends the Episcopal Manifesto and the legitimacy and impartiality of the lay judge, Lushington, in the Court of Arches trial, claiming the authority of the bishops to judge theologically what might be determined differently in a court of law; he then turns to Powell's essay.]

We may venture to believe that no very strong sensation would have been excited in the public mind by a layman who in our day should have revived the speculations of Spinoza and Hume on the absolute impossibility, or the incredibility of miracles. . . . But just for this reason the reproduction of these opinions in the work of a clergyman, could hardly fail to excite general surprise. . . . And this difficulty is increased when we find that the writer, in whose view the study of the "evidence of Christianity" must lead every duly cultivated mind to reject the belief in supernatural interposition, appears altogether to ignore the existence of any but secondary, or . . . natural causes in the world (16) . . . . "The *miracles* are merged in the *doctrines* with which they are connected. . . " [Powell ¶135]. But an "alleged miracle" is not the less a physical event because connected with religious doctrine. It cannot on that account be less capable of investigation by reason. If it is "accepted on religious grounds," it is accepted *as* a physical event, and only by those who do not admit that as such it is incredible . . . . A different question arises as to the miracles which were simply manifestations of the divine character of the Founder of our religion. . . . When the miraculous portions of the Gospel history are expunged, there will remain only a meagre outline of our Lord's life, ending with his death. . . . All beyond this would be involved in obscurity, and would only afford occasion for doubtful conjectures. When the most original and trustworthy accounts of His life had been so disfigured by fiction, no reliance could be placed on reports contained in them, of any declarations which He had made concerning Himself (21–22). . . . I have not thought myself precluded from bringing out the real character of the Essay which strikes most directly at the root of revealed religion, by the author's removal from the sphere of personal controversy. He indeed has passed beyond the reach, not only of ecclesiastical censure, but of literary criticism. But this is by no means the case with his writings; though to some it has appeared a reason for refraining from pronouncing a decided judgment on his Essay. It can never cease to occupy the foremost place in every general survey of the volume (25–26). . . .

The opening [essay] on the Education of the World . . . is in fact a Lecture on the Philosophy of History from the Christian point of view, and with special reference to Christianity. It was perhaps not altogether a happy thought to ground a theory on the analogy . . . between the development of the race and that of the individual (26–27). . . . All this was no doubt written with a view to edification; but language more directly suggestive of the most perplexing doubts, could hardly have been employed. It is not easy to understand on what ground a man of mature intellect can be required or expected to view an object in the same light in which it appeared to him in his youth; or why he should be better satisfied, if he was reminded that youth is the age most susceptible of lively impressions. That, to his riper judgment, might be exactly the reason why he should be no longer governed by them. . . . They must think it strange that they should be asked to recognize our Lord's Divinity, not upon any evidence directly offered to themselves, but on the ground of an impression made by His example on witnesses who, through the general imperfection of their development, were much less capable of accurately discerning correct inferences from the seen to the unseen . . . . If of this Essay nothing more can be fairly said, than that it opens the broadest room for an assault on the foundations of historical Christianity, without setting up any defence against it, this would not be enough to describe the bearing of some of the others on the same question (26–29).

The [third] Essayist adverts to a doubt which some may feel as to his author's [Bunsen's] claim to the name of Christian, notwithstanding the orthodoxy of his language: for he exposes himself, it is said, to the charge of "using Evangelical language in a philosophical sense." But in the critic's own opinion, the philosophical opinion is simply the "reasonable" sense. He himself thinks it "possible to defend our traditional theology, if stated reasonably" [Williams ¶24]. . . . For when he has occasion to allude to the sources from which his author's speculations on the Trinity may seem to have been drawn, he admits that they have a Sabellian or almost a Brahmanical sound [Williams ¶32]. . . . That they have any affinity to those of a School of much more recent date, and much nearer home,—not of Ptolemais or Benares, but of Berlin,—he entirely ignores. . . . But how far such liberty [of rejecting orthodox doctrine] may be rightfully claimed, or such laxity as to the Articles [of Religion] consistently exercised, by a Clergyman of the Church of England, is certainly a different question; one in which the example of the illustrious foreigner can afford no guidance to persons placed in entirely different relations (33–34). . . .

The most remarkable Essay in the volume is one which might have been entitled "a plea for National Churches established on comprehensive principles." We must all sympathize with the writer's [Wilson's] object, so far as it is to vindicate the national character of our own Church, among others, against those who deny the lawfulness of any established Church, and we may fully assent to his general position, that the Apostolical Churches, though differing from it as to their relation to the State, were not more exclusive in principle, and were constantly tending toward that outward form into which they were finally brought by the recognition which they received from the Civil Power. . . . The Essay is chiefly occupied with a statement . . . of the conditions on which a National Church, such as our own, may hope to endure and prosper (35). . . . [After criticizing Wilson's view of the liberty of thought and speech of the English clergy with respect to the Bible, the articles, and the liturgy, his view of the limitations on the speculative teachings of the church on matters of doctrine, and his view of ideology, Thirlwall concludes his discussion of the essay.]

The drift of the whole scheme is to bring the Church down to the religious level of those who hold least of Christian doctrine; or—as this class is assumed to include the most enlightened minds in the nation—to lift the Church up to their intellectual level. . . . This Essay is the practical complement of that which, by its absolute rejection of all supernatural interposition [Powell's], subverts the historical basis of Christianity. The one prepares us for a loss which it represents as inevitable, the other offers the compensation of an ideal to be substituted for the historical reality. That it retains any thing which would be inconsistent with the principle by which all that, in our traditional belief, is derived from such interposition, is referred to the evolution of merely natural causes, is nowhere intimated by a single word, and is a supposition at variance with the whole tenor of the Essay. It begins and ends with a speculation on the future state. . . .The solution of the difficulty is found in the uselessness of creeds; and the Essay, as we have seen, is chiefly occupied with the exposure of their worthlessness and noxiousness, and with practical suggestions for getting rid of them. It turns out, indeed, that even within the pale of Christianity the like difficulty arises as with regard to the unconverted heathen, and that we cannot be content with believing that the Judge of all the earth will do right, unless we determine . . . what it is right for Him to do (46–49).
. . .

Of the three remaining Essays, one is the work of a layman, and therefore, even if it had been distinguished from the rest by the boldness of its speculations, it would not have been liable to the censure which they have incurred. . . . The author has used his privilege with moderation. If he had been a clergyman, he would have had the same right to criticize the speculations of other authors, on what he calls the Mosaic Cosmogony; and the conclusion to which he is led does not differ essentially from one which has been since proposed by a clergyman of unimpeached orthodoxy [G. Rorison in *Replies to "Essays and Reviews"* 1862]. . . . Still less would anyone question the right of a clergyman to take a survey of the "tendencies of religious thought in England" in the last century, or, . . . of the Theory of Belief in the Church of England. . . . The general tendency of the investigation is to raise a doubt whether any of those on which it has been supposed to rest is sufficiently firm; any one who should look for a hint to supply the defect would be utterly disappointed. This indeed is quite in accordance with the principles laid down in the previous Essays, but is not sufficient to charge the author with the responsibility of maintaining them.

The same remark will apply to the last Essay in the volume. The subject of which it treats, "the Interpretation of Scripture," is indeed of vast range, and in itself of all but the very highest importance: but by the side of those which are discussed in other parts of the volume, it sinks into comparative insignificance. . . . The view of the question [of inspiration] taken in the Essay may be that which those who reject supernatural revelation are forced to take; but it does not follow that the author is by his theory of inspiration at all committed to their denial of revelation. . . . There is no visible organ of our Church competent to define that which hitherto has been left undetermined on this point [of inspiration] (49–50). . . .

Looking at the volume as a whole, I do not understand how any one reading it with common attention can fail to observe, notwithstanding the variety of topics and of treatment, that all is the product of one school. . . . The only question is as to the character of the school to which it belongs; and that this, so far as it may be inferred from the work, is mainly negative, is acknowledged by its warmest and ablest apologist [Stanley in *The Edinburgh Review*]. . . . I have been led to a very different conclusion; that the negation does reach to the very essence and foundation of Christian faith; that after the principles laid down in this work have been carried to their logical result, that which is left will be something to which the name of Christianity cannot be applied without a straining and abuse of language. It will be no longer a religion, and will not yet have become a philosophy (51). . . . The ideal sketched in this volume of a National Church, without a theology, without a confession, without a creed, with no other basis of united worship than a system of universal equivocation, has probably struck many with surprise at its extravagance. The scheme by which it is to be realized seems to exhibit an incongruity, almost amounting to direct opposition, between the means and the end. It aims at the cementing of religious unity, by a process apparently tending to the most complete disintegration of all religious communion. It proposes to attract larger congregations to our services, by extinguishing as much as possible the devotional element in them, and turning our churches into lecture-rooms, for the inculcation of ethical commonplace, as to which there is supposed to be no room for any difference of opinion in the audience. . . . But whatever may be the merits of the scheme, here is the fact, that it has been put forth by a clergyman of no mean ability and of considerable Academical reputation. And then, though among ourselves it is still only in the state of a crude project, it is not a mere dream. . . . Any proceeding which looked like the beginning of a movement for carrying it into effect, would be regarded by the great body of English Churchmen with suspicion and alarm (54–55). . . . [Thirlwall then discusses Colenso's *Pentateuch* for the remainder of the charge (55–85).]

(Connop Thirlwall, *A Charge Delivered to the Diocese of St. David's . . . at His Eighth Visitation October 1863*, 1863, 1–132)

The Episcopal Manifesto
(12 February 1861)

[The Episcopal Manifesto was first published in the *Times* (16 Feb. 1861, 10). It consisted of a letter from the archbishop of Canterbury dated 12 February, and was signed by twenty-five bishops. The letter is framed by a letter from William Robert Fremantle, a clergyman from Oxfordshire.

The Episcopal Manifesto responds to the "Protest of the Clergy," in widespread circulation since November 1860 (see below), and uses similar phrases and ideas concerning the clerical writers and their transgression of the formularies. The immediate occasion was a series of addresses sent to the archbishop of Canterbury from the gatherings of local clergy at their semiannual deanery meetings. The two archbishops and seventeen bishops met at Lambeth Palace in London on 1 February when the addresses were read and discussed (Letter 41). The choice of possible actions was between outright condemnation (urged by J. B. Sumner and Wilberforce, as well as Hampden, who said "we ought to prosecute," it being "a question of Christianity or no Christianity") and a more moderate declaration of doctrine (urged by Tait, who also said that Pattison's essay was "unobjectionable," Temple's contained nothing heretical, and Jowett's could only be answered by an elucidation of the doctrine that he neglects). Thirlwall and C. R. Sumner raised the possibility of legal advice, and Thirlwall "strongly deprecated any discussion in Convocation," the governing body of the Church of England, meeting in two houses, the lower house of clergy, and the upper house of bishops. After being prorogued in 1717 over a dispute about royal authority, Convocation did not resume sittings until 1852 (Letter 41).

Wilberforce drafted a response overnight, and the next day it was accepted. A manuscript draft by Wilberforce exists in the Tait papers at Lambeth, entitled "Proposed answer drawn up by Bp. of Oxford" (MS. Tait 80, fols. 13–14). It is dated 2 February 1861 and contains slight variations in phrasing, especially in the conclusion; it is to this document that Wilberforce refers in his diary entry of the same date (Letter 42). Such was what Thirlwall called "the secret history of the episcopal letter" (Thirlwall 1881, 235). From these documents it is clear that Wilberforce was the driving force in drafting the manifesto and in carrying it forward to publication and circulation.

The publication of the Episcopal Manifesto in the *Times* with the brief framing letter of Fremantle caused something of a puzzled sensation: many wondered why an episcopal pronouncement of such importance would be communicated to an obscure Oxfordshire clergyman. Even some of the published signatories were upset, since some of the bishops who had not been present (such as Henry Phillpotts of Exeter) found their names affixed to a document they had not seen. News that the bishops had had such a discussion was revealed by Montagu Villiers (bp. of Durham) in his letter to the *Times* of 11 February (Letter 45). Stanley wrote privately to Tait that undertakings in earlier private discussion between himself and Tait had been broken (Letters 54–55), and under the pseudonym of "Anglicanus" Stanley wrote to the *Times* (Letter 58). Temple wrote in dismay to Wilberforce and Phillpotts, and almost certainly to each signer of the Manifesto asking each to cite the offending passages in his essay (Letters 63–64). In anger he wrote to Tait as their long-standing friendship almost ended over what he saw as duplicity against himself and Jowett (Letters 65–70; 72, 76, 80, 82, 85–86). The Manifesto also ensured that the matter was discussed in detail in Convocation (Letter 78). The name "Episcopal Manifesto" was conferred on the document by Stanley in his review of *Essays and Reviews* in the *Edinburgh* (Apr. 1861), in which he also attacks its validity (1861a, 469–70). Nor was he alone; the Cambridge philosopher and educational reformer Henry Sidgwick asserted that what was wanted was "not a condemnation, but a refutation" because "the age when ecclesiastical censures were sufficient . . . has passed away" and "the thinking laity of England" will not be "satisfied by an *ex cathedra* shelving of the question" that does not take seriously the Essayists' "belief in the advantage of perfectly open discussion and perfectly impartial investigation" (Letter 62).

When Temple was appointed bishop of Exeter in 1869, the Episcopal Manifesto was reprinted in a four-page leaflet, along with Temple's letters addressed to the previous bishop of Exeter, Henry Phillpotts, concerning his signing of the manifesto. Phillpotts's replies were also included. This publication, printed by Baxter of Oxford, sets out Temple's implication in *Essays and Reviews* and his censure by the House of Bishops; it was very likely instigated by Pusey and his associates. A copy was sent to Gladstone, and is dated by him "Oct. 69" and is marked for his *Essays and Reviews* file (Hawarden, Glynne-Gladstone MSS. 1648). For other discussions of the context of the Episcopal Manifesto see Ellis 1980, 163–70; and Altholz 1994, 52–58.]

Sir,—I have had the honour to receive the enclosed reply to an address presented to His Grace the Archbishop of Canterbury.

As this important document contains the unanimous testimony of the Archbishops and Bishops of the Provinces of Canterbury and York, the only name lacking that of Worcester, who is as yet unconsecrated, you may think it deserving a place in your paper.

I am, Sir, your obliged servant,

Claydon Rectory, Feb. 13. W. R. Fremantle

Lambeth, Feb. 12.

Rev. Sir,—I have taken the opportunity of meeting many of my episcopal brethren in London, to lay your address before them.

They unanimously agree with me in expressing the pain it has given them than any clergyman of our Church should have published such opinions as those concerning which you have addressed us.

We cannot understand how their opinions can be held consistently with an honest subscription to the formularies of our Church, with many of the fundamental doctrines of which they appear to us essentially at variance.

Whether the language in which these views are expressed is such as to make their publication an act which could be visited in the ecclesiastical courts, or to justify the synodical condemnation of the book which contains them is still under our gravest consideration. But our main hope is our reliance on the blessing of God in the continued and increasing earnestness with which we trust that we and the clergy of our several dioceses may be enabled to teach and preach that good deposit of sound doctrine which our Church has received in its fulness, and which we pray that she may, through God's grace, ever set forth as the uncorrupted Gospel of our Lord Jesus Christ.

I remain, rev. Sir, your faithful servant,
J. B. CANTUAR [Canterbury]. [Sumner]

Rev. W. Fremantle.

I am authorized to append the following names:—

C. J [*sic* T]. EBOR [York: Longley], A. C. LONDON [Tait], H. M. DUNELM [Durham: Villiers], C. R. WINTON [Winchester: Sumner], H. EXETER [Phillpotts], C [*sic* G]. PETERBOROUGH [Davys], C. ST. DAVID'S [Thirlwall], A. T. CHICHESTER [Gilbert], J. LICHFIELD [Lonsdale], S. OXON [Oxford: Wilberforce], T. ELY [Turton], T. V. ST. ASAPH [Short], J. P. MANCHESTER [Lee], R. D. HEREFORD [Hampden], J. CHESTER [Graham], A. LLANDAFF [Ollivant], R. J. BATH AND WELLS [Eden], J. LINCOLN [Jackson], C. GLOUCESTER & BRISTOL [Baring], W. SARUM [Salisbury: Hamilton], R. RIPON [Bickersteth], J. T. NORWICH [Pelham], J. C. BANGOR [Campbell], J. ROCHESTER [Wigram], S. CARLISLE [Waldegrave].

[In a letter to the *Times* (18 Feb. 1861) A. C. Tait advises that "there is a typographical error," the substitution of "their opinions" for "these opinions," one which, as he maintains to Stanley, "materially alters its tone" (Letters 55–56). In the Tait papers, the Wilberforce draft reads "these" (Lambeth MS. Tait 80, fol. 13); the last sentence begins: "But our main hope for the prevention of these evils is under the blessing of God" (fol. 14).

The Episcopal Manifesto was also printed four days later in the High Church weekly, the *Guardian*. Instead of Fremantle's letter, the letter introducing the Manifesto is from Henry Blackstone Williams, rural dean of Dorchester, once again a rather indirect source for the Manifesto, and one differing from the report in the *Times*. He does, however, make the immediate occasion clearer by alluding to a letter of November 1860, signed by all of the clergy of the rural deanery except one, assuring the archbishop of "our unfeigned attachment to the doctrines and disciplines of the Church" and expressing alarm at "the spread of rationalistic and semi-infidel doctrines among the beneficed clergy of the realm." It was to such deanery addresses that the Episcopal Manifesto was a direct reply. The deanery of Dorchester submitted the following address:

We wish to make known to your Grace and to all the Bishops the alarm

> we feel at some late indications of the spread of rationalistic and semi-infidel doctrines among the beneficed clergy of the realm. We allude especially to the denial of the atoning efficacy of the Death and Passion of our Blessed Saviour Jesus Christ, both God and Man, for us men and for our salvation, and to the denial also of a Divine Inspiration, peculiar to themselves alone, of the Canonical Scriptures of the Old and New Testament.
>
> We would earnestly beseech your Grace and your Lordships, as faithful stewards over the House of God, to discourage by all means in your power the spread of speculations which would rob our countrymen, more especially the poor and unlearned, of their only sure stay and comfort for time and for eternity. And to this end we would more especially and most earnestly beseech you, in your Ordinations, to "lay hands suddenly on no man" [1 Tim. 5:22] till you have convinced yourselves (as far as human precaution can secure it) that each Deacon, who, in reply to the question, "Do you unfeignedly believe all the Canonical Scriptures of the Old and New Testament?" answers "I do believe them," *speaks the truth* as in the sight of God (*Guardian*, 20 Feb. 1861, 166–67; and Davidson and Benham 1891, 1:281–83).

In the Court of Arches, Williams's legal representative, Dr. Deane, referred on 13 December 1861 to the Episcopal manifesto in scathing terms: "Shortly after that . . . came the letter which I will call the Fremantle letter. Of that I will only say that I hope the person, whoever he may be, who may hereafter write the lives of the Bishops and Archbishops of England, will not think it necessary to say very much of the notice which was taken of that letter." At a later point in his address, on 13 January 1862, he refers to it again, more trenchantly: "I do not know in the whole of my reading a more unbecoming or a more cowardly act than the writing of that letter. . . . Who are the writers of that letter? Persons who by their very Office are Judges of the land in matters of this kind. . . . write a letter condemning . . . and they never call before them the writers of the [essays]. . . . It is one of the most indiscrete, nay . . . one of the most unbecoming and indecent things that a body of men, Judges by the Law of the land over these particular subjects, ever yet committed. . . . What they are now doing is merely lynch law" (British Library, Salisbury v. Williams in the Court of Arches BL 5155 K.11, 1: fol. 5; 3: fol.5). Meanwhile, the Clergy of the Lower House of Convocation debated the issue at length, covering the extremes from no action to synodical condemnation, urged by R. W. Jelf, who three years later saw his wish fulfilled. The Lower House resolved on 26 February to support the Episcopal Manifesto on a motion of Christopher Wordsworth:

> That the clergy of the Lower House of Convocation of the Province of Canterbury, having agreed to the unanimous censure which has been already pronounced and published by the Archbishops and Bishops of both provinces on certain opinions contained in a book entitled *Essays and Reviews*, entertain

an earnest hope that, under the Divine blessing, the faithful zeal of the Christian Church may be enabled to counteract the pernicious influences of the erroneous opinions contained in the said volume (*Chronicle of Convocation* 1859–64:1861, 364–413; *Guardian* 27 Feb. 1861, 188–95).

Finally, the Convocation of the Province of York met on March 21 and concurred with "unfeigned satisfaction" in the content of the Episcopal Manifesto that the archbishop of York and bishops of the northern province had already signed, concluding: "We hold it a solemn duty—distinguishing between the evidences for a revelation of which man is fully capable of judging, and the contents of a revelation of many of which man may be wholly incompetent to judge—to record our utter rejection, nay, our unfeigned abhorrence, of the principle referred to (Williams's 'verifying faculty'), as well as of other kindred principles characteristic of the volume" (*Record*, 25 Mar. 1861, 2).]

The Pastoral Letter of the Irish Archbishops
(8 March 1861)

[The archbishops of Armagh and Dublin, Lord John George Beresford and Richard Whately, following the lead of the English archbishops and bishops, sent a pastoral letter to all of their bishops asking that they inform their clergy concerning the dangerous threat to religious belief posed by *Essays and Reviews*. The letter was published in the *Times* on 8 Mar. 1861, 5.]

The Irish Archbishops on "Essays and Reviews"

The Archbishops of Armagh and Dublin have addressed the following letter to the bishops of their provinces on the subject of the *Essays and Reviews*:

RIGHT REV. BRETHREN,— Our attention has been called to a protest which has been issued by the prelates in England in reference to a publication entitled *Essays and Reviews*, the production of professed members, most of them clergymen of our Church, and yet setting forth views manifestly at variance with its principles. We cannot doubt your strong disapprobation of the disingenuousness of such conduct. Even supposing the doctrines of our Church to be as unsound as we firmly believe them to be the reverse, still, it is directly opposed to the most obvious principles of morality for persons to continue professed members of the Church, and perhaps enjoying its emoluments, while assailing those doctrines. With respect to the publication in question we have not hitherto deemed it necessary to take any public steps, considering that the writers were in English dioceses, and that the respective diocesans would be likely to take such measures, either by ecclesiastical censure or otherwise, as the case might appear to them to call for; and we believe that it is but very recently that the matter has obtained any considerable notoriety in this portion of the Church. But now that this publication is obtaining much circulation, we feel it necessary to call your attention to it, with a view to your putting your clergy specially on their guard against the possible inroads of erroneous and strange doctrines in the new form. As to the best mode of your doing this, your own judgement and knowledge of the circumstances in each locality will be a sufficient guide. With earnest prayers for the Divine guidance to ourselves and to you in all matters, and more especially in this difficult conjuncture,

We remain, Right Rev. Brethren, your &c.,

J. G. ARMAGH [Beresford]. R. DUBLIN [Whately].

The Proposed Declaration of Support by F. J. A. Hort
(12 February 1861)

[In a letter to Brooke Foss Westcott, his collaborator in the Greek edition of the New Testament (1881, 2 vols.), on 12 February 1861, Fenton John Anthony Hort proposed "a suggested declaration" to counteract the impact of the "Protest of the Clergy" on which it is modeled.

Hort had been invited by Williams (both were Cambridge graduates) to contribute to *Essays and Reviews*, but he declined. Although in general sympathy with a number of the aims as he then understood them, he was apprehensive about "serious differences between us on the subject of authority, and especially the authority of the Bible" and so declined (Letter 11). When the volume was published he wrote an appreciative letter about it to his friend John Ellerton (Letter 19) and as the crisis about the volume deepened, a letter of support to Pattison (Letter 57). After proposing the "declaration of support," which came to naught, he, Westcott, and Lightfoot discussed editing a "mediating volume" to be called *Revelation and History* (Letters 51–52), but it too came to nothing.]

WE, the undersigned clergymen of the Church of England, desire to protest publicly against the violent and indiscriminate agitation now being directed against a book called *Essays and Reviews*, and against the authors of it. Believing that the suppression of free criticism must ultimately be injurious to the cause of truth and religion, we especially regret the adoption of a harsh and intolerant policy, which tends to deter men of thought and learning from entering the ministry of the Church, and to impel generous minds into antagonism to the Christian faith (Hort 1896, 1:439).

"The Protest of the Clergy" Presented to the Archbishop of Canterbury at Lambeth (13 March 1861)

[The "Protest of the Clergy" (sometimes called "the Oxford Manifesto") dates from the gathering of almost 1,500 clergy who held the Oxford M. A. (and so were members of Convocation) in Oxford on 7 December 1860. Convocation met to elect a new Professor of Sanskrit. The choice was between F. Max Müller and M. Monier Williams, the former a distinguished German philologist and layman, sympathetic with the Broad Church, and a friend of Bunsen, Stanley, and Jowett, who had published on Sanskrit, and the latter a conservative clergyman. Williams won by a comfortable majority, but not without bitter words about Germanism, biblical criticism, and high feelings, and with, as Stanley reported, the first concerted meeting of the clergy to prepare a protest:

> On that occasion, when the University lost the services of the most eminent scholar within her walls, there was arrayed against him a vast mass of the Conservative elements of the country, both theological and political. The well-known anathema issued on that occasion against "the intellectuals," a fit precursor of the swarm of curses which have followed in its wake, admirably expressed the feeling of many who recorded their vote. . . against the illustrious German philologer. In the fermentation naturally engendered by the victorious combination of bodies of men for any common purpose arose, it is said, the first distinct conception of an organised attack on the volume with which Professor Müller's friends or country had been connected in the public mind. A meeting was held before the final dispersion of the electors, in one of the Oxford hotels; and there was breathed the earliest whisper of a demonstration against the book, which still remained in the modest obscurity of a small second edition (Stanley 1861a, 465).

Pusey was almost certainly instrumental in the organization and conduct of this meeting, as may be evidenced from his name affixed prominently to the earliest versions of it as a signatory. It was widely circulated over the next several months, eventually garnering seventy-six pages of signatures appended to it, approximately 8,500 clergy, with their institutional positions affixed by title and location (Liddon 1897, 4:43). The honorary secretaries who undertook the compilation of the list were Drs. Alexander McCaul, Low Church rector of St. Magnus Martyr in the City of London and professor of Hebrew at King's College, London, and William J. Irons, High Church incumbent of Brompton. Various versions of the list were printed in stages of final preparation from mid-February until it was eventually presented at Lambeth on 12 March 1861 (*Guardian*, 13 Mar. 1861, 250; cf. Ellen

Williams 1874, 2:30). Ellen Williams claims that there were 10,000 signatures; Liddon's is the more accurate figure. Two copies of the "Protest of the Clergy" are in the Bodleian Library. The earlier one is tipped into a copy of the first edition of *Essays and Reviews* and bears a printed outside address to "Rev. Doctors M'Caul and Irons, St. Dunstan's Vestry, Fleet-street, London E. C." As a recruitment document it begins by listing names hierarchically: five deans, two heads of colleges, one each at Oxford and Cambridge, three Oxford professors (Heurtley, Ogilvie, and Pusey), 20 archdeacons, W. J. Trower (subdean of Exeter, and bishop of Glasgow and Galloway, 1848–63) and 96 incumbents or clerical fellows of colleges. The other copy consists of the full document as presented at Lambeth with the complete list of signatories and the pages of extracts from the essays.

The "Protest" was printed in the *Guardian* on 20 February 1861, 165, and in the *Times* under the heading "'Important Clergy' to *The Times*" on 26 February 1861, 5, with the heading: "The following address has been signed by the Deans of Carlisle, Lincoln, Ripon, St. Asaph, and Bangor, Dr. Pusey, Regius Professor of Hebrew at Oxford; Archdeacons Denison, Macdonald, Moore, Atherton, and Clive; Bishop Trower, Chancellor Bird, and a large number of other clergymen holding important positions in the church, and will be presented to the Archbishop of Canterbury in the course of a few days." A comment was also added at the end of the "Protest": "A long string of extracts from the *Essays and Reviews* will accompany the memorial." In the printed versions of the "Protest" there is an extensive list of names, followed by two foolscap-size pages of "erroneous and strange doctrines," printed extracts from *Essays and Reviews*. It was alleged that many of the signatories were "men who had never seen the book, and knew it only through these [printed extracts], or through the *Quarterly Review* and newspaper notices" (Ellen Williams 1874, 2:30). Since by the end of January there were in circulation only 3,750 copies of *Essays and Reviews*, there can be little doubt that the extracts were the first direct encounter many of the 8,500 signers had with the volume.]

To the Most Reverend Father in God, John Bird,
Lord Archbishop of Canterbury, Primate of
All England, and Metropolitan.

May it please Your Grace,

We the undersigned, Clergy of the United Church of England and Ireland, respectfully request your Grace's attention to certain opinions contained in a Volume of 'Essays and Reviews' recently published, the tendency of which, as it appears to us, is to annihilate the authority of the Bible as the Inspired Word of God—to reject all Miracles (not excepting those of our Blessed Lord) as incapable of proof and repugnant to reason—and, in one instance at least, to undermine faith in God as the Creator.

These opinions have been promulgated, with one exception, by Clergymen of our Church, holding positions of great trust, and possessing opportunities favourable in no ordinary degree for the diffusion of error.

We therefore earnestly entreat your Grace to take counsel with the other members of the Episcopate, and to devise such measures as may, with God's blessing, "banish and drive away" from our Church all such "erroneous and strange doctrines."

The opinions against which we protest, as being repugnant to the natural meaning of our formularies and inconsistent with the teaching of the Church of England, are expressed in the accompanying extracts from the Essays to which we refer.

We have the honour to be,

Your Grace's obedient, humble Servants,

[A news item in the *Times* (13 Mar. 1861, 5) reported on the delivery of the "Protest of the Clergy" to Lambeth, and again reprinted the text of the "Protest":

> His Grace the Archbishop of Canterbury has appointed to-day (Wednesday) to receive an address on the subject of "Essays and Reviews," signed by clergymen of all parties in the Church—for example, Archdeacon Denison, Archdeacon Law, Archdeacon Ullerton, Archdeacon Grant, the Dean of Lincoln, the Dean of Ripon, the Dean of St. Asaph, Dr. Pusey, the Rev. Canon Heurtley, Margaret Professor of Divinity at Oxford; Professor Espin of Birmingham; Canon Dale, Canon Champneys, Dr. Irons of Brompton; the Dean of Carlisle, Dr. Cotton, Provost of Worcester College, Oxford; Bishop Trower, Chancellor Bird, Dr. Ogilvie, Archdeacon Allen, Dr. M'Neile, Dr. M'Caul, the Rev. John Keble, Dr. Maron, Dr. Moberley, Archdeacon Clive, Archdeacon Burney, the Rev. C. P. Golightly, the Rev. J. S. Jenkinson, vicar of Battersea; the Rev. W. Gresley, of Boyne-hill; the Rev. J. F. Lingham, rector of Lambeth; the Rev. Prebendary Burgess, rector of Upper Chelsea; the Rev. Hugh Stowell; the Rev. A. D. Wagner, incumbent of St. Paul's, Brighton; Canon Brodrick, Canon Carus, the Rev. E. Auriol, M.A., rector of St. Dunstan-in-the-West; the Rev. Sir C. Hardinge, the Rev. Sir H. Thompson, Archdeacon Hankinson, and Archdeacon Garbett. The address, which is said to bear the signatures of upwards of 6,000 English clergymen, is as follows:—[The "Protest" is reprinted] . . . It may be stated that during the present week meetings of the archbishops and bishops of both provinces of Canterbury and York, with a view to determine what course their Lordships will recommend to be taken in reference to the volume which has given rise to so much discussion, will take place.

The following passages were cited in a two-page Appendix attached to the Oxford Protest; they were also printed in the *Guardian*. One is from Temple, four from

Williams, three from Powell, seven from Wilson, one from Goodwin, one from Pattison, and three from Jowett. Each of the passages cited from Williams was cited in the charges in the Court of Arches. The second Powell passage contains the only reference in the volume to Darwin; the final word in the third Powell quotation substitutes "science" (as in the 2d ed.) for "reason" (in the 1st ed.). The second to fourth extracts from Wilson, as well as the sixth and seventh, were cited in the Court of Arches. The second passage cited from Jowett was cited in the Synodical Condemnation of 1864. In each case the extract was printed in full, though some were only a sentence long; all were taken entirely out of context. The page number was given for the first edition, here replaced with paragraph numbers:

Temple	"It is a history. . . . duty to disobey."	¶53
Williams	"Baron Bunsen notices. . . . remotely to Israel."	¶7
	"When the fierce ritual. . . . his righteousness."	¶10
	"The Bible is, before. . . . true hearts for ever."	¶24
	"Again, on the side of. . . . witness in ourselves."	¶28
Powell	"The first dissociation. . . the same direction."	¶102
	"Yet it is now acknowledged. . . powers of nature."	¶126
	"In nature and from nature. . . beyond science."	¶131
Wilson	"Previous to the time. . . . for the Roman."	¶31 note
	"Under the terms of the sixth. . . . and importance."	¶38
	"Many evils have flowed. . . . scripturalism."	¶39
	"There is no book. . . . truth within."	¶39
	"The like ill consequences. . . . and opinion."	¶41
	"But it by no means. . . . reasonably exercised."	¶73
	"For relations which may repose. . . . the literalist."	¶75
Goodwin	"It would have been well. . . . no part of revelation."	¶4
Pattison	"The career of the evidential. . . . bygone age."	¶s 38–39
Jowett	"No one would interpret. . . . the date (Isa. xlv. 1)."	¶13
	"Nor for any of the higher. . . coming of Christ."	¶15
	"The best informed. . . . origin of man."	¶18]

The Scientists' Testimonial
(February-March 1861)

[This testimonial was instituted in late February 1861, devised and compiled by the astronomer and mathematician Sir John Lubbock in opposition to the Episcopal Manifesto. In Lubbock's papers in the British Library (MS. ADD. 49,639 [Avebury papers], fol. 29) a printed clipping of the *Times* letter from Fremantle including the Episcopal Manifesto is filed directly before a printed copy of the Scientists' Testimonial on blue paper. The Testimonial is addressed "To the Rev. Dr. Temple" as the first of the Essayists in the volume, and at the time supposed by many to be the editor. On 25 February 1861 William Spottiswoode visited Jowett in Oxford, and showed the testimonial to him and to Stanley. Stanley thought the Testimonial "very good," declaring that the bishops would not try either synodical censure or the ecclesiastical courts; he was wrong on both counts (Letter 74). Among those who refused to sign were J. F. W. Herschel (who had not read *Essays and Reviews*), J. C. Adams, Charles Kingsley, and Thomas Vernon Wollaston (BL MS. ADD. 49,639, fols. 30–54). It is not clear whether T. H. Huxley signed, as Ellis claims (1980, 108). Although a copy of the testimonial is among the Huxley Papers at Imperial College, London (MS. v. 22. 63), there is no letter of agreement from him in the Avebury papers (Letters 75, 77, 84, 87–88, and 90). The Scientists' Testimonial was twice printed in the *Guardian*, first on 20 March 1861 when the second and third paragraphs were quoted in a letter of attack on the Essayists by C. A. Heurtley; he claims the document is "being circulated for signature" and those who believe its contents will "learn to doubt everything, to believe nothing" (271–72). On 27 March 1861 the entire document was printed as a news item with the heading: "The following address to Dr. Temple has been withdrawn from circulation" (294). In neither case was any signature attached. In the copy in the Avebury papers "English" is added in ink to the printed text before "Bishops." In the printed copy in the Huxley papers, there is no such MS. emendation, nor is the word in the *Guardian* on 27 March. It is also printed in Hutchinson 1914, 1:57–58.]

To The Rev. Dr. Temple.

WE the undersigned have read with surprise and regret a letter in which the Archbishop of Canterbury and the other English Bishops have severely censured the Volume of Articles entitled *Essays and Reviews.*

Without committing ourselves to the conclusions arrived at in the various Essays, we wish to express our sense of the value which is to be attached to enquiries conducted in a spirit so earnest and reverential, and our belief that such enquiries must tend to elicit truth, and to foster a spirit of sound religion.

Feeling as we do that the discoveries in science, and the general progress of thought, have necessitated some modification of the views generally held on theological matters, we welcome these attempts to establish religious teaching on a firmer and broader foundation.

While admitting that each writer in the *Essays and Reviews* is responsible only for the opinions expressed by himself, we address to you, as author of the first article, this expression of our sympathy and our thanks.

[The Testimonial was eventually concurred in or signed by:

George Biddell Airy, F.R.S., Astronomer-Royal, Plumian Professor of Astronomy, Cambridge

Charles Spence Bate, F.R.S., zoologist

George Bentham, Fellow and President of the Linnaean Society, botanist

George Busk, F.R.S., Hunterian Professor, and President of the Royal College of Surgeons
William Benjamin Carpenter, F.R.S., Fullerian Professor of Physiology, Royal Institution
Charles Darwin, F.R.S., naturalist
Thomas Graham, F.R.S., chemist, Master of the Mint
Leonard Horner, F.R.S., President of the Geological Society
John Lubbock, F.R.S., astronomer, mathematician, and banker
Charles Lyell, F.R.S., geologist
William Spottiswoode, F.R.S., mathematician and physicist.]

The Oxford "Protest Against the Prosecution of Professor Jowett" (4 March 1863)

[The "Protest" was published in the *Times* (4 Mar. 1863), 5. It was followed with 393 names of graduates of Oxford and members of the university, and included a number of Jowett's former pupils. Among the signatories were G. G. Bradley, headmaster of Marlborough; both G. C. Brodrick and W. H. Fremantle, who published *Judgments of the Judicial Committee of the Privy Council in Ecclesiastical Cases Relating to Doctrine and Discipline* (1865); Lewis Campbell, Jowett's biographer; John Earle, professor of Anglo-Saxon, Oxford; Frederic Harrison; Thomas Hughes, author of *Tom Brown's Schooldays*; Godfrey Lushington, the son of Stephen Lushington, Judge in the Court of Arches who condemned Williams and Wilson; F. D. Maurice; Herman Merivale (recently professor of political economy, Oxford); H. H. Milman, dean of St. Paul's; John Morley, successively editor of the *Fortnightly*, *Macmillan's*, and the *Pall Mall Gazette*; Francis Turner Palgrave, author of *The Golden Treasury*; J. Percival, headmaster of Clifton College; William Spottiswoode, the Queen's Printer; and Frederick Temple, one of the Essayists and headmaster of Rugby.]

Protest Against the Prosecution of Professor Jowett

WE, the undersigned Non-resident Graduates and Members of the University of Oxford, desire to draw public attention to the proceedings lately instituted against the Regius Professor of Greek in the Court of the Vice-Chancellor.

This Court has hitherto been almost exclusively occupied in determining cases of small debts between tradesmen and members of the University. It is now for the first time transformed into a tribunal for the punishment of heresy. Mr. Jowett, whose zeal and fidelity as a Professor and a College Tutor are undisputed, is the first person against whom the powers of the Court are invoked. He is not accused of any offence committed in either of his offices. He is charged with having expressed erroneous opinions in a Commentary published seven years ago in London, and in a contribution to another work published two years ago, also in London. A certain number of delegates, who are selected by the Proctors of each year, and who may even be appointed, as in the present case, after the institution of the proceedings, compose the Court of Appeal.

This jurisdiction may or may not exist. That question will be decided by the ordinary tribunals. We disclaim any desire to interfere with it, or to pass any judgment on the opinions imputed to Mr. Jowett; but, in the interests of policy and justice, we protest against this prosecution on the following grounds:—

(1.) Because its object is to drive from the University a man whose services Oxford has miserably rewarded, but can ill afford to lose.
(2.) Because the constitution and procedure of this particular tribunal are at once obsolete and oppressive. It may be put in motion by any person against any resident member of the University on account of any works published, or any opinions expressed, in any place or at any distance of time.
(3.) Because the institution of any Court of Heresy in the University must create feuds and suspicions, fatal to both social peace and to intellectual progress. [The names of the signatories follow.]

"Declaration on the Inspiration of the Word of God, and the Eternity of Future Punishment, by Clergymen of the United Church of England and Ireland," or the Oxford Declaration of the Clergy (1864)

[On 8 February 1864 Lord Westbury pronounced the acquittal of Williams and Wilson in their appeal to the Judicial Committee of the Privy Council. The next day Pusey wrote to Phillpotts of Exeter and followed that with a letter to Keble explaining how the decision affected the doctrine of plenary inspiration and the possibility of punishment for the reprobate as "everlasting" (Letter 215). He was also beginning another campaign in the press, abandoning the *Guardian*, the High Church weekly where he often published, in favor of the Low Church paper the *Record*. He wrote to Wilberforce and Gladstone about his concerns, organizing support around the two aspects of the issue—doctrinal matters, and the rivalry of church vs. state control over definitions of faith. H. P. Liddon, Pusey's biographer, records that on 21 February Wilberforce responded to Pusey, enclosing documents from two Oxfordshire clergy on both matters. One was from William Robert Fremantle, who had been instrumental in the Episcopal Manifesto, a proposal for a declaration on "the Divine authority of the Canonical Scriptures as being the Word of God, and in the certainty of the Everlasting Punishment of the wicked" (Liddon 1897, 4:53). The other enclosure was a draft memorial to the queen asking her to issue a commission to inquire into the powers and functions of the Judicial Committee. Wilberforce particularly asked Pusey to take up the former, to serve on a committee, and to "do your utmost to weld together for this purpose the two great sections of the Church, High and Low; and that at all events the protest and declaration should be numerously signed" (Liddon 1897, 4:53). Pusey wrote to the *Record* appealing for "one united action on the part of every clergyman and lay member of the Church," and one of the results was the consolidation of the relationship between Pusey and his cousin the evangelical leader Lord Shaftesbury that would be renewed in 1869 over the appointment of Temple to Exeter (Letters 223, 225).

On 25 February many of what Jowett called the "Country Clergy" (Letter 221), who had waited the required term and paid the required fee to be granted the M.A. and so were eligible to vote in Convocation, the large governing body of Oxford University, arrived to vote on changes in the examination statutes, general regulations governing requirements and examinations for degrees (Letter 221). After the meeting of Convocation, posters informed the clergy of the meeting in the Holywell Music Room concerning the decision in the Judicial Committee. The committee for the declaration, including Pusey, W. R. Fremantle as secretary, and George Anthony Denison, presented Pusey's rewording which the meeting approved and began to collect signatures. Subsequently it was printed and sent to the newspapers and to each of the 24,800 clergy in England and Ireland, importuning them to sign "for the love of God." The printed form of the declaration is a pamphlet with the names attached, consisting of an address from the committee to the bishops and archbishops, the declaration, and the printed names on 63 pages (Bodley 100 f. 143 [25]).]

Address to the Archbishops and Bishops of the United Church of England and Ireland

Most Reverend and Right Reverend Fathers in God,

We, the Members of the Committee appointed at a meeting held at Oxford to draw up a statement setting forth the clear and consistent teaching of the Church of England and Ireland on matters upon which such clearness and consistency of teaching have been gravely questioned, have now the honour to present to your Lordships a declaration of firm belief that the Church maintains without reserve or qualification the Inspiration and Divine Authority of the whole

Canonical Scriptures as not only containing but being the Word of God, and also teaches the eternal punishment of the wicked.

My Lords, we undertook the work entrusted to us under a sense of many and deep responsibilities; we were called upon to act with decision in matters of difficulty and importance which were heavily oppressing the minds of Churchmen, and we did not venture to issue the Declaration until we had obtained the counsel and sanction of a large number of the Clergy of England and Ireland.

We cannot draw our labours to a close without first of all expressing before your Lordships and the Clergy here assembled, that we are heartily thankful to ALMIGHTY GOD, because the task imposed upon us has been carried through to the end with perfect unanimity on our part, and because the weight of it has been greatly relieved by expressions of cordial assent and by hearty co-operation on the part of a large number of the Clergy who have affixed their signatures. We can assure your Lordships that large as this number is, it by no means represents the whole of those who unswervingly hold the several Articles of Faith, the truth of which this Declaration seeks to affirm. Beyond the public means of communication, we know through a large correspondence, that there are, beside the number of names appended to the Declaration, some thousands of the Clergy whose faith it equally expresses. They assure us they were deterred from signing it, not by any doubt as to the Faith of the Church of England or their own, but by various natural and legitimate considerations. Indeed, when we consider the novelty of the course which the necessity of the case suggested, in order to reassure the lay members of our Church of the faith of their Clergy, we have reason to be thankful to ALMIGHTY GOD for the great success with which He has been pleased to bless it.

We trust that the Declaration has had some force in removing the misgivings of many as to the authoritative teaching of the Church on matters of such vital moment to men's souls as the accepting or denying the Inspiration of the Holy Scriptures, and also the eternity of the punishment pronounced upon the cursed. We further trust, that as expressing the conviction of so large a body of the Clergy it will strengthen your Lordships' hands in any future measure which you may devise for guarding the Faith of the Church. As we commenced our work with humble prayer for Divine guidance, so we close it with fervent joy and thankfulness that we have been allowed to promote the glory of our LORD. The acceptance which this document has met with, affords an assurance that the Church of England can give to all her members throughout the length and breadth of the land a witness that the true Faith of CHRIST, which is her life, is upheld in her by her Divine LORD, and that her Clergy, who bind themselves to it, evince that obligation by a faithful, open, and unreserved acceptance of the doctrine of the Church as set forth in her Creeds, Articles, and other Formularies.

C. C. CLERKE, D.D., Archdeacon of Oxford, *Chairman.*
R. L. COTTON, D.D., Provost of Worcester College.
G. A. DENISON, M.A., Archdeacon of Taunton.

W. R. Fremantle, M.A., Rector of Claydon, *Secretary*.
F. K. Leighton, D.D., Warden of All Souls' College.
J. C. Miller, D.D., St. Martin's, Birmingham.
E. P. Pusey, D.D., Regius Professor of Hebrew.

We, the undersigned Presbyters and Deacons in Holy Orders of the Church of England and Ireland, hold it to be our bounden duty to the Church and to the souls of men, to declare our firm belief that the Church of England and Ireland, in common with the whole Catholic Church, maintains without reserve or qualification the Inspiration and Divine Authority of the whole Canonical Scriptures as not only containing but being the Word of God; and further teaches, in the words of our Blessed Lord, that the "punishment" of the "cursed," equally with the "life" of the "righteous," is "everlasting."

[This declaration is followed by 58 pages of signatories, or, according to Owen Chadwick, 10,906 names (1966–70, 1:84). Some printed versions include the following reply made by Archbishop Longley when he received the Declaration on 12 May 1864, along with five other bishops (*Guardian*, 18 May 1864, 476).]

The Archbishop of Canterbury answered the Oxford Declaration in the following statement:

Rev. and Dear Brethren,

We accept this Declaration as a renewed expression of your belief in those doctrines of the Church to which it refers. It is satisfactory to receive your assurance that there are some thousands of the Clergy who, agreeing with you in the substance of the Declaration, hesitated to sign it only by reason of its form and circumstances. This assurance strengthens our conviction that the Clergy of our Church will never be disposed to propagate opinions which tend to subvert the fundamental doctrines of Christianity.

We shall ever feel it to be our duty to maintain the authoritative teaching of the Church, humbly trusting that we may receive guidance from above, and be endued with strength and wisdom to promote the glory of God and the welfare of His Church through Jesus Christ our Lord.

[One copy at Lambeth Palace contains a letter from W. R. Fremantle to Stanley dated 26 March: "The Declaration speaks for itself. If it contravened the sentence of the Judicial Committee I for one could not have signed it. As an expression of individual opinion upon two most grave questions, which persons who are ignorant of the extent of the authority of the court might misunderstand to the immanent peril of their souls, I in common with a large number of the clergy to whom is committed the cure of souls and for whom we shall have to render an account at the day of Judgment, have felt it to be my duty for the love of God not only to sign the declaration but to take an active part in urging my brethren to do likewise" (Lambeth H 5155 /7). The publication of the declaration caused a new outbreak of pamphlets and letters to the editors. Legal opinions concerning the possibility that the clergy who signed were impeaching the judgment of the Judicial Committee and so of the queen in Council brought other legal opinions to the contrary. Pusey and F. D. Maurice carried on a public debate in the *Times* (Letters 229 and 232–36). It was well known that many thousands were signing the Declaration, and no doubt the impetus so generated had an impact on the April discussions in the Convocation of Canterbury and the final decision to approve synodical condemnation on 24 June.

In the Tait Papers in Lambeth Palace Library there are manuscript lists of all of the beneficed clergy in the Diocese of London who signed and who did not sign the Oxford Declaration, as well as Tait's personal summation of the data:

Number of Clergy in the Diocese of London		1,106
Number of Clergy who have signed		422
Number of Clergy who have not signed		684
Number of clergy in England (about)		22,509
Number of clergy in Ireland		2,296
		24,805
Number of clergy in England who signed	9,675	
Number of clergy in Ireland who signed	1,231	
	10,906	
Number who have not signed		13,899

Deans		
in England who signed		[8 out of 30]
York, Carlyle, Exeter, Peterborough, Gloucester, Lincoln (Dr. Jeune), Norwich, St. Asaph		
in Ireland		12
Oxford Heads who signed		13 [out of 24]
Cambridge Heads		3 [out of 16]
Oxford Professors		9 [out of 40]
Cambridge		none [out of 29]
[London] Rural Deans	who signed	8
	who did not sign	19

(Lambeth Palace Library, Tait Papers, MS. 291, fol. 305; fols. 310–345v)

Tait's calculations indicate the careful handling of these matters required by the ecclesiastical authorities as his decision to support or condemn is perhaps determined less by doctrine than by counting heads. He reported on these figures in detail to Convocation in the debate on the Synodical Condemnation (*Chronicle of Convocation* 21 June 1864, 1663–64).

Tait, Thirlwall, Stanley, and others repudiated the methods of collecting the signatures for the "melancholy Declaration" under the pressure of "a kind of moral torture," whereby signing "for the love of God" carried an unfair corollary: the imputation that not signing was a rejection of the love of God (*Guardian*, 27 Apr. 1864).

A parallel declaration of support and thanks to the archbishops of Canterbury and York for their dissenting voices in the decision of the Judicial Committee of the Privy Council garnered 137,000 lay signatures, and it was presented to the archbishops on 16 March 1864 (Davidson and Denham 1891, 1:318). For other discussions of the Declaration on the Inspiration of the Word of God see Stanley 1864; Liddon 1897, 4:47–62; Ellis 1980, 192–94; and Altholz 1994, 117–19.]

The Declaration of Students of the Natural and Physical Sciences
(16 April 1864 to May 1865)

[The Declaration on the Inspiration of the Word of God was a model for other declarations such as that begun by a group of London chemists on 16 April 1864 who by 21 April had 28 signatures when Christopher Wordsworth presented it in the lower House of Convocation (*Chronicle of Convocation* 1859–64:1864, 1577). When printed for general circulation, the final paragraph (given below) was omitted as being too closely directed toward the condemnation of *Essays and Reviews* in Convocation. The organizers were six London chemists associated with or students of the Royal College of Chemistry and from a variety of religious backgrounds: Alexander William Gillman, Herbert McLeod, John Stenhouse, Charles Edward Groves, David Howard, and Capel Henry Berger, with Berger very likely the chief instigator. A member of the London Plymouth Brethren, Berger organized the printing, collecting, and preservation of the documents and signed certificates, and his son presented copies to Cambridge and Oxford libraries (Brock and Macleod 1976, 61). Copies were sent to the members of the scientific societies of London (numbering about 5,000 people) but many reacted against the declaration as imposing a new article of faith or test of scientific and religious orthodoxy. The statement was a carefully worded and traditional expression of the "two-book" theory, the book of nature and the book of scripture, as set out in the seventeenth century by such writers as Thomas Browne in *Religio Medici* (1643). The "practical meaning" of this Declaration, as the *Saturday Review* observed, "was to give a general endorsement to the traditional interpretation of the book of Genesis," leaving "the Nicene Creed and the Apostles' Creed . . . wholly unaffected" (24 Sept. 1864, 396). The flat rejection of the declaration as "a new verbal test of religious partisanship" by Sir John Herschel, the astronomer, was widely circulated in the *Times* (20 Sept. 1864) and elsewhere, and the mathematician Augustus De Morgan called it "an awkward attempt to saturate sophism with truism" (*Athenaeum*, 19 Nov. 1864). When the Declaration was published in May 1865 for twopence, the names of 717 scientists were attached, including Philip Henry Gosse (who belonged to the same Plymouth Brethren group in London as Capel Berger), Sir David Brewster, James Prescott Joule, and the geologist, Adam Sedgwick. The signatories included, according to Brock and MacLeod's careful calculations, 65 out of 605 Fellows of the Royal Society, only about one out of nine who published scientific work. In many respects the controversy engendered by this Declaration was more widespread than the comment elicited by the Scientists' Testimonial. The Declaration pushed debate about *Essays and Reviews* further in the direction of arguments about the compartmentalization of knowledge and the nature of free inquiry, as well as the possible grounds for the reconciliation of supposed differences between science and religion. For a detailed examination of the context and signatories see Brock and Macleod 1976.]

The Declaration of Students of the Natural and Physical Sciences

WE, the undersigned Students of the Natural Sciences, desire to express our sincere regret, that researches into scientific truth are perverted by some in our own times into occasion for casting doubt upon the Truth and Authenticity of the Holy Scriptures. We conceive that it is impossible for the Word of God, as written in the book of nature, and God's Word written in Holy Scripture, to contradict one another, however much they appear to differ. We are not forgetful that Physical Science is not complete, but is only in a condition of progress, and that at present our finite reason enables us only to see as through a glass darkly [1 Cor. 13:12]; and we confidently believe, that a time will come when the two records will be seen to agree in every particular. We cannot but deplore that Natural Science should be looked upon with suspicion by many who do not make a study of it, merely on account of the unadvised manner in which some are placing it in opposition to Holy Writ. We believe that it is the duty of every Scientific Student to investigate nature simply for the purpose of elucidating truth, and that if he finds that some of his results appear to be in contradiction to the Written Word, or rather to his own *interpretations* of it, which may be erroneous, he should not presumptuously affirm that his own conclusions must be right, and the statements of Scripture wrong; rather, leave the two side by side till it shall please God to allow us to see the manner in which they may be reconciled; and, instead of insisting upon the seeming differences between Science and the Scriptures, it would be as well to rest in faith upon the points in which they agree.

WE therefore pray, that the Bishops and Clergy in Convocation assembled, and of the Church of England, will do all in their power to maintain a harmonious alliance between Physical Science and Revealed Religion.

The Archbishops' Pastoral Letters
(1864)

[A pastoral letter is a formal communication from a bishop to the clergy and laity of his diocese, taking the form of letter sent to all clergy to be read from the pulpit on a specified Sunday. The pastoral letter of the archbishop of Canterbury, Charles Thomas Longley, dated 14 March 1864 from his London residence at Lambeth Palace, discusses the trials and appeals of Rowland Williams and H. B. Wilson. He declares that he supports both their convictions in the Court of Arches as well as his own position in the Judicial Committee where he dissented only from the acquittal of Williams and Wilson concerning their position on the inspiration of the Bible. Of course Longley is justifying himself to his clergy and people after the fact. He could not offer a minority report in the Judicial Committee stating why he dissented on inspiration but agreed with acquittal on the other charges. It is a problematic line for him to pursue, given the fact that he had been a member of the Judicial Committee. In effect he is breaking rank and proprieties here in justifying a dissenting opinion for which he was one of the legal judges. He is declaring his opposition to one aspect of the acquittal as were all of the clergy who were simultaneously signing the Oxford Declaration. Stanley's review of Longley's and Thomson's pastorals makes precisely this point: "The two Primates . . . have given some countenancy to the insubordination of their flocks against the constituted authority of the Church"; while Longley's position "if consistently followed out, would place the Church of England outside the law, and in opposition to the law. . . . The archbishop is himself *extra legem* when he takes upon himself to assert that doctrines are necessarily held by the Church of England, which it has been expressly decided by the Sovereign and Head of the Church, acting upon the advice of a Committee of Councillors of whom the Archbishop was himself one, are not necessary to be so held" (1864, 282). On 21 June 1864, during debate in the Upper House of Convocation on the Synodical Condemnation, Longley went much further in defending himself than in his pastoral letter by an extreme assertion that fulfilled Stanley's fears: "I do not acquiesce in the terms of the judgment, and therefore I am not responsible for the words [of acquittal]" (*Chronicle of Convocation* 1859–64: 21 Apr. 1864, 1666). See also Letters 243–45.]

Charles Thomas Longley, Archbishop of Canterbury
A Pastoral Letter (1864)

Brethren—

I was in nowise called upon to attempt any justification of inspiration, seeing that the Church had not thought fit to prescribe one. . . . [But] the Church authoritatively declares Holy Scripture to be identical with all those Canonical Books . . . that it is "The Word of God," and "God's Word written." . . . By the term "Canonical Books" is meant, Books which lay down a rule of faith authoritatively. . . . On examining the charge . . . brought against Mr. Wilson, I find an assertion on his part, that in what he calls the "pivot Article of the Church" *viz* the Sixth Article of Belief, the expression "Word of God" does not appear, and he would seem to infer hence, that the Church never calls Holy Scripture by that name; that this term is not applied collectively to the Books of the Old and New Testament. But in the Twentieth Article, Holy Scripture is styled "God's Word written;" it is spoken of as "Holy Writ;" phrases corresponding exactly with the term Holy Scripture in the Sixth Article, in which it is declared to be co-extensive with the Canonical Books of the Old and New Testament, and in the Ordering of Priests the Church styles the Bible "the Word of God." The term Canonical as I have stated before is applied to all the contents of the Bible except the Apocryphal Books, denotes that they have the property of a Canon; *i.e.* "regulative," furnishing a Rule of Faith, competent to be applied to the establishing of doctrine. Thus, according to the mind of the Church, the terms "Holy Scripture," "the Canonical Books of the Old and New Testament," "the Word of God," and "God's Word written," appear to be equivalent.

How far is the language of Mr. Wilson reconcilable with that of the Church on these points? (4–5) . . . The view I have taken of the claim which the whole of the Holy Scripture has to be taken as the Word of God cannot interfere with the right of discussing questions as to various readings, or the genuineness of a disputed text; for this is no more than to argue that a given text or reading is not a part of any Canonical Book. But such an argument on the part of a clergyman is a widely different thing from his assertion that a portion of the Bible which he has acknowledged to belong to a Canonical Book is not the Word of God. Without any such latitude as this, there is ample room for fair criticism; but criticism in the case of a minister of our Church must have its limits; inasmuch as he has bound himself to adhere to the plain meaning of the articles and formularies. You will, I am persuaded, feel convinced that it cannot be agreeable to the mind of the Church that you should transgress these limits. For the Church prescribes order and not confusion; but what would not be the amount of confusion if it were left to each minister to proclaim from his pulpit which portion of the Bible was the Word of God and which not? And would not such licence on the part of the clergy prove the bondage of the laity, who would thus be left without redress against such a dangerous innovation? (6–7)

Nor do I conceive that the Church has any more sure warrant for belief in the eternal happiness of the saved than it has for belief in the eternal suffering of the lost. . . . There was so much obscurity in the forms of expression used by Mr. Wilson [that the passages cited could not sustain the charge]. . . . Our certainty of never-ending bliss for penitent believers is gone, if the word bears not the same signification [for] the everlasting suffering of the lost" (10–12).

(Charles Thomas Longley. *A Pastoral Letter Addressed to the Clergy and Laity of his Province by Charles Thomas, Archbishop of Canterbury*, 1864)

William Thomson, Archbishop of York
A Pastoral Letter (1864)

[A similar form was used by William Thomson, archbishop of York, for expressing his reasons for dissenting from the decision of the Judicial Committee. His pastoral letter, dated April 1864, was published first in the *Guardian* (11 May 1864, 461–62), and separately as a pamphlet. Like Longley in Convocation, Thomson expressed himself more strongly in public addresses, as when he claimed to the Church Missionary Society on 2 May 1864 that although the judgment of the Judicial Committee has "some colour from authority," true authority lay elsewhere: "The real authority of the Church of England is the voice of the clergy of the Church of England," a reference to the clergy signatures on the Declaration on the Inspiration of the Word of God and the Synodical Condemnation (*Guardian*, 11 May 1864).]

Brethren—

THE RESULT of the proceedings before the Privy Council in the two cases of the "Bishop of Salisbury *v.* Williams" and "Fendall *v.* Wilson," has caused great perplexity and dismay throughout the Church. . . .

My position, as a member of the Privy Council, necessarily limits me in discussing what is inaccurately called the Judgment. I do not indeed admit the doctrine which has been advanced, that the clergy in general are forbidden by the Oath of Supremacy to discuss the reasons of the Committee of Privy Council for the advice it has tendered to the Crown. Those who take this view are perhaps unaware that the Judgment (so called) which has excited so much discussion is an entirely different document from the Report to the Crown, upon which the real Judgment is founded; that the so-called Judgment is a statement for the guidance of the suitors and the public of the grounds upon which the advice to the Crown will be based, which statement never reaches the Crown at all; and that the Report to the Crown happily omits the grounds of the advice, and confines itself to advising briefly what the Judgment should be. . . . The clergy are happily not placed under the intolerable restraint that a number of theological statements, drawn up in fact by a committee with a majority of eminent laymen, and partly repudiated by two of the three professed theologians that compose the minority, are removed from the sphere of theological discussion and placed under the protection of the Oath of Supremacy. If a Committee of the Privy Council of the Queen imparts to the suitors and to the public the grounds of the advice it means to tender, the public and the suitors will form an opinion as to whether her Majesty is likely to be rightly or wrongly advised. . . . And whilst the Oath of Supremacy binds us to regard the Judgment of the Crown as final and decisive between the parties, it does not impose on the clergy the distasteful duty of imputing to the Crown propositions or reasoning which their own studies enable them to recognize as defective, which may happen to be corrected in some future case, which emanate not from the Crown but from responsible servants of her Majesty, and which are not even submitted to the Crown after being delivered to the public (2, 6–8). . . .

These remarks seem necessary, because, in spite of the explicit disclaimer in the "Judgment," many persist in treating it as an examination and acquittal of the whole work called *Essays and Reviews*.

There are only two points in the "Judgment" to which these remarks do not apply, and about which after all these limitations the mind of the Church is reasonably disquieted. I mean the inspiration and authority of Holy Scripture. and the eternity of the punishment of the wicked.

Upon the former of these points, the authority of Scripture, I must not shrink from saying that a doctrine has found some countenance from the "Judgment," which no article or formulary of any Church whatever has before adopted—namely, that the Bible is called the Word of God, not because it is, but because it contains, the Word of God. . . . One appellant then maintains that the Bible is not the Word of God, and the other that it is the word of devout men. These two doctrines are opposed not merely to one or more statements of our Church, but to those statements which are the very foundation of its teaching. . . . The Church has laid down no theory of inspiration; she has always had in her bosom teachers of at least two different theories. But she does lay down that the declarations of Scripture are intelligible, are self-consistent, are of supreme authority. If the Bible is not the Word of God, but contains the Word of God as the greater contains the less, every one of these predicates falls to the ground. There is no touchstone which shall test for us whether a given passage is part of the Word of God or of the word of man therewith entangled: and so we can no longer depend on understanding the will of God from the Bible. Passages may admit of a contrary interpretation if some are and some are not of divine origin; and therefore the Bible would cease to be self-consistent. And that book can no longer be of supreme authority in controversies of faith; we should either be without an authority, from our inability to discern and disentangle the divine and human portions. or the supreme authority would be that power which claimed to teach us what was divine and what was human (15–18). . . .

The charge against one appellant on the subject of eternal punishment did not seem to me to be sustained. On the one hand, the Church, in adopting the word everlasting to express the word that may also be rendered eternal, has cut off, for all purposes of law, some metaphysical speculations to which the original word has been subjected. Everlasting must mean lasting for ever, never coming to an end. The Church of England believes in a life that lasts for ever for the good, and in an everlasting punishment for the wicked.

But, on the other hand, the appellant explained to the Court that the "all" of whom he predicated salvation at the last did not include all men without exception; that he divided men into three classes—the utterly reprobate, the good, and a middle class of undeveloped or "germinal souls;" and it was this middle class whose characters at the hour of death did not mark them either as good or bad, of whom he hoped that they might hereafter be developed into something higher, and might be made fit for the bosom of the Father. Although this was not a formal retraction of anything he had advanced, yet as the words employed would bear that construction, with a little allowance for incautious writing, it did not seem to be right to inflict a heavy penalty for maintaining that all would be saved, in the face of a declaration that he meant "all the good and all the undeveloped," to the exclusion of the reprobate. The charge fell to the ground if the writer's own explanation was to be taken. . . .

I beseech my brethren of the clergy to beware of exceeding or departing from the statements of Scripture upon this awful subject. We are in the hands of a just God, who has revealed in Holy Writ His way of dealing with His creatures so far as we need to know it for a guide to our faith and a motive to practical duties. Let us rest in that revelation. (21–23)

(William Thomson. *A Pastoral Letter to the Clergy and Laity of the Province of York by William, Lord Bishop of York, Primate of England and Metropolitan*, 1864)

[The precise distinction concerning good or bad advice upon which Thomson bases his argument derives from the legal view of Sir Hugh Cairns, who was solicited by Pusey to comment on the legal force of the judgment of the Judicial Committee. Cairns and Sir Roundell Palmer, the attorney-general, delivered their reply that Pusey published as *Case as to the Legal Force of the Judgment of the Judicial Committee* (1864). Thomson argues that the judgment of Lord Westbury is merely "a statement for the guidance of the suitors and the public of the grounds upon which the advice to the Crown will be based" and that the real "Judgment" is the decision of the Crown to support or dismiss the summary report submitted to her. In his review of the Pastorals in the *Edinburgh Review*, Stanley comments:

> Some colour has been given to this extraordinary doctrine by the tenor of a legal opinion emanating from the very high authority of Sir Roundell Palmer and Sir Hugh Cairns, who appear to have held that, although it might be a breach of the Oath of Supremacy to impugn the Queen's Order in Council, the reasons assigned by the Lords of the Judicial Committee for their Report are not entitled to the same measure of deference. So that the Church and the country would be left in this absurd predicament—that the formal judgment of the Supreme Head of the Church in England should be unassailable, but that the grounds on which that judgment rests may be impugned and rejected altogether! What would the Archbishop have said if the judgment of the Lords had gone the other way? If the appellants, for example, had been acquitted on technical grounds alone, while the opinions expressed in their writings had been condemned with all the rigour of archiepiscopal censures: should we then have been told that the decision of the Crown was alone final and decisive, and that the reasoning by which that advice was justified may be set aside by the

private judgment of any individual? (1864, 284).

Stanley then demonstrates how such a view cannot be supported on the basis of the Privy Council Act in making a "Report or Recommendation" that is normally called "the Judgment." He quotes the actual words of the decision of the queen in Council to adopt and sanction the recommendation of the Judicial Committee. Stanley then addresses the manner in which the judgment of the Judicial Committee is reached. It is not "the production of any single hand" but is "revised by every member of the Board; in this very case of 'Essays and Reviews,' repeated meetings of the Committee were held for this purpose, at which the two Archbishops were present. The question is not what are the individual opinions of the several members of the Committee, but what is the collective advice to be tendered by the Committee as a body to the Sovereign. This it is that gives to the Judgments of the Privy Council their high authority. In no other Court in this realm are the Judgments prepared with the same amount of caution and collective weight; and to leave that weight unimpaired, it is expressly provided by one of the standing rules of the Council, that 'no publication is afterwards to be made by any man how the particular voices and opinions went'—a rule of the greatest value to a tribunal thus constituted" (1864, 285). Stanley had perhaps consulted Tait concerning some of these details or got the information from Henry Reeves, the clerk of the Privy Council and editor of his article in the *Edinburgh*. They would otherwise have been difficult for him to ascertain (see "Trials and Appeals"). His telling attack on the premises of Thomson's argument also had wide circulation in the *Edinburgh*, but because it was not published until well after the Pastorals were issued in March and April, it had no impact on the Synodical Condemnation that was issued in June.]

The Synodical Condemnation by the Convocation of Canterbury (21–22 June 1864)

[In the aftermath of the acquittal of Williams and Wilson by the Judicial Committee of the Privy Council, clerical members of the Lower House of the Convocation of Canterbury demanded synodical action to redress what they saw as a betrayal of the church by the highest secular court in England, a betrayal concurred in by Bishop Tait and the two archbishops who sat on the Judicial Committee for the appeals. Similar demands for censure were made in the Upper House of bishops. After extensive debate through the meetings in April 1864 the Upper House resolved to set up a committee, comprised of the archbishop of Canterbury and the rest of the house of bishops to report an the proposed condemnation (see the discussion in "Trials and Appeals"). Wilberforce's motion of synodical condemnation followed upon the receiving and adopting of the formal report that had been printed and circulated earlier to the bishops. It was printed in the *Chronicle of Convocation* (1859–64:1864, Session 66, 1656–59). The report, set in the format of a formal motion, was divided into five sections (Roman numerals) each with sub-sections, arranged by the Greek alphabet. Under several of the headings specific passages from *Essays and Reviews* were cited, as listed below, with references here to the corresponding paragraph number in the specified essay.]

THAT THE BOOK contains false and dangerous statements, and reasonings at variance with the teaching of the Church of England, and deserving the condemnation of the Synod.

The grounds for their judgment are as follow:—

I. They consider that a tendency to unsettle belief in the revelation of the Gospel pervades the book, especially in the following points:—

α. They are of the opinion that the arguments and assertions of the third Essay [by Baden Powell] deny, by necessary consequence, the supernatural origin of Christianity; that they strike at the root of all revealed religion, and are irreconcilable with the very existence of the Church of Christ.

β. The possibility of miracles, as historical facts, and the purpose of miracles, as evidences of the truth of revelation, appear to your committee to be absolutely denied in the following among other passages:

"To conclude. . . . inculcated" [Baden Powell, ¶s 132–133].

"What is alleged. . . . commonly discredited" [Baden Powell, ¶s 29–31].

The committee regret to add that the argument of the first Essay [by Frederick Temple, ¶33], by denying the probability of the recognition of the Divinity of our Lord in the more matured age of the world, appears to them to involve a similar denial of all miracles as historical facts: for it is asserted that "the faculty of faith has turned inwards, and cannot now accept any outer manifestations of the truth of God" [Frederick Temple, ¶33].

γ. In the second Essay [by Rowland Williams] the committee notice a prevailing attempt to explain away supernatural agency, even when its presence is directly asserted in Holy Scripture. That which is explicitly declared to be the immediate intervention of God is here attributed to the mere action of the human mind. The following, amongst other passages, appears to involve directly this false teaching:—

"When the fierce ritual of Syria . . . than sacrifice" [Rowland Williams, ¶10].

The fourth Essay [by H. B. Wilson] contains the same false teaching in its suggestion that the instances of supernatural interference recorded in the Bible may be safely rejected as facts, provided that we retain the ideas which would have been awakened by the knowledge of such alleged facts, if they had been real.

"The ideologian. . . . particular events" [H. B. Wilson, ¶75].

Further, it is suggested that this principle may be applied even to the historical record of the life of our blessed Lord, and that liberty must be left to all as to the extent in which they may apply it—

"But it by no means follows. . . . reasonably exercised" [H. B. Wilson, ¶119].

δ. As respects the Prophecies of the Old Testament, it appears to the committee that prophecy, in the sense of "literal prognostication" [Rowland Williams, ¶13] or the direct prediction of future events, is greatly disparaged, if not absolutely denied, in this volume.

After the recital of several particulars, it is said—

"When so vast an induction. . . . Neckar" [Rowland Williams, ¶14].

"Why he should add. . . . requires proof" [Rowland Williams, ¶15].

"There are many quotations. . . . our own day" [Benjamin Jowett, ¶73].

II. Besides this general teaching, which the committee consider as striking at the root of all revelation, they have found frequent contradictions of the particular truths of the Christian faith, or insinuations of their falsehood. These they cannot wholly pass over; but as they understand that the duty imposed on them is to advise on the liability of the book to Synodical censure, and not to enumerate all its errors, they will name only a few of those which appear to them to be amongst the most dangerous.

They observe throughout the book a mode of treating the Holy Scripture which subverts the authority it has always possessed in the Church as the inspired Word of God.

α. Thus the tendency of the last Essay [by Benjamin Jowett] is to teach that the statements of Holy Scripture are not to be accepted as conveying what the words themselves appear plainly to convey, but that allowance is to be made for a rhetorical element even in those passages in which the final issues of infinite justice are specified with more than usual distinctness.

This allegation appears to be justified by the following passage:—

"When we pass. . . . altogether a reality" [Benjamin Jowett, ¶65].

β. Thus, again, they find it laid down that there is in man a verifying faculty resident in himself, by virtue of which he may reject such portions of Holy Scripture as may appear to him incredible or wrong—

"Again, on the side of external criticism. . . . law of harmony" [Rowland Williams, ¶28].

The following passage affords a practical example of the proposed exercise of this assumed verifying faculty in reference not merely to narratives or precepts, but to a most important matter of doctrine:—

"First, if our traditions. . . . every man a liar" [H. B. Wilson, ¶10].

The following startling passage, in attempting to reconcile the exercise of this faculty with the teaching of our own Articles [of Religion], shows how large is the licence which is here claimed:—

"Under the terms of the. . . . of many events" [H. B. Wilson, ¶38].

γ. Again, it appears to be distinctly affirmed that the Evangelists and Apostles never intimate that a supernatural gift of inspiration was bestowed upon them, nor claim for themselves immunity from error in their writings:—

"Nor for any of the higher. . . . error or infirmity" [Benjamin Jowett, ¶15].

δ. Beyond this, a direct charge of inexactness in recording our Lord's words is brought against St. John, the other three Gospels being held to "embody more exact traditions of what He actually said than the fourth does;" and it is further intimated that an "admixture of legendary matter or embellishment in their narratives" is present in the four Gospels [H. B. Wilson, ¶21 and note].

III. Again, your committee consider that a private opinion upon the mysterious subject of the issues of "the great adjudication," which is at variance with the words of Holy Scripture, with the language of at least one of the creeds, and with the words of the Commination Service, is set forth in the following passage:

"The Christian Church can only tend. . . . according to his Will" [H. B. Wilson, ¶81].

IV. Nor are the highest doctrines of the faith exempt from this erroneous treatment. Thus, in speaking of the Holy Trinity, the second Essayist [Rowland Williams] applies the term Person only to God the Father, to the exclusion of the Son and the Holy Ghost. His words are—

"Being, becoming . . . and Spirit" (Rowland Williams, ¶32].

Nor is this an accidental opposition, for he says again—

"The Divine consciousness or wisdom . . . image of the Father" [Rowland Williams, ¶32].

In these passages, which stand in immediate connection, it seems to be clearly intimated that Christ was a Person only in His humanity, in place of the true doctrine that Christ, being a Divine Person from all eternity, took in time the manhood into God.

V. Further, your committee consider the fourth Essay [by H. B. Wilson] to advance the proposition that men may, as the condition of being invested with the office of teachers in the Church, subscribe to articles of religion without believing them to be true [¶s 36, 40]. This your committee judge to be a false and immoral position, sanctioning dishonesty in making the most solemn engagements, by claiming for the subscribers to articles the right either to teach that which they do not believe, or to teach the contrary of that to the truth of which they have declared their assent.

On all which grounds your committee report that this book does, in their judgment, merit the condemnation of this Synod.

(*Chronicle of Convocation* 1859–64: 21 June 1864, Session 66, 1656–59)

[After lengthy debate at the April and June 1864 meetings of Convocation, the report was received and approved, allowing the bishop of Oxford (Samuel Wilberforce) to move the following resolution on 22 June 22 1864:]

That the Upper House of Convocation, having received and adopted the report of the committee of the whole house appointed by them to examine the volume entitled *Essays and Reviews*, invite the Lower House to concur with them in the following judgement:—"That this Synod, having appointed committees of the Upper and Lower Houses to examine and report upon the volume entitled *Essays and Reviews*, and the said committees having severally reported thereon, doth hereby synodically condemn the said volume, as containing teaching contrary to the doctrine received by the United Church of England and Ireland, in common with the whole Catholic Church of Christ."

Chronicle of Convocation 1859–64: 21–22 June 1864, 1655, 1657, and 1683.

[The resolution was seconded by the bishop of Gloucester and was "agreed to—dissentient, the Bishops of London and Lincoln." The motion was then sent to the Lower House where, on a motion of George Anthony Denison to concur, making the condemnation the act of the entire synod, it was passed after three days of debate. Pusey and others brought forward the implications of this Synodical Condemnation during the controversy over Temple's appointment as bishop of Exeter in 1869 (Letter 317).]

A Subscription for Henry Bristow Wilson
(1866)

[In 1866 repairs were urgently needed in the Parish Church of Great Staughton, Huntingdonshire, where Henry Bristow Wilson had been appointed in 1850 and where he spent the remainder of his life after the trial and appeal resulting from *Essays and Reviews*. At the time of his prosecution in the Court of Arches his parishioners rallied round him, so that the local newspaper, *St. Neot's Chronicle*, reported: "We understand much sympathy is expressed by the parishioners with the Rev. H. B. Wilson in his present position in the Ecclesiastical courts, and confident hopes are entertained that he will be enabled successfully to resist his prosecutors" (8: No. 349 [1 Mar. 1862]: 1). In 1866 Wilson's friends, prompted by his long-time friend and defender, R. B. Kennard, circulated a subscription, first for the costs of the repairs to the church building, and then, more generally, as a testimonial to Wilson for his contribution to "English Theology." The subscription was circulated in December 1866 as a single sheet. A copy is inserted in

Baden Powell's copy of *Essays and Reviews* in the Bodleian Library, shelfmark Baden Powell 122.]

December, 1866

FRIENDS of the Rev. H. B. WILSON, B.D., finding that the expense of restoring his Parish Church at Great Staughton will be about £300 more than the sum already subscribed, are desirous of taking this opportunity of testifying to their regard for him by forming a Special List of Subscribers to be presented to him as an expression of their appreciation of the great services which he has rendered to the cause of true Religion and sound learning; more particularly by his Bampton Lectures, 1851 (which, through his exposition of the principles of "Christian Communion," and of the true ideal of a National Church, have added a gift of lasting value to English Theology); by his contribution to the "Oxford Essays," of 1857, and to the "Essays and Reviews," of 1860; and, above all, by "the masterly, yet dignified and pathetic, argument with which he pleaded for his own freedom, and for the freedom of the English Church" (see *Edinburgh Review*, July 1864, p. 271), before the Privy Council in the "Essays and Review" [*sic*] Case, 1863.

The General Subscription List for re-roofing the Church and restoration of the interior is given below (the restoration of the external walls and windows having been principally provided by the Church Rate).

General List

D. Onslow, Esq. Staughton House	£	150
Mr. Duberly, Gaynes Hall		50
Captain Duberly		250
Miss Duberly		25
Rev. H. B. Wilson		70
[and seven others]		
	£	605

The following Subscriptions have been already given for this SPECIAL LIST and further Subscriptions to it will be received by the Dean of Westminster [A. P. Stanley], The Deanery, Westminster S. W., the Rev. R. B. Kennard, Marnhull Rectory, Blandford, or by W. Henry Domville, Esq., 6 New Square, Lincoln's Inn, London, W. C. to the latter of whom it is requested letters may be addressed and cheques or post office orders may be made payable.

Special List

Thos. H. Bastard, Esq. £	5	Sir John Lubbock, Bart. £	5
Charles Buxton, Esq. M. P.	10	Rev. Henry Mills	1
A Clergyman	2	E. V. Neale, Esq.	5
E. Charles, Esq.	2	Rev. R. J. Simpkinson	1
W. H. Domville, Esq.	5	Very Rev. A. P. Stanley	5
Captain Harnham, R. N.	10	W. Unwin, Esq.	1
H. Huth, Esq.	5	E. P. Wolstoneholm, Esq.	2.2
Rev. Prof. Jowett	10	John Westlake, Esq.	10
Rev. R. H. Johnson	5	Others	1.15
Rev. R. B. Kennard	10	A Widow's Mite	3

The Rugby Testimonial for Temple

[On 26 October 1869 the Rugby Testimonial was presented to Temple in appreciation for his contribution to the life of Rugby school and town.]

On Thursday afternoon [26 Oct. 1869] a number of gentlemen of Rugby waited upon the Rev. Dr. Temple, at the School-house, to present to the rev. gentleman an address which had been signed by many townspeople, of all ranks and classes. The deputation consisted of the following gentlemen:—The Rev. Canon Moultrie, Rector; the Rev. T. F. Collins, Vicar of New Bilton; General Younghusband, Mr. W. S. H. Fitzroy, Colonel Vicars, the Rev. C. T. Arnold, the Rev. P. Bowden Smith, the Rev. C. B. Hutchinson, Mr. T. N. Hutchinson, Mr. Maude, Mr. Kitchener, Mr. Trott, Mr. Edmunds, Mr. Elkington, Mr. Markham, Mr. W. Gilbert, Mr. S. Garratt, and Mr. T. C. Lewis.

The Rev. Canon Moultrie said,—Dr. Temple, in presenting to you the address with which this deputation is charged, I wish to say on my own part as little as possible. From the signatures affixed to it you will perceive that it represents the sentiments entertained towards yourself by a very large number of persons belonging respectively to every social class in Rugby, and holding among themselves many different shades of opinion; nor have the projectors of the address endeavoured to increase the already large number of signatures by qualifying the expression of those sentiments, so as to render it, in existing circumstances, meaningless. Neither, as an evidence of personal feeling towards yourself, will you, I think, be displeased to learn that, numerous in all classes as are those who concur in this manifestation of perfect confidence in you as a man, a Christian, and a Bishop-Elect of the Church of England, of no class have the members come forward so eagerly to bear their part in it as that of the labourers and mechanics. If we had taken steps to circulate the document actively among them, I believe that scarcely one of their names would have failed to appear among the signatures. I will now, with your permission, read the address:—

To the Rev. Frederick Temple, D.D., Bishop-Designate of Exeter.
Reverend Sir,—

We, the undersigned inhabitants of Rugby, desire to offer our congratulations on the honour which our Most Gracious Majesty has been pleased to confer upon you by appointing you to the See of Exeter. At the same time we cannot but express the regret we feel at the severance of the tie which has for so many years connected you with our great school and town. Under your able superintendence Rugby School has maintained the foremost place among the public schools of England, while both school and town are alike indebted to the judgment, firmness, and enlightened liberality of your character, as well as to the Christian charity, benevolence, and philanthropy of your every-day life. Untiring energy and determined perseverance have enabled yourself and all who have come within the sphere of your influence to carry on the great work of social progress in various ways, to the general benefit of all classes of the community.

We rejoice to think that you leave us only at the call of duty to occupy a position of more extended responsibility in the ministry of the Church to which you are so warmly attached, and which you have so faithfully served. That you will carry to your new duties the same zeal, integrity, Christian liberality, enlightened toleration, and earnest piety which we have admired in you here we cannot doubt, and we earnestly hope and pray that the Almighty God will bless your future endeavours to do Him service, for His dear Son, Jesus Christ's sake.

John Moultrie, Rector of Rugby, and Hon. Canon of Worcester Cathedral.

About 200 signatures of all classes in Rugby were attached to the address.

The Rev. Dr. Temple said,—Mr. Moultrie and gentlemen, I cannot say much in answer to all you have said, or in answer to the address; because, although an address at such a time is usually called one of congratulation, I cannot say that it is a great matter of congratulation with me that I should be receiving an address from my fellow-townsmen on the occasion of my going away from them. It is to me a very real wrench, for certainly I do not think any other man could have met with more generosity or more kindness than I have received from my fellow-townsmen and all who know me here in Rugby during the 12 years I have been at the head of Rugby School. I cannot remember one instance of any person belonging to the town saying an unkind word to me, or an unkind thing about me. Wherever I have been, and whenever I have met my fellow-townsmen, I have always found the most generous construction placed upon everything I did. I have had a hearty and warm appreciation of every effort I have made in any way to serve the interests of the town, and I have found the most entire willingness to believe that if I made mistakes they were honest ones, and were those of a conscientious man, who cannot always do what is right, although he may do his very best to see it and to do it. I can assure you it is with very great reluctance, and only from a feeling of duty, that I consented to leave here at all, and when at first the Prime Minister asked if I should be willing to accept a bishopric, I answered that, though I thought it to be my duty to accept it if it was offered to me, yet I should be glad to remain where I was while the energy was in me to do the work, and afterwards to retire to some quiet country living, in which I might pass the rest of my days. I said this because I felt it very warmly, and, as a considerable interval elapsed before the offer was made, I had hopes that Mr. Gladstone had reconsidered the whole matter, and I should remain here. But when the offer was made, I thought I was bound to go, and I knew many who thought I was wanted elsewhere. I thought it my duty to take the position to which I was called, both by the authorities of the State and by the number of people who seemed to think I should be more useful there than here. But in doing so I don't expect again to have such a thoroughly enjoyable 12 years as I have had here. I know I shall meet with many kind friends, for I have many such in Devon now, which is to me an old county, in which I passed my childhood. I shall meet with many friends, but I don't expect I shall meet with the same complete happiness of life I have had here. It is, of course, impossible that I should have close around me those whose hearts are open to me as mine is open to them; to have constantly working with me men bound by ties of the warmest friendship and closest intimacy, and to have the most friendly relations with all my neighbours on every side. Here I have never once met with misconstruction, and it is too much to expect, nay, it is impossible, that this should be my lot hereafter. I need hardly tell you that wherever I go I shall not forget Rugby, and all the kindness I have received, and which has brought you here to-day. I shall not forget that I have been accompanied by such very good wishes from men of all ranks, not excepting those whose good wishes all my life I have felt as if I could value more than any other, the good wishes of the poor; and I hope that when you can give me nothing more than good wishes, those good wishes may still take the form sometimes of prayer to God, that I may be helped by Him to do my work elsewhere, as you have helped me to do my work here.

(*Times* 30 Oct. 1869, 5; reprinted from the *Rugby Advertiser*)

Petitions and Protests against the Appointment of Frederick Temple as Bishop of Exeter

[Beginning in October 1869 with the announcement of Temple's appointment to the See of Exeter, there began a series of protests, petitions, and condemnations, issued by individuals and by various groups of concerned clergy and lay people. Many letters were sent on the letterhead of the "Committee for Opposing the

Appointment of the Reverend Dr. Temple to the See of Exeter" of which Bishop W. J. Trower (subdean of Exeter) was the chairman, and for which E. B. Pusey was active in helping it organize. They prepared "A Petition to the Primates and Bishops of England against the Consecration of Dr. Temple as Bishop of Exeter."

John W. Burgon, for instance, had printed an eight-page "Protest Against Dr. Temple's Consecration to the Office of a Bishop in the Church of Christ," dated 12 November 1869, in which he called the proposed consecration "so great a scandal and calamity" (BL, MS. Add. 44,423 [Gladstone Papers], fols. 85–88). A "Second Protest" of eight pages was published by Burgon on 4 December 1869 (fols. 267–70). A "Memorial" from the High Church association, the English Church Union, was sent to Wilberforce on 8 December 1869. It consisted of a printed document from the members of 82 branches of the Church Union and was addressed to the archbishop of Canterbury protesting Temple's appointment and election. Another document is a printed protest dated 14 October 1869 by George Anthony Denison, a High Church defender of orthodoxy.]

"Pro Deo et Ecclesia"
To the Very Rev. Dean, and the Rev. the Chapter,
of the Cathedral Church of Exeter
The Memorial of the Undersigned, GEORGE ANTHONY DENISON, M.A.
Vicar of East Brent, Archdeacon of Taunton

SHEWETH

I. That it is currently reported and believed that the REV. FREDERIC TEMPLE, D.D., Head Master of Rugby School, has been recommended by the Prime Minister for the vacant See of Exeter.

II. That your Memorialist, in 1861, moved for a Committee of the Lower House of Convocation of Canterbury to examine and report upon the book called "Essays and Reviews"; and that he was Chairman of the Committee.

III. That it appeared to him then, as it appears now, that the Essay of DR. TEMPLE, being the Prefatory Essay of the book, has passages heretical in terms; and further, that it contains the substance of the entire volume.

IV. That it was, and is, impossible for him to come to any conclusion other than that the volume so disposed and arranged, that the remaining Six "Essays" or "Reviews" should proceed to develope in detail the principles laid down and indicated in the Prefatory "Essay" of DR. TEMPLE; the several subjects being assigned to the several writers by an anonymous EDITOR, conversant with, and perhaps initiating, the entire scheme; and that, all necessity of inter-communication between the several writers being thus avoided, each one of them was enabled to say that he was answerable for his own "essay," or "Review," only.

V. That your Memorialist has shewn by an Analysis of the volume, published by him in 1861, that it is impossible to come reasonably to any conclusions about the structure and composition of the volume other than that herein stated above. The Analysis was endorsed by men of high position and great ability in sections of the Church not agreeing with that section to which your Memorialist belongs.

VI. That your Memorialist has not at hand the records of the Convocation, so as to enable him to go here into the details of proceedings in the two Houses of Convocation upon the book: but that he is able to state that the Lower House at his instance, condemned the book upon the Report of its Committee.

VII. That Dr Temple has not recalled his Essay: nor retracted the heretical passages in it; nor disclaimed sympathy with the other "Essays" and "Reviews" being its complement and development: nor even expressed publicly his sorrow for having written it to be published.

VIII. That, regard being had to the facts herein above stated, your Memorialist is compelled to say, that, if the appointment of Dr Temple to the See of Exeter, or any other See of the Church of England, shall be carried out, a direct and intolerable offense and treason will have been committed against Christ and His Church; and that thereupon it will become the duty of every Churchman to labour actively and steadily to dissolve all connection between the Church and the State.

Your Memorialist therefore respectfully prays that you will withhold your official sanction of, and concurrence in, such appointment.

(BL, MS. Add. 44,611 [Gladstone Papers] fol. 92)

[Similar petitions were sent to Queen Victoria by the rural dean (Henry Burton) and clergy of Shrewsbury (21 Oct. 1869) and the Parish of Heyham, Kent (29 Oct. 1869), amongst many others (BL, MS. Add. 44,798 [Gladstone Papers], fols. 124–25). A typical protest addressed to Queen Victoria was sent to the Home Office, responsible for patronage appointments. It is date-stamped 1 November 1869.]

To the Queen's Most Excellent Majesty

May it please Your Majesty,
The humble petition of the undersigned inhabitants of Bourton, in the county of Berkshire, sheweth

That there is a current report which has neither been contradicted nor doubted up to the present time, that the Premier has recommended the Rev. Frederic [*sic*] Temple, D.D. Master of Rugby School for the Bishopric of Exeter which is now vacant.

That D[r] Temple was one of the seven authors of a book called Essays and Reviews, which, soon after its publication, was protested against by 12,000 of the clergy & unanimously by all the bishops & archbishops.

That this book was translated into one or more of the languages of India, with the avowed object of keeping back the natives from becoming Christians.

That it is evident that Dr Temple is not sorry for his authorship of a part of the book, nor for the sanction which he has given to the whole of it, from the fact that there have been many editions of the Essays & Reviews, in every one of which Dr Temple's own Essay appears unpurged from errors, in every one of which likewise Dr Temple continues to throw the shield of his name over the more outspoken and fully developed errors of the other six Essayists.

That two bishops (if not more) have strongly urged Dr Temple to express his regret in the share which he has had in the writing and publishing of this book, but that he still, up to the present time, has shown no sign of sorrow whatever, at all events in public, for having undermined, & for having helped others to undermine the belief of his fellow men in the great truths & doctrines which are made known to us in the Holy Scriptures.

That of the same Holy Scriptures, Dr Temple must declare solemnly (to the Archbishop in the presence of two other Bishops), (if he be consecrated to the See of Exeter) that he will instruct the people committed to his charge.

That (on the same supposition) he must likewise solemnly declare that he will faithfully exercise himself in the same Holy Scriptures, & call upon God by prayer for the true understanding of the same; so that he may be able by them to teach & exhort with wholesome doctrine, & to withstand & convince the gainsayers; and that he will be ready with all faithful diligence, to banish & drive away all erroneous and strange doctrine contrary to God's word, & both privately & openly to call upon and encourage others to do the same.

That in making these solemn promises, he must again & again, seven times, invoke the grace & help of that God whom he has so grievously insulted, and who has said that he will not hold him guiltless that taketh his name in vain.

That if Dr Temple be raised to the See of Exeter, there is every reason to believe that both he, & others directly or indirectly encouraged by him, will sow broad cast the seeds of infidelity, not only in Devonshire, but throughout the kingdom.

That the petitioners therefore most humbly & most dutifully & loyally, yet most earnestly beseech & implore Your Majesty to issue your Royal Command that some clergyman more worthy than Dr Temple should be appointed to the See of Exeter.

And the petitioners will ever pray for every blessing temporal & eternal on Your Majesty & on the Royal Family.

[Signed by the Vicar, John Batchelor Kearney, the churchwardens of Bourton, and thirteen others] (BL, MS. Add. 44,798 [Gladstone Papers], fols. 130–31)

[Another typical petition is a deanery protest from the diocese of Exeter.]

14 Dec. 1869

THAT THE APPOINTMENT, election, & proposed consecration of Dr. Temple to the Bishopric of this Diocese is regarded with deep sorrow & apprehension; because, as one of the acknowledged & persistent authors of the Book entitles

"Essays and Reviews," he is lying under the following Sentence of Condemnation, pronounced by the Authority of the Church in Convocation, viz . . . teaching contrary to the Doctrines received by the United Church of England and Ireland.

(Oxford, Bodley MS. Eng. th. d. 21, fol. 101)

Temple's Address to the Upper House of Convocation on 11 February 1870

[From the second week of October 1869, public and private pressure had been mounting on Temple as bishop designate of Exeter to distance himself from *Essays and Reviews* in various ways, such as by renouncing its theology, declaring his own orthodoxy, or giving the assurance that he would not allow the republication of the volume with his essay in it. Furthermore, the old and false rumor resurfaced that Temple was actually the editor. Publicly Temple remained silent, but privately he denied his editorship in a letter to Cook (Letter 282); simultaneously he concurred in republication when prompted by Wilson. Only after he was duly consecrated and had taken his place in the February 1870 meeting of Convocation was he finally pushed into speaking. One of the members of the Lower House, Philip Freeman, after a motion censuring Temple had failed, attempted to smooth ruffled tempers by declaring that Temple had agreed not to republish the offending essay, based on information Freeman had from Cook. In the ensuing uproar, Temple was compelled to make the following statement in the Upper House of Convocation on 11 February 1870.]

I SHOULD very much have preferred letting this matter wait until hereafter, because it is almost impossible to express precisely in words that which a man feels and thinks in such a matter as this. He must, to a very great extent, let his life and his actions speak for him, and then his words will receive their natural interpretation; whereas I, new to the Episcopal office, and new to this House, can of course convey my meaning by words and words only, and they must be interpreted as best they can. . . . I cannot help regretting that, by a most unfortunate blunder of my own, the necessity is apparently laid upon me of speaking now. . . . The fact is, that a little while ago I had occasion to tell an intimate friend—a layman, of whose opinion I think very highly—that I had come to the conclusion that I would not republish my Essay. . . . Now, so long as there was any legal right at stake, it seemed to me the strongest of all possible duties that I should not sacrifice any such right in any way whatever, either directly or indirectly. . . . But after I had become Bishop of Exeter, and when this matter was pressed very earnestly upon me, and pressed upon me by some who certainly shared with me a conviction of the necessity of great liberty of opinion, I thought that at any rate I might do this without injustice to any one—I might yield to those who felt the matter so keenly, by, so far as I was concerned, withdrawing the Essay from publication. . . . But in telling a friend or two of my intention, I had not thought about Convocation at all, and it certainly never occurred to my mind that the announcement would first be made in Convocation, and would thus have an appearance of being intended to avoid or prevent any such discussion as might arise either in the Upper House or in the Lower House. On the contrary, I think that if there is any place where such discussion may well be held, it is in these two Houses. . . . I felt certainly that the publication of one essay amongst others was a thing which might be allowed to Frederick Temple, but which was not, therefore, to be allowed to the Bishop of Exeter. . . . The Bishop of Exeter would be required, of course, to be more guarded in everything that he did, and would be required to see not only that what he himself published was what he approved, but also that everything else that was published with it, and might be confounded with it, was also approved; because it would be inevitable that his position would give it a kind of authority that it would not have of itself. . . .

One reason I have already dealt with—my great reason for withdrawing my Essay from future publication; but there was another. . . . When I was originally asked to join in writing for such a volume, my reason for agreeing to join was that I could not help being very much struck with the extraordinary reticence which then prevailed among the younger University men at both Universities, but especially at Oxford, and which seemed to me to be doing most serious mischief to their characters. . . . Men were unwilling to express doubts and perplexities which it was certainly far better that they should express. Such things, when they are kept in, always have a kind of importance which is quite inconsistent with their true value. Men magnify them; they brood over them and fancy they are very great; while, if they would only put them into words, in many cases they themselves would immediately begin to see how very much less their importance was than they had thought. . . . I think there is a much more reasonable and better tone in discussing great questions in consequence of the publication of that book. But when this matter came before me at the beginning of this year and I had to consider the whole subject—I thought that that work had really been done, and that to persist in the publication of the book now was not to persist in advocating certain principles, but to persist in maintaining a particular discussion of those principles which, as it seemed to me, instead of assisting the cause, had begun to hinder it. . . .

A great deal has been said about the mischief which that book has done, and I think that I am bound to say something on that point; and something, also, on the other side. I am not prepared to deny that the book has done mischief. . . . The fact is, that in all these cases a mischief of the kind which the Bishop of Lichfield [Dr. Selwyn] describes is almost a necessary accompaniment of the progress of investigation; but as God has made us, it is simply impossible to stop that progress, and I, for my part, certainly cannot conceive how any one can think it desirable to stop it. . . . I am quite sure that the belief in the most fundamental points, if once it were supposed to be absolutely free from all investigation and from all question, would begin to lose its real vitality, and a belief without vitality seems to me to be not merely a negation, but a most positive and real mischief. . . . I do not mean that the necessity of free inquiry has no limits; far from it—but that in a Church like ours it is of the essence of the health of the Church that those limits should be as wide as it is possible, with any reasonable regard to community of spirit. . . .

But I wish to say a word or two more, as it seems to me to be a fitting opportunity to do so, on the general question. . . . It seems to me that, whether we like it or not, we are of necessity involved in what Dr. Arnold spoke of some years ago,—namely, the general discussion, all over the Christian world, of the degree and limits of the inspiration of the Bible. It is a question of absolutely enormous importance. The progress of discovery and historical research has made it quite impossible for us to leave it alone; it is forced upon us on every side. It is quite impossible that this great discussion should really come to a worthy end unless it is conducted with real freedom on the part of those who take any real share in it. . . . For my part, therefore, I think that such a discussion ought to be allowed the greatest freedom that can possibly be given it, consistent with the acknowledgment of the Bible as the supreme revelation, and with a reverent—a really reverent—spirit in the treatment of all subjects connected with it. . . . It would seem to me to be monstrous to discourage such a man as Dr. Arnold, or the late Dean of S. Paul's [Dr. Milman], because in many cases the conclusions to which they arrived were very different from those which are ordinarily accepted. It is not whether a man comes to this conclusion or to that, but it is with what temper, with what spirit, with what feelings he enters on the discussion. . . . I will conclude by saying that I am quite sure that no one has a more real reverence for God's Word, or a more entire desire to make it the guide of his life, than I have myself; and that there is no one who feels more confident that the result of the freest inquiry in a reverent spirit will be to uphold the dignity and honour of that Word.

(*Chronicle of Convocation,* 11 Feb. 1870; Sandford 1906, 1:302–5)

4 Trials and Appeals, 1861 to 1864: "Erroneous, Strange, and Heretical Doctrines"

Only two of the Essayists, Williams and Wilson, were clearly vulnerable to formal charges of heresy under the existing ecclesiastical law, and they were the ones first singled out for prosecution. By the time that the proceedings were set in motion Powell was already dead (on 11 June 1860), and was castigated in the grave for "denying Miracles" by Robert Phillimore, one of the lawyers prosecuting Williams and Wilson, and E. B. Pusey claimed that Powell was even then facing his own trial "before a higher Tribunal" (*Case Whether Professor Jowett* 1862, 3). Goodwin by 1861 applied for a judgeship abroad through Lord John Russell (see Letter 142), but as a layman he was not subject to the Church Discipline Act. The remaining three were in teaching positions. Temple, "as a Queen's Chaplain, was not subject to ecclesiastical or academical discipline" (Ellis 1980, 178), but as headmaster of Rugby he had to justify himself to the boys and masters and to the governors of the college, but, until 1869 he was not formally implicated, notwithstanding the many pamphlet attacks that were leveled against him.[1] Pattison held a nominal parochial living in the gift of Lincoln College of which he was the head, or "Rector," from January 1861 so that his position insulated him, but his essay was deemed historical and therefore not open to doctrinal censure. Even so he had been attacked by the provost of Oriel College, Edward Hawkins, and by E. B. Pusey who in a sermon in the University Church advised undergraduates to avoid him (Ellis 1980, 179). Jowett, as Regius Professor of Greek, did not hold a parochial appointment but was a fellow of Balliol College: his prosecution in the only court available to charge him formally, that of the University, was brought forward in 1863, after a measure of legal success had been gained against Williams and Wilson in the Court of Arches.

Legal proceedings for heresy were thus initiated against three of the Essayists, two of whom could be arraigned by the episcopal authorities in the ecclesiastical courts, seeking dismissal for Williams and Wilson from their parochial responsibilities for heretical writing; and in Williams's case it seemed that his position as professor of Hebrew at St. David's College, Lampeter, was under attack if not in formal jeopardy from the trial. After Williams and Wilson were condemned, proceedings were also initiated against Jowett in the Chancellor's Court at Oxford. In the charges of heresy brought against Williams and Wilson in the Court of Arches in 1861, it is repeatedly stated in the Articles of Charge that in *Essays and*

Reviews each "maintained or affirmed, erroneous strange or heretical doctrines, positions or opinions, contrary to the doctrine and teaching of the United Church of England and Ireland as by law established or to the Statutes Constitutions Canons Ecclesiastical of the Realm or against the peace and unity of the Church." Jowett was charged with heresy for the theological position of *Essays and Reviews*, as well as *The Epistles of St. Paul* (1855). In all three cases, the establishment position lost: the secular and academic legal apparatuses refused to enforce the ecclesiastical judgment of heresy, in effect ruling that such a judgment was outside their jurisdiction.

Heresy is always defined by the orthodox from a position of power in which they determine who is beyond the pale of right belief. Heresy, in this sense, tests the limits and conventions of orthodoxy by pushing on those boundaries. But in similar fashion, heresy is not just the holding of unpopular or unconventional views: to be heretical, the opinions must contradict a doctrine that has been legally and bindingly defined as orthodox, on which truth claims have been established by a formal institutional process. In a widely accepted definition of heresy as "a religious error held in wilful and persistent opposition to the truth after it has been defined and declared by the church in a authoritative manner" (Schaff 1883–93, 2:512–16), the notion of "truth" precedes its position in institutional authority—in the heresy trials around *Essays and Reviews*, "truth" is fractured as the different levels of institutional authority cannot agree as to its constitution in an "authoritative manner." As the documents summarized and commented upon in this section will demonstrate, this gap between "truth" and its institutional constitution can be mapped out in complex ways.

These issues were brought sharply into focus by the Articles of Charge against Williams and Wilson, and they were so constructed as to implicate the other Essayists as well as those directly accused. To the prosecutors, the statements in the Preface to *Essays and Reviews* that each writer was responsible for his own essay only and all wrote "in entire independence of each other" were manifest lies since the whole of the volume was intended, the accusers argued, by the Essayists acting together to undermine the faith of the clergy and people of England. Accordingly, the whole of the volume was appended to the documents submitted to the ecclesiastical court, even though specific passages in the essays by Williams and Wilson, and the Preface, were cited. Hence, the trial implicated the other Essayists in the condemnation of the two, by means of guilt by association, as the *Times* said, on the principle of *noscitur a sociis* [he is known by his friends, by the company he keeps; 22 Oct. 1869, 6–7]. The condemnation in the public press and in the sustained and extended pamphlet attacks, without the need of due legal process, attacked all seven Essayists seriatim. This attack was extended to Jowett within the legal framework of the academy: to do so, Jowett's commentary on St. Paul, published five years earlier, was also cited as heretical.

A "That Stately March of Ecclesiastical Litigation": Williams and Wilson on Trial for Heresy in the Court of Arches

On 20 May 1861, the *Guardian* carried the news that Walter Kerr Hamilton, bishop of Salisbury, was initiating legal proceedings against Dr. Rowland Williams: "There are few probably who will not regret this . . . we regret it strongly" (497); the report also quoted the *Standard*: "We regret that the Bishop of Salisbury has determined to prosecute Dr. Rowland Williams. . . . His essay is the worst of the whole seven—it is the only one in the volume which has not one single redeeming feature—it is destitute of originality, clumsy, and ill-written" (500). Despite the wish of the *Guardian* that *Essays and Reviews* should "sink into deserved oblivion" (501), the prelates, the press, and the public were not ready to let it disappear. On 23 May, Hamilton announced his suit against Williams in the *Times* and the legal proceedings were duly set in motion, leading to the much-publicized reporting of Williams's case in the Court of Arches, the ecclesiastical court of the archbishop of Canterbury in December 1861 and January 1862.[2] With less newspaper coverage, the trial of H. B. Wilson in a separate but related proceeding brought by the Rev. James Fendall of the Diocese of Ely, with the secret financial backing of Samuel Wilberforce, bishop of Oxford, began in February 1862. On 25 June 1862 the judge of the ecclesiastical court, Dr. Stephen Lushington, delivered his "interlocutory" judgment, pronouncing on the merits of all of the charges in both cases, instructing that some of the charges against Williams and Wilson had to be reformulated. Those reformulations were submitted on 12 September, but the brief hearing on them was deferred until 15 December when Lushington convicted both Williams and Wilson of heresy and delivered his sentence depriving them of their ecclesiastical positions and incomes, inhibiting them from functioning as clergymen, and silencing them on doctrinal matters. So began what A. P. Stanley called the Essayists' "public prosecution, . . . that stately march which seems to belong to ecclesiastical litigation" (1864, 268). The trial filled the other Essayists with gloom, and the procedures of the courts were also matters of concern, as Jowett wrote at this time to Gilbert Elliot: "A law court is better for justice than Convocation but a law court easily gets inspired in these questions by public opinion. None of the ordinary rules of law are applicable: the judge does what he likes & the world calls this common sense. Still I hope that a Protestant judge will pause before he determines that the evidences, prophecies, etc. are a fiction (for that is what the decision would involve) to be maintained not by weapons of reason & argument but by the authority of the Court" (Balliol, MS. Jowett F4, fol. 9).

The Court of Arches was the church court of the ecclesiastical province of Canterbury. Its powers, dating from the Middle Ages, were confirmed and extended in 1840 in the Church Discipline Act. The court was empowered to hear cases of doctrine and discipline that were referred to it from the diocesan courts or, in some important cases, by a particular bishop. To do so a bishop would send a Letter of Request asking that the judge of the Court of Arches (whose title of "Official Principal" was by custom often changed to "Dean of the Arches"), appointed for life, hear the case and render a verdict. The Court of Arches followed the conventions of civil law, conducting the whole proceeding through the legal representatives of the prosecutors and the defendants, so that neither Hamilton nor Fendall, Williams nor Wilson, could speak or give evidence. The dean of the Arches alone was responsible for the judgment: there was no tribunal of judges nor a jury. Appeals against the decision of the Court of Arches were addressed to the king or queen in Council, and were heard before the Judicial Committee of the Privy Council until 1963. Hence, in 1860 the Court of Arches was a legal part of the judicial system of England, and the judgments of the dean of the Arches were binding in law; for instance, he only could order the deprivation of a clergyman from his benefit or parochial appointment in the Province of Canterbury. Furthermore, the Court of Arches, and ecclesiastical and canon law generally, was not a part of the common law of England but part of the traditional civil law, derived from Roman civil law and from the canon law of the medieval church. Lawyers in the ecclesiastical courts were required to be laymen, and at least the principal lawyers in ecclesiastical cases were to be doctors in civil law. Ecclesiastical lawyers were a select body of experts in civil law; they had their own association, Doctors' Commons (that also included lawyers for the High Court of Admiralty) with a magnificent library containing a rich collection of patristic, medieval, Reformation, and English theology, on which they drew in preparing their cases from authorities, rather than from precedent as in the common law. Their membership also included a group of proctors (the equivalent of solicitors in the courts of common law) who assisted in the preparation of cases in the ecclesiastical and admiralty courts. By the Court of Probate Act of 1857 matters of wills and probates, as well as matrimonial cases, were transferred, and the other ecclesiastical cases were opened up to the whole bar; in 1861 the library of Doctors' Commons was sold, and the buildings demolished (see Desmond Bowen 1968, 90–96).

The Court of Arches trial of Williams and Wilson was held in the Rolls Court, Westminster, part of the nineteenth-century buildings (now demolished) adjoining Westminster Hall and the Houses of Parliament that were erected to accommodate the chief courts of England from 1825 to 1882 when the new Royal Courts of Justice opened in the Strand.

Hence, it was exactly when the *Essays and Reviews* case came forward that there was some turmoil in the jurisdiction, administration, and practice of the ecclesiastical courts and their officials. The courts were now open to lawyers trained in the common law, unfamiliar with canon law and the procedures of ecclesiastical juris-

Figure 13. Stephen Lushington (1862). Painting by William Holman Hunt. Courtesy of the National Portrait Gallery, London.

diction which, until 1857, had been the prerogative of a small group of experts, numbering only about twenty-four. One of these was the 80-year-old former head of Doctors' Commons, the dean of Arches, Dr. Stephen Lushington, who had had a long legal career as a judge of the Admiralty Court, a Privy Councillor, and from 1858 as the judge in the Court of Arches (see fig. 13). The trial also had on both sides former members of Doctors' Commons, Dr. (later Sir) Robert Phillimore, acting for the prosecutors Hamilton and Fendall, and Dr. (later Sir) James Parker Deane, acting for Williams and Wilson. It was into these treacherous legal waters, where only highly technical expertise could possibly avert threatening disaster, that the Essayists were now swept.

I The Letters of Request and the Articles of Charge

THE "Letters of Request" in the case of Rowland Williams consisted of a large vellum manuscript document sent from Hamilton to Lushington.[3] Hamilton cited the Church Discipline Act, alleging that Williams had perpetrated a "scandal or offence against the Laws Ecclesiastical."[4] Hamilton later explained that he had not tried Williams in his own diocesan court before citing him before the Court of Arches because the bishop had already been involved in signing the condemnatory letter from the archbishop of Canterbury of 16 February 1861 and because he wished to have the case heard under the general Ecclesiastical law.[5] In the "Letters of Request" Hamilton alleged that "within the last two years [Williams had] written, printed, published, dispersed, and set forth . . . in a book entitled 'Essays and Reviews' a certain Article or Review with divers notes thereto entitled 'Bunsen's Biblical Researches,'" in which he "maintained and affirmed certain erroneous, strange, and heretical doctrines, positions, and opinions contrary and repugnant to the Doctrine and teaching of the said United Church of England and Ireland as by law established and thereby contravening the statutes constitutions and canons Ecclesiastical of the Realm and against the Peace and Unity of the Church." That is, he was alleged to have published opinions that contradicted the Formularies of the Church of England,[6] taken in their "literal and grammatical sense" a phrase that would be returned to over and over in the ensuing trials and appeals.[7] The Letters of Request formally requested Lushington to convene the Court of Arches and summon Williams "to answer to certain Articles, heads, positions, or interrogatories touching and concerning his Soul's health and the lawful correction and reformation of his manners and excesses and more especially for having printed . . . the said book entitled 'Essays and Reviews.'" It was signed and sealed in wax by Hamilton on 1 June 1861. Similar documents were prepared against Wilson. A vellum document, the "Decree by Letters of Request" accusing Henry Bristow Wilson and summoning him to trial, was sent by Lushington's court following the acceptance of the Letters of Request from Thomas Turton, bishop of Ely, on 16 December 1861, on behalf of the Rev. James Fendall, who was named as the "promoter," or

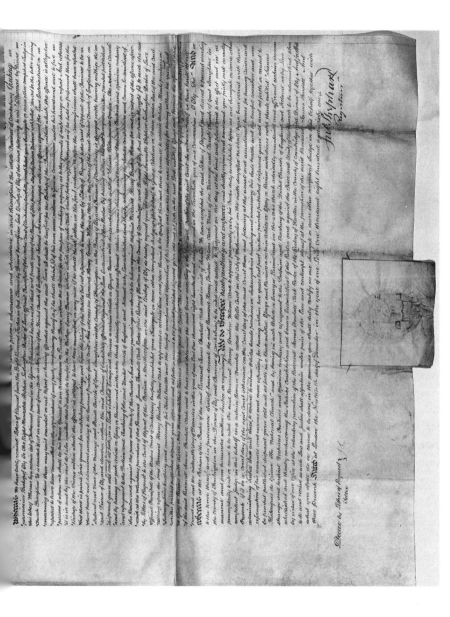

Figure 14. "Decree by Letters of Request," arraigning H. B. Wilson for trial for heresy in the Court of Arches (1861). Courtesy of Lambeth Palace Library.

accuser, of the case against Wilson (see fig. 14).[8] On 19 December, Lushington commented to his daughter, Alice: "These Essays & Reviews are horrible—a *fresh* prosecution this morning of Mr. Wilson" (Waddams 1992, 315).

Accompanying the Letters of Request were the "Articles of Charge" quoting the passages from the essays that were brought before the court as constituting an offense against the ecclesiastical law, together with statements of the doctrinal positions that were infringed.[9] These "Articles of Charge" (not to be confused with the "Thirty-nine Articles of Religion") were twenty-two in number for Williams, nineteen for Wilson. A distinction can be drawn between formal and substantive "Articles of Charge," between those that identify the defendants and the offending essays and those that allege heresy. The first six "Articles of Charge" concerned the identification of each defendant and the fact that each had subscribed to the Thirty-nine Articles, *The Book of Common Prayer*, and the Ordinal, or ordination services, in *The Book of Common Prayer*; the legality of the ordination and benefices held by each; the legality of the institution of each into their present incumbencies; the fact of the publication of the disputed essays; the fact that the essays had passed through nine editions with "no other preface or introduction than the aforesaid one ['To the Reader'] has been prefixed thereto or printed or published"; and the fact that each essay "has not during the nine editions aforesaid undergone any or at least any material or substantial alteration." The final five charges in both cases concern the annexing of a copy of the text of the charged essay; the admission of authorship; the fact that each is "an ecclesiastical person"; that the accused affirms "certain strange and heretical doctrines"; and that their arguments are "public and notorious," the object of a "public voice, fame, and report." The other charges are the substantive ones on which the accusation of heresy rested; they cite the passages charged for "erroneous strange and heretical doctrines," specifying the parts of the Thirty-nine Articles, and of the *BCP* and other documents, that are alleged to have been contravened.

The substantive "Articles of Charge" on which the trials of Williams and Wilson were conducted in the Court of Arches may be summarized in the following table. It indicates the number of the Article of Charge, the cited passage to which reference is made in the essays (indicated by paragraphs and quotations) and the grounds or basis for the doctrine that is alleged to have been transgressed in the Anglican Formularies. Reference is made to the Articles of Religion, to the *BCP*, the Ordinal in the *BCP*, *The Book of Homilies*, and the Constitutions and Canons of 1603. Passages from the Bible are also cited as having legal authority because they are included in readings from the gospels, epistles and other lections authorized for specific days of the church year in the *BCP*. The court's disposition of each Article of Charge in the interlocutory judgment is also indicated as admitted, rejected, withdrawn, or reformed (that is, to be revised and resubmitted before the final judgment was delivered). The passages cited in the Articles of Charge are marked in this edition of *Essays and Reviews*, following the twelfth edition.

Articles of Charge in the Court of Arches Preferred against both Williams and Wilson

Article 5

Cited Passage: Preface: "To the Reader"

Grounds for this Article of Charge: In argument this preface is said to constitute collaboration, or mutual knowledge on the part of the Essayists; and the fact that it has not been changed through nine editions shows no evidence that any of the Essayists is prepared to withdraw any passage, or distance himself from any other essayist. This article was admitted by Dr. Lushington, not on the grounds of collaboration, but as an assertion that each writer was responsible "only for his own contribution," and so went on to the Privy Council, though "of very slight importance." Admitted.

Articles of Charge in the Court of Arches Preferred against Williams

Article 7

Cited Passages: ¶10 "As in his *Egypt* . . . we breathe"; ¶28 "If we would . . . development"; ¶24 "But, if such . . . confirmed."

Grounds: Williams is alleged to have contravened the Thirty-nine Articles, especially 6, 7, 20; the clause in the Nicene Creed asserting "that the Holy Ghost spake by the Prophets"; the Epistle for Christmas Day (Heb 1:1), and the Epistle for Epiphany (Eph. 3:1 ff.) in the *BCP*. This Article of Charge alleges that Williams "did advisedly maintain and affirm that the Bible or Holy Scripture is an expression of devout reason and the written voice of the congregation, not the word of God, nor containing any special revelation of His truth or of His dealings with mankind, nor the rule of our faith." Reformed.

Article 8

Cited Passages: ¶13 "In our own country . . . lowered"; Williams's notes 50–51 in ¶13; ¶14 "To this . . . ignorance"; ¶14 "He may read . . . Neckar"; ¶15 "Great then is Baron . . . proof"; ¶16 "The most brilliant . . . people"; ¶s 17, 18 "This is an imperfect . . . Israel"; ¶19 "If any sincere Christian . . . prophecy."

Grounds: Contravention of the Thirty-nine Articles (6, 7), the Gospel for Monday in Easter Week (Luke 24:13) and the Epistle and Gospel for Tuesday in Easter Week (Acts 13:26; Luke 24: 36). This Article of Charge alleges that Williams holds that in the Old Testament "there is with the possible exception of one two or three doubtful passages no element of divinely inspired prediction or prognostication for future persons or events." Rejected.

Article 9

Cited Passages: ¶22 "In distinguishing . . . the case"; ¶s 22, 23 "The truth seems. . . . theories."

Grounds: Contravention of the Thirty-nine Articles (6) and of the vows required of deacons in the ordinal: "Do you unfeignedly believe [all] the Canonical Scriptures of the Old and New Testaments?" This Article of Charge alleges that Williams did "maintain that the Prophet Jonah was not a real historical person and that the Canonical Book written by him and incorporated in the Old Testament was not really written by him and has not any authority binding upon the Church." REJECTED.

ARTICLE 10
Cited Passages: ¶29 "Our author then. . . . St. Peter"; Williams's note 121 in ¶29.
Grounds: Contravention of the Thirty-nine Articles (6) and the Epistle for All Saints Day (Rev. 7:2 ff.). This Article of Charge alleges that Williams did "maintain that the portion of Holy Scripture usually called the Revelation of Saint John the Divine, the Epistle to the Hebrews and the Epistle usually called the [Second] Epistle of Saint Peter are not respectively parts of Holy Scripture whose authority is binding upon the Church." REJECTED.

ARTICLE 11
Cited Passages: ¶7 "Our deluge. . . . genealogies"; ¶7 "Baron Bunsen. . . . to Israel"; ¶8 "So in the passage. . . . accounts"; ¶10 "When the fierce . . . themselves."
Grounds: Contravention of the Thirty-nine Articles (6, 7), the first lection for Evensong for 1st Sunday in Lent (Gen. 22) and the second Lesson for Morning Prayer for All Saints (Heb. 11:33 ff), and the Ordinal vows for Deacons. REJECTED.

ARTICLE 12
Cited Passages: ¶27 "Propitiation would . . . hearts"; ¶31 "Salvation. . . . ritual."
Grounds: Contravention of the Thirty-nine Articles (2, 31) and of the Prayer of Consecration at Holy Communion in the *BCP*. This Article of Charge alleges that Williams did "affirm that Christ did not suffer nor was crucified dead and buried to reconcile His Father to us nor to be a sacrifice for the original guilt as well as for the actual sin of man. That the offering of Christ is not the perfect redemption, propitiation and satisfaction for the sins of the whole world both original and actual." REFORMED.

ARTICLE 13
Cited Passage: ¶31 "The first Christians. . . . with it."
Grounds: Contravention of the Thirty-nine Articles (27). This Article of Charge alleges that Williams did maintain "that the element of water is not a divinely ordained means by which we receive the Spiritual grace in the Sacrament of Baptism." REJECTED.

ARTICLE 14
Cited Passage: ¶27 "Thus the incarnation . . . holiness."

Grounds: Contravention of the Thirty-nine Articles (2). This Article of Charge alleges that Williams did maintain "that the incarnation of Our Lord Jesus Christ was purely spiritual, and that the Son of God did not take man's nature in the womb of the blessed Virgin." REJECTED.

ARTICLE 15
Cited Passage: ¶26 "For, though. . . . of our hearts."
Grounds: Contravention of the Thirty-nine Articles (11). This Article of Charge alleges that Williams did maintain "that Justification by faith means only the peace of mind or sense of divine approval which comes of trust in a righteous God and that Justification is a verdict of forgiveness upon our repentance and of acceptance upon the offering of our hearts." ADMITTED.

ARTICLE 16
Cited Passage: ¶s 36, 37 "So, when he asks. . . . thank I GOD."
Grounds: No contravention of the Thirty-nine Articles is specified. This Article of Charge alleges that Williams did "maintain" an "adherence to and assent in the substance of all the said Article" to agree with the opinions of Baron Bunsen. ADMITTED.

ARTICLE 17
Cited Passage: [none specified]
Grounds: No contravention of the Thirty-nine Articles is specified. This Article of Charge delivers a summary condemnation of the whole essay: "The manifest tendency scope object and design of the whole essay is to inculcate a disbelief in the Divine inspiration and authority of the Holy Scriptures . . . [;] to reduce [them] . . . to the level of a mere human composition such as the writings of Luther and of Milton[;] to deny that the Old Testament contains prophesies or predictions of the Saviour and other persons and events[;] to deny that the Prophets—speaking under the special inspiration of the Holy Spirit foretold the truth and genuineness of the historical portions of the Old Testament . . . [; to deny] the truth and reality of the miracles recorded as facts in the Old and New Testaments[;] to deny or interpret by a meaning at variance with that of the Church the Doctrines of Original Sin, of Infant Baptism, of Justification by Faith, of Atonement and Propitiation by the death of our Saviour, and of the Incarnation of the Lord." REJECTED.

ARTICLES OF CHARGE IN THE COURT OF ARCHES PREFERRED AGAINST WILSON
ARTICLE 7
Cited Passages: ¶s 21, 22 "But although. . . . universe"; ¶65 "Speculative. . . . life in man"; ¶78 "Jesus Christ. . . . the Church."
Grounds: Contravention of the Thirty-nine Articles (2, 3, 4, 31), the Nicene and Athanasian Creeds, the Exhortation at Holy Communion, and the Collect (or prayer) for Easter Day. This Article of Charge alleges that Wilson did "declare and

affirm that our Saviour Christ was and is a mere teacher of morality and a moral reformer, and not also the revealer of God's scheme of redemption of mankind from sin and misery, and not the person through whose human life, suffering, death, and resurrection that scheme of redemption and salvation is wrought out." REJECTED.

ARTICLE 8
Cited Passages: ¶s 37, 38, 39 "It has been . . . truth within."
Grounds: Contravention of the Thirty-nine Articles (6, 7, 20), the Nicene Creed, the Ordinal for Priests ["take thou authority to preach the word of God"], and the *Book of Sermons or Homilies* [Homily on those "which take offence at certain places of the Holy Scriptures"]. This Article of Charge alleges that Wilson did affirm "that the Scriptures of the Old and New Testament were not written under the inspiration of the Holy Spirit, and that they were not necessarily at all, and certainly not in parts, the word of God." REFORMED.

ARTICLE 9
Cited Passages: ¶38 "The Protestant. . . . importance"; ¶s 70–75 "It is sometimes. . . . literalist."
Grounds: Contravention of the Thirty-nine Articles (6, 7), the Apostles', Nicene, and Athanasian Creeds, and the following passages of scripture: Matt. 4, 10, 12, 22, 23, 24; and Luke 25. This Article of Charge alleges that Wilson did affirm "that a Clergyman of the said Church is at liberty to hold and promulgate a metaphorical or ideal interpretation in respect of any part of the Scriptures of the Old and New Testament, as to him shall seem meet; and to deny the reality of any of the facts narrated in the said Scriptures." REJECTED.

ARTICLE 10
Cited Passage: ¶44–48 "As far. . . . the greater."
Grounds: No contravention of the Thirty-nine Articles is specified. Contravention of the 36th of the Constitutions and Canons of 1603 [subscription to three articles, concerning the king as the "supreme governor" and to the *BCP* and the Thirty-nine Articles as containing "nothing contrary to" but as "agreeable to the Word of God"] required of such as are to be made ministers. This Article of Charge alleges that Wilson did affirm "that it is lawful for a clergyman of the said church to subscribe the said articles of religion, receiving and understanding them in a sense other than the plain literal meaning of the words and sentences used in the said Articles." REJECTED.

ARTICLE 11
Cited Passage: ¶51 "We have spoken. . . . Personalities."
Grounds: No contravention of the Thirty-nine Articles is specified. Contravention of the 36th of the Constitutions and Canons of 1603. The Article of Charge alleges

that Wilson did affirm "that it is lawful for a clergyman of the said church himself to disbelieve the doctrines contained in the five first of the said Articles of Religion, and in his public teaching to evade or pass by the facts and truths of the said five Articles asserted." REJECTED.

ARTICLE 12
Cited Passages: ¶10 "But with respect . . . a liar'"; ¶16 "Moreover . . . result."
Grounds: Contravention of Thirty-nine Articles (9, 18). The Article of Charge alleges that Wilson did affirm "that every person born into this world does not deserve God's wrath and damnation, and that the condition of men in a future state of existence will be determined by their moral conduct, exclusive of their religious belief." REFORMED.

ARTICLE 13
Cited Passage: ¶22 "And these words . . . moral."
Grounds: Contravention of the Thirty-nine Articles (6). This Article of Charge alleges that Wilson did affirm "that the second Epistle, which in the authorised English Version of the New Testament bears the name of the Apostle St. Peter, was not the work of that Apostle." WITHDRAWN.

ARTICLE 14
Cited Passage: ¶81 "The Christian. . . . his Will."
Grounds: No contravention of the Thirty-nine Articles is specified. Contravention of the Apostles', Nicene, and Athanasian Creeds, the Absolution in Morning Prayer, the Catechism in *BCP*, the Order for the Burial of the Dead, and the Commination against Sinners. This Article of Charge alleges that Wilson did affirm "that after this life and at the end of the existing order of things on this Earth, there will be no judgment of God, awarding to those Men whom he shall then approve, everlasting life or eternal happiness, and to those men whom he shall then condemn, everlasting death or eternal misery." ADMITTED.

II "No Legal Subterfuge . . . No Excuse for Misrepresenting": The Prosecution and Defense of Williams and Wilson

THE TWO CASES were heard separately in the Court of Arches, but the same lawyers acted for both Williams and Wilson, and followed similar lines of defense. So too, the prosecution lawyers followed similar attacks against both Essayists. The case of Williams was heard on 19, 20, and 21 December 1861 and 7–11, 13, and 16 January 1862. Wilson's was heard on 22, 24–25 February and 3 March 1862.[10] The lawyers for the defendants were Dr. James Parker Deane and James Fitzjames Stephen, and for the prosecutors, Dr. Robert Phillimore, John

Duke Coleridge, and M. C. M. Swabey.[11] The legal arguments were complicated and lengthy, with lawyers on both sides producing substantial books consisting of their speeches: Stephen's *Defence of the Rev. Rowland Williams, D.D. in the Arches' Court of Canterbury* (1862) and, on the other side, *Speech of Robert Phillimore . . . in the Case of "The Office of the Judge Promoted by the Bishop of Salisbury Against Williams" . . . and the Criminal Charges against Dr. R. Williams* (1862). Deane and Stephen made use of Williams's own privately published pamphlet *Hints to My Counsel in the Court of Arches* (1861), prepared for their advice and circulated only "for the use of personal friends, or of those who had taken particular interest in the proceedings" (Ellen Williams 1874, 2:53). Williams's *Hints to My Counsel* was written out of his concern that when the matter came to trial in the Court of Arches all theological points would be subsumed under legal and technical matters concerning the relation of his explicit words with the statements in the Formularies, and, even more worrying to him, to the niceties of the historical contexts and meanings of the Articles of Religion (matters in which H. B. Wilson reveled). Instead, Williams wished to direct attention to the theological issues and points of biblical interpretation that he was alleged to have transgressed. He addresses these matters in his instructions to his lawyers in the opening paragraphs:

> Dr. Rowland Williams, Defendant, leaves the technical part of his case to his Counsel, with this remark—No legal subterfuge, such as enabled a heterodox Archdeacon to escape at Bath, must here prejudice the truth.[12] No such plea as the differences between copies of our Articles at different dates must be employed. The Defendant accepts the Articles as they are, and claims to teach by them with fidelity and clearness unsurpassed by living man. . . .
>
> No method of removing a false tradition is more proper or more effective than analytical reviews of great authors who throw light around the subject; and the reviewers' selection of an author implies sympathy, but not identification. . . . The doctrines of the Defendant are so known from his own works, that there is no excuse for misrepresenting them (Ellen Williams 1874, 2:53–54).

Phillimore began the proceedings by reading into the court records the Articles of Charge against Williams and asked that they be admitted. Deane objected to admission of the articles, on the grounds that they impugn a cleric and scholar of undoubted renown, that they arise from a book that had been before the public "for a considerable time before any particular notice was taken of it," and that only after articles attacking it in the *Westminster Review* and the *Quarterly Review* and discussion amongst graduates of Oxford gathered there to elect the Professor of Sanskrit did the prosecution come forward, "influenced by pressure from without" (*Times,* 20 Dec. 1861, 8).

In the first few minutes of his address, Deane quoted Williams's opening statement, declaring that he would not adopt "any legal subterfuge" in dealing with "a thorough inquiry into the passages cited," despite the fact that the framers of the Articles of Charge had wrenched them from context and "mixed up passages taken from different parts of the essay." Lushington would have to decide "more as a literary critic than as an ecclesiastical judge" in dealing with advances in science and philology (*Times,* 20 Dec. 1861, 8). The next day Deane concluded his arguments, drawing a distinction between what Williams argued on his own and what he imputed to or cited from Baron Bunsen. In addition, Deane indicated the range of meaning, interpretation, and application of the word *inspiration*, pointing out that, following the position of Bishop Lowth, biblical and literary criticism generally had to distinguish between the words "genuine," "authentic," and "canonical": the first applies to what is "written by the person whose name it bore"; the second means "having authority as distinguished from apocryphal," while the third is used "in divinity [for] a collection of writings having Divine authority." Such a distinction allowed Deane to raise questions concerning matters of attribution, reliability of text and particular readings with respect to their "genuineness," and finally to matters of canonicity and its implications, for all of which he gave examples and raised questions, prompting Lushington to protest that he hoped he would not be obliged "to try these grave questions in divinity" (*Times*, 21 Dec. 1961, 11).

It was Williams's contention that the extracting of his remarks, such as in the "Oxford Manifesto" of March 1861 and as in the Articles of Charge, misrepresented his arguments by removing the context of the review and also tended to identify completely his views with those of Bunsen. In *Hints to My Counsel* Williams then sets out his purpose in writing the review of Bunsen's works, using the rhetorical device of foregrounding his own intentionality at the beginning of almost every sentence, so as to draw the sharpest distinction between his contentions, which he states as clearly as possible: "The Defendant . . . wishes to see bridged that chasm between the learned and the unlearned, which in England is so wide as to prejudice Christian ingenuousness. He feels ashamed that the world should often go before the Church, not only in intelligence, but in good works of freedom and humanity. He aims at reconciling the old conflict between Science and Faith, and thinks such reconciliation impossible, so long as men oppose Faith to Reason. . . . He thinks the elaborate skill of fence, for which too many of our great Divines are no less famous than Diplomatists, is a fitter accomplishment for politicians, than for Christian pastors. Still more he deprecates, whatever tends, by making the Clergy ignorant and time-serving, to lessen their just influence with the laity, and impair the moral weight of their doctrines" (Ellen Williams 1874, 2:25–26). Turning particularly to the uses for which his opponents had used the notion of prophecy, Williams excoriates both a literalist typological reading, as well as the unhistorical use of prophecy as predictive of subsequent, and even current, events: "He thinks the dominant tradition about Prophecy, from the violence which it does to the natural and historical sense of the Old Testament, disgraceful to the Clergy by whom it is taught, and dangerous to the Religion which it supports. He refuses absolutely, for his own part, to base the Everlasting Gospel upon calumny of the Hebrew race, and wild perversion of their Sacred Literature. Nor will he assist a misguided administration to retain forged texts in our Bibles, to mistranslate passages bearing on doctrines which divide men, to misrepresent the historical arrangement of parts of the Old Testament, and to build on such misrepresentation false theories of Prophecy, false foundations of faith, and false weapons for the partisan" (Ellen Williams 1874, 2:26). Williams then addresses more generally other matters that he considers abuses that are either mandated by the *BCP* or supported by the episcopacy and that are condoned by the Clergy, such as the required recitation of the "*Quicunque Vult*," or Athanasian Creed, thirteen times a year on specified holy days, with its condemnatory anathemas against those who do not hold a prescribed view of the Trinity ("an assurance that Milton and Sir Isaac Newton, Channing and Dr. Watts, have 'without doubt perished everlastingly,' when their names live in the hearts of men, and doubtless their spirits in the hands of God");[13] or the inability of the clergy to adapt the *BCP*; or the movement toward ecumenical reunion of the churches (Ellen Williams 1874, 2:26–27).

Turning to the issue of biblical inerrancy, Williams draws distinctions between historical truth and "the essentials of our faith": "He questions no historical fact of Holy Scripture, which he has not already found questioned by authority higher than his own; but he considers the essentials of our faith so independent of historical accidents, that he will accept whatever version of the latter is maintainable on evidence, and still uphold our faith as unimpaired by the result. He confesses that whatever doctrine, whether Prophetical, Moral, or Religious, is forced on men by external command, without authority of persuasion, or fitness, seems to him so far wrongly presented, and to fail in the vital characteristics of a Revelation. For the Gospel of Christ seems to him the emancipation of the human mind; and whoever violates the reasonable course of thought, or corrupts it, so far undoes the work of Christ in the world, and violates the liberty of the soul" (Ellen Williams 1874, 2:27–28).

Williams concludes by asserting his alignments, and by outlining three options before the Church of England—the drift toward Rome through ritualism, the drift toward secularism through acquiescence in the materialism of the times, or the acceptance of new knowledge to renew the church (Ellen Williams 1874, 2:28–29).

Making detailed use of Williams's *Hints*, his lawyers presented his case, one that was marked particularly with "the brilliance of Stephen's plea" (Colaiaco 1983, 174). Stephen presented his argument to the court beginning on 21 December, concluding on 8 January 1862. He opened with a dramatic question: "Did the law of England forbid the clergy of the Church of England to use their minds?" (*Times*, 23 Dec. 1861, 9). He was thereby collapsing the prosecution's Articles of Charge into an assertion that all of them relate to matters that are open questions: "All questions relating to the mode, the extent, the nature, and the effect on the books of the Bible of the inspiration of those books; all questions of criticism; and all questions of interpretation; are by law open questions, which the clergy, by their ordination vow, 'to be diligent in such studies as help to the knowledge of Holy Scriptures,' are bound in conscience to consider" (James Fitzjames Stephen 1862, xli). Hence, he is maintaining not only that such matters are open questions in point of fact, but further that the clergy are required by law to study the Bible in the light of such a consideration. Stephen then arranges his defense of Williams according to ten "propositions," increasingly narrowing the focus of his attention on the legal issues and their implications in allowing freedom of opinion with respect to biblical inspiration.

First Stephen argues that the issue before the court is not the doctrinal position of Williams nor a question of whether his opinions accord with either theological truth or the Bible taken as a whole, or, as argued by the prosecutors, with the biblical passages in the *BCP* selected to be read for particular days. Instead the court is only concerned with his legal position as a clergyman, bound by the laws of the church and the realm, and what he might legally be required to hold and teach, according to "the law upon this subject . . . found in the Thirty-nine Articles, the Rubrics, and Formularies" (1862, xli). The court has to decide whether Williams is constrained by law from expressing his opinions, not whether he is correct in them. Hence, matters left as open questions in the Formularies, such as inspiration and interpretation, cannot be made the basis of disciplining or convicting him. The law is the one that Williams had subscribed to at his ordination—and the law that governs the church in such matters—the Articles of Religion and the Formularies. Hence, this stage of the argument is an effort clearly to delimit the matters before the court to those legal documents and to exclude the Bible. Williams cannot, according to Stephen, be held to be accountable to the text of the Bible as to a legal document, but only to specific pronouncements concerning the Bible in the Articles of Religion and the Formularies.

Stephen's second proposition is that the Formularies do not prescribe the way in which the Bible "contains" the matters necessary to salvation, and hence it is open for a clergyman to hold that the Bible "contains" but does not "constitute" the word of God: "Protestant Christians *must* believe either that the Bible *contains*, or that it *constitutes* the Christian revelation. In the first case, they *may* believe that the Bible is fallible; but in either case, they *must* believe that the revelation is of Divine authority, and that so much of the Bible as constitutes that revelation, whether it be the whole or a part, is also of Divine authority" (1862, xli–xlii; 64).

The third proposition concerns the "general doctrine of the nature and authority of the Bible" under which questions are raised concerning its canonicity, authorship, and inspiration (in whole or in part), its criticism (including questions of "original" texts, languages, and dating), and its interpretation (including general hermeneutics, genres, and semantics). Stephen contends in his fourth proposition that the matter of canonicity is dealt with in three Articles of Religion (6, 7, and 20), but they "leave open the questions of inspiration, criticism, and interpretation" (1862, xliii). The fifth proposition sets out the view that the ordination vow of "unfeigned belief in the canonical Scriptures" has no "dogmatic authority." That is, it states a matter of belief, but does not test the orthodoxy of belief, and leaves open the same issues as the fourth proposition. Stephen makes the further point that "there is a considerable difference between unfeignedly believing canonical Scriptures, and unfeignedly believing the authorized version" (1862, 53). The former belief refers to the "original books," raising a host of problems about the origin and the originality of the "original books." In any case, the ordination vow cannot refer to "the authorized version, which, you will observe, is not even a transcript of the Jewish interpretation of the Hebrew text, but a translation of a commentary on such of the MS. of the Old Testament as were in existence 1350 years after the Old Testament canon was closed," according to the account of Robert Lowth (1862, 50–51). Stephen also draws distinctions between different kinds of belief, and different objects of belief: "to believe in a history is one thing, to believe in a poem is another. . . . The assertion 'I believe in Gibbon's *History*,' conveys one idea; the assertion 'I believe in Virgil's *Aeneid*,' conveys quite a different idea. . . . In church we all say, 'I believe' in the Apostles' Creed: we know what that means, I believe every proposition which it contains. . . . But suppose a man says, 'I believe in the 109th Psalm?' What does that mean? . . . It is not a subject of belief, it is not a thing a person can believe. My lord, a vast proportion of the Bible consists of matters of that kind" (1862, 54–55). Stephen points to the fallacy of equivocation here: the term *believe* is used with different meanings and objects and only by using "believe" in an equivocal sense could the term be used for all cases. A further fallacy is imputed to the prosecutors, the fallacy of division—that what is true of the whole (that the Bible is inspired and the proper object of belief in general) is also true of each and every part (that every part is inspired and the proper object of belief in particular). Further problems concerning the legitimacy of "belief" as a mode of affirmation arise over the Bible as a compilation of different genres, some poetry, some prose, some historical books, some devotional, some making extensive, some little use of metaphors. Are metaphors and other figures of speech to be taken literally, allegorically, or in some other sense? On these questions, as on all matters concerning inspiration, criticism, and interpretation, Stephen argues that the Articles of Religion are silent, allowing for diverse views: "There is a dilemma, between the horns of which I leave my friends [the prosecutors] to take their choice. Either the subject was not contemplated [by the framers of the Articles] at all, and if so, Dr. Williams is using a liberty of which he has never been deprived, or the subject was contemplated and it was knowingly passed over; and if so, he is using a liberty which was expressly and designedly conferred upon him" (1862, 65).

Stephen's sixth proposition argues that the Articles of Religion were framed deliberately to leave such matters open as he shows by comparing the Thirty-nine Articles with the historical conditions of their reaffirmation after the Presbyterian Westminster Confession of 1643 on the one hand and the Roman Catholic creed of Pius IV (promulgated in the last session of the Council of Trent, 1562–63) on the other. This argument is based on the Puritan revision of the sixth Article of Religion in the Westminster Confession of 1643 in which it is specifically asserted that the Bible constitutes entirely the word of God. The reratification of the Articles of Religion in 1662 did not sanction this view of inspiration in the Westminster Confession, despite the urging of the Presbyterian sympathizers in Convocation, enabling Stephen to argue that the notion of inspiration was a matter of opinion, undecided by the pronouncements of the Articles of Religion (1862, 66, 107).

Corroboration of this view is asserted in Stephen's propositions seven to ten, in which the views of "eminent divines" are adduced from the seventeenth to the nineteenth centuries on the openness of opinion allowed concerning biblical inspiration, criticism, and interpretation. Such views were particularly salient during "the Deistical controversy of the latter part of the seventeenth century and the whole of the eighteenth century," in which appeals to the general veracity of the Bible, though not to its literal truth in all respects, were defended "on the ground that the substantial truth of its contents was proved by historical and other evidence" (1862, xliv). Included in that "other evidence" was science: "Eminent divines . . . of the eighteenth and nineteenth centuries further exercised the same liberty by maintaining, that in all matters of science, science and not Scripture is the test of truth; and that in case of a difference between them, science is to be believed in preference to Scripture" (1862, xliv). The "twenty-three eminent divines" (1862, 182) cited by Stephen include Alford, Baxter, Berkeley, Burnet, Butler, Chillingworth, Heber, Hooker, Horsley, Marsh, Sumner, Jeremy Taylor, Tholuck, Tillotson, Tomline, Warburton, Whately, Whewell, and Thomas Wilson (1862, 111 ff.). All held that inspiration was a matter of opinion, not of dogmatic and prescribed belief. Further, even if the most extreme argument advocating plenary inspiration were the prescribed view, it would require specifying the "exact volume" that is so inspired: "Unless you specify the exact volume to which it applies, if you leave open the question of literary criticism, you leave open every question which could possibly arise if the question of inspiration were open" (1862, 185).

In the last part of his address to the Court of Arches, Stephen repudiates the view that Williams's comments on Bunsen can be taken as his own views, and denigrates the practice of Williams's prosecutors in garbling passages, and citing only very short passages at that, upon which to condemn him for major heresies: "Altogether, they extract three capital heresies from nine lines of print. Remember the case of *Burder* v. *Heath*. Recollect your own observations upon the difficulty you found in extracting Mr. Heath's views even from an isolated sermon upon the point in question, and then say whether it is possible to ascertain what Dr. Williams's views upon these all-important subjects are from little incidental remarks like these about another man's writings" (1862, 286–87).[14] Stephen outlines Williams's admiration, summation, and qualifications of Bunsen's position, "a very eminent writer who is charged with using evangelical language in a philosophical sense," concluding: "The real reason why he is prosecuted is simply that he insists that these subjects shall be discussed, and that an appeal shall be made to reason and conscience upon them. The prosecutors treat as a criminal a man who maintains that such a discussion ought to take place, simply because they dislike, and perhaps dread it" (295).

In his peroration, Stephen adopts a different tone, moving his argument to the Whig and Broad Church platform of rights and freedoms, and especially the right for freedom of inquiry. The account in the *Times* is even more dramatic than that in the (possibly reworked) published version: "There was no doubt that his Lordship's judgment could shut the mouths of the clergy. He could say, "Whoever doubts whether Daniel wrote *Daniel* must be silent, or lose his living." But could he shut the mouths of the laity? Would any one in this age and country dare to suggest that the Christian religion, and its vehicle the Bible, were not to be criticized at all? Could you silence literature? Could you silence science? Could you silence history? Can you send every man to the stake or the gallows who doubts the authorship of the Book of Daniel? . . . The clergy of the Church of England have freedom; they possess the only freedom worth having—namely, freedom secured by law. . . . And it is the exercise of this freedom which I defend here to-day" (*Times*, 9 Jan. 1862, 11–12; cf. Stephen 1862, 324–26). Accordingly, he renames the case as one of "constructive heresy," drawing a political comparison between the Arches trial and the high treason trials of 1794, in which the agitation for universal suffrage was interpreted as a move toward democracy, itself considered to be envisioning or compassing the death of the king, and imposing the tyranny of mass and despotic rule and the loss of freedom. Just as those accused of treason helped the push toward electoral reform (and were acquitted) so Williams, accused of heresy, is helping the move toward reform in the Church of England (and should be acquitted).[15] It is on this argument concerning freedom and tyranny that Stephen concludes that the case is one concerning political and religious liberty, concerning freedom of interpretation without let or hindrance: "It is the cause of learning, of freedom, and of reason—the learning of the most learned, the freedom of the freest, and the reason of the most rational church in the world" (Stephen 1862, 331).

Phillimore's presentation of the bishop of Salisbury's case against Williams followed that of Stephen; it took three days to deliver, 9–11 January 1862, and was published in a volume where the address occupied 175 pages.[16] He begins, like Stephen, by summarizing "the real issue before your lordship," the undermining of popular religion by *Essays and Reviews*:

> Is it competent to beneficed clergymen, with the cure of souls, who have subscribed the Articles and Formularies of the Church of England . . . to dispose of all the prophesies of the Old Testament; and by what they are pleased to call a "verifying faculty," to deny all miracles of the New? That, my lord, I say, stripped of its technicalities and of the cloud of verbiage which has been thrown over it, will be found to be the real issue which your lordship has to try; and it is one, the importance of which to the Church . . . I admit cannot be surpassed. . . . It is said that this volume of *Essays and Reviews*, which I now hold in my hand, was an innocent publication—a kind of closet speculation—which never would have obtained any notoriety or done any injury, if the Bishop of Salisbury had not instituted this suit against Dr. Williams. . . . No fair mind can close this volume without feeling it to be at bottom in direct antagonism to the whole system of popular belief. . . . In object, in spirit, and in method, in details no less than in general design, this book is incompatible

> with the religious belief of the mass of the Christian public, and the broad principles on which the Protestantism of Englishmen rests. (Phillimore 1862, 1–3).

Like Deane, Phillimore alludes to Harrison's *Westminster Review* article, but does so to show the impact of *Essays and Reviews* on the reading public. Furthermore, he alludes to the popularity of the book, and the potential damage it could do, provoking an exchange with Deane on the matter of publications and circulation. The *Times* reports that Phillimore "believed that the book had been circulated in a cheap form throughout the manufacturing districts, and that the poison of the work was influencing the minds of the artisans," to which Deane replied: "We . . . even employed a detective to inquire whether any true or garbled copies of this book had been published in the manufacturing districts, and we found that not one copy had been so circulated at Leeds." Phillimore then qualified his statement: "I have been informed that the Essays have been circulated in a cheap form, and sold for 1d. each among the artisans of Leeds," and again Deane denied the allegation (*Times*, 10 Jan. 1862, 9). The full version of Phillimore's speech records that he accepted Deane's intervention at face value, denied that he claimed that "editions of the book" were circulating at Leeds, and that he referred to circulation through the "secularist's lending library" (Phillimore 1862, 11–12). Phillimore's general appeal was to mass circulation and so to potential widespread damage from "the virus and the poison . . . being poured into the veins of the manufacturing artisans of this country," to universal condemnation, citing the reprobation of the houses of bishops from both the ecclesiastical provinces of Canterbury and of York, and to standards of orthodoxy in the Formularies. The Formularies were not merely imposed from without, but were subscribed to by every clergyman at the time of ordination; the obligations for conformity to their doctrinal standards was not only a condition for ordination but was also a condition for holding continuing appointment and office in the church. An effort to demonstrate the general "scope and tendency of the work" as a whole, the show the "co-operation between the writers" and to "illustrate the meaning of Dr. Williams from other Essays in the book," was disallowed.

Phillimore warns the court that if the Essayists and Reviewers have their way "the Hebrew Scriptures will take their place upon the bookshelf of the learned, beside the Arabian and Sanscrit poets" (1862, 4). The reason he gives is that "the whole scheme of salvation has to be entirely rearranged and altered": "Divine rewards and punishments, the Fall, original sin, the vicarious penalty, and salvation by faith are all, in the natural sense of the terms, repudiated as immoral delusions. Miracles, inspiration, and prophecy, in their plain and natural sense, are denounced as figments or exploded blunders. The Mosaic history dissolves into a mass of ill-digested legends, the Mosaic ritual into an Oriental system of priestcraft, and the Mosaic origin of the earth and man, sinks amidst the rubbish of rabbinical cosmogonies" (1862, 4). Such arguments from Phillimore depend, as Deane pointed out, on gross misrepresentations of what they had argued, that passages twenty pages apart had been connected together, and that an intervening passage had been transposed to the end (as in the 7th Article of Charge, concerning Williams ¶s 10, 28, and 24, cited in that sequence; see Ellen Williams 1870, 2:60).

On the central issue of inspiration, Phillimore asserted at length that the Church of England held the notion of plenary inspiration (see Jowett ¶s 14, 15, and notes): "The plenary inspiration of the Bible was the doctrine of the Church but in a different sense from that contended by the defendant. Inspiration, when applied to the Holy Scriptures, meant the action of the Holy Ghost upon the mind, different and distinct, not only in degree . . . but also in kind. . . . It was necessary for Dr. Williams to show that it was the mind of the Holy Ghost, expressed in the same way, which appeared in the works of Milton and Luther" (*Times*, 11 Jan. 1862, 9; see also Phillimore 1862, 174–75).

Like Deane and Stephen, and according to the standards of evidence and conventions of argument used in causes pleaded in the ecclesiastical courts, Phillimore "referred to and commented at considerable length on the writings of the other authorities that had been relied upon by the defendant, including Burnet, Barrow, and Tillotson. He also read several extracts from *Lectures on Inspiration* by Canon [Christopher] Wordsworth, which had been published since the *Essays and Reviews* had appeared, and also from the Bishop of London's [Tait's] work entitled *Dangers and Safeguards*. . . . He maintained that a clergyman within the Church could not treat the Bible in the same manner as he could criticize *Homer* or *Herodotus*" (*Times*, 11 Jan 1862, 9). The last remark contains, perhaps, a jab at Jowett, for arguing that the Bible is to be read like any other book.

Phillimore's next line of argument is to draw Williams into the net of German rationalism and then to align its terms (and those of Williams) with those of the English deists to demonstrate the scepticism of this entire drift in theology. The ideas in *Essays and Reviews* are not new; they "were of English origin and when discarded here were adopted in Germany, and now they had returned to us in a new form" (*Times*, 11 Jan. 1862, 9). A skillful gesture, it amounts to condemnation by guilt of association rather than demonstration of the error of Williams's own writings. By alluding to Bishops Pearson, Lowth, Marsh and others, already used in Williams's defense by Stephen, Phillimore shows how the same authorities and arguments, given this sketch of history, can be used against him. He then presents detailed evidence concerning specific points of biblical interpretation concerning each of the Articles of Charge.

Phillimore's peroration alludes again to the two major points of his argument, "the great subject of the authority and inspiration of 'God's Word written'" and "the Cardinal catholic doctrines of the Church of Christ," both of which he alleges Williams has denied. Phillimore denies again the supposition that his prosecution of the case is the result of "vulgar clamour" and attests to the widespread disapprobation of *Essays and Reviews* by reference to the episcopal censure and "nearly ten thousand of the clergy, whose petition I now hold in my hand." He concludes with an attack on Williams's learning ("a revival of the exploded heresies and discarded trash of the early heretics"), once again drawing the connections between it and sceptical deism and German rationalism, and the appeal to the Formularies as a bulwark against heresy and defense against "the most dishonest subterfuges, and the most palpable sophistry" (Phillimore 1862, 175). The last phrase, of course, adverts to the opening of Deane's speech (and to Williams's *Hints*) concerning the use of "no legal subterfuge," implicating both Williams and his lawyers in the slur.

On 11 January 1862 John Duke Coleridge continued to present the bishop of Salisbury's case against Williams, reiterating the impossibility of distinguishing Williams's views from those of Bunsen, stressing inspiration and the fact that "the Bible was in some sense different from all other books in the world." On inspiration Coleridge was slightly more liberal than Phillimore's "plenary inspiration": "Inspiration meant the communication of something to a person, of which we could not obtain the knowledge by the mere force of reason. Inspiration was what we call that quality which renders the writers of the Canonical Books infallible. He was not contending for verbal or literal inspiration of Holy Scripture, which meant that the very words were dictated by the Holy Ghost. But, as a rule of faith and practice, we take the Bible as an infallible authority" (*Times*, 12 Jan. 1862, 11).

On the charges concerning the repudiation of prophecy, Coleridge "quoted at great length from the sermons of Bishop [Samuel] Horsley, who regarded the predictive element of prophesy as one of the great pillars of the Christian Church, in opposition to the theory propounded in Dr. Williams's Essay, that the Messianic prophecies were melting away in the crucible of German literature." Williams's views on the book of Daniel are the subject of particular scorn: "He was not entitled to say that the Book of Daniel was written many years after the events therein foretold had occurred; that, in fact, the book was a literary trick and a forgery" (*Times*, 14 Jan. 1962, 9).

Coleridge concluded by uttering mock disbelief at what he would have heard in the proceedings, "that the Scripture may be questioned, and its exposition doubted, the prophecies denied, the Sacraments ridiculed, the authority of the Canon questioned, and that the man who does all this may remain a clergyman of the Church of England." He is following, and will lead others to follow, the path to "a despairing atheism" (*Times*, 14 Jan. 1862, 9).

After a brief foray by Maurice Swabey on Williams's apparent rejection of the historical veracity of the gospel narratives, Deane replied for the defense, first attacking the Episcopal manifesto as unfair, by condemning without a hearing and without citing offending passages and arguing infringements. Second he noted that subscription did not involve the present authorized version of scripture, as counsel for the bishop of Salisbury suggested, since the canon was framed before the AV was translated. Third, doctrine had nothing to do with prophecy, he argued, according to the conventional division of divinity as a field of knowledge into three sections, doctrine, ritual, and evidences: prophecy falls within the last category, not the first. Just as the prosecutors had backed away from verbal inspiration, it might be that they would concede there are different views of prophecy, Deane suggested.

As part of the subfield of divinity called "evidence," prophecy was open to examination and criticism. On the matter of inspiration, it was not a question of what definition of inspiration various divines had held, but whether Williams had infringed the doctrinal position set out in the Articles of Religion and the Formularies. Authorities might be attested who could explain such doctrinal positions, but it was a matter of determining Williams's views in relation to alleged infringements of specific documents that was at issue.

After dealing with a series of particular Articles of Charge, accusations, and points of interpretation regarding specific passages of scripture, Deane turned to the question of whether only a literal interpretation of the Bible was the prescribed position of the Church of England. Even on a literal level, he argued, William's position is acceptable and within the tolerated limits of faith and practice. For instance, when Williams asks questions concerning possible natural causes for alleged divine interventions into natural history that are represented as historical fact, the asking of such questions is not in itself heretical: "Dr. Williams did not entertain any doubts as to the truth of the history contained in the Old Testament; but he inquired whether the events brought about by the providence of God—the Deluge, for instance—could not be accounted for by the operation of fixed and immutable laws. That was not heresy" (*Times*, 17 Jan. 1862, 11). Deane here is at best literal, at worst disingenuous. Saying that Williams "did not entertain any doubts" may be literally true with respect to what he wrote concerning the "history" of the Old Testament; but the question of whether the flood is a historical event remains, and the asking of questions about it certainly implies doubts concerning its historicity, if not its providential cause. If it be taken as a natural phenomenon, or as a phenomenon in nature, then the issue of divine agency as a cause remains, but not the matter of history. Such precise and close reasoning is characteristic of Deane's other refutations of the arguments of Phillimore and Coleridge.

Wilson's section of the trial came before Lushington first on 23 January, but the session was brief, in which Deane asked for further time to consider the articles of charge. He was granted a week, and within that time had to declare whether or not he was opposing them (*Times*, 24 Jan. 1862, 9). Having done so, he began the hearing on 22 February 1862. Because so many of the arguments concerning Williams applied also to Wilson, his case was heard in only five days of debate rather than the nine days given to Williams. As before, Phillimore began by reading the nineteen Articles of Charge, both formal and substantive, and asked the court to admit them, to each of which Stephen objected. He began arguing the case in Wilson's defense by going over each of the charges and adding to the citations he had made in the case of Williams other sources and precedents more directly applicable to the detail of Wilson's argument. Deane returned to the Court of Arches on 24 February, and subjected James Fendall, the promoter of the case against Wilson, to his share of ad hominem argument: "He [Deane] remarked upon the length of time that had elapsed before this suit had been instituted by the voluntary promoter, and was at a loss to understand how the prosecution had been delayed. He supposed the heresy complained of was so shadowy and ideal that it had escaped the grasp of Mr. Fendall, and that it was so subtle and volatile that it was unsusceptible of chymical analysis" (*Times*, 25 Feb. 1862, 12). Having dealt, like Stephen, with the charges in detail he concluded with the necessity of measuring the cited passages against the standards of the Formularies: "You charge me with only thoughts or opinions by selecting passages from different parts of the essay; but you must bring my doctrine face to face with the doctrine of the Church, and, failing your doing that, your prosecution, whether brought by Bishop or voluntary promoter, must fail, and for all the vexation you have brought upon the Church you, and you only, are responsible" (*Times*, 25 Feb. 1862, 12).

Phillimore's reply rejected the notion that a clergyman might, as he alleged Wilson had, "select for himself that part of the Bible was the Word of God, what the 'dark patches of human passions and error' as the defendant had said" [Wilson ¶39] (*Times*, 26 Jan. 1862, 11). As with Williams, Phillimore drew Wilson as part of an international theological conspiracy: "Ideology, the substitution of ideas for facts, has led to admitted infidelity in Germany, under Strauss, and this defendant had adopted Strauss's principles, though he had stopped short, for the present, of their entire application. . . . The doctrines of Christianity were inseparable from the facts of Christianity; but the system of ideology rendered Our Lord and the Evangelists imposters" (*Times*, 26 Jan. 1862, 11). When Lushington asked whether, given the liberty of criticism the church allowed, if a clergyman might doubt that one verse or one chapter has divine authority, might he doubt a whole book of the Bible, and where might the line be drawn. To this question Swabey replied "that criticism must be restricted, that it must be confined to the examination of manuscripts and editions. But ideology was a system which differed entirely from the legitimate criticism permitted by the Church of England to its members" (*Times*, 26 Jan. 1862, 11). The same questions were repeated on 3 March, together with a question concerning miracles: "If one miracle may be construed allegorically, why not all?" (*Times*, 4 Mar. 1862, 11). Phillimore in turn responded by attacking the "foreign name of ideology": "As to miracles, the Church had not sanctioned at all the use of ideology in their interpretation," apparently conflating the notion of ideology and allegorical interpretation: "Individual divines might have occasionally, under the pressure of a supposed difficulty in comprehending a particular miracle in a literal sense, chosen to interpret it allegorically. But even they had never claimed the general right of putting an ideological interpretation on all miracles when a plain and literal reading sufficed for the interpretation of them" (*Times*, 4 Mar. 1862, 11). After further explanation along the same lines, Lushington again intervened, and declared that since Phillimore had not indicated where the line was to be drawn between allowing the allegorical interpretation of one miracle, and of all, he would have to draw it himself.

The final speech was that of Deane, once more asserting, as he did for Williams, that the passages selected for interrogation had been removed from their context "so as to make them appear to be connected passages." He denied that

Wilson had rejected the doctrines of inspiration, the incarnation, the resurrection, and went over again each of the accusations. Lushington reserved his judgment, finally delivering it as an "interlocutory judgment" on 25 June, asking that a number of the Articles of Charge be revised, some be rejected, and some sustained before he delivered his final judgment.

A month before Lushington delivered his judgment, and just two weeks before he left Lampeter College, Williams preached his farewell sermon, on a text from Psalm 119:161–63: "Princes have persecuted me without a cause; but my heart standeth in awe of thy word." He published it with the title, *Persecution for the Word* (1862), and hoped for a good result: "What will be the result of this suit, undertaken in order to procure the falsification of literature, brought forward under untrue pretexts, supported by dislocated quotations, pleaded with rude unfairness, and painfully procrastinated beyond its natural occasion? I trust, even surrounded by all arts of chicane, to reap from the God of justice, a reward for the many years in which I have taught faithfully the doctrines of my own Church, in an easy bursting of this episcopal bubble" (43). But the episcopal bubble had a tough skin.

III "Not a Court of Divinity, but a Court of Ecclesiastical Law": The Interlocutory Judgment

On 25 June 1862, Dr. Lushington delivered the "interlocutory," or provisional, judgment concerning the admissibility of the "Articles of Charge" in the cases of both Williams and Wilson. This judgment was published as *Essays and Reviews. Judgment Delivered on the 25th of June 1862 in the Case of the Bishop of Salisbury versus Williams, and in the Case of Fendall versus Wilson*, a document of 44 pages in which Lushington discusses the implications and merits of the cases in general and in detail. It was also published in the *Times* (26 June 1862, 9). Although he could not deliver his final judgment until he examined the reformed articles and heard arguments on them, it was the interlocutory judgment that dealt in substance with the main charges against Williams and Wilson. The final judgment confirmed the decisions made on specific articles in the interlocutory judgment.

In the case of Williams, Lushington retained the formal Articles of Charge (1–6 and 18–22), but rejected all of the others, except Articles 7, 12, 15, and 16. He admitted 15 and 16, but required that 7 and 12 be "reformed" or reformulated.[17] In the case of Wilson, Lushington retained the formal articles (1–6 and 15–19) but rejected four of the eight remaining substantive charges (7, 9, 10, 11). One "Article of Charge" against Wilson (13) was withdrawn during argument; Lushington admitted one (14), and ordered that the remaining two be reformed (8, 12).[18] Hence, of the original substantive charges, four remained against Williams, three against Wilson.

Both parties were given permission to appeal at this stage to the Judicial Committee of the Privy Council, but neither side elected to do so, reserving that option until Lushington delivered his final judgment: the prosecutors because they wished to have the case settled in the ecclesiastical rather than in the secular courts which they distrusted ever since the sensational Gorham judgment, notwithstanding the decision in the Heath judgment that supported the condemnation from the Court of Arches; the defendants because they already knew that many of the charges had already been dismissed against them, and they hoped that more would be dismissed.[19]

Lushington's opening paragraph sets out the circumstances under which the case came before the Court of Arches, and explains why he delayed his judgment until the case of *Burder v. Heath* was dealt with by the Judicial Committee of the Privy Council, since it too concerned the case of a clergyman who maintained doctrine alleged to be at variance with the Anglican Formularies. That case together with the case of *Gorham v. the Bishop of Exeter* (1848–50) were important precedents for Lushington. He cites *Burder v. Heath* to determine "that the Articles should specify, on the one hand, the opinions which the clerk [in Holy Orders] has advisedly maintained; on the other the doctrines of the Church which the opinions are alleged to contravene, and the particular Articles or portions of the Formularies which contain these doctrines" (4). Lushington returns over and over again to this decision.[20]

Lushington's Judgment in the Case against Williams

Turning immediately to the case of Williams, Lushington frames his treatment of the individual charges of heresy by dealing first with the general objections to the Articles of Charge raised by Williams's lawyers. In answering their objections, Lushington draws a distinction between the technical requirements of administering ecclesiastical law and speculative "theological questions" (13): he asserts that his only concern is to test the passages cited in the "Articles of Charge" against the legal Formularies. In this narrowing of his duties, he relies upon precedents in the judgments on appeals in ecclesiastical cases already heard by the Judicial Committee of Privy Council. He also asserts the right of private judgment on the part of clergy, provided such opinion, if contrary to the Formularies, be kept to oneself. At the same time, despite his protestations of adopting a dispassionate stance whose "duty" is "only to administer the law" (8), he often has "no hesitation in declaring my opinion" (11), sometimes in direct criticism of the accused.

Lushington summarizes Williams's lawyers' objections as "of a threefold character": "that divers opinions are imputed to Dr. Williams which he has not maintained; . . . that the opinions imputed to him have been submitted to a test not warranted by Ecclesiastical Law, viz. extracts from the Bible; [and] . . . that the opinions which the Articles may show Dr. Williams to have maintained are not opinions forbidden to a Clergyman to hold and publish" (4).

To the first objection Lushington replies by tackling the generic differences between the other essays in *Essays and Reviews* that argue specific positions on the part of their authors and the instance of Williams, who presents his argument in the form of a review of the writings of Bunsen: "I must hold that it is not competent to the reviewer, when he either states or professes to give the substance of unsound doctrine from the work reviewed, to leave his own opinion in the dark. . . . After many perusals of the Essay,[21] after carefully considering the arguments of his Counsel, I think this Review does prove a general but not indiscriminate approval of the opinions quoted from the work of Baron Bunsen,—a general adoption, with particular exceptions. . . . Surely it was his [Williams's] duty to have taken care that he did not so arrange his quotations and shape his observations as to leave it in doubt, whether he, a Clergyman of the Church of England, approved of what may be found to be repugnant to the doctrines as by law established" (4–5).

The second objection, addressing the general question of the legitimate tests for doctrinal orthodoxy in ecclesiastical law, is treated extensively by Lushington. His precedent is the Gorham case: "What has the Court got to try? Theological error in its general sense,—*i.e.* whether Dr. Williams is sound or unsound in his theological views; whether he has maintained doctrine inconsistent with the true doctrine of the Christian faith? Certainly not. The issue is, Has Dr. Williams promulgated doctrines at variance with the doctrines of the Church, as declared in the Articles and Formularies?" (5–6). Lushington argues that neither popular outcry nor episcopal censure can be legitimate tests for doctrinal orthodoxy: "The Court cannot pretend ignorance of the great excitement created by the publication of this volume; but the effect of such excitement upon the mind of the Court ought to be this only: to induce me to exercise all the care and vigilance in my power, and to preserve a perfectly equal and dispassionate mind, looking only to ascertain the law, and justly administer it. It has been said that this volume has been censured by the whole Episcopal Bench. Be it so. I cannot accede to the argument, that the mind of the Court should be influenced by that circumstance. Individually, I should receive with the highest respect the opinion of the Right Rev. Prelates; as a Judge, I can be guided by nothing but judicial authority. This is not a Court of Divinity, but a Court of Ecclesiastical Law" (6). Given this distinction between theology and law, Lushington denies the admissibility of the theological writings of Anglican or other divines as expert witnesses either for or against the accused: "I, as Judge of the Arches Court, cannot take for my guide the authority of even the most learned and orthodox divines of our Church. But so it is: it follows as a consequence of the duty of the Court as defined in the Gorham Judgment. . . . I shall neither form my opinion upon the authority of any of the eminent divines, whose works have been brought to the attention of the Court, nor quote any passages from their writings which might support my conclusions, nor attempt to grapple with the various citations from learned works, which might appear to conflict with them" (6–7). Doctrinal orthodoxy, then, is to be tested only against "the Articles of Religion, the Formularies, and the Canons, interpreted according to legal construction" (7), an interpretation, he asserts, that is derived from their "plain literal and grammatical sense" (11–12), in the words of the "Royal Declaration." Furthermore, he draws a distinction between private opinion and public pronouncement. Private opinion on any matter is left to one's own conscience; the courts can only deal with public pronouncements: "There is no inquisitorial power" (7).

Citing the judgment in the case of *Gorham v. the Bishop of Exeter* as precedent, Lushington agrees that "all theological questions not determined by the Articles or Liturgy are open questions" (9), despite the fact that "in a book like the 'Essays and Reviews' there may be much that, in the private opinion of the Court, excites deep regret and is deserving of censure, and yet the law of the Church may not reach it" (9). He continues: "With respect to the construction to be put upon the Articles and Liturgy I again have the advantage of the authority of the Gorham case [where the judgment of the Privy Council states:] 'The rules to be applied are the rules by law applicable to the construction of all written instruments. The consideration of external and historical facts is to be imported only so far as is necessary to understand the subject matter and the meaning of the words employed. We seek the plain literal and grammatical sense.' To the same effect is the higher authority of the King's Declaration" (11–12).[22] On the question of whether reference could be made in either prosecution or defense to the Bible, Lushington cites the Judicial Committee in the Heath judgment: "'It would be a departure from our duty if we were to admit any discussion as to the conformity or nonconformity of the Articles of Religion, or any of them, with the Holy Scriptures'" (12). Lushington applies this principle to Williams: "Pressed by these reasons, and urged by every motive to preserve peace in the Church, I will not be tempted, in the trial of any accusation against a Clergyman, to resort to Scripture as the standard by which the doctrine shall be measured; and I may with perfect truth add, that, were such a task imposed upon me, the want of theological knowledge would incapacitate me from adequately discharging it. The Articles [of Charge] then must be reformed by striking out all reference to extracts from the Bible found in the Prayer Book" (12–13).

The third objection, that "opinions maintained by him [Williams] are not such as are forbidden to a Clergyman to hold and publish," is said by Lushington to be "of momentous importance to the Clergy and the Laity," since it concerns "the question of the authority . . . to be ascribed by the Clergy to the Bible, and the limits within which the Clergy are restricted in publishing opinions immediately connected with Holy Writ" (13). But according to Lushington, he is not free to consider in general questions of "Inspiration, Miracles and Prophecies, the limits of Criticism and Interpretation" (13) but must deal with them only in the consideration of the particular Articles of Charge. In addressing this issue, Lushington sets out "a few general remarks," noting that the legal position on Holy Scripture is defined in Articles 6, 7, and 20 of the Articles of Religion, and in the question in the Ordination of Deacons: "Do you unfeignedly believe all the Canonical Scriptures of the Old and New Testament?" Lushington argues that this question must be considered "with reference to the subject matter, and that is the whole Bible," bearing in mind "the great number of these Books; the extreme antiquity of some; that our Scriptures must necessarily consist of copies and translations; that they embrace almost every possible variety of subject, parts being all-important to the salvation of mankind, and parts being historical and of a less sacred character, certainly not without some element of allegory and figures" (14–15). Thus, discussing the Bible as "canonical Scriptures" raises broad theological questions that Lushington wishes to separate from matters of ecclesiastical law.

However important these questions may be in theology, they are set aside as not covered by the Articles of Religion and so are irrelevant to the Articles of Charge. These questions are treated by Lushington in order: the relations between the ordination oath of the clergy and personal belief (14–15), biblical inspiration as a matter of legal doctrine (15–16), the right of clergy to offer criticism as distinguished from interpretation (16), the authorship of the various biblical books (16), and canonicity (16–17). Lushington limits his consideration to the technical definition of the meaning of the words "canonical Scriptures" in the ordination vow, and "Holy Scripture" in the Articles of Religion. He acknowledges the importance of the subject matter to religion and society in general, but again rejects such a discussion for these cases, limiting his definition: "The expressions 'God's Word written' and 'Scripture' are in this Article [20] plainly identical. . . . It is no part of my duty to define it [inspiration], and I shall not attempt to do so; but . . . I hold that in the phrases 'God's Word written' and 'the Holy Scripture containeth all things necessary to salvation' is necessarily implied the doctrine that in all matters necessary for salvation the Holy Scriptures emanated from the extraordinary and preternatural interposition of the Almighty,—the special mode and limit unknown to man" (15). By these definitions Lushington holds that "any Clergyman who advisedly maintains, whether in direct or indirect language, that the Holy Scriptures proceed from the same mental powers as have produced other works, or *vice versâ*, even with the qualification that these powers in the one case and the other differ in degree, impairs the Divine authority of Holy Scriptures, does in fact maintain that the Bible is not God's Word written, but is the work of man, and thereby contravenes the Sixth and Twentieth Articles of Religion" (16).

Before addressing the individual substantive Articles of Charge, Lushington considers Williams's "right of criticism," drawing a distinction between criticism and interpretation, tolerating a wide view of criticism concerning biblical texts and disputed authorship, and by-passing the issue of differing interpretations: "By criticism, as distinguished from interpretation, I mean examining and determining the text of Scripture. . . . As a matter of fact, learned divines, of whose orthodoxy I believe there is no reason to doubt, have come to the conclusion that certain verses or parts have been erroneously introduced, and are not really entitled to keep their place in Scripture. I am of opinion that . . . the law would not require me to hold persons coming to similar conclusions guilty of any Ecclesiastical offence. . . . I think it could not be permitted to Clergymen to reject the whole of one of the Books of Scripture . . . . Under the same head comes the discussion as to the authorship of the various Books . . . . I think it is open for the Clergy to maintain that any Book in the Bible is the work of another author than him whose name it bears, provided that they conform to the Sixth Article by admitting that the Book is an inspired writing and canonical" (16).

These opening remarks, the summation of Williams's lawyers' objections under three headings, enable Lushington to set out his own presuppositions, and his own manner of procedure. He first concludes that Williams must be held responsible for indicating where his views differ from those of Bunsen, and if he does not do so, then he is to be held as guilty if the arguments, whether his or Bunsen's, are deemed heretical by the legal criteria. Second he agrees at least in substantial part with Williams's lawyers' objections, in that popular outrage and episcopal censure cannot be a valid ground for condemnation under ecclesiastical law, nor is any such evidence admissible. Further, the passages of the Bible adduced in the Articles of Charge and alleged to have been rejected by Williams cannot be regarded as a legal test of religious orthodoxy. He also rejects as irrelevant all arguments based on theological precedent and the views of experts, all citation of the fathers of the church or Anglican divines. At the same time, Lushington clearly indicates the basis of his own judgment, declaring that, on the precedent of two famous cases, *Burder v. Heath* and *Gorham v. the Bishop of Exeter*, ecclesiastical law must proceed on the criminal charge of heresy only according to infringements of the Articles of Religion and the Formularies. Third, by assessing the implications of the Deacon's ordination oath concerning Holy Scripture, Lushington is able to set aside many disputed theological matters concerning inspiration, interpretation, and criticism, while insisting that the notion of the Bible as the word of God is a matter on which the Court can deliver a judgment.

Having disposed of these objections of Williams's lawyers, Lushington then proceeds to deal with each of the Articles of Charge in succession, beginning after the technical and formal articles (relating to the authors of *Essays and Reviews* and its publication history), with Articles 5 and 6.

ARTICLES 5 AND 6. Article 5, concerning the Preface "To the Reader," raises the question of why no changes were made during the "nine editions" up to the time of the trial. Lushington rejects Hamilton's lawyers' argument that despite the words of the Preface the book was planned as a collaboration and that Williams was at least guilty by association with the views of others in the volume: "there is no attempt in these proceedings to charge Dr. Williams with any responsibility for the writings of other persons." Lushington concludes that the fifth Article of Charge is "of slight importance" but also that it indicates "the adherence of Dr. Williams to the original design: it constitutes a history of the case. This Article does not conclude with any charge. In one sense, it is beneficial to the party accused; for the Introduction distinctly sets forth the avowal that each writer was responsible, or at least intended to be so, only for his own contribution. I shall admit the Article, and also, for similar reasons, the one next following it" (18). Article 6 concerns the publication history during which the essay has not undergone substantial alteration.

Article 7. After declining to comment on several of the sentences cited from ¶10 of William's review of Bunsen, Lushington considers the Bible as the word of God, denying that the passage cited from ¶28 impugns the Articles of Religion on this point. The passage concerns the "verifying faculty" that allows clergy the "liberty to reject parts of Scripture upon their own opinion that the narrative is inherently incredible, to disregard precepts in Holy Writ because they think them evidently wrong" (19). Lushington then turns to Williams's two phrases concerning the Bible as the "expression of devout reason" and as "the written word of the congregation" cited in the seventh article of charge. To Lushington the first phrase "is inconsistent with the doctrine that it was written by the interposition of God; which doctrine, I have said, is an indispensable part of the Sixth Article. It appears to me, that if the Bible in matters essential to salvation be declared to have emanated from Divine power, all suppositions inconsistent with that declaration are necessarily excluded. If it be God's Word written, as said in the Twentieth Article, it is not the expression of devout reason." On the second phrase Lushington comments:

> It is not a denial that the Bible is inspired, but it alleges that it is the written voice of the congregation. . . . It is not in my province to say whether this was the earliest creed of the Church. I have to look to the doctrine of the Church of England only; and, so far as my knowledge extends, there is not to be found in the Articles or in the Formularies a single syllable consistent with the assertion that the Bible is the written voice of the congregation. The doctrine of the Church of England is expressed in the Twentieth Article, that the Bible is the written Word of God. . . .
>
> I hold that the Sixth and Seventh Articles of Religion impose the obligation of acknowledging that the Bible, in matters essential to salvation, is the written Word of God; that it was written by the interposition of the Almighty, supernaturally brought to operate. I hold that, to declare the Bible to be an expression of devout reason,—to be the written voice of the congregation,—is a violation of the Sixth and Seventh Articles of Religion. I think such positions are substantially inconsistent with the all-important doctrine imposed by law, that the Bible is God's Word written.
>
> This article must be reformed. (19–20)

Article 8: On the charge that Williams has denied the "element of divinely inspired prediction or prognostication of future persons or events" in prophecy, Lushington rules:

> Such charge extends to all predictions, whether Messianic or otherwise. As I have said, I think, upon consideration of the whole extract, that, though there may be some very doubtful passages, it does not clearly appear that Dr. Williams has asserted so general a denial, and therefore I need say no more as to the charge in its full bearing. I must, however, consider the charge of denying *Messianic* predictions. . . . The doctrine usually maintained is, that the prophecies are beyond doubt Messianic; not that every prophecy is Messianic

> . . . but the doctrine is, that there is ample and incontestable proof that an adequate portion of the prophecies is Messianic; that the great events of our Lord appearing on earth, and many of the other facts connected with the appearance, are foretold by the prophets through the aid of the Holy Spirit. . . . But this is not the question which the law directs me to consider. The true question is, Has Dr. Williams in these passages contravened any of the Articles of Religion or the Liturgy as cited?
>
> Now admitting that Dr. Williams . . . has denied Messianic prophecy, I cannot find in the Articles of Religion quoted, viz. the Sixth and Seventh, any direct mention of Messianic prophecy, or undoubted reference to it. . . . Though I think Dr. Williams's opinion militates against one of the most important doctrines held by the most venerated divines of the Church, I cannot come to the conclusion that the Articles of Religion or the Liturgy have in this respect been violated. I must, therefore, reject this Article (21–22).

ARTICLE 9: On the authorship of the books of the Bible, specifically the passages relating to the books of Daniel and Jonah, Lushington considers whether Williams has contravened the Articles of Religion by asserting that the book of Daniel was not written by Daniel, that it was written to encourage the uprising against Antiochus Epiphanes, that it contains no literal prediction, and that clergy should not persist in finding in it such common errors. While admitting that all these views "may be wholly erroneous" (23), Lushington finds than none of them contravenes the Articles of Religion, and so this charge must be rejected.

ARTICLE 10: On Williams's denial of the canonicity of specific books of the Bible, Lushington finds that in asserting that they are "genuine," Williams is asserting their canonicity, the only matter covered in the Sixth Article of Religion, and quite irrespective of matters of dating, or the dating of particular passages. Furthermore, the denial of the Pauline authorship of the Epistle to the Hebrews, or the assertion that it is "post apostolic," is not to deny its canonicity; nor is the denial of the Petrine attribution of the Second Epistle of St. Peter a denial of canonicity, nor is an assertion about "an incorrect and unfounded comparison of what is found in the Apocalypse [with historical data] . . . a rejection of the Apocalypse from the Canon." He concludes: "The whole is a matter of interpretation; and questions of interpretation . . . I have no authority to investigate" (24–25). Hence, this Article of Charge is rejected.

ARTICLE 11: The charge of reading "historical facts" in the Bible in a "wholly figurative sense, and in a non-natural sense," is adjudged by Lushington as a matter "not struck at by the Sixth and Seventh Articles of Religion" (26):

> A general averment that the statements of Holy Scripture as to historical facts may be read and understood in a wholly figurative sense, cannot be deemed a violation of the declaration of belief in the truth of Scripture. To put a

> particular construction, however erroneous or absurd, on a part of Holy Scripture, cannot in a criminal case be deemed a contradiction of the Deacon's declaration of his belief in the truth of Holy Scripture. It is a denial of the truth of ordinary, or what may be called orthodox, interpretation, but not of the truth of the writing itself. The limits of my duty, as prescribed by the Privy Council, forbid me to enter into questions of interpretation, or to constitute myself a judge in any question of divinity, or as to what is the most correct construction of any part of the Bible, save with reference only to the Articles of Religion and the Formularies cited; and in the passages I have commented upon there is no repugnance to them . . . . The examination of such questions is not within my jurisdiction. I reject this Article (26–27).

ARTICLE 12: To the charge of denying the efficacy of the actions of Christ in his passion and resurrection, and hence of holding defective views of the atonement, Lushington contrasts Williams's use of the word "propitiation" (in ¶27) as "the recovery of that Peace which cannot be, while Sin divides us from the Searcher of hearts" with that used in Article 31 as the "oblation by Christ finished upon the Cross for sin" (27). He finds that Williams's view is "inconsistent with and contrary to the Thirty-first Article" (27). Concerning the matters of defective or corrupt views of the atonement in ¶31, the comments on reconciliation and transubstantiation appear to Lushington, following the arguments of Williams's Counsel, to be those of the Roman Catholic Church rather than those of the established church. Accordingly Lushington asked that this Article be reformed.

ARTICLE 13: On the charge of defective views of baptismal regeneration, Lushington accepts Williams's assertions as historical rather than doctrinal or statements of opinion. Lushington asserts that they do not contain a denial of original sin and that the references to St. Augustine are too general to be adequately documented. Even if they were documented, he argues, they would have to show that a contradiction of St. Augustine is identical with contradicting an Article of Religion: "In any view of the case, the inferences are too doubtful to allow me to come to the conclusions which, by the arguments on behalf of the prosecution, I am called upon to form. The Article must therefore be rejected" (29).

ARTICLE 14: Rejecting the charge that Williams has a defective view of the incarnation when set against the second Article of Religion, Lushington finds that the comparison made by Williams of Bunsen's view of the incarnation with that of Paul is "not an unfair quotation, or rather expression of the substance, of what St. Paul wrote, with one exception . . . the omission of the concluding words, 'by the resurrection from the dead.' . . . I am of the opinion that the omission of the reference to the resurrection does not appear to be necessarily either intentional or culpable; and I must reject the Article" (30).

ARTICLE 15: At issue is Williams's assertion in ¶26 that "justification by faith" means "only the peace of mind or sense of Divine approval which comes of trust in a righteous God; and that 'justification is a verdict of forgiveness upon our repentance, and of acceptance upon the offering of our hearts'" (30). Lushington claims: "The words are suggested by Dr. Williams as words which Baron Bunsen might speak in reply to a charge of using evangelical language in a philosophical sense. But looking to the whole context, I cannot doubt that Dr. Williams employs these words as a form of declaring his own sentiments. He is therefore responsible for them" (31). Lushington admits this Article of Charge as "repugnant to the Eleventh Article" of Religion, in that justification is not "for the merit of our Lord by faith, but a 'fiction of merit by transfer,'" an idea "wholly inconsistent with the Eleventh Article" (31).

ARTICLE 16: Referring to Williams's peroration and eulogistic poem on Bunsen that close his essay, Lushington admits this Article, in that in general Williams "approves and adopts the opinions of Baron Bunsen" (31).

ARTICLE 17: This Article of Charge contends that Williams's intent in "the tendency, object, and design of the whole Essay is to inculcate a disbelief of the Divine inspiration and orthodoxy of the Holy Scriptures; to deny the truth of parts thereof, and to deny the doctrines of original sin, justification by faith, atonement, propitiation, and the incarnation" (31). Since this charge requires consideration of the whole Essay and a general condemnation, "without any reference to any particular Articles of Religion," Lushington finds that it is "without precedent" and cannot be considered in light of the principles laid down by the Judicial Committee of the Privy Council in the case of *Burder v. Heath*, namely, "that the words or writings of the person accused must be pleaded; that the meaning, which they are alleged by the prosecution to convey, must be pleaded; and the particular Articles of Religion, or parts of them, asserted to be contravened, must be pleaded also. None of these things are done . . . and therefore I consider I am bound to reject it" (31–32).

Lushington, therefore, has rejected seven of the substantive Articles of Charge against Williams, has admitted two (15 and 16) and has ordered two (7 and 12) to be reformed before he hears them finally and pronounces on them in his final judgment. Williams and his lawyers were left with four major charges to argue in at least a summary fashion before the final judgment, though fundamentally Williams had already been found guilty of them in some sense, since it was admitted that there were grounds for accepting the articles, or demanding that they be reformulated in ways to make them stick. They dealt with the inspiration of the prophets and the nature of the Bible as the word of God (seventh article of charge), the atonement (twelfth article of charge), the definition of justification by faith (fifteenth article), and a general adherence to and approval of the theology and writings of Baron Bunsen (sixteenth article). The prospects of his being condemned seemed all too certain.

Lushington's Judgment in the Case against Wilson

Lushington asserts that the "same general rules and principles" for evidence and pleading must obtain in the case against Wilson as are already set out in the interlocutory judgment on Williams: "For this case and the previous one, though they may differ altogether as to the contents of the particular Articles [of Charge], yet are subject to precisely the same general rules and principles. These rules I have already fully considered and have nothing to add" (33). They had served to prepare for the condemnation of Williams, and, it was apparent, would now also work against Wilson. Lushington then moves immediately to discuss the specific Articles of Charge against Wilson.

Article 7: Addressing this charge against Wilson concerning the person, nature, and work of Christ, Lushington comments:

> To deny that our Saviour was the revealer of God's scheme of redemption, and the person through whose life, death, and resurrection redemption is wrought out, is to deny the very foundation of the Christian religion itself. There could be no heavier charge preferred against a Clergyman of the Church of England than this. But if such be the nature of the charge, it behooves a Court of Justice most seriously to consider whether it is satisfactorily established by the alleged proofs.
>
> I turn, then, to Mr. Wilson's own words. It is, indeed, to be regretted that Mr. Wilson in his Essay has frequently expressed himself in language so ambiguous as to admit of opposite constructions. He says that "the source of religion is in the heart." This is an expression capable of more than one meaning: in one sense it may be true; but it is false, if it be construed to deny that religion does not arise from other causes (33).

Similarly Lushington finds that other passages are open to divers and often contradictory meanings, and so cannot find any "repugnancy to the Articles and Formularies. On the whole, therefore, I come to the conclusion, that as a criminal charge this Article cannot be supported" (35).

Article 8: This article of charge deals with the related matters of the inspiration and interpretation of the Bible. Concerning the question of inspiration, Lushington refers to the comments he already made on the case of Williams: "I must declare my opinion to be, that the true construction of those Articles [of Religion] is, that the Scriptures, so far as relates to matters concerning salvation, were written by the Divine interposition of God, and that in a manner different from the ordinary agency of Providence, but I cannot go the length of saying that all parts of what are termed the Holy Scriptures were, without exception, so written" (35). In this qualification Lushington draws a distinction between what in the Bible is deemed necessary to salvation and what is not necessary. The Articles [of Religion] assert that the Bible "containeth" what is necessary to salvation, without specifying specific passages, but is silent on what in the Bible is not necessary to salvation. Hence, Lushington has nothing more to say about the "Divine interposition" concerning the scriptures than what the Articles of Religion affirm. But Wilson, in the cited passage, "expressing the opinion which he himself holds, denies that the Bible was written by the special interposition of the Almighty power; and . . . such doctrine cannot be reconciled with the Sixth and Twentieth Articles" (36). Other parts of the cited passage relate to what Lushington designates "interpretation," "the right of accepting, literally or allegorically, as parable, poetry, or legend, many of the facts recorded in Scripture" (36). Such matters of interpretation are beyond the Court's competence. Lushington ordered this Article of Charge to be reformed.

ARTICLE 9: At issue is Wilson's use of the terms *Idealist* and *Ideology*, whether Wilson "maintained that a Clergyman of the Church of England is at liberty to hold and promulgate a metaphysical or ideal interpretation in respect of any part of the Scriptures, as to him shall seem meet, and to deny the reality of any of the facts contained in the Scriptures" (36).[23] Although Lushington admits: "I am not sure that I distinctly comprehend the true meaning to be ascribed to the word 'Idealist' and the word 'Ideology.' They are terms with which I am not familiar." Despite self-professed unfamiliarity with the terms, Lushington does not cavil at a definition that opposes an "idealist" interpretation with a "literal and grammatical" one: "an Idealist claims the right of interpreting Scripture contrary to the rule prescribed by law for interpreting the Articles of Religion,—contrary, that is, to the usual meaning, the literal and grammatical sense,—and of saying, 'This or that narrative is an allegory, a parable, poetry, or a legend'" (37). With scarcely concealed regret, he is forced to reject the article: "I plainly see to what fearful consequences this doctrine may be carried; but, provided that the doctrines of the Articles of Religion and the Formularies are not contravened, the law lays down no limits of construction, no rule of interpretation for the Scriptures. My authority cannot reach this case. Accordingly I reject the Article" (37).

ARTICLE 10: Concerning Wilson's argument on subscription to the Articles of Religion, "receiving and understanding them in a sense other than the plain literal meaning thereof, . . . an offence contrary to the Thirty-sixth of the Canons of 1603" (37), Lushington summarizes Wilson's position: "It is to affirm that a Clergyman may subscribe to the Articles without any regard to the plain literal meaning thereof, and at the same time repudiate the essential doctrines contained therein. . . . So in this instance, it is one thing to violate the Thirty-sixth Canon, another to advise others to do it. Mr. Wilson has not violated the Thirty-sixth Canon; he has conformed to it, though he may have advised others to evade it. The Thirty-sixth Canon punishes only those who have disobeyed it, viz. the Bishops who admit a Clerk who has not conformed to its directions. I cannot satisfy my mind that Mr.

Wilson has committed any breach of the Thirty-sixth Canon itself; and as that is the only charge contained in this Article, I cannot admit the Article" (38–39).

ARTICLE 11: This Article of Charge deals with the matter of clerical subscription to the Thirty-nine Articles of Religion. It is affirmed that Wilson in the cited passage in ¶51 holds, in the words of the Article of Charge, that "it is lawful for a Clergyman of the Church of England himself to disbelieve the doctrines contained in the first five of the Articles of Religion, and in his public teaching to evade or pass by the facts and truths in the said first five Articles asserted; and that the said doctrine is contrary to the law of the Church as contained in the Thirty-sixth Canon" (39). Lushington responds: "The Clergy are bound by the King's Declaration to take the Articles in their literal and grammatical sense; the first five Articles are the most important of all. Is it consistent with their literal and grammatical sense to pass them by? I think not. Is it consistent with the declaration that they are agreeable to the Word of God? If so, why pass by? . . . I think that the substance of what Mr. Wilson has written is this: to suggest modes by which the Articles subscribed may be evaded, contrary to the King's Declaration and the terms of subscription" (39–40).[24] As Lushington points out, however, he has to adjudicate not what Wilson is counseling, but whether Wilson actually followed in what he wrote the explicit requirements of the Thirty-sixth Canon: "Mr. Wilson, so far as he himself is concerned, has subscribed . . . agreeably to the Canon; whether in the sense required by the Canon, or with what qualification, I forbear to enquire, for I have no authority so to do; nor is it possible to investigate what Mr. Wilson's conceptions or opinions were at the time when he subscribed. . . . The short question therefore is, whether [Wilson] . . . has, by counseling others that they may subscribe . . . in a sense not consonant either to the King's Declaration or the . . . [Canon itself], committed an Ecclesiastical offence against this particular Canon. . . . I cannot come to the conclusion in the affirmative; the offence struck at by the Canon being of a totally different character. I must reject this Article" (40).

ARTICLE 12: On the universality of original sin and its deserving of damnation, and whether hope in salvation is possible for those who have never heard of Christ but who live moral lives according to the precepts of whatever religion they profess, Lushington divides his response into three parts. First he addresses the final disposition of those who have not heard of Christ: "I am unable to discover in these words any conflict with the Articles of Religion cited. I am bound to adopt a charitable construction. Mr. Wilson does not here say that the persons here spoken of would be saved by the law they profess; he neither avers nor denies that they will be saved by the name of Jesus Christ; but only says that 'they will be equitably dealt with.' This is no negative of the Eighteenth Article. To the salvation promised by our Saviour faith is indispensable; but the Article, as I understand it, is wholly silent as to the necessity of faith to persons who never could have had it" (41–42).

Second, when Wilson is alleged to make "a denial of any distinction between covenanted and uncovenanted mercies" (42), and so to assert by implication that salvation is available to all who live according to the religion they profess, Lushington concludes: "To deny any distinction appears to me to declare that a man may be saved by the law which he professeth. Whether this proposition be true or not, is not the question. I think the Eighteenth Article prohibits its being declared; and therefore I must come to the conclusion that the Article has been infringed" (42).

Third, on the universality of original sin and the deserving of damnation, as applicable to the "myriads of non-Christian races," Lushington refers to the Ninth Article of Religion:

> That Article does . . . apply to all mankind, and assumes that all men are descended from Adam; it declares that the corruption of original sin attaches upon all, and deserveth God's wrath and damnation; but I can nowhere find that it is said or implied that therefore persons who had no possibility of knowing the Christian faith would suffer the penalty denounced. The corruption of their nature does, according to the Article, deserve the penalty; but that such penalty will be exacted, when the means of attaining saving faith have not existed, I do not find. I think that this Article does not contain any such declaration. It leaves, as I conceive, all such questions wholly unresolved.
>
> There is a very wide difference, in my opinion, in saying that original sin deserveth God's wrath and damnation, and that the only means of escape therefrom promised by God is faith in Jesus Christ, and in saying that all who never heard the name of our Saviour will, by reason of original sin, be consigned to perdition. I hold that the Ninth Article is silent as to the last proposition; and therefore it is no violation of that Article to express an opinion upon the matter. The Article must be reformed (42–43).

Hence, Lushington's instruction is to have this Article of Charge reformed by striking out the passages specified in the first and third points from ¶s 10 and 16 of Wilson's essay, leaving the second point as the one that he admits.

ARTICLE 13: Concerning the genuineness, alleged authorship, and canonicity of specific books of the Bible, Lushington comments (as he did in his interlocutory judgment on Article 10 against Williams), on the effect of Wilson's words "the First or *genuine* Epistle of St. Peter": "I understand him to mean that it [the Second Epistle] was not written by St. Peter. It is a matter of notoriety that questions have been raised whether the Second Epistle was really written by St. Peter, and that no such question has ever been raised as to the First Epistle. I cannot on this ground alone hold that the Sixth Article of Religion has been infringed. To bring the Court to such a conclusion, there must be a repudiation of the Epistle from the Canon. It certainly might be a Canonical Book though not written by St. Peter. It might have been written by another under Divine guidance—the essential condition of canonicity" (43). This charge would have to be rejected on the basis of Lushington's distinction between genuineness (related to matters of authorship and attribution), which Wilson denies, and canonicity, as Lushington had defined it in the opening paragraphs of his judgment, ("I think that the meaning of the word 'Canonical' clearly appears upon the face of the Article [6] itself, namely, books whose authority was never doubted in the Church; and by 'authority' I mean Divine authority, for there is no other authority which by possibility could cause them to contain all things necessary for salvation"). On this point Wilson offers no view. During argument before the Court of Arches, it was agreed that this Article of Charge should be withdrawn.[25]

ARTICLE 14: At issue is the "great adjudication" of good and evil lives at the last judgment, involving, in Lushington's words, "questions of the most momentous character,—the future destiny of mankind" (43). Citing the "damnatory clause" from the Athanasian Creed as "most important to the present issue," Lushington comments: "I am of course aware of the controversies which have arisen upon the meaning to be attributed to these words; but I must construe them in their plain, literal, and grammatical sense, and that is clearly to assert that eternal life shall be the portion of the good, and everlasting fire the destiny of the bad" (43). Lushington alludes to similar assertions in the Catechism and in the Commination against Sinners in the *BCP*, both cited in the Article of Charge. Wilson's argument, on the other hand, declares according to Lushington "that a hope must be entertained of an intermediate state, and that finally all, both great and small, will escape everlasting condemnation. I cannot reconcile the opinions thus declared with the passages cited of the Creeds and Formularies, and I must admit the Article" (44).

In the case against Wilson, then, Lushington agreed to having one Article of Charge withdrawn (13), four rejected (7, 9, 10, and 11), one admitted (14). He ordered two to be reformed (8 and 12).

Lushington concludes the interlocutory judgment on both cases by declaring that he will allow "if asked . . . , either or both parties to appeal" (44),[26] and by making reference both to the current controversy over *Essays and Reviews* and to the grounds of precedent on which he was basing his decision: "I am aware that these Judgments will be severely canvassed by the Clergy and by others. Be it so; thereby it may be ascertained whether they are in accordance with Law; and accordance with Law ought to be the sole object of a Court of Justice. It may be, that on the present occasion some may think that, so far from having gone too far, I have taken too limited a view of powers entrusted to me, and consequently have failed to apply a remedy where a remedy might seem to be wanted. I can only say that I have shaped my course according to the authority I am bound to follow,—the authority of the Privy Council" (44).

Within two weeks of Lushington's interlocutory judgment, Williams wrote and dated a Postscript to his Lampeter farewell sermon, *Persecution for the Word*, and published both together. In it he writes what he might have argued in the Court of Arches in reply to Lushington's interlocutory judgment, had the civil law procedures allowed him to speak:

> It has been argued that the Bible must be the Word of God, because the Thirty-nine Articles make it so; but it is not so clear how this argument differs from the Hindù elephant resting on the tortoise, nor how it assists men who seek ground both for our Church, and for the Scripture to which she appeals, and who are engaged in seeking rest for the conscience of mankind. . . .
>
> The idea of a verifying faculty has been thought open to objection; yet it is not denied that the internal evidence of Scripture, which must be verified, is superior to the external evidence of tradition; while the credibility, if not the necessity, of a correspondence between our moral nature and the contents of Revelation, has been implied by the present Archbishop of Canterbury; affirmed expressly by Butler, and still more positively by Tertullian [reference cited as *Praxeas*, §16].
>
> It has been thought wrong to quote any text in a sense different from that of their adaptation in our Prayer-Book; but it is not shown how such a restriction could be made to embrace honestly Psalm lxviii . . . or others. . . .
>
> It has been found easy to show the possibility of miracles, when they were approached with hardly a grasp of the ideas of physical science: their fitness to bias the mind externally, where there was no adequate appreciation of the moral instincts; their actual occurrence, where investigation of their evidence was forbidden or neglected; the impossibility of accounting for their narration, where the mind of man, as imaginatively creative, and as gazing with awe-struck wonder on the Creator's works, was not taken into account; while the desire to associate them with moral lessons, and to give our faith a persuasive tone, could be ridiculed by those who base religion on power. But the mode of showing a skeptical astronomer, that his prejudices about the sun should yield to the contemporaneousness of the book of Joshua, has not yet been devised. . . .
>
> It is represented as a reproach, that I destroy Christianity, by giving all Hebrew prophecy a primary sense; and again, as a taunt, that Christianity is uninjured by me, since the second, or spiritual, sense remain. These two remarks are not thought inconsistent; or uncharitable.
>
> Again, it is charged, that I start with such a conviction of the impossibility of prophecy, that no evidence would prove it to me—a charge, not only groundless, but opposed to the certainty of my strongest prepossessions (1862, 22–23).

Williams refers to the comments from the *Book of Sermons or Homilies* concerning the word of God that were brought out against him by Phillimore and that Stephen tried hard to restate to Williams's advantage. He writes of "the first sentence of the Book of Homilies in which the Word of God is said *not* to be identical with Scripture, but to be *contained in* it" (62–63). Balancing his gains and losses he sees his victory as undeniable: "Whatever freedom I have claimed for Biblical investigation, and more than I have claimed (since the negative aspect of my prophetical standing-point seems, through misrepresentation, a little exaggerated by the Court), is judicially conceded as permissable in the Church of England; whereas the counter claim of an episcopate to exercise a falsifying influence over hermeneutics, in virtue of the supposed interest of dogmatic theology, is repudiated as illegal" (51–52). Nevertheless, his final conclusion is bitter:

> It was said by no less a loyalist than Lord Clarendon, that no man ever had to do with an ecclesiastical court, but he found in it more delay and less justice, than any civil court in the realm. As it was in the days of Clarendon, so is it now. . . . If the modern reading of "benefit of clergy" means, that we may be treated as felons, whenever we have a Tractarian bishop, or one who does not know the passages in Eusebius on the Canon, it is time that in theology, as in treason, a judge should enunciate legal principles, and a jury try questions of fact. . . . In matters of belief and literature, the ultimate court is that of moral opinion (63).[27]

IV Lushington's Final Judgment in the Court of Arches

The articles that Lushington required to be reformed were redrafted and renumbered according to his stipulation, and were resubmitted to the Court of Arches on 25 July (*Times*, 26 July 1862, 13) The defendants were given a month to answer. On 12 September 1862, Douglas Dubois, Williams's proctor, made the formal opposing statement:

> First [That the Rev. Rowland Williams] hath not in any or either of the passages cited from the said Article Essay or Review . . . advisedly or at all maintained or affirmed erroneous strange or heretical doctrines positions or opinions contrary and repugnant to the doctrine and teachings of the United Church of England and Ireland as by law established . . . .
>
> Second [On the Bible as the expression of devout reason, Williams's statement is] . . . not inconsistent with nor repugnant or contrary to the Bible or Holy Scriptures being the Word of God and containing a special revelation of the truth of his dealings with mankind and being the rule of our faith, but that the Bible being Divine in origin is rational in substance and that it is Divinely inspired though written (or even because written) through the agency of inspired men.
>
> Third [On justification] . . . The offering of Christ . . . [is] the perfect sacrifice propitiation and satisfaction for all the sins of the whole world and this was and is true. . . .
>
> Fourth [Williams] . . . disavows that Justification by faith means only the peace of mind or sense of Divine approval which comes of trust in a religious God
>
> (Lambeth, Arches H 887/4)

Similar documents were presented by Dubois stating Wilson's opposing statements:

> First [That the Rev. H. B. Wilson] . . . hath not in any or either of the passages

cited from the said Article Essay or Review, in the amended Articles brought in and admitted in this Cause on behalf of the Promoter, advisedly or at all maintained or affirmed erroneous strange or heretical doctrines positions or opinions contrary to the doctrine and teaching of the United Church of England and Ireland as by law established or to the Statutes Constitutions Canons Ecclesiastical of the Realm or against the peace and unity of the Church.

Secondly [On inspiration, Wilson] . . . does not declare or affirm the doctrine, that the Scriptures of the Old and New Testament were not written under the inspiration of the Holy Spirit or that the Holy Scriptures so far as relates to matters concerning Salvation were not written by the Divine interposition of God and that in a manner different from the ordinary agency of Providence. . . .

Third [On the future state of existence, Wilson] . . . does not declare or affirm the doctrine that the condition of men in a future state of existence will be determined by their moral conduct, according to the law or sect which they severally profess exclusive of their religious belief. . . .

Fourth [On the last judgment, Wilson] . . . does not declare or affirm the doctrine that after this life there will be no Judgment of God awarding to those men whom he shall then approve everlasting life and to those men whom he shall then condemn everlasting death and also the doctrine that there is an intermediate state . . .

(Lambeth, Arches H 888/6;
Oxford: Bodley, LEW. Eng. Ref 57b. Heresy 1, 16–17)

However, other than these formal statements of objection, "no evidence was adduced by either side" (William Brooke 1874, 93). The prosecutors asked that Williams and Wilson "be duly and canonically corrected and punished, according to the gravity of . . . [the] offence, and the exigency of the law; and that . . . [they] be condemned in the costs" (Lambeth, Arches 887/11; 888/11). In order to declare their innocence of the reformed Articles of Charge, and to establish their right to appeal (one which they had not taken up at the time of the interlocutory judgment), Williams and Wilson both formally rejected the accusations on 17 November and denied having "maintained or affirmed, erroneous strange or heretical doctrines, positions, or opinions, contrary to the doctrine and teaching of the United Church of England and Ireland, as by law established, or to the Statutes, Constitutions, or Canons Ecclesiastical of the Realm, or against the peace and unity of the Church" (Oxford: Bodley LEW. Eng. Ref. 57b Heresy 1 [1] and [2]; see also *Times* 18 Nov. 1862, 9; and 24 Nov. 1862, 10). The final judgment was then deferred until 15 December 1862, when the required formal proceedings occurred, without argument by Phillimore on the substance of the charges that had been fully dealt with in the interlocutory judgment, that, as Wilson wrote, had "the force and effect of a definitive Sentence" (Wilson 1863, viii). At the same time, Phillimore addressed the court on the fact that Williams had already been convicted of contravening the teachings of the church with respect to inspiration, propitiation, and justification, that such convictions were "of the very gravest importance to the Church of England," and "that a sentence expressive of the opinion of the supreme ecclesiastical court adequate to the offence must now be pronounced." He asked that "the Court in the most solemn manner and with the utmost earnestness . . . pass a sentence of suspension until the error be retracted" (*Times*, 16 Dec. 1862, 10).

Deane responded at considerable length, maintaining that in the light of the interlocutory judgment, there now was new material to be addressed, and once more he went over the sustained and Reformed Articles of Charge, showing from lengthy citation from Williams's essay how Williams held an acceptable view of inspiration, how Williams's views on propitiation were also not heretical, and did not accord with the views of Mr. Heath condemned by the Court of Arches and upheld by the Privy Council. Similarly, Stephen said that given the substance of the interlocutory judgment, he should refrain from addressing the substance of the charges, but should restrict himself to the mitigation of the sentence. However, he felt obliged to intervene once more, and did so on the same issue of liberty with which he had concluded his long address during the trial. Williams's offense, he maintained "was an offence only by virtue of special enactment, which imposed restraints on that general liberty of private judgment which the law conferred, and in respect to every action which it did not explicitly forbid, as the Gorham case proved, up to the point at which the law forbade further inquiry, it was not only the right, but the duty of the clergy to inquire. Hence, the offense of which Dr. Williams was convicted was that of an excessive exercise of a right in the highest degree beneficial to the public and to the cause of truth" (*Times*, 16 Dec. 1862, 10). Stephen's argument was extended so that the court had to examine the many charges on which Williams was acquitted as well as those of which he was convicted: "If the expressions held to be illegal were struck out, the substance of the *Essay* prosecuted was precisely the same. The substance of the *Essay*, so far as it referred to the Bible, was to contend that it was not infallible. The Court had affirmed their right to say so. The rest was a matter of expression. As to the other articles admitted, which referred to the doctrines of propitiation and justification, . . Dr. Williams's only fault was want of caution. His allegation showed that he did not agree with the opinions expressed in those passages, and he was ready to disavow the opinions or withdraw the passages in which they were contained" (*Times*, 16 Dec. 1862, 10). This, then, was Williams's partial retraction, offered orally, and relating only to those passages in his review where his opinions on propitiation and justification and those of Bunsen could be confused. The offer was rejected by the court.[28]

Lushington then delivered his brief final judgment. He asserted that nothing was added in argument that had not been stated before, that the retraction was not one that he could admit, being only a verbal retraction, and that he must abide by his interlocutory judgment, condemning as heretical the infringements of the Articles and Formularies. Williams was condemned for his views on biblical inspiration, the doctrine of propitiation, and justification by faith, and Wilson for his views on biblical inspiration, for drawing no distinction between "covenanted and uncovenanted mercies" whereby the condition of those after death will be determined according to their moral conduct relevant to the religion they profess (reformed article 12) and for rejecting the everlasting punishment of the wicked. Lushington explicitly did not accept Phillimore's recommendation that suspension should be until the heresies were retracted, "as that judgment might cause a retraction which did not come from the heart" (*Times*, 16 Dec. 1862, 10). Lushington then pronounced his sentence against each: each defendant was ordered to pay for the costs incurred in the Court of Arches trial, a considerable sum. More importantly, Lushington determined that each of the accused, now convicted as heretical, was to be "suspended for the space of one year to commence from the publication of such suspension from all discharge and function of his clerical office and the execution thereof namely from preaching the word of God[,] administering the Sacraments and celebrating all other duties and offices in his said Church or elsewhere within the Province of Canterbury and from the profits and benefits of the said Vicarage and . . . all other ecclesiastical dues rights and emoluments whatsoever belonging and appertaining to the said Vicarage . . . [and is also to be prohibited] from writing printing publishing or preaching or otherwise promulgating any erroneous strange or heretical doctrines in any way contrary or repugnant to the doctrine and teaching of the Church of England" (British Library P.P. 1316: Parliamentary Papers: Privy Council Cases: Appendix: Court of Arches). The suspensions were to be published on 28 December 1862.

Hence, in the final judgment of the ecclesiastical court Williams and Wilson were suspended "*ab officio et beneficio*" (from their offices and benefices), from all ecclesiastical functions. They were deprived for one year of all income and benefits and were ordered to pay all of the substantial court costs. They were effectively silenced and inhibited from publishing or speaking out on the condemned matters for one year. Immediately upon the pronouncement of the sentence, Williams and Wilson launched separate appeals to the Judicial Committee of the Privy Council, thereby staying the imposition of the sentence until the appeal was heard.[29]

Lushington's judgment was, in his words, "a warning . . . to other clergymen throughout the country," and it was "sufficiently severe" to Williams and Wilson to show how seriously they had erred (*Guardian*, 16 Dec. 1862, 3b). In his interlocutory judgment Lushington had frequently alluded to what a clergyman was allowed to profess and teach, and to the penalties for infringements. He was aware that his warning would be "severely canvassed by the Clergy and by others" (1862, 44). He had also made many disparaging comments on *Essays and Reviews* as a whole and on the limitations he was laboring under in restricting himself to the terms of the cited passages and the Formularies. But Williams and Wilson both recognized that a number of the charges against them had been rejected, and only four were sustained against Williams, three against Wilson. Both claimed to have won a measure of freedom for others in disputing doctrine. Hence, Stanley could call it "a victory so nearly complete and a punishment so slight" (1864, 268–72). But their victory was hollow in the face of being branded as heretics. The warning had teeth, not only the label of heretics: there was a heavy financial penalty in costs and loss of income. Indeed Hamilton, as Williams's accuser, had asked for a less severe sentence, specifically that the court suspend Williams only "until such time as he should retract his erroneous opinions" and "not to visit with any severity of punishment the individual" (see Waddams 1992, 333–40). Nonetheless, Lushington refused Williams's oral retraction and imposed a year's suspension. Their clerical orders, however, were not rescinded. In that respect, at least, Lushington's sentence was lenient and his judgment was widely accepted as liberal (see the *Times*, 27 June 1862). Others, however, were only too aware of the toll of the sentence on Williams and Wilson, and, indeed, Williams's wife claimed the whole process hastened his death. Meanwhile, events moved to the next legal theater, to the appeal to the Judicial Committee of the Privy Council.

B "This Great Appeal": Before the Judicial Committee of the Privy Council

In the fourteen months from Lushington's final judgment to the decision of the Privy Council on 8 February 1864, there was continuing public agitation because ecclesiastical matters were being dealt with in the secular courts. In this interim period many of the same participants in the *Essays and Reviews* controversy such as E. B. Pusey, F. D. Maurice, and George Anthony Denison continued to write and organize, maintaining the same ecclesiastical party alliances. In addition the controversy over Bishop Colenso refueled the debate about *Essays and Reviews*.

On 15 April 1863, what Stanley would later refer to as "this great appeal" and "this famous Judgment" (1864, 271, 274), was "assigned for hearing" (Wilson 1863, ix) at the Privy Council Chamber, Whitehall.[30] The hearings took place from 19 to 26 June 1863. After a period of intense but futile negotiating to try to bring all of the Privy Councillors into agreement, the judgment of Lord Westbury, the Lord Chancellor, was delivered on 8 February 1864 (for a contemporary portrait drawing of him engraved the next year, see fig. 15). For appeals concerning offenses against the ecclesiastical law, Privy Councillors serving on the Judicial Committee included the archbishops of Canterbury and York and the bishop of London. They sat as judges, not merely as assessors who could give expert opinion on ecclesiastical cases, as was later mandated by the Appellate Jurisdiction Bill of 1876. The appeals of Williams and Wilson were considered together by a large Committee: Lord Granville, the president of the Privy Council (present *pro forma* on the opening day of the appeal), the Lord Chancellor (Lord Westbury), Lord Cranworth and Lord Chelmsford (both former Lord Chancellors), Lord Kingsdown, the archbishop of

Figure 15. Lord Westbury (1865). Engraving by W. Walker & Sons of a chalk drawing by William Walker. Courtesy of the National Portrait Gallery, London.

Canterbury (Charles Thomas Longley), the archbishop of York (William Thomson), and the bishop of London (Archibald Campbell Tait). The Registrar of the Judicial Committee was Henry Reeve (see frontispiece).[31]

The fact that so large a committee was convened by Reeve indicated the importance of the appeal.[32] Tait had had a long association with Wilson stretching back to his leadership of the "Protest of the Four Tutors" at Oxford (1841). But their paths had diverged widely. Tait had voted in favor of the Episcopal Manifesto of 16 February 1861 condemning *Essays and Reviews.* He wrote in a private memorandum in 1863, "I have lately read over again with the utmost care Wilson's and Williams' essays before writing my memorandum for the judgment of their cases before the Privy Council. Williams' spirit seems to me even worse than I thought it on the former perusal" (Davidson and Benham 1891, 1:325). Tait was also a close friend of Temple and Jowett and had both of them to visit him at Fulham in January, 1861 to discuss *Essays and Reviews.* He also had a lengthy correspondence with Temple and with Stanley on the Episcopal Manifesto, and the "treachery," as Temple called it, of his putting his name to it (Davidson and Benham 1891, 1:284–301; Letters 54–56, 59, 65–67, 70, 76, 80, 82, 85–86). Longley and Thomson had already declared themselves on the subject of *Essays and Reviews.* Both had signed the Episcopal Manifesto. Longley had denounced the volume in his Charge of 1861. Thomson had edited a collection of essays, *Aids to Faith* (1861), that attacked the Essayists and Reviewers; he was, in turn, "rewarded" in December 1861, by being appointed bishop of Gloucester and Bristol, and within a year by the elevation to York, a point made by Stanley (1864, 271).

I "Pleading Their Own Case": The Essayists before the Judicial Committee

The hearings in the Privy Council Chamber, Whitehall, began on 19 June 1863, first to present the appeals, and then to begin the pleadings. Both Williams and Wilson chose to plead their own cases. In his review of the proceedings in the Judicial Committee, Stanley comments: "The appellants, exhausted by the expenses of the lawsuit, took what many thought the hazardous course of pleading their own case. . . . The defence of Mr. Wilson remains on record, he having taken the precaution of confining himself to a written statement. Whatever may be thought of the truth or falsehood of his theological tenets, there was, we believe, but one opinion amongst his friends and foes as to the force of the masterly, yet dignified and pathetic argument which he pleaded for his own freedom and for the freedom of the English Church against the new yoke which, as he contended, was for the first time attempted to be imposed" (1864, 271). Williams also presented his own defense to "gain for himself the power of explaining what he meant, and disclaiming what he did not mean, with the advantage which the technical theologian has from the use of his own language." Stanley also commented privately on the "favourable impression made upon the Privy

Council by [his] personal pleading before them" (Ellen Williams 1874, 2:138–39).

There was a preliminary skirmish in which the queen's advocate, Robert Phillimore, objected on the technical point that Williams and Wilson had not taken advantage of an appeal to the Judicial Committee immediately after the interlocutory judgment, thereby losing their right to further appeal. He argued they must confine their appeal to the punishment imposed. Furthermore, Phillimore asserted that if Williams and Wilson were allowed to proceed with arguments of substance, the respondents would reopen the whole case concerning the Articles of Charge rejected in the interlocutory judgment. The Judicial Committee appealed to Lushington as an ecclesiastical lawyer for his advice, immediately obtaining a reply affirming that Williams and Wilson acted properly and legally in deferring their appeals until the final sentence was pronounced by the Court of Arches, and that they should not be treated unfairly in the Judicial Committee by having less recourse to arguments on the substance of the reformed charges against them than if they had appealed after the interlocutory judgment.[33] The Judicial Committee concurred, giving Williams and Wilson leave to continue, but denying to the respondents the right to reopen arguments concerning articles already rejected by the interlocutory judgment.

Westbury, the Lord Chancellor, indicated that the Judicial Committee did not see that Wilson's distinction between covenanted and uncovenanted mercies was in contradiction to the Eighteenth Article of Religion, and that he need not argue it; only if Phillimore wished to press it would he have to respond in his reply. The charge (original article 12; reformed article 8) was thereupon withdrawn by the respondent James Fendall and his lawyers, leaving only two charges for Wilson to appeal. Similarly, in Williams's case Westbury indicated that the charge concerning propitiation need not be argued (original article 12; reformed article 8); nor was it contested and so was withdrawn, leaving only two substantive charges for him to address. The cited passage at the end of Williams's essay that Lushington admitted as the 16th Article of Charge (reformed article 10), showing that Williams and Bunsen agree on doctrinal points, was not addressed specifically by the Judicial Committee of the Privy Council in 1864, since no infringement of the Articles of Religion or the Formularies was specified. The Privy Council did, however, reject such an identification of Williams and Bunsen: "The words of Dr. Williams, which are included in this Charge, are part of a supposed defence of Baron Bunsen against the accusation of not being a Christian. It would be a severe thing to treat language used by an imaginary advocate as advised speaking or teaching by Dr. Williams" (Brodrick and Fremantle 1865, 284).

On hearing that these two Articles of Charge had been withdrawn, and that the heretical charges seemed to be were dwindling away, Pusey was concerned that acquiescence by the Judicial Committee, especially on the part of the episcopal members, might result in letting all of the charges slip. Pusey therefore tried to influence Tait directly during the Judicial Committee's deliberations, urging him toward a position upholding religious orthodoxy:

> I am afraid of lawyers and so I have ventured to write to your Lordship in what is a great crisis of the Church. . . . Since I heard the rumour of the impending judgment, the thought of it has haunted me. It is the greatest crisis the Church of England has ever gone through. For I, at least, see no way out of it, except that the Court must either affirm what has been a part of the faith from the first, or, if it makes the doctrines an open question, must tamper with words in a way which will throw uncertainty on every man's meaning, and sanction unbounded hypocrisy. . . . If the highest Court of Appeal allows our clergy to take the word "everlasting" in a sense contrary to its known English meaning, . . . how can our people believe that we mean anything which we say? . . . I yet hope that God will hear us, and that He will incline the hearts of the judges not to allow His truth to be denied (Davidson and Benham 1891, 1:314).

Williams and Wilson set out what they wanted in their appeal. They first asked that the interlocutory decree and the definitive sentence of the Court of Arches be reversed, that they "be dismissed from the suit and from all further observance of justice therein," and that the "Respondent be condemned in the costs"—that is, that the bishop of Salisbury and James Fendall assume responsibility for all of the legal costs in both the Arches Court and the appeal. Both Williams and Wilson cited the same two reasons: "First—Because the Appellant has not maintained and affirmed any doctrine contrary to or inconsistent with any of the Thirty-nine Articles of Religion, or contrary to or in derogation of the doctrine and teaching of the Church, as set forth in the Book of Common Prayer. Second—Because the passages extracted from the said Article, Essay, or Review, in the said reformed Articles, do not warrant the conclusions drawn from them by the said Judge, and do not contain doctrines directly contrary and repugnant to any of the Thirty-nine Articles of Religion, or contrary to or in derogation of the doctrines and teaching of the Church, as set forth in the Book of Common Prayer" (Brodrick and Fremantle 1865, 280). To these Williams added two further reasons: "Third—Because the said Judge has ignored the in-dwelling of the Holy Spirit in the Church of God, and has otherwise misapprehended the doctrines of the Church of England, as established by law. Fourth—Because the said Judge has neither adequately protected the doctrine of the Church of England on Holy Baptism, nor assigned the Appellant due redress and reparation for charges proved false or erroneous" (Ellen Williams 1874, 2:140).

Wilson began his appeal first, on 19 June, setting out elaborate precedents and arguing the historic nature of the case, alluding particularly in his opening statement to its irregularity in that he received no formal admonition from his bishop to refrain from a specified offense, as was required in ecclesiastical law. He claimed that his was "the first case, since the Restoration, of a beneficed Clergyman being suspended upon a proceeding, under the general Ecclesiastical Law, for erroneous doctrine. The sentence of suspension ought not to have been pronounced without previous Monition."[34] Wilson organized his appeal against each of the articles of charge according to four headings: "First, as to the application of the rule which the learned Judge [Lushington] laid down for his guidance to the charges alleged; secondly, as to the definition or exposition of doctrine which he set forth, as expressly and exclusively the doctrine of the Church of England on the subject of each particular charge; thirdly, whether the judgment corresponds with the charges contained in the complaint; and fourthly, I shall show that the passages in the Essay which are articled and condemned do not fairly bear the meaning affixed to them by the Court below, and do not contradict the doctrine of the Church of England, even if correctly laid down by the learned Judge" (Edmund Moore 1863–65, 2:396; *English Reports* 1901, 15:951; and *Times*, 20 June 1863, 7). Wilson continued through 20 June, concluding on 24 June after about an hour. Wilson's *A Speech Delivered before the Judicial Committee*, a volume of 152 pages with materials he had to omit through pressure of time, was published by Longman, who simultaneously issued the eleventh edition of *Essays and Reviews* in time for popular interest aroused by the appeal. Wilson alluded throughout to numerous passages from the theologians of the early Church, in both Greek and Latin, to English and continental theologians and lawyers of the Reformation, to biblical commentators old and recent, and to the previous judgments of the Judicial Committee as precedence. His learning and erudition were impressive and unquestioned. Many of his friends helped him carry into the council chamber the substantial library from which he cited his sources; in the *Illustrated Times* engraving (see frontispiece) the books surround his lawyers and their clerks.

Wilson's argument against the first charge against him, of denying biblical inspiration, hinges on his first heading, the application by Lushington of the rules and precedents guiding his decision.[35] In the Arches judgment the rules involved the technical and legal meaning that Lushington attached to the words in the King's Declaration (1628) requiring that the words of the Articles of Religion and the other Formularies are to be taken in clerical oaths before ordination in their "plain and full meaning . . . in the literal and grammatical sense." It was to this phrase that Lushington returned over and over again in his effort to assess the degree to which Wilson had transgressed the Articles and Formularies. Wilson counters with the historical precedent of how that phrase from the King's Declaration was interpreted by the Judicial Committee of the Privy Council in *Gorham v. the Bishop of Exeter*, on which Lushington himself sat as a Privy Councillor. Wilson argues: "There appears to have been implanted in the mind of the Judge [Lushington] a notion that the terms 'literal and grammatical,' in the Gorham Judgment, are opposed to 'figurative'; whereas I submit that they are rather to be considered as opposed to argumentative, deductive, or inferential. And if the latter view is the correct one, the learned Judge has misapplied this important rule or maxim in two ways; for he has both insisted on understanding obviously figurative and metaphorical words in a 'literal' sense, or as grammarians would say, as 'proper words,' and he has also drawn inferences and deductions from expressions in the Articles and Formularies, when he ought not to have gone beyond the meaning of the propositions contained in them as they stand" (Wilson 1863, 9). Wilson contends that the "literal and grammatical sense" allows the "figurative" as a legitimate reading. On the other hand, where he asserts a figurative reading (as in "everlasting fires"), in the sanctioned "literal and grammatical sense," he is actually condemned by Lushington, not for the figurative reading, but because he is arguing, deducing, or inferring a theological meaning that Lushington considers at odds with received Anglican doctrine, and so opposed to the "literal and grammatical sense." But such a reading, Wilson maintains, is not sanctioned by the historical use of the phrase "literal and grammatical sense."

To demonstrate his contention, Wilson first challenges Lushington's assertion that the Royal Declaration was of higher authority than the Gorham decision of the Privy Council, arguing that the Royal Declaration is only a historical document, useful as "evidence of practice" which allows "the greatest possible latitude" in the interpretation of "literal and grammatical sense," but not legally binding because never passed into law. The purpose of the Royal Declaration in 1628 was to conciliate, reconcile, and include in the established church the disputing Calvinists and Arminians: "Neither of these parties shall force upon the other, inferences which it disclaims; neither of you shall draw conclusions from the Articles in order to bring your adversaries into contradiction with them; you shall be content with them as they stand, even if you understand them in opposite senses, and you shall not argue the points to show that one of you is wrong and the other right" (cited in Wilson 1863, 10). The object of the King's Declaration was "to preserve peace in the Church"; the object of the Judicial Committee in *Gorham v. the Bishop of Exeter* was "to do justice, and in order thereto, to interpret a written instrument on legal principles" (11). In *Gorham v. the Bishop of Exeter* they held that where there was "a dubious interpretation" of an Article of Religion, the court must not "fix on one meaning" and exclude contrary ones (13). To Wilson, then, Lushington "affixed a meaning to the word 'literal' which does not seem to have been in the distinct contemplation of the Privy Council; and, secondly, has pushed his maxim of literal interpretation, as opposed to figurative, to a universality which no such rule of interpretation of language can possibly admit of, and which is obviously inapplicable to some (though but a few) expressions in the Articles of Religion themselves" (11–12). Wilson gives two examples of figurative expressions in the Articles and Formularies that cannot be taken literally, "sitting at the right hand of God" as a statement about literal seating arrangements, and "called of God" as implying "an audible voice, and therefore a miraculous interposition" (12). At issue is the historical purpose of the Articles of Religion, and the kinds of diverse political, ecclesiastical, theological positions involved in framing them. Such "historical and intrinsic evidence" can be imported not only "to aid literal and grammatical interpretation" as Lushington maintained, but also to determine "the intention with which they [the Articles] were framed," an appeal to historical context sanctioned by a number of cases, some in the House of Lords, to which Wilson alludes. He then elaborates the controversies of the sixteenth century, citing voluminous and scholarly authorities, including the debates of the Council of Trent, to show that the words "Holy Scripture containeth all things necessary to salvation" in the Sixth Article of Religion, which both Wilson and Williams are accused of having violated, relate to sixteenth-century controversies between the Church of England and the Church of Rome:

> The object of the 20th Article especially was to exclude traditions which the Church of Rome accepted and mixed up with the Scriptures. By the sufficiency of the Scriptures for man's salvation is, therefore, to be understood the sufficiency, not of the Scriptures, but of the doctrine the Scriptures contain; which doctrine is not to be deemed true because it is in a written book, but because it is of a Divine authority. . . . It concerns all to know whether the divine authority is henceforth to be applied to the Scriptures or to the doctrine; to the spirit or to the Book; to the divinely illuminated thought or to the work of the hand of man. Now the Church of England has nowhere acknowledged itself to be founded as a branch of Christ's Church on a written Book. It claims to be founded upon a person, and, undoubtedly, Christ had a Church before the New Testament was written (Edmund Moore 1863–65, 2:399–400).

Wilson, then, drawing on the language used by the Privy Council in *Gorham v. the Bishop of Exeter*, refers to the Articles of Religion as "a Code," and maintains that "the doctrine to which each Article is intended to apply, must be looked for in that particular Article, as if in a separate Act of Parliament, and must not be supplemented by inferences drawn from other Articles." But the Court of Arches has erred in deducing "a law of doctrine from the Articles which was beyond its province" (Edmund Moore 1863–65, 2:400).

Wilson's second heading of argument is the theological issue with which he was charged directly, denying the inspiration of the Bible. Again his method is to show that "the definition or exposition of doctrine which he [Lushington] set forth, as expressly and exclusively the doctrine of the Church of England," cannot be maintained. To do so he places his own position in a long and contested history of doctrinal debate, directing attention to widely dispersed European discussions concerning inspiration in the mid-seventeenth century around Hugo Grotius. In these debates theological opinion extended from a view of verbal inspiration that stressed the absolute purity of the Bible's diction in every respect to "the assistance merely of the Holy Spirit." Wilson traces the affiliations of the Arminians in Holland with English thought, giving four examples—John Jortin on the Book of Esther (that it "does not contain the name of God or one single pious or moral reflection"), Edmund Law and John Potter on inspiration as "a general superintendence of Scripture by Providence," and Henry Alford on Matthew's Gospel as based on a Hebrew original, and on the Sermon on the Mount as containing nothing miraculous, though translating it into Greek would seem to be "a miraculous account of a non-miraculous event" (Edmund Moore 1863–65, 2:401–2).

Wilson's third point in attacking Lushington's condemnation, whether "the judgment corresponds with the charges contained in the complaint," goes back to the original terms of the charge, that he did "advisedly declare and affirm in effect that the Holy Scriptures were not written under the inspiration of the Holy Spirit." Wilson objects to a charge based on the allegation that he declared and affirmed "in effect" a disbelief in inspiration, a charge that lacks "sufficient precision": "[The Article of Charge] could not stand without the words 'in effect,' for it is not even pretended that there are any words of mine at all resembling the proposition, 'that the Holy Scriptures were not given by the Inspiration of the Holy Spirit.' It cannot stand with them, for they confess a defect in the precision which is necessary to describe the Charge" (60). Further, the word "inspiration" is not used in the Formularies of the Church of England in reference to the inspiration of the Bible: "The word 'Inspiration' occurs only three times in any of the forms of the Church of England; once in the Collect for the fifth Sunday after Easter. . . ; again in the Collect [for purity] in the Communion service . . . ; and once in the Thirty-nine Articles, namely in the 13th . . . :—all of which passages relate to the divine influence or operation on the spiritual nature of the Christian upon its moral side. And there is no passage or phrase in any part of the Articles of Religion or Prayer Book, in the dogmatical, the instructional, or the devotional forms, in which the word 'Inspiration' occurs as designating the influence whereby the writers of the Scripture were fitted for their special work" (61). Wilson argues, then, that the word "inspiration" forced the charge "to hinge upon an ambiguous term—a term capable of being understood in many different senses—around which many controversies and various opinions have gathered in recent times. It is beyond the competence of the Court to fix its meaning; the learned Judge himself . . . said he did not define it, he did not feel able or authorised to fix a precise theological meaning to it" (Wilson 1863, 62). How then, Wilson asked, could he be condemned for holding a view which the court had resisted defining and over which there was such controversy?

The only occurrence of the word "inspiration" in the Authorized Version of the Bible is 2 Tim. 3:16: "All Scripture is given by the inspiration of God." On this passage Wilson comments:

> In this place the substantive—the abstract noun—which would correspond, as an English reader would expect, to our word Inspiration, is not used by the Apostle. There is no such Greek word in the New Testament as Θεοπνευστία [Gk. *Theopneustia,* inspiration by God]. And that being so, the caution of our Church is perfectly to be understood which has laid down no doctrine concerning "Inspiration"; but the incaution becomes equally manifest which, because the substantive "Inspiration" occurs in the English Version, has built upon it theories as to the mode in which the Scriptures . . . were written. No doubt in the phrase πᾶσα γραφὴ Θεόπνευστος [Gk. *pasa graphe Theopneustos,* every writing God-breathed] (2 Tim. iii. 16), the Apostle intended to refer the Scripture of the Old Testament to a divine origin or source; but neither to assert that it is characterised by all divine perfections, nor to describe the process or special operation whereby it was produced (63).

Wilson argues a precise grammatical, rhetorical, and theological point, that a parallel case, indeed the only parallel usage, supports his contention that a precise assertion of divine intervention into the natural order cannot be assumed by placing the agency of God as the prefix to the adjective:

> And that this adjective Θεόπνευστος cannot be taken, either as indicating infallibility in the subject to which it belongs, or as laying down that the Scripture was written by miraculous interposition or interruption of the providential order, is confirmed by an illustration from another word, the only other word similarly compounded with Θεος which is to be met with either in the New Testament or in the Septuagint Version of the Old. It likewise occurs only once. In 1 Thess. iv. 9, we read, "But as touching brotherly love ye need not that I write unto you, for ye yourselves are taught of God to love one another" . . . Θεοδίδακτοι [Gr. *Theodidaktoi*, taught by God] . . . Whether St. Paul here means that God had taught them through their natural sentiments, or by the precepts of the Gospel, we can neither suppose absolute perfection in those persons as the product of that divine teaching, nor is any miracle, immediate operation, or interposition, implied in the process (63–64).

Hence, Wilson concludes, on this point, that he has been charged with denying inspiration, "that I deny the Scripture to have been given in the way the Judge infers that it was given—which is in fact less like an erroneous doctrine than the other," the denial of inspiration itself: "In short, it comes round to this, that I am charged with denying Inspiration, and found to have said that Inspiration is not miraculous" (64; see also Jowett ¶s 14 and 15 and n. 25).

On the fourth heading of his argument, that "the passages in the Essay which are articled and condemned do not fairly bear the meaning affixed to them by the Court below, and do not contradict the doctrine of the Church of England, even if correctly laid down by the learned Judge," Wilson argues that his actual statements in this Essay that were cited before the Court of Arches and upon which he was condemned cannot be held to support the meaning accorded them concerning denial of inspiration that was found by Lushington. The Court of Arches found that to the general and universal premise "all scripture is inspired," Wilson had responded, "some scripture is not inspired," while he maintained that the word "inspiration" is wrong in the context, too fraught with ambivalent meanings, and does not occur in the Formularies. Hence, his argument must be rephrased as "parts of scripture contain the word of God" and so the Bible may be spoken of as "containing the word of God," but scripture is not coextensive with the word of God: "The charge against me alleges, that I have denied that the Scripture was 'not necessarily at all,' or 'certainly not in parts,' the word of God. Now, what I said was 'that the word of God is contained in Scripture, whence it does not follow that it is co-extensive with it'; in other words, that it certainly is in parts, though not necessarily everywhere, the word of God. . . . I believe that all that is essential to salvation is contained in the Holy Scriptures, but it does not necessarily follow that every line contains the word of God. The charge does not point out with sufficient distinctness the particular Article of religion which was offended against" (Edmund Moore 1863–65, 2:404). In his address to the Judicial Committee, Wilson also discussed briefly the matters concerning covenanted and uncovenanted mercies enabling salvation for those who live according the religion they profess, even though the charges that he had thereby contradicted the 18th Article of Religion were withdrawn by Lord Westbury.

Fendall's lawyers, arguing against Wilson's appeal, had the opportunity to respond at the end of Wilson's argument. Wilson's treatment addresses those issues that had remained in contention from the Court of Arches decision and that could be said by his opponents to have been left unargued and so unresolved. He was determined, therefore, to comment on them, as in a full defense, but also as a response to the theological position he was alleged by Lushington to have contravened. In his published response this summary statement occupies twelve pages, and follows the same four headings as in his response to the first charge concerning inspiration. Wilson argues that the 18th Article of Religion ("*Of obtaining eternal Salvation only by the Name of Christ*: they also are to be had accursed that presume to say, that every man shall be saved by the Law or Sect which he professeth, so that he be diligent to frame his life according to that Law, and the light of Nature. For Holy Scripture doth set out unto us only the Name of Jesus Christ, whereby men must be saved") was framed "in condemnation of an apostasy" such as that of the Anabaptists at the Reformation, "who had thrown all Christian forms and beliefs over; some of them stating that it was unimportant for salvation whether they professed the name of Christ or not." Its purpose was not to define for members of the Church of England what views they should hold of those who had never heard of Christianity. Further, the 18th Article was "singularly open with regard to the Calvinistic and Arminian doctrines. The Calvinistic doctrine was that nobody could be saved except under the promise, whereas the Arminian was that through uncovenanted mercies the heathen might be saved eventually" (Edmund Moore 1863–65, 405), the point Wilson expounded in his essay. Wilson contends, then, that Lushington erred in three ways in not considering sufficiently the theological purpose in and historical context of the 18th Article: first, in identifying Wilson's view with a too narrow definition of the Article; second, of inferring a single meaning from such terms as "uncovenanted mercies" when they are capable historically of diverse meanings; and finally of determining that the accepted or "exclusive" view of the Church of England is the Calvinistic or semi-Calvinistic one. This last view, Wilson argues, is a new position, unwarranted by historical precedents cited from Isaac Barrow, John Jortin, James Macknight, and Edmund Law.

The third Article of Charge against Wilson condemned him for alleging that there will be no judgment of God awarding everlasting life or eternal happiness to those whom God approves and everlasting death or eternal misery to those whom God condemns, and it is the last clause, that "I deny the everlasting misery of the wicked," that was the chief point of this charge (Edmund Moore 1863–65, 406). As before Wilson first examines the principles of interpretation appealed to in the

Court of Arches, namely, that the words of the Formularies are to be taken in their plain, literal, and grammatical sense. On the other hand, the Judicial Committee had laid it down as a principle of interpretation in *Gorham v. the Bishop of Exeter* that "if the expressions used in the Rubrics and Formularies are *ambiguous*, it is not to be concluded that the Church meant to establish indirectly as a doctrine that which it did not establish directly as such by an Articles of Faith—the code avowedly made for the avoiding of diversities of opinion, and for the establishing of consent touching true religion" (Wilson 1863, 90–91; see also Nias 1951, 99). Wilson contends that there is not only theological ambiguity concerning the future state of all persons, but that there is linguistic ambiguity concerning the terms used to express the theological doctrine of the last judgment and its effects, and that he has the Gorham judgment on his side. Two of the creeds speak of the "life everlasting" and not of eternal death, and the burial service in the *BCP* also refers to the "hope of everlasting life." Only the Athanasian Creed speaks of the wicked as being consigned to "the everlasting fire." Hence, the ambiguity of the terms is in the Formularies. But the problem is exacerbated in that Lushington conflated the meaning of several of the condemnatory terms into one exclusive doctrine: "It seems surprising that the ambiguousness of those Formularies should not have presented itself to the mind of the learned Judge, when he thus placed side by side the words 'everlasting fire' and 'everlasting death.' 'Everlasting fire,' indeed, and 'everlasting death' might coincide upon a literal principle of interpretation, if the fire were supposed to destroy and annihilate that which is committed to it. But this, though it might be consistent with a plain, literal, and grammatical sense of both Formularies, is not the plain, literal, and grammatical sense of the Judge, for the Charge is laid that I have denied the 'everlasting misery' of the wicked, and the Judge finds that Charge proved, upon these words of 'everlasting fire' in the Creed of St. Athanasius (Wilson 1863, 92).

According to Wilson "everlasting" and "eternal" "do not necessarily signify an 'absolute eternity' or an 'endless continuance'" either in the Hebrew or in Greek where they have diverse usage (Wilson cites Gen. 8:7, 13 concerning circumcision as "an everlasting covenant" and comments that "according to the New Testament, circumcision is abolished" as a mandate under the Christian dispensation). The terms may also refer to "the existence of the Supreme Being" and to the "prolonged existence of that which undoubtedly shall have an end, though distant" (Wilson 1863, 95–97). Accordingly, the application to them of "a literal and material sense of fire" and of "the modern metaphysical sense of eternity" by Lushington is without warrant.

Wilson questions whether such a restricted interpretation of the conflated meanings is the doctrine of the Church of England. By alluding to the Statute 1st Elizabeth c. 1, s. 36 that "no matter of religion should be adjudged Error or Heresy that has not been condemned as such by the Canonical Scriptures or the first four General Councils" (Edmund Moore 1863–65, 406–7), Wilson argues that everlasting punishment is not mentioned in the canons of the first four General

Councils (Nicaea, 325, Constantinople, 381, Ephesus, 431, and Chalcedon, 451), nor as a part of the doctrine of the Church of England in the Articles of Religion. Quite the reverse appears, on Wilson's evidence, to be the fact: "Opinions have been held at different periods, and by eminent persons—have been most widely spread at times—uncondemned by any authority which our Church has recognised—which now would be excluded by the decision of the learned Judge" (Wilson 1863, 98). Citing such authorities in the early church as Justin Martyr, Irenaeus, Clement of Alexandria, Gregory Nazianzen, Gregory of Nyssa, Ambrose, Jerome, and Augustine, Wilson brings forward a list of the major doctors of the eastern and western church to support his view that the notion of the damned burning forever in everlasting fire is a matter left to opinion rather than prescribed belief. Similarly, in the period of the Reformation he refers to the Roman Catholic doctrine of Purgatory and the limbo for unbaptized children (*limbo infantium*) as enunciated at the Council of Trent, to the Helvetic Confessions, the various stages in the composition of the Articles of Religion, and such English theologians as Tillotson, Whately, Jeremy Taylor, and his contemporary, Henry Hart Milman. But just as everlasting punishment is not a mandatory doctrine of the first four centuries, or of the Roman Catholic, Reformation, or post-Reformation churches, so too the reverse doctrine, that of "universal restitution," is neither prescribed nor proscribed. The view, following Peter's words in Acts 3:19–21 concerning repentance and the "restitution of all things," that there might be "a termination of the sufferings of those who are condemned," is both an allowed opinion, founded on this biblical text, and is also not a position "excluded from the Church of England" (Edmund Moore 1863–65, 407). Hence, Lushington was, according to Wilson, wrong in condemning him for the statements of hope for all human beings at the final judgment expressed in the last paragraph of his essay as a statement of belief in universal restitution. Wilson concludes he was in agreement with Samuel Horsley in arguing for the hopeful preparation of all for that event, but, even had he argued for universal restitution itself, such a view would not place him in conflict with the Church of England (Edmund Moore 1863–65, 408).

The queen's advocate, Robert Phillimore, speaking for the respondent, James Fendall, "acknowledged that the second of the foregoing Charges could not be sustained" (Wilson 1863, 151), thereby agreeing with Westbury and the majority view on the Judicial Committee that the distinction between covenanted and uncovenanted mercies was not in contravention of the 18th Article of Religion. At the same time Phillimore repeated the contention of the Court of Arches that the first and third Articles of Charge, concerning the "plenary inspiration" of the Bible and the punishment of the wicked in everlasting fire, were "the doctrine of the Church of England." In reply, Wilson again pointed out the different and contradictory meanings of "plenary" as "a literal inspiration or verbal dictation" or in the sense of "sufficient" (Wilson 1863, 152). And there his case rested while Williams's arguments were heard.

Williams began his appeal on June 24 and concluded it the next day. His own summary of his appeal was briefly put: "My argument was in two heads:– 1st. Any clergyman has a right to deny the 'preternatural interposition of Almighty power' in the composition of Holy Writ. 2nd. The Vicar of Broadchalke has not, in his Essay, denied it" (Ellen Williams 1874, 2:143). Considerably less brief were the 180 "closely-written pages" of the "carefully-drawn-up notes" for his appeal in which his argument was divided into two sections, the first dealing with the inspiration of the Bible, and the second with the doctrine of justification by faith. The third matter with which he was charged, the issue of propitiation, was stated by the Judicial Committee as unnecessary to be argued.

Williams does not repeat the ground covered by Wilson concerning the meaning of subscription to the Articles of Religion, the historical nature of the Articles in dealing with controversies concerning biblical inspiration at the time of the Henrician and Elizabethan Settlements, the use and meaning of the word "inspiration" and its Greek equivalent in the Bible, and so on. He takes a different line, based on the distinction between direct or particular inspiration and general inspiration, between inspiration as a condition in which the Bible as revelatory has a kind of ontological position, and inspiration as a notion that describes the agency of those who "wrote" the Bible in the sense of committing it to written form. By pursuing such a strategy Williams bypasses the difficult (and, for the appeal, irrelevant) question of the nature of the inspiration that might have been present in any oral forms of the Bible or its parts when they were circulating as part of a tradition before being committed to writing (see Jowett ¶s 14, 15, and notes).

According to Williams, the conclusion to be drawn from Lushington's judgment concerning inspiration is that "the Scriptures were written by the extraordinary and preternatural interposition of God," a view at variance with the position maintained in the Formularies concerning "the general inspiration of the Scripture" (Edmund Moore 1863–65, 408–9). In drawing this distinction, Williams fastens on Lushington's verb "written." While maintaining the notion that the Bible is "the work of Jehovah," he argues that the mode or agency of its becoming "written" is an open question: "I maintain that any Clergyman of the Church of England has a right to controvert the doctrine" articulated in Lushington's judgment, "that the Holy Scripture is written by inspiration." In support of his position, like the arguments of Wilson on inspiration, Williams adduces St. Jerome to argue for "a liberal interpretation" of inspiration, namely, "that the Scriptures are a revelation of God, and were inspired by the Holy Spirit, but they were committed to writing by those who were liable to human error." Williams maintains two propositions: "First, that the Scriptures contain the work of the Eternal Spirit; secondly, that they were written, not by passionless machines, but by conscious writers and spiritual men, and that, therefore, they are necessarily an expression of devout reason." He then adds a further consideration, one rejected by Lushington, that the Bible is "the written voice of the congregation," again supporting his view by citations from such English doctrinal statements as John Pearson's *Exposition of the Creed* (1659) and Richard Laurence's Bampton Lectures on *Those Articles of the*

Church of England which the Calvinists Improperly Consider as Calvinistical (1804).

Williams then states his own position on inspiration: "There may be, in my Review, a tendency to minimise the difference between ordinary and extraordinary inspiration, but there is no denial of the general inspiration. I hold that the minds of the sacred writers were inspired by the Holy Spirit, and that the same Holy Ghost now dwells in the Church, and works in men's minds, supernaturally in the offices of salvation; that, in considering the difficulties which attend the works of fallible men, aid may be obtained by a comparison with the ordinary operation of the Holy Ghost; and that Divines should treat inspiration as analogous to or homogeneous with the operations of the Holy Ghost in all ages" (Edmund Moore 1863–65, 409–10). But even when considered in relation to the "strongest sense" of inspiration, that advanced by Lushington in his interlocutory judgment that the Bible is the result of "an extraordinary and preternatural interposition of God," Williams contends, while protesting against this notion, that "there is nothing in my Essay in any way irreconcilable with that doctrine." He does not argue that parts of the Bible are legendary, but he surveyed the "legendary element in Scripture" on the grounds that such a conclusion was "a consequence which might possibly arise." In Williams's view, nothing should be wrongly protected from intellectual inquiry out of a doctrinal predisposition or a false piety. On this point he concludes his treatment of inspiration: "As others made physical science free, so I claim for Biblical criticism absolute freedom" (Edmund Moore 1863–65, 410).

Williams only refers passingly to the matter of "propitiation": "The second question, with respect to 'propitiation,' I pass over, in obedience to an intimation from your Lordships that that part of the case had better be postponed till after the argument of the Queen's Advocate," a comment that became controversial when the issue of the decision of the Judicial Committee was discussed in the Upper House of Convocation and reported in the press.[36]

On the charge of heretical views of justification, Williams denies that his words were fairly interpreted. Lushington alleged that he held "justification by faith" to mean "only that peace of mind or sense of divine approval, which comes of trust in a righteous God." Williams argues that by restricting the meaning of justification to "only" this view, the Court of Arches wrongfully limited his assertion to that one view and ruled out other views which he might possibly hold, or did argue, or that were compatible with it. Again, as with inspiration, Williams is precise in his statement of his theological position: "I contend that justification means forgiveness of sins, and forgiveness of sins is emphatically a Christian doctrine. On the divine side, justification is the verdict of forgiveness, and on the human side the realization of forgiveness; and I contend that there is no Heresy in using the word in both senses. The introduction of the word 'only' into the charge is not justified in anything to be found in my Essay, and is a limitation which wholly misrepresented my meaning" (Edmund Moore 1863–65, 410–11). Among the broad range of authorities Williams cites in detail in support of his position are Jeremy Taylor's *Unum Necessarium* (1655), Gilbert Burnet's *Exposition of the XXIX Articles* (1699),

Robert Nelson's *Life of Dr. George Bull* (1713), Richard Whately's *Essays on Some of the Difficulties in the Writings of St. Paul* (1828), and R. D. Hampden's Bampton Lectures on *The Scholastic Philosophy Considered in Relation to Christian Theology* (1832).

On 26 June Robert Phillimore replied to Wilson and to Williams, and in addition John Duke Coleridge replied to Williams. Phillimore rejected Wilson's claim that he should have received an admonition before being charged on the grounds that such a procedure, as advocated in "some ancient Canons," has "never been followed here" (Edmund Moore 1863–65, 412). Phillimore summarizes the charges against both Williams and Wilson maintaining that both are guilty of the same two heresies: "I mean the denial of the inspiration of Scripture, and of a future judgment and everlasting rewards and punishments" (413). He too appeals to the legal precedent of *Gorham v. the Bishop of Exeter*, that the views of those charged with heresy are to be shown as contrary to the Articles of Religion and the Anglican Formularies. Phillimore contends that both "altogether deny the plenary inspiration of the Holy Scriptures" though in different ways. Wilson contends that "the Scriptures of the Old and New Testament were not written under the inspiration of the Holy Spirit, and were not necessarily at all, and certainly not in parts, the word of God." Williams affirms the Bible to be "an expression of devout reason" and the "written voice of the congregation" and "not the word of God" (413–14). On the second point Wilson, according to Phillimore, maintains that the future state of people after the final judgment "will be determined by their moral conduct according to the law and sect they severally profess, exclusive of their religious belief," and even contends that "there will be no final judgment, a doctrine also contrary to the teaching of the Church in her Creeds and Formularies." To Phillimore, Williams "denies the sacrificial atonement of our Saviour Christ," maintaining "that justification by faith means only the peace of mind, or sense of Divine approval which comes of trust in a righteous God" (414). Against such alleged heresies, Phillimore asserts what he considers the orthodox view concerning inspiration: "Now, I say, that a Clergyman of the Church of England has no right to question the inspiration of Scripture, in any degree whatever, the inspiration of Scripture being the law of the Church of England. . . . Now, I maintain that that passage [the sixth Article of Religion] . . . does not apply merely to the doctrines contained in the Holy Scripture, but to the historical facts from which those doctrines are derived. Thus the Divinity of our Lord is proved, among other things, by the historical fact of His resurrection; and I say, emphatically, that a Clergyman, an ordained Minister of the Church, has no right to say, 'I believe in the Divinity of our Lord, which is a doctrine of Faith, but I question the facts which support or are in aid of that Divinity, though they are stated in the Bible'" (414–15).

Phillimore's strategy is to oversimplify his assertions, thereby increasing the restrictive aspect of Wilson's and Williams's views, and turning their questions into strong negatives assertions. For instance, Williams actually wrote, "Why may not justification by faith have meant the peace of mind, or sense of Divine approval, which comes of trust in a righteous God . . . ?" (Williams ¶26); Phillimore turns Williams's question into an assertion, and adds that his view means "only" that.

He bolsters his argument with extensive citation from divines from the Reformation to the present, defending the notion of plenary inspiration as the exclusive view of the Church of England and its Formularies. Phillimore also attempts to incorporate the whole of the Bible as part of the evidence against Williams and Wilson (part of the original Articles of Charge, then under appeal), showing how the reading and teaching of it is enjoined by the Formularies:

> That Book [the *BCP*] contains the doctrines as well as the Formularies of the Church, and the object of the Calendar and Rubrics, as shown by the preface to the reformed Book [of 1662], is that the whole of the Bible, which is thus incorporated into the Book of Common Prayer, should be read during the year. . . . The reading of Scripture is especially enjoined in the 1st Homily, and all such portions as are contained in the Lessons, the Epistles, and Gospels are obligatory on the Clergy by the subscription required from them by the 36th Canon. That the Bible was so intended to be included in the Ritual of the Church is manifest from the notes on the Book of Common Prayer left by Bishop Cosin, who was one of those employed by Convocation to draw up the Prayer Book. . . . These authorities prove the proposition I set out with, contending for, namely, the plenary inspiration of the Holy Scriptures; and that the Church had a distinct meaning in choosing portions of those Scriptures for certain great historical and Scriptural events (417–19).

Despite the agreed-upon proposal from the Judicial Committee that the charge against Williams concerning propitiation should be withdrawn from the appeal, Phillimore addresses it. He repeats the charges concerning justification, and concludes by maintaining that the Appellants were "justly and properly condemned" with a "lenient" sentence and a "mild punishment" (420). Coleridge in his address maintains that Williams "adopts Baron Bunsen's opinions as his own" and then elaborates the relations between Williams's (or Bunsen's) views and those of the Articles of Religion.

After these responses from the lawyers, Wilson concluded by asking for reversal of the judgment of the Court of Arches and costs. But he spoke at too great length leaving Williams only a half-hour to conclude his case. As his wife reports, he "rose at once, and, speaking at railway speed, compressed into forty minutes a speech described as 'clever and brilliant,' which ought to have occupied an hour. As he concluded, as much of a low murmur of applause among the bystanders, as could be permitted in the presence of that August tribunal, made itself heard." (Ellen Williams 1874, 2:143–44). Subsequently, Wilson published his appeal and Williams assisted the court reporters to compile an accurate version of his address.[37] There the matter rested for the members of the Judicial Committee to consider the merits of the appeal and to prepare their response.

II The Preparation of the Decision

According to one of the historians of the Judicial Committee, the procedures of the Judicial Committee from 1833 to 1876 involved first the hearing of the appeal and then, "after preliminary discussion . . . the Councillors would disperse and the individual deputed for the purpose would prepare a draft judgment. This was printed, confidentially, and distributed to the members who had heard the appeal. In difficult cases, other members' comments on the draft were also circulated . . . . Sometimes several conferences were required, and two or three revisions of the judgment printed" (Peter Howell 1979, 198). He reports that for most decisions of the Judicial Committee "few printed drafts have been kept" (198, n. 379). However, an important and substantial collection of memoranda, letters, and printed documents concerning the *Essays and Reviews* appeal, dating from September 1863 to February 1864, has survived. In the seven months between the hearings of Williams and Wilson before the Judicial Committee and the delivery of the final judgment by Westbury on 8 February 1864, an elaborate series of exchanges among the Privy Councillors was conducted, showing the construction of the final text of the judgment through a process of five "revises" or revisions.[38] Furthermore, while it was customary for decisions of the Judicial Committee of the Privy Council to be unanimous, and for the votes of particular Councillors on particular issues to be secret, the decision in the *Essays and Reviews* appeal involved a formally split opinion, with the two archbishops dissenting in a minority position concerning the inspiration of the Bible in the charges against Williams and Wilson. From Tait's annotations we know in detail their precise opinions and the way in which the wording of the majority judgment was negotiated, chiefly by Tait and the secular Lay Lords, but with all Councillors able to add comments and proposals for final wording.

There was at least one preliminary discussion, very likely immediately following the presentations by Williams and Wilson. At this discussion it was agreed that Tait should prepare the first memorandum and the two archbishops should be the next to respond. In effect this opening statement of the argument sounds out the episcopal views on the issues of the appeal, informs the Lay Lords, and in large measure sets the tone and boundaries for the final judgment.

Tait initiates the negotiations with a printed "Confidential" memorandum to his fellow Privy Councillors dated "September 1863," to which he has added in his hand-written annotation: "This was the first paper circulated amongst the judges."[39] Tait's memorandum begins, in a manner similar to the demurs of Lushington, by articulating the limits of the proceedings: "I take it for granted that this Court is in no way concerned with the general scope and tendency of the book called 'Essays and Reviews.' However unsound and dangerous the book may be, it is not, as a volume, before the Court. Neither have we to do even with the whole Essays of the two authors who are the Appellants in this case. Our attention must be entirely limited to the passages impugned in those articles of charge which have been admitted by the Court below [the Court of Arches]" (Lambeth, MS. Tait 291, fol. 246). Tait then indicates a further narrowing in dealing with the specifics of the charges against Williams and Wilson:

> It will be obvious that, in the first of these extracts, Dr. Williams is, as he says in express terms, setting forth the opinion of Baron Bunsen. I therefore very much doubt how, in a penal prosecution, he can be held responsible for advisedly maintaining and affirming an opinion which he thus distinctly quotes and refers to as the opinion of another. . . . That the Bible may be read with reason in freedom is, I presume, a position which no Protestant will dispute, and which, therefore, may be dismissed; what is meant by saying that it is an expression of devout reason? . . . I know not where in the passages libelled Dr. Williams has asserted that the Bible is not the Word of God and that it does not contain any special revelation of God's truth nor of his dealings with mankind, and that it is not the rule of our faith. Greatly as I dislike and object to many of Dr. Williams' statements, I find nothing in them to justify this accusation. Such is my view as to the first charge against Dr. Williams, that which refers to Holy Scripture. . . . [On Wilson:] I cannot aver that there is any formal statement in the Articles or formularies that every particle of writing contained in Holy Scripture is, in a strict sense, the word of God [fols. 246v–48v].

He concludes his first memorandum:

> I am of opinion, therefore that, with reference both to the case of Dr. Williams and that of Mr. Wilson, the Appeal must be sustained, and the Judgment of the Court below reversed.
>
> Such a decision cannot, with fairness, be construed into any approval of the two Essays in which the inculpated passages occur. This Court, I repeat, it must be understood, has nothing to do with the general scope or tendency of these Essays. Certain very meagre extracts from them retained in the reformed Articles of Charge are alone before the Court, and the Court is called to decide simply on the question whether these short extracts can fairly be considered as advised and deliberate contradictions of the Articles or other formularies of the Church (Lambeth, MS. Tait 291, fol. 252v).

Westbury, speaking for the Lay Lords, responds in a candid letter to Tait, dated 5 September 1863. He indicates clearly that early on he and Tait form a united front with the other Lay Lords against the two archbishops, differing from them chiefly on biblical inspiration as a legal definition on which to deny the appeals:

> It seemed to be the understanding of all the Lay Lords & was also the understanding of the two Archbishops that the three Prelates sh^{d} first commit to writing & send to the Lay Lords their view separately of the Judgment that ought to be given on the several reformed articles of charge . . . . I must entirely agree with yr Lordship that there is not a single charge that can be maintained. It is a very lamentable thing that such an outcry sh^{d} have been raised in the Church against publications so futile & puerile & powerless as are the Essays

> & Reviews. They have been invested with an importance & character that nothing contained in them deserves.
>
> But for the names of the writers the compositions wld hardly have been noticed.
>
> Further, it is a very lamentable thing, that the Bp of Salisbury sh[d] have been advised to initiate the process, *& to persevere* in it after Lushington's Judgment.
>
> His advisors ought to have seen that if the principles referred to in that judgment had been duly applied, the whole of the passages libelled must have been treated as not containing any criminal matter.
>
> In confidence I must say to you that I fear we shall have some trouble. All the Lay Lords are, as I believe, of your mode of thinking and feel bound to allow the appeal, but I think the Primate is simply afraid of entertaining or rather arousing such an opinion, & it seems to me that his Grace of York has confused perceptions which will not be clear either to himself or to others.
>
> In the present state of the world, there is no dogma so mischievous & repulsive as that of plenary inspiration.
>
> I hope we shall agree on a very short Judgment, simply stating the Law as now settled by decision, namely, that the passages libelled must be shewn clearly to include or embody some doctrine or position contrary to the Articles or Book of Common Prayer, & that we do not find any passage which plainly & necessarily answers that description (Lambeth, MS. Tait 80. fols. 95–98v).

On 15 October Longley's "opinion" is printed and circulated, beginning in a manner very different from Tait:

> I agree with the Judge of the Court below that in this matter this Court has merely to ascertain the true construction of the Articles of Religion and of the Formularies, according to the plain, literal, and grammatical sense, on the one hand; and on the other to interpret according to the dictates of reason and common sense, the real meaning of the language which the Appellants have been charged with using, and then to decide, according to the rules by law applicable to the construction of all written documents, whether the statements of the Appellants are or are not consistent with these Articles and Formularies.

When Longley addresses the specific charges against Williams and Wilson his disagreements with Tait are stated explicitly:

> I cannot think that such a defence [of Williams as simply quoting Bunsen] can reasonably be argued in his favor; for no clergyman surely is justified in quoting and publishing erroneous doctrine, if he quotes it in such a way as to convey clearly that he approves of it; because then he avows and adopts it. No one can read Dr. Williams' 'Essay' without collecting that approval as clearly as if there had been a distinct expression of it. . . . Holy Scripture is treated of in the Articles as an unimpeachable authority for the final establishing of doctrine, whereas no such authority can reside in the "expression of devout reason," in the "record of the experience of spiritual giants." I feel no hesitation in delivering it

> as my opinion that the Judgment of the Court below should be affirmed.

He also agrees with Lushington's judgment against Williams on justification. Turning to Wilson's views on plenary inspiration, Longley lays out a categorical distinction between the twentieth Article of Religion and Wilson's position:

> In truth, the inconsistency appears to me to be so great as to amount to a strict logical contradiction, thus—
>
> | Holy Scripture is God's Word written | Some parts of Holy Scripture are not God's Word written. |
> |---|---|
>
> The universal affirmative contradicted by the particular negative.

Longley's conclusion is directly opposed to the position of Tait and Westbury:

> It is not our business to give any definition of inspiration, nor is this at all necessary for the decision of this Appeal. But I do conceive that we are bound by the most solemn obligations to maintain at its exact level that estimation in which Holy Scripture is held by our Church, as shown by the tenor of her Articles and Liturgy, and to beware lest we sanction a decision which shall detract one jot or tittle from the authority with which it is invested according to their language.
>
> This authority we cannot fail seriously to impair if by our Judgment we shall suffer a Clergyman of our Church to place Holy Scripture, as in the passage quoted from Dr. William's [*sic*] Essay, on a level with any "expression of devout reason," with "the written voice of the congregation," or with any "record of spiritual giants," or allow it to be said, as it has been by Mr. Wilson, that there are parts of Holy Scripture which are not "God's Word written."
>
> For the above reasons I hold that the Judgment of the Court below should be affirmed in both cases (Lambeth, MS. Tait 291, fols. 261–66v).

Tait replies to Longley on 3 November in a letter marked "Private and Confidential." He regrets their differences of opinion and seeks doctrinal common ground and conciliatory wording: "I feel no sympathy with the two appellants as to the tone of the Essays and the inferences that may be gathered from them; but I do not as at present informed see that either of them in the matter of inspiration has distinctly committed himself to heresy on this—1st that Bunsen may be held to be a Christian in so far as he holds the P[rotestan]t Bible is the record of an inspired Church—and also that the Scriptures contain a human element as well as that divine element in which all things necessary to salvation are set before us. I am becoming much afraid that we may cast a strong blow in the way of belief at all. . . ." He also states more fully his views on Wilson and his discussion of inspiration: "Scripture is given by inspiration of God, therefore all statements of Mr. Wilson that are indirect respecting physical science [in the Bible] are infallibly covered—and that when these passages of Scripture which St. Paul tells us came from himself and not from God are directly and essentially from God" (Lambeth, MS. Tait 80, fols. 99–102).

Longley's letter of reply on 11 November claims that he has followed the precedents of the cases on which he sat, especially the Heath case which "seemed to lay down the principle that where the language of the defendant was clearly inconsistent and irreconcilable with, not the Articles only, but the Formularies also of the Church, the party was amenable to the censure of the Court—it is this view of the matter which prevents me from considering that the fear of making a new article should forbid my supporting the judgment of Dr. Lushington. If the Law of the Church laid down that the 39 Articles alone were the criteria of orthodoxy, there would be reason in the apprehension—but the Prayer Book, together with the Creeds, the Catechism, are criteria; and they are also to be consulted in cases of this sort." To Longley, "Dr. Williams must be held to declare as his own opinion that the Bible is no more than the expression of devout reason; & that this position is inconsistent with the statement of our Church that the Bible is the Word of God and a Rule of Faith. I do not consider that this view at all implies or requires the belief that all statements, however indirect respecting physical science in the Bible must be infallibly correct. . . . I naturally apprehend most serious consequences from any decision on the part of the Highest Ecclesiastical Tribunal, which shall put the Bible on a level with the works of devout men, in the use of their reason, and this deprives it of all authority as a rule of Faith & Morals" (Lambeth, MS. Tait 80, fols. 102–5v).

The archbishop of York's printed opinion was very likely the next one to be circulated, since, as Westbury said in commenting on the agreed procedures, the three prelates were to set out their views first (the memorandum is annotated by Tait: "no date:—but it was not issued one of the first"). Extending Longley's argument, Thomson disagrees with Lushington's judgment in that it is not sufficiently condemnatory. To Thomson, Williams is "endorsing Bunsen" while Wilson supports the "fallibility of the Scriptures." To demonstrate Wilson's rejection of scriptural infallibility, Thomson discusses the patristic use of the term "canonical" as referring to "the *rule* of faith," then applies it to the body of scriptural writings, and then to the notion of the "word of God": "Upon the whole, I have no doubt that the plain meaning of the passage articled is, that the Bible cannot properly be called by us the Word of God—which is contrary to the 6th, 20th, and other Articles; that the Word of God is something contained in Scripture, but not co-extensive with it, which is contrary to the 20th Article . . . and which has received a very strained and unnatural interpretation from . . . the Court below" (Lambeth, MS. Tait 291, fols. 267–69).

From the first exchanges of memoranda, the two archbishops are agreed in identifying Williams's argument with that of Bunsen; and in condemning both Williams and Wilson for declaring that in some sense the Bible is fallible or is not in its entirety the infallible word of God.

As Westbury indicated, the three Lay Lords were from the beginning in agreement: the confidential memoranda from Lords Chelmsford, Kingsdown, and Cranworth demonstrate that they are in favor of granting the appeals. Chelmsford writes: "At all events, looking to the whole passage, and considering that Dr. Williams is not expressing his own views but exhibiting those of Bunsen, I can find no satisfactory ground for saying that he ought to be taken to have advisedly affirmed that the Bible is not the Word of God. . . . I think that none of the charges against Dr. Williams are proved. . . . It is one thing directly to affirm or maintain a doctrine and another to express a hope that it may be true. . . . [Wilson] is charged with advisedly affirming opinions contrary to the teaching of the Church, and in support of the charge the passage in question is adduced, which is not the affirmation of an opinion. I think the Judgment against Mr. Wilson ought also to be reversed. I think no costs" (Lambeth, MS. Tait 291, fols. 270v–271).

Kingsdown, like Chelmsford, reminds the other Privy Councillors that "at the close of our discussion it was suggested, we should avoid as far as possible all theological discussion. . . . [But] I do not see how this is possible in any great degree": "We are to construe the Articles [of Religion] as the Act of Parliament of the Church. It seems to me that upon the same principle [of making use of legal mechanisms such as judges, due process, and judgments] we may accept the opinions of the Heads of the Church and other eminent persons, as showing the construction put upon doubtful expressions of a theological character . . . by persons not accused of want of orthodoxy. The opinions of eminent members of the Church may be regarded as *responsa prudentum* [informed opinions], or as explanations by skillful persons of [the] terms of art[icles]." According to Kingsdown, Lushington in his judgment protested his theological ignorance too loudly, and laid too great claim to legal objectivity: "Dr. Lushington has laid himself open to observation in some degree in his judgment by professing an ignorance with which he is not justly chargeable." At the same time, in Kingsdown's opinion, Lushington did not allow sufficient tolerance for a clergyman to cite "erroneous opinions" without openly disavowing them: "Dr. Lushington lays down the law too strictly when he says that a clergyman must not quote erroneous opinions without stating that he dissents from them . . . . He must be shown to have affirmed and maintained them." Kingsdown agrees with Tait: "I agree with the Bishop of London that the first [passage cited] is a mere statement of what Bunsen thought," and therefore is not censurable. Similarly, he finds that in Wilson's passages there is "nothing contrary to the 6th Article [of Religion]." Kingsdown concludes his memorandum in agreement with Tait and Westbury: "The Judgement appealed from must be reversed. This of course will include that portion which awards costs below against the Appellants. But I think that the Appellants by these publications have given sufficient excuse for the prosecutions, and that there ought to be no costs on either side, either of the Appeal or in the Court below" (Lambeth, MS. Tait 291, fols. 273–75v). In other words, although Kingsdown supports the appeal, he is in favor of making each party pay for costs in both the Arches trial and the appeal, because there were sufficient grounds for charges to be brought in the Court of Arches. On the matter of costs, as we shall see, there was a compromise in the final judgment.

Lord Cranworth's opinion follows, setting out his view building on the opinions of Tait and the other two Lay Lords as "Heads for Consideration as the

Foundation of a Judgment," amounting to what was in effect the first formal draft of the final judgment. On the question of whether "Dr. Williams does expressly or impliedly affirm that these books are not *God's word written* or . . . *the word of God*," Cranworth asserts his opinion: "Dr. Williams certainly does not, in terms, say that these canonical books are not the word of God." In asserting that they are the expression of devout reason and the written voice of the congregation, Cranworth asks whether "these statements necessarily imply that they are not what the Articles declare them to be?—I cannot . . . find in [them] anything amounting to the expression of an opinion that the Bible is not the word of God." Cranworth also rejects the decision of the Court of Arches on Williams's view of justification. Concerning Wilson he asserts that "the sacred books are not throughout so inspired as to contain nothing which may legitimately be canvassed and questioned as being of human and not of divine origin." On the matter of the eternity of punishment for the wicked, Cranworth writes: "It cannot . . . be said that in the passage in question Mr. Wilson declares or affirms any doctrine. He must, I think, be taken to express a hope as to what may, after the final judgment, be the lot of those who are not then admitted to eternal happiness. . . . But he does not declare or affirm his opinion that such will be the case." On the question of contravening a specific phrase in the Athanasian Creed, Cranworth distinguishes between a literal and a figurative meaning: to him the Creed refers to everlasting fire as "physical heat occasioning combustion," and yet in that creed there is nothing to say that "those who shall be doomed to everlasting fire will be kept everlastingly alive, or even that they will be kept everlastingly in the everlasting fire." To Cranworth, then, the notion of hope that Wilson expresses, must be allowed. Hence, Cranworth concludes (like Tait, Westbury, and the other Lay Lords), that the charges against both Williams and Wilson cannot be sustained, and the appeal must be granted (Lambeth, MS. Tait 291, fols. 276–83).

III The Judgment of the Lord Chancellor

After each of the Privy Councillors had expressed his opinions in memoranda for and against the appellants, the collaborative effort continued in an effort to reach a final decision. Five confidential drafts or "revises" of the final judgment were printed and circulated, some with annotations, in the three-month period from November 1863 to February 1864. The first draft was that of Cranworth, substantially revised by Lord Westbury in the "second revise" as "Notes of Judgment in the two Appeals of Mr. Wilson and Dr. Williams: by the Lord Chancellor. For the Consideration of other Members of the Committee." Three subsequent revisions indicate that each member of the Judicial Committee had opportunity, often taken up, of adding to or amending the judgment.[40] As Lord Chancellor, Westbury delivered the final decision. He was respected for both his piety and his learning, qualifications for the niceties of this case. The respectful account accompanying the caricature of him in *Vanity Fair* entitled "An eminent Christian man" alludes to "the great legal knowledge and the broad clear intellect which made Lord Westbury the best Lord Chancellor of modern times" (15 May 1869, 390; see fig. 16). But it is clear from the revises that Tait took a leading role in the argument and wording of the judgment.[41] The final judgment, delivered by Lord Westbury, was subsequently published as *Judgment of the Lords of the Judicial Committee of the Privy Council upon the Appeals of Williams v the Lord Bishop of Salisbury, and Wilson v Fendall, from the Court of Arches: Delivered 8th February, 1864*.[42]

Stanley was present in the Privy Council chambers for the judgment "to which the Church, not of England only, but of foreign nations also, had been looking forward with intense expectation": "No one who was present can forget the interest with which the audience in that crowded Council Chamber listened to sentence after sentence as they rolled along from the smooth and silvery tongue of the Lord-Chancellor, enunciating with a lucidity which made it seem impossible that any other statement of the case was conceivable, and with a studied moderation of language which, at times, seemed to border on irony—first the principles on which the judgment was to proceed, and then the examination, part by part, and word by word, of each of the three charges that remained, till, at the close, not one was left, and the appellants remained in possession of the field" (Stanley 1864, 271–72).

The final judgment begins by setting out first its limitation to a consideration of the passages brought, admitted in, and condemned by the Court of Arches, then the need for precision and definition in dealing with such criminal charges, especially in the Articles of Religion and the formularies, the fact that some matters are left open in those documents, and the question of how far those accused are guilty of breaches of doctrine:

[General Remarks][43]

> These Appeals do not give to this Tribunal the power, and therefore it is no part of its duty, to pronounce any opinion on the character, effect, or tendency of the publications known by the name of "Essays and Reviews." Nor are we at liberty to take into consideration, for the purposes of the prosecution, the whole of the Essay of Dr. Williams or of the Essay of Mr. Wilson. A few short extracts only are before us,[44] and our Judgment must by law be confined to the matter which is therein contained. If, therefore, the Book, or these two Essays, or either of them as a whole, be of a mischievous and baneful tendency, as weakening the foundations of Christian belief, and likely to cause many to offend, they will retain that character, and be liable to that condemnation, notwithstanding this our Judgment.
>
> These prosecutions are in the nature of criminal proceedings, and it is necessary that there should be precision and distinctness in the accusation.
>
> The Articles of Charge must distinctly state the opinions which the Clerk has advisedly maintained, and set forth the passages in which those opinions

Figure 16. "An Eminent Christian Man" (Lord Westbury). Lithograph by "Ape" (Carlo Pellegrini) in *Vanity Fair* (15 May 1869). Courtesy of Victoria University Library, Toronto.

are stated; and further, the Articles must specify the doctrines of the Church which such opinions or teaching of the Clerk are alleged to contravene, and the particular Articles of Religion or portions of the Formularies which contain such doctrines.

The accuser is, for the purpose of the charge, confined to the passages which are included and set out in the Articles [of Charge] as the matter of the accusation;[45] but it is competent to the accused party to explain from the rest of his work the sense or meaning of any passage or word that is challenged by the accuser.

With respect to the legal tests of doctrine in the Church of England, by the application of which we are to try the soundness or unsoundness of the passages libelled, we agree with the learned Judge in the Court below that the Judgment in the Gorham case is conclusive:—

"This Court has no jurisdiction or authority to settle matters of faith, or to determine what ought in any particular to be the doctrine of the Church of England. Its duty extends only to the consideration of that which is by law established to be the doctrine of the Church of England, upon the true and legal construction of her Articles and Formularies."

By the rule thus enunciated it is our duty to abide.

Our province is, on the one hand, to ascertain the true construction of those Articles of Religion and Formularies referred to in each charge, according to the legal rules for the interpretation of statutes and written instruments; and, on the other hand, to ascertain the plain grammatical meaning of the passages which are charged as being contrary to or inconsistent with the doctrine of the Church, ascertained in the manner we have described.

It is obvious that there may be matters of doctrine on which the Church has not given any definite rule or standard of faith or opinion—there may be matters of religious belief on which the requisition of the Church may be less than Scripture may seem to warrant—there may be very many matters of religious speculation and inquiry on which the Church may have refrained from pronouncing any opinion at all.

On matters on which the Church has prescribed no rule, there is so far freedom of opinion that they may be discussed without penal consequences. Nor in a proceeding like the present, are we at liberty to ascribe to the Church any rule or teaching which we do not find expressly and distinctly stated, or which is not plainly involved in or to be collected from that which is written.

With respect to the construction of the passages extracted from the Essays of the accused parties, the meaning to be ascribed to them must be that which the words bear, according to the ordinary grammatical meaning of language.

That only is matter of accusation which is *advisedly* taught or maintained by a clergyman in opposition to the doctrine of the Church. The writer cannot in a proceeding such as the present be held responsible for more than the conclusions which are directly involved in the assertion he has made.[46]

With these general remarks we proceed to consider in the first place the Charges against Dr. Williams.

All the Charges against Dr. Williams were rejected by the learned judge in the Court below, or given up at the hearing before us, except the Charges contained in the 7th and 15th Articles.

[Seventh Article—Inspiration][47]

The 7th Article, as reformed, sets forth certain passages extracted from pages 60 and 61, and from pages 77 and 78 [Williams ¶s 10, 24], of the volume containing Dr. Williams's Essay, and charges that in the passages so extracted Dr. Williams has advisedly maintained and affirmed that the Bible or Holy Scripture is an expression of devout reason, and the written voice of the congregation—not the Word of God, nor containing any special revelation of His truth or of His dealings with mankind, nor the rule of our faith.

Dr. Williams has nowhere in terms asserted that Holy Scripture is not the Word of God; and the accusation therefore must mean that by calling the Bible "an expression of devout reasons and therefore to be read with reason in freedom," and stating that it is "the written voice of the congregation," Dr. Williams must be taken to affirm that it is not the Word of God.

Before we examine the meaning of these expressions it is right to observe what Dr. Williams has said on the subject of Holy Scripture in the second of the passages included in this Charge. Dr. Williams there refers to the teaching of the Church in her Ordination Service as to the abiding influence of "the Eternal Spirit," and then uses these words, "If such a Spirit did not dwell in the Church the Bible would not be inspired"; and again, "The Sacred Writers acknowledge themselves men of like passions with ourselves, and we are promised illumination from the Spirit that dwelt in them."

Dr. Williams may not unreasonably contend that the just result of these passages would be thus given:— "The Bible was inspired by the Holy Spirit that has ever dwelt and still dwells in the Church, which dwelt also in the Sacred Writers of Holy Scripture, and which will aid and illuminate the minds of these who read Holy Scripture trusting to receive the guidance and assistance of that Spirit."[48]

The words that the Bible is an expression of devout reason, and therefore to be read with reason in freedom,[49] are treated in the charge as equivalent to these words:—"The Bible is the composition or work of devout or pious men and nothing more;" but such a meaning ought not to be ascribed to the words of a writer who, a few lines further on, has plainly affirmed that the Holy Spirit dwelt in the Sacred Writers of the Bible. This context enables us to say that the words "an expression of devout reason, and therefore to be read with reason in freedom," ought not to be taken in the sense ascribed to them by the accusation.

In like manner we deem it unnecessary to put any interpretation on the words "written voice of the congregation," inasmuch as we are satisfied that whatever may be the meaning of the passages included in this Article, they do not, taken collectively, warrant the charge which has been made that Dr. Williams has maintained the Bible not to be the Word of God, nor the Rule of Faith.

[Fifteenth Article: Atonement][50]

We pass on to the remaining charge against Dr. Williams, which is contained in the 15th Article of Charge. The words of Dr. Williams, which are included in this Charge, are part of a supposed defence of Baron Bunsen against the accusation of not being a Christian. It would be a severe thing to treat language used by an imaginary advocate as advised speaking or teaching by Dr. Williams. Against such a general charge as that of not being a Christian,[51] topics of defence may be properly urged, although not in conformity with the doctrines of the Church of England.

But, even if Dr. Williams be taken to approve of the arguments which he uses for this supposed defence, it would, we think, be unjust to him to take his words as a full statement of his own belief or teaching on the subject of Justification.

The XIth Article of Religion, which Dr. Williams is accused of contravening, states, "We are accounted righteous before God only for the merits of our Lord and Saviour Jesus Christ, by faith, and not for our own works or deservings." The Article is wholly silent as to the merits of Jesus Christ being transferred to us. It asserts only that we are justified for the merits of our Saviour by faith, and by faith alone. We cannot say therefore that it is penal in a Clergyman to speak of merit by transfer as a fiction, however unseemly that word may be when used in connexion with such a subject.[52]

It is fair, however, to Dr. Williams to observe that in the argument at the Bar he repudiated the interpretation which had been put on these words, that "the doctrine of merit by transfer is a fiction," and he explained fiction as intended by him to describe the phantasy in the mind of an individual that he has received or enjoyed merit by transfer.[53]

Upon the whole we cannot accept the interpretation charged by the Promoter as the true meaning of the passages included in this 15th Article of Charge, nor can we consider those passages as warranting the specific charge, which, in effect, is that Dr. Williams asserts that justification by faith means *only* the peace of mind or sense of Divine approval which comes of trust in a righteous God. This is not the assertion of Dr. Williams.

We are therefore of opinion that the Judgment against Dr. Williams must be reversed.

We proceed to consider the Charges against Mr. Wilson.

These have been reduced to the 8th and 14th Articles of Charge. The other Articles of Charge were either rejected by the Court below, or have been abandoned at the hearing before this Tribunal.

[Eighth Article: Inspiration][54]

On[55] the 8th Article of Charge an extract of some length is made from Mr. Wilson's Essay, and the accusation is, that in the passage extracted Mr. Wilson has declared and affirmed *in effect* that the Scriptures of the Old and New Testament were not written under the inspiration of the Holy Spirit, and that they were not necessarily at all, and certainly not in parts, the Word of God; and then reference is made to the VIth and XXth Articles of Religion, to part of the Nicene Creed, and to a passage in the Ordination of Priests in the Book of Common Prayer.

This Charge therefore involves the proposition, "That it is a contradiction of the doctrine laid down in the VIth and XXth Articles of Religion, in the Nicene Creed, and in the Ordination Service of Priests, to affirm that any part of the Canonical Books of the Old Testament, upon any subject whatever, however unconnected with religious faith or moral duty, was not written under the inspiration of the Holy Spirit."[56]

The proposition or assertion that every part of[57] the Scriptures was written under the inspiration of the Holy Spirit is not to be found either in the Articles or in any of the Formularies of the Church. But in the VIth Article it is said that Holy Scripture containeth all things necessary to salvation, and the Books of the Old and New Testament are therein termed Canonical. In the XXth Article, the Scriptures are referred to as "God's Word written"; in the Ordination Service, when the Bible is given by the Bishop to the Priest, it is put into his hands with these words, "Take thou authority to preach the Word of God"; and in the Nicene Creed are the words, "the Holy Ghost who spake by the Prophets."

We are confined by the Articles of Charge to the consideration of these materials, and the question is, whether in them the Church has affirmed that every part of every Book of Scripture was written under the inspiration of the Holy Spirit, and is the Word of God.

Certainly, this doctrine is not involved in the statement of the VIth Article, that Holy Scripture containeth all things necessary to salvation. But inasmuch as it doth so from the revelations of the Holy Spirit, the Bible may well be denominated "Holy," and said to be "the Word of God," "God's Word written," or "Holy Writ"; terms which cannot be affirmed to be clearly predicated of every statement and representation contained in every part of the Old and New Testament.

The framers of the Articles have not used the word "inspiration" as applied to the Holy Scriptures; nor have they laid down anything as to the nature, extent, or limits of that operation of the Holy Spirit.

The caution of the framers of our Articles forbids our treating their language as implying more than is expressed; nor are we warranted in ascribing to them conclusions expressed in new forms of words involving minute and subtle matters of controversy.[58]

After an anxious consideration of the subject, we find ourselves unable to say that the passages extracted from Mr. Wilson's Essay, and which form the subject of this Article of Charge, are contradicted by or plainly inconsistent with, the Articles or Formularies to which the Charge refers, and which alone we are at liberty to consider.[59]

[Fourteenth Article of Charge: On Future Punishment][60]

We proceed to the remaining Charge against Mr. Wilson, namely, that contained in the 14th Article.

The Charge is, that in the portion of his Essay which is set out in this Article, Mr. Wilson has advisedly declared and affirmed, *in effect*, that after this life and at the end of the existing order of things on this earth there will be no judgment of God, awarding to those men whom He shall then approve everlasting life or eternal happiness, and to those men whom He shall then condemn everlasting death or eternal misery; and this position is affirmed to be contrary to the three Creeds, the Absolution, the Catechism and the Burial and Commination Services.

In the first place we find nothing in the passages extracted which in any respect questions or denies that at the end of the world there will be a judgment of God awarding to those men whom He shall approve everlasting life or eternal happiness; but with respect to a judgment of eternal misery, a hope is encouraged by Mr. Wilson that this may not be the purpose of God.

We think that it is not competent to[61] a clergyman of the Church of England to teach or suggest that a hope may be entertained of a state of things contrary to what the Church expressly teaches or declares will be the case; but the Charge is, that Mr. Wilson advisedly declares that after this life there will be no judgment of God awarding either eternal happiness or eternal misery,—an accusation which is not warranted by the passage extracted. Mr. Wilson expresses a hope that at the day of judgment those men who are not admitted to happiness may be so dealt with as that "the perverted may be restored," and all, "both small and great, may ultimately find a refuge in the bosom of the Universal Parent." The hope that the punishment of the wicked may not endure to all eternity is certainly not at variance with anything that is found in the Apostles' Creed, or the Nicene Creed, or in the Absolution, which forms part of the Morning and Evening Prayer, or in the Burial Service. In the Catechism the child is taught that in repeating the Lord's Prayer he prays unto God "that He will keep us from all sin and wickedness, and from our ghostly enemy, and from everlasting death"; but this exposition of the Lord's Prayer cannot be taken as necessarily declaring anything touching the eternity of punishment after the resurrection.

There remain the Commination Service and the Athanasian Creed. The material passage in the Commination Service is in these words: "O terrible voice of most just judgment which shall be pronounced upon them, when it shall be said unto them, Go, ye cursed, into the fire everlasting which is prepared for the devil and his angels." In like manner the Athanasian Creed declares that they that have done evil shall go into everlasting fire. Of the meaning of these words "everlasting fire," no interpretation is given in the Formularies which are referred to in the Charge. Mr. Wilson has urged in his defence that the word "everlasting" in the English translation of the New Testament, and of the Creed of St. Athanasius, must be subject to the same limited interpretation which some learned men have given to the original words which are translated by the English word "everlasting," and he has also appealed to the liberty of opinion which has always existed without restraint among very eminent divines upon this subject.

It is material to observe that in the Articles of King Edward VI., framed in 1552, the Forty-second Article was in the following words:—

> "'*All men shall not bee saved at the length.*'—Thei also are worthie of condemnation who indevoure at this time to restore the dangerouse opinion, that al menne, be thei never so ungodlie, shall at lengtht bee saved, when thei have suffered paines for their sinnes a certain time appoincted by God's justice."

This Article was omitted from the Thirty-nine Articles of Religion in the year 1562, and it might be said that the effect of sustaining the Judgment of the Court below on this charge would be to restore the Article so withdrawn.

We are not required, or at liberty, to express any opinion upon the mysterious question of the eternity of final punishment, further than to say that we do not find in the Formularies, to which this Article refers, any such distinct declaration of our Church upon the subject as to require us to condemn as penal the expression of hope by a clergyman, that even the ultimate pardon of the wicked, who are condemned in the day of judgment, may be consistent with the will of Almighty God.

[Concluding Remarks]

We desire to repeat that the meagre and disjointed extracts which have been allowed to remain in the reformed Articles, are alone the subject of our Judgment. On the design and general tendency of the book called "Essays and Reviews," and on the effect or aim of the whole Essay of Dr. Williams, or the whole Essay of Mr. Wilson, we neither can nor do pronounce any opinion. On the short extracts before us, our Judgment is that the Charges are not proved.

Their Lordships, therefore, will humbly recommend to Her Majesty that the sentences be reversed, and the reformed Articles rejected in like manner as the rest of the original Articles were rejected in the Court below, namely,

> without costs; but inasmuch as the Appellants have been obliged to come to this Court, their Lordships think it right that they should have the costs of this Appeal.
>
> I am desired by the Archbishop of Canterbury and the Archbishop of York to state that they do not concur in those parts of this Judgment which relate to the 7th Article of Charge against Dr. Williams, and to the 8th Article of Charge against Mr. Wilson.[62]

The Judgment is unusual in that it not only records that the decision was not unanimous but it also identifies the two archbishops as the dissenters and specifies two points of dissent. The preparation of the judgment involved the circulation of elaborate memoranda and opinions to try to arrive at a consensus before the five revises produced the final judgment. Peter Howell indicates that dissension in decisions of the Judicial Committee was unusual: it was particularly important for the Judicial Committee to try to arrive at a unanimous decision, since the Committee represented the final court of appeal: "From the Committee's foundation, its members took particular pains to resolve their differences before delivering judgment" (1979, 198). According to a procedural rule of 1627, "when there was a difference of opinion there was to be a division, but . . . judgment was to [be] given for the whole, and . . . it was not to be divulged how the several opinions went" (quoted in Peter Howell 1979, 200). The Registrar of the Judicial Committee at the time of Westbury's judgment, Henry Reeve, argued that in general this rule bound the proceedings of the Committee, but occasionally a division on a judgment was intimated: "In a few instances, the dissenting member(s) added a brief comment, although this was comparatively rare" (Peter Howell 1979, 201). Westbury himself later commented on this matter in a note in his diary in 1866: "The influence and weight of the judgments of the Final Court of Appeal are much impaired whenever there is an avowed difference of opinion among its members. In some cases, however, it is necessary not to appear to concur in what you believe to be an erroneous interpretation of the law" (Peter Howell 1979, 203).

The Court of Arches trial was costly; the decision there condemned Williams and Wilson to pay the whole costs of the proceedings: hence, their friends had established the "*Essays and Reviews* Defence Fund."[63] They were relieved of a considerable portion of these costs when the Judicial Committee ruled that each party in the Arches trial pay its own costs. Further, Williams and Wilson were awarded costs in the appeal under the stipulations of an Order-in-Council of 13 June 1853: "An Appellant who shall succeed in obtaining a reversal or material alteration of any judgment, decree, or order appealed from, ought to be entitled to recover the costs of the Appeal from the Respondent, except in cases in which the Lords of the Judicial Committee may think fit otherwise to direct" (Peter Howell 1979, 211). Such costs would include the printing of documents by the government printer, legal fees (though both Williams and Wilson elected to plead their own cases, though they consulted lawyers and were supported by them in the appeal, as the frontispiece shows), and the fees of the Privy Council Office that were deliberately fixed, according to a schedule, at a low rate: "Thenceforth [from 1853] the parties' London agents' sole remuneration in Conciliar business was calculated according to the scale of fees settled by the Judicial Committee, and even in complex cases they were, as a result, fortunate to receive £100," while the Privy Council Office fees "rarely amounted to more that £10 in any one case" (Peter Howell 1979, 210).

However, the costs for the trial and appeal to Hamilton and Fendall were very considerable. Hamilton had to pay the very moderate costs of Williams's appeal before the Privy Council, amounting to £186. 14s (moderate because Williams pleaded his own case), as well as his own costs for legal counsel and court costs in both the Court of Arches and the Judicial Committee, amounting to the staggering sum of £2,308. A subscription fund had been set up early in the proceedings managed by his archdeacons who collected about a third of the sum from the clergy of his diocese, no inconsiderable strain on their already limited resources, with donations also from other bishops and the general public. The *Guardian* reported that by May 25 Hamilton's costs had been met and no further contributions were needed.[64] However, the secretary for Fendall's subscription fund wrote: "Will you allow me to state that 450*l.* are still needed to reimburse Mr. Fendall for costs in the parallel proceedings of "Fendall *v.* Wilson" and appeal? More than 800*l.* have been already received, and it is hoped that the balance will be shortly made up by further subscriptions" (*Guardian*, 8 June 1864, 547). That is, the total cost for Fendall of his share of the Court of Arches trial, including court fees and legal fees, and for half of the Privy Council costs (court fees and his lawyers, since Williams and Wilson did not have to pay for the appeal), amounted to £1,250.

Neither of the archbishops was present for the reading of the final judgment. Wilson appears to have attended. Williams was in Bognor Regis, a seaside resort in the south of England, recovering from a serious fall in his library; when he returned to his parish he was welcomed with flags, church bells, and a service of thanksgiving. On 1 March 1864 the judgment was reported for royal assent to the queen in Council at Windsor Castle by Lord Westbury and Lord Granville, the president of the Privy Council, with others:

> Her Majesty having taken the said Report into consideration was pleased by and with the advice of her Privy Council to approve thereof and of what is therein recommended and to order as it is hereby ordered that the same be duly and punctually observed complied with and carried into execution, whereof all persons whom it may concern are to take notice and govern themselves accordingly (British Library: P.P. 1316).

Westbury's judgment earned him a mock epitaph (widely current in legal circles and cited in his biography) that summarized the judgment from the point of view of a cynical and secular wit: "He dismissed Hell with costs, and took away from orthodox members of the Church of England their last hope of everlasting damnation" (Atlay 1906–8, 2:264).

IV Reaction to the "Magna Charta of . . . the Church"

THE PRESS covered the legal proceedings of the trials and appeals from the initial stages to the final judgments. The dailies as well as the *Guardian* (High Church) and the *Record* (Evangelical) weeklies published detailed, often verbatim, reports. Throughout the controversy liberal opinion questioned the efficacy of taking any legal action, and even the *Guardian* had doubted the wisdom of proceeding to court to settle matters of doctrine. The *Athenaeum*, at the beginning of the Arches trial, reviewed the Articles of Charge and the Charge of the bishop of Salisbury to his Clergy (8 Aug. 1861), asking "In the name of common sense, what does the Bishop of Salisbury suppose he is to gain? He extends and intensifies the power of the heretical opinion: the consequence is, that others of the clergy begin to teach it. . . . Our main object is to secure the literary freedom of the clergy. So long as we are allowed to think that they speak their full thoughts and show their full counsel, we read their writings with interest, and weigh their arguments with respect. Should we be compelled to look upon them as unable to reason with us as free men with free men, we shall turn with contempt from the tongue-tied, thought-muzzled slaves of a code of inferences" (No. 1764; 17 Aug. 1861, 209) After Westbury's judgment, Stanley summarized the whole process in the *Edinburgh Review* (July 1864). He too castigated the bishop of Salisbury and James Fendall for bringing the suits in the first place, outlined all the points that Lushington had allowed and which were now free to debate with impunity in the Church of England, and then related the final points made in appeal to recent trials and to church politics: "[These trials and appeals are] the most important event which has taken place in the English Church since the Gorham Judgment. As the Gorham Judgment established beyond question the legal position of the Puritan or so-called evangelical party in the Church of England; as the Denison Judgment would, had it turned on the merits of the case instead of a technical flaw, have established the legal position of the High Church or Sacramental party; so the Judgment in the case of Mr. Wilson and Dr. Williams established the legal position of those who have always claimed the right of free inquiry and latitude of opinion equally for themselves and for both the other sections of the Church" (Stanley 1864, 268–72).

Pusey had been active throughout the proceedings in the Judicial Committee in writing to Keble and to Tait (as well as many other correspondents), but after the decision was announced Pusey abandoned the High Church *Guardian,* that he considered to have capitulated, and began to develop support among Low Church opponents of the Essayists through their journal, the *Record.* He also promoted the efforts for a national referendum among the clergy, later issued as the "Declaration of the Clergy," and sought legal advice from the attorney-general, Sir Roundell Palmer, and from Sir Hugh Cairns about the legal force of the judgment upon the relations of church and state concerning doctrinal matters. Their reply, published and commented on by Pusey as *Case as to the Legal Force of the Judgment of the Privy*

Council (1864), indicated that the judgment only dealt with the narrow matters that it addressed concerning the views about inspiration and eternal punishment that were not legally binding upon clergymen. To Stephen this pamphlet was "a virulent personal attack" on Westbury, and in turn Stephen castigated Pusey for having "poisoned the springs of English justice for ages in all matters of faith" by his "almost grotesque" inability to comprehend fundamental legal principles or to distinguish between "moral obligations [and] legal ones" (1864c, 644, 646, 656). Once again the pages of the daily and weekly press were filled with letters to the editors and more pamphlets were issued. The *Record* had been particularly critical of Tait's siding with the Law Lords in the acquittal. Following the release of the judgment, the two archbishops commented that Tait's decision was "disastrous to his own reputation. It has awakened mingled shame and indignation, not only among the dignitaries and clergy of the Church, but, we may add, the laity, always excepting the minority of the clergy, who may be called latitudinarians, and that section of the laity who may be termed free thinkers" (Davidson and Benham 1891, 1:317–18). And once again lawyers on both sides published assessments of the legal and doctrinal impact of the judgment on the relations between church and state (Stephen 1864a and 1864b and Swabey 1864). By Hamilton's and Fendall's lawyers the blame was laid on Lushington in the Court of Arches for drawing his line too tightly according to the precedent of *Gorham v. the Bishop of Exeter* in not allowing the full discussion of the doctrinal implications, but only dealing with the narrower matter of the fit between specified passages from the essays in relation to the precise words of the Formularies; he thereby also tied the hands of the Judicial Committee which, as an inadequate court of appeal in doctrinal matters (according to Swabey) could not speak for the teaching of the church. Williams and Wilson's lawyer, Stephen, hailed the judgment as the "Magna Charta of honest inquiry in the Church" and as the only appropriate decision that the Judicial Committee could reach given the legal relations of church and state, and (adopting the language of Wilson) the role of the Church of England as by law established as the national church (James Fitzjames Stephen 1864a, 440).

V "A Sentence So Oily and So Saponaceous": The Synodical Condemnation

THE ACQUITTAL of *Essays and Reviews* before the Judicial Committee galvanized opposition among the clergy and most of the bishops. Those previously on the theological sidelines were forcibly made aware that theological niceties were being decided by the lay Law Lords (with the support of Tait), over the heads of the dissenting and mildly protesting archbishops of Canterbury and York. Amidst cries of Erastianism, the Convocation of Canterbury convened just three days after Westbury's decision. There were immediate demands for synodical condemnation.

As early as the end of January, Wilberforce knew from Longley in secret the details of the judgment, that it would be "as bad as can be"; he wrote to Henry

Phillpotts another "secret" letter: "Now *what* are we to do. As the question may rise next Tuesday at Lambeth I venture to ask you if you are not able to attend to give me such suggestions as may guide my course" (Bodley, MS. Wilberforce c.5, fol. 196; 29 Jan. 1863). The judgment was delivered on 8 February. The Convocation of the Province of Canterbury met on 11 February, and in the Lower House of Clergy, George Anthony Denison, the long-standing enemy of *Essays and Reviews*, had prepared a "gravamen," a formal ecclesiastical complaint from the Lower House to the Upper House of Bishops respecting a matter of disorder in the church. He reviewed the earlier efforts to bring about a synodical condemnation, from the time of the bishops' report on *Essays and Reviews* dating from March 1861, "whether there are sufficient grounds for proceeding to a Synodical judgment upon the book" (*Chronicle of Convocation* 1859–64, 1864, 863). The report of 18 June 1861 was immediately followed on 21 June with a resolution from the Lower House asserting that there were such grounds; the action of the Upper House on 9 July 1862 was to adjourn the procedure, because the matter was then before the Court of Arches; the bishops should not pronounce on the book's heterodoxy when it was possible that they would have to sit on the Judicial Committee when the decision from the Court of Arches would be appealed. Since the appeal was concluded, no episcopal conscience could now be compromised, so Denison represented it.

When Convocation reconvened in April 1864, it was abundantly clear that the old move for a synodical condemnation would be urged vigorously by Denison and others in the Lower House, and by Wilberforce in the Upper. It was no surprise, then, when Wilberforce brought forward a petition from the clergy and laity of the diocese of Norwich urging the bishops to "proceed to a judgment upon such statement[s] of . . . *Essays and Reviews* as do deny or impugn the faith of the Church of England." In bringing it forward, Wilberforce articulated the distinction upon which the following debate was to be based: "I believe that it is the legal and special function of this Synod to be able to condemn books, leaving the question of the treatment of the writers of those books to the criminal courts" (*Chronicle of Convocation* 1859–64, 19 Apr. 1864, 1461). In a sense he is appealing to one of the old notions of the Inquisition (that originally dealt with the index of prohibited books)—that the Holy Office had the right to deal with the state of the soul of the heretic, but the punishment of the body was to be left to the secular arm. Here he is drawing a distinction between synodical condemnation of a book for doctrinal error and the punishment of individual heretics as criminals before the legal courts. Subsequently, the matter was greatly simplified into "examining the book" not "trying the man" (*Chronicle of Convocation* 1859–64, 24 June 1864, 1832). Also on 19 April, in the Lower House, Christopher Wordsworth presented a petition dated 16 April 1864 from Rowland Williams asking that "before judgment pass on any book or proposition for which he is responsible, he may be allowed an opportunity of hearing all the objections to it, and of answering them in general and in particulars," on the grounds that "the principles of justice in all nations require no man to be condemned without a chance of a hearing." The next day forty members of the Lower House sent to the bishops a gravamen asking for a synodical condemnation; it was presented to the bishops by Wilberforce, who argued that the decision in the Privy Council was too seriously limited to legal interpretations based on narrow definitions of adherence to the literal text of the Formularies, ignoring the doctrinal questions upon which the issue of heresy depended. He urged Convocation to address now the doctrinal questions of heresy that the Privy Council had declared beyond their terms of reference: "They have no means of interpreting the propositions raised in the action by the context of the work quoted, though they have power to refer to the context to explain any points raised against the accusation; and . . . they have no power of referring to God's Word, to the doctrines of the Holy Catholic Church, to the six General Councils, or to those things in which, as we consider, are to be found the rules of heresy in this realm of England; but . . . they are limited strictly by the letter of the formularies" (*Chronicle of Convocation* 1859–64, 20 Apr. 1864, 1490). Wilberforce thereupon moved that a committee be struck, empowered to report "whether or not this house ought to proceed to Synodical judgment . . . [and] to prepare the grounds on which the house should proceed" (1494). In the Lower House it was agreed that there was no point in hearing from Rowland Williams until some motion concerning him or *Essays and Reviews* came before the House for debate (*Chronicle of Convocation* 1859–64, 20 Apr. 1864, 1495–96). Debate on Wilberforce's motion covers almost fifty pages of the *Chronicle of Convocation* (1859–64, 21 Apr., 1528–75).

The bishops' debate was begun by Connop Thirlwall (St. David's) on the difference between the doctrine of the church and private opinion on a matter of traditional belief often discussed but which cannot be called a doctrine. His point is that if Convocation defines a formal theological matter it would be tending to the definition of a "new article of faith," in Tait's words (1547). To the end of the debate in June, Tait and Thirlwall remained in opposition to the condemnation. Alfred Ollivant (Llandaff), a supporter of the condemnation, nevertheless declared himself against precise definition: "I should be extremely sorry myself to see any strict definition given of the meaning of the word 'inspiration.'. . . I should greatly regret if a more strict definition were given as to that or any other point which the Church of England has in its wisdom left undefined and unexplained" (1543). Both Jackson (Lincoln) and Lonsdale (Lichfield) did not want the book "disinterred" but wanted to abandon it "in the oblivion into which it has nearly fallen" (1555–56). But when the vote on establishing a committee to report on the proposed condemnation was called, only eleven bishops were present, including the archbishop in the chair, and the vote was evenly divided; Longley cast the deciding vote in favor of Wilberforce's motion, whereupon Wilberforce moved that the archbishop and bishops of the province of Canterbury form the committee, which was agreed. Tait wrote on behalf of the Committee to the legal advisors Sir Hugh Cairns and John Rolt asking whether Convocation was inhibited by statute "from proceeding to pronounce Synodical condemnation upon a Book,—not intending to proceed against the Author,—or without receiving the special Royal Licence for the purpose?" They received the lawyers' opinion that no statute inhibited them from acting (Lambeth, MS. Tait 291, fol. 396).

Strengthened by this legal opinion, Wilberforce, on 21 June 1864 at the next meeting of Convocation, presented the report to the Upper House. It has five parts and a number of subsections. In each of the subsections, specific passages are quoted at full length from five of the Essayists, excluding Goodwin and Pattison (for the document see Manifestos).

The debate on this report in the Upper House takes up almost thirty pages of the *Chronicle of Convocation*. Tait began by asserting that he did not attend any of the meetings of the committee. He argued that what was required at the moment was some effort to calm the public mind, but the report would only excite it further, despite the fact that "many of the errors of the book lie hidden within it, and are not likely to be much thought of again" (*Chronicle of Convocation* 1859–64, 21 June 1864, 1663). The popular agitation prompted by the Oxford Declaration of the Clergy that had gained almost 11,000 signatures involved, he reported, fewer than half of the clergy of England and Ireland, and it should not be allowed to force Convocation to act. Tait was answered by a number of speakers, including Thirlwall and Ollivant. Wilberforce concluded the debate with a lengthy commentary on the precedent for condemning those who reject the eternal punishment of the damned: "When . . . the general teaching of a large portion of the volume strikes at the root of all revelation—when the clergymen who have put that forward have escaped being silenced by the court of law before which they were brought, can there ever be a time for the Church, as a Church, to speak out, if that time has not arrived? That is all we ask you to do—state synodically, before Christendom, before this nation, and before God, that as a Church, by the Church's voice, we repudiate this false teaching" (1680–81). The report was received and adopted, whereupon Wilberforce moved the resolution of condemnation:

> That the Upper House of Convocation, having received and adopted the report of the committee of the whole house appointed by them to examine the volume entitled *Essays and Reviews*, invite the Lower House to concur with them in the following judgment:—"That this Synod, having appointed committees of the Upper and Lower Houses to examine and report upon the volume entitled *Essays and Reviews*, and the said committees having severally reported thereon, doth hereby synodically condemn the said volume as containing teaching contrary to the doctrine received by the United Church of England and Ireland, in common with the whole Catholic Church of Christ" (1683).

The motion carried in the Upper House, with Tait and Jackson of Lincoln voting against. The *Chronicle of Convocation* does not record the total vote, but the *Guardian* reported that only ten of the twenty-one members showed up to vote at the final condemnation, and so the vote must have been eight to two (29 June 1864, 621). But even this truncated action of the bishops alone was not sufficient for the condemnation to be the collective voice of the whole Synod.

On the same day, Denison moved that the Lower House "thankfully accept and concur in the condemnation of the book by the Upper House which has been based upon the said report" so the act of condemnation might be the collective act of Convocation (*Chronicle of Convocation* 1859–64, 21 June 1864, 1707). But Stanley was the vigorous leader of opposition to the condemnation and drove its supporters into theological confusion by quoting passages from *Essays and Reviews* alongside passages from *Aids to Faith* for which Wilberforce himself had written the preface, asking which was which, which heretical, which orthodox. Debate continued for seven and a half hours on 21 June, for the whole of 22 June, and finally on 24 June the debate concluded with a vote of 39 in favor, 19 against, and the resolution was communicated to the Upper House and was widely reported in the papers (*Chronicle of Convocation* 1859–64, 21–24 June 1864, 1704–1833).

Only after the vote did the issue resurface of Williams's right to be heard before condemnation was imposed. Christopher Wordsworth brought it forward with the awkward suggestion that consideration of Williams's request be a rider to the condemnation just passed. He admits the procedural peculiarity: "I grant that *prima facie* there appears to be something inconsistent and objectionable to proceed to a judgment and then to hear the party who is concerned" (*Chronicle of Convocation* 1859–64, 24 June 1864, 1830). He then explains that he had voted in favor of the condemnation with a mental "reservation": "I desired, on my own part, to suspend my sentence with regard to that particular essay" (1831), and proposes that the Upper House hear Dr. Williams, citing the precedent of Whiston in 1711. More disingenuously still, M. W. Mayow argued that "to take means by which Dr. Williams shall be heard before either house appears to me to implicate us in the supposition that we have been trying the man, not examining the book" (1832). Despite a motion to have Williams's petition read and acted upon, the Lower House refused to hear him.

Richard Monckton Milnes, Lord Houghton, raised the matter of the synodical condemnation in the House of Lords on 15 July, initiating a lively debate to which the Lord Chancellor, Westbury, responded, and to which the archbishop of Canterbury (Longley), and the bishops of London and Oxford (Tait and Wilberforce) replied. The exchanges were reported verbatim in the *Times* and in *Hansard*. Houghton began by pointing to a number of issues that were troubling: the dangers of the ecclesiastical censoring of books, the rights of citizens to freedom of expression, the doubtful validity of a synodical condemnation without a royal licence (that is, the synodical condemnation is technically an action that carries with it the privilege of the Crown), and the potential damage done to all of the writers, including those against whom no accusations of heresy had been alleged (such as Pattison) and the one who was a layman (Goodwin). Houghton relied on James Anthony Froude for some of his information, and so was able to allude to a range of historical precedent in cases of secular and ecclesiastical censorship, including the interference in publication by the Emperor Charles V and by Pope Alexander VI (Borgia). His interest, he declared, was "the freedom of opinion and the liberty of literature"; his worry was arbitrary censure for which this act would be a dangerous precedent (*Times*, 16 July 1864, 8). After outlining a series of cases of censure that Convocation had undertaken, including the instances against writings of Thomas Cranmer, a version of the *BCP*, and a translation of the Bible that was one of the bases for the AV, he asks whether Convocation has the right to take action without a royal licence against *Essays and Reviews*, and having done so, was that action both legal and privileged. Rejecting the notion that the condemnation was of a book and not the authors, he continued in a sentence that was prophetic of what would actually happen to Temple in 1869–70: "Let me suppose the case of one of those eminent writers rising to the highest position in the Church, and occupying a seat on the right rev. bench, would they not have this censure still hanging over them, diminishing their influence, and preventing them from occupying that position in the State to which by their talents they are entitled?" Finally, Houghton alludes to the refusal of Convocation to allow Williams to defend himself: "The fact that Dr. Williams, after having made a strong application to Convocation to be heard in his defence, was refused permission, and condemned unheard, I am sure will be repulsive to your lordships' sense of justice. (Hear, hear.) In a letter he has written to me, Dr. Williams complains of this act of injustice, and he says: 'The nature of a suit in the Ecclesiastical Courts is to deal only with legal issues. The defendants in such a suit are excluded from all the moral bearings which depend upon literary, scientific, or other research. Convocation, by refusing to hear me, has declared I shall be heard nowhere.' I feel deeply, not only this act of injustice, but also the mistake which Convocation has made in diverging from the path of useful and practical reform on which it has entered of late years to an attempt to limit freedom of expression and thought in this country" (*Times*, 16 July 1864, 8).

Westbury responded by heaping scorn upon the synodical condemnation of Convocation, upon the bishops who collaborated in it, upon their incomes, and finally upon the chief and well-known architect of the condemnation, Wilberforce, before he got to his substantive attack on the condemnation itself. Westbury begins by belittling the work of Convocation: when it is "harmlessly busy" it is ignored; when it gets "into mischief" it must be prorogued; when it exceeds its powers it must be tried and punished. On the question of the need for a licence from the Crown before condemnation, Westbury invokes the doctrine of the royal supremacy which, when usurped, might incur the penalties of *praemunire*.[65] He paints a fanciful picture of the archbishops and bishops hauled before the House of Lords in sackcloth and ashes, Longley being condemned in the same terms as were meted out to Williams and Wilson, "a year's deprivation of his benefice," and because he voted twice in Convocation, Westbury increased the punishment to two years. He imagines the delight of the chancellor of the Exchequer "to spread his net and in one haul take in 30,000*l*. from the highest dignitary, not to speak of the *oi polloi* [the rabble]—the bishops, deacons, archdeacons, canons, vicars, all included in one common crime, all subject to one common penalty! (Much laughter.)"

Turning from such general satiric conjecture, Westbury addresses the question of what a "synodical condemnation" might be by a direct attack against Wilberforce, pointing his invective with a series of well-aimed digs at the architect of the condemnation through references to his cognomen, "Soapy Sam": "I am extremely anxious to know . . . what the thing is which is called a synodical judgment. No criminal has been condemned. . . . But assuming that the report of the judgment which I have read is a correct one, I am happy to tell your lordships that what is called a synodical judgment is simply a series of well-lubricated terms—a sentence so oily and so saponaceous that no one could grasp it. (A laugh.) Like an eel, it slips through your fingers—it is simply nothing, and I am glad to tell my noble friend (Lord Houghton) that is literally no sentence at all. (Renewed laughter, and 'Hear.')" After quoting the sentence of condemnation, Westbury heaps scorn on the question of how a book, rather than its authors, could be an agent of criminal intent or doctrinal transgression: "As a judgment, this sentence has no meaning whatever; this judgment is no judgment at all." Notwithstanding such nugatory dismissals, Westbury was compelled to answer the technical legal question posed by Lord Houghton, of whether Convocation as a "debating society" had the right to proceed to such an action as synodical condemnation without royal licence, or some other permission. After citing the statutes, he concluded that "it is impossible that Convocation can exercise anything like this jurisdiction." His final scorn is reserved for Convocation's condemning Williams without hearing him: "I call upon the bishops . . . to pause for their own sake, even if they have no regard to the injustice, to the anomaly, to the unreasonable spectacle of condemning a man whom they have no power to convene, whom they have no authority to hear, and whom, when he presents himself as a suppliant, their own timidity and fear of going beyond their tether compel them to dismiss. (Hear, hear.)" (*Times*, 16 July 1864, 8).

Longley's reply consisted chiefly in asserting that the law officers of the Crown had given no advice on the legality of a synodical condemnation, and that the best legal advice he could get, from Cairns and Rolt, was that such a condemnation was legal. He indicated that the Judicial Committee itself had suggested that, in the judgment's words, "if . . . the book . . . be of a mischievous and baneful tendency, as weakening the foundations of Christian belief, and likely to cause many to offend, [it] will retain that character, and be liable to that condemnation, notwithstanding this our judgment." And finally Longley alludes to the seriousness of the crisis in the church prompted by the "combination" of the Essayists and Reviewers: "I ask your lordships whether since the Reformation there has been any crisis in the English Church of so grave a character as that through which it is now passing, and whether there is ever likely to occur in the next 200 or 300 years so serious a case or one calling so urgently upon Convocation, the Synod of the Church, to pronounce its opinion. (Hear, hear.) . . . I know that in the *Edinburgh Review* and elsewhere the charge of combination has been denied, but combination I must call it, and that there was concert between these clergymen I cannot but believe."

Tait's reply rejects Westbury's use of ridicule, rejects the applicability of precedent in determining the present case by referring again to the Whiston and Hoadley cases, and rejects the hyperbole of Longley concerning the seriousness of the present crisis and the resort to a synodical condemnation as an appropriate means of dealing with dissent. He also lays responsibility upon Westbury for giving appropriate advice to Convocation about its legal constraints: "It is all very well to call this [Convocation] a debating society, but it is a debating society which must meet. If, however, there is the slightest chance that the law may be violated by such a body it is undoubtedly necessary that the very highest legal authority should as soon as possible pronounce upon what is the law, and what is the course which each individual belonging to that assembly should take."

Wilberforce concluded the debate. First he corrected some points of fact in Houghton's argument; then he addressed the matter of the royal licence, drawing the conclusion that the licence referred to was the precedent of the case against William Whiston's *Primitive Christianity Revived* (1711) when Convocation was authorized by licence to meet and condemn him, and that "a legal jurisdiction existed in matters of heresy and the condemnation of heretics." Turning to Westbury, Wilberforce adopts the high road of injured righteousness, attacking Westbury's trivializing of a matter of urgent theological concern, and of his belittling remarks about the intention of Convocation, and of the supposed lack of seriousness in their form of debate: "When the highest representative of the law of England in your lordship's Court, upon a matter involving the liberties of the subject and the religion of the realm, and all those high truths concerning which this discussion is, can think it fitting to descend to a ribaldry in which he knows that he can safely indulge, because those to whom he addresses it will have too much respect for their character to answer him in like sort,—I say that this House has ground to complain of having its high character unnecessarily injured in the sight of the people of this land by one occupying so high a position within it. (Cheers.)" Wilberforce concludes his speech by stating that Convocation acted to preserve divine truth, that it moved to condemnation only after serious study and by citing offensive passages, and that it did not hear Williams because it was dealing with the book and not the man:

> But is it true that the individuals concerned had no opportunity of answering the charges which were made? Why, edition after edition of the work was published after the passages which were objected to were known, and if the writers wished to explain they had ample opportunity to do so. It is, I would add, one thing to condemn a man, and another to censure a book. . . . The book . . . cannot retract itself. (Hear, hear.) It cannot explain itself. It stands a *litera scripta*—a document in court which speaks on its own behalf. (Hear, hear.) . . . Here is the true question. We are set in trust in this land for this—that we may be the depository of the truth which God has revealed, as held by this reformed Church of England. Was it or was it not our duty, when we saw the peace of the Church assailed, to use the instrument which, as we

> believed and still believe . . . fairly was our right and, because it was our right, imposed upon us a corresponding duty? . . . I would rather subject myself, in the presence of my countrymen and of your noble House, to any amount of that invective and insinuation, and all these arts of I will not say what part of the Bar of England of which we have seen something to-night . . . than have to look back on my deathbed on myself as one of those who had not striven for the truth of our Established Church, and had not encountered, because I was afraid, personally, of the consequence, anything which the maintenance of that truth might entail. (Hear.)

Westbury briefly responded that Wilberforce "has in the same excited manner which characterized the greater portion of his speech . . . with much licence of language charged me with misrepresenting a passage in an Act of Parliament. His apology, I think, must be that he himself does not quite understand it." Westbury again returns to the rights of the Crown in all matters ecclesiastical and spiritual, but adds nothing new to the argument. In the words of the parliamentary reporter, "The subject then dropped" (*Times,* 16 July 1864, 8).

C Jowett's Trial in the Chancellor's Court at Oxford: An "Obscure and Obsolete Process"

FOUR MONTHS before Lushington's interlocutory judgment, Pusey had been planning a legal attack against Jowett—from 4 February 1862 when he had written concerning Jowett to Keble (Liddon 1893–97, 4:23; Geoffrey Faber 1957, 266). His proceedings against Jowett culminated in his trial in the Chancellor's Court at Oxford (presided over by the vice-chancellor or his designate, and so also often referred to as the Vice-Chancellor's Court). Jowett was charged on 7 February 1863:

> *For infringing the statutes and privileges* of the said University, by having, in the years 1859, 1860, 1861, and 1862, written, printed, published, given, sold, or set forth, . . . within the precincts of the University of Oxford and elsewhere a certain book, entitled *The Epistles of St. Paul* . . . : also in a book called *Essays and Reviews,* a certain article, essay, or review, with divers notes thereto, entitled 'On the Interpretation of Scripture;' and by having in such a book, and such article, essay, or review, respectively, advisedly promulgated, maintained, declared, and affirmed certain erroneous and strange doctrines, positions, or opinions contrary to and inconsistent with the doctrines of the Church of England, the Thirty-nine Articles of Religion, . . . and the Catholic faith: thereby contravening the laws and statutes of the said University, and against the peace and unity of the Church.[66]

The summons asked that Jowett be "duly corrected and punished according to the gravity of the offence and the exigency of the law and statutes of the University, and be inhibited from promulgating or publishing such erroneous doctrines or opinions." But this formal proceeding was already enmeshed in another controversy. Oxford's governing bodies had refused to increase the endowment of the Regius Professorship of Greek that Jowett held, to make it equivalent to the other Regius professorships. This refusal was tied to attacks on his orthodoxy that lasted eleven years, from the publication of *The Epistles of St. Paul* in 1855, that was exacerbated by the publication of *Essays and Reviews*, and that continued until February 1865, when the chair was finally endowed for £500. In 1871 he published the *Dialogues of Plato*; the caricature of him drawn by "Spy" (Leslie Ward), and published shortly after he issued the second edition of his Plato, summarizes his acclaim as Regius Professor by simply titling it "Greek" (see fig. 17).

These legal entanglements of Jowett are analogous to the cases against Williams and Wilson. All three, as a result of their publication in *Essays and Reviews*, were officially prosecuted by their opponents within the terms set out in their specific institutions. For Jowett that institution included all of the legal apparatuses of the University of Oxford, from the legislative Hebdomadal Council, to the larger meetings of all professors and heads of colleges, Convocation, and the vast assembly of all graduates holding the M.A., Congregation. These focused on the Chancellor's Court, but in each of them his "trials" were conducted without his making a single appearance to speak on his own behalf over an eleven-year period. In the case of Williams and Wilson the emphasis for the prosecution came down to specific charges concerning the inspiration of scripture and the ultimate destiny of the damned; in Jowett's case, the prosecution, led by Pusey, focused on his view of the atonement and biblical interpretation, but the charges were never brought to a focus with specific accusations tested by argument and law.

I "The Question of the Endowment of the Greek Chair"

Since the publication of Jowett's *The Epistles of St. Paul* in 1855, Pusey had been troubled by Jowett's theology, especially his views of the atonement and biblical inspiration, and so when Jowett was appointed Regius Professor of Greek in the same year that his book was published, and the issue of the endowment of the chair emerged, it was deeply stained, in Pusey's view, with heresy.

Five Regius Professorships were established by Henry VIII with a stipend of £40 a year, originally to be paid by Westminster Abbey. The Royal Exchequer eventually paid for the chairs in Medicine and Civil Law; the other three, in Divinity, Hebrew, and Greek were to be paid for by Christ Church, the college that Henry VIII provided for after the fall of Cardinal Wolsey, its original patron. Except for the Greek Professorship, all of these chairs were lucrative thanks to the incumbents' being entitled (under the instructions of James I and Charles I) to an

Figure 17. "Greek" (Benjamin Jowett). Lithograph by "Spy" (Leslie Ward) in *Vanity Fair* (26 Feb. 1876). Collection of William Whitla.

appointment as a canon at Christ Church, or to some other sinecure often held as part of a pluralism, the holding of more than one ecclesiastical office or living.[67] But the Greek Professorship was not so favored. When the incumbent died in June 1855, Jowett was appointed on behalf of the Crown by Lord Palmerston.[68] The announcement of Jowett's appointment was praised by his many friends, and he immediately embarked on an enthusiastic lecturing and tutoring schedule, beginning with undergraduate lectures on Plato's *Republic* that Walter Pater described as "fascinating . . . informal, unwritten, and seemingly unpremeditated," when Jowett "taught the University for nothing" (Abbott and Campbell 1897, 1:329–30). But the appointment also prompted the principal of Magdalen Hall, the evangelical layman Dr. J. D. Macbride and a Low Church clergyman, C. P. Golightly, to protest Jowett's appointment to the vice-chancellor of the university, Dr. R. L. Cotton, provost of Worcester College (Cotton was Pusey's brother-in-law, and an opponent of the University Commission for university reform of which Stanley was secretary, and that Jowett so strongly supported). Jowett was summoned to appear before Cotton to resubscribe to the Articles of Religion in a burlesque scene that Jowett described to Stanley as a "schoolboy degradation," and from Jowett's account it is clear that Dr. Heurtley, Lady Margaret Professor of Divinity, who was later to be involved with Pusey in the legal prosecution of Jowett, had on this occasion also written against him (Letter 1).

Jowett had received the honor of the appointment not only because of his accomplishments as a tutor in Greek but also as a political patronage reward for his work for university reform. For several years before 1855 he had been very active in supporting Gladstone (who was then M.P. for Oxford University) on the issue of university reform to abrogate the medieval statutes, reorganize university government, open scholarships and fellowships to free competition, end the religious tests, make the teaching, programs of study, and examinations far more rigorous and responsible, and adjust the university finances. A royal commission had been appointed by Lord John Russell in 1850, but the task was opposed on many sides on the basis of entrenched interest and profitable endowments; and college finances were not within its purview. Even the recent intellectual ferment of the Oxford Movement had, in the view of Goldwin Smith, blocked reform that "showed a tendency to recede when Tractarianism, having become dominant, betrayed its hostility to intellect and its determination to keep the endowments, consequently the tutorial staff, as close as possible to those whom it called *pauperes Christi* [the paupers of Christ]; in fact, to youths of inferior intellect and submissive character, such as ecclesiastical leadership requires" (1910, 100). A. P. Stanley was the secretary of the royal commission, assisted by Goldwin Smith as assistant secretary, and the members included Baden Powell, A. C. Tait, and H. G. Liddell (then headmaster of Westminster). Jowett was very active in supporting its work. Hence, the makeup of the commission marked it as liberal in politics and either Broad Church, or sympathetic to Broad Church positions, in churchmanship. Its conclusions (*Report of the Oxford University Commission*, 1852) eventually yielded the

Oxford Act (1854, 17 & 18 Vict. c. lxxxi), a measure that was subject to extensive intervention in its preparation and passage by many interested people within the university and throughout the country. Jowett's correspondence with Gladstone advocated direct legislation to enforce the colleges to comply with the reform measures, a procedure that eventually Gladstone rejected in favor of implementation by means of another commission. And again Jowett was involved. For all of this work on behalf of the university, Jowett was rewarded with the Regius Professorship, but the appointment also brought with it a share of hostility from those who opposed not only his theology but also his reforming zeal on behalf of higher education.

A year before Jowett was appointed to the Greek chair, the University Commission had asked the dean and Chapter of Christ Church to review the endowment of the professorships, to which they responded that their chief goal was to endow the Greek Professorship with a canonry at Christ Church (*Correspondence* 1854, 46).[69] However, rather than proceeding to endow the chair, they used the money from the canonry to support "Studentships" or scholarship students and fellows at Christ Church. Pusey was active in trying to increase the endowment, in fairness to Jowett as the holder of the professorship, but he wanted it to be clear that the stipend was for the chair and should not be understood as condoning Jowett's theology. In particular the raising of the stipend for the Greek Professorship should not, in Pusey's view, be seen as approval of Jowett's *The Epistles of St. Paul*, and especially the essay "On the Atonement and Satisfaction," which Pusey had already attacked in the published notes to the volume of two sermons he preached before the university in 1855 (*All Faith the Gift of God; Real Faith Entire*).[70] In May 1858, Pusey first mentioned the connection between the Greek Chair and Jowett's theology in a letter to Keble: "It is proposed to endow the Regius Professorship of Greek with £300. . . . It is the Professorship, not the Professor which is endowed. . . . It seems to me that we should be declaring ourselves indifferent as to Professor Jowett's misbelief if we make the grant" (Liddon 1897, 4:12). Oxford's Hebdomadal Council, which prepared university legislation, rejected the changing of the endowment. Pusey joined in the rejection but did not oppose the motion on theological grounds; rather because it would have brought the university into conflict with the Crown, whereby the university would be paying for what was a royal appointment, with no say in who might hold the chair. In the autumn of 1859 Stanley, then Professor of Ecclesiastical History and canon at Christ Church, urged that the council consider the matter again, and again Pusey wrote to Keble: "This is, of course, a personal act of favor to Jowett . . . . If a grant is made to him, we pledge ourselves to indifference as to religious belief for the future. It is possible that the grant may be stopped in Council; but [Robert] Scott [master of Balliol] and [William] Jacobson [Regius Professor of Divinity] are supporters of it, on the ground that we must separate the Professor from his creed. 'He works well as Greek Professor, therefore he is to be endowed'" (Liddon 1897, 4:13). Again the vote failed. Pusey continued to agitate for an increase in the endowment, but remained troubled. In early January 1860 he wrote to Keble that "the Jowett business much perplexes me" and proposed that if the university endowed the chair, then it should have a say in the appointment, and also should dissociate itself from sanctioning an incumbent's theological opinions, a suggestion that he wrote about to Gladstone during the next year (Liddon 1897, 4:14).

Pusey and Stanley both were elected in the autumn of 1860 to the Hebdomadal Council. Jowett recognized that there was "to be another battle at Oxford about the endowment of the Greek Professorship" (Letter 28). At a meeting of the Hebdomadal Council, Stanley claimed he had Wilberforce's support for an endowment of the Greek Professorship by the university rather than the Crown. Thereupon Pusey wrote to Wilberforce, stating "how matters now stand," namely, that the council objected to "a direct and personal augmentation of Professor Jowett's income," partly because the Crown should assume responsibility for those whom it appoints, but largely because of "the deeper ground . . . that since Professor Jowett is a sceptic, denying all which a Socinian denies, it would be very evil for the University to do any act which should look like personal favor to Professor Jowett." He sets out his scheme as proposed to Gladstone, and shows why he cannot support Stanley's proposal because it looks like favoritism toward Jowett and would be open to misconstruing as approval of his theology. In this letter of 31 October 1860, he sets out the important link between Stanley, the endowment of Jowett's chair, and *Essays and Reviews*: "The only real object of Professor Stanley's motion can be to make the vote one of confidence in Professor Jowett. Has your Lordship read the article on Neo-Christianity in the last *Westminster Review*, in which the reviewer clearly, though painfully, shows that the writers of the Essays teach the same as themselves [Stanley and Jowett], the human origin of the Bible and its absolute want of Authority? I doubt whether Professor Stanley is to be moved. But I write this to your Lordship that I may know what to say if your name should be quoted against me" (Letter 29). On 8 February 1861 Jowett wrote to Gilbert Elliot about a "new attempt" that Pusey had instigated to raise the endowment, but it was cumbersome, requiring government approval for the measure. Jowett feared defeat in the House of Commons. But Stanley, in an effort to move more quickly, argued that the chair should be endowed immediately, though for a lesser sum, perhaps hoping that the smaller expenditure could induce swifter passage of the measure. But he misjudged the council: it defeated his motion and approved Pusey's. In March, Jowett wrote to Emily Tennyson about the "tumult" and to Francis Turner Palgrave: "Many thanks to you for caring whether I am troubled about the 'persecution.' I think I am not deceiving myself in saying that I don't mind about it" (Letters 99–100). He was grateful for support such as that of Stanley (Letter 106) but it was not sufficient. On 7 May 1861 when the Hebdomadal Council's motion came before Convocation for legislative action it was defeated by 21 votes (91–70), although both Stanley and Pusey spoke in favor (*Times*, 8 May 1861, 12; see also Geoffrey Faber 1957, 227–28). Three years later Pusey was still angry about the defeat, and in a later controversy with F. D. Maurice in the *Times*, threw the result back at Jowett and his friends, whom he condemned "for their own apathy": "Professor Jowett's friends should remember that, but for their own apathy, or the opposition of some of them, Professor Jowett would have been endowed three years ago, when a statute, which also avoided the direct endowment, and on which I had been employed for a year, was lost in a *Convocation* of less than 200 by a majority of some 20. As it afterwards appeared, it could have been carried had Professor Jowett's friends thought the endowment of paramount moment, or used the very slightest exertion, or even if some had not opposed it" (*Times,* 15 Mar. 1864, 14).

But it was not only Pusey's motion that could suffer a close defeat; in the next round it was Stanley's turn. By October 1861 both Stanley and Pusey took up more entrenched positions on the Greek Professorship before the Hebdomadal Council. Stanley persuaded the council to approve his proposal, arguing that the university take over payment of the endowment for £300 until such time as the formal matter of appointment and permanent arrangement for stabilizing of the endowment (whether controlled by the Crown or the university) be set in place. On 20 November the matter came before the next body, Congregation, where the debate lasted for three hours. Stanley delivered a lengthy address in which he traced "the history of the question" from Jowett's appointment in 1855, his lecturing on "Plato, Homer, Sophocles, Aristophanes, and Thucyidides," the good attendance at Jowett's lectures of between 40 to 80 students, his assiduous revision of students' compositions, and the testimonials of his students who had won "numerous honours." Other professorships had been raised "to sums varying from 300*l.* a-year to 1,000*l.*" Stanley indicated the previous efforts to have the endowment increased, and outlined three possible objections: "1. That it was undesirable to increase the patronage of the Crown. 2. That the existing Professor's theological opinions made the endowment undesirable at present. 3. That if the statute were approved by Congregation, Convocation would throw it out" (*Times*, 21 Nov. 1861, 10).[71] In the subsequent debate, Edward Hawkins, provost of Oriel College, asserted that "it was new to him to hear that Professor Jowett at the time of his appointment expected an increase of his stipend. He thought that he had merely accepted it as a sort of feather in his cap" and asserted that "his great objection was the theological one" (*Times*, 21 Nov. 1861, 10). Pusey also opposed the statute: asserting that no estates had been conferred on Christ Church to supply the payment, he opposed the endowment "of the present holder on theological grounds," as the *Times* reported: "He thought Professor Jowett's contribution to *Essays and Reviews* most mischievous. He had looked for some recantation or explanation, but none had appeared, and in his opinion the second edition of the work was worse than the first. The present time was particularly ill-chosen for mooting the question, as, if the endowment were carried, it tended to prejudice the case now pending in the diocese of Salisbury. He thought the Liberal party ought not now to make an outcry about persecution, as they had been on the persecuting side on the occasion of 'Tract 90'" (21 Nov. 1861, 10).

Pusey was adamant that Stanley's proposal would result in confusion concerning future appointments to the chair, and that appointments by the Crown, independent of ecclesiastical authority, were no guarantee of religious orthodoxy. When one of the Students (or fellows) of Christ Church asserted that "the proper quarter from which to obtain the endowment was Christ Church, which had accepted an estate from the Crown chargeable with the stipend, and had actually proposed in 1854 to endow the Professorship," Pusey denied the assertion: "Christ Church had received no estate, but only the burden of making the payment. . . . Crown nominations were likely to be made on political grounds. Formerly such nominations were good, because the highest ecclesiastical advice was taken, but this practice had been discontinued" (*Times*, 21 Nov. 1861, 10).[72] Montague Bernard, later to be the assessor in the trial of Jowett, supported Stanley's motion as the best one possible at the moment, and one necessary on the grounds of "substantial justice"; notwithstanding the fact that he "disliked that theology [of Jowett's] . . . he did not think it advisable to discountenance unsound theology by means of bad morality" (*Times*, 21 Nov. 1861, 10). Charles Lutwidge Dodgson ("Lewis Carroll") attended Congregation on this occasion, and noted in his diary that "the speaking took up the whole afternoon." He also made his first speech in Congregation, against Stanley's proposal, urging that the endowment and Jowett's theological opinions should be kept separate (Carroll 1953, 165–66). Two days later Dodgson published "his earliest Oxford 'squib'" as a mock university notice on the "Endowment of the Greek Professorship" (Carroll 1954, 166; see Part 3, Satires). Stanley published his address to Congregation of 20 November 1861 (Stanley 1861b), but a week later the motion was defeated, as he had foreseen, in Congregation, by a close vote of 99 to 96 (Abbott and Campbell 1897, 1:305). Pusey also published his speech, though anonymously, castigating the Liberals for not having supported his earlier measure (Pusey 1861). In a letter to Frances Power Cobbe, Jowett commented that the defeat of Stanley's motion involved "deferring indefinitely the endowment. . . . I have therefore requested Dr. Stanley to take no further steps in the Council on the subject; it seems to me undignified to keep the University squabbling about my income" (Letter 140). A number of Jowett's friends, distressed that approval for increasing the endowment had failed, undertook two tasks. They (under the editorship of Stanley) compiled and published "without his sanction and knowledge" a book of extracts from his writings to dispel the idea that he was "an enemy of Christ" (Jowett 1861, 3). They also collected £2,000, equivalent to his proposed salary for the previous five years. Jowett appreciated the financial gesture but refused the gift in a letter to his friend R. R. W. Lingen (Letter 149). Here the veiled attacks on Jowett's orthodoxy rested, in the guise of squabbles about university legislation concerning the endowment of the Greek Chair—until the interlocutory decision of Dr. Lushington condemned Williams and Wilson on 25 June 1862.

II "The Prosecution Is Commenced": "The Rusty Engine of Intolerance"

On 9 October 1862 Jowett wrote to Florence Nightingale that he knew that Pusey had consulted Robert Phillimore, the queen's advocate, and the successful prosecutor of Williams and Wilson in the Court of Arches: "for some things I have said I may be liable to prosecution." But already the results of Phillimore's first inquiry, very likely at the instigation of Pusey, had been announced in the *Guardian*, prompting the replies of writers, including John Keble, exactly when Jowett was writing to Nightingale (Letter 158). Phillimore eventually was asked two questions about the possibility of bringing charges against Jowett in some university court, whether he "had so distinctly contravened the doctrines of the Church of England that a court of law would pronounce him guilty" and whether his "legal position" would permit a prosecution (Abbott and Campbell 1897, 1:310). The elaboration of an anonymous answer, couched in the terms of a legal case, consisted of thirty-four pages of quotations from Jowett's works and counterpassages from the Articles and Formularies that were presented to Phillimore and that were printed together with his legal opinion concerning the viability of such a case in the courts. The document's pseudo-legal title explains its purpose: *Case Whether Professor Jowett in his Essay and Commentary Has so Distinctly Contravened the Doctrines of the Church of England, That a Court of Law Would Pronounce Him Guilty; with the Opinion of the Queen's Advocate Thereon.* The Preface sets out the fate of the Essayists, noting that Powell was "removed before a higher Tribunal," Goodwin resigned his fellowship, Temple and Pattison said nothing that could be formally prosecuted, Williams and Wilson have been condemned, and Jowett alone is left. The framer of the document, very likely Pusey, full as it is with his arguments and phrases, claims that he seeks to know the legal position of the university concerning Jowett's views. The Preface, written after Phillimore had delivered his view that he considered Jowett susceptible to prosecution for having contravened the doctrines of the Church of England and the statutes of the university, holds that Jowett has compromised "both the source and the substance of the faith. In denying the supernatural inspiration of Holy Scripture, he takes away from those who trust him the groundwork of all faith. In denying the agreement of the Creeds with Holy Scripture, he throws a doubt on the whole contents of the faith. In denying the doctrine of the Atonement, he takes away the ground of our reconciliation with God" (*Case Whether Professor Jowett* 1862, 4). Pusey, then (for all of the evidence points to him as author), was preparing for the prosecution of a case against Jowett at the same time that the debates concerning the endowment of the Greek Chair were being conducted, and in which Pusey also played a prominent role. Throughout he was the defender of the "High Church" position, the name that stuck to him as in the title of the caricature in

Vanity Fair by "Ape" (Carlo Pellegrini) that appeared a year before Jowett's (see fig. 18).

The writer of the pamphlet argues that the problem is that Jowett is in a position of great influence:

> The Regius Professorship of Greek is the most influential in the University; for the knowledge of Greek is the most essential element for honor in the Oxford schools, and for most competitive examinations. Professor Jowett's avowed object is to propagate that inconsistent form of unbelief which he holds, not directly through his lectures, but using that influence which his station gives him. His influence in promoting scepticism among our talented young men, through the knowledge of his published unbelief, and through the suspicion of a yet further unbelief lurking behind, has already been very destructive. As the talented young men, influenced by him, become tutors in other colleges, the extent to which Oxford may become a destroyer of souls is incalculable. If the University pass this by, as a matter beyond her, parents will send any son to Oxford at the risk of the loss of his faith and of his soul (*Case Whether Professor Jowett* 1862, 5–6).

The body of the documents consists of seven charges against Jowett, citing specific passages drawn chiefly from his essay "On the Atonement" from *The Epistles of St. Paul*, and his contribution to *Essays and Reviews*. The first point concerns Jowett's view of the atonement. He attacked the medieval notion that the importance of the passion and death of Christ is to satisfy the just and deserved anger of a righteous God against human sin (the satisfaction theory), a view current amongst High Church theologians. At the same time he rejected the language of penal substitution, that Christ is the one selected for punishment as a substitution for all human beings, and as the vicarious sufferer he performs atonement, the view most popular amongst the evangelicals. Instead, Jowett posited an exemplarist view, in which Christ is a patient example of undeserved suffering, with which the individual believer can be identified mystically. To the writer of the *Case Whether Professor Jowett*, Jowett denies "the one meritorious sacrifice for sin" (1862, 7–19).

The second contention is that Jowett denies "the infallible authority of the Holy Scripture" (19), and the critique focuses largely on Jowett ¶s 13 and 15 to show that Jowett denies a supernatural view of inspiration: "Nor for any of the higher or supernatural views of inspiration is there any foundation in the Gospels or Epistles" (Jowett ¶15). The third argument is that he maintains that the language of the Creeds does not correspond with the language of the Bible, but that a change in intellectual, and especially in philosophical and historical, understanding accounts for the difference, citing Jowett ¶s 22 and 23 (24–25). In the fourth argument it is alleged that Jowett throws "doubt on the true Divinity of our Lord and the doctrine" stated in the Second Article of Religion (Jowett ¶23). The fifth argument against Jowett is that he argues that the "personality of the Holy Spirit" depends upon texts taken out of context (Jowett ¶s 27–28). The sixth charge is that Jowett holds the doctrine of original sin to be unscriptural (28–32), citing the last section

Figure 18. "High Church" (E. B. Pusey). Lithograph by "Ape" (Carlo Pellegrini) in *Vanity Fair* (2 Jan. 1875). Collection of William Whitla.

of Jowett ¶28, and sections from his essay "On the imputation of the sin of Adam" in *The Epistles of St. Paul.* The final charge is that Jowett denies the prophetical and typological meaning of the Hebrew Scriptures as referring to Christ, in contradiction to the Seventh Article of Religion, citing passages from *The Epistles of St. Paul.*

Phillimore's Opinion was dated 12 October 1862, indicating that the whole of the project against Jowett came into being after the interlocutory judgment against Williams and Wilson gave impetus for a further prosecution. It appears, then, that the *Case Whether Professor Jowett* was constructed in August and September, so that Phillimore could respond in early October. Jowett in his comment to Florence Nightingale on 9 October shows that he had already got wind of the procedure, and, indeed, it was already in the press and the first *Case Whether Professor Jowett* was in circulation and is referred to by correspondents in the *Guardian* (Letter 158). Phillimore's Opinion was based on the precedent of the interlocutory decision already pronounced against the Essayists in the Court of Arches: "First. With respect to the Doctrines of the Atonement, Satisfaction for Sin, Vicarious Suffering of our Saviour. I am of opinion that various passages in the Commentary, entitled, 'On Atonement and Satisfaction,' are plainly at variance with, and contradictory of the second, fifteenth, twenty-eighth and thirty-first of the Thirty-Nine Articles, and also with various portions of the Liturgy upon these subjects" (*Case Whether Professor Jowett* 1862, 35–36). Phillimore, in his turn, gives lengthy citations from Jowett's essay "On Atonement." He then follows the same course of action with respect to each of the other six allegations. In the second, he bases his position upon the decision of "the recent judgment of the Dean of the Arches in the case of the *Bishop of Sarum v. Williams*, and *Fendall v. Wilson*" (*Case Whether Professor Jowett* 1862, 38). According to Phillimore, then, Jowett has heretical views, or at least views which contradict the doctrine of the Church of England, with respect to the atonement, the inspiration of the Bible, the relation of the Creeds and Scripture, the divinity of Christ, the personality of the Holy Spirit, the doctrine of original sin, and the harmony of the Old and New testaments. For each doctrine, specific Articles of Religion or other passages of the Formularies are alluded to.

Having secured the opinion of Lushington on Jowett's doctrinal errors, Phillimore was asked for his opinion on the second question, the legal position of Jowett in the university and the possibility of his being prosecuted in the university court. A further document was published, *Case as to the Legal Position of Professor Jowett with the Opinion of the Queen's Advocate Thereon* (1862). This document follows a somewhat different course from the first. In the opening Notice there is a brief report on the points made in *Case Whether Professor Jowett*, indicating the findings of Phillimore and once more enumerating Jowett's alleged heresies. The Case for Opinion that follows cites the University of Oxford Statutes in Latin, particularly those concerning the rights of the chancellor, and of the vice-chancellor who has, in his absence, "all his functions, and, specifically, his judicial authority," and those statutes respecting the vice-chancellor's right and duty "to restrain books which propagate opinions contrary to sound doctrine" and "prohibiting Professors from teaching any thing directly or indirectly against the Catholic faith" (*Case as to the Legal Position* 1862, 6–7). When the case wound its way into the Chancellor's Court in February 1863, primary attention was given to these statutes by the vice-chancellor's delegated assessor, Montague Bernard. In the event that the Chancellor's Court should refuse to hear the case, Phillimore was asked whether it was his legal opinion whether he could be compelled to hear it by an instruction of the Court of Queen's Bench. A final matter involved the delicate question of timing, since the Church Discipline Act placed a time-limit of two years for a charge to be brought against any publication, a restriction not specified in the university statutes; furthermore, there was the issue of whether republication in numerous editions constitutes continuous publication and so continuous offense.

Phillimore responded that the Chancellor's Court would be bound to hear a case "containing charges of Heresy or of preaching doctrines contrary to the Church of England" and that he could be compelled by an order of *mandamus* from Queen's Bench to hear such a case. Secondly, he stated that continued publication constitutes continued offence and the Church Discipline Act should not affect "proceedings against a Professor before the Vice-Chancellor" (*Case as to the Legal Position* 1862, 10–11). This second Opinion is dated 30 October 1862, but from the correspondence from Keble and others in the *Guardian* it was not yet public by 9 November 1862 (Abbott and Campbell 1897, 1:310).

Strengthened by such a clear legal opinion, Pusey solicited and gained the support of Charles Ogilvie, the Regius Professor of Pastoral Theology, and C. A. Heurtley, Lady Margaret Professor of Divinity, who jointly brought forward to the Chancellor's Court charges against Jowett. Jowett knew that they were coming by 3 February, when he wrote to Stanley asking for advice about lawyers and other matters (Letter 171). On 7 February 1863 the chancellor, Lord Derby, instructed John Haines, the yeoman bedell of law, an Oxford functionary of the Chancellor's Court, to issue a "monition":

> We hereby authorise and command you . . . that you cite or cause to be cited the Reverend Benjamin Jowett . . . to appear before our Vice-Chancellor or his Assessor, on Friday the 13th of February, at the hour of twelve o'clock in the forenoon of the said day, in the Apodyterium of the Convocation House (being the accustomed place of judicature in our said University), then and there to answer to certain articles or interrogatories to be administered and objected to him by virtue of our office concerning the reformation and correction of his manners and excesses, but more especially *for infringing the Statutes and privileges* of the said University, by having . . . written, printed, published, given, sold, or set forth . . . within the precincts of the University of Oxford and elsewhere a certain book, entitled *The Epistles of St. Paul* . . . : also in a book called *Essays and Reviews*, a certain article . . . entitled, "On the Interpretation of Scripture;" and by having in [them] . . . affirmed certain erroneous and strange doctrines . . . contrary to and inconsistent with the doctrines of the Church of England, the Thirty-nine Articles of Religion, . . .

> and the Catholic faith; thereby contravening the laws and statutes of the said University, and against the peace and unity of the Church.

There follows a prayer as in the Court of Arches proceedings, a petition or formal request for a specific action to be taken: "On legal proof being made of the charges, the said Professor Jowett be duly corrected and punished according to the gravity of the offence and the exigency of the law and statutes of the University, and be inhibited from promulgating or publishing such erroneous doctrines or opinions" (*Pusey and Others v. Jowett* 1863, 2).[73] Jowett wrote, very likely to Stanley, for help, reporting that he has talked the matter over with Pattison, who "counsels submission [subscription?]. But submission appears to imply that the limits of the Ch. of England in the University are acknowledged to be narrowed & gives up all the legal difficulties." He asked whether he should put his case in the hands of Fitzjames Stephen, who had acted for Williams and Wilson, and even wondered if his old friend Bishop Tait would help (3 Feb. 1863, Balliol, MS. Jowett III S, fol. 109). On 11 February the legal prosecution was announced, and the next day it was reported in the *Times*: "An action has been commenced in the Chancellor's Court against the Rev. B. Jowett, M.A. . . . Regius Professor of Greek, on account of opinions expressed by him in his *Commentary on the Epistles to the Thessalonians* and other works. The appellants are the Rev. Dr. Pusey, Regius Professor of Hebrew; the Rev. Dr. Heurtley, Margaret Professor of Divinity; and the Rev. Dr. Ogilvy, Regius Professor of Pastoral Theology—all Canons of Christ Church" (12 Feb. 1863, 5). Hence, it was clear that Pusey and the other prosecutors of the case were using the same language as that used against Williams and Wilson in the Court of Arches in bringing a heresy charge, a point that was returned to in Jowett's trial.

On 13 February the trial in the Chancellor's Court began before Montague Bernard, the vice-chancellor's assessor.[74] The heresy charge was formally presented, and Jowett's lawyer, Henry A. Pottinger, responded that Jowett would "object to the jurisdiction of the Court and to the matter and form of the citation" (*Times*, 16 Feb. 1863, 6); at his request the trial was adjourned for a week. Jowett was aware that Pusey and the other prosecutors were "trying to smuggle in an ecclesiastical cause under colour of a breach of the Statutes of the University," as he wrote to Emily Tennyson (Letter 172). But he and his proctor were clear about their line of defense—to object to the jurisdiction of the Chancellor's Court in hearing the matter.

The next day, on 14 February, the *Times*, in a lead article of a column and a half, attacked Pusey, Heurtley, and Ogilvie for availing themselves of an archaic legal manoeuver, in hauling Jowett before a court "the jurisdiction of which has practically been confined to the recovery of small debts" (9). The article alleges that "the old statutes have been ransacked for prohibitions and mischievous doctrines" and what was found is "ludicrous vagueness and irrelevancy." Jowett was accused of teaching what is "contrary to the 'Catholic faith' or morality . . . and the doctrine and discipline of the Church of England," even in his lectures as Greek Professor, but the "vindictive persecutions" do not rest on that: "No extravagance of assumption, however, could reconcile us even hypothetically to the employment of this obscure and obsolete process, the very legality of which is questionable, against a man whose only offence is that he had published in London two works on Biblical criticism." The "obscure and obsolete process" was to bring about a theological condemnation for heresy when Jowett could not be cited before the Court of Arches—by the invoking of "a rusty engine of intolerance," namely the Caroline statutes of the university in the Chancellor's Court. The article is critical of the fact that no notion of limitations has been invoked allowing so long a time to have passed from the dates of original publication: "Two years and a half have elapsed since the publication of *Essays and Reviews*, and three years and a half since the last edition of Mr. Jowett's *Commentaries*; yet it is for expressions culled from these two books that it is now sought to punish him. If this rusty engine of intolerance be allowed to be used, any one still resident in Oxford who took part in the [Tractarian] controversies of twenty years ago may be brought to account for the language of some forgotten pamphlet or sermon, and a war of extermination may be opened between the two great Church parties on their old battle-ground." More particularly, the *Times* criticized the entire process as curtailing freedom of thought and expression in the university. Having pointed out that Ogilvie and Heurtley had both attacked Pusey, and the former had condemned Pusey's theological opinions formally, the *Times* continues by contrasting their litigious propensities with the eirenic actions of Jowett, who had argued on behalf of freedom of speech when Pusey and others were being attacked for their protests over the Hampden affair in 1845. Pusey's defense then was freedom of speech and the breadth of the Anglican Formularies, on which Jowett supported him, the very points upon which Jowett would plan his own defense. The editorial explicitly connects the prosecution in the Chancellor's Court and the Greek Professorship: it charges that Jowett's "salary was withheld out of an unworthy jealousy of his independence," leading now to this culmination of a "deadly blow," aimed by "a few infatuated dignitaries . . . these three Canons of Christ Church," not only at "the foremost Tutor of the foremost College in Oxford," but also "at the peace of the Church of England." A short leader in the *Daily News* praised Jowett as "one of the most eminent, learned, and useful men in the University" and regretted that he was "to be sacrificed to the theological hatred of the three Canons of Christ Church" (16 Feb. 1863).

Pusey replied to the *Times* with a long defense, the first of a series of six letters he wrote to the *Times* in the next month, trying to vindicate his position by stating his purpose. He aimed to bring "the theological teaching of Professor Jowett to a legal issue," but protested that "Prosecution is not persecution." Jowett was accused by Pusey of professing that he believes the Formularies, but writes to the contrary, as part of a "systematic attempt to revolutionize the Church of England." Pusey concluded with a sentence that left him open to attack: "It would be an evil day for England when it should be recognized that to appeal to the majesty of justice is to contravene truth and justice" (19 Feb. 1863, 6). To call the court usually given to "the recovery of small debts" by the grand title of "the majesty of justice," and to claim that smuggling in a heresy trial against a fellow Regius Professor by such backhanded tactics was such an appeal, could only prompt ridicule and satire, not least of which was one from Lewis Carroll (see "Satires").

Pusey's defense of his actions was attacked the next day by F. D. Maurice, and an exchange of public letters between them continued until 21 March. Maurice belittled Pusey's hauling of Jowett before a "Court for the adjudication of small debts," a reference to the major business treated by the court; Pusey, on the other hand, continued to appeal to the propriety and dignity of the Chancellor's Court. Other correspondents took part, as the scope of the Oxford trial's implications broadened to include, as the *Times* leader suggested, old legal and doctrinal controversies that brought High, Low, and Broad Church parties into conflict.

On the same day that the Pusey-Maurice exchange began, 20 February 1863, Jowett's trial was resumed in the Chancellor's Court, before "a large attendance of Doctors, Masters and others" (*Times*, 28 Feb. 1963, 12). The summary accounts in the *Times* and in Jowett's biography do little justice to the seriousness of the charges, the formality of the proceedings, and the scholarly range of reference in the legal arguments. As proctor (or legal counsel) for Jowett it was Pottinger's right to begin by answering the charges, or objecting to the jurisdiction of the court, and it was the right of the promoters of the case through their legal representative, Digby Latimer, to respond. But before these proceeding got under way there was a preliminary skirmish over whether the formal protest of the court's legal jurisdiction was in writing as the court required. Neither had done so, and had immediately to write it out. Like a reprimand for a schoolboy's not having written out his excuse, it was one of the few moments of trivial informality in the trial. Pottinger objected to the jurisdiction of the court in hearing the case under three headings: "First, that the Court has no jurisdiction in things *merè spirituales* [Lat. purely spiritual]. Secondly, that the Court is not furnished with the machinery and forms for such a prosecution. And, thirdly, that the Court has no jurisdiction over a Regius Professor" (*Pusey and Others v. Jowett* 1863, 4). Pottinger's first point hinged on whether the chancellor had the right to deal legally with spiritual or ecclesiastical causes, and to make this clear, Pottinger distinguished between two kinds of issues, those that have to do with "questions of heresy, questions of holy orders," and those questions that were often dealt with by the ecclesiastical courts having to do with what are often seen as civil infractions but are related to moral laws or the laws concerning marriage, such as "wills, marriage, drunkenness, profaneness, lewdness."

In tracing this distinction, Pottinger is at pains to show that the Chancellor's Court at Oxford has never dealt with heresy in hearing a case so as to impose a judgment, tracing matters back through the university archives, royal charters, and papal bulls to the time of Henry VI and earlier. Such rights were jealously guarded by the bishop of Lincoln and the archdeacon of Oxford who then had rights over the city and university of Oxford, and by a series of agreements from 1345 these were qualified, giving the clergy teaching in the university certain rights independent of ecclesiastical interference. Pottinger took considerable time to trace "the history of these matters down to the Reformation, showing that before the Reformation the University never claimed any jurisdiction in matters merely spiritual, and never exercised any" (*Pusey and Others v. Jowett* 1863, 11). He then traced matters concerning spiritual jurisdiction since the Reformation, citing a number of instances which he discussed in some detail (and agreed to provide dates, instances, and references to Bernard at his request), dismissing them as potential precedents: "These are the cases which I have found illustrating the way in which the University has dealt with heresy. From the earliest times they have not been tried by the [Chancellor's] Court; and when there is anything done by the University, it is merely a preliminary investigation, and the ultimate decision is by the Archbishop and Bishops. . . . I think I can now leave that part of my objection in your hands—that the Court has no jurisdiction, and never had jurisdiction in matters purely spiritual. The charge of teaching against the Articles and against the peace and unity of the Church, is manifestly intended to be a charge of heresy" (*Pusey and Others v. Jowett* 1863, 14).

Pottinger explains the second point of Jowett's objection, that "the Court is not provided with the machinery necessary for carrying on an ecclesiastical cause; I cannot call it a summons." He refers to the technical forms of the court, the legal format of the monition, the citing of infringements which must be answered, proper notification and the ability to hear pertinent evidence and address legal arguments to infringements that are specified in the convening documents, all part of the technical procedures, or machinery, of the court: "This I illustrate from the document before me [indicating the monition quoted above]. It is not a summons, because it is not addressed to the person summoned. It is not an ecclesiastical citation. It is not an office process, because it does not show what is the Statute [of the university] infringed. I know not what to make of it. It is addressed to a Bedell, and contains a prayer. It prays on legal proof, Professor Jowett may be punished. It is the most informal document that I ever saw. If nothing else can be produced it shows that we are not provided with a sufficient machinery" (*Pusey and Others v. Jowett* 1863, 14). The third objection relates to Jowett's appointment by the Crown as *regius* professor (that is, as professor appointed literally by the monarch), and not by the university: "The third reason why I object to the proceeding is, that the University has no authority to make Statutes regulating the conduct of a Regius Professor, or calling him into Court with reference to his teaching or doctrine. That is evident on the face of the thing; we [the university] have nothing to do with the appointment. They are entirely independent of the University, and we have no jurisdiction over them. . . . The University has no jurisdiction whatever as to the teaching, or even the morals of the Regius Professors" (*Pusey and Others v. Jowett* 1863, 14–15). Once again precedents were advanced concerning the treatment of regius professors, including more recent history when books and sermons by regius professors had been questioned concerning their orthodoxy, a reference to the disputes in 1836 concerning the Professor of Moral Theology, Renn Dickson Hampden, who was nominated for the position of Regius Professor of Divinity but whose theology in the Bampton lectures of 1832 and other works was suspect, leading Pusey, Newman, and other Tractarians to mount a substantial campaign against him by means of highly selective quotation, and others, like Baden Powell, to oppose Pusey and Newman in supporting Hampden. The pertinence of such an illustration in the present context, with a number of the same protagonists still involved, and Hampden himself as bishop of Hereford and one of the signers of the Episcopal Manifesto, would not have been lost on either the assessor or the spectators.[75]

Finally, upon being asked whether he had any further objections, he indicated that the "place where the offence is supposed to have been committed is not specified. . . . 'Oxford and elsewhere,' means all the world over. There is no definite place fixed, and we do not know upon that point that the Court has jurisdiction, or that it could take cognizance of this case, even if it had any spiritual jurisdiction at all" (*Pusey and Others v. Jowett* 1863, 16–17).

Arguing for the other side, Latimer retraced a good deal of the same history, and showed how the university statutes, quoted in their authoritative Latin form, applied or did not apply in each case, indicating that one route followed in the course of appeals was from the Chancellor's Court to Convocation and finally to the queen in person. His analysis shows, he contends, that here "there is a charge that a book has been written contrary to the Christian faith.—That the University has a jurisdiction in such matters is expressly mentioned. The Statute says that books of that kind are to be restrained" (*Pusey and Others v. Jowett* 1863, 19). Latimer, therefore, rejects Jowett's position that the court has no jurisdiction, and draws on the recent condemnation of *Essays and Reviews* in the Court of Arches two months earlier: "Lastly, I submit that by the decision of the superior courts, it has been shown that in a book called 'Essays and Reviews,' opinions have been expressed which are contrary to the true sense and meaning of the Articles of the Church of England, and dangerous to the Christian faith. . . . I think it cannot be doubted that such an offence, being proved to be an offence under the law of the land, it is an offence against the Statutes of the University, and then it comes to this, that for offences for which there is no special statute, and no special penalty appointed, the Chancellor may adjudicate in court or out of court as he sees fit. But how is he to punish and has he authority to do in ecclesiastical cases? The punishments are enumerated in the Statute. He is called upon to punish the different offences according to the nature of that particular offence, either by corporal punishment . . ." (*Pusey and Others v. Jowett* 1863, 19–20). At this point, the image of inflicting corporal punishment upon Jowett elicited such laughter from the spectators that Bernard had to reprimand them. Latimer continued: . . . [or] by a pecuniary fine, by suspension from degrees, by expulsion from the University, by ecclesiastical censure, or by any other rational method, according to the nature of the offence." On Pottinger's second point he contends that the machinery of the court might render it "less effective than it was in former times," but it is still sufficient. And on the third, concerning the nature of the appointment and answerability of regius professors, silence in the Statutes concerning them does not make them exempt from the normal legal conditions of the university.

In reply, Pottinger cites the Church Discipline Act of 1840 (3 & 4 Vict. c. 86, sec. 23) that no prosecution can be brought against a clergyman except under the provisions of the act, and the act disallows other kinds of powers which the Chancellor's Court might have had at one time, though he argued that it had never had or exercised such powers.

When the court reconvened the next day, on 27 January 1863, Bernard immediately began by sketching out what the processes of the Court had been to that point. Secondly, he set aside the fourth of Pottinger's objections, declaring that the reference to "Oxford and elsewhere" is "not too vague" since having committed the offence of writing and distributing the cited books "in Oxford" is "a sufficient specification" for his court to deal with the matter.

Bernard then addressed more fully Pottinger's second objection on the machinery of the court and the adequacy of its procedures according to civil law for dealing with the case. In doing so, he maintained both that the monition was quite proper and that the promoters of the case, Pusey, Heurtley, and Ogilvie, were quite correct in bringing the matter before him for adjudication: "The procedure by which Professor Jowett would be tried here is substantially the same as that by which he would be tried in the Court of Arches—a procedure not ill suited, as it appears to me, to a case in which there is likely to be no serious conflict of evidence; either party may apply for leave to be heard by council, which is never refused in a proper case. . . . I am of opinion that the promoters, having satisfied themselves that this case ought to be brought before a legal tribunal, are not to blame for resorting to this Court, which is the only Court open to them; and that I am not precluded by its defective constitution or procedure from entertaining their complaint" (*Pusey and Others v. Jowett* 1863, 26). On the matter of the status of Jowett as a regius professor and so exempt from the jurisdiction of the Chancellor's Court, Pottinger's third point, Bernard states:

> But what is a Regius Professor? He is a person nominated by the Crown to an office within the University, paid or endowed by the Crown, and charged with certain duties. The acceptance of the donation constitutes what may be described as a contract between the Crown and the University, which neither party is at liberty to alter without the consent of the other—or perhaps without the sanction of Parliament, which is the guardian of the rights of the Crown. The University cannot deprive a Professor of his office, cannot in the minutest particular vary the duties prescribed to him; but I see no reason to assume that it has ever, consciously or unconsciously, relinquished all jurisdiction over him as one of its own members.
>
> I may observe, that the Statutes which the promoters in this suit seek to enforce against the Regius Professor of Greek are part of a code which was compiled by Royal command, and was sent down to Oxford solemnly ratified and confirmed by Royal Letters Patent under the Great Seal; and that . . . had

> the legal force and effect of a Royal Charter. . . . It is enough for me to say that the law, in my opinion, traces no magic circle round him [Jowett], and clothes him with no absolute inviolability; and that the office held by Professor Jowett is not a bar to his being cited to appear in this suit (*Pusey and Others v. Jowett* 1863, 26–27).

The final and most important question, Pottinger's first point, remained as the sole deterrent to the continuation of the trial, the competence of the court to deal with matters of alleged heresy, murky waters into which Bernard was hesitant to plunge. On this matter Bernard first asserts that Jowett is bound by both the general law of the land as well as the Statutes of the University. Bernard increasingly narrows the field of applicability: within the general law of the land there is the ecclesiastical law, and the question is whether this matter is an offense against the ecclesiastical law that can be tried in this court.

It is at this point that Bernard draws explicit connections between the monition for Jowett and the Articles of Charge brought against Wilson and Williams in the Court of Arches: "A clergyman who advisedly maintains opinions contrary to the Thirty-nine Articles is undoubtedly guilty of an offence, both against the Act 13 Eliz. c. 12. and against the general ecclesiastical law, which is part of the law of the land. But this is not a proceeding under the Act of Elizabeth. Is it a proceeding under the general ecclesiastical law? There are some expressions in the citation from which I might infer that it is. Professor Jowett is charged . . . [in] language precisely the same as would have been employed if he had been cited in the Court of Arches. He is not however accused of contravening the laws ecclesiastical but the Statutes of the University. . . . But whatever the promoters may have intended, I am clearly of opinion that an offence against ecclesiastical law and against the peace and unity of the Church, committed by a clergyman, is one which, as such, I have no power to punish. Such an offence is punishable only by an Ecclesiastical Court and I have no powers to sit as an Ecclesiastical Judge in this case" (*Pusey and Others v. Jowett* 1863, 28). The remaining issue was whether Jowett had, under the terms of the monition, committed an offence against the University Statutes, and in a category with which the Chancellor's Court has to deal: "I am of opinion, that I have power to restrain judicially by banishment, or such other means as the Statutes arm me with the publication, by a resident Member of the University, of doctrines contrary to the Thirty-nine Articles, if it can be shown that this is a violation of the Statutes" (*Pusey and Others v. Jowett* 1863, 29–30). As the field of the court's legitimate jurisdiction narrowed, Jowett must have felt that the noose was indeed tightening more and more closely around his neck. Again, like both Pottinger and Latimer, Bernard traces the historic relations between the legal role of the chancellor of Oxford University, and especially of his court in relation to the other legal jurisdictions:

> Oxford herself, overflowing with busy intellects and restless spirits, has generally shared to the full—and more than shared—the religious movements which have agitated England: the Chancellor's power, regarded rather as a privilege than as a restraint, was controlled by the public opinion of a literary democracy,

> and, when exerted against heterodoxy, appears to have been commonly set in motion by interference from without. Archbishops, [Papal] Legates, Councils, the King himself, and in later times non-resident Chancellors, interfered from time to time to make the University authorities bestir themselves in this matter, without much regard, perhaps, to their legal or actual powers. They were ordered to imprison, to banish, to inquire frequently concerning the doctrine as well as morals of their scholars, and to proceed against the heretically disposed by admonition, excommunication, and otherwise—to search out and destroy heretical books (*Pusey and Others v. Jowett* 1863, 31).

Bernard refers to the heretical disputes of the past (those concerned, incidentally, with the translation of the Bible), those of the Lollards and the Wycliffites before the Reformation, and the disputes between the Puritans and the Royalists at the time of Charles I: "The personal orthodoxy of individuals was secured by imposing a religious test at matriculation and at the taking of every degree; the orthodoxy of the University pulpit by regulations rigidly, and often vexatiously enforced: any person who dogmatically maintained unsound doctrine in a public exercise in the Schools was refused his degree: the publication of libels against the established religion was prohibited on pain of banishment: books deemed seditious and dangerous were by direction of the Privy Council seized and burnt: College Tutors were ordered to instruct their pupils in approved books of divinity" (*Pusey and Others v. Jowett* 1863, 32). Just such prescriptive and repressive procedures, of course, were being invoked by Pusey and the other prosecutors of the case against Jowett, though Pusey denied in his letters that the *Times* was correct in calling his actions "vindictive prosecutions." Pusey and the others had felt the same measures directed against themselves at the time of the Hampden affair, and during the tumultuous days of the Oxford Movement, and were then concerned both with the injustice and intemperance of the attacks. But in the case of Jowett, as Bernard pointed out, there was no protest from his College concerning his improprieties with respect to his religious instruction of the students at Balliol, whatever the college authorities thought of his religious opinions.

A further question concerned the stipulations of the Latin Statutes that no professor is to teach, either directly or indirectly, or to assert dogmatically, what is rejected by the Catholic faith: "Do [these words] apply only to the Professor in his lecture-room, or do they include a book published by him quite independent of his professorial functions, and either wholly or partially foreign to the subject of his Chair? . . . I cannot doubt that it would be doing violence to these words to extend them to a book published by the Professor in his private capacity, and not used by him in his Professorial teaching. . . . It might in that case become necessary for me to determine whether Professor Jowett has in these books 'dogmatically asserted'—or . . . 'indirectly taught'—anything repugnant to the Catholic Faith" (*Pusey and Others v. Jowett* 1863, 35–36). One other Statute is alluded to, that concerning the authority and office of the vice-chancellor, who by these clauses has the duty to "banish or get banished from the University heretics, schismatics, and any other persons whomsoever holding erroneous opinions concerning the Catholic Faith and the doctrine and discipline of the English Church. And to this end they arm him with power to use a certain inquisitorial method for detecting heterodoxy, which however is only applicable to persons in Holy Orders" (*Pusey and Others v. Jowett* 1863, 37). At this point it certainly seems as though Bernard's lengthy statement concerning the increasing focus of his jurisdiction, and of his right on legal and historical grounds to hear the case, was moving toward the arguments on substance and preparing for the detailed submissions of the prosecutors. But in fact, at the same time that he was making his claim for his jurisdiction and stating his opinion concerning the proper procedures and purposes of the court, he was raising questions concerning exactly that jurisdiction and propriety, on point after point of which lengthy debate could proceed, both in the present case, and possibly on appeal.

Bernard now draws all of the lines of his argument together in the peroration. Throughout Pottinger and Latimer, as well as Bernard to this point, had argued the appropriateness of the Statutes in allowing or even requiring the chancellor or his assessor to deal with matters of heresy, but underlying these arguments there is the hitherto unspoken aspect of the vagueness of the charges of heresy brought against Jowett. Tying the interrogative nature of the claims on legal jurisdiction to the vagueness of the charges of heresy is Bernard's opening move in his peroration, and he does so in an unusual reference by alluding to a precedent in the ecclesiastical court of a then-current case, currently under appeal to the Judicial Committee:

> I have not however by any means exhausted the questions that would arise if I were to attempt to apply this Statute [on the powers and authority of the vice-chancellor]. No one, I suppose, can read it without being struck, not only with its vagueness, but by its sweeping and inquisitorial character. "What the law," says Dr. Lushington in The Bishop of Salisbury v Williams, "takes notice of in a clergyman, is not the opinions which he holds in private, but the opinions which he advisedly maintains and promulgates. I take it to be the undoubted law of England that, except on the occasions where examination of Clerks, by superior authority, is specifically directed by law, a person in Orders may hold what opinions he will, provided they are kept within his own breast. What opinions it is compatible with his own professions privately to entertain, is a matter to be settled by his own conscience, not by the law. There is no inquisitorial power" (*Pusey and Others v. Jowett* 1863, 38–39).

Bernard is citing part of the opening remarks concerning the case against Williams in Lushington's interlocutory judgment of 25 June 1862, some eight months earlier, again enabling him to draw a difficult distinction between the Chancellor's Court and the Court of Arches and a parallel between the prosecution of Jowett and those of Williams and Wilson. But the statute of the university requires only private opinion; no overt act is necessary:

> This Statute strikes, not at the public promulgation of opinions, but at the opinions themselves, and declares that it does so by expressly creating an

> inquisitorial power. The most trenchant weapon in the armoury of English law is the Statute of Treasons, which makes imagining the King's death a capital crime, but a crime to be proved by overt acts. No overt acts are required here. Again, a layman, out of Oxford, may practically express what opinions he pleases, provided he does not so express them as to shock and offend the religious feeling of the community. This Statute applies to laymen as well as clergymen, even though they may be mere residents in Oxford, taking no share in its educational work. The University Statutes, as they now stand, require no subscription to the Articles except on taking a degree, which confers a vote in Convocation. But a Bachelor of Arts, Law, Medicine, or Music, would be equally within the reach of this Statute. It could hardly be insisted that I was bound to lend the authority of this Court to proceedings against any layman residing here, who might have published a heterodox book in London. But, if not, this Statute is not imperative. And how is anybody to know whether he would be held amenable to it or not? Or how is anybody to know what acts will, and what will not, be deemed to bring him within the grasp of the law? (*Pusey and Others v. Jowett* 1863, 39).

Having cited the power of the chancellor, at the time of the confirmation of the Caroline Statutes under Laud, to silence "a heterodox preacher, which had been often exercised" and having indicated that the public press was then under the control of the Court of Star Chamber, Bernard indicates that books were burned, and nothing could be published in the university without the chancellor's licence; but the times and the practices of such authority have changed so that Bernard was "not convinced that . . . the publication of an unsound book [is] a punishable offence":

> If a law is imperative—if it clearly prohibits an act and attaches to it a penalty—a Judge has nothing to do but to execute the law; and, on proof of the act, to inflict the penalty. If a discretionary power be given to him, it should be one which he can exercise on clear and recognised principles. I think that these Statutes are not imperative; that the offence which they create, if at all, by implication merely, is not clearly defined; and that the power of the Court to deal with it is not clear. And if it be said that this power is necessary to vindicate the religious character of the University, or to preserve its connection with the Church; I must answer, that even these objects, sacred as they may be, and dear as they undoubtedly were to the framers of our Statutes, would not justify me in attempting to exert an authority which, in my opinion, is enveloped in so much uncertainty, and open to such powerful objections (*Pusey and Others v. Jowett* 1863, 40).

Again Bernard asserts that he has sought through the registers of the court back to 1600 to ascertain "whether there is any record within that period of a prosecution for errors of doctrine." The one case "appears to have been a criminal suit, instituted without a promoter, for a blasphemous libel, which is an offence at common law, punishable by fine and imprisonment. We may conclude therefore that since the adoption of the Caroline Code, and as far back as the search has gone, there has been no precedent for a prosecution of this nature. I shall not attempt to make one" (*Pusey and Others v. Jowett* 1863, 40–41).

Bernard's conclusion continues to assert the possible but contested right of the court to adjudicate in such a case, but he elects not to exercise any rights in dealing with it, except to dismiss it. In doing so he in effect rejects the charges against Jowett:

> On the whole, I am of opinion, that if I have jurisdiction in this matter, which is doubtful, it is a jurisdiction which the Statutes do not imperatively bind me to exercise, and which I ought not to exercise upon this citation. I ought not, therefore, to permit my office to be promoted—or, in less technical language, to allow the suit to proceed any farther. To admit this Protest, however, would be to declare that I have absolutely no jurisdiction in the matter; of which I am by no means satisfied. I shall adopt therefore the course which answers most directly to the opinion at which I have arrived. I shall reject the Protest; but I shall refuse to order Professor Jowett to appear, and shall refuse to admit articles on the part of the Promoters. The practical effect will be, to dismiss the Defendant. From that refusal the Promoters are of course at liberty to appeal; and I have the satisfaction of knowing that if I am wrong, I shall be set right; and that my error, if it be one, will do no serious injury to the University (*Pusey and Others v. Jowett* 1863, 41).

Hence, all of the objections of Pottinger on behalf of Jowett were set aside. Bernard's decision, therefore, was to admit nothing to be heard, nothing of the protest of Pottinger on behalf of Jowett, nothing of the articles charged by Pusey, Heurtley and Ogilvie, and nothing of Jowett himself, refusing to let him appear before him. The summary in the *Times* set the matter out clearly:

> Unless the citation alleged an offence with which he had the power to deal—a breach of some law which he was authorized to enforce—the suit fell to the ground. The Court had to enforce two bodies of law—the general law of the land and the particular laws of the University. It might be argued that Professor Jowett was charged with an offence against the ecclesiastical law, which was part of the law of the land; but, if so, this was an offence which, as such, he had no power to punish. The Church Discipline Act showed clearly that he had no jurisdiction. The question remained whether this was an offence against the statutes, and, if so, an offence with which he had authority to deal. . . . The learned Assessor proceeded to examine the University statute-book. There were three statues which might be thought to apply to the case,—that on the subject of tutors, that on professors, and that on the powers of the Vice-Chancellor. He held that the first of these might apply to such a case, but that in the present instance it would be improper to apply it, as no complaint had been made by the College, and there were no grounds to suspect collusion. The second, he thought, did not apply at all, as it was only intended to restrain the teaching of professors in their professorial character and in their dealings with

> their pupils. The third statute—that on the powers of the Vice-Chancellor—was very vague in its terms. . . . but he thought it left him a discretionary power, and in the exercise of this power he declined to go forward with the case. He should not call on the promoters to exhibit articles (*Times*, 28 Feb. 1863, 12; see also Abbott and Campbell 1897, 1:313).

These technical arguments concern the right of the case to proceed under the cited acts as well as the limits of the court's jurisdiction. Bernard refused to affirm that the Chancellor's Court clearly had no jurisdiction in the case, though he doubted that it had jurisdiction. In any event, he argued that the Statutes of Oxford University did not require absolutely that he hear the case. Hence, he rejected both the protest made in Jowett's defense as well as the articles of his accusers. The fact that Bernard would not call Jowett to appear nor allow him to appear meant that Jowett was denied the opportunity of making a defense, and so could not clear his name from allegations of heresy.

Only a mandamus from the Court of Queen's Bench could compel Bernard to hear the case, and that would have to be pursued by the promoters; or they could appeal the decisionb to a higher tribunal. The case concluded with Pottinger asking for the costs of the defense, but that too was denied, because "up to this time they could not be great" (*Times*, 28 Feb. 1863, 12).

Jowett was depressed by Bernard's legal arguments, as he said to one of his lawyers, Frederick W. Farrer: "In a walk with Jowett afterwards, he was very low at the decision. I remember his saying, 'You don't know Pusey; he has the tenacity of a bull-dog" (Abbott and Campbell 1897, 1:313). Two weeks later he had "heard nothing of an appeal & the time for appealing is past so that the only danger . . . is from the Court of the Queen's Bench" (4 Mar. 1863; Balliol, MS. Jowett F 4, fol. 9). On the same day, a testimonial on Jowett's behalf, signed by almost four hundred of his pupils and friends, was published in the *Times*. Without presuming to interfere with either the due process of law, or the adjudication of Jowett's orthodoxy, it protested against the use of the Chancellor's Court to try heresy as an effort to "drive from the University a man whose services Oxford has miserably rewarded, but can ill afford to lose" (see Manifestos). Eleven days later Jowett still did not know whether an appeal had been taken by Pusey and the other prosecutors to the Court of Queen's Bench, but his legal advice was that there was little chance of Pusey's getting a mandamus (Letter 196). To Emily Tennyson he wrote that he was "in a better plight" but was still fearful about "the appeal to the Queen's Bench, which is not very likely to succeed" (Letter 191).

On 1 April 1863 an article in the *Church and State Review* relates the aborted effort in the Chancellor's Court to "a denial of justice" and to yet another circulation of a petition at Oxford, sponsored by Dean Liddell and Stanley to abolish subscription to the Articles of Religion as a condition for matriculation. Furthermore, the article relates the "consequences of Professor Jowett's opinions" to "the heresy of Bishop Colenso," thereby putting the Oxford controversy into the wider political and ecclesiastical debates in England (*Pusey and Others v. Jowett* 1863,

164–66). Not until 8 May did Pusey, Ogilvie, and Heurtley write to the vice-chancellor, J. P. Lightfoot, abandoning their right to appeal to the Court of Queen's Bench, and the same day they sent a similar letter to the *Times*, published on 11 May. The same day Lightfoot sent the news to Jowett: "I have just received a letter signed by Drs Ogilvie and Pusey from which I make the following extract: 'We the promoters of a suit against Professor Jowett beg leave to inform you at the earliest possible moment that we have given up the intention of making application in the Court of Queen's Bench.'" According to Jowett's biographers, further procedural problems in following the seldom-used processes of the Chancellor's Court had led to their abandoning the case against him: "It appears that in their anxiety to follow Dr. Phillimore's first opinion, the three prosecutors overlooked a Statute (Tit. XVII. 18) which required them to appeal, if at all, to the House of Congregation; and they consulted counsel again as to the expediency of applying for a *mandamus*. Under all the circumstances the advice of Dr. Phillimore and Mr. J. D. Coleridge was adverse to their taking that step."[76] Jowett's heresy trial had collapsed but he had not been vindicated. There had been no discussion of his theological position, other than the continued attacks that raged in the periodicals and in pamphlets against the Essayists as Williams and Wilson prepared for their appeal in the Judicial Committee, heard a month later, in June 1863. Montague Bernard, however, sent a letter to the *Times* explaining that "on account of its importance" the precise nature of the case and its final disposition in his court should be known in the words of his own decision. He therefore asked the *Times* to print the concluding paragraphs verbatim, which they did on 13 May. In the meantime, on 11 May a leader in the *Times* reflected on the entire prosecution, indicating that it should never have been initiated and that it had turned public opinion against Pusey.

III "Look at the Greek Professor"

When it appeared clear in March 1863 that the decision in Jowett's trial would not be appealed by Pusey and his supporters, Stanley once again brought up in the Hebdomadal Council the matter of the endowment of the Greek Professorship, but the proposal, as in previous votes, was narrowly defeated. The following autumn Pusey brought forward his proposal to the council, that the Professorship be endowed with £400 to be paid by the university until permanent arrangements were made (like Stanley's earlier motion, though for a different sum). Pusey's proposal carried the proviso concerning Jowett "that the University shall be held to have pronounced no judgement upon his writings, in so far as they touch the Catholic Faith" (Abbott and Campbell 1897, 1:314). The motion succeeded in both the Hebdomadal Council and in Congregation; all that remained was for it to pass the vote to be held the following March in Convocation. Jowett was pleased, and wrote to Emily Tennyson on 21 Dec. 1863: "I mean to do a great deal more mischief now that they are going to give me some money," and on Christmas day he wrote to his mother that "there is a prospect of their paying me my income, with a chance of the arrears hereafter" (Abbott and Campbell 1897, 1:326).

Pusey's proposal for endowment came before Convocation on 8 March 1864, exactly one month after Lord Westbury had acquitted Williams and Wilson. Oxford was caught up in two other causes: one was the beginning of the Newman-Kingsley controversy that had been initiated publicly on 12 February by the publication by Newman of his correspondence with Kingsley and Kingsley's countercharge that Newman did not think that truth was a necessary virtue, eventually leading to the publication of *Apologia Pro Vita Sua* (1864). The other matter was the "Declaration on the Inspiration of the Word of God" to protest Westbury's judgment. In this climate concerning theological belief, with the threat of Rome on the one hand, and the Germans on the other, the endowment of the Greek professorship had little hope of a passing vote in Convocation. There was a concerted effort to bring in country clergy holding the M.A. to vote against the proposal. The opposition was led by George Anthony Denison. At the Oxford Convocation Denison spoke in Latin, and was shouted down; nevertheless, the motion was defeated by 72 votes, 467 to 395. The eighty-two-year-old Lushington came to Oxford "at great inconvenience to vote in favor of the salary" that was under proposal to be increased (Abbott and Campbell 1897, 1:315). Jowett wrote on 12 March to Emily Tennyson: "I am truly sorry that so kind a friend as you are should be disappointed. I believe the Judgement [in the Privy Council] was the cause of the result; if so, there is ample compensation" (Abbott and Campbell 1897, 1:326). In the first half of March F. D. Maurice and Pusey exchanged a series of letters in the *Times* on the Oxford "Declaration," in the course of which Maurice particularly attacked the request to sign "for the love of God." He declared that he "never would sign it . . . because the adjuration prefixed to this Declaration that 'for the love of God' we should put our names to it, received a very lucid explanation from the recent decision of the Oxford Convocation. It means, 'Young clergymen, poor curates, poor incumbents, sign, or we will turn the whole force of religious public feeling against you. Sign or we will starve you! Look at the Greek Professor. You see we can take that vengeance on those whom we do not like. You see that we are willing to take it, and that no considerations of faithful and devoted services will hinder us.' This is what is called signing 'for the love of God'" (Letter 235).

Again there are links in the public press between *Essays and Reviews* and the endowment of the Greek Professorship: in the *Times*, adjoining the Pusey-Maurice exchange from 4–15 March 1864 on the Oxford Declaration, are letters both attacking and defending Convocation's decision to reject the endowment for the Greek Professorship. During these debates the same columns juxtaposed discussion of Bishop Colenso's views concerning biblical inspiration and the reaction to those views on the part of the ecclesiastical and legal authorities, extending the scope of what the *Times* had earlier called the "war of extermination . . . between the two great Church parties on their old battle-ground (14 Feb. 1863, 9).

In the House of Lords Westbury initiated "An Act for the Better Endowment of the Regius Professor of Greek in the University of Oxford," proposing that the first available canonry should be annexed to the Greek Professorship. In Committee the bill was thrown out on 14 May, despite the charges by Westbury that the university had broken its clear commitments to the University Commission by not endowing the chair, an assertion denied on 23 May by the chancellor of the university, Lord Derby. The following October the vice-chancellor, Lightfoot, began yet another move to endow the chair for £400 from university funds, still making a reservation concerning Jowett's theological opinions; like so many of its precursors, the proposal was defeated in the Hebdomadal Council—by one vote. Although Jowett had been hailed before the Chancellor's Court on the accusation of heresy, and although the vice-chancellor himself was an advocate of his in increasing the endowment, the process seemed doomed to failure.

Not until the combined resources of the future Regius Professor of History and one of Jowett's former students could be brought to bear on a study of the historical documents concerning both the original bequest of property at the time of Henry VIII and also the undertaking of the dean and Chapter of Christ Church in 1854 did matters change. Edward Augustus Freeman published a letter in the *Daily News* and later issued a pamphlet in October 1864 setting out the documents whereby Christ Church undertook to pay for the Greek Professorship the sum of £400. His arguments were supported by the researches into Tudor land conveyances undertaken by Charles Isaac Elton, who showed that Christ Church indeed had the income from lands that had come into their possession through the gift of Henry VIII. Thereupon, despite the recalcitrance of the Chapter of Christ Church, the dean, Henry Liddell, forced them to comply on 14 February, only with "great difficulty" on the grounds of "expediency."[77] They then took the necessary steps to ensure that the salary be raised to £500; the decision was finally sent to the vice-chancellor on 17 February 1865. Two days later Jowett paid tribute to the work of Elton and others in forcing the hand of the Chapter of Christ Church: "I am greatly indebted to some of my young friends, who without my knowledge hunted this matter out and assailed the Dean and Chapter in the newspapers" (Abbott and Campbell 1897, 1:326). At just this time, in early March 1865, Lewis Carroll wrote and published a satiric account of how the controversy was settled, entitled *The New Method of Evaluation as Applied to π* (see Satires).

After more than ten years' struggle, Jowett was finally paid a stipend commensurate to his labors, and comparable to that of the other regius professors—and with no theological disapproval formally attached to his name. But the *odium theologicum* still hung about him. The university's legislative bodies had never passed an act that would redress the Tudor salary for the Greek Professor: vote after vote had failed at one or another level, and always because of suspicion, distrust, and dislike of Jowett's theological opinions. The trial of Jowett in the Chancellor's Court had been an effort to bring the charges of heresy, as evidenced in *The Epistles of St. Paul* and in *Essays and Reviews*, into the open and to have the theology of those books dealt with on legal grounds. But on procedural and technical points that trial was aborted, and Jowett's theology was never addressed. Subsequent debates in the legislative bodies at Oxford continued to punish him financially for his theological writings. Only when the appeal was made to history (to what the dean and Chapter of Christ Church had actually claimed they would do in arguments before the University Commissioners) and to property and income (regarding the donation of land and its revenues to Christ Church by Henry VIII) was there space for pressure to be exerted upon the Chapter of Christ Church. Still denying moral or legal responsibility, they finally acceded to historical argument and to public pressure, claiming the grounds of "expediency." The damage inflicted on Jowett was lasting; although he continued to preach in chapel, and occasionally elsewhere—including Westminster Abbey—he never again wrote on theology or biblical interpretation.

By 1865 the prosecution of the writers of *Essays and Reviews* had ended—at least temporarily. Through different routes the theological opponents had used what institutional might they could muster to attempt a condemnation, in the case of Williams and Wilson, through the ecclesiastical and legal courts, in the case of Jowett through the machinations of university politics and the university court, and through a Synodical Condemnation for the volume as a whole. In every case the translation from theology to other discourses did not work well for the opponents of *Essays and Reviews*: when charges had to be specified and theological points had to be spelled out in detail, they were found to have little weight in legal discourse.

The legal trials and theological disputes aroused by *Essays and Reviews* and by the Colenso affair increased the demand for a different kind of process for theological adjudication, a demand from various voices in the Anglican church, not least those of the colonial bishops who wished to have the security of their decisions endorsed by what appeared to be a more orthodox body than the Judicial Committee of the Privy Council. John Travers Lewis, the bishop of Ontario in Canada, took the initiative in persuading the House of Bishops of the Canadian Provincial Synod to address to Longley a request for what eventually turned out to be the first Lambeth Conference of bishops of the Anglican communion in 1867. Lewis and his associates wrote in 1865: "That in consequence of the recent decisions of the Judicial Committee of the Privy Council in the well-known case respecting the *Essays and Reviews*, and also in the case of the Bishop of Natal and the Bishop of Cape Town, the minds of many members of the church have been unsettled or painfully alarmed; and that doctrines hitherto believed to be scriptural, undoubtedly held by members of the Church of England and Ireland, have been adjudicated upon by the Privy Council in such a way as to lead thousands of our brethren to conclude that, according to this decision, it is quite compatible with membership in the Church of England to discredit the historical facts of Holy Scripture, and to disbelieve in the eternity of future punishment." Accordingly, the Canadian bishops asked Longley "to convene a national synod of the bishops of the Anglican Church at home and abroad . . . [to] take such counsel and adopt such measures as may be best fitted to provide for the present distress" (William Curtis 1942, 125–26). Hence, it was to address the double scourge of the *Essays and Reviews* scandal and the Colenso affair, especially concerning the manner in which each was disposed of in the Judicial Committee, that the Lambeth Conferences were inaugurated in 1867. But that debate of the bishops in reaffirming orthodoxies was not able to dispel absolutely the scent of heresy. It was sniffed out again when Temple was appointed to bishopric of Exeter in October 1869, and when once more the old arguments concerning the book's heterodoxy were paraded before the public; and when yet another edition, exonerated by the legal process but the object of a synodical condemnation, was published as the final one in England in the nineteenth century.

Essays and Reviews is the last case cited in the entry "Heresy" in the eleventh edition of the *Encyclopaedia Britannica* (13:362), published in 1911. Thus, for the purposes of this article at least, the Essayists and Reviewers join the eminent company of gnostics, Montanists, Monarchians, Arians, Pelagians, and other groups famous for challenging and transgressing the boundaries of orthodoxy. The fact that discussion of the volume is the last instance in the entry's final section, "Heresy according to the Law of England," speaks not only to the Anglocentricity of the *Encyclopaedia Britannica*, but also to the positioning of the volume as in some sense terminative in definitions and discussions of heresy. In fact, however, the *Essays and Reviews* trials were not the last heresy cases in England. The case of Charles Voysey was tried in the Chancery Court of the archbishop of York in 1869. Voysey had argued that the Church of England, on the basis of the successful *Essays and Reviews* appeal, was flexible on biblical inspiration, original sin, the atonement, and eternal punishment, but he extended the Essayists' views to deny the validity of all of these doctrines. Although defended by James Fitzjames Stephen, he was condemned in 1870 in a decision that was confirmed by the Privy Council in February 1871, with Tait as the episcopal member of the Judicial Committee (Crowther 1970, 127–37). There were other cases too, though of much less notoriety, such as that of *Ffoulkes v. Fletcher* at Oxford in 1886 (Owen Chadwick 1966–70, 2:453). Even the publication of *Lux Mundi* in 1889 under the editorship of Charles Gore, attempting to interpret "the revelation of God . . . [for] the modern generation," prompted renewed attacks as the ghosts of the *Essays and Reviews* heresy were summoned once more into life. Old opponents of *Essays and Reviews* like Denison and Liddon, preached against *Lux Mundi* and urged Convocation to condemn it, but more moderate voices prevailed. Not even another declaration on the infallibility of the Bible (Dec., 1891), signed by Goulburn, Denison and others, could carry widespread support. Critical scholarship on the Hebrew Scriptures was finally admitted as both useful and necessary (Desmond Bowen 1968, 172–78; Owen Chadwick 1966–70, 2:100–104). The *Lux Mundi* essayists could claim, from their liberal Catholic position, more inclusive allegiance than the Essayists of thirty years earlier, in defining "the real development of theology" as "the apprehension of the new social and intellectual movements of each age . . . able to assimilate all new material, to welcome and give its place to all new knowledge" (*Lux Mundi* [1889] 1891, ix). It is hard to imagine these reformulations of *Lux Mundi* without the victory of *Essays and Reviews* as both precedent and example.

As a moment of "crisis" (Ellis 1980, ix) or "controversy" (Altholz 1994, 1), the heresy trials of Williams, Wilson, and Jowett map out elaborately the means available to ecclesiastical orthodoxy to attempt to enforce opinion and interpretation; the fact that in each instance such legal recourse proved ultimately ineffective ensured that from this point on seeking doctrinal redress through the courts was largely abandoned.

At issue in the three heresy trials were a number of general problems: first, the question of what weight could be given to the rational and moral aspects of religion in the face of new knowledge and social conditions; second, how far the interpretation of the Bible could make use of the new critical and textual methods used in Germany for the interpretation of the Bible; third, the issue of the reformulation of doctrinal matters concerning the nature and work of Christ, the theology of the sacraments and the church, and the doctrines of sin, redemption, and the last judgment; fourth, the appropriate institutional and doctrinal relationship between the church and its theologians and theology, particularly in the matter of the swearing of doctrinal oaths by clergy at their ordination; fifth, the form and content of those oaths as legal documents involving clergy as state and church functionaries; sixth, the rights of clergy and laity to free inquiry on disputed matters of biblical interpretation and doctrine; seventh, the freedom to entertain positions on these matters that are at variance with accepted orthodoxies, and to express those positions by spoken and written word; eighth, the relevance of the historic political and doctrinal contexts of such sixteenth and seventeenth-century documents as the Articles of Religion and the *BCP* to which oaths of subscription were required; ninth, the function of language, history, interpretation, and precedent in ecclesiastical, legal, and other forms of public discourse; and finally, the relationships between the state and established religion, and the state and the universities. Attacks were levied against the volume concerning all of these issues in the public press and in the ecclesiastical courts.

The broad charges of heretical belief and teaching alluded to in the Articles of Charge brought before the ecclesiastical court, attempting to defend doctrinal orthodoxy and biblical literalism, had dwindled to legalistic distinctions based on a corresponding literalism—the "literal and grammatical sense" of the Articles of Religion, required by precedent in the cases heard in doctrinal controversies over the previous decade. In the Judicial Committee that literalism was redefined with a different result. While the general importance of the doctrinal positions being debated before the Judicial Committee must not be underestimated, since the implications of the appeal decision were great, the weight and concentration of the British legal system were brought to bear not on the whole theology of the Broad Church, nor on the general heterodoxy of some of its advocates, but upon another hermeneutical problem, the interpretation of the law. To many clergy the right of a secular part of the government to determine doctrinal issues, albeit with episcopal representatives sitting on the appeal, smacked of Erastianism. Within the church the trial and the appeal forced allegiances between the High Church and evangelical parties against the condemned and heretical position of the Broad Church Essayists and their supporters. And finally the ecclesiastical trial and its appeal involved a reconsideration of the historical context of the Articles of Religion and the Anglican Formularies, a history that was quite at variance with the issues raised by J. H. Newman's *Tract XC* (1841). That is, the Articles were not being interpreted as in accord with Catholic practice as distinct from late medieval accretions and post-Tridentine theology in the Roman Catholic Church, but as documents that deliberately take a via media between Rome and Geneva, and that can therefore be interpreted with a broad degree of latitude.

In an era that was conventional in religious practice, traditional in religious belief, and simultaneously riven with religious doubts and various forms of modern scepticism interacting with explosions in new knowledge, the heresy trials of the three Essayists were in large measure emblematic of taking the measure of a collective inner state, the nation's spiritual health and condition. The trials of the Essayists and Reviewers and the controversy provoked by the volume as a whole are representative not so much of a loss or crisis of faith, as contemporaries tended to describe it, as of a new and modern sociology of knowledge that holds religion, history, and science in a secular relationship, increasingly free of institutional constraints.

Notes to Trials and Appeals

1. See, for instance, the *Christian Observer,* Sept. 1860. Temple also advised the boys at Rugby not to read *Essays and Reviews,* which would lead them to "critical speculations before their time" (Sandford 1906, 1:220).

2. The Court of Arches is named after its former meeting place from at least 1272, the Church of St. Mary-le-Bow, or *Beata Maria de Arcubus* (Lat. Blessed Mary of the arches), in London; it now meets in the Library at Lambeth Palace, or Church House, Westminster. For general discussion concerning the Court of Arches, see Coote 1847; Dibdin 1882; and Waddams 1992. On the controversy concerning appeals to the Judicial Committee in ecclesiastical causes or cases see Peter T. Marsh 1969, 129 ff.

3. The official legal documents of the Court of Arches in the cases of Williams and Wilson are in the Library of Lambeth Palace, MSS. Arches H 888 (1–17) [Fendall vs. Wilson] and H 887 (1–17) [Salisbury vs. Williams]. Hamilton's "Letters of Request" (Lambeth, MS. Arches H 888/1) are written in a copperplate hand with very little punctuation; the editors have added commas according to the convention followed in the printed legal documents for these cases.

4. The Tractarian Walter Kerr Hamilton was appointed bp. of Salisbury in 1854. Stephen Lushington, M.P., lawyer, and judge, was eighty years old when he heard the case of Williams and Wilson. He was appointed dean of the Arches Court of Canterbury in 1858. He had served on the Judicial Committee of the Privy Council in the case of *Gorham v. the Bishop of Exeter* (1849–50) and after the *Essays and Reviews* case he was involved in the Privy Council appeal of Bishop Colenso (1864–65). For a biography of Lushington see Waddams 1992.

5. Hamilton wrote to the archdeacons of his diocese to that effect in 1864: "Having appended my name to the letter of the Archbishop, I thought it more advisable not to hear and try the case myself; and I much preferred to proceed under the general law of the Church, by which the Defendant, if found guilty, would not be deprived of a *locus poenitentiae,* as he would have been by the statute of Elizabeth" (Brodrick and Fremantle 1865, 251). Under the statute of 13 Eliz. c. 12 a clergyman convicted of maintaining unsound doctrine is immediately deprived of his benefice; under the general ecclesiastical law of 1840 such a debarment would not be in effect until all the avenues of appeal were exhausted.

6. The Formularies of the C. of E. consist of the documents that have legal and binding status on clergy and to some extent upon the laity. Their legal status is conferred by having been approved by Convocation and Parliament. References are made in the Williams and Wilson trial and appeal to the Thirty-nine Articles of Religion, to the *BCP* (1662), the Ordinal in the *BCP*, the *Book of Homilies,* and the *Constitutions and Canons of 1603.* Specific passages from the Bible are also cited as having legal authority because they are included in readings from the Gospels, Epistles and other lections authorized for specific days of the church year in the *BCP.* There was some legal question about the admission of the Elizabethan *Book of Homilies* and the biblical passages cited in the *BCP* as part of the Formularies; on the other hand, there was no question concerning the legal status and authority of the *BCP* and the *Constitutions and Canons* as well as the Articles of Religion.

The Thirty-nine Articles of Religion are a set of doctrinal statements that define the position of the Church of England within the doctrinal controversies of the sixteenth century. From the formulation of the Ten Articles (1536) to the Forty-two Articles (1553) there were at least five efforts to set out an agreed set of articles that were finally approved by Convocation in 1563, being passed by both the Upper House (bishops) and Lower House (representatives of the parochial clergy). They were slightly revised in 1571 and reapproved by the bishops and Parliament and received the royal assent of Elizabeth I in the same year.

The Articles of Religion distinguish the Anglican position from the then-current Roman Catholic views (especially concerning medieval Catholic practices and doctrines), as well as from Calvinist and Anabaptist dogmatic positions, while allowing a considerable doctrinal latitude to Anglican clergy through calculated ambiguity in phrasing, aimed at both the exclusion of rejected theological positions, and the inclusion of accepted and tolerated viewpoints. Clergy were required to subscribe to the Articles of Religion at ordination until 1865 when the requirement was changed to an affirmation that the doctrine of the C. of E. as set forth in the *BCP* and the Articles of Religion is agreeable to the Word of God; an undertaking was also required that candidates for ordination not teach in contradiction to these Formularies. Problems of definition concerning the meaning of the Articles of Religion were central to establishing religious orthodoxy and heretical infringements of approved doctrine. The Articles of Religion are normally printed at the end of the *BCP.*

The *Constitutions and Canons* consists of 151

canons drawn up by the C. of E. synod of 1603 and passed by the Convocation of Canterbury in 1604 and by York in 1606. They constitute the chief body of canonical law in the C. of E. They govern the conduct of services, the administration of sacraments, the duties of clergy, and the care and administration of parishes and dioceses. The 36th canon, concerning clerical subscription before ordination, was a matter of controversy during the nineteenth century. It reads in part: "No person shall hereafter be received into the Ministry, nor either by institution or collation admitted to any Ecclesiastical Living . . . except he be licensed either by the Archbishop, or by the Bishop of the diocese, where he is to be placed, under their hands and seals, or by one of the two Universities under their seal likewise; and except he shall first subscribe to these three Articles following. . . .

> I. That the King's Majesty, under God, is the only supreme Governor of this realm. . . . as well in all Spiritual or Ecclesiastical things or causes, as Temporal. . . .
>
> II. That the Book of Common Prayer, and of ordering of Bishops, Priests, and Deacons, containeth in it nothing contrary to the Word of God. . . .
>
> III. That he alloweth the Book of Articles of Religion . . . ; and that he acknowledgeth all and every the Articles therein contained, being in number nine and thirty, besides the Ratification, to be agreeable to the Word of God" (*Book of Sermons or Homilies* [1547, 1563] 1802, 536–37).

7. The "general," and "plain and full meaning" of the articles in their "literal and grammatical sense" was asserted in the Royal Declaration that was formerly prefixed to the publication of the Thirty-nine Articles in the *BCP*. "His Majesty's Declaration," or "The Royal Declaration" as it is sometimes known, was very likely drawn up by William Laud and was issued by Charles I in 1628, to be affixed to future publications of the Thirty-nine Articles, where it is still printed in official but not general-printing copies of the *BCP*. It mediates between radically opposed theological positions, such as those of the English Calvinists, some of whom favored either the rigorous Dutch Calvinism or the rejected Arminianism of the Synod of Dort (1618), and the High Church followers of Laud (see Hardwick 1904, 188–204):

> All Clergymen within Our Realm have always most willingly subscribed to the Articles established; which is an argument to Us, that they all agree in the true, usual, literal meaning of the said Articles; and that even in those curious points, in which the present differences lie, men of all sorts take the Articles of the Church of England to be for them; which is an argument again, that none of them intend any desertion of the Articles established.
>
> That therefore in these both curious and unhappy differences, which have for so many hundred years, in different times and places, exercised the Church of Christ, We will, that all further curious search be laid aside, and these disputes shut up in God's promises, as they be generally set forth to us in the holy Scriptures, and the general meaning of the Articles of the Church of England according to them. And that no man hereafter shall either print, or preach, to draw the Article aside any way, but shall submit to it in the plain and full meaning thereof: and shall not put his own sense or comment to be the meaning of the Article, but shall take it in the literal and grammatical sense.
>
> That if any publick Reader in either of Our Universities, or any Head or Master of a College, or any other person respectively in either of them, shall affix any new sense to any Article, or shall publickly read, determine, or hold any publick Disputation, or suffer any such to be held either way, in either the Universities or Colleges respectively; or if any Divine in the Universities shall preach or print any thing either way, other than is already established in Convocation with Our Royal Assent; he, or they the Offenders, shall be liable to Our displeasure, and the Church's censure in Our Commission Ecclesiastical, as well as any other: And We will see there shall be due Execution upon them.

It is upon this Royal Declaration that the ecclesiastical and secular courts base their appeal to the "literal and grammatical sense" of the articles and other Formularies of the church (for instance, in the Tenth Article of Charge against Wilson, and in Lushington's frequent use of the phrase in his judgment against Wilson). The legal status of the Royal Declaration was asserted by Lushington but was challenged by Wilson in his appeal before the Privy Council, arguing that it was an important interpretative and historical document, but not of binding authority like the Articles of Religion and the Formularies, or the precedents of decisions made in the Judicial Committee. Other viewpoints than the "literal and grammatical sense" are, according to Lushington, the results of "curious search," or private interpretation ("his own sense or comment") and result in what was determined in these cases to be "erroneous, strange, and heretical doctrines."

8. Thomas Turton was appointed bp. of Ely in 1845. The Rev. James Fendall, formerly a fellow of Jesus College, Cambridge, was rector of the village of Harlton in the diocese of Ely and at the time of the *Essays and Reviews* case he was proctor in Convocation for the clergy of the diocese (*Times*, 26 Feb. 1862, 11). He published a 96-page pamphlet attacking Jowett's essay, *Authority of Scripture: An Examination*

into the Principles and Statements Advances in Professor Jowett's Essay on the Interpretation of Scripture (1861). This treatise was reprinted the following year as part of *Faith and Peace: Being Answers to Some of the "Essays and Reviews,"* ed. George Anthony Denison.

The Decree by Letters of Request against Wilson (see fig. 14) reads: (punctuation added):

> STEPHEN LUSHINGTON, Doctor of Laws, Official Principal of the Arches Court of Canterbury lawfully constituted, To All and singular Clerks and literate persons whomsoever and wheresoever in and throughout the whole Province of Canterbury, Greeting.
>
> WHEREAS We have lately received Letters of Request from the Right Reverend Father in God Thomas, by Divine permission Lord Bishop of Ely, of the tenor following, to wit: "Thomas, by Divine permission Bishop of Ely, To The Right Honorable Stephen Lushington, Doctor of Laws, Official Principal of the Arches Court of Canterbury lawfully constituted, your Surrogate, or some other competent Judge in this behalf. Whereas by a certain Act of Parliament passed in the Session of Parliament holden in the third and fourth years of the Reign of Her present Majesty Queen Victoria intituled 'An Act for the better enforcing Church Discipline,' it is enacted that in every case of any Clerk in Holy Orders of the United Church of England and Ireland who may be charged with any offence against the Laws Ecclesiastical or concerning whom there may exist scandal or evil Report as having offended against the said Laws, It shall be lawful for the Bishop of the Diocese within which the offence is alleged or reported to have been committed, on the application of any party complaining thereof, or if he shall think fit of his own mere motion, to issue a Commission under his hand and seal to five persons of whom one shall be his Vicar General or an Archdeacon or Rural Dean within the Diocese for the purpose of making enquiry as to the grounds of such charge or report. And whereas it is in and by the said Act also enacted that it shall be lawful for the Bishop of any Diocese within which any such Clerk shall hold any preferment, or if he hold no preferment then for the Bishop of the Diocese within which the offence is alleged to have been committed, in any case if he shall think \fit/ either in the first instance or after the Commissioners shall have reported that there is primâ facie ground for instituting proceedings and before the filing of the Articles but not afterwards, to send the case by Letters of Request to the Court of Appeal of the Province to be there heard and determined according to the law and practice of such Court. And whereas the Reverend Henry Bristow Wilson, a Clerk in Holy Orders of the said United Church of England and Ireland, and Vicar of the Vicarage and Parish Church of Great Stoughton in the County of Huntingdon in the Diocese of Ely and Province of Canterbury, is charged with having within the said Diocese of Ely and elsewhere within the said Province of Canterbury offended against the Laws Ecclesiastical of this Realm by having within the last two years written, printed, published, dispersed, given, sold, and set forth, \or caused to be printed, published, dispersed, given, sold, and set forth,/ in a Book entitled Essays and Reviews a certain Article, or Essay, or Review, with divers notes thereto, entitled 'Séances Historiques de Genève—The National Church,' and by having in such Article, Essay, or Review and in the Notes thereto, advisedly maintained and affirmed certain erroneous, strange, and heretical Doctrines, Positions, and Opinions contrary and repugnant to the Doctrine and Teaching of the said United Church of England and Ireland as by Law established, and thereby contravening the Statutes, Constitutions, and Canons Ecclesiastical of the Realm and against the peace and Unity of the Church. And whereas proceedings are about to be taken against the said Reverend Henry Bristow Wilson for and in respect of the offence aforesaid at the voluntary promotion of the Reverend James Fendall, Clerk, Rector of the Rectory of Harlton in the County of Cambridge and Diocese of Ely. And we have thought fit to send the case by Letters of Request to the Court of Appeal of the Province. Now, therefore, we the said Bishop of Ely do hereby request you the said Right Honorable Stephen Lushington, Doctor of Laws, Official Principal of the Arches Court of Canterbury lawfully constituted, your Surrogate, or some other competent Judge in this behalf, to issue a Citation or Decree under Seal of the said Court calling upon the said Reverend Henry Bristow Wilson, Clerk, to appear at a certain time and place therein to be specified, then and there to answer to certain Articles, Heads, Positions, or Interrogatories touching and concerning his Soul's health and the lawful correction and reformation of his manners and excesses, and more especially for having within two years \last/ past written, printed, published, dispersed, given, sold, and set forth, or caused to be printed, published, dispersed, given, sold, and set forth, in the said Book entitled Essays and Reviews the aforesaid Article, or Essay, or Review, with divers Notes thereto, entitled 'Séances Historiques de Genève The National Church' to be administered to him by virtue of your Office at the

voluntary promotion of the said Reverend James Fendall, Clerk, and to hear and determine the said Cause according to the Law and Practise of the said Court. In witness whereof we have hereto set our hand and seal the sixteenth day of December, in the year of our Lord One thousand eight hundred and sixty one, and in the Twentieth year of our Consecration. —T Ely—\seal/."

AND WHEREAS at the Petition of the Proctor of the said Reverend James Fendall, Clerk, and in aid of Justice, We have accepted the said Letters of Request and decreed to proceed according to the tenor thereof and in pursuance thereof have decreed the said Reverend Henry Bristow Wilson, Clerk, Vicar of the Vicarage and Parish Church of Great Stoughton in the County of Huntingdon in the Diocese of Ely and Province of Canterbury, to be cited and called to \appear in/ Judgment on the day at the time and place and to the effect and in manner and form hereunder written (Justice so requiring). We do therefore hereby authorize and empower and strictly enjoin and command you jointly and severally peremptorily to cite or cause to be cited The said Reverend Henry Bristow Wilson, Clerk, to appear personally or by his Proctor duly constituted before us, our Surrogate, or some other competent Judge in this behalf, in a certain Room or Chamber called the Rolls Court in the City of Westminster on the sixth day after he shall have been served with these Presents if it be a Court day of the said Court; otherwise on the Court day of the said Court then next following at the usual and accustomed hours for hearing Causes and administering Justice then and there \to abide during the sitting of the Court; if necessary then and there/ to answer to certain Articles, heads, positions, or Interrogatories touching and concerning his Soul's health and the lawful correction and reformation of his manners and excesses and more especially for having within two years last past written, printed, published, dispersed, given, sold, and set forth, or caused to be printed, published, dispersed, delivered, given, sold, and set forth, in a Book entitled Essays and Reviews a certain Article, or Essay, or Review, with divers notes thereto, entitled "Séances Historiques de Genève The National Church" and by having in such Article, or Essay, or Review, and in the Notes thereto, advisedly maintained and affirmed certain erroneous, strange, and heretical Doctrines, Positions, and Opinions contrary and repugnant to the Doctrine and Teaching of the United Church of England and Ireland as by Law established and thereby contravening the Statutes, Constitutions, and Canons Ecclesiastical of the Realm and against the Peace and Unity of the Church; to be administered to him by virtue of our Office at the voluntary promotion of the Reverend James Fendall, Clerk, Rector of the Rectory of Harlton in the County of Cambridge and Diocese of Ely. And further, to do and receive as unto Law and Justice shall appertain under pain of the Law and contempt thereof at the promotion of the said Reverend James Fendall. And what you shall do or cause to be done in the premises you shall duly certify us, our Surrogate, or some other competent Judge in this behalf, together with these presents.

DATED at London the Nineteenth day of December, in the year of our Lord One thousand eight hundred and sixty one.

Decree by Letters of Request

Toller [Seal of the Court of Arches] Jn Shephard Registrar

(Lambeth MS Arches 888/17: Decree by Letters of Request)

9. Lambeth MS. Arches H.887/2: "The Office of the Judge Promoted by the Bishop of Salisbury ag[ains]t Williams"; Lambeth MS. Arches H. 888/2: "In the Arches Court of Canterbury/ The Office of the Judge promoted by Fendall ag[t] Wilson."

10. The complete MS. transcript of the Court of Arches proceedings against Williams in fair copy is bound in three folio volumes in the British Library as *Court of Arches: Bishop of Salisbury v. Williams*, shelfmark 5155 k.11 (1–3); the cases were reported extensively in the press. The *Times* gave detailed reports on the proceedings each day.

11. James Parker Deane, educated at Winchester and St. John's College, Oxford, was a specialist in civil and ecclesiastical law. James Fitzjames Stephen was educated at Eton, King's College, London, and Trinity College, Cambridge, where he was a member of the Cambridge Apostles; from 1858 to 1861 he was secretary for a royal commission on popular education and in 1869 was appointed a legal member of the council in India. He was a regular contributor to the *Saturday Review* and the *Pall Mall Gazette*. Dr. Robert Phillimore was educated at Christ Church, Oxford, trained in the civil and ecclesiastical law and was chancellor for the Diocese of Salisbury, eventually being appointed judge of the high court of admiralty in 1867. John Duke Coleridge was educated at Eton and Balliol, where he was a friend of Clough and Matthew Arnold. A common-law expert, he was appointed solicitor general and was knighted in 1868. Maurice Charles Merttins Swabey published an account of the decision in the Judicial Committee of the Privy Council in the *Quarterly Review* 115 (Apr. 1864): 529–80.

12. Williams refers to the protracted case of George Anthony Denison, whose examination of candidates for ordination at Bath in 1852 prompted

an ordinand to inform the bishop, Richard Bagot, of Denison's views of the real presence of Christ in the eucharist, resulting in applications to the bishop to prosecute for heresy. Like Bagot, his successor refused to hear the case, but an appeal to the abp. of Canterbury, John Bird Sumner, led to a commission of inquiry that found grounds to proceed. Sumner refused until compelled by a *mandamus* [Lat. we command], a writ issued by the Court of Queen's Bench to an inferior court instructing that a specific course of action be followed. In 1856 Sumner's court heard the case in Bath, with Lushington as his legal advisor. Denison was convicted of heterodoxy and was deprived of his living, and thereupon appealed to the Court of Arches. The dean of Arches, Sir John Dodson, refused to hear the case (an appeal from the abp. of Canterbury's decision to his own court), but was required to do so by another *mandamus*. He then threw the case out as invalid in that more than two years had elapsed from the alleged offence and the hearing of the prosecution. A further appeal took the case to the Judicial Committee in February, 1858, where the prosecution case collapsed and Denison won, escaping through a legal loophole (see Owen Chadwick 1966–70, 1:491–94). Denison was also prominent in anti–*Essays and Reviews* agitation, especially in Convocation, where he was the leader of the High Church party and spearheaded in the Lower House the Synodical Condemnation of the whole volume in 1864.

13. Each had unorthodox views of the Trinity. John Milton published his religious views in *De Doctrina Christiana* ([c. 1650] 1825) holding a subordinationist view that the persons of the Trinity are not co-eternal and co-equal, but that the Son is subordinate to the Father (see Hunter 1971 and Bauman 1987). Isaac Newton denied the doctrine of the Trinity as inaccessible to human reason. William Ellery Channing, one of the founders of Unitarianism, denied the doctrine of the Trinity. Isaac Watts opposed the use of the doctrine of the Trinity as a faith requirement imposed on dissenting clergy.

14. The passages from Williams's review of Bunsen and the articles of charge to which Stephen refers are as follows: on the atonement (12th Article of Charge) with citations from Williams's Essay ¶27 "Propitiation would be . . . hearts" and ¶31 "Salvation from evil . . . ritual"; on baptism (13th Article): ¶31 "the first Christians . . . it"; on the incarnation (14th Article): ¶27 "Thus the incarnation . . . holiness"; and on justification (15th article): ¶26 ("For, though he embraces. . . . of our hearts"). Stephen's reference to three heresies in nine lines refers to the first three of these categories. His reference to *Burder v. Heath* is to the case of 1861 presided over by Lushington concerning justification.

15. The treason trials involved Thomas Hardy, founder of the London Corresponding Society to promote parliamentary reform (1792), and John Horne Tooke. Hardy, Tooke, and others led protests outside Parliament, and inside supported Pitt against Fox, urging reform both of Parliament and of the electoral process. But in the context of republican fervor in France after the French Revolution, Hardy and Tooke were arrested, taken to the tower, and were charged with high treason, their trial lasting eight days. The jury deliberated for three minutes before acquitting them, persuaded by the arguments of Thomas Erskine, who two years earlier had defended Thomas Paine.

16. The title of Phillimore's volume erroneously states that he delivered his speech to the court in February instead of January 1862.

17. The editors follow Lushington 1862. The summaries of the trial printed in the standard legal reports of the Privy Council decision omit the 16th Article of Charge against Williams, one that Lushington says is "admissible" though "of very little importance" (see Brodrick and Fremantle 1865, 252; William Brooke 1874, 84; Edmund Moore 1863–65, 2:377–78, 390; *English Reports* 1901, 15:945, 949).

18. The editors follow Lushington 1862. In Lushington's *Judgment* the 13th Article of Charge is marked "[Withdrawn.]" In the official Arches document entitled "The Office of the Judge Promoted by Fendall Against Wilson," the 13th Article of Charge is crossed out, and a comment is added in the margin: "Withdrawn during argument by agreement" (Lambeth MS. Arches H 888/3, 10). The legal summaries misleadingly list this Article of Charge as rejected (see Brodrick and Fremantle 1865, 252; William Brooke 1874, 87; Edmund Moore 1863–65, 2:382, 390; *English Reports* 1901, 15:946; 949).

19. See Broderick and Fremantle 1865, 252. For *Gorham v. the Bishop of Exeter* see Wilson ¶76 and n. 124. Lushington was the only ecclesiastical lawyer on the Judicial Committee in that case.

20. On the Heath case see Williams ¶s 26 and 27 and nn. 108 and 110. The Heath case was important to Lushington on three grounds. First, he was the judge of the Court of Arches in both the Heath and the *Essays and Reviews* cases. Second, his interpretation of what was applicable in the case, namely, the contravention or derogation of specific doctrines in the Articles of Religion or other Formularies, was the basis of his judgment, and he ruled out all other materials. Third, the validity of his assessment of materials as admissible or inadmissible, and the limitation of charges to the Articles of Religion and other Formularies, were at issue in the appeal to the Judicial Committee of the Privy Council: if they concurred, then his interpretation of evidence was vindicated. Finally, to the prosecutors and opponents of Williams and Wilson, the disposition of the Heath case under Lushington gave them cause for hope. Even if there were an appeal to the Privy Council, they could, notwithstanding *Gorham v. the Bishop of Exeter*, legitimately expect a condemnation on such

precedent as the Heath case. But the grounds for the charges and the arguments advanced made the cases very different. See James Fitzjames Stephen 1862, 286.

21. Ellen Williams reports that Lushington read through *Essays and Reviews* "(literally) twenty times" (1874, 2:68).

22. In his self-defense before the Judicial Committee of the Privy Council, Wilson offers a critique of this passage in Lushington's Judgment, in which the same laws of interpretation are to be applied in this case as in the legal interpretation of all written documents, and in which the King's Declaration is supposedly of a higher authority than the legal decisions of the highest court of appeal, even in *Gorham v. the Bishop of Exeter*. Wilson argues that the King's Declaration has no "legal authority at all. It has not even the force of an ecclesiastical canon. . . . It stands on the footing of any other royal proclamation not supported by Act of Parliament." Even the decision in the Gorham case on which Lushington sat "did not refer to it as a legal authority, but only as a historical evidence; and, what is more remarkable, not as an evidence in favour of a strict literal interpretation, but as an evidence of a practice and understanding in the Church of England, favourable to latitude of opinion and interpretation. What they said was, 'Upon the points which were left open, differences of opinion could not be avoided, even amongst those who sincerely subscribed the Articles, and that such differences amongst such persons were thought consistent with subscription to the Articles, and were not contemplated with disapprobation, appears in a passage in the Royal Declaration'" (Wilson 1863, 9–10).

23. Lushington has changed "metaphorical" in the Article of Charge (Lambeth MS. Arches H888/3, fol. 8) to "metaphysical," a significant change, whether by intent or error, that shifts the emphasis away from an allegorical reading based on rhetorical figures in the Bible to a more philosophical, abstract, or "metaphysical" reading, allowing even wider latitude, perhaps, in interpretation.

24. The form of subscription in the 36th Canon, including the phrase "that he acknowledgeth all and every the Articles . . . being in number nine and thirty . . . to be agreeable to the Word of God," was required of all ordinands in the C. of E. This phrase was omitted when in 1865 subscription was amended to the lesser commitment of a Declaration of Assent to the *BCP*, the Ordinal, and the Thirty-nine Articles.

25. Lambeth Palace Library has several versions of the printed and reformed Articles of Charge, including the original of the Articles of Charge, MS. Arches H 888/2, printed for Wilson and for his legal counsel (a similar one was printed for Williams) and for the court officials, including Lushington. It is entitled "The Office of the Judge Promoted by Fendall against Wilson." Another document consisting of the same printed text (Lambeth MS. Arches H 888/3) is inscribed on the outside "Articles as Reformed, filed in Registry by Consent as duplicate originals. [signed] Chas. Toller, Proctor. Douglas Du Bois, Proctor." This document includes manuscript annotations beside each of the Articles of Charge, indicating their disposition in the interlocutory judgment, with scorings through the rejected charges, and some changes of wording to the charges that Lushington had required to be reformed in his Interlocutory Judgment. The Lambeth copies are those used in the Court of Arches, and hence were those used by Lushington, and the inscriptions are very likely those of the legal counsels prepared for the use of the court. The manuscript inscription beside the original thirteenth Article of Charge reads: "Withdrawn during argument by agreement" (10).

26. According to statute (3 and 4 Vict., c. 86, sec. 13) discretionary power was given to the judge to refuse or to allow an appeal from an interlocutory judgment in proceedings conducted under that statute.

27. Edward Hyde, first Lord Clarendon.The "Tractarian bishop" is Williams's prosecutor, Walter Kerr Hamilton, bp. of Salisbury. For Eusebius on the canonical books in the Bible see Wilson ¶49 and nn. 86 and 87.

28. The offer of retraction was not a withdrawing of his offending opinions or of all of the offending passages but only of the passages in his essay on justification and propitiation (¶s 26, 27) where the court identified his opinions with those of Bunsen as Stephen explained in a letter to the *Spectator*: "What I said was, that Dr. Williams was prepared to withdraw the passages in which the court had held that he had identified himself with Baron Bunsen. As Dr. Williams did not adopt Baron Bunsen's opinions, and had not intended to advance them as his own, as it was the province of the court to say what was the legal effect of his words, and as the court had said that the legal effect of his words was to adopt those opinions, I strongly advised him to take this course; but he never did retract, or authorize me to retract in his name, any opinion which he had advanced as his own, and one of the passages condemned by Dr. Lushington had no reference to Baron Bunsen. He refused explicitly to retract that passage" (quoted in Ellen Williams 1874, 2:78–79). Williams also explained what had transpired: "The offer was, to suppress in future editions two Bunsenian sentences, on 'Justification' and 'Propitiation,' which were unconnected with the main tenor of the Essay, and which had been held to entangle me in the Articles. The court did not entertain this offer, because the prosecutor's counsel was not satisfied with it. The offer did not comprehend any suppression of any part of my Essay upon Biblical Inspiration, or upon any question of Biblical criticism whatsoever" (Ellen Williams 1874, 2:81).

29. Although Williams and Wilson were not removed from their offices or benefices, Williams had already resigned from Lampeter College in the autumn of 1862. Despite the sentence that they should not publish heretical doctrines, the eleventh edition of *Essays and Reviews* was published in March 1863.

30. According to the current registrar of the Judicial Committee of the Privy Council, D. H. O. Owen, "An appeal is not admitted unless either leave to appeal has been granted by the Court appealed from or, in the absence of such leave, special leave to appeal has been granted by the Board. The Court appealed from will grant leave in cases where either the appellant has a right of appeal or the Court is satisfied that the case raises a point of general public interest" (1989, 6). The Judicial Committee functions under the statutory authority of the *Judicial Committee Act*, 1833. See Bentwich [1912] 1937; M. D. Stephen 1966; and Peter Howell 1979.

31. Richard Bethell, Lord Westbury, Lord Chancellor of England, was educated at Wadham College, Oxford, and was called to the bar in 1823; while serving as M. P. for Aylesbury (1851–59) he was appointed attorney-general (1856), shepherding several important legal measures through Parliament, including the Divorce and Matrimonial Causes Act of 1856; he was appointed Lord Chancellor in 1861. Robert Rolfe, Lord Cranworth, was a lawyer and former solicitor-general and Lord Chancellor; he served on the Judicial Committee from 1850 to 1868. Thomas Pemberton-Leigh, Lord Kingsdown, served on the Judicial Committee from 1843 to 1867. He attended some 704 sittings, had a vast experience in both civil and ecclesiastical matters that came before the Privy Council, and "since the early 1850s, had assumed Brougham's mantle as the guiding spirit in the Judicial Committee's deliberations" (Peter Howell 1979, 62). Sir Frederick Thesiger, Lord Chelmsford, formerly attorney-general and Lord Chancellor, served on the Judicial Committee from 1858 to 1876. Henry Reeve was not only the registrar of the Privy Council but also a distinguished man of letters, from 1855 the editor of the *Edinburgh Review*.

Stanley comments on the composition of the Lay Lords: "It appears that these Members of the Judicial Committee were summoned by Her Majesty's command, because they are the four acting Members of the Committee highest in rank; each of them has held or might have held the Great Seal; two are Equity and two may be considered Common lawyers [Court of Common Pleas]; two are Whigs and two are Tories. The Court was therefore constituted with the most rigorous impartiality; and the decision of the Lay Lords was unanimous" (1864, 270–71). Peter Howell writes: "On the first day of the hearing of the *Essays and Reviews* appeals, the Lord President (Granville) and the Archbishop of Canterbury faced each other at the head of the Council board. Lord Westbury L[ord]. C[hancellor]., who was 'virtually presiding', and who ultimately delivered the Committee's judgment on these appeals, was seated in the third place, i.e. next to the Lord President" (1979, 197). In some accounts of those present at the hearing (e.g., Brodrick and Fremantle 1865, 246), the name of Lord Granville, present in a pro forma capacity at the opening session on 19 June 1863, is omitted. He did not participate in the circulation of the written memoranda in preparation for the judgment but is stated as present in the convening documents, court records, and reports in the *Times* (20 June 1863, 7).

32. Peter Howell 1979, 189. *Gorham vs. the Bishop of Exeter* also had a large committee of similar composition.

33. Lushington's response is recorded in the Minute Book, Privy Council Office, 19 June 1863. Williams heaps sarcasm and irony on Phillimore's tactic, blaming his bishop, Walter Kerr Hamilton: "The other side endeavoured not only to exclude me from the literary portion of my Essay, the interpretation of Prophecy, the authorship of Daniel, 2nd Isaiah, and Hebrews, all of which it was natural for them to deprecate as for me to desire; but, incredible as it may sound, they asked the judges to let neither of the defendants touch the doctrinal merits of the propositions condemned by the Court below, and would have limited us to the discussion of the extent of penalty. Hence it may appear to others as much a matter of surprise as it does to myself for sorrow, that the Bishop [of Salisbury] should since have addressed his diocese on the great advantage gained to me by the narrowing the issue, which, it seems, his lordship was desirous to have widened; though his counsel so ill understood their employer's inclinations, that they did all in their power to get it narrowed" (Introduction to *Forty Minutes before the Privy Council*, quoted in Ellen Williams 1874, 2:142).

34. Quoted in Edmund Moore 1863–65, 2:396; and *English Reports* 1901, 15 (Privy Council 4), 951. *Gorham v. the Bishop of Exeter* did not involve a "beneficed Clergyman." Indeed, the procedural issue at dispute in that case was the refusal of the bp. of Exeter to institute him into his benefice or parish, on the grounds of Gorham's belief concerning baptismal regeneration.

35. After publishing in *Essays and Reviews* Wilson again wrote extensively on inspiration in the 75-page introduction to the anonymous *Brief Examination . . . Inspiration of the Scriptures*. His comments provoked the charge of pantheism in Wilberforce's charge of 1863 (see Wilson 1861 and Wilberforce 1863, 45–60).

36. In remarks made in Convocation, Longley suggested that Williams had offered arguments concerning propitiation and that he had so moderated his views and explained away his meaning that he enabled Longley to support a more merciful

sentence. His remarks were published in the *Guardian*, 29 June 1864. In a correspondence with Longley, Williams sets out the facts as he sees them: he did not speak at all before the Privy Council on propitiation because the charge was withdrawn; accordingly he had no opportunity of clarifying his views on the doctrine. The official records of the proceedings substantiate Williams's position. Longley is noncommittal in his response, but Williams pressed him, and eventually published his own reply in the *Record* (Letters 243–45).

37. See Wilson 1863. The court reporters could not keep up with Williams's delivery, and so he dictated it from memory the next day, corrected it for printing, and added his comments to it in *Forty Minutes before the Privy Council*, a document that Williams prepared for publication but never issued (see Ellen Williams 1874, 2:142).

38. Lambeth, MS. Tait 291, fols. 201–304. Most of the documents (fols. 246–304) are printed; many contain Tait's MS. annotations, corrections, and comments on the history of each document.

39. Lambeth, MS. Tait 291, fols. 246–52v. Tait's MS. note at the top of the first page indicates that he had loaned out the memorandum a year later: "Strictly private to be returned as soon as possible to the Bp. of London, 18 June, 1864." It was very likely loaned in connection with the debate on the Synodical Condemnation of the Convocation of the Province of Canterbury (pronounced on 24 June 1864) which Tait opposed. Drafts of these memoranda in Tait's hand are found at fols. 201–44. All of the circulated memoranda and opinions are printed on blue paper, numbered by folios throughout the volume; each printed memorandum also has printed page numbers specific to it. The documents are as follows:

fols. 246–52v	"Memorandum by the Bishop of London on the Appeals of Williams *v.* the Bishop of Salisbury and Wilson *v.* Fendall: September 1863. Confidential" [with annotations on fol. 246]
fols. 253–60v	[another copy of Tait's memorandum, with other MS. annotations in his hand]
fols. 261–66v	"Opinion of the Archbishop of Canterbury upon the Appeals of Williams . . . and Wilson" [dated in MS. at the beginning "Oct. 15, 1863" and in print at the end]
fols. 267–69v	"Opinion of the Archbishop of York upon the Appeals of Williams . . . and Wilson" [undated, but with a MS. note in Tait's hand: "no date:—but it was not issued one of the first"]
fols. 270–72	"Memorandum on the Appeals . . . by the Right Hon. Lord Chelmsford"
fols. 273–75v	"Memorandum on the Appeals . . . by the Right Hon. Lord Kingsdown"
fols. 276–83v	"Heads for Consideration as the Foundation of a Judgment . . . by the Right Hon. Lord Cranworth" [the first draft of the formal judgment]
fols. 284–88	"Notes of Judgment in the two appeals of Mr. Wilson and Dr. Williams: by the Lord Chancellor. For the consideration of the other Members of the Committee. {SECOND REVISE}" [undated, with a few MS. annotations and proposed changes in Tait's hand]
fols. 289–93	[ditto] "{THIRD REVISE}" [with many MS. annotations in Tait's hand]
fol. 294	"Amendment to be proposed by Lord Kingsdown. . . ."
fols. 295–99v	"Draft Judgment of the Lords of the Judicial Committee of the Privy Council . . . {FOURTH REVISE}" [includes Tait's marginal headings and a MS. note in Tait's hand: "This copy was used by the Bp of London at the delivery of the Judgment"]
fols. 300–304	[ditto; the revise number is not specified, though it appears to be the fifth and contains further revisions. Tait has added in MS. "This copy was used by the Bp"]

40. Lambeth, MS. Tait 291, fols. 284–304. Each of the revises, except the last, is printed with an indication of its place in the sequence. Pointed brackets here indicate special square brackets printed in the text to indicate the number of each revise.

41. Tait's biographers comment: "Bishop Tait took the utmost pains during the whole course of the trial, and a comparison of the judgment as finally pronounced, with the printed memorandum of opinion which he, like the other judges, had circulated beforehand among his colleagues, shows how large a share he had in giving shape to the decision" (Davidson and Benham 1891, 1:313).

42. Our copytext is the separate printing in the Privy Council Papers (British Library: Parliamentary Papers: P.P. 1316/1864), collated with the copy in Lambeth Palace Library (H 5155 [1]). Our annotation includes added and removed phrasing from the various preparatory revisions in MS. Tait 291, excluding those that have already been cited above in the circulated memoranda. The judgment is also reprinted in Brodrick and Fremantle 1865, 247–90; William Brooke 1874, 81–102; Edmund Moore 1863–65, 2:375–434; and *English Reports* 1901, 15: Privy Council 4:943–65. Summary accounts of the plead-

ings by Wilson and Williams, and the replies of Phillimore, Swabey, and Coleridge, are given in Edmund Moore 1863–65 and *English Reports* 1901.

43. These marginal headings were added by Tait in his copy of the "FOURTH REVISE" (Lambeth, MS. Tait 291, fols. 295–99v). They are not included in the printed judgment.

44. Tait adds in his hand in the "FOURTH REVISE": "in the Articles of Charge as reformed and considered by the Court below" (Lambeth, MS. Tait 291, fol. 295).

45. In Lord Westbury's "SECOND REVISE" the following passage, applying the same interpretive principle to the appellants' writings as was applied in the Court of Arches to the Articles of Religion, is added: "Further, in this penal proceeding we are not at liberty to put any interpretation on the words of the accused but that which is their plain and obvious meaning. Such is the law that regulates this form of procedure." Tait scores out this passage in his copy of the "SECOND REVISE"; it was not retained in the "THIRD REVISE" (Lambeth, MS. Tait 291, fols. 284–284v).

46. This paragraph dismisses the 5th Article of Charge in the cases of both Williams and Wilson that had been admitted by Lushington in the interlocutory judgment. It concerned the preface entitled "To the Reader," allegations of collaboration, imputations of responsibility on all of the Essayists for the contents of the whole book, and criticism that no disclaimer was printed in any edition. Except for this indirect reference, it is not addressed further by the Judicial Committee.

47. Article 7 in the Articles of Charge considered in the Court of Arches. In the "FOURTH REVISE," the copy he had before him at the delivery of the judgment, Tait annotates this section: "With this article the Archbishops dissented."

48. At this point in the "THIRD REVISE" the following paragraph was added. It first appears in "Heads for Consideration as the Foundation of a Judgment . . . by the Right Hon. Lord Cranworth." Tait edited the paragraph by striking out some passages (as indicated), and by emending or adding other wording (indicated by obliques \thus/):

> Dr. Williams' views are founded on the supposition that the Holy Spirit operated in the framing of the Sacred Volume, ~~and that is all which can be considered as declared by the Articles. \The Articles of Religion & doctrine of the Church of Eng. are silent as to/~~ How the Holy Spirit operated; to what extent the Sacred Writers were so guided as to enable them to avoid \all/ error; how far the same influence, ~~differing only in degree~~, may have continued to operate in later ages, are all questions untouched by the Articles, and as to which, therefore the present proceeding cannot be sustained. ~~Dr. Williams (though it may be fair to infer from the passage in question that he thinks the same Spirit which operated in the framing of the Sacred Volume has operated on succeeding writers) nowhere \does not/ affirms that the influence so exercised, has been the same in degree~~ (Lambeth, MS. Tait 291, fol. 279).

The whole of this passage was deleted in the "FOURTH REVISE."

49. The phrase "and therefore to be read with reason in freedom" was added by Tait in the "THIRD REVISE."

50. Tait adds in MS. to the "FOURTH REVISE": "On this Article all the Judges were agreed."

51. Tait added the phrase "as that of not being a Christian" in the "THIRD REVISE."

52. Williams later comments on justification as a "fiction" in his *Broadchalke Sermon-Essays* (1867), citing Luther, and applying his and Luther's views to the arguments of J. H. Newman (see Williams ¶26 and note).

53. Tait adds this entire paragraph in the "THIRD REVISE" (Lambeth, MS. Tait 291, fol. 291).

54. Tait adds in the "FOURTH REVISE": "On this Article the Archbishops dissented."

55. So in the copytext and at Lambeth. Later printed texts read "In" (Brodrick and Fremantle 1865, 285; Edmund Moore 1863–65, 2:429; William Brooke 1874, 98).

56. Tait annotates this paragraph in the "THIRD REVISE": "Lord Kingsdown's substitution."

57. Tait adds the phrase "every part of" in the "THIRD REVISE."

58. This paragraph was considerably reworked in the "THIRD REVISE" (Lambeth, MS. Tait 291, fol. 292).

59. This paragraph was added by Tait to the "THIRD REVISE" (Lambeth, MS. Tait 291, fol. 292).

60. Tait adds in the "FOURTH REVISE": "On this Article all the Judges were agreed." Responding to attacks from both the High and Low Church, Longley wrote in self-defense to the *Times*, stating that he assented to the reversal of this article "solely on technical grounds, inasmuch as the charge . . . was so worded that I did not think it could be borne out by the facts" (12 Mar. 1864).

61. Tait begins this paragraph in the "THIRD REVISE" with the words "We grant that it is a dangerous precedent" and then scores them out.

62. *Judgment of the Lords of the Judicial Committee. . . .* 1864, 3–11. Commenting on "Dissenting Opinion," the current registrar of the Privy Council writes: "It was not until 1966 that a dissenting opinion was allowed to be published. Up to that time the rule was strictly observed that the Judicial Committee, being a branch of the Privy Council and deliberations of the Privy Council being secret, no dissenting opinion should be published. There are surprisingly few dissenting judgments: and they are more often

the result of a disagreement over the conclusions to be drawn from the evidence than of a difference of construction or statutory interpretation. By convention, any member of the Board who concurs with the majority in the result but arrives at that result by a different route is not permitted to prepare a separate judgment" (H. D. O. Owen 1989, 6–7).

63. Early in the proceedings before the Court of Arches, when it became clear that there would be a series of trials, defense funds were established by the supporters of Williams and Wilson, and very likely organized by Stanley. By midsummer 1861 there were active Manchester and London committees, as the *Athenaeum* reported: "Manchester, we find, is stirring heartily in defence of that freedom of inquiry which is menaced by the proceedings of the Bishop of Salisbury. A committee to collect funds to assist Dr. Williams in his lawsuits has been formed, and is already in communication with the London Committee" (24 Aug. 1861, 253).

64. Pusey House: Hamilton Papers, Macdonald to Edward Hamilton 9 Apr. 1864; Honey to Hamilton 28 July 1864.

65. "*Praemunire*" (Lat. "Let [person such and such] be warned) refers to a class of offenses, often ecclesiastical, where there is an allegation of the usurpation of royal authority. The penalties of a *praemunire* include the loss of civil rights, property, goods, and possible imprisonment.

66. *Pusey and Others v. Jowett: The Argument and Decision as to the Jurisdiction of the Chancellor's Court at Oxford* (1863, 2). The charge is contained in the Summons issued by the chancellor, Edward Stanley, earl of Derby, to John Haines, Yeoman Bedell of Law at Oxford, ordering him to cite Jowett for the charge, and to convene the Chancellor's Court to hear it.

67. In 1864–65 a canonry at Christ Church was worth "about £1,500 yearly." And at the time when Jowett was prosecuted at Oxford, two of his accusers were frankly pluralist: Charles Atmore Ogilvie held the Chair of Pastoral Theology and the annexed canonry at Christ Church, as well as a further "£1,100 yearly from the living of Ross-on-Wye (in the gift of a bishop)"; Charles Abel Heurtley as Lady Margaret Professor of Divinity held the annexed canonry, and £500 from the living of Fenny Compton; Pusey, on the other hand, only had the canonry at Christ Church (Bill and Mason, 1970, 102).

68. Thomas Gaisford, Regius Professor of Greek, was also dean of Christ Church (both the College and Cathedral), from 1831, and so enjoyed, as he said, "considerable emolument" (Geoffrey Faber 1957, 222, n. 1). He published a number of editions of classical texts, but did not give a single lecture as Professor of Greek; nor did he take a single class with students. (See Abbott and Campbell 1897, 1:236–37). According to Geoffrey Faber the announcement of Jowett's appointment as his replacement was made in October 1854 (1957, 221–22).

69. On the role of Christ Church in university reform throughout this period, see Bill and Mason, 1970.

70. Pusey's "All Faith the Gift of God" was reprinted the next year as the first sermon in a collection very likely instigated by him. *Christian Faith and the Atonement* made its purpose clear in its subtitle: *Sermons Preached before the University of Oxford in Reference to the Views Published by Mr. Jowett and Others.* The volume contained, besides Pusey's sermon, others by Bishop Wilberforce and Pusey's eventual co-prosecutor in the trial of Jowett, Charles Heurtley. Another eventual opponent of Jowett and the other Essayists, E. M. Goulburn, also had a sermon included.

71. Stanley's printed speech puts a little differently the objections to granting Jowett an increased stipend: "1. The University should not grant money to a chair whose appointment rests with the Crown. 2. The Greek Professor is 'supposed to hold certain theological opinions which, it is said, the University would endorse by endowing the Chair.' 3. If resident members of the University approve the measure, non-resident members will later come to Convocation and throw it out." Stanley pleads for justice in granting "a salary long withheld" (Stanley 1861b, 9–11).

72. See also *Oxford Chronicle* of 23 Nov. 1861. Abbott and Campbell point out that in the appointment of Jowett ecclesiastical advice had been taken, in that Henry Liddell, dean of Christ Church, had been consulted by Lord Palmerston before Jowett was appointed. Indeed, Liddell had himself been nominated, but he declined and proposed Jowett's name, amongst others (1897, 1:305–6; see also H. L. Thompson 1899, 140).

73. A full account of the proceedings in the Chancellor's Court is contained in *Pusey and Others v. Jowett; the Argument and Decision as to the Jurisdiction of the Chancellor's Court at Oxford* (1863), a pamphlet of 41 pages selling for a shilling.

74. Montague Bernard was especially interested in ecclesiastical law. He was one of the founders of the High Church weekly, the *Guardian.* From 1852 he was Professor of International Law and Diplomacy at Oxford, and was a Fellow of All Souls' College. He was particularly instrumental in constructing Britain's neutral position in the American Civil War and was one of the signatories of the Treaty of Washington (1871).

75. The *Times* was not slow in drawing attention to the coincidence of 13 February (when the proceeding against Jowett began in the Chancellor's Court) and other dates in recent Oxford history. Indeed Stanley had also pointed out that a similar collection of passages from Hampden had been published to vindicate him from the attacks of Pusey and others: "Theological panic, like misfortune,

makes us acquainted with strange companions, and these discordant elements have been united by a common antipathy to religious freedom. It must be confessed, however, that the 13th of February was an inauspicious day to select for the first enterprise of this unnatural alliance. It was on the 13th of February, 1836, that the statute against Dr. Hampden was brought forward at the instigation of Dr. Pusey and his friends, who surely cannot look back with any pride to the result of their efforts to crush him. It was on the 13th of February, 1845, that the aggressors in the former proceeding would have been visited with a like disgrace, had not Professor Jowett and other liberal members of Convocation come forward with generous zeal to vindicate liberty of speech for their High Church opponents, and defeated the disabling statute" (*Times*, 14 Feb. 1863, 9).

76. Abbott and Campbell 1897, 1:313. Geoffrey Faber argues that John Duke Coleridge was brought in because he had become an authority in cases involving a *mandamus* (1957, 271).

77. Abbott and Campbell 1897, 1:320; on the cited documents see Abbott and Campbell 1897, 1:317–20. The "Regius Professorship of Greek, 1865" is treated in Bill and Mason (1970, 102–9) almost wholly in relation to the internal politics of Christ Church, the reform of the funding for its undergraduate and graduate studentships, and as part of the agitation for and against the "Christ Church, Oxford Act" of 1867. On 14 February the legal opinion of Sir Roundell Palmer and Sir Hugh Cairns that Christ Church was not formally obligated to pay for the Greek Professorship was presented to the chapter. Bill and Mason report that "the minute" from the Chapter Act Book "is exquisitely worded":

> After a long discussion of the subjects of the liability of the Dean and Chapter to make adequate provision for the Regius Professor of Greek, it was resolved, on an unanimously expressed opinion, that the Chapter is not held by any legal obligation to alter the original endowment of £40 a year. The Chapter was not so perfectly agreed as to the existence of moral obligation in the matter. The Chapter then took into consideration the question of expediency and it was resolved (1) that it was expedient to consider whether there be any mode of adequately endowing the Greek Chair which it might be advisable for the Chapter to adopt, and (2) that it would be a gracious act, and one relieving the University from a painful difficulty, if the Chapter were to augment the Professor's Stipend from funds at their command and (3) . . . that the Dean be requested to communicate to the Vice-Chancellor the result of this deliberation.
>
> For the carrying out these resolutions it was further resolved, that the sum of £460 be charged on the incomes of the Dean and Canons yearly to be levied in due proportions until or unless some other means be found to defray this charge (1970, 108–9).

5 Satires by Lewis Carroll and Others

When *Essays and Reviews* was a topic of public controversy from 1861 to 1864 and again in late 1869, the newspapers and periodical press were extremely active in fueling the debates not only with reviews, articles, and letters but also with satire, with mockery through comic verse and pastiche. These documents, often privately printed for a small circulation, are in many ways typical of Oxford donnish and undergraduate wit, drawing to some extent on university and religious slang of the kind indexed in John Camden Hotten's *The Slang Dictionary* (1864): "The *Universities of Oxford and Cambridge*, and the great public schools, are the hotbeds of fashionable Slang. . . . *Religious Slang*, strange as the compound may appear, exists with other descriptions of vulgar speech at the present day. *Punch*, a short time since, in one of those half-humorous, half-serious articles in which he is so fond of lecturing any national abuse or popular folly, remarked that Slang had 'long since penetrated into the Forum . . . *and even the pulpit itself*'" (48–49). One of its topics was *Essays and Reviews*.

The popular appetite for light satiric verse was met in part by the pen of "Expectans" whose *The Grievance and the Remedy* (1861), a poem in two cantos and 31 pages, attacked

That book which evil dares diffuse,
Entitled "Essays and Reviews."

Another example is the anonymous 4-page versified attack against the "Dim Smokified Seven," whose title echoed Aeschylus' *Seven against Thebes*:

Have you heard of the smokified Essays—
The Reviews and dim smokified Essays?
Each one a dull libel
'Gainst plain sense and the Bible—
The seven dim smokified Essays

ΕΠΤΑ ΜΥΟΠΕΣ ΚΑΠΝΙΖΟΜΕΝΟΙ or The Dim Smokified Seven. [1861?], 1.

William MacFarlane in his *Practical Letter* (1863) gives rare support to the Essayists and Bishop Colenso against the attacks of the bishops, ending up with a satire of William Cowper's hymn, "God moves in a mysterious way":

God moves in a transparent way
His wonders to perform:
He plants His roots into the ground
And sends out perfect form.

"Perfect form" was not the hallmark of most poetasters who wrote on *Essays and Reviews*. For instance, among these scarce pamphlets for a popular audience was *Quagmire Ahead* by "Truthful Diggins," published in 1864 in 28 pages on the current difficulties of the Church of England, including Bishop Colenso and *Essays and Reviews*:

But lo! a Bishop comes with line and rule
And says: "Forsooth, you *must* be a great fool
Thus to believe that all the Bible's true"
And this he will most deftly prove to you—
Will prove it to you well by line and measure,
And oft repeat it with the greatest pleasure:
And try his best without or awe or ruth
To overturn the great Immortal Truth.
Yet, after all, good friends, 'tis no great news!
The way was shown by "Essays and Reviews" (10).

Of a rather different order are the more sustained satires by Lewis Carroll, and those appearing in the pages of *Punch* and its short-lived rival, *Judy*.

Lewis Carroll
"Endowment of the Greek Professorship"

[Charles Lutwidge Dodgson (1832–1898) was a student at Rugby School (1846–48), and entered Christ Church, Oxford, as an undergraduate in January 1851. In 1852 he was elected by the Chapter, on Pusey's nomination, to a studentship. Dodgson received a first-class degree in mathematics and was appointed sublibrarian in 1855, continuing to lecture in mathematics until 1881. He was ordained deacon in the Church of England on 22 December 1861, but never proceeded to priest's orders. Under his pseudonym "Lewis Carroll" he published *Alice's Adventures in Wonderland* (1865) and *Through the Looking-Glass* (1871). As an amateur photographer he took pictures of many of the notable figures of his day, including one of A. P. Stanley (see fig. 3). His mathematical works include guidebooks for undergraduates in algebra and geometry, and *Euclid and His Modern Rivals* (1879), a defense of Euclid against non-Euclidean geometry; his logical works include *The Game of Logic* (1886) and *Symbolic Logic* (1896).

At Christ Church, Dodgson took part in the affairs of the college and of the university and showed an interest in the theological debates of his time, including those concerning Benjamin Jowett and the endowment of the Greek Professorship. On this matter Carroll published three items, and possibly a fourth, here for the first time attributed to him: a short satire in the form of a university notice in November 1861; a poem, "The Majesty of Justice" in March 1863; *The New Method of Evaluation as applied to Π* (1865), a pseudo-mathematical satire on the various methods proposed for raising the endowment of the Greek Professorship; and possibly an anonymous lampoon in *Punch* in the week of 28 February 1863. These contributions of Dodgson's cover the period of the debate in the legislative bodies of Oxford University as well as the period of time from the trial in the Chancellor's Court to the date when the endowment was finally raised in 1865.

In addition, Dodgson continued until 1876 to publish satirical references to Jowett and his circle, to the Greek Chair, and to *Essays and Reviews*, in a series of other poems and pamphlets, including "Examination Statute" (1864), "The Dynamics of a Parti-cle" (1865), "The Elections to the Hebdomadal Council" (1866), "The Deserted Parks" (1867), "The New Belfrey of Christ Church, Oxford" (1872), "The Blank Cheque, A Fable" (1874), and "The Professorship of Comparative Philology" (1876). For each of these documents see Carroll 1993.

The legislative bodies of Oxford University consist of the Hebdomadal Council (the representative council of Oxford University that meets once a week to initiate any matters of concern or legislation concerning the university), Congregation (the meeting of all resident masters, doctors, and professors of the university to discuss the matters referred to it by the Council), and Convocation (the legislative assembly of all members of the university qualified with the degree of M.A., a large body consisting of all holders of the degree wherever they were located who go to Oxford for the meetings; normally about 1,500 would attend to vote on matters brought before it). At the height of the debates in the Hebdomadal Council in November 1861, Stanley was successful in bringing a motion forward for debate in Congregation and made a long speech on this occasion. Dodgson attended the meeting of 20 November and spoke when Stanley's motion was presented. His diary entry reads:

> 20 Nov. 1861.—Promulgation, in Congregation, of the new statute to endow Jowett. The speaking took up the whole afternoon, and the two points at issue, the endowing a *Regius* Professorship, and the countenancing Jowett's theological opinions, got so inextricably mixed up that I rose to beg that they might be kept separate. Once on my feet, I said more than I first meant, and defied them ever to tire out the opposition by perpetually bringing the question on (*Mem*: if I ever speak again I will try to say no more than I had resolved before rising). This was my first speech in Congregation (Carroll 1993).

In reporting the debate, the *Times* noted that it "continued till dark" and that Dodgson voted against the new statute.

The next day a leaflet, "The Endowment of the Greek Professorship," signed with the initials of Drummond Percy Chase, principal of St. Mary's Hall, was circulated. It proposed two amendments to the statute, in effect suggesting a remodeling under the new Statute to be like that of the Corpus Professorship of Latin. The second amendment reads:

> That the Statute be framed creating an independent Professorship of Greek.
>
> That the Professor shall be appointed by a Board similar in constitution to that which appoints the Professor of Latin: but that the Corpus element be omitted, and the Professor of Latin be substituted for the Regius Professor of Greek.
>
> That all the conditions imposed by the promulgated Statute be retained except No. 7, which shall be either omitted, or altered by inserting after the word

"Professione" the words "nisi in eadem materia (Lat. except on the same matter)" (Carroll 1993, 2).

That is, Chase was proposing that the wording of the Latin Professorship statute be followed, but omitting all reference to the Corpus Professorship and presumably substituting the references to the Latin Professor with those for the Greek. The following day, 22 November, Dodgson published his anonymous satire on the debate in the format of another university circular.

Dodgson refers to John Conington who was appointed to the chair of Latin at Oxford in 1854, the year before Jowett's appointment in Greek. The Latin chair was established by Corpus Christi College. Dodgson also alludes to the popularity of American spiritualist mediums such as Margaret and Kate Fox and Daniel Dunglas Home who were then the rage in England. He puns on the name of Corpus Christi College, and the notion of omitting the "corpus element"—the bodily component of a professor. He suggests that only a professor who was a fellow of All Souls College (and so would be all soul, and no body) would meet the requirement of having omitted the "corpus element." The peculiar wording of Chase's amendment dealing with the substitution of language concerning the office of the Latin and Greek professorships enabled Dodgson to suggest that the actual substitution of incumbents, of Conington for Jowett, would remove the "vexed question" since Conington's theological views were not suspect.

The leaflet (here edited from British Library 8365.g.23) was not republished by Dodgson, but was reprinted in R. L. Green's edition of Carroll's *Diaries* (Carroll 1953, 1: 166) and Carroll 1993, 1–4. The Latin phrase, *vexata quaestio*, means a vexed question.]

Endowment of the Greek Professorship

In the Alternative Amendments recently proposed in a paper issued under the above heading, the attention of Members of Convocation is respectfully invited to the following passage.

After proposing the institution of an independent Professorship of Greek, the following words occur: "That the Corpus element be omitted, and the Professor of Latin be substituted for the Regius Professor of Greek."

Here are two propositions, startling in their novelty, and demanding serious and separate consideration.

The first, "That the Corpus element be omitted," is a condition never before annexed to a Professorship, and which indicates but too clearly the wide influence which the so-called "spiritualist" views have attained both in America and in this country.

It may no doubt be desirable that a Professor should be free from the petty cares and distracting influences which are inseparable from our corporal condition; still, as none but a member of All Souls can possibly fulfil the stringent requisition here proposed, Members of Convocation are respectfully reminded that to confine this piece of preferment within such narrow limits would be illiberal, if not unjust to other Colleges.

The second portion of the clause above quoted is as novel as the first, but so desirable an innovation, that it cannot be too widely known, or too heartily supported by Members of Convocation. There is no doubt that the substitution of Mr. Conington for Mr. Jowett would remove one of the most powerful elements of discord in this "*vexata quaestio*," and would probably tend to its speedy and peaceful settlement. The question whether Mr. Conington himself would consent to the change is one which has no doubt suggested itself to, and been fully considered by, the proposer of these amendments.

Nov. 22, 1861.

Lewis Carroll
"The Majesty of Justice"

[The exchange between E. B. Pusey and F. D. Maurice in the *Times* in February 1863 on the occasion of the trial of Jowett in the Chancellor's Court (and, in his absence, the Vice-Chancellor's Court, presided over by his assessor, Montague Bernard) prompted Pusey to assert that he was prosecuting the charges there as his only possible route to bring Jowett's theological opinions before "the majesty of justice" (Letters 175–76). The Chancellor's Court (see Part 2, Trials and Appeals) was usually used for the settling of small debt disputes concerning Oxford undergraduates and local merchants (as in the *Punch* satire below), and consequently was frequently referred to as Oxford's "small debts court," as Geoffrey Lushington explained in detail in his reply to Pusey (Letter 177). Pusey later explained that by the term *majesty of justice* he referred not only to the Chancellor's Court (a designation of that site of law that Maurice and others pilloried) but also to the final court of appeal from the vice-chancellor—through the Court of Queen's Bench to the Judicial Committee of the Privy Council. But the phrase stuck as a ridiculous term to use for the Oxford Chancellor's Court. Pusey had used a similar phrase in his *Minor Prophets* (1860): "They did violence to the majesty of the law . . . and then, through profaning it, did violence to man" (474).

Carroll's reference to the "articles" is a pun on the Thirty-nine Articles of Religion that Jowett was accused of violating. The entire meaning of the satire hinges upon the final word of the poem. The references to the "WIG" are in part a pun on Whig and Tory political and ecclesiastical positions and also to the slang use of the word, especially Oxford slang ("getting a wigging"), as a rebuke, scolding, or reprimand of the kind often administered in the Chancellor's Court to undergraduates for intemperate spending. A "wig" was also street and underworld slang for a judge in court. The phrase "wiggery" was used by Carlyle in *Past and Present* (1843) for the arid but costly formality of the judicial system. In the suppressed episode on "the wasp in a wig" from chapter 8 of *Through the Looking-Glass* (1875), printed in 1977 from the newly found galleys, Carroll's rude wasp tells his story in prose and a five-stanza poem that ends up with the phrase "Because I wear a yellow wig."

Carroll had met Jowett when he was staying with the Tennysons at Freshwater on the Isle of Wight in April 1862 (and very likely earlier at Oxford; see Carroll 1979, 1:57). It was on the occasion of the Jowett trial that Dodgson wrote his satirical poem "The Majesty of Justice. An Oxford Idyll." It first was published in *College Rhymes: Contributed by Members of the Universities of Oxford and Cambridge*, issued in Lent Term, 1863. The poem was published when Dodgson was just at the end of his editorship of the series, from 1 July 1861 to 25 March 1863, and was dated and signed using one of his pseudonyms, R. W. G. The poem has been reprinted frequently, as in the Nonesuch edition (Carroll 1939, 812–14). The text below follows *College Rhymes* (1863, 4:96–99).]

The Majesty of Justice
An Oxford Idyll

THEY passed beneath the College gate,
And down the High went slowly on;
Then spake the Undergraduate
To that benign and portly Don;
"They say that Justice is a Queen—
A Queen of awful Majesty—
Yet in the papers I have seen
Some things that puzzle me.

"A Court obscure, so rumour states,
There is, called 'Vice-Cancellarii,'
Which keeps on Undergraduates,
Who do not pay their bills, a wary eye.
A case, I'm told, was lately brought
Into that tiniest of places,
And 'Justice' in that case was sought—
As in most other cases.

"Well! Justice, as *I* hold, dear friend,
Is Justice, neither more or less:
I never dreamed it could depend
On ceremonial or dress.
I thought that her imperial sway

In Oxford surely would appear:
But all the papers seem to say
She's not majestic *here*."

The portly Don he made reply,
With the most roguish of his glances,
"Perhaps she drops her Majesty
Under peculiar circumstances."
"But that's the point!" the young man cried,
"The puzzle that I wish to pen you in—
How are the public to decide
Which article is genuine?

"Is't only when the court is large
That we for 'Majesty' need hunt?
Would what is Justice in a barge
Be something different in a punt?"
"Nay, nay!" the Don replied, amused,
"You're talking nonsense, sir! You know it!
Such arguments were never used
By any friend of Jowett."

"Then is it in the men who trudge
(Beef-eaters I believe they call them)
Before each wigged and ermined judge,
For fear some mischief should befall them?
If I should recognise in one
(Through all disguise) my own domestic,
I fear 'twould shed a gleam of fun
Even on the 'Majestic'!"

The portly Don replied "Ahem!
They can't exactly be its *essence*:
I scarcely think the want of them
The 'Majesty of Justice' lessens.
Besides, they always march awry;
Their gorgeous garments never fit:
Processions don't make Majesty—
I'm quite convinced of it."

"Then is it in the *wig* it lies,
Whose countless rows of rigid curls
Are gazed at with admiring eyes

By country lads and servant-girls?"
Out laughed that bland and courteous Don:
"Dear sir, I do not mean to flatter—
But surely you have hit upon
The essence of the matter.

"They will not own the Majesty
Of Justice, making monarchs bow,
Unless as evidence they see
The horsehair wig about her brow.
Yes, yes! *That* makes the silliest men
Seem wise; the meanest men look big:
The 'Majesty of Justice,' then,
Is seated in the WIG!"

OXFORD. *March 1863.* R. W. G.

Lewis Carroll
The New Method of Evaluation as Applied to Π

[The controversy about Benjamin Jowett's stipend as Regius Professor of Greek, established at £40 at the time of Henry VIII, continued from 1855 to 1865. E. B. Pusey and others refused to increase Jowett's stipend, as had happened with the other Regius Professorships, because of their disapproval of his alleged heterodox theology in *The Epistles of St. Paul* (1855). Jowett's supporter in the Oxford administrative establishment of the Hebdomadal Council was A. P. Stanley, who repeatedly raised the question of the stipend, to little avail.

In Carroll's *Diaries* there are several entries on the endowment of the Greek Professorship. E. B. Pusey and A. P. Stanley were two of the leading figures in Oxford's political and administrative life, and were usually on opposite sides politically, administratively, and ecclesiastically. Stanley had advocated a raise in Jowett's stipend from the time of his first appointment in 1855, and Pusey had resolutely opposed it on the grounds of Jowett's allegedly defective views concerning the atonement and biblical inspiration. But by 1861, although he was even more than ever convinced of Jowett's heterodoxy, he moved on 7 May a resolution to increase the stipends for a number of professorships, including Jowett's, making it clear that he was increasing the stipend for the chair, not for its incumbent, whose theology he was in no way approving. This move, like all those from both him and Stanley for the next four years, proved ineffective in gaining sufficient support to pass through all of the legislative processes.

On 18 November 1863, when Pusey was supporting the effort to raise the stipend through the debates in the Hebdomadal Council and was negotiating it through Congregation, having failed in his suit against Jowett before the Chancellor's Court, Carroll made a diary entry: "Wrote a paper on the subject of the Jowett endowment, which is again being agitated" (Carroll 1953, 1:207). But it is not clear to what he refers. In February 1865 the Chapter of Christ Church was forced to consider the evidence brought forward by Freeman and Elton in the *Times* concerning the historic and financial obligation of Christ Church to pay the stipend. On 14 February the Chapter acceded to moral suasion and the intimidating compulsion of the dean, Henry George Liddell, agreeing to raise Jowett's stipend from £40 to £500, the additional £460 levied against the stipends of the dean and canons of Christ Church. When appeals were made by the Students ("Fellows" are termed "Students" at Christ Church) to use this change as a precedent to remedy other underpaid College officers, Dodgson took part in the deliberations and also used the occasion as an opportunity to prepare a more elaborate account of the various methods proposed for raising Jowett's stipend. In his *Diaries* Dodgson notes on 3 March 1865: "A day or two ago an idea occurred to me of writing a sham mathematical paper on Jowett's case, taking π to symbolise his payment, and have jotted down a little of it." On 8 March Carroll returns to his composition: "Sat up and wrote out the paper *On the evaluation of π*, which I began last week"; and on 14 March he indicates that it was published: "Coming out of *The new method of Evaluation, as applied to π*. I had about 80 copies sent round to the Common Rooms" (Carroll 1993, 17–18). The published pamphlet in four pages bears the date of "March, 1865"; no author is given. It was reprinted as the third chapter to *The Dynamics of a Parti-cle* (June 1865), separately in 1874, and was issued in the same year as the first part of Carroll's *Notes by an Oxford Chiel.* The copytext for the version printed below is the pamphlet of 1865, printed from Oxford Bodley GA Oxon. c. 81. It is designated *1865*; variants from *Notes by an Oxford Chiel* are designated *1874*. Variants from Carroll 1993 are designated *1993*.[1]

The pun in the title refers, on the basis of the nursery rhyme printed on the title page, to the fact that the "pie" of the endowments for the regius professorships, and perhaps for other college and university officers (especially those at Christ Church), can be calculated according to this new method.]

The New Method of Evaluation As Applied to Π

The problem of evaluating π,[2] which has engaged the attention of mathematicians from the earliest ages, had, down to our own time, been considered as purely arithmetical. It was reserved for this generation to make the discovery that it is really a dynamical problem: and the true value of π, which appeared an "ignis fatuus" to our forefathers, has been at last obtained under pressure.[3]

The following are the main data of the problem:—

Let U = the University, G = Greek, and P = Professor.

Then GP = Greek Professor; let this be reduced to its lowest terms, and call the result J.

Also let W = the work done, T = the Times, p = the given payment, π = the payment according to T, and S = the sum required; so that π = S.

The problem is, to obtain a value for π which shall be commensurable with W.

In the early treatises on this subject, the mean value assigned to π will be found to be 40.000000. Later writers suspected that the decimal point had been accidentally shifted, and that the proper value was 400.00000: but, as the details of the process for obtaining it had been lost, no further progress was made in the subject till our own time, though several most ingenious methods were tried for solving the problem.

Of these methods we proceed to give some brief account. Those chiefly worthy of note appear to be Rationalisation, the Method of Indifferences, Penrhyn's Method, and the Method of Elimination.[4]

I. Rationalisation.

The peculiarity of this process consists in its affecting all quantities alike with a negative sign.[5]

To apply it, let H = High Church, and L = Low Church, then the geometric mean = $\sqrt{HL}$: call this "B" (Broad Church).

$$\therefore HL = B^2.$$

Also let x and y represent unknown quantities.

The process now requires the breaking up of U into its partial factions, and the introduction of certain combinations. Of the two principal factions thus formed, that corresponding with P presented no further difficulty, but it appeared hopeless to rationalise the other.[6]

A *reductio ad absurdum* was therefore attempted, and it was asked "Why should π *not* be evaluated?" The great difficulty now was, to discover y.[7]

Several ingenious substitutions and transformations were then resorted to, and it was at one time asserted, though never actually proved, that all the y's were on one side of the equation. However, as repeated trials produced the same irrational result, the process was finally abandoned.[8]

II. The Method of Indifferences.

This was a modification of "*the method of finite Differences*,"[9] and may be thus briefly described:—

Let E = Essays, and R = Reviews; then the locus of (E+R), referred to multilinear co-ordinates, will be found to be a superficies (i.e., a locus possessing length and breadth, but no depth). Let ν = novelty, and assume (E+R) as a function of ν.[10]

Taking this superficies as the plane of reference,[11] we get —

$$E = R = B$$
$$\therefore EB = B^2 = HL \text{ (by the last article.)}^{12}$$
$$\text{Multiplying by P,} \quad EBP = HPL.$$

It was now necessary to investigate the locus of EBP: this was found to be a species of Catenary, called the Patristic Catenary, which is usually defined as "passing through origen, and containing many multiple points." The locus of HPL will be found almost entirely to coincide with this.[13]

Great results were expected from the assumption of (E+R) as a function of ν: but the opponents of this theorem having actually succeeded in demonstrating that the ν-element did not even enter into the function, it appeared hopeless to obtain any real value of π by this method.

III. Penrhyn's Method.

This was an exhaustive process for extracting the value of π in a series of terms, by repeated divisions.[14] The series so obtained appeared to be convergent, but the residual quantity was always negative, which of course made the process of extraction impossible.

This theorem was originally derived from a radical series in Arithmetical Progression: let us denote the series itself by A. P., and its sum by (A. P.)S. It was found that the function (A. P.)S. entered into the above process, in various forms.[15]

The experiment was therefore tried of transforming (A. P.)S. into a new scale of notation: it had hitherto been, through a long series of terms, entirely in the senary, in which scale it had furnished many beautiful expressions: it was now transformed into the denary.[16]

Under this modification, the process of division was repeated, but with the old negative result: the attempt was therefore abandoned, though not without a hope that future mathematicians, by introducing a number of hitherto undetermined constants, raised to the second degree, might succeed in obtaining a positive result.[17]

IV. Elimination of J.

It had long been perceived that the chief obstacle to the evaluation of π was the presence of J, and in an earlier age of mathematics J would probably have been referred to rectangular axes, and divided into two unequal parts—a process of arbitrary elimination which is now considered not strictly legitimate.[18]

It was proposed, therefore, to eliminate J by an appeal to the principle known as "*the permanence of equivalent formularies*": this, however, failed on application, as J became indeterminate. Some advocates of the process would have preferred that

J should be eliminated "*in toto*."[19] The classical scholar need hardly be reminded that "*toto*" is the ablative of "*tumtum*," and that this beautiful and expressive phrase embodied the wish that J should be eliminated by a compulsory religious examination.[20]

It was next proposed to eliminate J by means of a "*canonisant*:" the chief objection to this process was, that it would raise J to an inconveniently high power, and would after all only give an irrational value for π.[21]

Other processes, which we need not here describe, have been suggested for the evaluation of π. One was, that it should be treated as a *given* quantity: this theory was supported by many eminent men, at Cambridge and elsewhere; but, on application, J was found to exhibit a negative sign, which of course made the evaluation possible.[22]

We now proceed to describe the modern method, which has been crowned with brilliant and unexpected success, and which may be defined as

V. Evaluation Under Pressure.

Mathematicians had already investigated the locus of HPL, and had introduced this function into the calculation, but without effecting the desired evaluation, even when HPL was transferred to the opposite side of the equation, with a change of sign. The process we are about to describe consists chiefly in the substitution of G for P, and the application of pressure.[23]

Let the function ϕ (HGL) be developed into a series, and let the sum of this be assumed as a perfectly rigid body, moving in a fixed line; let "μ" be the coefficient of moral obligation, and "*e*" the expediency. Also let "F" be a Force acting equally in all directions, and varying inversely as T:[24]

We have now to develop ϕ (HGL) by Maclaurin's Theorem.[25]

The function itself vanishes when the variable vanishes:

i.e. $\phi\ (o) = O.$
differentiating under pressure, $\phi\ '\ (o) = C$ (a prime constant).
let P = J, and we get $\phi\ ''\ (o) = 2.J.$
differentiating for H, $\phi\ '''\ (o) = 2.3.H.$
let L = S, and we get $\phi\ ''''\ (o) = 2.3.4.S.$
let G = P, and we get $\phi\ '''''\ (o) = 2.3.4.5.P.$
let P = J, and we get $\phi\ ''''''\ (o) = 2.3.4.5.6.J.$
after which the quantities recur in the same order.

The above proof is taken from the learned treatise "*Augusti de fallibilitate historicorum*," and occupies an entire chapter: the evaluation of π is given in the next Chapter.[26] The author takes occasion to point out several remarkable properties, possessed by the above series, the existence of which had hardly been suspected before.

The series is a function of both μ and of e: but, when it is considered as a body, it will be found that $\mu = 0$, and that e only remains.

We now have the equation[27]

$$\phi\ (HGL) = O + C + J + H + S + P + J.$$

The summation of this gave a minimum value for π: this, however, was considered only as a first approximation, and the process was repeated under pressure F, which gave to π a partial maximum value: by continually increasing F, the result was at last obtained, $\pi = S = 500.00000$.[28]

The result differs considerably from the anticipated value, namely 400.00000: still there can be no doubt that the process has been correctly performed, and that the learned world may be congratulated on the final settlement of this most difficult problem.[29]

March, 1865.

[Lewis Carroll?]
"Small Debts and Heresies Court"

[*Punch* satirized religious topics throughout its publication history. Most of the religious jibes in the 1860s are directed at Pope Pius IX and his efforts to establish the hierarchy in England: hence, the large number of "no Popery" jokes. But in the period of the first substantial attacks on *Essays and Reviews*, a column on topics of the day entitled "Essays and Remarks" ran from 12 April to 31 May 1862.

This short satire was prompted by Jowett's trial in the Chancellor's Court in Oxford. The first hearing was on 13 February, when the case was postponed for a week. Meanwhile the papers were full of letters, especially by Pusey defending his suit on moral and theological grounds. This satire in *Punch* (dated 28 Feb. 1863, 87, but issued earlier in the week), republished in the *Times* on 26 February 1863 (7), focuses on a charge frequently made in this correspondence, that the Chancellor's Court was entirely inappropriate for such a hearing.

The first case concerns the theft of, or nonpayment for, the tarts, and the legal statute *De Tartibus* (Concerning tarts). The school-boy Latin pun translates as "Tarts are prohibited to girls and boys," echoing Horace, *Odes*, III.1. The first part of the phrase was used by R. L. Stevenson as a title for his collection of essays and travel notes, *Virginibus Puerisque* (1881). The phrase is perhaps echoed in the 8th stanza of "The Majesty of Justice" (above). *Jam satis* (enough, already) is from Horace, *Odes*, I.2.1. In the strongly antisemitic second case, Rattlecash is reading the play of Aeschylus that provided the scornful designation of the Essayists and Reviewers as the "Seven against Christ."

In the "Pusey v. Jowett" case, there are a number of pertinent jokes concerning the "Majesty of Justice" that Pusey invoked; Jowett's name is made to rhyme with "blow it"; the satire refers to his well-known refusal of the £2,000 testimonial collected by Russell and Lingen; Jowett is threatened with possible translation to Natal, the see of Colenso, then in the newspapers and courts over heresy charges.

Pusey's and Newman's involvement over Tract XC in interpreting the Articles of Religion in a "natural sense" had been recently in letters to the newspapers by Newman, Pusey, and Maurice (Letters 176, 180, 184, and 186). *Punch* also made reference to the "non-natural sense" in a poem on 7 March 1863 (100), printed on the same page as the second part of the "Small Debts and Heresies Court" satire:

Newman on Deglutition

Not in a sense non-natural,
But literal and grammatical,
Did I profess the Articles to sign.
I said that they who framed 'em,
At opposite sides aimed 'em,
That both might swallow all the Thirty-nine.

Which must, the inference is,
Each have two different senses
And two grammatical, either preferred
Without equivocation.
This candid explanation
Seems satisfactory and not absurd.

The Latin tags are *oram populo* (in the public court) and *Accusare* . . . (No one must prosecute himself).

On the basis of five kinds of circumstantial evidence we conjecture that the author of this anonymous satire is Lewis Carroll. First, as evidenced by the previous three satires, Carroll was deeply interested in Jowett's case in Oxford debates (where he spoke on it) and in the Chancellor's Court. Second, Carroll had sent various early satires to contemporary papers and journals, and from 1856 he published a number in the *Comic Times* and its successor, the *Train*; he also published reviews and fantasy poems in the *Illustrated Times* and *All the Year Round* (see Sidney Herbert Williams and Madden 1970, 14–16). Furthermore, he knew Tom Taylor, the dramatist who also worked for *Punch*, and through whom he was introduced in 1864 to *Punch*'s John Tenniel concerning illustrations for *Alice*. Third, Carroll frequently wrote and published parodic dialogues similar to "Small Debts and Heresies Court" (see, for instance, Carroll 1993, 75–78; 83–100; and 110–16). Many of the chapters of the Alice books are also in a similar dialogue format. Fourth, the stylistic feature of the Latin pun is a parodic strategy frequently deployed by Carroll, as in "The Greek Professorship" and the *New Method of Evaluation as*

Applied to Π, and as scattered throughout his parodic writings (see, for instance Carroll 1993, 42–43, 50, 95, and 133). The specific Latin pun *jam satis* anticipates the discussion of "jam" by the White Queen and Alice in chapter 5, "Wool and Water" of *Through the Looking-Glass*. Fifth, in *Alice's Adventures in Wonderland* (1865) there is parody of a court-room proceeding in which the theft of tarts, as in case one of "Small Debts and Heresies Courts" is the focus. Just as in the *New Method of Evaluation as Applied to Π* the satire is grounded upon a nursery rhyme, so too in chapter 11 of *Alice's Adventures* is the parody an elaboration of a child's poem—the same nursery rhyme ("The Queen of hearts she made some tarts") as that upon which the first case of this satire is structured. The publication of the first Alice book and this satire are almost simultaneous: the trip with the Liddell children had taken place on 4 July 1862, and Carroll wrote it up as *Alice's Adventures Under Ground* on 10 February 1863, exactly contemporaneous with the Jowett trial. *Alice's Adventures in Wonderland* was expanded from the 1863 version and was published in 1865 with chapter 11, "Who Stole the Tarts." At least one critic, Shane Leslie (1933), has gone so far as to suggest, perhaps as a pastiche of an academic paper, that *Alice in Wonderland* and *Through the Looking-Glass* are almost *romans à clef* with sustained references to the Essayists and their opponents. Without going so far as to search out such direct allusions to *Essays and Reviews* in Carroll's best-known literary productions, the Alice books, it is plausible to conjecture on the basis of these five reasons that Carroll is the author of the following parody.]

Small Debts and Heresies Court

Oxford, Tuesday

THE ASSESSOR took his seat as usual, and the list of cases was called over.

PATTYPAN *v*. FLIRTINGTON.

The plaintiff, an Oxford confectioner, claimed £11 3*s*. 6*d*., from the defendant, a handsome young Undergraduate, for goods supplied.

Assessor. Now, FLIRTINGTON, how will you pay?

Mr. Flirtington. Well, you know, look here—

Assessor. I don't know, and you mustn't tell the Court to look here. The Court looks here, there, and everywhere, just as it pleases.

Mr. Flirtington. Well, I didn't think the bill had run up so high.

Plaintiff. I don't want to press the gentleman, Sir, but he won't pay any attention to me.

Assessor. You don't come here to get attention paid, but debts. What is this debt?

Plaintiff. Well, Sir, Mr. FLIRTINGTON is a gentleman of very pleasing manners, and partial to the fair sex, which is all [very, added in the *Times* text] right and becoming at his time of life, and whenever he meets any ladies of his acquaintance he says, O come into old PATTYPAN's and have some tarts."

Assessor. This is all wrong, FLIRTINGTON. Don't you know what the Statute *De*

Tartibus says—*virginibusque puerisque tartes prohibiti sunt*, eh?
Plaintiff. They were jam tarts, chiefly, Sir.
Assessor. That's worse—what does HORACE say about *jam satis*? You'll be plucked, Mr. FLIRTINGTON, one of these fine days. Well, pay £5 this week and the rest in a month. Call the next case.

SHOBBUS *v*. RATTLECASH.

The plaintiff, a Hebrew jeweller, sued the defendant, SIR LIONEL RATTLECASH, BARONET, for £23 10s., the price of some rings.
Assessor. Now, RATTLECASH, how will you pay?
Sir Lionel. Nohow, your Assessorship.
Assessor. Come, come, that sort of answer won't do. If you're a baronet, behave as such. What do you object to?
Sir Lionel. Him, you, them, everything.
Assessor. This Court has the power of transportation, SIR LIONEL.
Sir Lionel. Very glad to hear it. Transport SHOBBUS for the rest of his unnatural life.
Plaintiff. Vot for? He ad the rings; be-u-tiful rings, lovely, fresh from Paris, vorthy to be presented to the PRINCESS HALEXANDER.
Assessor (*smiling*). PARIS AND ALEXANDER—tautology, eh, SIR LIONEL? I hope you read your HOMER?
Sir Lionel. Know him by heart. The fact is this, your Assessorship. I was in my rooms, busily engaged in translating the *Seven against Thebes*—
Plaintiff. He vos lying on his sophy, smoking like a steam Ingine out of a hookey.
Sir Lionel. Translating mentally, Israelite. I always take baccy with my Greek. In he comes with a trayful of his trash, and as they looked very smart, and he didn't care when he was paid, I let him leave half a dozen of his rings. I meant 'em for my cousins, but they ain't worth giving to a lady.
Plaintiff. They're shplendid, contiguous rings, and might be given promiscuous to any of the aristoxy.
Sir Lionel. I should like him to take 'em back.
Assessor. Come, SHOBBUS, that's fair. Take 'em back, and give a receipt.
Plaintiff. I shan't, I von't, it ain't justice. I'm not going to take a pack of rings like that for £23 10s.
Assessor. Just now you said they were valuable; you can't blow hot and cold. Give them back, SIR LIONEL, and let the clerk take a note of the arrangement. Call the next case.

PUSEY *v*. JOWETT.

The prosecutor, the notorious author of Puseyism, brought the defendant, the celebrated theologian and Greek Professor, before the Court for heresy.

Assessor. Now, JOWETT, how will you pay?
Professor Jowett (*smiling*). Pay, Sir? I apprehend—

Assessor. No, Sir, you don't apprehend, you are apprehended. Well, we will make it as easy as we can for you, though I must say it is your own fault that you are in difficulties. If you had taken the money which EARL RUSSELL, and all the other eminent men subscribed as a testimony to your merit, you would not have been obliged to borrow of DR. PUSEY. What's the amount, and how can we arrange it?
Professor Jowett. I rather think, Sir, that it is as a heretic, and not as a debtor, that I have the honour to be present here.
Assessor. Eh? Heresy. Oh! Then you haven't to pay. It's somebody else to pay and no pitch hot. Well, this is the shop for justice of all kinds. Ain't you ashamed of yourself? I hope you are. STIGGINS (*to a messenger*), go and fetch me the Fathers, take seven cabs, and look alive. Now, DR. PUSEY, I suppose you don't want to be hard on him?
Dr. Pusey. Yes, Sir, I do, but only for his good. I did wrong things in my time. I taught hypocrisy and non-naturalism. I was an enemy to the Church. I was punished severely. I was suspended. It did me such a deal of good that I am now a model and a pattern, and I wish the same salutary process performed on him.
Assessor. Well, JOWETT, you say you are a heretic?
Professor Jowett. I say nothing of the kind, Sir.
Assessor. Blow it, JOWETT, you did say you appeared as a heretic. Come, don't evade, but say you are sorry, and that'll be orthodox, and we'll not hurt you, for you are a first-rate Greek professor, and all that. Declare that you agree to the Articles, and all the rest of it, and that you have been misunderstood. Don't let's have a scandal *coram populo*.
Professor Jowett. My dear Mr. Assessor, while—
Assessor. No, don't go into detail. *Accusare nemo se debet*. You had better do as I say. You'll be satisfied, DR. PUSEY?
Dr. Pusey. If he will recant everything that he has written or said for the last seven years, declare his full concurrence, in a natural sense, mind, to everything in the Rubric and Canons, and apologise for his troubling me and the Church, I shall be content.
Assessor. There, JOWETT, come! Nothing can be more liberal or gentlemanly. I adjourn the case for a week, to give you time to think of it. If you don't comply at the next hearing, I shall transport you—send you to Natal, perhaps. Go along, heretic. Call the next case.
The Court was occupied with similar trifling business until the time of its rising.

[A second satire in *Punch* in the week of 7 March 1863 (100) continued the hearing of the Pusey *v*. Jowett case. It alludes to the correspondence in the *Times* with such contributors as Francis Close, dean of Carlisle, and F. D. Maurice (Letters 186–87), punning on both of their names; *to morris* was Oxford slang for "to be off" or dance away. The phrase "I am the Church of England" echoes Louis XIV's "I am the State" and anticipates Pius IX's comment at the Vatican Council of 1869–70, "I am tradition." The satire also refers to Pusey's notorious phrase "the Majesty of Justice" on which Carroll based his satiric poem. The Latin phrase *locus standi* means place to stand, or standing in the court; *adsum* means present or I am here; and *amicus curiae* means a friend of the court, presenting advice apart from the litigants.]

Oxford, Tuesday.

The Assessor took his seat, as usual, and by special order made as reported in our last, the first cause called was

PUSEY *v.* JOWETT.

Assessor. Are the parties here?
Dr. Pusey. Here you are, Sir.
Assessor. I know I am, Sir; but that is no answer to my question. However, appearance cures all defects. Are you here JOWETT?
Professor Jowett. Adsum.
Assessor. Don't say that, it sounds like "handsome" when you've got a cold in your head. Now, listen to me.
Dr. Close. If you please, Sir, my name is CLOSE, and *I* want to speak.
Assessor. You have no *locus standi.*
Dr. Close. I should have plenty if you would only tell MR. MAURICE, here, not to keep shoving.
Assessor. MAURICE, morris. CLOSE, shut up. Now, parties in the cause, attend to me.
Dr. Close. But, Sir, I have no confidence—
Assessor. I should say, Sir, that you had a great deal, to venture to speak after I have told you to be quiet.
Dr. Close. But I don't like any of the parties, Sir, and I don't like tobacco, which is more. Next to heresy, I consider tobacco to be the root of all evil, and I have stated as much to my clergy. Now you have got a very good opportunity of putting down tobacco and heresy at the same time, and in the name of the Church of England I call on you to do it.
Assessor. And what right do you have to speak for the Church of England? I am the Church of England, and I'll let you know it, if I hear another word from you.
Dr Close. I like to be persecuted, and I tell you that I believe PUSEY, JOWETT and MAURICE to be all dangerous parties, and I am not sure that you are much better.
Assessor (*in a rage*). Lock up DR. CLOSE till the Court rises, and let him have no refreshment but a short pipe. (*The Dean is removed quoting texts violently*). Now, perhaps, I may be attended to.
Mr. Maurice. I want to be heard as *amicus curiae.*
Assessor. Will you be so good as to allow me to choose my own friends? Hold your tongue.
Mr. Maurice. In MACMILLAN'S *Magazine*—
Assessor. One of the very best of the day, and therefore I read it, and therefore you need not quote it. Will you be silent?

Mr. Maurice. Only a word. I advise you, Sir, not to decide this case. The fact is, that nobody ought to decide upon anything. There are two kinds of belief. One is the common, natural kind, which does very well indeed for inferior persons of all classes. The other is esoteric, and is for educated minds. Now—

Assessor. Would you like to know what *I* believe?

Mr. Maurice. Well, I don't know that it much matters, but you can explain.

Assessor. I believe that in five minutes you'll wish you hadn't spoken. Lock up MR. MAURICE till the Court rises, and let him have no refreshment but one of the Tract Society's publications. (MR. MAURICE *is removed, drawing distinctions neatly*). Now it's my turn.

Dr. Pusey (*blandly*). You will not forget, Sir, that in my letter in this case I described you as the Majesty of Justice.

Assessor. More shame for you for writing such unmitigated bosh. I'm an old Judge in the country, but you can't come over me. JOWETT, I told you last week that I thought PUSEY's proposition, that you should recant all that you have been teaching for seven years, and declare yourself orthodox, was a liberal and gentlemanly offer. Since that time I have been reading the Fathers. It was severe work, and I had to take my coat off to think the harder. I have come to the conclusion, and I believe that I shall be supported by the best theologians of present and past days, that different people have different ideas on different subjects, and therefore I dismiss the case, recommend you both to mercy, and give no costs. Now, if you'll come up to my rooms, I'll send for CLOSE and MAURICE, and stand beer all round.

The learned Judge's decision was greeted with much applause, which was immediately suppressed, and the Court rose.

Anon.
"A Word of Advice to the Bishops"

[The "Episcopal Manifesto" was published in the *Times* on 16 February 1861, and by the end of the month the newspapers were reporting the extensive debate amongst the bishops in the Upper House of Convocation. On 13 March 1861 the 8,500 signatures added to the "Protest of the Clergy" were presented to the archbishop of Canterbury at Lambeth. In the same issue that published "A Word of Advice" (16 Mar. 1861, 109), *Punch* also printed an imaginary debate in the House of Bishops, entitled "Prelates at Play, or Prolusiones Episcopales," in which Archbishop Longley proposes they play a game of "episcopal epigrams." In this imaginary debate, Wilberforce is satirized as "saponaceous Oxford," a reference to his designation as "Soapy Sam." *Punch* comments: "It is not often that Bishops trifle—except on serious subjects; still seldomer that they deign to exchange the dark dredging box, from which they besprinkle Essayists and Reviewers with pungent and bitter *Odium Theologicum*, for the Classic cyathus (wine-cup) flavoured with Attic salt" (113). It is in this context that *Punch* suggested that instead of condemnation from the bishops a better response might be refutation.]

Denounce Essayists and Reviewers,
Hang, quarter, gag or shoot them—
Excellent plans—provided that
You first of all refute them.

By all means let the Hangman burn
Their awful book to ashes,
But don't expect to settle thus
Their heterodox hashes.

Some heresies are so ingrained,
E'en burning won't remove them,
A shorter and an easier way
You'll find it—to disprove them.

Be this, right reverends, your revenge,
For souls the best of cure[s]—
Essay Essayists to upset,
And to review Reviewers.

Anon.
"A Clerical Congratulation"

[On 25 June 1862 Lushington delivered the interlocutory judgment against Williams and Wilson, ordering that some of the charges against them had to be reformed or revised. On 12 September 1862 the reformed Articles of Charge were presented in the Court of Arches, and, after formal presentations, the hearing was postponed until 15 December when Lushington would deliver his final judgment. The day after the reformed charges were presented, *Punch* printed a letter ostensibly from the Essayists and Reviewers (13 Sept. 1862, 113). St. James's Day is 25 July.]

Dear Punch,
There can be no doubt that the intellect of mankind is in a progressive state, and that we are much wiser than our forefathers.

This consideration has just been forced upon us, the undersigned, by the historical statements which have appeared in reference to the departure of the

Nonconformist clergy from the Church of England upon the Act of Uniformity coming into operation.

A couple of thousand clergymen (more or fewer) resigned their livings, because they would not say that they believed in the whole contents of the Prayer Book.

Since that time, Sir, intellect has advanced, and did those good, but narrow-minded men live in our days, the Church would not need to lose their services.

Suppose that some Essayists and Reviewers in the time of CHARLES THE SECOND had made it clear to these two thousand clergymen, that in solemnly declaring their belief in the contents of the Prayer Book, they only meant that they were complying with what was generally understood in society to be a mere form, and that they were at liberty to believe as much or as little as they liked, provided that they accepted the Prayer Book in the spirit of men of the world, and did not scandalise their parishes by any out-of-the-way doctrines.

Had there happily existed such teachers in the times of the Nonconformists, those men might just as well have remained in the Church, and taken her honours and emoluments, as

Your obedient Servants,

St. James's Day, 1862. The ESSAYISTS AND REVIEWERS

Anon.
"A Non-Natural Prosecution"

[This satire in *Punch* (28 Feb. 1863, 84) lampoons the notion of the "non-natural" sense of interpreting the Thirty-nine Articles from the Pusey-Maurice exchange in the *Times* referred to in the comment on Satire 4 above.]

THE FOLLOWING extract in a letter which has appeared in the *Times* is rather good:—

> "Yet there has been of late a most large and systematic claim put forth that we clergy not only should inquire, but that, although our inquiries should, unhappily, in the case of any of us, end in the loss of our faith, we should still continue to act as clergy. A claim has been made to affix new meanings to words, and so to subscribe our formularies in senses which they will not bear" [Pusey to the *Times* 17 Feb. 1863; Letter 175.]

The name subscribed to the epistle which contains the foregoing complaint is that of E. B. PUSEY; date, Christ Church. What! Can this be the reverend and celebrated DR. PUSEY, after whom mankind have nicknamed a sect? Is this the PUSEY supposed to have originated the Puseyites? And is it the Puseyite PUSEY who complains that "a claim has been made to affix new meanings to words, and to subscribe our formularies in senses which they will not bear?" There may possibly be a coolness exceeding that of the GRACCHI complaining of sedition. Surely we seem to remember that there were certain persons who used to stickle for the right of signing certain articles in a non-natural sense. Is PUSEY of the Puseyites the PUSEY who so speaks of this subterfuge as if he now considered it humbug?

E. B. PUSEY writes to the *Times* in justification of the part which he has taken as one of the prosecutors of PROFESSOR JOWETT on account of that Professor's theological opinions, raked up out of a book published several years ago. But, surely, there was a PUSEY, who, not much longer ago, was suspended at Oxford for teaching false doctrine. Was not that an E. B. PUSEY, too? Is JOWETT's prosecutor only a namesake of that PUSEY, or has DR. PUSEY suffered persecution and not learned mercy? In that case, has DR. PUSEY recanted his errors? Has he cried *peccavi*? If not, how can he walk into PROFESSOR JOWETT, and why does he not walk out of the Church?

Unhappily there is no way out of the Church that leads anywhere except to the workhouse—if, even, a Clergyman is eligible as an inmate of that asylum. Once a parson always a parson, though stripped of his preferment, and forbidden to get any other living. If JOWETT could legally get called to the Bar of judicature, or instal himself behind that of a public-house, or indeed take to any honest line of secular business, then PUSEY, before prosecuting him, should invite him to adopt that course, and set him the example of so doing.

Anon.
"De Haeretico Comburendo"

[This satire was published in *Punch* (7 Mar. 1863, 92). The title of the poem (Lat. concerning the burning of heretics) derives from the fourteenth-century Statute 2 Henry IV. c.15 on the procedures to be used for the treatment of heretics. It gave power to the diocesan bishop alone, without a synod to give a hearing or advice, to pronounce a sentence of heresy on an offender, and required the sheriff to burn the heretic without waiting for consent by the state or ruler. The act was specifically mentioned in the proceedings against Jowett in the Chancellor's Court in Oxford on 20 January 1863, as one of the reference points for the treatment of heresy. The Latin phrase *laudari a laudato* means to be praised by the praised; *accusari ab accusato*, to be accused by the accused; the Italian *con brio* means with brilliance.]

"DE HAERETICO COMBURENDO!"

A LITTLE book PROFESSOR JOWETT made,
And argued not as one of truth afraid;
But Oxford Dons alike fear truth and JOWETT,
Their late proceedings not a little show it.

Drone-like, in hopes this working-bee to drive
Out from the comfort of their close-packed hive,
To cut his honey off, votes every drone,
Gauging his love of lucre by their own.

"When *we* object to work, even for pay,
Much less will *he* toil, salary ta'en away;"
But, baffling calculation and conjecture,
Lo, JOWETT, without fee, still chose to lecture!

Puzzled to deal with this heresiarch awful,
Now fire and faggot are no longer lawful,
Failing Star-Chamber's aid, or Convocation's,
Still the Vice-Chancellor's Court admits citations!

'Tis true its usual work no higher mounts,
Than rapid undergraduates' "small accounts,"
But Charters give its Bench power to affix
  A brand on here—(as on other) ticks.

"Let PUSEY's voice bespeak our dread of truth,
And teach this vile perverter of our youth,
That if 'tis well '*laudari a laudato,*'
'Tis grievous '*accusari ab accusato,*'

"Still scarred with Oxford's missiles freely thrown,
What hand as PUSEY's fit to cast the stone?
What he may want in spirit or in skill,
He will make up in venom and ill-will."

It only needs to drive the lesson home,
That NEWMAN should be summoned back from Rome;
And HAMPDEN called in to complete the trio,
JOWETT's indictment to conduct "*con brio!*"

Oh, for a holocaust of heretics,
With Jowett in one common ban to mix,
For leave to burn, hang, quarter, disembowel,
MAURICE and WILLIAMS, TEMPLE, WILSON, POWELL!

To teach admiring minds these Acts who follow,
That Oxford toleration's wide of swallow,
As wide as from Geneva to Maynooth,
But one thing it *won't* tolerate—the truth!

Anon.
"Extremes Meet"

[One of several rivals to *Punch* was *Judy, or the London Serio-Comic Journal*, a weekly that ran from 1867 to 1907, published by Gilbert Dalziel. Accompanying the cartoon entitled "Extremes Meet" (see fig. 21), was a poem (*Judy* 27 Oct. 1869, 7). The "spoiler of the Irish Church" is Gladstone whose Act for the Disestablishment of the Irish Church (26 July 1869) terminated the status of the Anglican Church in Ireland as the state church on 1 January 1871. The act was bitterly resented by many Conservatives in England. Temple strongly supported the measure as did Pusey.

But Pusey opposed Temple's appointment to the see of Exeter. In "Extremes Meet" Pusey is a ritualist, or "Puseyite," holding a manual of ritual to identify him, and wearing a cope. His other "extreme" is Lord Shaftesbury, Anthony Ashley Cooper, 7th Earl Shaftesbury, the reformer of working-class factory conditions in the Ten Hours' Bill (1847) and the Factory Act (1874). He was a leading Evangelical and opponent of ritualism. They were in league to block Temple's appointment, the topic of the poem and cartoon. See Letters 223, 225, 287, 296, and 308.]

Extremes Meet

The spoiler of the Irish Church,
With victory elate,
Temple essays at once to raise
To the Episcopate.
Th'appointment rouses to the fight
The shepherd of each fold!
And even those that once were foes
The hand of friendship hold.
When High and Low their voices raise
In condemnation strong;
When sects unite, resolved to fight,
Against a mighty wrong;—
'Tis time the Nation's voice was heard
Condemning those who fain
The Church from State would separate,
And England's fair name stain.

Notes on Satires by Lewis Carroll and Others

1. Sidney Herbert Williams and Madan 1970, 26; see also Carroll 1993, 17–18; the pamphlet is reprinted in Carroll 1939, 1011–16; and in Carroll 1993, 19–25.

2. Between the title and the first line of the text *1874* adds:

"Little Jack Horner
Sat in a Corner
Eating a Christmas Pie."

In *1993* there are no quotation marks.

3. For "really" *1874* reads "in reality."

The constant ratio of the circumference of a circle to its diameter is indicated by the Greek letter π, first used (1706) for this ratio by William Jones (1675–1749) and made conventional (1737) by Leonhard Euler (1707–1783). The ratio was known to the Egyptians and Babylonians from about 2000 B.C.E., and to the Hebrews (1 Kings 7:23, 26). The Greek mathematician Archimedes (c. 287–212 B.C.E.), in his treatise *The Measurement of the Circle*, determined the value of π as greater than $3^{10}/_{71}$ and less than $3^{1}/_{7}$, calculated by inscribing polygons inside and outside the circumference of a circle. This computation continued with only slight modification until the advent of calculus in the eighteenth century. The decimal extension of π (3.14159265. . .) is infinite. For a historical and mathematical discussion see Beckmann 1971.

"Ignis fatuus" (Lat. foolish fire) means "Will-o-the-wisp" or swamp fire, an illusory beacon or goal.

The letters suggesting algebraic equations refer to the major protagonists of the Greek Professorship debate: U = Oxford University; GP = Greek Professor, namely, Benjamin Jowett [J], whose stipend was "reduced to its lowest terms." He was known at Oxford for being the first incumbent of the chair to give public lectures and to tutor students [W, "work done"]. The controversy was reported widely in the papers, including the *Times* [T]. The existing value for *p* (the given payment) is £40 per annum. The proper value for π, according to the *Times*, should be £400, the stipend paid to the other Regius Professors.

4. For "commensurable" *1993* reads "commensurate".

In *1874* the following sentence was added as a separate paragraph to this section: "We shall conclude with an account of the great discovery of our own day, the Method of Evaluation under Pressure."

5. The first method consists of rationalizing the calculation of π. As applied to Jowett and the endowment for the Greek chair, this method involves providing rational arguments either justifying why the inequalities exist or why they should be eliminated. When such arguments made in the Hebdomadal Council were not forthcoming, or proved unpersuasive, the Council voted (the *ys* or wise votes as yeas against the nays) as Carroll describes. The combination of High Church and Low Church voters on the council defeated the Broad Church supporters through "repeated trials" to no effect. That is, they voted "no," thereby giving a "negative sign" to any effort to rationalize the endowment for the Greek chair. "Rationalisation" also puns on "rationalism," the charge brought against Jowett, the other writers in *Essays and Reviews*, and his Broad Church supporters.

6. Carroll puns on mathematical "partial factions" (that is, fractions) for party factions, associated with High, Low, and Broad Church parties divided on the basis of their theology. "Combinations" was the term applied to the collaborators in *Essays and Reviews* in the Court of Arches, that they had combined in concert to present a consistent theology, and so all of their works should be condemned together, the point returned to in the Synodical Condemnation of 1864. In addition "combinations" refers to the alignment of High and Low Church parties (symbolized by the collaboration of Pusey and Heurtley, as well as Pusey and Shaftesbury at the time of the Oxford Declaration on the Inspiration of the Word of God in 1864) to defeat the proposals to raise the endowment for the Greek chair. Hence the algebraic equation, $HL - B^2$, places the High-Low combination on one side of the equation, and the Broad Church squared on the other.

7. Oxford University, as well as the C. of E., took sides concerning Jowett [J] and Pusey, here designated as P, and divided into factions according to Anglican party politics, with the alignment of High Church (Pusey, Keble, and Liddon, amongst others) and Low Church (Heurtley and Ogilvie) against Jowett and his Broad Church supporters. The algebraic signs *x* and *y* traditionally designate unknown quantities.

The repeated efforts to raise the endowment were problematic in their outcome because of the "unknown quantities" of voters for the meetings in the Hebdomadal Council, Convocation, and Congregation. "Repeated trials" refers both to these efforts through Oxford's governing bodies, the formal "trial" of Jowett in the Chancellor's court, and the trials of Williams and Wilson in the Court of Arches and their appeals to the Judicial Committee. "Corresponding with P" suggests the numerous letters of Pusey and his respondents in the public press (Letters 175–202).

8. For "resorted to, and" *1874* reads "resorted to with a view to simplifying the equation, and."

For "was finally abandoned." *1874* reads "was

finally abandoned. That the *y*'s were all on one side." Carroll repeatedly puns on *y* throughout this passage: "to discover *y* [why]. . . . the *y*'s [wise = yea or yes votes] were all on one side." He also puns on "process" as both mathematical procedure and legal action, especially pertinent because Jowett's prosecutors abandoned the legal "process" by not appealing Bernard's decision to the Court of Queen's Bench.

9. The second method of evaluating π presupposes that there will be no difference between the endowment of the Greek chair and the other Regius Professorships. As a version of the "method of finite Differences" it draws on the much-publicized difference between Jowett's £40 and the others' £400 or more.

10. In this section Carroll extends his satire by making reference to *Essays and Reviews*. The Essayists were accused of "co-ordinating" their writing during the Court of Arches trial that condemned Williams and Wilson in 1862.

Carroll refers to a popular point of attack against *Essays and Reviews*, that they have breadth (they are Broad Church or liberal) and are long, but have no theological depth. They were also attacked as abandoning traditional modes of interpretation and theological positions in favor of "novelty" or "neology."

"Superficies" has a technical meaning in geometry, exactly as Carroll gives it; it also refers to whatever is superficial or trivial. The Greek letter ν (*nu*), indicating a variable in mathematics, is punningly associated by Carroll with "novelty," the Greek letter standing for the initial letter of the English word, a practice Carroll follows throughout. The letter *v.* also stands in the Latin alphabet for *versus*, as in the title of a lawsuit ("Pusey *v.* Jowett"). A "difference" is the remainder left when one quality is subtracted from another: there is a "difference" between the salary of Jowett and that of the other Regius Professors. "Indifference" refers to the lack of concern that was attributed to Pusey and his supporters in not being concerned with the equitable treatment of Jowett.

11. By manipulating the letters as standing for items previously defined, and moving further in combining them into initials for the participants in the Oxford politics surrounding the endowment debate, Carroll develops a series of equations. They suggest the following correspondences:

[E] Essays = [R] Reviews = [B] a Broad Church production

∴ [EB] Essays and Reviews as a Broad Church production = [B^2] Broad Church Squared = [HL] High-Low (the coalition under Pusey and Heurtley that formed against Jowett).

Multiplying by [P] Professor, gives [EBP] Broad Church Essay by the Professor of Greek (and also the initials for his chief opponent, Edward Bouverie Pusey)

= [HPL] High Church / Professor / Low Church, (and also the initials for Pusey's chief disciple and eventual biographer Henry Parry Liddon).

Liddon (1829–1890) was a Student of Christ Church with Carroll. At the time of these debates Liddon was vice-principal of St. Edmund Hall, Oxford (1859–62), and prebendary of Salisbury (1864). Liddon usually sided with Pusey, and hence the equation EBP = HPL, but voted in the Hebdomadal Council against Pusey's motion to increase the stipend. Liddon and Dodgson traveled together to Russia in 1867.

12. The equation HL = B^2 was demonstrated in the "last article" or method, "Rationalisation." In Carroll's elaborate joke on reading pseudo algebra as representative of Oxford politics and theological controversy, the "last article" is the thirty-ninth of the Articles of Religion, "Of a Christian Man's Oath." It sets out under what conditions, especially doctrinal, it is allowable to swear an oath. It was this "Article" that permitted clergy to swear or subscribe to the Thirty-nine Articles at ordination. Jowett was required by those who doubted his orthodoxy to undertake such a subscription before the vice-chancellor in December 1855 (Letter 1).

13. In this paragraph the "locus," or location, of Pusey and Liddon is set out in terms of both their associations with Tractarianism (and especially with patristic theology) and with the Chapter of Christ Church which had for so long resisted raising Jowett's stipend. The comparison is decked out in mathematical language that is susceptible to doubles entendres throughout.

A "catenary" [Lat. *catena*, chain] in mathematics is the curve produced by a chain of uniform density hanging freely from two fixed points, whose description was investigated by Jacques Bernoulli in *Acta Eruditorum* (1691).

In theology a catena is a connected series of extracts, and the phrase "Patristic Catenary" is a translation of the Latin *catena patrum*, a series of quotations from the Church Fathers commenting on scripture or a doctrinal point. Pusey and others associated with J. H. Newman produced *The Library of the Fathers of the Catholic Church*, a collection of translations of early Christian writings in many volumes, the first being Pusey's translation of Augustine's *Confessions* (1838).

In a mathematical catenary, the lowest point of the curve is referred to as the "origin" (O). Carroll puns on the name of the early Christian writer Origen, referred to a number of times by the Essayists for his allegorical or mystical interpretations of the Bible. For example, Rowland Williams writes: "When Jerome Origenises, he is worse than Origen, because he does not, like that great genius, distinguish the historical from the mystical sense . . . . We are promised from Oxford farther elucidations of the Minor Prophets by the Regius Professor of Hebrew [Pusey], whose book seems launched sufficiently to catch the gales of friendship, without yet tempting out of harbour the blasts of criticism. Let us hope that, when the work appears, its interpretations may differ from those of a *Catena Aurea*, published under high auspices in the same university" (Williams ¶13 and note).

The reference to "multiple points" is perhaps an allusion to the many points of High Church doctrine tested and proved by reference to the Church Fathers or to Pusey's penchant for doctrinal elaboration in, for example, his many letters to the press on religious controversies. In any event, Pusey is identified with this effort to go back to "origins" in the Church Fathers as his "locus." Liddon did the same.

14. The third method of calculating the value of π refers to the efforts to increase the endowment of the Greek chair (that is, to divide the "pie") by Jowett's friend Arthur Penrhyn Stanley, referred to in this method by his initials, whereby "S" can also refer conveniently to the "sum" of the series, and the sum total of the increase in the endowment Stanley seeks. Stanley was Regius Professor of Ecclesiastical History from 1856 to 1864 and was a member of the Hebdomadal Council during the debates on this matter. Stanley repeatedly introduced proposals to increase the endowment for the Greek Professor; some of his motions passed that body, but before being accepted as statues they had to be approved by Congregation and Convocation.

Each stage required a "division," or vote; the "series of terms" refers to the many academic terms at Oxford through which this exercise was played out. While from time to time the series seemed possible of success ("convergent") the resident canons and Heads of Houses (the masters or principals of the various colleges, or the "residual quantity") always voted against such a proposal, and hence the "extraction" of an increase in the endowment proved impossible.

15. The "radical" series is appropriate here because of the application of the term in mathematics to the root of any number, and in geometry to the radius of a circle, both connected with the determination of π. The "Arithmetical Progression" would augment the sum paid to the Professor of Greek, and would divide the financial pie to ensure such a sum. Stanley and his Broad Church colleagues like Jowett and the Essayists were viewed as theological "radicals."

16. In mathematics "senary" refers to the number six, to a scale based on six, or to a series of six (particularly in the seventeenth century to the six days of creation); "denary" refers to the number 10, or signifies a number system based on 10. The phrases "senary" and "denary" refer to Stanley's publication of "scenery," or travel writings, especially *Scenes of Travel in Sinai and Palestine* (1856) and perhaps his *Lectures on the History of the Eastern Church* (1861), in which he set out the historic scenes especially concerning the Council of Nicaea (325). In addition, Stanley was well known for his "beautiful expressions" as a stylist in his writing and sermons. A further possible pun in "senary" involves the term for a diocese or "see." In 1863 and 1864 Stanley's name was often mentioned as a possible candidate for a bishopric; in 1864, however, he was appointed to the "denary," as dean of Westminster.

17. The mathematical phrase "raised to the second degree" (*OED*, s.v. "degree," meaning 12) is applied to those graduates of Oxford who, after obtaining the B.A. waited a specified number of terms, paid the required fee, and were then "raised to the second degree" of M.A., and as such were allowed to vote in Convocation. Only when there were sufficient Broad Church M.A. holders to be "constant" would the vote carry there—hence the projection of a long period of time.

18. The fourth method involves the removal of J[owett] from the calculations for a new value for π. That is, the matter of increasing the endowment for the Greek chair could be accomplished without theological compromise were he not the incumbent. Hence, Pusey's effort to have him removed through the charges in the Chancellor's Court. In this method Carroll satirizes the proceeding as though it were a medieval heresy trial, ending in the drawing and quartering or the burning of the heretic, thereby accomplishing the "elimination of J."

In mathematics, an "axis" (plural "axes") is the straight line that passes through parallel sections of a geometrical figure. The pun plays on this mathematical use in dividing the pie, and the notion of the ax used against heretics in "an earlier age." To eliminate J[owett], he could be cut in two unequal portions ("divided") by the ax, already metaphorically attempted in his heresy trial.

19. Formularies" refers to the "articles and formularies" of the C. of E.: the *BCP*, the Canons and Constitutions, and *The Book of Homilies*. In the legal actions against Williams and Wilson in the Court of Arches, they were alleged to have contravened the doctrines of the Formularies, as was Jowett in his trial before the Chancellor's Court.

20. *In toto* means in all, on the whole, entirely (Lat. *totus*, all, whole); the *OED* gives "tootoo" as a variant of "toto" as a reduplicated form of the English "too." While the false derivation of *toto* as the Latin ablative of *tumtum* is fictitious, assuming a Latin noun "tum," the ablative would presumably be "to" in the neuter singular of the second declension. The Latin temporal adverb *tum* (meaning "then") could be repeated at the beginning of clauses, *tum . . . tum . . .* , meaning "sometimes . . . sometimes. . ." or "now . . . now. . . ." *Tumtum* is also mid- to late-nineteenth-century slang for a monotonous rhythm. The term *Tumtum tree* was used later by Carroll in "Jaberwocky" in *Through the Looking-Glass* (1871).

The "compulsory religious examination" refers specifically to Jowett's trial before the Chancellor's Court. In addition, "a compulsory religious examination" has a more general application in that it was a requirement for Moderations and Final Schools Examinations at Oxford, in which candidates for all degrees were examined upon the Thirty-nine Articles of Religion, the Greek New Testament, Paley's *Evidences of Religion*, the Old and New Testaments, and the history of the church. Further, subscription to the articles, required of every Oxford undergraduate before matriculation under the Test Act of 1673, was only ended with the University Test Act of 1871. Subscription was also incumbent upon clergy before ordination and could be required of those in holy orders teaching at Oxford. Jowett was compelled to subscribe to the articles before the vice-chancellor, R. L. Cotton in December 1855.

21. A "canonizant" in mathematics is the "attributive of an equation by the solution of which a quantic [a rational, integral function of two or more variables] may be reduced to the 'canonical form'" (*OED*). Regius Professorships at Oxford, such as that in Hebrew (held by Pusey), were often supplemented by appointment as a canon at Christ Church Cathedral, to which Christ Church College was attached. To be "canonized" was the term used for enrolling a person in the calendar of saints, often jokingly or obsoletely used for the installation of a canon. Carroll proposes that if that were to happen in Jowett's case he would be put into a position of political power. In mathematics, a "power" is the product of multiplying a number into itself a specified number of times.

22. This passage is a reference to the subscription of £2,000 "given" by Jowett's friends to cover his lost income in the previous five years. Jowett declined the gift but was grateful for the support (Letter 149). "Cambridge and elsewhere" echoes the phrase in the monition or charge against Jowett in the Chancellor's court, "Oxford and elsewhere," describing where Jowett published his "heresies." It was this phrase that was vigorously attacked by his lawyer as vague and meaningless, though it was allowed by the assessor, Montague Bernard.

23. The final method of calculating the value of π depends upon public pressure in the press, the failure of all legal efforts to bring heresy charges, and the pressure within the university to address the inequality of the endowment for the Greek chair. In particular the personal pressure of the dean of Christ Church, H. G. Liddell (HGL), on the governing body, the Chapter, was decisive. He convinced the Chapter to accede to raising the endowment only when, as Pusey had argued before, the endowment should be for the Greek Professorship not for the incumbent, and could not be seen as condoning the theological views of Jowett. Hence the substitution of G[reek Professorship] for P [the professor].

The references throughout this section of Carroll's satire are to the letters to the *Daily News* by Edward Augustus Freeman (1823–1892), one of Jowett's former students, and later Regius Professor of Modern History at Oxford. In October 1864 his letters to the press showed that the documents submitted by the "Chapter" of Christ Church in 1854 to the Ecclesiastical Commissioners indicated their willingness to endow the Greek Professorship for £400 from their estates. When Pusey and others denied that estates were conveyed to Christ Church by Henry VIII for that purpose, that too was demonstrated in a letter to the *Times* by another of Jowett's students, Charles Isaac Elton (see Trials and Appeals).

24. For "Force" *1993* reads "force".

For "as T:" *1874* "let A = Able, and E = Enlightened."

The Greek letter phi (ϕ) is a mathematical symbol for a function, the letter mu (μ) a coefficient, and the letter *e* an exponential; here the "function" of Liddell was to ensure that the "rigid body" of the Chapter of Christ Church, which had hitherto moved in a fixed line concerning the Greek Professor's stipend, move from their fixed notion of not increasing the stipend. They were now forced by both moral obligation and public pressure, but still would not move. The argument from expedience finally was accepted, when Liddell's F[orce] was put on the whole Chapter, varying according to the accounts in the *Times* (T). Carrol's term "expediency" was the actual word invoked by the Chapter of Christ Church that allowed them to salve their collective conscience—and grant the stipend (see Trials, p. 802). After the function is expanded below, Carroll asserts that moral obligation is nothing (0) and only expediency remains.

The symbol "A" for "Able," added in *1874*, is a reference to Charles Abel Heurtley (1806–1895), Lady Margaret Professor of Divinity, who with Pusey and Ogilvie was one of the prosecutors of Jowett before the Chancellor's Court. In the debate in the newspapers, many writers called for Christ Church to fulfil its "moral obligation," trying to shame the intransigent Chapter (the "perfectly rigid body") into paying for the endowment. Eventually they took legal advice, and were informed that, notwithstanding the historical information adduced by Freeman and Elton, there was no "moral obligation" to increase the endowment. Liddell brought more pressure to bear, and eventually they agreed, on the basis of "expediency," so that a decision was sent to the vice-chancellor on 17 February 1865, informing him of their willingness to increase the endowment to £500.

25. Colin Maclaurin (1698–1746), Scottish mathematician, was elected professor of mathematics at Marischal College, Aberdeen, when he was 19 years of age. He became a fellow of the Royal Society in 1719, met Sir Isaac Newton, and published his

Geometria organica, sive descriptio linearum curvarum universalis (Organic geometry, according to the description of universal curved lines). His greatest work was *Treatise on Fluxions* (1742), an eighteenth-century name for calculus, that won (with Euler and Bernoulli) the prize offered by the French Academy of Sciences for an essay on tides. On Maclaurin see Tweedle 1915; and Turnbull 1951.

Carroll's example is a standard expansion of a function according to Maclaurin's theorem.

26. Lat. On the fallibility of the historians of Augustus. This fictitious title refers to Freeman's middle name as the historian who indicated the fallibility of the historians of the "Chapter" of Christ Church.

27. The expansion is roughly as follows: The ϕ (function) of HGL (Liddell) equals Oxford + Christ Church + Jowett + Heresy [?] + Stanley + Pusey + Jowett.

28. For "pressure F, which" *1874* reads "pressure EAF, which."

For "increasing F, the" *1874* reads "increasing EAF, the."

Carroll changed the reference to Liddell's F[orce] in *1865* to the initials of Freeman in *1874*.

The final division of the pie results in a stipend of £500 for the Greek Professorship.

29. The anticipated stipend for the Greek Professorship, one repeatedly brought forward by Pusey, was £400.

6 *Essays and Reviews* and Bishop Colenso's "Great Scandal"

JUST as *Essays and Reviews* was arousing clerical concern and episcopal ire in 1861, a colonial bishop, John William Colenso, bishop of Natal, raised the heretical stakes by publishing two controversial books in quick succession, *St. Paul's Epistle to the Romans* (1861) and *The Pentateuch and Book of Joshua Critically Examined* (1862). Both raised problems in the same fields as those provoked by *Essays and Reviews*: Jowett's and F. D. Maurice's views were seen to inspire the former, and Colenso himself claimed *Essays and Reviews* and Lushington's judgment prompted his publication of the latter. The deleterious effect of the *Essays and Reviews* infection became apparent to all and had even corrupted the teaching office of the church in its episcopacy.

John William Colenso (1814–1883) was a graduate and had been a fellow of St. John's College, Cambridge, and tutor of mathematics at Harrow and St. John's. He published a widely used school text, *Arithmetic, Designed for the Use of Schools* (1843), making his name a byword for factual accuracy. He was appointed bishop of the new province of Natal in Africa in 1853 and took up the task of translating the Bible into Zulu with the help of Zulu assistants who raised questions concerning belief in what they were translating. His missionary activities had forced him into contact with the issues of higher criticism. His book on Romans extended the lectures Colenso gave to his Mission workers in 1854, as "a deliberate statement of doctrinal policy made by the most important missionary in South Africa" (Hinchliff 1964, 79). Colenso's *Romans* follows the teaching of F. D. Maurice on the atonement in rejecting the penal substitution theory, "that Christ died in order to take upon himself the *punishment* due to human sin . . . to placate an angry Father" (Hinchliff 1964, 80). Simplifying Maurice, Colenso denied "that God really has any righteous anger against sin at all," only having Christ pay the "debt of nature which sin had the right to demand of Him" (Colenso [1861] 1863, 96 ff.). He argued: "The Apostle [Paul] does not say that *God is reconciled to us* by the Death of His Son, but that *we are reconciled to God*" (Colenso 1863, 108). In thus paying the debt to nature once, all people everywhere are redeemed, a position that was close to Wilson's at the end of his essay, and a position on which he was condemned in the Court of Arches. But behind that dispute were Jowett's writings in *The Epistles of St. Paul* on the atonement that seemed to many of Colenso's critics the closest and most dangerous parallel. Two of Colenso's clergy, the Evangelical, Archdeacon Fearne and the High Churchman, Dean James Green wrote to Colenso on 25 October protesting his views on atonement, submitting their correspondence to Bishop Robert Gray, Colenso's metropolitan. Gray was a "moderate Tractarian and a strong Tory" (Owen Chadwick 1966–70, 2:91), and hence opposed to Colenso on both doctrinal and political grounds.

Colenso was already involved in several fields of controversy: in 1857–58 a dispute had arisen between him and the High Church clergy of his diocese over the doctrine of the Real Presence of Christ in the Eucharist. The clergy wrote to Robert Gray about possible charges of heresy. Gray consulted with Wilberforce in England. A second controversy concerned Colenso's move to establish synodical government, in which he was resisted by fiercely independent congregations and clergy.

Between April and May 1862, Part 1 of Colenso's *The Pentateuch and Book of Joshua Critically Examined*, was "set up and roughly printed" in South Africa (Hinchliff 1964, 85). Its publication in England coincided with the tenth edition of *Essays and Reviews*. Colenso had begun his research on the Pentateuch in January 1861, reading, as he declares in his preface, *Essays and Reviews*, the responses to the essays (especially *Aids to Faith* and *Replies to Essays and Reviews*), and a substantial amount of German theology, including Hengstenberg's traditionalist *Dissertation on the Genuineness of the Pentateuch*, as well as Ewald's more radical studies. He read the German biblical critics, Wilhelm De Wette and his student Friedrich Bleek on the Old Testament, and completed his draft in February or March, just after Wilson's case was being heard in the Court of Arches. In May the Convocation of Canterbury met and planned an attack against Colenso for his views on atonement in *Romans*. Wilberforce led the attack against Colenso, supported by Hamilton of Salisbury and Sumner of Winchester, three bishops particularly active against *Essays and Reviews*. Tait advocated postponement of the debate. In an exchange of letters, Colenso refused to meet the English bishops together, only singly.

The English edition of the first part of Colenso's *Pentateuch* was published on 29 October 1862 by Longman, the same publishers as *Essays and Reviews*, selling 8,000 copies in three weeks, amounting to four editions.[1] In the preface Colenso mentions Lushington's interlocutory judgment of 25 June (1862–79, 1:xxiv, xxxiii) and argues that it gave him freedom under the Articles of Religion to qualify his subscription to the Anglican Formularies to "'unfeignedly believe all the Canonical Scriptures of the Old and New Testament,' which, with the evidence now before me, it is impossible wholly to believe in" (1862–79, 1:xii). Colenso distances himself from the Essayists: "There are not a few points, on which I differ strongly with these writers," but acknowledges his decisive debt to them: "After reading that article [by Wilberforce in the *Quarterly*], I felt more hopelessly than ever how hollow is the ground, upon which we have so long been standing, with reference to the subject of the Inspiration of Scripture" (1862–79, 1:9–11). In *The Pentateuch* Colenso takes up the matters where his expertise can be brought to bear—the citations of demographic statistics, pointing out the numerical incongruities to challenge the literalism and belief in factual inerrancy of each of the biblical writers who were "*preserved . . . from error of every kind in the records they made*," as John Henry Pratt argued in *Science and Scripture Not at Variance* (also cited by Goodwin in ¶43; see Colenso 1862–79, 1:4).

In the light of such assertions of biblical inerrancy, Colenso addresses the notorious question of whether the whole of Israel could be inside the tabernacle in the wilderness to witness the ceremonies in Lev. 8: 14. The courtyard, he determines, could only have held 5,000 people, but in Israel there were 600,000 men (Num. 2:32). Allowing "two feet in width for each full-grown man, nine men could just have stood in front of it [the door of the tabernacle]"; and if all the males obeyed "the Divine Summons" and stood "side by side, as closely as possible, in front, not merely of the *door*, but of the whole *end* of the Tabernacle, in which the door was, they would have reached, allowing 18 inches between each rank of nine men, for a distance of more than 100,000 feet,—in fact, nearly *twenty miles*!" (1862–79, 1:31–33). Furthermore, Colenso questioned the number of the Israelite males, since the total population, including women and children, must have been well over two million persons, a number inconceivable if descended in four generations (Gen. 15:16) from the seventy persons who accompanied Jacob into Egypt (Gen. 46:26; Exod. 1:5; Deut. 10:22), unless "each man had 46 children (23 of each sex), and each of these 23 sons had 46 children, and so on" (Colenso 1862–79, 1:105), or if Num. 3:43 were taken literally,"*every mother of Israel must have had on the average forty-two sons!*" (1:84).

Such simple calculations served to show that the assertions of the Pentateuch are on these points "impossible, *if we will take the data to be derived from the Pentateuch itself*" (1:100). Similarly, the number of tents to shelter so many people, amounting to an estimated 200,000 to be carried, and then pitched within an area of twelve square miles, must have involved immense crowding and hardships in daily living, such as "having to carry out their rubbish . . . and bring in their daily supplies of water and fuel, after first cutting down the latter where they could find it! Further, we have to imagine half a million of men going out daily . . . for a distance of *six miles*—to the suburbs for the common necessities of nature!" (1:40). The rituals too seemed impossible: the duties of the three priests (Aaron and his two sons, Num. 3:10) were onerous from the labors of offering and consuming the sin-offerings after childbirth (Lev. 12:6–7)—calculated by Colenso to have been for 250 births a day, each sacrifice requiring at least five minutes, for an improbable total of 42 hours a day, "without a moment's rest or intermission" (1:123–24), quite apart from the impossibility of procuring the pigeons or turtle-doves, or of each priests' eating at least eighty of them each day (1:128). At Passover when a lamb would be sacrificed for each group of about fifteen Israelites, and if each was slaughtered as the Law required only in the evening (Exod. 12:6), "for the two millions of people, each Priest must have had to sprinkle the blood of 50,000 lambs in about two hours, that is, at the rate of about *four hundred lambs every minute for two hours together*" (1:131).

Reviewers recoiled in horror both from such picayune critiques of the details of the Pentateuch, from the application of the arithmetical logic of the bishop to demographic probabilities and ritualistic observances. Some scoffed, others, accepting the arithmetic, argued like the *Spectator* that Colenso's argument was founded on "a series of exaggerated numbers" ("Dr. Colenso" 1862, 1251), or on a too-literalist reading of them (ironic, in the light of the widespread acceptance of verbal inerrancy amongst Low and High Church alike), because it is probable, they argued, that the numbers were symbolic, as maintained in the *Eclectic Review* of December 1862 ("Colenso" 1862, 509). By early February Colenso's *Pentateuch and Book of Joshua* had been widely reviewed and reviled, and the pages of the *Guardian*, the *Christian Remembrancer*, and other religious journals were filled with letters to the editors. Most reviewers linked Colenso's book to *Essays and Reviews* and speculated on the meaning of the trials in the Court of Arches (for instance, "Present Position" in *Fraser's Magazine*, Dec. 1862; and "Recent Latitudinarianism" in the *Christian Remembrancer* 1863).

Throughout the Colenso affair there was interaction between his work and *Essays and Reviews* on various levels. Stanley wrote to Jowett: "I saw Colenso . . . an excellent man, and an able book; but it is so written as to vex me a good deal. I have urged upon him, if possible, to write it more like a defence and less like an attack. . . . No man ought ever to write himself down as a heretic" (Prothero and Bradley 1893, 2:100). Jowett, who had "an active friendship" with Colenso, replied: "I think the tone is a good deal mistaken. But don't be hurt or pained by it. You work in one way, he in another, I perhaps in a third way. All good persons should agree in heartily sympathizing with the effort to state the facts of Scripture exactly as they are. Then you really seem like Athanasius against the whole Christian world, past and present" (Abbott and Campbell 1897, 1:301). But "good persons" were few; most were against "sympathizing with the effort" of Colenso; and he was quickly isolated, like Athanasius, *contra mundum*.[2]

Early notices of Colenso's book, like the *Athenaeum* of 1 November 1862, compared it with *Essays and Reviews* and predicted it would "arouse still wider attention and more fiery passions" ("Literature" 1862, 553). The same line is taken in the January issue of the *Christian Remembrancer* where *Essays and Reviews* and the Arches trial are considered in relation to current thought on inspiration, while Colenso's publication is said to show "that the previous lull in the storm was only delusive" ("Review" 1863, 25). On the other hand, Mark Pattison, reviewing Colenso in the *Westminster Review* in the same month, praised him for applying the same criteria for evaluating truth claims to religious texts as are commonly applied to literary and philosophical texts, for asking "Who the persons are that are speaking to us in those books? On what evidence is their authority grounded that they should be believed, whether they speak concerning God, or the world, or of history?" (Pattison 1863a, 58–59). Other writers, A. C. Swinburne, George Meredith, Charles Dickens, W. M. Thackeray, and George Eliot all sided with Colenso in comments in their correspondence (See Thrane 1956, 518–63; Reidy 1971, 283–362; and Varner 1974, 60–131). But the weight of opinion went the other way. A February review of the implications of the legal decisions concerning *Essays and Reviews* in the *Christian Remembrancer* argues that they permit other attacks on orthodox interpretation, like those of Colenso ("unfortunately . . . called to the office of Bishop"), whose book is a "great scandal" that presages further theological catastrophes ("Recent Latitudinarianism" 1863, 252).

In January 1863 Matthew Arnold opposed Pattison's arguments, drawing parallels between *Essays and Reviews* and Colenso's treatise on the Pentateuch in *Macmillan's*.[3] To Arnold, Colenso is a "scapegoat," "sent forth . . . into the wilderness, amidst a titter from educated Europe" (1960–77, 3:40), and his book is "a series of problems, the solution of each of which is meant to be the *reductio ad absurdum* of that Book of the Pentateuch which supplied its terms" (48). Besides ridiculing Colenso's methods and conclusions, Arnold mocks his sincerity and trivializes Colenso's appeal to biblical truths above arithmetical impossibilities as a useless palliative for the "troubled minds" unsettled by Colenso's arguments. Arnold rejects Colenso's references to his commentary on Romans as a valid explanation of Paul's advocacy of spiritual truths above apparent common sense.

To exemplify his efforts as a missionary bishop to teach his flock to recognize God's voice "not in the Bible only, but also out of the Bible,—not to us Christians only, but to our fellow-men of all climes and countries, ages and religions" (1862–79, 1:154), Colenso had referred to a statement of Cicero's recorded in Lactantius on the spiritual necessity of a moral law and to the spiritual aspirations in Sikh and Hindu scriptures. These references to Asian religions are derided by Arnold: when "the simple everyday Englishman . . . crawls from under the ruins [of the church], bruised, bleeding, and bewildered, and begs for a little spiritual consolation, the Bishop 'refers him' to his own Commentary on the Romans, two chapters of Exodus, a fragment of Cicero, a revelation to the Sikh Gooroos, and an invocation of Rám. This good Samaritan sets his battered brother on his own beast (the Commentary), and for oil and wine pours into his wounds the Hindoo prayer, the passage of Cicero, and the rest of it." To Arnold, Colenso has "failed to edify the little-instructed, to advance the lower culture of his nation. It is demanded of him, therefore, that he shall have informed the much-instructed, that he shall have advanced the higher culture of his nation or of Europe" (1960–77, 3:47).

After contrasting Colenso's book unfavorably to Spinoza's *Tractatus Theologico-Politicus* (1670; recently translated by Robert Willis in 1862), Arnold sets it down as a failure in company with *Essays and Reviews*: "Treating religious subjects and written by clergymen, the compositions in that volume have in general, to the eye of literary criticism, this great fault—that they tend neither to edify the many, nor to inform the few." Pattison's essay alone "offers to the higher culture of Europe matter new and instructive." Temple's essay "has this fault—that while it offers nothing edifying to the uninstructed, it offers to the instructed nothing which they could not have found in a far more perfect shape in the works of Lessing." Jowett's essay "contains nothing which is not given, with greater convincingness of statement and far greater fulness of consequence in Spinoza's seventh chapter, which treats of the Interpretation of Scripture." It has one quality, however, "which, at the tribunal of literary criticism, is sufficient to justify it—a quality which communicates to all works where it is present an indefinable charm, and which is always, for the higher sort of minds, edifying;—it has *unction*" (1960–77, 3:53–54). Not only is this comparison important for the ways that it connects Colenso to *Essays and Reviews* in the periodical press at the time of the legal proceedings but also, in a broader cultural context, it demonstrates clearly the transition in Arnold's criticism between the literary and the religious. Jowett's "indefinable charm" works because of his "*unction*," both a technical term used in the anointing of the sick or the service of ordination (Lat. *unctio*, to anoint with oil), as well as in deprecatory references to oiliness of manner, as applied to Dickens's Uriah Heep in *David Copperfield* (1849–50). To Arnold the notion of unction is extended from the religious to the literary and cultural spheres when oil combines with honey for sweetness and light as the governing metaphors for a renewed culture in the first chapter of *Culture and Anarchy* (1869).

Arnold's comments on *Essays and Reviews* set up elitist distinctions between "the many" who are to be edified and "the few" who are to be informed, between the "little-instructed" and the "much instructed," and between "the lower culture of his nation" and the "higher culture . . . of Europe." These, quite apart from his scathing remarks sneering at Colenso's sincerity and also at Sikh and Hindu religious traditions, provoked a counterreaction and considerable sympathy for Colenso. Arnold was attacked in "Mr. Matthew Arnold on the Aristocratic Creed" in the *Spectator* (27 Dec. 1862), in "The Educated Few" in the *Saturday Review* (17 Jan. 1863), and elsewhere. The editor of the *Examiner*, Henry Morley, wrote of the "displeasure with which Professor Arnold's article . . . is spoken of by liberal men of all shades of religious opinion" (17 Jan. 1863, 36).[4]

The next month, in February 1863, Arnold published "Dr. Stanley's Lectures on the Jewish Church," again in *Macmillan's*, where he commented once more on the Colenso affair, defending himself by contrasting the edifying and informing work of Stanley with Colenso's "octavo volume on the arithmetical difficulties of the Bible." Among the "difficulties" he cites is the fact that "only a certain number of people can stand in a doorway at once, and that no man can eat eighty-eight pigeons a day" (1960–77, 3:72–74). Again, Arnold's contrast between an acceptable liberalism and one that goes too far in its criticism of the Bible is heightened with references to *Essays and Reviews*: "Ah! these liberals!—the power for good they have had, and lost: the power for good they will yet again have, and yet again lose! Eternal bondsmen of phrases and catchwords, will they never arrive at the heart of any matter, but always keep muttering round it their silly shibboleths like an incantation? There is truth of science and truth of religion: truth of science does not become truth of religion until it is made to harmonise with it. Applied as the laws of nature are applied in the 'Essays and Reviews,' applied as arithmetical calculations are applied in the Bishop of Natal's work, truths of science, even supposing them to be such, lose their truth, and the utterer of them is not a 'fearless speaker of truth,' but, at best, a blunderer" (1960–77, 3:74). The notion of compartmentalized truths of science and of religion, and of the failure of the Essayists and Colenso to harmonize the former with the latter is a notable shifting of the grounds of criticism from his first article, one not likely to evade the eyes of his contemporaries, as W. R. Greg pointed out in a long and scathing attack on Arnold in "Truth *versus* Edification" in the *Westminster Review* (Apr. 1863).[5] Arnold's attack on Colenso in which *Essays and Reviews* figures as an important reference point demonstrates not only fractures in the culture of English liberalism but also the ways in which Arnold's position in modern literary institutions is a form of what Frank M. Turner calls "secularized Anglicanism" (1993, 44).

Other factions than Broad Church liberalism or the secularized Anglicanism of Arnold used comparisons between *Essays and Reviews* and Colenso to mark out their territory. Henry Manning, for instance, on the eve of being appointed Roman Catholic archbishop of Westminster, and himself a convert from Anglicanism at the time of the Gorham case, drew the connections even more stringently, connecting the Essayists and Colenso with popular doubt: "What Dr. Lushington declared it was lawful to do, Dr. Colenso did. . . . Dr. Colenso represents the religion of the majority of English laymen. He has addressed himself pointedly to them with a style of thought and writing which reminds me of Cobbett. And I believe that the confidence, and I must add the shallowness of his books make them singularly popular among men who have an impatience both of study and of the supernatural; and such, I fear, is the state of most educated English laymen" (Manning 1864b, 19–20). In the same year, Robert Browning linked *Essays and Reviews* and the Colenso affair in the penultimate verse of "Gold Hair":

> The candid incline to surmise of late
> That the Christian faith proves false, I find;
> For our Essays-and-Reviews' debate
> Begins to tell on the public mind,
> And Colenso's words have weight (ll. 141–45).

The connection between Colenso and *Essays and Reviews* was commonplace by 1864—undoubtedly because of actions taken against the volume and the South African bishop in the ecclesiastical and secular courts.

Public outcries and clerical distress had prompted the House of Bishops to act, and on 9 February 1863 a letter was sent to Colenso, signed by all forty-one English bishops, with Thirlwall alone not signing, advising that he resign his office, since *The Pentateuch and Book of Joshua* could, in the bishops' view, not be reconciled with the promises of the ordinal. Four days later Pusey and his co-promoters launched a suit against Jowett in the Chancellor's Court at Oxford, and again the newspapers were filled with correspondence on *Essays and Reviews*. Also during February, Colenso published Part 2 of *The Pentateuch*, at the same time as Lyell's *Antiquity of Man*, after which Lyell and Colenso became close friends (Hinchliff 1964, 105). In the February meetings of Convocation, George Anthony Denison, seconded by Alexander McCaul, requested that a committee investigate Colenso's teaching, and during the May meetings Convocation adopted the report, declaring that Colenso's *Pentateuch* undermines faith in the Bible as the word of God. On 18 May Colenso was cited in Cape Town to appear before the Gray, his metropolitan, at a meeting on 17 November "to answer certain charges of false, strange, and erroneous doctrine and teaching, preferred against [him]," specifying *Romans* and *Pentateuch*, Parts 1 and 2 (Hinchliff 1964, 115). Gray had consulted Sir Roundell Palmer and Dr. Robert Phillimore, both active in the prosecution of *Essays and Reviews*, who advised that action on a heresy charge could be taken against Colenso.

On 24 June 1863 Lord Kingsdown (who was also sitting on the Williams and Wilson case and who interrupted those hearings for the purpose) delivered the judgment of the Judicial Committee of the Privy Council in the case of *Long v. Archbishop Gray of Capetown*, a dispute concerning the jurisdiction of colonial bishops that was eventually appealed from the Supreme Court of the Cape Colony to the Judicial Committee. Kingsdown's judgment in favor of William Long, restoring to him his clerical income, removed by Gray, was based on the distinction between a bishop's authority as a bishop concerning the cure of souls and as a bishop in a particular jurisdiction concerning law and temporalities (Hinchliff 1964, 118–26). Wilberforce recommended a peaceful settlement by restoring Long, which Gray did. The issue of Gray's jurisdiction reappeared later in the Colenso affair concerning the matter of legitimate jurisdiction.

The trial of Colenso at the Synod of South African Bishops, called by Gray, lasted from 16 to 21 November 1863. By letter Colenso denied Gray's jurisdiction, refusing to attend in person. Colenso was arraigned *in absentia* on nine charges and presentations were made against him. The Synod formally declared the independence of the church in South Africa, not from the Anglican Formularies, but from the interpretations of the Formularies given by the English courts, and adjourned on the Colenso affair until December. On 16 December in the reconvened Bishop's Court Gray pronounced judgment against Colenso on all nine charges, depriving him of his office as a clergyman in the Province of South Africa, and giving him until 16 April to retract. The next day Gray reported the decision formally to the Synod, which agreed that if Colenso continued in his contumacy he should be excommunicated. Colenso appealed to the Privy Council, not under ecclesiastical causes, but, as Owen Chadwick puts it, "as a citizen of the empire who was wronged" (1966–70, 2:93). Colenso claimed that *Essays and Reviews* had been for him a source of inspiration and direction. As the manifesto of Broad Church theology, then, *Essays and Reviews* informed (to opponents, corrupted), the teaching function of the church, as its position was instrumental in Colenso's teaching role as a bishop. Broad Church theology had moved from debate in the common rooms of Oxford around clerical dining tables, to debate in Convocation, to relations between the established church and the state, and now, to matters of imperial jurisdiction.

In the aftermath of Westbury's judgment on 8 February 1864, Convocation debated both *Essays and Reviews* and the Colenso affair simultaneously; in March, Kingsley inaugurated his famous attack on J. H. Newman that prompted Newman's reply as *Apologia Pro Vita Sua*, raising all the possibilities of further secessions from the Church of England to Rome, as had happened earlier in the

Tractarian controversy after *Tract XC.* On 30 April, Colenso, having refused to retract his views, was the object of a proclamation that was read in the cathedral in Pietermaritzburg, South Africa, formally deposing him from his diocese. On 24 June came the synodical condemnation of *Essays and Reviews.* Three days later Colenso's appeal to the Privy Council was first heard, and then was then held over for six months until 14 December.

Stephen Lushington sat on the Judicial Committee in the Colenso appeal as did Westbury, but no bishop was a member since the Judicial Committee was not in this case acting as an ecclesiastical court but only was responding to an alleged wrong committed against a colonial subject. Gray's side was represented by Phillimore and Sir Hugh Cairns, both of whom were involved in the ongoing actions against *Essays and Reviews.* On 20 March 1865, Westbury delivered judgment in favor of Colenso, declaring that the proceedings of the Synod of the South African Bishops in Cape Town against him were of no effect, since the *Letters Patent* appointing him preceded those appointing Gray. The issue was not heresy, as with Williams and Wilson, but rather one of jurisdiction, as with the cases of William Long in the Judicial Committee and with Jowett in the Chancellor's Court in Oxford: that is, whether a valid court, in deposing Colenso from his diocese, had deprived him properly of his right to work and to receive a stipend for that work (Hinchliff 1964, 153; Owen Chadwick 1966–70, 2:93). At the June meetings of Convocation, Stanley defended the theological position of Colenso, citing in support of that position St. Gregory of Nyssa on eternal punishment, and William Law and St. Anselm on the atonement. Meanwhile Colenso prepared Part 5 of *The Pentateuch and Book of Joshua*, dating the preface 3 June 1865, and was at work on a new translation of the Bible with a commentary for which he was to be the general editor. In that role he approached H. B. Wilson as a potential contributor, but nothing came of the project (Hinchliff 1964, 165). In the autumn he set sail for South Africa, and on 4 November arrived in Durban. On 10 November he obtained an interdict to allow him to take possession of his cathedral, despite the blocking of his way by the churchwardens and the dean who ordered him to depart.

The power of the Privy Council seemed much diluted by the distance between London and Cape Town. Gray still felt that, having failed in the secular courts, he could exercise one of the few weapons left to the church in the case of those who lose out in heresy squabbles, even though Colenso had not been tried on that issue in England. Gray could proceed to excommunication. Hence, on 5 January 1866 he had the sentence of greater excommunication on Colenso read in the cathedral at Pietermaritzburg. In London the issue arose whether the Province of Canterbury would side with Gray or with the excommunicated heretic, though never tried and convicted on the charge, except in the South African Synod that he refused to attend. Although Wilberforce proposed that the Church of England was in communion with Gray and was not with Colenso, Tait and Thirlwall advocated only the first half of the statement, saying nothing about Colenso, and so it passed. Events continued at an impasse from 1866 for three years, several efforts having failed at finding a candidate in England to be consecrated as Colenso's replacement. In January 1869 W. K. Macrorie was consecrated bishop of Natal in Cape Town, in opposition to Colenso, still the legally constituted incumbent. At that point a schism began in the diocese of Natal, one that continued past Colenso's death on 20 June 1883, until and beyond Macrorie's resignation in June 1891. All parties agreed that a successor should be appointed by the archbishop of Canterbury, who consecrated A. H. Baynes, but even he could not finally overcome some resistance, and he resigned in 1901. When he left there were still clergy loyal to Colenso—two remaining by 1901. The schism was finally healed in 1911 when the bishop of Natal recovered the endowments of which Colenso had been the proprietor.

The entanglements between the Colenso affair and *Essays and Reviews* can be traced on many levels, particularly concerning the interconnections in convocation and the ecclesiastical and secular courts, as well as matters of biblical and literary interpretation. These interrelations on an institutional level, however, must be carefully distinguished. While both the Colenso affair and *Essays and Reviews* involve differences between higher critical hermeneutics opposed to literalism, and the opposition to that hermeneutics by the Anglican Establishment, Colenso and the Essayists overlap institutionally only in the debates concerning their beliefs in Convocation. Colenso was never tried in the Court of Arches, and his appeal before the Privy Council revolved entirely around his status as a subject of empire and the jurisdiction of his bishop. It was not a charge of heresy that brought him there; that charge was leveled by Gray in a subsequent phase. Whereas the *Essays and Reviews* controversy had more or less faded from public view after 1870, the Colenso affair, because of its institutional complications in the ecclesiastical politics of South Africa, continued into the twentieth century. Nevertheless, both cases represent an important juncture in the formulation of Broad Church liberalism, a juncture that, as we have seen with Matthew Arnold, is instrumental in dominant forms of cultural criticism and the reading of literature to the present.

Notes on Bishop Colenso's "Great Scandal"

1. Part 2 was published in late January 1863; parts 3 and 4 also in 1863; part 5 in 1865; part 6 in 1872; and part 7 in 1879.

2. F. D. Maurice, for instance, who had been an inspiration for Colenso and a frequent correspondent from 1853 when Colenso dedicated a volume of his sermons to him, wrote in September and October, 1862: "The pain which Colenso's book has caused me is more than I can tell you." It is probable that the anonymous "Professor of Divinity" referred to by Colenso in the opening pages of the Preface to *The Pentateuch* was Maurice. Conversations with him concerning the possibility of Colenso's resigning his bishopric doubled back to Maurice's questioning of his own implication in holding his position in the church as a sinecure when he felt he could speak more freely without it: "It has obliged me to consider my whole position at [the Chapel of St. Peter] Vere Street. I had long perceived that that was put in jeopardy by the recent decisions in Heath's case, and in Wilson's case. I had prepared myself for a prosecution, and had determined that when it came I would not go into the court, but would rather retire. . . . But I had meant to wait till the blow came. Now I see very clearly that I ought to anticipate it." And writing on 12 October 1862 to Charles Kingsley he goes over the same matters is great detail, concerning the effect of Lushington's interlocutory judgment together with "Colenso's act" which "though it clenched my resolution . . . only showed me what would have been best at all events" about his purpose in resigning. To Stanley he wrote: "The coincidence of the appearance of Colenso's book with the rehearing of Wilson's case has determined the time of my retirement from Vere St." (Maurice 1884, 2:425–29). Dissuaded by Tait and others from resigning—it would be misunderstood as concurring with the Essayists and attacking Colenso who did not intend to resign—he wrote again to Stanley: "I soon perceived that I had been about to injure Colenso when I fancied I was only injuring myself. Then it became clear to me that people did—as you said they would—utterly mistake my meaning and suppose me to be leaving the Church" (2:434).

3. Arnold's "The Bishop and the Philosopher" was first published in *Macmillan's* (Jan. 1863). Parts of the essay were extracted for use in combining it with another essay, "Spinoza and the Bible" for the second edition of *Essays in Criticism* (1869), which also included a revision of "Spinoza" from the first edition (1865). In the process of revision, Arnold "rigorously excluded every allusion to Colenso and to *Essays and Reviews*" (1960–77, 3:417). For a discussion of Arnold and Colenso see Varner 1974, 132–93.

4. Arnold's attack on Colenso is referred to twice by R. H. Super, his modern editor, as undertaken "from his love of sport" and as "game too easy for a real sportsman" because Colenso's book was "so patently stupid" (1960–77, 3:416–17). Arnold's racialist treatment of Colenso's references to comparative religion receive one sentence: "Arnold's precise references mock Colenso's pedantry." In the *Collected Works* there is one reference to the "controversy stirred up" by Arnold's first article (1960–77, 3:423), but no detailed discussion of the adverse critical reception of it by what Morley called "liberal men of all shades of religious opinion."

5. Arnold's first attack on Colenso is praised by his modern editor as "an important step in the development of Arnold's idea of the function of criticism" (1960–77, 3:417). Arnold returned to the reception of his critique of Colenso in "The Function of Criticism at the Present Time" (1864), first delivered as a lecture at Oxford, then published in *National Review*, and finally as the first essay in his *Essays in Criticism* (1864). He declared his "impenitence" for having published his earlier articles, continued to make the same distinctions between the "the multitude" and those with culture, and repudiated his alliances with the liberals. Colenso's book is still "blundering" and "reposes on a total misconception of the essential elements of the religious problem. Arnold rejects it in a version of his dictum concerning canonical exclusivity: "To criticism, therefore, which seeks to have the best that is known and thought on this problem, it is, however well meant, of no importance whatever" (1960–77, 3:276–78).

7 Temple and the Exeter Controversy of 1869–70: "A Sham . . . a Scandal and a Sacrilege"

In 1869 Henry Phillpotts, the bishop of Exeter since 1830, died at the age of 91. A High Churchman and a sympathizer with the Oxford Movement, he had been involved as the prosecutor in the Gorham case of 1847–50. He had also been instrumental in extending High Church standards of worship in his diocese and the levels of education among his clergy. Selecting a replacement was important and significant for Gladstone's first ministry, in showing how the Liberals would dispense ecclesiastical patronage to shift the balance of power in the House of Bishops and the House of Lords.

During the summer of 1869 Gladstone as prime minister had already offered Frederick Temple the deanery of Durham. It was a prestigious position and had an important attachment as well to the University of Durham, but he refused it. Jowett wrote to Florence Nightingale that he did well to reject it; but at the same time Jowett regretted that Temple did not speak out more for the Broad Church position in theology, and he noted that he "could have administered a great office" (Letter 266). The words were prophetic, for by October, Temple had accepted Exeter, but as the process began for the appointment to be confirmed formally, many of the same participants from the *Essays and Reviews* trials and appeals reappeared, some on the same side, others, like the ecclesiastical lawyer James Parker Deane on the other. He appeared for those who challenged Temple's appointment in what was, in miniature, yet another aborted trial, rather like Jowett's in the Chancellor's Court at Oxford. Deane labeled the proceedings to approve Temple "a sham . . . a scandal and a sacrilege" (*Times*, 9 Dec. 1969, 6).

Four bishoprics were available, Oxford (Wilberforce had been appointed recently by Gladstone to Winchester), Bath and Wells, Exeter, and Manchester (and early in October Carlisle also fell vacant). Gladstone gave the choice to Temple, who did not hesitate: "They know me and I know them" (Sandford 1906, 1:275). Gladstone wrote to Tait, who had become archbishop of Canterbury:

> You have been very kind in supplying me with information and advice, and I take the earliest opportunity of giving your Grace what will be before the world in a few days.
>
> The arrangements are —
>
> 1. Bishop of Oxford to Winchester.
> 2. Lord A. Hervey to Bath and Wells.

3. Dr. Temple to Exeter.
4. Mr. Mackarness to Oxford.

I am persuaded that these appointments will not meet with your Grace's disapproval, though I am not so sanguine as to believe that *one* of the three new names will pass without some noise (Benham 1891, 2:58).

Before the noise exploded, Stanley had been informed, and sent his congratulations on 6 October, and the next day Tait sent his good wishes (Letters 269–70). The day after, the *Times* leaked the information, reminding its readers of the *Essays and Reviews* controversy and noting that Temple "during the last general election, took an active part in Warwickshire in support of Mr. Gladstone's measure for the disestablishment of the Irish Church" (8 Oct. 1869, 10). Within a week many congratulations poured in, but the old ghost of *Essays and Reviews* had been raised by a letter to Temple from John Duke Coleridge, one of the lawyers prosecuting Williams and Wilson in the Court of Arches eight years earlier. Coleridge had asked Temple to dissociate himself in some way from the volume and the other writers, to which Temple replied that he could not "rightly or wisely make any public declaration about *Essays and Reviews*" (Letter 275). The argument he makes to Coleridge, that first, he is not responsible for the other essays, and second, to speak out now would amount to a condemnation, he would repeat many times in the following three months as friends and foes, bishops and politicians, urged him to distance himself from *Essays and Reviews.*

Wilberforce put the matter strongly; having first sent a warm letter of congratulations, his ensuing correspondence became more testy, until he finally declared his goal: "My earnest desire that you should, for the Church's sake and that of others, and, I might almost say especially, for the sake of Gladstone, separate yourself from what Convocation has condemned, seems to me not only not difficult of reconciliation with this feeling towards you, but to be its necessary consequence" (Letter 342). Similar entreaties had come from Harold Browne, bishop of Ely, and from Christopher Wordsworth, bishop of Lincoln, both of whom had written against *Essays and Reviews*, the former in *Aids to Faith*, the latter in *Replies to "Essays and Reviews."* To Wordsworth (who published the correspondence in the *Times*, 30 Nov. 1869) Temple replied that he was bound only to make the oaths declared by law; for them to demand and for him to acquiesce in undertaking other tests of faith, even at widespread public request, was neither required nor wise (Letters 324 and 332). To Philip Freeman, archdeacon of Exeter, he put the case even more clearly, arguing that to give in after such pressure to denounce *Essays and Reviews* would be to submit to a tyranny against liberty of free thought and opinion (Letter 288). Williams wrote Temple with his congratulations but also indicated that he was concerned about Temple's moral difficulty in making a private act of disclaimer; instead he proposed an alternative, though one that was not followed up: "I am quite ready to join in any reasonable act of joint and mutual disclaimer" (Letter 298). As early as the first week of November, Temple became the first of a new series of caricatures in *Vanity Fair* depicting the "Men of the Day." The lengthy caption to the lithograph alludes to the revived controversy: "He has displayed ability in the free handling of religious subjects, and has nevertheless been made a Bishop." In the attached commentary Temple's work at Rugby is highly praised, and *Essays and Reviews* is no impediment to the episcopal bench: "The only authority that has judged the matter has decided that there is no heresy at all in the work" (6 Nov. 1869, 260). See figure 19.

At the same time, in the first week of November, Temple was carrying on a correspondence with H. B. Wilson concerning the republication of *Essays and Reviews* in the thirteenth edition to capitalize on rejuvenated interest in it (Letters 314–16 and 319). On the one hand Temple was unwilling to isolate himself from old friends and collaborators; on the other, he could not be known publicly to have sanctioned republication. There was certainly profit to be made, and further circulation of the book might still advance the cause of Broad Church theology, but it was a dangerous route.

By the third week of October, opposition to Temple's appointment had coalesced around a long letter Pusey had written to the *Guardian* on 10 October concerning the "frightful enormity" that Gladstone had committed, namely, "the horrible scandal of the recommendation of the editor of the *Essays and Reviews* to be a Christian bishop" (Sandford 1906, 1:281), and another letter to the *Times* on 3 November 1869 (Letter 317). The false story of Temple's editorship was also printed in the *Record* (13 Oct. 1869). To his friend Frederic Cook in Exeter, Temple denied the allegations, but he could not do so publicly, either for his own sake, or to incriminate Wilson, who had guarded the secret so carefully: "I was not the editor, as I think you know; and I never saw any Essay but my own till the Book was published. I should not like to be quoted as saying this just now. But still it is a bare fact which you may as well know" (Letter 282).

Meanwhile Pusey combined his own High Church support with his traditional ecclesiastical rivals, the Low Church, and called forth a committee that issued an unparalleled joint announcement about 20 October:

> The Earl of Shaftesbury and the Rev. Dr. Pusey having consented to act in unison in using every effort to prevent the scandal to the Church caused by the Premier's nomination of Dr. Temple, clergymen and laymen willing to support their brethren in the Diocese of Exeter are requested to communicate without delay with the secretaries (Sandford 1906, 1:281).

Editorial lead articles repeating this information in the *Times* (22 Oct. 1869, 6–7) were followed by hot denials from Lord Shaftesbury (Letter 296) and others with whom the agitation was associated (Letter 297). To Pusey the argument was clear—if Temple be innocent, let him abjure what he then said, and his association with the book—he need not condemn what the others said, but he had to distance himself from their positions; otherwise how could one who had been condemned by the Lower House of Convocation and by the House of Bishops for heretical doctrine in a synodical censure be welcomed as a participant in that very House? The Synodical Condemnation of the book in 1864 had fallen on all of the Essayists

Figure 19. "He Has Displayed Ability in the Free Handling of Religious Subjects, and Has Nevertheless Been Made a Bishop" (Frederick Temple). Lithograph by "Coïdé" (James Jacques Tissot) in *Vanity Fair* (6 Nov. 1869). Courtesy of Victoria University Library, Toronto.

alike and without distinction; passages were cited from each of the essays on that occasion, as well as in the many other denunciations, and Temple's name was certainly not free of taint. But the action of the prime minister in passing over the condemnation by Convocation was to Pusey and others a reprehensible dismissal of the chief doctrinal and administrative agency of the church, functioning in fact as a body trying to regulate its own doctrine. Pusey therefore busied himself in an active campaign of attack. He wrote letters to the *Times* adding considerable fuel to the fire by casting sneering aspersions on Temple's motives: "What would be thought of any disavowal now? Simply that while it was a question only of Christian faith and of human souls Dr. Temple was silent, and that he spoke when it was the question of worldly preferment" (Letters 303, 304, 309, 317), an allegation that Alexander Ewing, the bishop of Argyle, called "monstrous" (Letter 313). In the popular mind, and very clearly also in fact, High Church and Low Church were now cooperating to blow up the appointment in a modern reinterpretation of Guy Fawkes (as in the pages of *Tomahawk*) as the "extremes meet" in the language of the comic press (*Judy*, 27 Oct. 1869). See figures 20 and 21 (and p. 841 for the poetic satire). To Pusey and his friends there were only two alternatives if the appointment proceeded: "secession or disestablishment" (*Guardian*, 27 Oct. 1869, 1188).

The correspondence in the pages of the *Guardian* was extensive and typical of the passions that the appointment aroused. It occupied more space throughout the four months from October 1869 to January 1870 than any other issue. On 20 October there were eighteen letters, three pages of three long columns each, nine columns in total. On 22 October there were fifteen letters occupying two and one-half pages. The issues of 10 November and 17 November have each a full three columns; 24 November, a full page, and on 29 December a half-page. The letters finally ceased on 23 March 1870, with a quibbling dispute between John W. Burgon and the dean of Exeter about letters sent to the dean by the archbishop of Canterbury in support of Temple's election. The legalistic and picayune tone and matter of this final stage in many way characterizes the correspondence throughout. Entrenched positions are used to fire at each other as Temple's appointment becomes the focus of a large set of issues: the constitution of the church and state and their respective powers in ecclesiastical matters; the fitness of Gladstone's nomination of Temple despite a significant body of complaint within the church; the apparent political contempt on the part of the government for the Synodical Condemnation; and the unusual alliance between the High Churchman Pusey and Lord Shaftesbury and the Evangelicals, who, rather than joining for such goals as Christian missions or social action, had united in a marriage of convenience for theological disputation, fighting a rear-guard action against *Essays and Reviews* and the still-rankling acquittal from the Judicial Committee. Many letters in the press derive from the diocese of Exeter; most are antagonistic, and they, like others, summon up the past by quoting "The Education of the World" against Temple to declare him a heretic, predicting that his election signifies the immanent end of the established church. He is particularly condemned for not dissociating himself from

Figure 20. "The Modern Guy Faux! or, A Diabolical Attempt to Blow up a Bishop." Caricature by Matt Morgan of E. B. Pusey and Lord Shaftesbury attempting to blow up Frederick Temple in the House of Lords in *Tomahawk* (6 Nov. 1869). Courtesy of the National Portrait Gallery, London.

Figure 21. "Extremes Meet." Caricature by William Henry Boucher of E. B. Pusey and Lord Shaftesbury in *Judy* (27 Oct. 1869). Courtesy of the British Library.

the other Essayists. If he be innocent, they claim, let him so declare himself; by remaining silent, he continues to align himself with the reprobate.

Nor were letters to the editors of the various papers the only literary outpourings of sentiment. Articles and editorials were published in both the secular and ecclesiastical press. But the tone was very different from the partisanship of 1860–64. In October the *Times*, in the first of three lead editorials, compared Temple's nomination to the precedent of appointing the doctrinally suspect Hampden to Hereford, and attacked Pusey, Shaftesbury, and the ever-vigilant Archdeacon Denison for improperly maligning a man who "has not been convicted of heresy [and who is] open to no suspicion of it" (22 Oct. 1869, 6–7). But when the attacks on Temple gained strength in the following fortnight (despite the fact that the *Times* had published a strong testimonial on Temple's behalf from the people of Rugby), the editorial view of the newspaper was even more sharply expressed, criticizing Pusey, whose "opposition, as it will actually be futile, is also uncalled for" (4 Nov. 1869, 7). After Temple's formal election, the *Times* in another leader praised the chapter of Exeter for voting for Temple by a majority and rebuked those who voted against him, including the subdean, Bishop Trower, who broke the law by doing so, but narrowly escaped the charge of *praemunire* (because of the majority support), as well as those who had so resolutely promoted this agitation "by means nothing less than shameful" (13 Nov. 1869, 8).

In the religious press, the *Guardian*, for example, printed columns of letters from Temple's opponents, but its editorial policy remained cool toward Pusey and his supporters. From late October to mid-December, the *Guardian* had four leading articles about Temple's nomination and subsequent election. These articles on the whole took two positions. First of all they rejected the attacks on Temple on the grounds that they were unjust toward him, and that they came at a very dangerous time in the politics of the Church of England, threatening her unity. In particular they focus on Pusey's letter to the *Times* of 3 November 1869 (Letter 317) in which he threatened or argued that Temple's nomination represented a potential secession or disestablishment of the church:

> Our readers will see elsewhere the results of the meeting held under the auspices of Lord Shaftesbury and Dr. Pusey, for the purpose of opposing the elevation of Dr. Temple to the Bench. Apart from a species of animosity against their proposed allies which characterises the Low Church leaders, there is, as far as at present appears, one great difference between their plans of campaign. Lord Shaftesbury and his friends merely oppose and protest. Dr. Pusey proclaims the alternative of "secession or disestablishment" (27 Oct. 1869, 1188).

The long leader then goes through the specific charges against Temple made by Pusey, most of them related to *Essays and Reviews*. It concludes: "The question is, whether it is right or wise to make this mistaken or blamable omission the foundation of such action as Dr. Pusey proposes to take upon it. To our minds, the question answers itself." The other leaders in the *Guardian* repeatedly defend

Temple on the basis of attacks made on him as a heretic because of his involvement in *Essays and Reviews*. They take the legal position that his heresy was unproved. He was not charged, and his complicity was unsubstantiated by the ecclesiastical courts:

> People as remote as possible from agreement with the spirit or object of the *Essays* feel, when the question is raised, the injustice done by labouring to charge Dr. Temple with a responsibility which does not really belong to him; and they are unable to find a sufficient ground for destroying the connection of Church and State in the appointment of a man of high character and great eminence against whom, after all, no tangible charge whatever of heterodoxy or scepticism can be made (20 Oct. 1869, 1149).

At one point the *Guardian* reprints an extensive quotation from their 1861 review of the original volume (on 17 Nov. 1869, 1282–84; quoting from 19 June 1861), where Temple and Pattison were separated from the other five Essayists on the basis of the orthodoxy of their arguments. In 1869 that view was still claimed to be viable.

The pamphleteers were also at work, dusting off their copies of *Essays and Reviews* to repeat the arguments of 1860–64. While they were now vindicated by the power of the earlier Synodical Condemnation, they remained deeply troubled that the very heresy that merited that episcopal censure now was not only tolerated by the bishops in silence but was actually rewarded by elevation to the purple. About fifteen tracts and pamphlets were published, of which those by Burgon (1870a and 1870b) and Denison (1869), long-standing participants in the *Essays and Reviews* agitation, were typical (see Altholz 1994, 185–86). Denison even republished in 1869 his *Analysis of "Essays and Reviews"* (1861) with a new preface.

Outside the realm of public controversy, there remained four legal and ecclesiastical requirements for Temple's nomination to Exeter to be concluded: his formal election, the confirmation of the election, his consecration, and his enthronement as bishop. The first three were each matters of intense public interest and controversy; the last was an acclamation, even though the aftermath of his appointment continued on into the debate in both houses of Convocation in 1870.

First the cathedral chapter of Exeter had to confirm the *congé d'élire* (Fr. permission to elect, a royal document whose authority dated from the time of William the Conqueror, whereby the Crown nominated bishops, and the cathedral chapter had the power to elect, later, by 25 Henry VIII, c. 20, the Annates Statute of 1534, the requirement to elect). The election, then, was a formal requirement under law, necessitating that either a majority of the chapter vote for Temple, or the queen would invoke a little-used right of appointment by letters patent, with the option of arresting the chapter under the charge of *praemunire* (Lat. fore-warn, a wide range of ecclesiastical and civil offenses, including, as here, the contravening of a royal prerogative). There was intense lobbying before the election on 11 November. Some two hundred of the clergy protested his nomination. Temple's friend Frederic Charles Cook, canon of Exeter, had been writing to many of them, including the chapter, trying to persuade them of Temple's orthodoxy and abilities. The former bishop's son was one of the members of that chapter, as was a fierce opponent of Temple's, the former bishop of Gibraltar, W. J. Trower, who had become subdean of Exeter under Phillpotts and who had performed most of Phillpotts's episcopal duties during the last years of his life. A fortnight before the election, the *Times* took the unusual step of publishing a leader that cited the historical precedent for such a controversy in an election, that of Renn Dickson Hampden to the diocese of Hereford in 1848, an issue that had put some of the same agitators on similar sides. The leader also instructed the Exeter chapter about their duties as electors and the dangers of *praemunire* (22 Oct. 1869, 6–7). On 11 November the vote was finally taken, with thirteen in favor, six against, and four absent. Immediately afterwards *Punch* in the issue of 13 November published three short squibs in prose and a satire in verse on the election, capping it off with a full-page caricature by John Tenniel showing Mr. Punch himself as a doctor dousing the ire of Pusey, infected with "*congé d'élire-ium*" (and trampling a copy of *Essays and Reviews* underfoot) while Gladstone with the authority of the royal proclamation confronts Shaftesbury, at whose feet is the evangelical *Record* (see fig. 22).

The second stage was the formal confirmation of the election in the church of St. Mary-le-Bow in London, on 8 December, at which representatives from the diocese of Exeter, on behalf of many others, protested, raising not only theological questions concerning the propriety of Temple's doctrine but even of the legitimacy of his birth (in the Ionian Islands, without the benefit of parish baptismal records): "They went so far as to render it necessary to summon Dr. Temple's elder sister, at short notice, to prove that he had been born in lawful wedlock" (Sandford 1906, 1:291). What was normally a ceremonial event became on this occasion an aborted effort to bring Temple to some kind of trial, to determine his orthodoxy, to have him recant of his past errors, and to force him to mend his ways in the future. The crowded church expected fireworks, but since the proceedings all took place in hushed whispers in the church choir, the spectators had to rely upon reports in the press to learn what had transpired. In fact, Dr. Deane, who had represented Williams and Wilson in the *Essays and Reviews* trial, was here brought in on the other side as a capable ecclesiastical lawyer, representing Bishop Trower and two clergy, A. A. Hunt and S. H. Walker. The *Times* printed an almost verbatim account of the proceedings (9 Dec. 1869, 6), *Punch* attacked Temple's opponents, especially Trower, in verse satires (18 Dec. 1869, 247; 25 Dec. 1869, 260), and the *Illustrated London News* printed a front-page drawing of the event (see fig. 23), showing Sir Travers Twiss as the archbishop of Canterbury's vicar-general at the head of the table set up in the choir, and Temple at the foot. Twiss was a prominent lawyer, Regius Professor of Civil Law at Oxford, and had been chancellor of the diocese of London before becoming vicar-general of the province of Canterbury. Hence, the terms in which he framed his response depended upon this background in civil and ecclesiastical law. The *Times* article includes Queen Victoria's letters patent concerning Temple's appointment, a description of the ceremonial, the ensuing legal arguments in which Bishop Trower and others voiced objections through their lawyers (amidst hisses), Deane's arguments concerning

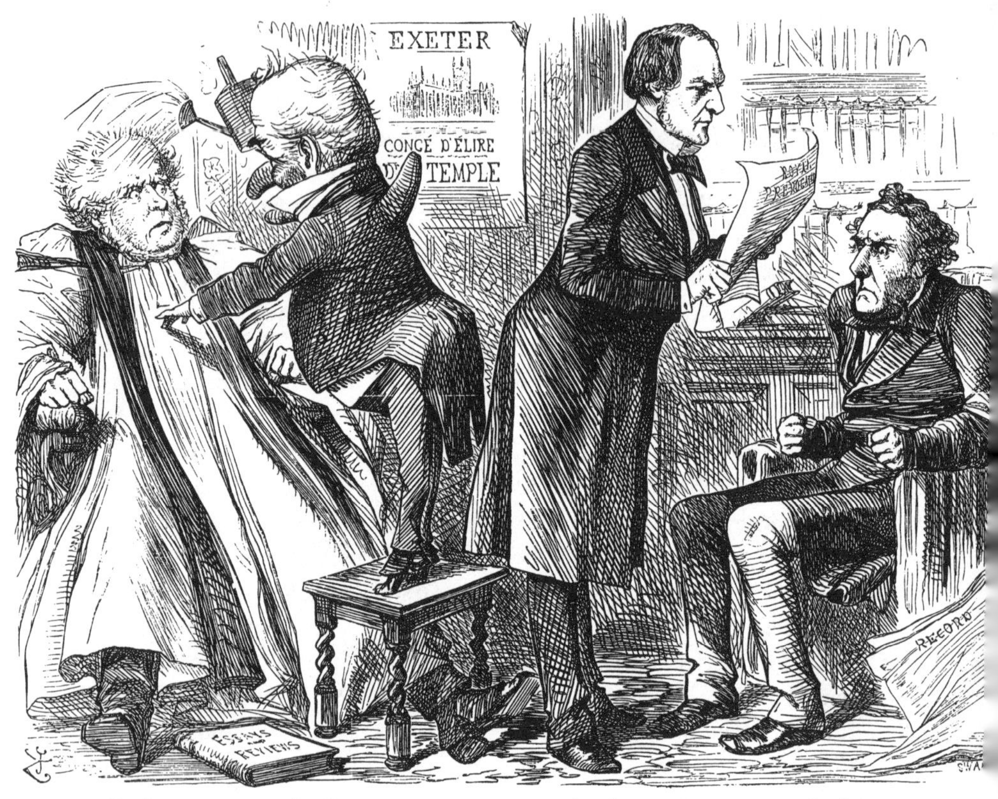

Dr. P—s—y. Dr. P—n—h. Dr. Gl—d—st—n. Ld. Sh—f—ts—b—y.

CONGÉ D'ÉLIRE-IUM. A CASE FOR THE DOCTORS.

Figure 22. "Congé d'élire-ium. A Case for the Doctors." Caricature by John Tenniel in *Punch* (13 Nov. 1869). Courtesy of the Robarts Library, University of Toronto.

Temple's unfitness to occupy the see (stifled applause), and the vicar-general's rejection of Deane's argument on the grounds that he had no power to "review the choice made by the Crown of Dr. Temple as a fit and proper person to be Bishop of the See of Exeter." Temple's election was therefore confirmed, and when he left the church he was "enthusiastically cheered."

The fact that the confirmation succeeded did not mean opposition ceased. The papers continued to parade learned legal arguments concerning the past records of some of Temple's opponents (Letters 336–37), and old foes, like Heurtley, entered again into the fray (Letter 338). Behind the scenes, Trower's "Committee for Opposing the Appointment of Dr. Temple" considered legal action, but they were in disarray. The committee's clerical secretary, J. L. Fish, wrote the day after the confirmation: "We are not advised to try the Court of Queen's Bench, as we did get a judgment [from Twiss], though unsatisfactory. We might appeal, with the certainty of defeat, and what Bp. Trower and others so much deprecate, viz. an authorized acquittal of Dr. Temple from the charge of heresy, as we should have to go to the Privy Council. The Dean of St. Paul's says that 3 bishops can easily be forced to consecrate" (Oxford Bodley MS. Eng. th. d. 21, fol. 39). The next day G. A. Denison listed Temple's seven deadly sins: "1. Temple in Writing; 2. Gladstone in Nominating; 3. Bishops, Clergy, & People in Acquiescing; 4. Dean & Chapter in Electing; 5. The Metropolitan in Confirming; 6. Archbishops & Bishops in Consecrating; 7. Synod in not Protesting" (Oxford Bodley MS. Eng. th. d. 21, fol. 54).

The consecration of Temple as bishop, the third event, was set for 21 December, but again there were difficulties, most not emerging until the congregation was waiting in Westminster Abbey for the ceremony. Temple, and two other bishops-elect, Lord Arthur Hervey of Bath and Wells and W. W. Stirling (first bishop of the Falkland Islands), gathered in the Jerusalem Chamber with the bishops who would be officiating at the consecration. Even they were problematical. John Jackson, recently appointed bishop of London, was acting on behalf of Archbishop Tait of Canterbury, who was sick. Jackson had publicly declared himself to be in favor of Temple, but wished that he would still distance himself from a book which caused "mischief" and earned "disapprobation" (Letter 339). Harold Browne, bishop of Ely, had conducted a correspondence with Temple to try to get him to dissociate himself from *Essays and Reviews*, but to no avail; now he conceded to proceed with the consecration (three bishops being required for the act), but would not fulfil the office of "presenting" Temple, justifying this nice distinctions in a letter to his archdeacons (Kitchin 1895, 324–25). Connop Thirlwall from St. David's agreed to act, as did Henry Philpott from Worcester. Wilberforce had been invited to assist in the consecration but declined (Letters 341–42), informing J. W. Burgon that he did so because of Temple's refusal to "clear himself" from complicity with *Essays and Reviews* (Bodley MS. Wilberforce d. 47).

Before the procession could move from the Jerusalem Chamber into the Abbey, formal protests were filed from eight bishops of the province of Canterbury, four of whom appeared, very likely organized by Christopher Wordsworth of Lincoln.

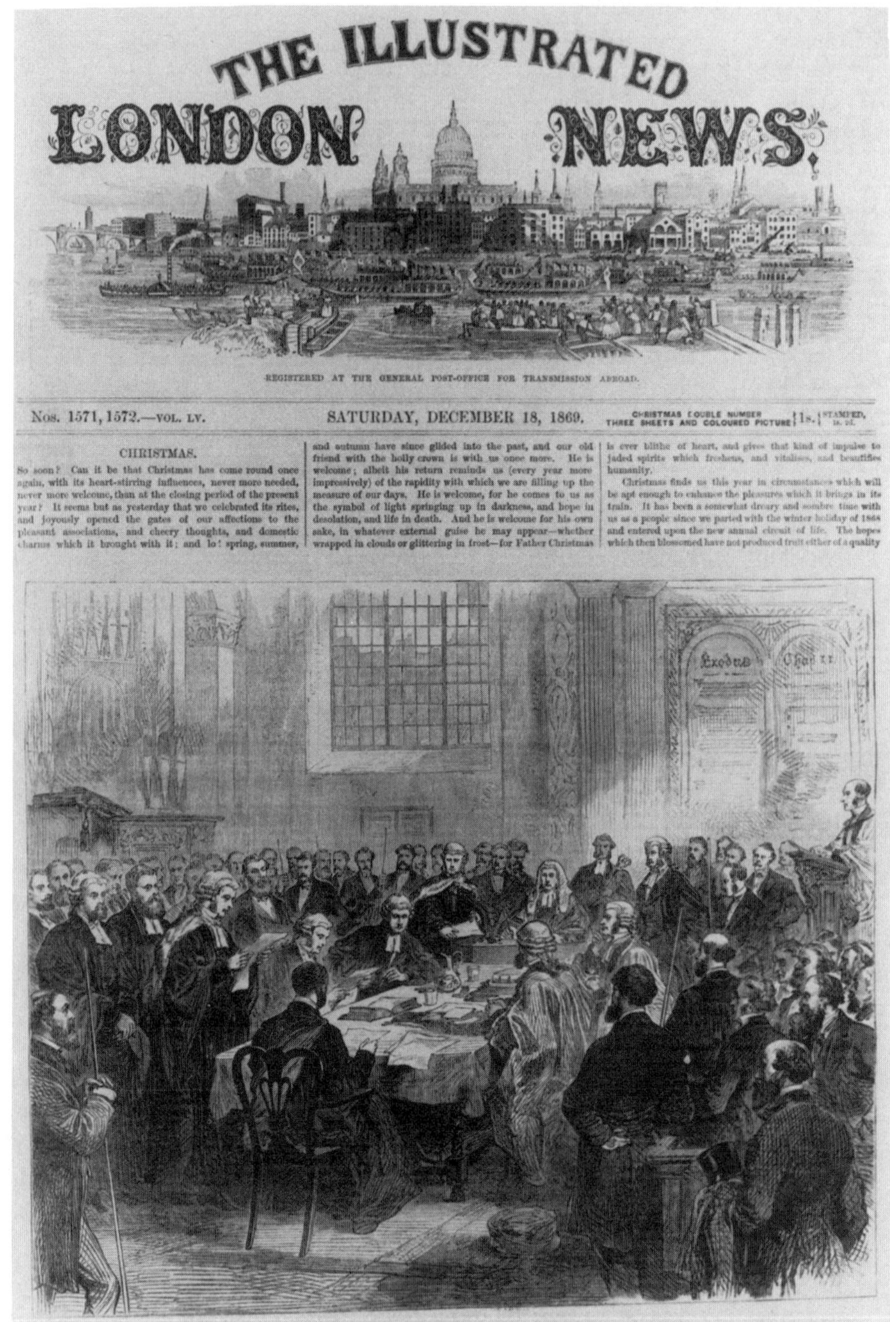

THE ILLUSTRATED LONDON NEWS.

REGISTERED AT THE GENERAL POST-OFFICE FOR TRANSMISSION ABROAD.

Nos. 1571, 1572.—VOL. LV. SATURDAY, DECEMBER 18, 1869. CHRISTMAS DOUBLE NUMBER THREE SHEETS AND COLOURED PICTURE 1s. STAMPED, 1s. 2d.

CHRISTMAS.

So soon? Can it be that Christmas has come round once again, with its heart-stirring influences, never more needed, never more welcome, than at the closing period of the present year? It seems but as yesterday that we celebrated its rites, and joyously opened the gates of our affections to the pleasant associations, and cheery thoughts, and domestic charms which it brought with it; and lo! spring, summer, and autumn have since glided into the past, and our old friend with the holly crown is with us once more. He is welcome; albeit his return reminds us (every year more impressively) of the rapidity with which we are filling up the measure of our days. He is welcome, for he comes to us as the symbol of light springing up in darkness, and hope in desolation, and life in death. And he is welcome for his own sake, in whatever external guise he may appear—whether wrapped in clouds or glittering in frost—for Father Christmas is ever blithe of heart, and gives that kind of impulse to jaded spirits which freshens, and vitalises, and beautifies humanity.

Christmas finds us this year in circumstances which will be apt enough to enhance the pleasures which it brings in its train. It has been a somewhat dreary and sombre time with us as a people since we parted with the winter holiday of 1868 and entered upon the new annual circuit of life. The hopes which then blossomed have not produced fruit either of a quality

Figure 23. Confirmation of Temple as Bishop of Exeter. Engraving in the *Illustrated London News* (18 Dec. 1869). Courtesy of the Robarts Library, University of Toronto. Permission of the Illustrated London News Picture Library.

Charles John Ellicott of Gloucester, who had also written against *Essays and Reviews* in *Aids to Faith*, objected that the consecration should not proceed until Temple "should declare his want of sympathy with the general contents and tendencies of the volume known as *Essays and Reviews*." He was followed by James Atlay of Hereford, George Augustus Selwyn of Lichfield (who declared he had not read, and had no intention of reading Temple's essay), and Christopher Wordsworth. The other protesting bishops were James Campbell of Bangor, Thomas Claughton of Rochester, William Connor Magee of Peterborough, and Rowland Williams's old enemy Alfred Ollivant of Llandaff (*Times*, 22 Dec. 1869, 3). Burgon, busy assembling a series of anti-Temple tracts and petitions, claimed Wilberforce wrote to him saying that he was like-minded with the protesters, giving a majority of nine bishops against the consecration, with only four for it and four neutral (Goulburn 1892, 2:36–38). The *Times*, however, reported that, in the Jerusalem Chamber, Jackson asserted that of the eighteen occupied sees in the province of Canterbury, a minority of eight bishops had protested. A week later the *Guardian* commented: "We are within a few steps of a serious schism" and face "as dangerous an internal division as ever threatened the unity of the English Church since the Reformation" (29 Dec. 1869, 1458).

Jackson had learned of the protest only three days earlier, on a Saturday, and had to contact the consecrators as well as seek legal advice. That he had done so carefully is clear from his judicious remarks reported in the *Times*, dealing in detail with the allegations of impropriety when there were dissenting bishops, according to the ancient canons from the Ecumenical Councils of Antioch and Nicaea, the legal requirements of the Church of England, and the penalties according to the statute of *praemunire*, each of which is cited or quoted. None of these supported the position of the objectors; further, Temple was blameless of life and had never been accused in any court, but was objected to "simply on account of his association with others." The sought-for delay of consecration until Temple could be examined (by whom? Jackson asked), was no remedy since no charges had been formally brought against Temple's essay, and the royal mandate to proceed with consecration should be obeyed. Each consecrating bishop was asked to affirm his consent and express his opinions before the move into the Abbey; all concurred, and the procession at last entered the Abbey and proceeded with the consecration. To the *Graphic* the event was worth a front-page drawing of the event on New Year's Day (see fig. 24).

Temple's enthronement, the fourth and final event, was set for 29 December. The *Times* had reported on Christmas Day that other journals stated that the opposition was regrouping: "It is a great mistake to suppose the opposition to Dr. Temple will now cease. It is true he has been consecrated and solemnly entrusted with the highest responsibilities in the Church, from which he can be released neither by his own desire nor by that of anyone else. It is true, also, that he has been confirmed in the temporal prerogatives of his see, and has done homage on his appointment. He has been opposed at his nomination, his election, his confirmation, his consecration, until no other ceremony remains at which he can be legally resisted. It might have been hoped that, after the opposition had been defeated at

THE GRAPHIC

AN ILLUSTRATED WEEKLY NEWSPAPER

OL. I—No. 5
red for Transmission Abroad]

SATURDAY, JANUARY 1, 1870

[PRICE SIXPENCE,
OR SEVENPENCE STAMPED

BISHOP TEMPLE

appointment of Dr. Temple to the See of Exeter has been criticised from us points of view, but there is one aspect of the nomination which has escaped e, but which is, nevertheless, of considerable interest. In Dr. Temple culminates the new race or what may be called high-pressure bishops. Forty c fifty years ago such prelates were unknown. In those quiet days, ecclesiasticall speaking, a bishop was regarded as an administrator, and little more. As a archdeacon was defined by Bishop Blomfield as a person who fulfilled archidia conal functions, so a bishop was held to be a person who fulfilled episcop

Figure 24. Consecration of Temple in Westminster Abbey. Engraving by Godefroy Durand in the *Graphic* (1 Jan. 1870). Courtesy of the Robarts Library, University of Toronto.

every point, and Dr. Temple had become one of the chief officers of the Church, his opponents would at length feel it their duty to submit to the deliberate judgment of the constituted authorities of the Church. . . . But it is nevertheless announced . . . that 'the gravest doubt rest, in the opinion of many best able to judge, as to the canonicity of his consecration, and the validity of the Orders which he may confer'" (*Times*, 25 Dec. 1869, 7). But the enthronement went off without any protest whatsoever, again being fully reported in the *Times* (30 Dec. 1869, 10). Bishop Trower absented himself from at least some of the festivities, and he is not reported in the *Times* account as having taken part in the enthronement, an act, along with the consecration, that he regarded as "the greatest sin" (Letter 253). Reports in the papers indicate that most of those who now were protesting were some 1,500 who signed the petitions: "Of these less than 700 are clergy, and of the clergy there are probably not 20 who are known beyond their own parishes. . . . Beyond these I cannot find the name of any layman of note; but I find whole columns filled with the names of labourers, blacksmiths, tavern keepers, tailors, shoemakers, hairdressers, beer retailers, and the like, with crowds of women in the same class of life. It is evident that in many parishes the incumbent went round and wrote down the names of his parishioners indiscriminately—young men and maidens, old men and children—just as they came" (*Times* 27 Dec. 1869, 8; Letter 344). As the writer commented, "the affair looks rather ugly."

Temple's remarks to Frederic Cook (Letter 282) concerning the fact that he was not the editor of the book were later amplified by Temple's private assertions to him that any future edition of *Essays and Reviews* would not contain his essay. Cook passed the information on to Philip Freeman, a member of the Lower House of Convocation. At the February 1870 meetings, the irascible archdeacon of Taunton, George Anthony Denison, so active in drawing up with Wilberforce the synodical condemnation of 1864, and a petitioner to the dean and chapter of Exeter protesting Temple's appointment five months earlier, once again introduced a motion of censure. In a palliative gesture when the motion failed, Freeman announced Temple had indicated he would not again republish the offending essay. The announcement immediately caused an uproar, as the supporters of Temple and the Essayists felt betrayed, while his enemies regarded it as an act of honesty too long delayed. The debate spilled over into the House of Bishops, and Temple was finally forced or shamed into stating his case in his own words (see the Manifestos).

And there the matter rested, or almost rested. Because Temple made his statement, Denison indicated that he would not make a fuss over the appointment of Temple as vice-president of the Society for the Propagation of the Gospel. Already Ellicott had written to Wilberforce on 9 December: "We must make a terrible stir about this S. P. G. or we are done" (Bodley MS. Wilberforce C.17, fol. 11), but done they were, since he was duly elected. Other and more notable preferments followed: Temple was appointed bishop of London in 1885, and archbishop of Canterbury in 1896, with scarcely a murmur of protest as *Essays and Reviews* had passed into approved, or at least accepted, pieties.

Appendixes

Appendix A: Publisher's Records

THE long-established London publishing house of Longman acquired the rights to *Essays and Reviews* in January 1861. William Longman, a senior member of the family firm, corresponded with Wilson concerning the details of the new contract and the editions (see Part 1, section 2 and Letter 35). The firm's extensive records have survived from the beginning of Thomas Norton Longman's direction in the late eighteenth century, and are housed in the publishing archives at the University of Reading. John Parker's records for the first three editions are not included in the collection. The Longman records include catalogues, ledgers, and many other records, as detailed by Alison Ingram in her *Index to the Archives of the House of Longman 1794–1814* (1981).

The ledgers and other documents relevant to the publication of *Essays and Reviews* are set out below, with brief headnotes to indicate the role of each ledger and the significance of the technical printing terminology and conventions (for further information on this terminology, see Beadnell 1859, Southward [1882] 1892, and Glaister 1960). The cost figures in every case refer to pounds, shillings, and pence. These documents are reproduced by the kind permission of The Longman Group UK Limited.

Impression Books (Reading: Longman Archive: Imp. 14, 15, 17)

The Impression Books give details of each edition, including date, edition number, size of book, and press run, as well as the Longman's costs of printing. *Essays and Reviews* entries include the costs for "Composition" (typesetting) and "Presswork" (printing) or other work for 28 shs (sheets, or 448 pages), at a rate of so many shillings per sheet (of sixteen pages), paid to the printers, Savill and Edwards. Extra costs were incurred for composing passages in Greek and Hebrew and for making corrections in the type when, after being locked up in formes, it had to be corrected against the corrections from the (proof-) "reader," comparing the author's copytext to a proof pulled from the formes. Coldpressing involved placing the printed and dried sheets in a screw or hydraulic press to remove the impressions made on the paper by the type. The cost for coldpressing was calculated according to the number of reams (R=500 sheets in the mid-nineteenth century) at a specified rate per ream. Finally the cost of the paper for the entire run is calculated at the cost per ream and size, either double demy (DDemy) or double foolscap (DFcap), paid to the paper supplier, Spalding and Co. Impression Books 14 and 15 are wholly in manuscript with both the category and the cost entered by the bookkeeper; Impression Book

17 is a printed document of compiled costing forms, with only the costs entered in the bookkeeper's manuscript hand.

THE FOURTH EDITION (Imp. 14, fol. 6):

[The fourth edition was the first issued by Longman after the purchase of *Essays and Reviews* from Parker, and so the whole of the text had to be reset, as costed in the impression-book accounts, along with other information such as the date and the size of the press run. Details of the changes introduced here, as in the other editions, are specified in Part 1, section 2 and the Textual Notes.]

January 1861 Essays and Reviews	8°	4th edition	N° 1000		
Composition and Presswork	28 shs @ 36/	Savill	50	8	0
Extra for Hebrew & Greek			1	17	6
Corrections			14		
Coldpressing	56 R/ @ 1/		2	16	0
28 R/ DDemy	@ 39/	Spalding	54	12	0
			110	7	6

THE FIFTH EDITION (Imp. 14, fol. 18ᵛ):

[After the run of the fifth edition, the type was left standing in formes ("standing matter") and was kept in the composing room storage until it was required for reprinting; since the type did not have to be distributed, the cost of distribution was deducted from the total costs of the run.]

February 1861 Essays and Reviews	demy 8°	5th ed	N° 2000		
Composition and Presswork	28 shs @ 48/6	Savill	67	18	0
Extra for Hebrew & Greek			1	17	6
Coldpressing	112 R/ 1/		5	12	0
56 R/ DDemy	@ 39/	Spalding	109	4	0
			184	11	6
Allowed for Standing matter			7		
			177	11	6

THE SIXTH EDITION (Imp. 14, fol. 18ᵛ):

[The sixth through ninth editions were printed from the type left standing in formes from the fifth edition. When it was imposed and proofs were pulled, it had to be proofed, read, and corrected to ensure that no errors or damage had occurred while the type was left standing. "Making good" refers to the work of the compositor in ensuring that the corrections the reader had marked are in fact completed and the required adjustments in the standing type have been completed (unlocking and relocking the formes or forms and correcting the impression). "Working" refers to the presswork. "Lifting the forms" refers to removing the formes from the press and cleaning them with lye and water, and allowing them to dry before either returning them to the composing room storage or preparing them for reprinting as happened between the sixth and seventh editions, printed on the same day. Nightwork upon the edition was overtime to get the job completed under the pressure of time.]

March, 1861 Essays and Reviews	demy 8°	6th ed	N° 3000		
Read, Correct &	28 shs standing				
making good	/ per sht	Savill	7	0	0
Working 84 R/ dble	@ 10/		42	0	0
Lifting the forms	@ 1000		3	18	0
Coldpressing and Cutting up	168 R/ 1/		8	8	0
Nightwork upon the Edition			2	10	0
84 R/ DDemy	@ 39/	[Spalding]	163	16	0
			227	12	0

The Seventh Edition (Imp. 14, fol. 19):
[The seventh edition was printed on the same day as the sixth edition, from the same standing matter, and so did not need to be proofread, corrected, or made ready. Again nightwork was charged to the run to complete the job as quickly as possible.]

March 1861 Essays and Reviews	demy 8°	7th ed	N° 3000		
Working	84 R/ dble @ 10/	Savill	42	0	0
Coldpressing and Cutting up	168 R/ @ 1/		8	8	0
Nightwork upon the ed.			2	10	0
84 R/ DDemy	@ 39/	Spalding	163	16	0
			216	14	0

The Eighth Edition (Imp. 14, fol. 19):
[The eighth edition was printed from standing matter two weeks after the seventh edition, and again required nightwork.]

March 1861 Essays and Reviews	demy 8°	8th ed	N° 3000		
Working	84 rms dble @ 10/	Savill	42	0	0
Coldpressing and Cutting up	168 R/ @ 1/		8	8	0
Nightwork upon the ed.			2	10	0
84 R/ DDemy	@ 39/	Spalding	163	16	0
			216	14	0

The Ninth Edition (Imp. 14, fol. 19):
[The ninth edition followed the eighth by two weeks, and again was printed from the same standing matter, but required no nightwork.]

March 1861 Essays and Reviews	demy 8°	9th ed	N° 3000		
Working	84 R/ dble @ 10/	Savill	42	0	0
Coldpressing and Cutting up	168 R/ @ 1/		8	8	0
84 R/ DDemy	@ 39/	Spalding	163	16	0
			214	4	0

THE TENTH EDITION; FIRST ISSUE (Imp. 14, fol. 85):
[The tenth edition was printed in a smaller format for a cheaper edition, necessitating a resetting of the whole text in small pica with smaller margins, numbering 528 pages and 16 pages of prelims and adverts. The corrections in signatures O and P occur in the middle of Wilson's essay, from ¶22 to the first two sentences of ¶53. The changes so introduced are included in the Textual Notes. The front and back paste-down endpapers in the tenth edition were printed with adverts.]

January 1862 Essays & Reviews	Fcap 8°	10th edit.	N° 1000		
Composition	16¾ shs @ 42/	Savill & Edwards	35	3	6
Extra for 13 pages small type			1	2	9
Extra for Greek & Hebrew			1	12	9
Corrections in Sigs O. P.			3	9	
Presswork	34 R/ @ 8/6		14	9	0
Coldpressing	34 R/ @ 1/		1	14	0
33½ R/ D Fcap	@20/	[Spalding?]	33	10	
End Papers Comp 2 pp Work & Press		Savill	1	1	
			88	16	0

THE TENTH EDITION; SECOND ISSUE (Imp. 14, fol. 102ᵛ):
[The second issue of the tenth edition was printed largely from standing matter from the first issue, though four sheets had to be reset, along with matter in Greek.]

March 1862 Essays & Reviews	fca 8°		N° 1000		
Composing 4 shs (12¾ shs standing) @ 42/		Savill & Edwards	8	8	0
Extra for Greek			5	6	6
Working	16¾ shs = 34 R/ @8/6		14	9	
Coldpressing	34 R/ @1/		1	14	0
33½ R/ D Fcap	@ 20/	[Spalding?]	33	10	
End Papers			1	1	0
			59	7	6

THE TENTH EDITION; THIRD ISSUE (Imp. 14, fol. 110):
[Like the second issue, the third was printed from the same standing matter, but with no new composition.]

April 1862 Essays & Reviews	fca 8°		N° 1000		
Working	16¾ shs = 34 R/ @8/6		14	9	0
		Savill & Edwards			
Coldpressing	34 R/ @1/		1	14	0
33½ R/ D Fcap	@ 20/	[Spalding?]	33	10	
End Papers			1	1	0
			50	14	0

THE ELEVENTH EDITION (Imp. 14, fol. 179ᵛ):
[The eleventh edition is not so marked in the Impression Book, but the fact that a

cost item is included for a new title indicates that the reset matter includes the new designation "The Eleventh Edition" and the new imprint for the addition of "Green" to the firm's name.]

March 1863 Essays & Reviews	fca 8°		N° 500		
Working and Pressing	16 3/4 shs = 17 R/ @ 10/6	Savill & Co	8	18	6
New Title			3	6	
16¾ R/ Fcap	@ 20/	[Spalding?]	16	15	0
			25	17	0

THE TWELFTH EDITION (Imp. 15, fol. 101v):

[The twelfth edition was reset, including for the first time long passages marked at the beginning of lines with single or double quotation marks, indicating that those passages were cited in the trials and appeals. The profit arrangements for this edition were also different.]

February 1865 Essays & Reviews fc 8°		12th Edit.	N° 1000		
Compos^n	16¾ shs @ 39/6	Savill	33	1	6
Extra for small type			2	2	0
Working	16¾ Shs = 34 R/ @ 8/6		14	9	0
Corrections			2	2	0
Coldpressing			1	14	0
33½ R/ D Fcap	@ 20/	[Spalding?]	33	10	0
Memo:— This edition on ½ profits			86	18	6

[THE THIRTEENTH EDITION] (Imp. 17, fol. 264):

[In this printed Impression Book each of the costing categories is set in type with only the applicable items entered by the bookkeeper in ink.]

1869 Nov 16 Essays & Reviews	Fcap 8°	N° 2000		
Composition	16¾ Shts. @ 2.4.0Spottiswoode	36	17	0
Stereotyping	Shts. @			
Corrections				
Small Letter &c.	Gk & Hebrew	1	10	0
Working	16¾ Shts.=68 Rms @ 8/	27	4	0
Coldpressing	67 Rms @ 1/	3	7	0
67 Rms D fcap	@ 28 D c 16/6 Do [?] [Spalding?]	55	5	6
		124	3	6

CHRONOLOGICAL REGISTERS (Reading: Longman Archives: 34)

[The Chronological Registers assign a folio to each publication and enter the data for each year in chronological order. The sixth and the seventh editions have the same date. The category "subscription" ("Subs") refers to the trade price of the book as sold to subscribing booksellers; it also was the rate on which the royalties were paid according to the contract between Wilson and Longman, twenty-five copies counting as twenty-four. This Register also notes the copyright copies sent to Stationers' Hall and to the copyright library, the British (Museum) Library. Two categories, "Customs" and "Abroad," have no entries for *Essays and Reviews* and so are omitted from this table.]

Essays & Reviews

[Date & Ed]	On Acct of	Sells	Subs	Sale	Bind	Stat Hall	Stat Hall	B. Museum
1861 Jan 29 4th ed 8° cl	L&Co	10/6	8/	7/6	cl 25/24			Feb 20
1861 Feb 19 5th ed 8° cl	L&Co	10/6				Mar 5		Mar 5
1861 Mar 8 6th ed 8° cl	L&Co	10/6						
1861 Mar 8 7th ed 8° cl	L&Co	10/6						
1861 Mar 22 8th ed 8° cl	L&Co	10/6	8/	7/6	cl 25/24			
1861 Apr 5 9th ed cl	L&Co	10/6		not to be registered		Apr 16		Apr 16
[Missing entry: 10th ed., 1st issue, Jan. 1862]								
1862 Mar 13 10th ed fc 8° cl [10th ed 2d issue]	L&Co	5–	3/10	3/1	cl see former edit.		Apr 4	Apr 4
1862 May 6 Fc 8°cl NE [10th ed 3d issue]	L&Co	5–	3/10	3/1	cl 25/24	see 9th ed		
[Missing entry: 11th ed. Mar. 1863]								
1865 [Feb 28?] 12th ed fc 8° cl	L&Co	5/	3/10	3/1	cl 25/24		Mar 23	Mar 23
[Missing entry: 13th ed., printed as 12th ed. Nov. 1869]								

Copyright Ledgers (Reading: Longman Archives: 52 Copyright 6 1851–73)

[This volume of Copyright Ledgers, the sixth in the series, covers the specified dates. It lists the term for the Longman share of the profits and the dated size of the print run.]
(Fol. 48v):

Essays & Reviews ~~1/3~~ [a reference to the Longman & Co share for all editions except the twelfth, scored out in ink, and written in below:]

1/2 of 12th Edit only

(Fol. 49):
Demy 8vo

1000	Jan 61	3000	Mar 61	3000 Mar 61
2000	Feb 61	3000	Mar 61	3000 Mar 61

Fcap 8°

1000	Jan 62	1000	Apr 62	1000 Feby 65
1000	Mar 62	500	Mar 63	2000 Nov 69

Divide Ledgers (Reading: Longman Archives: A3)

[The Divide Ledgers record various payments of from Longman to suppliers, here to Spalding and Co. for paper for *Essays and Reviews.*]

(Fol. 172):
Essays and Reviews
1861

Jan 31	To	28 R/ D Dmy	@	39/	Spalding & Co	54	12	0
Feb 7	"	28 R/ D°	@	39/	"	54	12	0
19	"	42 R/ D°	@	39/	"	81	18	0
21	"	14 R/ D°	@	39/	"	27	6	0
22	"	28 R/ D°	@	39/	"	54	12	0
[gap: then entries continue]								
Mch 2	To	56 R/ D Demy	@	39/	Spalding & Co	109	4	0
4	"	28 R/ D°	@	39/	"	54	12	0
12	"	56 R/ D°	@	39/	"	109	4	0
13	"	28 R/ D°	@	39/	"	54	12	0
18	"	84 R/ D°	@	39/	"	163	16	0

Stock and Cost Ledgers (Reading: Longman Archives D7 p. 1)

[These stock and cost ledgers (somewhat abbreviated) detail disposal of stock, including complimentary copies, copies to the copyright libraries, and stock on hand; they incorporate the size of printing runs and the total cost for printing and publishing ("P & P") from the impression books; they show the profit paid to the editor, H. B. Wilson, for dispersal by him to the other contributors, and what accrued to Longman.]

Col 1.	Essays and Reviews				Col 2.				
⅔ The Rev. H. B. Wilson, Great Staughton									
1861 Feb	1 copy to	John Bull							
	7	Sundries							
	1	H. Reeve Esq.							
		[Registrar of Judicial Committee of PC]							
	as 4th ed	B Museum							
		E. Walford Esq			[Added note:] 3 copies returned from Stationers' Hall				
	~~3 copies to Stat[ioners'] Hall~~								
	1	B Museum							
	1	Advocates' Libr'y							
	5 copies to	Stat Hall							
2½ per cent on 141.15.1 f[ro]m		427 sold L & Co							
Board 18 @ 7d					Totals [as opposite]				
Jan P & P	1000 Copies	4th edit		110 7 6					
Feb "	2000	5th		177 11 6					
Mar	3000	6th		227 12 0					
	3000	7th		216 14 0					
	3000	8th		216 14 0					
	3000	9th		214 4 0	15000				
Advertising				75 9 11				18	presented
Bal ⅔	Rev H. B. Wilson		2131.11.8		1626			1608	left since 1860
	⅓ L & C°		1065.15.9	3197 7 5		13374	Sold	25/24c	6/11 gns
				4440 10 0					4440 10 0

Oct 2½ [%]	Apl on 86.9.6	258 Sold	L & Co	
Dec 5	1 copy 8°	to Savill & Edwards for reprint		
[1862]				
Mar 15	1	J Wade Esq		
20	1	J Wade Esq		
	27	Sundries		
Post 8/v Printing [?] 5/2				
	22 copies 12° cl			
Apr 4	5 copies 12° cl	to Stat Hall		
Apl 2½ per cent on 22.10.1 for 149 Sold		L & Co 12 mo.		
June 13	1 copy 8°	to Rev. H. Roberts		
Board	2 8° Edit @ 7 cl			
"	34 Fcp 8° Edit @ 6d			
"	2 specimens			
Jan P & P	1000 copies	10th edit fc 8°	16 Imp 8°	88 16 0
Mch	1000	fc 8°	16 Imp	59 7 6
Apl	1000	fc 8°	16 Imp	50 14 0
June	Advertising		9 L 8	28 1 10
Bal	⅔ Rev H. B. Wilson		433. 9. 9	
	⅓ L & C°		216.14.11	650 4 8
				881 11 1

June	By				
1	608		Copies 8° gns	bro[ught] fwd	
			2	presented	
	43	copies	41	left June 1862	
	1565	Sold	25/24c		519 15 9
1862					
Apr 26	B Tauchnitz for right of translation into German				20 0 0
Jan	By				
	1000 copies Fcp 8°				
Mar	1000 copies				
	2000		34	Presented	
	1966	Sold	25/24c	3/1 gns	291 1 4
Apl By	1000	Copies	Fcp 8°		
	842	Copies left Inv 18/2			
	158	Sold	25/24c	3/1 gn	23 8 8
Amount short of Expenses Carried forward					27 5 4
					881 11 1

Date		Entry		£ s d
1862 [p. 174]				
June	To Amount short of Expenses			27 5 4
		1 copy 12° cl	to J. Pryse Esq	
[other data re inventories, etc]				
Mar P&P		500 copies 16 imp		25 17 0
June Bal	2/3	Rev. H. B. Wilson	74. 7. 2	
	1/3	L & Co	37. 3. 6	
				166 12 3
1864				
1865				
Mar 7		1 Copy	to Rev. H. B. Wilson	
Mar 23		5 copies	to Stat Hall	
April		[advertising data, etc.]		
June		[" " "]		
Feb		1000 Copies 12th Ed 15 Imp		86 18 6
		to Board 13 @ 6		
				115 7 9

Date		Entry			£ s d
1862					
June By		41 copies Bro fwd			
		& all copies Sold			
1862					
June By		842 Copies			
		500 Copies			
		1342 Copies	1	presented	
		310	309	Copies left	
		1032 Sold	25/24c @ 3/1 gns		152 15 7
					166 12 3
1864 By		166 Copies			
		& all sold	25/24c	3/1 gns	24 13 4
1865					
Jan By		1000 Copies Fc 12 edn			
			13	presented	
	889	876 June 1865			
	111	Sold 25/24			16 9 11
		Amt Short of expenses cd fwd			74 4 6
					115 7 9

1866

[June 1866-June 1868: continuing advertising expenses and inventory data, leaving 448 copies on hand in June 1868:]

[p. 332]

1868	[advertising data, etc]			
1869				
Nov 4	1 Copy	to Spottiswoode		
	[misc data and charges]			
2½ per cent on 20.3.11 for 136 Sold		L & Co		
P & P	2000 Copies 17 Imp 264			124 3 6
June	Advertising			3 9 4
	Bal ½ Author	78.19.8		
	½ L & Co	78.19.8		
			157 19 4	
				286 2 8

June 1868			
	549	Copies	
	448	left June 1868	
	101	Sold	
1869	448	Copies Fwd	
	331	Left June 1869	
	117	Sold	
June By	331	Copies	
Nov	2000	Copies	
	2331		
		1 presented	
	398	397 left June 1870	
	1933	Sold 25/24c 3/1 gns	
			286 2 8

1871 [June '71-June '74]

advertising and payments to author of

15	3	9	all at ½ author, ½ L & Co
6	15	8	
6	12	7	
	18	6	

[summary of stock:]

397	Copies June '70	192	copies June 71
192	left June 71	101	left June 72
205	sold	91	sold
101	copies June 72	12	copies June 73
89	sold	12	sold
12	left June 73	—	copies left June 74

Appendix B: Outlines of *Essays and Reviews*

1. Frederick Temple: "The Education of the World"

I. Introduction [¶s 1–6]
  A. Repetitive cycles of cause/effect in nature are mechanistic [1–2]
  B. Such cycles acceptable to mind, not spirit that demands purpose: seen in progress of individual
  and human race [3–4]
  C. Human Race a Colossal Man, temporally and developmentally [5–6]
II. The Model: Three Ages of the World: Child, Youth, Man with transitions by processes of training [7] and Trinitarian patterning [8]: [7–8]

Childhood	Positive Rules	Obedience	Law
Youth	Examples	Teaching	Son of Man
Manhood	Principles	Our Instructors	Gift of Spirit

III. First Stage: Child and Law [9–28]
  A. Analogy of education of Child: obedience, duty, intellect [9–11]
  B. Application of the Moral Analogy to the early history of the education of the world, constructed from the biblical accounts of "primitive" history: violence and division of nations in prehistory [12–14]; Jews and Mosaic Law, Prophets, Captivity [15–17]
  C. Application of Historical Analogy to Early Nations of World [18–27]

1. Judaea	Religion (Holiness)	Otherworldly Conscience a. Moral chastity (purity) [21]	Unity & Spirit of God [18–20]
2. Rome	Law (Justice)	Present b. Order and Organization of Government c. Law	Human will
3. Greece	Science & Art (Beauty)	All time d. Cultivation of Individual by Natural Faculties e. Reason and Taste	Reason and Taste
4. Asia	Mystery (Imagination)	Cycles f. Immortality of Soul g. Trinity	Otherworldly Spiritual Imagination

  D. Summary and Transition [28]
IV. Second Stage: Youth and Example [29–38]
  A. Analogy of education of youth: restraint & liberty, friendship; pleasure, joy, pain [29–32]
  B. Application of the Moral Analogy: to youthful history of the world, seen

in the transition from the Old to the New Testaments: meeting of law and Gospel in Jesus [33–34]

C. Application of the Historical Analogy in "three Companions" [34–38]

1. Greece and Rome [35]
2. Early Church [36]

V. Third Stage: Grown Man and Conscience [39–52]

A. Analogy of the education of grown man [39–40]

B. Application of the Moral Analogy to the history of the church in the fields of conduct and intellect [41–48]

C. Application of the Historical Analogy in the history of the church [49–54]

1. No further revelations after the Early Church [49]
2. Early Church [50]
3. Folk-Migrations [51]
4. Medieval discipline to free conscience (Luther) [52]

VI. Conclusion [53–58]

A. Role of right reading of the Bible in the education of world as authority [= law] in childhood of the individual and world [53]

B. The Bible as authority (Law) and as example (Jesus) in youth of individual and world, and as trainer of conscience (principles, Spirit) [54]

C. The Bible and toleration in maturity of individual and in history of the church to teach toleration [55]

D. Summation: Need is for study of the Bible [56–57] as the great teacher of all stages in history of human life or stages of development [58].

2. Rowland Williams: "Bunsen's Biblical Researches"

I. Introduction [¶s 1–5]

A. Analogy between gradualism in geology and continuous revelation of God in theology

1. Devotion turns present into sacred past [1]
2. Criticism turns past into harmony with present
3. But God remains and God's actions were/are true in past/present

B. Use "evidence" to test validity of revelation [2]

C. Enlarged idea of revelation [3]

D. Continuous, developing revelation in the Bible, the world—open to evidence from science, history—demands fair statement and evaluation [4]

E. Bunsen has been tracing this continuous revelation [5]

II. *Egypt's Place in Universal History* [6–9]

A. Bunsen's method: use of authorities [= history] and language origins [= philology] [6]

1. Ancient and contemporary authorities (Herodotus and Eratosthenes; Champollion, Young, and Lipsius)

2. Results: chronology of Egypt clear for 4,000 years B.C.E. concerning commerce, government, language, ethnography
3. Implications: requires 20,000 years of prehistoric preparation for the historical period on evidence of philology; linguistic distinctions in Indo-European family.

B. Comparative chronology: relation of chronologies of Babylon, Sidon, Assyria, Iran to Genesis, using Manetho [7]
1. Chronology from Exodus to the Temple [8]
2. Implications: rejection of temporal and authorial unity of the Pentateuch [9]

III. *God in History* [10–24]

A. The Bible as an "expression of devout reason": examples in narratives of Abraham, Moses, Elijah, Jeremiah [10]

B. Institutional and spiritual causes in the history of the Bible—e.g. sacerdotal in Mosaic books and spiritual and moral in continuous human nature—in Moses [11]

C. Survey of elements in the Bible that predate canonical text, with some reservations—but the weight of Bunsen's work convinces, despite adverse criticism in England [12]

D. Hebrew Prophecy and divine government [of history] [13–23]
1. General consideration of relations between prophecy and history [13–15]
   a. Prophecy is linked to historical events of the time of the prophet, and of the writing of the text—not to prognostication to specific events in later history. Authorities in biblical criticism cited [13]
   b. Predictive prophecy cannot be accepted in light of philological evidence of prophetic books [14]
   c. Bunsen's accomplishment—to show Hebrew Prophecy as witness to the continuous revelation of the kingdom of God [15]
2. Deutero-Isaiah as a specific example [16–21]
   a. Problems in Later (Deutero-) Isaiah [16–19]: (1) Isaiah 50–54; suffering servant as treated in text, Origen, Targum, commentators [16]; (2) Relation of Isa. 52–3 to Jeremiah [17–8]; (3) Relation of Isa. to New Testament Messiah [19]
   b. Implications of historical prophecy concerning: (1) anti-Semitism; (2) Christ; (3) Christian world [20]
   c. Possible author of Deutero-Isaiah is Baruch [21]
3. Prophet Daniel and Book of Daniel: distinctions on basis of textual/contextual problems concerning date (Babylonian Exile or Antiochus IV), canonical location (Hebrew or Greek canons), philological considerations [22]
4. Jonah as legend [23]

E. The Bible as the "written voice of the congregation" is continuous revelation as work of "Eternal Spirit": inspiration of spirit and instrumentality of the Bible in revelation: leads to inclusiveness of contemporary scholarship and use of reason in interpretation of the Bible in the church [24]

IV. *Hippolytus and His Age* [25–34]

A. Bunsen's belief in Christ leads him to harmonize early Church Fathers with evangelical school [25]

B. Christ as "moral saviour" is depicted in "reasonable" sense of the language in St. Paul and Gospels through development of terms of New Testament theology [26]

C. Key New Testament terms: justification, regeneration, resurrection, salvation, propitiation, eternal, hell, heaven, kingdom of God, divine will, and incarnation [27]

D. Two lines of inquiry: [28]

1. Subject matter of NT revelation
   a. spiritual affection
   b. metaphysical reasoning
   } both suggest revelation (like those of Christ) not confined to first 50 years
2. External Criticism
   a. canonical books } both prove illustrative principles true, but not negative
   b. patristic authors } proof of narratives as incredible or precepts as wrong
3. Therefore must verify authenticity in ourselves by use of reason [28]

E. Bunsen's argument in *Hippolytus* [29–34]

1. Treatment of the New Testament—traditional narrative and its development in Canon, place of John, Revelation, Hebrews [29]
2. Summary of implications of first 7 generations of Christendom from Peter and Paul to Hippolytus, concerning:
   a. Relation of religious feeling and intellect
   b. Christian freedom—controversy about doctrine at Councils, emergence of canon, liturgy [30]
3. "Reflection" of relation of feeling/intellect; controversy/freedom in later church history:
   a. Roman church vs early church
      "sacerdotalism" "heart purified by faith"
   b. Liturgy and sacraments: baptism and eucharist [31]
4. Doctrine: sin in Tertullian and deists; Trinity in pre-Augustinian theology and amongst contemporaries of Bunsen [32]
5. Hippolytus' assertion of freedom of will: implications to contemporaries [33]
6. Hippolytus advocates immortality of soul; comparison with Buddhism [34]

V. *Gesang- und Gebet-buch* (Song- and Prayer-Book) [35]

Theology tested in practice by hymns and liturgy

VI. Conclusion [36–37]
Other aspects of Bunsen could be mentioned: summary of his accomplishments [36] and poem of tribute [37].

3. Baden Powell: "On the Study of the Evidences of Christianity"

I. Introduction [¶s 1–15]
 A. General object: "Evidences of Revelation" as "external accessories" taking on a new form in light of new opinion and knowledge, and so it is opportune to examine "the existing state of these discussions" [1]
 B. Preliminary considerations [2–14]
  1. Need for "calm discussion" and toleration of diverse opinions [2–4]
  2. Roles of reason (for external fact) and feeling (moral and spiritual, for internal conviction) [5–8]
  3. "Common language" of orthodox theologians on evidence [9–14]
 C. Summary: present study is not "controversial . . . [but] purely contemplative and theoretical"; "to state, analyse, and estimate" the arguments for the evidences [15]
II. History and grounds of the discussion of the evidences: the arguments *for* miracles [16–53]
 A. Introduction: "Positive external Divine revelation" as basis for all systems of Christian belief [16]
 B. History [17–24]: The scope and character of evidences differ over time, and are conditioned by views of revelation, the kinds of objections to evidential arguments, and dominant ideologies [17]
 Historical survey (early church; medieval church; Reformation; modern times) [18–21]
  1. Protestantism and rise of metaphysical reasoning in response to deists [22]
  2. In past, "internal evidence" of miracles was allowed, but was subordinated to "external facts" of empirical data, dependent on the historic records [23]
  3. Today, a change from reliance on old authorities on evidence to Butler [24]
 C. Problematic "grounds" of religious belief, especially the validation of testimony
 Changes over time concerning tone and character [25–29] include: lack of consistency in objections [25]; reliability of witnesses about empirical evidence [26]; verification [27]; contamination by logic and rhetoric [28]; and contamination by antecedent conviction [29]

D. Miracles in the present day [30–40]
Example of the extraordinary and unaccountable fact that cannot be explained by present knowledge, but eventually will be explicable according to laws of nature [30]
  1. Miracles are not expected, but believed, so how to verify? [31–32]
  2. Example: glossolalia (speaking in tongues) among the Irvingites [33]
  3. Basis of proof lies in study of natural world and inductive logic, not Spinoza's tolerance of violations of natural law because we do not know all of nature [34–35]
  4. Present knowledge is at variance with traditional definition of miracle [36–40]

E. Summary: comparison of grounds for belief in testimony of witnesses concerning the miracles as evidence in gospels [41–53]
  1. Narrative and history: gospel testimony open to historical methods [41–44]
  2. Problems in method [45–48]: misapprehension of critical historical method [45]; dearth of study of laws of probability, antecedent credibility [46]; issue of antecedent incredibility at present time [47–48]
  3. Belief in miracles amongst theists and evidentialists as divine interposition in natural order depends on antecedent faith position regarding the nature and attributes of God [49–53]
  4. Summation: need for balance, toleration, patience [53]

III. Conditions for evidence: the purpose of miracles: testimony to evidence as a spur to faith: the argument *from* miracles [54–94]

A. Evidence is relative to: individual addressee [54–55] concerning faith position [54] and party [55]

B. Other considerations include technical distinctions in language of gospels [56–60]; terminology [56]; attraction [57–58] and rejection [59–60] to and by disbelievers

C. Moral evidence depends on addressee's moral and intellectual condition and is ineffective if the evidence is not appropriate to that condition [61–62]

D. Limited duration of evidence of gospel miracles [63–66] in Newman [63]; reformers [64]; missionaries [65]; and later rabbis [66]

E. Conditions of evidence from modern miracles as proof of Christianity as "Divine revelation" [67–70]; in Paley's school [67]; too great reliance on miracles as evidence [68]; relevance of internal or external conditions [69]; example from Paley [70]

F. Combination of external and internal evidence, with latter as test of former [71–86]
In the Bible [72–74]; English theologians [75–82]; German theologians [83–86]

G. Summary [87–94]: different assessments of conditions for evidentiary status of miracles exist [87]; such evidence, however regarded, must have reference to the "capacity and apprehension of the party addressed" [88]; objections of the more thoughtful [88] and of the shallow [89] must be answered differently over time [90] in balance of reason and faith [91], and in relation to dominant ideas of age [92–94]

IV. Evidence, the doctrine of revelation, and the spiritual nature of Christianity [95–130]

A. Evidence and the doctrine of revelation [95–100]

1. Claims of science concerning knowledge of matter, and of faith concerning knowledge of spirit [95]
2. Science uses reason to understand causation; faith to understand spiritual truth [96]
3. Appeal to evidence of miracles part of moral conviction [97–100]

B. Christianity as a spiritual religion in relation to physical sciences [101–8]; astronomy and geology [102–3]; discrepancies between physical and spiritual sciences and their distinct claims to truth [103–4]; external nature and evidence [105]; position of Paley in current debates [106–8]

C. Credibility of external facts as supported by testimony [109–26]: witnesses taken at face value [110]; conditioning of evidence by historical factors [112–13]; relation of scientific law to testimony [114–24]; and use of analogy in history [124], science [125], and ethnography [126]

D. Summary [127–130]:

1. Senses may be deceived; can be corrected by natural law and analogies [127]
2. Modern examples of deceptive nature of testimony when conditioned by prior belief [128]
3. Testimony is a blind guide and second hand [129] and so we can have no evidence of a deity working miracles because physical facts must be accommodated to natural laws [130]

V. Conclusion [131–37]

A. An alleged miracle can be either: a physical event verifiable by reason and laws of nature; or open to conviction by faith [131]

B. Miracle narratives are objects or "articles" of faith for the sake of the doctrine taught [132–35]; they are not "irresistible" but are subject to "trial of faith" [133]; miracles are "objects" not "evidences" of faith, in which miracles merge with doctrine [134]; evidence is relative to capacity of the addressee; hence its variety and strength [135]

C. So apostles were limited in knowledge and spiritual insight; there is no "infallible age"—even the apostolic age is suspect concerning testimony because of the accommodation of knowledge to age [136]

D. Hence "reason for the hope that is in us" is not restricted to compelling force of external evidence, but consists of what is appropriate in its accommodation to faith position of each person: principle of the accommodation of knowledge asserted [137].

4. H. B. Wilson: "Séances historiques de Genève—the National Church"

I. Introduction: contemporary Evangelical Church in Switzerland compared with England [¶s 1–5]
   A. Reorganization of Evangelical Church in Switzerland included lectures on historical Christianity [1]; on individualism in age of Constantine [1]; and multitudinism in age of Ambrose [2–3]
   B. Geneva's continuity with the past (Calvin) has implications about nationalism and the relations of church and state; and may be compared to England (continuities with the English and continental reformers) [4]
   C. In times of transition, there is a need to consider appropriate adaptations to changing conditions [5]

II. The effects and implications for the Christian church of religious doubts, modern scepticism, and questioning of Christianity in relation to its historic mission [6–15]
   A. Many evils are associated with Christianity, including religious doubts [6–9]; especially in England from sceptics, clergy, and laity [7], whose questions cannot be attributed to German rationalism but demand open discussion [8], in comparison to earlier debates [9]
   B. Modern sceptical movements arise from observation and thought based on new information about the world: millions of non-Christians raise for Christians questions of their relation to the gospel and their eventual moral treatment by God [10]
   C. Question of the eternal destiny of those who have not heard the Christian message [11–15], based on NT mandates in the context of the Roman Empire [12], the preparation of the Roman world for the gospel contrasted with conditions for Buddhism in India [13–14], and for Christianity in England [15]

III. Moral conduct of people in this world conditions their state in next world, according to the Bible, with implications for exclusionist Calvinist, Lutheran, and High Church theology [16] raising questions of Christianity's actions in relation to secular world [17] [16–25]
   A. Different responses [18–19] are based on history or doctrine [18], on external and visible (multitudinist) aspects or internal and invisible aspects (individualist), the former accused of doctrinal compromise with the state, the latter with exclusionary purity of personal morality, both shown as defective in apostolic Christianity [19]
   B. Study of apostolic churches does not substantiate some modern theological

positions, such as Lutheran view of justification or the explicit theology of the creeds [20]

C. Instead there is a different Christian principle: "the source of religion is in the heart" [21–23], involving the placing of morality before doctrine [21] as taught by Jesus and Paul [22–23]

D. Two conclusions: Moral life is as important as doctrinal belief and those defective in either should still be included in the church [24]

E. Hence apostolic church was multitudinist in including people with very different doctrines and inconsistent moral practice [25]

IV. Apostolic churches were multitudinist and national: extension to all nations and religions, and through religious history to include England [26–36]

A. Comparison of early church and Reformation churches: Constantine and Henry VIII [26]; Constantine allowed multitudinism generally, but also set doctrinal limitations at Nicaea [27]; similarly the Calvinistic churches (Geneva and Scotland) impose doctrinal limitations at variance with multitudinist principles that balance hierarchical order with congregational spirit [28]

B. Prejudices against nationalist churches [29–32]: state is demonic [29]; heathendom had national churches [30]; Judaism was exclusivist theocracy [31], defined figuratively [32]

C. All nations have a public religion developed from tendencies in their nationality: shown in history of Christian conversions through empire, Teutonic nations, and England, but may be multitudinist on civil side of state and exclusive doctrinally on religious side [33–36]

V. Condition of the Church of England as a national church founded on the "Word of God" raises many questions: above all, the phrase does not occur in the "pivot" doctrinal document, Article Six, and so is not a marker of doctrinal limitation, but should allow multitudinist freedom [37–58]

A. Analysis of negative and positive language of the Article: "no clause of creed, decision of council, tradition or exposition" is required to be believed unless it is biblical; also there is no requirement that everything biblical must be believed, or how the different Formularies are to be read [38–43]; literalism damages education [39]; Bible Society gives cheap Bibles without interpretation [40]; interpretation should be open, but there are questions on limits of legality of free interpretation [41–44]

B. Liberty of the clergy concerning private opinion is assured [44]

C. Restriction on liberty of clergy concerning expression of private opinion is restrained by subscription to the Thirty-nine Articles of Religion [45–58]; legal meaning of subscription is not defined [45]; it is determined by Canons 5 and 36 of the *Canons of 1603* [46] allowing broad latitude [47–50] as well as 13 Eliz. c. 12, which is also permissive [51]; hence the Articles allow inclusiveness in doctrine, and subscription should be abolished [52–58]

VI. The endowments of the national church: the "Nationalty" for the use and good of all; including property, rights of appointment, moral and spiritual endowments of all citizens are to be developed, along with the contribution of all to a biblical theology [59–71]

   A. Advantages and disadvantages of endowed and unendowed churches; to be nationally endowed benefits all, and prevents current inequity in clerical income [60–61]
   B. Moral and spiritual sides of national life develop into a church [62–69], to include all in both the state and the spiritual community [63]. Exclusion by doctrinal standards destroys the purpose of church and state [64] in which all should contribute to ethical development and biblical theology [65–69]
   C. Biblical theology benefits from the contribution of all in the national church [70–71]

VII. Ideology is the chief means of ensuring rational interpretation between the extremes of a complete rejection of all "historical residue" and a complete acceptance of everything on the basis of an "unquestioning" literalist biblicism with respect to (1) the interpretation of the Bible; (2) the doctrines of Christianity; and (3) the Formularies [72–77]

   A. Ideology accounts for the origin of parts of the Bible: criticism, avoiding Strauss's excesses [72]
   B. Ideology explains the Bible: exegesis, avoiding the excesses of Philo and Origen [73]
   C. For instance, the descent of humans from a historical Adam and Eve or the narrative of the legendary origins of the human race, elide the key point that brotherhood depends not on lines of descent but generic compatibility: shared human nature [74]
   D. The ideologian can accommodate differences in the interpretation of the Bible under the principle of the probability of evidence with respect to the meaning and ideas of the historical record, rather than relying on the empirical facticity of it [75]
   E. This principle applies to doctrines and Formularies (for instance, concerning the presence of Christ in the eucharist) [76] and the use of poetical language and figures of speech [77]

VIII. Conclusion: Christianity is not a theology of intellect or a historical fact, and so should not require uniformity of speculative doctrine [78–81]

   A. Pressing needs in personal and national life, such as the numbers untouched by religion, require no wasting of spiritual energy in presenting such an inclusive view of the national church to all [79]
   B. Calvinism and Augustinianism solve this problem unacceptably, distinguishing the elect from the reprobate by a theology of grace and election, limiting the church to the former, and condemning the rest to perdition [80]

C. Christianity in a national church cares for those committed to its care in this world, but those in the national church, and millions in the broader world, are not at the same state of religious development, and cannot be designated either elect or reprobate; in a future life all will have a place in the "bosom of the Universal Parent . . . according to his Will" [81].

5. C. W. Goodwin: "On the Mosaic Cosmogony"

I. Introduction: The Copernican System in conflict with revelation, recurs in Genesis–Geology conflict [¶s 1–8]
   A. In 16th-century revival of science, Roman Catholic Church opposed Galileo and Copernican system, and supported Ptolemaic system [1]
   B. In 17th century Protestants sympathetic to science, but helped over difficulty of inspiration by notion of separate spheres of knowledge [2]
   C. Once Copernican system is accepted, other difficulties between science and Gen. 1 dwindle [3]
   D. So should accept principle that things known to reason are not fit subjects for revelation [4]
   E. Difficulties of 16th century are recurrent in 19th century concerning geology and conflict with 6,000 year-old earth; and 6 days of creation vs. earth's immense age and long periods from first creation to appearance of humans [5]
   F. Despite attacks of scriptural geologists, antiquity of the earth is now widely accepted, and attention is now directed to reconciliation of Gen. 1. and geology [6]
   G. Summary: the Bible is a book of religious instruction, but is not "scientifically exact" and contains "erroneous views of nature"; conciliation theories differ and must be analyzed [7]

II. Astronomy [8–9]
   A. Account of astronomy places earth in relation to universe; and geology discusses surface and internal structure of earth: both must be surveyed [8]
   B. Copernican system described: earth, sun, moon, stars; use of telescope [9]

III. Geology: Geological periods described [10–15]
   A. Azoic period: early condition of the earth: fluid with intense heat; cooling, steam; condensation, rain, rivers [10]
   B. Palaeozoic period [11–13]
      1. Silurian system with remains of plant and animal life in strata [11]
      2. Upper strata of Silurian—fishes, first vertebrata [12]
      3 Carboniferous strata—luxuriant vegetation [13]
   C. Secondary period [14]
      1. Oolitic and
      2. Cretaceous systems: land animals; saurians in water; flying lizards [14]
   D. Tertiary period [15]

1 Animals to
2. Man [15]

IV. Genesis 1:1–2:3: Two Creation Narratives [16–27]

A. There are two creation narratives, Gen 1:1–2:3 and Gen.2:4–end; Goodwin will restrict this study to the first [16]
   1. Gen. 1:1: the word "created" (Heb. *bara*): whether out or nothing or out of pre-existent matter [17]
   2. Gen. 1:2: Creation out of what? the earth was "without form and void" (Heb. *tohu va-bohu*) [18]

B. The seven "days" of creation [19–24]
   1. Gen. 1:3–5: The First Day: light, earth and water, darkness and light; measurement of time before sun; also light before sun [19]
   2. Gen. 1:6–8: The Second Day: firmament of heaven and division of waters above and below it [20]
   3. Gen. 1:9–13: The Third Day: sea, dry land, plant life especially those for human food [21]
   4. Gen. 1:14–19: The Fourth Day: sun, moon, and measurement of time, stars [22]
   5. Gen. 1:20–23: The Fifth Day: fish and marine animals, birds [23]
   6. Gen. 1:24–31: The Sixth Day: living creatures, human beings in "likeness" of God; and food for humans [23]
   7. Gen. 2:1–3: The Seventh Day: Sabbath rest [24]

C. Comment on the narrative and implications of Genesis 1 and 2 [25–27]
   1. The narrative is not poetical, mystical, symbolical but descriptive [25]
   2. Second creation passage (Gen. 2:4 ff.) suggests mystical approach, but not first, nor is it interpreted so by the most allegorical of interpreters, Philo; so the order appears different from data of science [26]
   3. The problem of reconciling Genesis and geology is assumed by modern biblical apologists to consist in proving the Mosaic narrative is "essentially, and in fact true" although its truth was only imperfectly known until modern science supplied explanations [27]

V. Two Modes of Conciliation have been proposed: [28–67]

A. Chalmers-Buckland-Pratt and the "great gap" theory [29–48]
   1. Buckland's argument about gap in time between Gen. 1:1 and rest of narrative [29–37]
   2. Buckland is refuted by Miller: no evidence for a gap [37–39]
   3. Other arguments against Buckland: Buckland asserts that his concern is with interpretation not correctness of biblical record [40–43]
   4. Pratt supports Buckland: After a "previous convulsion in nature" the first four days involve a darkness of vapours [44]; Gen. 1 is not cosmology except verse 1, after which there are "infinite ages" to the narrative of creation just before humans [45]; the Bible is a record of appearances not scientific processes [46–47]

5. Argument against Pratt; Gen. 1 is wrong in fact; if only appearances are there, it can teach nothing [48]

B. Miller and the day-period theory [49–66]
   1. Theory is old, but is revived in Miller [49]
   2. Buckland's reasons for rejecting it in favor of Chalmers's great gap theory because plants and animals occur simultaneously [50]
   3. Pratt rejects day-period theory on same basis [51–53]
   4. Miller's argument and objections to it [54–66]: there is a general correspondence between geological divisions and sequence in Gen. 1: (1) Palaeozoic division (chiefly, not exclusively plants) [61]; (2) [Mesozoic] or Secondary division (fish and birds) [62]; and (3) [Cainozoic] or Tertiary division (animals) [62]. Problems involve dropping invertebrata and early fish from Palaeozoic division in favor of stress on plants; suppression of land reptiles in Secondary Division as though they are fish [63]; dealing with all plants as food, when some are fuel; and question of how plants survived without light [64–66]

C. Agreements among Buckland, Pratt, and Miller: both great-gap and day-period theories divest Genesis of accordance with geology and stress role of appearance [67]

VI. Conclusion: Implications for theories of revelation and inspiration [68–71]

A. Divine revelation is not given to teach physical science; but admitting errors in the Bible calls into question the idea of the Bible as divine revelation; God used "imperfectly informed men" with "partial" and "to some extent, erroneous" teaching to prepare for later and "higher knowledge"; contemporary scholars should recognize "their fallibility" [68]

B. The mission of the Hebrews was "to lay the foundation of religion upon the earth" and that should be studied, not what a revelation "ought" to be if we were to make one; the dogma that the Bible be "complete, perfect, and unimpeachable in all its parts" occupies the place of "modest enquiry after truth" that is followed in physical science at the "feet of nature" [69]

C. Providence has directed the Hebrew race, works, and books, but God did not communicate to "the writer of the Cosmogony" the knowledge of modern science; the theological geologists have not respected the Bible, but set it out as "a series of elaborate equivocations"; instead, if Gen. 1 is read as limited view of creation according to knowledge then available it has dignity and value [70]

D. Writer of Gen. 1 asserted as fact what was known to be only probability; his "one great truth" is the unity of creation and its subordination to one Lawgiver, not details of astronomy or geology; those who assert that Gen. 1 accords with scientific facts rob it of consistency and grandeur, both of which can be preserved if it is recognized as "a human utterance" used by Providence to educate the human race [71].

6. Mark Pattison: "Tendencies of Religious Thought in England, 1688–1750"

I Introduction: Historical periods and methods in English theology [¶s 1–11]
- A. The period 1714 to 1750 was one of peace, prosperity, and progress to the political philosopher [1] but of decay of religious morals to historian of religion [2]
- B. Cause and effect in history are read differently: historians stress the seventeenth century and resume with the Tractarians, omitting the eighteenth century; to Roman Catholic theology Christianity is withdrawn from human experience; in Protestant theology each individual balances probabilities with individual judgment; one must use inductive method to examine historical causes of the present in the 18th century [3]
- C. Causes of the "present" situation in religious thought: toleration between church and state, religious revival in Methodism and Evangelicalism, and supremacy of reason in Kant, Socinians and relations of deists [4]
- D. Chronological limits on "system" of religious opinion in England from the Restoration to the beginning of the Oxford Movement [5]
  Subdivisions into 2 periods, each with distinct method:
  1. 1688–1750, when the internal proofs of Christianity were stressed in the context of philosophical relations with reason; and
  2. 1750–1830 stressing the external proofs, the "evidences," in terms of apologetics [6]
- E. Problems with the second period concerning the method of studying it include lack of study of *Origines* [7]; and neglect of historical argument because of collapse of knowledge of classical learning in the universities, aversion to the past, and a revival of theology under Coleridge [8]
- F. The same problems do not apply to the methodology for studying the first period of the rational examination of the contexts of Christianity [9]
- G. But there is a neglect of theology proper in both methods [10]
- H. So the first period deserves study [11]

II. The deistical controversy and rational religion [12–39]
- A. Chronology:
  1. 1688–1699, Romanist Controversy
  2. 1720–1740, Deistical Controversy
  3. 1717, Bangorian Controversy [12]
- B. Period is marked by rationalism in religious thought: Examples [13–20]: Gibson [13]; Prideaux [14]; Tillotson [15]; Rogers [16]; Butler [17]; Foster [18]; Warburton [19]; and Locke [20]
- C. Intellectual process of religious argument in Natural Religion [21–24]: deists and Christians agree on the terminal point of the argument of

natural religion: to Christians that point is a bridge to revealed religion; to deists no such bridge is necessary, the natural law of right and duty being already seen perfectly in natural religion, as argued by Tindal [21]

D. Natural Religion is presumed to establish the necessity of revelation a priori with practical implications for morality: to deists the issue of future rewards and punishments; to Christians the language of the moralists [22–24]

E. Rhetorical basis of religious argument [25–34]:
   1. In pulpit rhetoric [25–26];
   2. In society, universities, and philosophy [27–28];
   3. In debates and apologies, like Butler as the synthesis of the age [29–32]

F. New foundation for theology after 1688 in the development of rationalism [35–39]: historical account (Laudian divines, Non-jurors, Puritans and Presbyterians, Independency and Dissent, Cambridge Platonists) [35]; rational, comprehensive, and utilitarian theology [36] with a loss of theological precision [37] while stressing common sense [38–39]

III. Characteristics and forms of theological debate [40–57]

A. Controversial polemic of rational religion [40–45]: lacks justice toward opponents [41]; exaggerates good and evil [42]; advocates internal evidences and judges external evidences [43–44], but remains partisan and fails to resolve issues [45]

B. Exceptions of successful polemic [46–49] include Butler [46], Bentley in his dispute with Collins [47–48], and differences between them and Bentley on Shaftesbury [49]

C. Power of public opinion [50–54] rejects attacks on Christianity by Mandeville, Bolingbroke, Toland, Collins; and legal attacks on grounds of religious libel [50]; public opinion aligns with religious orthodoxy [51]; meanwhile clergy were suspected of scepticism, and subjected to anti-clerical attacks [52–54]

D. Toward 1750, with mixing of French rationalism with English deism, attacks spread to all clergy of all religions [55] for virtues as well as vices, for "enthusiasm" by the strictly orthodox. Distinctions exist between faithful and faithless clergy [56], while Methodism spreads among the lower clergy [57]

IV. Role of theology and metaphysics in the new intellectual and moral climate [58–73]

A. Appeal of theology, both deist and orthodox, to "sound sense and common reason" in attacking moral depravity, rather than theological error. [58] Berkeley in *Alciphron* is an exception, taking on the deists' grounds for their morality as a religious moralist against the "corruption of manners" in first half of the eighteenth century [59]

B. Hartley sets out six attitudes that threaten Christianity [60–67]: the growth of atheism among governing bodies of state; sexual immorality in the upper classes; self-interest in public administrators; contempt of authority in all classes; worldly-mindedness of clergy, and neglect of their duties; and neglect of parents and magistrates regarding education of children

C. Reasons for "prevailing corruption" are attributed differently [68–69]:
   1. Non-jurors and High Churchmen attribute it to Toleration Act and latitudinarianism;
   2. Latitudinarian clergy blame freethinkers and Non-jurors;
   3. Freethinkers blame hypocrisy of clergy because of "passive obedience";
   4. Nonconformists blame conformity;
   5. Catholics blame Protestant Reformation;
   6. Warburton blames Walpole administration and clerical patronage;
   7. George II blames Methodism [68];
   8. Whewell blames low view of morality [69]

D. Cause and effect are reversed: corruption of morals was not caused by low doctrine of morality; instead moral consequences were preached as a remedy to licentiousness [70]; rational religion held it wiser to believe in Christianity than not, the argument of prudence

E. Results [71–73]:
   1. Failure of prudential ethics as restraining force on public morality is demonstrated by Evangelical and Methodist preaching: justification by works has failed; now advocate justification by faith [71]
   2. Hanoverian divines aware of this defect: the practical ineffectiveness of rational religion to correct morals; it plays into hands of those who reject reason as corrupted by the fall [72]
   3. Responses to the limitations of reason:
      a. Catholic response says defect of fallen reason is remedied by authority of the church;
      b. Protestants find such authority in the Bible
      c. Laudian divines sought authority in the church;
      d. Reformers in the Bible; the spirit within was basis for independency;
      e. Common Reason was the last court of appeal—occupied the theological interests of first half of eighteenth century [73]

V. Summary and Conclusion [74]

Discussion of present problems of relation of revelation to authority, inward light, reason, and scripture has its intellectual basis in the "past history of the Theory of Belief in the Church of England" [74].

7. Benjamin Jowett: "On the Interpretation of Scripture"

[Jowett's essay alone is divided into sections; the present editors have added a number for § 1 in the outline although he begins numbering only at § 2. In the first edition § 3 was misnumbered as a second §2, and thereafter the other section numbers follow; all have been corrected in this edition and outline. Hence the section numbers function like the Roman numerals in the outlines of the other essays, to mark off the main divisions of the argument].

§1 Introduction: Differences in interpretation result from different historical and sectarian causes; the remedy is a reformulated hermeneutics [¶s 1–13]

- A. General differences of opinion about the interpretation of the Bible are based on religion, nationality, and systems of knowledge [1]
- B. Particular differences in methods of interpretation [2–9] arise from:
  1. Claims for authority of the Bible derived from sectarian positions [2];
  2. Progress of the human mind [3];
  3. Differences between such fields of knowledge as religious and classical study [5–8], though the same rules apply to both [9]
- C. Thesis: the aim of critical interpretation is devoted to "the book itself [which] remains as at the first unchanged"; to recover the original meaning in its time and place of origin or reception; to use "a knowledge of the text itself"; to employ a theory of interpretation: "to read Scripture like any other book" [10] which would be aided by
- D. A history of interpretation [11–12]
- E. Current differences and uncertainty about the interpretation of the Bible arise from demands for truth claims in contemporary fields of knowledge (natural science, history, mathematics, theology) and party interests (concerning infallibility, prophecy, textual accuracy and especially the synoptic gospels, credal corruption, and theories of reservation) [13]

§2 Three preliminary problems interfere with interpretation of the Bible [14–38]

- A. Inspiration is both peacemaker and source of distrust: those who disagree about the word "inspiration" can agree about the thing it represents [14–21]
  1. "Inspiration" has many meanings (10 types are specified) [15]
  2. Two principles can clarify the problems of inspiration: the principle of progressive revelation in solving textual difficulties [16]; and inspiration must conform to the facts of history and science [17–19]
  3. Interpretation of the Bible has nothing to do with its inspiration [20]
  4. Theories of inspiration make interpretation apologetical and defensive [21]
- B. Accommodation as a possible solution to problems of interpretation [22–34] does so in two ways:
  1. By adapting the Bible to the creeds [22–24], and
  2. By adapting the Bible to language and practice of "our own age" [25–26]

  But such accommodation neglects the necessary distinction between the actual (= practice, action, fact) and the ideal (= doctrine, truth), in which some parts of the Bible are appropriated to bolster received opinions, as in the eight examples discussed [27–28], while other parts of the Bible dealing with matters out of harmony with the age are neglected, as in issues of poverty, class, position, wealth, swearing, keeping the Sabbath, and acting according to conscience [29–31]; in each case, the Bible is used to accommodate received opinion to orthodox doctrine, and for proof texts [32–34]

C. Question of whether there are single or plural meanings to passages or words in the Bible; and whether traditional modes of interpretation, literal, mystical, allegorical, illuminate them? [35–36]

D. Aim of essay is not to settle these problems, but to indicate that they must be settled as priorities before there can be agreement on the interpretation of the Bible [37–38]

§3 Biblical discrepancies must be addressed by interpretation; one primary rule; two secondary rules [39–56]

A. Any discussion of difficulties in the Bible requires appropriate interpretation for all readers [39–44]

B. The rules of interpretation [45–56]

1. One Primary Rule: "Interpret the Scripture like any other book" [45]
2. Two Secondary Rules:
   a. "To know the meaning": Scripture has one meaning, that of its first utterance, composition, or reception [46]
      This rule involves seven tertiary principles:
      (1) To "call up" the life of contemporaries;
      (2) To follow the language and argument;
      (3) To choose the more difficult reading or interpretation;
      (4) To refuse reading that accords only with accepted opinion;
      (5) To relate grammatical usage to author, state of language, and context;
      (6) To use texts that have been carefully edited to avoid erroneous readings;
      (7) To resist mistranslations that have become accepted in established texts

      The qualities of the interpreter include ability to perceive biblical truths not yet learned or hitherto ignored [47], and resistance to the notions that the Bible contains hidden truths, that biblical writers concealed secret meanings, or that the Bible's design or structure is different from other books in being mystical or arcane [48]
   b. "Interpret Scripture from itself" [49–56]: requiring the interpreter
      (1) To distinguish the different parts and kinds of biblical materials and time of writing to reject false harmonizations and forced parallels [49–50] or extraneous influences [51]

(2) But also to recognize continuity in design, arrangement, content of the Bible, and to note large historical or temporal gaps and patterns of theological growth or development [52–56]

§4 Linguistic problems in biblical interpretation: in the historic state of language and in figures of speech and modes of thought [57–70]

A. Problems in the languages of the Bible [57–61]:
   1. Hellenistic Greek at the time of the composition of the New Testament was decayed [57]; but the interpreter must know the original tongue for contexts and to avoid overloading meaning [58], or importing minutiae of classical scholarship [59], or overstressing mistranslations; instead the contextual study of key theological terms and comparisons with the LXX are promising approaches [60]
   2. The language of the Old Testament must also be studied to remove obscurities in translations. Decay is part of general changes in language and signals emergence of new forms [61]

B. The characteristics of New Testament Greek [62–63]

C. Logical and rhetorical character of New Testament Greek [64–69]
   1. Logical form of language, in figures of contrast, parallelism, comparison [64–65]
   2. Logical modes of thought relative to linguistic usage in specific historical periods [66–68]
   3. Figures of Speech, linguistic usage, and the representation of events in the real world [69]

D. Summary of § 4 [70]

§5 Many errors arise from confusion between the interpretation of the Bible to elicit the original meaning and the application of the Bible to contemporary circumstances [71–85]

A. Application replaces original meaning because of
   1. Religious use of the Bible to address present needs [71]
   2. Literary and educational uses of the Bible [72]

B. The question of the application of the OT to events and ideas in the NT in which original meaning is changed [73–74]; as a false precedent leading to abuses in historical examples and present circumstances

C. Raise the problem of what are proper limits on the application of biblical language and concepts to contemporary events or occasions, and the benefits of critical interpretation in dealing with such applications [75–78]

D. The application of the Bible to contemporary uses depends upon the unity of the Bible and unchanging "common element in human nature," the "first instincts of our being" concerning "truth and right" [79–80]

E. Universal applicability "to our own times" of three kinds of materials [81–85]: the words of Christ as in the parables [81–82]; the NT Epistles [83]; the OT [84–85]

§6 The relation of the interpretation of the Bible to theology and life [86–106]

A. Two preliminary remarks [86–87]

1. Change in modes of interpretation is a necessity, but original meaning is often at variance with conventional meaning [88] such as four-fold levels not currently tenable [89]; or interpretations based on history of biblical criticism [90]
2. Changes in the intellectual forms of Christianity contrast with "never-changing truth of the Christian life" [91]; and diminution of party differences over theology based on old interpretations [92]

B. Key question: what is possible effect of critical interpretation of the Bible on theology and life? [93] Results are unknown because human beings are subject to the conditions of time and space; but theological rivalries of past and present interfere with inquiry; can be overcome by associations on basis of "moral good and intellectual truth" [94]

C. Critical interpretation of the Bible can provide a basis for intellectual and moral reconciliation of denominational and other differences; and can contribute to other fields of action [95–101] through:

1. Overcoming divisions in Christianity [96] in part by critical interpretation of the Bible [97] as a means of promoting church union [98]
2. Work of Christian missions in using critical interpretation [99]
3. Liberal education in applying methods of classical scholarship to the Bible [100–101]
4. Sermons in using biblical terms with precise meaning [102]

D. Conclusion: The relation of the critical interpretation of the Bible to the role of the clergy in addressing these differences and challenges in various fields of activity raises four final considerations [103–6]:

1. Not all have necessary qualities to be critical interpreters of the Bible [103]
2. Interpreting the difficulties in the Bible raises opposition and attack, but is part of international project of clarification of the Bible [104]
3. Such attacks do not lessen the value of interpretation [105]
4. Resisting such attacks lays claim to higher purposes and ideals [106].

Appendix C: A Finding List for Letters and Diaries on *Essays and Reviews*

This finding list contains a selection of letters and diary entries on *Essays and Reviews*, set out in chronological order, to some of which reference is made by letter number elsewhere in this edition. When a document exists in both manuscript and published versions, we have cited the manuscript text. Following the letter numbers, the sender and recipient are specified, together with the date of the letter and the sources consulted, both in manuscript collections and more readily accessible newspapers and published biographies which may be referred to for the complete texts and more extensive correspondence.

1	Jowett to A. P. Stanley, 14 Dec. 1855	Abbott and Campbell 1897, 1:239–40
2	Wilson to Pattison, 27 Jan. 1858	Bodley, MS. Pattison 52, fol. 95
3	Wilson to Pattison, 19 Mar. 1858	Bodley, MS. Pattison 52, fol. 93
4	Wilson to Pattison, 28 Mar.1858	Bodley, MS. Pattison 52, fol. 44
5	John W. Parker to Pattison, 7 Apr. 1858	Bodley, MS. Pattison 52, fol. 55
6	Jowett to Stanley, 15 Aug. 1858	Balliol, MS. Jowett III S, fol. 89; Abbott and Campbell 1897, 1:275
7	Stanley to Jowett, 16 Aug. 1858	Balliol, MS. Jowett 410
8	Wilson to Pattison, 4 July 1859	Bodley, MS. Pattison 52, fol. 407
9	Wilson to Pattison, 27 Sept. 1859	Bodley, MS. Pattison 52, fol. 508
10	Wilson to Pattison, 3 Oct. 1859	Bodley, MS. Pattison 52, fol. 519
11	F. J. A. Hort to Williams, 21 Oct. 1858	Hort 1896, 1:399–401
12	Wilson to Pattison, 21 Nov. 1859	Bodley, MS. Pattison 52, fol. 551
13	Wilson to Pattison, 27 Mar. 1860	Bodley, MS. Pattison 53, fol. 138
14	H. P. Liddon to John Keble, 31 Mar. 1860	Johnston 1904, 63
15	Stanley to Pattison, [Apr. 1860?]	Bodley, MS. Pattison 112. f. 99
16	Williams's Journal Entry, 5 Apr. 1860	Ellen Williams 1874, 2:18
17	Jowett to Lewis Campbell, 16 Apr. 1860	Balliol, MS. Jowett F 12, fol. 3
18	John Chapman to Pattison, 17 Apr. 1860	Bodley, MS. Pattison 53, fol. 161
19	Hort to John Ellerton, 20 Apr. 1860	Hort 1896, 1:417
20	R. C. Christie to Pattison, 25 Apr. 1860	Bodley, MS. Pattison 53 fols. 174–75
21	Williams's Journal Entry, 2 June, 1860	Ellen Williams 1874, 2:18
22	Williams to A. Jessopp, 2 June 1860	Ellen Williams 1874, 2:90–91
23	Wilson to Pattison, 11 June 1860	Bodley, MS. Pattison 53, fol. 218
24	Chapman to Pattison, 23 July 1860	Bodley, MS. Pattison 53, fols. 244–45
25	Wilson to Pattison, 25 July 1860	Bodley, MS. Pattison 53, fols. 247–48
26	Jowett to Gilbert Elliot, 29 July 1860	Balliol, MS. Jowett F 4, fol. 1

27 Chapman to Pattison, 16 Aug. 1860 Bodley, MS. Pattison 53, fol. 277
28 Jowett to Anon., 27 Oct. 1860 Abbott and Campbell 1897, 1:322
29 E. B. Pusey to Bp. Wilberforce, 31 Oct. 1860 Liddon 1893–97, 4:15–16
30 Chapman to Pattison, 29 Nov. 1860 Bodley, MS. Pattison 53, fol. 406
31 Chapman to Pattison , 17 Dec. 1860 Bodley, MS. Pattison 53, fols. 433–34
32 Williams to Walker, Wise, & Co., 24 Dec. 1860 Ellen Williams 1874, 2:99–100
33 Jowett to Pattison, 1 Jan. 1861 [?] Bodley, MS. Pattison 54, fol. 217
34 A. C. Tait Journal Entry, 20 Jan. 1861 Davidson and Benham 1891, 1:281
35 Jowett to Anon., 22 Jan. 1861 Abbott and Campbell 1897, 1: 322–23
36 Wilson to Pattison, 28 Jan. 1861 Bodley, MS. Pattison 54, fols. 174–75
37 H. W. Fremantle to Pattison, 29 Jan. 1861 Bodley, MS. Pattison 54, fol. 183
38 Temple to Robert Scott, [undated; Feb. 1861?] Sandford 1906, 2:611
39 Temple's Address at Rugby, [Feb. 1861?] Sandford 1906, 1:221–25
40 Jowett to Stanley, [Feb. 1861?] Balliol, MS. Jowett III S, fol. 93; Abbott and Campbell 1897, 1:346–47
41 Wilberforce on Lambeth, Feb. 1861 Bodley, MS. Wilberforce 3. 13, fol. 103; meeting of Bishops partially printed in Ashwell and Wilberforce 1880–82, 3:2–3
42 Wilberforce Diary Entry, 2 Feb. 1861 Ashwell and Wilberforce 1880–82, 3:4
43 Williams to Pattison, 2 Feb. 1861 Bodley, MS. Pattison 54, fol. 236
44 R. D. Hampden to Tait, 4 Feb. 1861 Lambeth, MS. Tait 80, fol. 19
45 H. Montagu Villiers to Cox, 4 Feb. 1861 *Times*, 11 Feb. 1861, 9
46 Temple to Wilberforce, 6 Feb. 1861 Bodley, MS. Wilberforce C. 13, fol. 21
47 Jowett to Gilbert Elliot, 8 Feb. 1861 Balliol, MS. Jowett F 4, fol. 4; partially printed in Abbott and Campbell 1897, 1:322–23; 344–45
48 Temple to Scott, 12 Feb. 1861 Sandford 1906, 2:615–616
49 F. D. Maurice to Stanley, 12 Feb. 1861 Maurice 1884, 2:382–83
50 R. W. Jelf to Tait, 14 Feb. 1861 Lambeth, MS. Tait 80. fols. 15–16
51 Hort to B. F. Westcott, 15 Feb. 1861 Hort 1896, 1:440
52 Hort to John Ellerton, 15 Feb. 1861 Hort 1896, 1:442
53 "Rusticus" to the *Times*, 16 Feb. 1861 *Times*, 19 Feb. 1861, 3
54 Stanley to Tait, 16 Feb. 1861 Davidson and Benham 1891, 1:284
55 Tait to Stanley, 18 Feb. 1861 Davidson and Benham 1891, 1:285
56 Tait to the *Times*, 18 Feb. 1861 *Times*, 19 Feb. 1861, 3
57 Hort to Pattison, 18 Feb. 1861 Bodley, MS. Pattison 54, fol. 261
58 "Anglicanus" [Stanley] to the *Times*, 18 Feb. 1861 *Times*, 18 Feb. 1861, 12
59 Stanley to Tait, 19 Feb. 1861 Davidson and Benham 1891, 1:286
60 Temple to Scott, 19 Feb. 1861 Sandford 1906, 2:616
61 Williams's Journal Entry, 19 Feb. 1861 Ellen Williams 1874, 2:32
62 "A Cambridge Graduate" [Henry Sidgwick] to the *Times*, [undated] *Times*, 20 Feb. 1861, 12
63 Temple to Wilberforce, 20 Feb. 1861 Bodley, MS. Wilberforce 3. 13 fol. 23
64 Temple to Henry Phillpotts [bp. of Exeter], 21 Feb. 1861

Glynne-Gladstone Papers 1648 fol. 1; *Times*, 4 Mar. 1861, 10

65 Temple to Tait, 21 Feb. 1861 — Lambeth, MS. Tait 80, fol. 25; Davidson and Benham 1891, 1:287–88

66 Tait to Temple, 22 Feb. 1861 — Davidson and Benham 1891, 1:288–89

67 Temple to Tait, 22 Feb. 1861 — Davidson and Benham 1891, 1:289

68 Temple to Henry Phillpotts, 22 Feb. 1861 — *Times*, 4 Mar. 1861, 10

69 Temple to Robert Lawson, 22 Feb. 1861 — Sandford 1906, 1:220

70 Tait to Temple, 23 Feb. 1861 — Lambeth, MS. Tait 80, fol. 31; cf. Davidson and Benham 1891, 1:289–90

71 "Oxford Graduate" to the *Times*, 23 Feb. 1861 — *Times*, 23 Feb. 1861, 5

72 Temple to Tait, 25 Feb. 1861 — Lambeth, MS. Tait, fols. 37–40; Davidson and Benham 1891, 1:290–93

73 Henry Phillpotts to Temple, 25 Feb. 1861 — Glynne-Gladstone MSS 1648, fols.1–3; Times, 4 Mar. 1861, 10

74 William Spottiswoode to John Lubbock, 25 Feb. 1861 — BL, MS. Add. 49639 [Avebury Papers] fol. 28

75 Charles Lyell to Lubbock, 25 Feb. 1861 — BL, MS. Add. 49,639 [Avebury Papers] fols. 30–31

76 Tait to Temple, 27 Feb. 1861 — Davidson and Benham 1891, 1:294–97

77 William Carpenter to Lubbock, 27 Feb. 1861 — BL, MS. Add. 49,639 [Avebury Papers], fols. 32–33

78 "Anglicanus" [Stanley] to the *Times*, 28 Feb. 1861 — *Times*, 2 Mar. 1861, 9

79 "Cerdo" to the *Times*, 28 Feb. 1861 — *Times*, 28 Feb. 1861, 12

80 Temple to Tait, 1 Mar. 1861 — Davidson and Benham 1891, 1:297–98

81 Temple to Rugby Sixth Form, [Mar. 1861?] — Sandford 1906, 1:220

82 Tait to Temple, 2 Mar. 1861 — Davidson and Benham 1891, 1:298–99

83 Alexander Macmillan to Temple, 2 Mar. 1861 — Sandford 1906, 2:614

84 J. F. W. Herschel to Lubbock, 2 Mar. 1861 — BL, MS. Add. 49,639 [Avebury Papers], fols. 37–38

85 Temple to Tait, 3 Mar. 1861 — Davidson and Benham 1891, 1:299–300

86 Tait to Temple, 4 Mar. 1861 — Davidson and Benham 1891, 1:300–301

87 G. B. Airy to Lubbock, 4 Mar. 1861 — BL, MS. Add. 49,639 [Avebury Papers], fols. 39–40

88 J. C. Adams to Lubbock, 4 Mar. 1861 — BL, MS. Add. 49,639 [Avebury Papers], fols. 41–42

89 Charles Longley to Tait, 5 Mar. 1861 — Lambeth, MS. Tait 80, fol. 69

90 C. J. Bate to Lubbock, 6 Mar. 1861 — BL, MS. Add. 49,639 [Avebury Papers] fol. 51

91 Pusey to the *Guardian*, 6 Mar. 1861 — *A Letter on the "Essays and Reviews"* [reprinted from *Guardian* 6 Mar. 1861, 214–15]

92 Williams to Rev. Dr. G. J. Wild, 6 Mar. 1861 — Ellen Williams 1874, 2:100–101

93 J. H. Newman to Pattison, 7 Mar. 1861 — Bodley, MS. Pattison 54, fol. 275

94 Williams to R. B. Kennard, 8 Mar. 1861 — Ellen Williams 1874, 2:44–46
95 Temple to Scot, 14 Mar. 1861 — Sandford 1906, 2:614
96 Henry Phillpotts to Wilberforce, 14 Mar. 1861 — Bodley, MS. Wilberforce C. 5, fol. 194
97 Williams's Journal Entry, 20 Mar. 1861 — Ellen Williams 1874, 2:38–39
98 Stanley to Pattison, 22 Mar. 1861 — Bodley, MS. Pattison 54, fol. 293
99 Jowett to Francis Turner Palgrave, 22 Mar. 1861 — Balliol, MS. Jowett, F 10, fol. 57; Abbott and Campbell 1897, 1:347
100 Jowett to Palgrave, 22 Mar. 1861 — Abbott and Campbell 1897, 1:323
101 Temple to Lawson, 22 Mar. 1861 — Sandford 1906, 2:617
102 Alexander Grant to Pattison, 27 Mar. 1861 — Bodley, MS. Pattison 54, fol. 298
103 Wilson to Pattison, 1 Apr. 1861 — Bodley, MS. Pattison 54, fol. 306
104 Jowett to Gilbert Elliot, 1 Apr. 1861 — Balliol, MS. Jowett, F 4, fol. 5; partially printed in Abbott and Campbell 1897, 1:323; 347–48
105 Jowett to Miss [Margaret] Elliot, 1 Apr. 1861 — Abbott and Campbell 1897, 1:349
106 Jowett to Anon., 1 Apr. 1861 — Abbott and Campbell 1897, 1:323–24
107 Williams to a Former Pupil, 11 Apr. 1861 — Ellen Williams 1874, 2:101
108 Stanley to Pattison, 12 Apr. 1861 — Bodley, MS. Pattison 54, fol. 309
109 Jowett to Gilbert Elliot, 14 Apr. 1861 — Balliol, MS. Jowett F 4, fol. 7; Abbott and Campbell 1897, 1:349–50
110 Chapman to Pattison, 15 Apr. 1861 — Bodley, MS. Pattison 54, fol. 311
111 Jowett to Anon., 16 Apr. 1861 — Abbott and Campbell 1897, 1:324
112 Tait Diary Entry, 21 Apr. 1861 — Davidson and Benham 1891, 1:307
113 Jowett to Frederic Harrison, 23 Apr. 1861 — Abbott and Campbell 1899, 14–15
114 Jowett to Grant, 27 Apr. 1861 — Balliol, MS. Jowett F 10, fol. 7; Abbott and Campbell 1897, 1:351
115 Williams to a Friend, 27 Apr. 1861 — Ellen Williams 1874, 2: 39–40
116 Jowett to Harrison, 30 Apr. 1861 — Abbott and Campbell 1899, 15–16
117 Charles Kingsley to Williams, c. May 1861 — Ellen Williams 1874, 2:43
118 Jowett to Stanley, 9 May 1861 — Abbott and Campbell 1897, 1:324
119 Jowett to Robert B. D. Morier, 10 May 1861 — Balliol, MS. Jowett III M, fol. 10; partially printed in Abbot and Campbell 1899, 57–58
120 Williams to Anon., 13 May 1861 — Ellen Williams 1874, 2:40
121 Walter Kerr Hamilton to the *Dorset Country Chronicle*, 23 May 1861 — *Times*, 23 May 1861, 9
122 Williams to Kennard, 28 May 1861 — Ellen Williams 1874, 2:104–5
123 Jowett to Williams, c. June 1861 — Ellen Williams 1874, 2:40
124 Williams to "A Hebrew Friend," 1 June 1861 — Ellen Williams 1874, 2:105
125 Jowett to Margaret Elliot, 9 June 1861 — Balliol, MS. Jowett, F 4, fol. 8; partially printed in Abbott and Campbell 1897, 1:352
126 Williams to "A Churchman" in Manchester, 10 June 1861

Ellen Williams 1874, 2:46–47; partially printed in *Athenaeum*, 24 Aug. 1861, 253–54

127 Pusey to Hamilton, 22 June 1861 — Liddon 1893–97, 4:44
128 A "Hertfordshire Incumbent" to the *Times*, 2 July 1861 — *Times*, 3 July 1861, 12
129 Wilberforce to Alfred Ollivant, 3 July 1861 — Wilberforce 1970, 363–64
130 Stanley to Tait, 6 July 1861 — Davidson and Benham 1891, 1:308–9
131 Tait to Stanley, 8 July 1861 — Davidson and Benham 1891, 1:309–10
132 Stanley to Tait, 10 July 1861 — Davidson and Benham 1891, 1:310
133 Jowett to Stanley, [July/Aug. 1861?] — Abbott and Campbell 1897, 1:352–53
134 Jowett to Margaret Elliot, 4 Aug. 1861 — Balliol, MS. Jowett F 4, fol. 9; Abbott and Campbell 1897, 1:353–54
135 Williams Journal Entry, 16 Aug. 1861 — Ellen Williams 1874, 2:51
136 Wilson to Pattison, 25 Aug. 1861 — Bodley, MS. Pattison 54, fol. 409
137 Jowett to Florence Nightingale, 28 Aug. [1861] — Quinn and Prest 1987, 10–11
138 Wilberforce to James Fendall, 23 Oct. 1861 — Wilberforce 1970, 365–66
139 Williams's Journal Entry, 27 Oct. 1861 — Ellen Williams 1874, 2:51–52
140 Jowett to Frances Power Cobbe, Nov. 1861 — Abbott and Campbell 1897, 1:324–25; also in Cobbe 1894, 1:353
141 A. H. Layard to Lord John Russell, Nov. 1861 — BL, Layard Papers, MS. Add. 38,987, fol. 340–40v
142 Wilson to Pattison, 18 Nov. 1861 — Bodley, MS. Pattison 54, fol. 504
143 Wilson to Pattison, 23 Nov. 1861 — Bodley, MS. Pattison 54, fol. 511
144 Hort to Pattison, 28 Nov. 1861 — Bodley, MS. Pattison 54, fol. 515
145 Wilson to Pattison, 28 Nov. 1861 — Bodley, MS. Pattison 54, fol. 517
146 Stanley to Tait, 31 Dec. 1861 — Davidson and Benham 1891, 1:310–11
147 Chapman to Pattison, 3 Jan. 1862 — Bodley, MS. Pattison 55, fol. 3
148 Tait to Stanley, 6 Jan. 1862 — Davidson and Benham 1891, 1:311–12
149 Jowett to R. R. W. Lingen, 24 Jan. 1862 — Abbott and Campbell 1897, 1: 306–7
150 Wilberforce Diary Entry, 28 Jan. 1862 — Ashwell and Wilberforce 1880–82, 3:8
151 Jowett to Stanley, [1862] — Balliol, MS. Jowett III S, fol. 102; printed in Abbott and Campbell 1897, 1:325
152 Hort to John Ellerton, 1 May 1862 — Hort 1896, 1:454
153 Jowett to Nightingale, [c. July 1862] — Balliol, MS. Jowett III N, fol. 12; partially printed in Quinn and Prest 1987, 15–17
154 Jowett to Anon., 16 July 1862 — Balliol, MS. Jowett III C, fol. 11
155 Wilberforce to Fendall, 23 Aug. 1862 — Wilberforce 1970, 380
156 Williams to Kennard, 1 Sept. 1862 — Ellen Williams 1874, 2:131–32
157 Hort to Ellerton, 25 Sept. 1862 — Hort 1896, 1:457
158 Jowett to Nightingale, 9 Oct. 1862 — Quinn and Prest 1987, 24
159 "Another Member of Congregation" to the *Guardian*, 8 Nov. 1862 — *Guardian*, 12 Nov. 1862
160 "Another Resident" to the *Guardian*, 8 Nov. 1862 — *Guardian*, 12 Nov. 1862
161 Keble to the *Guardian*, 9 Nov. 1862 — *Guardian*, 12 Nov. 1862

162 "A Member of Convocation" to the *Guardian*, 17 Nov. 1862 — *Guardian*, 26 Nov. 1862
163 G. H. Curteis to the *Guardian*, 26 Nov. 1862 — *Guardian*, 26 Nov. 1862
164 Wilson to Pattison, 5 Dec. 1862 — Bodley, MS. Pattison 55, fol. 229
165 Williams to John Johnes, Jan. 1863 — Ellen Williams 1874, 2:65–67
166 James Fitzjames Stephen to *Spectator*, Jan. 1863 — Ellen Williams 1874, 2:78–79
167 Wilberforce to Fendall, 18 Jan. 1863 — Wilberforce 1970, 388–89
168 Williams to *Daily News*, 17 Jan. 1863 — Ellen Williams 1874, 2:80–81
169 Williams to Anon., 19 Jan. 1863 — Ellen Williams 1874, 2:82
170 Jowett to Nightingale, Feb. 1863 — Quinn and Prest 1987, 26–27
171 Jowett to Stanley, 3 Feb. 1863 — Balliol, MS. Jowett III S, fol. 109; Abbott and Campbell 1897, 1:311–12
172 Jowett to Emily Tennyson, Feb. 1863 — Abbott and Campbell 1897, 1:325
173 Williams to Anon., 3 Feb. 1863 — Ellen Williams 1874, 2:82
174 Williams to J. W. Colenso, 9 Feb. 1863 — Ellen Williams 1874, 2:175–77
175 Pusey to the *Times*, 17 Feb. 1863 — *Times*, 19 Feb. 1863, 6
176 Maurice to the *Times*, 19 Feb. 1863 — *Times*, 20 Feb. 1863, 9
177 Godfrey Lushington to the *Times*, 19 Feb. 1863 — *Times* 21 Feb. 1863, 12
178 "A [London] Protestant" to the *Times*, 19 Feb. 1863 — *Times*, 23 Feb. 1863, 5
179 "M.A. (of Balliol)" to the *Times*, [undated] — *Times*, 23 Feb. 1863, 5
180 Pusey to the *Times*, 20 Feb. 1863 — *Times*, 23 Feb. 1863, 5
181 Maurice to the *Times*, [undated] — *Times*, 24 Feb. 1863, 9
182 "Anglicanus" [Stanley] to the *Times*, 23 Feb. 1863 — *Times*, 24 Feb. 1863, 9
183 "A Looker-On" to the *Times*, [undated] — *Times*, 25 Feb. 1863, 5
184 J. H. Newman to the *Times*, 24 Feb. 1863 — *Times*, 26 Feb. 1863, 9
185 Pusey to the *Times*, 25 Feb. 1863 — *Times*, 26 Feb. 1863, 9
186 Maurice to the *Times*, 26 Feb. 1863 — *Times*, 27 Feb. 1863, 9
187 Francis Close to the *Times*, 26 Feb. 1863 — *Times*, 26 Feb. 1863, 9
188 "Oldest Lay Professor in the University of Oxford" [Charles Daubeny] to the *Times*, [undated] — *Times*, 3 Mar. 1863, 7
189 Pusey to the *Times*, 3 Mar. 1863 — *Times*, 4 Mar. 1863, 9
190 Jowett to Gilbert Elliot, 4 Mar. 1863 — Balliol, MS. Jowett F 4, fol. 15; partially printed in Abbott and Campbell 1897, 1:362
191 T. D. MacBride to the *Times*, 6 Mar. 1863 — *Times*, 9 Mar. 1863, 12
192 "Oxoniensis" to the *Times*, 11 Mar. 1863 — *Times*, 12 Mar. 1863, 10
193 Jowett to Emily Tennyson, 12 Mar. 1863 — Abbott and Campbell 1897, 1:325–26
194 "An Oxford Liberal" to the *Times*, 12 Mar. 1863 — *Times*, 13 Mar. 1863, 12
195 "Oxford Resident" to the *Times*, 13 Mar. 1863 — *Times*, 14 Mar. 1863, 7
196 Jowett to Margaret Elliot, 15 Mar. 1863 — Balliol, MS. Jowett F 4, fol. 16; printed in Abbott and Campbell 1897, 1:313
197 Pusey to the *Times*, 16 Mar. 1863 — *Times* 17 Mar. 1863, 5
198 "Oxoniensis" to the *Times*, 20 Mar. 1863 — *Times*, 20 Mar. 1863, 10

199 Pusey to the *Times*, 20 Mar. 1863 — *Times*, 21 Mar. 1863, 11
200 Pusey to Tait, 3 May 1863 — Lambeth, MS. Tait 80, fols. 93–94
201 Ogilvie, Pusey, and Heurtley to the *Times*, 8 May 1863 — *Times*, 11 May 1863, 9
202 Montague Bernard to the *Times*, 10 May 1863 — *Times*, 12 May 1863, 14
203 J. P. Lightfoot to Jowett, 11 May 1863 — Balliol, MS. Jowett, IV A 19, fol. 10
204 Brooks and Du Bois to the *Times*, 11 June 1863 — *Times*, 12 June 1863, 11
205 Williams to Colenso, 1 July 1863 — Ellen Williams 1874, 2:177
206 Pusey to Tait, 6 Dec. 1863 — Lambeth, MS. Tait 80, fol. 107–8
207 Pusey to Tait, 25 Dec. 1863 — Lambeth, MS. Tait 80, fols. 108–11
208 Edward Hawkins to Pattison, 31 Dec. 1863 — Bodley, MS. Pattison 112, fol. 72
209 Hawkins to Pattison, 7 Jan. 1864 — Bodley, MS. Pattison 112, fol. 74
210 Williams to Colenso, 22 Jan. 1864 — Ellen Williams 1874, 2:178–80
211 Wilberforce to Henry Phillpotts, 29 Jan. 1864 — Bodley, MS. Wilberforce C. 5, fol. 196
212 Pusey to Keble, 29 Jan. 1864 — Liddon 1893–97, 4:46
213 Pusey to Tait, 2 Feb. 1864 — Lambeth, MS. Tait 80, fols. 112–15; Davidson and Benham 1891, 1:314
214 Brooks and Du Boy [i. e. Du Bois] to the Times, 3 Feb. 1864 — *Times*, 4 Feb. 1864, 12
215 Pusey to Keble, 10 Feb. 1864 — Liddon 1893–97, 4:48–49
216 Pusey to Wilberforce, 13 Feb. 1864 — Liddon 1893–97, 4:52–53
217 Pusey to Gladstone, 18 Feb. 1864 — Liddon 1893–97, 4:83–84
218 Williams to a Former Pupil, 19 Feb. 1864 — Ellen Williams 1874, 2:181
219 Pusey to Liddon, 22 Feb. 1864 — Liddon 1893–97, 4:86
220 Pusey to Stanley, 23 Feb. 1864 — Liddon 1893–97, 4:63–64
221 Jowett to Gilbert Elliot, 24 Feb. 1864 — Balliol, MS. Jowett F 4, fol. 15
222 Stanley to Pusey, 25 Feb. 1864 — Liddon 1893–97, 4:64
223 Shaftesbury to Pusey, 26 Feb. 1864 — Liddon 1893–97, 4:51
224 Williams to His Sister, 28 Feb. 1864 — Ellen Williams 1874, 2:145
225 Pusey to Shaftesbury, 28 Feb. 1864 — Liddon 1893–97, 4:51–52
226 Pusey to Wilberforce, 28 Feb. 1864 — Liddon 1893–97, 4:54–56
227 Pusey to Stanley, 28 Feb. 1864 — Liddon 1893–97, 4:65
228 Longley to the *Times*, 4 Mar. 1864 — *Times*, 12 Mar. 1864, 11
229 Maurice to the *Times*, 4 Mar. 1864 — *Times*, 5 Mar 1864, 10
230 Pusey to Stanley, 5 Mar. 1864 — Liddon 1893–97, 4:66
231 Wilberforce to H. J. Pye, 7 Mar. 1864 — Wilberforce 1970, 395–96
232 Pusey to the *Times*, 7 Mar. 1864 — *Times*, 8 Mar. 1864, 12
233 Maurice to the *Times*, 8 Mar. 1864 — *Times* 9 Mar. 1864, 9
234 Pusey to the *Times*, [undated] — *Times*, 11 Mar. 1864, 5
235 Maurice to the *Times*, [undated] — *Times* 12 Mar. 1864, 14
236 Pusey to the *Times*, [undated] — *Times* 15 Mar. 1864, 14
237 Williams to His Sister, 17 Mar. 1864 — Ellen Williams 1874, 2:155–56
238 Williams [to Christopher Wordsworth], 16 Apr. 1864

Chronicle of Convocation 19 Apr. 1864, 1478–79; Ellen Williams 1874, 2:156–58

239 Williams to W. K. Hamilton, 18 Apr. 1864 — Ellen Williams 1874, 2:166–69
240 Gladstone to Tait, 25 Apr. 1864 — Lambeth, MS. Tait 81, fols. 190v–96a
241 Pusey to Keble, June 1864 — Liddon 1893–97, 4:86
242 Williams to Lord Houghton, 26 June 1864 — Ellen Williams 1874, 2:162–63
243 Williams to Longley, 2 July 1864 — Ellen Williams 1874, 2:170–71
244 Longley to Williams, 6 July 1864 — Ellen Williams 1874, 2:171–72
245 Williams to Longley, 8 July 1864 — Ellen Williams 1874, 2:172–74
246 Phillpotts to Wilberforce, 10 July 1864 — Bodley, MS. Wilberforce C5 fol. 200
247 Longley to Williams, 15 July 1864 — Ellen Williams 1874, 2:174
248 Jowett to Stanley, 17 July 1864 — Balliol, MS. Jowett III S fol. 115; Abbott and Campbell 1897, 1:368
249 Jowett to Nightingale, [Sept. 1864] — Quinn and Prest 1987, 35
250 Pusey to the *Times*, [undated; Sept. 15, 1864?] — *Times*, 16 Sept. 1864, 10
251 Keble to the *Times*, 20 Sept. 1864 — *Times*, 22 Sept. 1864, 7; partially printed in Liddon 1893–97, 4:90–91
252 Pusey to the *Times*, [undated] — *Times*, 22 Sept. 1864, 9
253 Pusey to Keble, 25 Sept. 1864 — Liddon 1893–97, 4:91–92
254 Pusey to Keble, Oct. 1864 — Liddon 1893–97, 4:93
255 Wilson to W. Longman, 27 Nov. 1864 — Reading, MS. Longman 43, fol. 2
256 Jowett to Nightingale, 28 Dec. 1864 — Quinn and Prest 1987, 39
257 Pusey to Gladstone, 21 Feb. 1865 — Liddon 1893–97, 4:94
258 Jowett to Emily Tennyson, 27 Feb. 1865 — Abbott and Campbell 1897, 1:373
259 Jowett to Pattison, 26 Dec. 1866 — Bodley, MS. Pattison 56, fol. 380
260 Wilson to Pattison, 4 Nov. 1867 — Bodley, MS. Pattison 112, fol. 86
261 Jowett to Nightingale, 9 Nov. 1868 — Quinn and Prest 1987, 154
262 Temple to Frederic Charles Cook, [Feb. 1869?] — Sandford 1906, 2:605
263 Jowett to Nightingale, 2 July 1869 — Quinn and Prest 1987, 170
264 Jowett to Nightingale, 15 July 1869 — Quinn and Prest 1987, 171
265 Jowett to Nightingale, 25 July 1869 — Quinn and Prest 1987, 174
266 Jowett to Nightingale, 1 Aug. 1869 — Quinn and Prest 1987, 175
267 Harold Browne to Temple, Oct. 1869 — Sandford 1906, 1:276
268 Wilberforce to Temple, Oct. 1869 — Sandford 1906, 1:277
269 Stanley to Temple, 6 Oct. 1869 — Sandford 1906, 1:277
270 Tait to Temple, 7 Oct. 1869 — Sandford 1906, 1:275–76
271 E. W. Benson to Temple, 7 Oct. 1869 — Sandford 1906, 1:276
272 Temple to Scott, 8 Oct. 1869 — Sandford 1906, 2:619–620
273 Jowett to Nightingale, 8 Oct. 1869 — Quinn and Prest 1987, 178
274 Thomas Hughes to Temple, 9 Oct. 1869 — Sandford 1906, 1:277
275 Temple to John Duke Coleridge, 11 Oct. 1869 — Sandford 1906, 1:285
276 Edward Henry Bradby to Temple, 11 Oct. 1869 — Sandford 1906, 1:277–78
277 Matthew Arnold to Temple, 12 Oct. 1869 — Sandford 1906, 1:278–79

278 Scott to Temple, 12 Oct. 1869 — Sandford 1906, 2:620
279 Temple to Scott, 13 Oct. 1869 — Sandford 1906, 2:620–621
280 Scott to Temple, 14 Oct. 1869 — Sandford 1906, 2:622
281 Benson to the *Times*, 16 Oct. 1869 — *Times* 22 Oct. 1869, 6
282 Temple to Cook, 16 Oct. 1869 — Sandford 1906, 1:285–86
283 Stafford Northcote to Temple, 17 Oct. 1869 — Sandford 1906, 1:283–84
284 Browne to Temple, 18 Oct. 1869 — Sandford 1906, 1:282
285 James Bryce to Temple, 18 Oct. 1869 — Sandford 1906, 1:278
286 "A London Clergyman" to the *Times*, 20 Oct. 1869 — *Times* 21 Oct. 1869, 4
287 "A London Vicar" to the *Times*, 20 Oct. 1869 — *Times* 21 Oct. 1869, 4
288 Temple to Philip Freeman, [undated after 20 Oct. 1869] — Sandford 1906, 1:286–87
289 Temple to Scott, 21 Oct. 1869 — Sandford 1906, 2:622
290 Temple to Bryce, 21 Oct. 1869 — Sandford 1906, 1:278
291 Francis Close to the *Times*, 21 Oct. 1869 — *Times* 23 Oct. 1869, 10
292 Lord Nelson to the *Times*, 21 Oct. 1869 — *Times* 23 Oct. 1869, 10
293 "Member of the Chapter of Exeter" to the *Times*, 21 Oct. 1869 — *Times* 23 Oct. 1869, 10
294 J.L. Fish and John Boodle to the *Times*, 21 Oct. 1869 — *Times* 22 Oct. 1869, 6
295 Malcolm MacColl to the *Times*, 21 Oct. 1869 — *Times* 22 Oct. 1869, 6
296 Lord Shaftesbury to the *Times*, 22 Oct. 1869 — *Times* 23 Oct. 1869, 10
297 Daniel Wilson to the *Times*, 22 Oct. 1869 — *Times*, 23 Oct. 1869 10
298 Williams to Temple, 23 Oct. 1869 — Ellen Williams 1874, 2:291–92
299 Daniel Moore to the *Times*, 23 Oct. 1869 — *Times* 25 Oct. 1869, 9
300 Hugh McNeile to the *Times*, 23 Oct. 1869 — *Times* 26 Oct. 1869, 5
301 Hort to Benson, 23 Oct. 1869 — Sandford 1906, 1:288–89
302 Lord Nelson to the *Times*, 24 Oct. 1869 — *Times* 26 Oct. 1869, 5
303 W. C. Lake to the *Guardian*, [25 Oct. 1969] — *Times* 1 Nov. 1869, 12
304 Pusey to the *Times*, 25 Oct. 1869 — *Times* 26 Oct. 1869, 5
305 John Wall Buckley to the *Times*, 25 Oct., 1869 — *Times* 27 Oct. 1869, 4
306 John Downwall to the *Times*, 27 Oct. 1869 — *Times* 28 Oct. 1869, 10
307 H. Brandreth to the *Times*, [undated] — *Times* 28 Oct. 1869, 10
308 Shaftesbury to Gladstone; Gladstone to Shaftesbury in the *Times*, 26, 30 Oct. 1869 — *Times* 5 Nov. 1869, 7
309 "A London Clergyman" to the *Times*, 28 Oct. 1869 — *Times* 29 Oct. 1869, 8
310 John MacNaught to the *Times*, 28 Oct. 1869 — *Times* 29 Oct. 1869, 8
311 "Oxoniensis" to the *Times*, 29 Oct. 1869 — *Times* 30 Oct. 1869, 5
312 C.G.P. to the *Times*, 30 Oct. 1869 — *Times*, 2 Nov. 1869, 6
313 Alexander Ewing to the *Times*, 30 Oct. 1869 — *Times* 3 Nov. 1869, 4
314 Wilson to Longman, 1 Nov. 1869 — Reading, MS. Longman 43, fol. $3–3^{v}$
315 Wilson to Longman, 2 Nov. 1869 — Reading, MS. Longman 43 [unnumbered]
316 Wilson to Longman, 2 Nov. 1869 — Reading, MS. Longman 43, fols. $4–4^{v}$
317 Pusey to the *Times*, [undated, 2 Nov. 1869?] — *Times* 3 Nov. 1869, 8

318 Jowett to Morier, 3 Nov. 1869 — Balliol, MS. Jowett III M fol. 32
319 Wilson to Longman, 4 Nov. 1869 — Reading, MS. Longman 43, fol. 5
320 "A Hertfordshire Incumbent" to the *Times*, 5 Nov. 1869 — *Times* 6 Nov. 1869, 9
321 Wilson to Pattison, 6 Nov. 1869 — Bodley, MS. Pattison 112, fol. 92
322 Wilson to Longman, 12 Nov. 1869 — Reading, MS. Longman 43, fol. 6–6v
323 C. Wordsworth to Temple, 13 Nov. 1869 [see Letter 332]
324 C. Wordsworth to Temple, 13 Nov. 1869 — Sandford, 1906, 1:292–93
325 "A Layman" to the *Times*, [undated] — *Times* 16 Nov. 1869, 6
326 Jowett to Nightingale, 18 Nov. 1869 — Quinn and Prest 1987, 181
327 Temple to Burgon, 18 Nov. 1869 — Bodley, MS. Eng. th d. 21, fol. 5
328 Edward Parry to the *Times*, 19 Nov. 1869 — *Times* 22 Nov. 1869, 7
329 Wilson to Longman, 21 Nov. 1869 — Reading, MS. Longman 43, fols. 7–7v
330 Wilson to Longman, 23 Nov. 1869 — Reading, MS. Longman 43, fol. 8
331 Lord John Russell to Temple, 26 Nov. 1869 — Sandford 1906, 1:279
332 C. Wordsworth / Temple in the *Times*, [30 Nov. 1869] — *Times* 2 Dec. 1869, 7
333 William Thomson to bp. of Victoria in the *Times*, [30 Nov. 1869] — *Times* 4 Dec. 1869, 8
334 Jowett to Campbell, Dec. 1869 — Abbott and Campbell 1899, 181–82
335 C. Wordsworth to Temple, 9 Dec. 1869 — *Times* 11 Dec. 1869, 5
336 MacColl to the *Times*, 11 Dec. 1869 — *Times* 15 Dec. 1869, 4
337 "A Member of Convocation" to the *Times*, [undated, 12 Dec. 1869?] — *Times* 13 Dec. 1869, 6
338 Heurtley to the *Times*, 14 Dec. 1869 — *Times* 16 Dec. 1869, 3
339 John Jackson to C. Wordsworth, 15 Dec. 1869 — *Times* 16 Dec. 1869, 3
340 Wilson to Longman, 17 Dec. 1869 — Reading, MS. Longman 43, fol. 9
341 Temple to Wilberforce, 18 Dec. 1869 — Bodley, MS. Wilberforce C. 17 fol. 21
342 Wilberforce to Temple, 20 Dec. 1869 — Sandford 1906, 1:282–83
343 W. J. Trower to the Mayor and Corporation of Exeter, 20 Dec. 1869 — *Times* 27 Dec. 1869, 7
344 "A London Clergyman" to the *Times*, [undated, Dec. 25, 1869?] — *Times* 27 Dec. 1869, 8
345 Jowett to Nightingale, 31 Dec. 1869 — Quinn and Prest 1987, 182
346 Williams to his Sister-in-law, 8 Jan. 1870 — Ellen Williams 1874, 2:366–68
347 Wilson to Longman, 10 Jan. 187 — Reading, MS. Longman 43, fols. 10–10v
348 Jowett to Edward Caird, 28 Jan. 1870 — Balliol, MS. Jowett F 13, fol. 3; Abbott and Campbell 1897, 1:441–43
349 Wilson to Pattison, 7 Feb. 1870 — Bodley, MS. Pattison 112, fol. 94
350 Wilson to Longman, 14 Feb. 1870 — Reading, MS. Longman 43, fols. 11–11v
351 Jowett to Fanny Campbell, Feb. or Mar. 1870 [?] — Balliol, MS. Jowett III C fol. 40
352 Jowett to Caird, 24 Feb. 1870 — Balliol, MS. Jowett, F 13, fol. 4; Abbott and Campbell 1897, 1:443–44

353 Jowett to Morier, 10 Apr. 1870 — Balliol, MS. Jowett III M fol. 35
354 Jowett to Stanley, 23 July 1873 — Abbott and Campbell 1899, 186–87
355 Jowett to Nightingale, 18 Aug. 1873 — Quinn and Prest 1987, 245
356 Jowett to Nightingale, 4 Dec. 1873 — Quinn and Prest 1987, 249
357 Jowett to Lady Wemyss, 25 Feb. 1890 — Balliol, MS. Jowett, F 12, fol. 56
358 Jowett to Lady Wemyss, 25 Apr. 1891 — Balliol, MS. Jowett, F 12, fol. 57
359 Henrietta G. Baden Powell to Abbott, 15 Apr. 1894 — Balliol, MS. Jowett II A 21, fol. 11

Appendix D: A Bibliography of Responses to *Essays and Reviews*

[*Essays and Reviews* was appraised in well over sixty different notices in a wide range of journals in England and Ireland. Periodicals such as the *Guardian* and the *Record* gave separate reviews to individual essays. Others such as the *Christian Remembrancer* published lengthy articles on the entire volume, some over sixty pages. By the end of 1861, a different phase in reviewing was reached: general assessments of the essays and the volume as a whole had, by and large, concluded in the periodical press. The new phase consisted of pamphlets, tracts, and published sermons, as well as more ephemeral leaflets and broadsides. Early in 1862, the first separate volumes against *Essays and Reviews* were published. The trials of Williams and Wilson in the Court of Arches and their appeal before the Privy Council launched a new wave of periodical interest and a fresh outpouring of pamphlets until 1865. Finally, Temple's appointment as bishop of Exeter provoked not only another series of tracts and pamphlets, but also led to the reissuing of writings from almost a decade earlier.]

Periodical Reviews, 1860–65

Bannerman, James. "Recent Rationalism in the Church of England." *North British Review* 33 (Aug. 1860): 217–55.

"Broad Church Theology." *Christian Observer* 60 (May 1860): 398.

"Bunsen and His English Admirers." *Journal of Sacred Literature* 12 (Oct. 1860): 233–36.

[Cox, George William.] "Eternal Punishment." *National Review* 16 (Jan. 1863): 88–116.

"The Credibility of Miracles." *Evangelical Magazine* n.s. 3 (May 1861): 296.

D. E. F. G. [Goodwin, Harvey.] "A Letter on *Essays and Reviews*." *Macmillan's Magazine* 4 (May 1861): 41–48.

"Dr. Temple's Place amongst the Oxford Essayists." *Christian Observer* 60 (Sept. 1860): 632–37.

"Ecclesiastical Court Proceedings." *Christian Remembrancer* 44 (Apr. 1864): 471–500.

"The Essays and Reviews." *Jewish Chronicle and Hebrew Observer* (8 Mar. 1861): 2.

"Essays and Reviews—The Broad Church." *Christian Reformer* 16 (Oct. 1860): 598.

"The Essays and Reviews:—The Conversion Mania." *Jewish Chronicle and Hebrew Observer* (22 Mar. 1861): 3.

"*Essays and Reviews*—Remorseless Criticism." *Dublin University Magazine* 57 (Apr.

1861): 387–404.
"Evidences of Christianity." [A Review of Powell]. *Christian Remembrancer* 41 (July 1861): 149–78.
[Froude, J. A.] "A Plea for the Free Discussion of Theological Difficulties." *Fraser's Magazine* 68 (Oct. 1863): 277–91.
Harrison, Frederic. "Neo-Christianity." *Westminster Review* 146 (Oct. 1860): 293–332. Repr. 1907. "Septem Contra Fidem." In *The Creed of a Layman: Apologia Pro Fide Mea*. London: Macmillan. 95–157.
"Indications of Antagonism in *Essays and Reviews*." *Dublin University Magazine* 57 (May 1861): 515–30.
"The Late Judgment of the Privy Council." *Dublin Review* 3 (July 1864): 1–26.
"The Latest Theology." *Literary Gazette* 91 (14 Apr. 1860): 459–60.
A Lay Churchman. "The Law and the Church." *Macmillan's Magazine* 9 (Mar. 1864): 440–45.
[Leader] *Record* (27 Aug. 1860): 2.
"Modern Sceptical Writers—'Essays and Reviews.'" *Journal of Sacred Literature* 13 (Apr. 1861).
"Modern Sceptical Writers—On the Interpretation of Scripture, by Professor Jowett." *Journal of Sacred Literature* 13 (Apr. 1861): 98–112.
"Mosaic Cosmogony." *Christian Remembrancer* 41 (Apr. 1861): 402–23.
"The New Essayists: Dr. Temple." *Ecclesiastic* 22 (May 1860): 229.
"The New Essayists: Dr. Williams and Others." *Ecclesiastic* 22 (June 1860): 245–60.
"Open Teaching in the Church of England." *Spectator* (7 Apr. 1860): 331–33.
Oxenham, H. N. "The Neo-Protestantism of Oxford." *Rambler* 27 (Mar. 1861): 287–314.
"The Oxford Clergymen's Attack on Christianity." *North American Review* 92 (Jan. 1861): 177–216.
"The Oxford Essayists—Their Relation to Christianity and to Strauss and Baur." *British and Foreign Evangelical Review* (1861): 407–30.
"The Oxford School." *Eclectic Review* 4 (July 1860): 1–12.
"The Oxford School. No. II." *Eclectic Review* 4 (Aug. 1860): 113–26.
Pope, William Burt. "The Oxford Essayists." *London Review* 14 (July 1860): 512–36.
"The Question of Law between the Bishop of Sarum and Mr. Williams." *National Review* 14 (Jan. 1862): 91–113.
"Rebellion in the Church." *Jewish Chronicle and Hebrew Observer* (28 Dec. 1860): 7.
"Remarks on the Theory of Dr. Temple's Essay on 'The Education of the World' in 'Essays and Reviews.'" *Journal of Sacred Literature* 14 (Oct. 1861): 13–30.
"[Review of] *Essays and Reviews*." *Athenaeum* (27 Oct. 1860): 546–49.
"[Review of] *Essays and Reviews*." *Christian Observer* (June 1860): 372–98.
"[Review of] *Essays and Reviews*." *Christian Remembrancer* 40 (Oct. 1860): 327–85.
"[Review of] *Essays and Reviews*." *Freeman* (27 June 1860).
"[Review of] *Essays and Reviews*." *Guardian* (23 May 1860): 473–75.

"[Review of] *Essays and Reviews.*" *Inquirer* (7 July 1860).
"[Review of] *Essays and Reviews.*" *National Reformer* (1 Dec. 1860): 1–2.
"[Review of] *Essays and Reviews.*" *National Reformer* (22 Dec. 1860): 1–2.
"[Review of] *Essays and Reviews.*" *Press* (21 Apr. 1860): 385–86.
"[Review of] *Essays and Reviews.*" *Primitive Baptist Magazine* (July 1860).
"[Review of] *Essays and Reviews.*" *Record* (21 May 1860): 2.
"[Review of] *Essays and Reviews.*" *Record* (8 June 1860): 2.
"[Review of] *Essays and Reviews.*" *Record* (3 Oct. 1860): 4.
"[Review of] *Essays and Reviews.*" *Record* (10 Oct. 1860): 4.
"[Review of] *Essays and Reviews.*" *Record* (16 Nov. 1860): 4.
"[Review of] *Essays and Reviews.*" *Saturday Review* 11 (2 Mar. 1861): 211–12.
"[Review of] *In the Arches Court of Canterbury. The Office of the Judge . . . Articles of Accusation* and *Charge Delivered by the Lord Bishop of Salisbury, August 8, 1861.*" *Athenaeum* (17 Aug. 1861): 208–9.
"[Review of] *Inspiration and Interpretation: Seven Sermons Preached before the University of Oxford; with Preliminary Remarks: Being an Answer to a Volume Entitled 'Essays and Reviews.'*" *Athenaeum* (7 Sept. 1861): 312.
[Review of Powell and Pattison]. *Record* (21 Sept. 1860).
"[Review of] *Replies to Essays and Reviews.*" *Gentleman's Magazine* 212 (Feb. 1862): 204–6.
[Review of Temple]. *Record* (1 June 1860).
[Review of Williams]. *Record* (12 Sept. 1860).
[Review of Williams]. *Record* (14 Sept. 1860).
[Review of Wilson]. *Record* (28 Sept. 1860).
Rogers, Henry. "Freedom of Religious Opinion—Its Conditions and Limits." *North British Review* 35 (Aug. 1861): 157–86.
[Russell, C. W.] "Anglican Neo-Christianity: The *Essays and Reviews* (Part I)." *Dublin Review* 49 (Feb. 1861): 457–502.
[———.] "The Convocation on *Essays and Reviews* (Part II)." *Dublin Review* 50 (May 1861): 242–59.
"The 'Six Days' of Genesis: 1. *Essays and Reviews.*" *Brownson's Quarterly Review* 25 (Apr. 1863): 204–27.
[Stanley, Arthur Penrhyn.] "*Essays and Reviews.*" *Edinburgh Review* 113 (Apr. 1861): 461–500.
[———.] "*Aids to Faith* and *Replies to 'Essays and Reviews.'*" *Fraser's Magazine* 66 (Aug. 1862): 200–206.
[———.] "The Three Pastorals." *Edinburgh Review* 120 (July 1864): 268–307.
[———.] "Theology of the Nineteenth Century." *Fraser's Magazine* 71 (Feb. 1865): 252–68.
[Stephen, James Fitzjames.] "The Law and the Church." *Macmillan's Magazine.* 9 (Mar. 1864): 440–45.
[———.] "The Privy Council and the Church of England." *Fraser's Magazine* 69

(May 1864): 521–37.

[———.] "Dr. Pusey and the Court of Appeal." *Fraser's Magazine* 70 (Nov. 1864): 644–62.

[———.] "What Is the Law of the Church of England?" *Fraser's Magazine* 71 (Feb. 1865): 225–41.

[Swabey, M. C. Merttins.] "The Privy Council Judgment." *Quarterly Review* 115 (Apr. 1864): 529–80.

"Table-Talk." *Guardian* (4 Apr. 1860): 1.

[Tayler, J. J.] "Old Creeds and New Beliefs." *National Review* 12 (Jan. 1861): 151–89.

[Taylor, Isaac.] "Present Movement in the Church of England." *North British Review* 34 (May 1861): 281–329.

[———.] "The Church of England—Respondent." *North British Review* 36 (May 1862): 273–313.

"Theodore Parker and the Oxford Essayists." *Christian Observer* 60 (July 1860): 486.

"The Truth and Its Defenders." [Lead Article]. *Literary Churchman* (16 Apr. 1861): 145–46.

"Toleration within the Church of England." *Fraser's Magazine* 63 (Apr. 1861): 483–92.

[Vaughan, Robert.] "The New Move in Oxford." *British Quarterly Review* 33 (Jan. 1861): 3–80.

Watson, W. D. "*Essays and Reviews*." *Fraser's Magazine* 62 (Aug. 1860): 228–42.

[Wilberforce, Samuel.] "*Essays and Reviews*." *Quarterly Review* 109 (Jan. 1861): 248–306.

[———.] "*Aids to Faith*." *Quarterly Review* 112 (Oct. 1862): 445–99.

Separate Publications: Books and Pamphlets

[Almost 400 separate responses to *Essays and Reviews* were published, independently of the numerous reviews and lead articles in the newspapers. Some were ephemeral leaflets, but others were substantial volumes issued by well-known publishers. They began during 1860 in the leaflets circulated for signature, such as the "Protest of the Clergy," and in prefaces to works written with other aims in mind, such as George Moberly's book on the beatitudes. During the first year of the publication of *Essays and Reviews*, the first separate pamphlets were also issued, such as those by Gresley and Pears. In 1861 there was a large production, some gathering together the essays that had appeared earlier in journals, such as Irons's compilation of his essays published in the *Literary Churchman*. The publications continued for most of the decade. We have not explicated pseudonyms, but have cross-listed them to the first words of their titles for easier identification; the authors of some pseudonymous works have now been identified, and are here properly attributed.]

Absolom, Charles Severn. 1861. *The Authors of Essays and Reviews Judged Out of Their Own Mouth.*

———. 1861. *Dr. Temple's Essay Examined.*

———. 1861. *Jesus Christ and the Authors of Essays and Reviews Contrasted in Their Estimate of Old Testament Scripture.*

Aikman, William Robertson. 1861. *The Last Regret; or, the Power of Divine Regeneration. A Poem: Illustrative of Truths of Inspiration, Assailed in a Late Work Entitled "Essays and Reviews." By a Soldier of the Cross.*

Ainslie, Robert. 1861. *Discourses on the "Essays and Reviews" Delivered in Christ Church, New Road, Brighton; Reprinted from the "Brighton Observer."*

———. 1861. *Three Discourses Supplemental to the Eight on the "Essays and Reviews," in Answer to the Question, What Is It That a Clergyman of the Church of England Is Required to Believe? Reprinted from the Brighton Observer.*

American Layman. See Close, Francis.

"Another Gospel" Examined: or, a Popular Criticism of Each of the Seven "Essays and Reviews." 1861.

An Answer to the "Essays and Reviews," Showing the Fallacy in Believing the Scriptures Are Not Written by Divine Inspiration. Also, Proving the Truth of Their Position in the Final Restitution of Man. 1862.

An Answer to Frederick Temple's Essay on "The Education of the World." By a Working Man. 1861.

An Answer to the Questions Raised by the "Essays and Reviews," Being a Sermon [on Heb. 12:1] *on Faith, Preached in Rochford Church, on Sunday, July 24, 1864.* 1864.

"Archeionoi, M. H. M." 1861. *Exposition of the Book Entitled "Essays and Reviews": Being the Substance of Three Lectures Delivered in the Wesleyan Methodist Chapel, the Primitive Methodist Chapel, and the Parochial School House, Crook, on the Evenings of September 19th, 21st, and 28th, 1861, by* 'Αρχηΐωνοι, *M. H. M., Lecturer to the Colliers, and Publicans and Sinners of Crook, Co. Durham.*

A. V. (M.A.). See *"Essays and Reviews." Thoughts on Miracles.*

Barker, Joseph. 1863. *An Essay on the Celebrated "Essays and Reviews," with Remarks on the Reception the Work Has Met with from the Church and the State, and the Lessons to be Drawn Therefrom.*

Baylay, Charles Frederick Rogers. 1861. *Essays and Reviews Compared with Reason and Revelation.*

Bayley, Jonathan. 1862. *Twelve Discourses on the Essays and Reviews by Seven Clergymen of Oxford.*

Beard, John Relly. 1861. *The Progress of Religious Thought as Illustrated in the Protestant Church of France; Being Essays and Reviews, Bearing on the Chief Religious Questions of the Day* [extracted from the "Revue de Théologie"], *Translated from the French; with an Introductory Essay on "The Oxford Essays & Reviews" by the Editor, J. R. Beard.*

Bernard, H. H. 1862. *Cambridge Free Thought and Letters on Bibliolatry Translated from G. E. Lessing.*

Bickersteth, Edward. 1861. *A Charge Delivered at His Fifth Visitation of the Archdeaconry of Buckingham, in June, 1861.*

Bickersteth, Robert. 1861. *A Charge Delivered to the Clergy of the Diocese of Ripon, at His Triennial Visitation, October, 1861, by Robert, Lord Bishop of Ripon.*

Blakelock, Ralph. 1861. *Observations on the Rev. Dr. Temple's Essay on the Education of the World. Being a Paper Read at a Meeting of the Ingworth and Repps Clerical Society.*

Booth, James. 1861. *The Bible and Its Interpreters: Being the Substance of Three Sermons Preached in the Parish Church of St. Ann, Wandsworth.*

Bosanquet, James Whatman. 1866. *Messiah the Prince; or, The Inspiration of the Prophecies of Daniel. Containing Remarks on the Views of Dr. Pusey, Mr. Desprez, and Mr. Williams, concerning the Book of Daniel, Together with a Treatise on the Sabbatical Years and Jubilees.*

———. 1869. *Messiah the Prince: or, the Inspiration of the Prophecies of Daniel, Containing Remarks on the Views of Dr. Williams.* 2d ed.

Bray, Charles. 1862. *Modern Protestantism: A Few Words on "Essays and Reviews." By a Layman.*

———. 1870. *Modern Protestantism: A Few Words on "Essays and Reviews." By the Author of the "Philosophy of Necessity."* 2d ed.

A Brief Examination of Prevalent Opinions on the Inspiration of the Scriptures of the Old and New Testaments. By a Lay Member of the Church of England. With an Introduction by the Rev. Henry Bristow Wilson. 1861.

Brock, William. 1864. *Infidelity in High Places. A Sermon Preached in the Parish Church of Bishop Waltham, on Sunday, February 28th, 1864, in Consequence of the Late Judgment in "Essays and Reviews" . . . With a letter to the . . . Lord Bishop of London, on the Doctrine of the Very Rev. A. P. Stanley.*

———. 1865. *Infidelity in High Places. A Sermon Preached . . . in Consequence of the Late Judgment in "Essays and Reviews." With a letter to the Right Reverend the Lord Bishop of London, on the Doctrine of the Very Rev. A. P. Stanley.* 4th ed.

Brownjohn, Simeon Dowell. 1896. *To His Grace the Lord Archbishop of York, Primate of England. A Protest.*

———. 1897. *The Cause and Purport of the Protest against the Confirmation of the Election of Dr. Frederick Temple to the See of Canterbury.*

Buchanan, James. 1861. *The "Essays and Reviews" Examined; A Series of Articles Contributed to the "Morning Post." Revised and Corrected by the Author. With Preface, Introduction, and Appendix, Containing Notes and Documents.*

Bullock, Charles. 1861. *"Essays and Reviews": The False Position of the Authors: An Appeal to the Bible and the Prayer-Book. A Lecture.*

Burgon, John William. 1861. *Inspiration and Interpretation: Seven Sermons Preached before the University of Oxford; with Preliminary Remarks: Being an Answer to a Volume Entitled "Essays and Reviews."*

———. 1870. *Dr. Temple's "Explanation" Examined.*

———. 1870. *Protests of the Bishops against the Consecration of Dr. Temple to the See of Exeter: Preceded by a Letter to the Right Hon. Right Rev. John Jackson, D.D., Bishop of London.*

Burnside, William Smyth. 1861. *The Lex Evangelica: or, Essay for the Times, Proving That Holy Scripture Is the Only Infallible Interpreter to Reason, in Search after Religious Truth. Being a Reply to a Recent Publication Entitled "Essays and Reviews."*

Cairns, John. 1861. *Oxford Rationalism and English Christianity*. 2d ed.

Cambridge M.A. See *Rhymes for the Times.*

Campbell, John. 1861. *The Conquest of England: Letters to the Prince Consort on Popery, Puseyism, Neology, Infidelity, and the Aggressive Policy of the Church of Rome.*

A Canadian Layman. See *Essays and Reviews Considered.*

Candy, Thomas Henry. 1861. *The Antidote; or, An Examination of Mr. Pattison's "Essay on the Tendencies of Religious Thought."*

Carr, Edward Henry. 1861. *Of Miracles. An Argument in Reply to the 3rd of the "Essays and Reviews," Being a Lecture Delivered in Trinity Chapel, Conduit St., Hanover Sq., March 14th, 1861.*

Carroll, Lewis. 1861. *Endowment of the Greek Professorship.*

———. 1865. *The New Method of Evaluation as Applied to Π.*

Case as to the Legal Force of the Judgment of the Privy Council in re Fendall v. Wilson; with . . . A preface by E. B. Pusey. 1864. 2d ed.

Case as to the Legal Position of Professor Jowett: with the Opinion of the Queen's Advocate Thereon. 1862.

Case Whether Professor Jowett in His Essay and Commentary Has So Distinctly Contravened the Doctrines of the Church of England, That a Court of Law Would Pronounce Him Guilty; with the Opinion of the Queen's Advocate Thereon. 1862.

Catholicity and Reason: A Few Considerations on "Essays and Reviews." 1861.

Cazenove, John Gibson. 1861. *On Certain Characteristics of Holy Scripture, with Special Reference to "An Essay on the Interpretation of Scripture" Contained in "Essays and Reviews." Reprinted, with Additions, from "The Christian Remembrancer," January, 1861.*

Challenge to Dr. Temple, in a Letter from a Godfather, on the Subject of His Essay, "The Education of the World." By a Clergyman (H.M.). 1861.

Challis, James. 1861. *Creation in Plan and in Progress.*

Chapman, Rev. J. 1861. *The Foundations of the Temple: The Fall of Man, Being a Reply to Essays and Reviews.*

Chrétien, C. P. 1861. *Evidences for Those Who Think and Feel More Than They Can Read.* ["Tracts for Priests and People," no. VIII].

The Church as It Is: With Special Reference to the Judgment of the Final Court of Appeal; in the Cases of Gorham v. the Bishop of Exeter; Williams, Appellant v. the Lord Bishop of Salisbury, Respondent; and Wilson, Appellant v. Fendall, Respondent. By a Worcester Vicar. [1864 ?].

Church Reform and True Christianity. 1867.
A Clergyman. See *Forgiveness after Death*.
A Clergyman (H. M.). See *Challenge to Dr. Temple*.
Close, Francis. Ed. 1861. *A Critical Examination of the "Essays and Reviews." By an American Layman. Edited by the Dean of Carlisle*.
Conington, John. 1863. *The University of Oxford and the Greek Chair*. 1863.
Cookesley, William Gifford. 1869. *A Letter to the Clergy of Bedfordshire on the Nomination of Dr. Temple to the See of Exeter*.
Cooper, Robert Jermyn. 1861. *A Brief Defence of the Bible against the Attacks of Rationalistic Infidelity: An Inquiry in Reference to Certain "Rationalist" Opinions, Especially Those Contained in the Volume "Essays and Reviews."*
Cowie, B. M. 1861. *An Address on the Chief Points of Controversy between Orthodoxy and Rationalism*.
Cruise, T. F. 1861. *Letter to a Rural Dean on Neology*.
Cumming, John. 1861. *The Atonement, in Its Two-fold Aspect, Toward English "Essays and Reviews" and Romish "Decrees and Canons."*
———. 1861. *The Bible: As Treated by the Essayists and Reviewers*.
———. 1861. *Popular Lectures on "The Essays and Reviews," Delivered in Various Places, and Addressed to the Common People*.
———. 1861. *Precious Truths Persecuted by the Essayists and Reviewers*.
——— and Richard Paul Blakeney. 1861. *The Education of the World, Dr. Temple's Essay on, Considered. With Some Notice of Mr. Pattison's Essay*.
———. 1861. *Modern Infidelity and Rationalism Exposed and Refuted, in Answer to the Essays and Reviews*. [Protestant Reformation Society Tracts].
———. 1861. *Mosaic Cosmogony. A Vindication of the Scripture Narrative, in Answer to Mr. Goodwin in His Essay on the Above Subject*.
———. 1861. *The Right Way, and a Way Which Seemeth Right: or, A Warning to Essayists and Reviewers*.
———. 1861. *Scripture, and Chronology, Egyptology, Glottology, and Ethnology, etc. in Answer to Mr. Williams in His Review on the Above Subjects*.
———. 1861. *Scripture Interpretation and Inspiration, Considered, in Answer to Mr. Jowett in His Essay on the Above Subject*.
———. 1861. *Scripture Miracles Vindicated, in Answer to Mr. Powell in His Essay on the Above Subject*.
———. 1861. *Scripture Prophecies Vindicated, in Answer to Mr. Williams in His Review on the Above Subject*.
———. 1861. *The Theology of the Church of England Vindicated, in Answer to Mr. Wilson in His Essay on the Above Subject*.
Dalton, G. W. 1861. *Notes on Neology: An Appeal to Antiquity on Behalf of the Authenticity of Holy Scripture, as Against the Oxford "Essays and Reviews."*
Danger to the Bible from Licentious Criticism: Letters to Sons in the University. By Presbyter Septuagenarius. 1861.

Darby, John Nelson. 1862. *Dialogues on the Essays and Reviews. By One Who Values Christianity for Its Own Sake, and Believes in It as a Revelation from God.* 2 vols.

———. 1863. *Dialogues on the Essays and Reviews. By One Who Values Christianity for Its Own Sake, and Believes in It as a Revelation from God.* 2d ed.

———. [1870 ?]. *Dialogue on Dr. Temple's Essay, with Preface in Reference to the Recent Sermon and Speech of the Lord Bishop of Exeter.*

Daubeny, C. G. B. 1861. *A Few Words of Apology for the Late Professor Baden Powell's Essay "On the Study of the Evidences of Christianity," Contained in the Volume Entitled "Essays and Reviews," by a Lay Graduate.*

Davies, John Llewelyn. 1861. *The Signs of the Kingdom of Heaven: An Appeal to Scripture upon the Question of Miracles.* ["Tracts for Priests and People," no. IV].

———. 1862. *The Spirit Giveth Life.* ["Tracts for Priests and People," no. XI].

——— and Francis Garden. 1862. *The Death of Christ: A Review of the Bishop of Gloucester and Bristol's Essay in "Aids to Faith."* ["Tracts for Priests and People," no. XIII].

Davis, Charles Henry. 1861. *Anti-Essays: The "Essays and Reviews" of 1860 Fallacious and Futile, "At Variance with Each Other and Mutually Destructive."*

Dayman, Edward Arthur. 1861. *Modern Infidelity. A Sermon, Preached in the Church of St. Peter and St. Paul, Blandford, at the Third Visitation of the Right Reverend Walter Kerr, Lord Bishop of Salisbury, Aug. 17, 1861.*

The Debate in the House of Lords on the Power of Convocation, July 15th, 1864, with an Introduction and the Judgment of the Privy Council in "Essays and Reviews." 1864.

Declaration on the Inspiration of the Word of God and the Eternity of Future Punishment by the Clergymen of the United Church of England and Ireland. 1864.

A Defence of Mr. Gladstone's Church Policy in the Matter of "the See of Exeter." By an Ex-Incumbent of the Anglican Establishment. 1869.

Denison, George Anthony. 1861. *Analysis of "Essays and Reviews."*

———. 1862. *Faith and Peace. Being Answers to Some of the "Essays and Reviews," by the Following Writers. William Edward Jelf. . . James Wayland Joyce . . . James Fendall . . . William Lee . . . Edgar Huxtable . . . With a Preface by the Venerable Archdeacon Denison.*

———. 1864. *Professor Jowett and the University of Oxford. A Letter . . . to Edward Bouverie Pusey.*

———. 1867. *Faith and Peace.* 2d ed.

———. 1869. *Analysis of "Essays and Reviews."* 2d ed.

———. 1869. *The Synod of Canterbury and "The Bishop of Exeter": A Letter, Addressed to the Ven. the Prolocutor of the Lower House . . . December 22, 1869 . . .* [with an] *"Appendix. The Declaration and Protest of George Anthony Denison . . . Read in the Parish Church of East Brent . . . December 19th, 1869."*

Denison, William Thomas. 1862. *Remarks on "Essays and Reviews."*

Desprez, Philip Charles Soulbieu. 1865. *Daniel; or, The Apocalypse of the Old*

Testament . . . With an Introduction by Rowland Williams.
Doctor of Divinity. See *An Hour with the Bishops.*
Doubting Disciple. See *Things That I Doubt.*
Drummond, Robert Blackley. 1861. *Free Thought v. Dogmatic Theology: Being Two Lectures on "Essays and Reviews," Delivered in St. Mark's Chapel, Edinburgh.*
Dublin Clergyman. See *What Does the Church.*
Duncan, David. 1861. *"Essays and Reviews." A Lecture Delivered at the Manchester Friends' Institute on the 12th of the 4th Month, 1861.*
———. 1861. *"Essays and Reviews." A Lecture Delivered at the Manchester Friends' Institute on the 12th of the 4th Month, 1861.* 2d ed.
Eden, Robert J. 1861. *The Charge of the Right Honourable Lord Bishop of Bath and Wells at His Third Visitation, in May 1861.*
ΕΠΤΑ ΜΥΟΠΕΣ ΚΑΠΝΙΖΟΜΕΝΟΙ; or, The Dim Smokified Seven. [1861 ?].
An Essay on Church Revision by a Late Etonian. 1864.
The "Essays and Reviews" and the People of England: A Popular Refutation of the Principal Propositions of the Essayists. With an Appendix, Containing the Protest of the Bishops and Clergy, the Proceedings in Convocation, and All the Documents and Letters Connected with the Subject. 1861.
Essays and Reviews Considered by a Canadian Layman. 1862.
Essays and Reviews. Examination of Mr. Baden Powell's Tractate on Miracles. Reprinted from the "Christian Examiner." 1861.
"Essays and Reviews." The False Position of the Authors: An Appeal to the Bible and the Prayer Book. 1861.
"Essays and Reviews." Thoughts on Miracles, Suggested by the Late Rev. Baden Powell's "Essay on the Study of the Evidences of Christianity." By A. V. (M.A.). 1861.
Ex-Incumbent of the Anglican Establishment. See *A Defence.*
Expectans. See *The Grievance and the Remedy.*
Fendall, James. 1861. *Authority of Scripture. An Examination into the Principles and Statements Advanced in Professor Jowett's Essay on the Interpretation of Scripture.* Repr. in Denison, George Anthony 1862.
Fitzgerald, John F. G. Purcell. 1861. *What Is the Faith of the Essayists and Reviewers?*
———. 1870. *A Letter of Earnest Remonstrance to the Rt. Hon. W. E. Gladstone, M.P., First Lord of the Treasury, etc., upon His Appointment of a Co-writer with Infidels to a Christian Bishopric.*
Forbes, Granville Hamilton. 1861. *No Antecedent Impossibility in Miracles. Some Remarks on the Essay of the Late Rev. Baden Powell and J. S. Mill on "The Study of the Evidences of Christianity," in a Letter by a Country Clergyman.*
———. 1861. *No Antecedent Impossibility in Miracles. Some Remarks on the Essay of the Late Rev. Baden Powell and J. S. Mill on "The Study of the Evidences of Christianity," in a Letter by a Country Clergyman.* 2d ed.
Forgiveness after Death: Does the Bible or the Church of England Affirm It to Be Impossible? A Review of the Alleged Proofs of the Hopelessness of the Future State. By a Clergyman. 1862.

Forster, Charles. 1861. *Spinoza Redivivus; or, The Reappearance of His School and Spirit, in the Volume Entitled "Essays and Reviews." A Sermon* [on 2 Tim. 3:16, 17].

The Further Revision of the Liturgy with Reference to the Clergy, "Essays and Reviews." 1861.

Garbett, Edward. 1861. *The Bible and Its Critics: An Enquiry into the Objective Reality of Revealed Truths.* [The Boyle Lectures for 1861].

Garden, Francis. 1861. *The Atonement as a Fact and as a Mystery.* ["Tracts for Priests and People," no. III].

Giffard, Francis Osbern. 1861. *Worn-out Neology; or, Brief Strictures upon the Oxford Essays and Reviews. By the Author of the Hartley Whitney Tracts.*

Girdlestone, Charles. 1861. *Negative Theology: An Argument for Liturgical Revision.*

Girdlestone, Edward. 1861. *Remarks on "Essays and Reviews," 1860.*

Gooch, Charles. 1861. *An Examination of Dr. R. Williams's Review of Bunsen's Biblical Researches.*

———. 1861. *An Examination of Dr. Temple's Essay on the Education of the World.*

———. 1861. *An Examination of the Late Professor Powell's Essay on the Study of the Evidences of Christianity.*

———. 1862. *The Record of Creation, Considered in an Examination of Mr. Goodwin's Essay on Mosaic Cosmogony.*

———. 1862. *Remarks on the Grounds of Faith, Suggested by Mr. Pattison's Essay on the Tendencies of Religious Thought.*

———. 1863. *Interpretation of Scripture.*

Gordon, Osborne. 1861. *A Sermon Preached in the Cathedral Church of Christ in Oxford, on Easter Day, 1861.*

Graduate of Oxford. See *Subscription to Articles.*

Gresley, William. 1860. *Idealism Considered; Chiefly with Reference to a Volume of "Essays and Reviews" Lately Published.*

———. 1861. *Idealism Considered; Chiefly with Reference to a Volume of "Essays and Reviews" Lately Published.* 2d ed.

The Grievance and the Remedy. An Essay in Verse, Essaying to Review Thoughts Suggested by Reading Address, Analysis, Animadversion, Answer, Caution . . . Sermon, Treatise, and Other Publications concerning "Essays and Reviews." By Expectans. 1861.

Griffin, John Nash. 1862. *Seven Answers to the Seven Essays and Reviews. Reprinted from the "London Review." . . . with an Introduction, by the Right Hon. J. Napier.*

Grindle, Edmund Samuel. 1869. *Episcopal Inconsistency; or, Convocation, the Bishops, and Dr. Temple. A Letter to the Archbishops and Bishops of the Church of England, Together with an Account of the Proceedings in Convocation with Regard to "Essays and Reviews," and Extracts from the Speeches of the Bishops, Taken Verbatim from the "Chronicle of Convocation."*

Grote, John. 1862. *Essays and Reviews. An Examination of Some Portions of Dr. Lushington's Judgment on the Admission of the Articles in the Cases of the Bishop of Salisbury v. Williams and Fendall v. Wilson. With Remarks on the Bearing of Them on the Clergy.*

Gurney, Archer. 1864. *The Faith against Free-Thinkers.*

Hamilton, Walter Kerr. 1861. *A Charge Delivered to the Clergy and Churchwardens of the Diocese of Salisbury at His Triennial Visitation, in August 1861.*

Hancock, Thomas. 1870. *A Bishop Must Have the Good Report of Those Who Are without the Church. A Sermon* [on 1 Tim. 3:7] *Preached on the Sunday after the Confirmation of Dr. Temple . . . (Dec. 12th, 1869).*

Hansell, Edward Halifax. 1861. *Notes on the First Essay in the Series Called "Essays and Reviews."*

Harris, Henry. 1861. *Scepticism and Revelation.*

Hawkins, Edward. 1861. *The Province of Private Judgment and the Right Conduct of Religious Inquiry: A Sermon* [on Acts 17:11–12] *Preached before the University of Oxford, April 21, 1861.*

Hayward, Savill. [1861 ?]. *The Essays and Reviews. A Dialogue Thereupon.*

———. 1863. *The Essays and Reviews: A Dialogue.*

Heard, John Bickford. 1862. *New Wine in Old Bottles; Being a Reply to the "Essays and Reviews."*

Hebert, Charles. 1861. *Neology Not True, and Truth Not New: Three Short Treatises concerning the Rev. F. D. Maurice's Vere St. Sermons, the Rev. Prof. Jowett's Doctrine on "The Righteousness of God," the Rev. J. L. Davies' Reply to "Atonement by Propitiation." With That Treatise Also, and a Summary of the Atonement Controversy. Third Edition, with a Post Script, and a Concise Account of the "Essays and Reviews."*

Heurtley, Charles Abel. 1861. *The Inspiration of Holy Scripture. Constancy in Prayer.*

Hoare, Edward. 1861. *Inspiration: Its Nature and Extent.*

Honest Man. See *Must We Burn Our Bibles?*

Hooper, Francis John Bodfield. 1861. *Reply to Dr. Wild and the "Edinburgh": A Defence of the Bishops and the Memorialists, in a Letter to the Rev. G. J. Wild, LL.D. Containing a Reply to His "Brief Defence of the 'Essays and Reviews,'" and an Answer to Certain Statements in the "Edinburgh Review," No. 230.*

Houghton, William. 1863. *Rationalism in the Church of England. An Essay (Reprinted from the "Ecclesiastic"), Revised and Enlarged, with an Appendix on "Essays and Reviews."*

An Hour with the Bishops about the "Essays and Reviews." Is Apostolical Succession a Safeguard against Error? By a Doctor of Divinity. 1861.

Hughes, Thomas. 1861. *Religio Laici.* ["Tracts for Priests and People," no. I].

Hume, Charles. 1861. *A Letter to a Friend on the Essays and Reviews.*

Humperley, John Bues. 1861. *Exoneravi Animam; or, One Radical Reformer's Way of Thinking: Containing a Few Suggestions Touching the Essays & Reviews, as Appreciated by Convocation, and the Discrepancy between Genuine Jesusism and Vulgar Christianity, Still Requiring Reformation.*

Hutton, Richard H. 1862. *The Incarnation and Principles of Evidence.* ["Tracts for

Priests and People," no. XIV].

Huxtable, Edgar. 1861. *The Sacred Record of Creation Vindicated and Explained, in Answer to the Essay "On the Mosaic Cosmogony," in the Volume of "Essays and Reviews."* Repr. in Denison, George Anthony 1862.

Irons, William J. 1861. *The Reviewers Reviewed and the Essayists Criticised: An Analysis and Confutation of Each of the Seven "Essays and Reviews." Reprinted from the "Literary Churchman."*

Jackson, John. 1861. *A Charge Delivered to the Clergy and Churchwardens of the Diocese of Lincoln, at His Triennial Visitation, in October, 1861 by John Jackson, D.D. Bishop of Lincoln.*

Jelf, Richard William. 1861. *Specific Evidence of Unsoundness in the Volume Entitled "Essays and Reviews," Submitted to the Lower House of Convocation, February 26th, 1861, on Moving an Address to the Upper House with a View to Synodical Censure.*

———. 1861. *Supremacy of Scripture. An Examination into the Principles and Statements Advanced in the Essay on the Education of the World. In a Letter to the Rev. Dr. Temple.* Repr. in Denison, George Anthony 1862.

Jenkins, Robert Charles. 1861. *Scriptural Interpretation. The Essay of Professor Jowett Briefly Considered, in a Letter to the Rev. Professor Stanley, D.D.*

———. 1861. *A Word on Inspiration. Being a Second Letter on the Essay of Professor Jowett Addressed to the Rev. Professor Stanley, D.D.*

Jones, Harry. 1861. *Conscience versus the Quarterly. A Plea for Fair Play towards the Writers of the Essays and Reviews.*

Jowett, Benjamin. 1861. *Statements of Christian Doctrine and Practice, Extracted from the Published Writings of the Rev. Benjamin Jowett, M.A.* [Compiled by A. P. Stanley].

Joyce, James Wayland. 1861. *The National Church. An Answer to an Essay on "The National Church" by Henry Bristow Wilson, D.D., Being no. 4 in a Volume Entitled "Essays and Reviews."* Repr. in Denison, George Anthony 1862.

[Keane, William.] 1869. *Protest against Dr. Temple's Consecration to the Bishopric of Exeter.*

Kennard, Robert Bruce. 1861. *Essays and Reviews. A Protest Addressed to the Right Reverend the Lord Bishop of Salisbury on the Appearance of the "Episcopal Manifesto." With a Letter to the Rev. Rowland Williams, D.D. and an Appendix Containing Extracts from Each of the Seven Essays and Reviews Exhibiting the General Character and Spirit of the Work.*

———. 1861. *Essays and Reviews. A Protest*. 2d ed.

———. 1863. *"Essays and Reviews." Their Origin, History, General Character and Significance, Persecution, Prosecution, the Judgment of the Arches Court,—Review of Judgment.*

———. 1864. *The Late Professor Powell and Dr. Thirlwall on the Supernatural. A Letter to the Right Reverend the Lord Bishop of St. David's in Reference to His Recent Remarks on Baden Powell's Essay "On the Study of the Evidences of*

Christianity."

———. 1866. *The Unity of the Material & Spiritual Worlds. A Sermon Preached before the University of Oxford, on the 21st Sunday after Trinity, October 21st, 1866.*

———. 1888. *In Memory of . . . Henry Bristow Wilson. A Sermon* [on Matt. 25:21] *Preached . . . August 19, 1888.*

The Last Resort; or, The Power of Divine Regeneration. A Poem: Illustrative of the Truth of Inspiration, Assailed in a Late Work Entitled "Essays and Reviews," by a Soldier of the Cross. 1861.

Late Etonian. See *An Essay on Church Revision.*

Lay Graduate. See Daubeny, C. G. B.

A Layman. See Bray, Charles.

Lee, William. 1861. *On Miracles. An Examination of the Remarks of Mr. Baden Powell on the Study of the Evidence of Christianity, Contained in the Volume Entitled "Essays and Reviews."* Repr. in Denison, George Anthony 1862.

Leichel, C. P. 1861. *The Christian Miracles: A Sermon Preached in St. George's Church, Belfast, on April 28, 1861, in Answer to the Rev. Baden Powell's Contribution to "Essays and Reviews."*

A Letter to the . . . Bishop of Exeter, on the Subject of the First Sermon Preached by Him in the Cathedral Church of His Diocese. By One of His Lordship's Clergy. 1870.

Liddell, Hon. Robert. 1864. *The Inspiration of the Holy Scripture, as Not Merely Containing, but Being, the Word of God. A Sermon* [on 2 Tim. 3:16]. *(With Reference to the Recent Judgment in the Court of Privy Council).*

Liddon, Henry Parry. 1864. *The Whole Counsel of God: or, The Duty of the Clergy as Teachers of the People, with Particular Reference to the Recent Judgment in the Case of "Essays and Reviews." A Sermon* [on Acts 20:27] *Preached . . . at the General Ordination of the Lord Bishop of Salisbury.*

Lloyd, Julius. 1861. *Abraham's Faith. A Sermon on Present Controversies.*

Longley, Charles Thomas. 1864. *A Pastoral Letter Addressed to the Clergy and Laity of His Province by Charles Thomas, Archbishop of Canterbury.*

Loughnan, Timothy. 1861. *"Essays and Reviews." An Answer to Certain Statements in the Essay Entitled "On the Study of the Evidences of Christianity"; Being the Substance of a Sermon Preached at Queen Square Chapel, Bath, on Sunday, January 27th, 1861.*

Ludlow, J. N. and F. D. Maurice. 1861. *The Sermon of the Bishop of Oxford on Revelation and the Layman's Answer.* ["Tracts for Priests and People," no. VI].

———. 1861. *Two Lay Dialogues.* ["Tracts for Priests and People," no. VII].

——— and Francis Garden. 1861. *Dissent and the Creeds.* ["Tracts for Priests and People," no. IX].

Lushington, Right Hon. Stephen. 1862. *Essays and Reviews. Judgment Delivered on the 25th of June 1862, in the Case of the Bishop of Salisbury versus Williams, and in the Case of Fendall versus Wilson, by the Rt. Hon. Stephen Lushington, D.C.L.,*

Dean of the Arches.

Lyttleton, G. W. 1864. *The Final Court of Appeal in Causes Affecting the Doctrine of the Church of England: A Letter Addressed to the Chairman of a Clerical Meeting, on the Best Mode of Amending the Present Law . . . to Which Is Prefixed, a Statement of Reasons for Seeking an Alteration of the Law by the Rev. R. Seymour.*

Lyttleton, W. H. 1862. *The Testimony of Scripture to the Authority of Conscience and of Reason.* ["Tracts for Priests and People," no. XII].

M.A. of Cambridge. See *A Reply.*

McCaul, Alexander. 1861. *Rationalism and Deistic Infidelity: Three Letters to the Editor of "The Record" Newspaper.*

———. 1861. *Some Notes on the First Chapter of Genesis, with Reference to Statements in "Essays and Reviews."*

———. 1862. *Testimonies to the Divine Authority and Inspiration of the Holy Scriptures, as Taught by the Church of England, in Reply to the Statements of Mr. James Fitzjames Stephen.*

MacClellan, John Brown. 1870. *The Fourth Nicene Canon and the Election and Consecration of Bishops; with Special Reference to the Case of Dr. Temple, an Appendix to a Letter to the Lord Bishop of Ely.*

MacFarlane, William. 1863. *A Practical Letter to the Citizens of the World on the Civil Wars among the Bishops and Clergy.*

McIlvain, Charles Petit. 1865. *Rationalism as Exhibited in the Writings of Certain Clergymen of the Church of England. A Letter to the Clergy and Candidates for Holy Orders of the Protestant Episcopal Church in the United States, Set Forth by Direction of the House of Bishops at the late General Convention.*

Main, Robert. 1862. *A Letter from the Radcliffe Observer on the "Essays and Reviews."*

Manning, Henry Edward. 1864. *The Crown in Council on the Essays and Reviews: A Letter to an Anglican Friend.*

Margoliouth, Moses. 1861. *The End of the Law: Two Sermons* [on Rom. 10:4 and Isa. 53:12] *Preached at St. Edmund the King's Church, Lombard Street. To Which Is Added a Letter, with Numerous Notes, to the Rev. William J. C. Lindsay . . . Being a Preliminary Examination of the "Essays and Reviews."*

Marshall, John George. 1862. *Answers to "Essays and Reviews."*

Maurice, Frederick Denison. 1861. *The Mote and the Beam: A Clergyman's Lessons from the Present Panic.* ["Tracts for Priests and People," no. II].

Meignan, Guillaume René. 1861. *Une Crise religieuse en Angleterre. (Essays and Reviews.)* [A religious crisis in England].

Member of Congregation. See *A Reply to Professor Conington.*

Miall, Edward. [1853] 1861. *Bases of Belief.* 3d ed.

Miller, Henry. 1861. *The Question of Inspiration Plainly Stated, in Reference to Certain Views Put Forth by the Authors of the Book Termed "Essays and Reviews."*

Miller, John Cale. 1861. *Bible Inspiration Vindicated: An Essay on "Essays and Reviews."*

Milton's Prophecy of "Essays and Reviews," and His Judgment on Prosecution of Them.

Extracted from the "Areopagitica: A Speech to the Parliament of England for the Liberty of Unlicensed Printing," . . . to Which Is Added an Extract from the Charge Delivered to His Clergy in 1861, by Walter Kerr, Bishop of Salisbury, on "Unity with the Bishop of Rome." 1861.

Moberly, George. 1860. *Sermons on the Beatitudes, with Others Mostly Preached before the University of Oxford; to Which Is Added a Preface Relating to the Recent Volume of "Essays and Reviews."*

———. 1861. *Some Remarks on "Essays and Reviews": Being the Revised Preface to the Second Edition of "Sermons on the Beatitudes."*

Must We Burn Our Bibles? A Few Honest Words about the "Essays and Reviews"; Addressed to Honest People by an Honest Man. 1861.

Must We Burn Our Bibles? 1862. 2d ed.

Napier, Joseph. 1863. *The Miracles. Butler's Argument on Miracles, Explained and Defended: with Observations on Hume, B. Powell, and J. S. Mill. To Which is Added a Critical Dissertation by H. L. Mansel.*

Newton, Benjamin Willis. 1864. *Remarks on "Mosaic Cosmogony," Being the Fifth of the "Essays and Reviews." Extracted from the Third Number of "Occasional Papers on Scriptural Subjects."*

———. 1866. *The Judgment of the Court of Arches and of the Judicial Committee of the Privy Council, in the Case of Rowland Williams, D.D., One of the Writers in "Essays and Reviews," Considered.*

———. 1882. *Remarks on "Mosaic Cosmogony" Being the Fifth of the "Essays and Reviews." Extracted from the Third Number of "Occasional Papers on Scriptural Subjects."* 3d ed.

Observations on a Lecture Delivered at the Manchester Friends' Institute by David Duncan, Entitled "Essays and Reviews." 1861.

O'Conor, William Anderson. 1861. *Miracles Not Antecedently Incredible. An Examination of Professor Powell's Argument in "Essays and Reviews": Being a Paper Read before the Manchester Clergy Society, and Published at Their Request.*

Owen, John. 1870. *The Ideal of a Christian Minister. A Sermon* [on 2 Tim. 2:15] *Preached . . . Jan. 30, 1870, on the Death of Dr. Rowland Williams.*

———. 1873. *The Use of Memorials. Being a Sermon* [on Gen. 35:19–20] *Preached . . . September 28th, 1873, on the Uncovering of the Memorial Window to the Rev. Dr. Rowland Williams.*

Parker, Franke. 1865. *A Light Thrown upon Thucydides, To Illustrate the Prophecy of Daniel as to the Coming of the Messiah: in Remarks on Dr. Pusey's Daniel the Prophet, and in Reply to Dr. Hincks on the Metonic Cycle and Calippie Period. To Which is Added, a Review of Dr. Temple's Essay on the Education of the World.*

Parker, William Henry. 1861. *Brief Remarks on the Rev. Dr. Temple's Essay, on the "Education of the World." A New Edition.*

Parry, Henry. 1864. *The Whole Counsel of God: or the Duty of the Clergy as Teachers of the People, with Particular Reference to the Recent Judgment in the Case of "Essays and Reviews." A Sermon Preached in the Abbey of St. Mary's, Sherborne, on the Second Sunday in Lent, Feb. 21, 1864, at the General Ordination of the Lord Bishop of Salisbury* .

Paul, C. Kegan and J. N. Langley. 1861. *On Terms of Communion.* ["Tracts for Priests and People," no. V].

Pears, S. A. 1860. *The Weapons of Our Warfare. A Sermon Preached on 12 June, 1860.*

Phillimore, Robert. 1862. *Speech of Robert Phillimore, D.C.L., Q.C., in the Case of "The Office of the Judge Promoted by the Bishop of Salisbury against Williams." Delivered on the 9th, 10th, and 11th of February, 1862, and the Criminal Articles against Rowland Williams.*

Philpott, Henry. 1862. *A Charge Delivered to the Clergy and Churchwardens of the Diocese of Worcester at His Primary Visitation in August 1862.*

Plumptre, Edward H. 1861. *Dangers Past and Present. A Sermon Preached before the University of Oxford, on Easter Tuesday, 1861.*

Porteous, George B. 1861. *Essays and Reviews; an Oration.*

Pratt, John Henry. [1856] 1861. *Scripture and Science Not at Variance; with Remarks on the Historical Character, Plenary Inspiration, and Surpassing Importance, of the Earlier Chapters of Genesis.* 4th ed.

———. 1871. *Scripture and Science Not at Variance; with Remarks on the Historical Character, Plenary Inspiration, and Surpassing Importance, of the Earlier Chapters of Genesis.* 6th ed.

Presbyter Septuagenarius. See *Danger to the Bible.*

The Present Crisis. A Letter to the Lord Bishop of London by One of His Clergy, upon the Recent Judgment in "Essays and Reviews." 1864.

Pusey, Edward Bouverie. 1861. *A Letter on the "Essays and Reviews." Reprinted from the "Guardian."*

———. 1864. *Dr. Pusey on the Privy Council Judgment. To the Editor of the "Record."*

Pusey and Others v. Jowett. The Argument and Decision as to the Jurisdiction of the Chancellor's Court at Oxford. 1863.

Pye, Henry John. 1864. *Convocation. A Sermon* [on Song of Solomon 6:10], *on the Late Synodical Condemnation of the Essays and Reviews.*

Quagmire Ahead by "Truthful Diggins." 1864.

Reichel, Charles Parsons. 1861. *The Christian Miracles: A Sermon* [on John 20:30–31] *Preached in St. George's Church, Belfast . . . on April 28, 1861, in Answer to the Rev. Baden Powell's Contribution to "Essays and Reviews."*

A Reply to the "Essays and Reviews": or, Christianity Vindicated from the Sceptical Attacks of the Septem Contra Christum. By an M.A. of Cambridge. 1861.

A Reply to the Letter Entitled "The Suppression of Doubt Is Not Faith" by One Who Doubts Not, but Fully Believes That the Bible Is the Word of God. 1861.

A Reply to Professor Conington's Pamphlet on the Greek Professorship at Oxford by a Member of Congregation. 1863.

Replies to "Essays and Reviews." . . . with a Preface by the Lord Bishop of Oxford; and Letters from the Radcliffe Observer and the Reader in Geology in the University of Oxford. 1862. [With essays by J. E. M. Goulburn, H. J. Rose, C. A. Heurtley,

W. J. Irons, V. G. Rorison, A. W. Haddan, and C. Wordsworth].

Replies to "Essays and Reviews." 2d ed. 1862.

Rhymes for the Times, or the Bible and the Church's Present Trial, by a Cambridge M.A. 1869.

Robins, Sanderson. 1862. *A Defence of the Faith.*

Rowley, Adam Clarke. 1864. *A Pamphlet on the Judgement of the Privy Council, in the Case of "Essays and Reviews."*

Russell, Arthur Tozer. 1862. *A Letter to the Right Rev. the Lord Bishop of Oxford, upon the Defence of the "Essays and Reviews" in the April Number of the "Edinburgh Review," 1861.*

Rust, Cyprian Thomas. 1861. *"Essays and Reviews." A Lecture Delivered before the Norwich Church of England Young Men's Society, March 18, 1861.*

Sangar, James Mortimer. 1869. *Sacrilege! "Who Is on the Lord's Side?" A Word with Bishops, Clergy, and People about the Proposed Consecration to the See of Exeter of One of the "Septem Contra Christum."*

Savile, Bourchier Wrey. 1862. *Revelation and Science in Respect to Bunsen's Biblical Researches, the Evidences of Christianity, and the Mosaic Cosmogony: with an Examination of Certain Statements put Forth by the Remaining Authors of Essays and Reviews.*

Savill, Hayward. [1861 ?]. *The Essays and Reviews. A Dialogue Thereupon.*

Seeley, Robert Benton. 1862. *Is the Bible True? Seven Dialogues between James White and Edward Owen, concerning the "Essays and Reviews." By the Author of "Essays on the Church."*

Selwyn, Sydney George. [1869 ?]. *A Few Plain Reasons Why Dr. Temple Ought Not to Be a Bishop.*

Sewell, William. 1861. *A Letter on the Inspiration of Holy Scripture, Addressed to a Student.*

Seymour, R. See Lyttleton, G. W.

Shelley, Frances. 1861. *Thoughts on the Doubts of the Day.*

Simon, Thomas Collyns. 1861. *An Answer to the Essays and Reviews.*

———. 1862. *The Philosophical Answer to the Essays and Reviews.*

Smith, Goldwin. 1861. *The Suppression of Doubt Is Not Faith. By a Layman.*

Snell, John Howe. 1861. *What Is the End? or Observations on the Temple-Jowett Essays and Reviews.*

Soldier of the Cross. See *The Last Resort.*

Stephen, James Fitzjames. 1862. *Defence of the Rev. Rowland Williams, D.D. in the Arches' Court of Canterbury.*

Subscription to Articles: Is It Truth or a Mockery? Considered in Reference to "Essays and Reviews" by a Graduate of Oxford. 1861.

Sumner, John Bird. 1861. *Evidence of Christianity, Derived from Its Nature and Reception. New Edition, Revised with Reference to Recent Objections.* [1st ed. 1824].

Tait, Archibald Campbell. 1861. *The Dangers and Safeguards of Modern Theology,*

Containing "Suggestions Offered to the Theological Students under Present Difficulties.

Taylor, James. 1861. *The "Essays and Reviews," Examined, on the Principles of Common Sense . . . By One Who Wishes to Ascertain What Is the "True Faith of a Christian."*

Theological Tracts for the Times. 1861.

Things That I Doubt: Dedicated to the Authors of "Essays and Reviews" by a Doubting Disciple. 1861.

Thirlwall, Connop. 1860. *A Letter to the Rev. R. Williams . . . in Answer to His "Earnestly Respectful" Letter to the Lord Bishop of St. David's: with an Appendix, Containing an Extract from the Bishop's Charge of 1857. By C. Thirlwall.*

———. 1861. *"Essays and Reviews" Anticipated: Extracts from a Work* ["A Critical Essay on the Gospel of St. Luke, by F. Schleiermacher"] *Published in the Year 1825. Attributed to the Lord Bishop of St. David's.*

———. 1863. *A Charge Delivered to the Clergy of the Diocese of St. David's, by Connop Thirlwall, D.D., Bishop of St. David's, at His Eighth Visitation, October, 1863.*

Thompson, Robert Anchor. 1864. *A Letter to the Rev. W. R. Fremantle and the Oxford Committee.*

Thomson, William. Ed., 1861. *Aids to Faith: A Series of Theological Essays. By Several Writers. Being a Reply to "Essays and Reviews."* [With essays by H. L. Mansel, William Fitzgerald, A. McCaul, F. C. Cook, George Rawlinson, Edward Harold Browne, William Thomson, and Charles John Ellicott].

———. 1862. *Aids to Faith*. 3d ed.

———. 1864. *A Pastoral Letter to the Clergy and Laity of the Province of York by William, Lord Bishop of York, Primate of England and Metropolitan.*

———. 1864. *A Pastoral Letter to the Clergy and Laity of the Province of York*. 2d ed.

To the Most Reverend Father in God, John Bird, Lord Archbishop of Canterbury . . . We the Undersigned, Clergy of the United Church of England and Ireland. 1861. [The "Protest of the Clergy," 13 Mar. 1861].

Troughton, Ellis J. 1861. *Essays and Reviews.*

Trower, Walter John. 1869. *A Letter to the Right Rev. the Bishop of Moray and Ross, Primus of the Scottish Episcopal Church, Explanatory of Opposition to the Election of Rev. Dr. Temple, as Bishop of Exeter . . . with an Appendix.*

"Truthful Diggins." See *Quagmire Ahead.*

Truths Out of the Earth. Bible Chronology Verified, by a Military Officer, a Pilgrim from the Last Century. 1861.

Tyrwhitt, Richard St. John. 1861. *Concerning Doubt.*

Waldegrave, Samuel. 1861. *The Charge Delivered in October, 1861, at His Primary Visitation, by the Honourable and Right Rev. Samuel Waldegrave, D.D. Lord Bishop of Carlisle.*

Walther, David. 1861. *On Qualification for Religious Enquiry Compared with the Trifling of Essayists and Reviewers. . . Read at the Christian Union Institute.*

———. 1861. *Some Notice of Prof. Baden Powell's Essay.*

Weir, Archibald. 1861. *Revelation and Belief: A Word of Counsel to the Laity in the Present Theological Crisis. A Sermon.*

What Does the Church of England Say About I. The Authority of Scripture; II. The Sacrifice of Jesus Christ; and III. The Eternity of Future Punishment? Being a Series of Quotations from the Book of Common Prayer, the XXXIX Articles, and the Homilies of the Church of England, by a Dublin Clergyman. 1864.

Whately, Richard. 1861. *Danger from Within: A Charge Delivered at the Annual Visitation of the Dioceses of Dublin and Glandelagh, and Kildare. June 1861, by Richard Whately, D.D. Archbishop of Dublin.*

Wigram, Joseph Cotton. 1864. *A Charge Delivered to the Clergy and Churchwardens in the Diocese of Rochester in November, 1864.*

Wilberforce, Samuel. 1860. *A Charge Delivered at the Triennial Visitation of the Diocese, November, 1860.*

———. 1861. *The Revelation of God the Probation of Man. Two Sermons* [on John 12:37 and 20:27].

———. 1863. *A Charge Delivered to the Diocese of Oxford at His Sixth Visitation, November, 1863.*

Wild, George John. 1861. *A Brief Defence of the "Essays and Reviews": Showing, by Extracts from Their Works, That Similar Doctrines Have Been Maintained by Eminent Divines and Living Dignitaries of Our Church.*

Williams, Rowland. 1860. *An Earnestly Respectful Letter to the Lord Bishop of St. David's, on the Difficulty of Bringing Theological Questions to an Issue, with Special Reference to His Lordship's Charge of 1857, and His Forthcoming Charge of 1860.*

———. 1861. *A Critical Appendix upon the Bishop of St. David's Reply, by the Author of "An Earnestly Respectful Letter" to His Lordship.*

———. 1862. *Persecution for the Word. With a Postscript on the Interlocutory Judgement and the Present State of the Case.*

———. 1866. *The Hebrew Prophets, Translated Afresh from the Original . . . by Rowland Williams.* 2 vols.

Wilson, Henry Bristow. 1861. *Three Sermons Composed for Delivery at the Opening of New Organ at St. Chrysostom's Church, Everton . . . May 24, and . . . 26, 1861.*

———. 1863. *A Speech Delivered before the Judicial Committee of Her Majesty's Most Honourable Privy Council in the Case of Wilson v. Fendall on Appeal from the Arches Court of Canterbury.*

Wilson, Daniel. 1861. *The Inspired Scriptures, Not Man's "Verifying Faculty," the Final Ground of Appeal in Matters of Faith. A Sermon* [on Tim. 3:16] *Preached . . . in Reference to a Work Entitled "Essays and Reviews."*

The Witness of Prophecy. 1861.

Woodgate, Henry Arthur. 1861. *"Essays and Reviews" Considered in Relation to the Current Principles & Fallacies of the Day.*

Woodward, F. B. 1864. *Court of Last Appeal: A Letter to the Lord Bishop of Salisbury.*

Worcester Vicar. See *The Church as It Is.*

Wordsworth, Christopher. 1861. *The Inspiration of the Bible.*

———. 1861. *The Interpretation of the Bible.*

Working Man. See *An Answer to F. Temple's Essay.*

Wratislaw, Albert Henry. 1864. *A Plea for the Ancient Charitable Foundation of Rugby School. In Reply to the Report of the Public School Commissioners, with a Few Remarks upon That of the Headmaster to the Trustees.*

Young, John Radford. 1861. *The Mosaic Cosmogony Not "Adverse to Modern Science;" Being an Examination of the Essay of C. W. Goodwin, M.A., with Some Remarks on the Essay of Professor Powell, as Published in "Essays and Reviews."*

Works Cited

Manuscripts

Among the chief collections used are the following:

London:
- The British Library (Gladstone, Lubbock, and Privy Council papers)
- Lambeth Palace Library (Tait, Longley, Golightly, and Court of Arches papers)
- Imperial College of Science and Technology (Huxley papers)

Oxford:
- The Bodleian Library (Pattison, Wilberforce, and Oxford Diocesan papers)
- Balliol College Library (Jowett papers)
- Pusey House (Pusey and Hamilton papers)

Reading:
- University of Reading (Longman Publishing Archives)

Hawarden, Wales
- Clwyd Record Office (Glynne-Gladstone papers)

General Reference Books

The editors have consulted the following reference books for standard information. Where we have quoted or wish to draw particular attention to a source we have used the abbreviations specified.

The Anchor Bible Dictionary. 1992. Ed. David Noel Freedman. 6 vols. New York: Doubleday.

Allgemeine deutsche Biographie. 1875–1912. 56 vols. Leipzig: Duncker.

Ante-Nicene Fathers. [1867–83] 1885. Ed. Alexander Roberts and James Donaldson. 10 vols. [*ANF*]

Biographie universelle. 1843–65. Ed. M. Michaud. 45 vols.

British Library General Catalogue of Printed Books to 1975. 1979–87. 360 vols. London: Bingley. [*BLC*]

The Catholic Encyclopedia. 1907–12. 15 vols. New York: Encyclopedia Press.

Dictionary of American Biography. 1928–37. Ed. Allen Johnson and Dumas Malone. 20 vols. New York: Scribners.

A Dictionary of Biblical Tradition in English Literature. 1992. Ed. David Lyle Jeffrey. Grand Rapids: Eerdmans.

Dictionary of the History of Ideas: Studies of Selected Pivotal Ideas. 1973. Ed. Philip P. Wiener. 5 vols. New York: Scribner. [*DHI*]

Dictionary of National Biography. 1908–9. Ed. Leslie Stephen and Sidney Lee. 22 vols. London: Smith, Elder. [*DNB*]

Dictionnaire de la Bible. 1912-28. Ed. Fulcran-Grégroire Vigoureux. 5 vols. in 10. Paris: Letouzey et Ané.

Encyclopaedia Britannica. 1875–99. 9th ed. 25 vols.

———. 1910–11. 11th ed. 29 vols. [*EB*]

Encyclopaedia Judaica. 1971–72. 16 vols. New York: Macmillan.

Encyclopaedia Metropolitana. [1817–45] 1849. Ed. Edward Smedley, Hugh James Rose, and Henry John Rose. 26 vols.

Encyclopedia of Religion and Ethics. 1908–26. Ed. James Hastings. 13 vols. New York: Scribners. [*ERE*]

Harper's Bible Commentary. 1988. Ed. James L. Mays. San Francisco: Harper & Row.

Harper's Bible Dictionary. 1985. Ed. Paul J. Achtemeier. San Francisco: Harper.

The New Jerome Bible Commentary. 1990. Ed. Raymond E. Brown, Joseph A. Fitzmyer, and Roland E. Murphy. Englewood Cliffs: Prentice-Hall. [*JBC*]

Library of the Fathers of the Holy Catholic Church, Anterior to the Division of the East and West. 1839-85. Ed. E. B. Pusey, John Keble, and J. H. Newman. 48 vols.

The Loeb Classical Library. 1912– . 450 vols. Cambridge: Harvard Univ. Press. [*Loeb*]

Melton, J. Gordon. Ed. 1987. *The Encyclopedia of American Religions: Religious Creeds*. Detroit: Gale.

National Union Catalogue, Pre-1965 Imprints. 1968–81. 754 vols. London: Mansell.

New Catholic Encyclopedia. 1967. 15 vols. New York: McGraw-Hill.

The Oxford English Dictionary. 1989. 2d ed. 20 vols. Oxford: Clarendon Press. [*OED*]

The Oxford Classical Dictionary. 1970. Ed. N. G. L. Hammond and H. H. Scullard. 2d ed. Oxford: Clarendon Press.

The Oxford Dictionary of the Christian Church. [1959–61] 1983. Ed. F. L. Cross and E. A. Livingstone. 2d ed. London: Oxford Univ. Press.

A Select Library of the Nicene and Post-Nicene Fathers of the Christian Church. 1886–90. Ed. Philip Schaff and Henry Wace. 1st Series. 14 vols. [*NPNF1*]

A Select Library of the Nicene and Post-Nicene Fathers of the Christian Church. 1890–1900. Ed. Philip Schaff. 2d Series. 14 vols. [*NPNF2*]

Wellesley Index to Victorian Periodicals, 1824–1900. 1966–89. Ed. Walter E. Houghton, Esther Rhoads Houghton, and Jean Harris Slingerland. 5 vols. Toronto: Univ. of Toronto Press.

Printed Works Cited

Aarsleff, Hans. [1966] 1983. *The Study of Language in England, 1780–1860.* Minneapolis: Univ. of Minnesota Press.

Abbott, Evelyn, and Lewis Campbell. 1897. *The Life and Letters of Benjamin Jowett, M.A., Master of Balliol College, Oxford.* 2 vols.

———. 1899. *Letters of Benjamin Jowett, M. A., Master of Balliol College, Oxford.*

Abraham, William J. 1981. *The Divine Inspiration of Holy Scripture.* Oxford: Oxford Univ. Press.

Abrams, M. H. 1953. *The Mirror and the Lamp: Romantic Theory and the Critical Tradition.* New York: Oxford Univ. Press.

———. 1971. *Natural Supernaturalism: Tradition and Revolution in Romantic Literature.* New York: Norton.

Achtemeier, Paul J. 1980. *The Inspiration of Scripture: Problems and Proposals.* Philadelphia: Westminster Press.

Acton, Lord. 1986. *Selected Writings of Lord Acton.* Ed. J. Rufus Fears. 3 vols. Indianapolis: Liberty Classics.

Addison, Joseph. [1737] 1811. "Of the Christian Religion." In *The Works of the Right Honourable Joseph Addison.* Ed. Richard Hurd. 6 vols. 6:255–97.

Ahlström, Gosta W. 1986. *Who Were the Israelites?* Winona Lake: Eisenbrauns.

Aland, Kurt, and Barbara Aland. 1987. *The Text of the New Testament: An Introduction to the Critical Editions and to the Theory and Practice of Modern Textual Criticism.* Trans. Erroll F. Rhodes. Grand Rapids: Eerdmans.

Alexander, Philip. 1993. "Jewish Interpretation." In Metzger and Coogan 1993, 305–10.

Alford, Henry. [1849] 1863. *The Greek Testament.* 5th ed. 4 vols.

———. 1868. "Memoirs of Baron Bunsen." *Contemporary Review* 8 (May): 114–38.

Allen, Don Cameron. 1964. *Doubt's Boundless Sea.* Baltimore: Johns Hopkins Univ. Press.

Allen, Peter. 1985. "S. T. Coleridge's *Church and State* and the Idea of an Intellectual Establishment." *Journal of the History of Ideas* 46:89–106.

Alt, Albrecht. 1966. *Essays on Old Testament History and Religion.* Oxford: Blackwell.

Altholz, Josef L. 1966. *The Churches in the Nineteenth Century.* Indianapolis: Bobbs-Merrill.

———. 1976. "The Warfare of Conscience with Theology." *The Mind and Art of Victorian England.* Ed. Josef L. Altholz. Minneapolis: Univ. of Minnesota Press. 58–78.

———. 1977. "Periodical Origins and Implications of *Essays and Reviews.*" *Victorian Periodicals Newsletter* 10:140–54.

———. 1982a. "The Mind of Victorian Orthodoxy: Anglican Responses to 'Essays and Reviews,' 1860–1864." *Church History* 51:186–97.

———. 1982b. "Publishing History of *Essays and Reviews.*" *Notes and Queries* 29:312–13.
———. 1986. "Early Periodical Responses to 'Essays and Reviews.'" *Victorian Periodicals Review* 19:50–56.
———. 1989. *The Religious Press in Britain, 1760–1900*. New York: Greenwood.
———. 1994. *Anatomy of a Controversy: The Debate over "Essays and Reviews," 1860–1864*. Aldershot: Scolar Press.
Altick, Richard D. 1957. *The English Common Reader: A Social History of the Mass Reading Public, 1800–1900*. Chicago: Univ. of Chicago Press.
Altizer, Thomas J. J., et al. 1982. *Deconstruction and Theology*. New York: Crossroad.
Ambrose. 1961. *Saint Ambrose: Hexameron, Paradise, and Cain and Abel.* Trans. John J. Savage. New York: Fathers of the Church.
———. 1963. *Saint Ambrose: Theological and Dogmatic Works.* Trans. Roy J. Deferrari. Washington: Catholic Univ. of America Press.
Anderson, Benedict. 1991. *Imagined Communities*. London: Verso.
Anderson, Hugh. 1976. *The Gospel of Mark*. London: Oliphants.
Anderson, Marvin W. 1987. "Theodore Beza: Savant or Scholastic." *Theologische Zeitschrift* 43:320–32.
Anderson, Olive. 1967. "War Finance." In *A Liberal State at War: English Politics and Economics during the Crimean War.* London: Macmillan. 190–228.
Anderson, Patricia J., and Jonathan Rose. Eds. 1991. *British Literary Publishing Houses, 1820–1880*. Detroit: Gale Research.
Ankarloo, Bengt, and Gustav Henningsten. Eds. 1990. *Early Modern Witchcraft.* Oxford: Oxford Univ. Press.
The Apostolic Fathers. 1947. Trans. Francis X. Glimm, Joseph M.-F. Marique, and Gerald G. Walsh. New York: Cima.
Arieli, Yehoshua. 1964. *Individualism and Nationalism in American Ideology.* Cambridge: Harvard Univ. Press.
Armstrong, Anthony. 1973. *The Church of England, the Methodists, and Society, 1700–1850*. London: Univ. of London Press.
Arnold, Matthew. 1960–77. *The Complete Prose Works of Matthew Arnold.* Ed. R. H. Super. 11 vols. Ann Arbor: Univ. of Michigan Press.
Arnold, Thomas. [1832] 1844. "An Essay on the Right Interpretation and Understanding of Scripture." In Thomas Arnold 1844, 2:374–425.
———. [1833] 1962. *Principles of Church Reform.* Ed. M. J. Jackson and J. Rogan. London: SPCK.
———. 1836. "The Oxford Malignants and Dr. Hampden." *Edinburgh Review* 63 (Apr.): 225–39.
———. 1838–1842. *The History of Rome.* 3 vols.
———. 1844. *Sermons.* 4 vols.
———. 1845. *Fragments on Church and State.*
———. 1874. *Sermons.* 5 vols.

Arnstein, Walter L. 1965. *The Bradlaugh Case: A Study in Late Victorian Opinion and Politics*. Oxford: Clarendon Press.

Ashmun, Margaret Eliza. 1931. *The Singing Swan: An Account of Anna Seward and Her Acquaintance with Dr. Johnson, Boswell, and Others of Their Time*. New Haven: Yale Univ. Press.

Ashwell, A. R., and R. G. Wilberforce. 1880–82. *The Life of Samuel Wilberforce*. 3 vols.

Athanasius. 1854. *The Festal Letters of S. Athanasius*. Trans. Henry Burgess. Vol. 38 in *A Library of the Fathers of the Holy Catholic Church*.

Atlay, J. 1906–8. *The Victorian Chancellors*. 2 vols. London: Smith, Elder.

Auberlen, Karl August. 1856. *The Prophecies of Daniel and the Revelations of St. John Viewed in Their Mutual Relations . . . with an Appendix by M. Fr. Roos*. Trans. Adolph Sapir.

Augustine, St. 1964. *The Essential Augustine*. Ed. Vernon J. Bourke. New York: Mentor-Omega.

Aulen, Gustaf. 1951. *Christus Victor: An Historical Study of the Three Main Types of the Idea of Atonement*. New York: Macmillan.

Bacon, Francis. [1605] 1973. *The Advancement of Learning*. Ed. G. W. Kitchin. London: Dent.

———. [1620] 1855. *The Novum Organon, or A True Guide to the Interpretation of Nature*. Trans. G. W. Kitchin.

———. 1858–74. *The Works of Francis Bacon*. Ed. James Spedding, Robert Leslie Ellis, and Douglas Denon Heath. 14 vols.

Badger, Kingsbury. 1945. "Mark Pattison and the Victorian Scholar." *Modern Language Quarterly* 6:423–47.

Bagehot, Walter. 1965–86. *The Collected Works of Walter Bagehot*. Ed. Norman St. John-Stevas. 15 vols. London: The Economist.

Baird, William. 1992. *History of New Testament Research: From Deism to Tübingen*. Minneapolis: Fortress.

Bakewell, Robert. [1813] 1833. *An Introduction to Geology: Intended to Convey a Practical Knowledge of the Science, and Comprising the Important Recent Discoveries; with Explanations of Facts and Phenomena Which Serve to Confirm or Invalidate the Various Geological Theories*. 2d American ed. Ed. Benjamin Silliman.

Balfour, John Hutton. 1854. *Class Book of Botany, Being an Introduction to the Study of the Vegetable Kingdom*.

———. 1855. *A Manual of Botany: Being an Introduction to the Structure, Physiology, and Classification of Plants*. 3d ed. Ed. Joseph Williams.

Balguy, Thomas. 1785. *Discourses on Various Subjects*.

Bannerman, James. 1860. "Recent Rationalism in the Church of England." *North British Review* 33 (Aug.): 217–55.

Barber, Lynn. 1980. *The Heyday of Natural History, 1820–1870*. New York: Doubleday.

Barnes, Barry, and Stephen Shapin. Eds. 1979. *Natural Order: Historical Studies of Scientific Culture*. London: Sage.

Barnes, James J. 1964. *Free Trade in Books: A Study of the London Book Trade since 1800*. Oxford: Clarendon Press.

Barnes, Timothy David. 1981. *Constantine and Eusebius*. Cambridge: Harvard Univ. Press.

Barney, Stephen A. Ed. 1991. *Annotation and Its Texts*. New York: Oxford Univ. Press.

Barni, Jules Romain. 1850. *Philosophie de Kant. Examen de la Critique du jugement.*

Barr, James. 1961. *The Semantics of Biblical Language*. Oxford: Oxford Univ. Press.

———. 1977. *Fundamentalism*. London: SCM Press.

———. 1982. "Jowett and the 'Original Meaning' of Scripture." *Religious Studies* 18:433–37.

———. 1983. "Jowett and the Reading of the Bible 'Like Any Other Book.'" *Horizons in Biblical Theology* 4/5:1–44.

Barthélemy-Madaule, Madeleine. [1979] 1982. *Lamarck the Mythical Precursor*. Trans. M. H. Shank. Boston: MIT Press.

Bassnett-McGuire, Susan. 1991. *Translation Studies*. London: Routledge.

Bauman, Michael. 1987. *Milton's Arianism*. New York: Lang.

Beadnell, Henry. 1859. *A Guide to Typography in Two Parts, Literary and Practical, or, the Reader's Handbook and the Compositor's Vade Mecum*. 2 vols.

Beard, J. R. Ed. 1845. *Voices of the Church, in Reply to Dr. D. F. Strauss.*

Beare, Francis Wright. 1962. *The Earliest Records of Jesus: A Companion to "The Synopsis of the First Three Gospels" by Albert Huck*. New York: Abingdon.

Beardslee, William A. 1989. "Recent Literary Criticism [of the New Testament]." In Epp and MacRae 1989, 175–98.

Beattie, J. M. 1986. *Crime and the Courts in England, 1660–1800*. Princeton: Princeton Univ. Press.

Beausobre, Isaac de. 1734–39. *Histoire critique de Manichée et du Manichéïsme*. 2 vols.

Beck, George Andrew. Ed. 1950. *The English Catholics, 1850–1950*. London: Burns Oates.

Beckmann, Petr. 1971. *A History of π (PI)*. Boulder: Golem Press.

Bede. 1969. *Bede's Ecclesiastical History of the English People*. Ed. Bertram Colgrave and R. A. B. Mynors. Oxford: Clarendon Press.

Beegle, Dewey M. 1979. *Scripture, Tradition, and Infallibility*. Ann Arbor: Pryor Pentengill.

Benko, Stephen. 1984. *Pagan Rome and the Early Christians*. Bloomington: Indiana Univ. Press.

Bennett, G. V. 1975. *The Tory Crisis in Church and State, 1688–1730: The Career of Francis Atterbury, Bishop of Rochester*. Oxford: Clarendon Press.

Bentley, James. 1978. *Ritualism and Politics in Victorian Britain: The Attempt to Legislate for Belief.* Oxford: Oxford Univ. Press.

Bentley, Richard. [1836] 1966. *The Works of Richard Bentley, D.D.* Ed. Alexander Dyce. 3 vols. Repr. New York: AMS Press.

Bentwich, Norman DeMattos. [1912] 1937. *The Privy Council in Judicial Matters in Appeals from Courts of Civil, Criminal, and Admiralty Jurisdiction and in Appeals from Ecclesiastical and Prize Courts; with the Statutes, Rules, and Forms of Procedure.* 3d ed. London: Sweet & Maxwell.

Berchman, Robert M. 1984. *From Philo to Origen: Middle Platonism in Transition.* Chico: Scholars Press.

Berger, Peter L. 1979. *The Heretical Imperative: Contemporary Possibilities of Religious Affirmation.* New York: Anchor / Doubleday.

Berkeley, George. 1948–56. *The Works of George Berkeley, Bishop of Cloyne.* Ed. A. A. Luce and T. E. Jessop. 9 vols. London: Nelson.

Best, Geoffrey F. A. 1964. *Temporal Pillars: Queen Anne's Bounty, the Ecclesiastical Commissioners, and the Church of England.* Cambridge: Cambridge Univ. Press.

———. 1967. "Popular Protestantism in Victorian Britain." In Robson, Robert. 1967, 115–42.

Bethune, John Elliot Drinkwater. 1829. *The Life of Galileo Galilei.*

Betz, Hans Dieter. 1985. *2 Corinthians 8 and 9: A Commentary on Two Administrative Letters of the Apostle Paul.* Philadelphia: Fortress.

Beyer, Klaus. 1968. *Semitische Syntax im Neuen Testament.* Göttingen: Vandenhoeck & Ruprecht.

Beveridge, William. 1709. *Private Thoughts upon Religion.*

Biagini, Eugenio F., and Alastair J. Reid. Eds. 1991. *Currents of Radicalism: Popular Radicalism, Organised Labour, and Party Politics in Britain, 1850–1914.* Cambridge: Cambridge Univ. Press.

Biagioli, Mario. 1993. *Galileo, Courtier.* Chicago: Univ. of Chicago Press.

Bickerman, Elias J. 1988. *The Jews in the Greek Age.* Cambridge: Harvard Univ. Press.

Bigg, Charles. 1886. *The Christian Platonists of Alexandria: Eight Lectures.*

Bildiss, Michael D. 1970. *Father of Racist Ideology: The Social and Political Thought of Count Gobineau.* London: Weidenfeld & Nicolson.

———. 1976. "The Politics of Anatomy: Dr. Robert Knox and Victorian Racism." *Proceedings of the Royal Society of Medicine* 69:245–50.

———. 1979. *Images of Race.* New York: Holmes & Meier.

Bill, E. G. W., and J. F. A. Mason. 1970. *Christ Church and Reform, 1850–1867.* Oxford: Clarendon Press.

Billington, Louis. 1986. "The Religious Periodical and Newspaper Press, 1770–1870." In Harris and Lee 1986.

Biographica Britannica; or The Lives of the Most Eminent Persons Who Have Flourished in Great Britain and Ireland. [1747–66] 1778–93. 2d ed. 5 vols.

Birch, Samuel. 1872. "The Progress of Biblical Archaeology: An Address." *Transactions of the Society of Biblical Archaeology.* 1.

Bird, Isabella. 1860. "Religious Revivals." *Quarterly Review* 107:148–68.

Birks, Thomas Rawson. [1847] 1869. *Church and State: or, National Religion and Church Establishments.*

"Bishop Colenso on the Pentateuch." 1863. *National Review* 16 (Jan.): 1–27.

Black, Henry Campbell. [1891] 1990. *Black's Law Dictionary.* 6th ed. St. Paul: West Publishing.

Black, M. H. 1963. "The Printed Bible." In *The Cambridge History of the Bible.* Ed. S. L. Greenslade. Cambridge: Cambridge Univ. Press. 1:408–75.

Blackstone, William. [1765–69] 1876. *The Commentaries on the Laws of England.* Adapted Robert Malcolm Kerr. 4th ed. 4 vols.

———. [1764–70] 1979. *The Commentaries on the Laws of England.* 4 vols. Chicago: Univ. of Chicago Press. Facsimile of 1st ed.

Blake, Robert. 1967. *Disraeli.* New York: St. Martin's.

Blench, J. W. 1964. *Preaching in England in the Late Fifteenth and Sixteenth Centuries: A Study of English Sermons, 1450–c. 1600.* Oxford: Blackwell.

Boak, Arthur E. R. 1955. *Manpower Shortage and the Fall of the Roman Empire in the West.* Ann Arbor: Univ. of Michigan Press.

Book of Sermons or Homilies Appointed to be Read in Churches. [1547, 1563] 1802.

Booth, Stephen Paul. 1969. "*Essays and Reviews*: The Controversy as Seen in the Correspondence and Papers of Dr. E. B. Pusey and Archbishop Archibald Tait." *Historical Magazine of the Protestant Episcopal Church* 38:259–79.

Bostock, David. 1986. *Plato's "Phaedo."* Oxford: Clarendon Press.

Boswell, James. [1791] 1936. *Boswell's Life of Johnson.* Ed. George Birkbeck Hill. 6 Vols. Oxford: Clarendon Press.

Botterweck, G. Johannes, and Helmer Ringgren. 1874–86. *Theological Dictionary of the Old Testament.* Trans. John T. Willis. 6 vols.

Bousma, William James. 1988. *John Calvin: a Sixteenth-Century Portrait.* Oxford: Oxford Univ. Press.

Bowen, Catherine Shober Drinker. 1957. *The Lion and the Throne: The Life and Times of Sir Edward Coke.* Boston: Little, Brown.

Bowen, Desmond. 1968. *The Idea of the Victorian Church: A Study of the Church of England, 1833–1889.* Montreal: McGill Univ. Press.

Boyce, George, James Curran, and Pauline Wingate. Eds. 1978. *Newspaper History from the Seventeenth Century to the Present Day.* London: Constable.

Bradley, James E. 1990. *Religion, Revolution, and English Radicalism: Nonconformity in Eighteenth-Century Politics and Society.* Cambridge: Cambridge Univ. Press.

Brake, Laurel, Aled Jones, and Lionel Madden. Eds. 1990. *Investigating Victorian Journalism.* London: Macmillan.

Brandon, S. G. F. 1965. *History, Time, and Deity.* Manchester: Manchester Univ. Press.

Brantlinger, Patrick. 1988. *Rule of Darkness: British Literature and Imperialism, 1840–1914.* Ithaca: Cornell Univ. Press.

Breech, James. 1983. *The Silence of Jesus: The Authentic Voice of the Historical Man.* Philadelphia: Fortress.

Brent, Richard. 1987. *Liberal Anglican Politics: Whiggery, Religion, and Reform, 1830–1841*. Oxford: Clarendon Press.

Brewster, David. 1854. Review of "Works on Mental Philosophy, Mesmerism, Electro-Biology, &c." [28 books]. *North British Review* 22 (Nov.): 179–224.

A Brief Summary in Plain Language of the Most Important Laws concerning Women. 1854.

Briggs, Asa. Ed. 1974. *Essays in the History of Publishing: In Celebration of the 250th Anniversary of the House of Longman, 1724–1974*. London: Longmans.

Bright, John. 1959. *A History of Israel*. Philadelphia: Westminster Press.

Brink, C. O. 1986. *English Classical Scholarship: Historical Reflections on Bentley, Porson, and Housman*. Cambridge: James Clarke.

Brodrick, George C., and William H. Fremantle. Eds. 1865. *A Collection of the Judgments of the Judicial Committee of the Privy Council in Ecclesiastical Cases Relating to Doctrine and Discipline*.

Bromiley, Geoffrey. Ed. 1982. *The International Standard Bible Encyclopedia*. 4 vols. Grand Rapids: Eerdmans.

Brooke, John Hedley. 1985. "The Relations between Darwin's Science and His Religion." In *Darwinism and Divinity*. Ed. John Durant. Oxford: Blackwell. 40–75.

———. 1991. *Science and Religion: Some Historical Perspectives*. Cambridge: Cambridge Univ. Press.

Brooke, William G. Ed. 1874. *Six Judgments of the Judicial Committee of the Privy Council in Ecclesiastical Cases, 1850–1872*.

Brown Colin. 1984. *Miracles and the Critical Mind*. Devon: Eerdmans.

Brown, J. Mellor. 1838. *Reflections on Geology*.

Brown, Samuel. 1851. "Animal Magnetism." *North British Review* 15 (May): 133–59.

Brown, Schuyler. 1989. "Philology." In Epp and MacRae 1989, 127–47.

Brown, Stewart J. 1982. *Thomas Chalmers and the Godly Commonwealth in Scotland*. Oxford: Oxford Univ. Press.

Browne, Edward Harold. 1862. "Inspiration." In Thomson 1861, 287–321.

———. 1871. *The Holy Bible*.

———. 1882. *An Exposition of the Thirty-Nine Articles, Historical and Doctrinal*. 12th ed.

Brueggemann, Walter. 1982. *Genesis*. Atlanta: John Knox Press.

Bruns, Gerald L. 1992. *Hermeneutics, Ancient & Modern*. New Haven: Yale Univ. Press.

Buchanan, James. 1861. *The "Essays and Reviews" Examined; A Series of Articles contributed to the "Morning Post."* 1861.

Buck, Charles. 1851. *A Theological Dictionary*.

Buckland, William. 1823. *Reliquae Diluvianae, or Observations on the Organic Remains Contained in Caves, Fissures, and Diluvial Gravel, and on Other Geological Phenomena, Attesting to the Action of a Universal Deluge*.

———. 1833. *Geology and Mineralogy Considered with Reference to Natural Theology*.

2 vols. [A Bridgewater Treatise].

Bugg, George. 1826. *Scriptural Geology; or, Geological Phenomena Consistent Only with the Literal Interpretation of the Sacred Scriptures, upon the Subjects of the Creation and Deluge; in Answer to an "Essay on the Theory of the Earth," by M. Cuvier . . . and to Professor Buckland's Theory of the Caves, as Delineated in His "Reliquae Diluvianae."* 2 vols.

Bull, George. [1685] 1851. *Defensio Fidei Nicaenae: A Defence of the Nicene Creed.* 2 vols.

Bullard, J. V. 1934. *Constitutions and Canons Ecclesiastical 1604: Latin and English.* London: Faith Press.

Bullett, Gerald. 1951. *Sydney Smith: A Biography and a Selection.* London: Michael Joseph.

Bullinger, E. W. [1898] 1968. *Figures of Speech Used in the Bible.* Grand Rapids: Baker.

Bullock, F. W. B. 1955. *A History of Training for the Ministry of the Church of England . . . from 1800 to 1874.* St. Leonards-on-Sea: Budd & Gilliatt.

Bunsen, Christian C. J., baron von. 1845–57. *Aegeptens Stelle in der Weltgeschichte.* 5 vols. Translated as Bunsen 1848–67.

———. 1847. *The Constitution of the Church of the Future. A Practical Explanation of the Correspondence with the Right Honourable William Gladstone, on the German Church, Episcopacy, and Jerusalem.*

———. 1848–67. *Egypt's Place in Universal History.* 5 vols. Trans. Charles H. Cottrell. [vol. 1, 1848; vol. 2, 1854; vol. 3, 1859; vol. 4, 1860; vol. 5, 1867]; 2d English ed. 1867, with additions by Samuel Birch.

———. 1852a. *Hippolytus und seine Zeit.* 2 vols. Translated as Bunsen 1852b.

———. 1852b. *Hippolytus and His Age, or, the Doctrine and Practice of the Church of Rome under Commodus and Alexander Severus: and Ancient and Modern Christianity and Divinity Compared.* Trans. Charles H. Cottrell. 4 vols.

———. 1854. *Christianity and Mankind, Their Beginnings and Prospects.* 7 vols. [*Hippolytus and His Age.* Vols. 1, 2. 2d ed.; *Outlines of the Philosophy of Universal History, Applied to Language and Religion.* Vols. 3, 4.; *Analecta Ante-Nicaena.* Vols. 5–7].

———. 1857. *Gott in der Geschichte.* 3 vols. Translated as Bunsen 1868–70.

———. 1868–70. *God in History; or, the Progress of Man's Faith in the Moral Order of the World.* Trans. Susanna Winkworth. 3 vols.

Bunsen, Frances von. 1868. *A Memoir of Baron Bunsen.* 2 vols.

Burgon, J. W. 1861. *Inspiration and Interpretation.*

———. 1870a. *Dr. Temple's "Explanation" Examined.*

———. 1870b. *Protests of the Bishops against the Consecration to the See of Exeter.*

Burke, Edmund. [1790] 1969. *Reflections on the Revolution in France.* Ed. Conor Cruise O'Brien. Harmondsworth: Penguin.

———. 1844. *Correspondence.* Ed. Charles William, Earl Fitzwilliam, and Sir Richard Bourke. 4 vols.

Burn, Richard. [1760] 1842. *The Ecclesiastical Law*. Ed. Robert Phillimore. 4 vols.

Burnet, Gilbert. [1699] 1819. *An Exposition of the XXXIX Articles of the Church of England.*

———. [1724–33] 1823–33. *History of His Own Time*. Ed. M. J. Routh. 7 vols.

———. 1737. *A Defence of Natural and Revealed Religion: Being an Abridgment of the Sermons Preached at the Lecture Founded by the Hon. Robert Boyle*. 4 vols.

Burrow, J. W. 1966. *Evolution and Society: A Study in Victorian Social Theory*. London: Cambridge Univ. Press.

———. 1967. "The Uses of Philology in Victorian England." In Robson, Robert. 1967. 180–204.

———. 1981. *A Liberal Descent: Victorian Historians and the English Past*. Cambridge: Cambridge Univ. Press.

Burrows, Mark S., and Paul Rorem. Eds. 1991. *Biblical Hermeneutics in Historical Perspective*. Grand Rapids: Eerdmans.

Burrows, Millar. 1940. "Levirate Marriage in Israel." *Journal of Biblical Literature* 59:23–33.

———. 1951. "The Semitic Background of the New Testament." *Bible Translator* 2:67–73.

Burrows, Montagu. 1860. *Pass and Class: An Oxford Guide-Book through the Courses of Literae Humaniores, Mathematics, Natural Science, and Law and Modern History*.

Burtchaell, James Tunstead. 1969. *Catholic Theories of Biblical Inspiration since 1810: A Review and Critique*. Cambridge: Cambridge Univ. Press.

Burton, John Hill. 1846. *Life and Correspondence of David Hume*. 2 vols.

Bury, J. B. 1928. *The Invasions of Europe by the Barbarians*. London: Macmillan.

Butler, Joseph. [1736] 1855. *The Analogy of Religion to the Constitution and Course of Nature*. Ed. Joseph Angus.

———. 1853. *Some Remains (Hitherto Unpublished) of Joseph Butler*. Ed. Edward Steere.

———. 1896. *The Works of Joseph Butler, D.C.L.* Ed. W. E. Gladstone. 2 vols.

Butler, Perry. 1982. *Gladstone, Church, State, and Tractarianism: A Study of His Religious Ideas and Attitudes, 1809–1859*. Oxford: Clarendon Press.

Butterfield, Herbert. 1931. *The Whig Interpretation of History*. London: Bell.

Byrne, Peter. 1989. *Natural Religion and the Nature of Religion: The Legacy of Deism*. London: Routledge.

Cairns, John. 1852. "Infallibility of the Bible and Recent Theories of Inspiration." *North British Review* 18 (Nov.): 138–85.

Calamy, Edmund. [1702] 1713. *An Abridgment of Mr. Baxter's History of His Life and Times, and the Continuation . . . to . . . 1711*. 2 vols.

Call, W. M. W. 1861. "Bible Infallibility—'Evangelical Defenders of the Faith.'" *Westminster Review* 75 (Jan.): 89–114.

Calvin, John. [1536] 1957. *Institutes of the Christian Religion*. Trans. Henry Beveridge. 2 vols. Grand Rapids: Eerdmans [Originally published by the Calvin

Translation Society. 3 vols. 1845–46].

———. [1539] 1973. *Calvin's Commentaries: The Epistles of Paul the Apostle to the Romans and to the Thessalonians.* Trans. Ross MacKenzie. Grand Rapids: Eerdmans.

———. [1546] 1976. *Calvin's Commentaries: The First Epistle of Paul the Apostle to the Corinthians.* Trans. John W. Fraser. Grand Rapids: Eerdmans.

Cambridge Essays. 1855.

Cambridge Essays. 1856.

Cambridge Essays. 1857.

Cambridge Essays. 1858.

Campbell, Lewis. Ed. 1871. *Sophocles: The Plays and Fragments.* Vol. 1.

———. Ed. 1881. *Sophocles.* Vol. 2.

Cameron, Nigel M. de S. 1987. *Biblical Higher Criticism and the Defense of Infallibilism in 19th Century Britain.* Lewiston: Edwin Mellen Press.

———. Ed. 1992. *Universalism and the Doctrine of Hell: Papers Presented at the Fourth Edinburgh Conference in Christian Dogmatics.* Grand Rapids: Baker Book House.

Cannon, Walter F. 1960. "The Uniformitarian-Catastrophist Debate." *Isis* 51 (Mar.): 38–55.

Cantor, Geoffrey N. 1991. *Michael Faraday: Sandemanian and Scientist: A Study of Science and Religion in the Nineteenth Century.* Basingstoke: Macmillan.

Capes, Frederick. 1852. "China—Its Civilization and Religion." *British Quarterly Review* 16 (Nov.): 396–418.

———. 1857. "Chinese Life and Manners." *Rambler* 20 (Nov.): 354–68.

———. 1858. "China." *Rambler* 22 (Nov.): 345–68.

Capes, J. M. 1849. "The Duties of Journalists." *Rambler* 3 (Jan.): 329.

Cardona, G., H. M. Hoenigswald, and A. Senn. Eds. 1970. *Indo-European and the Indo-Europeans.* Philadelphia: Univ. of Pennsylvania Press.

Carlyle, Thomas. [1833–34] 1937. *Sartor Resartus: The Life and Opinions of Herr Teufelsdröckh.* Ed. Charles Frederick Harrold. New York: Odyssey Press.

———. [1841] 1993. *On Heroes, Hero-Worship, & the Heroic in History.* Notes and Introduction by Michael K. Goldberg. Berkeley: Univ. of California Press.

———. [1843] 1977. *Past and Present.* Ed. Richard D. Altick. New York: New York Univ. Press.

———. 1896–99. *The Works of Thomas Carlyle.* 30 vols. Ed. H. D. Traill.

Carné, Louis Joseph Marie de. 1859. *La Monarchie française au dix-huitième siècle.* 2 vols.

Carpenter, William Benjamin. 1845. Review of *Vestiges of the Natural History of Creation* [by Robert Chambers]. *British and Foreign Medical Review* 19:155–81.

———. 1853. "Electro-biology and Mesmerism." *Quarterly Review* 93 (Sept.): 501–57.

———. 1857. "The Literature of Spirit-Rapping." *National Review* 4:131–51.

———. 1858. "Spirits and Spirit-Rapping." *Westminster Review* 60:29–60.

Carroll, Lewis. [1865] 1992. *Alice in Wonderland.* Ed. Donald J. Gray. New York: Norton. 2d ed.

———. [1899] 1961. *The Unknown Lewis Carroll.* Ed. Stuart Dodgson Collingwood. New York: Dover.

———. 1939. *The Complete Works of Lewis Carroll.* Intro. Alexander Woollcott. London: Nonesuch.

———. 1953. *The Diaries of Lewis Carroll.* Ed. Roger Lancelyn Green. 2 vols. London: Cassell.

———. 1979. *The Letters of Lewis Carroll.* Ed. Morton N. Cohen. 2 vols. London: Macmillan.

———. 1993. *The Oxford Pamphlets, Leaflets, and Circulars of Charles Lutwidge Dodgson.* Vol. 1 of *The Pamphlets of Lewis Carroll.* Ed. Edward Wakeling. Charlottesville: Univ. Press of Virginia.

Carruthers, Robert. 1857. *The Life of Alexander Pope.*

Carson, D. A., and J. D. Woodbridge. Eds. 1983. *Scripture and Truth.* Grand Rapids: Zondervan.

Cashdollar, Charles D. 1989. *The Transformation of Theology, 1830–1890.* Princeton: Princeton Univ. Press.

Case as to the Legal Position of Professor Jowett with the Opinion of the Queen's Advocate Thereon. 1862.

Case Whether Professor Jowett in His Essay and Commentary Has So Distinctly Contravened the Doctrines of the Church of England, That a Court of Law Would Pronounce Him Guilty; with the Opinion of the Queen's Advocate Thereon. 1862.

Catchpole, David R. 1993. *The Quest for Q.* Edinburgh: T. & T. Clark.

Caygill, Howard. 1989. *Art of Judgement.* Oxford: Basil Blackwell.

Cazenove, John Gibson. 1861. *On Certain Characteristics of Holy Scripture, with Special Reference to "An Essay on the Interpretation of Scripture" Contained in "Essays and Reviews." Reprinted, with Additions, from "The Christian Remembrancer," January, 1861.*

Cesarani, David. 1994. *The Jewish Chronicle and Anglo-Jewry, 1841–1991.* Cambridge: Cambridge Univ. Press.

Chadwick, Henry. 1967. *The Early Church.* Harmondsworth: Penguin.

Chadwick, Owen. Trans. and ed. 1954. *Alexandrian Christianity.* Philadelphia: Westminster Press.

Chadwick, Owen. 1966–70. *The Victorian Church: An Ecclesiastical History of England.* 2 vols. London: A. & C. Black.

Chalmers, Thomas. 1814. *On the Miraculous and Internal Evidences of the Christian Revelation, and the Authority of Its Records.*

———. 1836. *Natural Theology.* 2 vols.

Chambers, Robert. [1844] 1969. *Vestiges of the Natural History of Creation.* Ed. Gavin de Beer. Leicester: Leicester Univ. Press.

———. [1844] 1994. *Vestiges of the Natural History of Creation.* Ed. James A.

Secord. Chicago: Univ. of Chicago Press.

Chandos, John. Ed. 1971. *In God's Name: Examples of Preaching in England from the Act of Supremacy to the Act of Uniformity, 1534–1662*. London: Hutchinson.

Cheetham, Nicolas. 1983. *Keepers of the Keys: A History of the Popes from St. Peter to John Paul II*. New York: Scribner.

Cheney, Edward. 1855. "The Feast of the Conception." *Quarterly Review* 97 (June): 143–83.

Chéruel, Pierre Adolphe. 1864. *Saint-Simon considéré comme historien de Louis XIV*.

Cheyne, A. C. Ed. 1985. *The Practical and the Pious: Essays on Thomas Chalmers (1780–1847)*. Edinburgh: Saint Andrew Press.

Chichester, Edward. 1821. *Deism Compared with Christianity; Being an Epistolary Correspondence, Containing all the Principal Objections against Revealed Religion, with the Answers Annexed*. 3 vols.

Chilton, Bruce D. Ed. and trans. 1987. *The Isaiah Targum*. In McNamara et al. 1987–94. Vol. 11.

Christian Faith and the Atonement: Sermons Preached before the University of Oxford, in Reference to the Views Published by Mr. Jowett and Others. 1856.

"The Christian Sabbath: Its History and Authority." 1857. *London Quarterly Review* 8 (July): 395–430.

Le Christianisme au quatrième siècle: Constantin, Ambroise, Augustin. Séances historiques (Seconde Série) données à Genève en Mars 1858 par MM. de Gasparin, Bungener et de Pressensé. 1858.

Christianity and Paganism, 350–750: The Conversion of Western Europe. 1986. Ed. J. N. Hillgarth. Philadelphia: Univ. of Pennsylvania Press.

Christensen, Merton A. 1954. "The Impact of Biblical Criticism upon English Literary Thought from 1800 to 1875." Ph.D. diss., University of Maryland.

Christianson, Paul. 1978. *Reformers and Babylon: English Apocalyptic Visions from the Reformation to the Eve of the Civil War*. Toronto: Univ. of Toronto Press.

Chronicle of Convocation. 1859–64.

Church, R. W. 1891. *The Oxford Movement: Twelve Years, 1833–1845*.

Cicero. 1848. *The Republic*. Trans. Walter Keyes.

Clark, G. Kitson. 1962. *The Making of Victorian England*. London: Methuen.

———. 1973. *Churchmen and the Condition of England: A Study in the Development of Social Ideas and Practices from the Old Regime to the Modern State*. London: Methuen.

Clark, J. C. D. 1985. *English Society, 1688–1832: Ideology, Social Structure, and Political Practice during the Ancien Regime*. Cambridge: Cambridge Univ. Press.

Clark, Kenneth W. 1957. "The Transmission of the New Testament." In *The Interpreter's Bible*. Ed. George Arthur Buttrick. 12 vols. 12:617–27.

Clarke, M. L. 1959. *Classical Education in Britain: 1500–1900*. Cambridge: Cambridge Univ. Press.

———. 1974. *Paley: Evidences for the Man*. Toronto: Univ. of Toronto Press.

Clifford, Alan C. 1990. *Atonement and Justification: English Evangelical Theology,*

1640–1790. Oxford: Clarendon Press.

[Close, Francis]. 1861. *A Critical Examination of the Essays and Reviews. By an American Layman. Ed. by the Dean of Carlisle.*

Coats, George W. 1983. *Genesis with an Introduction to Narrative Literature*. Grand Rapids: Eerdmans.

Cobbe, Frances Power. 1894. *The Life of Frances Power Cobbe, by Herself.* 2 vols.

Cockshut, Anthony O. J.1959. *Anglican Attitudes: A Study of Victorian Religious Controversies*. London: Collins.

———. Ed. 1966. *Religious Controversies of the Nineteenth Century: Selected Documents*. Lincoln: Univ. of Nebraska Press.

———. 1964. *The Unbelievers: English Agnostic Thought, 1848–1890*. London: Collins.

Codex Sinaiticus and the Simonides Affair: An Examination of the Nineteenth Century Claim. 1982. Thessalonike: Patriarchikon Hidyrma Paterikon Meleton.

Coggins, R. J., and J. L. Houlden. Eds. 1990. *A Dictionary of Biblical Interpretation*. London: SCM Press.

Cohen, Philip. Ed. 1991. *Devils and Angels: Textual Editing and Literary Theory*. Charlottesville: Univ. Press of Virginia.

Coke, Edward. 1826. *The Reports of Sir Edward Coke, Knt.* Ed. John Henry Thomas and John Farquhar Fraser. 6 vols.

Colaiaco, J. A. 1983. *James Fitzjames Stephen and the Crisis of Victorian Thought*. New York: St. Martin's.

Cole, Henry. 1834. *Popular Geology Subversive of Divine Revelation.*

Colenso, John William. [1861] 1863. *St. Paul's Epistle to the Romans: Newly Translated, and Explained from a Missionary Point of View.*

———. 1862–79. *The Pentateuch and Book of Joshua Critically Examined.* 7 parts.

"Colenso on the Pentateuch." 1862. *Eclectic Review* n.s. 3 (Dec.) 506–24.

Coleridge, Henry Nelson. [1830] 1834. *Introduction to the Study of the Greek Classic Poets.*

Coleridge, S. T. [1809] 1969. *The Friend.* Ed. B. E. Rooke. In *The Collected Works of Samuel Taylor Coleridge*. Vols. 4 and 5. Princeton: Princeton Univ. Press.

———. [1817] 1983. *Biographia Literaria.* Ed. James Engell and W. Jackson Bate. In *The Collected Works of Samuel Taylor Coleridge*. Vols. 7 and 8. Princeton: Princeton Univ. Press.

———. 1825. *Aids to Reflection in the Formation of a Manly Character.*

———. [1829] 1976. *On the Constitution of the Church and State.* Ed. John Colmer. In *The Collected Works of Samuel Taylor Coleridge*. Vol. 10. Princeton: Princeton Univ. Press.

———. 1836–39. *The Literary Remains of Samuel Taylor Coleridge*. Ed. H. N. Coleridge. 4 vols.

———. [1840] 1988. *Confessions of an Inquiring Spirit.* Philadelphia: Fortress.

College Rhymes: Contributed by Members of the Universities of Oxford and Cambridge. 1860–73. 14 vols.

Collette, Charles Hastings. 1860. *Dr. Wiseman's Popish Literary Blunders Exposed.*

Conacher, J. B. 1959. "Party Politics in the Age of Palmerston." In *1859: Entering an Age of Crisis.* Ed. Philip Appleman et al. Bloomington: Indiana Univ. Press. 163–80.

Conrad, Joseph. [1897] 1979. *The Nigger of the "Narcissus."* Ed. Robert Kimbrough. New York: Norton.

Constitution on Divine Revelation. 1870. [Papal Encyclical of Pius IX].

Conybeare, W. J. 1853. "Church Parties." *Edinburgh Review* 98 (Oct.): 273–342.

———. 1854. "Vestries and Church-Rates." *Edinburgh Review* 100 (Oct.): 305–47.

———. 1855. "The Neology of the Cloister." *Quarterly Review* 98 (Dec.): 148–89.

Coode, John. 1853. "The Income Tax." *Edinburgh Review* 97 (Apr.): 531–84.

Cook, Chris, and Brendan Keith. 1984. *British Historical Facts, 1830–1900.* London: Macmillan.

Cook, F. C. Ed. 1871–88. *The Holy Bible . . . with an Explanatory and Critical Commentary . . . by Bishops and Other Clergy of the Anglican Church.* 12 vols.

Cook, Stanley A. [1923] 1928. "Chronology: I. Mesopotamia." *The Cambridge Ancient History.* Ed. J. B. Bury, S. A. Cook, and F. E. Adcock. 2 vols. Cambridge: Cambridge Univ. Press. 1:145–56.

Coote, H. C. 1847. *Practice of the Ecclesiastical Courts.*

Coote Robert B., and Keith W. Whitelam. 1987. *The Emergence of Early Israel in Historical Perspective.* Sheffield: Almond.

Correspondence Respecting the Proposed Measures of Improvement in the Universities and Colleges of Oxford and Cambridge. 1854.

Corsi, Pietro. [1983] 1988. *The Age of Lamarck.* Trans. Jonathan Mandelbaum. Berkeley: Univ. of California Press.

———. 1988. *Science and Religion: Baden Powell and the Anglican Debate, 1800–1860.* Cambridge: Cambridge Univ. Press.

Courtade, G. 1945. "Inspiration et Inérrance." *Dictionnaire de la Bible.* Supplement. 4:482–559.

Cox, Harold, and John E. Chandler. 1925. *The House of Longman.* London: Longmans Green.

Cox, J. 1982. *The English Churches in a Secular Society, Lambeth 1870–1930.* Oxford: Oxford Univ. Press.

Coyne, George V., Michael Heller, and Joseph Zycinski. Eds. 1985. *The Galileo Affair: A Meeting of Faith and Science.* Vatican City: Vatican Observatory.

Cranston, Maurice. 1957. *John Locke: A Biography.* London: Longmans.

Cross, Frank More. 1992. "The Text behind the Text of the Hebrew Bible." *Understanding the Dead Sea Scrolls.* Ed. Hershel Shanks. New York: Random House. 139–56.

Crosse, Andrew. 1836–37. "On the Production of Insects by Voltaic Electricity." *Annals of Electricity, Magnetism, and Chemistry* 1:242–44.

Crowe, Michael J. 1986. *The Extraterrestrial Life Debate, 1750–1900: The Idea of a Plurality of Worlds from Kant to Lowell.* Cambridge: Cambridge Univ. Press.

Crowther, M. A. 1970. *Church Embattled: Religious Controversy in Mid-Victorian England.* London: David & Charles, Archon Books.
Crystal, David. 1987. *The Cambridge Encyclopedia of Language.* Cambridge: Cambridge Univ. Press.
Culican, William. 1965. *The Medes and Persians.* New York: Praeger.
Culler, A. Dwight. 1985. *The Victorian Mirror of History.* New Haven: Yale Univ. Press.
Cundall, H. M. 1906. *Birket Foster, R.W.S.* London: Adam & Charles Black.
Cunningham, Adrian. 1973. "Myth, Ideology, and Lévi-Strauss: The Problem of the Genesis Story in the Nineteenth Century." In *The Theory of Myth: Six Studies.* Ed. Adrian Cunningham. London: Sheed & Ward. 132–76.
Curtis, L. P., Jr. 1968. *Anglo-Saxon and Celts: A Study of Anti-Irish Prejudice in Victorian England.* Bridgeport: Conference on British Studies.
Curtis, William Redmond. 1942. *The Lambeth Conferences: The Solution for Pan-Anglican Organization.* New York: Columbia Univ. Press.
Darwin, Charles. [1859] 1964. *On the Origin of Species by Charles Darwin: A Facsimile of the First Edition.* Intro. Ernst Meyr. Cambridge: Harvard Univ. Press.
Daube, David. 1956. *The New Testament and Rabbinic Judaism.* London: Athlone.
Davidson, Randall Thomas, and William Benham. 1891. *Life of Archibald Campbell Tait, Archbishop of Canterbury.* 2 vols.
Davidson, Samuel. 1848–51. *An Introduction to the New Testament.* 3 vols.
Davies, Horton. 1986. *Like Angels from a Cloud: The English Metaphysical Preachers, 1588–1645.* San Marino: Huntingdon Library.
Davies, Julian. 1992. *The Caroline Captivity of the Church: Charles I and the Remoulding of Anglicanism, 1625–1641.* Oxford: Clarendon Press.
Davies, Rupert, and Gordon Rupp. 1965–88. *The Methodist Church in Great Britain.* 4 vols. London: Epworth Press.
Davies, W. D. 1955. *Paul and Rabbinic Judaism: Some Rabbinic Elements in Pauline Theology.* London: SPCK.
Davis, S. T. 1977. *The Debate about the Bible: Inerrancy versus Infallibility.* Philadelphia: Westminster Press.
Davis, Tom. 1977. "The CEAA and Modern Textual Editing." *Library.* 5th Series. 32:61–74.
Dawson, David. 1992. *Allegorical Readers and Cultural Revision in Ancient Alexandria.* Berkeley: Univ. of California Press.
Dawson, Warren R. 1934. *Charles Wycliffe Goodwin, 1817–1878: A Pioneer in Egyptology.* Oxford: Oxford Univ. Press.
Day, P. W. 1964. *Matthew Arnold and the Philosophy of Vico.* Auckland: Univ. of Auckland Press.
Deák, Esteban. 1977. *Apokatastasis: The Problem of Universal Salvation in Twentieth Century Theology.* Ph.D. diss. St. Michael's College, Toronto: Institute of Christian Thought.

Dean, Dennis R. 1981. "'Through Science to Despair?': Geology and the Victorians." In Paradis and Postlewait 1981, 111–36.

———. 1991. "John W. Parker." In Anderson and Rose 1991, 233–36.

De Groot, Hans B. 1969. "Baden Powell, Scientist, and Theologian: A Bibliographical Note." *Victorian Periodicals Newsletter* 5–6:16–18.

Delaire, Justin B., and William S. Sarjeant. 1975. "The Earliest Discoveries of Dinosaurs." *Isis* 66:5–25.

Delaura, David J. 1969. *Hebrew and Hellene in Victorian England: Newman, Arnold, and Pater*. Austin: Univ. of Texas Press.

Delitzsch, Franz. [1871] 1988. *The Psalms*. 3 vols. Grand Rapids: Eerdmans.

Denison, George Anthony. 1861. *Analysis of "Essays and Reviews."*

Denton, W. 1876. *A Commentary on the Acts of the Apostles*. 2 vols.

Denzinger, H. 1960. *The Church Teaches: Documents of the Church in English Translation*. St. Louis: Herder. Trans. of *Enchiridion Symbolorum definitionum et Declarationum de Rebus Fidei et Morum*.

Derrida, Jacques. [1967] 1976. *Of Grammatology*. Trans. Gayatri Chakravorty Spivak. Baltimore: Johns Hopkins Univ. Press.

———. 1991. "This Is Not an Oral Footnote." In Barney 1991, 192–205.

Desmond, Adrian. 1984. *Archetypes and Ancestors: Palaeontology in Victorian London, 1850–1875*. Chicago: Univ. of Chicago Press.

Despres, Philip Charles Soulbieu. 1854. *Apocalypse Fulfilled: or, an Answer to Apocalyptic Sketches by Dr. Cumming*.

Detweiler, Robert. Ed. 1982. *Semeia*. Vol. 23. *Derrida and Biblical Studies*.

De Wette, Wilhelm Martin Leberecht. [1817] 1843. *Einleitung in das Alte Testament*. Trans. Theodore Parker as *Introduction to the Old Testament*.

Dey, Lala Kalyan Kumar. 1975. *The Intermediary World and Patterns of Perfection in Philo and Hebrews*. Cambridge, MA: Society of Biblical Literature.

Dibdin, Lewis T. 1882. *Church Courts*.

Dickens, Charles. [1853] 1971. *Bleak House*. Harmondsworth: Penguin.

———. [1854] 1975. *Hard Times*. Harmondsworth: Penguin.

———. [1857] 1988. *Little Dorrit*. Harmondsworth: Penguin.

Dickinson, H. T. 1970. *Bolingbroke*. London: Constable.

———. 1979. *Liberty and Property: Political Ideology in Eighteenth-Century England*. London: Methuen.

———. 1985. *British Radicalism and the French Revolution, 1789–1815*. London: Basil Blackwell.

Digby, Anne, and Peter Searby. 1981. *Children, School, and Society in Nineteenth-Century England*. London: Macmillan.

Dillenberger, John, and Claude Welch. 1954. *Protestant Christianity Interpreted through Its Development*. New York: Scribner.

Disraeli, Benjamin. 1904. *The Works of Benjamin Disraeli Earl of Beaconsfield*. 20 vols. New York: M. Walter Dunne.

D'Orbigny, Alcide Dessalines. 1849. *Prodrome de Paléontologie Stratigraphique*

universelle des animaux mollusques & rayonnés. 3 vols.
Donne, W. B. 1857. "China and the Chinese." *Westminster Review* 67 (Apr.): 526–57.
Dooley, Allan C. 1992. *Author and Printer in Victorian England.* Charlottesville: Univ. Press of Virginia.
Dorner, Isaac August. 1885. *System of Christian Doctrine.* 2 vols.
Dörries, Hermann. 1960. *Constantine and Religious Liberty.* New Haven: Yale Univ. Press.
Douglas, John. [1752] 1824. *The Criterion; or, Rules by Which the True Miracles Recorded in the New Testament Are Distinguished from the Spurious Miracles of the Pagans and Papists.* Ed. W. Marsh.
Dumont, Louis. 1982. "A Modified View of Our Origins: The Christian Beginnings of Modern Individualism." *Religion* 12:1–27.
Dowling, Linda. 1982. "Victorian Oxford and the Science of Language." *PMLA* 97:160–78.
———. 1986. *Language and Decadence in the Victorian Fin de Siècle.* Princeton: Princeton Univ. Press.
Downey, James. 1969. *The Eighteenth Century Pulpit: A Study of the Sermons of Butler, Berkeley, Secker, Sterne, Whitefield, and Wesley.* Oxford: Clarendon Press.
"Dr. Colenso on the Arithmetic of the Pentateuch." 1862. *Spectator* (8 Nov.): 1250–52.
Drake, Stillman. 1990. *Galileo: Pioneer Scientist.* Toronto: Univ. of Toronto Press.
Driscoll, John T. 1911. "Miracles." *The Catholic Encyclopedia.*
Drummond, James. 1888. *Philo Judaeus: or, the Jewish-Alexandrian Philosophy in Its Development and Completion.*
Drury, John. Ed. 1989. *Critics of the Bible, 1724–1873.* Cambridge: Cambridge Univ. Press.
Dryden, John. 1958. *The Poems of John Dryden.* Ed. James Kinsley. 4 vols. Oxford: Clarendon Press.
Dugmore, C. W. 1942. *Eucharistic Doctrine in England from Hooker to Waterland.* London: SPCK.
———. Ed. 1944. *The Interpretation of the Bible.* London: SPCK.
Dyer, G. J. 1964. *Limbo: Unsettled Questions.* New York: Sheed & Ward.
Dyer, Thomas Henry. 1855. *The Life of John Calvin: Compiled from Authentic Sources, and Particularly from His Correspondence.*
Eagles, John. 1851. "What Is Mesmerism?" *Blackwood's Magazine* 70 (July): 70–83.
Eagleton, Terry. 1983. *Literary Theory: An Introduction.* Oxford: Basil Blackwell.
———. 1991. *Ideology: An Introduction.* London: Verso.
Edwards, John. 1695. *Some Thoughts concerning the Several Causes and Occasions of Atheism, Especially in the Present Age, with Some Brief Reflections on Socinianism and on a Late Book* [by John Locke] *Entitled: "The Reasonableness of Christianity as Delivered in the Scriptures."*

Eisen, Sydney, and Bernard Lightman. 1984. *Victorian Science and Religion: A Bibliography.* Hamden: Archon.

Ellens, Jacob P. 1983. "The Church-Rate Conflict in England and Wales, 1832–1868." Ph.D. diss., University of Toronto.

Ellicott, C. J. 1856. *A Critical and Grammatical Commentary on the Pastoral Epistles with a Revised Translation.*

———. 1861. "Scripture, and Its Interpretation." In Thomson 1861, 371–469.

Elliott-Binns, L. E. 1953. *The Early Evangelicals: A Religious and Social Study.* London: Lutterworth Press.

Ellis, Ieuan Pryce. 1971. "'Essays and Reviews' Reconsidered." *Theology* 74:394–404.

———. 1980. *Seven against Christ: A Study of "Essays and Reviews."* Leiden: E. J. Brill.

———. 1986. "Dean Farrar and the Quest for the Historical Jesus." *Theology* 89: 108–15.

Elwin, Whitwell. 1857. "Travels in China—Fortune and Huc." *Quarterly Review* 102 (July): 126–65.

Emerson, Ralph Waldo. [1841] 1979. "Spiritual Laws." In *The Collected Works of Ralph Waldo Emerson.* Ed. Alfred R. Ferguson and Jean Ferguson Carr. 4 vols. Cambridge: Belknap Press. 2:75–96.

Emil, Henry Paul. 1849. *The Life and Times of John Calvin, the Great Reformer.*

Empson, William. 1831. "Pretended Miracles." *Edinburgh Review* 53 (June): 261–305.

Engen, Rodney K. 1985. *Dictionary of Victorian Wood Engravers.* Cambridge: Chadwyck-Healey.

The English Reports. 1901. Vol. 15: Privy Council. Edinburgh: William Green & Sons.

———. 1907. Vol. 79: King's Bench Division. Edinburgh: William Green & Sons.

Epp, Eldon J., and George W. MacRae. Eds. 1989. *The New Testament and Its Modern Interpreters.* Philadelphia: Fortress [The Society of Biblical Literature].

Erasmus, Desiderius. [1511] 1971. *Praise of Folly and Letter to Martin Dorp, 1515.* Trans. Betty Radice. Harmondsworth: Penguin.

Erlanger, Rachel. 1988. *The Unarmed Prophet: Savonarola in Florence.* New York: McGraw-Hill.

Essays and Reviews. 1860.

Faber, Geoffrey. [1933] 1954. *Oxford Apostles: A Character Study of the Oxford Movement.* London: Faber & Faber.

———. 1957. *Jowett: A Portrait with Background.* London: Faber & Faber.

Faber, George Stanley. 1842. *The Primitive Doctrine of Election: or an Historical Inquiry into the Ideality and Causation of Scriptural Election, as Received and Maintained in the Primitive Church of Christ.* 2d ed.

Fairbairn, Patrick. [1845–47] 1882. *The Typology of the Scriptures Viewed in Connection with the Whole Series of the Divine Dispensations.* 6th ed. 2 vols.

Fairweather, E. R. 1956. *A Scholastic Miscellany: Anselm to Ockham.* Philadelphia: Westminster Press.

Fantoli, Annibale. 1994. *Galileo: For Copernicanism and for the Church*. Trans. George V. Coyne. Vatican City: Vatican Observatory.

Faraday, Michael. 1854. "Observations on Mental Education." In *Lectures on Education Delivered at the Royal Institute of Great Britain*. 39–88.

Farmer, William R. 1964. *The Synoptic Problem: A Critical Analysis*. New York: Macmillan.

Farrar, A. S. 1856. *Hints to Students Reading for Classical Honours in the University of Oxford*.

Favaro, Antonio. 1907. *Galileo e l'Inquisizione: Documenti del Processo Galileiano esistenti nell'Archivio del S. Uffizio e nell'Archivio segreto vaticano*. Firenze: G. Barbèra.

Fichte, Johann Gottlieb. [1804] 1845–46. "Die Grundzüge des gegenwärtigen Zeitalters." In *Sämmtliche Werke*. 8 vols.

———. [1804] 1977. "Die Grundzüge des gegenwärtigen Zeitalters." Trans. William Smith as *The Characteristics of the Present Age*, (1844) 1889. Repr. in *Significant Contributions to the History of Psychology, 1750–1920*. 1977. Ed. Daniel F. Robinson. Washington, D.C.: University Publications of America.

Finocchiaro, Maurice A. 1989. *The Galileo Affair: A Documentary History*. Berkeley: Univ. of California Press.

Fischer, Ernst Kuno Berthold. [1852–72] 1872–82. *Geschichte der neuern Philosophie*. 6 vols.

Fitzgerald, John Percival. 1870. *A Letter of Earnest Remonstrance to the Rt. Hon. W. E. Gladstone, M.P., First Lord of the Treasury, etc. upon His Appointment of a Co-Writer with Infidels to a Christian Bishopric*.

Fitzgerald, William, Whitwell Elwin, and Richard Whately. 1859. "[Review of] *The Order of Nature*. By Baden Powell." *Quarterly Review* 106 (Oct.): 420–54.

Fletcher, Angus. 1974. *Allegory: The Theory of a Symbolic Mode*. Ithaca: Cornell Univ. Press.

Forbes, Duncan. 1952. *The Liberal Anglican Idea of History*. Cambridge: Cambridge Univ. Press.

Force, James E., and Richard H. Popkin. 1990. *Essays on the Context, Nature, and Influence of Isaac Newton's Theology*. Dordrecht: Kluwer.

Foucault, Michel. 1973. *The Order of Things: An Archaeology of the Human Sciences*. New York: Vintage.

Fox, Robin Lane. 1992. *The Unauthorized Version: Truth and Fiction in the Bible*. New York: Knopf.

Foxe, John [1562–63] 1570. *Acts and Monuments of Matters Happening in the Church*.

Francis, Mark. 1974. "The Origins of Essays and Reviews: An Interpretation of Mark Pattison in the 1850's." *Historical Journal* 17:797–811.

Freeman, E. A. [1860] 1871. "The Continuity of English History." In *Historical Essays: First Series*. 40–52. [Review of Vaughan's *Revolutions in English History*. *Edinburgh Review* 112 (July 1860)].

Frei, Hans W. 1974. *The Eclipse of Biblical Narrative: A Study in Eighteenth and*

Nineteenth Century Hermeneutics. New Haven: Yale Univ. Press.

Froude, James Anthony. 1851. "Materialism: Miss Martineau and Mr. Atkinson." *Fraser's Magazine* 43 (Apr.): 418–34.

———. [1863] 1877. "A Plea for the Free Discussion of Theological Difficulties." *Short Studies on Great Subjects*. 1:166–96.

Frye, Northrop. 1982. *The Great Code: The Bible and Literature*. New York: Harcourt Brace Jovanovich.

Funk, Robert W. 1991. *The Gospel of Mark: Red Letter Edition*. Sonoma: Polebridge Press.

——— Roy W. Hoover, and the Jesus Seminar. 1993. *The Five Gospels: The Search for the Authentic Words of Jesus*. New York: Macmillan.

Galileo. 1957. *Discoveries and Opinions of Galileo*. Trans. Stillman Drake. New York: Doubleday Anchor.

Gamble, Richard C. Ed. 1992. *Calvin's Work in Geneva*. New York: Garland.

Gardiner, Samuel Rawson. 1906. *The Constitutional Documents of the Puritan Revolution, 1625–1660*. Oxford: Clarendon Press.

Gardner, Helen. 1952. *John Donne: The Divine Poems*. Oxford: Clarendon Press.

Gasquet, Francis Aidan. [1887] 1889. *Henry VIII and the English Monasteries*. 4th ed.

Gaussen, Louis. [1842] 1888. *"Theopneustia": The Plenary Inspiration of the Holy Scriptures*. Trans. David Scott.

Gaye, Russell Kerr. 1904. *The Platonic Conception of Immortality and Its Connexion with the Theory of Ideas*. London: Clay.

Geike, Archibald. [1897] 1905. *The Founders of Geology*. 2d ed. Repr. 1962. New York: Dover.

Geisler, Norman L. Ed. 1979. *Inerrancy*. Grand Rapids: Zondervan.

Gehman, Henry S. 1951. "The Hebraic Character of Septuagint Greek." *Vetus Testamentum* 1:81–90.

Gervinus, Georg Gottfried. 1842. *Handbuch der Geschichte der poetischen Nationallitteratur der Deutschen*.

Gesenius, Heinrich Friedrich Wilhelm. 1846. *Gesenius's Hebrew and Chaldee Lexicon to the Old Testament Scriptures*. Trans. Samuel Prideaux Tregelles.

Gibbon, Edward. [1796] 1962. *Autobiography of Edward Gibbon as Originally Edited by Lord Sheffield*. London: Oxford Univ. Press.

———. [1776–88] 1858. *The History of the Decline and Fall of the Roman Empire*. Ed. H. H. Milman. 6 vols.

Gibson, Edgar C. S. 1915. *The Thirty-Nine Articles of the Church of England*. London: Methuen.

Gibson, Edmund. 1730. *The Bishop of London's Second Pastoral Letter to the People of His Diocese; Particularly, to Those of the Two Great Cities of London and Westminster. Occasioned by Some Late Writings in Which It Is Asserted "That Reason Is a Sufficient Guide in Matters of Religion, without the Help of Revelation."*

Gieseler, Johann Karl Ludwig. 1827. *Lehrbuch der Kirchengeschichte*. 6 vols. Trans.

Samuel Davidson and John Winstanley Hull. *A Compendium of Ecclesiastical History*. 1846–65. 5 vols.

Gilbert, A. D. 1976. *Religion and Society in Industrial England: Church, Chapel, and Social Change, 1740–1914*. London: Longman.

Gilley, Sheridan. 1981. "The Huxley-Wilberforce Debate: A Reconsideration." In Robbins 1981, 325–40.

——— and Ann Loades. 1981. "Thomas Henry Huxley: The War between Science and Religion." *Journal of Religion* 61:285–308.

Gillispie, Charles Coulston. 1959. *Genesis and Geology: A Study in the Relations of Scientific Thought, Natural Theology, and Social Opinion in Great Britain, 1790–1850*. New York: Harper & Row.

Gilmour, Ian. 1992. *Riots, Risings, and Revolution: Governance and Violence in Eighteenth-Century England*. London: Hutchinson.

Gilson, Étienne. 1940. *The Mystical Theology of Saint Bernard*. Trans. A. H. C. Downes. London: Sheed & Ward.

Gladstone, W. E. 1841. *The State in Its Relations with the Church*. 4th ed. 2 vols.

[———]. 1857. "The Bill for Divorce." *Quarterly Review*. 102 (July): 252–88. [Published anonymously].

———. 1858. *Studies on Homer and the Homeric Age*. 3 vols.

———. 1890. *Landmarks of Homeric Study*.

Glaister, Geoffrey Ashall. 1960. *The Glossary of the Book*. London: Allen & Unwin.

Glover, Willis Borders. 1954. *Evangelical Nonconformists and Higher Criticism in the Nineteenth Century*. London: Independent Press.

Gloyn, C. K. 1942. *The Church in the Social Order*. Forest Grove: Pacific Univ. Press.

Gobineau, Joseph Arthur de. 1853–54. *Essai sur l'Inégalité des races humaines*. 4 vols. Trans. H. Holz as *The Moral and Intellectual Diversity of Races* (1856).

Goguel, Maurice. 1964. *The Primitive Church*. Trans. H. C. Snape. London: Allen & Unwin.

Goldberg, David Theo. Ed. 1990. *Anatomy of Racism*. Minneapolis: Univ. of Minnesota Press.

Goodwin, John. [1670] 1867. *Πλήρωμα τό πνευματικων, or Being Filled with the Spirit*.

Goodwin, Harvey. 1856. *The Doctrines and Difficulties of the Christian Faith*. [Hulsean Lectures for 1855].

Goree, William Balfour. 1980. "The Cultural Bases of Montanism." Ph.D. diss., Baylor University.

Goulburn, E. M. 1861. *"The Education of the World" and Also a Review of Lessing's "The Education of the Human Race" from the German of Gotthold Ephraim Lessing*.

———. 1892. *John William Burgon, Late Dean of Chichester*. 2 vols.

Gorham v. the Bishop of Exeter: The Judgment of the Judicial Committee of the Privy Council, Delivered March 8, 1850, Reversing the Decision of Sir. H. J. Fust. 1850.

Gould, Stephen J. 1979. *Ever since Darwin: Reflections in Natural History*. New York: Norton.

———. 1981. *The Mismeasure of Man*. New York: Norton.

Gowan, Donald E. 1986. *Eschatology in the Old Testament*. Philadelphia: Fortress Press.

Gramsci, Antonio. 1971. *Selections from the Prison Notebooks*. Trans. Quintin Hoare and Geoffrey Nowell-Smith. New York: International Press.

Grant, Anthony. 1853. "Religion of the Chinese Rebels." *Quarterly Review* 94 (Dec.): 171–95.

Grant, Robert M. [1848] 1965. *The Bible in the Church: A Short History of Interpretation*. New York: Macmillan.

———. 1952. *Miracle and Natural Law in Graeco-Roman and Early Christian Thought*. Amsterdam: North Holland Publishing.

——— with David Tracy [1948] 1984. *A Short History of the Interpretation of the Bible*. 2d ed. London: Adam & Charles Black.

Green, Thomas. 1755. *A Dissertation on Enthusiasm; Shewing the Danger of Its Late Increase, and the Great Mischief It Has Occasioned, Both in Ancient and Modern Times, with an Examination of the Claims in General Now Laid to Immediate Revelations, Calls, Gifts, or Extraordinary Communications of the Spirit.*

Green, V. H. H. 1957. *Oxford Common Room: A Study of Lincoln College and Mark Pattison*. London: Edwin Arnold.

Greene, J. C. 1981. *Science, Ideology, and World View: Essays in the History of Evolutionary Ideas*. Berkeley: Univ. of California Press.

Greetham, D. C. 1988. "Textual and Literary Theory: Redrawing the Matrix." *Studies in Bibliography* 42:1–24.

Greg, William Rathbone. [1848] 1875. *The Creed of Christendom: Its Foundation Contrasted with Its Superstructure.*

———. 1853. "Life and Times of Madame de Staël." *North British Review* 20:1–36.

———. 1860. "British Taxation." *Edinburgh Review* 111 (Jan.): 236–72.

———. 1863. "Truth *versus* Edification." *Westminster Review* 79 (Apr.): 503–16.

Grimm, Friedrich Melchior von. 1880. *Mémoire historique sur l'origine et les suites de mon attachement pour l"impératrice Cathérine II jusqu'au décès de sa majesté impériale.*

Grote, John. 1856. "Old Studies and New." In *Cambridge Essays* 1856, 64–114.

Guerlac, Henry. 1961. *Lavoisier—The Crucial Year*. Ithaca: Cornell Univ. Press.

Gundry, Robert H. 1993. *Mark: A Commentary on His Apology for the Cross*. Grand Rapids: Eerdmans.

Gunkel, Hermann. [1926] 1967. *The Psalms: A Form-Critical Introduction*. Trans. Thomas M. Horner. Philadelphia: Westminster.

Hackwood, Frederick William. 1912. *William Hone: His Life and Times*. New York: Franklin.

Hahn, Roger. 1967. *Laplace as a Newtonian Scientist*. William Andrews Clark Memorial Library, Univ. of California.

Haig, Alan. 1984. *The Victorian Clergy*. London: Croom Helm.
Haight, George S. 1969. *George Eliot and John Chapman, with Chapman's Diaries*. Hamden: Archon Books.
Hall, F. W. [1913] 1970. *A Companion to Classical Texts*. Chicago: Argonaut.
Hall, Francis J. 1923. *The Being and Attributes of God*. Vol. 5 of *Dogmatic Theology*. New York: Longmans, Green.
———. 1933. *Theological Outlines*. New York: Moorhouse-Gorham.
Hallam, Henry. [1827] 1842. *The Constitutional History of England from the Accession of Henry VII to the Death of George II*. 2 vols.
———. 1837–39. *Introduction to the Literature of Europe in the 15th, 16th, and 17th Centuries*. 4 vols.
Haller, William. 1938. *The Rise of Puritanism: Or the Way to the New Jerusalem as Set Forth in Pulpit and Press from Thomas Cartwright to. . . John Milton*. New York: Columbia Univ. Press.
Halpern, Baruch. 1983. *The Emergence of Israel in Canaan*. Chico: Scholars Press.
———. 1988. *The First Historians: The Hebrew Bible and History*. San Francisco: Harper & Row.
Hamlin, Christopher. 1985. "Providence and Putrefaction: Victorian Sanitarians and the Natural Theology of Health and Disease." *Victorian Studies* 28:381–411.
Hammond, Peter C. 1977. *The Parson and the Victorian Parish*. London: Hodder & Stoughton.
Hampden, Renn Dickson. 1827. *Essays on the Philosophical Evidence of Christianity*.
Hannah, J. 1863. *The Relation between the Divine and Human Elements in Holy Scripture*. [The Bampton Lectures for 1863].
Hanson, R. P. C. 1959. *Allegory and Event: A Study of the Sources and Significance of Origen's Interpretation of Scripture*. London: SCM Press.
Haran, M. 1978. *Temples and Temple Service in Ancient Israel*. Oxford: Clarendon Press.
Harding, Anthony John. 1985. *Coleridge and the Inspired Word*. Kingston: McGill-Queen's Univ. Press.
Hardwick, Charles. 1904. *A History of the Articles of Religion*. London: Bell.
Harris, Horton. 1973. *David Friedrich Strauss and His Theology*. Cambridge: Cambridge Univ. Press.
Harris, John. 1846. *The Prae-Adamite Earth, Contributions to Theological Science*.
Harris, Michael. 1986. "Introduction: the Nineteenth Century." In Harris and Lee 1986.
Harris, Michael, and Alan Lee. Eds. 1986. *The Press in English Society from the Seventeenth to Nineteenth Centuries*. Rutherford: Fairleigh Dickinson Univ. Press.
Harrison, Frederic. 1860. "Neo-Christianity." *Westminster Review* 146 (Oct.): 293–332; repr. in Harrison 1907, 95–157.
———. 1907. *The Creed of a Layman: Apologia Pro Fide Mea*. London: Macmillan.
———. 1911. *Autobiographic Memoirs*. 2 vols. London: Macmillan.

Harrison, J. F. C. 1965. *Society and Politics in England, 1780–1960*. New York: Harper & Row.

Harrison, Royden. 1968. Afterword. In Samuel Smiles. *Self-Help*. London: Sphere Books.

Hart, J. 1977. "Religion and Social Control in the Mid-Nineteenth Century." *Social Control in Nineteenth-Century Britain*. Ed. A. P. Donajgrodzki. London: Croom Helm.

Harvey, B. Peter. 1990. *An Introduction to Buddhism: Teachings, History, and Practices*. Cambridge: Cambridge Univ. Press.

Harvie, C. 1976. *The Lights of Liberalism: University Liberals and the Challenge of Democracy, 1860–86*. London: Allen Lane.

Hatch, Edwin. 1889. *Essays in Biblical Greek*.

Hayes, Carlton J. H. 1966. *Essays on Nationalism*. New York: Russell & Russell.

Hayward, Abraham. 1859. "The Church Rate Question." *Edinburgh Review* 109 (Jan.): 66–85.

Heales, A. 1872. *The History and Law of Church Seats or Pews*. 2 vols.

Hedge, Frederic H. 1860. *Recent Inquiries in Theology, by Eminent English Churchmen; Being "Essays and Reviews.*

Heeney, Brian. 1976. *A Different Kind of Gentleman: Parish Clergy as Professional Men in Early and Mid-Victorian England*. Camden: Archon Books.

Hegel, Georg Wilhelm Friedrich. [1807] 1834–44. *Phenomenologie des Geistes*. Vol. 2 in *Werke*. 20 vols.

———. [1807] 1977. *Phenomenology of Spirit*. Trans. A. V. Miller. Oxford: Oxford Univ. Press.

———. [1832] 1881. *Lectures on the Philosophy of History*. Trans. J. Sibree. First published in 1857.

———. [1832] 1985. *Lectures on the Philosophy of Religion*. Ed. Peter C. Hodgson. 3 vols. Berkeley: Univ. of California Press.

———. 1874. *The Logic of Hegel, Translated from the Encyclopaedia of the Philosophical Sciences, with Prolegomena*. Ed. William Wallace.

Heineman, F. H. 1950. "John Toland and the Age of Reason." *Archiv für Philosophie* 4:33–66.

Helmstadter, Richard J., and Bernard Lightman. 1990. *Victorian Faith in Crisis: Essays on Continuity and Change in Nineteenth-Century Religious Belief*. Stanford: Stanford Univ. Press.

Henaut, Barry W. 1993. *Oral Tradition and the Gospels: The Problem of Mark 4*. Sheffield: JSOT Press.

Hendrickx, Herman. 1987. *The Miracle Stories of the Synoptic Gospels*. London: Geoffrey Chapman.

Hengel, Martin. 1981. *The Atonement: A Study of the Origins of the Doctrine in the New Testament*. London: SCM Press.

———. 1989. *The Johannine Question*. Trans. John Bowden. London: SCM Press.

Hepworth, Brian. 1978. *Robert Lowth*. Boston: Twayne.

Herbert, Edward [Lord Herbert of Cherbury]. [1624] 1937. *De Veritate, prout distinguitur a revelatione, a verisimili, a possibili, et a falso*. Trans. Meyrick H. Carré. Bristol: Bristol Univ. Press.

Herder, J. G. 1833. *The Spirit of Hebrew Poetry*. Trans. J. Marsh. 2 vols.

Herrmann, Siegfried. 1975. *A History of Israel in Old Testament Times*. London: SCM Press.

Hettner, Hermann Julius Theodor. 1856–70. *Geschichte der Deutschen Literatur im achtzehnten Jahrhundert*. 3 vols.

Heurtley, Charles. 1845. *Justification*.

Hey, John. [1796] 1841. *Lectures in Divinity Delivered in the University of Cambridge*. 3d ed. 2 vols.

Heyck, T. W. 1982. *The Transformation of Intellectual Life in Victorian England*. London: Croom Helm.

Hickson, W. E. 1850. "Septenary Institutions: Jewish Sabbaths; Jewish Scriptures; the Christian Sabbath." *Westminster Review* 53 (Oct.): 153–206.

Higonnet, Patrice L. R. 1989. *Sister Republics: The Origins of the French and American Republics*. Cambridge: Harvard Univ. Press.

Hill, Christopher. 1956. *Economic Problems of the Church from Archbishop Whitgift to the Long Parliament*. Oxford: Clarendon Press.

———. [1961] 1969. *The Century of Revolution: 1603–1714*. London: Sphere.

———. 1986. *The Collected Essays of Christopher Hill*. 3 vols. Amherst: Univ. of Massachusetts Press.

Hill, Christopher, and Edmund Dell. Eds. 1949. *The Good Old Cause: The English Revolution of 1640–60: Its Causes, Course, and Consequences*. London: Lawrence & Wishart.

Himmelfarb, Gertrude. 1968. *Darwin and the Darwinian Revolution*. New York: Norton.

Himrod, David Kirk. 1977. "Cosmic Order and Divine Activity: A Study in the Relation between Science and Religion, 1850–1950." Ph.D. diss., University of California, Los Angeles.

Hinchliff, Peter Bingham. 1964. *J. W. Colenso, Bishop of Natal*. London: Nelson.

———. 1984. "Jowett and Gore: Two Balliol Essayists." *Theology* 87:251–59.

———. 1987. *Benjamin Jowett and the Christian Religion*. Oxford: Oxford Univ. Press.

Hobsbawm, E. J. 1974. "From Social History to History of Society." In *Essays in Social History*. Ed. M. W. Flinn and C. T. Smout. Oxford: Oxford Univ. Press. 1–22.

———. [1975] 1979. *The Age of Capital: 1848–1875*. New York: New American Library.

———. 1992. *Nations and Nationalism since 1780: Programme, Myth, Reality*. 2d ed. Cambridge: Cambridge Univ. Press.

Hodgkin, Thomas. 1967. *Italy and Her Invaders*. London: Russell & Russell.

Hogan, James C. 1991. *A Commentary on the Plays of Sophocles*. Carbondale:

Southern Illinois Univ. Press.

Holbach, Paul Heinrich Dietrich, baron d'. [1770] 1868. *La Système de la nature.* Trans. H. D. Robinson. *The System of Nature or Laws of the Moral and Physical World.* 2 vols. Repr. 1970. New York: Burt Franklin.

Holland, Henry. 1852. "Meteors, Aerolites, Shooting Stars." *Quarterly Review* 92 (Dec.): 77–106.

Hone, Anne. 1982. *For the Cause of Truth: Radicalism in London, 1796–1821.* Oxford: Clarendon Press.

Hook, Walter Farquhar. 1852. *A Church Dictionary.*

Hooker, Richard [1594–1662] 1954. *Of the Laws of Ecclesiastical Polity.* Ed. Christopher Morris. 2 vols. London: Dent (Everyman).

Horne, Thomas Hartwell. [1818] 1828. *An Introduction to the Critical Study and Knowledge of the Holy Scriptures.* 6th ed. 4 vols.

———. [1818] 1872. *An Introduction to the Critical Study and Knowledge of the Holy Scriptures.* Ed. John Ayre and Samuel Prideaux Tregelles. 13th ed. 4 vols.

Horsley, Samuel. 1810–22. *Sermons.* Ed. Heneage Horsley. 4 vols.

Horstman, Allen. 1985. *Victorian Divorce.* London: Croom Helm.

Hort, Arthur Fenton. 1896. *Life and Letters of Fenton John Anthony Hort.* 2 vols.

Hort, Fenton John Anthony. 1856. "Coleridge." In *Cambridge Essays* 1856, 292–351.

Hotten, John Camden. 1864. *The Slang Dictionary.*

Howell, Peter Anthony. 1979. *The Judicial Committee of the Privy Council, 1833–1876: Its Origins, Structure, and Development.* Cambridge: Cambridge Univ. Press.

Howell, Wilbur Samuel. 1971. *Eighteenth-Century British Logic and Rhetoric.* Princeton: Princeton Univ. Press.

Howsam, Leslie. 1991. *Cheap Bibles: Nineteenth-Century Publishing and the British and Foreign Bible Society.* Cambridge: Cambridge Univ. Press.

Huc, Evariste R. 1857. *Christianity in China, Tartary, and Thibet.*

Huck, Albert. 1892. *A Synopsis of the First Three Gospels.*

Hughes, Geoffrey. 1991. *Swearing: A Social History of Foul Language, Oaths, and Profanity in English.* Oxford: Basil Blackwell.

Hume, David. [1748] 1964. *An Enquiry concerning Human Understanding.* Vol. 4 in *Philosophical Works.* Ed. T. H. Green and T. H. Grose. Aalen: Scientia Verlag.

———. [1748] 1985. "Of the Original Contract." In *Essays Moral, Political, and Literary.* Ed. Eugene F. Miller. Indianapolis: Liberty Classics. 465–88.

———. [1776] 1826. *My Own Life.*

Hundert, E. J. 1994. *The Enlightenment's Fable: Bernard Mandeville and the Discovery of Society.* Cambridge: Cambridge Univ. Press.

Hunt, William. 1983. *The Puritan Moment: The Coming of Revolution in an English County.* Cambridge: Harvard Univ. Press.

[Hunt, William Holman.] 1969. *William Holman Hunt: An Exhibition Arranged by the Walker Art Gallery*. Liverpool: Walker Art Gallery.

Hunter, William B. Ed. 1971. *Bright Essence: Studies in Milton's Theology*. Salt Lake City: Univ. of Utah Press.

Huss, John. [1413] 1974. *The Church*. Trans. David S. Schaff. Westport: Greenwood.

Hutchinson, H. G. 1914. *Life of Sir John Lubbock*. 2 vols. London: Macmillan.

Hutten, Ulrich von. [1515] 1909. *Epistolae Obscurorum Virorum ad Dominus Magistrum Ortvinum Gratium*. Trans. and ed. Francis Griffin Stokes. *Letters of Obscure Men*. London: Chatto & Windus.

Huxley, Thomas Henry. 1865. "On the Methods and Results of Ethnology." *Fortnightly Review* 1 (June 15): 257–77.

Hyatt, J. Philip. 1964. *The Heritage of Biblical Faith: An Aid to Reading the Bible*. St. Louis: Bethany Press.

The Idea of a National Church: (Considered in Reply to Mr. Wilson). 1861 [?]. [Anonymous pamphlet].

Imlah, Ann G. 1966. *Britain and Switzerland, 1845–60: A Study of Anglo-Swiss Relations during Some Critical Years for Swiss Neutrality*. Hamden: Archon.

The Independent Whig: or, a Defence of Primitive Christianity, and of Our Ecclesiastical Establishment, against the Exorbitant Claims and Encroachments of Fanatical and Disaffected Clergymen. 1753. Ed. Thomas Gordon. 8th ed. 4 vols.

Ingram, Alison. 1981. *Index to the Archives of the House of Longman, 1794–1914*. Cambridge: Chadwyck-Healey.

Innes, William C. 1983. *Social Concern in Calvin's Geneva*. Alison Park: Pickwick.

Irons, W. J. Ed. 1850. *The Judgments on Baptismal Regeneration*.

Irving, Edward. 1829. *The Church and State Responsible to Christ and to One Another: A Series of Discourses on Daniel's Vision of the Four Beasts*.

Irving, Washington. [1822] 1977. *Bracebridge Hall, or The Humourists*. Ed. Herbert F. Smith. Boston: Twayne.

Jacob, J. R. 1977. *Robert Boyle and the English Revolution: A Study in Social and Intellectual Change*. New York: Franklin.

Jacyna, L. S. 1981. "The Physiology of Mind, the Unity of Nature, and the Moral Order in Victorian Thought." *British Journal for the History of Science* 14:109–32.

Jagersma, Henk. 1986. *A History of Israel from Alexander the Great to Bar Kochba*. Philadelphia: Fortress.

Jamieson, Robert. 1868–71. *A Commentary, Critical, Experimental, and Practical, on the Old and New Testaments*. 6 vols.

Jann, Rosemary. 1985. *The Art and Science of Victorian History*. Columbus: Ohio State Univ. Press.

Jebb, R. C. [1882] 1889. *Bentley*. Vol. 13 in *English Men of Letters*. Ed. John Morley.

———. 1907. *Essays and Addresses*. Cambridge: Cambridge Univ. Press.

Jedin, Hubert. 1961. *A History of the Council of Trent*. Trans. Ernest Graf. 2 vols. London: Thomas Nelson.

Jeffery, Arthur. 1956. Introduction and Exegesis to *The Book of Daniel.* In *The Interpreter's Bible.* New York: Abingdon. 6:340–549.

Jeffrey, David Lyle. Ed. 1992. *A Dictionary of Biblical Tradition in English Literature.* Grand Rapids: Eerdmans.

Jelf, William Edward. 1861. *Supremacy of Scripture: An Examination into the Principles and Statements Advanced in the Essay on the Education of the World in a Letter to the Reverend Dr. Temple.*

Jensen, J. Vernon. 1991. *Thomas Henry Huxley.* Newark: Univ. of Delaware Press.

Jeremias, Joachim. 1960. *Infant Baptism in the First Four Centuries.* London: SCM Press.

Jerome. 1965. *The Apology against the Books of Rufinus.* Trans. John N. Hritzu. In *Saint Jerome: Dogmatic and Polemical Works.* Washington: Catholic Univ. of America Press.

Johnson, Samuel. 1905. *Lives of the English Poets.* Ed. George Birkbeck Hill. 3 vols. Oxford: Clarendon Press.

Jolley, Nicholas. 1978. "Leibniz on Locke and Socinianism." *Journal of the History of Ideas* 39:233–50.

Jones, A. H. M. 1948. *Constantine and the Conversion of Europe.* London: Hodder & Stoughton.

Jones, G. 1980. *Social Darwinism and English Thought: The Interaction between Biological and Social Theory.* Brighton: Harvester Press.

Jones, Gareth Stedman. 1983. "Rethinking Chartism." In *Studies in English Working Class History, 1832–1982.* Cambridge: Cambridge Univ. Press. 90–179.

Jones, Richard Foster. 1975. *Ancients and Moderns: A Study of the Rise of the Scientific Movement in Seventeenth-Century England.* Gloucester: Peter Smith.

Jordanova, L. J., and Roy S. Porter. Eds. 1979. *Images of the Earth: Essays in the History of the Environmental Sciences.* Chalfont St. Giles: British Society for the History of Science.

Joubert, Louis. 1860. "Maintenon, Françoise d'Aubigne, Marquise de." In *Nouvelle Biographie Générale.* 32:926.

Jowett, Benjamin. [1855] 1859. *The Epistles of St. Paul to the Thessalonians, Galatians, and Romans.* 2d ed. 2 vols.

———. 1861. *Statements of Christian Doctrine and Practice, Extracted from the Published Writings of the Rev. Benjamin Jowett, M.A.* [Compiled by A. P. Stanley].

———. [1871] 1875. *The Dialogues of Plato, Translated into English with Analysis and Introductions.* 2d ed. 5 vols.

———. 1895. *College Sermons.* Ed. W. H. Fremantle.

———. 1899. *Sermons Biographical and Miscellaneous.* Ed. W. H. Fremantle.

———. 1901. *Sermons on Faith and Doctrine.* Ed. W. H. Fremantle. London: John Murray.

———. 1902a. *Select Passages from the Introductions to Plato.* Ed. Lewis Campbell. London: John Murray.

———. 1902b. *Select Passages from the Theological Writings of Benjamin Jowett.* Ed. Lewis Campbell. London: John Murray.

———. 1906. *The Interpretation of Scripture and Other Essays.* London: George Routledge & Sons.

———. 1907. *Scripture and Truth: Dissertations by the late Benjamin Jowett.* Intro. Lewis Campbell. London: Henry Frowde.

Joyce, James Weyland. 1861. *The National Church: An Answer to an Essay on "The National Church" by Henry Bristow Wilson, D.D.*

Judgment of the Lords of the Judicial Committee of the Privy Council upon the Appeals of Williams v the Lord Bishop of Salisbury, and Wilson v Fendall, from the Court of Arches: Delivered 8th February, 1864. 1864.

Kant, Immanuel. [1798] 1979. *Streit der Facultäten.* Trans. Mary J. Gregor. *The Conflict of the Faculties.* New York: Abaris Books.

———. 1903–80. *Gesammelte Schriften.* 29 vols. Berlin: Royal Prussian Academy.

———. 1988. *Kant Selections.* Ed. and trans. Lewis White Beck. New York: Macmillan.

———. 1992. *Lectures on Logic.* Trans. J. Michael Young. Cambridge: Cambridge Univ. Press.

Kantorowicz, Ernst Hartwig. 1957. *The King's Two Bodies: A Study in Medieval Political Theology.* Princeton: Princeton Univ. Press.

Katz, Peter. 1973. *The Text of the Septuagint: Its Corruptions and Their Emendations.* Cambridge: Cambridge Univ. Press.

Kaye, J.W. 1857. "India." *Edinburgh Review* 106 (Oct.): 544–94.

Keble, John. 1833. "Adherence to the Apostolical Succession the Safest Course." In *Tracts for the Times* 1833–41, no. IV.

———. 1848. *Sermons, Academical and Occasional.* 2d ed.

———. 1879–80. *Sermons for the Christian Year.* 7 vols.

Kee, Howard Clark. 1983. *Miracle in the Early Christian World.* New Haven: Yale Univ. Press.

———. 1986. *Medicine, Miracle, and Magic in New Testament Times.* Cambridge: Cambridge Univ. Press.

Kelber, Werner H. 1982. *The Oral and the Written Gospel: The Hermeneutics of Speaking and Writing in the Synoptic Tradition, Mark, Paul, and Q.* Philadelphia: Fortress.

Kelly, J. N. D. 1950. *Early Christian Creeds.* London: Longmans Green.

———. 1964. *The Athanasian Creed.* London: Adam & Charles Black.

Kennard, R. B. 1863. *"Essays and Reviews": Their Origin, History, General Characteristics, and Significance.*

———. 1888. *In Memory of the Rev. Henry Bristow Wilson . . . A Sermon Preached in the Parish Church of Great Staughton, on Sunday, August 19, 1888.*

Kennedy, George A. 1983. *Greek Rhetoric under Christian Emperors.* Princeton: Princeton Univ. Press.

Kenney, E. J. 1974. *The Classical Text: Aspects of Editing in the Age of the Printed*

Book. Berkeley: Univ. of California Press.

Kent, C. 1979. *Brains and Numbers: Elitism, Comtism, and Democracy in Mid-Victorian England*. Toronto: Univ. of Toronto Press.

Kent, John. 1978. *Holding the Fort: Studies in Victorian Revivalism*. London: Epworth Press.

Kidd, John. 1815. *A Geological Essay on the Imperfect Evidences in Support of a Theory of the Earth*.

Kiernan, V. G. [1969] 1972. *The Lords of Human Kind: Black Man, Yellow Man, and White Man in an Age of Empire*. Harmondsworth: Penguin.

King, Ross W. A. 1992. "Fair Prospects: Analogy and the Ideology of Order from Pope to Wordsworth." Ph.D. diss., York University.

Kingsley, Henry. 1867. *Silcote of Silcotes*. 3 vols.

Kinns, Samuel. 1882. *Moses and Geology; or, the Harmony of the Bible with Science*.

Kirby, Ethyn Williams. 1939. "Sermons before the Commons, 1640–42." *American Historical Review* 44:538–48.

Kirby, William. 1835. *On the Power, Wisdom, and Goodness of God as Manifested in the Creation of Animals and in their History, Habits, and Instincts*.

Kirwan, Richard. [1799] 1978. *Geological Essays*. New York: Arno Press.

Kitchin, G. W. 1895. *Edward Harold Browne, D.D., Lord Bishop of Wincester*.

Kittel, Gerhard, and Gerhard Friedrich. Eds. 1964–76. *Theological Dictionary of the New Testament*. 10 vols. Trans. and ed. Geoffrey W. Bottomley. Grand Rapids: Eerdmans.

Kitto, John. Ed. 1864. *A Cyclopaedia of Biblical Literature*. Enlarged by Alexander William Lindsay. 3d ed. 3 vols.

Knight, David M. 1972. *Natural Science Books in English, 1600–1900*. New York: Praeger.

Knight, Douglas A., and Gene M. Tucker. Eds. 1985. *The Hebrew Bible and Its Modern Interpreters*. Philadelphia: Fortress.

Knox, Robert. 1850. *The Races of Men: A Fragment*.

Koester, Helmut. 1990. *Ancient Christian Gospels: Their History and Development*. London: SCM Press.

Korshin, Paul J. 1982. *Typologies in England, 1650–1820*. Princeton: Princeton Univ. Press.

Kraus, Hans-Joachim. 1987–89. *Psalms*. 2 vols. Minneapolis: Augsburg.

Kugel, James L., and Rowan A. Greer. 1986. *Early Biblical Interpretation*. Philadelphia: Westminster Press.

Kuhn, Thomas S. 1962. *The Structure of Scientific Revolutions*. Chicago: Univ. of Chicago Press.

Kümmel, Werner Georg. 1972. *The New Testament: The History of the Investigation of Its Problems*. Trans. S. McLean Gilmour and Howard C. Kee. Nashville: Abingdon.

Lake, Peter. 1988. *Anglicans and Puritans? Presbyterianism and English Conformist Thought from Whitgift to Hooker*. London: Unwin Hyman.

Lake, Philip. 1896. "The Work of the Portuguese Geological Survey." *Science Progress* 5:439–53.
Lamarck, Jean-Baptiste Pierre Antoine De Monet, chevalier de. 1815–22. *Histoire naturelle des animaux sans vertèbres*. 6 vols.
Lampe, G. W. H. Ed. 1954. *The Doctrine of Justification by Faith*. London: A. R. Mowbray.
———. 1965. "Miracles and Early Christian Apologetic." In *Miracles* 1965, 205–18.
Landauer, Bella Clara. 1926. *Printers' Mottoes*. New York: Privately Printed [Douglas C. McMurtrie].
Landow, George P. 1971. *The Aesthetic and Critical Theories of John Ruskin*. Princeton: Princeton Univ. Press.
———. 1979. *William Holman Hunt and Typological Symbolism*. New Haven: Yale Univ. Press.
———. 1980. *Victorian Types, Victorian Shadows: Biblical Typology in Victorian Literature, Art, and Thought*. Boston: Routledge & Kegan Paul.
Lang, Bernhard. 1983. *Monotheism and the Prophetic Minority: An Essay in Biblical History and Sociology*. Sheffield: Almond Press.
Langbain, John. 1976. *Torture and the Law of Proof*. Chicago: Univ. of Chicago Press.
Larson, Edward J. 1985. *Trial and Error: The American Controversy over Creation and Evolution*. New York: Oxford Univ. Press.
"The Latest Theology." 1860. *The Literary Gazette* 91 (14 Apr.): 459–60.
Laud, William. [1639] 1849. *A Relation of the Conference between William Laud, Late Archbishop of Canterbury, and Mr. Fisher the Jesuit*. [Library of Anglo-Catholic Theology].
Laurence, Richard. [1804] 1853. *An Attempt to Illustrate Those Articles of the Church of England Which the Calvinists Improperly Consider as Calvinistical*.
Laurent, François. 1850–70. *Histoire du droit des gens et des relations internationales: Études sur l'histoire de l'humanité*. 18 vols.
Lawler, Edwina G. 1986. *David Friedrich Strauss and His Critics: The Life of Jesus Debate in Early Nineteenth-Century German Journals*. New York: Lang
Lawrie, James. 1964. "Hugh Miller: Geologist and Man of Letters." *Proceedings of the Royal Institution of Great Britain* 40:92–103.
Lawson, Annette. 1988. *Adultery: An Analysis of Love and Betrayal*. New York: Basic Books.
Layard, Austen Henry. 1849. *Nineveh and Its Remains: With an Account of a Visit to the Chaldaean Christians of Kurdistan, and the Yezidid, or Devil-Worshippers; and an Inquiry into the Manners and Arts of the Ancient Assyrians*. 2 vols.
Leach, Edmund. 1987. "Fishing for Men on the Edge of the Wilderness." In *The Literary Guide to the Bible*. Ed. Robert Alter and Frank Kermode. Cambridge: Harvard Univ. Press. 579–99.
Lecky, W. E. H. 1878–90. *The History of England in the Eighteenth Century*. 8 vols.
Lee, Alan. 1978. "The Structure, Ownership and Control of the Press, 1855–1914."

In Boyce, Curran, and Wingate 1978, 117–29.

Lee, William. 1857. *The Inspiration of Holy Scripture, Its Nature and Proof.*

Leeming, Bernard. 1960. *Principles of Sacramental Theology*. London: Longmans.

Lefevere, André. 1992. *Translating Literature: Practice and Theory in a Comparative Literature Context*. New York: Modern Language Association.

Leitch, Vincent B. 1983. *Deconstructive Criticism: An Advanced Introduction*. New York: Columbia Univ. Press.

Leibniz, Gottfried Wilhelm. 1710. *Essais de Théodicée sur la bonté de Dieu, la liberté de l'homme, et l'origine du mal.*

Le Mahieu. Dan Lloyd. 1976. *The Mind of William Paley*. Lincoln: Univ. of Nebraska Press.

Leslie, Shane. 1933. "Lewis Carroll and the Oxford Movement." *London Mercury* 28:233–39.

Lessing, Gotthold Ephraim. 1853–57. *Sämmtliche Schriften*. 12 vols.

———. [1777–80] 1858. *Die Erziehung des Menschengeschlechts*. Trans. D. W. Robertson. *The Education of the Human Race*.

Lessnoff, Michael H. 1986. *Social Contract*. London: Macmillan.

Levine, Joseph M. 1991. *The Battle of the Books: History and Literature in the Augustan Age*. Ithaca: Cornell Univ. Press.

Levine, Michael P. 1989. *Hume and the Problem of Miracles: A Solution*. Dordrecht: Kulwer Academic Publishers.

Lewis, C. S. 1960. *The Four Loves*. London: Collins.

Lewis, Gillian. 1985. "Calvinism in Geneva in the Time of Calvin and Beza, 1541–1608." In *International Calvinism*. Ed. Menna Prestwich. Oxford: Clarendon Press. 39–70.

Lewis, Jack P. 1991. *The English Bible from KJV to NIV: A History and Evaluation*. Grand Rapids: Baker House.

Lichtheim, George. 1967. "Oriental Despotism." In *The Concept of Ideology*. New York: Vintage Books. 62–93.

Lichtenberger, F. 1889. *History of German Theology in the Nineteenth Century*.

Liddon, Henry Parry. 1893–97. *Life of Edward Bouverie Pusey*. Ed. J. O. Johnston, Robert J. Wilson, and W. C. E. Newbolt. 4 vols.

———. [1870] 1904. *Some Elements of Religion: Lent Lectures, 1870*. London: Longmans, Green.

Lightfoot, John. 1822–25. *The Whole Works of John Lightfoot*. Ed. John Rogers Pitman. 13 vols.

Lightman, Bernard. 1979. "Henry Longueville Mansel and the Genesis of Victorian Agnosticism." Ph.D. diss., Brandeis University.

———. 1987. *The Origins of Agnosticism: Victorian Unbelief and the Limits of Knowledge*. Baltimore: Johns Hopkins Univ. Press.

Lindberg, David C., and Ronald L. Numbers. Eds. 1986. *God and Nature: Historical Essays on the Encounter between Christianity and Science*. Berkeley: Univ. of California Press.

"Literature." 1862. *The Athenaeum* (1 Nov.): 553–54.
Littré, Maximilien Paul Émile. 1875. *Littérature et histoire.*
Livingston, James C. 1974a. *The Ethics of Belief: An Essay on the Victorian Religious Conscience.* Talahassee: American Academy of Religion.
———. 1974b. "The Religious Creed and Criticism of Sir James Fitzjames Stephen." *Victorian Studies* 20:279–300.
Livingstone, David N. 1992. "The Preadamite Theory and the Marriage of Science and Religion." *Transactions of the American Philosophical Society.*
Lloyd, T. O. 1984. *The British Empire 1558–1983.* Oxford: Oxford Univ. Press.
Locke, John. [1690] 1975. *An Essay concerning Human Understanding.* Ed. Peter H. Nidditch. Oxford: Clarendon Press.
———. [1693] 1989. *Some Thoughts concerning Education.* Ed. John N. and Jean S. Yolton. Oxford: Clarendon Press.
———. [1695] 1958. *The Reasonableness of Christianity with a Discourse of Miracles and Part of a Third Letter concerning Toleration.* Ed. I. T. Ramsay. London: A. & C. Black.
———. [1695] 1965. *The Reasonableness of Christianity as Delivered in the Scriptures.* Ed. George W. Ewing. Washington: Regnery Gateway.
———. 1976–89. *The Correspondence of John Locke.* Ed. E. S. De Beer. 8 vols. Oxford: Clarendon Press.
Longenecker, Richard N. 1975. *Biblical Exegesis in the Apostolic Period.* Grand Rapids: Eerdmans.
Longley, Charles Thomas. 1864. *A Pastoral Letter Addressed to the Clergy and Laity of His Province by Charles Thomas, Archbishop of Canterbury.*
Longstaff, Thomas R. W. 1988. *The Synoptic Problem: A Bibliography, 1716–1988.* Macon: Mercer Univ. Press.
Lovejoy, A. O. 1932. "The Parallel of Deism and Classicism." *Modern Philology* 29:281–99.
Lubac, Henri de. 1959. *Exégèse médiévale: les quartres sens de l'écriture.* Paris:Aubier. 4 vols.
Lucas, E. V. 1907. *A Swan and Her Friends.* London: Methuen.
Lucas, J. R. 1979. "Wilberforce and Huxley: A Legendary Encounter." *Historical Journal* 22:313–30.
Luce, Arthur Aston. 1934. *Berkeley and Malebranche: A Study in the Origins of Berkeley's Thought.* Oxford: Clarendon Press.
Lushington, Stephen. 1862. *Essays and Reviews. Judgment Delivered on the 25th of June 1862, in the Case of the Bishop of Salisbury versus Williams, and in the Case of Fendall versus Wilson, by the Rt. Hon. Stephen Lushington, D.C.L., Dean of the Arches.*
Luther, Martin. 1856. *The Table Talk of Martin Luther.* Trans. and ed. William Hazlitt. With "The Life of Martin Luther" by Alexander Chalmers.
———. 1883–1995. *Luthers Werke.* 66 vols. Weimar: H. Böhlaus.
———. 1932. *Works of Martin Luther.* 6 vols. Philadelphia: Muhlenberg Press.

———. 1955–86. *Collected Works of Martin Luther*. Ed. Jaroslav Pelikan and Helmut T. Lehmann. 55 vols. St. Louis: Concordia Publishing House.

———. 1961. *Sermons on the Gospel of John, Chapters 14–16*. In Luther 1955–86, vol. 24.

Lux Mundi: A Series of Studies in the Religion of the Incarnation. [1889] 1891.

Lyall, William R. 1840. *Propaedeia Prophetica: The Preparation of Prophecy; or Use and Design of the Old Testament Examined.*

Lyell, Charles. 1830–33. *The Principles of Geology*. 3 vols.

Macaulay, Thomas Babington. [1843] 1850. "Life and Writings of Addison." In *Critical and Historical Essays*. 681–724.

———. [1849–55]. 1913. *The History of England from the Accession of James the Second.* Ed. Charles Harding Firth. 6 vols. London: Macmillan.

———. 1972. *Selected Writings*. Ed. John Clive and Thomas Pinney. Chicago: Univ. of Chicago Press.

Macdonald, Donald. 1856. *Creation and the Fall: A Defence and Exposition of the First Three Chapters of Genesis.*

MacHaffie, B. Z. 1981. "'Monument Facts and Higher Critical Fancies': Archaeology and the Popularization of Old Testament Criticism in Nineteenth-Century Britain." *Church History* 50:316–28.

Machin, G. I. T. 1978. *Politics and the Churches in Great Britain, 1832–1868*. Oxford: Clarendon Press.

———. 1987. *Politics and the Churches in Great Britain, 1868–1921*. Oxford: Clarendon Press.

Mack, Edward Clarence. 1971. *Public Schools and British Opinion since 1860: The Relationship between Contemporary Ideas and the Evolution of an English Institution*. Westport: Greenwood Press.

———. 1973. *Public Schools and British Opinion, 1780 to 1860: An Examination of the Relationship between Contemporary Ideas and the Evolution of an English Institution*. Westport: Greenwood Press.

Mackintosh, James. 1851. *The Miscellaneous Works of the Right Honourable Sir James Mackintosh.*

Maclean, Charles. 1977. *The Wolf Children.* London: Allen Lane.

Maclure, Millar. 1958. *The Paul's Cross Sermons, 1534–1642*. Toronto: Univ. of Toronto Press.

MacMullen, Ramsay. 1984. *Christianizing the Roman Empire (A.D. 100–400)*. New Haven: Yale Univ. Press.

Macnaught, John. 1856. *The Doctrine of Inspiration: Being an Inquiry concerning the Infallibility, Inspiration, and Authority of Holy Writ.*

Madigan, Patrick. 1988. *Christian Revelation and the Completion of the Aristotelian Revolution*. Langham: Univ. Press of America.

Magnus, Philip. 1954. *Gladstone: A Biography*. London: John Murray.

[Main, Robert]. 1861. *A Letter from the Radcliffe Observer on the "Essays and Reviews."*

Maine, Henry. [1861] 1931. *Ancient Law: Its Connection with the Early History of Society and Its Relation to Modern Ideas.* London: Oxford Univ. Press.
Maistre, Joseph Marie de. 1821. *Les Soirées de Saint-Pétersbourg, ou Éntretiens sur le gouvernement temporel de la Providence.* 2 vols.
Maloney, Elliott C. 1981. *Semitic Interference in Marcan Syntax.* Chico: Scholars Press.
Malson, Lucien. 1972. *Wolf Children.* London: New Left Books.
Malthus, T. R. [1798] 1973. *An Essay on the Principle of Population.* London: Dent.
Mangenot, E. 1923. "Inspiration de l'Écriture." *Dictionnaire de Théologie Catholique.* 7:2067–2266.
Manning, Henry Edward. 1864a. *The Convocation and Crown in Council.*
———. 1864b. *The Crown in Council on the "Essays and Reviews": A Letter to an Anglican Friend.*
Mansel, Henry L. 1858. *The Limits of Religious Thought Examined.*
Mantell, Gideon Algernon. 1850. *A Pictorial Atlas of Fossil Remains.*
———. 1857. *The Wonders of Geology.* Ed. T. Rupert Jones. 7th ed. 2 vols.
Marsden, George M. 1980. *Fundamentalism and American Culture: The Shaping of Twentieth-Century Evangelicalism, 1870–1925.* New York: Oxford Univ. Press.
Marsh, Herbert. 1823. "Dissertation on the Origin and Composition of the First Three Canonical Gospels." In Michaelis 1823, 3:167–409.
Marsh, Peter T. 1969. *The Victorian Church in Decline: Archbishop Tait and the Church of England, 1868–1882.* London: Routledge.
———. 1979. *The Conscience of the Victorian State.* Brighton: Harvester Press.
Marshall, Dorothy. 1962. *Eighteenth Century England.* London: Longmans.
Martin, Louis Henri. 1837–65. *Histoire de France depuis le temps le plus recules jusqu'en 1789.* 4th ed. 16 vols.
Martineau, Harriet. 1854. "Results of the Census of 1851." *Westminster Review* 61 (Apr.): 323–57.
———. 1858a. "China: Past and Present." *Westminster Review* 69 (Apr.): 370–401.
———. 1858b. "The Last Days of Church-Rates." *Westminster Review* 70 (July): 30–52.
Martz, Louis L. 1954. *The Poetry of Meditation.* New Haven: Yale Univ. Press.
Mason, R. 1977. *The Books of Haggai, Zechariah, and Malachi.* Cambridge: Cambridge Univ. Press.
Mason, Steven Neil. 1991. *Flavius Josephus on the Pharisees: A Composition-Critical Study.* Leiden: E. J. Brill.
Masson, David Mather. 1856. "Samuel Rogers and His Times." *North British Review* 25 (Aug.): 399–436.
———. 1859–80. *The Life of John Milton.* 6 vols.
———. 1865. *Recent British Philosophy: A Review.*
Maurice, Frederick Denison. 1835. *Subscription No Bondage, or the Practical Advantages Afforded by the Thirty-Nine Articles of Religion as Guides in All*

Branches of Academical Education. Published with the pseudonym "Rusticus."

———. [1838] 1858. *The Kingdom of Christ: or, Hints to a Quaker Respecting the Principles, Constitution, and Ordinances of the Catholic Church*. Ed. Alec R. Vidler. London: SCM Press.

———. 1847. *The Religions of the World and Their Relations to Christianity: The Boyle Lectures*.

———. 1861. "Baron Bunsen." *Macmillan's Magazine* 3 (Mar.): 372–82

———. 1868. "Baron Bunsen." *Macmillan's Magazine* 18 (June): 144–50.

———. 1884. *The Life of Frederick Denison Maurice, Chiefly Told in His Own Letters*. Ed. Frederick Maurice. 2 vols.

Maxwell, William Stirling. 1855. "The Law of Marriage and Divorce." *Fraser's Magazine* 52 (Aug.): 149–51.

Mays, James L. 1988. *Harper's Bible Commentary*. San Francisco: Harper & Row.

McCarthy, Patrick Joseph. 1964. *Matthew Arnold and the Three Classes*. New York: Columbia Univ. Press.

McCrum, Michael. 1989. *Thomas Arnold, Headmaster: A Reassessment*. Oxford: Oxford Univ. Press.

McDannell, Coleen, and Bernhard Lang. 1988. *Heaven: A History*. New York: Vintage.

McGann, Jerome J. 1983. *A Critique of Modern Textual Criticism*. Chicago: Univ. of Chicago Press.

McGrath, Alister E. 1986. *Iustitia Dei: A History of the Christian Doctrine of Justification*. 2 vols. Cambridge: Cambridge Univ. Press.

———. 1990. *A Life of John Calvin: A Study in the Shaping of Western Culture*. Oxford: Basil Blackwell.

McKenzie, D. F. 1986. *Bibliography and the Sociology of Texts*. London: The British Library.

McKim, Donald K. Ed. 1986. *A Guide to Contemporary Hermeneutics: Major Trends in Biblical Interpretation*. Grand Rapids: Eerdmans.

McLachlan, H. John. 1951. *Socinianism in Seventeenth-Century England*. London: Oxford Univ. Press.

McNamara, Martin, Kevin Cathcart, and Michael Maher. Eds. 1987–94. *The Aramaic Bible: The Targums*. 19 vols. Wilmington: Michael Glazier.

McNeil, J. T. 1974. *The Celtic Churches: A History, A.D. 200–1200*. Chicago: Univ. of Chicago Press.

McQuire, Ann Marie. 1983. "Valentinus and the *Gnostike Hairesis*: An Investigation of Valentinus's Position in the History of Gnosticism." Ph.D. diss., Yale University.

Mede, Joseph. 1677. *The Works of the Pious and Profoundly-Learned Joseph Mede*.

Meeks, Wayne A. Ed. 1972. *The Writings of St. Paul*. New York: Norton.

Merrill, Walter M. 1949. *From Statesman to Philosopher: A Study in Bolingbroke's Deism*. New York: Philosophical Library.

Metzger, Bruce M. 1992. *The Text of the New Testament: Its Transmission,*

Corruption, and Restoration. New York: Oxford Univ. Press.

Metzger, Bruce M., and Michael D. Coogan. Eds. 1993. *The Oxford Companion to the Bible*. New York: Oxford Univ. Press.

Meyboom, Hajo Uden. 1993. *A History and Critique of the Origin of the Marcan Hypothesis, 1835–1866: A Contemporary Report*. Louvain: Peeters.

Miall, Edward. 1862. *Title-Deeds of the Church of England to Her Parochial Endowments*.

Michaelis, Johann David. [1750] 1793–1801. *Einleitung in die göttlichen Schriften des Neue Bandes*. Trans. Herbert Marsh. *Introduction to the New Testament*. 6 vols.

———. 1823. Trans. Herbert Marsh. *Introduction to the New Testament*. 4th ed. 4 vols.

Middleton, Anne. 1990. "Life in the Margins, or, What's an Annotator to Do?" In Oliphant and Bradford 1990, 167–83.

Mill, J. S. 1963–91. *Collected Works of John Stuart Mill*. Ed. John M. Robson. 33 vols. Toronto: Univ. of Toronto Press.

Millar, Oliver. 1977. *The Queen's Pictures*. New York: Gallery.

Miller, Edward. 1878. *The History and Doctrines of Irvingism*. 2 vols.

Miller, Hugh. [1847] 1850. *The Foot-Prints of the Creator: or, the Asterolepis of Stromness*.

———. 1857. *The Testimony of the Rocks; or, Geology in Its Bearings on the Two Theologies, Natural and Revealed*.

Miller, J. 1973. *Popery and Politics in England, 1660–88*. Cambridge: Cambridge Univ. Press.

Miller, J. M., and John H. Hayes. 1986. *A History of Ancient Israel and Judah*. Philadelphia: Fortress.

Miller & Richards Typefounders Catalogue. 1873. In *Specimens of Book Newspaper Jobbing and Ornamental Types*. 1974. Owston Ferry, Lincolnshire: Bloomfield Books. [Facsimile reprint].

Millhauser, Milton. 1954. "The Scriptural Geologists: An Episode in the History of Opinion." *Osiris* 11: 65–86.

———. 1959. *Just Before Darwin: Robert Chambers and "Vestiges."* Middletown: Wesleyan Univ. Press.

Mills, Dennis, and Carol Pearce. 1989. *People and Places in the Victorian Census*. Cambridge: Cambridge Group for the History of Population and Social Structure. Historical Geography Research Series, no. 23.

Milman, Henry Hart. 1855. *History of Latin Christianity down to the Death of Pope Nicholas V*.

Milton, John. 1931–38. *The Works of John Milton*. Ed. Frank M. Patterson. 13 vols. New York: Columbia Univ. Press.

———. [1651] 1932. *Defensio Prima*. In Milton 1931–38. Vol. 7.

Miracles: Cambridge Studies in their Philosophy and History. 1965. Ed. C. F. D. Moule. London: Mowbray.

Mitchell, W. Fraser. 1962. *English Pulpit Oratory from Andrewes to Tillotson: A Study of Its Literary Aspects*. New York: Russell & Russell.

Monk, James H. 1830. *The Life of Richard Bentley . . . with an Account of His Writings*.

Monotheism. 1985. Ed. Claude Geffré and Jean-Pierre Jossua. Edinburgh: Clark.

Montaigne, Michel de. 1965. *The Complete Essays of Montaigne*. Trans. Donald M. Frame. Stanford: Stanford Univ. Press.

Monter, William E. [1967] 1975. *Calvin's Geneva*. Huntingdon: Krieger.

Montesquieu, Charles de Secondat, baron de. [1748] 1973. *De l'Esprit des lois*. 2 vols. Paris: Éditions Garnier Frères.

Monypenny, W. F., and G. E. Buckle. 1910–20. *The Life of Benjamin Disraeli, Earl of Beaconsfield*. 6 vols. London: John Murray.

Moore, A. L. 1966. *The Parousia in the New Testament*. Leiden: E. J. Brill.

Moore, Edmund F. 1863–65. *Report of Cases Heard and Determined by the Judicial Committee and the Lords of Her Majesty's Most Honourable Privy Council*. New Series. Vol. 2, pt. 3.

Moore, J. R. 1979. *The Post-Darwinian Controversies: A Study of the Protestant Struggle to Come to Terms with Darwin in Great Britain and America, 1870–1900*. Cambridge: Cambridge Univ. Press.

———. Ed. 1988. *Sources*. Vol. 3 in Parsons 1988.

———. Ed. 1989. *History, Humanity, and Evolution*. Cambridge: Cambridge Univ. Press.

Moore, Stephen D. 1989. *Literary Criticism and the Gospels: The Theoretical Challenge*. New Haven: Yale Univ. Press.

———. 1992. *Mark and Luke in Poststructuralist Perspectives: Jesus Begins to Write*. New Haven: Yale Univ. Press.

Morgan, Caesar. 1853. *An Investigation of the Trinity of Plato and of Philo Judaeus, and of the Effects Which an Attachment to Their Writings Had upon the Principles and Reasonings of the Fathers of the Christian Church*.

Morgan, Robert, and John Barton. 1988. *Biblical Interpretation*. Oxford: Oxford Univ. Press.

Morley, Henry. 1863. "The Bishop and the Professor." *Examiner* (17 Jan.): 36.

Morley, John. 1872. *Voltaire*.

———. 1873. *Rousseau*. 2 vols.

———. 1903. *The Life of William Ewart Gladstone*. 3 vols. London: Macmillan.

Mossner, Ernest Campbell. 1936. *Bishop Butler and the Age of Reason: A Study in the History of Thought*. New York: Macmillan.

———. 1980. *The Life of David Hume*. Oxford: Clarendon Press.

Moule, C. F. D. 1953. *An Idiom Book of New Testament Greek*. Cambridge: Cambridge Univ. Press.

———. 1965. "The Vocabulary of Miracle." In *Miracles* 1965, 235–38.

Moulton, James Hope. 1909. *A Grammar of New Testament Greek*. 3d ed. 3 vols. Edinburgh: T. & T. Clark.

Mouw, Richard. 1982. "Individualism and Christian Faith." *Theology Today*

38:450–57.

Moyser, G. Ed. 1985. *Church and Politics Today: The Role of the Church of England in Contemporary Politics*. Edinburgh: T. & T. Clark.

Mozley, J. B. [1855] 1883. *A Treatise on the Augustinian Doctrine of Predestination.*

———. 1862. *The Baptism Controversy.*

Mueller, William A. 1953. *Church and State in Luther and Calvin: A Comparative Study*. Nashville: Broadman Press.

Mueller-Vollmer, Kurt. 1986. *The Hermeneutics Reader: Texts of the German Tradition from the Enlightenment to the Present*. Oxford: Basil Blackwell.

Müller, K. O. 1847. *History of the Literature of Ancient Greece, to the Period of Isocrates*. Trans. George Cornwall Lewis.

Müller, Friedrich Max. 1859. *History of Ancient Sanskrit Literature So Far as It Illustrates the Primitive Religion of the Brahmans.*

———. 1861. *Lectures on the Science of Language*. 2 vols.

———. 1876. *Chips from a German Workshop: Essays on Literature, Biography, and Antiquities*. 4 vols.

———. 1901. *My Autobiography: A Fragment*. New York: Scribners.

———. 1902. *The Life and Letters of the Right Honourable Friedrich Max Müller*. London: Longmans, Green.

Muller, Richard A. 1985. *Dictionary of Latin and Greek Theological Terms Drawn Principally from Protestant Scholastic Theology*. Grand Rapids: Baker Book House.

Neal, Daniel. [1732–38] 1822. *History of the Puritans, 1517–1688*. Ed. Joshua Toulmin. 5 vols.

Neale, E. Vansittart. 1856. "Buddhism: Mythical and Historical." *Westminster Review* 66 (Oct.): 296–331.

———. 1860. "Buddha and Buddhism." *Macmillan's Magazine* 1 (Apr.): 439–48.

Neale, John Mason. 1856. *Mediaeval Preachers and Mediaeval Preaching.*

Neander, August. [1825–52] 1850–58. *Allgemeine Geschichte der christlichen Religion und Kirche*. Trans. J. Torrey. *General History of the Christian Religion and Church*. 6 vols.

———. 1858. *Lectures on the History of Christian Dogmas*. Ed. J. L. Jacobi. Trans. J. E. Ryland. 2 vols.

Neil, W. 1963. "The Criticism and Theological Use of the Bible, 1700–1950." In *The Cambridge History of the Bible*. Ed. S. L. Greenslade. Cambridge: Cambridge Univ. Press. 4:238–93.

Neill, Stephen. 1964a. *A History of Christian Missions*. Harmondsworth: Penguin.

———. 1964b. *The Interpretation of the New Testament, 1861–1961*. London: Oxford Univ. Press.

Neufeld, Ephraim. 1944. *Ancient Hebrew Marriage Laws*. New York: Longmans, Green.

Newman, Francis W. 1845a. "[Review of Chambers's] *Vestiges of the Natural History of Creation*." *Prospective Review* 1:49–82.

———. 1845b. "[Review of Chambers's] *Explanations: A Sequel to the Vestiges of the Natural History of Creation.*" *Prospective Review* 2:33–44.

———. 1850. *Phases of Faith, or Passages from the History of My Creed.*

———. 1862. "Essays and Reviews: Dr. Lushington's Judgment." *Westminster Review* 78 (Oct.): 301–15.

Newman, John Henry. [1825–26; 1842–43; 1870] 1969. *Two Essays on Biblical and on Ecclesiastical Miracles.* Westminster: Christian Classics.

———. 1833a. "Thoughts on the Ministerial Commission." In *Tracts for the Times* 1833–41, no. I.

———. 1833b. "The Episcopal Church Apostolical." In *Tracts for the Times* 1833–41, no. VII.

———. 1833c. "On the Apostolical Succession in the English Church." In *Tracts for the Times* 1833–41, no. XV.

———. 1833d. "On Arguing concerning the Apostolical Succession." In *Tracts for the Times* 1833–41, no. XIX.

———. 1833e. *The Arians of the Fourth Century.*

———. [1834–43] 1891. *Parochial and Plain Sermons.* 8 vols.

———. 1836a. "On the Introduction of Rationalistic Principles into Religion." In *Tracts for the Times* 1833–41, no. LXXIII.

———. 1836b. "Apostolical Tradition." *British Critic* 20:166–99.

———. 1838. "Lectures on the Scripture Proof of the Doctrines of the Church." In *Tracts for the Times* 1833–41, no. LXXXV.

———. [1840] 1948. "Catholicity of the Anglican Church." In *Essays and Sketches.* Ed. Charles Frederick Harrold. 3 vols. New York: Longmans, Green. 2:41–134.

———. [1841] 1865. *Tract XC. Remarks on Certain Passages in the XXIX Articles.*

———. 1843. *Essay on the Miracles Recorded in Ecclesiastical History.*

———. 1850. *Lectures on Certain Difficulties Felt by Anglicans in Submitting to the Catholic Church.*

———. 1859. "On Consulting the Faithful in Matters of Doctrine." *Rambler* 24 (July): 198–230.

———. [1852] 1976. *The Idea of a University.* Ed. I. T. Ker. Oxford: Oxford Univ. Press.

———. [1861] 1979. "The Inspiration of Scripture, 1861." In *The Theological Papers of John Henry Newman on Biblical Inspiration and on Infallibility.* Ed. J. Derek Holmes. Oxford: Clarendon Press. 72–83.

———. [1864] 1967. *Apologia Pro Vita Sua, Being a History of His Religious Opinions by John Henry Cardinal Newman.* Ed. Martin J. Svaglic. Oxford: Clarendon Press.

———. [1884] 1967. "On the Inspiration of Scripture." *Nineteenth Century* 15:185–99. Repr. in *On the Inspiration of Scripture.* Ed. J. Derek Holmes and Robert Murray. London: Geoffrey Chapman.

———. 1991. *John Henry Newman: Sermons 1824–1843.* Ed. Placid Murray. New York: Oxford Univ. Press.

Newsome, D. 1966. *The Parting of Friends*. London: John Murray.

———. 1961. *Godliness and Good Learning: Four Studies in a Victorian Ideal*. London: John Murray.

Newsome, James D. 1979. *By the Waters of Babylon: An Introduction to the History and Theology of the Exile*. Edinburgh: Clark.

Nias, J. C. S. 1951. *Gorham and the Bishop of Exeter*. London: SPCK.

Nicholls, David. 1967. *Church and State in Britain*.

Nicholson, Ernest W. 1967. *Deuteronomy and Tradition*. Oxford: Blackwell.

Nichols, Stephen G. 1991. "On the Sociology of Medieval Manuscript Annotation." In Barney 1991, 43–73.

Nickelsburg, George W. E., Jr. 1972. *Resurrection, Immortality, and Eternal Life in Intertestamental Judaism*. Cambridge: Harvard Univ. Press.

Niebuhr, H. Richard. 1941. *The Meaning of Revelation*. New York: Macmillan.

Nietzsche, Friedrich. 1968. *Basic Writings of Nietzsche*. Trans. Walter Kaufmann. New York: Modern Library.

Nightingale, Florence. 1989. *Ever Yours, Florence Nightingale: Selected Letters*. Ed. Martha Vicinus and Bea Nergaard. London: Virago.

Nimmo, D. 1981. "Learning against Religion, Learning as Religion: Mark Pattison and the Victorian Crisis of Faith." In *Studies in Church History*. Ed. Keith Robbins. vol. 17. Oxford: Oxford Univ. Press.

Nisard, Jean Marie Désiré. 1855. *Études sur la renaissance: Erasme, Thomas Morus, Mélanchthon*.

Non-Beneficed Clergyman. 1833. *Letter to the Archbishop of Canterbury on Church Reform*.

Norman, Edward. 1976. *Church and Society in England, 1770–1970: A Historical Study*. Oxford: Clarendon Press.

———. 1984. *The English Catholic Church in the Nineteenth Century*. Oxford: Clarendon Press.

Norris, Thomas J. 1977. *Newman and His Theological Method: A Guide for the Theologian Today*. Leiden: E. J. Brill.

Noth, Martin. 1962. *Exodus: A Commentary*. Philadelphia: Westminster Press.

Nott, Josiah Clark. [1849] 1969. *Two Lectures on the Connection between the Biblical and Physical History of Man*. New York: Negro Universities Press.

——— and G. R. Gliddon. 1854. *Types of Mankind: Ethnological Researches*.

Nygren, Anders. 1932. *Agape and Eros: A Study of the Christian Idea of Love*. Trans. P. S. Watson. 3 vols. London: SPCK.

Oechsli, Wilhelm. 1922. *History of Switzerland, 1499–1914*. Trans. Eden and Cedar Paul. Cambridge: Cambridge Univ. Press.

Oesterley, W. O. E. 1955. *The Psalms*. London: SPCK.

O'Higgins, James. 1970. *Anthony Collins: The Man and His Works*. The Hague: Martinus Nijhoff.

Oliphant, Dave, and Robin Bradford. Eds. 1990. *New Directions in Textual Studies*. Austin: Univ. of Texas Press.

Oliphant, Margaret. 1858. "Edward Irving." *Blackwood's Magazine* 84 (Nov.): 567–86.

———. 1862. *The Life of Edward Irving.* 2 vols.

———. 1868. "Bunsen." *Blackwood's Magazine.* 104:285–308.

Oliver, W. H. 1978. *Prophets and Millennialists: The Uses of Biblical Prophecy in England from the 1790s to the 1840s.* Oxford: Oxford Univ. Press.

Ollard, S. L. 1963. *A Short History of the Oxford Movement.* London: Faith Press.

Ollivant, Alfred. 1857. *A Charge Delivered to the Clergy of the Diocese of Llandaff, at His Third Visitation, August, 1857; with an Appendix, containing Notes Chiefly upon Spiritualism and a Volume Entitled "Rational Godliness."*

Oort, Johannes van. 1991. *Jerusalem and Babylon: A Study into Augustine's City of God and the Sources of His Doctrine of the Two Cities.* Leiden: E. J. Brill.

Opfell, Olga S. 1982. *The King James Bible Translators.* Jefferson: McFarland.

Orr, J. E. 1949. *The Second Evangelical Revival in Britain.* London: Morgan, Marshall & Scott.

Ospovat, Alexander M. 1967. "The Place of the 'Kureze Klassifikation' in the Work of A. G. Werner." *Isis* 58:90–95.

———. 1969. "Reflections on A. G. Werner's 'Kurze Klassifikation.'" In Schneer 1969, 242–57.

Outlaw, Lucius. 1990. "Toward a Critical Theory of 'Race.'" In Goldberg 1990, 58–82.

Overton, John H. 1886. *The Evangelical Revival in the Eighteenth Century.*

Overton, John H., and Frederic Relton. 1906. *The English Church from the Accession of George I to the End of the Eighteenth Century.* London: Macmillan.

Owen, H. D. O. 1989. "The Judicial Committee of the Privy Council." Privy Council Office. Mimeograph pamphlet.

Owen, Ralph Albert Dornfeld. 1924. *Christian Bunsen and Liberal English Theology.* Montpelier: Capitol City Press.

Owen, Richard. 1860. "[Review of] *On the Origin of Species* by Charles Darwin." *Edinburgh Review* 111 (Apr.): 487–532.

Oxford Essays. 1855.

Oxford Essays. 1856.

Oxford Essays. 1857.

Oxford Essays. 1858.

"The Oxford School." 1860a. *Eclectic Review* 4 (July): 1–12.

"The Oxford School.—No. II." 1860b. *Eclectic Review* 4 (Aug.): 113–26.

Page, David. 1859. *Handbook of Geological Terms.*

Paine, Thomas. 1989. *Political Writings.* Ed. Bruce Kuklick. Cambridge: Cambridge Univ. Press.

Paley, William [1794] 1850. *A View of the Evidences . . . and the Horae Paulinae.* Ed. Robert Potts.

———. [1794] 1851. *Evidences of Christianity.*

———. [1794] 1859. *A View of the Evidences of Christianity.* With Annotations by

Richard Whately.
———. [1802] *Natural Theology, or Evidences of the Existence and Attributes of the Deity Collected from the Appearances of Nature.*
———. 1819. *The Works of William Paley, D.D.* 5 vols.
Palmer, William. 1848. "On Tendencies towards the Subversion of Faith." *English Review* 10:428–41.
Pals, D. L. 1982. *The Victorian Lives of Jesus.* San Antonio: Trinity Univ. Press.
Paradis, James, and T. Postlewait. Eds. 1981. *Victorian Science and Victorian Values.* New York: New York Academy of Science.
Parker, Theodore. 1853. *Sermons on Theism, Atheism, and the Popular Theology.*
Parkin, Tim G. 1992. *Demography and Roman Society.* Baltimore: Johns Hopkins Univ. Press.
Parrot, A. 1957. *The Temple of Jerusalem.* London: SCM.
Parsons, Gerald. Ed. 1988. *Religion in Victorian Britain.* 4 vols. Manchester: Manchester Univ. Press.
Pascal, Blaise. 1978. *Great Shorter Works of Pascal.* Trans. Émile Cailliet and John C. Blankenagel. Westport: Greenwood Press.
Pateman, Carole. 1985. *The Problem of Political Obligation: A Critique of Liberal Theory.* Berkeley: Univ. of California Press.
Pater, Walter. [1893] 1980. *The Renaissance: Studies in Art and Poetry. The 1893 Text.* Ed. Donald L. Hill. Berkeley: Univ. of California Press.
Paton, J. B. 1858. "Inspiration of Scripture: Current Theories." *London Review* 10:285–343.
Patrick, Simon. 1846–49. *A Critical Commentary and Paraphrase on the Old and New Testament . . . by Patrick, Lowth, Arnald, Whitby, and Lowman.* 5 vols.
Patterson, R. H. 1859. "The Castes and Creeds of India." *Blackwood's Magazine* 85 (Mar.): 308–34.
Pattie, Frank A. 1994. *Mesmer and Animal Magnetism: A Chapter in the History of Medicine.* New York: Edmonston.
Pattison, Mark. 1853. "Diary of Casaubon." Review of *Ephemerides Isaaci Casauboni* (1851) and *Le Triumvirat Littéraire au XVI Siècle. . .* par M. Charles Nisard. *Quarterly Review* 93 (Sept.): 462–500.
———. 1855. "Oxford Studies." In *Oxford Essays* 1855.
———. 1857. "Present State of Theology in Germany." *Westminster Review* 67:327–63.
———. 1863a. "Bishop Colenso on the Pentateuch." *Westminster Review* 79 (Jan.): 57–76.
———. 1863b. "Life of Bishop Warburton." *National Review* 17:61–102.
———. 1875. *Isaac Casaubon: 1559–1614.*
———. 1881. [Review of] *The Provincial Letters of Pascal. Academy* 452 (1 Jan.): 1.
———. 1885a. *Memoirs.*
———. 1885b. *Sermons.*
———. 1889. *Essays by the Late Mark Pattison, Sometime Rector of Lincoln College.*

Collected by Henry Nettleship. 2 vols.

———. 1901. "Life of St. Edmund, Archbishop of Canterbury." Vol. 6 in *The Lives of the English Saints*. Philadelphia: J. B. Lippincott.

Peacocke, A. R. 1979. *Creation and the World of Science: The Bampton Lectures, 1978*. Oxford: Clarendon Press.

Pearson, John. [1659] 1849. *An Exposition of the Creed*. Ed. Temple Chevallier.

Pedersen, Holger. [1931] 1967. *The Discovery of Language: Linguistic Science in the Nineteenth Century*. Trans. John Webster Spargo. Bloomington: Indiana Univ. Press.

Pedersen, Olaf. 1991. *Galileo and the Council of Trent*. Vatican City: Vatican Observatory.

Pelikan, Jaroslav. 1959. *Luther the Expositor: Introduction to the Reformer's Exegetical Writings*. St. Louis: Concordia Publishing House.

Penn, Granville. 1822. *Comparative Estimate of the Mineral and Mosaic Geologies*.

Petty, J. 1860. *The History of the Primitive Methodist Connexion from Its Origin to the Conference of 1859*.

Pfleiderer, Otto. 1893. *Development of Theology*. 2d ed.

Phillimore, Robert. 1862. *Speech of Robert Phillimore, D.C.L., Q.C., in the Case of "The Office of the Judge Promoted by the Bishop of Salisbury against Williams." Delivered on the 9th, 10th, and 11th of February, 1862; and the Criminal Articles against Dr. R. Williams*.

Phillips, Roderick. 1988. *Putting Asunder: A History of Divorce in Western Society*. Cambridge: Cambridge Univ. Press.

Phillpotts, Henry. 1847. *Reply to Lord John Russell on the Bishops' Remonstrance against the Hampden Appointment*.

Philo, Judaeus. 1854. *The Works of Philo Judaeus*. Trans. C. D. Yonge. 4 vols.

Pickering, Samuel F., Jr. 1993. *Moral Instruction and Fiction for Children, 1749–1820*. Athens: Univ. of Georgia Press.

Pine-Coffin, R. S. 1961. Introduction to Augustine. *Confessions*. Harmondsworth: Penguin. 11–18.

Polizzotto, Lorenzo. 1994. *The Elect Nation: The Savonarola Movement in Florence, 1494–1545*. New York: Oxford Univ. Press.

Pope, Alexander. 1766. *The Works of Alexander Pope. With His Last Corrections, Additions, and Improvements. Together with a Commentary and Notes of His Editor*. Ed. William Warburton. 9 vols.

———. 1853. *The Poetical Works of Alexander Pope*. Ed. Robert Carruthers. 4 vols.

———. 1953–69. *The Twickenham Edition of the Poems of Alexander Pope*. Ed. Maynard Mack. 11 vols. London: Methuen.

Pope, William Burt. 1860. "The Oxford Essayists." *London Review* 14 (July): 512–36.

Porter, Roy. 1977. *The Making of Geology: Earth Science in Britain 1660–1815*. Cambridge: Cambridge Univ. Press.

Powell, Baden. 1824. "Review of *Discourses on Prophesy* by John Davison." *The British Critic* 22:368–89.

———. 1838. *Connexion of Natural and Divine Truth.*

———. 1844. "The Oxford Controversy: Anglo-Catholicism." *British and Foreign Review.* 16:528–59.

———. 1847. "The Study of the Christian Evidences." *Edinburgh Review* 86 (Oct.): 397–418.

———. 1855. *Essays on the Spirit of the Inductive Philosophy, the Unity of Worlds, and the Philosophy of Creation.*

———. 1857. "The Burnett Prizes: The Study of the Evidences of Natural Theology." In *Oxford Essays.* 168–203.

———. 1859a. *The Order of Nature Considered in Reference to the Claims of Revelation.*

———. 1859b. "Testimony: Its Posture in the Scientific World." *Chambers' Edinburgh Journal.* 1–24.

Powell, H. Gordon. 1966. "'Ecce Homo': The Historical Jesus in 1865." *London Quarterly and Holborn Review* 35:52–56.

Pratt, John H. 1836. *Mathematical Principles of Mechanical Philosophy.* Revised as *A Treatise on Attractions, La Place's Functions, and the Figure of the Earth* (1860).

———. [1856] 1859. *Scripture and Science Not at Variance; with Remarks on the Historical Character, Plenary Inspiration, and Surpassing Importance, of the Earlier Chapters of Genesis.* 3d ed.

———. [1856] 1861. *Scripture and Science Not at Variance; with Remarks on the Historical Character, Plenary Inspiration, and Surpassing Importance, of the Earlier Chapters of Genesis.* 4th ed.

———. [1856] 1871. *Scripture and Science Not at Variance; with Remarks on the Historical Character, Plenary Inspiration, and Surpassing Importance, of the Earlier Chapters of Genesis.* 6th ed.

"The Present Position of the Church of England." 1862. *Fraser's Magazine* 66 (Dec.): 695–709.

Preus, Robert. [1953] 1957. *The Inspiration of Scripture: A Study of the Theology of the Seventeenth Century Lutheran Dogmaticians.* 2d ed. Edinburgh: Oliver & Boyd.

Prichard, James Cowles. 1826. *Physical Researches into the History of Man.* 5 vols.

———. 1847. *Reports of the British Association.*

Printing and the Mind of Man. 1963. London: Bridges & Sons.

Prochaska, Frank K. 1980. *Women and Philanthropy in Nineteenth-Century England.* Oxford: Clarendon Press.

Prothero, R. E., and G. Bradley. 1893. *The Life and Correspondence of Arthur Penrhyn Stanley, D.D.* 2 vols.

Prout, William. 1834. *Chemistry, Meteorology, and the Function of Digestion Considered with Reference to Natural Theology.* [A Bridgewater Treatise].

Pugh, R. K. 1957. "The Episcopate of Samuel Wilberforce." D.Phil. diss., Oxford University.

Pusey, Edward Bouverie. 1828. *An Historical Enquiry into the Probable Causes of the Rationalist Character Lately Predominant in the Theology of Germany.*

———. 1835. "Scriptural Views of Holy Baptism." In *Tracts for the Times* 1833–41, nos. LXVII–LXIX.

———. [1855] 1883. *The Doctrine of the Real Presence.*

———. 1860. *The Minor Prophets with a Commentary.*

———. 1861. *With Whom Lies the Responsibility of the Approaching Conflict as to the Greek Chair?* [published under the pseudonym "Pacificus"]

———. 1864. *Daniel the Prophet.*

Pusey and Others v. Jowett; The Argument and Decision as to the Jurisdiction of the Chancellor's Court at Oxford. 1863.

"Pusey and Others *v.* Jowett." 1863. *The Church and State Review* (1 Apr.): 164–66.

Quinn, Vincent, and John Prest. Eds. 1987. *Dear Miss Nightingale: A Selection of Benjamin Jowett's Letters to Florence Nightingale, 1860–1893.* Oxford: Clarendon Press.

Rack, H. 1976. "'Christ's Kingdom Not of This World': The Case of Benjamin Hoadly versus William Law Re-Considered." *Studies in Church History* 12:275–91.

Raitt, Jill. 1981. "Theodore Beza." In *Shapers of Religious Tradition in Germany, Switzerland, and Poland, 1560–1600.* Ed. Jill Raitt. New Haven: Yale Univ. Press. 89–104.

Ramm, A. 1985. "Gladstone's Religion." *Historical Journal* 28:327–40.

Rankin, H. D. 1987. *Celts and the Classical World.* London: Croom Helm.

Ratcliff, E. C. 1953. *The Coronation Service of Queen Elizabeth II.* Cambridge: Cambridge Univ. Press.

Rawlinson, George. [1859] 1860. *The Historical Evidence of the Truth of the Scripture Records, Stated Anew, with Special Reference to the Doubts and Discoveries of Modern Times.* [Annotated by A. N. Arnold].

Reader, W. J. 1966. *Professional Men: The Rise of the Professional Classes in Nineteenth-Century England.* London: Weidenfield & Nicolson.

Reardon, Bernard M. G. 1960. "'Essays and Reviews': A Centenary of Anglican Liberalism." *Quarterly Review* 298:301–8.

———. [1971] 1980. *Religious Thought in the Victorian Age: A Survey from Coleridge to Gore.* London: Longman.

"Recent Latitudinarianism." 1863. *The Christian Remembrancer* 45 (Feb.): 225–55.

Redford, Donald B. 1992. *Egypt, Canaan, and Israel in Ancient Times.* Princeton: Princeton Univ. Press.

Redgrave, Samuel. 1878. *A Dictionary of Artists of the English School.*

Redwood, John. 1976. *Reason, Ridicule, and Religion: The Age of Enlightenment in England, 1660–1750.* London: Thames & Hudson.

Reedy, Gerard. 1977. "Socinians, John Toland, and the Anglican Rationalists." *Harvard Theological Review* 70:285–304.

Rees, Abraham. 1819. *Cyclopedia.*

Reese, James M. 1970. *Hellenistic Influence on the Book of Wisdom and Its Consequences.* Rome: Biblical Institute Press.

Redordi, Pietro. [1983] 1987. *Galileo Heretic.* Trans. Raymond Rosenthal. Princeton: Princeton Univ. Press.

Reid, Thomas. [1764] 1970. *An Inquiry into the Human Mind.* Ed. Timothy Duggan. Chicago: Univ. of Chicago Press.

Reider, Joseph. 1937. *Deuteronomy with Commentary.* Philadelphia: The Jewish Publication Society of America.

Reidy, James Edward. 1971. "The Higher Criticism in England and the Periodical Debate of the 1860's." Ph.D. diss., University of Minnesota.

Rémusat, Charles de. 1856. *L'Angleterre audix-huitième siècle.* 2 vols.

Renan, Joseph Ernest. 1859. *Essais de morale et de critique.*

Replies to "Essays and Reviews." 1862.

Reston, James. 1994. *Galileo: A Life.* New York: Harper Collins.

"[Review of] *Essays and Reviews.*" 1860. *Athenaeum* (27 Oct.): 546–49.

"[Review of] Essays and Reviews." 1860. *Christian Remembrancer* 40 (Oct.): 327–85.

"Review of *Essays and Reviews,* the *[Westminster] Confession of Faith,* and William Lee's *The Inspiration of Scripture.*" 1863. *Christian Remembrancer* 119 (Jan.): 25–60.

"Reviews. *Essays and Reviews.*" 1860. *Guardian* (23 May): 473–75.

Reynolds, H.R. 1859. "The Buddhist Pilgrims." *British Quarterly Review* 30 (Oct.): 391–425.

Reynolds, Jan. 1984. *Birket Foster.* London: B. T. Batsford.

Rhoads, David M. 1976. *Israel in Revolution: 6–74 C.E.: A Political History Based on the Writings of Josephus.* Philadelphia: Fortress.

Riley, Patrick. 1982. *Will and Political Legitimacy: A Critical Exposition of Social Contract Theory in Hobbes, Locke, Rousseau, Kant, and Hegel.* Cambridge: Harvard Univ. Press.

Robbins, Keith. Ed. 1981. *Religion and Humanism.* Oxford: Basil Blackwell.

———. 1988. *Nineteenth-Century Britain: Integration and Diversity.* Oxford: Clarendon Press.

Robertson, D. W. 1963. *A Preface to Chaucer.* Princeton: Princeton Univ. Press.

Robertson, Frederick William. 1855–63. *Sermons Preached at Brighton.* 4 series.

Robertson, J. M. 1929. *A History of Freethought in the Nineteenth Century.* 2 vols. London: Watts.

Robinson, Hastings. 1833. *Church Reform on Christian Principles.*

Robinson, J. A. T. 1976. *Redating the New Testament.* London: SCM Press.

Robinson, Thomas L. 1992. *The Biblical Timeline.* London: Merehurst.

Robson, John M. 1990. "The Fiat and Finger of God: The Bridgewater Treatises." In Helmstadter and Lightman 1990, 71–125.

Robson, Robert. 1967, *Ideas and Institutions of Victorian Britain: Essays in Honour of George Kitson Clark.* London: Bell.

Rogers, Henry. 1852. *The Eclipse of Faith; or, A Visit to a Religious Sceptic.*

———. 1853. "Marriage with a Deceased Wife's Sister." *Edinburgh Review* 97 (Apr.): 315–41.

Rogers, Jack B., and Donald K. McKim. 1979. *The Authority and the Interpretation of the Bible: An Historical Approach.* San Francisco: Harper & Row.

Rogers, Nicholas. 1989. *Whigs and Cities: Popular Politics in the Age of Walpole and Pitt.* Oxford: Clarendon Press.

Rogers, Samuel. 1856. *Recollections of the Table-Talk of Samuel Rogers to Which Is Added Porsoniana.*

Rogerson, John. 1984. *Old Testament Criticism in the Nineteenth Century: England and Germany.* London: SPCK.

Rogerson, John, Christopher Rowland, and Barnabas Lindars. 1988. *The Study and Use of the Bible.* Grand Rapids: Eerdmans.

Roget, Peter Mark. 1834. *Animal and Vegetable Physiology Considered with Reference to Natural Theology.* [A Bridgewater Treatise].

Rollinson, P. 1981. *Classical Theories of Allegory and Christian Culture.* Pittsburg: Duquesne Univ. Press.

Rose, Elliot. [1962] 1989. *A Razor for a Goat.* Toronto: Univ. of Toronto Press.

———. 1975. *Cases of Conscience: Alternatives Open to Recusants and Puritans under Elizabeth I and James I.* Cambridge: Cambridge Univ. Press.

Rose, Hugh James. 1825. *The State of the Protestant Religion in Germany.*

———. 1834. *The Study of Church History Recommended.*

Rossi, Paolo. 1984. *The Dark Abyss of Time: The History of the Earth and the History of Nations from Hooke to Vico.* Trans. Lydia G. Cochrane. Chicago: Univ. of Chicago Press.

Rottman, John Michael. 1987. "Prophecy and Ecstasy in Two Heterodox: Gnosticism and Montanism." M.A. diss., University of Toronto.

Rousseau, Jean-Jacques. [1763] 1964. "Lettres écrites de la Montagne." Vol. 3 in *Oeuvres Complètes de Jean-Jacques Rousseau.* Ed. Bernard Gagnebin et Marcel Raymond. Paris: Pléiade.

Row, C. A. 1864. *The Nature and Extent of Divine Inspiration, as Stated by the Writers, and Deduced from the Facts, of the New Testament.*

Rowell, Geoffrey. 1974. *Hell and the Victorians: A Study of the Nineteenth-Century Theological Controversies concerning Eternal Punishment and the Future Life.* Oxford: Clarendon Press.

Rowland, Beryl. 1978. *Birds with Human Souls: A Guide to Bird Symbolism.* Knoxville: Univ. of Tennessee Press.

Rowley, H. H. 1935. *Darius the Mede and the Four World Empires in the Book of Daniel.* Cardiff: Univ. of Wales Press.

Royle, Edward. 1971. *Radical Politics, 1790–1900: Religion and Unbelief.* London: Longman.

———. 1974. *Victorian Infidels: The Origins of the British Secularist Movement, 1791–1866.* Manchester: Manchester Univ. Press.

———. Ed. 1976. *The Infidel Tradition from Paine to Bradlaugh.* London: Macmillan.

——— and James Walvin. 1982. *English Radicals and Reformers, 1760–1848.*

Brighton: Harvester.
Rudolph, Erwin P. 1992. "Perfection." In Jeffrey 1992, 601–3.
Rudwick, Martin J. S. 1972. *The Meaning of Fossils: Episodes in the History of Palaeontology*. London: Macdonald.
———. 1985. *The Great Devonian Controversy: The Shaping of Scientific Knowledge among Gentlemanly Specialists*. Chicago: Univ. of Chicago Press.
Rupke, Nicolaas A. 1983. *The Great Chain of History: William Buckland and the English School of Geology (1814–1849)*. Oxford: Clarendon Press.
———. 1994. *Richard Owen: Victorian Naturalist*. New Haven: Yale Univ. Press.
Rupp, Gordon. 1986. *Religion in England, 1688–1791*. Oxford: Clarendon Press.
Ruse, Michael. 1979. *The Darwinian Revolution: Science Red in Tooth and Claw*. Chicago: Univ. of Chicago Press.
———. 1982. *Darwinism Defended: A Guide to the Evolution Controversies*. Reading: Addison-Wesley.
———. 1989. *The Darwinian Paradigm: Essays on History, Philosophy, and Religious Implications*. London: Routledge.
Ruskin, John. 1903–12. *The Works of John Ruskin*. Ed. E. T. Cook and Alexander Wedderburn. 39 vols. London: George Allen.
Rypins, Stanley. 1951. *The Book of Thirty Centuries: An Introduction to Modern Study of the Bible*. New York: Macmillan.
Said, Edward W. [1978] 1979. *Orientalism*. New York: Vintage.
"St. Elmo's Fire." 1845. *Penny Magazine* 14 (Mar. 22): 106–7.
Saint-Simon, Louis de Rouvroy, duc de. 1856–58. *Mémoirs complets et authentiques du duc de Saint-Simon sur le siècle de Louis XIV et la Régence*. Ed. Pierre Adolphe Chéruel. 12 vols.
Sainte-Beuve, Charles-Augustin. [1845] 1869. "Madame de Staël." In *Portraits de Femmes*. 81–156.
———. 1850. *Causeries de Lundi*. 5th ed. 16 vols.
———. 1863–70. *Nouveaux Lundis*. 13 vols.
Salevouris, Michael J. 1982. *"Riflemen Form": The War Scare of 1859–1860*. New York: Garland.
Sanday, William. 1876. "On the Nature and Development of Monotheism in Israel." *Theological Review* 55 (Oct.): 486–99.
———. [1893] 1896. *Inspiration*. 3d ed. [The Bampton Lectures for 1893].
Sandeen, Ernest R. 1970. *The Roots of Fundamentalism: British and American Millenarianism, 1800–1930*. Chicago: Univ. of Chicago Press.
Sander, Nicolas. [1585] 1877. *Rise and Growth of the Anglican Schism*. Trans. David Lewis.
Sanders, Charles Richard. 1942. *Coleridge and the Broad Church Movement*. Durham: Duke Univ. Press.
Sanders, E. P., and Margaret Davies. 1989. *Studying the Synoptic Gospels*. Philadelphia: SCM Press.
Sandford, E. G. Ed. 1906. *Memoirs of Archbishop Temple by Seven Friends*. 2 vols.

London: Macmillan.

———. 1907. *The Exeter Episcopate of Archbishop Temple, 1869–1885*. London: Macmillan.

Sandmel, Samuel. 1979. *Philo of Alexandria: An Introduction*. New York: Oxford Univ. Press.

Sandys, John Edwin. 1908. *A History of Classical Scholarship*. 3 vols. Cambridge: Cambridge Univ. Press.

Schaff, Philip. Ed. [1877] 1983. *The Creeds of Christendom, with a History and Critical Notes*. 6th ed. 3 vols. Grand Rapids: Baker Book House.

———. 1883–93. *History of the Christian Church*. 12 vols.

Schinder, Thomas F. 1989. *Ethics, the Social Dimension: Individualism and the Catholic Tradition*. Wilmington: M. Glazier.

Schlegel, Friedrich von. [1808] 1849. "On the Indian Language, Literature, and Philosophy." *The Aesthetic and Miscellaneous Works of Frederick Von Schlegel*. Trans. E. J. Millington. 425–526.

Schleiermacher, Friedrich D. E. [1817] 1825. *A Critical Essay on the Gospel of St. Luke*. Trans. Connop Thirlwall; repr. 1861 as *"Essays and Reviews" Anticipated*.

———. [1821–22] 1928. *The Christian Faith*. Trans. H. R. Mackintosh and J. S. Stewart. Edinburgh: T. & T. Clark.

———. [1838] 1977. *Hermeneutics: The Handwritten Manuscripts*. Ed. Heinz Kimmerle. Trans. James Duke and Jack Forstman. Missoula: Scholars Press.

Schneer, Cecil J. Ed. 1969. *Toward a History of Geology*. Cambridge: MIT Press.

Schweitzer, Albert. 1912. *Paul and his Interpreters: A Critical History*. London: Adam & Charles Black.

Schwengler, Albert. [1848] 1868. *Handbuch der Geschichte der Philosophie im Umriss*. Trans. James Hutchison Stirling as *Handbook of the History of Philosophy*.

Scotland, N. A. D. 1990. "*Essays and Reviews* (1860) and the Reaction of Victorian Churches and Churchmen." *Downside Review* 108 (Apr.): 146–56.

Scott, P. 1973. "The Business of Belief: The Emergence of 'Religious' Publishing." In *Sanctity and Secularity: The Church and the World*. Ed. D. Baker. Oxford: Blackwell. 213–24.

Scott, Walter. 1827. *The Lives of the Novelists*.

Secord, James A. 1982. "King of Siluria: Roderick Murchison and the Imperial Theme in Nineteenth-century British Geology." *Victorian Studies* 25:413–42.

———. 1986. *Controversy in Victorian Geology: The Cambrian-Silurian Dispute*. Princeton: Princeton Univ. Press.

———. 1989. "'Behind the Veil': Robert Chambers and *Vestiges*." In Moore 1989, 165–94.

Seeley, Henry Govier. 1870. *The Ornithosauria: An Elementary Study of the Bones of Pterodactyls*.

———. 1901. *Dragons of the Air. An Account of the Extinct Flying Reptiles*. London: Methuen.

Seifrid, Mark A. 1992. *Justification by Faith: The Origins and Development of a*

Central Pauline Theme. Leiden: E. J. Brill.

Sermons or Homilies Appointed to Be Read in Churches in the Time of Queen Elizabeth of Famous Memory, in Two Parts [1547, 1563] 1802.

Service, Elman R. 1985. *A Century of Controversy: Ethnological Issues from 1860 to 1960*. Orlando: Academic Press.

Sevenster Jan N. 1968. *Do You Know Greek? How Much Greek Could the First Jewish Christians Have Known?* Leiden: E. J. Brill.

Sewall, William. 1838. "Animal Magnetism." *British Critic* 24 (Oct.): 301–47.

Seynaeve, Jaak. 1953. *Cardinal Newman's Doctrine on Holy Scripture According to His Published Works and Previously Unedited Manuscripts*. Louvain: Publications Universitaires.

Shaffer, Elinor S. 1975. *"Kubla Khan" and "The Fall of Jerusalem": The Mythological School in Biblical Criticism and Secular Literature, 1770–1880*. Cambridge: Cambridge Univ. Press.

Shaftesbury, earl of. [Anthony Ashley Cooper]. [1711] 1714. *Characteristics of Men, Manners, Opinions, Times*. 3 vols. Repr. 1968. London: Gregg International.

———. [1711] 1728. *Characteristics of Men, Manners, Opinions, Times*. 3 vols.

Shanley, Mary Lyndon. 1989. *Feminism, Marriage, and the Law in Victorian England, 1850–1895*. Princeton: Princeton Univ. Press.

Shannon, Richard. 1982. *Gladstone*. London: Hamilton.

Shaw, W. David. 1987. *The Lucid Veil: Poetic Truth in the Victorian Age*. London: Athlone Press.

Shepherd, Massey H., Jr. 1968. "Before and after Constantine." In *The Impact of the Church upon Its Culture: Reappraisals of the History of Christianity*. Ed. Jerald C. Brauer. Chicago: Univ. of Chicago Press. 17–38.

Sherlock, William. [1689] 1703. *A Practical Discourse concerning Death*. 12th ed.

Sherwood, Morgan B. 1969. "Genesis, Evolution, and Geology in America before Darwin: The Dana-Lewis Controversy, 1856–1857." In Schneer 1969, 305–17.

Shillingsburg, Peter L. 1975. "Detecting the Use of Stereotypes." *Editorial Quarterly* 1:2–3.

Shirley, Walter Augustus. 1847. *The Supremacy of Holy Scripture*. [The Bampton Lectures for 1847].

Simkins, Ronald A. 1994. *Creator and Creation: Nature in the Worldview of Ancient Israel*. Peabody: Hendrickson.

Simpson, Richard. 1858. "Modern Individualism." *Rambler* 21 (June): 390–99.

Singh, J. A. L., and Robert M. Zingg. 1966. *Wolf Children and Feral Man*. New York: Harper & Row.

Sisson, C. H. Ed. 1976. *The English Sermon*. 3 vols. Cheadle: Carcanet Press.

Smalley, Beryl. 1964. *The Study of the Bible in the Middle Ages*. South Bend: Univ. of Notre Dame Press.

Smiles, Samuel. [1859] 1906. *Self-Help*. London: John Murray.

Smith, E. A. 1993. *A Queen on Trial: The Affair of Queen Caroline*. Dover: A. Sutton.

Smith, F. B. 1967. "The Atheist Mission, 1840–1900." In Robson, Robert. 1967, 205–35.

Smith, George. 1844. *The Religion of Ancient Britain: or, A Succinct Account of the Several Religious Systems Which Have Obtained in This Island from the Earliest Times to the Norman Conquest.*

Smith, Goldwin. 1910. *Reminiscences.* New York: Macmillan.

Smith, Ulrich. 1944. *The Prophecies of Daniel and the Revelation.* Nashville: Southern Publishing.

Smith, William Henry. 1845. "[Review of Chambers's] *Vestiges of the Natural History of Creation.*" *Blackwood's Magazine* 57 (Apr.): 448–460.

Smolar, Leivy, and Moses Aberbach. 1983. *Studies in Targum Jonathan to the Prophets.* New York: Ktav.

Soames, Henry. 1830. *An Enquiry into the Doctrines of the Anglo-Saxon Church.*

Sommerville, C. John. 1992. *The Discovery of Childhood in Puritan England.* Athens: Univ. of Georgia Press.

Southward, John. [1882] 1892. *Practical Printing: A Handbook of the Art of Typography.* Ed. Arthur Powell. 4th ed.

Sowers, Sidney G. 1965. *The Hermeneutics of Philo and Hebrews: A Comparison of the Interpretation of the Old Testament in Philo Judaeus and the Epistle to the Hebrews.* Richmond: John Knox Press.

Spadafora, David. 1990. *The Idea of Progress in Eighteenth-Century Britain.* New Haven: Yale Univ. Press.

Sparrow, J. H. A. 1967. *Mark Pattison and the Idea of a University.* London: Cambridge Univ. Press.

Speakman, Colin. 1982. *Adam Sedgwick: Geologist and Dalesman, 1785–1873.* Heathfield, East Sussex: Geological Society of London.

Speller, J. L. 1979. "Alexander Nicoll and the Study of German Biblical Criticism in Early Nineteenth-Century Oxford." *Journal of Ecclesiastical History* 30:451–59.

Spencer, Herbert. 1858–63. *Essays: Scientific, Political, and Speculative.* 3 vols.

Spinka, Matthew. 1968. *John Huss: A Biography.* Princeton: Princeton Univ. Press.

Spinoza, Benedict de. [1670] 1951. *Tractatus Theologico-Politicus.* Trans. R. H. M. Elwes. New York: Dover.

Spurgeon, Charles Haddon. 1856. *Sermons.* 20 vols.

Stackhouse, Thomas. [1737] 1816. *New History of the Holy Bible from the Beginning of the World to the Establishment of Christianity.* Ed. George Gleig. 3 vols.

Stafford, Robert A. 1989. *Scientist of Empire: Sir Roderick Murchison, Scientific Exploration, and Victorian Imperialism.* Cambridge: Cambridge Univ. Press.

Stanley, A. P. 1844. *Life and Correspondence of Thomas Arnold, D.D.* 2 vols. 2d ed.

———. 1846. *Sermons on the Apostolic Age.*

———. 1855. *The Epistles of St. Paul to the Corinthians: With Critical Notes and Dissertations.* 2 vols.

———. [1856] 1860. *Sinai and Palestine in Connection with Their History.*

[———.] 1861a. "Essays and Reviews." *Edinburgh Review* 113 (Apr.): 461–500; reprinted in Stanley 1870, 46–96.

———. 1861b. *A Speech Delivered in the House of Congregation, Nov. 20, 1861 on the Endowment of the Regius Professorship of Greek.*

———. [1861] 1924. *Lectures on the History of the Eastern Church.* London: Dent.

———. 1863–76. *Lectures on the History of the Jewish Church.* 3 vols.

[———.] 1864. "The Three Pastorals." *Edinburgh Review* 120:268–307.

[———.] 1865. "The Theology of the Nineteenth Century." *Fraser's Magazine* 71:252–68.

———. 1870. *Essays Chiefly on Questions of Church and State from 1850 to 1870.*

Steinmetz, David C. 1986. "The Superiority of Precritical Exegesis." In McKim 1986, 65–77.

Stepan, Nancy. 1982. *The Idea of Race in Science: Great Britain, 1800–1950.* London: Macmillan.

———. 1990. "Race and Gender: The Role of Analogy in Science." In Goldberg 1990, 38–58.

[Stephen, James]. 1839. "The Practical Works of Richard Baxter." *Edinburgh Review* 70 (Oct.): 181–220.

Stephen, James Fitzjames. 1862. *Defence of the Rev. Rowland Williams, D.D. in the Arches' Court of Canterbury.*

[———.] 1864a. "The Law and the Church." *Macmillan's Magazine* 9 (Mar.): 440–45.

[———.] 1864b. "The Privy Council and the Church of England." *Fraser's Magazine* 69 (May): 521–37.

[———.] 1864c. "Dr. Pusey and the Court of Appeal." *Fraser's Magazine* 70 (Nov. 1864): 644–62.

Stephen, Leslie. 1870. "The Broad Church." *Fraser's Magazine* 20:311–25.

———. [1876] 1962. *History of English Thought in the Eighteenth Century.* 2 vols. New York: Harcourt, Brace & World.

Stephen, M. D. 1966. "Gladstone and the Composition of the Final Court in Ecclesiastical Causes, 1850–1873." *Historical Journal* 9:191–200.

Stephens, W. B. 1987. *Education, Literacy, and Society, 1830–70: The Geography of Diversity in Provincial England.* Manchester: Manchester Univ. Press.

Stern, Ephraim. Ed. 1993. *The New Encyclopedia of Archaeological Excavations in the Holy Land.* New York: Simon & Schuster.

Stevenson, J. Ed. 1957. *A New Eusebius: Documents Illustrative of the History of the Church to A. D. 337.* London: SPCK.

Stevenson, John. 1989. "Popular Radicalism and Popular Protest, 1789–1815." In *Britain and the French Revolution, 1789–1815.* Ed. H. T. Dickinson. New York: St. Martin's. 61–83.

Stewart, Dugald. 1854–60. *The Collected Works of Dugald Stewart.* Ed. Sir William Hamilton. 11 vols.

"Stones, Meteoric." 1849. *Encyclopaedia Metropolitana* 25:81–90.

Storm, Melvin B. 1987. "Excommunication in the Life and Theology of the Primitive Christian Communities." Ph.D. diss., Baylor University.

Strauss, David Friedrich. [1835] 1846. *Leben Jesu.* Trans. George Eliot as *The Life of Jesus, Critically Examined.* 2 vols.

Strauss, Leo. [1930] 1965. *Spinoza's Critique of Religion.* Trans. E. M. Sinclair. New York: Schocken Books.

Strawson, William. 1968. "The *London Quarterly and Holborn Review,* 1853–1968." *Church Quarterly* 1:41–52.

Streeter, Burnett Hillman. 1929. *The Primitive Church Studied with Special Reference to the Origins of the Christian Ministry.* London: Macmillan.

———. 1932. *The Buddha and the Christ.* London: Macmillan.

Stromberg, Roland N. 1954. *Religious Liberalism in Eighteenth-Century England.* Oxford: Oxford Univ. Press.

Strong, Roy. 1978. *Recreating the Past: British History and the Victorian Painter.* New York: Thames & Hudson.

Stuart, Moses. 1832. "Are the Same Principles of Interpretation to Be Applied to the Scripture as to Other Books?" *Biblical Repository* 2:124–37.

Stunt, Timothy. 1981. "Geneva and British Evangelicals in the Early Nineteenth Century." *Journal of Ecclesiastical History* 32:35–46.

Subscription and Assent to the Thirty-nine Articles: A Report of the Archbishop's Commission on Christian Doctrine. 1968. London: SPCK.

Sullivan, Harry R. 1983. *Frederic Harrison.* Boston: Twayne.

Sullivan, Robert E. 1982. *John Toland and the Deist Controversy: A Study in Adaptation.* Cambridge: Harvard Univ. Press.

Sully, James. 1876. "Hartmann's Philosophy of the Unconscious." *Fortnightly Review* 20 (Aug.): 242–62.

"Sunday in Great Britain." 1856. *Westminster Review* 65 (Apr.): 426–56.

Sussman, Herbert L. 1968. *Victorians and the Machine: The Literary Response to Technology.* Cambridge: Cambridge Univ. Press.

Swabey, Maurice. 1864. "The Privy Council Judgment." *Quarterly Review* 115 (Apr.): 529–80.

Swart, K. W. 1962. "'Individualism' in the Mid-Nineteenth Century (1826–1860)." *Journal of the History of Ideas* 23:77–90.

Swanston, Hamish F. G. 1966. *Ideas of Order: Anglicans and the Renewal of Theological Method in the Middle of the Nineteenth Century.* Assen: Gorcum.

Sykes, Norman. 1966. "The Duke of Newcastle as Ecclesiastical Minister." In *Essays in Eighteenth-Century History from the English Historical Review.* Ed. Rosalind Mitchison. New York: Barnes & Noble. 145–70.

Symonds, Henry Edward. 1933. *The Council of Trent and Anglican Formularies.* London: Oxford Univ. Press.

Tagliacozzo Giorgio, and Donald P. Verene. Eds. 1976. *Gianbattista Vico's Science of Humanity.* Baltimore: Johns Hopkins Univ. Press.

Talbot, C. H. 1954. *The Anglo-Saxon Missionaries in Germany.* London: Sheed &

Ward.

Tanselle, G. Thomas. 1976. "The Editorial Problem of Final Authorial Intention." *Studies in Bibliography* 29:167–211.

———. 1980. "Recent Editorial Discussion and the Central Questions of Editing." *Studies in Bibliography* 34:23–65.

———. 1991. "Textual Criticism and Literary Sociology." *Studies in Bibliography* 44:83–143.

Taplin, Oliver. 1989. *Greek Fire.* London: Jonathan Cape.

Taylor, Jeremy. 1847–54. *The Whole Works of the Right Rev. Jeremy Taylor.* Ed. Reginald Heber and Charles Page Eden. 10 vols.

Taylor, M. M. 1992. *Man versus the State: Herbert Spenser and Late Victorian Individualism.* Oxford: Oxford Univ. Press.

Temple, Frederick. 1860. *The Present Relations of Science and Religion. A Sermon* [on Eccles. 1:17] *Preached on Act Sunday, July 1, 1860, before the University of Oxford during the Meeting of the British Association.*

———. [1861–71] 1896. *Sermons Preached in Rugby School Chapel in 1858, 1859, 1860.*

———. 1899. *Helps to Godly Living, Being Devotional Extracts from the Writings . . . of the Right Hon. and Most Rev. Frederick Temple.*

Thiessen, Gerd. 1983. *The Miracle Stories of the Early Christian Tradition.* Ed. John Riches. Trans. Francis McDonagh. Philadelphia: Fortress.

Thirlwall, Connop. 1863. *A Charge Delivered to the Clergy of the Diocese of St. David's by Connop Thirlwall . . . at His Eighth Visitation October 1863.*

———. 1877. *Remains Literary and Theological of Connop Thirlwall.* Ed J. J. Stewart Perowne. 2 vols.

———. 1881. *Letters Literary and Theological of Connop Thirlwall.* Ed. J. J. S. Perowne and L. Stokes.

Thirlwall, John Connop, Jr. 1936. *Connop Thirlwall, Historian and Theologian.* London: SPCK.

Thomas à Kempis. [1471] 1874. *The Imitation of Christ.* Trans. W. Benham.

Thomas Aquinas. [1265–] 1962–64. *Summa Theologica.* Trans. Thomas Gilby. 60 Vols. London: Blackfriars.

Thomas, C. 1981. *Christianity in Roman Britain to A. D. 500.* Berkeley: Univ. of California Press.

Thompson, David M. 1978. "The Religious Census of 1851." In *The Census and Social Structure: An Interpretative Guide to Nineteenth Century Census for England and Wales.* Ed. Richard Lawton. London: Frank Cass. 241–86.

Thompson, E. P. [1963] 1968. *The Making of the English Working Class.* Harmondsworth: Penguin.

Thompson, H. L. 1899. *Memoir of Henry George Liddell.*

Thompson, Kenneth A. 1970. *Bureaucracy and Church Reform: The Organizational Response of the Church of England to Social Change, 1800–1965.* Oxford: Oxford Univ. Press.

Thomson, Ethel H. 1919. *The Life and Letters of William Thomson, Archbishop of*

York. London: John Lane.

Thomson, J. A. F. 1965. *The Later Lollards: 1414–1520*. London: Oxford Univ. Press.

Thomson, William. Ed. 1861. *Aids to Faith: A Series of Theological Essays*.

———. 1864. *A Pastoral Letter to the Clergy and Laity of the Province of York by William, Lord Bishop of York, Primate of England and Metropolitan*.

Thrane, James Robert. 1956. "The Rise of Higher Criticism in England, 1800–1870." Ph.D. diss., Columbia University.

Throckmorton, Burton H. Ed. 1979. *Gospel Parallels: A Synopsis of the First Three Gospels*. 4th ed. Nashville: Thomas Nelson.

Thucydides. 1881. *Thucydides Translated into English*. Trans. Benjamin Jowett. 2 vols.

Tillotson, John. 1820. *The Works of John Tillotson*. With Life by Thomas Birch. 10 vols.

Tjernagel, Neelaks S. 1965. *Henry VIII and the Lutherans: A Study in Anglo-Lutheran Relations from 1521–1547*. St. Louis: Concordia Publishing House.

Tocqueville, Alexis de. [1835–39] 1899. *Democracy in America*. Trans. Henry Reeve.

Todd, Margo. 1987. *Christian Humanism and the Puritan Social Order*. Cambridge: Cambridge Univ. Press.

Toland, John. 1696. *Christianity Not Mysterious*. 2d ed.

———. 1747. *The Miscellaneous Works of Mr. John Toland*. 2 vols.

Toohey, Timothy J. 1987. "Blasphemy in Nineteenth-Century England: The Pooley Case and Its Background." *Victorian Studies* 30:315–33.

Topham, Jonathan R. 1993. "'An Infinite Variety of Arguments': *The Bridgewater Treatises* and British Natural Theology in the 1830s." Ph.D. diss., University of Lancaster.

Tov, Emanuel. 1992. *Textual Criticism of the Hebrew Bible*. Minneapolis: Fortress.

Tracts for the Times. 1833–41. 6 vols.

Tregelles, Samuel Prideaux. 1854. *An Account of the Printed Text of the Greek New Testament; with Remarks on Its Revision upon Critical Principles*.

Trembath, Kern Robert. 1987. *Evangelical Theories of Biblical Inspiration: A Review and Proposal*. New York: Oxford Univ. Press.

Trench, R. C. [1846] 1856. *Notes on the Miracles of Our Lord*. 5th ed.

———. 1851. *St. Augustine as an Interpreter of Scripture*.

Trigg, Joseph Wilson. 1983. *Origen: The Bible and Philosophy in the Third-Century Church*. Atlanta: Knox.

Tuckett, Christopher Mark. 1993. *The Revival of the Griesbach Hypothesis: An Analysis and Appraisal*. Cambridge: Cambridge Univ. Press.

Tulloch, John. 1872. *Rational Theology and Christian Philosophy in England in the Seventeenth Century*. 2 vols.

Turnbull, Herbert Westren. 1951. *Bi-centenary of the Death of Colin Maclaurin*. Aberdeen: Aberdeen Univ. Press.

Turner, Frank M. 1974a. *Between Science and Religion: The Reaction to Scientific Naturalism in Late Victorian England*. New Haven: Yale Univ. Press.

———. 1974b. "Rainfall, Plagues, and the Prince of Wales: A Chapter in the Conflict of Religion and Science." *Journal of British Studies* 13:46–65.

———. 1978. "The Victorian Conflict between Science and Religion: A Professional Dimension." *Isis* 69:356–76.

———. 1981. *The Greek Heritage in Victorian Britain.* New Haven: Yale Univ. Press.

———. 1993. *Contesting Cultural Authority: Essays in Victorian Intellectual Life.* Cambridge: Cambridge Univ. Press.

——— and J. Von Arx. 1982. "Victorian Ethics of Belief: A Reconsideration." *The Secular Mind: Transformations of Faith in Modern Europe.* Ed. W. W. Wager. London: Holmes & Meier. 83–101.

Turner, Nigel. 1963. *Syntax.* Vol. 3 in *A Grammar of New Testament Greek* [by James Hope Moulton]. Edinburgh: T. & T. Clark.

Turner, Sharon. 1832–37. *The Sacred History of the World, as Displayed in the Creation and Subsequent Events to the Deluge. Attempted to be Philosophically Considered in a Series of Letters to a Son.* 3 vols.

Tweedle, C. 1915. "Colin Maclurin." *Proceedings of the Royal Society of Edinburgh* 36:87–150.

Tyacke, Nicholas. 1987a. "The Rise of Arminianism Reconsidered." *Past and Present* 115 (May): 201–16.

———. 1987b. *Anti-Calvinist: The Rise of English Arminianism c. 1590–1640.* Oxford: Clarendon Press.

Tyndall, John. 1874. "Address Delivered before the British Association at Belfast." *Academy* 120 (22 Aug.): 209–17.

Typology: From the Late Middle Ages to the Present. 1977. Ed. Earl Miner. Princeton: Princeton Univ. Press.

Ueberweg, Friedrich. 1863–66. *Grundriss der Geschichte der Philosophie von Thales bis auf die Gegenwart.* 3 vols. Trans. G. S. Morris. 1872–74. *A History of Philosophy from Thales to the Present Time.* 2 vols.

Vaillancourt, Jean-Guy. 1980. *Papal Power: A Study of Vatican Control over Lay Catholic Elites.* Berkeley: Univ. of California Press.

Van Helden, Albert. 1974. "The Telescope in the Seventeenth Century." *Isis* 65:38–58.

———. 1977. *The Invention of the Telescope.* Philadelphia: American Philosophical Society.

———. 1985. *Measuring the Universe: Cosmic Dimensions from Aristarchus to Halley.* Chicago: Univ. of Chicago Press.

Van Seters, John. 1966. *The Hyksos.* New Haven: Yale Univ. Press.

———. 1983. *In Search of History.* New Haven: Yale Univ. Press.

Varner, Leo Bentley. 1974. "The Literary Reception of Bishop Colenso: Arnold, Kingsley, Newman, and Others." Ph.D. diss., University of Illinois, Urbana-Champaign.

Vawter, Bruce. 1972. *Biblical Inspiration.* Philadelphia: Westminster Press.

Venuti, Lawrence. Ed. 1992. *Rethinking Translation: Discourse, Subjectivity, Ideology*. London: Routledge.

Véra, Augusto. 1861. *L'héglianisme et la philosophie*.

Verene, Donald P., Michael Mooney, and Giorgio Tagliacozzo. Eds. 1976. *Vico and Contemporary Thought*. Atlantic Highlands: Humanities Press.

Villemain, Abel-François. 1829. *Cours de la littérature française: tableau du Dix-huitième siècle*. 4 vols.

Vincent of Lerins. [434] 1914. *The Commonitory of St. Vincent of Lerins*. Trans. T. Herbert Bindley. London: SPCK.

Vinet, Alexandre Rodolphe. 1849. *An Essay on the Profession of Personal Religious Conviction: and upon the Separation of Church and State, Considered with Reference to the Fulfilment of that Duty*. Trans. Charles Theodore Jones.

———. 1855. *L'Éducation, la famille et la société*.

Vogeler, Martha S. 1979. "More Light on *Essays and Reviews*: The Role of Frederic Harrison." *Victorian Periodicals Review* 12:105–17.

———. 1984. *Frederic Harrison: The Vocations of a Positivist*.

Voltaire, Marie François Arouet. [1732] 1972. *Zaïre*. Ed. Claude Blum. Paris: Librairie Larousse.

Von Arx, J. 1985. *Progress and Pessimism: Religion, Politics, and History in Late Nineteenth Century Britain*. Cambridge: Harvard Univ. Press.

Waddams, S. M. 1992. *Law, Politics, and the Church of England: The Career of Stephen Lushington, 1782–1873*. Cambridge: Cambridge Univ. Press.

Walker, Williston. [1893] 1960. *The Creeds and Platforms of Congregationalism*. Boston: Pilgrim Press.

Wallace-Hadrill, J. M. 1952. *The Barbarian West, 400–1000*. London: Hutchinson.

———. 1988. *Bede's Ecclesiastical History of the English People: A Historical Commentary*. Oxford: Oxford Univ. Press.

Walsh, Walter. 1898. *The Secret History of the Oxford Movement*. 3d ed.

———. 1900. *The History of the Romeward Movement in the Church of England, 1833–1864*. London: James Nisbet.

Warburton, William. 1789. *Tracts by Warburton, and a Warburtonian; not Admitted into the Collections of their Respective Works*. Ed. Samuel Parr.

———. 1811. *The Works of the Right Reverend William Warburton*. With a Life by Richard Hurd. 12 vols.

Ward, Benedicta. 1982. *Miracles and the Medieval Mind: Theory, Record, and Event, 1000–1215*. Philadelphia: Univ. of Pennsylvania Press.

Ward, William George. 1844. *The Ideal of a Christian Church*.

Ward, W. R. 1965. *Victorian Oxford*. London: Frank Cass.

Warfield, B. B. [1940] 1960. *The Inspiration and Authority of the Bible*. Philadelphia: Presbyterian & Reformed Publishing Company.

———. 1982. "Inspiration." In *The International Standard Bible Encyclopedia*. Ed. Geoffrey Bromiley. Grand Rapids: Eerdmans. 2:839–49.

Waring, E. Graham. Ed. 1967. *Deism and Natural Religion: A Source Book*. New York: Ungar.

Warton, Joseph. [1757–82] 1806. *An Essay on the Genius and Writings of Pope*. 2 vols.

Waterland, Daniel. 1843. *The Works*. Ed. William Van Mildert. 6 vols.

Watkins, Henry William. 1890. *Modern Criticism Considered in Relation to the Fourth Gospel, Being the Bampton Lectures for 1890*.

Watson, William Davy. 1860. "*Essays and Reviews*." *Fraser's Magazine* 62 (Aug.): 228–42.

Weekes, William Henry. 1843. "Details of an Experiment, in Which Certain Insects, Known as Acarus Crossii, Appeared Incident to the Long Continued Operation of Voltaic Current." *Proceedings of the London Electrical Society*. 240–47.

Wegg-Prosser, F. R. 1889. *Galileo and His Judges*.

Weinfeld, Moshe. 1991. *Deuteronomy 1–11: A New Translation with Introduction and Commentary*. New York: Doubleday.

Weinsheimer, Joel. 1991. *Philosophical Hermeneutics and Literary Theory*. New Haven: Yale Univ. Press.

Weiss, Bernhard. 1887. *A Manual of Introduction to the New Testament*. Trans. A. J. K. Davidson. 2 vols.

Welch, Adam C. 1932. *Deuteronomy: The Framework to the Code*. Oxford: Oxford Univ. Press.

Wesley, John. 1909–16. *The Journal of the Rev. John Wesley*. Ed. Nehemiah Curnock. 8 vols. London: Robert Culley.

———. 1961. *Wesley's Standard Sermons*. Ed. Edward H. Sugden. 5th ed. 2 vols. London: Epworth Press.

Westcott, Brooke Foss. [1851] 1888. *An Introduction to the Study of the Gospels*.

——— and Fenton John Anthony Hort. 1881. *The New Testament in the Original Greek*. 2 vols.

Westermann, Claus. 1984. *Genesis 1–11: A Commentary*. Trans. John J. Scullion. London: SPCK.

Westermarck, Edward. [1908] 1917. *The Origin and Development of Moral Ideas*. 2 vols. London: Macmillan.

Westfall, Richard S. 1989. *Essays on the Trial of Galileo*. Vatican City: Vatican Observatory.

Whately, Richard. 1826. *Elements of Logic*.

———. 1828. *Elements of Rhetoric*.

———. [1828] 1845. *Essays (Second Series) on Some of the Difficulties in the Writings of the Apostle Paul and in Other Parts of the New Testament*. 5th ed.

———. 1830. *The Errors of Romanism Traced to Their Origin in Human Nature*.

———. 1831. *Introductory Lectures on Political Economy*.

———. 1838. *Lectures on Christian Evidences*.

———. [1841] 1842. *The Kingdom of Christ Delineated, in Two Essays on Our Lord's Own Account of His Person and of the Nature of His Kingdom, and on the*

Constitution, Powers, and Ministry of a Christian Church, as Appointed by Himself.

———. 1854. *On the Origin of Civilization. A Lecture by His Grace the Archbishop of Dublin to the Young Men's Christian Association.*

Wheeler, Michael. 1990. *Death and the Future Life in Victorian Literature and Theology.* Cambridge: Cambridge Univ. Press.

Whewell, William. 1833. *Astronomy and General Physics Considered with Reference to Natural Theology.* [A Bridgewater Treatise].

———. 1837. *History of the Inductive Sciences.* 3 vols.

———. [1840] 1857. *The Philosophy of the Inductive Sciences.* 2 vols.

———. 1852. *Lectures on the History of Moral Philosophy in England.*

———. [1852] 1862. *Lectures on the History of Moral Philosophy in England.* 2d ed.

———. 1857. *Supplementary Volume to the Second Edition of the History of the Inductive Sciences.*

White, Hayden. 1973. *Metahistory: The Historical Imagination in Nineteenth-Century Europe.* Baltimore: Johns Hopkins Univ. Press.

White, James [Theocritus Brown]. 1837. "Animal Magnetism in London in 1837." *Blackwood's Magazine* 42 (Sept.): 384–93.

White, Peter O. G. 1960. "*Essays and Reviews.*" *Theology* 63 (Feb.): 46–53.

———. 1983. "The Rise of Arminianism Reconsidered." *Past and Present* 101 (Nov.): 34–54.

———. 1987. "A Rejoinder." *Past and Present* 115 (May): 217–29.

———. 1992. *Predestination, Policy, and Polemic: Conflict and Consensus in the English Church from the Reformation to the Civil War.* Cambridge: Cambridge Univ. Press.

White, R. J. 1957. *Waterloo to Peterloo.* Harmondsworth: Penguin.

Whitelocke, Bulstrode. [1682] 1853. *Memorials of the English Affairs from the Beginning of the Reign of Charles the First to the Happy Restoration of King Charles the Second.*

The Whole Duty of Man Laid Down in a Plain and Familiar Way for the Use of All but Especially the Meanest Reader with Private Devotions for Several Occasions. [1658] 1842. Ed. William Bentinck Hawkins.

Wigmore-Beddoes, D. G. 1971. *Yesterday's Radicals: A Study of the Affinity between Unitarianism and Broad Church Anglicanism in the Nineteenth Century.* Cambridge: James Clarke.

Wilberforce, Robert Isaac, and Samuel Wilberforce. 1838. *The Life of William Wilberforce.* 5 vols.

[Wilberforce, Samuel]. 1860. *A Charge Delivered at the Triennial Visitation of the Diocese, November, 1860.*

———. 1861. "Essays and Reviews." *Quarterly Review* 109 (Jan.): 248–306.

———. 1863. *A Charge Delivered to the Diocese of Oxford at His Sixth Visitation, November, 1863.*

———. 1874. *Essays Contributed to the Quarterly Review.* 2 vols.

———. 1970. *The Letterbooks of Samuel Wilberforce, 1843–1868.* Ed. R. K. Pugh. Vol. 47 in *Publications of the Oxfordshire Record Society.*

Wilbur, E. M. 1952. *A History of Unitarianism.* 2 vols. Cambridge: Harvard Univ. Press.

Wild, G. 1861. *A Brief Defence of "Essays and Reviews."*

Wilken, Robert L. 1988. "The Bible and Its Interpreters: Christian Biblical Interpretation." In Mays 1988, 57–64.

Wilkins, Eliza Gregory. [1917] 1980. *"Know Thyself" in Greek and Latin Literature.* Chicago: Ares Publishers.

Wilkins, John. 1675. *Of the Principles and Duties of Natural Religion.*

Willey, Basil. 1956. *More Nineteenth Century Studies: A Group of Honest Doubters.* New York: Columbia Univ. Press.

Williams, Ellen. 1874. *The Life and Letters of Rowland Williams, D.D.* 2 vols.

Williams, Jacqueline A. 1988. *Biblical Interpretation in the Gnostic Gospel of Truth.* Atlanta: Scholars Press.

Williams, Raymond. 1958. *Culture and Society: 1780–1950.* New York: Harper.

———. 1976. *Keywords.* London: Fontana.

———. 1981. *Culture.* London: Fontana.

Williams, Rowland. 1855. *Rational Godliness after the Mind of Christ and the Written Voices of His Church.*

———. 1856. *Lampeter Theology Exemplified in Extracts from the Vice-Principal's Lectures, Letters, and Sermons.*

———. 1857. *Christian Freedom in the Council of Jerusalem. A Discourse [on Acts xv. 5, 7, 10, 13, 19–23, 28] Preached before the University of Cambridge on Commencement Sunday, 1857; a Discourse with Some Review of Bishop Ollivant's Charge.*

———. 1860. *An Earnestly Respectful Letter to the Lord Bishop of St. David's, on the Difficulty of Bringing Theological Questions to an Issue, with Special Reference to His Lordship's Charge of 1857, and His Forthcoming Charge of 1860.*

———. 1862. *Persecution for the Word. With a Postscript on the Interlocutory Judgment and the Present State of the Case.*

———. 1867. *Broadchalke Sermon-Essays on Nature, Mediation, Atonement, Absolution.*

Williams, Sidney Herbert, and Falconer Madan. 1970. *The Lewis Carroll Handbook.* London: Dawsons.

Williamson, Eugene La Coste. 1961. "Significant Points of Comparison between the Biblical Criticism of Thomas and Matthew Arnold." *PMLA* 76:539–43.

———. 1964. *The Liberalism of Thomas Arnold: A Study of his Religious and Political Writings.* University: Univ. of Alabama Press.

Williamson, Ronald. 1970. *Philo and the Epistle to the Hebrews.* Leiden: E. J. Brill.

Willis, Kirk. 1988. "The Introduction and Critical Reception of Hegelian Thought in Britain, 1830–1900." *Victorian Studies* 32:85–111.

[Willmott, Robert Eldridge Aris]. 1836. *Conversations at Cambridge.*

Wilson, Daniel. 1828. *The Evidences of Christianity.* 2 vols.

Wilson, Henry Bristow. 1851. *The Communion of Saints: An Attempt to Illustrate the True Principles of Christian Union.*

———. 1857. "Schemes of Christian Comprehension." In *Oxford Essays* 1857, 94–128.

———. 1860. "Vedic Religion." *Westminster Review* 73 (Apr.): 333–63.

———. 1861. Introduction. *A Brief Examination of Prevalent Opinions on the Inspiration of the Scriptures of the Old and New Testaments. By a Lay Member of the Church of England.* vi–lxxi.

———. 1862. "Contemporary Literature. Theology and Philosophy." *Westminster Review* 78 (Oct.): 511–29.

———. 1863. *A Speech Delivered before the Judicial Committee of Her Majesty's Most Honourable Privy Council in the Case of Wilson v. Fendall on Appeal from the Arches Court of Canterbury.*

Wilson, Thomas. 1852. *The Letter and Spirit of Scripture.*

Winstanley, D. A. 1947. *Later Victorian Cambridge.* Cambridge: Cambridge Univ. Press.

Wolf, F. A. [1795] 1985. *Prolegomena to Homer.* Trans. Anthony Grafton, Glenn W. Most, and James E. G. Zetzel. Princeton: Princeton Univ. Press.

Woodgate, Henry Arthur. 1861. *"Essays and Reviews" Considered in Relation to the Current Principles & Fallacies of the Day.*

Wordsworth, Christopher. [1848] 1851. *On the Inspiration of Holy Scripture; or, on the Canon of the Old and New Testament.* 2d ed. [The Hulsean Lectures, 1847–48].

———. 1849a. *Lectures on the Apocalypse; Critical, Expository, and Practical.* 2d ed.

———. 1849b. *The Apocalypse, or, Book of Revelation; the Original Greek Text.*

———. 1850. *Is the Church of Rome the Babylon of the Book of Revelation? An Essay Derived in Part from the Author's Lectures on the Apocalypse.*

———. 1861. *The New Testament . . . in the Original Greek with Introductions and Notes.*

———. 1862. "On the Interpretation of Scripture." In *Replies to "Essays and Reviews"* 1860, 409–98.

Wordsworth, William. 1974. *The Prose Works of William Wordsworth.* Ed. W. J. B. Owen and Jane Worthington Smyser. 3 vols. Oxford: Oxford Univ. Press.

Wright, Mrs. John. 1854. *The Globe Prepared for Man: A Guide to Geology.*

Wright, T. R. 1986. *The Religion of Humanity: The Influence of Comtean Positivism on Victorian England.* Cambridge: Cambridge Univ. Press.

Wright, Thomas. 1851. "The Romans in Britain." *Edinburgh Review* 94 (July): 177–204.

Wybrow, Cameron. 1991. *The Bible, Baconianism, and Mastery over Nature: The Old Testament and Its Modern Misreading.* New York: Lang.

Wyttenbach, Daniel. 1823. *Vita Danielis Wyttenbachii.* Ed. Willem Leonard Mahne.

Yeo, R. 1984–85. "Science and Intellectual Authority in Mid-Nineteenth Century Britain: Robert Chambers and 'Vestiges of the Natural History of Creation.'"

Victorian Studies 28:5–31.

Yoder, Albert C. 1971. *Concepts of Mythology in Victorian England.* Ann Arbor: University Microfilms.

Young, Frances M. 1983. *From Nicaea to Chalcedon: A Guide to the Literature and Its Background.* Philadelphia: Fortress Press.

Young, George. 1838. *Scriptural Geology.*

Young, Michael. 1958. *The Rise of Meritocracy.* London: Thames & Hudson.

Young, Robert M. 1980. "Natural Theology, Victorian Periodicals, and the Fragmentation of a Common Context." *Darwin to Einstein: Historical Studies on Science and Belief.* Ed. C. Chant and J. Fauvell. London: Open Univ. Press. 69–107.

Zeller, Eduard. [1844–52] 1856–68. *Die Philosophie der Griechen in ihrer geschichtlichen Entwicklung.* 3 vols. in 5. Trans. Sarah Frances Alleyne as *History of Greek Philosophy.* 1881. 2 vols.

———. 1874. *Strauss in seinem Leben und seinen Schriften.*

Index of Biblical Passages

This index uses the standard AV titles and order for the books of the Bible. General references to each book are given first in the index after each book's title. For additional references to dating, authorship, and other questions see book titles in the Index of Subjects.

OLD TESTAMENT

APOCRYPHA

NEW TESTAMENT

Index of Persons

Throughout these indexes *Essays and Reviews* is abbreviated as *E&R*. Illustrations appear in italics. Nationality is English unless specified otherwise.

Abelard, Peter (1079–1142), French philosopher and theologian, 434, 482, 542

Abercrombie, John (1780–1844), Scottish physician, 259, 272

Abishag the Shunamite, biblical character, 188, 212

Abraham, Hebrew patriarch, 184–87, 208–9, 211, 499, 552, 560, 568

Acton, John Emerich Edward Dalberg, Lord (1834–1902), historian, 326

Adam (in Genesis), 184, 280, 306, 377, 562

Adams, J. C. (1819–1892), F.R.S., astronomer, discoverer of Neptune, 658

Addison, Joseph (1672–1719), essayist, 390, 417–18, 433, 447, 451

Aeschylus (525–456 B.C.E.), Greek dramatist, 171, 498, 512, 541, 567, 578, 818, 830

Abgar V (1st cent.?), king of Edessa, 417, 447

Agrippa von Nettesheim, Henry Cornelius (1486–1535), German writer and physician, 418, 448

Ahaz (735–715 B.C.E.), king of Judah, 190, 212, 215, 217

Airy, Sir George Biddell (1801–1892), F.R.S., Astronomer-Royal, 380, 658

Alcaeus (7th cent. B.C.E.), Greek lyric poet, 540

Alcman (7th cent. B.C.E.), Greek lyric poet, 540

Alexander of Hales (1170–1245), English Franciscan theologian and teacher at Paris, 628, 634

Alexander, St. (d. 328), bp. of Alexandria, 321–22

Alexander the Great (356–323 B.C.E.), king of Macedon, 146, 171, 193, 220, 576–77, 581

Alexander VI (Rodrigo Borgia) (1431–1503), pope, 771

Alford, Henry (1810–1871), dean of Canterbury and NT critic: anticipates *E&R*, 40; on Aramaic gospels, 566; on baptism, 561; on dating of Gospels, 575; edition of NT, 120; on Epistle to Hebrews, 319; on Epistle of James, 320; on Johannine question, 319; on last judgment, 554; on love, 567; on Luke, 580; on MSS. of NT, 555; on Matthew, 739; reviews Bunsen, 60; on righteousness, 582; on spirit, 175; mentioned, 160, 550, 705

Allestree, Richard (1619–1681), Laudian divine, 172

Ambrose, St. (339–397), bp. of Milan and doctor of the church: Bungener on, 275, 311; on creation, 351–52; *Hexameron*, 376; mentioned, 169, 213, 497, 555–56, 565, 744

Anaximander of Miletus (c. 610–545 B.C.E.), Greek philosopher, 540

Anaximenes of Miletus (fl. 550 B.C.E.), Greek philosopher, 540

Andrewes, Lancelot (1555–1626), bp. of Winchester and translator of the Bible, 382, 436, 442, 445, 543, 589

Anne (1665–1714), queen of Great Britain and Ireland, 264, 442

Annet, Peter (1693–1769), deist, 449

Anselm of Canterbury, St. (c. 1033–1109), abbot of Bec, abp. of Canterbury, and philosopher, 40, 178, 228, 434, 628, 634, 855

Antiochus IV Epiphanes (215–163 B.C.E.), Seleucid king of Syria, 171, 190, 193–94, 217, 220–21, 719

Antoninus Liberalis (2d cent.), Greek grammarian and mythographer, 411, 444

Apelles (4th cent. B.C.E.), Greek painter, 221–22

Apollonius of Rhodes (3d cent. B.C.E.), Greek epic poet, 576

Apollos (1st cent.), Alexandrian Jewish convert to Christianity, 226

Aquinas, Thomas. *See* Thomas Aquinas

Aratus (3d cent. B.C.E.), Greek court poet, 168

Archimedes (287–212. B.C.E.), Greek mathematician, 180, 842

Aristarchus (c. 217–145 B.C.E.), Alexandrian Homeric critic, 226

Aristobulus II (2d cent. B.C.E.), Alexandrian Jewish commentator on the Pentateuch, 576

Aristophanes (c. 457–c. 385 B.C.E.), Greek comic poet, 781

Aristotle (384–322 B.C.E.), Greek philosopher: on the beautiful, 146; and Butler, 406; *Ethics*, 129; four causes of, 538; on friendship, 173; and logic, 444, 552; and Pattison, 95; *Politics*, 107, 166; and theology, 305; mentioned, 120, 152, 174, 272, 411, 444, 491, 518, 556

Arius (c. 250–c. 336), Alexandrian deacon and heretic, 171, 323. *See also* Arianism; Constantine; Nicaea, Council of

Arminius, Jacobus (1560–1609), Dutch Reformed theologian, 335

Arnauld, Antoine (1612–1694), French Jansenist theologian, 546

Arnold, Matthew (1822–1888), poet and essayist: attacks Colenso, 851–53; on Butler, 468; on culture, 126, 339; *Culture and Anarchy*, 169, 178, 557, 558–59, 560, 852; on Dissenters, 323–24; on education, 571, 593; "Equality," 166; on *E&R*, 851–53, 857; on facts, 262; on Hebraism and Hellenism, 169; on Homer, 226, 539, 542, 556, 577, 585; on Jowett, 851–52; on Pattison, 851; in Pattison's annotations, 462; on Stanley, 852–53; on Temple, 851; mentioned, 7, 165, 273, 632, 635, 810

Arnold, Thomas (1795–1842), headmaster of Rugby and historian: anticipates *E&R*, 40; on apostolic succession, 324–25; on Articles of Religion, 333–34; on church and state, 78–79, 324, 326; and class, 340; on clerical abuses, 451;

Saadiah, Gaon (882–942), Jewish theologian and biblical translator, 191, 219

Sacheverell, Henry (c. 1674–1724), Anglican divine and pamphleteer: on passive obedience, 452–53; in Pattison's annotations, 474; sermons, 472; mentioned, 450

Saint-Simon, duc de (Louis de Rouvroy) (1675–1755), French diplomat: in Pattison's annotations, 459

Sainte-Beuve, Charles Augustin de (1804–1869), French literary critic: in Pattison's annotations, 459–62, 469–70; on zeal, 450

Samuel (11th century B.C.E.), Hebrew prophet, 527

Sanday, William (1843–1920), Lady Margaret professor of divinity at Oxford, 546, 549

Sanders, Nicholas (1530–1581), Roman Catholic controversialist and professor of theology at Louvain, 323

Sappho (7th cent. B.C.E.), Greek lyric poet, 540

Sardanapalus, legendary monarch of Assyria, 209

Sargon II (c. 721–705 B.C.E.), king of Assyria, 553

Savonarola, Girolamo (1452–1498), Florentine Dominican friar and reformer, 424, 451

Scaliger, Joseph Justus (1540–1609), French classicist and professor at Leiden, 578

Schelling, Friedrich Wilhelm Joseph von (1775–1854), German idealist philosopher and professor at Jena and Würzburg, 23, 69, 130, 231, 262

Schlegel, Karl Wilhelm Friedrich von (1772–1829), German romantic philosopher and critic, 205

Schleiermacher, Friedrich Daniel Ernst (1768–1834), German theologian, philosopher, and professor at Berlin: *Discourses on Religion*, 539; on hermeneutics, 111–12, 115, 117, 543, 572; on infancy narratives, 489, 554; on inspirations, 550; on Luke, 320, 643; on miracles, 245, 266; on salvation, 343; mentioned, 54, 79, 130, 445, 469

Schliemann, Heinrich (1822–1890), German archaeologist and discoverer of Troy, 575

Schmidt, Wilhelm Adolf (1812–1887), German professor of history at Jena: in Pattison's annotations, 476

Schwegler, Albert (1819–1857), German patristic scholar and professor of history at Tübingen: in Pattison's annotations, 465

Scott, John (1639–1695), Anglican divine, 402, 440

Scott, Robert (1811–1887), lexicographer, Dean Ireland's professor of exegesis at Oxford, and master of Balliol College, Oxford, 779

Scott, Thomas (1747–1821), Anglican divine and biblical commentator, 540

Scott, Sir Walter (1771–1832), Scottish novelist and poet, 16, 273, 543, 563, 589

Scott, William, Lord Stowell (1745–1836), M.P., Admiralty and ecclesiastical judge, 297, 335

"Search, John." *See* Whately, Richard

Seckendorf, Veit Ludwig von (1626–1692), German statesman and scholar, 267

Sedgwick, Adam (1785–1873), F.R.S., professor of geology at Cambridge, 90, 381, 666

Seeley, Sir John Robert (1834–1895), historian and professor of modern history at Cambridge, 4, 7

Selden, John (1584–1654), antiroyalist jurist and legal scholar, 401, 440

Selwyn, George Augustus (1809–1878), bp. of Lichfield, 871

Semiramis (Sammuramat) (late 9th cent. B.C.E.), regent of Assyria, 185, 209

Semler, Johann Salomo (1725–1791), German Lutheran biblical critic and professor of theology at Halle, 55, 432, 548, 552, 629

Seneca, Lucius Annaeus, the younger (4 B.C.E.–65), Roman Stoic moralist and playwright, 128, 387, 417, 431, 447, 573, 592

Servetus, Michael (1511–1553), Spanish physician and theologian, 313

Sesostris I (d. 1928 B.C.E.), 2d pharaoh of the 12th dynasty of Egypt, 185, 209

Sety I (1291–1279 B.C.E.), pharoah of the 19th dynasty of Egypt, 169

Seward, Anna ("Swan of Lichfield") (1747–1809), poet, 414, 446

Shaftesbury, Lord (Anthony Ashley Cooper), third earl of (1671–1713), moral philosopher: and atheism, 419–20, 448; and Butler, 407, 443; and controversial theology, 445; and enthusiasm, 451; as "genius," 448; on miracles, 268; and morality, 398, 438, 440; mentioned, 461, 471

Shaftesbury, Lord (Anthony Ashley Cooper), seventh earl of (1801–1885), Whig M.P. and social reformer: illustrations, 862, *863*, *864*, *868*; opposes Temple as bp. of Exeter, 860–68; mentioned, 661, 841

Shakespeare, William (1564–1616), dramatist: *As You Like It*, 271, 576; *Coriolanus*, 339; *Hamlet*, 171, 178, 546, 577; *Henry V*, 592; *Julius Caesar*, 165; *King Lear*, 317; *Macbeth*, 386; *Merchant of Venice*, 317; *Midsummer Night's Dream*, 317, 539; *Romeo and Juliet*, 177, 592; *Tempest*, 592; *Troilus and Cressida*, 563; mentioned, 152, 174, 447, 514, 520, 541

Shalmaneser V (727–722 B.C.E.), king of Assyria, 169

Sharp, John (1645–1714), abp. of York: in Pattison's annotations, 473–74; and preaching, 402, 440

Shelley, Mary Wollstonecraft (1797–1851), novelist, 210

Shem, eldest son of Noah, 208

Sherlock, Thomas (1678–1761), bp. of London: and Bangorian controversy, 436, 446; *Tryal of the Witnesses*, 411, 415, 434, 444, 446; mentioned, 100

Sherlock, William (c. 1641–1707), dean of St. Paul's: and Athanasianism, 433; Pope on, 400, 439; and preaching, 393, 436; and Socinianism, 432; mentioned, 565, 634

Index of Subjects

Victorian Literature and Culture Series

Daniel Albright
Tennyson: The Muses' Tug-of-War

David G. Riede
Matthew Arnold and the Betrayal of Language

Anthony Winner
Culture and Irony: Studies in Joseph Conrad's Major Novels

James Richardson
Vanishing Lives: Style and Self in Tennyson, D. G. Rossetti, Swinburne, and Yeats

Jerome J. McGann, Editor
Victorian Connections

Antony H. Harrison
Victorian Poets and Romantic Poems: Intertextuality and Ideology

E. Warwick Slinn
The Discourse of Self in Victorian Poetry

Linda K. Hughes and Michael Lund
The Victorian Serial

Anna Leonowens
The Romance of the Harem
Edited by Susan Morgan

Alan Fischler
Modified Rapture: Comedy in W. S. Gilbert's Savoy Operas

Emily Shore
Journal of Emily Shore
Edited by Barbara Timm Gates

Richard Maxwell
The Mysteries of Paris and London

Felicia Bonaparte
The Gypsy-Bachelor of Manchester: The Life of Mrs. Gaskell's Demon

Peter L. Shillingsburg
Pegasus in Harness: Victorian Publishing and W. M. Thackeray

Angela Leighton
Victorian Women Poets: Writing against the Heart

Allan C. Dooley
Author and Printer in Victorian England

Simon Gatrell
Thomas Hardy and the Proper Study of Mankind

Jeffrey Skoblow
Paradise Dislocated: Morris, Politics, Art

Matthew Rowlinson
Tennyson's Fixations: Psychoanalysis and the Topics of the Early Poetry

Beverly Seaton
The Language of Flowers: A History

Barry Milligan
Pleasures and Pains: Opium and the Orient in Nineteenth-Century British Culture

Ginger S. Frost
Promises Broken: Courtship, Class, and Gender in Victorian England

Linda Dowling
The Vulgarization of Art: The Victorians and Aesthetic Democracy

Tricia Lootens
Lost Saints: Silence, Gender, and Victorian Literary Canonization

Matthew Arnold
The Letters of Matthew Arnold, vols. 1–4
Edited by Cecil Y. Lang

Edward FitzGerald
Edward FitzGerald, Rubáiyát of Omar Khayyám: *A Critical Edition*
Edited by Christopher Decker

Christina Rossetti
The Letters of Christina Rossetti, vols. 1–2
Edited by Antony H. Harrison

Barbara Leah Harman
The Feminine Political Novel in Victorian England

John Ruskin
The Genius of John Ruskin: Selections from His Writings
Edited by John D. Rosenberg

Antony H. Harrison
Victorian Poets and the Politics of Culture: Discourse and Ideology

Judith Stoddart
Ruskin's Culture Wars: Fors Clavigera *and the Crisis of Victorian Liberalism*

Linda K. Hughes and Michael Lund
Victorian Publishing and Mrs. Gaskell's Work

Linda H. Peterson
Traditions of Victorian Women's Autobiography: The Poetics and Politics of Life Writing

Gail Turley Houston
Royalties: The Queen and Victorian Writers

Laura C. Berry
The Child, the State, and the Victorian Novel

Barbara J. Black
On Exhibit: Victorians and Their Museums

Annette R. Federico
Idol of Suburbia: Marie Corelli and Late-Victorian Literary Culture

Talia Schaffer
The Forgotten Female Aesthetes: Literary Culture in Late-Victorian England

Julia F. Saville
A Queer Chivalry: The Homoerotic Asceticism of Gerard Manley Hopkins

Victor Shea and William Whitla, Editors
Essays and Reviews: The 1860 Text and Its Reading